Prentice Hall

LITERATURE
Timeless Voices, Timeless Themes

Copper

Bronze

Silver

Gold

Platinum

The American Experience

The British Tradition

SERIES AUTHORS

The series authors guided the direction and the philosophy of Prentice Hall Literature: Timeless Voices, Timeless Themes. Working closely with the development team, they contributed to the pedagogical integrity of the program and to its relevance for today's teachers and students.

Heidi Hayes Jacobs

Department of Curriculum and Teaching
Teachers College
Columbia University
New York, New York
Heidi Hayes Jacobs has served as an educational consultant to over 1,000 schools nationally and internationally. A frequent contributor to professional journals, she has published two best-selling books through ASCD: Interdisciplinary Curriculum: Design and Implementation *and* Mapping the Big Picture: Integrating Curriculum and Assessment K–12. *She has been on the faculty of Teachers College, Columbia University, since 1981, and her years as a teacher of high-school, middle-school, and elementary-school students in Utah, Massachusetts, and New York provide the fundamental background of her experience.*

Richard Lederer

Author, speaker, columnist, and teacher
San Diego, California
Richard Lederer celebrates the English language as the best-selling author of more than ten books, including Anguished English *and* The Miracle of Language. *He writes a syndicated weekly column, "Looking at Language," and he is the* Grammar Grappler *for* Writer's Digest. *His work has also appeared in publications such as* The New York Times, Sports Illustrated, National Review, *and* Reader's Digest. *Well-known as a speaker and a presenter, Lederer has entertained and informed a wide variety of audiences, including the National Council of Teachers of English. For many years, he taught English at St. Paul's School in Concord, New Hampshire.*

Sharon Sorensen

Author, speaker, and consultant
Mt. Vernon, Indiana
An educator with more than thirty years of classroom experience, Sharon Sorensen has taught both secondary language arts and language arts methods at the university level. She has also published over eighty articles and has authored or co-authored more than twenty-five books on writing, writing process, and the teaching of writing, including How to Write Short Stories, How to Write Research Papers, *and* Webster's New World Student Writing Handbook. *She and her husband live in a self-created wildlife sanctuary in rural Indiana, where they are active in the National Audubon Society.*

PROGRAM ADVISORS

The program advisors provided ongoing input throughout the development of Prentice Hall Literature: Timeless Voices, Timeless Themes. Their valuable insights ensure that the perspectives of teachers throughout the country are represented within this literature series.

Diane Cappillo

Language Arts Department Chair
Barbara Goleman Senior High School
Miami, Florida
Past President of the Dade County Council of Teachers of English.

Anita Clay

English Instructor
Gateway Institute of Technology
St. Louis, Missouri
Former Middle School Team Leader; Former Chair, High School English Department.

Mary Curfman

Teacher of English
Clark County School District
Las Vegas, Nevada

Ellen Eberly

Teacher of Language Arts
Catholic Memorial
West Roxbury, Massachusetts

Nancy M. Fahner

Language Arts Instructor
Ingham Intermediate School District
Mason, Michigan
Recipient of Charlotte, Michigan, Teacher of the Year Award, 1992. Curriculum Coordinator for School-to-Work Program.

Terri Fields

Language Arts and Communication Arts Teacher, Author
Sunnyslope High School
Phoenix, Arizona
Recipient of Arizona Teacher of the Year and U.S. WEST Outstanding Arizona Teacher awards.

Susan J. Goldberg

Teacher of English
Westlake Middle School
Thornwood, New York
President, Westchester Council of English Educators. President-Elect, New York State English Council.

Argelia Arizpe Guadarrama
Secondary Curriculum Coordinator
Phar–San Juan–Alamo Independent School District
San Juan, Texas
Recognized by Texas Education Agency for work on Texas Assessment of Academic Skills.

V. Pauline Hodges, Ph.D.
Teacher and Educational Consultant
Forgan High School
Forgan, Oklahoma
President, National Rural Education Association. Former Language Arts Coordinator, Jefferson County, Colorado.

Jennifer Huntress
Secondary Language Arts Coordinator
Putnam City Schools
Oklahoma City, Oklahoma
National trainer for writing evaluation, curriculum integration, and alternative assessment strategies.

Angelique McMath Jordan
Teacher of English
Dunwoody High School
Dunwoody, Georgia
Teacher of the Year at Dunwoody High School, 1991.

Thomas S. Lindsay
Assistant Superintendent
Mannheim School District 83
Franklin Park, Illinois

Carol McKee
Middle School Language Arts Research Teacher
Fayette County Public Schools
Lexington, Kentucky
Past President, Kentucky Middle School Association.

Nancy L. Monroe
Teacher of English and ACT Preparation
Bolton High School
Alexandria, Louisiana
Past President of the Rapides Council of Teachers of English and the Louisiana Council of Teachers. National Advanced Placement Consultant.

Rosemary A. Naab
Chair, English Department
Archbishop Ryan High School
Archdiocese of Philadelphia
Philadelphia, Pennsylvania
English Curriculum Committee. Awarded Curriculum Quill Award by the Archdiocese of Philadelphia.

Ann Okamura
Teacher of English
Laguna Creek High School
Elk Grove, California
Participant in the College Board Pacesetters Program. Formerly K–12 District Resource Specialist in Writing, Competency Assessment, Foreign Languages, and the Elk Grove Writing Project. Fellow in the San Joaquin Valley Writing Project and the California Literature Project.

Scott Phillips
Teacher of English
Ford Middle School
Allen, Texas
District Curriculum Committee Member.

Jonathan L. Schatz
Teacher of English/Team Leader
Tappan Zee High School
Orangeburg, New York
Creator of a literacy program to assist students with reading in all content areas.

John Scott
Teacher of English
Hampton High School
Hampton, Virginia
Recipient of the Folger Shakespeare Library Renaissance Forum Award. Participant in four National Endowment for the Humanities teacher programs.

Ken Spurlock
Assistant Principal
Boone County High School
Florence, Kentucky
Former Teacher of English at Holmes High School and District Writing Supervisor. Twice elected President of Kentucky Council of Teachers of English.

Joan West
Teacher of English
Oliver Middle School
Broken Arrow, Oklahoma
Runner-up, Middle Grades Teacher of the Year.

Rick Wormeli
Teacher of English
Rachel Carson Middle School
Herndon, Virginia
Disney's Outstanding English Teacher of the Year, 1996.

CONTRIBUTING WRITERS

Elaine Epstein
Former Teacher of English
Lynbrook High School
Lynbrook, New York

Bruce Goldstone
Children's Book Author
New York, New York

W. Frances Holder
Former Teacher of English
Palos Verdes United School District
Palos Verdes, California

Emily Hutchinson
Former Teacher of English
Jordan High School
Los Angeles, California

Howard Kutcher
Teacher of English
Conrad Middle School
Red Clay Consolidated School District
Wilmington, Delaware

Lisa Moore
Former Teacher of English
Wayland High School
Wayland, Massachusetts

Jacqueline M. Regan
Former Teacher of English
Newington High School
Newington, Connecticut

Stacey Sparks
Former Librarian
Cuyahoga County Public Library System
Cuyahoga County, Ohio

MULTICULTURAL REVIEW BOARD

Jocelyn Chadwick-Joshua
Director of American Studies
The Dallas Institute of Humanities and Culture
Dallas, Texas

Clara M. Chu
Assistant Professor, Department of Library
   and Information Science
University of California at Los Angeles
Los Angeles, California

Nora A. Little Light Bird
Department of Special Education
Montana State University
Billings, Montana

K. Tsianina Lomawaima
Associate Professor, American Indian Studies
University of Arizona
Tucson, Arizona

Larry L. Martin
Chair of History, Geography,
   and International Studies
Coppin State College
Baltimore, Maryland

Sunita Sunder Mukhi
Program Associate
Cultural Programs Division
Asia Society
New York, New York

Julio Noboa Polanco
Professor, Department of Teaching
The University of Northern Iowa
San Antonio, Texas

Alfredo Sámano
Educational Consultant
Region 4, Education Service Center
Houston, Texas

A. J. Williams-Meyers
Professor, Black Studies Department
SUNY–College at New Paltz
New Paltz, New York

Prentice Hall
LITERATURE
Timeless Voices, Timeless Themes

SILVER

PRENTICE HALL
Upper Saddle River, New Jersey
Needham, Massachusetts

ACKNOWLEDGMENTS

Grateful acknowledgment is made to the following for permission to reprint copyrighted material:

Albion Books "How to Be Polite Online" from *Netiquette:* by Virginia Shea. Copyright © 1994 by Virginia Shea. Used Courtesy of Albion.com (www.albion.com).

Arte Público Press "Baseball" by Lionel G. García from *I Can Hear the Cowbells Ring* (Houston: Arte Público Press—University of Houston, 1994). "Old Man" by Ricardo Sánchez from *Selected Poems* (Houston: Arte Público Press—University of Houston, 1985). Reprinted by permission of the publisher.

Brent Ashabranner "The Vision of Maya Ying Lin" by Brent Ashabranner from *Always to Remember*. Copyright © 1988 by Brent Ashabranner. Reprinted by permission of the author.

The Estate of Yoshiko Uchida "Tears of Autumn" from *The Forbidden Stitch* by Yoshiko Uchida. Copyright © 1989 by Yoshiko Uchida. Reprinted by permission of the author's estate.

Borden Publishing Company From "Hokusai: The Old Man Mad About Drawing," reproduced by permission of the publisher, from *The Drawings of Hokusai* by Stephen Longstreet, published by Borden Publishing Co., Alhambra, California.

Brandt & Brandt Literary Agents, Inc. "Western Wagons" by Stephen Vincent Benét, from *A Book of Americans* by Rosemary and Stephen Vincent Benét (Holt, Rinehart & Winston, Inc.). Copyright © 1937 by Rosemary and Stephen Vincent Benét. Copyright renewed © 1964 by Thomas C. Benét, Stephanie B. Mahin, and Rachel Benét Lewis. "Johnny Appleseed" by Stephen Vincent Benét, from *A Book of Americans* by Rosemary and Stephen Vincent Benét (Holt, Rinehart & Winston, Inc.). Copyright © 1933 by Rosemary and Stephen Vincent Benét. Copyright renewed © 1961 by Rosemary Carr Benét. Reprinted by permission of Brandt & Brandt Literary Agents, Inc.

Clarion Books/Houghton Mifflin Company Excerpt from "Emancipation" from *Lincoln: A Photobiography*. Copyright © 1987 by Russell Freedman. Reprinted by permission of Clarion Books/Houghton Mifflin Company. All rights reserved.

Frances Collin, Literary Agent "Shooting Stars" from *This World of Wonder* by Hal Borland (J.B. Lippincott), copyright © 1972, 1973 by Hal Borland. Reprinted by permission of Frances Collin, Literary Agent.

Don Congdon Associates, Inc. "The Drummer Boy of Shiloh" by Ray Bradbury. Copyright © 1960 by Curtis Publishing Co., renewed 1988 by Ray Bradbury. Reprinted by permission of Don Congdon Associates, Inc.

Doubleday, a division of Bantam Doubleday Dell Publishing Group Inc. "The Bat," copyright 1938 by Theodore Roethke, from *The Collected Poems of Theodore Roethke* by Theodore Roethke. Used by permission of Doubleday, a division of Bantam Doubleday Dell Publishing Group Inc. "A Retrieved Refor-mation" from *Roads of Destiny* by O. Henry.

Dutton Signet, a division of Penguin Putnam Inc. "A Horseman in the Sky" by Ambrose Bierce, from *In the Midst of Life* by Ambrose Bierce, afterword by Morris Cunliffe. Copyright © 1961 by the New American Library of World Literature, Inc. From *A Walk In the Woods* by Lee Blessing. Copyright © 1986 by Lee Blessing. Used by permission of Dutton Signet, a division of Penguin Putnam Inc.

Farrar, Straus & Giroux, Inc. "Charles" from *The Lottery* by Shirley Jackson. Copyright © 1948, 1949 by Shirley Jackson, and copyright renewed © 1976, 1977 by Laurence Hyman, Barry Hyman, Mrs. Sarah Webster and Mrs. Joanne Schnurer. Excerpt from *The Right Stuff* by Tom Wolfe. Copyright © 1979 by Tom Wolfe. "Animal Craftsmen" from *Nature by Design* by Bruce Brooks. Copyright © 1992 by Educational Broadcasting Corporation and Bruce Brooks. "The Day I Got Lost" from *Stories for Children* by Isaac Bashevis Singer. Copyright © 1984 by Isaac Bashevis Singer. Used by permission of Farrar, Straus & Giroux, Inc. Reprinted by permission of Farrar, Straus & Giroux, Inc.

Farrar, Straus & Giroux, Inc., and Faber and Faber "Solar" from *Collected Poems* by Philip Larkin. Copyright © 1988, 1989 by the Estate of Philip Larkin. Reprinted by permission.

Free Spirit Publishing Inc. "Saving the Wetlands" excerpted from *Kids With Courage,* by Barbara A. Lewis, © 1992. Used with permission from Free Spirit Publishing Inc., Minneapolis, MN; 1-800-735-7323; www.freespirit.com. All Rights Reserved.

Chris Granstrom From "How to Tell a Good Story" by Chris Granstrom featured in *Country Journal,* Nov/Dec 1997. © Chris Granstrom. Used by permission of the author.

Graywolf Press "One Time," copyright 1982, 1998 by the Estate of William Stafford. Reprinted from *The Way It Is: New & Selected Poems* by William Stafford with the permission of Graywolf Press, Saint Paul, Minnesota.

(Acknowledgments continue on page 995.)

Looking at Universal Themes

Coming of Age

Unit 2

Looking at Universal Themes

Meeting Challenges

Looking at Universal Themes

Quest for Justice

Contents ◆ *ix*

Unit 4

Looking at Universal Themes

From Sea to Shining Sea

Looking at Universal Themes

Extraordinary Occurrences

PART 1: THE EXTRAORDINARY IN THE ORDINARY

PART 2: STRANGE DOINGS

Unit

6

Looking at Literary Forms

Short Stories

Unit 8

Looking at Literary Forms

Drama

Looking at Literary Forms

Poetry

Looking at Literary Forms

The American Folk Tradition

Complete Contents by Genre

SHORT STORY

NONFICTION

Complete Contents by Genre

NONFICTION (CONTINUED)

DRAMA

POETRY

Complete Contents by Genre

POETRY (CONTINUED)

MYTHS, TALES, AND LEGENDS

Complete Contents by Theme

COMING OF AGE

MEETING CHALLENGES

QUEST FOR JUSTICE

Complete Contents by Theme

Complete Contents by Theme

THE ENVIRONMENT AND YOU (CONTINUED)

A WORLD OF PEOPLE

Relationships

Appreciating Others

HEROES AND ADVENTURES

Heroes

Conflicts and Challenges

Prentice Hall

LITERATURE

Timeless Voices, Timeless Themes

The Cat, Robert Vickrey, Licensed by VAGA, New York

Coming of Age

Laughter, tears, failure, and triumph are part of every life. These experiences are part of growing up and part of growing older. Along with the characters and authors in this unit, experience what it's like to travel on the road of life—finding adventure and friendship, and gaining insights about life along the way.

Guide for Reading

Meet the Author:

Ray Bradbury (1920–   )

Ray Bradbury grew up in Waukegan, Illinois, and later moved with his family to California. As a teenager, he read science-fiction stories and soon began writing his own.

The young writer eventually became an award-winning science-fiction author, known for such works as *The Martian Chronicles*.

Time Travel Bradbury often travels to the future in his stories, setting them on Mars or Venus. Occasionally, however, he shifts his time-travel machine into reverse and heads for the past. This story, for instance, takes place in Shiloh, Tennessee, on the eve of a great Civil War battle.

Timeless Themes Although Bradbury travels in time to find his stories, his themes are timeless. His themes include the need to be true to oneself and the importance of accepting others. "The Drummer Boy of Shiloh" deals with growing up during a crisis.

THE STORY BEHIND THE STORY

This story began with the poetic words of its title. Many years ago, Bradbury read the death notice of an actor whose grandfather had been "the drummer boy of Shiloh." This phrase inspired him to write his tale. Before he began to write, he went to the Los Angeles library to look up the weather conditions during the Battle of Shiloh.

◆ LITERATURE AND YOUR LIFE

CONNECT YOUR EXPERIENCE

Everyone has felt the last-minute jitters. You're about to take the big test, step up to the plate with runners on base, or go on a first date. Your heart is racing and your breathing is shallow. You've survived these moments. However, suppose you were about to risk your life in battle. In this story, you'll discover how the jitters feel when your life is at stake.

THEMATIC FOCUS: Arriving at Understanding

Often, the most trying experiences teach us valuable lessons. As you read, note what, if anything, the character learns from going into battle.

◆ Background for Understanding

HISTORY

This story is about a Civil War drummer boy. Drummer boys went with troops into battle, pacing their drumbeats to the speed of the attack. They didn't carry rifles or other weapons. The boy in the story is fourteen, and at least one real-life drummer boy was only thirteen. There was no age requirement for drummer boys because the job supposedly didn't involve combat. In reality, it involved great risk. Because few parents allowed their children to take that risk, drummer boys were usually orphans or runaways.

The Drummer Boy of Shiloh

Drummer Boy, Julian Scott, N.S. Mayer

◆ Literary Focus

HISTORICAL SETTING

You study the past, but your history books probably don't give you a true sense of what it was actually like to *live* in an earlier era. In a story with a **historical setting,** however, you can see places and events from history through the eyes of fictional characters. As you share their experiences, you'll discover what it might have been like to live through the events yourself.

In this story, you'll keep watch with a boy on the eve of his first Civil War battle. You'll feel his fear and see the "familiar shadows" of soldiers lying exhausted around him.

◆ Build Vocabulary

WORD PART: *bene-*

Bradbury writes that for many Civil War soldiers, their youth was their "benediction." This word, which means "blessing," contains the word parts *bene-,* meaning "well" or "good," and *diction,* which means "saying."

WORD BANK

Look over these words from the story. Which word means "fastened or made firm"? Check the Build Vocabulary box on page 5 to see if you chose correctly.

benediction
riveted
compounded
resolute

Reading for Success

Literal Comprehension Strategies

When you watch television, you can put your brain to bed, leave your finger on the remote, and channel-surf. Reading is different. It's more rewarding than television, but it's also more work. These strategies will help you train your mind to connect with the page.

Break down long sentences.
▶ Read long sentences in meaningful groups of words, not word by word. Often punctuation will guide you to words that work together as a unit. Notice, for example, how the words before the first comma combine to answer the question *when:*

> In the April night, more than once, blossoms fell from the orchard trees. . . .

▶ Read through the sentence quickly to find the subject—the person, place, thing, or idea that the sentence is discussing. Then, decide what the sentence is saying about the subject.

Use context clues.
Use the context, or the surroundings, of an unfamiliar word to find clues to its meaning. As the passage below indicates, words similar or opposite in meaning can help you understand the unfamiliar word:

> . . . forty thousand men, exhausted by nervous expectation, unable to sleep for romantic dreams of battles yet unfought, lay crazily askew in their uniforms.

The word *askew* may be unfamiliar to you, but the word *crazily* suggests something "crooked" or "out of order." Men lying askew must therefore be lying "in a crooked way."

Reread or read ahead.
▶ Reread passages that confuse you until you understand them.
▶ If rereading doesn't clarify a passage, read ahead. You may find the answer in the next few sentences or paragraphs.

Paraphrase.
▶ Restate a sentence or paragraph in your own words to be sure you understand it.

As you read Ray Bradbury's "The Drummer Boy of Shiloh," look at the notes in the boxes. The notes demonstrate how to apply these strategies to a work of literature.

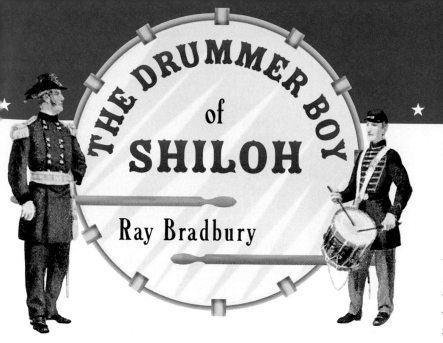

THE DRUMMER BOY of SHILOH

Ray Bradbury

★ ★ ★ ★ ★ ★ ★ ★ ★ ★ ★

In the April night, more than once, blossoms fell from the orchard trees and lit with rustling taps on the drumskin. At midnight a peach stone left miraculously on a branch through winter, flicked by a bird, fell swift and unseen, struck once, like panic, which jerked the boy upright. In silence he listened to his own heart ruffle away, away—at last gone from his ears and back in his chest again.

After that, he turned the drum on its side, where its great lunar face peered at him whenever he opened his eyes.

His face, alert or at rest, was solemn. It was indeed a solemn time and a solemn night for a boy just turned fourteen in the peach field near the Owl Creek not far from the church at Shiloh.[1]

". . . thirty-one, thirty-two, thirty-three . . ."

Unable to see, he stopped counting.

> **Break down this long sentence** and you'll discover that its subject is "forty thousand men." The sentence tells you how these men lay.

Beyond the thirty-three familiar shadows, forty thousand men, exhausted by nervous expectation, unable to sleep for romantic dreams of battles yet unfought, lay crazily askew in their uniforms. A mile yet farther on, another army was strewn helter-skelter,

turning slow, basting themselves[2] with the thought of what they would do when the time came: a leap, a yell, a blind plunge their strategy, raw youth their protection and <u>benediction</u>.

Now and again the boy heard a vast wind come up, that gently stirred the air. But he knew what it was—the army here, the army there, whispering to itself in the dark. Some men talking to others, others murmuring to themselves, and all so quiet it was like a natural element arisen from South or North with the motion of the earth toward dawn.

What the men whispered the boy could only guess, and he guessed that it was: "Me, I'm the one, I'm the one of all the rest who won't die. I'll live through it. I'll go home. The band will play. And I'll be there to hear it."

Yes, thought the boy, that's all very well for them, they can give as good as they get!

For with the careless bones of the young men harvested by night and bindled[3] around campfires were the similarly strewn steel bones of their rifles, with bayonets fixed like eternal lightning lost in the orchard grass.

Me, thought the boy, I got only a drum, two sticks to beat it, and no shield.

There wasn't a man-boy on this ground tonight who did not have a shield he cast, <u>riveted</u> or carved himself on his way to his

---

1. **Shiloh** (shī´ lō): Site of a Civil War battle in 1862; now a national military park in southwest Tennessee.

2. **basting themselves:** Here, letting their thoughts pour over them as they turn in their sleep.
3. **bindled** (bin´ dəld) *adj.*: Bedded.

◆ **Build Vocabulary**

benediction (ben´ ə dik´ shən) *n.*: Blessing

riveted (riv´ it əd) *adj.*: Fastened or made firm

▲ **Critical Viewing** Does the drummer boy in this photograph seem to want to "hide inside himself"? Explain. [**Assess**]

first attack, compounded of remote but nonetheless firm and fiery family devotion, flag-blown patriotism and cocksure immortality strengthened by the touchstone of very real gunpowder, ramrod, Minié ball[4] and flint. But without these last, the boy felt his family move yet farther off away in the dark, as if one of those great prairie-burning trains had chanted them away never to return—leaving him with this drum which was worse than a toy in the game to be played tomorrow or some day much too soon.

The boy turned on his side. A moth brushed his face, but it was a peach blossom. A peach blossom flicked him, but it was a moth. Nothing stayed put. Nothing had a name. Nothing was as it once was.

If he lay very still, when the dawn came up and the soldiers put on their bravery with their caps, perhaps they might go away, the war with them, and not notice him lying small here, no more than a toy himself.

"Well, now," said a voice.

The boy shut up his eyes, to hide inside

---

4. **Minié** (min´ ē) **ball:** Cone-shaped rifle bullet that expands when fired.

himself, but it was too late. Someone, walking by in the night, stood over him.

"Well," said the voice quietly, "here's a soldier crying *before* the fight. Good. Get it over. Won't be time once it all starts."

And the voice was about to move on when the boy, startled, touched the drum at his elbow. The man above, hearing this, stopped. The boy could feel his eyes, sense him slowly bending near. A hand must have come down out of the night, for there was a little *rat-tat* as the fingernails brushed and the man's breath fanned his face.

"Why, it's the drummer boy, isn't it?"

The boy nodded, not knowing if his nod was seen. "Sir, is that *you*?" he said.

"I assume it is." The man's knees cracked as he bent still closer.

He smelled as all fathers should smell, of salt sweat, ginger tobacco, horse and boot leather, and the earth he walked upon. He had many eyes. No, not eyes—brass buttons that watched the boy.

He could only be, and was, the general.

"What's your name, boy?" he asked.

"Joby," whispered the boy, starting to sit up.

"All right, Joby, don't stir." A hand pressed his chest gently, and the boy relaxed. "How long you been with us, Joby?"

"Three weeks, sir."

"Run off from home or joined legitimately, boy?"

Silence.

"Fool question," said the general. "Do you shave yet, boy? Even more of a fool. There's your cheek, fell right off the tree overhead. And the others here not much older. Raw, raw, the lot of you. You ready for tomorrow or the next day, Joby?"

"I think so, sir."

"You want to cry some more, go on ahead. I did the same last night."

"*You*, sir?"

> Use **context clues** to see that *legitimately* means "lawfully." The words "run off from home" provide a clue.

"It's the truth. Thinking of everything ahead. Both sides figuring the other side will just give up, and soon, and the war done in weeks, and us all home. Well, that's not how it's going to be. And maybe that's why I cried."

"Yes, sir," said Joby.

The general must have taken out a cigar now, for the dark was suddenly filled with the smell of tobacco unlit as yet, but chewed as the man thought what next to say.

"It's going to be a crazy time," said the general. "Counting both sides, there's a hundred thousand men, give or take a few thousand out there tonight, not one as can spit a sparrow off a tree, or knows a horse clod from a Minié ball. Stand up, bare the breast, ask to be a target, thank them and sit down, that's us, that's them. We should turn tail and train four months, they should do the same. But here we are, taken with spring fever and thinking it blood lust, taking our sulfur with cannons instead of with molasses, as it should be, going to be a hero, going to live forever. And I can see all of them over there nodding agreement, save the other way around. It's wrong, boy, it's wrong as a head put on hindside front and a man marching backward through life. More innocents will get shot out of pure enthusiasm than ever got shot before. Owl Creek was full of boys splashing around in the noonday sun just a few hours ago. I fear it will be full of boys again, just floating, at sundown tomorrow, not caring where the tide takes them."

The general stopped and made a little pile of winter leaves and twigs in the darkness, as if he might at any moment strike fire to them to see his way through the coming days when the sun might not show its face because of what was happening here and just beyond.

> **Read ahead** to find out what the general means when he says "It's going to be a crazy time."

◆ Build Vocabulary

compounded (käm pound´ əd) *adj.*: Mixed or combined

resolute (rez´ ə l$\overline{oo}$t´) *adj.*: Showing a firm purpose; determined

The boy watched the hand stirring the leaves and opened his lips to say something, but did not say it. The general heard the boy's breath and spoke himself.

"Why am I telling you this? That's what you wanted to ask, eh? Well, when you got a bunch of wild horses on a loose rein somewhere, somehow you got to bring order, rein them in. These lads, fresh out of the milkshed, don't know what I know, and I can't tell them: men actually die, in war. So each is his own army. I got to make *one* army of them. And for that, boy, I need you."

"Me!" The boy's lips barely twitched.

"Now, boy," said the general quietly, "you are the heart of the army. Think of that. You're the heart of the army. Listen, now."

And, lying there, Joby listened. And the general spoke on.

If he, Joby, beat slow tomorrow, the heart would beat slow in the men. They would lag by the wayside. They would drowse in the fields on their muskets. They would sleep forever, after that, in those same fields—their hearts slowed by a drummer boy and stopped by enemy lead.

But if he beat a sure, steady, ever faster rhythm, then, then their knees would come up in a long line down over that hill, one knee after the other, like a wave on the ocean shore! Had he seen the ocean ever? Seen the waves rolling in like a well-ordered cavalry charge to the sand? Well, that was it, that's what he wanted, that's what was needed! Joby was his right hand and his left. He gave the orders, but Joby set the pace!

> **Paraphrase** the general's description of what will happen if Joby beats a sure rhythm.

So bring the right knee up and the right foot out and the left knee up and the left foot out. One following the other in good time, in brisk time. Move the blood up the body and make the head proud and the spine stiff and the jaw <u>resolute</u>. Focus the eye and set the teeth, flare the nostrils and tighten the hands, put steel armor all over the men, for blood moving fast in them does indeed make men feel as if they'd put on steel. He must keep at it, at it! Long and steady, steady and long! Then, even though shot or torn, those wounds got in hot blood—in blood he'd helped stir—would feel less pain. If their blood was cold, it would be more than slaughter, it would be murderous nightmare and pain best not told and no one to guess.

The general spoke and stopped, letting his breath slack off. Then, after a moment, he said, "So there you are, that's it. Will you do that, boy? Do you know now you're general of the army when the general's left behind?"

The boy nodded mutely.

"You'll run them through for me then, boy?"

"Yes, sir."

"Good. And, maybe, many nights from tonight, many years from now, when you're as old or far much older than me, when they ask you what you did in this awful time, you will tell them—one part humble and one part proud—'I was the drummer boy at the battle of Owl Creek,' or the Tennessee River, or maybe they'll just name it after the church there. 'I was the drummer boy at Shiloh.' Good grief, that has a beat and sound to it fitting for Mr. Longfellow. 'I was the drummer boy at Shiloh.' Who will ever hear those words and not know you, boy, or what you thought this night, or what you'll think tomorrow or the next day when we must get up on our legs and *move!*"

The general stood up. "Well, then. Bless you, boy. Good night."

"Good night, sir." And tobacco, brass, boot polish, salt sweat and leather, the man moved away through the grass.

Joby lay for a moment, staring but unable to see where the man had gone. He swallowed. He wiped his eyes. He cleared his throat. He settled himself. Then, at last, very slowly and firmly, he turned the drum so that it faced up toward the sky.

He lay next to it, his arm around it, feeling the tremor, the touch, the muted thunder as, all the rest of the April night in the year 1862, near the Tennessee River, not far from the Owl Creek, very close to the church named Shiloh, the peach blossoms fell on the drum.

Guide for Responding

◆ LITERATURE AND YOUR LIFE

Reader's Response Do you think Joby should have enlisted as a drummer boy? Why or why not?

Thematic Focus What new understanding of himself and his role does Joby get from the general?

☑ Check Your Comprehension

1. How old is the drummer boy?
2. What is the boy thinking about as he lies in the orchard?
3. What frightens him about the coming battle?
4. Why did the general cry the night before?
5. Why does the general say he needs Joby?

◆ Critical Thinking

INTERPRET

1. In what ways is Joby like and unlike the other soldiers? **[Compare and Contrast]**
2. Why do you think the general stops to talk to Joby? **[Infer]**
3. In what way is Joby "the heart of the army"? **[Interpret]**
4. How do you think Joby feels after his talk with the general? Explain. **[Draw Conclusions]**

EVALUATE

5. Is the role of the drummer boy as crucial as the general says? Explain. **[Evaluate]**

APPLY

6. The writer Mark Twain once said, "Courage is resistance to fear, mastery of fear—not absence of fear." How does this quotation apply to the story? **[Apply]**

Guide for Responding (continued)

◆ Reading for Success

LITERAL COMPREHENSION STRATEGIES

Review the reading strategies and the notes that show how to understand a writer's words and messages. Then, apply the strategies to answer the following:

1. Break down the sentence on page 8 that begins, "And, maybe, many nights . . ." What is the subject? What key words tell what the subject will do?
2. Use context clues to find the meaning of *tremor* on page 8. Explain how you figured out the meaning.
3. Paraphrase the paragraph on page 7 that begins, "'Why am I telling you . . .'" What is the paragraph's basic meaning?

◆ Build Vocabulary

USING THE WORD PART *bene-*

In your notebook, explain how the word part *bene-* ("well" or "good") contributes its upbeat meaning to each italicized word:

The general showed Joby the *benefit* that the soldiers would receive from his drumming. In that sense, the general's visit to Joby was more than *beneficial*. It was a *benediction*.

SPELLING STRATEGY

When adding *-ed* to a two-syllable word, don't double the final consonant if the stress is on the first syllable:

riv´ et + -ed = riveted

On your paper, add *-ed* to the following verbs:

1. travel   2. hinder   3. label

USING THE WORD BANK

On your paper, write the word closest in meaning to that of the first word.

1. benediction: (a) curse, (b) wealth, (c) blessing
2. riveted: (a) fastened, (b) drilled, (c) split
3. compounded: (a) flattened, (b) complicated, (c) mixed
4. resolute: (a) determined, (b) absolute, (c) calm

◆ Literary Focus

HISTORICAL SETTING

Bradbury creates a **historical setting,** a place and time from history, by using such diverse details as peach blossoms and bayonets. However, it takes more than details—even accurate ones—to bring the past to life. The real emotions of made-up characters give added truth to the story.

1. Identify three additional details from the Civil War era. Then, explain your choices.
2. The general blesses Joby as he leaves. How does this expression of feeling give added truth to the details of the general's appearance?

◆ Build Grammar Skills

NOUNS

Nouns are words that name a person, animal, place, thing, or idea. In just the first three paragraphs of "The Drummer Boy of Shiloh," Bradbury uses nouns that name each.

Person	boy	**Thing**	branch
Animal	bird	**Idea**	silence
Place	field		

Practice On your paper, rewrite each sentence, underlining the nouns. Then, tell whether each noun is a person, animal, place, thing, or idea.

1. The young drummer boy felt solemn.
2. The soldiers camped in a field near the Owl Creek.
3. A moth brushed his face and landed on a branch.
4. The soldiers dreamed of battles.
5. Raw youth was their protection.

Writing Application Rewrite each sentence, replacing the italicized nouns with nouns of the same kind. For example, replace a person with a person and a thing with a thing. Be sure the new sentence makes sense.

1. The *boy* was camped near the *creek*.
2. The *blossom* fell onto the *drum*.
3. How could the *moth* understand the boy's *nervousness*?

Build Your Portfolio

 Idea Bank

Writing

1. **Diary Entry** As Joby, write a diary entry in which you respond to what the general has just said to you.

2. **Job Manual** Review the general's description of a drummer boy's duties. Then, write a brief manual that will teach new drummer boys how to perform their job. Divide your information into categories, such as *duties* and *qualifications*. **[Career Link]**

3. **News Article** You're a reporter for a newspaper and have overheard the general speaking to Joby. Write an article about this scene that will appeal to your readers. **[Career Link]**

Speaking and Listening

4. **Retelling** Imagine you're Joby as an old man. Tell your grandchildren the story of what happened to you on the night before the Battle of Shiloh. Perform this retelling for the class. **[Social Studies Link; Performing Arts Link]**

5. **Debate [Group Activity]** Form two groups and debate this proposition: that the age of enlistment in the armed forces should be lowered to sixteen. Have a panel of students judge the outcome based on the content of the argument and the skill of the presentation. **[Social Studies Link]**

Projects

6. **Report on the Civil War** Write a report for your classmates on the roles that teenagers played in the Civil War—as drummer boys, bugle boys, and soldiers. **[Social Studies Link]**

7. **Time Capsule [Group Activity]** With a group, prepare a time capsule to be opened in a hundred years. List items you'd include to give people of the future a picture of our time. Also, write brief explanations to go with each of the items. **[Social Studies Link]**

 Writing Mini-Lesson

Letter Home From a Soldier

Some soldiers camping near Joby that night must have been writing letters home. Step into the shoes of one of those soldiers and write a letter home to your anxious family. Combine your deep feelings with accurate historical details to give your letter the ring of truth.

Writing Skills Focus: Show, Don't Tell

Make your letter lively by **showing** feelings and events, not just telling about them. Notice how Bradbury doesn't tell you that the boy is nervous. Instead, he shows you the boy's nervous behavior:

Model From the Story

At midnight a peach stone left miraculously on a branch through winter, flicked by a bird . . . struck once, like panic, which jerked the boy upright.

Prewriting Imagine yourself as a soldier in camp on the eve of a Civil War battle. Jot down what you might be thinking, seeing, hearing, smelling, tasting, and touching. Also, jot down ideas and feelings to tell your parents.

Drafting Put yourself in the time and place described in "The Drummer Boy of Shiloh," and begin drafting. Use vivid descriptions and stories to show your parents what's happening at camp and how much you miss them.

> ◆ **Grammar Application**
>
> Circle the nouns in your letter. Where appropriate, replace general nouns with more specific ones.

Revising Reread your draft critically. Take out references to items, like appliances, that wouldn't have existed in 1862. Find passages in which you just tell your parents what's happening or how you feel. Revise these passages by adding examples or stories to show what you mean.

PART **1** $\mathscr{A}\!\textit{rriving}$
at Understanding

Untitled, Jim Lang, Stockworks

Guide for Reading

Meet the Author:

Shirley Jackson (1919–1965)

As the mother of four energetic children, Shirley Jackson once said that she wrote because "It's the only chance I get to sit down." As a writer, she produced mainly two types of stories—spine-tingling tales of supernatural events and hilarious stories about daily life. She made a joking reference to her contrasting styles by giving her family stories titles that sound as if they were horror tales: *Life Among the Savages* and *Raising Demons*.

From Family Stories to Horror Stories In all, Jackson wrote fifty-five short stories, several articles and other nonfiction works, two family books, a play, seven novels, and some poetry. Among her novels are the horror and suspense classics *The Haunting of Hill House* (1959) and *We Have Always Lived in the Castle* (1962). Author Dorothy Parker once wryly commented that Jackson "restores my faith in terror and dread."

THE STORY BEHIND THE STORY

Many fictional stories enlarge real characters and events. Often the characters and events come from the writer's own life. Shirley Jackson collected countless ideas from her four children. The main character in "Charles" is patterned after Jackson's son Laurie.

◆ LITERATURE AND YOUR LIFE

CONNECT YOUR EXPERIENCE

"The dog did it!" "Not me—my invisible twin!" You have probably heard the amazing excuses children use to cover up bad behavior. What outrageous excuses have you given or heard? In "Charles," you'll read about a young boy who comes up with a unique way to cover for his bad behavior.

THEMATIC FOCUS: Arriving at Understanding

As you read "Charles," ask yourself who's learned more—Laurie, the main character, or his parents.

◆ Background for Understanding

SCIENCE

School can be a place of fun as well as a place of learning, as the photograph at right suggests. Laurie, the boy in "Charles," is just beginning kindergarten, adjusting to a new school environment. Some experts believe that children's play—both make-believe and group-oriented—can help children adjust to such new situations. In "Charles," you'll meet a boy who focuses on just one type of play and causes mayhem in the classroom.

◆ Build Vocabulary

WORD ROOTS: -cred-

The word root -cred- means "believe." With the prefix in-, which makes what follows negative or opposite, the word *incredulous* means "not willing to believe." Adding the suffix -ly creates the adverb *incredulously*.

WORD BANK

Which words on the list might describe how something is done? Check the Build Vocabulary boxes on pages 15 and 17 to see if you chose correctly.

renounced
insolently
elaborately
simultaneously
incredulously

◆ Charles ◆

◆ Literary Focus

POINT OF VIEW

Every story is told by someone—either by a narrator outside the story or by a character in the story. The vantage point or perspective from which a story is told is referred to as its **point of view.** "Charles" is told from the point of view of a character in the story, the main character's mother.

◆ Reading Strategy

BREAK DOWN LONG SENTENCES

Have you ever gotten lost in the middle of a sentence? When you come across a long sentence, it can be helpful to **break it down**. Begin by reading the sentence in meaningful sections, not word by word. Look for natural breaks, signaled by punctuation. Then, look for main parts in each section of a long sentence.

You can use a chart like this one:

What is the sentence about?	What does the sentence say about the subject?
Laurie (her son)	Started kindergarten Renounced overalls Began wearing jeans

Charles

Shirley Jackson

The day my son Laurie started kindergarten he <u>renounced</u> corduroy overalls with bibs and began wearing blue jeans with a belt; I watched him go off the first morning with the older girl next door, seeing clearly that an era of my life was ended, my sweet-voiced nursery-school tot replaced by a long-trousered, swaggering[1] character who forgot to stop at the corner and wave good-bye to me.

He came home the same way, the front door slamming open, his cap on the floor, and the voice suddenly become raucous[2] shouting, "Isn't anybody *here?*"

At lunch he spoke <u>insolently</u> to his father, spilled his baby sister's milk, and remarked that his teacher said we were not to take the name of the Lord in vain.

"How *was* school today?" I asked, elaborately casual.

"All right," he said.

"Did you learn anything?" his father asked.

Laurie regarded his father coldly. "I didn't learn nothing," he said.

"Anything," I said. "Didn't learn anything."

"The teacher spanked a boy, though," Laurie said, addressing his bread and butter. "For being fresh," he added, with his mouth full.

"What did he do?" I asked. "Who was it?"

Laurie thought. "It was Charles," he said. "He was fresh. The teacher spanked him and made him stand in a corner. He was awfully fresh."

"What did he do?" I asked again, but Laurie slid off his chair, took a cookie, and left, while his father was still saying, "See here, young man."

The next day Laurie remarked at lunch, as soon as he sat down, "Well, Charles was bad again today." He grinned enormously and said, "Today Charles hit the teacher."

"Good heavens," I said, mindful of the Lord's name, "I suppose he got spanked again?"

"He sure did," Laurie said. "Look up," he said to his father.

"What?" his father said, looking up.

◆ Build Vocabulary

renounced (ri nounst´) *v.*: Gave up

insolently (in´ sə lənt lē) *adv.*: Boldly disrespectful in speech or behavior

---

1. **swaggering** (swag´ ər iŋ) *v.*: Strutting; walking with a bold step.
2. **raucous** (rô´ kəs) *adj.*: Boisterous; disorderly.

"Look down," Laurie said. "Look at my thumb. Gee, you're dumb." He began to laugh insanely.

"Why did Charles hit the teacher?" I asked quickly.

"Because she tried to make him color with red crayons," Laurie said. "Charles wanted to color with green crayons so he hit the teacher and she spanked him and said nobody play with Charles but everybody did."

The third day—it was Wednesday of the first week—Charles bounced a see-saw on to the head of a little girl and made her bleed, and the teacher made him stay inside all during recess. Thursday Charles had to stand in a corner during story-time because he kept pounding his feet on the floor. Friday Charles was deprived of blackboard privileges because he threw chalk.

On Saturday I remarked to my husband, "Do you think kindergarten is too unsettling for Laurie? All this toughness, and bad grammar, and this Charles boy sounds like such a bad influence."

"It'll be all right," my husband said reassuringly. "Bound to be people like Charles in the world. Might as well meet them now as later."

On Monday Laurie came home late, full of news. "Charles," he shouted as he came up the hill; I was waiting anxiously on the front steps. "Charles," Laurie yelled all the way up the hill, "Charles was bad again."

"Come right in," I said, as soon as he came close enough. "Lunch is waiting."

"You know what Charles did?" he demanded, following me through the door. "Charles yelled so in school they sent a boy in from first grade to tell the teacher she had to make Charles keep quiet, and so Charles had to stay after school. And so all the children stayed to watch him."

"What did he do?" I asked.

"He just sat there," Laurie said, climbing into his chair at the table. "Hi, Pop, y'old dust mop."

"Charles had to stay after school today," I told my husband. "Everyone stayed with him."

"What does this Charles look like?" my husband asked Laurie. "What's his other name?"

"He's bigger than me," Laurie said. "And he doesn't have any rubbers and he doesn't ever wear a jacket."

Monday night was the first Parent-Teachers meeting, and only the fact that the baby had a cold kept me from going; I wanted passionately to meet Charles's mother. On Tuesday Laurie remarked suddenly, "Our teacher had a friend come to see her in school today."

"Charles's mother?" my husband and I asked simultaneously.

"Naaah," Laurie said scornfully. "It was a man who came and made us do exercises, we had to touch our toes. Look." He climbed down from his chair and squatted down and touched his toes. "Like this," he said. He got solemnly back into his chair and said, picking up his fork, "Charles didn't even *do* exercises."

"That's fine," I said heartily. "Didn't Charles want to do exercises?"

"Naaah," Laurie said. "Charles was so fresh to the teacher's friend he wasn't *let* do exercises."

"Fresh again?" I said.

"He kicked the teacher's friend," Laurie said. "The teacher's friend told Charles to touch his toes like I just did and Charles kicked him."

"What are they going to do about Charles, do you suppose?" Laurie's father asked him.

Laurie shrugged elaborately. "Throw him out of school, I guess," he said.

Wednesday and Thursday were routine; Charles yelled during story hour and hit a boy in the stomach and made him cry. On Friday Charles stayed after school again and

---

◆ **Build Vocabulary**

simultaneously (sī′ məl tā′ nē əs lē) *adv.*: At the same time

▲ **Critical Viewing** Examine the expressions on these children's faces. Which of them might have a personality like that of Charles? [**Connect**]

so did all the other children.

With the third week of kindergarten

◆ **Reading Strategy**
Break down this long sentence into sections. What is each section about?

Charles was an institution in our family; the baby was being a Charles when she cried all afternoon; Laurie did a Charles when he filled his wagon full of mud and pulled it through the kitchen; even my husband, when he caught his elbow in the telephone cord and pulled the telephone, ashtray, and a bowl of flowers off the table, said, after the first minute, "Looks like Charles."

During the third and fourth weeks it looked like a reformation in Charles; Laurie reported grimly at lunch on Thursday of the third week, "Charles was so good today the teacher gave him an apple."

"What?" I said, and my husband added warily, "You mean Charles?"

"Charles," Laurie said. "He gave the crayons around and he picked up the books afterward and the teacher said he was her helper."

"What happened?" I asked incredulously.

◆ **Build Vocabulary**

incredulously (in krej′ oo ləs lē) *adv.*: With doubt or disbelief

"He was her helper, that's all," Laurie said, and shrugged.

"Can this be true, about Charles?" I asked my husband that night. "Can something like this happen?"

"Wait and see," my husband said cynically.[3] "When you've got a Charles to deal with, this may mean he's only plotting." He seemed to be wrong. For over a week Charles was the teacher's helper; each day he handed things out and he picked things up; no one had to stay after school.

"The PTA meeting's next week again," I told my husband one evening. "I'm going to find Charles's mother there."

"Ask her what happened to Charles," my husband said. "I'd like to know."

"I'd like to know myself," I said.

On Friday of that week things were back to normal. "You know what Charles did today?" Laurie demanded at the lunch table, in a voice slightly awed. "He told a little girl to say a word and she said it and the teacher washed her mouth out with soap and Charles laughed."

"What word?" his father asked unwisely, and Laurie said, "I'll have to whisper it to you, it's so bad." He got down off his chair and went around to his father. His father bent his head down and Laurie whispered joyfully. His father's eyes widened.

"Did Charles tell the little girl to say *that?*" he asked respectfully.

"She said it *twice,*" Laurie said. "Charles told her to say it *twice.*"

"What happened to Charles?" my husband asked.

"Nothing," Laurie said. "He was passing out the crayons."

Monday morning Charles abandoned the little girl and said the evil word himself three or four times, getting his mouth washed out with soap each time. He also threw chalk.

My husband came to the door with me that evening as I set out for the PTA meeting. "Invite her over for a cup of tea after the meeting," he said. "I want to get a look at her."

"If only she's there," I said prayerfully.

"She'll be there," my husband said. I don't see how they could hold a PTA meeting without Charles's mother."

At the meeting I sat restlessly, scanning each comfortable matronly face, trying to determine which one hid the secret of Charles. None of them looked to me haggard enough. No one stood up in the meeting and apologized for the way her son had been acting. No one mentioned Charles.

◆ Literary Focus
Why do you think no one mentions Charles at the PTA meeting?

After the meeting I identified and sought out Laurie's kindergarten teacher. She had a plate with a cup of tea and a piece of chocolate cake; I had a plate with a cup of tea and a piece of marshmallow cake. We maneuvered[4] up to one another cautiously, and smiled.

"I've been so anxious to meet you," I said. "I'm Laurie's mother."

"We're all so interested in Laurie," she said.

"Well, he certainly likes kindergarten," I said. "He talks about it all the time."

"We had a little trouble adjusting, the first week or so," she said primly, "but now he's a fine little helper. With occasional lapses, of course."

"Laurie usually adjusts very quickly," I said. "I suppose this time it's Charles's influence."

"Charles?"

"Yes," I said, laughing, "you must have your hands full in that kindergarten, with Charles."

"Charles?" she said. "We don't have any Charles in the kindergarten."

---

4. maneuvered (mə nōō´ vərd) *v.*: Moved in a planned way.

---

3. cynically (sin´ i klē) *adv.*: With disbelief as to the sincerity of people's intentions or actions.

School experiences like those in "Charles" are often funny and memorable. In Bill Watterson's popular comic strip, he often uses Calvin's school experiences as humorous subject matter.

Calvin and Hobbes

by Bill Watterson

1. Why do you think the substitute teacher went home at noon?
2. In what ways is Calvin, the boy in the cartoon, similar to Laurie, the boy in "Charles"?

Guide for Responding

◆ LITERATURE AND YOUR LIFE

Reader's Response Were you surprised to learn that Charles and Laurie were the same person? Why or why not?

Thematic Focus What lesson do you think the narrator learns about her son?

☑ Check Your Comprehension

1. Why does Charles become a well-known character to the family?
2. Give three examples of Charles's bad behavior at school.
3. Give three examples of Laurie's bad behavior at home.
4. What does Laurie's mother discover about her son at the PTA meeting?

◆ Critical Thinking

INTERPRET

1. How do you think Laurie feels when he starts kindergarten? **[Infer]**
2. How is Charles's behavior at school similar to Laurie's at home? **[Compare and Contrast]**
3. Why do you think Laurie invented Charles? **[Draw Conclusions]**
4. How do you think Laurie will react after his parents learn his secret? **[Infer]**

EVALUATE

5. Does Laurie deserve to be punished, or has he learned his lesson? **[Make a Judgment]**

APPLY

6. How would this story be different if Laurie were entering high school? **[Hypothesize]**

◆ Guide for Responding (continued)

◆ Reading Strategy

BREAK DOWN LONG SENTENCES

Like many stories, "Charles" contains some long, difficult sentences. It's helpful to **break down the sentences** to identify basic parts. Once you've done that, you can reread to get the full picture.

Divide each long sentence into sections. Tell what each section is about (the subject) and what the rest of the section says about the subject.

1. For over a week Charles was the teacher's helper; each day he handed things out and he picked things up; no one had to stay after school.
2. "We had a little trouble adjusting, the first week or so," she said primly, "but now he's a fine little helper."

◆ Build Vocabulary

USING THE WORD ROOT -cred-

Jackson uses the adverb *incredulously* to show the narrator's disbelief: "'What happened?' I asked incredulously." Use the meaning of the word root *-cred-* to define these words. Use a dictionary to check your definitions.

1. incredible   2. credible   3. credence

SPELLING STRATEGY

You can change most adjectives to adverbs by adding *-ly*. When you add *-ly,* do not change the spelling of the adjective.

vicious → viciously   absolute → absolutely
ideal → ideally   respectful → respectfully

Copy each adjective. Then write the adverb form.

1. close   2. regal   3. fortunate   4. jealous

USING THE WORD BANK

On your paper, complete the paragraph sensibly, using the Word Bank. Use each word only once.

Tia's teacher, Mr. Acevedo, stared at her paper _____?_____. The page was covered with drawings but no words. "I have _____?_____ language in favor of Art," Tia declared. Mr. Acevedo laughed, but he refused to accept the paper. Tia stamped her foot _____?_____ and _____?_____ started to pout.

◆ Literary Focus

POINT OF VIEW

"Charles" is told from the **point of view** of Laurie's mother. It is through her eyes that the story unfolds; we learn information only as Laurie's mother learns it.

1. How does Laurie's mother learn about Charles and his doings?
2. How would "Charles" be different if it were told from Laurie's point of view?
3. Explain how the point of view from which "Charles" is told helps contribute to the surprise ending.

◆ Build Grammar Skills

COMMON AND PROPER NOUNS

Nouns may be common or proper. **Common nouns** name any person, place, thing, or idea. **Proper nouns** name a particular person, place, thing, or idea. Capitalize proper nouns wherever they appear. Do not capitalize common nouns unless they begin a sentence.

Example: Charles bounced a see-saw on to
the head of a little girl. . . .

Practice Write the sentences on your paper. Underline common nouns and circle proper nouns.

1. Laurie regarded his father coldly.
2. "What does this Charles look like?" my husband asked Laurie.
3. On Friday of that week things were back to normal.
4. He got down off his chair and went around to his father.
5. No one stood up in the meeting and apologized for the way her son had been acting.

Writing Application Rewrite each sentence, fixing capitalization in common and proper nouns.

1. Edward is to begin Kindergarten.
2. Listen to the Crossing Guard's directions.
3. On tuesday, we're going on a field trip.

Build Your Portfolio

 Idea Bank

Writing

1. **Description** Using details from the story, write a description of Charles and his behavior at school.

2. **Letter** Write a letter from Laurie's teacher to his family, describing his behavior at school. Describe Laurie's actions, and tell how they affect the class.

3. **Problem-and-Solution Essay** Laurie's naughty behavior poses a problem to his teacher and his parents. Write a problem-and-solution essay in which you lay out steps they could take in handling the situation.

Speaking and Listening

4. **Retelling** Imagine that you are Laurie several years after the story takes place. Now you are in the eighth grade, telling a story about your own childhood. Tell the story of "Charles" from your new point of view. **[Performing Arts Link]**

5. **Advisory Panel [Group Activity]** With a group of classmates, form an advisory panel to discuss how to deal with children who misbehave, like Charles. Hold your discussion in front of the class.

Projects

6. **Multimedia Display [Group Activity]** With a group, collect kindergarten stories and pictures from classmates and peers. Working together, design and assemble the stories into a multimedia display about childhood memories. **[Media Link]**

7. **Comic Strip** Create a comic strip featuring Charles as a main character. What humorous activities might you show Charles doing? Use speech balloons to indicate dialogue. **[Art Link]**

 Writing Mini-Lesson

Humorous Description

If this story were true, Laurie's parents would probably have plenty of stories to tell about their son's mischief. Think back to your own childhood, and write a humorous description of a childhood event. Include details that will bring the description to life for your readers. As you develop your description, focus on creating a light and humorous tone.

Writing Skills Focus: Appropriate Tone

Tone refers to a writer's attitude toward his or her subject. Choose words carefully, and use exaggeration to create a humorous **tone** for your description. In the following example, words were changed and one detail was exaggerated to change the tone from neutral to humorous.

Neutral Tone: He swallowed the uncooked pasta.

Humorous Tone: He downed the entire box of macaroni.

Prewriting Decide on the childhood event you will describe. List the characters involved; jot down notes about who they are and their actions and responses. You may also plan out the series of events you're going to describe.

Drafting Begin your draft by telling the story. Be sure that you set the scene, and include all the characters and events from your Prewriting notes.

Revising Review your draft to be sure that the characters are fully described and that the events are clear. Read it aloud, and listen for comic words and rhythms. You can often change the tone of a passage by replacing one or two words.

> ◆ **Grammar Application**
> Reread your draft to be sure that you've capitalized proper nouns but not common nouns.

Guide for Reading

Meet the Author:

Maya Angelou (1928–   )

Born Marguerite Johnson in St. Louis, Missouri, Maya Angelou received her unusual first name from her brother, Bailey, who referred to her as "mya sister." Maya and Bailey were raised by their grandmother, who owned a country store in rural Arkansas.

Overcoming Obstacles Growing up in the segregated South did not prevent Maya Angelou from breaking through the barriers of racism and poverty to remarkable achievements in many areas. She has been a streetcar conductor in San Francisco, a journalist, an actor, a civil rights worker, a teacher, and a poet.

A Presidential Commission In 1992, Maya Angelou was asked by President-elect Bill Clinton to write a poem for his inauguration. In January 1993, Angelou read "On the Pulse of Morning" for an appreciative President and an admiring nation.

THE STORY BEHIND THE STORY

I Know Why the Caged Bird Sings is a true account of Maya Angelou's humble beginnings. The excerpt included here tells how her life was influenced by a remarkable woman named Mrs. Flowers.

The publication *I Know Why the Caged Bird Sings* places Angelou among the first African American women to hit the bestseller list. Her story later became a screenplay that aired as a television special.

◆ LITERATURE AND YOUR LIFE

CONNECT YOUR EXPERIENCE

In this true-life story, a young girl is taken under the wing of a very special person. Perhaps you, too, have received guidance from a special person—a parent, sibling, coach, or friend—who helped you to develop self-esteem.

THEMATIC FOCUS: Arriving at Understanding

As you read, take note of how Mrs. Flowers, a friend of Angelou's family, helped Angelou to appreciate her own abilities.

◆ Background for Understanding

HISTORY

When Angelou was growing up in Arkansas in the 1930's and 1940's, blacks and whites lived apart and attended separate schools. In addition, blacks were excluded from many social facilities and barred from all-white restaurants. As an African American woman, Angelou experienced both racial and gender discrimination, yet with the help of Mrs. Flowers, she learned to rise above it.

◆ Build Vocabulary

RELATED WORDS: FORMS OF *tolerate*

The verb *tolerate* means "to accept." Other forms of *tolerate* include *tolerance, tolerable,* and *intolerant,* which is used in the story and means "not accepting others' ideas."

WORD BANK

Which words from the list do you think are adjectives? Why? Check the Build Vocabulary boxes on pages 25, 27, and 28 to see if you chose correctly.

fiscal
taut
benign
infuse
intolerant
couched

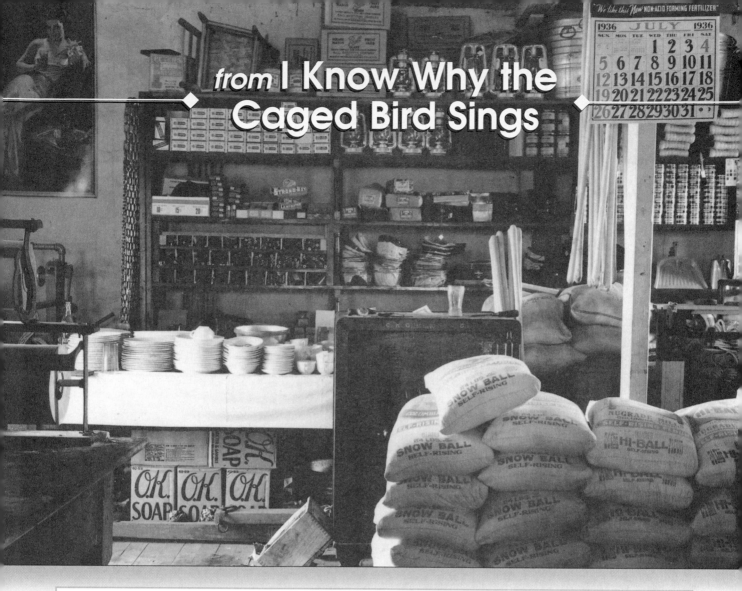

from I Know Why the Caged Bird Sings

◆ Literary Focus

MEMOIR

A **memoir** is a form of autobiographical writing—true writing from a person's own life—that deals with the writer's memory of someone or of a significant event. In this excerpt from *I Know Why the Caged Bird Sings*, Angelou writes about her memories of working in the family store, like the one in the photograph.

◆ Reading Strategy

REREAD OR READ AHEAD

Reading can be a many-step process. On a first reading, you may miss details or have questions about what's happening. It makes sense, then, to go back and **reread** a passage to clarify details. Sometimes you may need to **read ahead** to find answers to questions or to understand why an author is presenting certain information.

A chart like the one below can help you note when to reread or read ahead to find an answer.

Reading	Rereading	Reading Ahead
Take notes Ask questions	Clarify details	Find answers

from
I Know Why the Caged Bird Sings

Maya Angelou

We lived with our grandmother and uncle in the rear of the Store (it was always spoken of with a capital s), which she had owned some twenty-five years.

Early in the century, Momma (we soon stopped calling her Grandmother) sold lunches to the sawmen in the lumberyard (east Stamps) and the seedmen at the cotton gin (west Stamps). Her crisp meat pies and cool lemonade, when joined to her miraculous ability to be in two places at the same time, assured her business success. From being a mobile lunch counter, she set up a stand between the two points of <u>fiscal</u> interest and supplied the workers' needs for a few years. Then she had the Store built in the heart of the Negro area. Over the years it became the lay center of activities in town. On Saturdays, barbers sat their customers in the shade on the porch of the Store, and troubadours[1] on their ceaseless crawlings through the South leaned across its benches and sang their sad songs of The Brazos[2] while they played juice harps[3] and cigar-box guitars.

The formal name of the Store was the Wm. Johnson General Merchandise Store. Customers could find food staples, a good variety of colored thread, mash for hogs, corn for

---

1. **troubadours** (troo′ bə dôrz′) *n.*: Traveling singers.
2. **The Brazos** (bräz′ əs): Area in central Texas near the Brazos River.
3. **juice** (joos) **harps:** Small musical instruments held between the teeth and played by plucking.

▲ **Critical Viewing** The town in this painting is similar to the town of Stamps, as described by Angelou. What might it be like to grow up in a town like this? **[Speculate]**

chickens, coal oil for lamps, light bulbs for the wealthy, shoestrings, hair dressing, balloons, and flower seeds. Anything not visible had only to be ordered.

◆ **Reading Strategy**
Who is meant by the pronoun *we*? Reread to find out.

Until we became familiar enough to belong to the Store and it to us, we were locked up in a Fun House of Things where the attendant had gone home for life. . . .

Weighing the half-pounds of flour, excluding the scoop, and depositing them dust-free into the thin paper sacks held a simple kind of adventure for me. I developed an eye for measuring how full a silver-looking ladle of flour, mash, meal, sugar or corn had to be to push the scale indicator over to eight ounces or one

pound. When I was absolutely accurate our appreciative customers used to admire: "Sister Henderson sure got some smart grandchildrens." If I was off in the Store's favor, the eagle-eyed women would say, "Put some more in that sack, child. Don't you try to make your profit offa me."

Then I would quietly but persistently punish myself. For every bad judgment, the fine was no silver-wrapped kisses, the sweet chocolate drops that I loved more than anything in the world, except Bailey. And maybe canned pineapples. My obsession with pineapples nearly drove me mad. I dreamt of the

◆ **Build Vocabulary**
fiscal (fis´ kəl) *adj.*: Having to do with finances

from *I Know Why the Caged Bird Sings* ◆ 25

days when I would be grown and able to buy a whole carton for myself alone.

Although the syrupy golden rings sat in their exotic cans on our shelves year round, we only tasted them during Christmas. Momma used the juice to make almost-black fruit cakes. Then she lined heavy soot-encrusted iron skillets with the pineapple rings for rich upside-down cakes. Bailey and I received one slice each, and I carried mine around for hours, shredding off the fruit until nothing was left except the perfume on my fingers. I'd like to think that my desire for pineapples was so sacred that I wouldn't allow myself to steal a can (which was possible) and eat it alone out in the garden, but I'm certain that I must have weighed the possibility of the scent exposing me and didn't have the nerve to attempt it.

Until I was thirteen and left Arkansas for good, the Store was my favorite place to be. Alone and empty in the mornings, it looked like an unopened present from a stranger. Opening the front doors was pulling the ribbon off the unexpected gift. The light would come in softly (we faced north), easing itself over the shelves of mackerel, salmon, tobacco, thread. It fell flat on the big vat of lard and by noontime during the summer the grease had softened to a thick soup. Whenever I walked into the Store in the afternoon, I sensed that it was tired. I alone could hear the slow pulse of its job half done. But just before bedtime, after numerous people had walked in and out, had argued over their bills, or joked about their neighbors, or just dropped in "to give Sister Henderson a 'Hi y'all,'" the promise of magic mornings returned to the Store and spread itself over the family in washed life waves. . . .

When Maya was about ten years old, she returned to Stamps from a visit to St. Louis with her mother. She had become depressed and withdrawn.

For nearly a year, I sopped around the house, the Store, the school and the church, like an old biscuit, dirty and inedible. Then I met, or rather got to know, the lady who threw me my first lifeline.

Mrs. Bertha Flowers was the aristocrat[4] of Black Stamps. She had the grace of control to appear warm in the coldest weather, and on the Arkansas summer days it seemed she had a private breeze which swirled around, cooling her. She was thin without the <u>taut</u> look of wiry people, and her printed voile[5] dresses and flowered hats were as right for her as denim overalls for a farmer. She was our side's answer to the richest white woman in town.

Her skin was a rich black that would have peeled like a plum if snagged, but then no one would have thought of getting close enough to Mrs. Flowers to ruffle her dress, let alone snag her skin. She didn't encourage familiarity. She wore gloves too.

I don't think I ever saw Mrs. Flowers laugh, but she smiled often. A slow widening of her thin black lips to show even, small white teeth, then the slow effortless closing. When she chose to smile on me, I always wanted to thank her. The action was so graceful and inclusively <u>benign</u>.

She was one of the few gentlewomen I have ever known, and has remained throughout my life the measure of what a human being can be. . . .

One summer afternoon, sweet-milk fresh in my memory, she stopped at the Store to buy provisions. Another Negro woman of her health and age would have been expected to carry the paper sacks home in one hand, but Momma said, "Sister Flowers, I'll send Bailey up to your house with these things."

She smiled that slow dragging smile, "Thank you, Mrs. Henderson. I'd prefer Marguerite, though." My name was beautiful when she said it. "I've been meaning to talk to her, anyway." They gave each other age-group looks.

---

4. **aristocrat** (ə ris´ tə krat) *n.*: Person belonging to the upper class.
5. **voile** (voil) *n.*: Light cotton fabric.

Momma said, "Well, that's all right then. Sister, go and change your dress. You going to Sister Flowers's. . . ."

There was a little path beside the rocky road, and Mrs. Flowers walked in front swinging her arms and picking her way over the stones.

She said, without turning her head, to me, "I hear you're doing very good school work, Marguerite, but that it's all written. The teachers report that they have trouble getting you to talk in class." We passed the triangular farm on our left and the path widened to allow us to walk together. I hung back in the separate unasked and unanswerable questions.

"Come and walk along with me, Marguerite." I couldn't have refused even if I wanted to. She pronounced my name so nicely. Or more correctly, she spoke each word with such clarity that I was certain a foreigner who didn't understand English could have understood her.

◆ **Literary Focus**
What does this passage reveal about Angelou's personality?

"Now no one is going to make you talk— possibly no one can. But bear in mind, language is man's way of communicating with his fellow man and it is language alone which separates him from the lower animals." That was a totally new idea to me, and I would need time to think about it.

"Your grandmother says you read a lot. Every chance you get. That's good, but not good enough. Words mean more than what is set down on paper. It takes the human voice to <u>infuse</u> them with the shades of deeper meaning."

I memorized the part about the human voice infusing words. It seemed so valid and poetic.

She said she was going to give me some books and that I not only must read them, I must read them aloud. She suggested that I

◆ **Build Vocabulary**
taut (tôt) *adj.*: Tightly stretched
benign (bi nīn´) *adj.*: Kindly
infuse (in fyo͞oz´) *v.*: Put into

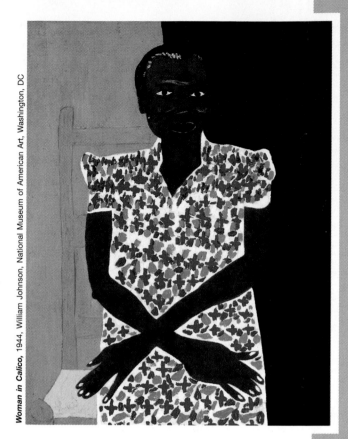

Woman in Calico, 1944, William Johnson, National Museum of American Art, Washington, DC

▲ **Critical Viewing** Reread the description of Mrs. Flowers on page 26. How well does this painting capture her essence? Explain. [Assess]

try to make a sentence sound in as many different ways as possible.

"I'll accept no excuse if you return a book to me that has been badly handled." My imagination boggled at the punishment I would deserve if in fact I did abuse a book of Mrs. Flowers'. Death would be too kind and brief.

The odors in the house surprised me. Somehow I had never connected Mrs. Flowers with food or eating or any other common experience of common people. There must have been an outhouse, too, but my mind never recorded it.

The sweet scent of vanilla had met us as she opened the door.

"I made tea cookies this morning. You see, I had planned to invite you for cookies and lemonade so we could have this little chat. The lemonade is in the icebox."

It followed that Mrs. Flowers would have ice on an ordinary day, when most families in our town bought ice late on Saturdays only a few times during the summer to be used in the wooden ice cream freezers.

She took the bags from me and disappeared through the kitchen door. I looked around the room that I had never in my wildest fantasies imagined I would see. Browned photographs leered or threatened from the walls and the white, freshly done curtains pushed against themselves and against the wind. I wanted to gobble up the room entire and take it to Bailey, who would help me analyze and enjoy it.

"Have a seat, Marguerite. Over there by the table." She carried a platter covered with a tea towel. Although she warned that she hadn't tried her hand at baking sweets for some time, I was certain that like everything else about her the cookies would be perfect.

They were flat round wafers, slightly browned on the edges and butter-yellow in the center. With the cold lemonade they were sufficient for childhood's lifelong diet. Remembering my manners, I took nice little ladylike bites off the edges. She said she had made them expressly for me and that she had a few in the kitchen that I could take home to my brother. So I jammed one whole cake in my mouth and the rough crumbs scratched the insides of my jaws, and if I hadn't had to swallow, it would have been a dream come true.

As I ate she began the first of what we later called "my lessons in living." She said that I must always be <u>intolerant</u> of ignorance but understanding of illiteracy. That some people, unable to go to school, were more educated and even more intelligent than college professors. She

encouraged me to listen carefully to what country people called mother wit. That in those homely sayings was <u>couched</u> the collective wisdom of generations.

When I finished the cookies she brushed off the table and brought a thick, small book from the bookcase. I had read *A Tale of Two Cities* and found it up to my standards as a romantic novel. She opened the first page and I heard poetry for the first time in my life.

"It was the best of times and the worst of times . . ." Her voice slid in and curved down through and over the words. She was nearly singing. I wanted to look at the pages. Were they the same that I had read? Or were there notes, music, lined on the pages, as in a hymn book? Her sounds began cascading gently. I knew from listening to a thousand preachers that she was nearing the end of her reading, and I hadn't really heard, heard to understand, a single word.

"How do you like that?"

It occurred to me that she expected a response. The sweet vanilla flavor was still on my tongue and her reading was a wonder in my ears. I had to speak.

I said, "Yes, ma'am." It was the least I could do, but it was the most also.

"There's one more thing. Take this book of poems and memorize one for me. Next time you pay me a visit, I want you to recite."

I have tried often to search behind the sophistication of years for the enchantment I so easily found in those

◆ Build Vocabulary

intolerant (in tä´ ər ənt) *adj.*: Not able or willing to accept

couched (koucht) *v.*: Put into words; expressed

gifts. The essence escapes but its aura[6] remains. To be allowed, no, invited, into the private lives of strangers, and to share their joys and fears, was a chance to exchange the Southern bitter wormwood[7] for a cup of mead with Beowulf[8] or a hot cup of tea and milk with Oliver Twist. When I said aloud, "It is a far far better thing that I do, than I have ever done . . ."[9] tears of love filled my eyes at my selflessness.

---

6. **aura** (ôr´ ə) *n.*: Atmosphere or quality.
7. **wormwood** (wʉrm´ wo͝od´) *n.*: Plant that produces a bitter oil.
8. **Beowulf** (bā´ ə wo͝olf): Hero of an old Anglo-Saxon epic. People in this poem drink mead, (mēd), a drink made with honey and water.
9. **"It is . . . than I have ever done"**: Speech from *A Tale of Two Cities* by Charles Dickens.

On that first day, I ran down the hill and into the road (few cars ever came along it) and had the good sense to stop running before I reached the Store.

I was liked, and what a difference it made. I was respected not as Mrs. Henderson's grandchild or Bailey's sister but for just being Marguerite Johnson.

Childhood's logic never asks to be proved (all conclusions are absolute). I didn't question why Mrs. Flowers had singled me out for attention, nor did it occur to me that Momma might have asked her to give me a little talking to. All I cared about was that she had made tea cookies for *me* and read to *me* from her favorite book. It was enough to prove that she liked me.

Guide for Responding

◆ LITERATURE AND YOUR LIFE

Reader's Response Does Mrs. Flowers remind you of anyone you know? Explain.

Thematic Focus What does Maya learn about herself as a result of her visit with Mrs. Flowers?

Thank-You Note As the character Marguerite, write a thank-you note to Mrs. Flowers following the visit.

☑ Check Your Comprehension

1. Describe how the "Store" came into existence.
2. According to Mrs. Flowers, for what two reasons is language important?
3. Although Marguerite reads a great deal, what does she not do?
4. What does Mrs. Flowers tell Marguerite in the first of her "lessons in living"?
5. Mrs. Flowers makes cookies and reads to Marguerite. What do these actions prove to Marguerite?

◆ Critical Thinking

INTERPRET

1. What can you tell about Marguerite's character from her actions at the Store? **[Infer]**
2. Why does Mrs. Flowers tell Marguerite to read aloud and in as many different ways as possible? **[Interpret]**
3. How do you think Marguerite changes as a result of her meetings with Mrs. Flowers? **[Draw Conclusions]**
4. Why has Mrs. Flowers remained "the measure of what a human being can be"? **[Interpret]**

APPLY

5. Mrs. Flowers throws Marguerite a "lifeline" by talking and reading with her. In what other ways do people offer "lifelines"? **[Relate]**

EXTEND

6. Angelou's memoir takes place during a time in which segregation laws governed most of the South. How might Angelou's self-esteem have been affected by those laws? **[Social Studies Link]**

Guide for Responding (continued)

◆ Reading Strategy

REREAD OR READ AHEAD

Rereading can help you answer questions or clear up confusing issues. Another strategy for clearing up confusion or piecing together meaning is to **read ahead** with a specific purpose in mind.

1. Give two questions or details that you clarified by rereading.
2. What question or piece of information made sense to you after you read ahead?

◆ Build Vocabulary

USING FORMS OF *tolerate*

Knowing that *tolerate* means "to recognize someone else's beliefs or actions," you can determine the meaning of its related forms. Complete the following sentences with an appropriate related word.

intolerant tolerance tolerable tolerant

1. Mrs. Flowers suggested that Marguerite show ____?____ toward people who are illiterate, but to always be ____?____ of ignorance.
2. Marguerite's working at the store was ____?____, but Mrs. Flowers was ____?____ and helped her realize that she was special.

SPELLING STRATEGY

In some words, like *benign,* the *īn* sound is spelled *ign,* with a silent *g.* Complete each of the following with an *ign* word that fits the definition.

1. A pattern or arrangement of parts: ____?____
2. To give out as a task, such as homework: ____?____
3. A publicly displayed board: ____?____

USING THE WORD BANK

In your notebook, write the word from the Word Bank that best completes each sentence.

1. The rope was pulled ____?____ to secure the boxes of goods.
2. For ____?____ reasons, the Store was open late.
3. Mrs. Flowers used lemons to ____?____ her tea.
4. Although stern, Mrs. Flowers was also____?____.
5. Her voice was ____?____ with wisdom.
6. Marguerite learned not to be ____?____ of those who are unschooled.

◆ Literary Focus

MEMOIR

This **memoir** focuses on a significant person and a significant event in Maya Angelou's life—Mrs. Flowers and her positive influence on young Marguerite.

1. Why is Angelou's description of life at the Store important to the introduction of Mrs. Flowers?
2. Why is Angelou so impressed with Mrs. Flowers? How does she describe her?
3. Why does the visit to Mrs. Flowers's house remain so memorable to Angelou?

◆ Build Grammar Skills

PLURAL AND POSSESSIVE NOUNS

Plural and possessive nouns are sometimes confused. A **plural noun** indicates more than one person, place, thing, or idea. Most plural nouns end with the letter *-s.*

Plural Nouns: On *Saturdays, barbers* sat their *customers* in the shade on the porch. . . .

A **possessive noun** shows ownership, belonging, or other close relationship. A possessive noun can be **singular,** ending in *-'s,* or **plural,** usually ending in *-s'.*

Singular Possessive: If I was off in the *Store's* favor, the eagle-eyed woman would . . .

Plural Possessive: "[S]he . . . supplied the *workers'* needs for a few years."

Practice In your notebook, identify whether each italicized noun is plural or possessive.

1. *Mrs. Flowers's* home smelled like vanilla.
2. The *pictures'* torn edges and fading colors made their appearance threatening.
3. *Marguerite's* shyness showed when she first visited Mrs. Flowers.
4. The only *words* she uttered during her visit were "yes, ma'am."
5. Take this book of *poems* and memorize one.

Writing Application Write a paragraph using the plural of the nouns *store, owner,* and *customer.* Then, write a paragraph making these nouns plural and possessive.

Build Your Portfolio

 ## Idea Bank

Writing

1. **Journal Entry** Write a journal entry that Maya Angelou might have written after her visit with Mrs. Flowers. Include a description of how she felt during and after the visit.

2. **Memoir Poem** Choose a significant event in your life to describe in a poem. Choose details that express emotion as well as tell your story.

3. **Analysis** Write a brief analysis. In it, point out which details about Mrs. Flowers's home and her treatment of Angleou indicate the writer's feeling about that fateful visit.

Speaking and Listening

4. **Oral Interpretation [Group Activity]** Mrs. Flowers says that the way in which words are spoken can help determine their meaning. Working with a group of classmates, choose a passage from the story to read aloud. Each member should read the passage to the class, stressing different words.

5. **Oral Tribute** Put yourself in Angelou's shoes, and deliver an oral tribute about Mrs. Flowers to your class. Use details from the story to help you to describe her. **[Performing Arts Link]**

Projects

6. **Advertisement** Create a poster advertising the Wm. Johnson General Merchandise Store. List the merchandise mentioned in the selection, and emphasize its importance as a center of activity for this rural town in Arkansas. **[Art Link]**

7. **Photo Essay [Group Activity]** With a group, compile a photo essay of the rural South in the 1930's and 1940's. Photocopy the photographs, and write explanatory captions for them. Display your photo essay in the classroom. **[Social Studies Link]**

 ## Writing Mini-Lesson

Personal Memoir About a Turning Point

Angelou's visit with Mrs. Flowers was a turning point in her life—one that changed her outlook and future behavior. Cast your thoughts back to a time when you experienced a turning point of some kind. Then, write a memoir that describes the event. Personalize the memoir by choosing details that infuse the writing with your personality.

Writing Skills Focus: Elaborate to Make Writing Personal

Include details that explain why the event you're describing was so significant. For example, in the following passage, Angelou makes her writing personal by describing why her visit with Mrs. Flowers was a turning point.

Model From the Story

I was liked, and what a difference it made. I was respected not as Mrs. Henderson's grandchild or Bailey's sister but for just being Marguerite Johnson.

Prewriting List specific details that describe your turning point. Include explanations of how events and people made you feel and why. Then, organize the details into a sequence.

Drafting Use your organized list as the basis for drafting your memoir. As you write, include transitions, such as *after that* and *to our surprise,* that make connections between ideas clear.

Revising Revise your personal memoir by looking for places where adding personal details will help you reveal your feelings and emotions at the time of the event.

> ◆ **Grammar Application**
> Check all words that end in *-s*. Do not use apostrophes to make a word plural. Use apostrophes only to show possession.

Guide for Reading

Meet the Authors:

Robert Frost (1874–1963)

One of the high points for poetry in the twentieth century was Robert Frost's reading of his poem "The Gift Outright" at the inauguration of President John F. Kennedy. Many of Frost's poems are set in or are about some aspect of rural New England, and they contain the same rhythms as everyday spoken English.

Walter de la Mare (1873–1956)

British poet and novelist Walter de la Mare has been called the "last poet of the Romantic tradition." De la Mare believed that the world beyond human experience could best be understood through the imagination. His poetry has a sense of magic about it, with subject matter that includes childhood, nature, dreams, and the uncanny.

Dorothy Parker (1893–1967)

A poet, short-story writer, and famed wit, Dorothy Parker has written many poems that comment on departed and departing love and various kinds of suitors. In New York literary circles, Parker was known as a member of the Algonquin Round Table. This group of writers lunched regularly at the Algonquin Hotel in the 1920's, trading brilliant insults and witty observations.

◆ LITERATURE AND YOUR LIFE

CONNECT YOUR EXPERIENCE

Making simple decisions, like choosing a fork in the road like the one in this photograph, may inspire you to think about life—where you've been, the choices you've made, and what the future holds. In these poems, the speakers reflect upon their lives and how they've chosen to live them.

THEMATIC FOCUS: Arriving at Understanding

As you read, think about the lessons people learn from important life decisions.

◆ Background for Understanding

SCIENCE

In "All But Blind," the speaker compares himself to creatures that are blind or have poor vision: moles, bats, and barn owls. Moles are small furry blind animals who live underground. Bats, although not blind, have very poor eyesight. Barn owls have eyes that are much smaller than those of other types of owls, leading some to believe that they lack adequate vision.

◆ Build Vocabulary

WORD ROOTS: -verg-

The word root -verg- means "to bend or turn." When preceded by the prefix di- from dis-, meaning "apart," you can figure out that diverged, as used in "The Road Not Taken," means "bending apart."

WORD BANK

Which word from the list might mean "burning without flame"? Check the Build Vocabulary box on page 36 to see if you chose correctly.

diverged
blunders
smoldering
lilting

The Road Not Taken ◆ All But Blind ◆ The Choice ◆

◆ Literary Focus

THE SPEAKER IN A POEM

The **speaker in a poem** is the voice assumed by the writer of the poem. Sometimes the speaker is the poet; sometimes the speaker is a character the poet has created. This character may not even be human. It could be a lamp, a butterfly, a princess in disguise, or a tree. Don't be fooled by the use of the pronoun "I" in a poem: This does not always mean that the poem's speaker is the author.

◆ Reading Strategy

PARAPHRASE

Most poems contain language unlike everyday speech. To better understand poetry, **paraphrase,** or restate the lines in your own words.

Original: All but blind/In his chambered hole/Gropes for worms/The four-clawed Mole.

Paraphrase: The nearly blind mole searches for worms in his underground cave.

Apply this technique to other lines in the poems, filling out a chart like the one below.

Poem Title	Original Lines	Paraphrased Lines
The Road Not Taken	as just as fair	just as nice
All But Blind		
The Choice		

The Road

Robert Frost

Two roads <u>diverged</u> in a yellow wood,
And sorry I could not travel both
And be one traveler, long I stood
And looked down one as far as I could
5   To where it bent in the undergrowth;

Then took the other, as just as fair,
And having perhaps the better claim,
Because it was grassy and wanted wear;
Though as for that, the passing there
10   Had worn them really about the same,

And both that morning equally lay
In leaves no step had trodden black.
Oh, I kept the first for another day!
Yet knowing how way leads on to way,
15   I doubted if I should ever come back.

I shall be telling this with a sigh
Somewhere ages and ages hence:
Two roads diverged in a wood, and I—
I took the one less traveled by,
20   And that has made all the difference.

◆ **Build Vocabulary**
diverged (dī vʉrjd´) *v.*: Branched off

Not Taken

Guide for Responding

◆ Literature and Your Life

Reader's Response Do you think the speaker made a wise choice? Explain.

Thematic Focus At what understanding did the speaker arrive?

Journal Writing In your journal, write about a time you made a decision like the one the speaker made.

☑ Check Your Comprehension

1. Where is the speaker standing when he has to make his decision?
2. In what way are the roads similar and different?
3. Which road did the speaker choose to take?
4. What reason does the speaker give for choosing one road over the other?

◆ Critical Thinking

INTERPRET

1. What can you determine about the speaker's character in the first five lines of the poem? **[Infer]**

2. Find two details suggesting that the speaker feels his decision is significant. **[Connect]**

3. What do the two roads symbolize, or stand for? **[Interpret]**

4. Explain the message or theme of the poem. **[Analyze]**

EVALUATE

5. The poem's speaker senses that his decision was important. Do you agree? Explain. **[Make a Judgment]**

APPLY

6. An old proverb states that opportunity never knocks twice. How does this saying relate to the poem? **[Apply]**

All But Blind

Walter de la Mare

All but blind
   In his chambered hole
Gropes for worms
   The four-clawed Mole.

5 All but blind
   In the evening sky
The hooded Bat
   Twirls softly by.

All but blind
10   In the burning day
The Barn-Owl <u>blunders</u>
   On her way.

And blind as are
   These three to me,
15 So, blind to Some-One
   I must be.

◆ **Build Vocabulary**

blunders (blun′ dərz) *v.*: Moves clumsily or carelessly

smoldering (smōl′ dər iŋ) *adj.*: Burning or smoking without flame

lilting (lilt′ iŋ) *adj.*: Singing or speaking with a light, graceful rhythm

The Choice
Dorothy Parker

He'd have given me rolling lands,
   Houses of marble, and billowing farms,
Pearls, to trickle between my hands,
   Smoldering rubies, to circle my arms.
5 You—you'd only a lilting song.
   Only a melody, happy and high,
You were sudden and swift and strong,—
   Never a thought for another had I.

He'd have given me laces rare,
10   Dresses that glimmered with frosty sheen,
Shining ribbons to wrap my hair,
   Horses to draw me, as fine as a queen.
You—you'd only to whistle low,
   Gaily I followed wherever you led.
15 I took you, and I let him go,—
   Somebody ought to examine my head!

Guide for Responding

◆ LITERATURE AND YOUR LIFE

Reader's Response With which poem's speaker would you rather converse? Why?

Thematic Focus Describe the understanding arrived at by each of the speakers.

☑ Check Your Comprehension

1. In "All But Blind," to what three animals does the speaker compare himself?
2. (a) In "The Choice," what are the two choices the speaker had? (b) What choice did the speaker make?
3. What evidence is there that the speaker in "The Choice" is not sure she made the right decision?

◆ Critical Thinking

INTERPRET

1. (a) Who might be the "Some-One" referred to in line 15 of "All But Blind"? (b) What does the reference reveal about the speaker's world view? **[Interpret]**
2. What do the details in "The Choice" reveal about the speaker's personality? **[Infer]**
3. What might have happened to make her question her decision? **[Speculate]**

COMPARE LITERARY WORKS

4. Examine the last lines in "The Road Not Taken" and in "The Choice." How would the emotional impact of each poem differ if the last lines were switched? **[Hypothesize]**

Guide for Responding (continued)

◆ Reading Strategy

PARAPHRASE

This **paraphrase,** or restatement, of lines 5–8 from "The Choice" may lead you to recognize the main, or key, idea in the passage.

Original: You—you'd only a lilting song./Only a melody, happy and high,/You were sudden and swift and strong,—/Never a thought for another had I.

Paraphrase: The only thing you had was your joyous attitude. You were like a whirlwind that drove thoughts of all other boyfriends out of my head.

1. (a) Paraphrase any passage of "The Road Not Taken." (b) What important ideas were you able to identify through paraphrasing?
2. (a) Paraphrase any passage of "All But Blind." (b) What is the passage about (the subject)? What does it say about the subject?

◆ Build Grammar Skills

GENERAL AND SPECIFIC NOUNS

Nouns name people, places, things, or ideas. **General nouns,** like *tree* and *flower,* convey broad information. **Specific nouns,** like *elm* and *willow* or *daisy* and *violet,* convey more precise information. Although it's not necessary to use only specific nouns in your writing, you should recognize that they give writing clarity.

Practice Divide your paper into two columns. Write the general nouns in one column and the corresponding specific nouns in the other.

planet, flower, car, daisy, sedan, Jupiter, holiday, musician, rose, convertible, Thanksgiving, cellist, Mercury, guitarist

Writing Application On your paper, revise each sentence, replacing the italicized general noun with a more specific noun.

1. They served *beverages* at the dance.
2. The *tree* will be chopped down.
3. For her eighteenth birthday party, she wore her grandmother's *jewelry.*
4. *Insects* are annoyingly persistent.
5. She listens to *music* all day.

◆ Literary Focus

THE SPEAKER IN A POEM

When you read poetry, be alert to the **speaker,** the character or voice assumed by the poet. The thoughts, attitude, and character of the speaker give meaning to a poem.

1. Describe the speaker's attitude or philosophy in "The Road Not Taken."
2. In "All But Blind," the speaker reveals his view of life. Describe his view, and explain how it gives the poem its meaning.
3. If you assume that the speaker of "The Choice" is Dorothy Parker herself, what do you think she values most?

◆ Build Vocabulary

USING THE WORD ROOT -verg-

The word root *-verg-,* meaning "to bend or turn" and found in *diverged,* also appears in *converge,* the opposite of *diverge.* The prefix *con-* means "together." What does *converge* mean?

Complete the following sentences using a form of *converge* or *diverge.*

1. The two groups plan to _____?_____ at noon.
2. Because of the boulder, the stream _____?_____.

SPELLING STRATEGY

When adding *-ing* to a verb to make an adjective, keep this in mind: If a verb has more than one syllable, ends in a consonant, and is not accented on the last syllable, just add *-ing.*

smolder + -ing = smoldering

On your paper, add *-ing* to the following.

1. travel   2. gallop   3. billow   4. administer

USING THE WORD BANK

On your paper, replace each italicized word or phrase with the correct Word Bank word.

1. Through the *smoking* pile of leaves a bear *stumbles.*
2. On the tree branch that *curved in two directions,* a robin ceased her *melodic* song.

Build Your Portfolio

 ## Idea Bank

Writing

1. **List** List the qualities of each suitor in "The Choice." You might have to "read between the lines" of the poem to determine the character of each suitor.

2. **Dialogue** Imagine that you are hiking with the speaker of "The Road Not Taken." You have just come to the place described in the poem. Write the dialogue you might have with the speaker about which road to take.

3. **Compare and Contrast** The speakers of these poems have distinct personalities and attitudes. Choose two of the poems, and write an essay in which you compare and contrast the poems and the speakers.

Speaking and Listening

4. **Dramatic Scene [Group Activity]** The speaker of "The Road Not Taken" is satisfied with his life choice, whereas the speaker in "The Choice" is not so sure she chose wisely. With a classmate, prepare and present a scene in which the two speakers discuss their feelings. **[Performing Arts Link]**

5. **Speech** In "The Road Not Taken," the speaker is convinced that he made a sound decision in choosing a path. Transform the poem into a persuasive speech, and deliver it to the class. **[Performing Arts Link]**

Projects

6. **Final Words** An obituary is a notice of someone's death that includes a brief biography. With two classmates, write obituary notices for each poem's speaker. Tailor the notices to the speakers' personalities as closely as possible.

7. **Illustration** Illustrate a scene from one of the poems. Write a caption for your art, as if it were appearing in a book or being displayed on a museum wall. Display your work in class. **[Art Link]**

 ## Writing Mini-Lesson

Persuasive Essay

Like the speakers in "The Road Not Taken" and "The Choice," you make decisions every day. Although some decisions affect only yourself, sometimes you need the cooperation of others in order to make a change or take a step. Think about a path you'd like to take that involves the agreement of others. Then, write a persuasive essay to convince them to support you.

Writing Skills Focus: Supporting Your Argument

Persuasive writing usually contains an argument, a set of reasons for doing or believing something. To make your argument forceful, **support it** by giving reasons why one particular choice is better than another.

Here, the speaker in Frost's poem explains why he chose one path over another.

Model From the Poem
Then took the other, as just as fair,
And having perhaps the better claim,
Because it was grassy and wanted wear;

Prewriting Choose a two-sided issue about which you feel strongly. Jot down arguments that support your position on the issue.

Drafting Begin your persuasive essay by stating what you want to do and why you deserve your readers' support. Then, develop and support your argument by giving reasons, facts, and examples.

Revising Look for places in which your argument can be strengthened. For example, you may want to add facts and details or choose more powerful words.

> ◆ **Grammar Application**
> Read through your draft, underlining general nouns and circling specific nouns. Consider whether you can strengthen your argument by replacing some general nouns with specific ones.

Guide for Reading

Meet the Author:

John Seabrook (1959–)

John Seabrook grew up in the tomato farm community of Salem, New Jersey. Years later, he was to write an article about a new industry, biotechnology, and the process scientists used to develop a new supermarket tomato. Almost as an afterthought, he included some comments on his boyhood connection to tomatoes. The positive reaction to that article helped Seabrook realize that science writers need to tell their audiences why they are interested in a subject and show how it affects them.

THE STORY BEHIND THE STORY

Bill Gates (1955–) is the chief executive officer and co-founder of Microsoft Corporation, the world's largest computer software company. His phenomenal success and astounding wealth have made him a legendary figure in the business world. When John Seabrook began writing this article for *The New Yorker,* he attempted to contact Gates by e-mail, not knowing whether or not he'd get a response. To his surprise, he got an immediate reply and was able to conduct the interview almost entirely through e-mail correspondence.

◆ LITERATURE AND YOUR LIFE

CONNECT YOUR EXPERIENCE

Although virtually everyone loves getting cards and letters in the mail, many people don't write letters, preferring the quickness of making phone calls. Recently, however, letter writing has undergone a renewed popularity due to the emergence of e-mail—electronic mail.

THEMATIC FOCUS: Arriving at Understanding

In "E-Mail from Bill Gates," John Seabrook interviews the computer industry's biggest player, Bill Gates, in an effort to understand e-mail and its impact on our lives.

◆ Background for Understanding

TECHNOLOGY

In "E-Mail from Bill Gates," John Seabrook conducts an interview with Bill Gates, head of Microsoft Corporation, via e-mail. E-mail stands for electronic mail, which is relayed through telephone lines. Messages that used to take weeks to arrive by traditional mail can now be sent round the world in minutes. This new technology also allows for attachments of files, making it possible for many people to work from their homes.

◆ Build Vocabulary

PREFIXES: *inter-*

The prefix *inter-,* meaning "between," appears in the word *interaction,* which means "actions that have an effect on each other."

WORD BANK

Which word from the list means "in a spontaneous way"? Check the Build Vocabulary box on page 44 to see if you chose correctly.

| interaction |
| misinterpret |
| intimate |
| etiquette |
| spontaneously |

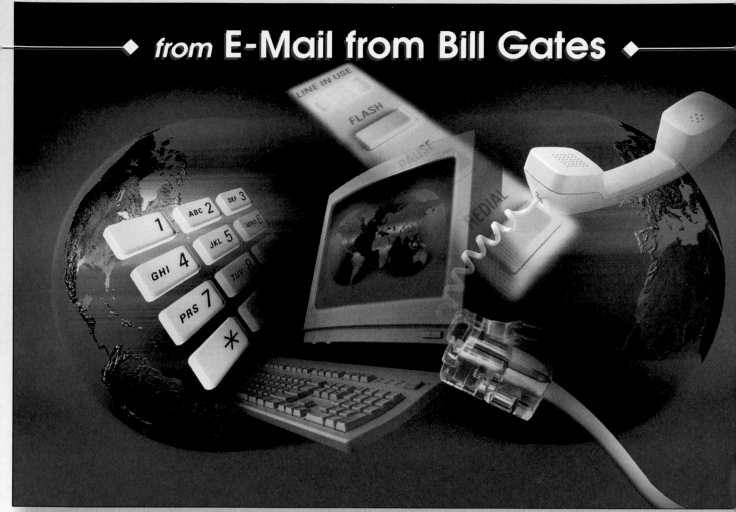

from E-Mail from Bill Gates

◆ Literary Focus

MAGAZINE ARTICLE

A **magazine article** is a short work of non-fiction that gives information. Some articles are human-interest stories that give insights on interesting people and their accomplishments. Other articles explain or investigate specific subjects, like the behavior of bees or a new technology.

This magazine article by John Seabrook does both: It profiles a fascinating person who is at the cutting edge of the new technology, and, at the same time, it provides knowledge on a scientific subject.

◆ Reading Strategy

CONTEXT CLUES

While reading, you may occasionally encounter unfamiliar words. By using **context clues,** examining the surrounding text, you may be able to make an informed guess about the meaning of words new to you.

As you read, use a chart like the one below to record unknown words and guess at their meanings. When you've finished reading, use a dictionary to see if you were on target.

Word	Clue	Predicted Meaning
nevertheless	wasting money/ logged on again	"anyway" or "in spite of"

ADDRESS | **SEND** | **REPLY** | **DELETE** JOHN SEABROOK

from E-Mail *from* Bill Gates

At the moment, the best way to communicate with another person on the information highway[1] is to exchange electronic mail: to write a message on a computer and send it through the telephone lines into someone else's computer. In the future, people will send each other sound and pictures as well as text, and do it in real time,[2] and improved technology will make it possible to have rich, human electronic exchanges, but at present E-mail is the closest thing we have to that. Even now, E-mail allows you to meet and communicate with people in a way that would be impossible on the phone, through the regular mail, or face to face, as I discovered while I was working on this story. Sitting at my computer one day, I realized that I could try to communicate with Bill Gates, the chairman and co-founder of the software giant Microsoft, on the information highway. At least, I could send E-mail to his electronic address, which is widely available, not tell anyone at Microsoft I was doing it, and see what happened. I wrote:

---

1. **information highway:** Network of computers and file servers that allows for the rapid exchange of electronic information.
2. **real time:** Accessing of information or exchange of data that requires no downloading of files.

Dear Bill,

I am the guy who is writing the article about you for The New Yorker. It occurs to me that we ought to be able to do some of the work through e-mail. Which raises this fascinating question—What kind of understanding of another person can e-mail give you? . . .

You could begin by telling me what you think is unique about e-mail as a form of communication.

John

I hit "return," and the computer said, "mail sent." I walked out to the kitchen to get a drink of water and played with the cat for a while, then came back and sat at my computer. Thinking that I was probably wasting money, I nevertheless logged on again and entered my password. "You have mail," the computer said.

I typed "get mail," and the computer got the following:

From: Bill Gates <billg@microsoft.com>
Ok, let me know if you get this email.

According to my computer, eighteen minutes had passed between the time I E-mailed Bill and he E-mailed me back. His message said:

E-mail is a unique communication

vehicle for a lot of reasons. However email is not a substitute for direct interaction. . . .

There are people who I have corresponded with on email for months before actually meeting them—people at work and otherwise. If someone isn't saying something of interest its easier to not respond to their mail than it is not to answer the phone. In fact I give out my home phone number to almost no one but my email address is known very broadly. I am the only person who reads my email so no one has to worry about embarrassing themselves or going around people when they send a message. Our email is completely secure. . . .

Email helps out with other types of communication. It allows you to exchange a lot of information in advance of a meeting and make the meeting far far more valuable. . . .

Email is not a good way to get mad at someone since you can't interact. You can send friendly messages very easily since those are harder to misinterpret.

We began to E-mail each other three or four times a week. I would have a question about something and say to myself, "I'm going to E-mail Bill about that," and I'd write him a message and get a one- or two-page message back within twenty-four hours, sometimes much sooner. At the beginning of our electronic relationship, I would wake up in the middle of the night and lie in bed wondering if I had E-mail from Bill. Generally, he seemed to write messages at night, sleep (maybe), then send them the next morning. We were

◆ Build Vocabulary

interaction (in´ tər ak´ shən) *n*.: Actions that affect each other

misinterpret (mis´ in tʉr´ prit) *v*.: To understand or explain incorrectly

intimate (in´ tə mət) *adj*.: Private or personal

etiquette (et´ i kit) *n*.: Rules for behavior

intimate in a curious way, in the sense of being wired into each other's minds, but our contact was elaborately stylized, like ballroom dancing.

In some ways, my E-mail relationship with Bill was like an ongoing, monthlong conversation, except that there was a pause after each response to think; it was like football players huddling up after each play. There was no beginning or end to Gates' messages—no time wasted on stuff like "Dear" and "Yours"—and I quickly corrected this etiquette breach in my own messages. Nor were there any fifth-grade-composition-book standards like "It may have come to your attention that" and "Looking forward to hearing from you." Social niceties are not what Bill Gates is about. Good spelling is not what Bill Gates is about, either. He never signed his messages to me, but sometimes he put an "&" at the end, which, I learned, means "Write back" in E-mail language. After a while, he stopped putting the "&," but I wrote back anyway. He never addressed me by name. Instead of a letterhead, there was this:

Sender: billg@microsoft.com
Received: from netmail.microsoft.com by dub-img-2.compuserve.com (5.67/5.930129sam) id AA03768; Wed, 6 Oct 93 14:00:51-0400
Received: by netmail.microsoft.com (5.65/25—eef) id AA27745; Fri, 8 Oct 93 10:56:01-0700
Message-Id: <9310081756.AA27745@netmail.microsoft.com>
X-Msmail-Message-Id: 15305A55
X-Msmail-Conversation-Id: 15305A55
From: Bill Gates <billg@microsoft.com>
To: 73124.1524@CompuServe.COM

I sometimes felt that this correspondence was a game I was playing with Gates through the computer, or maybe a game I was playing against a computer. What is the right move? What question will get me past the dragon and into the wizard's star chamber, where the rich information is stored? I had no idea where Gates was when he wrote to me, except that once he told me he was on a "think week" at his family's summer place on Hood Canal. I could not tell whether he was impatient or bored with my questions and was merely answering them because it served his interest. Because we couldn't talk at the same time, there was little chance for the conversation to move spontaneously. On the other hand, his answers meant more, in a certain way, being written, than answers I would have received on the phone. I worried that he might think I was being "random" (a big putdown at Microsoft) because I jumped from topic to topic. I sometimes wondered if I was actually communicating with Bill Gates. How hard would it be for an assistant to write these messages? Or for an intelligent agent to do it?

I wrote a message titled "What motivates you?":

> You love to compete, right? Is that where your energy comes from—love of the game? I wonder how it feels to win on your level. How much do you fear losing? How about immortality—being remembered for a thousand years after you're dead—does that excite you? How strong is your desire to improve people's lives (by providing them with better tools for thinking and communicating)? Some driven people are trying to heal a wound or to recover a loss. Is that the case with you?

Gates wrote back:

> Its easy to understand why I think I have the best job around because of day to day enjoyment rather than some grand long term deep psychological explanation. It's a lot of fun to work with very smart people in a competitive environment. . . . We get to hire the best people coming out of school and give them challenging jobs. We get to try and figure out how to sell software in every part of the world. Sometimes our ideas work very well and sometimes they work very poorly. As long as we stay in the feedback loop and keep trying it's a lot of fun.
>
> It is pretty cool that the products we work on empower individuals and make their jobs more interesting. It helps a lot in inventing new software ideas that I will be one of the users of the software so I can model what's important. . . .
>
> Just thinking of things as winning is a terrible approach. Success comes from focusing in on what you really like and are good at—not challenging every random thing. My original vision of a personal computer on every desk and every home will take more than 15 years to achieve so there will have been more than 30 years since I first got excited about that goal. My work is not like sports where you actually win a game and its over after a short period of time.
>
> Besides a lot of luck, a high energy level and perhaps some IQ I think having an ability to deal with things at a very detailed level and a very broad level and synthesize[3] between them is probably the thing that helps me the most. This allows someone to take deep technical understanding and figure out a business strategy that fits together with it.
>
> It's ridiculous to consider how things will be remembered after you are dead. The pioneers of personal computers including Jobs, Kapor, Lampson, Roberts, Kaye,[4] are all great people but I don't think any of us will merit an entry in a history book.

---

3. **synthesize:** To form by bringing together separate parts.
4. **Jobs, . . . Kaye:** Pioneers in technology.

◆ Build Vocabulary

spontaneously (spän tā′ nē əs lē) *adv.:* Resulting from a natural feeling

I don't remember being wounded or losing something big so I don't think that is driving me. I have wonderful parents and great siblings. I live in the same neighborhood I grew up in (although I will be moving across the lake when my new house is done). I can't remember any major disappointments. I did figure out at one point that if I pursued pure mathematics it would be hard to make a major contribution and there were a few girls who turned me down when I asked them out.

At the end of one message, I wrote:

This reporting via e-mail is really fascinating and I think you are going to come across in an attractive way, in case you weren't sure of that.

Gates wrote:

I comb my hair everytime before I send email hoping to appear attractive. I try and use punctuation in a friendly way also. I send :) and never :(.

Guide for Responding

◆ LITERATURE AND YOUR LIFE

Reader's Response Would you like to meet Bill Gates? Why or why not?

Thematic Focus What did you learn about both e-mail and Bill Gates from reading this article?

☑ Check Your Comprehension

1. Who are the two people exchanging e-mail messages in this article?
2. What does Seabrook learn about the etiquette of sending and receiving e-mail?
3. What does Gates say about his motivation for success that might help other people achieve their goals?

◆ Critical Thinking

INTERPRET

1. What does Seabrook accomplish by letting Gates speak for himself? **[Analyze]**
2. How do Seabrook's and Gates's e-mail messages change over time? **[Analyze]**
3. Does the author learn what he had hoped to learn about Bill Gates? **[Draw Conclusions]**
4. Would you include Gates in a history book? **[Make a Judgment]**

EXTEND

5. What skills do you think are needed by people who work in the computer field? **[Career Link]**

Guide for Responding (continued)

◆ Reading Strategy

CONTEXT CLUES

When reading a science article like "E-Mail from Bill Gates," it's helpful to identify **context clues,** clues in the surrounding text, to figure out the meaning of unfamiliar words.

1. What context clues help you understand the italicized term in this passage? "[O]ur contact was *elaborately stylized,* like ballroom dancing."
2. (a) With which words or phrases in the article were you unfamiliar? (b) What context clues helped you guess at their meanings?

◆ Build Vocabulary

USING THE PREFIX *inter-*

The prefix *inter-* means "between." Write the word that should appear in each blank by adding *inter-* to these words: state, connection, national.

1. E-mail can help you establish an ____?____ with faraway friends.
2. Instead of airmail, you can send an ____?____ e-mail.
3. To get from Texas to Arizona, take the ____?____ highway.

SPELLING STRATEGY

The suffix sound *shun* is often spelled *-tion.* Before adding the suffix, you will probably have to drop the final letter of the base word.

interact + -tion = interaction

On your paper, add *-tion* to the following verbs.

1. create   2. connect   3. designate   4. reflect

USING THE WORD BANK

On your paper, write the antonym, or opposite, of each first word.

1. misinterpret: (a) understand, (b) explain, (c) true
2. interaction: (a) play, (b) independence, (c)collaboration
3. etiquette: (a) program, (b) rules, (c) incorrectness
4. spontaneously: (a) quickly, (b) hesitantly, (c) accidentally
5. intimate: (a) close, (b) personal, (c) public

◆ Literary Focus

MAGAZINE ARTICLE

Magazine articles are short nonfiction works meant to inform and entertain. In "E-Mail from Bill Gates," John Seabrook does both: He publishes the actual e-mail messages that he received from Bill Gates to make his point about e-mail as a communications tool.

1. List two facts you learned about e-mail.
2. Why do you think Seabrook printed the e-mail identification you see on page 43?
3. Would you describe this article as more informative or more entertaining? Why?

◆ Build Grammar Skills

CONCRETE AND ABSTRACT NOUNS

In his article, Seabrook often gives information about technology by using concrete nouns. A **concrete noun** names a place or thing that you can perceive with your senses. You can touch a *computer* and type a *message.* An **abstract noun** names an idea, concept, belief, or quality—something that can't be touched. When Seabrook talks about ideas or relationships, he often uses abstract nouns, such as *understanding.*

Practice   Copy the following sentences. Decide whether the nouns in italics are concrete or abstract. Underline each concrete noun. Draw two lines under each abstract noun.

1. I had a *question* about *something.*
2. In the *future, people* will send each other *sound* and *pictures.*
3. *E-mail* is not a good *way* to get mad at *someone.*
4. How strong is your *desire* to improve people's *lives?*
5. I can't remember any major *disappointments.*

Writing Application   Write a paragraph about technology using both concrete and abstract nouns. Underline concrete nouns and circle abstract nouns.

Build Your Portfolio

 ## Idea Bank

Writing

1. **Letter to the Author** In a letter to John Seabrook, tell him why you appreciated "E-Mail from Bill Gates." Include any questions about technology or Bill Gates that you would like him to answer.

2. **Advertisement** Write an advertisement that might have appeared to introduce a technological product such as the telephone or the radio when it was first made available to the public. **[Science Link]**

3. **Cause-and-Effect Essay** In this article, Seabrook and Gates discuss the impact of technology on our lives. Choose one technological breakthrough and write a cause-and-effect essay in which you examine its effect on daily life.

Speaking and Listening

4. **Dialogue [Group Activity]** With a classmate, convert the series of e-mail letters between Bill Gates and John Seabrook into a traditional conversation. Perform their dialogue for the class. **[Performing Arts Link]**

5. **Interview** Interview a science teacher to learn how technology has changed and will change our lives. Publish both your questions and the teacher's answers.

Projects

6. **Internet Exploration** Write a report on how to send and receive e-mail, how to download files sent by e-mail, and how to create an e-mail address book. Present your information to the class. If possible, use a computer to demonstrate your knowledge. **[Science Link]**

7. **Diagram** Do research to find out how e-mail is relayed from one computer to another. Make a diagram, with explanatory captions to show how the system works.

 ## Writing Mini-Lesson

Comparison of Forms of Communication

In this article, John Seabrook uses comparisons and contrasts to show how e-mail is similar to and different from other forms of communication. Choose two forms of communication, such as the telephone and e-mail, and write a short essay comparing and contrasting them.

Writing Skills Focus: Transitions That Show Relationships

Help make your essay clear by using **transitions that show relationships.** Transitions such as *similarly, in addition, too,* and *likewise* signal that things are alike. Transitions such as *whereas, despite,* and *however* signal differences. Notice how Seabrook uses a transitional phrase to show relationships.

Model From the Article

[T]here was little chance for the conversation to move spontaneously. *On the other hand,* his answers meant more, in a certain way. . . .

Prewriting Choose the two forms of communication you will compare and contrast. List the ways in which your subjects are alike and different.

Drafting Organize your essay in a way that is easy to follow. You might want to discuss each type of communication separately, or you might want to discuss each similarity and difference in turn. As you draft the body, be specific about the ways in which your subjects are alike and different.

Revising Reread your draft carefully. Look for passages that are confusing or weak, and revise them. Add transitions to make sense out of confusing passages.

> ◆ **Grammar Application**
> Look for places where adding a concrete noun would clarify your comparisons.

CONNECTING LITERATURE TO SOCIAL STUDIES

THE FIRST AMERICANS

The Girl Who Hunted Rabbits *Zuñi Legend*

Understanding the World Growing up and learning about the world go hand in hand. From continent to continent, throughout the centuries, folk tales and songs have chronicled the achievements, hopes, and dreams of the young. Many wonderful tales of youth come to us from Native American literature.

Native Americans
Native American civilizations provide the longest continuous record of human habitation on the North American continent. Evidence of native peoples dates back 5,000 years to Bat Cave, New Mexico.

The Zuñi From the tenth century to the present, the Zuñi have lived in the Four Corners area, where the states of Colorado, Utah, New Mexico, and Arizona now meet. A story is told of a Spanish explorer who first sighted a Zuñi pueblo village and thought he had found the fabled Seven Cities of Cibola. In fact, the explorer may have interrupted an important ceremony; he was killed by the Zuñi.

Voices of the Past "The Girl Who Hunted Rabbits" is a legend, a story passed down orally from generation to generation and partially based on truth. It tells of a Zuñi girl who goes out alone to hunt. The girl's courage and bravery embody the qualities held in admiration by those of the Zuñi culture.

Native American Culture Areas

Inuit
Kutchin
ARCTIC OCEAN
Tlingit
Arctic
Inuit
Northwest Coast
Subarctic
Beaver
Bella Coola
Cree
Kwakiutl
PACIFIC OCEAN
Blackfoot
Chippewa
Algonquin
Plateau
Huron
Nez Percé
Crow
Mandan
Iroquois
Coos
Eastern Woodlands
Dakota
Leni-Lenape
Pomo
Cheyenne
Miami
ATLANTIC OCEAN
Great Basin
Great Plains
Shoshone
Arapaho
Shawnee
Osage
Navajo
Cherokee
California
Hopi Pueblo (Zuñi)
Comanche
Southeast
Southwest
Natchez
Apache
Calusa
Gulf of Mexico
Middle America
Maya
Aztec

0   500   1000 Miles
0   500   1000 Kilometers

130°W   110°W   90°W   80°W   70°W

The Girl Who Hunted Rabbits

Zuñi Legend

It was long ago, in the days of the ancients, that a poor maiden lived at "Little Gateway of Zuñi River." You know there are black stone walls of houses standing there on the tops of the cliffs of lava, above the narrow place through which the river runs, to this day.

In one of these houses there lived this poor maiden alone with her feeble old father and her aged mother. She was unmarried, and her brothers had all been killed in wars, or had died gently; so the family lived there helplessly, so far as many things were concerned, from the lack of men in their house.

It is true that in making the gardens—

Connecting Literature to Social Studies
Which details supply information about the value and importance of land cultivation in relation to hunting?

the little plantings of beans, pumpkins, squashes, melons, and corn—the maiden was able to do very well; and thus mainly on the products of these things the family were supported. But, as in those days of our ancients we had neither sheep nor cattle, the hunt was depended upon to supply the meat; or sometimes it was procured by barter of the products of the fields to those who hunted mostly. Of these things this little family had barely enough for their own subsistence; hence, they could not

procure their supplies of meat in this way.

Long before, it had been a great house, for many were the brave and strong young men who had lived in it; but the rooms were now empty, or at best contained only the leavings of those who had lived there, much used and worn out.

One autumn day, near wintertime, snow fell, and it became very cold. The maiden had gathered brush and firewood in abundance, and it was piled along the roof of the house and down underneath the ladder which descended from the top. She saw the young men issue forth the next morning in great numbers, their feet protected by long stockings of deerskin, the fur turned inward, and they carried on their shoulders and stuck in their belts stone axes and rabbit sticks. As she gazed at them from the roof, she said to herself, "O that I were a man and could go forth, as do these young men, hunting rabbits! Then my poor old mother and father would not lack for flesh with which to duly season their food and nourish their lean bodies." Thus ran her thoughts, and before night, as she saw these same young men coming in, one after another, some of them bringing long strings

◆ **Build Vocabulary**

procured (prō kyoord') *v.*: Obtained by some effort

of rabbits, others short ones, but none of them empty-handed, she decided that she would set forth on the morrow to try what luck she might find in the killing of rabbits herself.

It may seem strange that, although this maiden was beautiful and young, the youths did not give her some of their rabbits. But their feelings were not friendly, for no one of them would she accept as a husband, although one after another of them had offered himself for marriage.

Fully resolved, the girl that evening sat down by the fireplace, and turning toward her aged parents, said, "O my mother and father, I see that the snow has fallen, whereby easily rabbits are tracked, and the young men who went out this morning returned long before evening heavily laden with strings of this game. Behold, in the other rooms of our house are many rabbit sticks, and there hang on the walls stone axes, and with these I might perchance strike down a rabbit on his trail, or, if he runs into a log, split the log and dig him out. So I have thought during the day, and have decided to go tomorrow and try my fortunes in the hunt."

"*Naiya*, my daughter," quavered the feeble, old mother, "you would surely be very cold, or you would lose your way, or grow so tired that you could not return before night, and you must not go out to hunt rabbits."

Connecting Literature to Social Studies
What does the parents' reaction to the girl's wish to go hunting tell us about the gender roles of the Zuñi Indians?

"Why, certainly not," insisted the old man, rubbing his lean knees and shaking his head over the days that were gone. "No, no; let us live in poverty rather than that you should run such risks as these, O my daughter."

But, say what they would, the girl was determined. And the old man said at last, "Very well! You will not be turned from your course. Therefore, O daughter, I will help you as best I may." He hobbled into another room, and found there some old deerskins covered thickly with fur; and drawing them out, he

moistened and carefully softened them, and cut out for the maiden long stockings, which he sewed up with <u>sinew</u> and the fiber of the yucca[1] leaf. Then he selected for her from among the old possessions of his brothers and sons, who had been killed or perished otherwise, a number of rabbit sticks and a fine, heavy stone ax. Meanwhile, the old woman busied herself in preparing a lunch for the girl, which was composed of little cakes of cornmeal, spiced with pepper and wild onions, pierced through the middle, and baked in the ashes. When she had made a long string of these by threading them like beads on a rope of yucca fiber, she laid them down not far from the ladder on a little bench, with the rabbit sticks, the stone ax, and the deerskin stockings.

That night the maiden planned and planned, and early on the following morning, even before the young men had gone out from the town, she had put on a warm, short-skirted dress, knotted a <u>mantle</u> over her shoulder and thrown another and larger one over her back, drawn on the deerskin stockings, had thrown the string of corncakes over her shoulder, stuck the rabbit sticks in her belt, and carrying the stone ax in her hand sallied[2] forth eastward through the Gateway of Zuñi and into the plain of the valley beyond, called the Plain of the Burnt River, on account of the black, roasted-looking rocks along some parts of its sides. Dazzlingly white the snow stretched out before her—not deep, but unbroken—and when she came near the cliffs with many little canyons in them, along the northern side of the valley, she saw many a trail of rabbits running out and in among the rocks and between the bushes.

Warm and excited by her <u>unwonted</u> exercise, she did not heed a coming snowstorm, but ran about from one place to another, following the trails of the rabbits, sometimes up into the canyons where the forests of pine and

---

1. **yucca** (yuk´ ə) *n*.: Desert plant with stiff leaves and white flowers.
2. **sallied** (sal´ ēd) *v*.: Set out energetically.

cedar stood, and where here and there she had the good fortune sometimes to run two, three, or four rabbits into a single hollow log. It was little work to split these logs, for they were small, as you know, and to dig out the rabbits and slay them by a blow of the hand on the nape of the neck, back of the ears; and as she killed each rabbit she raised it reverently to her lips, and breathed from its nostrils its expiring breath[3] and, tying its legs together, placed it on the string, which after a while began to grow heavy on her shoulders. Still she kept on, little heeding the snow which was falling fast; nor did she notice that it was growing darker and darker, so intent was she on the hunt, and so glad was she to capture so many rabbits. Indeed, she followed the trails until they were no longer visible, as the snow fell all around her, thinking all the while, "How happy will be my poor old father and mother that they shall now have flesh to eat! How strong will they grow! And when this meat is gone, that which is dried and preserved of it also, lo! another snowstorm will no doubt come, and I can go out hunting again."

At last the twilight came, and, looking around, she found that the snow had fallen deeply, there was no trail, and that she had lost her way.

True, she turned about and started in the direction of her home, as she supposed, walking as fast as she could through the soft, deep snow. Yet she reckoned not rightly, for instead of going eastward along the valley, she went southward across it, and entering the mouth of the Descending Plain of the Pines, she went

on and on, thinking she was going homeward, until at last it grew dark and she knew not which way to turn.

"What harm," thought she, "if I find a sheltered place among the rocks? What harm if I remain all night, and go home in the morning when the snow has ceased falling, and by the light I shall know my way?"

So she turned about to some rocks which appeared, black and dim, a short distance away. Fortunately, among these rocks is the cave which is known as Taiuma's[4] Cave. This she came to, and peering into that black hole, she saw in it, back some distance, a little glowing light. "Ha, ha!" thought she, "perhaps some rabbit hunters like myself, belated yesterday, passed the night here and left the fire burning. If so, this is greater good fortune than I could have looked for." So, lowering the string of rabbits which she carried on her shoulder, and throwing off her mantle, she crawled in, peering well into the darkness, for fear of wild beasts; then, returning, she drew in the string of rabbits and the mantle.

Behold! there was a bed of hot coals buried in the ashes in the very middle of the cave, and piled up on one side were fragments of broken wood. The girl, happy in her good fortune, issued forth and gathered more sticks from the cliffside, where dead pines are found in great numbers, and bringing them in little armfuls one after another, she finally succeeded in gathering a store sufficient to keep the fire burning brightly all the night through. Then she drew off her snow-covered stockings of deerskin and the bedraggled mantles, and, building a fire, hung them up to dry and sat down to rest herself. The fire burned up and glowed brightly, so that the whole cave was as light as a room at night when a dance is being celebrated. By and by, after her clothing had dried, she spread a mantle on the floor of the cave by the side of the fire, and, sitting down, dressed one of her rabbits and roasted it, and, untying the string of corncakes her mother

---

3. **expiring** (ik spīr´ iŋ) **breath:** Dying breath.

◆ Build Vocabulary

sinew (sin´ yōō) *n.*: Tendon; band of fibrous tissue that connects muscles to bones or other parts and can also be used as thread for sewing

mantle (man´ təl) *n.*: Sleeveless cloak or cape

unwonted (un wän´ tid) *adj.*: Not usual

bedraggled (bi drag´ əld) *adj.*: Dirty and wet

---

4. **Taiuma's** (tī ōō´ məz)

The Girl Who Hunted Rabbits ◆ 51

had made for her, feasted on the roasted meat and cakes.

She had just finished her evening meal, and was about to recline and watch the fire for awhile, when she heard away off in the distance a long, low cry of distress—*"Ho-o-o-o thlaia-a!"*

"Ah!" thought the girl, "someone, more belated than myself, is lost; doubtless one of the rabbit-hunters." She got up, and went nearer to the entrance of the cavern.

"Ho-o-o-o thlaia-a!" sounded the cry, nearer this time. She ran out, and, as it was repeated again, she placed her hand to her mouth, and cried, as loudly as possible, *"Li-i- thlaia-a!"* ("Here!")

The cry was repeated near at hand, and presently the maiden, listening first, and then shouting, and listening again, heard the clatter of an enormous rattle. In dismay and terror she threw her hands into the air, and,

---

▼ **Critical Viewing** Does the girl in the painting seem to have the same qualities as the maiden in the story? Explain. **[Interpret]**

Indian Girl, Robert Henri, Indianapolis Museum of Art

crouching down, rushed into the cave and retreated to its farthest limits, where she sat shuddering with fear, for she knew that one of the Cannibal Demons of those days, perhaps the renowned Atahsaia[5] of the east, had seen the light of her fire through the cave entrance, with his terrible staring eyes, and assuming it to be a lost wanderer, had cried out, and so led her to guide him to her place of concealment.

On came the Demon, snapping the twigs under his feet and shouting in a hoarse, loud voice, *"Ho lithlsh tâ ime!"* ("Ho, there! So you are in here, are you?") *Kothl!* clanged his rattle, while, almost fainting with terror, closer to the rock crouched the maiden.

The old Demon came to the entrance of the cave and bawled out, "I am cold, I am hungry! Let me in!" Without further ado, he stooped and tried to get in; but, behold! the entrance was too small for his giant shoulders to pass. Then he pretended to be wonderfully civil, and said, "Come out, and bring me something to eat."

"I have nothing for you," cried the maiden. "I have eaten my food."

"Have you no rabbits?"

"Yes."

"Come out and bring me some of them."

But the maiden was so terrified that she dared not move toward the entrance.

"Throw me a rabbit!" shouted the old Demon.

The maiden threw him one of her precious rabbits at last, when she could rise and go to it. He clutched it with his long, horny hand, gave one gulp and swallowed it. Then he cried out, "Throw me another!" She threw him another, which he also immediately swallowed; and so on until the poor maiden had thrown all the rabbits to the <u>voracious</u> old monster. Every one she threw him he caught in his huge, yellow-tusked mouth, and swallowed, hair and all, at one gulp.

"Throw me another!" cried he, when the last

---

5. **Atahsaia** (ah´ tə sī´ ə)

had already been thrown to him.

So the poor maiden was forced to say, "I have no more."

"Throw me your overshoes!" cried he.

She threw the overshoes of deerskin, and these like the rabbits he speedily <u>devoured</u>. Then he called for her moccasins, and she threw them; for her belt, and she threw it; and finally, wonderful to tell, she threw even her mantle, and blanket, and her overdress, until, behold, she had nothing left!

Now, with all he had eaten, the old Demon was swollen hugely at the stomach, and, though he tried and tried to squeeze himself through the mouth of the cave, he could not by any means succeed. Finally, lifting his great flint ax, he began to shatter the rock about the entrance to the cave, and slowly but surely he enlarged the hole and the maiden now knew that as soon as he could get in he would devour her also, and she almost fainted at the sickening thought. Pound, pound, pound, pound, went the great ax of the Demon as he struck the rocks.

> **Connecting Literature to Social Studies**
> What details reveal the maiden's belief in folklore?

In the distance the two war-gods were sitting in their home at the Shrine amid the Bushes beyond Thunder Mountain, and though far off, they heard thus in the middle of the night the pounding of the Demon's hammer ax against the rocks. And of course they knew at once that a poor maiden, for the sake of her father and mother, had been out hunting—that she had lost her way and, finding a cave where there was a little fire, entered it, rebuilt the fire, and rested herself; that, attracted by the light of her fire, the Cannibal Demon had come and besieged her retreat,[6] and only a little time hence would he so enlarge the entrance to the cave that he could squeeze even his great overfilled paunch through it and come at the maiden to destroy her. So, catching up their wonderful weapons,

these two war-gods flew away into the darkness and in no time they were approaching the Descending Plain of the Pines.

Just as the Demon was about to enter the cavern, and the maiden had fainted at seeing his huge face and gray shock of hair and staring eyes, his yellow, protruding tusks, and his horny, taloned hand, they came upon the old beast. Each one hitting him a blow with his war club, they "ended his daylight," and then hauled him forth into the open space. They opened his huge paunch and withdrew from it the maiden's garments, and even the rabbits which had been slain. The rabbits they cast away among the soap-weed plants that grew on the slope at the foot of the cliff. The garments they spread out on the snow, and cleansed and made them perfect, even more perfect than they had been before. Then, flinging the huge body of the giant Demon down into the depths of the canyon, they turned them about and, calling out gentle words to the maiden, entered and restored her. She, seeing in them not their usual ugly persons, but handsome youths, was greatly comforted; and bending low, and breathing upon their hands, thanked them over and over for the rescue they had brought her. But she crouched herself low with shame that her garments were but few, when, behold! the youths went out and brought in to her the garments they had cleaned, restoring them to her.

Then, spreading their mantles by the door of the cave, they slept there that night, in order to protect the maiden, and on the morrow wakened her. They told her many things, and showed her many things which she had not known before, and counseled her thus, "It is not fearful that a maiden should marry; therefore, O maiden, return unto thy people in the Village of the Gateway of the River of Zuñi.

---

6. **besieged** (bi sējd´) **her retreat:** Attacked her place of refuge.

◆ Build Vocabulary

voracious (vô rā´ shəs) *adj.*: Eager to devour large quantities of food

devoured (di vourd´) *v.*: Ate greedily

This morning we will slay rabbits unnumbered for you, and start you on your way, guarding you down the snow-covered valley. When you are in sight of your home we will leave you, telling you our names."

So, early in the morning the two gods went forth, flinging their sticks among the soap-weed plants. Behold! as though the soap-weed plants were rabbits, so many lay killed on the snow before these mighty hunters. And they gathered together great numbers of these rabbits, a string for each one of the party. When the Sun had risen clearer in the sky, and his light sparkled on the snow around them, they took the rabbits to the maiden and presented them, saying, "We will carry each one of us a string of these rabbits." Then taking her hand, they led her out of the cave and down the valley, until, beyond on the high black mesas[7] at the Gateway of the River of Zuñi, she saw the smoke rise from the houses of her village.

---

7. **mesas** (mā´ səz) *n.*: Small mountains with flat tops and steep sides.

Then turned the two war-gods to her, and they told her their names. And again she bent low, and breathed on their hands. Then, dropping the strings of rabbits which they had carried close beside the maiden, they swiftly disappeared.

Thinking much of all she had learned, she continued her way to the home of her father and mother. As she went into the town, staggering under her load of rabbits, the young men and the old men and women and children beheld her with wonder; and no hunter in that town thought of comparing himself with the Maiden Hunter of Zuñi River. The old man and the old woman, who had mourned the night through and sat up anxiously watching, were overcome with happiness when they saw their daughter had returned.

> **Connecting Literature to Social Studies**
> What conclusion can you draw from the fact that the huntsmen of the town would not compare themselves with the Maiden Hunter?

Guide for Responding

◆ LITERATURE AND YOUR LIFE

Reader's Response Do you admire the actions of the girl in the story? Why or why not?

Thematic Focus What does the girl in the story learn about herself and the world?

☑ Check Your Comprehension

1. For what reasons does the girl go hunting?
2. Why do the girl's parents at first resist her plans?
3. How is the girl rescued?
4. How do the villagers regard the girl when she returns?

◆ Critical Thinking

INTERPRET

1. Why do the girl's parents help her when they really do not want her to go hunting? **[Speculate]**
2. For what reason do the war gods help the girl? **[Connect]**
3. Why does the girl see the two war gods as handsome youths? **[Draw Conclusions]**
4. What does the girl learn from the war gods? **[Interpret]**

EVALUATE

5. Was the girl's decision to spend the night in a cave a wise one or a foolish one? Explain. **[Make a Judgment]**

CONNECTING LITERATURE TO SOCIAL STUDIES

"The Girl Who Hunted Rabbits" gives insights into the culture of the Zuñi Native Americans from the Southwest. For example, the girl who hunts rabbits displays attitudes and behaviors that are valued by the Zuñi, such as courage, skill at hunting, and strength of purpose.

1. Judging from "The Girl Who Hunted Rabbits," what can you learn about the place of women in Zuñi culture?
2. What can you determine about the climate and terrain of Zuñi territory?
3. What might the Demon represent in "The Girl Who Hunted Rabbits"?

 Idea Bank

Writing

1. **List of Clues** Read through "The Girl Who Hunted Rabbits," and make a list of the clues in the story that give information about Zuñi society and culture.

2. **Letter** Write a letter to the girl in "The Girl Who Hunted Rabbits." Explain how the legends and heroes of your ancestors are similar to and different from those of the Zuñi. You may want to include a chart that shows how categories such as clothing and food differ between your culture and that of the Zuñis.

3. **Cause and Effect** Analyze Zuñi traditions using clues in "The Girl Who Hunted Rabbits." Then, write a cause-and-effect essay showing how Zuñi traditions, such as hunting, cause the girl in the story to take certain actions.

Speaking and Listening

4. **Music Connection** Find several pieces of music that enhance "The Girl Who Hunted Rabbits." Play the music for the class as you read the story aloud.

Projects

5. **Art** Make an illustrated map of the landscape described and places named in "The Girl Who Hunted Rabbits." Indicate the maiden's path, and illustrate scenes along the way. **[Art Link]**

6. **Encyclopedia Entry** With a group of students, do research about the Zuñi people. Create an illustrated encyclopedia entry, giving information about where they live (then and now), their beliefs and social structure, and their customs. **[Social Studies Link]**

Further Reading, Listening, and Viewing

- *Gluskabe Stories,* Audio Edition, by Joseph Bruchac
- *The Apaches* by Virginia Driving Hawk Sneve
- *A Narrative of the Captivity and Restoration of Mrs. Mary Rowlandson* by Mary Rowlandson

Personal Narrative

Writing Process Workshop

Like the writers in this unit, you are a storyteller. When you tell a friend about what happened to you on your vacation or describe the time you won a T-ball competition, you're telling a **personal narrative,** a story that relates a real-life experience from your point of view. Personal narratives bring past events to life through action, description, and dialogue. Write a personal narrative about an important experience you've had.

The following skills, introduced in this section's Writing Mini-Lessons, will help you write your personal narrative.

Writing Skills Focus

▶ **Use an appropriate tone** to describe the people and events in your narrative. (See p. 21.)
▶ **Elaborate to make writing personal.** Include details that reveal your ideas about people, places, and events. (See p. 31.)
▶ Connect the events in your narrative using **transitions.** (See p. 47.)

MODEL FROM LITERATURE

from *I Know Why the Caged Bird Sings* by Maya Angelou

Weighing the half-pounds of flour, excluding the scoop, and depositing them dust-free into the thin paper sacks held a simple kind of adventure for me. ① I developed an eye for measuring how full a silver-looking ladle of flour, mash, meal, sugar or corn had to be to push the scale indicator over to eight ounces or one pound. When I was absolutely accurate ② our appreciative customers used to admire: "Sister Henderson sure got some smart grandchildrens." ③

① Specific incidents bring Angelou's personal experience to life.
② The transition word *when* makes the logical connection clear.
③ This line of dialogue gives the narrative a warm, homey tone.

Prewriting

Choose a Topic Your memory is probably the best place to search for a topic for your personal narrative. Recall holidays, birthdays, school trips, or even what you did this morning to find an experience to describe in a personal narrative. You may also select from among these topic ideas:

> ### Topic Ideas
> - A misunderstanding between you and a friend
> - The best vacation ever
> - Getting a pet

Create a Timeline Make a chronological list of events you want to include in your story by filling in a timeline like this one:

| Arrived at school. | Met Johnny for lunch. | Spilled pudding. | Slipped in spill. | Missed bus home. |

Drafting

Tell the Story As you draft, check off events on your timeline. By doing this, you'll be sure to include all the specific incidents of the narrative.

Elaborate to Personalize Your Writing Consider how you would describe the events of your narrative to a close friend. Elaborate on the events with specific details and personal observations. Personalizing your narrative in this way will bring your reader closer to the events as you experienced them.

Choose an Appropriate Tone One way to make your personal narrative memorable is to give it an appropriate tone, or to convey your attitude about the event. To do this, choose words and phrasing that support or mirror the emotional impact of the scene you're describing.

Serious Tone: His face fell when I said I have to move to another town.

Humorous Tone: His jaw hit the floor when I said "I'm outta here."

APPLYING LANGUAGE SKILLS: Writing Realistic Dialogue

Realistic dialogue captures the way people really speak. In casual speech, people use informal language and contractions rather than phrasing that would be expected in formal writing.

Formal Phrasing
"I will buy you some french-fried potatoes."

Realistic Dialogue
"I'll get you some fries."

Practice For each statement below, write a line of dialogue.

1. Filip tells you after class that he can't come to the meeting after school today.
2. Mother asked Alonso to bring home a gallon of milk from the store.
3. Stan asked Wendy why she wasn't at the Fun Fair on Saturday.

Writing Application As you edit, revise your dialogue to make it realistic.

Writer's Solution Connection Writing Lab

To learn more about realistic dialogue, see the interactive models on improving dialogue in the Revising and Editing section of the Narration tutorial.

Applying LANGUAGE SKILLS: Common and Proper Nouns

Proper nouns name specific people, places, and things; they should be capitalized. Common nouns, which name general people, places, and things, are not capitalized unless they begin a sentence.

Common Nouns

state, store, girl

Proper Nouns

Arkansas, Marguerite

Practice Rewrite the following, correcting capitalization as needed.

1. The pueblo peoples live in the area of the country now known as the four corners.
2. I remember my family's trip to the grand canyon.
3. Stories of the exchange student from turkey taught us a lot about our life in the united states.
4. Moving to indiana changed melanie's life.

Writing Application Check your draft to be sure you've capitalized proper nouns but not common nouns.

Writer's Solution Connection Language Lab

For more practice with proper nouns, complete the Language Lab lesson Proper Nouns in the Capitalization unit.

Revising

Make Connections Look over your draft. Have you described events so they are clear and detailed? Have you used transitions to indicate how events are related?

> **Transitions Showing Time Order:** *first, then, next, now, after, before, while, during, when*

> **Transitions Showing Importance:** *although, however, yet, despite, even though*

Add Dialogue to Make Characters Memorable In the real-life event you're describing, conversation probably took place. Instead of telling what people said, bring their actual words to life by adding dialogue.

> **Telling:** Mike promised he'd never go there again.

> **Dialogue:** "I'll never, ever go there again!" Mike sobbed.

REVISION MODEL

Working after school at the library made a big difference in my life. I learned to smile at people and look them in the eye as I helped them locate and check out books. I

① *My cheery "How can I help you?" usually won me smiles at the kids' corner.*

② *most of all*

learned to work quickly and efficiently to keep the check-out line moving. ~~The yuckiest~~ part of the job was stocking

③ *My least favorite*

shelves at the end of the day, but knowing that was the last thing to do before I could go home made even that part tolerable.

① I added dialogue to help make events more personal.
② Adding a transition connects ideas in my narrative.
③ I changed the beginning of this sentence to match the tone of the rest of the piece.

Publishing and Presenting

▶ **Classroom** One way to share your personal narrative is to read it aloud to your classmates. You may want to work with fellow classmates to arrange a reading of your personal narratives to a class of younger students.

▶ **E-mail** Share your narrative by e-mailing it to a close friend or relative.

Real-World Reading Skills Workshop

Strategies for Success

In a typical week, you probably skim through magazines or news articles, glance at posters and advertisements, and read through menus or sales catalogs. You probably won't be tested on the meaning of these pieces of writing. You will, however, benefit by learning to recognize the author's purpose behind each piece and to read appropriately. The tips at the right will help you identify an author's purpose.

These wool-lined leather mountain boots are a "must-have" for serious hikers.
Lovingly crafted from all-natural materials, these boots cradle your feet while allowing them to breathe.
Skid resistant and waterproof.
Available in Butter, Toffee, and Mocha colors.
Specify size when ordering.

Men's Boots: $89.99 plus tax and shipping
Women's Boots: $79.99 plus tax and shipping

How to Read Magazine and News

Articles Most magazine and news articles are meant to inform, to entertain, or to persuade. Look at the title of the article, and skim the first paragraph to get a hint about the author's purpose. Once you've determined the author's purpose, adjust your reading accordingly. For example, if the article is meant to entertain, you can read quickly for enjoyment. If, however, the author wants to convince you of something, read critically, questioning his or her ideas.

How to Read Advertisements, Brochures, Catalogs, and Menus Writers of advertisements, brochures, catalogs, and menus want you to buy their products or services. If you're an interested customer, read carefully and critically before buying. For example, in a catalog description of an item, separate factual details, such as "solid oak" or "$1.99 plus tax," from persuasive details, such as "lovely" or "inexpensive."

How to Read Posters and Flyers Most posters and flyers are meant to inform or persuade. If the poster or flyer is meant to inform, skim it to find such important information as dates, times, and maps. If the poster or flyer is persuasive, read it more critically, questioning the information that is given.

Apply the Strategies

Read the catalog entry at the left, and answer the following questions.

1. What is the author's purpose?
2. Should you read this piece carefully and critically, or should you read for enjoyment? Explain why.

Nouns

Grammar Review

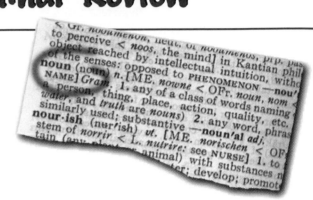

Nouns are words that refer to people, places, things, and ideas or qualities. They are the building blocks of nearly everything we say.

Person	general, teacher, Bill Gates
Place	home, kindergarten, Texas
Thing	drum, pearl, e-mail
Idea or quality	fear, childhood, communication

You can put nouns into these categories:

Common	uniform, store, computer (See p. 20.)
Proper	Shiloh, Charles, Macintosh (See p. 20.)
Concrete	peach, woods, rabbit (See p. 46.)
Abstract	taste, imagination, technology (See p. 46.)
Plural	drums, desks, lunches, cookies (See p. 30.)
Possessive Singular	the general's coat (See p. 30.)
Possessive Plural	the armies' strategies (See p. 30.)

Practice 1 On your paper, write the nouns in each sentence that follows. Label each as common or proper; then label them as concrete or abstract.

1. How did the students respond to the story set during the Civil War?

2. On Fridays, her sister helped out in the grocery store.

3. The little boy has great concentration.

4. The kindergarten students went to see bats and monkeys at the Harris Zoo.

5. When do you think Senator Lee will talk about progress?

Practice 2 Create plurals and possessives of the given nouns according to the directions after each word.

1. march (plural)

2. building (possessive, singular)

3. teacher (possessive, plural)

4. brother (possessive, plural)

5. dress (possessive, plural)

Grammar in Writing

✔ *Nouns can sharpen your writing. Whenever possible, choose nouns that are specific.*

General: The gym teacher loved sports.

Specific: The gym teacher loved soccer, tennis, and baseball.

✔ *Be careful not to use apostrophes when you make nouns plural. Use apostrophes only when you make nouns possessive.*

PART 2 *Seasons and Cycles*

Late September Afternoon, Viola's Field, 1997, Jim Schantz, Pucker Gallery

Guide for Reading

Meet the Author:

Pearl S. Buck (1892–1973)

The first woman ever to win both the Pulitzer Prize and the Nobel Prize, Pearl S. Buck grew up in China, where her parents were missionaries. Like many of her books, Buck's Pulitzer Prize-winning novel, *The Good Earth*, is set in China. However, Buck also wrote novels, short stories, and essays that are set in the United States. "Christmas Day in the Morning," for example, takes place on a small American dairy farm.

At Home in Two Cultures Following her childhood in China, Buck attended college in the United States. She later went back to China to teach. Eventually, Buck returned to American shores, finally settling in Bucks County, Pennsylvania. There she became active in promoting women's rights and child welfare, and in condemning racism.

THE STORY BEHIND THE STORY

Like the main character in "Christmas Day in the Morning," Buck, too, had an experience of giving the gift of love at Christmas. When she was fifteen years old and living in China, that country experienced a terrible famine. Rather than spending money on a holiday feast for themselves, Buck's family bought rice for the starving peasants. They spent all of Christmas Day feeding hungry families.

◆ LITERATURE AND YOUR LIFE

CONNECT YOUR EXPERIENCE

Not all gifts come in brightly wrapped packages, like those in the photograph at right. Some gifts come in the form of kindness and caring. Take a moment to recall the best gift you ever gave and the best one you ever received. In "Christmas Day in the Morning," you'll learn about a precious gift that one boy gives to his dad.

THEMATIC FOCUS: Seasons and Cycles

As you read this story, look for ways in which the Christmas season—a time of gift giving—comes to hold special meaning for the main character.

◆ Background for Understanding

SOCIAL STUDIES

Small family dairy farms, like the one in "Christmas Day in the Morning," once were commonplace in America. Because they were not automated, as most dairy farms are today, all chores had to be done by hand. Not only did the cows have to be milked, they had to be moved from pasture to pasture and cared for when ill.

◆ Build Vocabulary

RELATED WORDS: FORMS OF *finite*

Pearl Buck describes the main character's children as showing "infinite gentleness." The word *infinite* is a form of the word *finite,* which means "having a beginning and an end." Coupled with the prefix *-in,* meaning "without" or "not," it means "having no limits or end."

WORD BANK

Preview these words from the selection. Which word do you think means "calmly"? Check the Build Vocabulary box on page 67 to see if you chose correctly.

infinite
brisk
loitering
placidly
acquiescent

◆ Christmas Day in the Morning ◆

◆ Literary Focus

FLASHBACK

A **flashback** is a scene within a story that interrupts the sequence of events to relate events that occurred in the past. Flashbacks allow writers to present two different time frames simultaneously, enabling readers to compare and contrast the present and the past. In "Christmas Day in the Morning," Pearl Buck uses a flashback to show why the main character, Robert, who is now a grandfather, has had special feelings about Christmas since he was fifteen years old.

◆ Reading Strategy

IDENTIFY SEQUENCE OF EVENTS

The **sequence of events** in a story is the order in which things happen. Authors use time-order words like *first, before, later,* and *eventually* to let you know which events happened first, next, and last. These signal words are especially important in stories that shift backward or forward in time.

To keep track of the story events, create a timeline like the one below. Chart the key events that happen in the present time and in the flashback.

Timeline

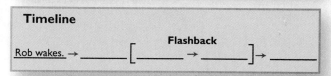

Christmas Day

in the Morning
Pearl S. Buck

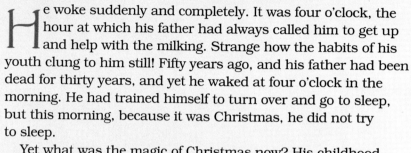

He woke suddenly and completely. It was four o'clock, the hour at which his father had always called him to get up and help with the milking. Strange how the habits of his youth clung to him still! Fifty years ago, and his father had been dead for thirty years, and yet he waked at four o'clock in the morning. He had trained himself to turn over and go to sleep, but this morning, because it was Christmas, he did not try to sleep.

Yet what was the magic of Christmas now? His childhood and youth were long past, and his own children had grown up and gone. Some of them lived only a few miles away but they had their own families, and though they would come in as usual toward the end of the day, they had explained with <u>infinite</u> gentleness that they wanted their children to build Christmas memories about *their* houses, not his. He was left alone with his wife.

Yesterday she had said, "It isn't worthwhile, perhaps—"

And he had said, "Oh, yes, Alice, even if there are only the two of us, let's have a Christmas of our own."

Then she had said, "Let's not trim the tree until tomorrow, Robert—just so it's ready when the children come. I'm tired."

He had agreed, and the tree was still out in the back entry.

Why did he feel so awake tonight? For it was still night, a clear and starry night. No moon, of course, but the stars were extraordinary! Now that he thought of it, the stars seemed always large and clear before the dawn of Christmas Day. There was one star now that was certainly larger and brighter than any of the others. He could even imagine it moving, as it had seemed to him to move one night long ago.

He slipped back in time, as he did so easily nowadays. He was fifteen years old and still on his father's farm. He loved his father. He had not known it until one day a few days before Christmas, when he had overheard what his father was saying to his mother.

◆ Build Vocabulary

infinite (in´ fə nit) *adj.*: Extending beyond measure or comprehension

---

◀ **Critical Viewing** What in this painting creates a feeling of expectation? **[Interpret]**

Christmas Snow, 1984, David Armstrong, North Mountain Press, Inc.

"Mary, I hate to call Rob in the mornings. He's growing so fast and he needs his sleep. If you could see how he sleeps when I go in to wake him up! I wish I could manage alone."

"Well, you can't, Adam." His mother's voice was brisk. "Besides, he isn't a child anymore. It's time he took his turn."

"Yes," his father said slowly. "But I sure do hate to wake him."

When he heard these words, something in him woke: his father loved him! He had never thought of it before, taking for granted the tie of their blood. Neither his father nor his mother talked about loving their children—they had no time for such things. There was always so much to do on a farm.

◆ **Reading Strategy**
Which signal words in this paragraph indicate the sequence of events?

Now that he knew his father loved him, there would be no more loitering in the mornings and having to be called again. He got up after that, stumbling blind with sleep, and pulled on his clothes, his eyes tight shut, but he got up.

And then on the night before Christmas, that year when he was fifteen, he lay for a few minutes thinking about the next day. They were poor, and most of the excitement was in the turkey they had raised themselves and in the mince pies his mother made. His sisters sewed presents and his mother and father always bought something he needed, not only a warm jacket, maybe, but something more, such as a book. And he saved and bought them each something, too.

He wished, that Christmas he was fifteen, he had a better present for his father. As usual he had gone to the ten-cent store and bought a tie.

◆ **Build Vocabulary**

brisk (brisk) *adj.*: Quick in manner

loitering (loit´ ər iŋ) *n.*: Lingering in an aimless way

placidly (plas´ id lē) *adv.*: In a calm way

◀ **Critical Viewing** How would you describe the boy's mood? In what way does it resemble young Rob's mood in the days before Christmas? [Analyze]

It had seemed nice enough until he lay thinking the night before Christmas, and then he wished that he had heard his father and mother talking in time for him to save for something better.

He lay on his side, his head supported by his elbow, and looked out of his attic window. The stars were bright, much brighter than he ever remembered seeing them, and one star in particular was so bright that he wondered if it were really the Star of Bethlehem.

"Dad," he had once asked when he was a little boy, "what is a stable?"

"It's just a barn," his father had replied, "like ours."

Then Jesus had been born in a barn, and to a barn the shepherds and the Wise Men had come, bringing their Christmas gifts!

The thought struck him like a silver dagger. Why should he not give his father a special gift too, out there in the barn? He could get up early, earlier than four o'clock, and he could creep into the barn and get all the milking done. He'd do it alone, milk and clean up, and then when his father went in to start the milking, he'd see it all done. And he would know who had done it.

He laughed to himself as he gazed at the stars. It was what he would do, and he mustn't sleep too sound.

He must have waked twenty times, scratching a match each time to look at his old watch—midnight, and half past one, and then two o'clock.

At a quarter to three he got up and put on his clothes. He crept downstairs, careful of the creaky boards, and let himself out. The big star hung lower over the barn roof, a reddish gold. The cows looked at him, sleepy and surprised. It was early for them too.

"So, boss," he whispered. They accepted him placidly and he fetched some hay for each cow and then got the milking pail and the big milk cans.

He had never milked all alone before, but it seemed almost easy. He kept thinking about his father's surprise. His father would come in and call him, saying that he would get things started while Rob was getting dressed. He'd go to the barn, open the door, and then he'd go to get the two big empty milk cans. But they wouldn't be waiting or empty; they'd be standing in the milkhouse, filled.

"What the—" he could hear his father exclaiming.

He smiled and milked steadily, two strong streams rushing into the pail, frothing and fragrant. The cows were still surprised but acquiescent. For once they were behaving well, as though they knew it was Christmas.

The task went more easily than he had ever known it to before. Milking for once was not a chore. It was something else, a gift to his father who loved him. He finished, the two milk cans were full, and he covered them and closed the milkhouse door carefully, making sure of the latch. He put the stool in its place by the door and hung up the clean milk pail. Then he went out of the barn and barred the door behind him.

Back in his room he had only a minute to pull off his clothes in the darkness and jump into bed, for he heard his father up. He put the covers over his head to silence his quick breathing. The door opened.

"Rob!" his father called. "We have to get up, son, even if it is Christmas."

"Aw-right," he said sleepily.

"I'll go on out," his father said. "I'll get things started."

The door closed and he lay still, laughing to himself. In just a few minutes his father would know. His dancing heart was ready to jump from his body.

The minutes were endless—ten, fifteen, he did not know how many—and he heard his father's footsteps again. The door opened and he lay still.

"Rob!"

"Yes, Dad—"

"You son of a—" His father was laughing, a queer sobbing sort of a laugh. "Thought you'd fool me, did you?" His father was standing beside his bed, feeling for him, pulling away the cover.

◆ Build Vocabulary

acquiescent (ak´ wē es´ ənt) *adj.*: Agreeing without protest

"It's for Christmas, Dad!"

He found his father and clutched him in a great hug. He felt his father's arms go around him. It was dark and they could not see each other's faces.

"Son, I thank you. Nobody ever did a nicer thing—"

"Oh, Dad, I want you to know—I do want to be good!" The words broke from him of their own will. He did not know what to say. His heart was bursting with love.

"Well, I reckon I can go back to bed and sleep," his father said after a moment. "No, hark—the little ones are waked up. Come to think of it, son, I've never seen you children when you first saw the Christmas tree. I was always in the barn. Come on!"

He got up and pulled on his clothes again and they went down to the Christmas tree, and soon the sun was creeping up to where the star had been. Oh, what a Christmas, and how his heart had nearly burst again with shyness and pride as his father told his mother and made the younger children listen about how he, Rob, had got up all by himself.

"The best Christmas gift I ever had, and I'll remember it, son, every year on Christmas morning, so long as I live."

They had both remembered it, and now that his father was dead he remembered it alone: that blessed Christmas dawn when, alone with the cows in the barn, he had made his first gift of true love.

◆ **Literary Focus**
How do you know that this is the end of the flashback?

Outside the window now the great star slowly sank. He got up out of bed and put on his slippers and bathrobe and went softly upstairs to the attic and found the box of Christmas-tree decorations. He took them downstairs into the living room. Then he brought in the tree. It was a little one—they had not had a big tree since the children went away—but he set it in the holder and put it in the middle of the long table under the window. Then carefully he began to trim it.

It was done very soon, the time passing as quickly as it had that morning long ago in the barn. He went to his library and fetched the little box that contained his special gift to his wife, a star of diamonds, not large but dainty in design. He had written the card for it the day before. He tied the gift on the tree and then stood back. It was pretty, very pretty, and she would be surprised.

But he was not satisfied. He wanted to tell her—to tell her how much he loved her. It had been a long time since he had really told her, although he loved her in a very special way, much more than he ever had when they were young.

He had been fortunate that she had loved him—and how fortunate that he had been able to love! Ah, that was the true joy of life, the ability to love! For he was quite sure that some people were genuinely unable to love anyone. But love was alive in him, it still was.

It occurred to him suddenly that it was alive because long ago it had been born in him when he knew his father loved him. That was it: love alone could waken love.

And he could give the gift again and again. This morning, this blessed Christmas morning, he would give it to his beloved wife. He could write it down in a letter for her to read and keep forever. He went to his desk and began his love letter to his wife: *My dearest love . . .*

When it was finished he sealed it and tied it on the tree where she would see it the first thing when she came into the room. She would read it, surprised and then moved, and realize how very much he loved her.

He put out the light and went tiptoeing up the stairs. The star in the sky was gone, and the first rays of the sun were gleaming in the sky. Such a happy, happy Christmas!

Guide for Responding

◆ LITERATURE AND YOUR LIFE

Reader's Response What do you think of Rob's gift to his father?

Thematic Focus In what way does "Christmas Day in the Morning" reveal cycles of life?

Group Discussion With a group of classmates, explore the saying "It is better to give than to receive." Use events in the story as examples.

☑ Check Your Comprehension

1. Why does young Rob's father wake him every morning at four o'clock?
2. What happens to make Rob realize that he loves his father?
3. What gift does young Rob first plan to give his father? Why does he alter his plan?
4. How does Rob's father show his gratitude for Rob's gift?
5. What gift does Robert, as an adult, first plan to give his wife? What does he do to enhance his gift?

◆ Critical Thinking

INTERPRET

1. What is special about the gift young Rob gives his father? How does giving it make Rob feel? **[Connect]**
2. How are Rob's feelings about the gift similar to his father's feelings? How are they different? **[Compare and Contrast]**
3. At the beginning of the story, the adult Robert wakes up and wonders what happened to the magic of Christmas. (a) How do his feelings change by the end of the story? (b) What has brought about the change? **[Draw Conclusions]**
4. In what ways other than by giving gifts does Robert show his "ability to love"? Explain. **[Interpret]**

EVALUATE

5. Do you agree with the statement "Love alone could waken love"? **[Criticize]**

APPLY

6. What are "gifts of true love," such as the ones Robert gives? **[Define]**

Guide for Responding (continued)

◆ Literary Focus

FLASHBACK

Flashbacks, which interrupt story events to reveal events that happened in the past, may help you gain insight into a story. They can give you a broader view of the story's events or help you understand a character's actions.

1. When does the flashback begin in "Christmas Day in the Morning"?
2. How do you know when the flashback is over?
3. What insights about Robert do you gain from the flashback?

◆ Build Vocabulary

USING FORMS OF *finite*

The adjective *finite*, meaning "with a beginning and end," can stand alone or combine with prefixes and suffixes to make related words. On your paper, write the form(s) of *finite* that answers each question.

infinity infinitesimal infinite finite infinitely

1. Which two words are antonyms, or opposites?
2. Which word means "too small to be measured"?
3. Which word is an adverb?
4. Which noun means "the state of being infinite"?

SPELLING STRATEGY

The letter combination *qu* usually makes the *kw* sound. In words like *acquiescent,* the *c* preceding the *qu* is sometimes mistakenly dropped because it is unvoiced. On your paper, fill in the following, using words that begin with the letters *acqu.*

1. Someone you've met is an ____?____.
2. When a defendant is not guilty, you ____?____ him or her.
3. When you buy something, you ____?____ it.

USING THE WORD BANK

On your paper, write the word that is opposite in meaning to the first word.

1. brisk: (a) clever, (b) curt, (c) slow
2. infinite: (a) endless, (b) limited, (c) tiny
3. loitering: (a) littering, (b) dawdling, (c) moving
4. acquiescent: (a) watery, (b) dull, (c) argumentative
5. placidly: (a) turbulently, (b) nicely, (c) meanly

◆ Reading Strategy

IDENTIFY SEQUENCE OF EVENTS

Sometimes an author will interrupt a story's regular **sequence of events** to tell about something that happened before the story began. As you read, look for clues, like "He slipped back in time," that indicate a time change.

Tell whether each event takes place in the past, in the flashback, or in the present.

1. Rob realizes his father loves him.
2. Rob writes a love letter to his wife.
3. Rob remembers his gift to his father.
4. Rob decides to get up early and milk the cows.

◆ Build Grammar Skills

PRONOUNS AND ANTECEDENTS

A **pronoun** takes the place of a noun or another pronoun. Some common pronouns are *we, you, he, she, it, we, they, us, mine, their,* and *who.* An **antecedent** is the word or group of words that a pronoun replaces. In these sentences from the story, the pronoun *he* replaces the antecedent *Rob.*

I hate to call *Rob* in the mornings. *He's* growing so fast and *he* needs his sleep.

Practice Copy the following sentences. Underline each pronoun and draw an arrow to its antecedent.

1. Adam hated to wake his son.
2. When Rob heard his father's words, he became filled with love.
3. The cows were in their stalls.
4. When the tree was trimmed, it glistened.
5. When she saw the gift, Robert's wife cried.

Writing Application Rewrite the following sentences, replacing repeated nouns with pronouns.

1. Adam and Mary discussed what to do about the chores on Adam and Mary's farm.
2. Rob remembered that on that past Christmas Rob gave his father a special gift.
3. Because Alice didn't feel well, Robert wanted to surprise Alice by trimming the tree.

Build Your Portfolio

 ## Idea Bank

Writing

1. **Letter From Robert** Write a letter from Robert to his children, expressing his thoughts on the night before Christmas.

2. **Book-Jacket Copy** Write an attention-grabbing summary of "Christmas Day in the Morning" for a book jacket. Don't give away the whole story, but provide enough information to interest potential readers.

3. **Essay** How would "Christmas Day in the Morning" be different if it had contained no flashback but told the story of Rob from his youth to old age? Explain your ideas in an essay. Use details from the story to support your ideas.

Speaking and Listening

4. **Speech** As Rob, prepare a one-minute speech about the meaning of the Christmas season. Practice reading your speech aloud before presenting it to the class.

5. **Modern Scene [Group Activity]** With a group, create a script for a dramatic scene based on events from "Christmas Day in the Morning" but set in a modern setting of your choice. Rehearse your scene, and then perform it for the class. **[Performing Arts Link]**

Projects

6. **Holiday Spirit [Group Activity]** Work with a group of classmates to create a multimedia presentation about various holidays celebrated by diverse cultures. For example, you might compare and contrast Christmas, Hanuka, and Kwanzaa. **[Social Studies Link]**

7. **Comic Strip** Create a comic strip about an important event in a character's life. In your comic strip, include a flashback scene. You may want to refer to actual comic strips to get ideas about formatting. **[Art Link]**

 ## Writing Mini-Lesson

Fictional Narrative Containing a Flashback

In "Christmas Day in the Morning," Robert lets his thoughts wander back to a memorable Christmas on which he gave a very special gift. Write a story of your own, containing a flashback in which your main character relives an incident from the past.

Writing Skills Focus: Use Transitions

Use **transitions** like *after a while, before,* and *earlier* to show what happens first, next, and last. Also, use transitions to indicate to readers where the flashback begins, as Pearl Buck does in the following example.

Model From the Story

He slipped back in time, as he did so easily nowadays. He was fifteen years old and still on his father's farm.

Prewriting Sketch out the form your narrative will take—who the characters are and what happens. Make a timeline showing the order of events and where you will insert the flashback.

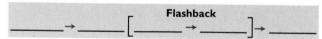

Drafting Now, write the story, weaving together plot events and developing your characters. Use transitions as you write, indicating the sequence of story events.

Revising Where necessary, add description to your narrative to strengthen characters and setting. Insert transitions wherever the time order of plot events is unclear. Also, be sure that you've begun your flashback with a transition.

◆ **Grammar Application**
If you've used a particular noun repeatedly, replace the noun with a pronoun.

Guide for Reading

Meet the Authors:

Leo Tolstoy (1828–1910)

Leo Tolstoy, a Russian writer, is regarded by many experts to be one of the world's finest novelists. He developed a taste for literature as a boy, when he discovered the joys of reading the folk tales of his native land, poems about Russian heroes, and stories from the Bible.

THE STORY BEHIND THE STORY

In "The Old Grandfather and His Little Grandson," Tolstoy stresses the importance of providing care and showing respect for the elderly. Because Tolstoy lost both parents to illness when he was still a boy, he probably felt very strongly that parents were to be valued and loved.

Amy Ling (1939–   )

Amy Ling is fascinated by China. She was born in that country and spent six years there before coming with her family to the United States. In the 1960's, she visited her grandmother in Taiwan, an island off the coast of China. She describes the dramatic meeting in "Grandma."

Ricardo Sánchez (1941–1995)

Born in El Paso, Texas, Ricardo Sánchez had roots in Spanish Mexican, North American, and Native American cultures. Most of his work, including "Old Man," is an exploration and celebration of his rich heritage. That's why he often used both English and Spanish words in his writing.

◆ LITERATURE AND YOUR LIFE

CONNECT YOUR EXPERIENCE

The painting at the right might be described as showing a circle of life in which people old and young dance together. In the world around you, what might symbolize a circle of life? The writers in this section focus on their relatives and ancestors—and how those people contributed to their lives.

THEMATIC FOCUS: Seasons and Cycles

What do these writers suggest about the gifts that people from different stages in life can give to one another?

◆ Background for Understanding

SOCIAL STUDIES

In "Grandma," the poem's speaker tells of visiting her grandmother in Taiwan. Taiwan, formed by islands off the coast of China, has a rich and interesting history. Over the centuries, it has been occupied by Portugal, China, Holland, and Japan. Today, it is an independent nation inhabited largely by people who fled from mainland China when the communist forces won control of the Chinese government.

◆ Build Vocabulary

SYNONYMS FOR *rivulets*

English is rich in synonyms—words that express the same meaning in slightly different ways. For example, *rivulets* ("little streams") has the synonyms *brooks, streams,* and *creeks.*

WORD BANK

Which word from the list might describe a well-made table? Check the Build Vocabulary box on page 75 to see if you chose correctly.

scolded
sturdy
rivulets
furrows
supple
stoic

The Old Grandfather and His Little Grandson
Grandma ◆ Old Man

Second Circle Dance, Phoebe Beasley

◆ Literary Focus
SENSORY LANGUAGE

Reading a work of literature can allow you to step through a door into a new world. Writers enable you to picture this new world clearly by using **sensory language**—language that captures sights, sounds, smells, tastes, and sensations of touch. As you read these works, take full advantage of the sensory language by reading them with your senses as well as with your mind. For example, use Tolstoy's description of the grandfather to see him sitting at the table, "old" and blind and "toothless."

◆ Reading Strategy
RELATE TO WHAT YOU KNOW

Your own memories and observations help you to appreciate the sensory language in a literary work. Similarly, you can better understand the characters and situations if you **relate them to what you know.** Consider what you've learned through experience, as well as the knowledge you've gained from school and other sources. Use a reader's journal like this one to help you make connections to these selections.

Passage	⟶	What I Know
The grandfather had become very old. His legs would not carry him....		My grandfather recently fell and broke his hip.

The Old Grandfather and His Little Grandson

Leo Tolstoy

The grandfather had become very old. His legs would not carry him, his eyes could not see, his ears could not hear, and he was toothless. When he ate, bits of food sometimes dropped out of his mouth. His son and his son's wife no longer allowed him to eat with them at the table. He had to eat his meals in the corner near the stove.

One day they gave him his food in a bowl. He tried to move the bowl closer; it fell to the floor and broke. His daughter-in-law <u>scolded</u> him. She told him that he spoiled everything in the house and broke their dishes, and she said that from now on he would get his food in a wooden dish. The old man sighed and said nothing.

A few days later, the old man's son and his wife were sitting in their hut, resting and watching their little boy playing on the floor. They saw him putting together something out of small pieces of wood. His father asked him, "What are you making, Misha?"

The little grandson said, "I'm making a wooden bucket. When you and Mamma get old, I'll feed you out of this wooden dish."

The young peasant and his wife looked at each other, and tears filled their eyes. They were ashamed because they had treated the old grandfather so meanly, and from that day they again let the old man eat with them at the table and took better care of him.

◀ **Critical Viewing** How do the details in this painting symbolize, or represent, the story's message? [Interpret]

Woman with White Kerchief (Uygur), Lunda Hoyle Gill

▶ **Critical Viewing** Compare and contrast the woman in this painting with Grandma, as described in the poem. **[Compare and Contrast]**

Grandma

Amy Ling

If you dig that hole deep enough
you'll reach China, they used to tell me,
a child in a backyard, Allentown, Pa.
Not strong enough to dig that hole,
5   I waited twenty years
then sailed back
half way around the world.

In Taiwan I first met Grandma.
Before she came to view I heard
10   her slippered feet softly measure
the tatami[1] floor with even step.
The aqua paper door slid open
and there, breathless, I faced
my five foot height, my sturdy legs and feet,
15   my square forehead, high cheeks, and wide-set eyes.
My image stood before me
acted on by fifty years;
here in my past was my future.

She smiled, stretched her arms
20   to take to heart the eldest daughter
of her youngest son a quarter century away.
She spoke a tongue I knew no word of
and I was sad I could not understand,
but I could hug her.

◆ **Build Vocabulary**

scolded (skōld´ əd) *v.*: Criticized harshly

sturdy (stʉr´ dē) *adj.*: Firm; strong

―――――――――――――――――

1. **tatami** (tə tä´ mē) *adj.*: Woven of rice straw.

Old Man

Ricardo Sánchez

El Pan Nuestro (Our Daily Bread), c. 1905, Ramon Frade, Instituto de Cultura Puertorriquena, San Juan

▲ **Critical Viewing** Does this painting effectively convey an old man "wise with time"? Explain. [Make a Judgment]

remembrance (smiles/hurts sweetly)
           October 8, 1972

    old man
    with brown skin
    talking of past
        when being shepherd
5   in utah, nevada, colorado and
           new mexico
    was life lived freely;

    old man,
        grandfather,
    wise with time
10   running <u>rivulets</u> on face,
    deep, rich <u>furrows</u>,
        each one a legacy,
    deep, rich memories
    of life . . .
15   "you are indio,[1]

        among other things,"
    he would tell me
        during nights spent
    so long ago
20   amidst familial gatherings
    in albuquerque . . .

    old man, loved and respected,
    he would speak sometimes
    of pueblos,[2]
25   san juan, santa clara,
        and even santo domingo,
    and his family, he would say,
    came from there:
        some of our blood was here,
30   he would say,
        before the coming of coronado,[3]

---

1. **indio** (ēn´ dyō) *n.*: Indian; Native American.

2. **pueblos** (pweb´ lōz) *n.*: Here, Native American towns in central and northern New Mexico.
3. **coronado** (kô rô nä´ dô): Coronado explored what is today the American Southwest.

◆ Build Vocabulary

rivulets (riv´ yoo lits) *n.*: Little streams
furrows (fur´ ōz) *n.*: Deep wrinkles
supple (sup´ əl) *adj.*: Flexible and pliant
stoic (stō´ ik) *adj.*: Calm and unbothered in spite of suffering

other of our blood
   came with los españoles,[4]
and the mixture
35 was rich,
   though often painful . . .
old man,
who knew earth
   by its awesome aromas
40 and who felt
the heated sweetness
   of chile verde [5]
by his supple touch,
gone into dust is your body
45   with its stoic look and resolution,
but your reality, old man, lives on
in a mindsoul touched by you . . .

Old Man . . .

---

4. **los españoles** (lōs es pä nyōl´ es) *n.*: The Spaniards.
5. **chile verde** (chē´ le vehr´ dē) *n.*: Green pepper.

Beyond Literature

Social Studies Connection

Caring for the Elderly Social scientists study aging trends to help us plan for the future. The average human life span has greatly increased due to advances in medical care and living conditions. It will take careful economic and social planning to ensure that we are able to care for the large numbers of elderly citizens living in our society.

Cross-Curricular Activity
Science Do research on average life expectancy rates from the 1700's onward. Create a chart showing the average life span for men and women throughout the years.

Guide for Responding

◆ LITERATURE AND YOUR LIFE

Reader's Response Which person in these works do you admire most? Why?

Thematic Focus What do these works suggest about the bond between a grandparent and a grandchild?

☑ Check Your Comprehension

1. How do the old man's son and his wife treat the grandfather in "The Old Grandfather . . ."?
2. Describe how and why the couple changes their behavior at the end of "The Old Grandfather . . ."
3. Describe the meeting between Ling and her grandmother in "Grandma."
4. To whom does Sánchez address his poem?
5. What did the old man teach Sánchez about their shared heritage?

◆ Critical Thinking

INTERPRET
1. Why does the boy's response to his father's question in "The Old Grandfather . . ." make his parents feel "ashamed"? **[Interpret]**
2. Why is Ling's meeting with her grandmother so important to her? **[Draw Conclusions]**
3. In what way do lines 46–47 sum up the meaning of "Old Man"? **[Analyze]**

EVALUATE
4. Can children in real life teach grown-ups, as the grandson does in "The Old Grandfather . . ."? Why or why not? **[Make a Judgment]**

COMPARE LITERARY WORKS
5. What similar attitudes toward older people do "The Old Grandfather . . ." and "Grandma" express? **[Compare and Contrast]**

Guide for Responding (continued)

◆ Reading Strategy

RELATE WHAT YOU KNOW

By **relating what you know** to these works, you brought the gift of your own life to the writers' words. Describe an experience of your own that helped you understand each of these situations:

1. "The Old Grandfather . . .": adults learning from a child
2. "Grandma": seeing yourself in an older relative
3. "Old Man": feeling grateful to an older person

◆ Build Vocabulary

USING SYNONYMS FOR *rivulets*

Synonyms express different shades of the same basic meaning. For example, although *rivulets, brooks, streams,* and *creeks* are synonyms, streams are larger than creeks, which are larger than both rivulets and brooks. Also, *brook* suggests a more lively body of water than *rivulet* does.

On your paper, choose one synonym to complete each sentence. Then, explain your choice.

1. All day, he listened to the babbling (rivulet, brook).
2. He liked to swim across the (creek, brook).
3. Row, row, row your boat, gently down the (rivulet, stream).

SPELLING STRATEGY

When spelling most two-syllable words with a consonant sound in the middle after a short vowel sound, double the middle consonant:

   supple: (short *u* sound followed by *p* sound)
   brittle: (short *i* sound followed by *t* sound)

On your paper, correct any misspelled words.

1. furow   2. battle   3. litle   4. beter

USING THE WORD BANK

On your paper, write the word closest in meaning to the first word.

1. scolded: (a) praised, (b) criticized, (c) scalded
2. sturdy: (a) strong, (b) flimsy, (c) intelligent
3. rivulets: (a) oceans, (b) fasteners, (c) brooks
4. furrows: (a) wrinkles, (b) creeks, (c) holes
5. stoic: (a) pained, (b) unbothered, (c) unconscious
6. supple: (a) rigid, (b) tasty, (c) flexible

◆ Literary Focus

SENSORY LANGUAGE

In these works, the **sensory language**—language appealing to the senses—helps you experience what the writers describe. In "Grandma," for example, you can hear the grandmother approach before you actually see her: "her slippered feet softly measure/the tatami floor with even step."

1. Find two more sensory details in "Grandma," one appealing to sight and one to touch.
2. Explain how details appealing to the senses of smell and touch enhance "Old Man."

◆ Build Grammar Skills

PERSONAL PRONOUNS

Speakers or writers use **personal pronouns** to refer to themselves (first person), the person spoken to (second person), or the person spoken about (third person).

	Singular	Plural
First Person	I, me, my, mine	we, us, our, ours
Second Person	you, your, yours	you, your, yours
Third Person	he, him, his, she, her, hers, it, its	they, them, their, theirs

Practice   On your paper, identify the personal pronouns in these sentences.

1. His legs would not carry him.
2. She told him that he spoiled everything in the house and broke their dishes.
3. Before she came into view, I heard her slippered feet.
4. "You are indio, among other things," he would tell me.
5. Gone into dust is your body with its stoic look.

Writing Application   Write sentences that include the personal pronoun in the form indicated.

1. A description of a family having dinner with an older relative (third-person plural)
2. Something a granddaughter might say to her grandmother (second-person singular)
3. A statement a grandfather might make to describe his family (first-person plural)

Build Your Portfolio

 ## Idea Bank

Writing

1. **Descriptive Close-up** Focus on the hands or face of a person who is dear to you. Then, use sensory details to describe your close-up picture for a reader.

2. **Proposal for a Reunion** In a letter to family members, propose a family reunion that they can attend. Suggest a place, ways to get there, and activities that everyone would enjoy.

3. **Folk Tale** Write a brief tale like Tolstoy's, focusing on an elderly person. Make sure that the characters and plot of the tale teach a lesson about growing older or about the relationships between different generations.

Speaking and Listening

4. **Storytelling Circle [Group Activity]** With several classmates, exchange stories in front of the class about older family members or friends who have inspired you. Include details to help listeners visualize the person you are describing.

5. **Dialogue With Yourself** Imagine that you could travel forward in time and meet yourself as an older person. Act out both sides of that dialogue for your classmates, playing yourself as you are now and yourself as you will become. **[Performing Arts Link]**

Projects

6. **Life Dance [Group Activity]** With several classmates, create and perform a dance illustrating the different stages of life. Show through movement what it's like to be a child, a teenager, an adult, and an elder. **[Performing Arts Link]**

7. **Community-Service Report** Volunteer to help out at a home for older people in your community. Then, give an oral report on your experiences to the class. You may want to explain the training and skills required in caring for the elderly. **[Social Studies Link]**

 ## Writing Mini-Lesson

Description of an Older Person

All the authors in this group paint a portrait of an older person. Follow their lead by writing your own description of a senior citizen. Your subject can be someone you know well, someone you've observed from a distance, or a character from a novel. Whether your subject is real or fictional, describe this person as an individual and not as a "typical" older person.

Writing Skills Focus: Use Precise Language

Use **precise language,** terms that convey a detailed impression, to describe your subject. For example, notice how precise Amy Ling is in her self-description in "Grandma:"

> ***Model From the Poem***
> my five foot height, my sturdy legs
>   and feet,
> my square forehead, high cheeks,
>   and wide-set eyes.

Prewriting Once you've chosen your subject, gather details that describe his or her appearance, habits, and qualities.

Drafting Begin your description by showing your subject in action, or hook readers by revealing an intriguing or mysterious aspect of your subject. As you draft, refer to the descriptive details you gathered in Prewriting.

Revising Replace general terms with precise language that describes your subject as an individual. For example, instead of calling a man *pleasant,* you might say that he has *an amused glint in his eye.*

◆ **Grammar Application**

In reviewing your draft, make sure readers can tell to whom each personal pronoun refers.

Guide for Reading

Meet the Authors:

Hal Borland (1900–1978)

Born in Sterling, Nebraska, Hal Borland became a naturalist, a person who studies animals and plants. Borland loved and respected the outdoors. He once said that "if you would know strength and patience, welcome the company of trees." The National Audubon Society honored him by creating the Hal Borland Trail in Connecticut.

As a writer, Borland wore many hats: He wrote documentary film scripts, radio scripts, and other pieces of non-fiction. He also worked as a reporter for the *Denver Post* and the *Brooklyn Times*. "Shooting Stars" blends his fascination with nature and his ability to report facts in a clear, appealing way.

Garrison Keillor (1942–   )

Every Saturday night, more than two million public radio listeners tune in to Garrison Keillor's show, "A Prairie Home Companion." The variety show includes music, comedy sketches, and Keillor's dryly amusing monologue, "The News From Lake Wobegon." A member of the Radio Hall of Fame and author of several books of humorous and insightful commentary, Keillor often focuses on life in the imaginary yet universal midwestern town of Lake Wobegon.

◆ LITERATURE AND YOUR LIFE

CONNECT YOUR EXPERIENCE

From Halley's Comet to clothing styles, virtually everything in the universe fits into a season or cycle. Chances are, a style considered "out" now will be "in" again soon. In these essays, two writers observe two very different kinds of cycles.

THEMATIC FOCUS: Seasons and Cycles

As you read, ask: Why are seasons and cycles reassuring or comforting to people?

◆ Background for Understanding

CULTURE

Decades are often given a "personality" in hindsight. For example, the sixties are remembered as a time of social and political change. During this turbulent decade, a strong youth movement rebelled against established social rules and staged protests on college campuses across the nation. Many aspects of culture—from fashion and music to film and writing—also departed from traditional formats and styles. In "Something From the Sixties," Garrison Keillor offers a glimpse of what sixties clothing styles were like.

◆ Build Vocabulary

PREFIXES: *extra-*

In his essay, Keillor describes the extravagance of an outfit. Notice how the prefix *extra-*, meaning "outside" or "beyond," combines with the root *vagant*, meaning "to wander," to create a term meaning "to go outside the norm."

WORD BANK

Which word from the list means "to circle an orb"? Check the Build Vocabulary box on page 82 to see if you chose correctly.

orbit
friction
constellation
descended
extravagance

Shooting Stars
◆ Something From the Sixties ◆

◆ Literary Focus
FIRST-PERSON NARRATIVE

A **first-person narrative** is an account of a writer's own experience. It is written in the first person, which is signaled by the narrator's use of the pronoun "I." In a first-person narrative, the author gives his reactions to and reflections on the meaning of an event, often revealing his or her personal viewpoint, as Hal Borland does in this statement:

> I once watched the August Perseids with an astronomer on a hilltop in open country, and in two hours we counted almost a thousand meteors.

Unfamiliar Word	Word Parts	My Definition

◆ Reading Strategy
WORD IDENTIFICATION

Narratives by people with different backgrounds from your own are likely to include unfamiliar words. When you encounter an unfamiliar word, you can apply **word identification** to unlock its meaning. Break the word into its syllables or parts, and look for something familiar in it.

Unfamiliar Word: periodically
Familiar Word Part: period
Possible Definition: happening at different periods

Use a chart like the one to the left to identify word meanings as you read.

SHOOTING STARS

Hal Borland

Most clear, dark nights you can see a shooting star, as we call it, if you keep looking. Those shooting stars are meteors. They are points of light that suddenly appear in the sky, like distant stars, race across the darkness, usually toward the horizon, and disappear.

For a long time nobody knew what a meteor was. But finally those who study stars and the sky decided that a meteor is a piece of a comet that exploded long ago. Those pieces are still wandering about the universe in huge, looping paths that follow the original comet's orbit. There are uncounted pieces of such comets out there in the depths of space. Periodically clusters of them come close to the earth's orbit, or path around the sun. Most meteors are small, probably only a few inches in diameter, but when they enter the earth's atmosphere the friction makes them white-hot. Then they look big as stars streaking across the darkness.

There are half a dozen meteor showers each year. Each is named after the constellation from which it appears to come. The biggest of all, the Perseids, named for the constellation of Perseus, occurs on the 10th, 11th, and 12th of August. The next largest, the Leonids, named for the constellation of Leo, comes on the nights of November 14, 15, and 16. Another, the Andromedids, which is not quite so big, comes from November 17 through 23. There are other meteor showers in December, January, April, May, and July, but none of them is as big as those in August and November.

Most people watching meteors will be satisfied if they see ten or twenty in an hour of watching. On special occasions, however, the meteors seem to come in droves. The most remarkable meteor shower I ever heard of was seen by a distinguished astronomer, Professor Denison Olmstead, of New Haven,

Connecticut, on the night of November 12, 1833. He was watching the Leonids, which seem to come from directly overhead and race downward toward the horizon in all directions. He reported that meteors fell "like flakes of snow." He estimated that he saw 240,000 meteors in nine hours that night. He said they ranged in size from mere streaks of light to "globes of the moon's diameter." If he had not been a notable astronomer whose accuracy was beyond question, such statements would seem ridiculous. But there is no reason to doubt what he reported. He had seen one of the most unusual meteor showers ever reported. What he watched should be called a meteor storm rather than a shower.

I once watched the August Perseids with an astronomer on a hilltop in open country, and in two hours we counted almost a thousand meteors. That was the most I ever saw at one time. And we were bitten by one mosquito for every meteor we saw. After that I tried watching for meteors in November, when there were no mosquitoes. But the most I ever saw in November was about one hundred meteors in two hours of watching.

The amazing thing about these meteor showers is that they come year after year. Professor Olmstead saw all those Leonids in November of 1833, but if you watch for meteors this year you almost certainly will see them on the same nights he saw them. They will come

---

◆ Build Vocabulary

orbit (ôr´ bit) *n.*: Path a planet or other celestial body takes moving around another celestial body

friction (frik´ shən) *n.*: Rubbing of one object against another

constellation (kän´ stə lā´ shən) *n.*: Collection of stars

next year, the year after that, and for countless years more. Your grandfather saw them, and your grandchildren will see them if they look for them.

Occasionally a meteor reaches the earth. Then it is called a meteorite and it is valued as a sample of the vast mystery of the deep space in the sky. Scientists examine it, try to guess what it was to begin with, where it came from, what it is like out there. Nobody ever learned very much from the meteorites except that they often contain a great deal of nickel and iron.

Only a few large meteorites have struck the earth. The largest we know about fell in Arizona many centuries ago and made what is now called Meteor Crater, a hole about a mile across and 600 feet deep. Some Indian legends of the Southwest tell of a big fire that fell from the sky and ate a huge hole in the earth, so this big meteorite may have fallen since man first arrived in America, perhaps twenty-five thousand years ago.

Other big meteorites have fallen, in ancient times, in Texas, in Argentina, in northern Siberia, in South-West Africa, and in Greenland. A meteorite weighing more than thirty-six tons was found in Greenland and now can be seen in the Hayden Planetarium in New York City. Millions of meteors have flashed across the night sky, but only a few large meteorites have ever reached the earth. Never in all the centuries of written history has there been a report of anyone being struck by a meteorite.

Beyond Literature

Science Connection

The Hubble Telescope In the 1600's, Galileo invented the first telescope, which created magnified views of celestial bodies. Throughout the years, telescopes have improved, becoming more accurate and powerful. In 1990, the Hubble Space Telescope was launched by the space shuttle *Discovery*. Because it is outside our atmosphere, it can collect undistorted light. The Hubble broadcasts the clearest pictures of the universe yet seen.

Cross-Curricular Activity
Science Create an astral journal by viewing the night sky and making specific observations about its appearance.

Guide for Responding

◆ LITERATURE AND YOUR LIFE

Reader's Response What do you think is the most beautiful part of the night sky?

Thematic Focus In what way does the idea of seasons and cycles apply to meteor showers?

☑ Check Your Comprehension

1. What are meteors?
2. Why are meteorites valued so highly?
3. What was the effect of the largest meteorite that fell to Earth?

◆ Critical Thinking

INTERPRET
1. Why do scientists observe meteors? **[Interpret]**
2. What might be learned from studying meteorites? **[Speculate]**
3. What does Borland say to encourage his readers to become amateur observers? **[Analyze]**

APPLY
4. Will astronomers 100 years from today still study meteors? Explain. **[Speculate]**

EXTEND
5. What characteristics do you think a professional astronomer should have? **[Science Link]**

Something From the Sixties

Garrison Keillor

▲ **Critical Viewing** What can you learn of the sixties by studying the fashions of the time? **[Interpret]**

About five o'clock last Sunday evening, my son burst into the kitchen and said, "I didn't know it was so late!" He was due at a party immediately—a sixties party, he said—and he needed something from the sixties to wear. My son is almost fifteen years old, the size of a grown man, and when he bursts into a room glassware rattles and the cat on your lap grabs on to your knees and leaps from the starting block. I used to think the phrase "burst into the room" was only for detective fiction, until my son got his growth. He can burst in a way that, done by an older fellow, would mean that angels had <u>descended</u> into the front yard and were eating apples off the tree, and he does it whenever he's late—as being my son, he often is. I have so little sense of time that when he said he needed something from the sixties it took me a moment to place that decade. It's the one he was born toward the end of.

I asked, "What sort of stuff you want to wear?"

He said, "I don't know. Whatever they wore then."

We went up to the attic, into a long, low room under the eaves where I've squirreled away some boxes of old stuff; I dug into one box, and the first thing I hauled out was the very thing he wanted. A thigh-length leather vest covered with fringe and studded with silver, it dates from around 1967, a fanciful time in college-boy fashions. Like many boys, I grew up in nice clothes my mother bought, but was meanwhile admiring Roy Rogers, Sergeant Rock, the Cisco Kid, and other sharp dressers, so when I left home I was ready to step out and be somebody. Military Surplus was the basic style then—olive drab, and navy-blue pea jackets—with a touch of Common Man in the work boots and blue work shirts, but if you showed up in Riverboat Gambler or Spanish Peasant or Rodeo King nobody blinked, nobody laughed. I haven't worn the vest in ten years, but a few weeks ago, seeing a picture of Michael Jackson wearing a fancy band jacket like the ones the Beatles wore on the cover of "Sgt. Pepper," I missed the fun I used to have getting dressed in the morning. Pull on the jeans, a shirt with brilliant-red roses, a pair of Red Wing boots. A denim jacket. Rose-tinted glasses. A cowboy hat. Or an engineer's cap. Or, instead of jeans, bib overalls. Or white trousers with blue stripes. Take off the denim jacket, take off the rose shirt, try the neon-green bowling shirt with "Moose" stitched on the pocket, the black dinner jacket. Now the dark-green Chinese Army cap. And an orange tie with hula dancers and palm trees.

Then—presto!—I pulled the rose shirt out. He put it on, and the vest, which weighs about fifteen pounds, and by then I had found him a hat—a broad-brimmed panama that ought to make you think of a cotton planter enjoying a Sazerac on a veranda in New Orleans. I followed him down to his bedroom, where he admired himself in a full-length mirror.

"Who wore this?" he asked.

I said that I did.

"Did you really? This? You?"

Yes, I really did. After he was born, in 1969, I wore it less and less, finally settling down with what I think of as the Dad look, and now I would no sooner wear my old fringed vest in public than walk around in a taffeta tutu. I loved the fact that it fitted him so well, though, and his pleasure at the heft and extravagance of the thing, the poses he struck in front of the mirror. Later, when he got home and reported that his costume was a big hit and that all his friends had tried on the vest, it made me happy again. You squirrel away old stuff on the principle of its being useful and interesting someday; it's wonderful when the day finally arrives. That vest was waiting for a boy to come along—a boy who has a flair for the dramatic, who bursts into rooms—and to jump right into the part. I'm happy to be the audience.

◆ **Build Vocabulary**

descended (dē send´ id) *v.*: Came down

extravagance (ek strav´ ə gəns) *n.*: A spending of more than is necessary; wastefulness

Guide for Responding

◆ LITERATURE AND YOUR LIFE

Reader's Response Would you like to wear the vest described in "Something From the Sixties"? Why or why not?

Thematic Focus Why do you think old clothing styles come back in fashion?

Sketch Make a sketch of the vest described in the story.

☑ Check Your Comprehension

1. Why does the narrator's son want to borrow some clothing?
2. What clothing do the father and son find in the attic?
3. How successful is the son's costume at the party?

◆ Critical Thinking

INTERPRET

1. What is the narrator's attitude toward his past style of dress? **[Interpret]**
2. Why is the narrator's son surprised that his father wore such dramatic clothing? **[Infer]**
3. What does the final sentence reveal about the narrator's current attitude toward fashion? **[Draw Conclusions]**

APPLY

4. How might the narrator respond if his son began wearing extravagant clothing? **[Hypothesize]**

COMPARE LITERARY WORKS

5. How does the idea of cycles of events connect these two essays? Are the cycles described in both predictable? **[Interpret]**

Guide for Responding (continued)

◆ Reading Strategy

WORD IDENTIFICATION

Apply **word identification** to unlock the meaning of unfamiliar words. Break unfamiliar words into parts, looking for familiar words or word parts within them that will help you determine the word's meaning.

1. Which word part in the word *astronomer* gives a clue to its meaning?
2. Explain how you would use word identification to make sense of these words:
   a. glassware   **b.** fanciful   **c.** nobody

◆ Build Vocabulary

USING THE PREFIX *extra-*

Knowing that the prefix *extra-* means "outside" or "beyond," figure out the meaning of each word. Then, use a dictionary to check your definitions.

1. extraordinary   3. extraterrestrial
2. extracurricular   4. extrasensory

SPELLING STRATEGY

The s sound is sometimes spelled *sc*, as in *descended*. On your paper, write the words in each sentence that use the *sc* spelling for the s sound.

1. The scientist studied the ascent of the missile.
2. The scene was lit by a crescent moon.
3. Scented candles were popular in the sixties.

USING THE WORD BANK

Write the word from the Word Bank that best completes each sentence. Use each word only once.

1. The sun ____?____ behind the hills.
2. The ____?____ of the colorful display seemed almost overdone.
3. Can you identify the ____?____ of Orion?
4. The moon's ____?____ circles the Earth.
5. While entering the atmosphere, ____?____ eroded the surface of the meteorite.

◆ Literary Focus

FIRST-PERSON NARRATIVE

Both essays in this section are **first-person narratives,** accounts of events from the authors' lives. They are told from the first-person point of view. Some first-person narrators act as on-the-scene reporters, sticking to the facts, whereas others reveal their personal reactions to the events.

1. At what point in "Shooting Stars" does it become clear that it is a first-person narrative and not a purely factual report? Explain.
2. (a) Which narrative is primarily reporting? (b) Which is primarily a personal recounting of a true-life event? How can you tell?
3. Which piece would be more greatly altered if it were rewritten to be a newspaper report? Why?

◆ Build Grammar Skills

INDEFINITE PRONOUNS

An **indefinite pronoun** refers to a person, place, or thing that is not specifically named. Indefinite pronouns are singular or plural.

Singular: *another, anyone, anything, each, either, everyone, everything, much, neither, no one, nothing, one, someone, something*

Plural: *both, few, several, many*

Singular or Plural: *all, any, most, none, some*

Practice Write each sentence on your paper. Then, circle each indefinite pronoun.

1. Everything is ready for the meteor watch.
2. Few appear in March.
3. In August and November, most of the meteors fall.
4. Something unexpected often happens.
5. The spectacular sight surprised many of us.

Writing Application Write four sentences about "Something From the Sixties." Include at least one indefinite pronoun in each sentence.

Build Your Portfolio

 ## Idea Bank

Writing

1. **Thank-You Note** Imagine that you are the son in "Something From the Sixties." Write a thank-you note to your father for letting you borrow his old clothing.

2. **Poem** Write a poem about shooting stars or some other element of the night sky. Create word images to represent the pictures that you see in your mind's eye.

3. **Essay** Write an essay in which you explore a cycle or season. For example, you might describe the phases of the moon, a comet's orbit, or the northern lights. **[Science Link]**

Speaking and Listening

4. **Debate [Group Activity]** Hold a class debate about the idea that "clothes make the man." Appoint a moderator to make sure that the debate rules are followed and that everyone has a turn to voice an opinion.

5. **Radio Monologue** Garrison Keillor's essay is like a written version of his radio monologues—oral narratives about his life. Write a radio monologue of your own. Then, record and play it for the class. **[Performing Arts Link]**

Projects

6. **Social Research** Conduct research to find out about events like the civil rights marches and the moon landing that took place during the sixties. Consider how this period of history affected the decades that followed. **[Social Studies Link]**

7. **Meteor Presentation [Group Activity]** Work in a group to create a presentation on meteors. You might focus on the Perseids, Leonids, and the Andromedids, or you might focus on meteorites that have hit the Earth. Create charts and illustrations to make your presentation visually interesting. **[Science Link]**

 ## Writing Mini-Lesson

Extended Definition

Hal Borland's "Shooting Stars" is an extended definition of the title topic—meteors. An extended definition is a full exploration of a single topic. Choose a topic to explore fully in an extended definition. You might write about a scientific term, such as *supernova* or *black hole,* or a fashionable item, such as *high tops.*

Writing Skills Focus: Audience

Always consider the **audience** for whom you are writing. You need to provide information and speak in language that's appropriate for their level of understanding.

Model From "Shooting Stars"

But finally those who study stars and the sky decided that a meteor is a piece of a comet that exploded long ago. Those pieces are still wandering about the universe in huge, looping paths that follow the original comet's orbit.

Prewriting Conduct research in a variety of sources to gather information about your topic. Think about who your audience is and what information they'll need to know. Jot down examples, and draw diagrams they'll find useful.

Drafting Begin with a basic definition of the term. Then, extend your definition by describing a different aspect of your main topic in each paragraph.

Revising Test your writing on an audience by reading your draft aloud to a partner. Have him or her identify the points that need to be made more clear or expanded upon.

> ◆ **Grammar Application**
> If you've used indefinite pronouns, be sure that your audience will understand to what they refer.

Guide for Reading

Meet the Authors:

Walt Whitman (1819–1892)

American poetry was born with Walt Whitman's *Leaves of Grass* (1855). Whitman, a New Yorker who worked at a variety of jobs, created bold new poems to suit a new country. He discarded the regular rhythms and rhymes of British poetry in favor of his own invented rhythms and unrhymed lines.

Langston Hughes (1902–1967)

Langston Hughes was the first African American to get the rhythm and feel of "blues" music into his poems. He came of age during the Harlem Renaissance of the 1920's. This renaissance, "rebirth," was a flowering of African American writers, musicians, and painters in New York City's Harlem.

Alfred, Lord Tennyson (1809–1892)

Born in rural England, Tennyson left home as a teenager to attend Cambridge University. While at Cambridge, Tennyson won a university prize for poetry, his first step on the way to becoming a famous poet. In 1850, Queen Victoria appointed him Poet Laureate of England.

THE STORY BEHIND THE POEM

"Ring Out, Wild Bells" is part of the long poem "In Memoriam, A.H.H." This poem's title means "In Memory," and Tennyson wrote it in memory of his close friend Arthur Henry Hallam, who died in 1833. The section "Ring Out, Wild Bells" marks the third New Year's holiday after his friend's death.

◆ LITERATURE AND YOUR LIFE

CONNECT YOUR EXPERIENCE

Just as the moon has cycles or phases, so does life itself. Think for a moment about various cycles you've observed. For example, think about the seasons, the school year, birthdays, and so on. In these poems, the speakers all make observations about life's patterns.

THEMATIC FOCUS: Seasons and Cycles

As you read, compare each speaker's thoughts about life's patterns to your own observations.

◆ Background for Understanding

CULTURE

"Ring Out, Wild Bells" captures the English tradition of ringing bells to express New Year's hopes. Here are other customs for welcoming the New Year:

- Scandinavia—skiing with torches
- Southern India—boiling new rice
- Bangladesh—worshiping the river Ganges
- Southern United States—eating black-eyed peas
- China—going to theatrical performances

◆ Build Vocabulary

SUFFIXES: *-or*

The prefix *-or* signals that a word means "a person or thing that does something." In "Poets to Come," Whitman addresses future *orators,* "people who give public speeches." *Orators* combines *orate,* "to give a speech," and *-or.*

WORD BANK

Which word from the list is often paired with *trouble* and has a similar meaning? Check the Build Vocabulary box on page 92 to see if you chose correctly.

orators
indicative
sauntering
strife

Poets to Come ◆ Winter Moon
◆ Ring Out, Wild Bells ◆

◆ Literary Focus

REPETITION IN POETRY

Songwriters and poets hate to waste good words. That's why they use **repetition** in their works, returning again and again to a haunting word or phrase with a special meaning. Repetition is also an excellent way of tying a poem together. The familiar phrase is like a melody that keeps reappearing.

Pay special attention to repeated words and phrases in these poems. Notice their sounds and rhythms as well as their meanings. Then, ask yourself how these repetitions capture, in a tiny space, a whole world of thought and feeling.

◆ Reading Strategy

READ POETRY ACCORDING TO PUNCTUATION

Every poem comes equipped with a set of instructions on how to read it. Those instructions are its **punctuation** marks. You don't automatically stop at the ends of lines, but you do pause briefly for commas and stop for end marks like periods and exclamation points.

As you read, make sure you're clear about the poet's reading instructions. Copy a poem on your paper, and put little Post-it reminders near punctuation marks. Here's an example:

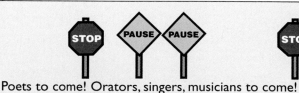

Poets to come! Orators, singers, musicians to come!

POETS TO COME
Walt Whitman

Poets to come! <u>orators</u>, singers, musicians to come!
Not to-day is to justify me and answer what I am for,
But you, a new brood, native, athletic, continental,
   greater than before known,
Arouse! for you must justify me.

5   I myself but write one or two <u>indicative</u> words for
   the future,
I but advance a moment only to wheel and hurry
   back in the darkness.

I am a man who, <u>sauntering</u> along without fully
   stopping, turns a casual look upon you and then
   averts his face,
Leaving it to you to prove and define it,
Expecting the main things from you.

◆ **Build Vocabulary**

orators (ôr´ ət ərz) *n*.: Public speakers

indicative (in dik´ ə tiv) *adj*.: Giving a
suggestion; showing

sauntering (sân´ tər iŋ) *v*.: Walking
slowly and confidently

WINTER MOON
Langston Hughes

How thin and sharp is the moon tonight!
How thin and sharp and ghostly white
Is the slim curved crook of the moon tonight!

Guide for Responding

◆ LITERATURE AND YOUR LIFE

Reader's Response Do you feel that Whitman and Hughes are speaking directly to you in their poems? Why or why not?

Thematic Focus How does each poet mark the present moment as special?

Speech Make up and deliver a brief speech in which you respond to the message that Whitman delivers to you.

☑ Check Your Comprehension

1. Whom is Whitman addressing in "Poets to Come"?
2. What is Whitman asking his audience to do?
3. How does Whitman describe himself?
4. Describe the sight that catches Hughes's eye in "Winter Moon."

◆ Critical Thinking

INTERPRET

1. What does Whitman mean in "Poets to Come" when he asks future poets to "justify" him? **[Draw Conclusions]**
2. What does the phrase "hurry back in the darkness" mean? **[Interpret]**
3. (a) In "Winter Moon," what phrase is repeated? (b) To what effect? **[Interpret]**
4. What qualities of the moon appeal to Hughes? **[Connect]**

EVALUATE

5. In "Poets to Come," Whitman directly addresses future readers. Is this device effective? Why or why not? **[Criticize]**

COMPARE LITERARY WORKS

6. Does "Winter Moon" reveal that Hughes was one of the "poets to come" who listened to Whitman? Explain. **[Connect]**

Ring Out, Wild Bells

Alfred, Lord Tennyson

Ring out, wild bells, to the wild sky,
    The flying cloud, the frosty light:
    The year is dying in the night;
Ring out, wild bells, and let him die.

5   Ring out the old, ring in the new,
      Ring, happy bells, across the snow:
      The year is going, let him go;
Ring out the false, ring in the true.

Ring out the grief that saps[1] the mind,
10   For those that here we see no more;
      Ring out the feud of rich and poor,
Ring in redress[2] to all mankind.

Ring out a slowly dying cause,
    And ancient forms of party <u>strife</u>;
15   Ring in the nobler modes[3] of life,
With sweeter manners, purer laws.

Ring out the want, the care, the sin,
    The faithless coldness of the times;
    Ring out, ring out thy mournful rhymes,
20   But ring the fuller minstrel[4] in.

Ring out false pride in place and blood,
    The civic[5] slander and the spite;
    Ring in the love of truth and right,
Ring in the common love of good.

25   Ring out old shapes of foul disease;
      Ring out the narrowing lust of gold;
      Ring out the thousand wars of old,
Ring in the thousand years of peace.

◆ Build Vocabulary

strife (strīf) *n.*: Conflict

---

1. **saps** (saps) *v.*: Drains; exhausts.
2. **redress** (ri dres′) *n.*: The righting of wrongs.
3. **modes** (mōdz) *n.*: Ways; forms.
4. **fuller minstrel** (min′ strəl) *n.*: Singer of the highest rank.
5. **civic** (siv′ ik) *adj.*: Of a city.

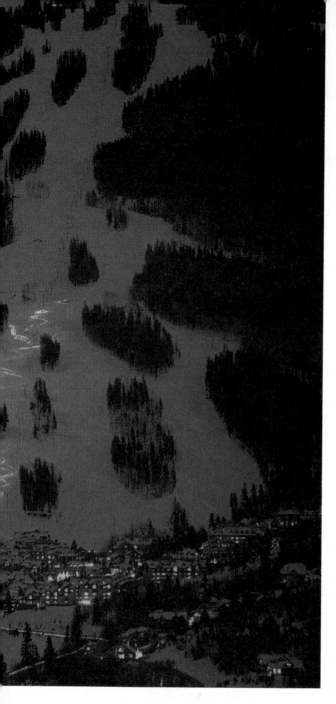

▲ **Critical Viewing** In what ways does this photograph capture the spirit of the poem? [Interpret]

Guide for Responding

◆ **LITERATURE AND YOUR LIFE**

Reader's Response What is a New Year's hope that you have expressed?

Thematic Focus Why is New Year's Eve a time when people focus on the past and the future?

New Year's Ceremony With several classmates, create a New Year's ceremony that would help people feel good about the coming year.

Journal Writing Jot down in your journal some New Year's resolutions you've made over the years.

☑ **Check Your Comprehension**

1. List five things the poet wants to "ring out."
2. Name five things that the poet wants to "ring in."

◆ Critical Thinking

INTERPRET
1. How does the poet seem to feel about the past? **[Infer]**
2. Explain what the poet hopes the future will bring. **[Interpret]**
3. In what way is this poem about more than the passing of the old year? **[Draw Conclusions]**

EVALUATE
4. Would it be appropriate to read this poem aloud at a modern New Year's Eve celebration? Why or why not? **[Make a Judgment]**

EXTEND
5. What do you think would bring a "thousand years of peace" to today's world? Explain. **[Social Studies Link]**

COMPARING LITERARY WORKS
6. How are the messages or themes of "Poets to Come" and "Ring Out, Wild Bells" similar and different? **[Compare and Contrast]**

Guide for Responding (continued)

◆ Reading Strategy

READ POETRY ACCORDING TO PUNCTUATION

By **reading according to punctuation,** you used commas and end marks in these poems as guides to pauses and stops. In line 3 of "Ring Out, Wild Bells," each comma and semicolon signals a pause. The colon, however, that ends line 2 and the period that ends line 4 signal stops.

1. Explain where you would pause and where you would stop in lines 21–24 of "Ring Out, Wild Bells."
2. Which of these poems calls for no pauses and just two stops? Explain.
3. How many brief pauses are there in the final stanza of "Poets to Come"? How do you know?

◆ Build Vocabulary

USING THE SUFFIX -or

Use your knowledge of the suffix -or ("the person or thing that does something") to explain the meaning of the italicized words:

A new movie featured a fight among the *Terminator*, the *Eliminator*, and the *Hesitator*. While the Hesitator was waiting, the first two guys destroyed each other. Then the movie *projector* caught on fire. I had to stop applauding to dial the emergency *operator*.

SPELLING STRATEGY

When adding a suffix beginning with a vowel to words ending in e, drop the e in the new word:

advise + -or = advisor   race + -ial = racial

On your paper, spell the word that results from combining these words and suffixes:

1. create + -or   3. senate + -or
2. face + -ial   4. machine + -ist

USING THE WORD BANK

On your paper, answer these true-or-false questions. Then, explain your answers.

1. The best *orators* usually win debates.
2. A jogger in action is an example of *sauntering*.
3. The color red on a sign is usually *indicative* of a warning.
4. *Strife* is what ends when a war begins.

◆ Literary Focus

REPETITION IN POETRY

Repetition makes poems easy to remember by adding to the verbal "music," linking the different sections of a poem, and revealing key ideas.

1. In "Poets to Come," how does the repetition of the pronouns *I* and *you* tie the poem together and emphasize its meaning?
2. Extend "Winter Moon" by two lines, repeating and adding to what Hughes says. Help readers see and feel a winter moon.
3. Explain how stanzas in "Ring Out, Wild Bells" use repetition in different ways.

◆ Build Grammar Skills

INTENSIVE PRONOUNS

Intensive pronouns are formed by combining the personal pronoun and the suffix -self or -selves:

myself; ourselves; yourself, yourselves; herself, himself, itself; themselves

Intensive pronouns emphasize the person's role or indicate that a person performs an action alone:

Emphasizes Person: "I *myself* but write one or two . . ."

Indicates Person Acts Alone: I'll do it *myself*, thanks.

Practice On your paper, identify the intensive pronoun in each sentence. Then, indicate whether it stresses the person performing the act or the idea that the person performs the action alone.

1. I myself read "Poets to Come."
2. Did you yourself see the winter moon?
3. They themselves heard the New Year's bells.
4. Whitman himself addresses future poets, without a backup chorus of voices.
5. Should we ourselves ring those bells?

Writing Application On your paper, fill in each blank with a suitable intensive pronoun.

1. I _____?_____ was born on January fifth.
2. Have you _____?_____ seen a crescent moon?
3. They made the poetry book _____?_____.

Build Your Portfolio

Idea Bank

Writing

1. **Description** As Hughes does in "Winter Moon," write a brief sentence describing something. Then, in a follow-up sentence, repeat your description and add to it.

2. **Pattern Poem** Write a poem expressing your wishes for the New Year. Follow the pattern in Tennyson's poem, telling the bells to "ring out" some things and "ring in" others.

3. **Critical Interpretation** Interpret the lyrics of your favorite song, explaining the message they contain. Show how the songwriter has used repetition to convey important thoughts and feelings.

Speaking and Listening

4. **New Year's Speech** As a class, imagine you are having dinner with a group of friends on New Year's Eve. Give a brief speech expressing your good wishes for your friends and your hopes for the new year.

5. **Poetry Reading** Read these poems aloud for your classmates. Before reading, prepare rehearsal copies of the poems by marking where you will pause, stop, or emphasize a key word. **[Performing Arts Link]**

Projects

6. **Multimedia Presentation** Choose a holiday that marks an anniversary or a change in seasons. Then, give a presentation explaining how the same type of holiday is celebrated in different cultures. If possible, include photographs, film clips, diagrams, recorded interviews, and samples of food. **[Social Studies Link; Media Link]**

7. **Report [Group Activity]** Work with a group to prepare a multimedia report on the phases of the moon. You may create a chart showing the monthly changes in the moon's appearance—from new moon to full moon. You may also want to explore the moon's effect on the tides. **[Science Link]**

Writing Mini-Lesson

Script for a Time-Capsule Video

"Poets to Come" is like a time-capsule message to people living in the future. Suppose you could write the script for a video that would be placed into a time capsule. Your purpose would be to give teenagers living a hundred years from now a sense of our life today.

Writing Skills Focus: Use the Right Format

When writing a script, **use the right format** to set up dialogue, directions, and camera shots:

- To show dialogue, capitalize the character's name, put a period after it, and then write the character's words.

TEENAGER. Let me tell you about our music. . . .

- To show directions and camera shots, use brackets and put text in italics.

TEENAGER. [*Standing in CD store*] [*Long shot down the aisle*] Let me tell you about our music. . . .

Prewriting Think what teenagers of the future will want to know, and outline the topics you'll cover, like sports or music. Also, decide on the order in which you'll present these topics.

Drafting Convey as much information as possible through images and sequences of images. Use dialogue or voice-over, a person speaking off camera, to enhance and summarize the visual "story."

◆ **Grammar Application**
Use intensive pronouns in the camera directions to indicate that someone performs an action alone.

Revising Add information that future teenagers would want to know. Wherever necessary, add directions for characters and the camera. Review the formatting guidelines to be sure your script conforms.

Description

Writing Process Workshop

In this unit, the writers use descriptive language to bring to life a meteor shower, a special Christmas, and a hopeful New Year's Eve. Descriptive writing can appear in any type of writing—from poetry to essays—but no matter where it is used, it conveys vivid impressions through sensory details. Think about a person, place, thing, or experience that calls to mind vivid memories, and share those vivid impressions by writing a piece of description.

Use the skills in the Writing Mini-Lessons introduced in this section to help you.

Writing Skills Focus

▶ **Use transitional words** and phrases to weave together your description. (See p. 71.)

▶ **Use precise language** to create a main impression of your topic. (See p. 79.)

▶ Use details and language that **your audience** will understand and appreciate. (See p. 87.)

Garrison Keillor uses these skills in "Something From the Sixties."

MODEL FROM LITERATURE

from "Something From the Sixties" by Garrison Keillor

About five o'clock last Sunday evening, ① my son burst into the kitchen and said, "I didn't know it was so late!" He was due at a party immediately—a sixties party, he said—and he needed something from the sixties to wear. My son is almost fifteen years old, the size of a grown man, ② and when he bursts into a room glassware rattles and the cat on your lap grabs on to your knees and leaps from the starting block. ③

① This transitional phrase leads into the story.

② Precise details like these give necessary information about the son.

③ This colorful example amuses the audience.

Prewriting

Choose a Topic Spend some time jotting down observations about things, people, events, and ideas. Circle three or four you like. Jot down a one- or two-word impression for each. Then, choose the one that would make the best topic for a description.

Make a Sunburst Diagram Collect precise details about your topic using a sunburst diagram.

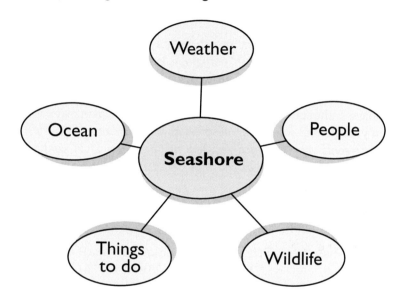

Identify Your Audience Who will read your description? Jot down notes about your readers' familiarity with your subject and the style of language they'll respond to and enjoy. For example, will they better appreciate humor or sincerity? Will technical descriptions or slang confuse them?

Description Writing Tip Try closing your eyes to re-create an image in your mind. Imagine or recall the sight, sound, scent, taste, and feel of your topic before you write about it.

Drafting

Create a Main Impression As you draft, focus on capturing the essence, or most important quality, of your subject.

Write for Your Audience Draft your description using words and a writing style that will interest and appeal to your readers.

Use Transitional Words Connect your thoughts and ideas by using transitional words and phrases like *first, not only,* and *before you knew it.*

APPLYING LANGUAGE SKILLS: Using Sensory Words

Using words that appeal to the five senses will make your description more interesting.

Neutral Words:
I like summer.

Sensory Words:
I like the *smell* of cook-outs, the *sounds* of cardinals, and the *taste* of fresh strawberries that summer brings.

Notice how the sentence with sensory details captures the smell, sound, and taste of a summer day.

Practice On your paper, rewrite each sentence, providing sensory descriptive words for the sense in parentheses.

1. There was an odor coming from the trunk. (smell)
2. We sat in the attic, listening to the rain. (sound)
3. Hank lifted out the vest. (touch)

Writing Application As you draft, use sensory words to make your description more alive and realistic.

Writer's Solution Connection
Writing Lab

For help with sensory words, use the Sensory Word Bin in the Prewriting sections of the Description tutorial.

APPLYING LANGUAGE SKILLS: Avoiding Fragments

A fragment is a group of words, written as a sentence, that does not express a complete thought. Avoid fragments in your writing. Correct them by adding words to make a complete thought.

Fragment:

A slight twig over the expanding tide

Complete Thought:

The bridge looked like a slight twig over the expanding tide.

Practice On your paper, rewrite these fragments as complete thoughts.

1. The small island surrounded by water.
2. Riding their rafts in on the tide.
3. Dolphins in the sea.
4. Each evening, clambakes.
5. Was the best vacation ever.

Writing Application Review your description, and correct any sentence fragments.

Writer's Solution Connection
Language Lab

For help identifying and correcting fragments, complete the lesson on Sentence Fragments in the Sentence Errors unit.

Revising

Read Your Description Aloud Listening to your words read aloud can help you to identify unwanted repetition, bland words, mistakes, sentence fragments, and other errors.

Use a Checklist Go back to the Writing Skills Focus on the first page of this lesson, and use the items as a checklist to evaluate and revise your description.

▶ Have I used precise language? *Overuse of adjectives and adverbs may indicate that you need to choose a more precise noun or verb.*

▶ Do transitions connect the thoughts and ideas within the description? *Review each paragraph in your description. Be sure that you've linked your thoughts by using transitions to lead into and out of each paragraph.*

▶ Have I chosen details and a style that are appropriate for my audience? *Read your description aloud to someone who represents your audience. Ask him or her to point out confusing or dull passages so that you may revise them.*

REVISION MODEL

I didn't even notice the bridge because the neap tide was ①
~~In a way, though, the~~ ②
out. The bridge is interesting. It's wooden, short, and plain
connects two sand dunes. ③
and just ~~goes over some sand~~. The tide began coming in,
spectacular
and it was really ~~neat~~. No cars can cross that bridge until

the tide goes back out!

① The writer deleted this term because it's not important and might confuse the audience.
② This transitional phrase leads into the main idea of the sentence.
③ The vague phrase "just goes over some sand" was replaced with a more precise description.

Publishing and Presenting

▶ **Classroom** Illustrate your description with your own drawing or design, or with a picture you've found. Display your description in the classroom.

▶ **E-mail** Consider e-mailing your description to a relative or friend.

Real-World Reading Skills Workshop

Strategies for Success

You may have noticed that when you read things out of idle curiosity or for pleasure, you skim the text quickly. When you read things to find specific information that you will be tested on, however, you read slowly and carefully. This is called adjusting your reading rate, and you can use this strategy to help you read different kinds of texts.

The following strategies will help you adjust your reading rate according to your purpose and the level of difficulty of the writing.

- ▶ **Identify Your Reading Goals** If you are reading for entertainment, you don't need to read carefully and slowly. If, however, you're reading in order to learn something, you should read more slowly and carefully.
- ▶ **Preview Headings and Captions** Headings, subheads, and captions will give you clues about the subject matter of the writing.
- ▶ **Skim a Text for Difficulty** Quickly skim the text of the writing, looking for the types of words used. If the text appears to have technical or sophisticated ideas, read it slowly. If the text contains simple language and ideas, you can read it more quickly.

✔ Here are other situations in which you adjust your reading rate for the situation:
- ▶ Selecting a suitable book for a friend
- ▶ Reading a long reference article
- ▶ Searching through Web sites on the World Wide Web

Apply the Strategies

1. How would you read the following article "Great Pastas," judging from the headings you see?

2. Skim the text. How would you describe the level of difficulty of this article?

3. If you came across this article in a magazine, how would you read it if:

   a. You had little interest in cooking

   b. You were writing a report for school about Italian foods

   c. You planned to make pasta that evening

Great Pastas

Pasta is one of the easiest, most nutritious meals you can make. With sauces ranging from oil and garlic to meat and vegetable, you can eat pasta every day of the week and not become bored.

Following are some popular pasta types:

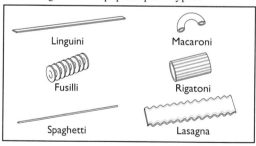

Linguini

Macaroni

Fusilli

Rigatoni

Spaghetti

Lasagna

Basic Cooking Instructions

For each pound of pasta, bring two quarts of water to a rolling boil in a covered pot. If desired, add a teaspoon of vegetable oil and a pinch of salt to the water. Add dry pasta and allow pasta to boil uncovered, stirring occasionally. After approximately 8 to 10 minutes, test pasta for doneness. When done, pour into colander and strain out the water. Toss pasta with your favorite sauce.

Pronouns are words that take the place of nouns or groups of words acting as nouns. They are used in order to avoid repetition of nouns. The word or group of words a pronoun replaces is called its **antecedent.**

> antecedent
> *Andrea* attended night-school classes.
> pronoun
> During the day, *she* worked.

Personal pronouns refer to the person speaking (first person), the person spoken to (second person), and the person spoken about (third person).

	Singular	**Plural**
First Person	I, me, my, mine	we, us, our, ours
Second Person	you, your, yours	you, your, yours
Third Person	he, him, his, she, her, hers, it, its	they, them, their, theirs

Indefinite pronouns—such as *another, anybody, neither, each, everything, several,* and *many*—refer to people, places, or things in general. Some indefinite pronouns are used without antecedents.

With Antecedent: Of the candidates, *none* was qualified.

Without Antecedent: *Everyone* was nice.

Grammar in Writing

✔ *Use pronouns to avoid repeating nouns unnecessarily. Be sure each pronoun has a clear antecedent.*

✔ *Add emphasis to a noun by using an intensive pronoun within the same sentence.*

nominal adjective "our"] —pro·nom'i·nal·ly *adv.* pro·noun (prō'noun') *n.* [altered (infl. by NOUN) < pronomen < *pro,* for + *nomen,* NOUN] *Gram.* any relationship or signal words that assume the fu within clauses or phrases while referring to othe the sentence or in other sentences: *I, you, them, it,* *myself, anybody,* etc. ... pronouns

An **intensive pronoun** ends in -*self* or -*selves* and adds emphasis to a noun or pronoun in the same sentence.

Example: I, *myself,* prefer to stand.

Practice 1 Locate the pronouns in each sentence, and label each as a personal pronoun, an indefinite pronoun, or an intensive pronoun.

1. She preferred watching shooting stars herself.

2. Both Bill and Rita enjoy the holidays.

3. They went to a costume party together.

4. Do your grandparents live nearby?

5. Our New Year's Eve celebration was a hit.

6. Nothing in memory was more fun.

7. He, himself, said he will visit soon.

Practice 2 Rewrite this paragraph, replacing repeated nouns with an appropriate pronoun.

In the nineteenth century, few people owned cameras. Cameras were too costly. Not many people could go to photographers because photographers charged too much. During the Civil War, young soldiers wanted to be photographed in uniform. Some merchants knew this. Merchants sold inexpensive copies of photographs of soldiers. A private with little cash would buy a picture of someone who looked like the private. Then, the private sent this picture home.

Speaking, Listening, and Viewing Workshop

Participating in a Group

Sometimes problems and tasks are more easily solved or accomplished by a group of people working together than by an individual tackling them alone. Often, you will find that talking out ideas with others helps you think more clearly, just as your response to other people's ideas can help them organize their thoughts. For a group to work effectively, though, there are certain ground rules that should be observed. Following are suggestions that will help you work effectively in a group.

- **Clearly state the group's purpose.** Once you have a purpose, you can keep the discussion focused.
- **Take turns speaking while others listen.** If everyone speaks at once, no one is heard and no progress is made toward reaching an understanding.
- **Record ideas as they are stated.** Assign one person to be responsible for taking notes as ideas are discussed.
- **Be sure everyone is heard.** A moderator, or discussion leader, can ensure that everyone's ideas are heard. No one person should be allowed to dominate the discussion.
- **Make a contribution.** It's your responsibility as a group member to voice your ideas. Don't let others do the work.

- **Respond to what others say.** Politely voice your agreements and disagreements to what others say. Sometimes solutions come out of conflict.

Apply the Strategies

Form groups of three or more to address one of the following tasks. Then, use the checklist that follows to assess your group's performance.

1. A hospital or nursing home in your community is in need of student volunteers. Devise a recruitment plan that will persuade students to donate their free time.

2. The boys' and girls' soccer teams are arguing over who gets to use the school's playing field. With the group, come up with a compromise plan.

Use a Checklist

✔ *When your group has completed its task, complete a checklist such as the following to decide whether you have worked effectively as a group.*

- ▶ *Did we define our task clearly?*
- ▶ *Was attention given to each speaker?*
- ▶ *Did we keep a record of the ideas presented?*
- ▶ *Was everyone given a chance to contribute?*
- ▶ *Did we complete our task successfully?*

What's Behind the Words

Vocabulary Adventures With Richard Lederer

Origins of Calendar Words

Long before we humans knew that time was a way of measuring the Earth's circle around the sun—back in the days when we believed that the Earth was flat and the sun moved across its face—we became filled with fear as the days grew short.

As the winter darkness engulfed our lives, we invoked the ancient gods with bonfires, feasts, and dances in the hope of charming the sun back to Earth. Slowly, over time, we learned that the sun always does return to warm the face of the Earth, and we grew to understand that time is a tide that ebbs and flows like the sea.

The First Calendar

It wasn't long before units of time, like the year, became standard. A year is about 365 days, 5 hours, 48 minutes, and 46 seconds. The word *calendar*, used to mark years, comes from the Latin, in which the first day of each Roman month was called the *kalends*. Interest on loans was due on the first day of each month, and the record of interest days was called a *calendarium*.

People throughout the years have adapted and used the calendarium to track the passage of years. When the Anglo Saxons, from whose language English is descended, wanted names for their days, they substituted their own gods for the Roman ones.

ACTIVITY 1 Unlike the days of our week, the names of our months descend directly from Latin. Create a chart like the one below to explain how each month got its name.

ACTIVITY 2 Write an essay explaining how the four seasons acquired their names.

ACTIVITY 3 Our word *day* comes from an Indo-European base *dhegwh-*, meaning "the time when the sun shines." *Month* comes to us through the Old English *mona,* meaning both "a measure of time" and "moon." What is the source or origin of each of the following words that describe time?

1. chronological
2. cycle
3. eon
4. epoch
5. season
6. solstice
7. temporal
8. week

January

Sunday	Monday	Tuesday	Wednesday	Thursday	Friday	Saturday
Sunday is "sun's day." In Old English, it is *Sunnan daeg*, taken from the Latin *Dies solis*.	**Monday** is "moon's day," from *Monan daeg*, the Old English translation of the Latin *Lunse dies*, "day of the moon."	**Tuesday** is "Tiw's day," honoring Tiw, an Anglo-Saxon god of war and a son of Woden.	**Wednesday** is "Woden's day," dedicated to Tiw's father, Woden, who was chief of the Anglo-Saxon gods.	**Thursday** is "Thunor's day." Thunor, another of Woden's sons, also known by his Norse name of Thor, was the Anglo-Saxon god of thunder.	**Friday** is "Frig's day." Frig was the wife of Woden and the Anglo-Saxon goddess of marriage.	**Saturday** is from the Latin "Saturn's day," the only day of our week not fashioned from an Anglo-Saxon word or god. Saturn (*Cronus* in Greek) was the father of Jove (*Zeus* in Greek).

Extended Reading Opportunities

Novels and other full-length works sometimes explore "coming of age"—what it's like to grow up or to arrive at some new understanding about the world or yourself. Following are a few possibilities for extending your exploration of this theme.

Suggested Titles

Johnny Tremain
Esther Forbes

Johnny Tremain is set in pre-Revolutionary New England, and it is an example of historical fiction. Following a serious accident, a young apprentice silversmith, Johnny Tremain, is swept up into the colonists' rebellion against the British. Tremain participates in the Boston Tea Party and the Battle of Lexington—events that prompted the Revolutionary War. During his escapades, Tremain meets such notable figures as Paul Revere, Samuel Adams, and John Hancock.

A Gathering of Days
Joan W. Blos

This story is told through the entries of a young girl's journal. Born to the rigors of life on a small New Hampshire farm, thirteen-year-old Catherine Hall is keeping house for her widowed father and younger sister as she begins her journal in 1830. Her father's remarriage introduces a new mother and brother into her home, the plight of a runaway slave opens her eyes to injustice, and the death of her best friend through illness introduces her to grief.

M.C. Higgins, the Great
Virginia Hamilton

This story revolves around fifteen-year-old M.C., eldest boy of the Higgins family. M.C. longs to move from Sarah Mountain because their property is threatened by a sliding spoil heap left over from a strip mine, but M.C.'s father won't move from the land of his ancestors. By the story's end, M.C. convinces his father to take action about the spoil heap. In doing so, M.C. brings together the Higgins family and the neighboring Killburn family, from whom they had always been estranged.

Other Possibilities

Dicey's Song	Cynthia Voight
Picture Bride	Yoshiko Uchida
Dogsong	Gary Paulsen

The Idleness of Sisyphus, 1981, Sandro Chia, Museum of Modern Art

Meeting Challenges

From taking your first steps, to learning to ride a two-wheeled bicycle, to graduating with honors, to curing cancer or eliminating world hunger—challenges occur throughout life. Some challenges make headlines; others are personal. In these stories, poems, and essays, you'll meet people who encounter challenges of all types and meet them head on.

Guide for Reading

Meet the Author:

Mark Twain (1835–1910)

As a boy growing up in Hannibal, Missouri, Mark Twain was enchanted by the Mississippi River, which ran through town. Born Samuel Langhorne Clemens, he took his pen name from a riverman's call, "By the mark—twain," which means "the water is two fathoms (twelve feet) deep."

Real-Life Inspirations Although Twain traveled all over the United States and worked as a printer, prospector, reporter, editor, and lecturer, his boyhood experiences on the Mississippi River were the strongest influences on his most memorable writing. In *The Adventures of Tom Sawyer,* Twain draws on his early life in Hannibal to write a coming-of-age story about a boy in a small Missouri town. In his novel *The Adventures of Huckleberry Finn,* Twain tells about a boy and a runaway slave who travel down the Mississippi together.

THE STORY BEHIND THE STORY

At age twenty-two, Twain became an apprentice riverboat pilot. Being an apprentice involved on-the-job training, learning a skill or trade from someone practicing the skill or trade. Sometimes apprentices were badly treated by their masters. In "Cub Pilot on the Mississippi," Twain tells the true story of how he dealt with the cruel treatment he received from Pilot Brown, a master riverboat pilot.

◆ LITERATURE AND YOUR LIFE

CONNECT YOUR EXPERIENCE

At one time or another, most people face a conflict with another person. Have you ever encountered a schoolyard bully or someone whose behavior was impossible to ignore? What did you do about the situation? In "Cub Pilot on the Mississippi," you'll find out how young Mark Twain dealt with an ill-tempered boss.

THEMATIC FOCUS: Meeting Challenges

Mark Twain meets the challenge of dealing with a bully while learning to become a riverboat pilot. What might be difficult about both of these challenges?

◆ Background for Understanding

SOCIAL STUDIES

In "Cub Pilot on the Mississippi," Mark Twain shares his memories of being an apprentice pilot on a Mississippi steamboat. In the 1800's, steamboats like the ones shown on the facing page appeared on the nation's waterways, carrying goods and people from port to port. Especially on the wide, long Mississippi River, people could travel quickly and sometimes luxuriously. However, there were also dangers. Fires broke out, boilers burst, hidden rocks had to be avoided, and ever-changing currents had to be negotiated.

◆ Cub Pilot on the Mississippi ◆

The Champions of the Mississippi, Currier & Ives

◆ Literary Focus

CONFLICT BETWEEN CHARACTERS

Like short stories, many pieces of nonfiction involve a **conflict,** or struggle between opposing forces. Sometimes the conflict is between two characters and may be caused by a difference in ideas or personalities. In "Cub Pilot on the Mississippi," Twain describes the conflict between himself and Pilot Brown, the steamboat pilot for whom he works. As you read, list the differences that develop the conflict between Twain and Brown.

DIFFERENCES	
Twain	**Brown**
Young; inexperienced	Older; experienced

◆ Build Vocabulary

RELATED WORDS: FORMS OF *judge*

In this story, you'll encounter the word *judicious,* which is part of a word family related to *judge.* The root is an important clue to the meaning of *judicious,* which is "having or showing good judgment."

WORD BANK

Which word on this list has a beginning sound like *hint* and means "hint"? Check the Build Vocabulary box on page 114 to see if you chose correctly.

furtive
pretext
intimation
judicious
indulgent
emancipated

*R*eading for Success

Interactive Reading Strategies

You get more out of life when you really live it—laughing with friends, standing up for what you believe in, learning something new. The same is true when you read. The more you read interactively—questioning, comparing, reading for specifics, and responding—the more you'll enjoy and remember your reading. Use these strategies to interact with your reading.

Set a purpose.

Decide what you want to get from a piece of literature before you begin to read. Then, look for details that help you meet this purpose. For example, you might read "Cub Pilot on the Mississippi" to find out about life as a riverboat pilot. To achieve this purpose, look for details that describe Twain's experiences on the job.

Purpose	**Details**
To learn about being a riverboat pilot	Apprenticeships last for years

Use your prior knowledge.

Your prior knowledge is what you already know. As you read, apply this knowledge to make connections with what the author is saying.

Ask questions.

Don't blindly accept characters' actions and statements. Question their motives and judgment. Question why the writer gives you certain information. Then, read on to find out what happens.

Story Text: I still remember the first time I ever entered the presence of that man.

Question: Why is the encounter so memorable?

Respond.

Allow yourself to respond to characters and situations. Become angry, become amazed, become enthralled. Root for your hero, and hiss at the villain. Then, examine why each character provokes a specific emotional response from you. You may want to keep a reader's response journal, in which you record your reactions to characters, events, and ideas.

As you read "Cub Pilot on the Mississippi," look at the notes in the boxes along the sides of the pages. The notes demonstrate how to apply these strategies to a work of literature.

The Great Mississippi Steamboat Race, 1870, Currier & Ives

▲ **Critical Viewing** What do the details in this painting reveal about steamboat travel? **[Analyze]**

CUB PILOT ON THE MISSISSIPPI

— Mark Twain —

During the two or two and a half years of my apprenticeship[1] I served under many pilots, and had experience of many kinds of steamboatmen and many varieties of steamboats. I am to this day profiting somewhat by that experience; for in that brief, sharp schooling, I got personally and familiarly acquainted with about all the different types of human nature that are to be found in fiction, biography, or history.

The fact is daily borne in upon me that the average shore-employment requires as much as forty years to equip a man with this sort of an education. When I say I am still profiting by this thing, I do not mean that it has constituted me a judge of men—no, it has not done that, for judges of men are born, not made. My profit is various in kind and degree, but the feature of it which I value most is the zest which that early experience has given to my later reading. When I find a well-drawn character in fiction or biography I generally take a warm personal interest in him, for the reason that I have known him before—met him on the river.

> Your **purpose** for reading this may be to discover what characters Twain has "met . . . on the river."

The figure that comes before me oftenest, out of the shadows of that vanished time, is that of Brown, of the steamer *Pennsylvania*. He was a middle-aged, long, slim, bony,

---

1. apprenticeship (ə pren′ tis ship) *n.*: Time a person spends working for a master craftsperson in a craft or trade in return for instruction.

smooth-shaven, horse-faced, ignorant, stingy, malicious, snarling, fault-hunting, mote-[2] magnifying tyrant. I early got the habit of coming on watch with dread at my heart. No matter how good a time I might have been having with the off-watch below,

This statement prompts the question "Why does he dread coming on watch?"

and no matter how high my spirits might be when I started aloft, my soul became lead in my body the moment I approached the pilothouse.

I still remember the first time I ever entered the presence of that man. The boat had backed out from St. Louis and was "straightening down." I ascended to the pilothouse in high feather, and very proud to be semiofficially a member of the executive family of so fast and famous a boat. Brown was at the wheel. I paused in the middle of the room, all fixed to make my bow, but Brown did not look around. I thought he took a <u>furtive</u> glance at me out of the corner of his eye, but as not even this notice was repeated, I judged I had been mistaken. By this time he was picking his way among some dangerous "breaks" abreast the wood-yards; therefore it would not be proper to interrupt him; so I stepped softly to the high bench and took a seat.

There was silence for ten minutes; then my new boss turned and inspected me deliberately and painstakingly from head to heel for about—as it seemed to me—a quarter of an hour. After which he removed his countenance[3] and I saw it no more for some seconds; then it came around once more, and this question greeted me: "Are you Horace Bigsby's cub?"[4]

▲ **Critical Viewing** Imagine the activity that might be occurring in this scene. Why were riverboats important to the life of Mississippi towns like this? [**Analyze**]

"Yes, sir."

After this there was a pause and another inspection. Then: "What's your name?"

I told him. He repeated it after me. It was probably the only thing he ever forgot; for although I was with him many months he never addressed himself to me in any other way than "Here!" and then his command followed.

"Where was you born?"

"In Florida, Missouri."

A pause. Then: "Dern sight better stayed there!"

By means of a dozen or so of pretty direct questions, he pumped my family history out of me.

2. **mote** (mōt) *n.*: Speck of dust.
3. **countenance** (koun′ tə nəns) *n.*: Face.
4. **cub** (kub) *n.*: Beginner.

◆ **Build Vocabulary**

furtive (fur′ tiv) *adj.*: Sly or done in secret

Looking down the Mississippi River at Hannibal, MO, George L. Crosby, Mark Twain Home and Museum

round upon me again—and then what a change! It was as red as fire, and every muscle in it was working. Now came this shriek: "Here! You going to set there all day?"

I lit in the middle of the floor, shot there by the electric suddenness of the surprise. As soon as I could get my voice I said apologetically: "I have had no orders, sir."

"You've had no *orders*! My, what a fine bird we are! We must have *orders*! Our father was a *gentleman* —and *we've* been to *school*. Yes, *we* are a gentleman, *too*, and got to have *orders*! ORDERS, is it? ORDERS is what you want! Dod dern my skin, *I'll* learn you to swell yourself up and blow around *here* about your dod-derned *orders*! G'way from the wheel!" (I had approached it without knowing it.)

I moved back a step or two and stood as in a dream, all my senses stupefied by this frantic assault.

"What you standing there for? Take that ice-pitcher down to the texas-tender![7] Come, move along, and don't you be all day about it!"

The moment I got back to the pilothouse Brown said: "Here! What was you doing down there all this time?"

"I couldn't find the texas-tender; I had to go all the way to the pantry."

"Derned likely story! Fill up the stove."

I proceeded to do so. He watched me like a cat. Presently he shouted: "Put down that shovel! Derndest

The leads[5] were going now in the first crossing. This interrupted the inquest.[6] When the leads had been laid in he resumed:

"How long you been on the river?"

I told him. After a pause:

"Where'd you get them shoes?"

I gave him the information.

"Hold up your foot!"

I did so. He stepped back, examined the shoe minutely and contemptuously, scratching his head thoughtfully, tilting his high sugar-loaf hat well forward to facilitate the operation, then ejaculated, "Well, I'll be dod derned!" and returned to his wheel.

What occasion there was to be dod derned about it is a thing which is still as much of a mystery to me now as it was then. It must have been all of fifteen minutes—fifteen minutes of dull, homesick silence—before that long horse-face swung

Footnotes are useful if you have no **prior knowledge** about a particular reference.

---

5. **leads** (ledz) *n.*: Weights that were lowered to test the depth of the river.

6. **inquest** (in´ kwest) *n.*: Investigation.

7. **texas-tender:** The waiter in the officers' quarters. On Mississippi steamboats, rooms were named after the states. The officers' area, which was the largest, was named after what was then the largest state, Texas.

▲ **Critical Viewing** Put yourself in the place of this pilot. What challenges does the river pose? **[Assess]**

numskull I ever saw—ain't even got sense enough to load up a stove."

All through the watch this sort of thing went on. Yes, and the subsequent watches were much like it during a stretch of months. As I have said, I soon got the habit of coming on duty with dread. The moment I was in the presence, even in the darkest night, I could feel those yellow eyes upon me, and knew their owner was watching for a pretext to spit out some venom on me. Preliminarily he would say: "Here! Take the wheel."

The examples of Brown's behavior support your **purpose** of learning about characters met on the river.

Two minutes later: "*Where* in the nation you going to? Pull her down! pull her down!"

After another moment: "Say! You going to hold her all day? Let her go—meet her! meet her!"

Then he would jump from the bench, snatch the wheel from me, and meet her himself, pouring out wrath upon me all the time.

George Ritchie was the other pilot's cub. He was having good times now; for his boss, George Ealer, was as kind-hearted as Brown wasn't. Ritchie had steered for Brown the season before; consequently, he knew exactly how to entertain himself and plague me, all by the one operation. Whenever I took the wheel for a moment on Ealer's watch, Ritchie would sit back on the bench and play Brown, with continual ejaculations of "Snatch her! Snatch her! Derndest mudcat I ever saw!" "Here! Where are you going *now*? Going to run over that snag?" "Pull her *down*! Don't you hear me? Pull her *down*!" "There she goes! *Just* as I expected! I *told* you not to cramp that reef. G'way from the wheel!"

So I always had a rough time of it, no matter whose watch it was; and sometimes it seemed to me that Ritchie's good-natured badgering was pretty nearly as aggravating as Brown's dead-earnest nagging.

I often wanted to kill Brown, but this would not answer. A cub had to take everything his boss gave, in the way of vigorous comment and criticism; and we all believed that there was a United States law making it a penitentiary offense to strike or threaten a pilot who was on duty.

However, I could *imagine* myself killing Brown; there was no law against that; and that was the thing I used always to do the moment I was abed. Instead of going over my river in my mind, as was my duty, I threw business aside for pleasure, and killed Brown. I killed Brown every night for months; not in old, stale, commonplace ways, but in new and picturesque ones—ways that were sometimes surprising for freshness of design and ghastliness of situation and environment.

> **Ask** why Twain provides this information about killing Brown. Watch for a connection to the action later on.

Brown was *always* watching for a pretext to find fault; and if he could find no plausible pretext, he would invent one. He would scold you for shaving a shore, and for not shaving it; for hugging a bar, and for not hugging it; for "pulling down" when not invited, and for *not* pulling down when not invited; for firing up without orders, and *for* waiting for orders. In a word, it was his invariable rule to find fault with *everything* you did and another invariable rule of his was to throw all his remarks (to you) into the form of an insult.

One day we were approaching New Madrid, bound down and heavily laden. Brown was at one side of the wheel, steering; I was at the other, standing by to "pull down" or "shove up." He cast a furtive glance at me every now and then. I had long ago learned what that meant; viz., he was trying to invent a trap for me. I wondered what shape it was going to take. By and by he stepped back from the wheel and said in his usual snarly way:

"Here! See if you've got gumption enough to round her to."

This was simply *bound* to be a success; nothing could prevent it; for he had never allowed me to round the boat to before; consequently, no matter how I might do the thing, he could find free fault with it. He stood back there with his greedy eye on me, and the result was what might have been foreseen: I lost my head in a quarter of a minute, and didn't know what I was about; I started too early to bring the boat around, but detected a green gleam of joy in Brown's eye, and corrected my mistake. I started around once more while too high up, but corrected myself again in time. I made other false moves, and still managed to save myself; but at last I grew so confused and anxious that I tumbled into the very worst blunder of all—I got too far *down* before beginning to fetch the boat around. Brown's chance was come.

His face turned red with passion; he made one bound, hurled me across the house with a sweep of his arm, spun the wheel down, and began to pour out a stream of vituperation[8] upon me which lasted till he was out of breath. In the course of this speech he called me all the different kinds of hard names he could think of, and once or twice I thought he was even going to swear—but he had never done that, and he didn't this time. "Dod dern" was the nearest he ventured to the luxury of swearing.

Two trips later I got into serious trouble. Brown was steering; I was "pulling down." My younger brother Henry appeared on the hurricane deck, and shouted to Brown to

---

8. **vituperation** (vī too′ pə rā′ shən) *n.:* Abusive language.

◆ **Build Vocabulary**

pretext (prē′ tekst) *n.:* False reason or motive used to hide a real intention

stop at some landing or other, a mile or so below. Brown gave no intimation that he had heard anything. But that was his way: he never condescended to take notice of an underclerk. The wind was blowing; Brown was deaf (although he always pretended he wasn't), and I very much doubted if he had heard the order. If I had had two heads, I would have spoken; but as I had only one, it seemed judicious to take care of it; so I kept still.

Presently, sure enough, we went sailing by that plantation. Captain Klinefelter appeared on the deck, and said: "Let her come around, sir, let her come around. Didn't Henry tell you to land here?"

"*No*, sir!"

"I sent him up to do it."

"He *did* come up; and that's all the good it done, the dod-derned fool. He never said anything."

"Didn't *you* hear him?" asked the captain of me.

Of course I didn't want to be mixed up in this business, but there was no way to avoid it; so I said: "Yes, sir."

I knew what Brown's next remark would be, before he uttered it. It was: "Shut your mouth! You never heard anything of the kind."

I closed my mouth, according to instructions. An hour later Henry entered the pilothouse, unaware of what had been going on. He was a thoroughly inoffensive boy, and I was sorry to see him come, for I knew Brown would have no pity on him. Brown began, straightway: "Here! Why didn't you tell me we'd got to land at that plantation?"

"I did tell you, Mr. Brown."

"It's a lie!"

I said: "You lie, yourself. He did tell you."

◆ Build Vocabulary

intimation (in´ tə mā´ shən) *n*.: Hint or suggestion

judicious (jōō dish´ əs) *adj*.: Showing sound judgment; wise and careful

indulgent (in dul´ jənt) *adj*.: Very mild and tolerant; not strict or critical

Brown glared at me in unaffected surprise; and for as much as a moment he was entirely speechless; then he shouted to me: "I'll attend to your case in a half a minute!" then to Henry, "And you leave the pilothouse; out with you!"

It was pilot law, and must be obeyed. The boy started out, and even had his foot on the upper step outside the door, when Brown, with a sudden access of fury, picked up a ten-pound lump of coal and sprang after him; but I was between, with a heavy stool, and I hit Brown a good honest blow which stretched him out.

I had committed the crime of crimes—I had lifted my hand against a pilot on duty! I supposed I was booked for the penitentiary sure, and couldn't be booked any surer if I went on and squared my long account with this person while I had the chance; consequently I stuck to him and pounded him with my fists a considerable time. I do not know how long, the pleasure of it probably made it seem longer than it really was; but in the end he struggled free and jumped up and sprang to the wheel: a very natural solicitude, for, all this time, here was this steamboat tearing down the river at the rate of fifteen miles an hour and nobody at the helm! However, Eagle Bend was two miles wide at this bank-full stage, and correspondingly long and deep: and the boat was steering herself straight down the middle and taking no chances. Still, that was only luck—a body *might* have found her charging into the woods.

Perceiving at a glance that the *Pennsylvania* was in no danger, Brown gathered up the big spyglass, war-club fashion, and ordered me out of the pilothouse with more than ordinary bluster. But I was not afraid of him now; so, instead of going, I tarried, and criticized his grammar. I reformed his ferocious speeches for him, and put them into good English, calling his attention to the advantage of pure English over the

> **Respond** to Twain's answer to Brown. Did you expect Twain to stand his ground?

dialect of the collieries[9] whence he was extracted. He could have done his part to admiration in a crossfire of mere vituperation, of course; but he was not equipped for this species of controversy; so he presently laid aside his glass and took the wheel, muttering and shaking his head; and I retired to the bench. The racket had brought everybody to the hurricane deck, and I trembled when I saw the old captain looking up from amid the crowd. I said to myself, "Now I *am* done for!" for although, as a rule, he was so fatherly and indulgent toward the boat's family, and so patient of minor shortcomings, he could be stern enough when the fault was worth it.

> You might be **asking** what the captain will do to Twain.

I tried to imagine what he *would* do to a cub pilot who had been guilty of such a crime as mine, committed on a boat guard-deep[10] with costly freight and alive with passengers. Our watch was nearly ended.

> Use your **prior knowledge** or experience to understand Twain's nervousness when confronted with a figure of authority.

I thought I would go and hide somewhere till I got a chance to slide ashore. So I slipped out of the pilothouse, and down the steps, and around to the texas-door, and was in the act of gliding within, when the captain confronted me! I dropped my head, and he stood over me in silence a moment or two, then said impressively: "Follow me."

I dropped into his wake; he led the way to his parlor in the forward end of the texas. We were alone now. He closed the afterdoor, then moved slowly to the forward one and closed that. He sat down; I stood before him. He looked at me some little time, then said: "So you have been fighting Mr. Brown?"

I answered meekly: "Yes, sir."

"Do you know that that is a very serious matter?"

"Yes, sir."

"Are you aware that this boat was plowing down the river fully five minutes with no one at the wheel?"

"Yes, sir."

"Did you strike him first?"

"Yes, sir."

"What with?"

"A stool, sir."

"Hard?"

"Middling, sir."

"Did it knock him down?"

"He—he fell, sir."

"Did you follow it up? Did you do anything further?"

"Yes, sir."

"What did you do?"

"Pounded him, sir."

"Pounded him?"

"Yes, sir."

"Did you pound him much? that is, severely?"

"One might call it that, sir, maybe."

"I'm deuced glad of it! Hark ye, never mention that I said that. You have been guilty of a great crime; and don't you ever be guilty of it again, on this boat. *But*—lay for him ashore! Give him a good sound thrashing, do you hear? I'll pay the expenses. Now go—and mind you, not a word of this to anybody. Clear out with you! You've been guilty of a great crime, you whelp!"[11]

I slid out, happy with the sense of a close shave and a mighty deliverance; and I heard him laughing to himself and slapping his fat thighs after I had closed his door.

When Brown came off watch he went straight to the captain, who was talking with some passengers on the boiler deck, and demanded that I be put ashore in New Orleans—and added: "I'll never turn a wheel on this boat again while that cub stays."

The captain said: "But he needn't come round when you are on watch, Mr. Brown."

"I won't even stay on the same boat with him. One of us has got to go ashore."

---

9. **collieries** (kal´ yər ēz) *n.*: Coal mines.
10. **guard-deep:** Here, a wooden frame protecting the paddle wheel.

---

11. **whelp** (hwelp) *n.*: Here, a disrespectful young man.

"Very well," said the captain, "let it be yourself," and resumed his talk with the passengers.

During the brief remainder of the trip I knew how an <u>emancipated</u> slave feels, for I was an emancipated slave myself. While we lay at landings I listened to George Ealer's flute, or to his readings from his two Bibles, that is to say, Goldsmith and Shakespeare, or I played chess with him—and would have beaten him sometimes, only he always took back his last move and ran the game out differently.

◆ **Build Vocabulary**

emancipated (i man´ sə pā´ təd) v.: Freed from the control or power of another

Beyond Literature

Science Connection

River Navigation In the early nine-teenth century, the Mississippi River was navigable by small boats only. They faced dangerous rapids, rocks, and snags. Snags are submerged trees that are not always visible from the surface.

Steamboats could not use this major waterway until it was cleared of snags. In the 1820's, riverboat builder Henry Shreve invented a boat to pull up and remove snags. The boat had two hulls, with a heavy iron wedge between them. To remove a snag, the boat rammed the wedge into the submerged tree. The powerful boat engine operated lifting machinery that hoisted the large, sodden trunks. By 1830, the snag boats, called "Uncle Sam's Tooth Pullers," had cleared the Mississippi River for navigation.

Cross-Curricular Activity

Boat Diagram Use reference sources to find out about the snag boats that cleared the Mississippi. Then, create a diagram that shows how the boats worked. Label the parts of your diagram.

Guide for Responding

◆ LITERATURE AND YOUR LIFE

Reader's Response Do you think that Mark Twain could have resolved the conflict with Brown in another way? Why or why not?

Thematic Focus What challenges does a steamboat pilot face?

Role Play With a partner, role-play a conversation between Mark Twain and his brother Henry about Mr. Brown.

☑ Check Your Comprehension

1. About how old is Twain at the time the story takes place?
2. Why is Twain in the pilothouse with Mr. Brown?
3. Whom does Twain try to defend when he hits Brown?
4. Why does Twain feel like "an emancipated slave" at the end?

◆ Critical Thinking

INTERPRET

1. In what ways was Brown's treatment of the young Twain unfair? **[Support]**
2. How do you know that Brown treated other cub pilots the same way he treated Twain? **[Deduce]**
3. How does the captain feel about Mr. Brown? What evidence supports your answer? **[Draw Conclusions]**
4. What do Twain's answers to the captain suggest about Twain's character? **[Infer]**

EVALUATE

5. From what you learn about him in the story, do you think Twain will make a good riverboat captain? **[Evaluate]**

EXTEND

6. What kinds of skills do you think would be necessary to pilot a riverboat? **[Career Link]**

Guide for Responding (continued)

◆ Reading for Success

INTERACTIVE READING STRATEGIES

Review the reading strategies on page 108 and notes that show how to interact with the text. Then, apply them to answer these questions.

1. (a) What was your purpose for reading? (b) What details in the text helped you fulfill your purpose?
2. (a) What was your response to Twain's method of resolving the conflict with Brown? (b) Was the captain's reaction to Twain's confession what you expected? Explain.
3. Using your own experience with bullies as a guide, advise Twain on how to deal with them in the future.

◆ Build Vocabulary

USING FORMS OF *judge*

The word family that includes *judicious, judgment,* and *judicial* descends from the verb *judge,* meaning "to decide [in a court of law]." Correctly complete each sentence, using *judicious, judgment,* or *judicial.*

1. I wouldn't want to make a _____?_____ about that.
2. She was a _____?_____ referee.
3. The Supreme Court is a _____?_____ branch of government.

SPELLING STRATEGY

The *shus* sound at the end of a word may be spelled in different ways. One way to spell it is *cious,* as in *judicious.*

Rewrite these words to end in the *shus* sound.

1. lush   2. grace   3. malice

USING THE WORD BANK

On your paper, write the word closest in meaning to the Word Bank word.

1. pretext: (a) pretend, (b) excuse, (c) scholarly
2. indulgent: (a) soft, (b) greedy, (c) tolerant
3. judicious: (a) wise, (b) critical, (c) lawful
4. emancipated: (a) fled, (b) freed, (c) tied
5. furtive: (a) random, (b) curious, (c) secretive
6. intimation: (a) hint, (b) caution, (c) mild

◆ Literary Focus

CONFLICT BETWEEN CHARACTERS

The **conflict between characters** in this story propels the plot, or the story's action. The struggle between Twain and Brown escalates until it is finally resolved at the story's conclusion.

1. List three occasions in the story during which Twain and Mr. Brown are involved in conflict.
2. (a) Why does Twain always come to the pilot-house with "dread at my heart"? (b) Why doesn't Twain, the cub pilot, defy Mr. Brown sooner?
3. How is the conflict between Twain and Mr. Brown finally resolved?

◆ Build Grammar Skills

VERBS AND VERB PHRASES

A **verb** is a word that expresses an action or the fact that something exists.

> I *closed* my mouth, according to instructions.
> My profit *is* various in kind and degree.

A **verb phrase** consists of a main verb and its helping verbs. In the following sentence, *closed* is the main verb; *had* is the helping verb.

> I *had closed* my mouth.

Common Helping Verbs:
be, been, am, are, is, was, were, do, does, did, have, has, had, can, could, will, would, may, might, shall, should, must

Practice Copy the following passages from the story. Circle the verb phrases. Then, underline each helping verb once and each main verb twice.

1. Then he would jump from the bench . . .
2. The racket had brought everybody to the hurricane deck . . .
3. He would scold you for shaving a shore . . .
4. I had long ago learned what that meant . . .
5. I could feel those yellow eyes upon me . . .

Writing Application Write a paragraph about what it might have been like to be a riverboat pilot. In the paragraph, use the verbs *concentrate* and *steer,* along with the helping verbs *would* and *have.*

Build Your Portfolio

 ## Idea Bank

Writing

1. **Journal Entry** Write a journal entry that Mark Twain might have written about the outcome of his conflict. The journal entry should be dated the night of Twain's conversation with the captain.

2. **Character Sketch** Write a character sketch of Mark Twain, cub pilot, based on his actions and comments within the story.

3. **Essay on Humor** In an essay, write about Mark Twain's use of humor in "Cub Pilot on the Mississippi." Discuss his use of dialogue and dialect, and explain how he uses humor to engage the reader in this story.

Speaking and Listening

4. **Dramatic Reading [Group Activity]** With several classmates, prepare and deliver a dramatic reading of part of the story. Use the tone, volume, and inflection of your voices to highlight changes in character or mood. **[Performing Arts Link]**

5. **Talk-Show Interview [Group Activity]** With a group, produce a talk show on the subject of fighting, featuring Mark Twain as a guest. The talk-show host should interview Twain and find out his views on fighting as a means of solving a conflict. Choose several other characters to participate in the talk show to offer views that are different from Twain's. **[Media Link]**

Projects

6. **Timeline** Research Twain's life and achievements. Then, create an illustrated timeline of his life. Post your finished product in the classroom. **[Literature Link; Art Link]**

7. **Transportation Brochure** Create a brochure that encourages people to travel on the Mississippi steamboats of the 1800's. Do research to make your brochure seem authentic. Display your brochure in the classroom. **[Social Studies Link]**

 ## Writing Mini-Lesson

Anecdote

Like Mark Twain, we all have stories to tell about our lives. Choose a memorable experience, and write an **anecdote,** a brief true account of something meaningful that happened to you. The following may help you organize your anecdote.

Writing Skills Focus: Introduction, Body, Conclusion

Using an **introduction, body,** and **conclusion** will give your anecdote structure and shape. In his introduction, Twain reveals that he learned a lesson about human character when he was a cub pilot. In the body of the story, he relates events that illustrate that lesson. In the conclusion, Twain wraps up the story, revealing his feelings about the incident.

Prewriting Take notes about the most dramatic aspects and colorful details of the event you've chosen. Jot down bits of dialogue you might include in your anecdote.

Drafting Capture readers' interest in the introduction, tell your story in the body, and describe what you learned or how you changed in the conclusion. Consider using dialogue to make the people and situations in your anecdote come alive.

◆ **Grammar Application**

Choose a paragraph of your narrative. In each sentence, identify the verb or verb phrases.

Revising Reread your draft, and make sure it has a beginning, a middle, and an ending. Revise by adding details about characters or events that will make the importance of the story more clear. Proofread to correct errors in grammar, spelling, and punctuation.

Blazing Trails

The Parkman Outfit–Henry Chatillon, Guide and Hunter, N.C. Wyeth, Wells Fargo & Co.

Guide for Reading

Meet the Author:

Arthur C. Clarke (1917–)

This writer has always been ahead of his time. As a twenty-eight-year-old scientist, Clarke outlined ideas for a worldwide satellite system. Today, we rely on satellites to transmit radio and television communication signals. One common satellite orbit is even named in Clarke's honor.

From Scientist to Author Clarke built on his career as a scientist by writing science fiction. The author of more than seventy books, he has presented many versions of what our future might hold. Many of his stories have inspired motion pictures. The most famous is *2001: A Space Odyssey*.

Clarke has said that his curiosity about the future keeps him going. How would he like to be remembered? He suggests this simple epitaph: "He never grew up; but he never stopped growing."

THE STORY BEHIND THE STORY

"The Secret" is set in a human colony on the moon. Clarke believes that with efficient research, human colonies in space will someday be an affordable reality. He says, "There's no reason why, in the next century, it should cost more to go to the Moon than it costs to fly around the world today."

◆ Literature and Your Life

CONNECT YOUR EXPERIENCE

You might keep a personal diary or mark a letter "confidential." Most people feel the need to keep some things private. Yet many journalists believe that all information should be accessible to the public. In "The Secret," a character struggles over whether or not to publish an intriguing discovery.

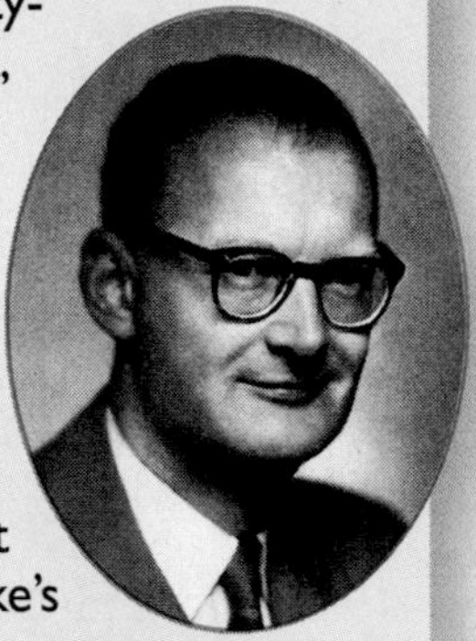

THEMATIC FOCUS: Blazing Trails

What are the advantages of being the first person to discover something? What are possible disadvantages?

◆ Background for Understanding

SCIENCE

"The Secret" takes place in a colony on the moon. Although it may be hard to believe, the idea of living in a space colony is not as far-fetched as it might seem. In fact, for years, astronauts like the one in the photograph have conducted ongoing experiments to learn about living in space. For example, they evaluate how the human body adapts to extreme changes in atmosphere and gravity. Information collected in space is then analyzed on Earth; the results help scientists develop new strategies for survival in space.

◆ Build Vocabulary

WORD PART: *micro*

The word *microbes,* meaning "small form of life" or "tiny organism," contains the word parts *micro,* meaning "small," and *bio* (*be*), meaning "life."

WORD BANK

Which word from this list means "radiating or branching out from the center"? Check the Build Vocabulary box on page 125 to see if you chose correctly.

receding
competent
microbes
hemisphere
radial
heedless
implications
looming

◆ The Secret ◆

◆ Literary Focus

SCIENCE FICTION

Science fiction combines elements of fiction and fantasy with scientific fact. This type of writing is most effective when the writer creates a believable setting and characters, and balances new ideas with familiar details. Arthur C. Clarke has said that "the only way of discovering the limits of the possible is to venture a little way past them into the impossible." As you read "The Secret," think about which elements are "possible" and which approach the "impossible."

◆ Reading Strategy

ASK QUESTIONS

Most writers don't spell out everything for readers. It's up to you to **ask questions** about characters' actions, the meaning of events, and why certain details are included. For example, consider this opening sentence:

> Henry Cooper had been on the Moon for almost two weeks before he discovered that something was wrong.

After reading this, you might ask: "Who's Henry Cooper? What's he doing on the moon?" As you read, record questions and answers in a chart like this one.

Questions	Answers
Who is Henry Cooper? Why is he on the moon?	**He's a journalist.**

THE
SECRET

Arthur C. Clarke

Henry Cooper had been on the Moon for almost two weeks before he discovered that something was wrong. At first it was only an ill-defined suspicion, the sort of hunch that a hard-headed science reporter would not take too seriously. He had come here, after all, at the United Nations Space Administration's own request. UNSA had always been hot on public relations—especially just before budget time, when an overcrowded world was screaming for more roads and schools and sea farms, and complaining about the billions being poured into space.

So here he was, doing the lunar circuit for the second time, and beaming back two thousand words of copy a day. Although the novelty had worn off, there still remained the wonder and mystery of a world as big as Africa, thoroughly mapped, yet almost completely unexplored. A stone's throw away from the pressure domes, the labs, the spaceports, was a yawning emptiness that would challenge humankind for centuries to come.

Some parts of the Moon were almost too familiar, of course. Who had not seen that dusty scar on the Mare Imbrium, with its gleaming metal pylon and the plaque that announced in the three official languages of Earth:

ON THIS SPOT
AT 2001 UT
13 SEPTEMBER 1959
THE FIRST MAN-MADE OBJECT
REACHED ANOTHER WORLD

Cooper had visited the grave of Lunik II— and the more famous tomb of the men who had come after it. But these things belonged to the past; already, like Columbus and the Wright brothers,[1] they were receding into history. What concerned him now was the future.

When he had landed at Archimedes Spaceport, the Chief Administrator had been obviously glad to see him, and had shown a personal interest in his tour. Transportation, accommodation, and official guide were all arranged. He could go anywhere he liked, ask any questions he pleased. UNSA trusted him, for his stories had always been accurate, his attitudes friendly. Yet the tour had gone sour; he did not know why, but he was going to find out.

He reached for the phone and said: "Operator? . . . Please get me the Police Department. I want to speak to the Inspector General."

Presumably Chandra Coomaraswamy possessed a uniform, but Cooper had never seen him wearing it. They met, as arranged, at the entrance to the little park that was Plato City's chief pride and joy. At this time in the morning of the artificial twenty-four-hour "day" it was almost deserted, and they could talk without interruption.

As they walked along the narrow gravel paths, they chatted about old times, the friends they had known at college together, the latest developments in interplanetary politics. They had reached the middle of the park, under the exact center of the great blue-painted dome, when Cooper came to the point.

"You know everything that's happening on the Moon, Chandra," he said. "And you know that I'm here to do a series for UNSA—hope to make a book out of it when I get back to Earth. So why should people be trying to hide things from me?"

It was impossible to hurry Chandra. He always took his time to answer questions, and his few words escaped with difficulty around the stem of his hand-carved Bavarian[2] pipe.

"What people?" he asked at length.

"You've really no idea?"

The Inspector General shook his head.

"Not the faintest," he answered; and Cooper knew that he was telling the truth. Chandra might be silent, but he would not lie.

"I was afraid you'd say that. Well, if you don't know any more than I do, here's the only clue I have—and it frightens me. Medical Research is trying to keep me at arm's length."

"Hmmm," replied Chandra, taking his pipe from his mouth and looking at it thoughtfully.

---

1. **Columbus . . . Wright brothers:** Christopher Columbus (16th c. Italian navigator) and Orville and Wilbur Wright (19th c. American inventors of the airplane) were great explorers, the former of land and the latter of air.

2. **Bavarian** (bə ver´ ē ən) adj.: Of or related to Bavaria, a region in Germany.

"Is that all you have to say?"

"You haven't given me much to work on. Remember, I'm only a cop; I lack your vivid journalistic imagination."

"All I can tell you is that the higher I get in Medical Research, the colder the atmosphere becomes. Last time I was here, everyone was very friendly, and gave me some fine stories. But now, I can't even meet the Director. He's always too busy, or on the other side of the Moon. Anyway, what sort of man is he?"

"Dr. Hastings? Prickly little character. Very competent, but not easy to work with."

"What could he be trying to hide?"

"Knowing you, I'm sure you have some interesting theories."

"Oh, I thought of narcotics, and fraud, and political conspiracies—but they don't make sense, in these days. So what's left scares the heck out of me."

Chandra's eyebrows signaled a silent question mark.

"Interplanetary plague," said Cooper bluntly.

"I thought that was impossible."

"Yes—I've written articles myself proving that the life forms of other planets have such alien chemistries that they can't react with us, and that all our microbes and bugs took millions of years to adapt to our bodies. But I've always wondered if it was true. Suppose a ship has come back from Mars, say, with something *really* vicious—and the doctors can't cope with it?"

There was a long silence. Then Chandra said: "I'll start investigating. *I* don't like it, either, for here's an item you probably don't know. There were three nervous breakdowns in the Medical Division last month—and that's very, very unusual."

He glanced at his watch, then at the false sky, which seemed so distant, yet was only two hundred feet above their heads.

"We'd better get moving," he said. "The morning shower's due in five minutes."

The call came two weeks later in the middle of the night—the real lunar night. By Plato City time, it was Sunday morning.

"Henry? . . . Chandra here. Can you meet me in half an hour at air lock five? . . . Good. I'll see you."

This was it, Cooper knew. Air lock five meant they were going outside the dome. Chandra had found something.

The presence of the police driver restricted conversation as the tractor moved away from the city along the road roughly bulldozed across the ash and pumice. Low in the south, Earth was almost full, casting a brilliant blue-green light over the infernal landscape. However hard one tried, Cooper told himself, it was difficult to make the Moon appear glamorous. But nature guards her greatest secrets well; to such places men must come to find them.

The multiple domes of the city dropped below the sharply curved horizon. Presently, the tractor turned aside from the main road to follow a scarcely visible trail. Ten minutes later, Cooper saw a single glittering hemisphere ahead of them, standing on an isolated ridge of rock. Another vehicle, bearing a red cross, was parked beside the entrance. It seemed that they were not the only visitors.

Nor were they unexpected. As they drew up to the dome, the flexible tube of the air-lock coupling groped out toward them and snapped into place against their tractor's outer hull. There was a brief hissing as pressures equalized. Then Cooper followed Chandra into the building.

The air-lock operator led them along curving corridors and radial passageways toward the center of the dome. Sometimes they caught glimpses of laboratories, scientific instruments, computers—all perfectly ordinary, and all deserted on this Sunday morning. They must have reached the heart of the building, Cooper told himself, when their guide ushered them into a large circular chamber and shut the door softly behind them.

It was a small zoo. All around them were cages, tanks, jars containing a wide selection of the fauna and flora of Earth. Waiting at its center was a short, gray-haired man, looking very

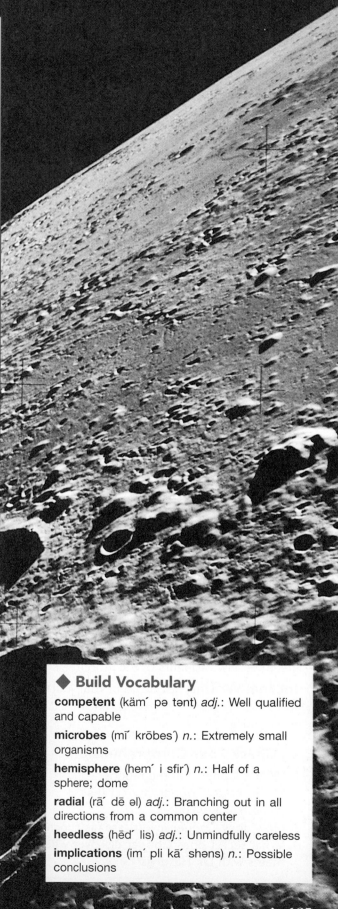

worried, and very unhappy.

"Dr. Hastings," said Coomaraswamy, "meet Mr. Cooper." The Inspector General turned to his companion and added, "I've convinced the Doctor that there's only one way to keep you quiet— and that's to tell you everything."

"Frankly," said Hastings, "I'm not sure if I care anymore." His voice was unsteady, barely under control, and Cooper thought, Hello! There's another breakdown on the way.

The scientist wasted no time on such formalities as shaking hands. He walked to one of the cages, took out a small bundle of fur, and held it toward Cooper.

"Do you know what this is?" he asked abruptly.

"Of course. A hamster—the commonest lab animal."

"Yes," said Hastings. "A perfectly ordinary golden hamster. Except that this one is five years old—like all the others in this cage."

"Well? What's odd about that?"

"Oh, nothing, nothing at all . . . except for the fact that hamsters live for only two years. And we have some here that are getting on for ten."

For a moment no one spoke; but the room was not silent. It was full of rustlings and slitherings and scratchings, of faint whimpers and tiny animal cries. Then Cooper whispered, "My God—you've found a way of prolonging life!"

"No," retorted Hastings. "We've not found it. The Moon has given it to us . . . as we might have expected, if we'd looked in front of our noses." He seemed to have gained control over his emotions—as if he was once more the pure scientist, fascinated by a discovery for its own sake and <u>heedless</u> of its <u>implications</u>.

"On Earth," he said, "we spend our whole lives fighting gravity. It wears down our muscles, pulls our stomachs out of shape. In seventy years, how many tons of blood does the heart lift through how many miles? And all that work, all that strain is reduced to a sixth here on the Moon, where a one-hundred-and-eighty-pound human weighs only thirty pounds?"

"I see," said Cooper slowly.

◆ **Literary Focus**
How does Clarke use facts to make his science-fiction story believable?

◆ **Build Vocabulary**

competent (käm′ pə tənt) *adj.*: Well qualified and capable

microbes (mī′ krōbes′) *n.*: Extremely small organisms

hemisphere (hem′ i sfir′) *n.*: Half of a sphere; dome

radial (rā′ dē əl) *adj.*: Branching out in all directions from a common center

heedless (hēd′ lis) *adj.*: Unmindfully careless

implications (im′ pli kā′ shəns) *n.*: Possible conclusions

"Ten years for a hamster—and how long for a man?"

"It's not a simple law," answered Hastings. "It varies with the sex and the species. Even a month ago, we weren't certain. But now we're quite sure of this: on the Moon, the span of human life will be at least two hundred years."

"And you've been trying to keep this a secret!"

"You fool! Don't you understand?"

"Take it easy, Doctor—take it easy," said Chandra softly.

With an obvious effort of will, Hastings got control of himself again. He began to speak with such icy calm that his words sank like freezing raindrops into Cooper's mind.

"Think of them up there," he said, pointing to the roof, to the invisible Earth, whose looming presence no one on the Moon could forget. "Six billion of them, packing all the continents to the edges—and now crowding over into the sea beds. And here—" he pointed to the ground—

"only a hundred thousand of us, on an almost empty world. But a world where we need miracles of technology and engineering merely to exist, where a man with an IQ of only a hundred and fifty can't even get a job.

"And now we find that we can live for two hundred years. Imagine how they're going to react to that news! This is your problem now, Mister Journalist; you've asked for it, and you've got it. Tell me this, please—I'd really be interested to know—*just how are you going to break it to them?*"

He waited, and waited. Cooper opened his mouth, then closed it again, unable to think of anything to say.

In the far corner of the room, a baby monkey started to cry.

◆ Build Vocabulary

looming (lo͞om′ iŋ) *adj.*: Ominous and awe-inspiring

Guide for Responding

◆ LITERATURE AND YOUR LIFE

Reader's Response Do you think Cooper should write about the secret or hide this information from people on Earth? Why?

Thematic Focus How will this situation affect the new residents of the moon?

Journal Writing Jot down in your journal notes that Cooper may have taken while investigating "the secret."

☑ Check Your Comprehension

1. Why is Cooper on the moon?
2. What makes Cooper suspect that something is wrong?
3. How does Cooper investigate his hunch?
4. What secret does Cooper discover when he meets with Dr. Hastings?

◆ Critical Thinking

INTERPRET

1. How is Cooper's profession important to the story? **[Connect]**
2. Why is Dr. Hastings discouraged? **[Infer]**
3. How can the secret be interpreted as both good news and bad news? **[Interpret]**
4. What hard question does Cooper face once he learns the secret? **[Speculate]**

EVALUATE

5. What makes a good reporter? Judging from details in the story, do you think that Cooper is a good reporter? Explain. **[Assess]**

APPLY

6. Do you think this story supports or discourages the idea of human colonies in space? Explain. **[Generalize]**

For more than a century, ideas about space travel have inspired writers of novels, scripts, poems, and songs. Arthur C. Clarke writes often about everyday life set on other planets or on our moon. In this song, rock star David Bowie explores another aspect of space travel—its very real dangers.

1. What message does the song convey?
2. In what ways does Major Tom blaze a trail?
3. Would you describe this song as science fiction or realistic? Explain.

SPACE ODDITY
David Bowie

Ground Control to Major Tom,
Ground Control to Major Tom,
Take your protein pills and put
    your helmet on.
Ten
5 Ground Control to Major Tom
    Nine, Eight, Seven
Commencing countdown, engines
    on *Six, Five, Four*
Check ignition and may God's love
    be with you *Three, Two, One*
Liftoff

This is Ground Control to Major Tom,
10 You've really made the grade
And the papers want to know whose
    shirts you wear
Now it's time to leave the capsule if
    you dare.

"This is Major Tom to Ground Control
I'm stepping through the door
15 And I'm floating in a most peculiar
    way
And the stars look very different
    today.

For here
Am I sitting in a tin can
Far above the world,
20 Planet Earth is blue
And there's nothing I can do.

Though I'm past one hundred
    thousand miles,
I'm feeling very still,
And I think my spaceship knows
    which way to go.
25 Tell my wife I love her very much
    she knows."

Ground Control to Major Tom
Your circuit's dead, there's
    something wrong.
Can you hear me, Major Tom?
Can you hear me, Major Tom?
30 Can you hear me, Major Tom?
Can you . . .

"Here I am floating round my tin can,
Far above the Moon,
Planet Earth is blue
35 And there's nothing I can do."

Guide for Responding (continued)

◆ Reading Strategy

ASK QUESTIONS

After reading a story, think about the **questions** you asked and answered while reading. If any questions remain unanswered, piece together details from the story to find answers.

1. Why do you think Clarke chose to title his story "The Secret"? What other titles might you suggest for this story?
2. Why does Chandra help Cooper?
3. Why do you think Dr. Hastings revealed the secret to Cooper?

◆ Build Vocabulary

USING THE WORD PART *micro*

Many words combine *micro* with various word parts. Determine the meanings of the following words by analyzing the word parts.

1. microscopic   2. microwave   3. microfilm

SPELLING STRATEGY

When adding *-ing* to words that end with *-cede*, drop the e and then add the ending.

recede + -ing = receding

On your paper, add *-ing* to the following words.

1. precede   2. accede   3. concede

USING THE WORD BANK

In your notebook, write the letter of the word or phrase that is most nearly the same in meaning as the Word Bank word.

1. competent: (a) simple, (b) attractive, (c) able
2. receding: (a) tiring, (b) surging, (c) decreasing
3. heedless: (a) unmindful, (b) cautious, (c) sly
4. implications: (a) possible effects, (b) facts, (c) styles
5. hemisphere: (a) pyramid, (b) cube, (c) dome
6. radial: (a) from outside to inside, (b) from outer space, (c) from a central point
7. microbes: (a) scientists, (b) tiny forms of life, (c) substances
8. looming: (a) glowing, (b) appearing, (c) building

◆ Literary Focus

SCIENCE FICTION

"The Secret" is a **science-fiction** story set in the distant future. Like many science-fiction stories, it combines scientific fact with familiar details to make this future believable.

1. List elements in the story that are based on scientific fact.
2. What changes does Clarke suggest will happen between the present and the time of the story?
3. Do you think the story would be as effective if all the characters were from other planets? Explain.

◆ Build Grammar Skills

ACTION VERBS AND LINKING VERBS

An **action verb** expresses action:

He *walked* to one of the cages.
He *waited*, and *waited*.

A **linking verb** expresses a state of being. Linking verbs include forms of the verb *to be* as well as *seem, appear, look, feel, become, sound, stay, remain,* and *grow*. To determine whether a verb is an action or a linking verb, replace it with a form of *to be*. If the sentence still makes sense, it is a linking verb.

I thought that *was* impossible.

Practice Copy the following sentences. Underline each verb. Above each verb, write *AV* if it is an action verb and *LV* if it is a linking verb.

1. The space colony orbits Mars.
2. Last year was the settlement's first anniversary.
3. Radiation shields protected the inhabitants.
4. Life became routine for the colonists.
5. They remain optimistic about their future.

Writing Application Follow the directions for each item.

1. Use two action verbs in a sentence about a space colony.
2. Use a linking verb in a sentence about a planet.
3. Use an action verb to describe an action performed by Cooper.

Build Your Portfolio

 ## Idea Bank

Writing

1. **Advertisement** Create an advertisement to attract new colonists to the moon settlement. Use information from the story to describe the colony.

2. **News Article** Imagine that you are Cooper. Write an article informing people on Earth about the discovery at the moon colony.

3. **Critical Response** Write a response to the story in which you examine how effectively Clarke has developed the story's characters and setting.

Speaking and Listening

4. **Telephone Call** Imagine that Cooper calls a friend on Earth using a satellite phone. Role-play the conversation between the two characters. Will Cooper reveal the secret? **[Performing Arts Link]**

5. **Radio Review** Prepare a brief radio review of "The Secret." Provide enough information to interest listeners in the story, but don't give away too much. **[Media Link]**

Projects

6. **Space Settlement [Group Activity]** With a small group, design your own space settlement. Present your drawings, ideas, and plans to the class. You may want to visit this Web site to get information and ideas: http://science.nas.nasa.gov/ Services/Education/SpaceSettlement/index.html. **[Science Link]**

7. **Comic Book** Work with a team to create a comic book based on "The Secret." Each team member should have a specific job, such as artist, author, or colorist. First, work together to outline your ideas. Decide how many pages your comic will contain and how many frames will appear on each page. Display the finished product in the classroom. **[Art Link]**

 ## Writing Mini-Lesson

Story Continuation

What might happen after "the secret" is revealed? What if "the secret" is never revealed? Write a continuation of the story. In your story, include science-fiction elements of scientific fact and fantasy.

Writing Skills Focus: Sequence of Events

Stories contain a sequence of events, the order in which things happen. In this passage from "The Secret," transitions make the sequence of events clear.

Model From the Story
Presently, the tractor turned aside from the main road to follow a scarcely visible trail. *Ten minutes later,* Cooper saw a single glittering hemisphere ahead of them. . . .

Prewriting Reread the story, and decide what will happen next. Use a story chart like the one below to organize your ideas.

Characters:
Setting:
Events:
Outcome:

Drafting Use your story chart to describe what happens after "The Secret" ends. Keep the original story nearby, and use it to help you with characters and details. Create a sequence of events, and use transitions to show the order in which things happen.

Revising Will readers be able to follow your new ending? Make sure you have used transitions to make the sequence of events clear. Look for places where the addition of science-fiction details will make the futuristic setting more vivid.

> ◆ **Grammar Application**
> Replace some linking verbs with action verbs to make your story more dramatic.

Guide for Reading

Meet the Author:

Ann Petry (1912–1997)

Growing up in Old Saybrook, Connecticut, in a predominantly white community, Ann Petry sometimes encountered racism during her childhood. Her family, however, provided her with a caring and protective environment, and Petry became inspired by tales told to her by her mother of the strength and courage of her ancestors.

A Writer's Life Petry began writing while in high school, but she went on to get a degree as a pharmacist. Following her marriage to George D. Petry, a mystery writer, Petry herself refocused her attention and energy on writing. She became a reporter for the New York City newspapers *The Amsterdam News* and the *People's Voice* before she went on to write novels and short stories. Her first novel, *The Street*, was set in New York's Harlem.

THE STORY BEHIND THE STORY

Petry believed that it is impossible to understand the present without a knowledge of the past. Harriet Tubman, a historical hero, became a particular object of Petry's admiration. She pays tribute to Tubman in the biography *Harriet Tubman: Conductor of the Underground Railroad*, from which this selection is taken.

◆ LITERATURE AND YOUR LIFE

CONNECT YOUR EXPERIENCE

Climbing on the roof to get a Frisbee is taking a foolish risk, but is climbing on the roof to rescue a kitten as foolish? Think about risks you've taken and whether or not taking those risks was justified. In the following story, you'll read about Harriet Tubman, a woman who broke the law and risked her life—but for a worthy cause.

THEMATIC FOCUS: Blazing Trails

As you read the story, identify the trails that Tubman blazed and the risks she took.

◆ Background for Understanding

HISTORY

The narrative you're about to read tells the story of Harriet Tubman. She was one of the leading forces behind the Underground Railroad, a network of people who helped enslaved Africans escape from the South in the mid-1800's. Led by abolitionists—people against slavery—the Underground Railroad hid, fed, and sometimes supplied money to runaway slaves. Tubman made nineteen trips on this "railroad," during which she brought 300 people North to freedom.

◆ Build Vocabulary

WORD ROOTS: -fug-

In "Harriet Tubman: Guide to Freedom," you'll learn how Tubman guided *fugitives* to freedom. The word *fugitives*, meaning "persons running from the law," is built on the word root *-fug-*, meaning "to flee."

fugitives
incentive
disheveled
guttural
mutinous
cajoling
indomitable
fastidious

WORD BANK

Which word from the list means "rebellious" or "engaged in mutiny"? Check the Build Vocabulary box on page 137 to see if you chose correctly.

Harriet Tubman: Guide to Freedom

Harriet Tubman Quilt made by the Negro History Club of Marin City and Sausalito, designed by Ben Irvin, Atlanta University Center, Robert W. Woodruff Library

◆ Literary Focus

THIRD-PERSON NARRATIVE

A narrative is a story. All narratives, both fiction and nonfiction, have narrators who describe the action. When the narrator is outside the story, the story is a **third-person narrative.** The narrator uses third-person pronouns to refer to the character. Although not part of the action, the narrator can provide details, dialogue, and even sometimes the characters' thoughts, as if he or she were there, to bring the characters' experiences to life.

◆ Reading Strategy

SET A PURPOSE FOR READING

Just as you have reasons for seeing a movie—to be entertained, to be scared, to learn something—you should have a reason, or **purpose,** for reading literature. For example, your purpose in reading this selection might be to learn about Harriet Tubman. To further define this purpose, you might ask *who, what, when, where, why,* and *how* questions like the ones in the chart below. You can then fill in answers to these questions as you read.

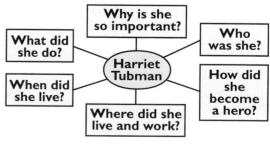

HARRIET TUBMAN:
Guide to Freedom
ANN PETRY

Along the Eastern Shore of Maryland, in Dorchester County, in Caroline County, the masters kept hearing whispers about the man named Moses, who was running off slaves. At first they did not believe in his existence. The stories about him were fantastic, unbelievable. Yet they watched for him. They offered rewards for his capture.

They never saw him. Now and then they heard whispered rumors to the effect that he was in the neighborhood. The woods were searched. The roads were watched. There was never anything to indicate his whereabouts. But a few days afterward, a goodly number of slaves would be gone from the plantation. Neither the master nor the overseer had heard or seen anything unusual in the quarter. Sometimes one or the other would vaguely remember having heard a whippoorwill call somewhere in the woods, close by, late at night. Though it was the wrong season for whippoorwills.

Sometimes the masters thought they had heard the cry of a hoot owl, repeated, and would remember having thought that the intervals between the low moaning cry were wrong, that it had been repeated four times in succession instead of three. There was

never anything more than that to suggest that all was not well in the quarter. Yet when morning came, they invariably discovered that a group of the finest slaves had taken to their heels.

Unfortunately, the discovery was almost always made on a Sunday. Thus a whole day was lost before the machinery of pursuit could be set in motion. The posters offering rewards for the fugitives could not be printed until Monday. The men who made a living hunting for runaway slaves were out of reach, off in the woods with their dogs and their guns, in pursuit of four-footed game, or they were in camp meetings[1] saying their prayers with their wives and families beside them.

Harriet Tubman could have told them that there was far more involved in this matter of running off slaves than signaling the would-be runaways by imitating the call of a whippoorwill, or a hoot owl, far more involved than a matter of waiting for a clear night when the North Star was visible.

◆ **Reading Strategy**
How do these details help you achieve your purpose?

---

1. **camp meetings:** Religious meetings held outdoors or in a tent.

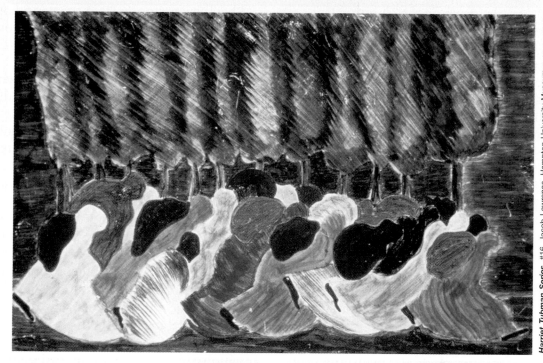

Harriet Tubman Series, #16, Jacob Lawrence, Hampton University Museum

In December 1851, when she started out with the band of fugitives that she planned to take to Canada, she had been in the vicinity of the plantation for days, planning the trip, carefully selecting the slaves that she would take with her.

She had announced her arrival in the quarter by singing the forbidden spiritual[2] —"Go down, Moses, 'way down to Egypt Land"—singing it softly outside the door of a slave cabin, late at night. The husky voice was beautiful even when it was barely more than a murmur borne on the wind.

Once she had made her presence known, word of her coming spread from cabin to cabin. The slaves whispered to each other, ear to mouth, mouth to ear, "Moses is here." "Moses has come." "Get ready. Moses is back again." The ones who had agreed to

▲ **Critical Viewing** This painting depicts fugitive slaves fleeing north. Why might the artist have chosen not to include details showing faces and clothing? [**Draw Conclusions**]

go North with her put ashcake and salt herring in an old bandanna, hastily tied it into a bundle, and then waited patiently for the signal that meant it was time to start.

There were eleven in this party, including one of her brothers and his wife. It was the largest group that she had ever conducted, but she was determined that more and more slaves should know what freedom was like.

She had to take them all the way to Canada. The Fugitive Slave Law[3] was no longer a great many incomprehensible

---

2. **forbidden spiritual:** In 1831, a slave named Nat Turner encouraged an unsuccessful slave uprising in Virginia by talking about the biblical story of the Israelites' escape from Egypt. Afterwards, the singing of certain spirituals was forbidden, for fear of encouraging more uprisings.

3. **Fugitive Slave Law:** This part of the Compromise of 1850 held that escaped slaves, even if found in free states, could be returned to their masters. As a result, fugitives were not safe until they reached Canada.

◆ **Build Vocabulary**
fugitives (fyoo′ ji tivs′) *n.*: People fleeing

words written down on the country's law-books. The new law had become a reality. It was Thomas Sims, a boy, picked up on the streets of Boston at night and shipped back to Georgia. It was Jerry and Shadrach, arrested and jailed with no warning.

She had never been in Canada. The route beyond Philadelphia was strange to her. But she could not let the runaways who accompanied her know this. As they walked along she told them stories of her own first flight, she kept painting vivid word pictures of what it would be like to be free.

But there were so many of them this time. She knew moments of doubt when she was half-afraid, and kept looking back over her shoulder, imagining that she heard the sound of pursuit. They would certainly be pursued. Eleven of them. Eleven thousand dollars' worth of flesh and bone and muscle that belonged to Maryland planters. If they were caught, the eleven runaways would be whipped and sold South, but she—she would probably be hanged.

◆ Literary Focus
What insight into Tubman's thoughts does the narrator provide?

They tried to sleep during the day but they never could wholly relax into sleep. She could tell by the positions they assumed, by their restless movements. And they walked at night. Their progress was slow. It took them three nights of walking to reach the first stop. She had told them about the place where they would stay, promising warmth and good food, holding these things out to them as an incentive to keep going.

When she knocked on the door of a farmhouse, a place where she and her parties of runaways had always been welcome, always been given shelter and plenty to eat, there was no answer. She knocked again, softly. A voice from within said, "Who is it?" There was fear in the voice.

She knew instantly from the sound of the voice that there was something wrong. She said, "A friend with friends," the password on the Underground Railroad.

The door opened, slowly. The man who stood in the doorway looked at her coldly, looked with unconcealed astonishment and fear at the eleven disheveled runaways who were standing near her. Then he shouted, "Too many, too many. It's not safe. My place was searched last week. It's not safe!" and slammed the door in her face.

She turned away from the house, frowning. She had promised her passengers food and rest and warmth, and instead of that, there would be hunger and cold and more walking over the frozen ground. Somehow she would have to instill courage into these eleven people, most of them strangers, would have to feed them on hope and bright dreams of freedom instead of the fried pork and corn bread and milk she had promised them.

They stumbled along behind her, half-dead for sleep, and she urged them on, though she was as tired and as discouraged as they were. She had never been in Canada but she kept painting wondrous word pictures of what it would be like. She managed to dispel their fear of pursuit, so that they would not become hysterical, panic-stricken. Then she had to bring some of the fear back, so that they would stay awake and keep walking though they drooped with sleep.

Yet during the day, when they lay down deep in a thicket, they never really slept, because if a twig snapped or the wind sighed in the branches of a pine tree, they jumped to their feet, afraid of their own shadows, shivering and shaking. It was very cold, but they dared not make fires because someone would see the smoke and wonder about it.

She kept thinking, eleven of them. Eleven thousand dollars' worth of slaves. And she had to take them all the way to Canada.

Sometimes she told them about Thomas Garrett, in Wilmington. She said he was their friend even though he did not know them. He was the friend of all fugitives. He called them God's poor. He was a Quaker and his speech was a little different from that of other people. His clothing was different, too. He wore the wide-brimmed hat that the Quakers wear.

She said that he had thick white hair, soft, almost like a baby's, and the kindest eyes she had ever seen. He was a big man and strong, but he had never used his strength to harm anyone, always to help people. He would give all of them a new pair of shoes. Everybody. He always did. Once they reached his house in Wilmington, they would be safe. He would see to it that they were.

She described the house where he lived, told them about the store where he sold shoes. She said he kept a pail of milk and a loaf of bread in the drawer of his desk so that he would have food ready at hand for any of God's poor who should suddenly appear before him, fainting with hunger. There was a hidden room in the store. A whole wall swung open, and behind it was a room where he could hide fugitives. On the wall there were shelves filled with small boxes—boxes of shoes—so that you would never guess that the wall actually opened.

While she talked, she kept watching them. They did not believe her. She could tell by their expressions. They were thinking. New shoes, Thomas Garrett, Quaker, Wilmington—what foolishness was this? Who knew if she told the truth? Where was she taking them anyway?

That night they reached the next stop—a farm that belonged to a German. She made the runaways take shelter behind trees at the edge of the fields before she knocked at the door. She hesitated before she approached the door, thinking, suppose that he, too,

should refuse shelter, suppose—Then she thought, Lord, I'm going to hold steady on to You and You've got to see me through—and knocked softly.

She heard the familiar <u>guttural</u> voice say, "Who's there?"

She answered quickly, "A friend with friends."

He opened the door and greeted her warmly. "How many this time?" he asked.

"Eleven," she said and waited, doubting, wondering.

He said, "Good. Bring them in."

He and his wife fed them in the lamplit kitchen, their faces glowing, as they offered food and more food, urging them to eat, saying there was plenty for everybody, have more milk, have more bread, have more meat.

They spent the night in the warm kitchen. They really slept, all that night and until dusk the next day. When they left, it was with reluctance. They had all been warm and safe and well-fed. It was hard to exchange the security offered by that clean, warm kitchen for the darkness and the cold of a December night.

Harriet had found it hard to leave the warmth and friendliness, too. But she urged them on. For a while, as they walked, they seemed to carry in them a measure of contentment; some of the serenity and the cleanliness of that big warm kitchen lingered on inside them. But

> ◆ **Literature and Your Life**
> The fugitives find it hard to leave the safe warmth for the cold December night. Have you ever experienced a similar feeling? Explain.

◆ **Build Vocabulary**

incentive (in sent′ iv) *n*.: Something that stimulates one to action; encouragement

disheveled (di shev′ əld) *adj*.: Untidy; messy

guttural (gut′ ər əl) *adj*.: Made in back of the throat

as they walked farther and farther away from the warmth and the light, the cold and the darkness entered into them. They fell silent, sullen, suspicious. She waited for the moment when some one of them would turn <u>mutinous</u>. It did not happen that night.

Two nights later she was aware that the feet behind her were moving slower and slower. She heard the irritability in their voices, knew that soon someone would refuse to go on.

She started talking about William Still and the Philadelphia Vigilance Committee.[4] No one commented. No one asked any questions. She told them the story of William and Ellen Craft and how they escaped from Georgia. Ellen was so fair that she looked as though she were white, and so she dressed up in a man's clothing and she looked like a wealthy young planter. Her husband, William, who was dark, played the role of her slave. Thus they traveled from Macon, Georgia, to Philadelphia, riding on the trains, staying at the finest hotels. Ellen pretended to be very ill— her right arm was in a sling, and her right hand was bandaged, because she was supposed to have rheumatism. Thus she avoided having to sign the register at the hotels for she could not read or write. They finally arrived safely in Philadelphia, and then went on to Boston.

No one said anything. Not one of them seemed to have heard her.

Harriet Tubman Series, #20, Jacob Lawrence, Hampton University Museum, Hampton, Virginia

---

▲ **Critical Viewing** Judging from the details in this painting, what can you infer about the relationship among the fugitives by the journey's end? **[Infer]**

She told them about Frederick Douglass, the most famous of the escaped slaves, of his eloquence, of his magnificent appearance. Then she told them of her own first vain effort at running away, evoking the memory of that miserable life she had led as a child, reliving it for a moment in the telling.

But they had been tired too long, hungry too long, afraid too long, footsore too long. One of them suddenly cried out in despair, "Let me go back. It is better to be a slave than to suffer like this in order to be free."

She carried a gun with her on these

---

4. **Philadelphia Vigilance Committee:** Group of citizens who helped escaped slaves. Its secretary was a free black man named William Still.

trips. She had never used it—except as a threat. Now as she aimed it, she experienced a feeling of guilt, remembering that time, years ago, when she had prayed for the death of Edward Brodas, the Master, and then not too long afterward had heard that great wailing cry that came from the throats of the field hands, and knew from the sound that the Master was dead.

One of the runaways said, again, "Let me go back. Let me go back," and stood still, and then turned around and said, over his shoulder, "I am going back."

She lifted the gun, aimed it at the despairing slave. She said, "Go on with us or die." The husky low-pitched voice was grim.

He hesitated for a moment and then he joined the others. They started walking again. She tried to explain to them why none of them could go back to the plantation. If a runaway returned, he would turn traitor, the master and the overseer would force him to turn traitor. The returned slave would disclose the stopping places, the hiding places, the cornstacks they had used with the full knowledge of the owner of the farm, the name of the German farmer who had fed them and sheltered them. These people who had risked their own security to help runaways would be ruined, fined, imprisoned. She said, "We got to go free or die. And freedom's not bought with dust."

This time she told them about the long agony of the Middle Passage on the old slave ships, about the black horror of the holds, about the chains and the whips. They too knew these stories. But she wanted to remind them of the long hard way they had come, about the long hard way they had yet to go. She told them about Thomas Sims, the boy picked up on the streets of Boston and sent back to Georgia. She said when they got him back to Savannah, got him in prison there, they whipped him until a doctor who was

standing by watching said, "You will kill him if you strike him again!" His master said, "Let him die!"

Thus she forced them to go on. Sometimes she thought she had become nothing but a voice speaking in the darkness, cajoling, urging, threatening. Sometimes she told them things to make them laugh, sometimes she sang to them, and heard the eleven voices behind her blending softly with hers, and then she knew that for the moment all was well with them.

She gave the impression of being a short, muscular, indomitable woman who could never be defeated. Yet at any moment she was liable to be seized by one of those curious fits of sleep, which might last for a few minutes or for hours.[5]

Even on this trip, she suddenly fell asleep in the woods. The runaways, ragged, dirty, hungry, cold, did not steal the gun as they might have, and set off by themselves, or turn back. They sat on the ground near her and waited patiently until she awakened. They had come to trust her implicitly, totally. They, too, had come to believe her repeated statement, "We got to go free or die." She was leading them into freedom, and so they waited until she was ready to go on.

Finally, they reached Thomas Garrett's house in Wilmington, Delaware. Just as Harriet had promised, Garrett gave them all new shoes, and provided carriages to take them on to the next stop.

---

5. **sleep . . . hours:** When she was about 13, Harriet accidentally received a severe blow on the head. Afterwards, she often lost consciousness and could not be awakened until the episode was over.

◆ Build Vocabulary

mutinous (myoot′ ən əs) *adj.*: Rebellious

cajoling (kə jōl′ iŋ) *v.*: Coaxing or persuading gently

indomitable (in däm′ it ə bəl) *adj.*: Not easily discouraged

By slow stages they reached Philadelphia, where William Still hastily recorded their names, and the plantations whence they had come, and something of the life they had led in slavery. Then he carefully hid what he had written, for fear it might be discovered. In 1872 he published this record in book form and called it *The Underground Railroad.* In the foreword to his book he said: "While I knew the danger of keeping strict records, and while I did not then dream that in my day slavery would be blotted out, or that the time would come when I could publish these records, it used to afford me great satisfaction to take them down, fresh from the lips of fugitives on the way to freedom, and to preserve them as they had given them."

William Still, who was familiar with all the station stops on the Underground Railroad, supplied Harriet with money and sent her and her eleven fugitives on to Burlington, New Jersey.

Harriet felt safer now, though there were danger spots ahead. But the biggest part of her job was over. As they went farther and farther north, it grew colder; she was aware of the wind on the Jersey ferry and aware of the cold damp in New York. From New York they went on to Syracuse, where the temperature was even lower.

In Syracuse she met the Reverend J.W. Loguen, known as "Jarm" Loguen. This was the beginning of a lifelong friendship. Both Harriet and Jarm Loguen were to become friends and supporters of Old John Brown.[6]

From Syracuse they went north again, into a colder, snowier city—Rochester. Here they almost certainly stayed with Frederick Douglass, for he wrote in his autobiography:

> ◆ **Reading Strategy**
> What do you learn about Tubman in this passage?

"On one occasion I had eleven fugitives at the same time under my roof, and it was necessary for them to remain with me until I could collect sufficient money to get them to Canada. It was the largest number I ever had at any one time, and I had some difficulty in providing so many with food and shelter, but, as may well be imagined, they were not very <u>fastidious</u> in either direction, and were well content with very plain food, and a strip of carpet on the floor for a bed, or a place on the straw in the barnloft."

Late in December 1851, Harriet arrived in St. Catharines, Canada West (now Ontario), with the eleven fugitives. It had taken almost a month to complete this journey; most of the time had been spent getting out of Maryland.

That first winter in St. Catharines was a terrible one. Canada was a strange frozen land, snow everywhere, ice everywhere, and a bone-biting cold the like of which none of them had ever experienced before. Harriet rented a small frame house in the town and set to work to make a home. The fugitives boarded with her. They worked in the forests, felling trees, and so did she. Sometimes she took other jobs, cooking or cleaning house for people in the town. She cheered on these newly arrived fugitives, working herself, finding work for them, finding food for them, praying for them, sometimes begging for them.

Often she found herself thinking of the beauty of Maryland, the mellowness of the soil, the richness of the plant life there. The climate itself made for an ease of living that could never be duplicated in this bleak, barren countryside.

In spite of the severe cold, the hard work, she came to love St. Catharines, and the other towns and cities in Canada where black men lived. She discovered that freedom meant more than the right to change jobs at will, more than the right to keep the money that one earned. It was the right to vote and to sit on juries. It was the right to

---

6. **John Brown:** White abolitionist (1800–1859) who was hanged for leading a raid on the arsenal at Harpers Ferry, Virginia, as part of a slave uprising.

be elected to office. In Canada there were black men who were county officials and members of school boards. St. Catharines had a large colony of ex-slaves, and they owned their own homes, kept them neat and clean and in good repair. They lived in whatever part of town they chose and sent their children to the schools.

When spring came she decided that she would make this small Canadian city her home—as much as any place could be said to be home to a woman who traveled from Canada to the Eastern Shore of Maryland as often as she did.

In the spring of 1852, she went back to Cape May, New Jersey. She spent the summer there, cooking in a hotel. That fall she returned, as usual, to Dorchester County, and brought out nine more slaves, conducting them all the way to St. Catharines, in Canada West, to the bone-biting cold, the snow-covered forests—and freedom.

She continued to live in this fashion, spending the winter in Canada, and the spring and summer working in Cape May, New Jersey, or in Philadelphia. She made two trips a year into slave territory, one in the fall and another in the spring. She now had a definite crystallized purpose, and in carrying it out, her life fell into a pattern which remained unchanged for the next six years.

◆ Build Vocabulary

fastidious (fas tid′ ē əs) *adj.*: Refined in an oversensitive way, so as to be easily disgusted or displeased

*G*uide for Responding

◆ LITERATURE AND YOUR LIFE

Reader's Response Would you have trusted Harriet Tubman to take you on a long, difficult journey? Why or why not?

Thematic Focus What aspects of Harriet Tubman's character might inspire a young person to follow a difficult path today?

Journal Writing Write a journal entry in which you list the main concerns that Harriet Tubman might have had in conducting a group north on the Underground Railroad.

☑ Check Your Comprehension

1. What part does Tubman play in the Underground Railroad?
2. How does Harriet Tubman announce her arrival in the headquarters late at night?
3. Summarize the general sequence of events in traveling on the Underground Railroad.
4. Why was no fugitive allowed to turn back?

◆ Critical Thinking

INTERPRET

1. (a) What kinds of stories does Tubman tell the fugitives? (b) Why does she tell them these stories? **[Analyze]**
2. Why did Tubman never admit she was afraid? **[Draw Conclusions]**
3. Explain one of the several possible meanings of Tubman's statement "We live free or die." **[Interpret]**

EVALUATE

4. Is Harriet Tubman justified in threatening to take the life of the man who wants to turn back? Explain. **[Make a Judgment]**

EXTEND

5. What modern figures share qualities with Harriet Tubman? Explain. **[Social Studies Link]**

Guide for Responding (continued)

◆ Reading Strategy

SET A PURPOSE FOR READING

Setting a purpose helps you focus your reading to find information or note particular kinds of details. With your purpose in mind—to learn about Harriet Tubman—answer the following.

1. How did having a purpose focus your reading?
2. List three things you learned from the story that helped you to achieve your purpose.

◆ Build Vocabulary

USING THE WORD ROOT -fug-

Write a sentence explaining how the word root -fug- contributes to the meaning of each word. Use a dictionary to help you.

1. subterfuge
2. refuge
3. centrifugal

SPELLING STRATEGY

In the word *incentive,* the s sound is spelled with a c. Because there is no rule that tells you when to spell the s sound with a c, try remembering this little tip: An *incentive* to work might involve *cents*.

Other words in which the s sound is spelled c include *recent, decent,* and *century*. Use each of these words in a sentence to practice spelling the s sound with a c.

USING THE WORD BANK

On your paper, match each Word Bank word with the word closest in meaning.

1. guttural	a. escapees
2. disheveled	b. gruntlike
3. incentive	c. unconquerable
4. fugitives	d. picky
5. mutinous	e. encouragement
6. cajoling	f. rebellious
7. indomitable	g. messy
8. fastidious	h. coaxing

◆ Literary Focus

THIRD-PERSON NARRATIVE

In a **third-person narrative,** the narrator tells the story but does not participate in it. Most biographies, like the one from which this true-life story comes, are third-person narratives. To make third-person narratives interesting, many biographers, like Petry, use dialogue and reveal the thoughts of the subject.

1. Cite an example of dialogue within the narrative.
2. Locate a passage in which Petry reveals the inner thoughts of Harriet Tubman.
3. How would this story be different if it were written by someone whom Tubman led on the Underground Railroad?

◆ Build Grammar Skills

TRANSITIVE AND INTRANSITIVE VERBS

A verb is **transitive** when it expresses an action directed toward a person or thing; the action passes from the doer to the receiver of the action. The person or thing receiving the action is the object of the verb.

verb ⟶ ⟵ object
Transitive: They never *saw* him.

A verb is **intransitive** when it expresses action (or tells something about the subject) without passing the action to the receiver.

Intransitive: They *did* not *believe* in his existence.

Practice Identify each verb as transitive or intransitive in your notebook. If the verb is transitive, identify its object.

1. At night she guided the fugitives.
2. She knocked on the farmhouse door.
3. One fugitive pleaded to go back.
4. They arrived safely in Philadelphia.
5. The abolitionist gave them food and money.

Writing Application Write sentences that contain transitive and intransitive verbs, as indicated.

1. *run,* intransitive
2. *hide,* transitive
3. *whistle,* transitive
4. *arrive,* intransitive

Build Your Portfolio

 ## Idea Bank

Writing

1. **Diary Entry** Write a diary entry that Harriet Tubman might have recorded on the day she arrived in Canada with her group of fugitives.

2. **Biographical Description** Write a short biographical description of Harriet Tubman, using information revealed in this selection. **[Social Studies Link]**

3. **Dramatization** Write a dramatic scene based on the selection. Describe the setting, and create dialogue and stage directions actors could use to perform the scene. **[Performing Arts Link]**

Speaking and Listening

4. **Speech** Write and deliver a speech in which you praise Harriet Tubman and others associated with running the Underground Railroad. You may do research to gather details for your speech.

5. **Debate [Group Activity]** Form two teams to debate the following issue: Harriet Tubman was taking part in an illegal activity. Were her actions justified? You may appoint a classmate to act as moderator, who times the teams' responses and ensures that rules of debate are followed.

Projects

6. **Research Project [Group Activity]** Work with a group to create a map showing the Underground Railroad routes, the approximate location of safe houses, final destinations, and other relevant information. Display your map in the classroom. **[Social Studies Link]**

7. **Fugitive Slave Laws** Do research to find out about the Fugitive Slave Laws—when they were passed, who supported them, and who opposed them. Then, report to your class on your findings. **[Social Studies Link]**

 ## Writing Mini-Lesson

Spoken Introduction

Heroes like Harriet Tubman deserve awards, tributes, and banquets to honor their work. Imagine that you are a speaker at an awards banquet and your role is to acknowledge the achievements of Harriet Tubman. In your speech, let the audience know why she's such an inspiration to you.

Writing Skills Focus: Give Specific Examples

An introduction that includes **specific examples** has more meaning than one that consists of generalizations—broad, vague statements.

General: "She is an extraordinary person."
Specific: "Harriet Tubman's extraordinary efforts to help escaped Africans find a new life in the North deserve admiration."

Prewriting Gather details about Harriet Tubman that you'd like to include in your acknowledgment. Include biographical information as well as specific examples of how she influenced your own life.

Drafting Begin with an attention-grabbing statement. You might pose a question, state a fact, or cite a stunning statistic. Use specific examples to support statements you make about Tubman. Conclude by "introducing" her to your audience.

Revising Read your draft to a classmate, and ask for suggestions about how to make it more interesting and clear. Add specific examples wherever your draft is vague. Proofread carefully to eliminate errors in grammar, punctuation, and spelling.

> ◆ **Grammar Application**
> Read through your speech. Circle transitive verbs and underline intransitive verbs.

Guide for Reading

Meet the Authors:

Joaquin Miller (1839–1913)

Joaquin Miller was born near Liberty, Indiana, though he once claimed that his cradle was "a covered wagon pointed West." A man of vision and energy, Miller is credited with helping to establish a pony express route between Idaho and Washington. Later in life, as a tribute to Mexican bandit Joaquin Murrietta, Miller changed his given name, Cincinnatus Hiner Miller, to Joaquin Miller.

Stephen Vincent Benét
(1898–1943)

A poet, short-story writer, and dramatist, Stephen Vincent Benét had his first collection of poetry published when he was only seventeen years old. *John Brown's Body,* his epic poem, won the Pulitzer Prize in 1928.

Roberto Félix Salazar

In his writing, Roberto Félix Salazar aims to dramatize his Mexican American heritage as well as challenge his readers' assumptions about the nation's beginnings.

THE STORY BEHIND "THE OTHER PIONEERS"

According to Philip Ortego, a professor of Chicano Studies, "The Other Pioneers" was written to remind Mexican Americans and others that the first pioneers to settle the Southwest had Spanish names—and that their descendants still do, although they are American citizens.

◆ LITERATURE AND YOUR LIFE

CONNECT YOUR EXPERIENCE

If you've ever moved to a new home, changed schools, or traveled to new places, you understand the thrill of going someplace you've never been before. The poems that follow celebrate those who took risks to explore and settle a new land.

THEMATIC FOCUS: Blazing Trails

As you read these poems, imagine what it was like to be an explorer or early pioneer.

◆ Background for Understanding

SOCIAL STUDIES

"Columbus," "Western Wagons," and "The Other Pioneers" celebrate the discovery and settlement of what is now the West Indies and North America. The map on the facing page shows trails to the West that were used by pioneers described in "Western Wagons." Also shown is the Republic of Texas, where the "other pioneers" described by Roberto Félix Salazar settle after crossing the Rio Grande from Mexico.

◆ Build Vocabulary

ANTONYMS: *wan* AND *swarthy*

In "Columbus," Joaquin Miller uses antonyms, words that have opposite meanings. *Wan* means "pale and sickly," and its antonym *swarthy* means "being of a dark color or complexion."

WORD BANK

Look over these words from the poems. They are all descriptive words. Which word do you think describes something coming unfolded? How do you know? Check the Build Vocabulary box on page 144 to see if you chose correctly.

mutinous
wan
swarthy
unfurled
stalwart

Columbus ◆ Western Wagons
◆ The Other Pioneers ◆

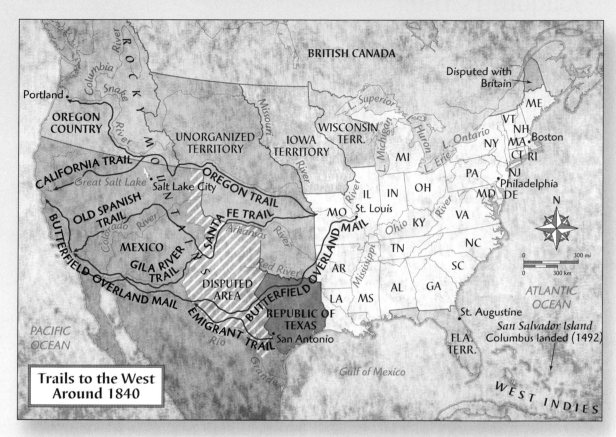

Trails to the West
Around 1840

◆ Literary Focus
STANZAS IN POETRY

These poems are organized in **stanzas,** groups of lines that form units in a poem, just as paragraphs form units of prose. The stanzas in a poem are separated by spaces. Some poems have stanzas of matching length, rhythms, and rhyme schemes, and some poems have stanzas that do not match at all. Stanzas often focus on a single topic. As you read these poems, fill out a chart like this one to keep track of the stanzas.

Poem	Number of Stanzas	Number of Lines in Each	Rhyming Words
Columbus			
Western Wagons			
The Other Pioneers			

◆ Reading Strategy
RELATE TO WHAT YOU KNOW

One way to understand a poem is to **relate** what the poet is saying to what you know.

In "Columbus," Joaquin Miller describes Columbus's voyage of discovery. You may know that Columbus sailed for America in the late 1400's. Knowing the dangers of sea voyages during that time period, you can better understand the courage and determination of Columbus and the fear of the crew.

As you read these poems, relate what the poets are saying to what you already know about history and human nature.

Columbus

Joaquin Miller

Behind him lay the gray Azores,[1]
Behind the Gates of Hercules;[2]
Before him not the ghost of shores;
Before him only shoreless seas.
5   The good mate said: "Now must we pray,
For lo! the very stars are gone.
Brave Adm'r'l, speak; what shall I say?"
"Why, say: 'Sail on! sail on! and on!'"

"My men grow <u>mutinous</u> day by day;
10   My men grow ghastly <u>wan</u> and weak."
The stout mate thought of home; a spray
Of salt wave washed his <u>swarthy</u> cheek.
"What shall I say, brave Adm'r'l, say,
If we sight naught[3] but seas at dawn?"
15   "Why, you shall say at break of day:
'Sail on! sail on! sail on! and on!'"

They sailed and sailed, as winds might blow,
Until at last the blanched mate said:
"Why, now not even God would know
20   Should I and all my men fall dead.
These very winds forget their way,
For God from these dread seas is gone.
Now speak, brave Adm'r'l; speak and say—"
He said: "Sail on! sail on! and on!"

25   They sailed. They sailed. Then spake[4] the mate:
"This mad sea shows his teeth to-night.
He curls his lip, he lies in wait,
With lifted teeth, as if to bite!
Brave Adm'r'l, say but one good word:
30   What shall we do when hope is gone?"
The words leapt like a leaping sword:
"Sail on! sail on! sail on! and on!"

Then, pale and worn, he kept his deck,
And peered through darkness. Ah, that night
35   Of all dark nights! And then a speck—
A light! A light! A light! A light!
It grew, a starlit flag <u>unfurled</u>!
It grew to be Time's burst of dawn.
He gained a world; he gave that world
40   Its grandest lesson: "On! sail on!"

---

1. Azores (ā´ zôrz): Group of Portuguese islands in the North Atlantic west of Portugal.

2. Gates of Hercules (gāts uv hʉr´ kyə lēz´): Entrance to the Strait of Gibraltar, between Spain and Africa.

3. naught (nôt) *n.*: Nothing.

4. spake (spāk) *v.*: Old-fashioned word for "spoke."

◆ **Build Vocabulary**

mutinous (myo͞ot´ ən əs) *adj.*: Rebellious

wan (wän) *adj.*: Pale

swarthy (swôr´ thē) *adj.*: Having a dark complexion

unfurled (un fʉrld´) *adj.*: Unfolded

The Landing of Columbus, 1876, Currier & Ives, Museum of the City of New York

▲ **Critical Viewing** What qualities of Columbus depicted in the poem are revealed or suggested by the figure of Columbus, standing at the front of the boat in this painting? What qualities are not shown? **[Compare and Contrast]**

Guide for Responding

◆ LITERATURE AND YOUR LIFE

Reader's Response Would you like to have been on Columbus's voyage? Explain.

Thematic Focus What personal qualities of Columbus are suited to a trailblazer?

Journal Writing As the first mate, write a journal entry about the voyage to the "New World."

☑ Check Your Comprehension

1. In "Columbus," who is the "Brave Adm'r'l"? What does he say each time to the mate?
2. What seems to frighten the mate in each of the first four stanzas?

◆ Critical Thinking

INTERPRET

1. (a) To what does Miller compare the sea in lines 26-28 of "Columbus"? (b) What is the effect of the comparison? **[Interpret]**
2. What is the light sighted in the last stanza of "Columbus"? **[Interpret]**
3. What is the "grandest lesson"? **[Interpret]**
4. Compare and contrast the mate and Adm'r'l in "Columbus." **[Compare and Contrast]**
5. In what ways is this poem about the value of determination and courage? **[Analyze]**

EVALUATE

6. In "Columbus," is the explorer portrayed as brave or stubborn? Explain. **[Evaluate]**

Western Wagons

Stephen Vincent Benét

They went with axe and rifle, when the trail was
   still to blaze,
They went with wife and children, in the prairie-
   schooner days,
With banjo and with frying pan—Susanna, don't
   you cry!
For I'm off to California to get rich out there or die!

5   We've broken land and cleared it, but we're tired
   of where we are.
They say that wild Nebraska is a better place
   by far.
There's gold in far Wyoming, there's black earth
   in Ioway,
So pack up the kids and blankets, for we're moving
   out today!

The cowards never started and the weak died on
   the road,
10   And all across the continent the endless campfires
   glowed.
We'd taken land and settled—but a traveler
   passed by—
And we're going West tomorrow—Lordy, never ask
   us why!

We're going West tomorrow, where the promises
   can't fail.
O'er the hills in legions, boys, and crowd the
   dusty trail!
15   We shall starve and freeze and suffer. We shall die,
   and tame the lands.
But we're going West tomorrow, with our fortune
   in our hands.

A New Beginning, Duane Bryers, Courtesy of the artist

▲ Critical Viewing What do the expressions on the faces of the couple in the painting reveal about their emotions? [Infer]

Guide for Responding

◆ LITERATURE AND YOUR LIFE

Reader's Response Does the life of a westward pioneer appeal to you? Explain.

Thematic Focus Would you describe these pioneers as trailblazers or adventure seekers— or both?

Travel List Imagine that you're about to embark on a journey west in a covered wagon. Make a list of the supplies you'd need to take along.

✓ Check Your Comprehension

1. With what items did these pioneers travel?
2. What are the destinations of the people in "Western Wagons"?

◆ Critical Thinking

INTERPRET

1. What is meant by the phrase "when the trail was still to blaze"? [Interpret]
2. What circumstances might have prompted the pioneers to seek a better life? [Speculate]
3. Is the thrill of blazing trails or the need for a better home the driving force in the pioneers' lives? [Draw Conclusions]

EVALUATE

4. Are these pioneers foolish in their quest for riches and adventure? Explain. [Make a Judgment]

COMPARE LITERARY WORKS

5. Compare and contrast the motivation and character of Columbus with that of the pioneers in "Western Wagons." [Compare and Contrast]

The Other Pioneers

Roberto Félix Salazar

Now I must write
Of those of mine who rode these plains
Long years before the Saxon[1] and the Irish came.
Of those who plowed the land and built the towns
5   And gave the towns soft-woven Spanish names.
Of those who moved across the Rio Grande
Toward the hiss of Texas snake and Indian yell.
Of men who from the earth made thick-walled homes
And from the earth raised churches to their God.
10 And of the wives who bore them sons
And smiled with knowing joy.

They saw the Texas sun rise golden-red with
   promised wealth
And saw the Texas sun sink golden yet, with
   wealth unspent.
"Here," they said. "Here to live and here to love."
15 "Here is the land for our sons and the sons of
   our sons."
And they sang the songs of ancient Spain
And they made new songs to fit new needs.
They cleared the brush and planted the corn
And saw green stalks turn black from lack of rain.
20 They roamed the plains behind the herds
And stood the Indian's cruel attacks.
There was dust and there was sweat.
And there were tears and the women prayed.

And the years moved on.
25 Those who were first placed in graves
Beside the broad mesquite[2] and the tall nopal.[3]
Gentle mothers left their graces and their arts
And <u>stalwart</u> fathers pride and manly strength.
Salinas, de la Garza, Sánchez, García,
30 Uribe, Gonzáles, Martinez, de León:[4]
Such were the names of the fathers.
Salinas, de la Garza, Sánchez, García,
Uribe, Gonzáles, Martinez, de León:
Such are the names of the sons.

1. **Saxon** (sak´ sən) n.: English.

2. **mesquite** (mes kēt´) n.: Thorny tree or shrub common in the southwestern United States and Mexico.

3. **nopal** (nō´ pəl) n.: Cactus with red flowers.

4. **Salinas** (sä lē´ näs), **de la Garza** (dā lä gär´sä), **Sánchez** (sän´ chās), **García** (Gär sē´ ä), **Uribe** (o͞o rē´ bā) **Gonzáles** (gōn sä´ lās), **Martinez** (mär tē´ nās), **de León** (dā lā ōn´)

◆ **Build Vocabulary**

stalwart (stôl´ wərt) adj.: Resolute; firm; unyielding

▲ **Critical Viewing** This painting depicts San Antonio, Texas, in the mid 1800's. What does the painting reveal about the climate and living conditions there? **[Infer]**

East Side Main Plaza, San Antonio, Texas, 1844, William G.M. Samuel, Courtesy of Bexar County and the Witte Museum, San Antonio, Texas

Guide for Responding

◆ LITERATURE AND YOUR LIFE

Reader's Response What feelings toward the pioneers does the poem evoke in you? Why?

Thematic Focus In what ways did these "other pioneers" blaze trails?

Letter Write a letter to one of the "other pioneers." In it, ask questions about their experiences in settling the region that is now Texas.

☑ Check Your Comprehension

1. Who are the "other pioneers"?
2. When did they ride the plains?
3. What did they accomplish?

◆ Critical Thinking

INTERPRET

1. From what country did the "other pioneers" come? **[Interpret]**
2. Why might the pioneers have chosen to settle in a new land? **[Infer]**
3. What does the repetition of family names in the final lines of the poem signify? **[Analyze]**

EVALUATE

4. How would you describe the speaker's attitude toward his ancestors? **[Assess]**

APPLY

5. The poem describes the pioneers' legacy to their children. What do you think is the most valuable thing a parent can leave to a child? **[Generalize]**

Guide for Responding (continued)

◆ Reading Strategy

RELATE TO WHAT YOU KNOW

Relating to what you know helps you understand literature. Use your own experience and knowledge to answer the following:

1. How does your previous knowledge of Christopher Columbus compare with the way he's described in "Columbus"?
2. Why might the pioneers in "Western Wagons" have traveled with an axe and a rifle?
3. What do you know about Texas that makes "The Other Pioneers" easier to understand?

◆ Build Vocabulary

USING THE ANTONYMS *wan* AND *swarthy*

Joaquin Miller uses the antonyms *wan* and *swarthy* in "Columbus." If you know that *wan* means "pale," you can guess that *swarthy* means "having a dark complexion."

Copy the following sentences on your paper. Fill in each blank with *wan* or *swarthy*.

1. The sickly child looked pale and _____?_____.
2. The old sailor had a _____?_____ complexion because of years spent in the sun and wind.

SPELLING STRATEGY

When adding *-ous* to a word that ends in *y*, follow these rules. Drop the *y* if the sound it represents disappears: mutiny + -ous = mutinous

Keep the *y* or change it to *e* or *i* if the sound it represents remains: harmony + -ous = harmonious

On your paper, add *-ous* to these words.

1. joy
2. victory
3. larceny
4. beauty
5. glory
6. bounty

USING THE WORD BANK

On your paper, write the letter of the word that has the opposite meaning of the Word Bank word.

1. mutinous: (a) silly, (b) rebellious, (c) obedient
2. wan: (a) swarthy, (b) pale, (c) wanting
3. swarthy: (a) true, (b) complicated, (c) wan
4. unfurled: (a) folded, (b) opened, (c) hidden
5. stalwart: (a) strong, (b) weak, (c) heavy

◆ Literary Focus

STANZAS IN POETRY

Stanzas are groupings of two or more lines in poetry. In some poems, each stanza has the same line length, rhythm, and rhyme pattern. In "Columbus," for example, each stanza has eight lines and a repeated rhyme pattern (the last word in every other line rhymes). Like paragraphs in prose, stanzas in poetry mark changes in thought or emphasis.

1. Compare the first and last stanzas of "Columbus." What is alike about them, and what is different?
2. (a) How many stanzas are in "Western Wagons"? (b) Do they repeat a rhyme pattern?
3. Examine the stanzas in "The Other Pioneers." Explain the main thought in each.

◆ Build Grammar Skills

COMMONLY CONFUSED VERBS: *lie* AND *lay*

The verbs *lie* and *lay* are often confused, especially in speech. *Lie* means "to rest or recline." Its forms are *lie, lay,* and (*have* or *had*) *lain. Lie* is intransitive; it does not pass action to a receiver: The sailors *lie* in their bunks.

Lay means "to put or set something down." Its forms are *lay, laid,* and (*have* or *had*) *laid.* The verb *lay* is transitive: It always passes its action to a receiver: Please *lay* the supplies in the wagon.

These words are frequently confused because the past of *lie* is the same as the present of *lay.* Miller uses the past form of *lie* in this line from "Columbus": Behind him *lay* the great Azores . . .

Practice Copy the following sentences. Choose the correct form of the verb.

1. The tired traveler wanted to (lie, lay) down.
2. First, she (lay, laid) the baby down for a nap.
3. She had to (lie, lay) a blanket over the baby.
4. She had (lain, laid) her head on the pillow for only five minutes before she fell asleep.
5. After she had (lain, laid) down, she felt better.

Writing Application Complete the following.

1. Write a sentence using the past tense of *lay.*
2. Write a sentence using the past tense of *lie.*

Build Your Portfolio

 Idea Bank

Writing

1. Letter Put yourself in the place of a pioneer described in "Western Wagons" or "The Other Pioneers." Write a letter to someone you had to leave behind as you traveled to another area. Tell about your adventures along the way.

2. Dialogue Imagine that you are one of the sailors growing "mutinous day by day" in "Columbus." Write the dialogue you might have with another sailor about the voyage.

3. Comparison-and-Contrast Essay In a brief essay, compare and contrast the reasons or motives behind Columbus's exploration and the westward pioneers' travels. Use lines from the poems for support.

Speaking and Listening

4. Skit With a classmate, take on the roles of Columbus and the first mate. Using "Columbus" as a guide, write and perform a skit for the class. **[Performing Arts Link]**

5. Oral Presentation Find out about the early settlement of any area named in "Western Wagons" or "The Other Pioneers." Make an oral presentation to your class on one aspect of this settlement that interests you. **[Social Studies Link]**

Projects

6. Living History [Group Activity] With a group of classmates, reenact a scene that might have taken place during the early settlement of the Americas. Use props to make your scene come to life. Each group member should be responsible for a different task, such as checking historical accuracy, obtaining props, or writing dialogue. **[Social Studies Link]**

7. Book Cover Design and create a book cover for a collection of poems in which "Columbus," "Western Wagons, " and "The Other Pioneers" might appear. **[Art Link]**

 Writing Mini-Lesson

Speech

The characters in these poems are courageous trailblazers. (Some of them are named in history books, and some remain nameless, yet all are worthy of remembrance.) One way we remember such people is by naming places, such as schools and parks, after them. Write a speech in which you give reasons for naming a place after an explorer or a hero.

Writing Skills Focus: Support Ideas With Reasons

Your goal is to convince your audience of something. To make your speech persuasive, **support your ideas with reasons.** To do this, find facts through library research and on-line sources. In the following, Stephen Vincent Benét gives reasons why the pioneers were admirable.

Model From "Western Wagons"
We shall starve and freeze and suffer. We shall die, /and tame the lands.

Prewriting Decide which hero or explorer you would like to honor. Gather facts about that person's achievements.

Drafting Begin by naming the place and the person whom you want to honor. Develop and support your ideas by giving facts about the person's life. Conclude by restating your main points.

◆ **Grammar Application**

In your speech, use the verb *lie* or *lay*. Make sure you have used it correctly.

Revising Deliver your speech to a classmate. Ask him or her to point out places where additional facts would strengthen your argument. Add information to support your ideas.

Guide for Reading

Meet the Author:

Jack London (1876–1916)

Jack London was the highest paid, most popular novelist and short-story writer of his day. His exciting tales of adventure and courage were inspired by his own challenging experiences. At age seventeen, London sailed with a seal-hunting ship to Japan and Siberia. On his return, he became involved with a band of oyster thieves. When caught, he worked with the local coastal patrol to catch other such outlaws.

Capturing Adventures in Print At the age of nineteen, London returned to high school and vowed to become a writer. He eventually wrote more than fifty books, including novels, short stories, and nonfiction. His best-known works create vivid pictures of strong characters facing the challenges of nature—from Buck the dog in *Call of the Wild* to the ruthless Wolf Larson of *The Sea Wolf.*

THE STORY BEHIND THE STORY

London spent the winter of 1897 in the Yukon Territory of northwest Canada. Along with thousands of others, he journeyed to the Klondike region of the Yukon in search of gold. Although he did not find the valuable mineral, he did find an important source of inspiration. The cold, stark climate of the Yukon became the backdrop for many of his stories, including "Up the Slide."

◆ LITERATURE AND YOUR LIFE

CONNECT YOUR EXPERIENCE

Think about times you've gotten in over your head. For example, you may have taken a bike ride that turned into a marathon after you got lost, or you may have gone swimming in the ocean and gotten caught in the undertow. In "Up the Slide," a young man sets out to do something simple that turns into a hair-raising, life-threatening adventure.

THEMATIC FOCUS: Blazing Trails

The young man in London's story was one of many prospectors who blazed a trail into Canada's frigid Yukon Territory in search of gold. What risks might these trailblazers have faced?

◆ Background for Understanding

GEOGRAPHY

The Yukon Territory is in the northwestern corner of Canada, just beside Alaska. The climate there is one of the most challenging on Earth. It is part of the subarctic climate zone, where temperatures have been known to plunge to -80°F. Because of its northern position on the globe, daylight hours vary greatly—from more than twenty hours a day in summer to only a few hours in winter.

◆ Build Vocabulary

RELATED WORDS: FORMS OF *exhaust*

The main character in "Up the Slide" becomes *exhausted* by his struggles against the elements. *Exhausted* is a form of the verb *exhaust,* meaning "to tire completely." Related forms are *exhaustion* (noun) and *exhausting* (adjective).

WORD BANK

Which words from the story might have opposite meanings? Check the Build Vocabulary box on page 158 to see if you chose correctly.

exhausted
thoroughly
manifestly
exertion
maneuver
ascent
descent

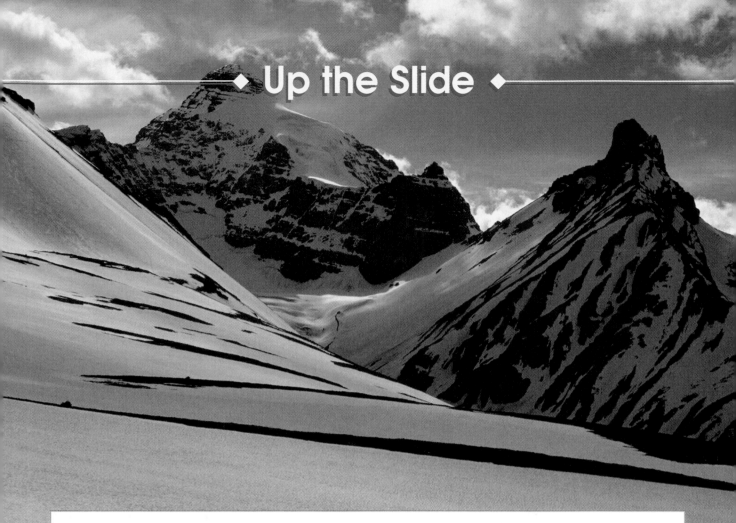

◆ Up the Slide ◆

◆ Literary Focus

CONFLICT WITH NATURE

A **conflict** is a struggle between opposing forces. In literature, a conflict may be between characters, within a character's mind, or between a character and some force of nature. In "Up the Slide," the primary conflict is between a character, Clay Dilham, and nature—the cold, icy conditions of the Yukon. You can get an idea of what Clay faces from this photograph of Yukon wilderness.

◆ Reading Strategy

PREDICT

As you read an adventure story like "Up the Slide," you keep wondering what will happen. You can **predict,** or make educated guesses about, story events based on clues in the story that suggest a certain outcome. You might also base a prediction on your own experience in a similar situation. After you make a prediction, read on to see how your prediction matches the actual outcome. Use a chart like this one to record your ideas.

Story Event or Clue	Prediction	Actual Outcome
Each step became more difficult and perilous, and he was faint from exertion and from lack of Swanson's dinner.	He will collapse and have to be rescued.	

Up the SLIDE

Jack London

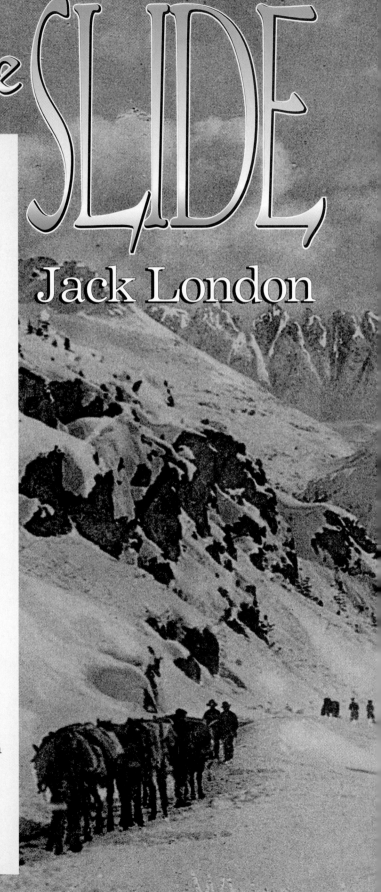

When Clay Dilham left the tent to get a sled-load of firewood, he expected to be back in half an hour. So he told Swanson, who was cooking the dinner. Swanson and he belonged to different outfits, located about twenty miles apart on the Stewart River, but they had become traveling partners on a trip down the Yukon to Dawson[1] to get the mail.

Swanson had laughed when Clay said he would be back in half an hour. It stood to reason, Swanson said, that good, dry firewood could not be found so close to Dawson; that whatever firewood there was originally had long since been gathered in; that firewood would not be selling at forty dollars a cord if any man could go out and get a sled-load and be back in the time Clay expected to make it.

Then it was Clay's turn to laugh, as he sprang on the sled and *mushed* the dogs on the river-trail. For, coming up from the Siwash village the previous day, he had noticed a small dead pine in an out-of-the-way place, which had defied discovery by eyes less sharp than his. And his eyes were both young and sharp, for his seventeenth birthday was just cleared.

A swift ten minutes over the ice brought him to the place, and figuring ten minutes to get the tree and ten minutes to return made him certain that Swanson's dinner would not wait.

Just below Dawson, and rising out of the Yukon itself, towered the great Moosehide Mountain, so named by Lieutenant Schwatka long ere[2] the Yukon became famous. On the river side the mountain was scarred and gul-

---

1. **Yukon** (yo͞o´ kän) **. . . Dawson** (dô´ sən): The Yukon River is in the Yukon Territory of northwestern Canada, and Dawson is a town nearby.
2. **ere** (er) *prep.*: Archaic for *before.*

lied and gored; and it was up one of these gores or gullies that Clay had seen the tree.

Halting his dogs beneath, on the river ice, he looked up, and after some searching, rediscovered it. Being dead, its weatherbeaten gray so blended with the gray wall of rock that a thousand men could pass by and never notice it. Taking root in a cranny, it had grown up, <u>exhausted</u> its bit of soil, and perished. Beneath it the wall fell sheer for a hundred feet to the river. All one had to do was to sink an ax into the dry trunk a dozen times and it would fall to the ice, and most probably smash conveniently to pieces. This Clay had figured on when confidently limiting the trip to half an hour.

He studied the cliff <u>thoroughly</u> before attempting it. So far as he was concerned, the longest way round was the shortest way to the tree. Twenty feet of nearly perpendicular climbing would bring him to where a slide sloped more gently in. By making a long zigzag across the face of this slide and back again, he would arrive at the pine.

Fastening his ax across his shoulders so that it would not interfere with his movements, he clawed up the broken rock, hand and foot, like a cat, till the twenty feet were cleared and he could draw breath on the edge of the slide.

The slide was steep and its snow-covered surface slippery. Further, the heelless, walrus-hide shoes of his *muclucs* were polished by much ice travel, and by his second step he realized how little he could depend upon them for clinging purposes. A slip at that point meant a plunge over the edge and a twenty-foot fall to the ice. A hundred feet farther along, and a slip would mean a fifty-foot fall.

He thrust his mittened hand through the snow to the earth to steady himself, and went on. But he was forced to exercise such care that the first zigzag consumed five minutes. Then, returning across the face of the slide toward the pine, he met with a new difficulty. The slope steepened considerably, so that little snow collected, while bent flat

◆ **Build Vocabulary**

exhausted (eg zôst´ əd) *v.*: Used up; expended completely

thoroughly (thʉr´ ō lē) *adv.*: Accurately and with regard to detail

beneath this thin covering were long, dry last-year's grasses.

◆ **Literary Focus**
In what ways is the slide an opposing force to Clay?

The surface they presented was as glassy as that of his muclucs, and when both surfaces came together his feet shot out, and he fell on his face, sliding downward and convulsively clutching for something to stay himself.

This he succeeded in doing, although he lay quiet for a couple of minutes to get back his nerve. He would have taken off his muclucs and gone at it in his socks, only the cold was thirty below zero, and at such temperature his feet would quickly freeze. So he went on, and after ten minutes of risky work made the safe and solid rock where stood the pine.

A few strokes of the ax felled it into the chasm, and peeping over the edge, he indulged a laugh at the startled dogs. They were on the verge of bolting when he called aloud to them, soothingly, and they were reassured.

Then he turned about for the trip back. Going down, he knew, was even more dangerous than coming up, but how dangerous he did not realize till he had slipped half a dozen times, and each time saved himself by what appeared to him a miracle. Time and again he ventured upon the slide, and time and again he was balked when he came to the grasses.

He sat down and looked at the treacherous snow-covered slope. It was <u>manifestly</u> impossible for him to make it with a whole body, and he did not wish to arrive at the bottom shattered like the pine tree.

But while he sat inactive the frost was stealing in on him, and the quick chilling of his body warned him that he could not delay. He must be doing something to keep his blood circulating. If he could not get down by going down, there only remained to him to get down

◆ **Build Vocabulary**
manifestly (man´ ə fest´ lē) *adv.*: Clearly
exertion (eg zʉr´ shən) *n.*: Energetic activity; effort

by going up. It was a herculean task, but it was the only way out of the predicament.

From where he was he could not see the top of the cliff, but he reasoned that the gully in which lay the slide must give inward more and more as it approached the top. From what little he could see, the gully displayed this tendency; and he noticed, also, that the slide extended for many hundreds of feet upward, and that where it ended the rock was well broken up and favorable for climbing. . . .

So instead of taking the zigzag which led downward, he made a new one leading upward and crossing the slide at an angle of thirty degrees. The grasses gave him much trouble, and made him long for soft-tanned moosehide moccasins, which could make his feet cling like a second pair of hands.

◆ **Reading Strategy**
Clay encounters problem after problem. What do you predict will happen?

He soon found that thrusting his mittened hands through the snow and clutching the grass roots was uncertain and unsafe. His mittens were too thick for him to be sure of his grip, so he took them off. But this brought with it new trouble. When he held on to a bunch of roots the snow, coming in contact with his bare warm hand, was melted, so that his hands and the wristbands of his woolen shirt were dripping with water. This the frost was quick to attack, and his fingers were numbed and made worthless.

Then he was forced to seek good footing, where he could stand erect unsupported, to put on his mittens, and to thrash his hands against his sides until the heat came back into them.

This constant numbing of his fingers made his progress very slow; but the zigzag came to an end finally, where the side of the slide was buttressed by a perpendicular rock, and he turned back and upward again. As he climbed higher and higher, he found that the slide was wedge-shaped, its rocky buttresses pinching it away as it reared its upper end. Each step increased the depth which seemed to yawn for him.

While beating his hands against his sides he turned and looked down the long slippery slope, and figured, in case he slipped, that he would be flying with the speed of an express train ere he took the final plunge into the icy bed of the Yukon.

He passed the first outcropping rock, and the second, and at the end of an hour found himself above the third, and fully five hundred feet above the river. And here, with the end nearly two hundred feet above him, the pitch of the slide was increasing.

Each step became more difficult and perilous, and he was faint from exertion and from lack of Swanson's dinner. Three or four times he slipped slightly and recovered himself; but, growing careless from exhaustion and the long tension on his nerves, he tried to continue with too great haste, and was rewarded by a double slip of each foot, which tore him loose and started him down the slope.

On account of the steepness there was little snow; but what little there was was displaced by his body, so that he became the nucleus of a young avalanche. He clawed desperately with his hands, but there was little to cling to, and he sped downward faster and faster.

The first and second outcroppings were below him, but he knew that the first was almost out of line, and pinned his hope on the second. Yet the first was just enough in line to catch one of his feet and to whirl him over and head downward on his back.

The shock of this was severe in itself, and the fine snow enveloped him in a blinding, maddening cloud; but he was thinking quickly and clearly of what would happen if he brought up head first against the outcropping. He twisted himself over on his stomach, thrust both hands out to one side, and pressed them heavily against the flying surface.

This had the effect of a brake, drawing his head and shoulders to the side. In this position he rolled over and over a couple of times, and then, with a quick jerk at the right moment, he got his body the rest of the way round.

And none too soon, for the next moment his feet drove into the outcropping, his legs doubled up, and the wind was driven from his stomach with the abruptness of the stop.

There was much snow down his neck and up his sleeves. At once and with unconcern he

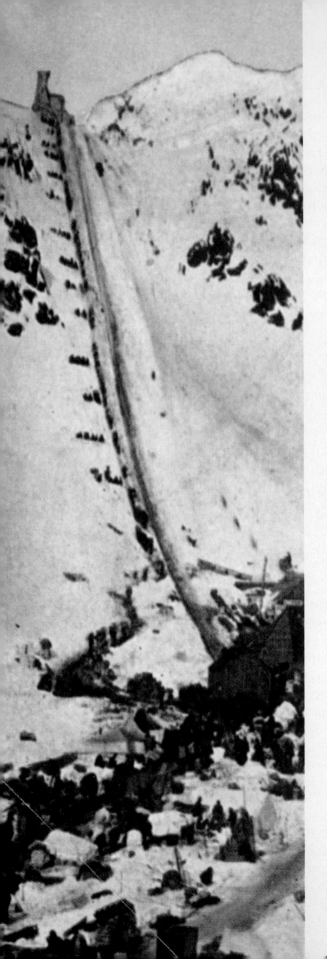

shook this out, only to discover, when he looked up to where he must climb again, that he had lost his nerve. He was shaking as if with a palsy, and sick and faint from a frightful nausea.

Fully ten minutes passed ere he could master these sensations and summon sufficient strength for the weary climb. His legs hurt him and he was limping, and he was conscious of a sore place in his back, where he had fallen on the ax.

In an hour he had regained the point of his tumble, and was contemplating the slide, which so suddenly steepened. It was plain to him that he could not go up with his hands and feet alone, and he was beginning to lose his nerve again when he remembered the ax.

Reaching upward the distance of a step, he brushed away the snow, and in the frozen gravel and crumbled rock of the slide chopped a shallow resting place for his foot. Then he came up a step, reached forward, and repeated the <u>maneuver</u>. And so, step by step, foot-hole by foot-hole, a tiny speck of toiling life poised like a fly on the face of Moosehide Mountain, he fought his upward way.

Twilight was beginning to fall when he gained the head of the slide and drew himself into the rocky bottom of the gully. At this point the shoulder of the mountain began to bend back toward the crest, and in addition to its being less steep, the rocks afforded better handhold and foothold. The worst was over, and the best yet to come!

The gully opened out into a miniature basin, in which a floor of soil had been deposited, out of which, in turn, a tiny grove of pines had sprung. The trees were all dead, dry and seasoned, having long since exhausted the thin skin of earth.

Clay ran his experienced eye over the timber, and estimated that it would chop up into fifty cords at least. Beyond, the gully closed in and became barren rock again. On every hand was barren rock, so the wonder was small that the trees had escaped the eyes

◄ **Critical Viewing** What does this photograph reveal about the hardships endured by gold prospectors in the Yukon? [Connect]

◆ **Build Vocabulary**

maneuver (mə nōṓ vər) *n.*: Series of planned steps

ascent (ə sent́) *n.*: The act of climbing or rising

descent (dē sent́) *n.*: The act of climbing down

of men. They were only to be discovered as he had discovered them—by climbing after them.

He continued the <u>ascent</u>, and the white moon greeted him when he came out upon the crest of Moosehide Mountain. At his feet, a thousand feet below, sparkled the lights of Dawson.

But the <u>descent</u> was precipitate and dangerous in the uncertain moonlight, and he elected to go down the mountain by its gentler northern flank. In a couple of hours he reached the Yukon at the Siwash village, and took the river-trail back to where he had left the dogs. There he found Swanson, with a fire going, waiting for him to come down.

And although Swanson had a hearty laugh at his expense, nevertheless, a week or so later, in Dawson, there were fifty cords of wood sold at forty dollars a cord, and it was he and Swanson who sold them.

Beyond Literature

Social Studies Connection

The Klondike Gold Rush History's largest gold discovery took place in August 1896 near a remote Klondike river, Dawson's Creek. News of the discovery didn't reach the world until the spring of 1897, when a Seattle newspaper headline trumpeted the discovery of "more than a ton of gold," divided among 68 miners!

The news triggered the last great gold rush. An estimated 100,000 people began the trek, but only about 30,000 actually made it to Dawson's Creek. Once there, few of the prospectors found gold, and the few who did often lost their fortunes as quickly.

Cross-Curricular Activity
Historic Newspaper What might a newspaper of the time have said about the Gold Rush in the spring of 1898? Work with a team to create a historic newspaper that focuses on the Klondike Gold Rush.

Guide for Responding

◆ LITERATURE AND YOUR LIFE

Reader's Response Do you think the risks that Clay took were reasonable or foolish? Why?

Thematic Focus Is it more important for trailblazers to be lucky or skillful? Explain.

Group Activity With a few classmates, jot down some ways in which you would adjust to life in the harsh and frozen Yukon.

☑ Check Your Comprehension

1. Why is Clay so confident at the beginning of his journey?
2. What events reduce his confidence?
3. How does Clay escape his difficult position?
4. What surprise does Clay discover at the end of his adventure?

◆ Critical Thinking

INTERPRET
1. Why does London begin the story with a description of Clay and Swanson's disagreement? **[Speculate]**
2. How is Clay's age reflected in his actions? **[Deduce]**
3. Identify three specific skills Clay possesses that aid his survival. **[Infer]**

EVALUATE
4. Based on his actions in the story, for what specific jobs do you think Clay is suited? **[Assess]**

APPLY
5. How would this story be different if it were set in the jungle? **[Modify]**
6. What lesson does this story hold for readers who will never visit the Yukon? **[Generalize]**

Guide for Responding (continued)

◆ Reading Strategy

PREDICT

Predicting while you read keeps you involved in what you're reading. For example, in "Up the Slide," your predictions may become less optimistic with each challenge Clay faces. Uncertainty about Clay's fate increases your interest in the story.

1. Did you predict that Clay would survive? On what clues did you base your prediction?
2. What prediction would you make about Clay's future? Describe the story clues that support this prediction.

◆ Build Vocabulary

USING FORMS OF *exhaust*

Add forms of the word *exhaust* to your vocabulary. Copy the following sentences on your paper. Then, fill in each blank sensibly by adding *-ion, -ible,* and *-ed* to *exhaust.*

1. He was _____?_____ when he reached the top.
2. Because they had no wells, their water supply was _____?_____.
3. The hiker collapsed from _____?_____.

SPELLING STRATEGY

The long *o* sound is occasionally spelled *ough,* as in *thoroughly, dough,* and *though.* Copy the following sentences on your paper. Fill in the blank with a long *o* word from the words listed above.

1. We were _____?_____ exhausted by the journey.
2. _____?_____ it was still light, we went to bed.
3. He formed the _____?_____ into a loaf.

USING THE WORD BANK

Write the word from the Word Bank that best matches the meaning of the italicized word(s).

1. He felt *completely* ready for the climb.
2. His *upward journey* began at dawn.
3. Trembling from *effort,* he collapsed.
4. By noon, he felt surprisingly *tired.*
5. The *downward journey* was even more difficult.
6. Eventually, he devised a new *strategy* that he called "controlled sliding."
7. The strategy was *clearly* successful as he arrived back feeling alert and not at all tired.

◆ Literary Focus

CONFLICT WITH NATURE

The central **conflict,** or struggle, in "Up the Slide" occurs between Clay and an element of nature. As Clay struggles against the icy, rocky terrain and the bitter cold, his fate becomes uncertain and the suspense builds.

1. Explain how elements of nature oppose Clay's efforts to find firewood.
2. How is the conflict resolved?
3. Critics sometimes say that a story's setting is like another character. Do you think this idea applies to "Up the Slide"? Explain.

◆ Build Grammar Skills

ACTIVE AND PASSIVE VOICE

A verb is in the **active voice** when the subject of the sentence performs the action. It is in the **passive voice** when the subject receives the action. The passive voice uses a form of the helping verb *be.*

> **Active Voice:** Clay *threw* the ax.
> **Passive Voice:** The ax *was thrown* by Clay.

Practice In your notebook, indicate whether each verb is in the active or the passive voice.

1. Clay climbed the steep mountain.
2. The thin crust of ice was broken by his heavy feet.
3. In the moonlight, the icy surface glistened like crystal.
4. After the landslide, the snow settled in a large heap at the bottom of the basin.
5. Swanson was surprised by Clay.

Writing Application Rewrite the following passage, changing the passive voice to the active voice. Verbs in the passive voice are italicized.

The mountain *was climbed* by Clay. Although the parka covered Clay, the icy air *was felt* by him. The frigid temperature chilled his fingers and toes. Suddenly, the thin crust of ice *was broken* by his feet. A distant shout *was heard* faintly by the numbed climber. He *had been found* by the rescue party!

Build Your Portfolio

 ## Idea Bank

Writing

1. **Diary Entry** Write a diary entry that Clay might have composed after his difficult journey. Include details that show his feelings.

2. **Job Description** Write a job description for a gold prospector. Describe the skills necessary, as well as the types of challenges prospectors are likely to face. **[Career Link]**

3. **Modified Story** Rewrite "Up the Slide" using a different extreme climate, such as a desert or tropical rain forest. Keep the character of Clay the same, and describe a similar adventure.

Speaking and Listening

4. **Oral Interpretation** Choose an exciting part of "Up the Slide," and read it aloud. Change the speed, volume, and tone of your reading to create varied effects. Perform your reading for classmates. **[Performing Arts Link]**

5. **Casting Proposal** Choose an actor that you think should portray Clay Dilham in a film version of "Up the Slide." Imagine that your classmates are the film's producers. Make a speech to them about why this actor is perfect for the role. **[Media Link]**

Projects

6. **Multimedia Report [Group Activity]** Work with a group to create an exhibit highlighting the climate of the Yukon. Use visuals and texts that help your audience experience this unusual climate. **[Geography Link]**

7. **Author Research** Find out more about Jack London's life and works. Consult biographies, Internet sources, and London's own writings, such as the autobiographical novel *Martin Eden* or stories in "Tales of the Fish Patrol." Share your findings with the class, and identify the sources you used. **[Literature Link]**

 ## Writing Mini-Lesson

Report on the Yukon

The Yukon is a vast and fascinating region that inspired Jack London to write many of his best-known works. Write a research report about the Yukon, focusing on one specific topic that interests you. Use several reference sources to gain factual details for your report.

Writing Skills Focus: Narrowing a Topic

Narrow a broad topic like the Yukon by dividing it into subtopics. Reading in a general reference source, like an encyclopedia, can help you find different subtopics to consider.

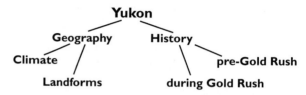

Prewriting Identify a specific topic that addresses a single key feature of the Yukon. Use a variety of sources, including nonfiction books, encyclopedias, and Internet sites to gather details.

Drafting Begin your research report with a clear statement of your topic. Present your facts in a logical order, and conclude with a brief summary or an appropriate conclusion.

Revising Check the facts in your report for accuracy. Wherever passages are unclear, reorganize the facts and edit out unnecessary words. Be sure that you've begun your report with a topic statement and ended with a conclusion that sums up the facts.

> ◆ **Grammar Application**
>
> Wherever you can, change statements in the passive voice to the active voice to give your report more impact.

CONNECTING LITERATURE TO SOCIAL STUDIES
THE COLONIAL ERA

The Pilgrims' Landing and First Winter *by William Bradford*

THE PILGRIMS Once the "New World" was discovered, it wasn't long before groups of Europeans braved the crossing of the Atlantic to settle on Roanoke Island, Jamestown, and Plymouth. Among the earliest English groups to settle in America were the Pilgrims. Many of the Pilgrims were members of the Puritan sect, a religious group unpopular in England because of their beliefs. They left England for Holland, hoping to be allowed to practice their religion freely in that country. However, things weren't much better for them in Holland, so they set sail for America.

The *Mayflower* Their ship, the *Mayflower,* arrived at Plymouth, Massachusetts, in November 1620. It had been a long, hard journey across the Atlantic. Many passengers died during the voyage, including the wife of William Bradford. Bradford became the first governor of Plymouth, the settlement formed by the Puritans. He wrote a book called *History of Plymouth Plantation*, from which this selection comes. This book is the source of most of what we know about the early Puritan settlement.

The Challenge of the New World The Puritans came to the "New World" so they could practice their religion freely. They expected life in America to be hard, but they did not realize how difficult it would be. The area they called New England was not very good for farming. The winter weather was much more fierce than weather in England or in Holland. They had left behind not only family and friends, but such necessities as medical care, housing supplies, and food. In addition, some of the natives—Indians—feared and distrusted these strangers, and there was the constant danger of fights. In this selection, William Bradford tells about some of the challenges the Puritans met when they first arrived on shore.

The First English Settlements

0   100   200 Miles
0 100   200 Kilometers

Pilgrims Going to Church, George Henry Boughton, Collection of The New-York Historical Society

▲ **Critical Viewing** What can you learn from this painting about the Pilgrims' first winter? [Analyze]

The Pilgrims' Landing and First Winter

William Bradford

Being thus arrived at Cape Cod the 11th of November, and necessity called them to look out a place for habitation (as well as the master's and mariners' importunity[1]); they having brought a large shallop[2] with them out of England, stowed in quarters in the ship, they now got her out and set their carpenters to work to trim her up; but being much bruised and shattered in the ship with foul weather, they saw she would be long in mending. Whereupon a few of them tendered themselves to go by land and discover those nearest places, whilst the shallop was in mending; and the rather because as they went into that harbor there seemed to be an opening some two or three leagues off, which the master judged to be a river. It was conceived there might be some danger in the attempt, yet seeing them resolute, they were permitted to go, being sixteen of them well armed under the conduct of Captain Standish, having such instructions given them as was thought meet.[3] They set forth the 15th of November; and when they had marched about the space of a mile by the seaside, they espied five or six persons with a dog coming towards them, who were savages; but they fled from them and ran up into the woods, and the English followed them, partly to see if they could speak with them, and partly to discover if there might not be

1. **importunity** (im pôr tōon′ i tē) *n.*: Urgent demands.
2. **shallop** (shal′ əp) *n.*: Small open boat.
3. **meet** (mēt) *adj.*: Old English word meaning "proper" or "fit."

more of them lying in ambush. But the Indians seeing themselves thus followed, they again forsook[4] the woods and ran away on the sands as hard as they could, so as they could not come near them but followed them by the track of their feet sundry miles and saw that they had come the same way. So, night coming on, they made their rendezvous and set out their sentinels,[5] and rested in quiet that night; and the next morning followed their track till they had headed a great creek and so left the sands, and turned another way into the woods. But they still followed them by guess, hoping to find their dwellings; but they soon lost both them and themselves, falling into such thickets as were ready to tear their clothes and armor in pieces; but were most distressed for want of drink. But at length they found water and refreshed themselves. . . .

Afterwards they directed their course to come to the other shore, for they knew it was a neck of land they were to cross over, and so at length got to the seaside and marched to this supposed river, and by the way found a pond of clear, fresh water, and shortly after a good quantity of clear ground where the Indians had formerly set corn, and some of their graves. And proceeding further they saw new stubble where corn had been set the same year; also they found where lately a house had been, where some planks and a great kettle was remaining, and heaps of sand newly paddled with their hands. Which, they digging up,

found in them divers[6] fair Indian baskets filled with corn, and some in ears, fair and good, of divers colours, which seemed to them a very goodly sight (having never seen any such before). This was near the place of that supposed river they came to seek, unto which they went and found it to open itself into two arms with a high cliff of sand in the entrance but more like to be creeks of salt water than any fresh, for aught[7] they saw; and that there was good harborage for their shallop, leaving it further to be discovered by their shallop, when she was ready. So, their time limited them being expired, they returned to the ship lest they should be in fear of their safety; and took with them part of the corn and buried up the rest. And so, like the men from Eshcol, carried with them the fruits of the land and showed their brethren; of which, and their return, they were marvelously glad and their hearts encouraged.

After this, the shallop being got ready, they set out again for the better discovery of this place, and the master of the ship desired to go himself. So there went some thirty men but found it to be no harbor for ships but only for boats. There was also found two of their houses covered with mats, and sundry of their implements in them, but the people were run away and could not be seen. Also there was found more of their corn and of their beans of various colours; the corn and beans they brought away, purposing to give them full satisfaction when they should meet with any of them as, about some six months afterward they did, to their good content.

---

4. **forsook** (fôr´ sook´) *v.*: Abandoned.
5. **sentinels** (sen´ ti nəls) *n.*: Guards.
6. **divers** (dī´ vərz) *adj.*: Diverse.

---

7. **aught** (ôt) *n.*: Anything.

Guide for Responding

◆ LITERATURE AND YOUR LIFE

Reader's Response Do you find the Puritans' actions sensible? Explain.

Thematic Focus What challenges did the Puritans face when they arrived in America?

☑ Check Your Comprehension

1. Why did several men volunteer to explore the land, instead of using the shallop?
2. What two reasons did the men have for following the Indians into the woods?
3. What items did the men find when they reached the Indian village?

◆ Critical Thinking

INTERPRET

1. What do the Puritans assume to be true about the Indians before the two groups have even met? **[Infer]**
2. How can you tell that the Indians were a civilized group of people? **[Draw Conclusions]**

3. What might the Puritans have done to keep the Indians from running away from them? **[Make a Judgment]**

EXTEND

4. What part or parts of this account might have inspired European readers to follow the Puritans to America? **[Social Studies Link]**

CONNECTING LITERATURE TO SOCIAL STUDIES

One reason people study history is to learn how the modern world got to be the way it is. For example, Americans often state that they prefer to depend on themselves, without help from government or other institutions. This is an attitude the Puritans brought with them from Europe.

1. What parts of Bradford's story show that the Puritans have admirable qualities?
2. What parts show that they have qualities that are not so admirable?
3. Which of these two sets of qualities have you seen in present-day Americans?

 Idea Bank

Writing

1. **Letter** As a passenger on the *Mayflower,* write a letter to a friend or relative in England. Describe your first few days in New England.
2. **Script** Imagine that one of the Puritans and one of the Indians can speak the same language. Write a script for a conversation that might take place when the two meet for the first time.
3. **Regulations** As an assistant to Governor Bradford, write a series of regulations showing the settlers how they must behave toward the Indians, who lived there before the Puritans arrived.

Speaking and Listening

4. **Discussion [Group Activity]** Role-play a discussion between one settler who wants to live peacefully with the Indians and one who wants to drive them away and use their land.

Projects

5. **Oral Report** Use encyclopedias and other reference works to learn details about how the Puritans lived. Present the information you find to the class in an oral report.
6. ***Mayflower* Illustration** Do research on the *Mayflower,* the Pilgrims' ship. Then, draw a realistic illustration of it and post it in the classroom. **[Art Link]**

Further Reading, Listening, and Viewing

- Gary D. Schmidt's *William Bradford, Plymouth's Faithful Pilgrim* is a biography of Bradford.
- Henri Nouwen's *A Pilgrim's Report* is an audio book about Pilgrim life.
- Lucille Recht Penner's *Eating the Plates: A Pilgrim Book of Food and Manners* gives information about the daily lives of the Pilgrims.

Historical Cause-and-Effect Essay

Writing Process Workshop

Many of the selections in this section take place in the past, during various periods of history. Often the events of history, such as the Yukon Gold Rush or the westward movement by settlers, cause other events to happen. When you write a **historical cause-and-effect essay,** you investigate a situation or event and then explore how and why that event occurred. The challenge is to find the causes behind the events.

Which puzzles of history interest you? Write a historical cause-and-effect essay that investigates one of them. Use the skills introduced in the Writing Mini-Lessons in this section to help you.

Writing Skills Focus

▶ **Narrow your topic** so that your cause-and-effect essay will be focused. (See p. 161.)

▶ **Create an introduction, body, and conclusion** that will state your topic in a captivating way, build a body of important details, and bring your essay to a satisfying close. (See p. 118.)

▶ **Follow a logical sequence of events** to help your readers see how one action or event is related to the next. (See p. 129.)

▶ **Support your statements with reasons.** (See p. 151.)

Ann Petry uses these skills in her account of Harriet Tubman.

Harriet Tubman Series, #28, Jacob Lawrence, Hampton University Museum

---

MODEL FROM LITERATURE

from *Harriet Tubman: Guide to Freedom* by Ann Petry

① But there were so many of them this time. She knew moments of doubt when she was half-afraid, and kept looking back over her shoulder, imagining that she heard the sound of pursuit. ② They would certainly be pursued. Eleven of them. Eleven thousand dollars' worth of flesh and bone and muscle that belonged to Maryland planters. ③ If they were caught, the eleven runaways would be whipped and sold South, but she—she would probably be hanged. ④

① This essay's topic is narrow. It focuses on Tubman's role in the Underground Railroad.

② In the body of her account, Petry provides important details.

③ Petry gives the reason (cause) the runaway slaves will be pursued.

④ Using a logical sequence of events, Petry clearly points out what will happen if they're caught.

Prewriting

Choose a Topic Why did the American colonies allow slavery in their new country? Which was more important—the discovery of penicillin or the computer chip? Which historical questions puzzle you? Choose one to investigate, and explain it in a cause-and-effect essay.

Review the Literary Selections to Find a Topic Think of the theme *blazing a trail*. Are there others who have blazed a trail you'd like to follow back to its source, perhaps colonists who went to Rhode Island or to Jamestown, Virginia?

Narrow Your Topic Once you've selected a topic, make sure it's narrow enough for you to cover in depth. Take time to jot down subtopics. Then, consider using one of the subtopics as your main topic. You may want to create a Topic Web like this:

Make a Cause-and-Effect Chain to Find Support A cause-and-effect chain will help you identify the support you'll need for your essay. Write the historical event at the end of a chain, then write the causes that led up to it.

History Writing Tip If you're writing about a different culture or era, don't assume that the people of that time or place had the same values and ideas that you have today. Try to put yourself in their shoes.

Drafting

Create an Introduction, Body, and Conclusion As you draft, structure your essay with an introduction, in which you introduce your topic. Then, write the body, in which you develop your ideas. In the conclusion, restate your main points.

Follow a Logical Organization Use an organization that will allow you to present your facts in the most effective way. A chronological organization will allow you to trace how each cause triggered each effect. Another possible organization is to pinpoint a major event (effect) and then examine the various causes that contributed to it.

Proceed Slowly and Carefully This is nonfiction—factual writing. You don't need to write quickly to get your ideas on paper. Follow your organization plan, and check off your notes as you include them in your first draft.

DRAFTING/REVISING

APPLYING LANGUAGE SKILLS: Using Correct Verb Forms

Some verb forms require the use of a helping verb, such as *will* or *had*. Be sure to include a helping verb with the past participle of a verb. Do not use a helping verb with the past form.

Incorrect:
He <u>had saw</u> the play.
He <u>seen</u> the play.

Correct:
He <u>saw</u> the play.
He <u>had seen</u> the play.

Practice On your paper, re-write this paragraph. Correct the verb forms of the under-lined verbs, if necessary.

After blasting off for the moon, Cooper <u>seen</u> something unusual. He <u>had knew</u> that the trip was risky, but never <u>guessed</u> it would be so dangerous.

Writing Application Review your essay to be sure you've correctly used verb forms.

Writer's Solution Connection Language Lab

For more practice with verb tenses, complete the lesson Using the Correct Verb Tense in the Using Verbs unit.

APPLYING LANGUAGE SKILLS: Using Active Voice

When the subject of a sentence performs the action of the verb, the verb is in the active voice. When the action is performed on the subject, the verb is in the passive voice. In your writing, use the active voice whenever possible. It is crisper and more direct than the passive voice.

Active Voice:
Harriet knocked on the door.

Passive Voice:
The door was knocked on by Harriet.

Practice Rewrite these sentences. Change passive voice to active voice.

1. The flowers were sent by the family.
2. The photos were developed by the lab.
3. The letter was signed by the President.
4. The meal was eaten by the hungry cat.

Writing Application As you draft, use the active voice where possible.

Writer's Solution Connection Writing Lab

For more practice with the active voice, see the Revising section of the Narration tutorial.

Revising

Consult With a Peer Reviewer Ask a peer to review your essay and answer questions such as these:
- ▶ Is the essay logical and interesting?
- ▶ Do the cause-and-effect statements make sense? Is the connection between the cause(s) and effect(s) clear?
- ▶ Are there factual errors?

Use your reviewers' responses to help you revise.

Use a Checklist Use the Writing Skills Focus points on the first page of this lesson as a checklist to evaluate and revise your essay.

Review Your Organizational Strategy Reread your essay, paying close attention to its organization. Add transitions where necessary to link your ideas. Change the order of details that seem to be "out of place."

Delete Unnecessary Details As you review your draft, remove details that do not contribute to the main points in your essay.

REVISION MODEL

Harriet Tubman was a great person. ① who helped bring slavery to its knees with her work on the Underground Railroad. Because of her work, many slaves were freed. ② escaped herself, found a route to Canada, and helped many others escape. She found a route to help escaped slaves to Canada and she escaped herself. ③ Her work will never be forgotten.

① The writer adds reasons to support her statements.
② These facts are presented in chronological order.
③ This added sentence makes the essay's conclusion more satisfying.

Publishing and Presenting

- ▶ **Classroom** Display your historical cause-and-effect essays on a timeline.
- ▶ **Social Studies Classroom** Read your historical essay to your social studies class.
- ▶ **Internet** Post your essay on a Web site devoted to the same historical period.

Real-World Reading Skills Workshop

Strategies for Success

Suppose you want to find information about a historical figure, such as Benjamin Rush, in your social studies book. Use the following strategies to conduct a quick and effective search for specific information.

Check the Index A book's index provides a specific listing of information found in it. If any information about your topic is in the book, it will be listed in the index.

Look for Related Topics You may find specific information about your topic by looking under related headings in the table of contents. For example, you might find information about Benjamin Rush under the related topic Revolutionary Figures.

Skim Subheads Subheads usually appear in boldface type. They reveal the main point of a book's section or chapter. Skim subheads to see if any of the material is related to your topic.

Scan Maps Maps provide many types of specific information, such as geographical features, population density, place names and locations, distances between points, and so on. Scan maps to see what kind of information they offer.

Apply the Strategies

Examine the sample table of contents, and answer these questions:

1. If you wanted to find out whether Benjamin Rush was a signer of the Declaration of Independence, which chapter would you turn to?

2. Which chapter might give you more in-depth information about Benjamin Rush? How can you tell?

3. If you wanted to find out whether Benjamin Rush's portrait appears in the book, where would you look? Why?

Table Of Contents

Unit 1 The Revolutionary Period

Index

✔ You may also find specific information in
- ▶ Guide books for historic sites
- ▶ Biographical dictionaries
- ▶ Magazines

A **verb** is a word used to express action or a state of being. A verb may appear in a **verb phrase,** which consists of a main verb and at least one helping verb. The following chart gives the characteristics of verbs.

verb (verb) *n.* a word that shows action or a condition of being: some verbs are used to link a subject with words that tell about the subject, or to help other verbs show special features [In "The children ate early" and "Cactuses grow slowly," the words "ate" and "grow" are *verbs*. In "He is asleep," the word "is" is a linking *verb*. In "Where have you gone?", the word "hav...

Action Verbs (see p. 128)	Express action: I *moved* quickly.
Linking Verbs (see p. 128)	Express a state of being: She *became* suspicious.
Transitive Verbs (see p. 140)	Express action directed toward a person or thing: She *caught him* as he stumbled.
Intransitive Verbs (see p. 140)	Express action without passing the action to a receiver: Tubman *whistled* softly.
Active Voice (see p. 160)	The subject of the sentence performs the action: *Columbus sailed* the ocean.
Passive Voice (see p. 160)	The subject of the sentence receives the action: *America was discovered* by Columbus.

Practice 1 On your paper, identify the verb or verb phrase in each sentence. Tell whether the verb is an action or a linking verb. For each action verb, tell if it's transitive or intransitive.

1. She was trained to survive subzero conditions.

2. He climbed the icy mountain.

3. They crawled slowly in the darkness.

4. They grew confident because of success.

5. They called to one another with joy.

Practice 2 Rewrite the following paragraph, changing passive voice verbs to active voice wherever appropriate.

The reporter was awakened by the telephone's ring. The telephone was answered by him. The person on the other end was upset and scared. "Is it true?" was asked by the caller. "Is what true?" the reporter asked wearily. "Is it true that you can live forever on the moon?" The bed was collapsed on by the stunned reporter. "Who told?" he thought.

Grammar in Writing

✔ *Use the active voice when you write. Reserve the use of passive voice for emphasizing the receiver of the action rather than the performer of the action or when the doer of the action is unknown.*

✔ *Use* lie *and* lay *correctly.* Lay *means "to put something down."* Lie *means "to place yourself in a horizontal position."*

PART 2 *Facing Hard Questions*

The Letter, Tim Solliday, Courtesy of the artist

Guide for Reading

Meet the Authors:

Anton Chekhov (1860–1904)

Chekhov's short stories and plays present such a detailed and precise view of Russian life that some critics believe they contain more information than nonfiction works.

Chekhov was trained as a doctor, and many reviewers feel that his medical training greatly influenced his writing. Although his ideas are sharply analytical, his tone is always compassionate. Chekhov's understanding of people is reflected in the humor and emotion of "The Ninny."

Neil Simon (1927–   )

Neil Simon has entertained millions of people with his plays and films. His ability to depict human frailty with hilarious one-line gags has brought him tremendous success.

Simon grew up in Washington Heights, a section of New York City. Many of his plays, from "The Odd Couple" to "Broadway Bound," take place in his chaotic and crazy version of New York.

"The Governess" is taken from *The Good Doctor*, a collection of Simon's adaptations of Chekhov's stories.

◆ LITERATURE AND YOUR LIFE

CONNECT YOUR EXPERIENCE

An old expression says that "the squeaky wheel gets the grease." People use it to stress the importance of speaking up for yourself. Think of situations in which you've either spoken up for yourself, or decided it was wiser to stay silent.

In "The Ninny" and "The Governess," a retelling of "The Ninny," you'll learn how a governess reacts to unfair treatment from her employer.

THEMATIC FOCUS: Facing Hard Questions

As you read, ask yourself if you would have reacted as the governess did when faced with hard questions.

◆ Background for Understanding

HISTORY

In nineteenth-century Europe, most upper-class families hired governesses for their children. Governesses taught lessons, monitored safety, and provided moral instruction. The life of a governess was often lonely because she belonged to neither the servant class nor the upper class. "The Ninny" and "The Governess" are two works about one particular governess.

◆ Build Vocabulary

SUFFIXES: -ment

The suffix -ment can be added to some verbs to create nouns. For example, the verb *baffle* means "to confuse." The noun *bafflement* means "a state of confusion."

WORD BANK

Which word from the list is the opposite of *superior*? Check the Build Vocabulary box on page 176 to see if you chose correctly.

bitter
timidly
inferior
discrepancies
discharged
guileless
bafflement

The Ninny ◆ The Governess

The Rev. and Mrs. Palmer-Lovell with their daughters Georgina and Christina, Augustus Egg. Phillips, the International Fine Art Auctioneers, UK

◆ Literary Focus
CHARACTERS' MOTIVES

People in real life rarely act without a cause or reason. The same is true in literature. **Characters' motives** are the reasons behind their actions. Some motives are obvious. For example, a character's motive for scolding a child is that the child misbehaved. Sometimes, however, motives are hidden and must be guessed at by the reader.

As you read "The Ninny" and "The Governess," look for clues to the employer's motives.

◆ Reading Strategy
QUESTION CHARACTERS' ACTIONS

Characters in literature usually act and react as real people do. To get a deeper understanding of characters, **question their actions**—what the characters do and say. For example, after an important event, ask yourself, "Why did the character do this?" Your answers can help you to understand a character's motives.

Character	What the Character Said or Did	Why?
The Mistress	She calls Julia.	To review her salary

The Ninny

Anton Chekhov

Translated by Robert Payne

The Governess, 1844 (detail), Richard Redgrave, Victoria & Albert Museum, London, UK

Just a few days ago I invited Yulia Vassilyevna, the governess[1] of my children, to come to my study. I wanted to settle my account with her.

"Sit down, Yulia Vassilyevna," I said to her. "Let's get our accounts settled. I'm sure you need some money, but you keep standing on ceremony and never ask for it. Let me see. We agreed to give you thirty rubles a month, didn't we?"

"Forty."

"No, thirty. I made a note of it. I always pay the governess thirty. Now, let me see. You have been with us for two months?"

"Two months and five days."

"Two months exactly. I made a note of it. So you have sixty rubles coming to you. Subtract nine Sundays. You know you don't tutor Kolya on Sundays, you just go out for a walk. And then the three holidays . . ."

Yulia Vassilyevna blushed and picked at the trimmings of her dress, but said not a word.

"Three holidays. So we take off twelve rubles. Kolya was sick for four days—those days you didn't look after him. You looked

---

▲ **Critical Viewing** Judging by the expression on the governess's face, do you think her life is a happy one? **[Draw Conclusions]**

after Vanya, only Vanya. Then there were the three days you had toothache, when my wife gave you permission to stay away from the children after dinner. Twelve and seven makes nineteen. Subtract. . . . That leaves . . . hm . . . forty-one rubles. Correct?"

Yulia Vassilyevna's left eye reddened and filled with tears. Her chin trembled. She began to cough nervously, blew her nose, and said nothing.

"Then around New Year's Day you broke a cup and saucer. Subtract two rubles. The cup cost more than that—it was an heirloom, but we won't bother about that. We're the ones who pay. Another matter. Due to your carelessness Kolya climbed a tree and tore his coat. Subtract ten. Also, due to your carelessness the chambermaid ran off with Vanya's boots. You ought to have kept your eyes open. You get a good salary. So we dock off five more. . . . On the tenth of January you took ten rubles from me."

"I didn't," Yulia Vassilyevna whispered.

"But I made a note of it."

"Well, yes—perhaps . . ."

"From forty-one we take twenty-seven. That leaves fourteen."

Her eyes filled with tears, and her thin, pretty little nose was shining with perspiration. Poor little child!

"I only took money once," she said in a trembling voice. "I took three rubles from your wife . . . never anything more."

"Did you now? You see, I never made a note of it. Take three from fourteen. That leaves eleven. Here's your money, my dear. Three, three, three . . . one and one. Take it, my dear."

I gave her the eleven rubles. With trembling fingers she took them and slipped them into her pocket.

"*Merci*," she whispered.

I jumped up, and began pacing up and down the room. I was in a furious temper.

"Why did you say '*merci*'?" I asked.

"For the money."

"Don't you realize I've been cheating you? I steal your money, and all you can say is '*merci*'!"

"In my other places they gave me nothing."

"They gave you nothing! Well, no wonder! I was playing a trick on you—a dirty trick. . . . I'll give you your eighty rubles, they are all here in an envelope made out for you. Is it possible for anyone to be such a nitwit? Why didn't you protest? Why did you keep your mouth shut? Is it possible that there is anyone in this world who is so spineless? Why are you such a ninny?"

She gave me a <u>bitter</u> little smile. On her face I read the words: "Yes, it is possible."

I apologized for having played this cruel trick on her, and to her great surprise gave her the eighty rubles. And then she said "*merci*" again several times, always <u>timidly</u>, and went out. I gazed after her, thinking how very easy it is in this world to be strong.

◆ **Build Vocabulary**

bitter (bit´ ər) *adj.*: Showing discomfort, sorrow, or pain

timidly (tim´ id lē) *adv.*: In a shy manner

Guide for Responding

◆ LITERATURE AND YOUR LIFE

Reader's Response What advice would you like to give the governess?

Thematic Focus Do you think that the governess answered the narrator's questions wisely? Explain.

Journal Writing Taking on the character of the governess, write a journal entry she might have written following this interview with her employer.

☑ Check Your Comprehension

1. Who narrates "The Ninny"?
2. How does the governess respond to each question?
3. What trick does the narrator reveal at the end of the story?

◆ Critical Thinking

INTERPRET

1. What strategies does the narrator use to decrease the governess's salary? **[Classify]**
2. Why does the narrator decide to play this trick? **[Infer]**
3. What does the governess's response to the trick suggest about her? **[Interpret]**

EVALUATE

4. Which character do you admire more at the end of the story? Why? **[Make a Judgment]**

APPLY

5. Suppose the narrator decided to give this story a moral. What moral might he have chosen? **[Generalize]**

The Governess
Neil Simon

MISTRESS. Julia! [*Calls again*] Julia!

[*A young governess,* JULIA, *comes rushing in. She stops before the desk and curtsies.*]

JULIA. [*Head down*] Yes, madame?

MISTRESS. Look at me, child. Pick your head up. I like to see your eyes when I speak to you.

JULIA. [*Lifts her head up*] Yes, madame. [*But her head has a habit of slowly drifting down again*]

MISTRESS. And how are the children coming along with their French lessons?

JULIA. They're very bright children, madame.

MISTRESS. Eyes up . . . They're bright, you say. Well, why not? And mathematics? They're doing well in mathematics, I assume?

JULIA. Yes, madame. Especially Vanya.

MISTRESS. Certainly. I knew it. I excelled in mathematics. He gets that from his mother, wouldn't you say?

JULIA. Yes, madame.

MISTRESS. Head up . . .

[*She lifts head up*]

That's it. Don't be afraid to look people in the eyes, my dear. If you think of yourself as <u>inferior</u>, that's exactly how people will treat you.

JULIA. Yes, ma'am.

MISTRESS. A quiet girl, aren't you? . . . Now then, let's settle our accounts. I imagine you must need money, although you never ask me for it yourself. Let's see now, we agreed on thirty rubles[1] a month, did we not?

JULIA. [*Surprised*] Forty, ma'am.

MISTRESS. No, no, thirty. I made a note of it. [*Points to the book*] I always pay my governess thirty . . . Who told you forty?

JULIA. You did, ma'am. I spoke to no one else concerning money . . .

MISTRESS. Impossible. Maybe you *thought* you heard forty when I said thirty. If you kept your head up, that would never happen. Look at me again and I'll say it clearly. *Thirty rubles a month.*

JULIA. If you say so, ma'am.

1. rubles (rōō′ bəlz) *n.*: Basic monetary unit of Russia.

◆ **Build Vocabulary**

inferior (in fir′ ē ər) *adj.*: Lower in status, order, or rank

discrepancies (di skrep′ ən sēz) *n.*: Differences; inconsistencies; lack of agreement

Woman in Chair, John Collier, Courtesy of the artist.

▲ **Critical Viewing** Do you think that, like the governess in the play, this woman is "afraid to look people in the eyes"? Explain. **[Interpret]**

MISTRESS. Settled. Thirty a month it is . . . Now then, you've been here two months exactly.

JULIA. Two months and five days.

MISTRESS. No, no. Exactly two months. I made a note of it. You should keep books the way I do so there wouldn't be these discrepancies. So—we have two months at thirty rubles a month . . . comes to sixty rubles. Correct?

JULIA. [*Curtsies*] Yes, ma'am. Thank you, ma'am.

MISTRESS. Subtract nine Sundays . . . We did agree to subtract Sundays, didn't we?

JULIA. No, ma'am.

MISTRESS. Eyes! Eyes! . . . Certainly we did. I've always subtracted Sundays. I didn't bother making a note of it because I always do it. Don't you recall when I said we will subtract Sundays?

◆ **Reading Strategy**
Wy doesn't Julia stand up for herself?

JULIA. No, ma'am.

MISTRESS. Think.

JULIA. [*Thinks*] No, ma'am.

MISTRESS. You weren't thinking. Your eyes were wandering. Look straight at my face and look hard . . . Do you remember now?

JULIA. [*Softly*] Yes, ma'am.

MISTRESS. I didn't hear you, Julia.

JULIA. [*Louder*] Yes, ma'am.

MISTRESS. Good. I was sure you'd remember . . . Plus three holidays. Correct?

JULIA. Two, ma'am. Christmas and New Year's.

MISTRESS. And your birthday. That's three.

JULIA. I worked on my birthday, ma'am.

MISTRESS. You did? There was no need to. My governesses never worked on their birthdays . . .

JULIA. But I did work, ma'am.

MISTRESS. But that's not the question, Julia. We're discussing financial matters now. I will, however, only count two holidays if you insist . . . Do you insist?

JULIA. I did work, ma'am.

MISTRESS. Then you *do* insist.

JULIA. No, ma'am.

MISTRESS. Very well. That's three holidays, therefore we take off twelve rubles. Now then, four days little Kolya was sick, and there were no lessons.

JULIA. But I gave lessons to Vanya.

MISTRESS. True. But I engaged you to teach two children, not one. Shall I pay you in full for doing only half the work?

JULIA. No, ma'am.

MISTRESS. So we'll deduct it . . . Now, three days you had a toothache and my husband gave you permission not to work after lunch. Correct?

JULIA. After four. I worked until four.

MISTRESS. [*Looks in the book*] I have here: "Did not work after lunch." We have lunch at one and are finished at two, not at four, correct?

JULIA. Yes, ma'am. But I—

MISTRESS. That's another seven rubles . . . Seven and twelve is nineteen . . . Subtract . . . that leaves . . . forty-one rubles . . . Correct?

JULIA. Yes, ma'am. Thank you, ma'am.

MISTRESS. Now then, on January fourth you broke a teacup and saucer, is that true?

◆ **Literary Focus**
What might be the Mistress's motive for deducting the money from Julia's salary?

◆ **Build Vocabulary**
discharged (dis chärjd´) *v.*: Relieved or released from something; fired

JULIA. Just the saucer, ma'am.

MISTRESS. What good is a teacup without a saucer, eh? . . . That's two rubles. The saucer was an heirloom. It cost much more, but let it go. I'm used to taking losses.

JULIA. Thank you, ma'am.

MISTRESS. Now then, January ninth, Kolya climbed a tree and tore his jacket.

JULIA. I forbid him to do so, ma'am.

MISTRESS. But he didn't listen, did he? . . . Ten rubles . . . January fourteenth, Vanya's shoes were stolen . . .

JULIA. But the maid, ma'am. You discharged her yourself.

MISTRESS. But you get paid good money to watch everything. I explained that in our first meeting. Perhaps you weren't listening. Were you listening that day, Julia, or was your head in the clouds?

JULIA. Yes, ma'am.

MISTRESS. Yes, your head was in the clouds?

JULIA. No, ma'am. I was listening.

MISTRESS. Good girl. So that means another five rubles off [*Looks in the book*] . . . Ah, yes . . . The sixteenth of January I gave you ten rubles.

JULIA. You didn't.

MISTRESS. But I made a note of it. Why would I make a note of it if I didn't give it to you?

JULIA. I don't know, ma'am.

MISTRESS. That's not a satisfactory answer, Julia . . . Why would I make a note of giving you ten rubles if I did not in fact give it to you, eh? . . . No answer? . . . Then I must have given it to you, mustn't I?

JULIA. Yes, ma'am. If you say so, ma'am.

MISTRESS. Well, certainly I say so. That's the point of this little talk. To clear these matters up. Take twenty-seven from forty-one, that leaves . . . fourteen, correct?

Woman Standing at Highboy, John Collier, Courtesy of the artist

▲ **Critical Viewing** The subject of this painting has her back turned to the viewer. In what way is the effect created suited for depicting "the governess"? **[Interpret]**

JULIA. Yes, ma'am. [*She turns away, softly crying*]

MISTRESS. What's this? Tears? Are you crying? Has something made you unhappy, Julia? Please tell me. It pains me to see you like this. I'm so sensitive to tears. What is it?

JULIA. Only once since I've been here have I ever been given any money and that was by your husband. On my birthday he gave me three rubles.

MISTRESS. Really? There's no note of it in my book. I'll put it down now. [*She writes in the book.*] Three rubles. Thank you for telling me. Sometimes I'm a little lax with my accounts . . . Always short-changing myself. So then, we take three more from fourteen . . . leaves eleven . . . Do you wish to check my figures?

JULIA. There's no need to, ma'am.

MISTRESS. Then we're all settled. Here's your salary for two months, dear. Eleven rubles. [*She puts the pile of coins on the desk.*] Count it.

JULIA. It's not necessary, ma'am.

MISTRESS. Come, come. Let's keep the records straight. Count it.

JULIA. [*Reluctantly counts it*] One, two, three, four, five, six, seven, eight, nine, ten . . . ? There's only ten, ma'am.

MISTRESS. Are you sure? Possibly you dropped one . . . Look on the floor, see if there's a coin there.

JULIA. I didn't drop any, ma'am. I'm quite sure.

MISTRESS. Well, it's not here on my desk, and I *know* I gave you eleven rubles. Look on the floor.

JULIA. It's all right, ma'am. Ten rubles will be fine.

MISTRESS. Well, keep the ten for now. And if we don't find it on the floor later, we'll discuss it again next month.

JULIA. Yes, ma'am. Thank you, ma'am. You're very kind, ma'am.

[*She curtsies and then starts to leave.*]

   MISTRESS. Julia!

[JULIA *stops, turns.*]

   Come back here.

[*She goes back to the desk and curtsies again.*]

   Why did you thank me?

JULIA. For the money, ma'am.

MISTRESS. For the money? . . . But don't you realize what I've done? I've cheated you . . . *Robbed* you! I have no such notes in my book. I made up whatever came into my mind. Instead of the eighty rubles which I owe you, I gave you only ten. I have actually stolen from you and you still thank me . . . Why?

JULIA. In the other places that I've worked, they didn't give me anything at all.

MISTRESS. Then they cheated you even worse than I did . . . I was playing a little joke on you. A cruel lesson just to teach you. You're much too trusting, and in this world that's very dangerous . . . I'm going to give you the entire eighty rubles. [*Hands her an envelope*] It's all ready for you. The rest is in this envelope. Here, take it.

JULIA. As you wish, ma'am. [*She curtsies and starts to go again.*]

MISTRESS. Julia!

[JULIA *stops.*]

Is it possible to be so spineless? Why don't you protest? Why don't you speak up? Why don't you cry out against this cruel and unjust treatment? Is it really possible to be so <u>guileless</u>, so innocent, such a—pardon me for being so blunt—such a simpleton?

JULIA. [*The faintest trace of a smile on her lips*] Yes, ma'am . . . it's possible.

[*She curtsies again and runs off. The* MISTRESS *looks after her a moment, a look of complete <u>bafflement</u> on her face. The lights fade.*]

◆ **Literature and Your Life**
Have you ever met someone who didn't stand up for himself or herself? Explain.

Guide for Responding

◆ LITERATURE AND YOUR LIFE

Reader's Response What did you think of the Mistress's behavior?

Thematic Focus How do people use questions to get the answers they want to hear?

Letter of Advice Write a letter to the governess in which you give her advice on how to stand up for herself.

☑ Check Your Comprehension

1. How are Julia and the Mistress related?
2. What happens to Julia's salary during the meeting?
3. How does Julia respond to the Mistress's actions?

◆ Critical Thinking

INTERPRET

1. How are the Mistress and Julia different? **[Compare and Contrast]**
2. In what way does the Mistress try to provoke a reaction from Julia? **[Infer]**
3. Do you think the Mistress is satisfied with her trick? **[Speculate]**
4. How does Neil Simon create humor in this situation? **[Analyze]**

APPLY

5. How can people learn to stand up for their rights? **[Apply]**

COMPARE LITERARY WORKS

6. Which version of this story do you think is more successful? Why? **[Assess]**

Guide for Responding (continued)

◆ Reading Strategy

QUESTION CHARACTERS' ACTIONS

Questioning characters' actions while reading can lead you to understand story events and characters' motives.

1. How does the narrator of "The Ninny" react when the governess says, "*merci*"?
2. Why might the narrator of "The Ninny" have chosen to act so unreasonably toward the governess?
3. In "The Governess," what does Julia's body language—her posture and movements—tell you about her character?

◆ Build Vocabulary

USING THE SUFFIX *-ment*

The suffix *-ment* can be added to verbs such as *entertain* to form nouns such as *entertainment*. On your paper, fill in the blank in the second sentence by adding *-ment* to a word from the first.

1. The mistress judged Julia. She passed _____?_____.
2. Julia is not encouraged. She needs _____?_____.

SPELLING STRATEGY

If a noun ends in a consonant and *y*, form the plural by changing the *y* to *i* and adding *-es*:

discrepancy → discrepancies

If a noun ends in a vowel and *y*, form the plural by adding *-s*.

buoy → buoys   Saturday → Saturdays

On your paper, write the plural of each noun.

1. opportunity   3. monkey
2. alloy   4. mercy

USING THE WORD BANK

In your notebook, match each Word Bank word with the word opposite in meaning.

1. bitter   a. boldly
2. discrepancies   b. similarities
3. timidly   c. happy
4. bafflement   d. hired
5. discharged   e. superior
6. guileless   f. understanding
7. inferior   g. sly

◆ Literary Focus

CHARACTERS' MOTIVES

You can understand **characters' motives**—the reasons for their actions—by reviewing what the characters say and do. In both versions of this story, the employer tricks the governess.

1. Who do you think is trickier, the narrator in "The Ninny" or the Mistress in "The Governess"? Why?
2. What motive does the governess give for saying "*merci*" in "The Ninny"?
3. What is the governess's motive for smiling at the end of each story?

◆ Build Grammar Skills

PRINCIPAL PARTS OF REGULAR VERBS

Every verb has four **principal parts**. A **regular verb** forms its past and past participle by adding *-d* or *-ed* to the base form. The following chart explains the principal parts of regular verbs.

Principal Part	Description	Examples
Base Form:	basic form	listen, care
Past:	adds *-ed* or *-d*	listened, cared
Present Participle:	adds *-ing*	listening, caring
Past Participle:	adds *-ed* or *-d*	listened, cared

Some spellings change when forming principal parts. You may need to drop the final *e* when adding *-ing*: *dare, dared, daring, dared*. Sometimes you need to double the final consonant when you add *-ed* or *-ing*: *wrap, wrapped, wrapping, wrapped*.

Practice On your paper, write the principal parts of each verb.

1. look 2. invite 3. subtract 4. trap 5. compel

Writing Application On your paper, write sentences about the story, using each verb in the principal part indicated. You will need a helping verb with present and past participles.

1. (*stare*; past)
2. (*listen*; base)
3. (*long*; present participle)
4. (*end*; past participle)

Build Your Portfolio

 ## Idea Bank

Writing

1. **Advertisement** Write an advertisement seeking a governess. Identify the job duties and list the qualities that a good governess should have.

2. **Letter of Resignation** Imagine that you are a governess who has decided to leave your current employer. Write a letter explaining why you are leaving.

3. **Interior Monologue** An interior monologue is a speech in which a character reveals his or her thoughts. Imagine what the governess is thinking during the scene you've just read, and write an interior monologue. **[Performing Arts Link]**

Speaking and Listening

4. **Dramatization** Work with a partner to perform "The Governess." First, rehearse to develop effective readings of each line. Then, present a script-in-hand performance for your class. **[Performing Arts Link]**

5. **Job Interview** Role-play the part of the narrator in "The Ninny" and interview several classmates for the job of governess. Then, explain which governess you would hire and why. **[Career Link]**

Projects

6. **Production Plan [Group Activity]** Working with a group of classmates, create a complete production plan for a stage version of "The Governess." Include casting suggestions, set designs, rehearsal schedule, as well as a poster and publicity materials. Each group member should be responsible for preparing one aspect of the production plan. **[Performing Arts Link]**

7. **Opinion Poll** Design and conduct a survey about work attitudes in your community. Ask questions, such as when, if ever, is it appropriate to speak up to your boss. Summarize your findings, and share the results with the class.

 ## Writing Mini-Lesson

Comparison of Stories

Neil Simon adapted Chekhov's short story "The Ninny" for the stage. He made several changes to the original story. Think about the alterations he made, and consider why he made each of them. Then, write an essay in which you compare and contrast the two versions of this story.

Writing Skills Focus: Organization

Organize your comparison-and-contrast essay clearly and effectively. For example, you might present all of the similarities in one section and describe all of the differences in another section. Another strategy is to focus each paragraph on one aspect of your subject, pointing out both similarities and differences.

Prewriting Gather details about each version of the story. Use a Venn diagram like the one below to record similarities and differences.

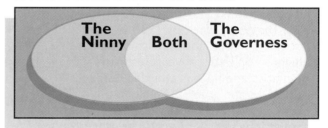

Drafting Follow your organizational plan. While drafting, refer to information you recorded in your Venn diagram. Use transitions, such as *in contrast, both, neither,* and *although,* to help readers follow your ideas.

Revising Give your paper to a writing partner to review. Ask for feedback on the clarity of your organization. Correct any errors in grammar and spelling.

> ◆ **Grammar Application**
> Make sure that you have formed principal parts of regular verbs correctly.

Guide for Reading

Meet the Author:

Langston Hughes (1902–1967)

Famed writer Langston Hughes was born in Joplin, Missouri. As a boy, his favorite destination was the library. He began writing poetry as a way of coping with an ever-changing home address and the difficulties of being a young African American in the early 1900's. His grandmother's stories about slavery and freedom, in which "always life moved, moved heroically toward an end," encouraged his love of words and understanding of African American history.

Literary Success Hughes attended Columbia University for a year. In 1926, he published his first collection of poetry, *The Weary Blues*. By 1930, he had become an internationally famous poet. Hughes was also a novelist, essayist, and dramatist, and he was awarded numerous prizes and grants. "Thank You, M'am" is one of Hughes's many stories about city life for African Americans.

THE STORY BEHIND THE STORY

Hughes felt it was important to write about the African American experience. In "Thank You, M'am," he writes about the dignity of the common people against the backdrop of Harlem. The characters in the story speak in urban dialect, using everyday speech and expressions.

◆ LITERATURE AND YOUR LIFE

CONNECT YOUR EXPERIENCE

Have you ever been surprised by someone's act of kindness and trust? Perhaps it came at a particularly significant point in your life and made a profound difference in the way you viewed the world. In "Thank You, M'am," a young boy is taught a lesson in kindness and trust by a woman he meant to rob.

THEMATIC FOCUS: Facing Hard Questions

As you read this story, think about the hard questions both the young boy and the woman must face.

◆ Background for Understanding

CULTURE

"Thank You, M'am" is set in Harlem, a community in New York City that became the center of African American intellectual and artistic life in the 1920's. As more and more people moved to Harlem, many single-family buildings were converted into small apartments to create more housing. The character Mrs. Jones lives in a "bedsit," or "kitchenette," which is even smaller than an apartment. It usually had just one room for both sleeping and living, plus a bath.

◆ Build Vocabulary

SUFFIXES: -able

The suffix *-able* means "capable of" or "like." When combined with the verb *present,* it forms a word meaning "good enough to be present in company."

WORD BANK

Which word on the list means the opposite of *trusted*? Check the Build Vocabulary box on page 189 to see if you chose correctly.

presentable
mistrusted
latching
barren
barely

◆ Thank You, M'am ◆

Empire State, Tom Christopher, Vicki Morgan Associates

◆ Literary Focus

THEME

The **theme** of a literary work is the underlying message or insight about life that it communicates. Although a theme may be stated directly in the text, it is more often presented indirectly. You can determine a story's theme by noticing details about the characters, the story's events and setting, and asking, "What aspect of life does the author want me to think about?"

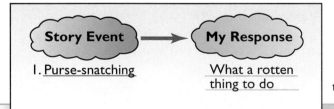

Story Event	→	My Response
1. Purse-snatching		What a rotten thing to do

◆ Reading Strategy

RESPOND TO CHARACTERS' ACTIONS

Reading stories is much more rewarding when you get involved. One way to do this is to **respond to the characters' actions** as you read. You may start rooting for one character or wishing another one would stop behaving in a certain way. You can ask questions like these to help you respond to a character's actions.

- Why does the character take this action?
- If I put myself in the character's shoes, what actions might I take?
- Does the character do or say anything that I can apply to my own life?

As you read, fill out a chart like the one to the left.

Thank You, M'am

LANGSTON HUGHES

She was a large woman with a large purse that had everything in it but hammer and nails. It had a long strap and she carried it slung across her shoulder. It was about eleven o'clock at night, and she was walking alone, when a boy ran up behind her and tried to snatch her purse. The strap broke with the single tug the boy gave it from behind. But the boy's weight, and the weight of the purse combined caused him to lose his balance. Instead of taking off full blast as he had hoped, the boy fell on his back on the sidewalk, and his legs flew up. The large woman simply turned around and kicked him right square in his blue-jeaned sitter. Then she reached down, picked the boy up by his shirt front, and shook him until his teeth rattled.

After that the woman said, "Pick up my pocketbook, boy, and give it here."

> ◆ **Reading Strategy**
> What is your response to the woman's actions?

She still held him. But she bent down enough to permit him to stoop and pick up her purse. Then she said, "Now ain't you ashamed of yourself?"

Firmly gripped by his shirt front, the boy said, "Yes'm."

The woman said, "What did you want to do it for?"

The boy said, "I didn't aim to."

She said, "You a lie!"

By that time two or three people passed, stopped, turned to look, and some stood watching.

"If I turn you loose, will you run?" asked the woman.

"Yes'm," said the boy.

"Then I won't turn you loose," said the woman. She did not release him.

"Lady, I'm sorry," whispered the boy.

"Um-hum! Your face is dirty. I got a great mind to wash your face for you. Ain't you got nobody home to tell you to wash your face?"

"No'm," said the boy.

"Then it will get washed this evening," said the large woman starting up the street, dragging the frightened boy behind her.

He looked as if he were fourteen or fifteen, frail and willow-wild, in tennis shoes and blue jeans.

The woman said, "You ought to be my son. I would teach you right from wrong. Least I can do right now is to wash your face. Are you hungry?"

"No'm," said the being-dragged boy. "I just want you to turn me loose."

"Was I bothering *you* when I turned that corner?" asked the woman.

"No'm."

"But you put yourself in contact with *me*," said the woman. "If you think that that contact is not going to last awhile, you got another thought coming. When I get through with you, sir, you are going to remember Mrs. Luella Bates Washington Jones."

Sweat popped out on the boy's face and he began to struggle. Mrs. Jones stopped, jerked him around in front of her, put a half nelson[1] about his neck, and continued to drag him up the street. When she got to her door, she dragged the boy inside, down a hall, and into a large kitchenette-furnished room at the rear of the house. She switched on the light and left the door open. The boy could hear other roomers laughing and talking in the large house. Some of their doors were open, too, so he knew he and the woman were not alone. The woman still had him by the neck in the middle of her room.

She said, "What is your name?"

▼ **Critical Viewing** Does the woman in the painting resemble Mrs. Jones as described in the story? Explain. **[Make a Judgment]**

Minnie, 1930, William Johnson, National Museum of American Art, Washington, DC

---

1. **half nelson:** Wrestling hold using one arm.

"Roger," answered the boy.

"Then, Roger, you go to that sink and wash your face," said the woman, whereupon she turned him loose—at last. Roger looked at the door—looked at the woman—looked at the door—*and went to the sink.*

"Let the water run until it gets warm," she said. "Here's a clean towel."

"You gonna take me to jail?" asked the boy, bending over the sink.

"Not with that face, I would not take you nowhere," said the woman. "Here I am trying to get home to cook me a bite to eat and you snatch my pocketbook! Maybe you ain't been to your supper either, late as it be. Have you?"

"There's nobody home at my house," said the boy.

"Then we'll eat," said the woman. "I believe you're hungry—or been hungry—to try to snatch my pocketbook."

"I wanted a pair of blue suede shoes," said the boy.

"Well, you didn't have to snatch *my* pocketbook to get some suede shoes," said Mrs. Luella Bates Washington Jones. "You could of asked me."

"M'am?"

The water dripping from his face, the boy looked at her. There was a long pause. A very long pause. After he had dried his face and not knowing what else to do dried it again, the boy turned around, wondering what next. The door was open. He could make a dash for it down the hall. He could run, run, run, run, *run!*

The woman was sitting on the day bed. After awhile she said, "I were young once and I wanted things I could not get."

There was another long pause. The boy's mouth opened. Then he frowned, but not knowing he frowned.

The woman said, "Um-hum! You thought I was going to say *but,* didn't you? You thought I was going to say, *but I didn't snatch people's pocketbooks.* Well, I wasn't going to say that." Pause. Silence. "I have done things, too, which I would not tell you, son—neither tell God, if He didn't already know. So you set down while I fix us something to eat. You might run that comb through your hair so you will look presentable."

In another corner of the room behind a screen was a gas plate and an icebox. Mrs. Jones got up and went behind the screen. The woman did not watch the boy to see if he was going to run now, nor did she watch her purse which she left behind her on the day bed. But the boy took care to sit on the far side of the room where he thought she could easily see him out of the corner of her eye, if she wanted to. He did not trust the woman *not* to trust him. And he did not want to be mistrusted now.

"Do you need somebody to go to the store," asked the boy, "maybe to get some milk or something?"

"Don't believe I do," said the woman, "unless you just want sweet milk yourself. I was going to make cocoa out of this canned milk I got here."

"That will be fine," said the boy.

She heated some lima beans and ham she had in the icebox, made the cocoa, and set the table. The woman did not ask the boy anything about where he lived, or his folks, or anything else that would embarrass him. Instead, as they ate, she told him about her job in a hotel beauty shop that stayed open late, what the work was like, and how all kinds of women came in and out, blondes, redheads, and brunettes. Then she cut him a half of her ten-cent cake.

"Eat some more, son," she said.

When they were finished eating she got up and said, "Now, here, take this ten dollars and buy yourself some blue suede shoes. And next time, do not make the mistake of latching onto *my* pocketbook *nor nobody else's*—because shoes come by devilish like that will burn your feet. I got to get my rest now. But from here on in, son, I hope you will behave yourself."

◆ Literary Focus
With what message does Mrs. Jones leave Roger? How does that contribute to the story's theme?

She led him down the hall to the front door and opened it. "Goodnight! Behave yourself, boy!" she said, looking out into the street.

The boy wanted to say something other than, "Thank you, m'am," to Mrs. Luella Bates Washington Jones, but although his lips moved, he couldn't even say that as he turned at the foot of the <u>barren</u> stoop and looked up at the large woman in the door. Then she shut the door.

◆ Build Vocabulary
presentable (prē zent´ ə bəl) *adj.*: In proper order for being seen, met, etc., by others
mistrusted (mis´ trust´ əd) *v.*: Doubted
latching (lach´ iŋ) *v.*: Grasping or attaching oneself to
barren (bar´ ən) *adj.*: Sterile; empty

Guide for Responding

◆ LITERATURE AND YOUR LIFE

Reader's Response Do you think Mrs. Jones is wise or foolish to trust Roger? Why?

Thematic Focus If you were Mrs. Jones, what is the hardest question you would have asked yourself about Roger? What is the main question Roger might have asked himself about his own actions?

☑ Check Your Comprehension

1. What does Mrs. Jones do when Roger tries to steal her purse?
2. What does she say she would teach Roger if he were her son?
3. What reason does Roger give for trying to steal her purse? How does Mrs. Jones respond to this reason?
4. Why does Mrs. Jones give Roger ten dollars?

◆ Critical Thinking

INTERPRET

1. Why doesn't Roger run away from Mrs. Jones's apartment at the first opportunity? **[Analyze]**
2. What does the following tell about Roger: "He did not trust the woman *not* to trust him. And he did not want to be mistrusted now." **[Infer]**
3. Why does Mrs. Jones trust Roger to sit alone with her purse? **[Deduce]**
4. At the end of the story, why does Roger want to say more than just "Thank you, m'am"? **[Interpret]**

EVALUATE

5. Do you think that Mrs. Jones did Roger a favor by not turning him over to the police? Explain. **[Make a Judgment]**

APPLY

6. Can you change someone's behavior through kindness and understanding? Explain. **[Generalize]**

Guide for Responding (continued)

◆ Reading Strategy

RESPOND TO CHARACTERS' ACTIONS

Responding to characters' actions involves you in a story and increases your appreciation of the story's characters, plot events, and theme.

1. What did you learn from a character in the story? Explain.
2. Describe your feelings about Mrs. Jones and Roger at the end of the story.

◆ Build Vocabulary

USING THE SUFFIX -able

The suffix -able can be added to some verbs, such as *present*, to form adjectives (descriptive words), like *presentable*. On your paper, complete these sentences sensibly by adding -able to one of the following words: *disagree, reason*

1. A _____?_____ encounter turned out well for both characters.
2. Roger's _____?_____ behavior once he was in the house surprised me.

SPELLING STRATEGY

The *miss* sound at the beginning of a word is spelled "mis." When adding *mis-* to a word, do not change the original spelling of the word:

mis- + spell = misspell

On your paper, add *mis-* to the following words.

1. speak   2. take   3. fortune   4. trust   5. step

USING THE WORD BANK

On your paper, rewrite the following sentences. Replace the italicized word or phrase with the appropriate word from the Word Bank.

1. The kitchenette was *empty* of furniture.
2. The boy *was suspicious* of kindness from adults.
3. After combing her hair and changing her shoes, she felt *she could go out in public*.
4. She felt someone *grasping* onto her arm to prevent her from stumbling.
5. There was so much clutter in the attic that there was *hardly* room to stand.

◆ Literary Focus

THEME

The **theme** of a story is its message about life or human nature. Often a character's actions and experiences will convey the story's theme.

1. How would you state the theme of "Thank You, M'am"? Is the theme stated directly or indirectly?
2. Which character expresses the theme? By what means?
3. Why is it possible that different readers may learn different lessons from the story?

◆ Build Grammar Skills

PRINCIPAL PARTS OF IRREGULAR VERBS

A verb's **principal parts** are the basic forms of a verb. An **irregular verb** forms its past and past participle in some other way than by adding -ed to the present or base form of the verb.

Below are listed some commonly used irregular verbs and their principal parts.

Present	Past	Past Participle
eat	ate	eaten
have	had	had
drink	drank	drunk
grow	grew	grown

Practice On your paper, replace each verb in parentheses with the correct form of the verb. Use the past participle after a helping verb.

1. By the time he awoke, the sun had (rise).
2. He (buy) a pair of blue suede shoes.
3. Mrs. Jones (speak) calmly but with authority.
4. She had (choose) to ignore his excuses.
5. He (steal) the purse to buy some shoes.

Writing Application Write a paragraph about the story using various principal parts of these irregular verbs: *see, hear, write, choose.*

Build Your Portfolio

 ## Idea Bank

Writing

1. **Letter** Write a letter from Mrs. Jones to an advice columnist, asking if she did the right thing in her treatment of Roger. Include specific questions in your letter.

2. **Sequel** Write a sequel to "Thank You, M'am," telling what happens when Roger and Mrs. Jones meet again.

3. **Speech** Imagine that Mrs. Jones has been invited to give a speech on the health and education of children at her local community center. Write a brief speech in which Mrs. Jones expresses her beliefs about how children should be treated.

Speaking and Listening

4. **Readers Theater [Group Activity]** With classmates, prepare and present a Readers Theatre version of "Thank You, M'am." Write a script and practice reading, putting emphasis on oral interpretation of the characters and their actions. **[Performing Arts Link]**

5. **Rap Song** Compose and perform a rap song that is inspired by your response to the story "Thank You, M'am." **[Music Link]**

Projects

6. **Multimedia Presentation [Group Activity]** Work with several classmates to create a multimedia presentation about Langston Hughes and his role in the Harlem Renaissance. Include photographs, music recordings, examples of art, and readings of poems and texts. Share your findings with the class.

7. **Painting or Drawing** Chose your favorite visual medium, and re-create a scene or a character from "Thank You, M'am." Give your finished work a title. Then, reveal to your class the feeling you tried to convey in your artwork. **[Art Link]**

 ## Writing Mini-Lesson

Letter of Guidance

Imagine that you are Roger twenty years after the story took place. Write a letter to a young relative who needs guidance and direction. In your letter, tell about your encounter with Mrs. Jones, sharing what you learned from it.

Writing Skills Focus: Give Necessary Background

In your letter, supply the **necessary background** about what happened to you in the past. For example, explain who you are, what you did, and how it affected you.

Model

When I was about your age, I tried to rob an older woman who taught me a valuable lesson about life.

Prewriting Begin by jotting down the advice you plan to give in the letter. Also, think about how Roger might have changed through the years and what he has made of his life.

Drafting Take on Roger's personality as you write the letter to your relative. Whenever necessary, give background information to support your points. Use the standard format for informal letters: Include a greeting, body, and closing.

Revising Review your letter, looking for places where you can add background information that will support your impression of Mrs. Jones or yourself as a young boy. Check your letter to be sure it's free of spelling, punctuation, and grammar errors.

◆ **Grammar Application**

Look at the irregular verbs you have used. Make sure that you have written the correct verb form and used the correct spelling.

Guide for Reading

Meet the Authors:

Adrienne Rich (1929–)

Born in Baltimore, Maryland, Adrienne Rich was educated at Radcliffe College. Her first volume of poetry, *A Change of World,* was published in 1951. Today, she is a widely published poet and essayist. She lives in California.

Emily Dickinson (1830–1886)

Known by her neighbors as the "moth of Amherst," Emily Dickinson dressed only in white after 1862. A recluse, she observed the life of Amherst, Massachusetts, her birthplace, from her upstairs bedroom window. After her death, nearly 1,800 of her poems, tied neatly in packets, were found in the house by her sister and later published.

Chief Seattle (1786?–1866)

Chief Seattle, whose ancestors came from several tribes in the Pacific Northwest, was born into Native American nobility. A warrior, Seattle led his last attack when he was almost sixty years old. He later became a diplomat and speaker.

Margaret Tsuda (1921–)

Margaret Tsuda, who obtained a degree in art history from the City University of New York, has written several essays on art. An admirer of Walt Whitman, Tsuda strives to find the "unusual in common, ordinary things" in her own poetry.

◆ Literature and Your Life

Connect Your Experience

Society has a great impact on our lives—from where and how we live to how we're regarded as individuals. In these selections, four writers voice their concerns about modern society. Two of the writers focus on maintaining individuality. The other two writers present heartfelt pleas about the importance of preserving nature's bounty in an increasingly developed world.

Thematic Focus: Facing Hard Questions

As you read these selections, think about what the speakers have to say about society and the individual.

◆ Background for Understanding

History

In 1854, when he met with the first governor of Washington Territory (now Washington State), Chief Seattle delivered the speech "This We Know." It has since become famous. Chief Seattle's purpose was to make a statement about Indian lands and traditions. The speech is now frequently quoted by environmentalists and Native American leaders.

◆ Build Vocabulary

Related Words: Forms of *evade*

The word *evade* means "to avoid something by cleverness or trickery." Knowing this, you can figure out the meaning of related words, like *evasion, evasive, evasively,* and *evasiveness.*

Word Bank

Review this list. Find a word embedded in *worthily* that suggests its meaning. Check the Build Vocabulary box on page 194 to see if you guessed correctly.

worthily
evade
discerning
prevail
assent
ancestors

Prospective Immigrants Please Note
◆ Much Madness is divinest Sense — ◆
This We Know ◆ Hard Questions

d, 1955, M.C. Escher, Cordon Art B.V.–Baarn-Holland

◆ Literary Focus
IMAGERY

Imagery refers to words and phrases that appeal to one or more of the five senses. The following line from "This We Know" includes images that appeal to the sense of sound.

> The water's murmur is the voice of my father's father.

Through vivid images, a writer draws you into a work of literature and enables you to see, hear, touch, taste, and smell what the characters are experiencing.

◆ Reading Strategy
USE YOUR SENSES

To appreciate the imagery in a poem, essay, or story, **use your senses** as you read. When a writer is describing the appearance of something, for example, see it in your mind. Then, close your eyes and imagine the smells, sounds, and other sensations that the writer describes. Draw from your own experiences to fill in details the writer may not have mentioned.

Keep track of the sensory images in these works by filling out a chart like the one below.

	Sight	Sound	Touch	Taste	Smell
Prospective Immigrants . . .					
Much Madness . . .					
This We Know					
Hard Questions					

PROSPECTIVE IMMIGRANTS PLEASE NOTE

Adrienne Rich

▲ **Critical Viewing** What might the people in the photograph be thinking about? How might they respond to Rich's words of caution? **[Speculate]**

Either you will
go through this door
or you will not go through.

5 If you go through
there is always the risk
of remembering your name.

Things look at you doubly[1]
and you must look back
and let them happen.

10 If you do not go through
it is possible
to live <u>worthily</u>

to maintain your attitudes
to hold your position
15 to die bravely

but much will blind you,
much will <u>evade</u> you,
at what cost who knows?

The door itself
20 makes no promises.
It is only a door.

---

1. doubly *adv.*: Twice; having more than one perspective.

Much Madness is divinest Sense —

Emily Dickinson

Much Madness is divinest Sense—
To a discerning Eye—
Much Sense—the starkest Madness—
'Tis[1] the Majority
5   In this, as All, prevail—
Assent—and you are sane—
Demur—you're straightway dangerous—
And handled with a Chain—

1. **'tis** (tiz): It is.

Guide for Responding

◆ LITERATURE AND YOUR LIFE

Reader's Response Dickinson defines madness as "divinest sense." How would you define it?

Journal Writing In your journal, jot down your thoughts on the importance of maintaining one's individuality.

☑ Check Your Comprehension

In "Much Madness is divinest Sense—," what does the poet say happens to those who don't go along with the majority?

◆ Critical Thinking

INTERPRET
1. What kind of behavior is considered insane, according to the speaker in "Much Madness . . ."? **[Analyze Causes and Effects]**

EVALUATE
2. Do you agree with the speaker's ideas in "Much Madness . . ."? Explain. **[Make a Judgment]**

Chief Seattle

This We Know

The President in Washington sends word that he wishes to buy our land. But how can you buy or sell the sky? The land? The idea is strange to us. If we do not own the freshness of the air and the sparkle of the water, how can you buy them?

Every part of this earth is sacred to my people. Every shining pine needle, every sandy shore, every mist in the dark woods, every meadow, every humming insect. All are holy in the memory and experience of my people.

◆ **Reading Strategy**
To what senses does the imagery in this paragraph appeal?

We know the sap which courses through the trees as we know the blood that courses through our veins. We are part of the earth and it is part of us. The perfumed flowers are our sisters. The bear, the deer, the great eagle, these are our brothers. The rocky crests, the juices in the meadow, the body heat of the pony, and man, all belong to the same family.

The shining water that moves in the streams and rivers is not just water, but the blood of our <u>ancestors</u>. If we sell you our land, you must remember that it is sacred. Each ghostly reflection in the clear water of the lakes tells of events and memories in the life of my people. The water's murmur is the voice of my father's father.

The rivers are our brothers. They quench our thirst. They carry our canoes and feed our children. So you must give to the rivers the kindness you would give any brother.

If we sell you our land, remember that the air is precious to us, that the air shares its spirit with all the life it supports. The wind that gave our grandfather his first breath also receives his last sigh. The wind also gives our children the spirit of life. So if we sell you our land, you must keep it apart and sacred, as a place where man can go to taste the wind that is sweetened by the meadow flowers.

Will you teach your children what we have

taught our children? That the earth is our mother? What befalls the earth, befalls all the sons of the earth.

This we know: The earth does not belong to man, man belongs to the earth. All things are connected like the blood which unites us all. Man did not weave the web of life, he is merely a strand in it. Whatever he does to the web, he does to himself.

One thing we know: Our god is also your god. The earth is precious to him and to harm the earth is to heap contempt on its creator.

Your destiny is a mystery to us. What will happen when the buffalo are all slaughtered? The wild horses tamed? What will happen when the secret corners of the forest are heavy with the scent of many men and the view of the ripe hills is blotted by talking wires? Where will the thicket be? Gone! Where will the eagle be? Gone! And what is it to say good-bye to the swift pony and the hunt? The end of living and the beginning of survival.

When the last Red Man has vanished with his wilderness and his memory is only the shadow of a cloud moving across the prairie, will these shores and forests still be here? Will there be any of the spirit of my people left?

We love this earth as a newborn loves its mother's heartbeat. So, if we sell you our land, love it as we have loved it. Care for it as we have cared for it. Hold in your mind the memory of the land as it is when you receive it. Preserve the land for all children and love it, as God loves us all.

As we are part of the land, you too are part of the land. This earth is precious to us. It is also precious to you. One thing we know: There is only one God. No man, be he Red Man or White Man, can be apart. We *are* brothers after all.

◆ Build Vocabulary

ancestors (an´ ses´ tərs) *n.*: People from whom one is descended

Beyond Literature

Social Studies Connection

History of Our National Parks

Artist and traveler George Catlin was one of the first people to envision a national park to protect America's wilderness. He hoped for "A nation's park, containing man and beast, in all the wild and freshness of their nature's beauty!" His dream became reality in 1872, when Congress created Yellowstone National Park.

In 1903, President Theodore Roosevelt established a Florida island as the first national wildlife refuge. The President asked his advisors, "Is there any law that will prevent me from declaring Pelican Island a Federal Bird Reservation?" When no law was discovered, he said, "Very well, then I so declare it." He also doubled the number of current national parks. The new additions included Mesa Verde, Colorado, and Crater Lake, Oregon.

In 1916, President Woodrow Wilson signed the Organic Act, which created the National Park Service. Today, the system of parks and refuges includes 376 areas covering a total of more than 83 million acres of protected land.

Cross-Curricular Activity

Parks Tour Use an atlas of the United States to plan a tour of at least three National Parks. Your itinerary should describe the parks you will visit, how you will explore them, and how long it will take to travel from one location to another. You may wish to work with a partner or team to plan a practical and efficient itinerary.

HARD
QUESTIONS

Margaret Tsuda

Why not mark out the land
into neat rectangles
squares and clover leafs?

5   Put on them cubes of
varying sizes
according to use—
dwellings
      singles/multiples
complexes
10   commercial/industrial.

Bale them together with
bands of roads.

What if a child shall cry
"I have never known spring!
15   I have never seen autumn!"

What if a man shall say
"I have never heard
silence fraught with living as
in swamp or forest!"
20   What if the eye shall never see
marsh birds and muskrats?

Does not the heart need
wildness?
Does not the thought need
25   something
to rest upon
not self-made by man,
a bosom
not his own?

◆ LITERATURE AND YOUR LIFE

Reader's Response Are the issues raised in Chief Seattle's speech still being raised today? Explain.

Thematic Focus In your opinion, who poses the harder questions—Chief Seattle or Margaret Tsuda? Explain.

☑ Check Your Comprehension

1. In "This We Know," what does Chief Seattle want the white settlers to do with the land?
2. What does Chief Seattle say is the relationship between people and the Earth?
3. In "Hard Questions," what is the poet's attitude about the development of wild land for human use?

◆ Critical Thinking

1. What does the speaker in "This We Know" think will happen to his people? **[Interpret]**
2. "This We Know" is generally regarded as a defense of Indian traditions and an argument in favor of environmentalism. Support this view with specific examples from the speech. **[Support]**
3. What does the speaker in "Hard Questions" mean when she asks "Does not the heart need wildness?" **[Interpret]**
4. How can lines 13–29 in "Hard Questions" be seen as the answers to the question in lines 1–3? **[Interpret]**

APPLY

5. What if the speaker in "Hard Questions" were to meet a city planner who was considering the development of a large tract of homes on a wild hillside? What advice do you think the speaker would give to the city planner? **[Hypothesize]**

COMPARE LITERARY WORKS

6. Find lines in "This We Know" that convey the same feelings and ideas as lines 13–29 in "Hard Questions." Explain your choice. **[Connect]**

Guide for Responding (continued)

◆ Reading Strategy

USE YOUR SENSES

To appreciate writer's imagery, **use your senses** as you read. Draw upon the details the writer provides, along with your own memories and associations, to picture in your mind what the writer is describing.

1. From "This We Know," list a word or phrase that appeals to each of the five senses.
2. Explain how personal experiences or things you've observed in the movies or on television helped you picture one or more of the images in Chief Seattle's speech.
3. Which poem appeals equally to the senses of sight and sound?

◆ Build Grammar Skills

VERB TENSES

The **tense** of a verb shows the time of action or the condition expressed by the verb. The three main verb tenses are present, past, and future. Here are the forms of the regular verb *own*. Other regular verbs use the same endings or helping words.

Present Tense: I own; you own; he, she, or it owns; we own; you own; they own

Past Tense: I owned; you owned; he, she, or it owned; we owned; you owned; they owned

Future Tense: I will own; you will own; he, she, or it will own; we will own; you will own; they will own

Practice Copy these sentences, writing the tense of the verb indicated in parentheses.

1. Now the sap (*course,* present) through the trees.
2. Tomorrow, what (*happen,* future) to the eagle?
3. Yesterday, the rivers (*quench,* past) our thirst.
4. Today, some people (*harm,* present) the Earth.
5. Next year, we still (*belong,* future) to the Earth.

Writing Application Write a paragraph about your high-school years. Use the future tense of the verbs *achieve, grow,* and *succeed.*

◆ Literary Focus

IMAGERY

Through **imagery,** writers paint vivid word pictures, making their writing interesting and memorable. In "This We Know," for example, Chief Seattle's imagery brings the beauty of nature to life for the reader.

1. (a) In "This We Know," find an example of imagery that indicates that the air itself is sacred. (b) Find an example of imagery that emphasizes the importance of natural bodies of water.
2. Explain how the individual images in "Hard Questions" combine to create one dominant image.

◆ Build Vocabulary

USING FORMS OF *evade*

Copy these sentences on your paper, filling in the blank with a form of *evade,* which means "to avoid."
evasion   evasive   evasiveness

1. His ____?____ maneuvers helped him escape.
2. Modern technology makes ____?____ difficult.
3. Her ____?____ makes her seem mysterious.

SPELLING STRATEGY

Ancestors has an *-or* suffix, which indicates that the word refers to a person who is or does something. Add *-or* to these verbs to create nouns that refer to persons or things that perform the action of the verb.

- If the root ends in a silent e, drop it before adding *-or:* imitate + *-or* = imitator
- If the root ends in a consonant, simply add *-or:* act + *-or* = actor

On your paper, add *-or* to these words.

1. operate   **2.** govern   **3.** invent   **4.** percolate

USING THE WORD BANK

On your paper, write the letter of the word or phrase closest in meaning to each Word Bank word.

1. discerning
2. prevail
3. assent
4. worthily
5. evade
6. ancestors

a. forebears
b. succeed
c. agree
d. well
e. showing good judgment
f. escape

Build Your Portfolio

 Idea Bank

Writing

1. **Journal Entry** Put yourself in the place of the speaker in "Much Madness is divinest Sense—." Write a journal entry in which you elaborate on what is "sanity" in the world and what is "madness."

2. **Public Service Announcement** Write the script for a public service announcement that will influence people to preserve the environment.

3. **Speech Analysis** News commentators frequently summarize and analyze the speeches of political figures and discuss their impact. Prepare a news commentary on Chief Seattle's speech "This We Know" for a television audience. **[Media Link]**

Speaking and Listening

4. **Committee Discussion [Group Activity]** As a group, take on the role of a committee that approves or disapproves of the land development projects described in "Hard Questions." Stage a working discussion on the subject.

5. **Dramatization** With a partner, act out a scene that might take place between two relatives or close friends, one of whom wants to make a big change in his or her life, whereas the other does not. **[Performing Arts Link]**

Projects

6. **Timeline** Create a timeline of the life of Chief Seattle. On the timeline, note his accomplishments. You may also want to display portraits of him at various stages of the timeline and show on a map where he lived. **[Media Link]**

7. **Sculpture** Design and create a clay or papier-mâché sculpture to represent any image or idea from "Much Madness is divinest Sense—," "This We Know," or "Hard Questions." **[Art Link]**

 Writing Mini-Lesson

Persuasive Appeal

The writers in this section all make persuasive appeals on issues about which they feel strongly. Choose a topic you have strong opinions about, and write a persuasive appeal. Your appeal should be in prose.

Writing Skills Focus: Clear Purpose

Always have a **clear purpose** in mind as you write. Because you will be writing a persuasive appeal, your purpose will be to persuade someone to agree with your thinking. To do so, give several examples that support your ideas. In the following passage, Chief Seattle gives an example to support his purpose:

Model From "This We Know"
What befalls the earth, befalls all the sons of the earth.

Prewriting Decide on an issue or problem that you feel needs to be addressed. Jot down reasons why you think as you do.

Drafting Begin your appeal with a dramatic statement that calls attention to the issue or problem about which you're writing. Then, develop and support your ideas with facts that inform or alert the reader about the situation.

Revising Reread to be sure your purpose is clear. Also, check to make sure you've clearly and effectively given examples that support the points you're making. Proofread carefully to correct errors in spelling, punctuation, and grammar.

> ◆ **Grammar Application**
> Reread your written advice to be sure that you have used appropriate verb tenses.

Guide for Reading

Meet the Author:

Daniel Keyes (1927–)

Daniel Keyes was raised in Brooklyn, New York. He has been a photographer, merchant seaman, and editor. His many works of fiction include the novels *The Touch* (1968) and *The Fifth Sally* (1980). Keyes has also written several nonfiction books, including *The Minds of Billy Milligan,* an in-depth portrait of a man with multiple-personality disorder. A sequel, *The Milligan Wars,* continues the harrowing account.

An Award-Winning Story "Flowers for Algernon," Keyes's best-known story, won the Hugo Award of the Science Fiction Writers of America in 1959. Inspired by its success, Keyes later expanded the story into a novel. Actor Cliff Robertson won an Academy Award for his portrayal of the title character in the film adaptation, *Charly.* The story was also adapted as a Broadway musical, *Charlie and Algernon.*

THE STORY BEHIND THE STORY

The idea for "Flowers for Algernon" came to Keyes after he met a mentally disadvantaged young man. Keyes began to wonder what would happen "if it were possible to increase human intelligence artificially." He points out that "Charlie Gordon (the main character in the story) is not real, nor is he based on a real person: he is imagined or invented, probably a composite of many people I know—including a little bit of me."

◆ LITERATURE AND YOUR LIFE

CONNECT YOUR EXPERIENCE

At some point or another in your life, you may have unfairly judged someone because he or she was different from you. In "Flowers for Algernon," the main character is unfairly judged and taunted by those around him. He decides to subject himself to scientific experimentation in an effort to become "like everyone else."

THEMATIC FOCUS: Facing Hard Questions

Shown at right is an EEG, a brain scan, that helps doctors understand how the brain works. How far should science go in "fixing" human capabilities and intelligence?

◆ Background for Understanding

SCIENCE

The story focuses on an experiment aimed at increasing a character's intelligence level. The most common measure of intelligence is the IQ (intelligence quotient). A person's IQ is determined by a test first developed at the turn of the twentieth century. An IQ of 100 is considered average. Recently, people have come to recognize that one test cannot accurately measure intelligence, and that people may have different types of ability.

◆ Build Vocabulary

WORD ROOTS: -psych-

The word root -psych- comes from the Greek word meaning "soul." In English word combinations, -psych- usually refers to the mind. For example, *psychology* is "the science of the mind."

WORD BANK

Which two words on the list contain the same root? What might the root mean? Check the Build Vocabulary boxes on pages 216 and 220 to see if you chose correctly.

psychology
tangible
specter
refute
illiteracy
obscure
syndromes
introspective

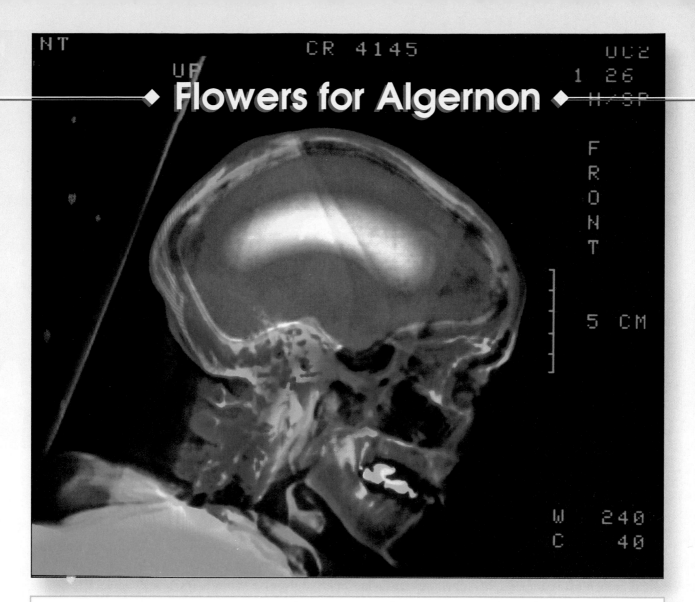

◆ Flowers for Algernon ◆

◆ Literary Focus

FIRST-PERSON POINT OF VIEW

Point of view refers to the vantage point from which a story is told. A story with a **first-person point of view** is told from the perspective of one of the characters, who uses the first-person pronoun "I." In "Flowers for Algernon," you'll learn about a fascinating scientific experiment through the eyes of the experiment's subject, Charlie Gordon. What he can tell you is limited to the things that he sees, feels, and thinks. For example, you will learn about other characters through Charlie's eyes.

◆ Reading Strategy

SUMMARIZE

When you **summarize,** you state in your own words the key ideas and details of a piece of writing. Summarizing sections of a story as you read will help you clarify and remember story events. As you read Charlie's progress reports in "Flowers for Algernon," summarize each report or each set of reports. Use a chart like the one below to keep track of your summaries.

Section of Story	Summary
Progress Report I	Says he wants to be smart. He gives his name and age.

Flowers for ALGERNON

Daniel Keyes

progris riport 1—martch 5 1965

Dr. Strauss says I shud rite down what I think and evrey thing that happins to me from now on. I dont know why but he says its importint so they will see if they will use me. I hope they use me. Miss Kinnian says maybe they can make me smart. I want to be smart. My name is Charlie Gordon. I am 37 years old and 2 weeks ago was my brithday. I have nuthing more to rite now so I will close for today.

♦ **Literary Focus**
How can you tell this story is told from a first-person point of view?

progris riport 2—martch 6

I had a test today. I think I faled it. and I think that maybe now they wont use me. What happind is a nice young man was in the room and he had some white cards with ink spillled all over them. He sed Charlie what do you see on this card. I was very skared even tho I had my rabits foot in my pockit because when I was a kid I always faled tests in school and I spilled ink to.

I told him I saw a inkblot. He said yes and it made me feel good. I thot that was all but when I got up to go he stopped me. He said now sit down Charlie we are not thru yet. Then I dont remember so good but he wantid me to say what was in the ink. I dint see nuthing in the ink but he said there was picturs there other pepul saw some picturs. I coudnt see any picturs. I reely tryed to see. I held the card close up and then far away. Then I said if I had my glases I coud see better I usally only ware my glases in the movies or TV but I said they are in the closit in the hall. I got them. Then I said let me see that card agen I bet Ill find it now.

I tryed hard but I still coudnt find the picturs I only saw the ink. I told him maybe I need new glases. He rote somthing down on a paper and I got skared of faling the test. I told him it was a very nice inkblot with littel points all around the eges. He looked very sad so that wasnt it. I said please let me try agen. Ill get it in a few minits becaus Im not so fast

Edited for this edition.

◀ **Critical Viewing** What impression of Charlie Gordon do you get from this scene from the movie? [Infer]

somtimes. Im a slow reeder too in Miss Kinnians class for slow adults but I'm trying very hard.

He gave me a chance with another card that had 2 kinds of ink spilled on it red and blue.

He was very nice and talked slow like Miss Kinnian does and he explained it to me that it was a *raw shok*.[1] He said pepul see things in the ink. I said show me where. He said think. I told him I think a inkblot but that wasnt rite eather. He said what does it remind you—pretend somthing. I closd my eyes for a long time to pretend. I told him I pretned a fowntan pen with ink leeking all over a table cloth. Then he got up and went out.

I dont think I passd the *raw shok* test.

progris report 3—martch 7

Dr Strauss and Dr Nemur say it dont matter about the inkblots. I told them I dint spill the ink on the cards and I coudnt see anything in the ink. They said that maybe they will still use me. I said Miss Kinnian never gave me tests like that one only spelling and reading. They said Miss Kinnian told that I was her bestist pupil in the adult nite scool becaus I tryed the hardist and I reely wantid to lern. They said how come you went to the adult nite scool all by yourself Charlie. How did you find it. I said I askd pepul and sumbody told me where I shud go to lern to read and spell good. They said why did you want to. I told them becaus all my life I wantid to be smart and not dumb. But its very hard to be smart. They said you know it will probly be tempirery. I said yes. Miss Kinnian told me. I dont care if it herts.

Later I had more crazy tests today. The nice lady who gave it me told me the name and I

---

1. raw shok: Misspelling of Rorschach (rôr´ shäk) test, a psychological test involving inkblots that the subject describes.

asked her how do you spellit so I can rite it in my progris riport. THEMATIC APPERCEPTION TEST.[2] I dont know the frist 2 words but I know what *test* means. You got to pass it or you get bad marks. This test lookd easy becaus I coud see the picturs. Only this time she dint want me to tell her the picturs. That mixd me up. I said the man yesterday said I shoud tell him what I saw in the ink she said that dont make no difrence. She said make up storys about the pepul in the picturs.

I told her how can you tell storys about pepul you never met. I said why shud I make up lies. I never tell lies any more becaus I always get caut.

She told me this test and the other one the raw-shok was for getting personalty. I laffed so hard. I said how can you get that thing from inkblots and fotos. She got sore and put her picturs away. I dont care. It was sily. I gess I faled that test too.

Later some men in white coats took me to a difernt part of the hospitil and gave me a game to play. It was like a race with a white mouse. They called the mouse Algernon. Algernon was in a box with a lot of twists and turns like all kinds of walls and they gave me a pencil and a paper with lines and lots of boxes. On one side it said START and on the other end it said FINISH. They said it was *amazed*[3] and that Algernon and me had the same *amazed* to do. I dint see how we could have the same *amazed* if Algernon had a box and I had a paper but I dint say nothing. Anyway there wasnt time because the race started.

One of the men had a watch he was trying to hide so I woudnt see it so I tryed not to look and that made me nervus.

Anyway that test made me feel worser than all the others because they did it over 10 times with difernt *amazeds* and Algernon won every time. I dint know that mice were so smart. Maybe thats because Algernon is a white mouse. Maybe white mice are smarter than other mice.

progris riport 4—Mar 8

Their going to use me! Im so exited I can hardly write. Dr Nemur and Dr Strauss had a argament about it first. Dr Nemur was in the office when Dr Strauss brot me in. Dr Nemur was worryed about using me but Dr Strauss told him Miss Kinnian rekemmended me the best from all the pepul who she was teaching. I like Miss Kinnian becaus shes a very smart teacher. And she said Charlie your going to have a second chance. If you volenteer for this experament you mite get smart. They dont know if it will be perminint but theirs a chance. Thats why I said ok even when I was scared because she said it was an operashun. She said dont be scared Charlie you done so much with so little I think you deserv it most of all.

So I got scaird when Dr Nemur and Dr Strauss argud about it. Dr Strauss said I had something that was very good. He said I had a good *motor-vation*.[4] I never even knew I had that. I felt proud when he said that not every body with an *eye-q*[5] of 68 had that thing. I dont know what it is or where I got it but he said Algernon had it too. Algernons *motor-vation* is the cheese they put in his box. But it cant be that because I didnt eat any cheese this week.

Then he told Dr Nemur something I dint understand so while they were talking I

◆ **Reading Strategy**
How would you summarize this entry of Charlie's progress report?

---

2. **THEMATIC** (thē mat′ ik) **APPERCEPTION** (ap′ ər sep′ shən) **TEST:** Personality test in which the subject makes up stories about a series of pictures.
3. **amazed:** A maze, or confusing series of paths. Often, the intelligence of animals is assessed by how fast they go through a maze.

4. **motor-vation:** Motivation, or desire to work hard and achieve a goal.
5. **eye-q:** IQ, or intelligence quotient. A way of measuring human intelligence.

wrote down some of the words.

He said Dr Nemur I know Charlie is not what you had in mind as the first of your new brede of intelek** (coudnt get the word) superman. But most people of his low ment** are host** and uncoop** they are usualy dull apath** and hard to reach. He has a good natcher hes intristed and eager to please.

Dr Nemur said remember he will be the first human beeng ever to have his intelijence trippled by surgicle meens.

Dr Strauss said exakly. Look at how well hes lerned to read and write for his low mentel age its as grate an acheve** as you and I lerning einstines therey of **vity without help. That shows the intenss motorvation. Its comparat** a tremen** achev** I say we use Charlie.

I dint get all the words and they were talking to fast but it sounded like Dr Strauss was on my side and like the other one wasnt.

Then Dr Nemur nodded he said all right maybe your right. We will use Charlie. When he said that I got so exited I jumped up and shook his hand for being so good to me. I told him thank you doc you wont be sorry for giving me a second chance. And I mean it like I told him. After the operashun Im gonna try to be smart. Im gonna try awful hard.

progris ript 5—Mar 10

Im skared. Lots of people who work here and the nurses and the people who gave me the tests came to bring me candy and wish me luck. I hope I have luck. I got my rabits foot and my lucky penny and my horse shoe. Only a black cat crossed me when I was comming

to the hospitil. Dr Strauss says dont be supersitis Charlie this is sience. Anyway Im keeping my rabits foot with me.

I asked Dr Strauss if Ill beat Algernon in the race after the operashun and he said maybe. If the operashun works Ill show that mouse I can be as smart as he is. Maybe smarter. Then Ill be abel to read better and spell the words

▲ **Critical Viewing** In what ways are Charlie and Algernon alike? [**Compare and Contrast**]

good and know lots of things and be like other people. I want to be smart like other people. If it works perminint they will make everybody smart all over the wurld.

They dint give me anything to eat this morning. I dont know what that eating has to do with getting smart. Im very hungry and Dr Nemur took away my box of candy. That Dr Nemur is a grouch. Dr Strauss says I can have it back after the operashun. You cant eat befor a operashun . . .

Progress Report 6—Mar 15

The operashun dint hurt. He did it while I was sleeping. They took off the bandijis from my eyes and my head today so I can make a PROGRESS REPORT. Dr Nemur who looked at some of my other ones says I spell PROGRESS wrong and he told me how to spell it and REPORT too. I got to try and remember that.

I have a very bad memary for spelling. Dr Strauss says its ok to tell about all the things that happin to me but he says I shoud tell more about what I feel and what I think. When I told him I dont know how to think he said try. All the time when the bandijis were on my eyes I tried to think. Nothing happened. I dont know what to think about. Maybe if I ask him he will tell me how I can think now that Im suppose to get smart. What do smart people think about. Fancy things I suppose. I wish I knew some fancy things alredy.

Progress Report 7—Mar 19

Nothing is happining. I had lots of tests and different kinds of races with Algernon. I hate that mouse. He always beats me. Dr Strauss said I got to play those games. And he said some time I got to take those tests over again. Thse inkblots are stupid. And those pictures are stupid too. I like to draw a picture of a man and a woman but I wont make up lies about people.

I got a headache from trying to think so much. I thot Dr Strauss was my frend but he dont help me. He dont tell me what to think or when Ill get smart. Miss Kinnian dint come to see me. I think writing these progress reports are stupid too.

Progress Report 8—Mar 23

Im going back to work at the factery. They said it was better I shud go back to work but I cant tell anyone what the operashun was for and I have to come to the hospitil for an hour evry night after work. They are gonna pay me mony every month for lerning to be smart.

Im glad Im going back to work because I miss my job and all my frends and all the fun we have there.

Dr Strauss says I shud keep writing things down but I dont have to do it every day just when I think of something or something speshul happins. He says dont get discoridged because it takes time and it happins slow. He says it took a long time with Algernon before he got 3 times smarter then he was before. Thats why Algernon beats me all the time because he had that operashun too. That makes me feel better. I coud probly do that *amazed* faster than a reglar mouse. Maybe some day

Ill beat Algernon. Boy that would be something. So far Algernon looks like he mite be smart perminent.

Mar 25 (I dont have to write PROGRESS REPORT on top any more just when I hand it in once a week for Dr Nemur to read. I just have to put the date on. That saves time)

We had a lot of fun at the factery today. Joe Carp said hey look where Charlie had his operashun what did they do Charlie put some brains in. I was going to tell him but I remembered Dr Strauss said no. Then Frank Reilly said what did you do Charlie forget your key and open your door the hard way. That made me laff. Their really my friends and they like me.

◆ **Literature and Your Life**
Have you ever witnessed cruel behavior like this?

Sometimes somebody will say hey look at Joe or Frank or George he really pulled a Charlie Gordon. I dont know why they say that but they always laff. This morning Amos Borg who is the 4 man at Donnegans used my name when he shouted at Ernie the office boy. Ernie lost a packige. He said Ernie what are you trying to be a Charlie Gordon. I dont understand why he said that. I never lost any packiges.

Mar 28 Dr Straus came to my room tonight to see why I dint come in like I was suppose to. I told him I dont like to race with Algernon any more. He said I dont have to for a while but I shud come in. He had a present for me only it wasnt a present but just for lend. I thot it was a little television but it wasnt. He said I got to turn it on when I go to sleep. I said your kidding why shud I turn it on when Im going to sleep. Who ever herd of a thing like that. But he said if I want to get smart I got to do what he says. I told him I dint think I was going to get smart and he put his hand on my sholder and said Charlie you dont know it yet but your getting smarter all the time. You wont notice for a while. I think he was just being nice to make me feel good because I dont look any smarter.

Oh yes I almost forgot. I asked him when I can go back to the class at Miss Kinnians school. He said I wont go their. He said that soon Miss Kinnian will come to the hospitil to start and teach me speshul. I was mad at her for not comming to see me when I got the operashun but I like her so maybe we will be frends again.

Mar 29 That crazy TV kept me up all night. How can I sleep with something yelling crazy things all night in my ears. And the nutty pictures. Wow. I dont know what it says when Im up so how am I going to know when Im sleeping.

Dr Strauss says its ok. He says my brains are lerning when I sleep and that will help me when Miss Kinnian starts my lessons in the hospitl only I found out it isnt a hospitil its a labatory. I think its all crazy. If you can get smart when your sleeping why do people go to school. That thing I dont think will work. I use to watch the late show and the late late show on TV all the time and it never made me smart. Maybe you have to sleep while you watch it.

Dr Strauss showed me how to keep the TV turned low so now I can sleep. I don't hear a thing. And I still dont understand what it says. A few times I play it over in the morning to find out what I lerned when I was sleeping and I dont think so. Miss Kinnian says Maybe its another langwidge or something. But most times it sounds american. It talks so fast faster then even Miss Gold who was my teacher in 6 grade and I remember she talked so fast I coudnt understand her.

I told Dr Strauss what good is it to get smart in my sleep. I want to be smart when Im awake. He says its the same thing and I have two minds. Theres the *subconscious* and the *conscious* (thats how you spell it). And one dont tell the other one what its doing. They dont even talk to each other. Thats why I dream. And boy have I been having crazy dreams. Wow. Ever since that night TV. The late late late late late show.

I forgot to ask him if it was only me or if everybody had those two minds.

(I just looked up the word in the dictionary Dr Strauss gave me. The word is *subconscious. adj. Of the nature of mental operations yet not present in consciousness; as, subconscious conflict of desires.*) There's more but I still dont know what it means. This isnt a very good dictionary for dumb people like me.

Anyway the headache is from the party. My frends from the factery Joe Carp and Frank Reilly invited me to go with them to Muggsys Saloon for some drinks. I dont like to drink but they said we will have lots of fun. I had a good time.

Joe Carp said I shoud show the girls how I mop out the toilet in the factory and he got me a mop. I showed them and everyone laffed when I told that Mr Donnegan said I was the best janiter he ever had because I like my job and do it good and never come late or miss a day except for my operashun.

I said Miss Kinnian always said Charlie be proud of your job because you do it good.

Everybody laffed and we had a good time and they gave me lots of drinks and Joe said Charlie is a card when hes potted. I dont know what that means but everybody likes me and we have fun. I cant wait to be smart like my best frends Joe Carp and Frank Reilly.

I dont remember how the party was over but I think I went out to buy a newspaper and coffe for Joe and Frank and when I came back there was no one their. I looked for them all over till late. Then I dont remember so good but I think I got sleepy or sick. A nice cop brot me back home. Thats what my landlady Mrs Flynn says.

But I got a headache and a big lump on my head and black and blue all over. I think maybe I fell. Anyway I got a bad headache and Im sick and hurt all over. I dont think Ill drink anymore.

April 6 I beat Algernon! I dint even know I beat him until Burt the tester told me. Then the second time I lost because I got so exited I fell off the chair before I finished. But after that I beat him 8 more times. I must be getting smart to beat a smart mouse like Algernon. But I dont *feel* smarter.

I wanted to race Algernon some more but Burt said thats enough for one day. They let me hold him for a minit. Hes not so bad. Hes soft like a ball of cotton. He blinks and when he opens his eyes their black and pink on the eges.

I said can I feed him because I felt bad to beat him and I wanted to be nice and make frends. Burt said no Algernon is a very spec- shul mouse with an operashun like mine, and he was the first of all the animals to stay smart so long. He told me Algernon is so smart that every day he has to solve a test to get his food. Its a thing like a lock on a door that changes every time Algernon goes in to eat so he has to lern something new to get his food. That made me sad because if he coudnt

lern he woud be hungry.

I dont think its right to make you pass a test to eat. How woud Dr Nemur like it to have to pass a test every time he wants to eat. I think Ill be frends with Algernon.

April 9 Tonight after work Miss Kinnian was at the laboratory. She looked like she was glad to see me but scared. I told her dont worry Miss Kinnian Im not smart yet and she laffed. She said I have confidence in you Charlie the way you struggled so hard to read and right better than all the others. At werst you will have it for a littel wile and your doing some- thing for sience.

We are reading a very hard book. I never read such a hard book before. Its called *Robin- son Crusoe*[6] about a man who gets merooned on a dessert Iland. Hes smart and figers out all kinds of things so he can have a house and food and hes a good swimmer. Only I feel sorry because hes all alone and has no frends. But I think their must be somebody else on the iland because theres a picture with his funny umbrella looking at footprints. I hope he gets a frend and not be lonly.

April 10 Miss Kinnian teaches me to spell bet- ter. She says look at a word and close your eyes and say it over and over until you re- member. I have lots of truble with *through* that you say *threw* and *enough* and *tough* that you dont say *enew* and *tew*. You got to say *enuff* and *tuff*. Thats how I use to write it before I started to get smart. Im confused but Miss Kinnian says theres no reason in spelling.

Apr 14 Finished Robinson Crusoe. I want to find out more about what happens to him but Miss Kinnian says thats all there is. *Why*

Apr 15 Miss Kinnian says Im lerning fast. She read some of the Progress Reports and she

---

6. **Robinson Crusoe** (kro͞o´ so): Novel written in 1719 by Daniel Defoe, a British author.

▲ **Critical Viewing** Compare and contrast your vision of Charlie as described in the story with these photographs showing the actor's portrayal of the character. [**Compare and Contrast**]

looked at me kind of funny. She says Im a fine person and Ill show them all. I asked her why. She said never mind but I shoudnt feel bad if I find out that everybody isnt nice like I think. She said for a person who god gave so little to you done more then a lot of people with brains they never even used. I said all my frends are smart people but there good. They like me and they never did anything that wasnt nice. Then she got something in her eye and she had to run out to the ladys room.

Apr 16 Today, I lerned, the *comma*, this is a comma (,) a period, with a tail, Miss Kinnian, says its importent, because, it makes writing, better, she said, somebody, coud lose, a lot of money, if a comma, isnt, in the, right place, I dont have, any money, and I dont see, how a comma, keeps you, from losing it,

But she says, everybody, uses commas, so Ill use, them too,

Apr 17 I used the comma wrong. Its punctuation. Miss Kinnian told me to look up long words in the dictionary to lern to spell them. I said whats the difference if you can read it anyway. She said its part of your education so now on Ill look up all the words Im not sure how to spell. It takes a long time to write that way but I think Im remembering. I only have to look up once and after that I get it right. Anyway thats how come I got the word *punctuation* right. (Its that way in the dictionary).

Miss Kinnian says a period is punctuation too, and there are lots of other marks to lern. I told her I thot all the periods had to have tails but she said no.

You got to mix them up, she showed? me" how. to mix! them(up,. and now; I can! mix up all kinds" of punctuation, in! my writing? There, are lots! of rules? to lern; but Im gettin'g them in my head.

One thing I? like about, Dear Miss Kinnian: (thats the way it goes in a business letter if I ever go into business) is she, always gives me' a reason" when—I ask. She's a gen'ius! I wish! I cou'd be smart" like, her;

(Punctuation, is; fun!)

April 18 What a dope I am! I didn't even understand what she was talking about. I read the grammar book last night and it explanes the whole thing. Then I saw it was the same way as Miss Kinnian was trying to tell me, but I didn't get it. I got up in the middle of the night, and the whole thing straightened out in my mind.

Miss Kinnian said that the TV working in my sleep helped out. She said I reached a plateau. Thats like the flat top of a hill.

After I figgered out how punctuation worked, I read over all my old Progress Reports from the beginning. Boy, did I have crazy spelling and punctuation! I told Miss Kinnian I ought to go over the pages and fix all the mistakes but she said, "No, Charlie, Dr. Nemur wants them just as they are. That's why he let you keep them after they were photostated, to see your own progress. You're coming along fast, Charlie."

That made me feel good. After the lesson I went down and played with Algernon. We don't race any more.

April 20 I feel sick inside. Not sick like for a doctor, but inside my chest it feels empty like getting punched and a heartburn at the same time.

I wasn't going to write about it, but I guess I got to, because its important. Today was the first time I ever stayed home from work.

Last night Joe Carp and Frank Reilly invited me to a party. There were lots of girls and some men from the factory. I remembered how sick I got last time I drank too much, so I told Joe I didn't want anything to drink. He gave me a plain coke instead. It tasted funny, but I thought it was just a bad taste in my mouth.

We had a lot of fun for a while. Joe said I should dance with Ellen and she would teach me the steps. I fell a few times and I couldn't understand why because no one else was dancing besides Ellen and me. And all the time I was tripping because somebody's foot was always sticking out.

Then when I got up I saw the look on Joe's face and it gave me a funny feeling in my stomack. "He's a scream," one of the girls said. Everybody was laughing.

Frank said, "I ain't laughed so much since we sent him off for the newspaper that night at Muggsy's and ditched him."

"Look at him. His face is red."

"He's blushing. Charlie is blushing."

"Hey, Ellen, what'd you do to Charlie? I never saw him act like that before."

I didn't know what to do or where to turn. Everyone was looking at me and laughing and I felt naked. I wanted to hide myself. I ran out into the street and I threw up. Then I walked home. It's a funny thing I never knew that Joe and Frank and the others liked to have me around all the time to make fun of me.

Now I know what it means when they say

> ◆ **Literary Focus**
> Explain how this episode would differ if it were told from someone else's point of view.

◆ **Build Vocabulary**

psychology (sī käl´ ə jē) n.: Science dealing with the mind and with mental and emotional processes

"to pull a Charlie Gordon."

I'm ashamed.

PROGRESS REPORT 11

April 21 Still didn't go into the factory. I told Mrs. Flynn my landlady to call and tell Mr. Donnegan I was sick. Mrs. Flynn looks at me very funny lately like she's scared of me.

I think it's a good thing about finding out how everybody laughs at me. I thought about it a lot. It's because I'm so dumb and I don't even know when I'm doing something dumb. People think it's funny when a dumb person can't do things the same way they can.

Anyway, now I know I'm getting smarter every day. I know punctuation and I can spell good. I like to look up all the hard words in the dictionary and I remember them. I'm reading a lot now, and Miss Kinnian says I read very fast. Sometimes I even understand what I'm reading about, and it stays in my mind. There are times when I can close my eyes and think of a page and it all comes back like a picture.

Besides history, geography and arithmetic, Miss Kinnian said I should start to learn a few foreign languages. Dr. Strauss gave me some more tapes to play while I sleep. I still don't understand how that conscious and unconscious mind works, but Dr. Strauss says not to worry yet. He asked me to promise that when I start learning college subjects next week I wouldn't read any books on psychology—that is, until he gives me permission.

I feel a lot better today, but I guess I'm still a little angry that all the time people were laughing and making fun of me because I wasn't so smart. When I become intelligent like Dr. Strauss says, with three times my I.Q. of 68, then maybe I'll be like everyone else and people will like me and be friendly.

I'm not sure what an I.Q. is. Dr. Nemur said it was something that measured how intelligent you were—like a scale in the drugstore weighs pounds. But Dr. Strauss had a big arguement with him and said an I.Q. didn't weigh intelligence at all. He said an I.Q. showed how much intelligence you could get, like the numbers on the outside of a measuring cup. You still had to fill the cup up with stuff.

Then when I asked Burt, who gives me my intelligence tests and works with Algernon, he said that both of them were wrong (only I had to promise not to tell them he said so). Burt says that the I.Q. measures a lot of different things including some of the things you learned already, and it really isn't any good at all.

So I still don't know what I.Q. is except that mine is going to be over 200 soon. I didn't want to say anything, but I don't see how if they don't know *what* it is, or *where* it is—I don't see how they know *how much* of it you've got.

Dr. Nemur says I have to take a *Rorshach Test* tomorrow. I wonder what *that* is.

April 22 I found out what a *Rorshach* is. It's the test I took before the operation—the one with the inkblots on the pieces of cardboard. The man who gave me the test was the same one.

I was scared to death of those inkblots. I knew he was going to ask me to find the pictures and I knew I wouldn't be able to. I was thinking to myself, if only there was some way of knowing what kind of pictures were hidden there. Maybe there weren't any pictures at all. Maybe it was just a trick to see if I was dumb enough too look for something that wasn't there. Just thinking about that made me sore at him.

"All right, Charlie," he said, "you've seen these cards before, remember?"

"Of course I remember."

The way I said it, he knew I was angry, and he looked surprised. "Yes, of course. Now I want you to look at this one. What might this be? What do you see on this card? People see all sorts of things in these inkblots. Tell me what it might be for you—what it makes you think of."

I was shocked. That wasn't what I had expected him to say at all. "You mean there are no pictures hidden in those inkblots?"

He frowned and took off his glasses. "What?"

"Pictures. Hidden in the inkblots. Last time you told me that everyone could see them and you wanted me to find them too."

He explained to me that the last time he had used almost the exact same words he was using now. I didn't believe it, and I still have the suspicion that he misled me at the time just for the fun of it. Unless—I don't know any more—could I have been *that* feeble-minded?

We went through the cards slowly. One of them looked like a pair of bats tugging at something. Another one looked like two men fencing with swords. I imagined all sorts of things. I guess I got carried away. But I didn't trust him any more, and I kept turning them around and even looking on the back to see if there was anything there I was supposed to catch. While he was making his notes, I peeked out of the corner of my eye to read it. But it was all in code that looked like this:

WF + A DdF-Ad orig. WF-A
SF + obj

The test still doesn't make sense to me. It seems to me that anyone could make up lies about things that they didn't really see. How could he know I wasn't making a fool of him by mentioning things that I didn't really imagine? Maybe I'll understand it when Dr. Strauss lets me read up on psychology.

April 25 I figured out a new way to line up the machines in the factory, and Mr. Donnegan says it will save him ten thousand dollars a year in labor and increased production. He gave me a $25 bonus.

I wanted to take Joe Carp and Frank Reilly out to lunch to celebrate, but Joe said he had to buy some things for his wife, and Frank said he was meeting his cousin for lunch. I guess it'll take a little time for them to get used to the changes in me. Everybody seems to be frightened of me. When I went over to Amos Borg and tapped him on the shoulder, he jumped up in the air.

People don't talk to me much any more or kid around the way they used to. It makes the job kind of lonely.

April 27 I got up the nerve today to ask Miss Kinnian to have dinner with me tomorrow night to celebrate my bonus.

At first she wasn't sure it was right, but I asked Dr. Strauss and he said it was okay. Dr. Strauss and Dr. Nemur don't seem to be getting along so well. They're arguing all the time. This evening when I came in to ask Dr. Strauss about having dinner with Miss Kinnian, I heard them shouting. Dr. Nemur was saying that it was *his* experiment and *his* research, and Dr. Strauss was shouting back that he contributed just as much, because he found me through Miss Kinnian and he performed the operation. Dr. Strauss said that someday thousands of neurosurgeons[7] might be using his technique all over the world.

Dr. Nemur wanted to publish the results of the experiment at the end of this month. Dr. Strauss wanted to wait a while longer to be sure. Dr. Strauss said that Dr. Nemur was more interested in the Chair[8] of Psychology at Princeton than he was in the experiment. Dr. Nemur said that Dr. Strauss was nothing but an opportunist who was trying to ride to glory on *his* coattails.

When I left afterwards, I found myself trembling. I don't know why for sure, but it was as if I'd seen both men clearly for the first time. I remember hearing Burt say that Dr. Nemur had a shrew of a wife who was pushing

---

7. **neurosurgeons** (noo′ rō sur′ jənz) *n.*: Doctors who operate on the nervous system, including the brain and spine.
8. **chair:** Professorship.

him all the time to get things published so that he could become famous. Burt said that the dream of her life was to have a big shot husband.

Was Dr. Strauss really trying to ride on his coattails?

April 28 I don't understand why I never noticed how beautiful Miss Kinnian really is. She has brown eyes and feathery brown hair that comes to the top of her neck. She's only thirty-four! I think from the beginning I had the feeling that she was an unreachable genius—and very, very old. Now, every time I see her she grows younger and more lovely.

We had dinner and a long talk. When she said that I was coming along so fast that soon I'd be leaving her behind, I laughed.

"It's true, Charlie. You're already a better reader than I am. You can read a whole page at a glance while I can take in only a few lines at a time. And you remember every single thing you read. I'm lucky if I can recall the main thoughts and the general meaning."

"I don't feel intelligent. There are so many things I don't understand."

She took out a cigarette and I lit it for her.

"You've got to be a *little* patient. You're accomplishing in days and weeks what it takes normal people to do in half a lifetime. That's what makes it so amazing. You're like a giant sponge now, soaking things in. Facts, figures, general knowledge. And soon you'll begin to

◀ **Critical Viewing** Does Charlie seem to have made progress, judging from the details in this photograph? Explain. [Interpret]

connect them, too. You'll see how the different branches of learning are related. There are many levels, Charlie, like steps on a giant ladder that take you up higher and higher to see more and more of the world around you.

"I can see only a little bit of that, Charlie, and I won't go much higher than I am now, but you'll keep climbing up and up, and see more and more, and each step will open new worlds that you never even knew existed." She frowned. "I hope . . . I just hope to God—"

"What?"

"Never mind, Charles. I just hope I wasn't wrong to advise you to go into this in the first place."

I laughed. "How could that be? It worked, didn't it? Even Algernon is still smart."

We sat there silently for a while and I knew what she was thinking about as she watched me toying with the chain of my rabbit's foot and my keys. I didn't want to think of that possibility any more than elderly people want to think of death. I *knew* that this was only the beginning. I knew what she meant about levels because I'd seen some of them already. The thought of leaving her behind made me sad.

I'm in love with Miss Kinnian.

PROGRESS REPORT 12

April 30 I've quit my job with Donnegan's Plastic Box Company. Mr. Donnegan insisted that it would be better for all concerned if I left. What did I do to make them hate me so?

The first I knew of it was when Mr. Donnegan showed me the petition. Eight hundred and forty names, everyone connected with the factory, except Fanny Girden. Scanning the list quickly, I saw at once that hers was the only missing name. All the rest demanded that I be fired.

Joe Carp and Frank Reilly wouldn't talk to me about it. No one else would either, except Fanny. She was one of the few people I'd known who set her mind to something and believed it no matter what the rest of the world proved, said or did—and Fanny did not believe that I should have been fired. She had been against the petition on principle and despite the pressure and threats she'd held out.

"Which don't mean to say," she remarked, "that I don't think there's something mighty strange about you, Charlie. Them changes. I don't know. You used to be a good, dependable, ordinary man—not too bright maybe, but honest. Who knows what you done to yourself to get so smart all of a sudden. Like everybody around here's been saying, Charlie, it's not right."

"But how can you say that, Fanny? What's wrong with a man becoming intelligent and wanting to acquire knowledge and understanding of the world around him?"

She stared down at her work, and I turned to leave. Without looking at me, she said: "It was evil when Eve listened to the snake and ate from the tree of knowledge. It was evil when she saw that she was naked. If not for that none of us would ever have to grow old and sick, and die."

Once again now I have the feeling of shame burning inside me. This intelligence has driven a wedge between me and all the people I once knew and loved. Before, they laughed at me and despised me for my ignorance and dullness; now, they hate me for my knowledge and understanding. What do they want of me?

◆ Build Vocabulary

tangible (tan´ jə bəl) *adj.*: That can be understood; definite; objective

specter (spek´ tər) *n.*: Disturbing thoughts

refute (ri fyo͞ot´) *v.*: Prove (an argument or statement) to be false by argument or evidence

They've driven me out of the factory. Now I'm more alone than ever before . . .

May 15 Dr. Strauss is very angry at me for not having written any progress reports in two weeks. He's justified because the lab is now paying me a regular salary. I told him I was too busy thinking and reading. When I pointed out that writing was such a slow process that it made me impatient with my poor hand writing, he suggested that I learn to type. It's much easier to write now because I can type nearly seventy-five words a minute. Dr. Strauss continually reminds me of the need to speak and write simply so that people will be able to understand me.

I'll try to review all the things that happened to me during the last two weeks. Algernon and I were presented to the American Psychological Association sitting in convention with the World Psychological Association last Tuesday. We created quite a sensation. Dr. Nemur and Dr. Strauss were proud of us.

I suspect that Dr. Nemur, who is sixty—ten years older than Dr. Strauss—finds it necessary to see tangible results of his work. Undoubtedly the result of pressure by Mrs. Nemur.

Contrary to my earlier impressions of him, I realize that Dr. Nemur is not at all a genius. He has a very good mind, but it struggles under the specter of self-doubt. He wants people to take him for a genius. Therefore, it is important for him to feel that his work is accepted by the world. I believe that Dr. Nemur was afraid of further delay because he worried that someone else might make a discovery along these lines and take the credit from him.

Dr. Strauss on the other hand might be called a genius, although I feel that his areas of knowledge are too limited. He was educated in the tradition of narrow specialization; the broader aspects of background were neglected far more than necessary—even for a neurosurgeon.

I was shocked to learn that the only ancient languages he could read were Latin, Greek and Hebrew, and that he knows almost nothing of mathematics beyond the elementary levels of the calculus of variations. When he admitted this to me, I found myself almost annoyed. It was as if he'd hidden this part of himself in order to deceive me, pretending—as do many people I've discovered—to be what he is not. No one I've ever known is what he appears to be on the surface.

Dr. Nemur appears to be uncomfortable around me. Sometimes when I try to talk to him, he just looks at me strangely and turns away. I was angry at first when Dr. Strauss told me I was giving Dr. Nemur an inferiority complex. I thought he was mocking me and I'm oversensitive at being made fun of.

How was I to know that a highly respected psychoexperimentalist like Nemur was unacquainted with Hindustani[9] and Chinese? It's absurd when you consider the work that is being done in India and China today in the very field of his study.

I asked Dr. Strauss how Nemur could refute Rahajamati's attack on his method and results if Nemur couldn't even read them in the first place. That strange look on Dr. Strauss' face can mean only one of two things. Either he doesn't want to tell Nemur what they're saying in India, or else—and this worries me—Dr. Strauss doesn't know either. I must be careful to speak and write clearly and simply so that people won't laugh.

May 18 I am very disturbed. I saw Miss Kinnian last night for the first time in over a week. I tried to avoid all discussions of intellectual concepts and to keep the conversation on a simple, everyday level, but she just stared at me blankly and asked me what I meant about the mathematical variance equivalent in Dorbermann's *Fifth Concerto.*

When I tried to explain she stopped me and

---

9. Hindustani (hin′ doo stä′ nē) *n.*: A language of northern India.

The boy stood there, dazed and frightened, holding the empty tray in his hand. The whistles and catcalls from the customers (the cries of "hey, there go the profits!" . . . "*Mazeltov!*" . . . and "well, *he* didn't work here very long . . ." which invariably seems to follow the breaking of glass or dishware in a public restaurant) all seemed to confuse him.

When the owner came to see what the excitement was about, the boy cowered as if he expected to be struck and threw up his arms as if to ward off the blow.

"All right! All right, you dope," shouted the owner, "don't just stand there! Get the broom and sweep that mess up. A broom . . . a broom, you idiot! It's in the kitchen. Sweep up all the pieces."

The boy saw that he was not going to be punished. His frightened expression disappeared and he smiled and hummed as he came back with the broom to sweep the floor. A few of the rowdier customers kept up the remarks, amusing themselves at his expense.

"Here, sonny, over here there's a nice piece behind you . . ."

"C'mon, do it again . . ."

"He's not so dumb. It's easier to break 'em than to wash 'em . . ."

As his vacant eyes moved across the crowd of amused onlookers, he slowly mirrored their smiles and finally broke into an uncertain

laughed. I guess I got angry, but I suspect I'm approaching her on the wrong level. No matter what I try to discuss with her, I am unable to communicate. I must review Vrostadt's equations on *Levels of Semantic Progression.* I find that I don't communicate with people much any more. Thank God for books and music and things I can think about. I am alone in my apartment at Mrs. Flynn's boarding house most of the time and seldom speak to anyone.

May 20 I would not have noticed the new dishwasher, a boy of about sixteen, at the corner diner where I take my evening meals if not for the incident of the broken dishes.

They crashed to the floor, shattering and sending bits of white china under the tables.

grin at the joke which he obviously did not understand.

I felt sick inside as I looked at his dull, vacuous smile, the wide, bright eyes of a child, uncertain but eager to please. They were laughing at him because he was mentally retarded.

And I had been laughing at him too.

Suddenly, I was furious at myself and all those who were smirking at him. I jumped up and shouted, "Shut up! Leave him alone! It's not his fault he can't understand! He can't help what he is! But . . . he's still a human being!"

The room grew silent. I cursed myself for losing control and creating a scene. I tried not to look at the boy as I paid my check and walked out without touching my food. I felt ashamed for both of us.

How strange it is that people of honest feelings and sensibility, who would not take advantage of a man born without arms or legs or eyes—how such people think nothing of abusing a man born with low intelligence. It infuriated me to think that not too long ago I, like this boy, had foolishly played the clown.

And I had almost forgotten.

I'd hidden the picture of the old Charlie Gordon from myself because now that I was intelligent it was something that had to be pushed out of my mind. But today in looking at that boy, for the first time I saw what I had been. *I was just like him!*

Only a short time ago, I learned that people laughed at me. Now I can see that unknowingly I joined with them in laughing at myself. That hurts most of all.

I have often reread my progress reports and seen the illiteracy, the childish naïvete,[10] the mind of low intelligence peering from a dark room, through the keyhole, at the dazzling light outside. I see that even in my dullness I knew that I was inferior, and that other people had something I lacked—something denied

me. In my mental blindness, I thought that it was somehow connected with the ability to read and write, and I was sure that if I could get those skills I would automatically have intelligence too.

Even a feeble-minded man wants to be like other men.

A child may not know how to feed itself, or what to eat, yet it knows of hunger.

This then is what I was like. I never knew. Even with my gift of intellectual awareness, I never really knew.

This day was good for me. Seeing the past more clearly, I have decided to use my knowledge and skills to work in the field of increasing human intelligence levels. Who is better equipped for this work? Who else has lived in both worlds? These are my people. Let me use my gift to do something for them.

Tomorrow, I will discuss with Dr. Strauss the manner in which I can work in this area. I may be able to help him work out the problems of widespread use of the technique which was used on me. I have several good ideas of my own.

There is so much that might be done with this technique. If I could be made into a genius, what about thousands of others like myself? What fantastic levels might be achieved by using this technique on normal people? On *geniuses*?

There are so many doors to open. I am impatient to begin.

PROGRESS REPORT 13

May 23 It happened today. Algernon bit me. I visited the lab to see him as I do occasionally, and when I took him out of his cage, he snapped at my hand. I put him back and watched him for a while. He was unusually disturbed and vicious.

◆ **Build Vocabulary**
illiteracy (il lit′ ər ə sē) *n.*: Inability to read or write

---

10. **naïvete** (nä ēv tā′) *n.*: Simplicity.

May 24 Burt, who is in charge of the experimental animals, tells me that Algernon is changing. He is less cooperative; he refuses to run the maze any more; general motivation has decreased. And he hasn't been eating. Everyone is upset about what this may mean.

May 25 They've been feeding Algernon, who now refuses to work the shifting-lock problem. Everyone identifies me with Algernon. In a way we're both the first of our kind. They're all pretending that Algernon's behavior is not necessarily significant for me. But it's hard to hide the fact that some of the other animals who were used in this experiment are showing strange behavior.

Dr. Strauss and Dr. Nemur have asked me not to come to the lab any more. I know what they're thinking but I can't accept it. I am going ahead with my plans to carry their research forward. With all due respect to both of these fine scientists, I am well aware of their limitations. If there is an answer, I'll have to find it out for myself. Suddenly, time has become very important to me.

May 29 I have been given a lab of my own and permission to go ahead with the research. I'm on to something. Working day and night. I've had a cot moved into the lab. Most of my writing time is spent on the notes which I keep in a separate folder, but from time to time I feel it necessary to put down my moods and my thoughts out of sheer habit.

I find the *calculus of intelligence* to be a fascinating study. Here is the place for the application of all the knowledge I have acquired. In a sense it's the problem I've been concerned with all my life.

May 31 Dr. Strauss thinks I'm working too hard. Dr. Nemur says I'm trying to cram a lifetime of research and thought into a few weeks. I know I should rest, but I'm driven on by something inside that won't let me stop. I've got to find the reason for the sharp regression in Algernon. I've got to know *if* and *when* it will happen to me.

June 4

LETTER TO DR. STRAUSS (*copy*)
Dear Dr. Strauss:
Under separate cover I am sending you a copy of my report entitled, "The Algernon-Gordon Effect: A Study of Structure and Function of Increased Intelligence," which I would like to have you read and have published.

As you see, my experiments are completed. I have included in my report all of my formulae, as well as mathematical analysis in the appendix. Of course, these should be verified.

Because of its importance to both you and Dr. Nemur (and need I say to myself, too?) I have checked and rechecked my results a dozen times in the hope of finding an error. I am sorry to say the results must stand. Yet for the sake of science, I am grateful for the little bit that I here add to the knowledge of the function of the human mind and of the laws governing the artificial increase of human intelligence.

I recall your once saying to me that an experimental *failure* or the *disproving* of a theory was as important to the advancement of learning as a success would be. I know now that this is true. I am sorry, however, that my own contribution to the field must rest upon the ashes of the work of two men I regard so highly.

Yours truly,
Charles Gordon

encl.: rept.

June 5 I must not become emotional. The facts and the results of my experiments are clear, and the more sensational aspects of my own rapid climb cannot obscure the fact that the tripling of intelligence by the surgical technique developed by Drs. Strauss and Nemur must be viewed as having little or no practical applicability (at the present time) to the increase of human intelligence.

As I review the records and data on Algernon, I see that although he is still in his physical infancy, he has regressed mentally. Motor activity[11] is impaired; there is a general reduction of glandular activity; there is an accelerated loss of coordination.

There are also strong indications of progressive amnesia.

As will be seen by my report, these and other physical and mental deterioration syndromes can be predicted with statistically significant results by the application of my formula.

The surgical stimulus to which we were both subjected has resulted in an intensification and acceleration of all mental processes. The unforeseen development, which I have taken the liberty of calling the "Algernon-Gordon Effect," is the logical extension of the entire intelligence speedup. The hypothesis here proven may be described simply in the following terms: Artificially increased intelligence deteriorates at a rate of time directly proportional to the quantity of the increase.

◆ **Reading Strategy**
How would you summarize this paragraph?

I feel that this, in itself, is an important discovery.

As long as I am able to write, I will continue to record my thoughts in these progress reports. It is one of my few pleasures. However, by all indications, my own mental deterioration will be very rapid.

I have already begun to notice signs of emotional instability and forgetfulness, the first symptoms of the burnout.

June 10 Deterioration progressing. I have become absent-minded. Algernon died two days ago. Dissection shows my predictions were right. His brain had decreased in weight and there was a general smoothing out of cerebral convolutions as well as a deepening and broadening of brain fissures.

I guess the same thing is or will soon be happening to me. Now that it's definite, I don't want it to happen.

I put Algernon's body in a cheese box and buried him in the back yard. I cried.

June 15 Dr. Strauss came to see me again. I wouldn't open the door and I told him to go away. I want to be left to myself. I have become touchy and irritable. I feel the darkness closing in. I keep telling myself how important this introspective journal will be.

It's a strange sensation to pick up a book that you've read and enjoyed just a few months ago and discover that you don't remember it. I remembered how great I thought John Milton[12] was, but when I picked up *Paradise Lost* I couldn't understand it at all. I got so angry I threw the book across the room.

I've got to try to hold on to some of it. Some of the things I've learned. Oh, God, please don't take it all away.

June 19 Sometimes, at night, I go out for a walk. Last night I couldn't remember where I lived. A policeman took me home. I have the strange feeling that this has all happened to me before—a long time ago. I keep telling myself I'm the only person in the world who can describe what's happening to me.

---

11. **motor activity:** Movement; physical coordination.

12. **John Milton:** British poet (1608–1674) who wrote *Paradise Lost*.

June 21 Why can't I remember? I've got to fight. I lie in bed for days and I don't know who or where I am. Then it all comes back to me in a flash. Fugues of amnesia.[13] Symptoms of senility—second childhood. I can watch them coming on. It's so cruelly logical. I learned so much and so fast. Now my mind is deteriorating rapidly. I won't let it happen. I'll fight it. I can't help thinking of the boy in the restaurant, the blank expression, the silly smile, the people laughing at him. No—please—not that again . . .

June 22 I'm forgetting things that I learned recently. It seems to be following the classic pattern—the last things learned are the first things forgotten. Or is that the pattern? I'd better look it up again . . .

I reread my paper on the "Algernon-Gordon Effect" and I get the strange feeling that it was written by someone else. There are parts I don't even understand.

Motor activity impaired. I keep tripping over things, and it becomes increasingly difficult to type.

June 23 I've given up using the typewriter completely. My coordination is bad. I feel that I'm moving slower and slower. Had a terrible shock today. I picked up a copy of an article I used in my research, Krueger's "Uber psychische Ganzheit," to see if it would help me understand what I had done. First I thought there was something wrong with my eyes. Then I realized I could no longer read German. I tested myself in other languages. All gone.

June 30 A week since I dared to write again. It's slipping away like sand through my fingers. Most of the books I have are too hard for me now. I get angry with them because I know that I read and understood them just a few weeks ago.

---

13. **Fugues** (fyo͞ogz) **of amnesia** (am neʹ zhə): Periods of loss of memory.

I keep telling myself I must keep writing these reports so that somebody will know what is happening to me. But it gets harder to form the words and remember spellings. I have to look up even simple words in the dictionary now and it makes me impatient with myself.

Dr. Strauss comes around almost every day, but I told him I wouldn't see or speak to anybody. He feels guilty. They all do. But I don't blame anyone. I knew what might happen. But how it hurts.

July 7 I don't know where the week went. Todays Sunday I know because I can see through my window people going to church. I think I stayed in bed all week but I remember Mrs. Flynn bringing food to me a few times. I keep saying over and over Ive got to do something but then I forget or maybe its just easier not to do what I say Im going to do.

I think of my mother and father a lot these days. I found a picture of them with me taken at a beach. My father has a big ball under his arm and my mother is holding me by the hand. I dont remember them the way they are in the picture. All I remember is my father arguing with mom about money.

He never shaved much and he used to scratch my face when he hugged me. He said he was going to take me to see cows on a farm once but he never did. He never kept his promises . . .

July 10 My landlady Mrs Flynn is very worried about me. She said she doesnt like loafers. If Im sick its one thing, but if Im a loafer thats another thing and she wont have it. I told her I think Im sick.

I try to read a little bit every day, mostly stories, but sometimes I have to read the same thing over and over again because I dont know what it means. And its hard to write. I know I should look up all the words in the dictionary but its so hard and Im so tired all the time.

► **Critical Viewing**
Charlie's boss says "Charlie Gordon, you got guts." How does this scene illustrate his comment? **[Support]**

Then I got the idea that I would only use the easy words instead of the long hard ones. That saves time. I put flowers on Algernons grave about once a week. Mrs. Flynn thinks Im crazy to put flowers on a mouses grave but I told her that Algernon was special.

July 14 Its sunday again. I dont have anything to do to keep me busy now because my television set is broke and I dont have any money to get it fixed. (I think I lost this months check from the lab. I dont remember)

I get awful headaches and asperin doesnt help me much. Mrs. Flynn knows Im really sick and she feels very sorry for me. Shes a wonderful woman whenever someone is sick.

July 22 Mrs. Flynn called a strange doctor to see me. She was afraid I was going to die. I told the doctor I wasnt too sick and that I only forget sometimes. He asked me did I have any friends or relatives and I said no I dont have any. I told him I had a friend called Algernon once but he was a mouse and we used to run races together. He looked at me kind of funny like he thought I was crazy.

He smiled when I told him I used to be a genius. He talked to me like I was a baby and he winked at Mrs Flynn. I got mad and chased him out because he was making fun of me the way they all used to.

July 24 I have no more money and Mrs Flynn says I got to go to work somewhere and pay the rent because I havent paid for over two months. I dont know any work but the job I used to have at Donnegans Plastic Box Company. I dont want to go back there because they all knew me when I was smart and maybe they'll laugh at me. But I dont know what else to do to get money.

July 25 I was looking at some of my old progress reports and its very funny but I cant read what I wrote. I can make out some of the words but they dont make sense.

Miss Kinnian came to the door but I said go away I dont want to see you. She cried and I cried too but I wouldnt let her in because I didnt want her to laugh at me. I told her I didn't like her any more. I told her I didn't want to be smart any more. Thats not true. I still love her and I still want to be smart but I had to say that so shed go away. She gave Mrs. Flynn money to pay the rent. I dont want that. I got to get a job.

Please . . . please let me not forget how to read and write . . .

July 27 Mr. Donnegan was very nice when I came back and asked him for my old job of janitor. First he was very suspicious but I told him what happened to me then he looked very sad and put his hand on my shoulder and said Charlie Gordon you got guts.

Everybody looked at me when I came downstairs and started working in the toilet sweeping it out like I used to. I told myself Charlie if they make fun of you dont get sore because you remember their not so smart as you once thot they were. And besides they were once your friends and if they laughed at you that doesnt mean anything because they liked you too.

One of the new men who came to work there after I went away made a nasty crack he said hey Charlie I hear your a very smart fella a real quiz kid. Say something intelligent. I felt bad but Joe Carp came over and grabbed him by the shirt and said leave him alone or Ill break your neck. I didnt expect Joe to take my part so I guess hes really my friend.

Later Frank Reilly came over and said Charlie if anybody bothers you or trys to take advantage you call me or Joe and we will set em straight. I said thanks Frank and I got choked up so I had to turn around and go into the supply room so he wouldnt see me cry. Its good to have friends.

July 28 I did a dumb thing today I forgot I wasnt in Miss Kinnians class at the adult center any more like I use to be. I went in and sat down in my old seat in the back of the room and she looked at me funny and she said Charles. I dint remember she ever called me that before only Charlie so I said hello Miss Kinnian Im ready for my lesin today only I lost my reader that we was using. She startid to cry and run out of the room and everybody looked at me and I saw they wasnt the same pepul who use to be in my class.

Then all of a suddin I rememberd some things about the operashun and me getting smart and I said holy smoke I reely pulled a Charlie Gordon that time. I went away before she come back to the room.

Thats why Im going away from New York for good. I dont want to do nothing like that agen. I dont want Miss Kinnian to feel sorry for me. Evry body feels sorry at the factery and I dont want that eather so Im going someplace where nobody knows that Charlie Gordon was once a genus and now he cant even reed a book or rite good.

Im taking a cuple of books along and even if I cant reed them Ill practise hard and maybe I wont forget every thing I lerned. If I try reel hard maybe Ill be a littel bit smarter then I was before the operashun. I got my rabits foot and my luky penny and maybe they will help me.

If you ever reed this Miss Kinnian dont be sorry for me Im glad I got a second chanse to be smart becaus I lerned a lot of things that I never even new were in this world and Im grateful that I saw it all for a littel bit. I dont know why Im dumb agen or what I did wrong maybe its becaus I dint try hard enuff. But if I try and practis very hard maybe Ill get a littl smarter and know what all the words are. I remember a littel bit how nice I had a feeling with the blue book that has the torn cover when I red it. Thats why Im gonna keep trying to get smart so I can have that feeling agen. Its a good feeling to know things and be smart. I wish I had it rite now if I did I woud sit down and reed all the time. Anyway I bet Im the first dumb person in the world who ever found out somthing importent for sience. I remember I did somthing but I dont remember what. So I gess its like I did it for all the dumb pepul like me.

Goodbye Miss Kinnian and Dr Strauss and evreybody. And P.S. please tell Dr Nemur not to be such a grouch when pepul laff at him and he woud have more frends. Its easy to make frends if you let pepul laff at you. Im going to have lots of frends where I go.

P.P.S. Please if you get a chanse put some flowrs on Algernons grave in the bak yard . . .

*G*uide for Responding

◆ LITERATURE AND YOUR LIFE

Reader's Response Was being part of the experiment good for Charlie? Explain.

Thematic Focus What difficult questions does Charlie face in this story?

☑ Check Your Comprehension

1. Why is Charlie keeping a journal?
2. Why does Miss Kinnian believe that Charlie should take part in this experiment?
3. (a) Why does Charlie believe he failed the Rorschach test? (b) What does he come to learn about the Rorschach test?
4. (a) How do Charlie's co-workers treat him after he becomes smart? (b) Why does Charlie leave his job?
5. Why does Charlie decide to leave New York?

◆ Critical Thinking

INTERPRET

1. Explain how Charlie's development parallels Algernon's. **[Compare and Contrast]**
2. How do the spelling, punctuation, and grammar in Charlie's reports contribute to your view of his progress? **[Infer]**
3. How is Charlie at the end of the story different from the way he was at the beginning? **[Compare and Contrast]**

EVALUATE

4. Do you think that Charlie was a good subject for this experiment? Explain. **[Make a Judgment]**

APPLY

5. As Charlie grows smarter, he asks questions. Explain why the ability to ask questions is an important part of intelligence. **[Apply]**

*G*uide for Responding *(continued)*

◆ Reading Strategy

SUMMARIZE

When you **summarize,** you restate key ideas and details in your own words. An effective written summary is brief and omits less significant details.

1. Summarize the progress report of March 6.
2. Write a summary of "Flowers for Algernon" to put on a book jacket.

◆ Build Vocabulary

USING THE WORD ROOT -*psych*-

When used in English words, the word root -*psych*- usually refers to the mind. Speculate about the meaning of each word below. Then, use a dictionary to check your definitions.

1. psychoanalysis   2. psychic   3. psychotherapist

SPELLING STRATEGY

In -*psych*-, the s sound is spelled *ps* and the *k* sound is spelled *ch*. Identify the words in these sentences that follow one of the two rules.

1. She used a pseudonym on her essay about chaos.
2. The chorus sang at the psychology convention.

USING THE WORD BANK

Write the word from the Word Bank that best completes each sentence. Use each word only once.

1. The doctor taught a _____?_____ course about common mental disorders.
2. In one case study, a man was haunted by the _____?_____ of growing older.
3. The doctor achieved concrete, _____?_____ results using psychotherapy.
4. No one could _____?_____ the success of the treatment.
5. No longer would rivals describe his studies and experiments as being _____?_____.
6. Another case was about a quiet, thoughtful _____?_____ woman.
7. She was troubled by her _____?_____, or inability to read and write.
8. Her condition did not exactly match any of the mental _____?_____ described in the textbooks.

◆ Literary Focus

FIRST-PERSON POINT OF VIEW

"Flowers for Algernon" is told from the **first-person point of view.** Charlie, the story's main character, serves as narrator. What you learn about people and events in the story is filtered through Charlie's eyes and mind.

1. What do you learn about Charlie's personality through his writing?
2. How does Charlie's condition change as the story progresses?
3. Why did Keyes use a first-person narrator rather than one who is not a story character?

◆ Build Grammar Skills

VERBS: PERFECT TENSES

In addition to the simple present, past, and future tenses, verbs have **perfect tenses.** Perfect verb tenses use *have, has,* or *had* with the past participle.

The **present perfect** tense shows an action that began in the past and continues into the present:

They *have wondered* about it for centuries.

The **past perfect** tense shows a past action that ended before another past action began:

The show *had ended* before we arrived.

The **future perfect** shows a future action that will have ended before another begins. This tense uses the helping verbs *will have:*

In ten years, they *will have finished* their work.

Practice Classify the verbs in each sentence as present perfect, past perfect, or future perfect:

1. We have started the experiment.
2. Last week's experiment has ended.
3. By next year, the scientists will have published the results.
4. Our publication had arrived before the experiment began.
5. It has taught readers throughout the world.

Writing Application Write a paragraph about the story, using the present perfect, past perfect, and future perfect tenses of the verb *improve.*

Build Your Portfolio

 ## Idea Bank

Writing

1. **Award Plaque** Create an award plaque for Charlie Gordon, honoring his contribution to science. Explain why he deserves to be remembered.

2. **Explanation** Write an essay explaining whether or not "Flowers for Algernon" is an appropriate and effective title.

3. **Journal Article** Imagine that you are Dr. Strauss or Dr. Nemur. Write an article about the experiment with Charlie. Describe the predicted and the actual outcomes, as well as what you have learned.

Speaking and Listening

4. **Dramatization [Group Activity]** Work with a group to dramatize a scene from the story. Develop dialogue and stage directions for your scene. Assign roles, rehearse, and perform your scene for the class. **[Performing Arts Link]**

5. **Debate** Hold a class debate on the topic of using IQ tests to measure intelligence. Choose teams for and against the topic. In your arguments, use specific details and support your generalizations. Present your arguments in front of a panel of student judges. **[Science Link]**

Projects

6. **Research Report** Use reference sources to find out about intelligence and how it is measured. Share your findings with the class, and talk about Charlie's intellectual growth and decline throughout the story. **[Science Link]**

7. **Audiovisual Interviews** Work with a partner and "hold" three interviews with Charlie. Choose three specific dates in the story on which a reporter might have interviewed Charlie. Practice your interviews, and record them on audio- or videotape. Play the results for the class. **[Media Link]**

 ## Writing Mini-Lesson

Observation Journal

Imagine that you are Miss Kinnian, observing Charlie's progress. Write several entries in her observation journal to describe the events from her point of view.

Writing Skills Focus: Details to Support Points

As you write, support your observations with specific **details.** Choose a variety of details to help readers understand each important event, as in this passage from the story.

Model From the Story

It happened today. Algernon bit me. I visited the lab to see him as I do occasionally, and when I took him out of his cage, he snapped at my hand. I put him back and watched him for a while. He was unusually disturbed and vicious.

Prewriting Choose a specific day or period of days to write about. Review Charlie's version in his progress reports. Then, jot down ideas about how Miss Kinnian's point of view would differ.

Drafting Begin each day's entry with a day and date. Start each paragraph with a simple description of an event. Then, expand the description with specific details that Miss Kinnian might observe and find significant.

Revising Read your entries to a classmate. Look for inconsistencies in point of view, as well as unsupported details. Does each journal entry have a main point that is supported by details?

> ◆ **Grammar Application**
>
> Check that your verb tenses are correct. Form present perfect, past perfect, and future perfect tenses using *has, had,* or *have* and the past participle of the verb.

Problem-and-Solution Essay

Writing Process Workshop

The selections in this part all deal with facing hard questions—when to speak up for oneself, what should be done to preserve our identities and the environment, and how far science should go in "fixing" what nature has given us. Very often the best way to face a hard question—and find an answer to it—is to set it down on paper. Write an essay that poses a problem and provides a solution to a hard question.

Use the skills in the Writing Mini-Lessons introduced in this section to help you.

Writing Skills Focus

▶ **Use an organizational strategy** that presents your problem and solution clearly. (See p. 183.)

▶ **Provide the necessary background** of your problem so all aspects of the situation are clear and the solution makes sense. (See p. 191.)

▶ Use relevant details to **support your points,** enabling your readers to see the depth of your problem and the logic of your solution. (See p. 227.)

WRITING MODEL

We were approaching bear country and needed to know what to do if we met a bear. We had a problem, though. ① Each guidebook offered different advice about bears: stay away from them altogether *or* it's okay to get close to bears as long as you don't separate the mother from its cub *or* make lots of noise near bears *or* be quiet. ② We were confused and a little scared. Our solutions seemed to be to skip the wilderness altogether or try to find a better guidebook. Then we heard a voice behind us, "Why not ask an expert?" ③ There sat the solution to our problem, a tanned and smiling park ranger. He stretched out and began, "Let me tell you about bears. . . ."

① The writer provides background information about the problem.

② These details support the statement that advice about bears was contradictory.

③ The essay is organized logically, identifying the problem first, giving possible solutions next, and then identifying the best solution.

Prewriting

Choose a Topic Your problem-and-solution essay might deal with a personal, local, or universal problem. For a personal topic, consider how you have mastered different situations. Look for a local topic in the editorial pages of your school and town newspapers. For a universal problem, listen to special reports on the evening news.

Make a Problem-and-Solution Diagram Create a diagram that shows the relationship between a problem and possible solutions.

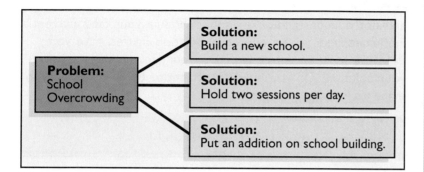

Choose an Organizational Plan Once you've gathered details for your problem-and-solution essay, decide on the best way to present them. Chronological, or time, order will be effective if your solution has many steps. Use order-of-importance organization if you're presenting several possible solutions and want to save the best for last. Use point-by-point organization if you want to discuss a problem that is complicated and has several separate solutions.

Drafting

Refer to Your Prewriting Notes and Diagrams As you draft, be sure you're on track by referring to the details you have gathered.

Begin by Providing Background Be sure your readers will be able to follow what you say by providing necessary background as you draft. You may want to place an asterisk beside words you'll need to define. When finished drafting, go back and insert definitions for those terms.

Support Your Points As you draft, include details that support the points you're making.

APPLYING LANGUAGE SKILLS: Avoiding Run-on Sentences

A run-on sentence is two or more complete sentences that are not properly joined or separated. You can correct run-on sentences by separating complete thoughts with a period (not a comma) or with a comma and conjunction such as *and, or, for, so, yet,* and *but.*

Run-on:

He hesitated a moment, he finally joined the others.

Correct:

He hesitated a moment, but he finally joined the others.

Practice On your paper, correct the run-on sentences.

1. She didn't know the way, she was determined to go on.
2. Harriet's challenge was great she had to get eleven slaves to Canada.
3. There were many dangers lurking everywhere, there were great friends along the way.

Writing Application Review your essay and correct run-on sentences.

Writer's Solution Connection
Writing Lab

For help choosing a topic, use the Inspirations for Writing in the tutorial for Exposition: Making Connections.

Writing Process Workshop

EDITING/PROOFREADING

APPLYING LANGUAGE SKILLS: Combining Sentences

Combine short, choppy sentences to make your writing smooth and clear. Use connecting words and phrases such as *in order, because,* and *who* to connect your sentences.

Short Sentences: Harriet Tubman risked her life. She wanted to save many slaves.

Combined Sentence: Harriet Tubman risked her life in order to save many slaves.

Practice On your paper, combine the short sentences into a longer, more logical and fluid one. Use the word provided to combine the sentences.

1. There were eleven fugitives. They all wanted to flee north. (*who*)
2. The slaves had nothing to eat. They had nowhere to sleep. (*and*)
3. They had to reach Canada. They faced death if they were captured in the United States. (*because*)

Writing Application As you draft, combine short choppy sentences.

Writer's Solution Connection Language Lab

For more practice combining sentences, complete the Combining Sentences lesson in the Styling Sentences unit.

Revising

Add Details Reread your draft critically. Add details wherever necessary to support your main points.

Do an Organization Check Read your paper critically. Circle or highlight in blue all the points that refer to the problem. Then, circle or highlight in red all the solution points. Make sure your points are all in the right places.

Use a Checklist Go back to the Writing Skills Focus on page 228, and use the items as a checklist to evaluate and revise your essay.

Do a Fact Check Have you used strong, undeniable facts and not opinions and/or assumptions? Are your facts current? For example, if you've quoted population figures, have you used the most recent census? Do your facts actually support your solution? Do you need to add more or different facts to make your essay stronger?

REVISION MODEL

① We wanted to learn about wolves in the wilderness, but we didn't want to be in any danger.
This time we went straight to the Park Service. We learned more about wolves than we ever could on our own. ② There was a program all about wolves as well as a guided hike.

③ It was called "Wolves: Myths and Realities," and it included a presentation about the wolves' lives. Then, we went by truck up into the mountains and hiked with the ranger near areas that wolves frequent. We saw a timber wolf.

① This sentence was added to provide necessary background.
② For better organization, this sentence was moved to the end to summarize the solution.
③ These details were added to support the main point.

Publishing and Presenting

▶ **Classroom** Share your problem-and-solution essays in class by reading them aloud.
▶ **Library** With your classmates, bind your essays together. Display a copy in your school library.
▶ **Letter** Enclose your problem-and-solution essay in a letter to a friend or relative.

Real-World Reading Skills Workshop

Strategies for Success

"All that glitters is not gold." This saying warns you to avoid accepting things at face value. This also holds true for things you read. Magazine and newspaper advertisements, political pamphlets, editorials, and even help-wanted advertisements may be deceptive in their wording. Rather than accepting everything you read as truth, challenge texts to determine whether they are unbiased and truthful.

Use Your Common Sense Give advertisements, editorials, and political pledges the reality test. Ask yourself: "Does this make sense? Have I ever heard of an offer this good or a promise so wonderful?" If the answer is no, beware.

Consider Motivation Think about why someone is paying for an ad or writing an editorial. What is it he or she is trying to accomplish? Is the writer working for your benefit or the employer's?

Look for Details Remember the first time you got a toy and expected it to do something, but all it did was lie in the box? Then, you learned it needed batteries to run. Details are like batteries—they are necessary. Make sure the details about the promise or the advertisement are included!

Check References Ask other people for their opinions about the product, candidate, or issue. Find out whether past promises or claims turned out to be true. You may also want to contact the Better Business Bureau to find out whether customers have lodged complaints about the company.

> **KIDS – Earn BIG BUCKS!!**
> Lots of money and not much work!
> Choose your hours.
> No experience needed.
> Call Pat at 878-2367 Today!!!
> Must be strong, healthy, and willing to follow directions.

Apply the Strategies

Read the advertisement above carefully. Then, answer the questions below.

1. What are the wages for this job?
2. What will you do to earn your money?
3. What is written in smaller print? Why, do you think, is it written this way?
4. What actual facts and details does this advertisement provide?
5. Using your common sense as a guide, is this a good job to have? Why or why not?

✔ Here are other situations in which challenging the text is important:
▶ Reading a campaign flyer
▶ Reading a newspaper editorial
▶ Reading a scientific report

Principal Parts and Verb Tenses

Grammar Review

A **verb** is a word that shows action or being. Verbs have four basic forms called the **principal parts.** The principal parts are the present (or base form), the present participle, the past, and the past participle.

A regular verb forms its past and past participle by adding -*ed* or -*d* to the present form (see p. 182). Irregular verbs form their past and past participle in different ways (see p. 190).

tense (tens) *n.* any of the forms of a verb that show the time of the action or condition [The present tense of the verb "talk" is "talk" or "talks"; the past tense is "talked", the future *tense* is "will talk."] [This word comes to us, through Old French, from Latin *tempus*, meaning "time."]

Present	Present Participle	Past	Past Participle
walk	walking	walked	(have) walked
draw	drawing	drew	(have) drawn

Verb Tense The **tense** of a verb shows the time of the action or condition expressed by the verb. You form the verb tenses by using the principal parts and helping verbs (see p. 200).

Present:	I walk
Past:	I walked
Future:	I will walk
Present Perfect:	I have walked
Past Perfect:	I had walked
Future Perfect:	I will have walked

Practice 1 For each of the following sentences, choose the correct verb from the choices in parentheses and write it on your paper.

1. Has she (got, gotten) up yet?

2. She had (run, ran) to the North before.

3. The fugitives (sang, sung) while fleeing.

4. The doorbell had already (rung, rang) twice before it was answered.

5. She must have (grown, grew) tired waiting.

6. She will be (remember, remembered) for all time.

7. I have always (thought, think) of her as a hero.

Practice 2 On your paper, write the required form of the verb in parentheses for the following sentences.

1. Her employer (*surprise,* past) the governess with the news.

2. The governess (*remain,* past) silent.

3. She may have (*wonder,* past participle) why her employer was being mean.

4. Charlie is (*worry,* present participle) about the tests.

5. Algernon (*die,* past) during the experiment.

Strategies for Success

How dull it would be if everyone had the same opinions, or if they liked the same color, the same dog, the same ice cream. People disagree; it's natural, normal, and can often be a useful tool for change and improvement. Problems arise, however, when disagreements lead to anger, disrespect, and resentment. Your task is to disagree reasonably, in an intelligent and mature way.

Listen Thoughtfully Many people are so eager to express their own opinions that they ignore what others are saying. *Before* you express your disagreement, listen thoughtfully.

Listen to Agree, Not to Disagree Listen to find points on which you agree. First, this will put you in a cooperative state of mind. Second, it will help you find a common ground, an idea on which you both agree.

Think Before You Speak This strategy helps you to order your thoughts so that when you do speak, your arguments are easier to follow, and it allows you time to collect your feelings. If you're angry or insulted, it allows you time to cool down.

Speak Slowly and in a Low Voice Nothing inflames a disagreement more than a loud, rapid-fire, high-pitched verbal attack. Speak in a way that encourages people to trust your judgment.

Use Common Sense and Facts Argue from a position of knowledge. Give reasons, and back up your reasons with facts. Make it clear why your opinion makes sense.

Inappropriate: That's a stupid idea.

Better: If you do it that way, it will cause other problems.

Apply the Strategies

With a partner, role-play these situations. Express your disagreement reasonably and maturely.

1. You believe that Ned doesn't do his share of the work in your science group, which makes you feel you have to do extra work. What would you say to express your opinion?

2. Each year, your class does a community service project. You and your friends want to work in the community food pantry. Kylee and her friends want to clean up the park. How would you express your disagreement?

Tips for Expressing Disagreement

- Before you disagree, listen.
- Never disagree in anger. Think before you speak.
- Never shout. Speak in a calm, confident, low-pitched voice.
- Disagree from a position of knowledge.
- Use common sense and facts.

What's Behind the Words

Vocabulary Adventures With Richard Lederer

Words Borrowed From Native Americans

The North American Indians, or Native Americans, were here long before any other group of people who are now living in the United States. The early colonists began borrowing words almost from the moment of first contact, and many of those words have remained in our everyday language. Native American names for animals (*moose*), plants (*hickory*), and Indian life (*tomahawk*) started to appear in our language soon after the colonists landed.

A Native Way of Life

Many Native American terms offer insight into the people and way of life of North American Indians:

People: *sachem* (Narraganset), *squaw* (Massachuset), *papoose* (Narraganset), *mugwump* (Natick)

Native American life: *moccasin* (Chippewa), *toboggan* (Algonquian), *wigwam* (Abenaki), *tepee* (Dakota), *pow-wow* (Narraganset), *wampum* (Massachuset), *hogan* (Navajo), *hickory* (Algonquian), *kayak* (Inuit)

ACTIVITY 1 Pronouncing many of the Native American words was difficult for the early explorers and settlers. In many instances, they shortened and simplified the names. Given the Native American names, identify the following animals:

1. apossoun (Don't play dead now.)
2. wuchak (How much wood?)
3. rahaugcum (Ring around the tail)
4. khalibu (Rudolph is one.)
5. seganku (What's black and white and stinks all over?)

ACTIVITY 2 The following food names originated as Native American words. Find out what kind of food each one is.

1. squash (Natick)
2. pecan (Algonquian)
3. hominy (Algonquian)
4. pone (Algonquian)
5. pemmican (Cree)
6. succotash (Narraganset)

The Poetry of Place Names

If you look at a map of the United States, you will realize how freely settlers used words of Indian origin to name states, cities, towns, mountains, lakes, rivers, ponds, and creeks. The people of Webster, Massachusetts (especially those who sell postcards), continue to take pride in a local lake named *Chargoggagogg-manchauggauggagogghaubunagungamaugg,* Nipmuck for "You fish on your side, I fish on my side, and nobody fish in the middle."

ACTIVITY 3 With help from an encyclopedia, find out which Native American tribes lived in your part of the country. Have their languages survived in many place names? Pick out five names of places in your state—cities, towns, mountains, or bodies of water—that have Native American names. Try to find their exact origins. What can you find out about the history of your state that will help explain why these names were chosen?

Extended Reading Opportunities

The many challenges that life brings and the struggles of those who must confront them are the basis for the works of literature in this unit. To further explore the theme of meeting challenges, choose from the following works.

Suggested Titles

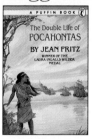

The Double Life of Pocahontas
Jean Fritz

Biographer Jean Fritz dispels the romantic stories surrounding Pocahontas. A Powhatan Indian, she befriended settler Captain John Smith and made him part of her tribe. She was permitted to move freely between the settlers and her tribe. When relations between the tribe and the settlers became tense, she was kidnapped in an attempt to negotiate peace. This biography portrays Pocahontas as a pawn between two worlds, a woman who pays a high price for keeping peace.

Across Five Aprils
Irene Hunt

Jethro Creighton lives on a farm in southern Illinois, a border state, during the Civil War. Although Jethro's town supports the Union, his family has divided loyalties—two of his brothers fight for the North and one fights for the South. When Jethro's father passes away, he must run the farm and take care of his family. Watching his family and country torn apart by war, Jethro grows too rapidly from boy to man.

Shark Beneath the Reef
Jean Craighead George

Fourteen-year-old Tomás Torres dreams of catching a great shark in the Sea of Cortez. He aspires to become a marine biologist, and his family supports this decision. When Tomás finds out that his family is having financial troubles, he wants to help them. Tomás is then confronted with deciding between going to high school or becoming a fisherman. His battle with a shark and voyage to self-discovery help him come to his decision.

Other Possibilities

Lyddie	Katherine Paterson
Among the Volcanoes	Omar Castenda
Lupita Mañana	Patricia Beatty

Trial by Jury, 1964, Thomas Hart Benton, Nelson-Atkins Museum of Art, Kansas City, Missouri;
© T.H. Benton and R.P. Benton Testamentary Trusts/Licensed by VAGA, New York, NY

Quest for Justice

I t's human nature to fight for what we believe is right. The quest for justice occurs in many forms and in many places—courtroom battles, drawing attention to world hunger, solving a dispute among friends. The selections in this unit explore the various ways in which people join the search for justice.

Guide for Reading

Meet the Author:

Walter Dean Myers (1937–   )

"I've got more ideas than I'll ever have time to write," says Walter Dean Myers. A native of West Virginia, Myers was raised in Harlem, an African American community in New York City. His foster parents, the Deans, encouraged him to read widely, and from them he developed a lifelong love of books.

Early Inspiration Early in his life, Myers realized the importance of quality education. The combination of education and love of words led young Myers to see writing as a way to overcome a serious childhood speech problem and his painful shyness. Langston Hughes, the renowned African American poet, encouraged Myers to try writing poetry.

Skill and Chance Myers's career as an author began almost by chance in 1969 when he entered a contest for minority writers. His story won the $500 prize. Since then, Myers has published more than forty works for young people, and he has won four Coretta Scott King Awards and two Newbery Honor Awards.

THE STORY BEHIND THE STORY

Long interested in and concerned by the injustices suffered by African Americans, Walter Dean Myers has focused much of his writing on their experiences. In "Brown *vs.* Board of Education," Myers writes about the historic Supreme Court decision and its effect on the nation.

◆ LITERATURE AND YOUR LIFE

CONNECT YOUR EXPERIENCE

When treated unfairly, you are likely to feel hurt and angry. Like the people in this essay, however, you can also take a positive step and work to change the situation.

THEMATIC FOCUS: Quest for Justice

The African American struggle for justice and racial equality has affected generations of Americans—from the schoolchildren who integrated the Little Rock, Arkansas, schools, shown on the facing page, to people of all ages, races, and economic backgrounds.

◆ Background for Understanding

HISTORY

Following the Civil War, Congress passed several laws protecting the civil rights of African Americans. However, those laws were often disregarded. In 1883, for example, the Supreme Court ruled that congressional acts to prevent racial discrimination were unconstitutional. The often-cited 1896 case of *Plessy* v. *Ferguson* upheld a law requiring "separate but equal" accommodations in railroad cars. For fifty years, that ruling was applied to segregate the races in transportation, hotels, restaurants, and even in the public schools. It wasn't until 1954, in *Brown* v. *Board of Education of Topeka,* that segregation in public schools was declared unconstitutional. Eventually, this decision broke down the "separate but equal" doctrine.

◆ Brown *vs.* Board of Education ◆

◆ Literary Focus

INFORMATIVE ESSAY

An **informative essay** is a short nonfiction piece that gives information about a topic, including facts, examples, and details. It may also present the writer's point of view or opinion about the topic. "Brown *vs.* Board of Education" informs us about the long struggle to desegregate public schools. Use an outline like the one below to record the information in the essay.

I. History of School Segregation
   A.
   B.
   C.
II. Thurgood Marshall's Life
   A.
   B.
   C.
III. The *Brown* vs. *Board of Education* Decision
   A.
   B.
   C.

◆ Build Vocabulary

PREFIXES: *in-*

In "Brown *vs.* Board of Education," attorney Thurgood Marshall argued that "there were *intangible* factors" which made segregated education unequal. In the word *intangible,* the prefix *in-* means "not." The word *intangible* is a combination of *in-,* "not," and *tangible,* "able to be touched or felt." Therefore, *intangible* means "cannot be touched or defined."

WORD BANK

Look over these words from the essay. Which one is something a jury might be doing? Check the Build Vocabulary box on page 245 to see if you chose correctly.

elusive
predominantly
diligent
intangible
unconstitutional
deliberating
oppressed

Reading for Success

Strategies for Constructing Meaning

To understand a piece of writing fully—especially nonfiction—you must put words and ideas together in your own mind, so that they have meaning for you. Use these strategies to help you construct meaning:

Make inferences.

Writers don't always tell you everything directly. Sometimes you must "read between the lines," or make inferences, to arrive at ideas the writer suggests but doesn't say. This includes looking beyond the literal meaning of the words to get a full picture of what the author means.
▶ Make an inference by considering the details that the writer includes or doesn't include.
▶ Think about what this choice of details tells you about the author's opinions or purpose in writing.

Determine cause and effect.

To better understand the information presented to you, look for relation-ships among ideas. Cause and effect is one kind of relationship. A *cause* makes something happen. An *effect* is what happens—the result. You will read in this selection that segregation caused black children to feel inferior to white chil-dren. The cause is segregation. The effect is a feeling of inferiority.

Identify important ideas.

In many nonfiction pieces, most paragraphs have a main idea that is either stated or implied. Main ideas are general statements supported by facts, examples, and details. To discover the important, or main, ideas, try these strategies:
▶ Answer the question, "What is the author's point?"
▶ Identify the supporting details for each main idea.

Interpret what you read.

Interpreting what you read will help make the information your own. To interpret, follow these steps:
▶ Restate in your own words what the author has written.
▶ Explain the importance of what the author is saying.

As you read "Brown *vs.* Board of Education," look at the notes in the boxes. They show you how to apply these strategies to your reading.

BROWN *vs.* BOARD OF EDUCATION

Walter Dean Myers

There was a time when the meaning of freedom was easily understood. For an African crouched in the darkness of a tossing ship, wrists chained, men with guns standing on the decks above him, freedom was a physical thing, the ability to move away from his captors, to follow the dictates of his own heart, to listen to the voices within him that defined his values and showed him the truth of his own path. The plantation owners wanted to make the Africans feel helpless, inferior. They denied them images of themselves as Africans and told them that they were without beauty. They segregated them and told them they were without value.

> You can **infer** from the images here that Myers believes the problems caused by slavery continued long after slavery had been abolished.

Slowly, surely, the meaning of freedom changed to an elusive thing that even the strongest people could not hold in their hands. There were no chains on black wrists, but there were the shadows of chains, stretching for hundreds of years back through time, across black minds.

* * *

From the end of the Civil War in 1865 to the early 1950's, many public schools in both the North and South were segregated. Segregation was different in the different sections of the country. In the North most of the schools were segregated *de facto*;[1] that is, the law allowed blacks and whites to go to school together, but they did not actually always attend the same schools. Since a school is generally attended by children living in its neighborhood, wherever there were predominantly African-American neighborhoods there were, "in fact," segregated schools. In many parts of the country, however, and especially in the South, the segregation was *de jure*,[2] meaning that there were laws which forbade blacks to attend the same schools as whites.

> This is an **important idea**—that segregation in schools was occurring in both the North and the South.

The states with segregated schools relied upon the ruling of the Supreme Court in the 1896 *Plessy vs. Ferguson* case for legal justification: Facilities that were "separate but equal" were legal.

In the early 1950's the National Association for the Advancement of Colored People (N.A.A.C.P.) sponsored five cases that eventually reached the Supreme Court. One of the cases involved the school board of Topeka, Kansas.

Thirteen families sued the Topeka school board, claiming that to segregate the children

---

1. *de facto* (dē fak´ tō): Latin for "existing in actual fact."

2. *de jure* (dē jʉr´ ə): Latin for "by right or legal establishment."

◆ Build Vocabulary

elusive (i lōō´ siv) *adj.*: Hard to grasp or retain mentally

predominantly (pri däm´ ə nənt lē) *adj.*: Mainly; most noticeably

▲ **Critical Viewing** What details in this photograph reveal that segregated education was "separate but not equal"? [Connect]

was harmful to the children and, therefore, a violation of the equal protection clause of the Fourteenth Amendment. The names on the Topeka case were listed in alphabetical order, with the father of seven-year-old Linda Brown listed first.

"I didn't understand why I couldn't go to school with my playmates. I lived in an integrated neighborhood and played with children of all nationalities, but when school started they went to a school only four blocks from my home and I was sent to school across town," she says.

For young Linda the case was one of convenience and of being made to feel different, but for African-American parents it had been a long, hard struggle to get a good education for their children. It was also a struggle waged by lawyers who had worked for years to

overcome segregation. The head of the legal team who presented the school cases was Thurgood Marshall.

* * *

The city was Baltimore, Maryland, and the year was 1921. Thirteen-year-old Thurgood Marshall struggled to balance the packages he was carrying with one hand while he tried to get his bus fare out of his pocket with the other. It was almost Easter, and the part-time job he had would provide money for flowers for his mother. Suddenly he felt a violent tug at his right arm that spun him around, sending his packages sprawling over the floor of the bus.

"Nigguh, don't you never push in front of no white lady again!" an angry voice spat in his ear.

Thurgood turned and threw a punch into the face of the name caller. The man charged into Thurgood, throwing punches that mostly missed, and tried to wrestle the slim boy to the ground. A policeman broke up the fight, grabbing Thurgood with one huge black hand and pushing him against the side of the bus. Within minutes they were in the local courthouse.

Thurgood was not the first of his family to get into a good fight. His father's father had joined the Union Army during the Civil War, taking the names Thorough Good to add to the one name he had in bondage. His grandfather on his mother's side was a man brought from Africa and, according to Marshall's biography, "so ornery that his owner wouldn't sell him out of pity for the people who might buy him, but gave him his freedom instead and told him to clear out of the county."

Thurgood's frequent scrapes earned him a reputation as a young boy who couldn't be trusted to get along with white folks.

His father, Will Marshall, was a steward at the Gibson Island Yacht Club near Baltimore, and his mother, Norma, taught in a segregated school. The elder Marshall felt he could have done more with his life if his education had been better, but there had been few opportunities available for African Americans when he had been a young man. When it was time for the Marshall boys to go to college, he was more than willing to make the sacrifices necessary to send them.

Young people of color from all over the world came to the United States to study at Lincoln University, a predominantly black institution in southeastern Pennsylvania. Here Marshall

◆ **Build Vocabulary**

diligent (dil′ ə jənt) *adj*.: Done with careful, steady effort; hardworking

majored in predentistry, which he found boring, and joined the Debating Club, which he found interesting. By the time he was graduated at the age of twenty-one, he had decided to give up dentistry for the law. Three years later he was graduated, first in his class, from Howard University Law School.

> This passage shows a **cause and effect.** Marshall became a lawyer as a result of his boredom with predentistry and his interest in debating.

At Howard there was a law professor, Charles Hamilton Houston, who would affect the lives of many African-American lawyers and who would influence the legal aspects of the civil rights movement. Houston was a

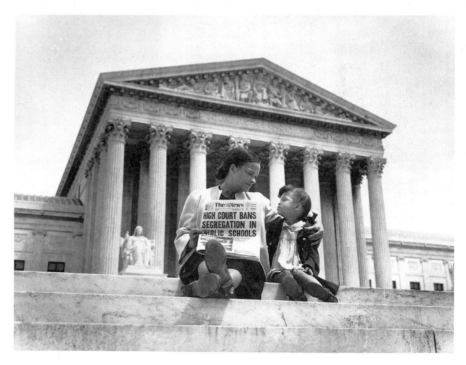

▲ **Critical Viewing** In this photograph, a woman explains the significance of the ruling to her young daughter. What does the newspaper the woman is holding tell you about the impact of the ruling? **[Connect]**

great teacher, one who demanded that his students be not just good lawyers but great lawyers. If they were going to help their people—and for Houston the only reason for African Americans to become lawyers was to do just that—they would have to have absolute understanding of the law, and be diligent in the preparation of their cases. At the time, Houston was an attorney for the

▲ **Critical Viewing** Thurgood Marshall is being sworn in as a Supreme Court justice as President Johnson looks on. What details show that this is a solemn, historic occasion? **[Interpret]**

N.A.A.C.P. and fought against discrimination in housing and in jobs.

After graduation, Thurgood Marshall began to do some work for the N.A.A.C.P., trying the difficult civil rights cases. He not only knew about the effects of discrimination by reading about it, he was still living it when he was graduated from law school in 1933. In 1936 Marshall began working full-time for the N.A.A.C.P., and in 1940 became its chief counsel.

It was Thurgood Marshall and a battery of N.A.A.C.P. attorneys who began to challenge segregation throughout the country. These men and women were warriors in the cause of freedom for African Americans, taking their battles into courtrooms across the country. They understood the process of American justice and the power of the Constitution.

In *Brown* vs. *Board of Education of Topeka*, Marshall argued that segregation was a violation of the Fourteenth Amendment—that even if the facilities and all other "tangibles" were equal, which was the heart of the case in *Plessy* vs. *Ferguson*, a violation still existed. There were <u>intangible</u> factors, he argued, that made the education unequal.

Everyone involved understood the significance of the case: that it was much more than whether black children could go to school with white children. If segregation in the schools was declared <u>unconstitutional</u>, then all segregation in public places could be declared unconstitutional.

Southerners who argued against ending school segregation were caught up, as then-

> Based on the words he uses, such as *warriors*, *cause*, and *battles*, you can **infer** that Myers considers Marshall and the other attorneys to be engaged in a heroic struggle.

Congressman Brooks Hays of Arkansas put it, in "a lifetime of adventures in that gap between law and custom." The law was one thing, but most Southern whites felt just as strongly about their customs as they did the law.

Dr. Kenneth B. Clark, an African-American psychologist, testified for the N.A.A.C.P. He presented clear evidence that the effect of segregation was harmful to African-American children. Describing studies conducted by black and white psychologists over a twenty-year period, he showed that black children felt inferior to white children. In a particularly dramatic study that he had supervised, four dolls, two white and two black, were presented to African-American children. From the responses of the children to the dolls, identical in every way except color, it was clear that the children were rejecting the black dolls. African-American children did not just feel separated from white children, they felt that the separation was based on their inferiority.

> This paragraph discusses a **cause-and-effect** relationship. Segregation was the cause of feelings of inferiority in African American children.

Dr. Clark understood fully the principles and ideas of those people who had held Africans in bondage and had tried to make slaves of captives. By isolating people of African descent, by barring them from certain actions or places, they could make them feel inferior. The social scientists who testified at *Brown* vs. *Board of Education* showed that children who felt inferior also performed poorly.

> The **main idea** of this paragraph—that Marshall and the N.A.A.C.P. won their case—is supported by such details as the Court's looking beyond the intentions of the Fourteenth Amendment and overturning *Plessy* vs. *Ferguson*.

The Justice Department argued that racial segregation was objectionable to the Eisenhower Administration and hurt our relationships with other nations.

* * *

On May 17, 1954, after deliberating for nearly a year and a half, the Supreme Court made its ruling. The Court stated that it could not use the intentions of 1868, when the Fourteenth Amendment was passed, as a guide to its ruling, or even those of 1896, when the decision in *Plessy* vs. *Ferguson* was handed down. Chief Justice Earl Warren wrote:

> We must consider public education in the light of its full development and its present place in American life throughout the nation. We must look instead to the effect of segregation itself on public education.

The Court went on to say that "modern authority" supported the idea that segregation deprived African Americans of equal opportunity. "Modern authority" referred to Dr. Kenneth B. Clark and the weight of evidence that he and the other social scientists had presented.

The high court's decision in *Brown* vs. *Board of Education* signaled an important change in the struggle for civil rights. It signaled clearly that the legal prohibitions that oppressed African Americans would have to fall. Equally important was the idea that the nature of the fight for equality would change. Ibrahima, Cinqué, Nat Turner, and George Latimer had struggled for freedom by fighting against their captors or fleeing from them. The 54th had fought for African freedom on the battlefields of the Civil War. Ida B. Wells had fought for equality with her pen. Lewis H. Latimer and Meta Vaux Warrick had tried to earn equality with their work. In *Brown* vs. *Board of Education* Thurgood Marshall, Kenneth B. Clark, and the lawyers and social scientists, both black and white, who helped them had

◆ Build Vocabulary

intangible (in tan´ jə bəl) *adj*.: Not able to be touched or grasped

unconstitutional (un´ kän stə to͞o´ shə nəl) *adj*.: Not in accordance with or permitted by the U.S. Constitution

deliberating (di lib´ ə rā tiŋ) *v*.: Thinking or considering very carefully and fully

oppressed (ə prest´) *adj*.: Kept down by cruel or unjust use of power

won for African Americans a victory that would bring them closer to full equality than they had ever been in North America. There would still be legal battles to be won, but the major struggle would be in the hearts and minds of people and "in that gap between law and custom."

> You can **interpret** this appointment to mean that Marshall had a successful law career.

In 1967 Thurgood Marshall was appointed by President Lyndon B. Johnson as an associate justice of the U.S. Supreme Court. He retired in 1991.

* * *

"I didn't think of my father or the other parents as being heroic at the time," Linda Brown says. "I was only seven. But as I grew older and realized how far-reaching the case was and how it changed the complexion of the history of this country, I was just thrilled that my father and the others here in Topeka were involved."

Beyond Literature

Social Studies Connection

The Role of the Supreme Court
Why was the Supreme Court of the United States charged with making a decision in the case of *Brown* vs. *Board of Education of Topeka*? Article III of the Constitution gives the Supreme Court the right to decide cases concerning constitutional issues, such as whether racially "separate but equal" schools are constitutionally legal. The Supreme Court also has the right of judicial review—the right to strike down a law made by Congress, a state, or a local government if that law violates the Constitution.

Cross-Curricular Activity
The Judges Supreme Court justices are appointed by the President of the United States. Find out who the current justices are and which President appointed each one.

Guide for Responding

◆ LITERATURE AND YOUR LIFE

Reader's Response How do you think the Supreme Court's decision in *Brown* vs. *Board of Education* has affected your life?

Thematic Focus In what ways was Marshall's quest for justice fulfilled?

Journal Writing Jot down in your journal some ways in which you have joined in a quest for justice.

☑ Check Your Comprehension

1. What were the main claims made by parents in the lawsuit against the Topeka school board?
2. Why were some people concerned about the *Brown* vs. *Board of Education* case, although these people had nothing to do with schools?
3. Name two significant changes in the nature of the African American struggle following *Brown* vs. *Board of Education*.

◆ Critical Thinking

INTERPRET

1. Why were so many people willing to fight against segregation in the schools? **[Analyze]**
2. What does Myers mean when he refers to "shadows of chains" in black minds? **[Interpret]**
3. What is the author's purpose in concluding with Linda Brown's comments about the impact of this case? **[Speculate]**

APPLY

4. Why is this Supreme Court case so important in American history? **[Apply]**

EVALUATE

5. Charles Hamilton Houston thought it was important for his students to become "great" lawyers. Do you agree or disagree? Explain. **[Make a Judgment]**

Guide for Responding (continued)

◆ Reading for Success

STRATEGIES FOR CONSTRUCTING MEANING

Review the reading strategies and the notes showing how to construct meaning. Then, apply them to answer the following.

1. What can you infer about Myers's opinion of Thurgood Marshall? Support your answer.
2. Identify three important ideas in this essay.
3. Interpret Myers's statement that the future "struggle would be in the hearts and minds of people and 'in that gap between law and custom.'" Do you agree with his opinion? Explain.

◆ Build Vocabulary Skills

USING THE PREFIX in-

The prefix in- usually means "not." On a sheet of paper, form words by adding in- to the following. Then, write a definition of each new word.

1. appropriate 2. capable 3. tolerant

SPELLING STRATEGY

You may have to drop or change a letter before adding -ed to form the past tense of a verb. When a verb ends in silent e, drop the e before adding -ed: escape + -ed = escaped. When a verb ends in a consonant and y, change the y to i and add -ed: solidify + -ed = solidified.

Add -ed to these verbs to form their past tense.

1. release 2. beautify 3. exchange 4. qualify

USING THE WORD BANK

On your paper, write the word that is closest in meaning to the Word Bank word.

1. elusive: (a) outstanding, (b) ungraspable, (c) frightening
2. predominantly: (a) mainly, (b) quickly, (c) unfairly
3. diligent: (a) respectful, (b) lazy, (c) hardworking
4. intangible: (a) weak, (b) concrete, (c) not solid
5. unconstitutional: (a) legal, (b) illegal, (c) illogical
6. deliberating: (a) considering, (b) noting, (c) waiting
7. oppressed: (a) cleansed, (b) beaten down, (c) hurried

◆ Literary Focus

INFORMATIVE ESSAY

An **informative essay** is a short nonfiction work that explains or gives information about a topic. The writer may also express a point of view or an opinion about the topic of the essay.

1. What are three main ideas that Myers wants his readers to know about the Brown vs. Board of Education decision?
2. How important does Myers think the Brown vs. Board of Education decision is? Find three examples that are evidence of his opinion.

◆ Build Grammar Skills

ADJECTIVES

Adjectives are words that modify, or describe, nouns or pronouns. They tell more about the nouns or pronouns they modify by answering the questions which, what kind, how many, or how much. In the following sentence, Myers uses adjectives to tell what kind of tug he felt and on which arm:

Suddenly he felt a *violent* tug at his *right* arm . . .

Practice Copy these sentences. Underline each adjective, and draw an arrow to the word it modifies. Then, tell what question it answers.

1. His mother taught in a segregated school.
2. Thurgood's frequent scrapes earned him a reputation.
3. Marshall graduated first in his law class.
4. Four dolls were presented to African American children.
5. The decision signaled an important change.

Writing Application On your paper, write this paragraph, replacing the blanks with adjectives.

The ____?____ child showed ____?____ interest in going to the ____?____ school. Her ____?____ friends went to the ____?____ school. A ____?____ counselor eased the ____?____ child's fears.

Build Your Portfolio

 ## Idea Bank

Writing

1. **Letter** Compose a letter to Linda Brown that expresses your feelings about what she and her family accomplished.

2. **Editorial** Write an editorial for your school newspaper in which you reveal your thoughts about a current issue in your community. **[Community Link]**

3. **Biography** Write a brief biography of Thurgood Marshall, Kenneth B. Clark, or another civil rights leader who was involved in the legal battle to end segregation in the public schools.

Speaking and Listening

4. **Drama [Group Activity]** Work with a small group to dramatize one event in Thurgood Marshall's life. You might choose the occurrence at the bus stop, his argument before the Supreme Court in "Brown vs. Board of Education," or another event you learn about through research. Allow each group member to play a part in your dramatization. **[Performing Arts Link]**

5. **Panel Discussion [Group Activity]** With a small group, prepare and present a panel discussion on the current status of the civil rights movement in the United States. Conduct research to learn about differing positions and views, and present your findings in your panel discussion. **[Social Studies Link]**

Projects

6. **Timeline** Research the history of the civil rights movement in the United States. Create an illustrated timeline of key events in the movement. **[Social Studies Link]**

7. **Collage** Photocopy photographs, news headlines, and magazine articles, and with them, create a collage that captures the essence of the civil rights movement. **[Art Link]**

 ## Writing Mini-Lesson

Personal Essay

"Brown vs. Board of Education" is an informative essay that conveys information, but it also expresses Myers's personal views. Write an essay that tells about your personal views on a topic that is currently in the news.

Writing Skills Focus: Strong Introduction

Use a **strong introduction** to grab your readers' interest. You might begin with a quotation, a question, a startling fact, or a brief story. Walter Dean Myers uses a startling image to capture his readers' attention:

Model From the Essay

There was a time when the meaning of freedom was easily understood. For an African crouched in the darkness of a tossing ship, wrists chained, men with guns stand on the decks above him, freedom was a physical thing, . . .

Prewriting Outline the most important ideas you want to communicate in your essay. Then, list a few details that will support each main idea.

Drafting Follow your outline to write your first draft. Begin with a strong introduction. Then, present your main points one by one. Remember that a personal essay is about your ideas and feelings. Make it personal and reflective of *you*.

Revising Review your introduction to be sure you opened in an interesting way. Will it make the reader want to continue reading?

> ◆ **Grammar Application**
> Add adjectives to your personal essay to create greater detail and add interest.

Taking a Stand

We Demand, Joe Jones, Butler Institute of American Art, Youngstown, Ohio

Guide for Reading

Meet the Author:

O. Henry (1862–1910)

O. Henry, who became one of America's best-known short-story writers, was born William Sydney Porter. His gift for storytelling was nurtured by his sister Evelina, who developed a game in which she would begin to tell a story and her brother would finish it. After his childhood in Greensboro, North Carolina, Porter moved to Texas in 1882. There, he worked as a ranch hand, a bank teller, a writer and publisher of a humor magazine, and a reporter for the *Houston Post*.

A Difficult Start O. Henry's career as a short-story writer did not start off well—in fact, it began in prison. In 1896, he was sent to jail for embezzling bank funds. During his three years in prison, he began to write short stories. Upon his release, William Sydney Porter adopted the pen name O. Henry. His stories, which show a keen understanding of human nature and often feature surprise endings, became very popular with magazine readers.

THE STORY BEHIND THE STORY

O. Henry spent much of his time in prison observing people and developing story lines. It was there that he heard of a bank robber and a safe cracker who inspired the character of Jimmy Valentine, the hero of "A Retrieved Reformation."

◆ LITERATURE AND YOUR LIFE

CONNECT YOUR EXPERIENCE

You may know, or have heard about, a person who has changed his or her life in a major way. A character in this story, caught in an unforeseen situation, decides to turn his life around completely.

THEMATIC FOCUS: Taking a Stand

In this story, a character takes a surprising stand and prepares to accept the consequences of his actions.

◆ Background for Understanding

HISTORY

"A Retrieved Reformation" takes place around the turn of the twentieth century in a town like the one on the facing page. The main character breaks into bank safes to steal money. At the time of the story, the locks, dials, and levers of most safes were located on the outside. Safe crackers developed special tools and techniques to punch out these parts. Today, safes are built with their locks and bolts on the inside, making them much harder to break into.

◆ Build Vocabulary

WORD ROOTS: -simul-

In this story, you'll encounter the word *simultaneously*. It contains the word root *-simul-*, which means "same." Therefore, events that happen simultaneously happen at the same time.

WORD BANK

Which word from the story means "full of virtue or goodness"? Check the Build Vocabulary box on page 253 to see if you chose correctly.

assiduously
virtuous
retribution
unobtrusively
simultaneously
anguish

◆ A Retrieved Reformation ◆

Young of the Town, 1933, Gerrit V. Sinclair, Williams American Art Galleries, Tennessee

◆ Literary Focus

SURPRISE ENDING

O. Henry is known for startling his readers with surprise endings. A **surprise ending** is one that's different from what the writer leads you to expect. Even though you often can't predict a surprise ending, writers make them believable by dropping a few hints about the ending without giving it away.

◆ Reading Strategy

ASK QUESTIONS

You will get a better understanding of what you read if you **ask questions** about the characters and events. You might ask why a character behaves in a certain way or what an action really means. Then, read on to find answers to your questions. Use a chart like the one below to list your questions and the answers you find as you read "A Retrieved Reformation."

Questions	Answers
What will Jimmy do when he gets out of prison?	

A Retrieved Reformation

O. HENRY

A guard came to the prison shoe-shop, where Jimmy Valentine was <u>assiduously</u> stitching uppers, and escorted him to the front office. There the warden handed Jimmy his pardon, which had been signed that morning by the governor. Jimmy took it in a tired kind of way. He had served nearly ten months of a four-year sentence. He had expected to stay only about three months, at the longest. When a man with as many friends on the outside as Jimmy Valentine had is received in the "stir" it is hardly worthwhile to cut his hair.

"Now, Valentine," said the warden, "you'll go out in the morning. Brace up, and make a man of yourself. You're not a bad fellow at heart. Stop cracking safes, and live straight."

"Me?" said Jimmy, in surprise. "Why, I never cracked a safe in my life."

"Oh, no," laughed the warden. "Of course not. Let's see, now. How was it you happened to get sent up on that Springfield job? Was it because you wouldn't prove an alibi for fear of compromising somebody in extremely high-toned society? Or was it simply a case of a mean old jury that had it in for you? It's always one or the other with you innocent victims."

"Me?" said Jimmy, still blankly <u>virtuous</u>. "Why, warden, I never was in Springfield in my life!"

"Take him back, Cronin," smiled the warden, "and fix him up with outgoing clothes. Unlock him at seven in the morning, and let him come to the

▲ **Critical Viewing** What details in this photograph reveal that it was taken long ago? **[Connect]**

bullpen.[1] Better think over my advice, Valentine."

At a quarter past seven on the next morning Jimmy stood in the warden's outer office. He had on a suit of the villainously fitting, ready-made clothes and a pair of the stiff, squeaky shoes that the state furnishes to its discharged compulsory guests.

The clerk handed him a railroad ticket and the five-dollar bill with which the law expected him to rehabilitate himself into good citizenship and prosperity. The

---

1. **bullpen** *n.*: Barred room in a jail, where prisoners are kept temporarily.

warden gave him a cigar, and shook hands. Valentine, 9762, was chronicled on the books "Pardoned by Governor," and Mr. James Valentine walked out into the sunshine.

Disregarding the song of the birds, the waving green trees, and the smell of the flowers, Jimmy headed straight for a restaurant. There he tasted the first sweet joys of liberty in the shape of a chicken dinner. From there he proceeded leisurely to the depot and boarded his train. Three hours set him down in a little town near the state line. He went to the café of one Mike Dolan and shook hands with Mike, who was alone behind the bar.

"Sorry we couldn't make it sooner, Jimmy, me boy," said Mike. "But we had that protest from Springfield to buck against, and the governor nearly balked. Feeling all right?"

"Fine," said Jimmy. "Got my key?"

He got his key and went upstairs, unlocking the door of a room at the rear. Everything was just as he had left it. There on the floor was still Ben Price's collar-button that had been torn from that eminent detective's shirt-band when they had overpowered Jimmy to arrest him.

◆ Reading Strategy
What is Valentine planning to do with the burglar's tools?

Pulling out from the wall a folding-bed, Jimmy slid back a panel in the wall and dragged out a dust-covered suitcase. He opened this and gazed fondly at the finest set of burglar's tools in the East. It was a complete set, made of specially tempered steel, the latest designs in drills, punches, braces and bits, jimmies, clamps, and augers,[2] with two or three novelties invented by Jimmy himself, in which he took pride. Over nine hundred dollars they had cost him to have made at —, a place where they make such things for the profession.

In half an hour Jimmy went downstairs and through the café. He was now dressed in tasteful and well-fitting clothes, and carried his dusted and cleaned suitcase in his hand.

"Got anything on?" asked Mike Dolan, genially.

"Me?" said Jimmy, in a puzzled tone. "I don't understand. I'm representing the New York Amalgamated Short Snap Biscuit Cracker and Frazzled Wheat Company."

This statement delighted Mike to such an extent that Jimmy had to take a seltzer-and-milk on the spot. He never touched "hard" drinks.

A week after the release of Valentine, 9762, there was a neat job of safe-burglary done in Richmond, Indiana, with no clue to the author. A scant eight hundred dollars was all that was secured. Two weeks after that a patented, improved, burglar-proof safe in Logansport was opened like a cheese to the tune of fifteen hundred dollars, currency; securities and silver untouched. That began to interest the rogue-catchers.[3] Then an old-fashioned bank-safe in Jefferson City became active and threw out of its crater an eruption of bank-notes amounting to five thousand dollars. The losses were now high enough to bring the matter up into Ben Price's class of work. By comparing notes, a remarkable similarity in the methods of the burglaries was noticed. Ben Price investigated the scenes of the robberies, and was heard to remark:

"That's Dandy Jim Valentine's autograph. He's resumed business. Look at that combination knob—jerked out as easy as pulling up a radish in wet weather. He's got the only clamps that can do it. And look how clean those tumblers were punched out! Jimmy never has to drill but one hole. Yes, I guess I want Mr. Valentine. He'll do his bit next time without any short-time or clemency foolishness."

Ben Price knew Jimmy's habits. He had learned them while working up the Springfield case. Long jumps, quick getaways, no confederates,[4] and a taste for good society—these

---

2. **drills . . . augers** (ô′ gərz) *n.:* Tools used in metalwork.

3. **rogue-catchers** *n.:* Police.
4. **confederates** (kən fed′ ər its) *n.:* Accomplices.

◆ **Build Vocabulary**

assiduously (ə sij′ o͞o wəs lē) *adv.:* Carefully and busily

virtuous (vʉr′ cho͞o wəs) *adj.:* Moral; upright

ways had helped Mr. Valentine to become noted as a successful dodger of <u>retribution</u>. It was given out that Ben Price had taken up the trail of the elusive cracksman, and other people with burglar-proof safes felt more at ease.

One afternoon, Jimmy Valentine and his suitcase climbed out of the mail hack[5] in Elmore, a little town five miles off the railroad down in the blackjack country of Arkansas. Jimmy, looking like an athletic young senior just home from college, went down the board sidewalk toward the hotel.

A young lady crossed the street, passed him at the corner and entered a door over which was the sign "The Elmore Bank." Jimmy Valentine looked into her eyes, forgot what he was, and became another man. She lowered her eyes and colored slightly. Young men of Jimmy's style and looks were scarce in Elmore.

▲ **Critical Viewing** What would appeal to Jimmy Valentine about this town? **[Deduce]**

Jimmy collared a boy that was loafing on the steps of the bank as if he were one of the stockholders, and began to ask him questions about the town, feeding him dimes at intervals. By and by the young lady came out, looking royally unconscious of the young man with the suitcase, and went her way.

"Isn't that young lady Miss Polly Simpson?" asked Jimmy, with specious guile.[6]

"Naw," said the boy. "She's Annabel Adams. Her pa owns this bank. What'd you come to Elmore for? Is that a gold watch chain? I'm going to get a bulldog. Got any more dimes?"

Jimmy went to the Planters' Hotel, registered as Ralph D. Spencer, and engaged a room. He leaned on the desk and declared his platform[7] to the clerk. He said he had come to Elmore to look for a location to go into business. How was the shoe business, now, in the town? He had thought of the shoe business. Was there an opening?

The clerk was impressed by the clothes and manner of Jimmy. He, himself, was something of a pattern of fashion to the thinly gilded[8] youth of Elmore, but he now perceived his shortcomings. While trying to figure out Jimmy's manner of tying his four-in-hand,[9] he cordially gave information.

Yes, there ought to be a good opening in the shoe line. There wasn't an exclusive shoe store in the place. The dry-goods and general stores handled them. Business in all lines was fairly good. Hoped Mr. Spencer would decide to locate in Elmore. He would find it a pleasant town to live in, and the people very sociable.

Mr. Spencer thought he would stop over in the town a few days and look over the situation. No, the clerk needn't call the boy. He would carry up his suitcase, himself: it was rather heavy.

Mr. Ralph Spencer, the phoenix[10] that arose

---

5. mail hack *n.*: Horse and carriage used to deliver mail.

6. specious guile (spē′ shəs gīl′) *n.*: Crafty, indirect way of obtaining information.

7. platform *n.*: Here, a statement of intention.

8. thinly gilded *adj.*: Coated with a thin layer of gold; here, appearing well dressed.

9. four-in-hand *n.*: Necktie.

10. phoenix (fē′ niks) *n.*: In Egyptian mythology, a beautiful bird that lived for about 600 years and then burst into flames. A new bird arose from its ashes.

from Jimmy Valentine's ashes—ashes left by the flame of a sudden and alterative attack of love—remained in Elmore, and prospered. He opened a shoe store and secured a good run of trade.

Socially he was also a success, and made many friends. And he accomplished the wish of his heart. He met Miss Annabel Adams, and became more and more captivated by her charms.

At the end of a year the situation of Mr. Ralph Spencer was this: he had won the respect of the community, his shoe store was flourishing, and he and Annabel were engaged to be married in two weeks. Mr. Adams, the typical, plodding, country banker, approved of Spencer. Annabel's pride in him almost equaled her affection. He was as much at home in the family of Mr. Adams and that of Annabel's married sister as if he were already a member.

One day Jimmy sat down in his room and wrote this letter, which he mailed to the safe address of one of his old friends in St. Louis:

Dear Old Pal:

I want you to be at Sullivan's place, in Little Rock, next Wednesday night, at nine o'clock. I want you to wind up some little matters for me. And, also, I want to make you a present of my kit of tools. I know you'll be glad to get them— you couldn't duplicate the lot for a thousand dollars. Say, Billy, I've quit the old business— a year ago. I've got a nice store. I'm making an honest living, and I'm going to marry the finest girl on earth two weeks from now. It's the only life, Billy—the straight one. I wouldn't touch a dollar of another man's money now for a million. After I get married I'm going to sell out and go West, where there won't be so much danger of having old scores brought up against me. I tell you, Billy, she's an angel. She believes in me; and I wouldn't do another crooked thing for the whole world. Be sure to be at Sully's, for I must see you. I'll bring along the tools with me.

Your old friend,
Jimmy.

On the Monday night after Jimmy wrote this letter, Ben Price jogged <u>unobtrusively</u> into Elmore in a livery buggy.[11] He lounged about town in his quiet way until he found out what he wanted to know. From the drugstore across the street from Spencer's shoe store he got a good look at Ralph D. Spencer.

"Going to marry the banker's daughter are you, Jimmy?" said Ben to himself, softly. "Well, I don't know!"

The next morning Jimmy took breakfast at the Adamses. He was going to Little Rock that day to order his wedding suit and buy something nice for Annabel. That would be the first time he had left town since he came to Elmore. It had been more than a year now since those last professional "jobs," and he thought he could safely venture out.

After breakfast quite a family party went downtown together—Mr. Adams, Annabel, Jimmy, and Annabel's married sister with her two little girls, aged five and nine. They came by the hotel where Jimmy still boarded, and he ran up to his room and brought along his suitcase. Then they went on to the bank. There stood Jimmy's horse and buggy and Dolph Gibson, who was going to drive him over to the railroad station.

All went inside the high, carved oak railings into the banking-room—Jimmy included, for Mr. Adams's future son-in-law was welcome anywhere. The clerks were pleased to be greeted by the good-looking, agreeable young man who was going to marry Miss Annabel. Jimmy set his suitcase down. Annabel, whose heart was bubbling with happiness and lively youth, put on Jimmy's hat, and picked up the suitcase. "Wouldn't I make a nice drummer?"[12] said Annabel. "My! Ralph, how heavy it is! Feels like it was full of gold bricks."

"Lot of nickel-plated shoehorns in there," said Jimmy, coolly, "that I'm going to return. Thought I'd save express charges by taking them up. I'm getting awfully economical."

---

11. **livery buggy** *n.*: Horse and carriage for hire.
12. **drummer** *n.*: Traveling salesman.

◆ Build Vocabulary

retribution (re´ trə byo͞o´ shən) *n.*: Punishment for wrong-doing

unobtrusively (un´ əb tro͞o´ siv lē) *adv.*: Without calling attention to oneself

▲ **Critical Viewing** Does the woman in this photograph share any qualitites with Annabel, as described in the story? Explain. **[Connect]**

The Elmore Bank had just put in a new safe and vault. Mr. Adams was very proud of it, and insisted on an inspection by everyone. The vault was a small one, but it had a new, patented door. It fastened with three solid steel bolts thrown <u>simultaneously</u> with a single handle, and had a time lock. Mr. Adams beamingly explained its workings to Mr. Spencer, who showed a courteous but not too intelligent interest. The two children, May and Agatha, were delighted by the shining metal and funny clock and knobs.

While they were thus engaged Ben Price sauntered in and leaned on his elbow, looking casually inside between the railings. He told the teller that he didn't want anything; he was just waiting for a man he knew.

Suddenly there was a scream or two from the women, and a commotion. Unperceived by the elders, May, the nine-year-old girl, in a spirit of play, had shut Agatha in the vault. She had then shot the bolts and turned the knob of the combination as she had seen Mr. Adams do.

The old banker sprang to the handle and tugged at it for a moment. "The door can't be opened," he groaned. "The clock hasn't been wound nor the combination set."

Agatha's mother screamed again, hysterically.

"Hush!" said Mr. Adams, raising his trembling hand. "All be quiet for a moment. Agatha!" he called as loudly as he could. "Listen to me." During the following silence they could just hear the faint sound of the child wildly shrieking in the dark vault in a panic of terror.

"My precious darling!" wailed the mother. "She will die of fright! Open the door! Oh, break it open! Can't you men do something?"

"There isn't a man nearer than Little Rock who can open that door," said Mr. Adams, in a shaky voice. "My God! Spencer, what shall we do? That child—she can't stand it long in there. There isn't enough air, and, besides, she'll go into convulsions from fright."

Agatha's mother, frantic now, beat the door of the vault with her hands. Somebody wildly suggested dynamite. Annabel turned to Jimmy, her large eyes full of <u>anguish</u>, but not yet despairing. To a woman nothing seems quite impossible to the powers of the man she worships.

"Can't you do something, Ralph—*try*, won't you?"

He looked at her with a queer, soft smile on his lips and in his keen eyes.

"Annabel," he said, "give me that rose you are wearing, will you?"

Hardly believing that she heard him aright, she unpinned the bud from the bosom of her dress, and placed it in his hand. Jimmy stuffed it into his vest pocket, threw off his coat and pulled up his shirt sleeves. With that act Ralph D. Spencer passed away and Jimmy Valentine took his place.

"Get away from the door, all of you," he commanded, shortly.

He set his suitcase on the table, and opened it out flat. From that time on he seemed to be unconscious of the presence of anyone else. He laid out the shining, queer implements swiftly and orderly, whistling softly to himself as he always did when at work. In a deep silence and immovable, the others watched him as if under a spell.

In a minute Jimmy's pet drill was biting smoothly into the steel door. In ten minutes— breaking his own burglarious record—he threw back the bolts and opened the door.

Agatha, almost collapsed, but safe, was gathered into her mother's arms.

Jimmy Valentine put on his coat, and walked outside the railings toward the front door. As he went he thought he heard a far-away voice that he once knew call "Ralph!" But he never hesitated.

At the door a big man stood somewhat in his way.

"Hello, Ben!" said Jimmy, still with his strange smile. "Got around at last, have you? Well, let's go. I don't know that it makes much difference, now."

And then Ben Price acted rather strangely.

"Guess you're mistaken, Mr. Spencer," he said. "Don't believe I recognize you. Your buggy's waiting for you, ain't it?"

And Ben Price turned and strolled down the street.

> ◆ **Literary Focus**
> In what way is this ending surprising?

◆ Build Vocabulary

simultaneously (sī´ məl tā´ nē əs lē) *adv.*: Occurring at the same time

anguish (aŋ´ gwish) *n.*: Great suffering from worry

*G*uide for Responding

◆ LITERATURE AND YOUR LIFE

Reader's Response Would you have done what Ben Price did? Explain.

Thematic Focus Why does Valentine take a stand that could alter the course of his life?

☑ Check Your Comprehension

1. Why is Jimmy Valentine in prison?
2. How does Valentine support himself after his release from prison?
3. Who is Ben Price?
4. At what point in the story does Valentine have a change of heart? What causes this change?

◆ Critical Thinking

INTERPRET

1. Find at least two details in the story that prove Valentine has really changed. **[Support]**
2. Why does Ben Price pretend not to know Valentine at the bank? **[Infer]**
3. In your opinion, does Price do the right thing? Explain. **[Draw Conclusions]**
4. Explain the meaning of the story's title. **[Interpret]**

APPLY

5. What message does this story suggest about life in general? **[Synthesize]**

Guide for Responding (continued)

◆ Reading Strategy

ASK QUESTIONS

Asking questions and then answering them helps you to remember details about a story's plot and its characters.

1. You may have questioned whether Jimmy's "new life" in Elmore would last. What details in the story led to your answer?
2. How does answering "Why does Ben Price let Jimmy go?" help you to understand the story?

◆ Build Vocabulary

USING THE WORD ROOT -simul-

Keeping in mind that the word root -simul-, as in simultaneously, means "same," match each word with its definition.

1. simulcast
2. simulate
3. simulation

a. to look or act the same
b. broadcast at the same time on radio and television
c. an imitation

SPELLING STRATEGY

When you add -ion to verbs that end in te, you drop the e before adding -ion:

contribute + -ion = contribution

On a piece of paper, write the noun forms of these verbs by adding the -ion suffix.

1. rehabilitate
2. relate
3. stimulate
4. promote

USING THE WORD BANK

On your paper, complete each sentence with one of the words in the Word Bank.

1. If you are studying ____?____, you are studying carefully.
2. Jimmy earned respect in Elmore by living a ____?____ life.
3. Detention is a type of ____?____.
4. An elephant cannot move ____?____.
5. Two things that occur at the same time happen ____?____.
6. Tears can be a sign of ____?____.

◆ Literary Focus

SURPRISE ENDING

To make a **surprise ending** believable, an author includes hints in the story that point to the ending without giving it away.

1. (a) How did you think the story would end? (b) Which clues led you to expect this ending?
2. (a) How did the story really end? (b) What clues did the author plant, leading to this ending?

◆ Build Grammar Skills

PLACEMENT OF ADJECTIVES

Adjectives make nouns and pronouns more vivid and precise by telling *what kind, which one,* or *how many.* An adjective may occupy one of several positions in relation to the word it modifies:

Before the modified word: The *dusty* case contained *expensive* tools.

After the modified word: The thief, *skilled* and *clever,* escaped with the money.

After a linking verb: The clerk thought the suitcase was *heavy.*

Practice Copy the following sentences. Underline each adjective, and draw an arrow to the noun it modifies.

1. "It's always one or the other with you innocent victims."
2. Young men of Jimmy's style and looks were scarce in Elmore.
3. Business in all lines was fairly good.
4. Mr. Adams, the typical, plodding, country banker, approved of Spencer.
5. In a minute Jimmy's pet drill was biting smoothly into the steel door.

Writing Application Write pairs of sentences in your notebook. In the first sentence, place the adjective before a noun it modifies. In the second sentence, use a linking verb and place the adjective after the noun or pronoun it modifies.

1. popular 2. honest 3. responsible 4. hilarious

Build Your Portfolio

 Idea Bank

Writing

I. Letter From Billy Answer the letter that Jimmy Valentine sends to his "Old Pal" Billy in St. Louis.

2. Another Surprise Ending Write a new ending for "A Retrieved Reformation." You might change the existing ending or continue the story by adding another episode that tells what happens next.

3. Essay Write a brief essay in which you identify the story's theme and explain how the theme is revealed. Use details from the story to support your points.

Speaking and Listening

4. Debate [Group Activity] Form two teams to debate the pros and cons of Ben Price's decision not to recognize Jimmy Valentine in the bank. Meet with your team to prepare your argument before conducting the debate.

5. Monologue If you were Annabel, how would you feel about Jimmy at the end of the story? Deliver a monologue, a dramatic speech, to share Annabel's inner thoughts and feelings with the class. **[Performing Arts Link]**

Projects

6. Comic Book Retell the story of Jimmy Valentine in comic-strip form. Draw cartoon frames with captions and speech balloons to re-create the most important events from the story. **[Art Link]**

7. Research Report Research the history of banks in the United States. Find answers to these questions: What services did the first banks provide? How was money stored? How are banks different today? Share your findings with your class. **[Social Studies Link]**

 Writing Mini-Lesson

Response to the Story

Do you agree that Ben Price should have let Jimmy go free at the end of the story? Write a response to the story in which you present your opinion of Price's action.

Writing Skills Focus: Support Through Examples

Strengthen your writing by **supporting your ideas with examples.** Notice how O. Henry gives specific examples to support his statement that Jimmy's tools are "the finest set of burglar's tools in the East."

Model From the Story

It was a complete set made of specially tempered steel, the latest designs in drills, punches, braces and bits, jimmies, clamps, and augers, with two or three novelties invented by Jimmy himself . . .

Prewriting Decide whether or not you think Ben Price should have let Jimmy go free. In your notebook, write three reasons for your opinion. Next to each reason, write an example from the story that supports it.

Drafting Begin by stating your position, either for or against Ben Price's action. Then, list your reasons, and give support for those reasons. You might present your strongest reason first or you might save it for last.

Revising Make sure you've supported your ideas with examples. If necessary, go back through the story to find additional examples. Proofread carefully to correct errors in grammar, spelling, and punctuation.

> ◆ **Grammar Application**
> Look for places where changing the placement of adjectives will add variety to your sentences.

Guide for Reading

Meet the Authors:

Russell Freedman (1929–   )

If you like to read biographies, you may be familiar with the work of Russell Freedman. His critically acclaimed non-fiction books for young people focus on great figures in American history, such as the Wright brothers and Eleanor Roosevelt.

Freedman was born and grew up in San Francisco, California. After his discharge from the army, he worked as a reporter and writer for the Associated Press. He published his first book in 1961 and has been a full-time writer ever since. *Lincoln: A Photobiography* won a Newbery Medal in 1988.

Walt Whitman (1819–1892)

Walt Whitman, one of America's greatest poets, began his career as a printer and journalist in New York City. During the Civil War, he worked in military hospitals in Washington, D.C. Although he never met President Lincoln, he often saw the President at a distance in Washington. Lincoln's death moved Whitman to compose two famous poems, "O Captain! My Captain!" and "When Lilacs Last in the Dooryard Bloom'd." Whitman became widely recognized as a poet who loved democracy and who championed the individual.

◆ Literature and Your Life

Connect Your Experience

Think of a leader you admire, someone who has the capacity to change the world for the better. This is the kind of leader Abraham Lincoln was. Lincoln, the subject of these two selections, is considered by many people to be among the greatest leaders of all time.

Thematic Focus: Taking a Stand

Doing what is right can be challenging. President Lincoln, for example, had to make an important decision about slavery. As you read "Emancipation," notice all the factors he had to consider in making his decision.

◆ Background for Understanding

History

Although President Lincoln is remembered as a great leader, he did not always have the full support of the American people. One reason is that Lincoln opposed slavery while many southern landowners supported it. A month after Lincoln's inauguration in 1861, eleven southern states left the Union to form their own Confederacy. Civil war broke out between the Union and the Confederacy. Slavery was one of the key issues of the war.

◆ Build Vocabulary

Suffixes: -ate

Lincoln feared that his decision might "alienate" certain people. The word *alienate* is derived from *alien,* an adjective meaning "opposed." The suffix *-ate* means "to make or apply." When you add *-ate* to *alien,* it becomes a verb meaning "to make unfriendly or opposed."

Word Bank

Which word from the list is related to the verb *humiliate*? Check the Build Vocabulary box on page 265 to see if you chose correctly.

alienate
compensate
shackles
peril
decisive
humiliating
exulting
tread

◆ Emancipation ◆
O Captain! My Captain!

Abraham Lincoln, George Peter Alexander Healy, In the Collection of The Corcoran Gallery of Art, Washington, DC

◆ Reading Strategy

DETERMINE CAUSE AND EFFECT

A **cause** is an action, event, or situation that makes something happen. An **effect** is the result produced by a cause. Historians agree that slavery was one of several causes of the Civil War. In "Emancipation," President Lincoln debates with himself whether he should abolish slavery and, if so, what the effect of his decision would be. As you read, look for cause-and-effect relationships among events.

◆ Literary Focus

HISTORICAL CONTEXT

The **historical context** of a literary work is the time period about which it is written or during which it is set. Knowing the events and issues of a period in history can help you understand references and ideas in a work of literature. For example, "O Captain! My Captain!" was inspired by the tragic death of President Lincoln and reflects the pain Americans experienced during the Civil War.

The timeline below shows events you will read about in these selections.

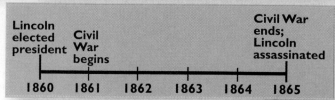

Lincoln elected president	Civil War begins				Civil War ends; Lincoln assassinated
1860	1861	1862	1863	1864	1865

Emancipation
from Lincoln: A Photobiography
Russell Freedman

President Abraham Lincoln was leading the country in 1862 during the Civil War. He was challenged to find the best means for preserving the Union. His troops had just been beaten in fierce battles in Virginia. He had tough military and political decisions to make.

The toughest decision facing Lincoln . . . was the one he had to make about slavery. Early in the war, he was still willing to leave slavery alone in the South, if only he could restore the Union. Once the rebellion was crushed, slavery would be confined to the Southern states, where it would gradually die out. "We didn't go into the war to put down slavery, but to put the flag back," Lincoln said. "To act differently at this moment would, I have no doubt, not only weaken our cause, but smack of bad faith."

Abolitionists were demanding that the president free the slaves at once, by means of a wartime proclamation. "Teach the rebels and traitors that the price they are to pay for the attempt to abolish this Government must be the abolition of slavery," said Frederick Douglass, the famous black editor and reformer. "Let the war cry be down with treason, and down with slavery, the cause of treason!"

But Lincoln hesitated. He was afraid to <u>alienate</u> the large numbers of Northerners who supported the Union but opposed emancipation. And he worried about the loyal, slaveholding border states—Kentucky, Missouri, Maryland, and Delaware—that had refused to join the Confederacy. Lincoln feared

---

◀ **Critical Viewing** This photograph shows enslaved African Americans bringing in cotton from the fields. How can you tell theirs was a life of hardship? **[Connect]**

that emancipation might drive those states into the arms of the South.

Yet slavery was the issue that had divided the country, and the president was under mounting pressure to do something about it. At first he supported a voluntary plan that would free the slaves gradually and <u>compensate</u> their owners with money from the federal treasury. Emancipation would begin in the loyal border states and be extended into the South as the rebel states were conquered. Perhaps then the liberated slaves could be resettled in Africa or Central America.

Lincoln pleaded with the border-state congressmen to accept his plan, but they turned him down. They would not part with their slave property or willingly change their way of life. "Emancipation in the cotton states is simply an absurdity," said a Kentucky congressman. "There is not enough power in the world to compel it to be done."

◆ **Literary Focus**
Which details in this paragraph reveal historical context?

Lincoln came to realize that if he wanted to attack slavery, he would have to act more boldly. A group of powerful Republican senators had been urging him to act. It was absurd, they argued, to fight the war without destroying the institution that had caused it. Slaves provided a vast pool of labor that was crucial to the South's war effort. If Lincoln freed the slaves, he could cripple the Confederacy and hasten the end of the war. If he did not free them, then the war would settle nothing. Even if the South agreed to return to the Union, it would start another war as soon as slavery was threatened again.

Besides, enslaved blacks were eager to throw off their <u>shackles</u> and fight for their own freedom. Thousands of slaves had already escaped from behind Southern lines. Thousands more were ready to enlist in the Union armies. "You need more men," Senator Charles Sumner told Lincoln, "not only at the North, but at the South, in the rear of the rebels. You need the slaves."

▲ **Critical Viewing** Here, an overseer watches over cotton-picking. Who do you think has an easier job—the overseer or the cotton pickers? [Make a Judgment]

All along, Lincoln had questioned his authority as president to abolish slavery in those states where it was protected by law. His Republican advisors argued that in time of war, with the nation in <u>peril</u>, the president *did* have the power to outlaw slavery. He could do it in his capacity as commander in chief of the armed forces. Such an act would be justified

◆ **Build Vocabulary**
alienate (āl´ yən āt´) *v.*: To make unfriendly; estrange
compensate (käm´ pən sāt´) *v.*: To repay
shackles (shak´ əls) *n.*: Metal fastenings, usually a linked pair for the wrists or ankles of a prisoner
peril (per´ əl) *n.*: Exposure to harm or injury; danger

as a necessary war measure, because it would weaken the enemy. If Lincoln really wanted to save the Union, Senator Sumner told him, he must act now. He must wipe out slavery.

The war had become an endless nightmare of bloodshed and bungling generals. Lincoln doubted if the Union could survive without

The First Reading of the Emancipation Proclamation before the Cabinet, Courtesy of the Library of Congress

▲ **Critical Viewing** This painting depicts President Lincoln presenting the Emancipation Proclamation to his Cabinet. Why is this occasion worthy of capturing in art? [Defend]

bold and drastic measures. By the summer of 1862, he had worked out a plan that would hold the loyal slave states in the Union, while striking at the enemies of the Union.

On July 22, 1862, he revealed his plan to his cabinet. He had decided, he told them, that emancipation was "a military necessity, absolutely essential to the preservation of the Union." For that reason, he intended to issue a proclamation freeing all the slaves in rebel states that had not returned to the Union by January 1, 1863. The proclamation would be aimed at the Confederate South only. In the loyal border states, he would continue to push for gradual, compensated emancipation.

Some cabinet members warned that the country wasn't ready to accept emancipation.

But most of them nodded their approval, and in any case, Lincoln had made up his mind. He did listen to the objection of William H. Seward, his secretary of state. If Lincoln published his proclamation now, Seward argued, when Union armies had just been defeated in Virginia, it would seem like an act of desperation, "the last shriek on our retreat." The president must wait until the Union had won a <u>decisive</u> military victory in the East. Then he could issue his proclamation from a position of strength. Lincoln agreed. For the time being, he filed the document away in his desk.

◆ **Reading Strategy**
According to William H. Seward, how would the timing of the proclamation change its effect?

A month later, in the war's second battle at Bull Run, Union forces commanded by General John Pope suffered another <u>humiliating</u> defeat. "We are whipped again," Lincoln moaned. He feared now that the war was lost. Rebel troops under Robert E. Lee were driving north. Early in September, Lee invaded Maryland and advanced toward Pennsylvania.

Lincoln again turned to General George McClellan—Who else do I have? he asked—and ordered him to repel the invasion. The two armies met at Antietam Creek in Maryland on September 17 in the bloodiest single engagement of the war. Lee was forced to retreat back to Virginia. But McClellan, cautious as ever, held his position and failed to pursue the defeated rebel army. It wasn't the decisive victory Lincoln had hoped for, but it would have to do.

On September 22, Lincoln read the final wording of his Emancipation Proclamation to his cabinet. If the rebels did not return to the Union by January 1, the president would free "thenceforward and forever" all the slaves everywhere in the Confederacy. Emancipation would become a Union war objective. As Union armies smashed their way into rebel territory, they would annihilate slavery once and for all.

The next day, the proclamation was released to the press. Throughout the North, opponents of slavery hailed the measure, and black people rejoiced. Frederick Douglass, the black abolitionist, had criticized Lincoln severely in the past. But he said now: "We shout for joy that we live to record this righteous decree."

When Lincoln delivered his annual message to Congress on December 1, he asked support for his program of military emancipation:

"Fellow citizens, *we* cannot escape history. We of this Congress and this administration, will be remembered in spite of ourselves. . . . In *giving* freedom to the *slave,* we *assure* freedom to the *free*—honorable alike in what we give, and what we preserve."

On New Year's Day, after a fitful night's sleep, Lincoln sat at his White House desk and put the finishing touches on his historic decree. From this day forward, all slaves in the rebel states were "forever free." Blacks who wished to could now enlist in the Union army and sail on Union ships. Several all-black regiments were formed immediately. By the end of the war, more than 180,000 blacks—a majority of them emancipated slaves—had volunteered for the Union forces. They manned military garrisons and served as front-line combat troops in every theatre of the war.

The traditional New Year's reception was held in the White House that morning. Mary appeared at an official gathering for the first time since Willie's death[1], wearing garlands in her hair and a black shawl about her head.

During the reception, Lincoln slipped away and retired to his office with several cabinet members and other officials for the formal signing of the proclamation. He looked tired. He had been shaking hands all morning, and now his hand trembled as he picked up a gold pen to sign his name.

Ordinarily he signed "A. Lincoln." But today, as he put pen to paper, he carefully wrote out his full name. "If my name ever goes into history," he said then, "it will be for this act."

---

1. **Mary appeared . . . Willie's death:** Mary Todd Lincoln was the President's wife. The couple's son William died in 1861 at the age of eleven.

◆ **Build Vocabulary**

decisive (di sī′ siv) *adj.*: Having the power to settle a question or dispute

humiliating (hyo͞o mil′ ē āt′ iŋ) *adj.*: Embarrassing; undignified

Guide for Responding

◆ LITERATURE AND YOUR LIFE

Reader's Response Did Lincoln end slavery at the right time? Support your answer.

Thematic Focus Does Freedman present Abraham Lincoln as a good leader? Explain.

☑ Check Your Comprehension

1. During the Civil War, what was the toughest decision facing Abraham Lincoln?
2. What consequences did he anticipate from certain northerners?
3. Name two reasons that Lincoln decided to attack the issue of slavery boldly.

◆ Critical Thinking

INTERPRET

1. Why did Lincoln worry about Kentucky, Missouri, Maryland, and Delaware? **[Infer]**
2. Explain Lincoln's reasoning when he finally decided to issue the Emancipation Proclamation. **[Infer]**
3. Why did Lincoln choose to end slavery after the battle of Antietam Creek? **[Speculate]**

EXTEND

4. If Lincoln were President today, what issues would he bring to national attention? Would they earn him national respect? **[Social Studies Link]**

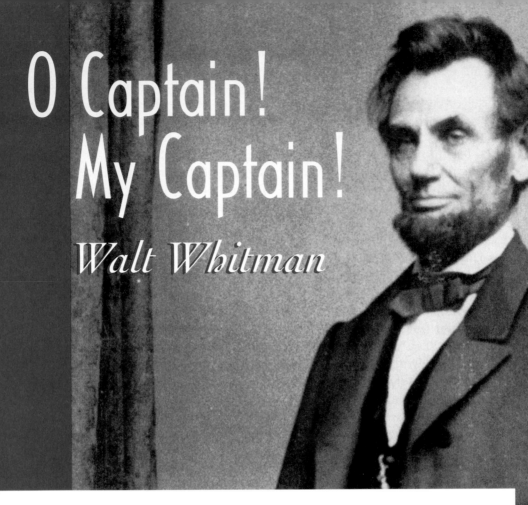

O Captain! My Captain!

Walt Whitman

O Captain! my Captain! our fearful trip is done,
The ship has weather'd every rack,[1] the prize we sought is won,
The port is near, the bells I hear, the people all <u>exulting</u>,
While follow eyes the steady keel,[2] the vessel grim and daring;
  But O heart! heart! heart!
    O the bleeding drops of red,
      Where on the deck my Captain lies,
        Fallen cold and dead.

O Captain! my Captain! rise up and hear the bells;
Rise up—for you the flag is flung—for you the bugle trills,
For you bouquets and ribbon'd wreaths—for you the shores a-crowding,
For you they call, the swaying mass, their eager faces turning;

---

1. **rack** *n.*: Great stress.
2. **keel** *n.*: Chief structural beam extending along the entire length of the bottom of a boat
or ship and supporting the frame.

▲ **Critical Viewing** In what ways does Lincoln, as
depicted in this photograph, exhibit leadership
qualities? **[Interpret]**

<pre>
          Here Captain! dear father!
            This arm beneath your head!
15   It is some dream that on the deck,
              You've fallen cold and dead.

          My Captain does not answer, his lips are pale and still,
          My father does not feel my arm, he has no pulse nor will,
          The ship is anchor'd safe and sound, its voyage closed and done,
20   From fearful trip the victor ship comes in with object won;
              Exult O shores, and ring O bells!
                But I with mournful <u>tread</u>,
                  Walk the deck my Captain lies,
                    Fallen cold and dead.
</pre>

◆ **Build Vocabulary**

exulting (ig zult´ iŋ) *v.*: Rejoicing
tread (tred) *n.*: Step

Guide for Responding

◆ LITERATURE AND YOUR LIFE

Reader's Response How does this poem affect you?

Thematic Focus "O Captain! My Captain!" mourns the death of President Lincoln. What kind of leader does Whitman consider Lincoln?

Discussion With a small group, create a list of the qualities that make a good leader. How close does Lincoln come to your standard?

☑ Check Your Comprehension

1. What has happened to the Captain? Why is this event unfortunate?
2. What is the other name the poet calls the Captain?

◆ Critical Thinking

INTERPRET

1. What pronoun does the poet use to modify the word *captain*? What is the significance of the pronoun? **[Interpret]**
2. In what ways does Lincoln's leadership of the country resemble a captain's role on a ship? **[Compare and Contrast]**
3. What is the mood of the poem? **[Interpret]**

EVALUATE

4. Do you think that the fate of a nation ever rests entirely on one person? Explain your answer. **[Make a Judgment]**

COMPARE LITERARY WORKS

5. Compare and contrast the portrayal of President Lincoln in these two selections. **[Compare and Contrast]**

Guide for Responding (continued)

◆ Reading Strategy

DETERMINE CAUSE AND EFFECT

A **cause** produces a result. An **effect** is the result of the cause. To identify an effect, ask yourself, "What happened?" To identify a cause, ask, "Why?"

1. What did Lincoln's Republican advisors say would be the effect if Lincoln ended slavery?
2. What caused Lincoln's delay in issuing the Emancipation Proclamation?
3. What event caused Lincoln to believe it was time to issue the Emancipation Proclamation?

◆ Build Vocabulary Skills

USING THE SUFFIX -ate

The suffix -ate is usually used to form verbs. Often it is added to a root word that cannot stand alone as an English word: *compensate, emancipate.* Sometimes it is added to a noun or adjective: alien + -ate = alienate. Complete these sentences by adding the suffix -ate to the word in parentheses.

1. The smell of food can make a hungry person _____?_____. (saliva)
2. Doctors _____?_____ children against measles and other diseases. (vaccine)

SPELLING STRATEGY

The egz sound at the beginning of some words, like *exult,* is spelled ex. Write the word that begins with ex that fits each of the following definitions.

exhibit   exert   exact

1. to present: _____?_____
2. to put forth great effort: _____?_____
3. very accurate: _____?_____

USING THE WORD BANK

On your paper, match each Word Bank word to its closest definition.

1. compensate	a. great rejoicing
2. peril	b. make unfriendly
3. decisive	c. step
4. humiliating	d. restraints
5. shackles	e. danger
6. tread	f. repay
7. exulting	g. crucial
8. alienate	h. hurtful to one's pride

◆ Literary Focus

HISTORICAL CONTEXT

The **historical context** is the time period about which a literary work is written or during which it is set. Besides historical people and events, historical context refers to attitudes and beliefs common during the time.

1. What political pressures did Lincoln feel during the Civil War?
2. Why was emancipation important not just morally, but politically as well? How does knowing this help you to understand Lincoln's action?
3. Why was Lincoln's death a tragedy for both the North and the South?

◆ Build Grammar Skills

ADVERBS

An **adverb** is a word that modifies, or describes, a verb, an adjective, or another adverb. Adverbs answer the questions *when, where, in what manner,* and *to what extent.* This example from "Emancipation" shows how adverbs can add detail and clarity to writing:

"If Lincoln *really* wanted to save the Union, . . . he must act *now.*"

(*Really* tells to what extent he wanted; *now* tells when he must act.)

Practice On your paper, copy the following sentences. Underline the adverb in each sentence, and draw an arrow to the word it modifies.

1. "To act differently at this moment would . . . smack of bad faith."
2. Thousands of slaves had already escaped. . . .
3. Lincoln carefully wrote out his full name.
4. Yesterday I read a poem by Walt Whitman.
5. It was more moving than another poem I read.

Writing Application Copy the sentences below. Add at least one adverb to each sentence.

1. Lincoln was cautious about freeing the slaves.
2. Many believed that slavery had caused the division between the North and the South.
3. Others expressed fear that the South would begin another war if Lincoln ended slavery.

Build Your Portfolio

 Idea Bank

Writing

1. Epitaph An epitaph is an inscription on a tomb. Write an epitaph for Lincoln's grave that tells what he did for his country.

2. Poem "O Captain! My Captain!" mourns a leader for whom the poet had great respect. Write a poem honoring a leader whom you admire.

3. Character Profile Write a short profile of Lincoln, describing the qualities he possessed that made him a great leader.

Speaking and Listening

4. Dramatic Reading Give a dramatic reading of the poem "O Captain! My Captain!" Use your voice and gestures to convey the emotion of the poem. **[Performing Arts Link]**

5. Dialogue [Group Activity] With a partner, write and perform a dialogue between Lincoln and Seward about when to issue the Emancipation Proclamation. Before you write, conduct library research to find out what the issues were. **[Social Studies Link]**

Projects

6. Multimedia Presentation Dramatize the life of Walt Whitman or Abraham Lincoln in a multimedia presentation. Research the individual's life, collecting pictures, quotations, and relevant maps and timelines. Then, weave these materials into a script, and present the biography to your class. **[Social Studies Link; Media Link]**

7. Picture Book [Group Activity] As a class, create an illustrated book about the Civil War period, with small groups responsible for each chapter. The book should provide background information and illustrations. It may include the following: interviews with soldiers, enslaved people, citizens, and political leaders; reports about battles; and information on home life. **[Social Studies Link]**

 Writing Mini-Lesson

Letter

Before telephones and e-mail were invented, people communicated by writing letters. Imagine that you are someone who has just been freed by the Emancipation Proclamation. Write a letter to a friend describing your feelings.

Writing Skills Focus: Descriptive Details

Express your deepest feelings by using **descriptive details** that convey your emotions. For example, saying "joyful tears flooded my face" does more to indicate happiness than "I cried." Notice how Freedman conveys Lincoln's tension and exhaustion in this detail:

Model From the Selection
". . . now his hand trembled as he picked up a gold pen to sign his name."

Prewriting Imagine that you are someone who was born into slavery. List the thoughts you might have had upon learning that you are now free. Jot down phrases that express your emotions. To add authenticity to your letter, conduct research to find out what life was like for enslaved people before and after the Emancipation Proclamation. Take notes on what you learn.

Drafting Use your notes to draft your letter. Reread your writing, and add vivid details to give emphasis to your emotions. Order events chronologically to create clarity.

Revising Make sure that your letter includes a heading, a salutation, body, closing, and signature. If you aren't sure about standard letter form, refer to the Writing Process Workshop on p. 285.

> ◆ **Grammar Application**
> Look for places where you can use adverbs to make a description more precise.

Guide for Reading

Meet the Authors:

Juan A.A. Sedillo (1902–1982)

A native of New Mexico, Juan A.A. Sedillo was a descendant of early Spanish colonists of the Southwest. In addition to being a writer, Sedillo served as a lawyer and judge, and held a number of public offices.

THE STORY BEHIND THE STORY

"Gentleman of Río en Medio" is based on an actual legal case that arose from a conflict over the value of a piece of property. Sedillo turned this case into a gentle tale that reveals the attitudes and culture of the people he knew so well.

Barbara A. Lewis (1943–   )

Barbara Lewis never expected to be a writer. While teaching sixth grade in her home state of Utah, her class began a campaign to get rid of a hazardous waste site. Lewis was so impressed by her students' efforts that she decided to write about them.

Inspiration Lewis believes that when it comes to taking social action, age doesn't matter. She wants young people to know that they can make a difference. To demonstrate this belief, she wrote *Kids With Courage,* a book that tells the stories of eighteen young people who spoke up for what they believed in.

◆ LITERATURE AND YOUR LIFE

CONNECT YOUR EXPERIENCE

Something that you find valuable may not be valuable to someone else. Each of these selections focuses on a person who finds value in nature—a value that is not shared by everyone.

THEMATIC FOCUS: Taking a Stand

As you read these selections, think about the different ways in which people can take a stand.

◆ Background for Understanding

SCIENCE

Wetlands are areas of land where the water level remains near or above the surface of the ground for most of the year. Types of wetlands include bogs, fens, marshes, and swamps. Wetlands are home to many types of plants and animals, including several endangered species. They also help control flooding by retaining large amounts of water. Although wetlands in the United States are protected by the Federal Clean Water Act and by various state and local laws, many environmentalists are asking for stronger laws to protect them.

◆ Build Vocabulary

WORD ROOTS: -num-

The old man in "Gentleman of Río en Medio" has *innumerable* kin. The word root -num- tells you that the meaning of this word is related to *number*. *Innumerable* means "too many to be counted."

WORD BANK

If you needed to reach an agreement or negotiate, which word from the list indicates something you might take part in? Check the Build Vocabulary box on page 273 to see if you chose correctly.

> negotiation
> gnarled
> innumerable
> broached
> petition
> wizened
> brandishing

Gentleman of Río en Medio
◆ Saving the Wetlands ◆

◆ Literary Focus
RESOLUTION OF A CONFLICT

In literature, as in life, a **conflict** is a struggle between opposing forces or a problem that must be solved. The **resolution** is the way that the conflict is solved, the final outcome. As you read, think about how the conflicts in these selections might be resolved. When you finish, ask yourself if each resolution satisfies you.

◆ Reading Strategy
MAKE INFERENCES

An **inference** is a reasonable conclusion you can draw from given facts or clues. Noticing details a writer shares with you helps you "read between the lines," or make inferences, about a character, a situation, or the way in which a conflict might be resolved. Use a chart like the one below to list details in the selections and the inferences you draw from them.

Detail	Inference
Don Anselmo carries a broken umbrella instead of a cane.	He has little money, or he is thrifty.

Gentleman of
Río en Medio
Juan A. A. Sedillo

The Sacristan of Trampas (detail), ca. 1915, Paul Burlin Museum of Fine Arts, New Mexico

*I*t took months of negotiation to come to an understanding with the old man. He was in no hurry. What he had the most of was time. He lived up in Río en Medio,[1] where his people had been for hundreds of years. He tilled the same land they had tilled. His house was small and wretched, but quaint. The little creek ran through his land. His orchard was gnarled and beautiful.

The day of the sale he came into the office. His coat was old, green and faded. I thought of Senator Catron,[2] who had been such a power with these people up there in the mountains. Perhaps it was one of his old Prince Alberts.[3] He also wore gloves. They were old and torn and his fingertips showed through them. He carried a cane, but it was only the skeleton of a worn-out umbrella. Behind him walked one of his innumerable kin—a dark young man with eyes like a gazelle.

The old man bowed to all of us in the room. Then he removed his hat and gloves, slowly and carefully. Chaplin[4] once did that in a picture, in a bank—he was the janitor. Then he handed his things to the boy, who stood obediently behind the old man's chair.

There was a great deal of conversation, about rain and about his family. He was very proud of his large family. Finally we got down to business. Yes, he would sell, as he had agreed, for twelve hundred dollars, in cash. We would buy, and the money was ready. "Don[5] Anselmo," I said to him in Spanish, "we have made a discovery. You remember that we sent that surveyor, that engineer, up there to survey your land so as to make the deed. Well, he finds that you own more than eight acres. He tells us that your land extends across the river and that you own almost twice as much as you thought." He didn't know that. "And now, Don Anselmo," I added, "these Americans are *buena gente*,[6] they are good people, and they are willing to pay you for the additional land as well, at the same rate per acre, so that instead of twelve hundred dollars you will get almost twice as much, and the money is here for you."

The old man hung his head for a moment in thought. Then he stood up and stared at me. "Friend," he said, "I do not like to have you speak to me in that manner." I kept still and let him have his say. "I know these Americans are good people, and that is why I have agreed to sell to them. But I do not care to be insulted. I have agreed to sell my house and land for twelve hundred dollars and that is the price."

I argued with him but it was useless. Finally he signed the deed and took the money but refused to take more than the amount agreed upon.

> **◆ Reading Strategy**
> What inference can you draw about Don Anselmo based on his refusal to accept more money?

Then he shook hands all around, put on his ragged gloves, took his stick and walked out with the boy behind him.

A month later my friends had moved into Río en Medio. They had replastered the old adobe house, pruned the trees, patched the fence, and moved in for the summer. One day they came back to the office to complain. The children of the village were overrunning their

---

1. **Río en Medio** (rē´ ō en mä´ dē ō)
2. **Senator Catron:** Thomas Benton Catron, senator from New Mexico, 1912–1917.
3. **Prince Alberts:** Long, double-breasted coats.
4. **Chaplin:** Charlie Chaplin (1889–1977), actor and producer of silent films in the United States.
5. **don:** Spanish title of respect, similar to *sir* in English.

6. *buena gente* (bwā´ nä hen´ tā): Spanish for "good people."

◀ **Critical Viewing** Does the man in this painting look like someone who would "bow to all of us in the room"? Why or why not? **[Infer]**

◆ Build Vocabulary

negotiation (ni gō´ shē ā´ shən) *n.*: Discussion to reach an agreement

gnarled (närld) *adj.*: Knotty and twisted

innumerable (i noo´ mər ə bəl) *adj.*: Too many to be counted

property. They came every day and played under the trees, built little play fences around them, and took blossoms. When they were spoken to they only laughed and talked back good-naturedly in Spanish.

I sent a messenger up to the mountains for Don Anselmo. It took a week to arrange another meeting. When he arrived he repeated his previous preliminary performance. He wore the same faded cutaway,[7] carried the same stick and was accompanied by the boy again. He shook hands all around, sat down

---

7. **cutaway** (kut´ ə wā´) *n.:* Coat worn by men for formal daytime occasions.

with the boy behind his chair, and talked about the weather. Finally I broached the subject. "Don Anselmo, about the ranch you sold to these people. They are good people and want to be your friends and neighbors always. When you sold to them you signed a document, a deed, and in that deed you agreed to several things. One thing was that they were to have the complete possession of the property. Now, Don Anselmo, it seems that every day the children of the village over-run the orchard and spend most of their time there. We would like to know if

◆ **Literary Focus**
Why does the narrator try to resolve the conflict in this way?

Springtime. c. 1928-29, Victor Higgins. Private collection, photo courtesy of the Gerald Peters Gallery, Santa Fe, NM.

▲ **Critical Viewing** Does this orchard seem "gnarled and beautiful" to you? **[Evaluate]**

you, as the most respected man in the village, could not stop them from doing so in order that these people may enjoy their new home more in peace."

Don Anselmo stood up. "We have all learned to love these Americans," he said, "because they are good people and good neighbors. I sold them my property because I knew they were good people, but I did not sell them the trees in the orchard."

This was bad. "Don Anselmo," I pleaded, "when one signs a deed and sells real property one sells also everything that grows on the land, and those trees, every one of them, are on the land and inside the boundaries of what you sold."

"Yes, I admit that," he said. "You know," he added, "I am the oldest man in the village. Almost everyone there is my relative and all the children of Río en Medio are my *sobrinos* and *nietos*,[8] my descendants. Every time a child

---

8. *sobrinos* (sō brē´ nōs) and *nietos* (nyā´ tōs): Spanish for "nieces and nephews" and "grandchildren."

has been born in Río en Medio since I took possession of that house from my mother I have planted a tree for that child. The trees in that orchard are not mine, *Señor*, they belong to the children of the village. Every person in Río en Medio born since the railroad came to Santa Fe owns a tree in that orchard. I did not sell the trees because I could not. They are not mine."

There was nothing we could do. Legally we owned the trees but the old man had been so generous, refusing what amounted to a fortune for him. It took most of the following winter to buy the trees, individually, from the descendants of Don Anselmo in the valley of Río en Medio.

◆ **Literature and Your Life**
Is there anything in your hometown that belongs to "the people," as trees do in Río en Medio? Explain.

◆ **Build Vocabulary**

broached (brōcht) *v.*: Started a discussion about a topic

---

*G*uide for Responding

◆ LITERATURE AND YOUR LIFE

Reader's Response If you had bought Don Anselmo's land, would you be satisfied with the way things turned out? Why or why not?

Thematic Focus Don Anselmo stands up for his beliefs, even though he loses money. Do you think he is foolish or admirable? Why?

☑ Check Your Comprehension

1. Why is Don Anselmo in no hurry to do things?
2. Why do the Americans want to pay more than originally agreed upon for the land?
3. Why does Don Anselmo refuse to accept more money?
4. According to Don Anselmo, who owns the trees?

◆ Critical Thinking

INTERPRET

1. (a) What is the role of the narrator in this story? (b) How does his behavior affect the outcome? **[Analyze]**
2. Don Anselmo talks about other topics before getting down to business. What does this tell you about him? **[Infer]**
3. Compare the attitudes of Don Anselmo and the Americans toward money and what it can buy. **[Compare and Contrast]**
4. What makes Don Anselmo the "Gentleman of Río en Medio"? **[Infer]**

APPLY

5. Put yourself in the Americans' place. How would you have solved their problem? **[Relate]**

Saving the Wetlands

Barbara A. Lewis

One day in 1987, Andy Holleman's family received a letter from a land developer. The letter announced the developer's plans to build 180 condominium[1] units near the Hollemans' home in Chelmsford, Massachusetts.

Twelve-year-old Andy snatched the letter and shouted, "He can't do that! He's talking about building right on top of the wetlands!"

Andy knew that several species living on that land were either endangered or on the Special Concern list of animals whose numbers are shrinking. He had spent much of his

---

1. **condominium** (kän′ də min′ ē əm) *n.*: Group of living units joined together; each unit is separately owned.

▲ **Critical Viewing** What might happen to deer like these if wetlands were to disappear? **[Speculate]**

---

free time roaming the area, watching great blue herons bend their long, delicate legs in marshy waters, seeing blue-spotted salamanders slither past shy wood turtles, and hearing the red-tailed hawk's lonely call—*cree, cree.* He often ripped off his baseball cap and waved to salute their graceful flight.

"Mom, you've got to take me to the library," Andy insisted. "I need to find out everything I can about the land. We've got to fight this."

Cheryl Holleman, a school nurse, dropped her son off at the library. There Andy examined the master plan for their town. He dug into the Annotated Laws[2] for the state. And he discovered that the condos would take up 16.3 acres of land, one-half of which would cover and destroy the wetlands. A new sewage treatment plant, oil from driveways, and fertilizer runoff could all pollute the water system or penetrate the soil, contaminating both water and land.

Andy also learned that the proposed development sat on a stream which led into Russell Mill Pond. The pond fed into town wells. So it was possible that Chelmsford's drinking water could be contaminated, too. "Our drinking water was already terrible enough," Andy says, grinning.

He had his ammunition, and he had to do *something.* He thought of all the living things whose habitats would be destroyed by the condos: the ladyslippers, mountain laurels, fringed gentians, foxes, and snakes. And he knew he could count on his parents' support. They had always encouraged him to respect the environment.

Even now, when Cheryl needs Andy to do a chore, she doesn't bother looking for him in front of the TV. She knows she'll find him sprawled half off his bed or stretched across the floor, reading. Andy devours Audubon books about wildlife. He loves author Gerald Durrell's *The Drunken Forest* and *Birds, Beasts, and Other Relatives.* Sometimes, of course, he sneaks in a Stephen King thriller.

Andy and his family have taken many nature walks in the wooded area

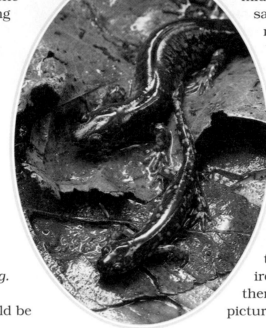

▲ **Critical Viewing** Why might salamanders like these depend on water for survival? [**Draw Conclusions**]

by Russell Mill Pond. It's something they enjoy doing together—Andy, Cheryl, his dad, David, and his younger brother and sister, Nicholas and Elizabeth.

Andy remembers sitting on the glacial rocks by the stream in the middle of winter, eating baloney sandwiches. In the warmer months, he and Nicholas and Elizabeth played tag in the stream, jumping on the slippery rocks, soaking their shoes, socks, and jeans. When fall came, they gathered brilliant red leaves from swamp maples and golden oak, while their mother picked dried grape vines for wreaths. The children took their leaves home, pressed them between waxed paper, ironed them flat, then hung them on doorknobs and from picture frames.

The wetlands area where the developer wanted to build held other memories for Andy. Sometimes he ice-skated on the pond. Sometimes he made important discoveries.

"Once I brought home a huge baby crow," he says. "A baby crow is called a 'fledgling,' and this one was just learning to fly. It had fallen out of the nest. So I fed him popcorn and water that night, and built him a perch.

"Mom wouldn't let me keep him in the house while I was at school. But that was okay. He was able to fly away the next day to return to his home in the swamp."

When Andy was eleven, he found a skunk caught in a steel-jaw trap, the kind that rips animals' legs apart. Since he had been swimming with a friend, Andy was wearing only his swim trunks and tattered sneakers—luckily, as it turned out.

He put on a diving mask, sneaked up

◆ **Reading Strategy**
What kind of relationship does Andy have with his family?

2. **Annotated** (an ō tāt´ əd) **Laws:** Laws with explanatory notes.

behind the skunk, pressed the release button on the trap, and grabbed the startled skunk by the tail. Then he carried him upside-down for a quarter of a mile—all the way to his house. He knew that skunks can't spray when held by the tail.

Small children trailed behind him, holding their noses and giggling. A neighbor telephoned Andy's mother and said, "Go outside and watch. And shut your windows and doors behind you. Don't ask me to explain. Just do it."

By the time Andy arrived home, he was leading twenty dancing, squealing children, like the Pied Piper. The skunk dangled from his hand at arm's length.

"This is one animal you're not going to keep, Andrew," his mom called in a shrill voice.

His father, who was home from his job as a medical technologist, phoned the local animal shelter for advice.

"They said we could either let the skunk go in the woods, or bring it in to the shelter," David Holleman told his son. "You'd better let him go and let nature take its course. There is no way you're putting that animal in my car, and you certainly can't hold him out the window by his tail the whole way to the shelter."

"I let him go," Andy recalls. "His leg wasn't too bad, so it would probably heal by itself. Everyone thought I smelled pretty skunky, though. I bathed in vinegar, which smelled just as

awful as the skunk to me. I finally came clean, but we had to throw my sneakers away."

Crows and skunks aren't the only creatures Andy has brought home from the wetlands. "My mother remembers an eighteen-inch snapping turtle which went to the bathroom all over the kitchen linoleum." He laughs. "I fed him raw hamburger."

Often Andy just wandered through the woods to think or to write a poem. Sometimes he sat quietly for hours, studying animal behavior. He spotted deer and red foxes. He captured salamanders, snakes, mice, and moles; after learning all he could from observing each animal, Andy carefully carried it back to its home in the woods.

◆ **Reading Strategy**
Infer why Andy wants people to come to the meeting.

The wetlands were too important to cover with concrete and steel. Andy couldn't allow Pontiacs and Toyotas to replace blue herons and shy wood turtles. He couldn't permit blaring car horns to muffle the *cree* of the redtailed hawk.

"So I drafted a <u>petition</u> for the residents to sign to try to stop the developer from building," Andy says. "I walked around the neighborhood and collected 180 signatures. I told everyone to come to the public town meeting scheduled with the developer. I also collected about fifty signatures from students in the neighborhood and at McCarthy Middle School."

Critical Viewing In what way are the animals pictured on these two pages alike? How are they different? [Compare and Contrast]

Only one or two people refused to sign the petition. "They acted like they thought I was too young, like I didn't know what I was doing. But almost everybody was really supportive."

Often Andy carried his petition around for an hour and collected only a few signatures—not because people didn't want to sign, but because they wanted to talk. They'd offer Andy a Coke and invite him in to discuss the problem. Andy spent a lot of time conversing with his neighbors.

An elderly lady named Agatha answered her door with long, bony fingers. Although she was <u>wizened</u> and thin with wild, white hair, Andy's enthusiasm breathed new life into her. She attended over forty meetings and became a real activist.

Once, on the way back from carrying his petition, Andy decided to detour through the swamp. He kicked up his heels with too much energy and tripped over a rotted log. He snatched helplessly at the pages of his petition as they tumbled into a muddy stream, but he managed to salvage them.

"It took a while for the pages to dry out," he recalls with a grin, "and then my mom had to iron them out flat. That's the last time I ever went through the swamp with something that wasn't waterproofed."

Andy sent copies of his petition to the Board of Selectmen,[3] the Conservation Commission, the Zoning Board of Appeals,[4] the Board of Health, and the land developer. He wrote letters to senators, representatives, and a TV anchorwoman. Although he received letters of support in return, no one did anything to help.

3. **Board of Selectmen:** Group of persons elected to manage town affairs.
4. **Zoning Board of Appeals:** Group of persons who review problems dealing with construction in business and residential areas.

"When I called the Massachusetts Audubon Society and told them my problem with the wetlands and that no one was really helping me, the woman gave me no sympathy," Andy says. "She just told me, 'That's no excuse for *you*,' and went right on giving information. I learned that when you really believe in something, you have to stand up for it no matter how old you are."

Slowly, Andy's neighbors joined in, neighbors he had contacted with his petition. They organized into the Concord Neighborhood Association and raised $16,000 to hire a lawyer and an environmental consultant to fight the development of the wetlands.

On the night of the town meeting with the developer, over 250 people showed up. The meeting had to be moved to the basement of the Town Hall to make room for the crowd. And when the developer stood up and announced that *he* was the one who had invited everyone, the residents disagreed, saying, "No, it was Andy Holleman who invited us here."

Andy had prepared a speech to give at the meeting. When it was time for him to speak, his stomach flipped, but he walked to the front of the room anyway, <u>brandishing</u> the brown shell of a wood turtle.

"You call yourself the Russell Mill Pond Realty Trust, Inc.," Andy began. "I don't understand how you can call yourself this when you're essentially polluting your own name."

◆ **Build Vocabulary**

petition (pə tish´ ən) *n.*: A formal document that makes a request, addressed to a person or group and often signed by a number of people

wizened (wiz´ ənd) *adj.*: Shriveled or withered

brandishing (bran´ dish iŋ) *v.*: Waving or exhibiting in a challenging way

The residents responded with thunderous applause. White-haired Agatha winked at him and motioned a thumbs-up.

Andy continued. "We need the wetlands to prevent flooding and to purify the water through the mud," he said. "We need the plants and the creatures living there."

Nobody won that night's debate. In fact, the meetings continued for ten months. There were at least two meetings every week and sometimes more. Andy and either his mom or his dad attended every meeting—and Andy *still* got high grades in school. He spoke at most of the meetings.

In one meeting with the Board of Health, the developer arose and announced, "I'm not going to argue hydro-geological[5] facts with a thirteen-year-old!" Andy's parents were angry, but Andy just shrugged his shoulders.

◆ Literary Focus
Is this a good way to resolve the conflict? Why or why not?

Nine months after the first meeting, an important test called a "deep-hole test" was conducted in the swamp. The purpose of the test was to find out how quickly a hole dug in the swamp would fill up with water. If it filled up very fast, that would be a sign that the land was not suitable for building.

The developer, members of the Concord Neighborhood Association, and state environmental officials gathered to observe the test. The hole was dug—and it filled with water almost immediately. Andy grinned clear around his head.

The developer tried to withdraw his application to build on the wetlands, but the Zoning Board of Appeals wouldn't let him. Legally, that wouldn't have solved the problem. Someone else could have applied for the same kind of project, and Andy and his neighbors would have had to start fighting all over again. Instead, the Board totally denied the application. Their refusal prevented anyone from trying to build a big development on the wetlands.

5. **hydro-geological** (hī´ drō jē ä lä´ jə kəl) *adj.*: Related to water and to the science of the nature and history of the Earth.

When they got the news, Andy and the Concord Neighborhood Association cheered. Their battle was over! And the wetlands were safe from large developers.

Soon after, the developer started building condos on an old drive-in movie lot—an acceptable site Andy had suggested in the beginning.

What did all of this mean to Andy? He became a celebrity. Even though he is modest and shy, he accepted invitations to speak at schools, community groups, and organizations. He received many awards, including the Young Giraffe Award for young people who "stick their necks out" for the good of others. His award was a free trip to the Soviet Union in July, 1990.

And what is Andy doing now? He's planning to go to college in a few years, where he'd like to study environmental law. Meanwhile, he's setting up a non-profit, tax-exempt fund to purchase the wetlands and any surrounding threatened land to preserve it forever. Then he can always wander by Russell Mill Pond, gathering autumn leaves from crimson swamp maples and golden oaks. He can watch the blue herons bend their long, delicate legs in marshy waters, and see blue-spotted salamanders slither safely past shy wood turtles. And he can hear the lonely *cree* of the red-tailed hawk as it soars freely, high above the pond, dipping its wings as if in salute to him. To Andy.

◀ **Critical Viewing** In what way is a red-tailed hawk like this strong? In what ways is it fragile? **[Classify]**

Beyond ◆ Literature

Science Connection

Saving the Earth Would you like to see a new swimming pool or baseball diamond or even a new school built in your community? It's not always so easy. Throughout the United States, the presence of wetlands affects whether undeveloped land may be developed. Wetlands—swamps, marshes, and some forests—are protected by law on both public and private property. We now recognize how vital they are to preserving the ecology. Their importance was not widely known, however, until the 1970's. By then, more than half of the nation's wetlands had been destroyed, resulting in erosion and flooding in many places. The decrease in wetlands has also decreased populations of waterfowl, fish, and shellfish. Protecting the remaining wetlands has become a critical national priority.

Cross-Curricular Activity
Observing Animal Life in Wetlands
If possible, visit wetlands located near you with a group of classmates. Watch closely to track the types of animal life you observe. Take notes so that you can make a chart or poster to show the animals you saw. If there are no wetlands close by, research wetlands to learn about the species that live in this environment in your state. Create a chart or poster based on your findings.

Guide for Responding

◆ LITERATURE AND YOUR LIFE

Reader's Response What part of the environment do you care about most? Would you mount a campaign to save it?

Thematic Focus Can you think of other instances when people have joined together to save something worth saving?

Brainstorm List some things in the natural environment near your home that are important to you.

☑ Check Your Comprehension

1. Why did Andy want to save the wetlands?
2. What was the first thing Andy did in his struggle against the developer?
3. What did Andy ask his neighbors to do?
4. In the end, were the developers able to build condominiums?

◆ Critical Thinking

INTERPRET
1. How does Andy transform his sense of outrage about the plan to build condominiums into action? **[Connect]**
2. Why does the author tell so much about Andy's experiences with the animals? **[Analyze]**
3. Do you think Andy's age worked for or against him in his campaign to stop the developers? Explain. **[Analyze]**

APPLY
4. Suppose Andy had lost his fight. What would have happened to the wildlife and the wetlands? **[Hypothesize]**

EXTEND
5. Andy learned a great deal in his campaign to save the wetlands. Identify several careers he might pursue using the knowledge and skills he gained. **[Career Link]**

Guide for Responding (continued)

◆ Reading Strategy

MAKE INFERENCES

An **inference** is an educated guess you make based on details in a story, essay, or article.

1. What can you infer about the Americans based on the fact that they offer more money for Don Anselmo's land?
2. Who is the narrator of "Gentleman of Río en Medio"? How can you tell?
3. List three inferences you can make about Andy based on his actions in "Saving the Wetlands."

◆ Build Vocabulary

USING THE WORD ROOT -num-

Words that contain the word root -num-, as in *innumerable,* are related in meaning to the word *number.* On a sheet of paper, write the word from the list below that best completes each sentence.

enumerate   numerator   innumerable

1. The sky was dotted with _____?_____ stars.
2. The _____?_____ is the top number in a simple fraction.
3. The teacher will _____?_____ the rules of the classroom.

SPELLING STRATEGY

The *n* sound you hear in *gnarled* is spelled with a silent *g* preceding the *n.* Unscramble these *gn* words. Then, refer to a dictionary to write a definition for each one.

1. wagn   2. tnag   3. hnags   4. mogen

USING THE WORD BANK

On your paper, write the word that is closest in meaning to the Word Bank word.

1. negotiation: (a) discussion, (b) argument, (c) opinion
2. gnarled: (a) angry, (b) intelligent, (c) twisted
3. innumerable: (a) countless, (b) difficult, (c) impossible
4. broached: (a) mentioned, (b) bejeweled, (c) followed
5. petition: (a) request, (b) reply, (c) complaint
6. wizened: (a) wise, (b) shriveled, (c) empty
7. brandishing: (a) waving, (b) bragging, (c) swaying

◆ Literary Focus

RESOLUTION OF A CONFLICT

The characters in these selections **resolve conflicts** over land use and ownership in very different ways. In each selection, the resolution depends on the attitudes of the key people and on the way in which their communities respond to them.

1. In "Gentleman of Río en Medio," how does Don Anselmo expect the Americans to behave when conflicts arise?
2. In "Saving the Wetlands," why does Andy assume from the start that there will be a conflict?
3. Identify winners and losers in each selection. Tell what each has gained or lost.

◆ Build Grammar Skills

ADVERBS MODIFYING ADJECTIVES AND ADVERBS

An **adverb** is a word that modifies or describes a verb. It can also modify an adjective or another adverb. The following adverbs are commonly used to modify adjectives and other adverbs: *too, so, very, quite, much, more, rather, usually, almost.*

. . . the old man had been *so* generous (*How generous?*)

Our drinking water was *already* terrible (*When was it terrible?*)

Practice On your paper, write each adverb, and tell whether the word it modifies is an adjective or an adverb.

1. Don Anselmo spoke very slowly.
2. Andy was an unusually persistent boy.
3. The developers were quite angry.
4. Andy's family rather consistently supported his efforts.
5. The developers were very aggressive.

Writing Application Copy the following sentences. Fill in each blank with an appropriate adverb.

1. Don Anselmo arrived _____?_____ late.
2. Andy thought the developers were _____?_____ unfair.
3. The Americans were _____?_____ patient.

Build Your Portfolio

 ## Idea Bank

Writing

1. **Advertisement** Write a real estate advertisement for the condominiums that the developers would have built on the wetlands if they had not been stopped.

2. **Letter to the Editor** Write a letter that Andy Holleman might have written to his local newspaper. Explain the threat to the wetlands, and ask people for help in the fight to stop the developers.

3. **Formula** If the Americans in Río en Medio came to you for advice about how much they should pay for each tree, what formula would you develop? Write a paragraph explaining the formula and why you think it is fair to all parties. **[Math Link]**

Speaking and Listening

4. **Speech** Imagine you live in Río en Medio. Deliver a speech to your "neighbors," praising Don Anselmo for his contributions to the village. Tape-record your speech so you can listen to it afterward. **[Performing Arts Link]**

5. **Debate [Group Activity]** With another classmate, research the subject of wetlands and environmental protection laws. Stage a debate with one of you playing the role of Andy Holleman and the other playing the role of a developer.

Projects

6. **Artwork** Draw or paint a portrait of Don Anselmo or a landscape showing the house and orchard the Americans bought from him. **[Art Link]**

7. **Community Action [Group Activity]** Identify an environmental problem in your community. With several classmates, work out a plan for solving the problem. Consult with your teacher or other adults about putting the plan into action. **[Science Link; Career Link]**

 ## Writing Mini-Lesson

Speech Supporting the Environment

When Andy Holleman gave his first speech at a town meeting, he spoke persuasively about an issue that meant a lot to him—saving the wetlands. Choose an environmental issue you care about, and write a short speech supporting that issue.

Writing Skills Focus: Persuasive Tone

The **tone** of a piece of writing is the writer's attitude toward his or her subject. As you write, choose words that will persuade your audience that the subject of your speech is important. Notice the tone that Andy's words convey at the town meeting:

Model From the Selection

"You call yourself the Russell Mill Pond Realty Trust, Inc.," Andy began. "I don't understand how you can call yourself this when you're essentially polluting your own name."

Prewriting Conduct research to learn the facts about both sides of your issue. Look for details, statistics, and quotations that support your position. Take careful notes on what you learn.

Drafting Begin by stating the issue and your position. Then, support your position with details you uncovered in your research. Use language that conveys the importance of your cause.

Revising Read your speech aloud to a friend to find out if your arguments are clear and convincing. If not, look for places where replacing a word or adding a fact will strengthen the persuasive tone of your speech.

> ◆ **Grammar Application**
> Make your writing more vivid and precise by adding adverbs to modify adjectives and other adverbs.

Letter to the Editor

Writing Process Workshop

One way newspaper and magazine readers can take a stand is by writing a **letter to the editor.** In this type of letter, you agree or disagree with an article or editorial and try to persuade others to do the same. Write a letter to the editor, responding to an issue about which you feel strongly. The following skills, introduced in this section's Writing Mini-Lessons, will help you.

Writing Skills Focus

▶ **Begin with a strong opening** to grab your readers' attention. (See p. 248.)

▶ **Support your points with examples, facts, statistics, and quotations** to strengthen your arguments. (See p. 259.)

▶ **Use descriptive details** that will help readers to see things from your point of view. (See p. 269.)

▶ **Adopt a persuasive tone** by using positive, emotionally charged language. (See p. 283.)

In this passage from a letter to the editor, the writer uses these skills to persuade readers to accept a particular point of view.

WRITING MODEL

Dear Editor:

Don't call me lazy! ① In a May 19 article "The Trouble With Teens," the writer stated that, "typical teenagers do nothing but skateboard and hang out at the mall." I strongly disagree, and here's why. In a survey conducted by eighth graders at Hanover Middle School, 65% of the students said that they participate in an after-school club or play on a sports team. ② . . . More importantly though, there is no "typical teenager," just as there is no "typical" adult. We are all individual and unique—just like you. ③

① The writer's strong beginning makes you want to read more.

② This statistic supports the writer's opinion with a fact.

③ The writer adopts a persuasive tone by comparing teenagers with adults.

Prewriting

Choose a Topic Choose an issue of current concern to focus on in your letter. For ideas, scan newspapers and magazines, watch television news shows, and talk to people in your community.

Gather Facts and Details Once you've decided on a topic, conduct research in the library or on the Internet to gather facts, details, statistics, and quotations that support your position. Take careful notes on what you learn.

Brainstorm for "Forceful Language" Jot down a list of forceful words, like those in this list, that you can use to make your argument persuasive and effective:

Weak	Forceful
should	must
probably	certainly
ask	implore
necessary	crucial

Drafting

Use the Correct Letter Form A letter to the editor follows the form of a business letter:

[Return Address ➞]	Your street address City, State, and Zip Code Date
Editor Title of publication Publication street address City, State, and Zip Code	**[⬅ Address of Editor at Publication]**
Dear Editor: Body of your letter	**[⬅ Greeting]**
[Closing ➞]	Sincerely, Your signature Your name

Write a Strong Opening Hook your readers right from the start by beginning your letter with a clever statement, a thought-provoking question, or a powerful quotation.

Adopt a Persuasive Tone Readers can be put off by a negative approach. If you make a criticism, state it fairly and simply. Then, explain an alternative, using positive, persuasive language.

APPLYING LANGUAGE SKILLS: Degrees of Comparison

The **comparative form** compares two items. It is formed by adding the ending -*er* or by beginning with the word *more*. The **superlative form** compares three or more items. It is formed by adding the ending -*est* or by beginning with the word *most*.

Comparative: Champ is the faster of the two horses, but Star is the more intelligent.

Superlative: Champ is the fastest horse I've ever seen, and Star is the most intelligent.

Practice On your paper, write the correct form of the adjective in parentheses.

1. Of all the kids on the team, Jen is the (*strong*).
2. Patrick probably throws (*hard*) than Stephen.
3. Chiara is (*graceful*) on the ice than Cerise.
4. Ana is the (*fast*) runner on the team.

Writing Application As you draft, be sure to use the correct degree of comparison.

Writer's Solution Connection
Writing Lab

For more help using degrees of comparison, see the Proofreading section of the Exposition: Making Connections tutorial.

APPLYING LANGUAGE SKILLS: Using Commas With Coordinate Adjectives

Coordinate adjectives are adjectives of equal rank that separately modify the noun they precede. The order of coordinate adjectives can be switched without changing the meaning of a sentence. Coordinate adjectives should be separated by commas.

Incorrect: The honest kind intelligent student was popular.

Correct: The honest, kind, intelligent student was popular.

Practice On your paper, add commas where necessary. Some sentences may be correct.

1. It was a terribly hot humid stormy day.
2. A huge old hungry alligator crawled out of the swamp.
3. The child played with his red and black tin soldiers.
4. The student pulled the screaming sobbing frightened child to safety.

Writing Application Review your letter, and make sure you've used commas correctly with coordinate adjectives.

Writer's Solution Connection Language Lab

For more practice in using commas correctly, refer to the lesson on Commas in the unit on Punctuation.

Revising

Work With a Peer Reviewer Ask a classmate to read and evaluate your letter, using the following checklist:
- ▶ What is the writer's position?
- ▶ Does the letter have a strong beginning?
- ▶ What descriptive details support the writer's position?
- ▶ Are ideas supported with facts, statistics, and examples?
- ▶ Does the language help persuade you to adopt the writer's point of view?

Use your reviewer's responses to these questions to help you improve your letter to the editor.

Verify the Format Before submitting your letter to the editor, check to be sure you've followed standard letter format.

Proofread Check your letter carefully to be sure it's free of errors in grammar, spelling, and punctuation.

REVISION MODEL

① desperately

Our schools need more money for the Performing Arts

② over 500

and Music departments. Last year, ~~many~~ students signed

② more than half

up for drama, band, and orchestra classes, but ~~a lot~~ had

to be turned away because there weren't enough classes

③ due to a shortage of teachers and classrooms

available. ~~Please support us.~~

④ We matter. We are the future. Support us now!

① Adding a forceful word increases the impact of this statement.

② The writer adds facts and statistics to support the argument.

③ This descriptive detail helps emphasize the writer's position.

④ This sentence was rewritten to convey a more persuasive, positive message.

Publishing and Presenting

- ▶ **Newspaper** Submit your letter to the editor for publication in your local newspaper.
- ▶ **School** Read your letter at a school meeting or assembly. If others agree with you, ask them to write their own letters to the editor in support of your position.

Real-World Reading Skills Workshop

Strategies for Success

In a newspaper or magazine, you'll sometimes come across an editorial, which expresses the writer's point of view on an issue. Analyze the writer's position before you agree or disagree with it.

Identify an Editorial Sometimes editorials are not identified as such. You must determine whether an article is news—fact, not opinion—or an editorial—primarily opinion.

Determine the Writer's Position Usually an editorial writer will quickly identify the subject and explain his or her position on it. Sometimes the writer will suggest a course of action that the reader should take.

Recognize the Writer's Bias A *bias* is a leaning toward a certain position; for example, a lawyer writing about unfair treatment of lawyers may be writing from a bias. Be aware of subtle forms of bias. Notice clues such as quotations from "my friends" or "my colleagues," or statements such as "Most thinking people agree . . ."

Separate Facts From Opinions Facts can be checked. When a writer uses vague generalizations, they often indicate opinions rather than facts.

Consider Opposing Positions Sometimes a writer will include an opposing idea in an editorial and then refute it. If the writer doesn't do this, the job is yours. Think of the opposing position, and decide whether the writer has dealt with it fairly. For example, did he or she include current and important facts?

Apply the Strategies

Read "Fireworks for Us." Then, analyze the writer's position by answering these questions:

1. Is this a news article or an editorial? What evidence do you have?

2. Explain the writer's position. Be specific.

3. Does the writer have a bias? Explain.

4. What facts does the writer present? Do you think they're reliable? Where might you check them?

5. Does the writer present an opposing view? If so, how does he deal with it?

6. Do you agree or disagree with the writer? Why?

Fireworks for Us
by Dale Croyle

All the other states in the USA are allowed to have fireworks except us, and, frankly, I think that stinks! We should be allowed to have fireworks too. On special occasions like the Fourth of July, our towns and cities have to pay professional companies to come and set off fireworks. My friend's father says that costs a lot of money. If individuals and minors were allowed to own and discharge fireworks, we'd save the state plenty. You may argue that people get hurt using fireworks. That's like saying skis aren't safe because some people have accidents. I say "Fireworks for Us," and so should YOU!

Dale Croyle is an eighth grader at Biegly Junior High.

✔ Here are other situations in which analyzing a position is important:
▶ Reading a letter to the editor
▶ Reading the text of a political speech
▶ Reading a petition you are asked to sign

Adjectives and Adverbs
Grammar Review

An **adjective** modifies or describes a noun or pronoun. Adjectives answer questions such as *which, what kind, how many,* or *how much.* (See page 247.)

Question	Example
Which?	*That* lawyer argued brilliantly.
What kind?	Lincoln was an *effective* president.
How many?	*Several* wetlands animals were endangered.
How much?	There was *enough* land for everyone.

Adjectives are located most commonly before the word they modify or after a linking verb. (See page 258.)

> *Three* egrets stood in the *shallow* water.
> Those birds are *beautiful.*

Question	Example
How?	The students felt *strongly* about ending segregation.
When?	I read the selection *yesterday.*
Where?	Jimmy Valentine put his tools *there.*
To what extent?	He *hardly* noticed that everyone was watching.

An **adverb** modifies a verb, an adjective, or another adverb. Adverbs answer the questions *how, when, where,* and *to what extent.* (See pages 268 and 282.)

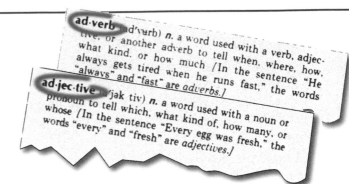

ad·verb (ad'vərb) *n.* a word used with a verb, adjective, or another adverb to tell when, where, how, what kind, or how much /In the sentence "He always gets tired when he runs fast," the words "always" and "fast" are adverbs.]

ad·jec·tive (ajak'tiv) *n.* a word used with a noun or pronoun to tell which, what kind of, how many, or whose /In the sentence "Every egg was fresh," the words "every" and "fresh" are adjectives.]

Practice 1 Copy these sentences. Underline each adjective once and each adverb twice. Draw arrows from the adjectives and adverbs to the words they modify.

1. Marshall, well-spoken and intelligent, happily joined the Debating Club.

2. The students enthusiastically supported the Supreme Court's decision.

3. Many of his stories have surprise endings.

4. The next morning, Lincoln delivered his proclamation.

5. We were very worried about the wetlands.

Practice 2 Rewrite this paragraph, filling in the blanks with adjectives or adverbs.

The (adjective) detective returned to his office. He sat (adverb) at his desk, feeling (adverb) (adjective) with himself. "I did a (adjective) thing today," he said (adverb) .

Grammar in Writing

- ✔ A proper adjective is formed from a proper noun: *American* author. A proper adjective begins with a capital letter.

- ✔ Many adverbs are formed by adding *-ly* to an adjective; for example, *happily carefully, strangely.*

PART **2** *Leading the Way*

Lightning Bolt, Paul Colon

Guide for Reading

Meet the Author:

Toni Cade Bambara (1939–1995)

Reading the work of Toni Cade Bambara, you can't help noticing the writer's interest in African American heritage and her concern for other people. As one critic noted, "Bambara tells me more about being black through her quiet, proud, silly, tender, hip, acute, loving stories than any amount of literary [discussion] could hope to do. . . . All of her stories share the affection that their narrator feels for the subject . . . "

Teacher and Writer A New York City native, Bambara was educated in Europe and the United States. She worked as a teacher, with pupils ranging from preschoolers to college students. She also wrote two collections of short stories—*Gorilla, My Love*, in which "Raymond's Run" appears, and *The Sea Birds Are Still Alive*—as well as a novel, *The Salt Eaters*.

THE STORY BEHIND THE STORY

In 1971, Bambara edited a collection of stories called *Tales and Stories for Black Folks*. In the preface to the book, she urges readers to take the stories "seriously as valuable lessons in human behavior and examples of living history." "Raymond's Run," about a young runner, appears in the section of the book entitled "Stories I Wish I Had Read Growing Up."

◆ LITERATURE AND YOUR LIFE

CONNECT YOUR EXPERIENCE

Have you ever competed in an athletic event or an academic contest that you just *had* to win? Squeaky, the main character in "Raymond's Run," always wants to come out on top. In this story, she learns an important lesson about what being a winner really means.

THEMATIC FOCUS: Leading the Way

In "Raymond's Run," notice how a sister leads the way for her brother.

◆ Background for Understanding

PHYSICAL EDUCATION

Runners, like Squeaky in "Raymond's Run," get a number of benefits from their running. Squeaky trains by doing breathing exercises and prancing and trotting to keep her legs strong. The more a runner trains, the stronger he or she becomes. Running strengthens the heart and the leg muscles and increases the circulation of oxygen through the bloodstream to the body's organs and tissues.

◆ Build Vocabulary

WORD PARTS: *scope*

In the story, Mr. Pearson "looks around the park for Gretchen like a periscope in a submarine movie." The word part *scope* means "an instrument for seeing." A periscope is an instrument used to see above the water from a submerged submarine.

WORD BANK

Which word from the story means "to show or make known, as by a sign"? Check the Build Vocabulary box on page 295 to see if you guessed correctly.

prodigy
signify
ventriloquist
periscope

◆ Raymond's Run ◆

◆ Literary Focus

MAJOR AND MINOR CHARACTERS

Characters are the people (or sometimes animals) who take part in a literary work. Most stories have both major and minor characters. A **major character** is the most important character in the story. This person often changes in a significant way as the story unfolds. **Minor characters** play lesser roles in the story's events but are necessary for the story to develop. In "Raymond's Run," Squeaky, the major character, tells the story.

◆ Reading Strategy

PREDICT

As you read a story, you may find yourself wondering what's going to happen. You can often **predict** the story events by paying attention to details the author provides. Your prediction is an informed guess based on story details. In "Raymond's Run," two characters compete in an important race. Keep track of details the author gives you about each character to see if you can predict what will happen. Use a chart like the one below to help you make predictions.

Story Text	Prediction
"I'm the fastest thing on two feet."	She will meet her match.

RAYMOND'S RUN

Toni Cade Bambara

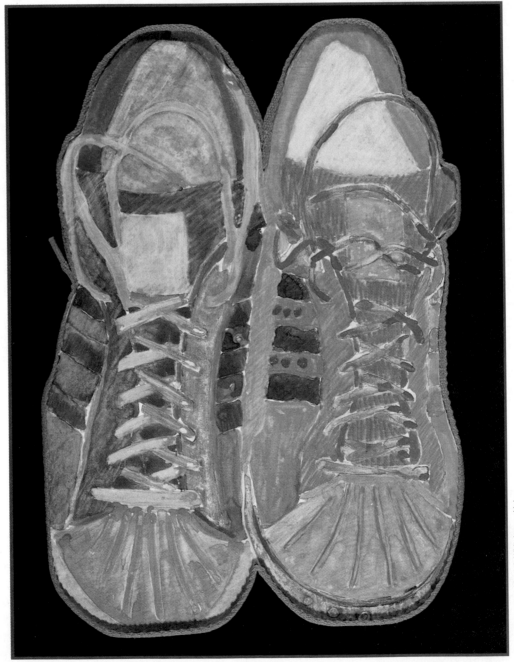

Shoe Series, #2, Marilee Whitehouse-Holm

I don't have much work to do around the house like some girls. My mother does that. And I don't have to earn my pocket money by hustling; George runs errands for the big boys and sells Christmas cards. And anything else that's got to get done, my father does. All I have to do in life is mind my brother Raymond, which is enough.

Sometimes I slip and say my little brother Raymond. But as any fool can see he's much bigger and he's older too. But a lot of people call him my little brother cause he needs looking after cause he's not quite right. And a lot of smart mouths got lots to say about that too, especially when George was minding him. But now, if anybody has anything to say to Raymond, anything to say about his big head, they have to come by me. And I don't play the dozens[1] or believe in standing around with somebody in my face doing a lot of talking. I much rather just knock you down and take my chances even if I am a little girl with skinny arms and a squeaky voice, which is how I got the name Squeaky. And if things get too rough, I run. And as anybody can tell you, I'm the fastest thing on two feet.

There is no track meet that I don't win the first place medal. I used to win the twenty-yard dash when I was a little kid in kindergarten. Nowadays, it's the fifty-yard dash. And tomorrow I'm subject to run the quarter-meter relay all by myself and come in first, second, and third. The big kids call me Mercury[2] cause I'm the swiftest thing in the neighborhood. Everybody knows that—except two people who know better, my father and me.

He can beat me to Amsterdam Avenue with me having a two fire-hydrant headstart and him running with his hands in his pockets and whistling. But that's private information. Cause can you imagine some thirty-five-year-old man stuffing himself into PAL[3] shorts to race little kids? So as far as everyone's concerned, I'm the fastest and that goes for Gretchen, too, who has put out the tale that she is going to win the first-place medal this year. Ridiculous. In the second place, she's got short legs. In the third place, she's got freckles. In the first place, no one can beat me and that's all there is to it.

I'm standing on the corner admiring the weather and about to take a stroll down Broadway so I can practice my breathing exercises, and I've got Raymond walking on the inside close to the buildings, cause he's subject to fits of fantasy and starts thinking he's a circus performer and that the curb is a tightrope strung high in the air. And sometimes after a rain he likes to step down off his tightrope right into the gutter and slosh around getting his shoes and cuffs wet. Or sometimes if you don't watch him he'll dash across traffic to the island in the middle of Broadway and give the pigeons a fit. Then I have to go behind him apologizing to all the old people sitting around trying to get some sun and getting all upset with the pigeons fluttering around them, scattering their newspapers and upsetting the waxpaper lunches in their laps. So I keep Raymond on the inside of me, and he plays like he's driving a stage coach, which is O.K. by me so long as he doesn't run me over or interrupt my breathing exercises, which I have to do on account of I'm serious about my running, and I don't care who knows it.

Now some people like to act like things come easy to them, won't let on that they practice. Not me. I'll high prance down 34th Street like a rodeo pony to keep my knees strong even if it does get my mother uptight so that she walks ahead like she's not with me, don't know me, is all by herself on a shopping trip, and I am somebody else's crazy child.

Now you take Cynthia Procter for instance. She's just the opposite. If there's a test tomorrow, she'll say something like, "Oh, I guess I'll play handball this afternoon and watch television tonight," just to let you know she ain't

---

1. **the dozens:** Game in which the players insult one another; the first to show anger loses.
2. **Mercury:** In Roman mythology, the messenger of the gods, known for great speed.

◀ **Critical Viewing** Most young people, not just athletes, wear athletic shoes. What do athletic shoes symbolize to you? **[Generalize]**

---

3. **PAL:** Police Athletic League.

▲ **Critical Viewing** Do you think the runners in this photograph love to race as much as Squeaky does? Why or why not? [**Speculate**]

thinking about the test. Or like last week when she won the spelling bee for the millionth time, "A good thing you got 'receive,' Squeaky, cause I would have got it wrong. I completely forgot about the spelling bee." And she'll clutch the lace on her blouse like it was a narrow escape. Oh, brother.

But of course when I pass her house on my early morning trots around the block, she is practicing the scales on the piano over and over and over and over. Then in music class she always lets herself get bumped around so she falls accidently on purpose onto the piano stool and is so surprised to find herself sitting there that she decides just for fun to try out the ole keys and what do you know—Chopin's[4] waltzes just spring out of her fingertips and she's the most surprised thing in the world. A regular <u>prodigy</u>. I could kill people like that.

I stay up all night studying the words for the spelling bee. And you can see me any time of day practicing running. I never walk if I can trot, and shame on Raymond if he can't keep up. But of course he does, cause if he hangs back someone's liable to walk up to him and get smart, or take his allowance from him, or ask him where he got that great big pumpkin head. People are so stupid sometimes.

So I'm strolling down Broadway breathing out and breathing in on counts of seven, which is my lucky number, and here comes Gretchen and her sidekicks—Mary Louise who used to be a friend of mine when she first moved to Harlem from Baltimore and got beat up by everybody till I took up for her on account of her mother and my mother used to sing in the same choir when they were young girls, but people ain't grateful, so now she hangs out with the new girl Gretchen and talks about me like a dog; and Rosie who is as fat as I am skinny and has a big mouth where Raymond is concerned and is too stupid to know that there is not a big deal of difference between herself and Raymond and that she can't afford to throw stones. So they are steady coming up Broadway and I see right away that it's going to be one of those Dodge City[5] scenes cause the street ain't that big and they're close to the buildings just as we are. First I think I'll step into the candy store and look over the new comics and let them pass. But that's chicken and I've got a reputation to consider. So then I think I'll just walk straight

---

4. **Chopin** (shō pan´): Frédéric François Chopin (1810–1849), Polish composer and pianist.

5. **Dodge City:** Location of the television program *Gunsmoke,* which often presented a gunfight between the sheriff and an outlaw.

on through them or even over them if necessary. But as they get to me, they slow down. I'm ready to fight, cause like I said I don't feature a whole lot of chit-chat, I much prefer to just knock you down right from the jump and save everybody a lotta precious time.

"You signing up for the May Day races?" smiles Mary Louise, only it's not a smile at all.

A dumb question like that doesn't deserve an answer. Besides, there's just me and Gretchen standing there really, so no use wasting my breath talking to shadows.

◆ **Literary Focus**
What do you learn about the major character, Squeaky, through her conversation with the minor characters Mary Louise, Gretchen, and Rosie?

"I don't think you're going to win this time," says Rosie, trying to signify with her hands on her hips all salty, completely forgetting that I have whupped her many times for less salt than that.

"I always win cause I'm the best," I say straight at Gretchen who is, as far as I'm concerned, the only one talking in this ventriloquist-dummy routine.

Gretchen smiles, but it's not a smile, and I'm thinking that girls never really smile at each other because they don't know how and don't want to know how and there's probably no one to teach us how cause grown-up girls don't know either. Then they all look at Raymond who has just brought his mule team to a standstill. And they're about to see what trouble they can get into through him.

"What grade you in now, Raymond?"

"You got anything to say to my brother, you say it to me, Mary Louise Williams of Raggedy Town, Baltimore."

"What are you, his mother?" sasses Rosie.

"That's right, Fatso. And the next word out

of anybody and I'll be *their* mother too." So they just stand there and Gretchen shifts from one leg to the other and so do they. Then Gretchen puts her hands on her hips and is about to say something with her freckle-face self but doesn't. Then she walks around me looking me up and down but keeps walking up Broadway, and her sidekicks follow her. So me and Raymond smile at each other and he says, "Gidyap" to his team and I continue with my breathing exercises, strolling down Broadway toward the ice man on 145th with not a care in the world cause I am Miss Quicksilver herself.

I take my time getting to the park on May Day because the track meet is the last thing on the program. The biggest thing on the program is the May Pole dancing, which I can do without, thank you, even if my mother thinks it's a shame I don't take part and act like a girl for a change. You'd think my mother'd be grateful not to have to make me a white organdy dress with a big satin sash and buy me new white baby-doll shoes that can't be taken out of the box till the big day. You'd think she'd be glad her daughter ain't out there prancing around a May Pole getting the new clothes all dirty and sweaty and trying to act like a fairy or a flower or whatever you're supposed to be when you should be trying to be yourself, whatever that is, which is, as far as I am concerned, a poor black girl who really can't afford to buy shoes and a new dress you only wear once a lifetime cause it won't fit next year.

I was once a strawberry in a Hansel and Gretel pageant when I was in nursery school and didn't have no better sense than to dance on tiptoe with my arms in a circle over my head doing umbrella steps and being a perfect fool just so my mother and father could come dressed up and clap. You'd think they'd know better than to encourage that kind of nonsense. I am not a strawberry. I do not dance on my toes. I run. That is what I am all about. So I always come late to the May Day program, just in time to get my number pinned on and lay in the grass till they announce the fifty-yard dash.

◆ **Build Vocabulary**

prodigy (präd´ ə jē) n.: A wonder; an unusually talented person

signify (sig´ nə fī) v.: To show or make known, as by a sign, words, etc.

ventriloquist (ven tril´ ə kwist) n.: Someone who speaks through a puppet or dummy

I put Raymond in the little swings, which is a tight squeeze this year and will be impossible next year. Then I look around for Mr. Pearson, who pins the numbers on. I'm really looking for Gretchen if you want to know the truth, but she's not around. The park is jam-packed. Parents in hats and corsages and breast-pocket handkerchiefs peeking up. Kids in white dresses and light-blue suits. The parkees unfolding chairs and chasing the rowdy kids from Lenox as if they had no right to be there. The big guys with their caps on backwards, leaning against the fence swirling the basketballs on the tips of their fingers, waiting for all these crazy people to clear out the park so they can play. Most of the kids in my class are carrying bass drums and glockenspiels[6] and flutes. You'd think they'd put in a few bongos or something for real like that.

Then here comes Mr. Pearson with his clipboard and his cards and pencils and whistles and safety pins and fifty million other things he's always dropping all over the place with his clumsy self. He sticks out in a crowd because he's on stilts. We used to call him Jack and the Beanstalk to get him mad. But I'm the only one that can outrun him and get away, and I'm too grown for that silliness now.

"Well, Squeaky," he says, checking my name off the list and handing me number seven and two pins. And I'm thinking he's got no right to call me Squeaky, if I can't call him Beanstalk.

"Hazel Elizabeth Deborah Parker," I correct him and tell him to write it down on his board.

"Well, Hazel Elizabeth Deborah Parker, going to give someone else a break this year?" I squint at him real hard to see if he is seriously thinking I should lose the race on purpose just to give someone else a break. "Only six girls running this time," he continues, shaking his head sadly like it's my fault all of New York didn't turn out in sneakers. "That new girl should give

◆ **Reading Strategy**
Predict what will happen in the race. On what details in the story do you base your prediction?

you a run for your money." He looks around the park for Gretchen like a periscope in a submarine movie. "Wouldn't it be a nice gesture if you were . . . to ahhh . . ."

I give him such a look he couldn't finish putting that idea into words. Grownups got a lot of nerve sometimes. I pin number seven to myself and stomp away, I'm so burnt. And I go straight for the track and stretch out on the grass while the band winds up with "Oh, the Monkey Wrapped His Tail Around the Flag Pole," which my teacher calls by some other name. The man on the loudspeaker is calling everyone over to the track and I'm on my back looking at the sky, trying to pretend I'm in the country, but I can't, because even grass in the city feels hard as sidewalk, and there's just no pretending you are anywhere but in a "concrete jungle" as my grandfather says.

The twenty-yard dash takes all of two minutes cause most of the little kids don't know no better than to run off the track or run the wrong way or run smack into the fence and fall down and cry. One little kid, though, has got the good sense to run straight for the white ribbon up ahead, so he wins. Then the second-graders line up for the thirty-yard dash and I don't even bother to turn my head to watch cause Raphael Perez always wins. He wins before he even begins by psyching[7] the runners, telling them they're going to trip on their shoelaces and fall on their faces or lose their shorts or something, which he doesn't really have to do since he is very fast, almost as fast as I am. After that is the forty-yard dash which I use to run when I was in first grade. Raymond is hollering from the swings cause he knows I'm about to do my thing cause the man on the loudspeaker has just announced the fifty-yard dash, although he

---

6. **glockenspiels** (gläk´ ən spēlz) *n.*: Musical instruments with flat metal bars that make bell-like tones when struck with small hammers.

7. **psyching** (sīk´ iŋ) *v.*: Slang for playing on a person's mental state.

might just as well be giving a recipe for angel food cake cause you can hardly make out what he's saying for the static. I get up and slip off my sweat pants and then I see Gretchen standing at the starting line, kicking her legs out like a pro. Then as I get into place I see that ole Raymond is on line on the other side of the fence, bending down with his fingers on the ground just like he knew what he was doing. I was going to yell at him but then I didn't. It burns up your energy to holler.

Every time, just before I take off in a race, I always feel like I'm in a dream, the kind of

◆ **Literature and Your Life**
How do you feel right before you compete?

dream you have when you're sick with fever and feel all hot and weightless. I dream I'm flying over a sandy beach in the early morning sun, kissing the leaves of the trees as I fly by. And there's always the smell of apples, just like in the country when I was little and used to think I was a choo-choo train, running through the fields of corn and chugging up the

▲ **Critical Viewing** What constitutes success in a race? Is the winner the only one who succeeds? Explain. [Define]

hill to the orchard. And all the time I'm dreaming this, I get lighter and lighter until I'm flying over the beach again, getting blown through the sky like a feather that weighs nothing at all. But once I spread my fingers in the dirt and crouch over the Get on Your Mark, the dream goes and I am solid again and am telling myself, Squeaky you must win, you must win, you are the fastest thing in the world, you can even beat your father up Amsterdam if you really try. And then I feel my weight coming back just behind my knees then down to my feet then into the earth and the pistol shot explodes in my blood and I am

◆ **Build Vocabulary**

periscope (per´ ə skōp) *n.*: An instrument containing mirrors and lenses, used to see objects not in a direct line from the viewer; often used in submarines to see objects above the water

▲ **Critical Viewing** Put yourself in the place of this race's winner. How must she feel? [Speculate]

off and weightless again, flying past the other runners, my arms pumping up and down and the whole world is quiet except for the crunch as I zoom over the gravel in the track. I glance to my left and there is no one. To the right a blurred Gretchen, who's got her chin jutting out as if it would win the race all by itself. And on the other side of the fence is Raymond with his arms down to his side and the palms tucked up behind him, running in his very own style, and it's the first time I ever saw that and I almost stop to watch my brother Raymond on his first run. But the white ribbon is bouncing toward me and I tear past it, racing into the distance till my feet with a mind of their own start digging up footfuls of dirt and brake me short. Then all the kids standing on the side pile on me, banging me on the back and slapping my head with their May Day programs, for I have won again and everybody on 151st Street can walk tall for another year.

"In first place . . ." the man on the loudspeaker is clear as a bell now. But then he pauses and the loudspeaker starts to whine. Then static. And I lean down to catch my breath and here comes Gretchen walking back, for she's overshot the finish line too, huffing and puffing with her hands on her hips taking it slow, breathing in steady time like a real pro and I sort of like her a little for the first time. "In first place . . ." and then three or four voices get all mixed up on the loudspeaker and I dig my sneaker into the grass and stare at Gretchen who's staring back, we both wondering just who did win. I can hear old Beanstalk arguing with the man on the loudspeaker and then a few others running their mouths about what the stopwatches say. Then I hear Raymond yanking at the fence to call me and I wave to shush him, but he keeps rattling the fence like a gorilla in a cage like in them gorilla movies, but then like a dancer or something he starts climbing up nice and easy but very fast. And it occurs to me, watching how smoothly he climbs hand over hand and remembering how he looked running with his arms down to his side and with the wind pulling his mouth back and his teeth showing and all, it occurred to me that Raymond would make a very fine runner. Doesn't he always keep up with me on my trots? And he surely knows how to breathe in counts of seven cause he's always doing it at the dinner table, which drives my brother George up the wall. And I'm smiling to beat the band cause if I've lost this race, or if me and Gretchen tied, or

◆ **Literary Focus**
What realization has Squeaky come to? How does this show that she is a major character?

even if I've won, I can always retire as a runner and begin a whole new career as a coach with Raymond as my champion. After all, with a little more study I can beat Cynthia and her phony self at the spelling bee. And if I bugged my mother, I could get piano lessons and become a star. And I have a big rep as the baddest thing around. And I've got a roomful of ribbons and medals and awards. But what has Raymond got to call his own?

So I stand there with my new plans, laughing out loud by this time as Raymond jumps down from the fence and runs over with his teeth showing and his arms down to the side, which no one before him has quite mastered as a running style. And by the time he comes over I'm jumping up and down so glad to see him—my brother Raymond, a great runner in the family tradition. But of course everyone thinks I'm jumping up and down because the men on the loudspeaker have finally gotten themselves together and compared notes and are announcing "In first place—Miss Hazel Elizabeth Deborah Parker." (Dig that.) "In second place—Miss Gretchen P. Lewis." And I look over at Gretchen wondering what the "P" stands for. And I smile. Cause she's good, no doubt about it. Maybe she'd like to help me coach Raymond; she obviously is serious about running, as any fool can see. And she nods to congratulate me and then she smiles. And I smile. We stand there with this big smile of respect between us. It's about as real a smile as girls can do for each other, considering we don't practice real smiling every day, you know, cause maybe we too busy being flowers or fairies or strawberries instead of something honest and worthy of respect . . . you know . . . like being people.

Guide for Responding

◆ LITERATURE AND YOUR LIFE

Reader's Response If you were Squeaky, how would you feel if you had lost the race?

Thematic Focus In what way does Squeaky show that she is "leading the way"?

Journal Writing Briefly write about a time when helping someone made you feel good.

☑ Check Your Comprehension

1. How did Squeaky get her nickname? Why is she also called Mercury?
2. What does Mr. Pearson want Squeaky to do in the race?
3. How does Squeaky feel before each race?
4. (a) What does Squeaky realize about herself at the end of the race? (b) What does she realize about Raymond?

◆ Critical Thinking

INTERPRET

1. How does Squeaky feel about taking care of Raymond? Support your answer. **[Analyze]**
2. What does Squeaky's behavior toward people who "talk smart" to her suggest about her? **[Interpret]**
3. How does Squeaky feel about the other girls in her class? Explain. **[Analyze]**
4. Explain the significance of the smile that Squeaky and Gretchen share. **[Interpret]**

EVALUATE

5. Is "Raymond's Run" a good title for this story? Explain. **[Assess]**

APPLY

6. Squeaky suggests that it is difficult for girls in our society to be "something honest and worthy of respect." Explain why you agree or disagree with her opinion. **[Relate]**

Guide for Responding *(continued)*

◆ Reading Strategy

PREDICT

When you **predict,** you look ahead to what will happen in a story, using details the author shares with you.

1. What details might lead you to predict that Squeaky and Gretchen would share a friendly moment at the end of the story?

2. Do you predict that Raymond will become a runner like Squeaky? Explain your answer.

◆ Build Vocabulary

USING THE WORD PART *scope*

The word part *scope* combines with other word parts to form nouns that name instruments for seeing. Use a dictionary to find the definitions of these words. What other *scope* words do you know?

1. periscope 2. telescope 3. microscope

SPELLING STRATEGY

In most words that end in *gy*, the vowel that precedes *gy* is *o*. Examples include *biology, physiology,* and *anthropology.*

However, in a few words, like *prodigy*, another vowel precedes *gy*. It is best to memorize these exceptions to the rule.

    stra**te**gy   el**e**gy   ef**fi**gy

On your paper, complete each sentence with the correct *gy* word.

    strategy   apology   psychology

1. I made an _____?_____ for my mistake.

2. My winning _____?_____ is to act like a pro.

3. I'll study _____?_____ when I get to high school.

USING THE WORD BANK

On your paper, match each word with its definition.

1. prodigy   **a.** person who speaks through a puppet or dummy

2. signify   **b.** instrument for seeing from a submarine

3. ventriloquist   **c.** child genius

4. periscope   **d.** show or make known

◆ Literary Focus

MAJOR AND MINOR CHARACTERS

In literature, the **major character** is the one who plays the largest role in the story and the one who changes the most. The **minor characters** have less significant roles. In "Raymond's Run," you see Squeaky, the major character, grow and change when she recognizes that her brother is a natural runner.

1. What changes do you see in Squeaky as the story progresses?

2. What role does Gretchen play in this story?

3. How is Raymond's role in the story different from Squeaky's role?

◆ Build Grammar Skills

PREPOSITIONS

A **preposition** is a word that relates the noun or pronoun that follows it to another word in the sentence. Prepositions often show relationships of time (*before, after*) and space (*beyond, behind*).

Here are some other common prepositions:

> about above across around as behind below beside between down for from in near of on over toward under up with

Some prepositions, like the following, consist of more than one word: *according to, ahead of, as of, because of, in front of,* and *instead of.*

Toni Cade Bambara uses the preposition *in* to relate the word *neighborhood* to *the swiftest thing:*

> . . . I'm the swiftest thing *in* the neighborhood.

Practice On your paper, underline the preposition in each sentence.

1. George runs errands for the big boys.

2. I'm standing on the corner.

3. Raymond was walking close by the wall.

4. Gretchen puts her hands on her hips.

5. Here comes Mr. Peabody with his clipboard.

Writing Application Copy this sentence three times, completing each version with a different preposition. Notice how the meaning of the sentence changes.

    The racers ran _____?_____ the fence.

Build Your Portfolio

 Idea Bank

Writing

1. Letter Write a letter from Gretchen to a friend. Describe Squeaky's victory in the race, along with your reaction.

2. Sequel A sequel is a continuation of a story. Write a sequel to "Raymond's Run" that tells what happens to Squeaky and Raymond in the weeks following the race.

3. Essay In an essay, trace the changes the main character, Squeaky, undergoes during the course of the story.

Speaking and Listening

4. Scene [Group Activity] In a small group, choose a scene from "Raymond's Run" to perform. Different group members can be responsible for writing dialogue, supplying or creating props and costumes, providing background music, and so on. Practice the scene before performing it for the class. **[Performing Arts Link]**

5. Telephone Conversation [Group Activity] With a partner, improvise a telephone conversation in which Squeaky asks Gretchen to help coach Raymond. **[Performing Arts Link]**

Projects

6. Map of the Setting [Group Activity] In a small group, create a map that shows where the events in "Raymond's Run" take place. You may wish to consult a map of New York City. You may also wish to add to your map any details mentioned in the story that would not be on a city map. **[Social Studies Link]**

7. Track and Running Bibliography Research to create a bibliography or listing of track and running magazines, books, and Web sites. Share your bibliography with the class. **[Technology Link; Sports Link]**

 Writing Mini-Lesson

Script for a Sportscaster

Squeaky's description of the May Day race makes you feel as if you were there—just as a good sportscast vividly captures the excitement of an athletic event. Write a script for a sportscaster. It can be about any sport you choose, but it should bring an athletic event to life for your audience.

Writing Skill Focus: Background Information

Include **background information,** such as facts, statistics, and interesting or unusual details, to bring the event to life. In this example from the story, Squeaky provides information that is both factual and amusing:

Model From the Story
The twenty-yard dash takes all of two minutes cause most of the little kids don't know no better than to run off the track . . .

Prewriting Recall a sports event that you have seen. List, in chronological order, the events that took place. Make notes about the human emotions that you observed. Research background information that your audience needs to know or that will enliven your script.

Drafting As you draft, include only the most interesting background information. Use a lively tone that conveys the excitement of the event.

> **Grammar Application**
> Use prepositions to add details to your sportscast script.

Revising Imagine that you are a sportscaster, and read your script aloud to a peer. Ask whether you have provided enough background information and if your sportscast is interesting and exciting. Revise according to the feedback you receive.

CONNECTIONS TO TODAY'S WORLD

In 1963, Eunice Kennedy Shriver organized an athletic tournament for mentally challenged young people. In 1968, that tournament became the Special Olympics. Today, thousands of Special Olympians, ages eight and up, compete in the World Summer and Winter Games.

The Special Olympics organization likes to say that it is "training for life." In fact, increased confidence, self-esteem, and social skills are the real gains—even more important to participants than the development of athletic skills.

THERE IS NO OFF-SEASON.

"*T*o provide year-round sports training and athletic competition in a variety of Olympic-type sports for individuals with mental retardation by giving them continuing opportunities to develop physical fitness, demonstrate courage, experience joy and participate in a sharing of gifts, skills and friendship with their families, other Special Olympics athletes and the community."

Special Olympics is "training for life."

You may have thought that Special Olympics was just a few days of games once or twice a year. But in reality, the training for competition is as important as the competition itself. Special Olympics involves individuals of all ages and ability levels—from people with low motor abilities to highly-skilled athletes who can compete in a higher level of sports both in and out of Special Olympics. To accommodate this range of skill levels, Special Olympics offers a wide variety of programs so athletes may choose those best suited to their abilities and interests.

Special Olympics is a year-round program, a lifetime of learning through sport. The mission of the Special Olympics movement has remained constant since Eunice Kennedy Shriver began the program and organized the first games in 1968.

1. What are the positive and negative outcomes from participation in competitive athletic programs? Do you think the outcomes are the same for mentally challenged people? Explain.
2. What does Special Olympics mean by the phrase "training for life"?
3. Do you think Raymond in "Raymond's Run" would benefit from a program like Special Olympics? Why or why not?

Guide for Reading

◆ LITERATURE AND YOUR LIFE

CONNECT YOUR EXPERIENCE

Sometimes ordinary people perform extraordinary acts. You probably read about or hear about these "everyday heroes" in newspapers, magazines, and on television. In these poems, you'll meet three people who became unlikely heroes.

THEMATIC FOCUS: Leading the Way

During the Revolutionary War, Paul Revere, pictured on the opposite page, risked his life to warn fellow colonists about the approaching British army. Think about what might inspire someone to lead the way—even if it means facing danger.

◆ Background for Understanding

HISTORY

Elizabeth Blackwell, the subject of the poem by Eve Merriam, was one woman who led the way for other women. In the nineteenth century, it was uncommon for women to consider a career in medicine. In fact, until little more than 150 years ago, no American medical college would admit female students. However, in 1847, Elizabeth Blackwell entered medical school. She graduated with high honors to become the first female medical doctor in the United States.

◆ Build Vocabulary

WORD ROOTS: -spec-

The word *spectral* in "Paul Revere's Ride" contains the word root -spec-, which is related to appearances. *Spectral* means "appearing ghostly."

WORD BANK

Which word from the poems might describe someone who steals into a room? Check the Build Vocabulary box on page 307 to see if you chose correctly.

stealthy
somber
impetuous
spectral
tranquil
aghast
horde

Paul Revere's Ride ◆ Barbara Frietchie
◆ Elizabeth Blackwell ◆

◆ Literary Focus

HEROIC CHARACTERS

A man risks his life for the good of his country. A woman braves danger to express her patriotism. A girl stubbornly refuses to give up her dream of helping others. These characters are **heroes** because their actions are inspiring and noble. They bravely struggle to overcome the obstacles and problems that stand in their way. As you read about these characters, keep track of their heroic qualities and actions on character wheels like the one below.

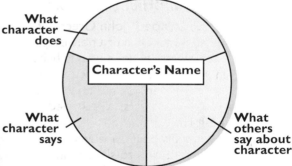

What character does

Character's Name

What character says

What others say about character

◆ Reading Strategy

INTERPRET THE MEANING

The characters in these poems all perform heroic deeds. You'll better understand the significance of their actions if you **interpret the meaning** behind the poets' words. First, use the images the poet includes to form a picture in your mind of what is being described. Next, ask yourself why the poet has chosen these specific images. Finally, explain the meaning and importance of these images.

Paul Revere's Ride

Henry Wadsworth Longfellow

Listen, my children, and you shall hear
Of the midnight ride of Paul Revere,
On the eighteenth of April, in Seventy-five;
Hardly a man is now alive
5   Who remembers that famous day and year.

He said to his friend, "If the British march
By land or sea from the town to-night,
Hang a lantern aloft in the belfry arch[1]
Of the North Church tower as a signal light,—
10 One, if by land, and two, if by sea;
And I on the opposite shore will be,
Ready to ride and spread the alarm
Through every Middlesex[2] village and farm,
For the country folk to be up and to arm."

15 Then he said, "Good night!" and with muffled oar
Silently rowed to the Charlestown[3] shore,
Just as the moon rose over the bay,
Where swinging wide at her moorings[4] lay
The *Somerset*, British man-of-war;[5]
20 A phantom ship, with each mast and spar[6]
Across the moon like a prison bar,
And a huge black hulk, that was magnified
By its own reflection in the tide.

Meanwhile, his friend, through alley and street,
25 Wanders and watches with eager ears,
Till in the silence around him he hears
The muster[7] of men at the barrack door,
The sound of arms, and the tramp of feet,
And the measured tread of the grenadiers,[8]
30 Marching down to their boats on the shore.

Then he climbed the tower of the Old
    North Church,
By the wooden stairs, with <u>stealthy</u> tread,
To the belfry-chamber overhead,
And startled the pigeons from their perch
35 On the <u>somber</u> rafters,[9] that round him made

◀ **Critical Viewing** How does this painting reinforce the legendary nature of Paul Revere's ride? [**Analyze**]

1. **belfry arch** (bel´ frē ärch): Curved top of a tower or steeple that holds the bells.

2. **Middlesex** (mid´ əl seks´): A county in Massachusetts.

3. **Charlestown**: Part of Boston on the harbor.
4. **moorings** (moor´ iηs) *n.*: Lines, cables, or chains that hold a ship to the shore.
5. **man-of-war:** Armed naval vessel; warship.
6. **mast and spar:** Poles used to support sails.

7. **muster** *n.*: An assembly of troops summoned for inspection, roll call, or service.
8. **grenadiers** (gren´ ə dirz´) *n.*: Members of a special regiment or corps.
9. **rafters** *n.*: Beams that slope from the ridge of a roof to the eaves and serve to support the roof.

◆ **Build Vocabulary**

stealthy (stel´ thē) *adj.*: Artfully sly and secretive

somber (säm´ bər) *adj.*: Dark and gloomy

Masses and moving shapes of shade,—
By the trembling ladder, steep and tall,
To the highest window in the wall,
Where he paused to listen and look down
40   A moment on the roofs of the town,
And the moonlight flowing over all.

Beneath, in the churchyard, lay the dead,
In their night-encampment on the hill,
Wrapped in silence so deep and still
45   That he could hear, like a sentinel's[10] tread,
The watchful night-wind, as it went
Creeping along from tent to tent,
And seeming to whisper, "All is well!"
A moment only he feels the spell
50   Of the place and the hour, and the secret dread
Of the lonely belfry and the dead;
For suddenly all his thoughts are bent
On a shadowy something far away,
Where the river widens to meet the bay,—
55   A line of black that bends and floats
On the rising tide, like a bridge of boats.

Meanwhile, impatient to mount and ride,
Booted and spurred, with a heavy stride
On the opposite shore walked Paul Revere.
60   Now he patted his horse's side,
Now gazed at the landscape far and near,
Then, <u>impetuous</u>, stamped the earth,
And turned and tightened his saddle-girth;[11]
But mostly he watched with eager search
65   The belfry-tower of the Old North Church,
As it rose above the graves on the hill,
Lonely and <u>spectral</u> and somber and still.
And lo! as he looks, on the belfry's height
A glimmer, and then a gleam of light!
70   He springs to the saddle, the bridle[12] he turns,
But lingers and gazes, till full on his sight
A second lamp in the belfry burns!

A hurry of hoofs in a village street,

---

10. sentinel (sen´ ti nəl) *n.*: Guard.
11. girth (gɘrth) *n.*: A band put around the belly of a horse
for holding a saddle.
12. bridle (brīd´ əl) *n.*: A head harness for guiding a horse.

◀ **Critical Viewing** Why would a church steeple like this one be ideal for a signal? [Connect]

75 A shape in the moonlight, a bulk in the dark,
    And beneath, from the pebbles, in passing, a spark
    Struck out by a steed flying fearless and fleet:
    That was all! And yet, through the gloom and the light,
    The fate of a nation was riding that night;
    And the spark struck out by that steed[13] in his flight,
80 Kindled the land into flame with its heat.
    He has left the village and mounted the steep,[14]
    And beneath him, tranquil and broad and deep,
    Is the Mystic,[15] meeting the ocean tides;
    And under the alders[16] that skirt its edge,
85 Now soft on the sand, now loud on the ledge,
    Is heard the tramp of his steed as he rides.

    It was twelve by the village clock,
    When he crossed the bridge into Medford[17] town.
    He heard the crowing of the cock,
90 And the barking of the farmer's dog,
    And felt the damp of the river fog,
    That rises after the sun goes down.

    It was one by the village clock,
    When he galloped into Lexington.[18]
95 He saw the gilded weathercock[19]
    Swim in the moonlight as he passed,
    And the meeting-house windows, blank and bare,
    Gaze at him with a spectral glare,
    As if they already stood aghast
100 At the bloody work they would look upon.

    It was two by the village clock,
    When he came to the bridge in Concord[20] town.
    He heard the bleating[21] of the flock,

◆ Build Vocabulary

impetuous
(im pech′ oo əs)
adj.: Done suddenly with little thought

spectral (spek′ trəl)
adj.: Phantomlike; ghostly

tranquil (tran′ kwil)
adj.: Quiet or motionless; peaceful

aghast (ə gäst′) *adj.*: Feeling great horror or dismay

---

13. **steed** *n.*: Horse, especially a high-spirited riding horse.
14. **steep** *n.*: Slope or incline having a sharp rise.
15. **Mystic** (mis′ tik): A river in Massachusetts.
16. **alders** (ôl′ dərz) *n.*: Trees and shrubs of the birch family.
17. **Medford**: A town outside Boston.
18. **Lexington**: A town in eastern Massachusetts, outside Boston.
19. **weathercock** (weth′ ər käk′) *n.*: Weathervane in the form of a rooster.
20. **Concord**: A town in eastern Massachusetts. The first battles of the Revolutionary War (April 19, 1775) were fought in Lexington and Concord.
21. **bleating** (blēt′ iŋ) *n.*: Sound made by sheep.

And the twitter of birds among the trees,
105 And felt the breath of the morning breeze
Blowing over the meadows brown.
And one was safe and asleep in his bed
Who at the bridge would be first to fall,
Who that day would be lying dead,
110 Pierced by a British musket-ball.

You know the rest. In the books you
      have read,
How the British Regulars fired and fled,—
How the farmers gave them ball for ball,
From behind each fence and farm-yard wall,
115 Chasing the red-coats down the lane,
Then crossing the fields to emerge again
Under the trees at the turn of the road,
And only pausing to fire and load.

So through the night rode Paul Revere;
120 And so through the night went his cry
      of alarm
To every Middlesex village and farm,—
A cry of defiance and not of fear,
A voice in the darkness, a knock at the door,
And a word that shall echo forevermore!
125 For, borne on the night-wind of the Past,
Through all our history, to the last,
In the hour of darkness and peril and need,
The people will waken and listen to hear
The hurrying hoof-beats of that steed,
130 And the midnight message of Paul Revere.

Guide for Responding

◆ LITERATURE AND YOUR LIFE

Reader's Response Does this poem capture the excitement of Revere's ride? Explain.

Thematic Focus List three qualities of leadership that Paul Revere shows.

Journal Writing In your journal, jot down some thoughts or feelings Revere may have had during his midnight ride.

☑ Check Your Comprehension

1. When does Paul Revere make his ride?
2. Explain the meaning of the signals used to communicate to Revere.
3. What does Revere do after seeing the signals?
4. Does Revere accomplish his purpose?

◆ Critical Thinking

INTERPRET

1. (a) To what is the *Somerset* compared in lines 15–23? (b) What is the effect of this image? **[Interpret]**
2. How do lines 78 through 80 express the importance the poet places on the ride? **[Analyze]**
3. Describe Paul Revere's character. **[Analyze]**
4. In what ways is this poem similar to and different from a short story? **[Compare and Contrast]**

EVALUATE

5. Do you think Revere's friend is also a hero? Explain. **[Make a Judgment]**

EXTEND

6. What does Longfellow mean when he says, "The fate of a nation was riding that night"? **[Social Studies Link]**

Barbara Frietchie

John Greenleaf Whittier

The Battle of Fredericksburg, 1862, Frederic Cavada, The Historical Society of Pennsylvania

▲ **Critical Viewing** This painting depicts the Battle of Fredericksburg. Does this painting help you understand what it was like to fight in such a battle? Why or why not? [**Assess**]

Up from the meadows rich with corn,
Clear in the cool September morn,

The clustered spires of Frederick[1] stand
Green-walled by the hills of Maryland.

5   Round about them orchards sweep,
Apple and peach tree fruited deep,

Fair as the garden of the Lord
To the eyes of the famished rebel <u>horde</u>,

1. **Frederick** (fred´ rik):
A town in Maryland.

◆ **Build Vocabulary**

horde (hôrd) *n.*: Large, moving group

On that pleasant morn of the early fall
10 When Lee[2] marched over the mountain wall;

Over the mountains winding down,
Horse and foot, into Frederick town.

Forty flags with their silver stars,
Forty flags with their crimson bars,

15 Flapped in the morning wind: the sun
Of noon looked down, and saw not one.

Up rose old Barbara Frietchie then,
Bowed with her fourscore[3] years and ten;

Bravest of all in Frederick town,
20 She took up the flag the men hauled down

In her attic window the staff she set,
To show that one heart was loyal yet.

Up the street came the rebel tread,
Stonewall Jackson[4] riding ahead.

25 Under his slouched hat left and right
He glanced; the old flag met his sight.

"Halt!"—the dust-brown ranks stood fast.
"Fire!"—out blazed the rifle-blast.

It shivered the window, pane and sash;[5]
30 It rent the banner with seam and gash.

Quick, as it fell, from the broken staff
Dame Barbara snatched the silken scarf.

She leaned far out on the window-sill,
And shook it forth with a royal will.

35 "Shoot, if you must, this old gray head,
But spare your country's flag," she said.

A shade of sadness, a blush of shame,
Over the face of the leader came;

The nobler nature within him stirred
40 To life at that woman's deed and word;

"Who touches a hair of yon gray head
Dies like a dog! March on!" he said.

2. Lee: Robert E. Lee, Commander in Chief of the Confederate army in the Civil War.

3. fourscore (fôr´ skôr´) *adj.*: Four times twenty; eighty.

4. Stonewall Jackson: Nickname of Thomas Jonathan Jackson, Confederate general in the Civil War.

5. sash (sash) *n.*: The frame holding the glass panes of a window.

All day long through Frederick street
Sounded the tread of marching feet:

45 All day long that free flag tost[6]
Over the heads of the rebel host.[7]

Ever its torn folds rose and fell
On the loyal winds that loved it well;

And through the hill-gaps sunset light
50 Shone over it with a warm good-night.

Barbara Frietchie's work is o'er,
And the Rebel rides on his raids no more.

Honor to her! and let a tear
Fall, for her sake, on Stonewall's bier.[8]

55 Over Barbara Frietchie's grave,
Flag of Freedom and Union, wave!

Peace and order and beauty draw
Round thy symbol of light and law;

And ever the stars above look down
60 On thy stars below in Frederick town!

6. tost (tôst) *v.*: Old-fashioned form of *tossed.*
7. host (hōst) *n.*: An army; a multitude or great number.

8. bier (bir) *n.*: A coffin and its supporting platform.

Guide for Responding

◆ LITERATURE AND YOUR LIFE

Reader's Response Would you have done what Barbara Frietchie did? Why or why not?

Thematic Focus In the poem, Barbara Frietchie acts alone—no one follows her actions. Do you consider her a leader? Why or why not?

☑ Check Your Comprehension

1. Describe the time and place of the poem.
2. What does Frietchie do before the soldiers arrive in town?
3. How does Frietchie meet Stonewall Jackson?
4. What is Jackson's response to Frietchie's actions?

◆ Critical Thinking

INTERPRET
1. Why does Barbara Frietchie do what she does? **[Analyze]**
2. Why do you think Stonewall Jackson orders his soldiers to fire on the flag? **[Speculate]**
3. What is the meaning of the last two lines of the poem? **[Interpret]**

EVALUATE
4. Was Jackson a good leader? Explain. **[Assess]**

COMPARE LITERARY WORKS
5. Compare and contrast the ways in which Paul Revere and Barbara Frietchie show their patriotism. **[Compare and Contrast]**

Elizabeth Blackwell

Eve Merriam

What will you do when you grow up,
nineteenth-century-young-lady?
Will you sew a fine seam and spoon dappled cream
under an apple tree shady?

5   Or will you be a teacher
in a dames' school
and train the little dears
by the scientific rule
that mental activity
10 may strain
the delicate female brain;
therefore let
the curriculum stress music, French,
   and especially
etiquette:[1]
15 teach how to set
a truly refined banquet.
Question One:
What kind of sauce
for the fish dish,
20 and pickle or lemon fork?
Quickly, students,
which should it be?

Now Elizabeth Blackwell, how about you?
Seamstress or teacher, which of the two?
25 You know there's not much else that a girl can do.
Don't mumble, Elizabeth. Learn to raise your head.
"I'm not very nimble with a needle and thread.
I could teach music—if I had to," she said,
"But I think I'd rather be a doctor instead."

30 "Is this some kind of joke?"
asked the proper menfolk.
"A woman be a doctor?

▲ **Critical Viewing** What do the details in this photograph of Blackwell reveal about the time in which she lived? **[Deduce]**

---

1. etiquette (et´ i kət) *n.*: Forms, manners, and ceremonies considered to be acceptable means of behavior.

Not in our respectable day!
A doctor? An M.D.! Did you hear what she said?
35   She's clearly and indubitably[2] out of her head!"
"Indeed, indeed, we are thoroughly agreed,"
hissed the ladies of society all laced in and prim,
"it's a scientific fact a doctor has to be a him.
Yes, sir,
40   'twould be against nature
if a doctor were a her."

hibble hobble bibble bobble
widdle waddle wag
tsk tsk
45   twit twit
    flip flap flutter
        mitter matter mutter
moan groan wail and rail
    Indecorous![3]
50   Revolting!!
        A *scandal*
            A SIN
their voices pierced the air like a jabbing hat-pin.
But little miss Elizabeth wouldn't give in.

55   To medical schools she applied.
In vain.
And applied again
and again
and again
60   and one rejection offered this plan:
why not disguise herself as a man?
If she pulled her hair back, put on boots
    and pants,
she might attend medical lectures in France.
Although she wouldn't earn a degree,
65   they'd let her study anatomy.

Elizabeth refused to hide
her feminine pride.
She drew herself up tall
(all five feet one of her!)
70   and tried again.
And denied again.
The letters answering no
mounted like winter snow.

▲ Critical Viewing This is an Elizabeth Blackwell Award, awarded by the American Medical Women's Association. On whom might such an award be bestowed? [Speculate]

---

2. indubitably (in dŏŏ′ bi tə blē) *adv.*: That cannot be doubted; unquestionably.
3. indecorous (in dek′ ə rəs) *adj.*: Improper; in poor taste.

Until the day
75 when her ramrod will
finally had its way.
After the twenty-ninth try,
there came from Geneva, New York
the reply
80 of a blessed
Yes!

Geneva,
Geneva,
how sweet the sound;
85 Geneva,
Geneva,
sweet sanctuary found . . .

. . . and the ladies of Geneva
passing by her in the street
90 drew back their hoopskirts[4]
so they wouldn't have to meet.

Psst, psst,
hiss, hiss
the sinister scarlet miss.
95 Avoid her, the hoyden,[5] the hussy,
lest we all be contaminated!
If your glove so much as touch her, my dear,
best to get it fumigated!

When Elizabeth came to table,
100 their talking all would halt;
wouldn't so much as ask her
please to pass the salt.

In between classes
without a kind word,
105 Elizabeth dwelt
like a pale gray bird.

In a bare attic room
cold as stone,
far from her family,
110 huddled alone

studying, studying
throughout the night

warming herself
with an inner light:

115 don't let it darken
the spark of fire;
keep it aglow,
that heart's desire:

the will to serve,
120 to help those in pain—
flickered and flared
and flickered again—

until
like a fairy tale
125 (except it was true!)
Elizabeth received
her honored due.

The perfect happy ending
came to pass:
130 Elizabeth graduated . . .
. . . at the head of her class.

And the ladies of Geneva
all rushed forward now to greet
that clever, dear Elizabeth,
135 so talented, so sweet!

Wasn't it glorious
she'd won first prize?

Elizabeth smiled
with cool gray eyes

140 and she wrapped her shawl
against the praise:

how soon there might come
more chilling days.

Turned to leave
145 without hesitating.

She was ready now,
and the world was waiting.

---

4. hoopskirts *n.*: Skirt worn over a framework of
hoops or rings, to make it spread out.
5. hoyden (hoĭ´ dən) *n.*: Tomboy.

Beyond Literature

Career Connection

Facts About Women in Medicine
A century ago, it was almost impossible for a woman to be accepted into a medical school in the United States. In the 1930's, only one hospital in ten would accept a female doctor to its staff. Forty years ago, people still found it difficult to imagine a female surgeon. Times have changed. Today, about one fifth of all doctors practicing medicine in the United States, more than 100,000, are women. By 2010, women are expected to make up about one third of the total number of physicians in practice.

Cross-Curricular Activity
Becoming a Doctor Find out what kind of education and training a person must have to prepare for a medical career. Research the qualifications for admission to medical school and the number of years of training it takes to become a physician. Share your findings with your class.

Guide for Responding

◆ LITERATURE AND YOUR LIFE

Reader's Response What would you like to say to the people who mistreated and misjudged Elizabeth Blackwell?

Thematic Focus What might have happened to Blackwell if she had been a follower rather than a leader?

Journal Writing Jot down a list of women who, like Blackwell, integrated what were previously male-dominated professions.

☑ Check Your Comprehension

1. What special purpose does Elizabeth Blackwell set for herself?
2. How do people respond when they know of Blackwell's ambitions?
3. What happens when Blackwell applies to medical school?
4. How do people treat Blackwell after she graduates from medical school?

◆ Critical Thinking

INTERPRET
1. Do you think Elizabeth Blackwell was a person easily discouraged? Explain. **[Support]**
2. What personality traits helped Blackwell to reach her goal? **[Analyze]**
3. What effect did people's opinions seem to have on Blackwell? **[Speculate]**
4. Explain what the following lines from "Elizabeth Blackwell" may mean: "and she wrapped her shawl/against the praise:/how soon there might come/more chilling days." **[Interpret]**

EVALUATE
5. Do you think Elizabeth Blackwell had the qualities necessary to become a successful doctor? Why or why not? **[Assess]**

APPLY
6. How have society's expectations changed for "twentieth-century-young-ladies"? **[Apply]**

Guide for Responding (continued)

◆ Reading Strategy

INTERPRET THE MEANING

One way to **interpret the meanings** of these poems about heroic characters is to analyze the images in them.

1. Describe how Paul Revere feels in lines 57–72 of "Paul Revere's Ride." What words and images convey this feeling?
2. List three images in "Barbara Frietchie" that convey Frietchie's character.
3. Compare and contrast Elizabeth Blackwell with the image of the "nineteenth-century-young-lady" described at the beginning of the poem.

◆ Build Vocabulary

USING THE WORD ROOT -spec-

The word root -spec- in spectral means "related to appearances or something seen." On your paper, match the words with their definitions.

1. spectacle
2. spectrum
3. inspect

a. colors in a series
b. look carefully at
c. an unusual sight

SPELLING STRATEGY

Sometimes the hard g sound is spelled gh, as in aghast. On your paper, fill in the blanks to write words that contain gh, pronounced as a hard g.

1. gh_s t
2. _ _oul
3. spa_ _etti

USING THE WORD BANK

On your paper, match each Word Bank word in Column A with a synonym in Column B.

Column A	Column B
1. stealthy	a. calm
2. somber	b. crowd
3. impetuous	c. secret
4. spectral	d. horrified
5. tranquil	e. impulsive
6. aghast	f. gloomy
7. horde	g. ghostly

◆ Literary Focus

HEROIC CHARACTERS

The subjects of these poems are all **heroic characters.** Their actions in the face of great obstacles are inspiring and noble.

1. What heroic traits does Paul Revere possess? Support your answer.
2. Why was Barbara Frietchie's action heroic?
3. Elizabeth Blackwell does not risk her life, but she is heroic nonetheless. Explain why.

◆ Build Grammar Skills

PREPOSITIONAL PHRASES

A **prepositional phrase** is a group of words beginning with a preposition and ending with a noun or a pronoun. A preposition is a word like of, between, or from that shows a relationship. The noun or pronoun in the phrase is called the object of the preposition. In this example from "Paul Revere's Ride," there are two prepositional phrases, each beginning with the preposition of. The two objects of the preposition are midnight ride and Paul Revere.

> Listen, my children, and you shall hear
> of the midnight ride of Paul Revere,

Practice Copy the following passages on your paper. Underline each prepositional phrase.

1. . . . in the silence around him he hears/The muster of men at the barrack door, . . .
2. Then he climbed the tower of the Old North Church, . . .
3. He heard the bleating of the flock, . . .
4. And felt the breath of the morning breeze/ Blowing over the meadows brown.
5. So through the night rode Paul Revere; . . .

Writing Application Write two sentences about Paul Revere's ride that contain at least three of the following prepositions:

on, across, until, during, of, like, at

Build Your Portfolio

 Idea Bank

Writing

1. **Movie Summary** Write a brief summary of "The Elizabeth Blackwell Story" for the back of a videocassette box.

2. **Character Sketch** Who was Paul Revere's friend and partner? Use your imagination to write a character sketch of this person.

3. **Report** Research one of the heroes in the poems, and write a report on his or her contributions to history. **[Social Studies Link]**

Speaking and Listening

4. **Retelling** Imagine that you are a Confederate soldier marching into Frederick, Maryland. Retell to the class the story of Barbara Frietchie from your point of view. **[Performing Arts Link]**

5. **Dramatic Reading** Prepare a dramatic reading of lines 111–130 from "Paul Revere's Ride." Use a tape recorder to practice reading rhythmically, to imitate the pace of the horse. Read the poem aloud to your class. **[Performing Arts Link]**

Projects

6. **Boston Area Map [Group Activity]** Work with a small group to research what actually happened on the night of April 18, 1775, and on the following day. Draw a map of Boston and the surrounding area, tracing the route of Paul Revere's ride and locating landmarks and places mentioned in the poem. **[Social Studies Link; Art Link]**

7. **Folk Ballad [Group Activity]** Set the words of "Barbara Frietchie" to music. Work with a partner to compose or to find a melody. Select the stanzas to include in your song. If possible, record the song for others to hear. **[Music Link]**

 Writing Mini-Lesson

"Eyewitness" Speech

Each of these poems gives a detailed report about an important event in American history. Write a speech that gives an "eyewitness" account of an important current event.

Writing Skills Focus: Appeal to Your Audience

A successful speech keeps the audience on the edge of their seats, waiting eagerly to hear more. To **appeal to your audience,** use words and phrases that will arouse people's emotions, amuse them, or cause them to think. Notice how these lines from "Barbara Frietchie" make you want to keep reading to find out what happens next:

Model From the Poem
"Shoot, if you must, this old gray head,
But spare your country's flag," she said.

Prewriting Choose a current event that interests you. Then, check newspapers, magazines, television news shows, and the Internet to find details about the setting, who was there, and what happened. Make an outline of your findings.

Drafting Using your outline, write your speech as if you were an on-the-scene observer of the events taking place. Include words and phrases that convey emotional impact, to hook your audience and hold their interest.

> ◆ **Grammar Application**
> Use prepositional phrases to add precise details and interest to your speech.

Revising Deliver your speech to several classmates. Ask if they feel as if they were present at the event you are describing. Revise any sections that your audience found dull or confusing.

CONNECTING LITERATURE TO SOCIAL STUDIES
THE REVOLUTIONARY PERIOD

Young Jefferson Gets Some Advice From Ben Franklin *by Thomas Jefferson*

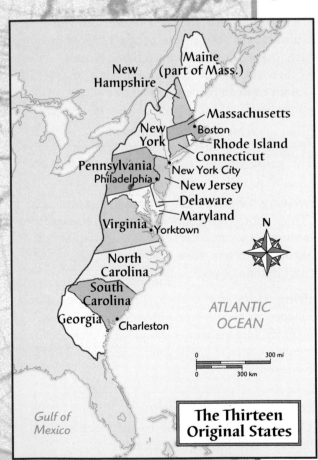

New Hampshire
Maine (part of Mass.)
Massachusetts
• Boston
New York
Rhode Island
Connecticut
Pennsylvania
• New York City
Philadelphia •
New Jersey
Delaware
Maryland
Virginia • Yorktown
North Carolina
South Carolina
Georgia • Charleston
ATLANTIC OCEAN
N
Gulf of Mexico

0   300 mi
0   300 km

The Thirteen Original States

AMERICA AS A COLONY To many people, the American Revolutionary period brings to mind a British government forcing Americans to live by laws that treated them unjustly. It's easy to forget that the people we think of as Americans were actually British citizens living in a British colony. Until the Revolutionary War, the British government had a legal right to pass laws that governed its citizens in America.

The Movement Toward Independence Some American colonists were talking about independence from England as early as the 1730's. However, for a long time after that, most colonists did not want to break away from England. They would have preferred to see the British government give more attention to their complaints about unfair treatment. It took many years to get most colonists to favor independence. Even in 1776, many were still opposed to the idea.

The Declaration of Independence In 1776, the Second Continental Congress met in Philadelphia to resolve the issue of independence. Thomas Jefferson, a delegate from Virginia, was chosen to write a declaration of independence, a document which would state the colonies' reasons for proclaiming their freedom from Britain. Once presented to the Congress, the document underwent many revisions at the suggestion and demand of various delegates. Jefferson was, understandably, upset at the amount of revision made to the document he wrote. In the passage that follows, Thomas Jefferson recalls advice that he received from elder statesman Benjamin Franklin during the process of the Declaration's revision.

Young Jefferson Gets Some Advice From Ben Franklin

THOMAS JEFFERSON

Thomas Jefferson, 3rd President of the United States, Museum of the City of New York

Benjamin Franklin (1706-1790), 19th century colored engraving

When the Declaration of Independence was under the consideration of Congress, there were two or three unlucky expressions in it which gave offense to some members. The words "Scotch and other foreign auxiliaries" excited the <u>ire</u> of a gentleman or two of that country. Severe <u>strictures</u> on the conduct of the British king, in negativing[1] our repeated repeals of the law which permitted the importation of slaves, were disapproved by some Southern gentlemen, whose reflections were not yet matured to the full <u>abhorrence</u> of that traffic.

> **Connecting Literature to Social Studies**
> What does this suggest about Jefferson's attitude toward laws allowing slavery?

---

1. **negativing** (neg´ ə tiv´ iŋ) *n.*: Vetoing; rejecting.

▲ **Critical Viewing** Name a character trait that you can infer about each of these men from these portraits. **[Infer]**

Altho' the offensive expressions were immediately yielded, these gentlemen continued their depredations[2] on other parts of the instrument. I was sitting by Dr. Franklin, who perceived that I was not insensible to these mutilations. "I have made it a rule," said he,

---

2. **depredations** (dep´ rə dā´ shəns) *n.*: Here, extremely harsh and destructive criticism.

◆ **Build Vocabulary**
ire (īr) *n.*: Anger; wrath
strictures (strik´ chərs) *n.*: Criticisms
abhorrence (əb hôr´ əns) *n.*: Loathing; disgust

"whenever in my power, to avoid becoming the draughtsman[3] of papers to be reviewed by a public body. I took my lesson from an incident which I will relate to you. When I was journeyman[4] printer, one of my companions, an apprentice Hatter, having served out his time, was about to open shop for himself. His first concern was to have a handsome signboard, with a proper inscription. He composed it in these words 'John Thomson, Hatter, makes and sells hats for ready money,' with a figure of a hat subjoined. But he thought he would submit it to his friends for their amendments. The first he showed it to thought the word 'Hatter,' tautologous,[5] because followed by the words 'makes hats' which show he was a Hatter. It was struck out. The next observed that the word 'makes'

might as well be omitted, because his customer would not care who made the hats. If good and to their mind, they would buy, by whomsoever made. He struck it out. A third said he thought the words 'for ready money' were useless as it was not the custom of the place to sell on credit. Every one who purchased expected to pay. They were parted with, and the inscription now stood 'John Thomson sells hats.' 'Sells hats' says his next friend? Why nobody will expect you to give them away. What then is the use of that word? It was stricken out, and 'hats' followed it, as there was one painted on the board. So his inscription was reduced ultimately to 'John Thomson' with the figure of a hat."

---

3. **draughtsman** (dräfts´ mən): Person who draws up legal documents, speeches, etc.
4. **journeyman:** Worker who has served his apprenticeship and thus qualifies to work at his trade.
5. **tautologous** (tô täl´ ə gəs) adj.: Redundant; repetitious.

◆ **Build Vocabulary**

inscription (in skrip´ shən) n.: Something written or engraved onto a surface

amendments (ə mend´ mənts) n.: Corrections of errors, faults, etc.

Guide for Responding

◆ **LITERATURE AND YOUR LIFE**

Reader's Response Do you think Franklin chooses an effective way to get his point across to Jefferson? Explain your answer.

Thematic Focus How does Franklin's advice show Franklin to be a leader?

☑ **Check Your Comprehension**

1. Name two complaints about the Declaration that Jefferson had to address.
2. Why does Franklin offer advice to Jefferson?
3. How does each comment reduce the content of John Thomson's sign?

◆ **Critical Thinking**

INTERPRET

1. Why were people from Scotland offended by a phrase in the Declaration of Independence? **[Infer]**
2. What is Jefferson's opinion of people who want to continue importing slaves into America? **[Infer]**

APPLY

3. What does Franklin's story suggest about the role of leaders in situations similar to the one faced by the colonists in 1776? **[Apply]**

CONNECTING LITERATURE TO SOCIAL STUDIES

Because most members of the Continental Congress considered Thomas Jefferson very intelligent, they chose him to write the first draft of the statement declaring the colonies' independence from England. When he had finished his draft, the Congress made several changes, most of which were meant to soften the language of the Declaration. Even though the members of the Congress were declaring the colonies independent, they were worried about offending the king and other members of the British government. Many years later, Jefferson wrote in his autobiography that these changes reflected the "pusillanimous [cowardly] idea that we had friends in England worth keeping terms with. . . ."

1. What does the disagreement about the Declaration's wording reveal about the group of men usually referred to as "the founding fathers"?

2. Explain why you believe Benjamin Franklin would or would not have approved of the changes made by the members of the Continental Congress.

 Idea Bank

Writing

1. **Letter** Pretend that you are John Thomson. Write a letter describing the sign you put outside your store. Explain why you did or did not accept the advice of your various friends.

2. **Article** As a newspaper reporter, write an article about the making of the Declaration of Independence.

3. **Biographical Report** Using various resources, research the life of Thomas Jefferson or Benjamin Franklin. Include your findings in a biographical report. You may also want to list in the report the various accomplishments of your subject.

Speaking and Listening

4. **Role Play** Prepare the story told by Benjamin Franklin so that you can deliver it to the class. Pretend that you are Franklin, and share the advice with another classmate who plays the role of Jefferson.

Project

5. **Research** Read the Declaration of Independence in an encyclopedia or a history book. Note the list of offenses that led the colonists to separate from England. Select two offenses, and explain how the king and his supporters would have reacted to the statement of these offenses.

Further Reading, Listening, and Viewing

- Margaret Cousins's *Ben Franklin of Old Philadelphia* (1987) tells about the amazing life of Benjamin Franklin.
- *1776* by Peter Stone is a movie musical that brings the actions of the Second Continental Congress to life.
- Richard Conrad Stein's *The Declaration of Independence* (1995) provides an in-depth look at this important document.

Guide for Reading

Meet the Author:

Brent Ashabranner (1921–   )

Brent Ashabranner knows what it's like to have good friends die in battle. He served in the military during World War II. That experience was one of the things that drew him to the story of the Vietnam Veterans Memorial.

Cultural and Social Issues Ashabranner found his creative voice when he began writing about places he knew and things he cared about. Born and raised in Oklahoma, he worked for a number of years as an advisor to the Peace Corps. Many of his books grew out of his experiences living in Africa, India, the Philippines, and Indonesia. In addition to writing about other cultures, Ashabranner writes about complex social issues, explaining them in ways young readers can understand. He has won acclaim for his books on migrant farm workers, Native Americans, and immigration policy.

THE STORY BEHIND THE STORY

Ashabranner, who lives in Washington, D.C., wanted to write about the Vietnam Veterans Memorial because "It will make us remember that war—any war, any time, any place . . . is about sacrifice and sorrow, not about glory and reward."

◆ LITERATURE AND YOUR LIFE

CONNECT YOUR EXPERIENCE

Maya Ying Lin designed the Vietnam Veterans Memorial, which honors the memory of every American killed or missing in the Vietnam War. Think of a person or group you would like to honor with a memorial. What would the memorial look like?

THEMATIC FOCUS: Leading the Way

The Vietnam Veterans Memorial might not exist if Jan Scruggs hadn't led the way—and rallied others, like Maya Ying Lin, to turn his dream into reality.

◆ Background for Understanding

HISTORY

In 1961, President John F. Kennedy sent 400 military advisors to help the South Vietnamese government fight against communist rebels supported by North Vietnam. By 1968, the U.S. had more than 500,000 troops in Vietnam. In the United States, the war sparked massive protests. When the war ended, the soldiers returned to a nation bitterly divided between those who supported the war and those who opposed it.

◆ Build Vocabulary

LATIN PLURAL FORMS

Before the Vietnam Veterans Memorial could be built, *criteria* for its design were established. *Criteria* is the plural form of *criterion*, which means "a standard by which something can be judged."

WORD BANK

Which word from the selection means "people who register"? Check the Build Vocabulary box on page 328 to see if you chose correctly.

criteria
registrants
harmonious
anonymously
eloquent
unanimous
prominent
conception

Always to Remember: The Vision of Maya Ying Lin

◆ Literary Focus

BIOGRAPHICAL PROFILE

A biography tells the full story of a person's life. A **biographical profile** is a shorter version, often focusing on one important event or achievement. "Always to Remember" is a profile that concentrates on aspects of architect Maya Lin's life that led to her design of the Vietnam Veterans Memorial. After reading a profile, you may want to learn more about the person by reading a full biography.

◆ Reading Strategy

IDENTIFY IMPORTANT IDEAS

When you read nonfiction, **identify the important ideas** by asking questions such as: Who is the subject of this selection? Why did this event occur? What points does the author want to make? Your answers will help you focus on the main ideas of the piece. Copy this chart. Then, as you read, jot down the most important information in each category.

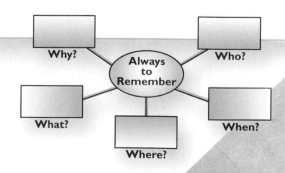

Why? — Always to Remember — Who?
What? — Where? — When?

Always to Remember:
The Vision of
Maya Ying Lin

Brent Ashabranner

"in honor and
recognition of the
men and women of
the Armed Forces of
the United States
who served in the
Vietnam War."

In the 1960's and 1970's, the United States was involved in a war in Vietnam. Because many people opposed the war, Vietnam veterans were not honored as veterans of other wars had been. Jan Scruggs, a Vietnam veteran, thought that the 58,000 U.S. servicemen and women killed or reported missing in Vietnam should be honored with a memorial. With the help of lawyers Robert Doubek and John Wheeler, Scruggs worked to gain support for his idea. In 1980, Congress authorized the building of the Vietnam Veterans Memorial in Washington, D.C., between the Washington Monument and the Lincoln Memorial.

The memorial had been authorized by Congress "in honor and recognition of the men and women of the Armed Forces of the United States who served in the Vietnam War." The law, however, said not a word about what the memorial should be or what it should look like. That was left up to the Vietnam Veterans Memorial Fund, but the law did state that the memorial design and plans would have to be approved by the Secretary of the Interior, the Commission of Fine Arts, and the National Capital Planning Commission.

What would the memorial be? What should it look like? Who would design it? Scruggs, Doubek, and Wheeler didn't know, but they were determined that the memorial should help bring closer together a nation still bitterly divided by the Vietnam War. It couldn't be something like the Marine Corps Memorial showing American troops planting a flag on enemy soil at Iwo Jima. It couldn't be a giant dove with an olive branch of peace in its beak. It had to soothe passions, not stir them up. But there was one thing Jan Scruggs insisted on: The memorial, whatever it turned out to be, would have to show the name of every man and woman killed or missing in the war.

The answer, they decided, was to hold a national design competition open to all Americans. The winning design would receive a prize of $20,000, but the real prize would be the

◀ **Critical Viewing** What does the pictured veteran's reaction to the memorial tell you about its effectiveness? [Draw Conclusions]

winner's knowledge that the memorial would become a part of American history on the Mall in Washington, D.C. Although fund raising was only well started at this point, the choosing of a memorial design could not be delayed if the memorial was to be built by Veterans Day, 1982. H. Ross Perot contributed the $160,000 necessary to hold the competition, and a panel of distinguished architects, landscape architects, sculptors, and design specialists was chosen to decide the winner.

▲ **Critical Viewing** What impact does the listing of names have on the viewer? **[Analyze]**

Announcement of the competition in October, 1980, brought an astonishing response. The Vietnam Veterans Memorial Fund received over five thousand inquiries. They came from every state in the nation and from every field of design; as expected, architects and sculptors were particularly interested. Everyone who inquired received a booklet explaining the <u>criteria</u>. Among the most important: The memorial could not make a political statement about the war; it must contain the names of all persons killed or missing in action in the war; it must be in harmony with its location on the Mall.

A total of 2,573 individuals and teams registered for the competition. They were sent photographs of the memorial site, maps of the area around the site and of the entire Mall, and other technical design information. The competitors had three months to prepare their designs, which had to be received by March 31, 1981.

Of the 2,573 <u>registrants</u>, 1,421 submitted designs, a record number for such a design competition. When the designs were spread out for jury selection, they filled a large airplane hangar. The jury's task was to select the design which, in their judgment, was the best in meeting these criteria:

• a design that honored the memory of those Americans who served and died in the Vietnam War.

• a design of high artistic merit.

• a design which would be <u>harmonious</u> with its site, including visual harmony with the Lincoln Memorial and the Washington Monument.

• a design that could take its place in the "historic continuity" of America's national art.

• a design that would be buildable, durable, and not too hard to maintain.

The designs were displayed without any indication of the designer's name so that they could be judged <u>anonymously</u>, on their design merits alone. The jury spent one week reviewing all the designs in the airplane hangar. On May 1 it made its report to the

◆ **Build Vocabulary**

criteria (krī tir´ ē ə) *n.*: Standards or tests by which something can be judged

registrants (rej´ is trənts) *n.*: People who register to participate in something

harmonious (här mō´ nē əs) *adj.*: Combined in a pleasing, orderly arrangement

Vietnam Veterans Memorial Fund; the experts declared Entry Number 1,026 the winner. The report called it "the finest and most appropriate" of all submitted and said it was "superbly harmonious" with the site on the Mall. Remarking upon the "simple and forthright" materials needed to build the winning entry, the report concludes:

This memorial, with its wall of names, becomes a place of quiet reflection, and a tribute to those who served their

▲ **Critical Viewing** What word would you use to describe the effect of this photograph? Explain your choice. [Defend]

◆ **Reading Strategy**
How does this passage convey the importance of the memorial to the American people?

nation in difficult times. All who come here can find it a place of healing. This will be a quiet memorial, one that achieves an excellent relationship with both the Lincoln Memorial and Washington Monument, and relates the visitor to them. It is uniquely horizontal, entering the earth rather than piercing the sky.

This is very much a memorial of our own times, one that could not have been achieved in another time and place. The designer has created an <u>eloquent</u> place where the simple meeting of earth, sky and remembered names contain messages for all who will know this place.

The eight jurors signed their names to the

report, a <u>unanimous</u> decision. When the name of the winner was revealed, the art and architecture worlds were stunned. It was not the name of a nationally famous architect or sculptor, as most people had been sure it would be. The creator of Entry Number 1,026 was a twenty-one-year-old student at Yale University. Her name—unknown as yet in any field of art or architecture—was Maya Ying Lin.

How could this be? How could an undergraduate student win one of the most important design competitions ever held? How could she beat out some of the top names in American art and architecture? Who was Maya Ying Lin?

The answer to that question provided some of the other answers, at least in part. Maya Lin, reporters soon discovered, was a Chinese-American girl who had been born and raised in the small midwestern city of Athens, Ohio. Her father, Henry Huan Lin, was a ceramicist of considerable reputation and dean of fine arts at Ohio University in Athens. Her mother, Julia C. Lin, was a poet and professor of

◆ **Build Vocabulary**

anonymously (ə nän´ ə məs lē) *adv.*: With the name withheld or secret

eloquent (el´ ə kwənt) *adj.*: Fluent, forceful, and persuasive

unanimous (yōō nan´ ə məs) *adj.*: Agreeing completely; united in opinion

▲ **Critical Viewing** What might this visitor to the memorial be doing? **[Speculate]**

Oriental and English literature. Maya Lin's parents were born to culturally <u>prominent</u> families in China. When the Communists came to power in China in the 1940's, Henry and Julia Lin left the country and in time made their way to the United States.

Maya Lin grew up in an environment of art and literature. She was interested in sculpture and made both small and large sculptural figures, one cast in bronze. She learned silversmithing and made jewelry. She was surrounded by books and read a great deal, especially fantasies such as *The Hobbit* and *Lord of the Rings*.[1]

But she also found time to work at McDonald's. "It was about the only way to make money in the summer," she said.

A covaledictorian at high school graduation,

◆ **Literary Focus**
Why does the author tell you about Maya Lin's parents?

Maya Lin went to Yale without a clear notion of what she wanted to study and eventually decided to major in Yale's undergraduate program in architecture. During her junior year she studied in Europe and found herself increasingly interested in cemetery architecture. "In Europe there's very little space, so graveyards are used as parks," she said. "Cemeteries are cities of the dead in European countries, but they are also living gardens."

In France, Maya Lin was deeply moved by the war memorial to those who died in the Somme offensive in 1916 during World War I.[2] The great arch by architect Sir Edwin Lutyens is considered one of the world's most outstanding war memorials.

Back at Yale for her senior year, Maya Lin enrolled in Professor Andrus Burr's course in funerary (burial) architecture. The Vietnam Veterans Memorial competition had recently been announced, and although the memorial would be a cenotaph—a monument in honor of persons buried someplace else—Professor Burr thought that having his students prepare

---

1. *The Hobbit* and *Lord of the Rings*: Mythical novels by the English author and scholar J.R.R. Tolkien (1892–1973), chronicling the struggle between various good and evil kingdoms for possession of a magical ring that can shift the balance of power in the world.

2. **Somme offensive** . . . : A costly and largely unsuccessful Allied offensive during World War I that sustained roughly 615,000 casualties of British and French troops.

a design of the memorial would be a worthwhile course assignment.

Surely, no classroom exercise ever had such spectacular results.

After receiving the assignment, Maya Lin and two of her classmates decided to make the day's journey from New Haven, Connecticut, to Washington to look at the site where the memorial would be built. On the day of their visit, Maya Lin remembers, Constitution Gardens was awash with a late November sun; the park was full of light, alive with joggers and people walking beside the lake.

"It was while I was at the site that I designed it," Maya Lin said later in an interview about the memorial with *Washington Post* writer Phil McCombs. "I just sort of visualized it. It just popped into my head. Some people were playing Frisbee. It was a beautiful park. I didn't want to destroy a living park. You use the landscape. You don't fight with it. You absorb the landscape. . . . When I looked at the site I just knew I wanted something horizontal that took you in, that made you feel safe within the park, yet at the same time reminding you of the dead. So I just imagined opening up the earth. . . ."

When Maya Lin returned to Yale, she made a clay model of the vision that had come to her in Constitution Gardens. She showed it to Professor Burr; he liked her <u>conception</u> and encouraged her to enter the memorial competition. She put her design on paper, a task that took six weeks, and mailed it to Washington barely in time to meet the March 31 deadline.

A month and a day later, Maya Lin was attending class. Her roommate slipped into the classroom and handed her a note. Washington was calling and would call back in fifteen minutes. Maya Lin hurried to her room. The call came. She had won the memorial competition.

◆ **Build Vocabulary**

prominent (präm´ ə nənt) *adj.*: Widely and favorably known

conception (kən sep´ shən) *n.*: An original idea, design, plan, etc.

Guide for Responding

◆ LITERATURE AND YOUR LIFE

Reader's Response How has this essay changed the way you think about memorials?

Thematic Focus Would there be a Vietnam Memorial today if Vietnam veteran Jan Scruggs had not spoken out? Why or why not?

☑ Check Your Comprehension

1. Why did people think that a Vietnam veterans memorial was needed?
2. Why did Maya Lin enter the design competition?
3. Give two reasons why her design won.

◆ Critical Thinking

INTERPRET

1. Why was it surprising that a twenty-one-year-old student beat architects and sculptors in the design competition? **[Draw Conclusions]**
2. In what ways does Maya Lin's design fit the criteria set forth by Scruggs, Doubeck, and Wheeler? **[Connect]**

APPLY

3. What lessons can Maya Lin's experience teach others about reaching for a goal? **[Apply]**

EXTEND

4. What are some things that architects do that you learned about from reading this article? **[Career Link]**

Guide for Responding (continued)

◆ Reading Strategy

IDENTIFY IMPORTANT IDEAS

The **important ideas** in "Always to Remember" reflect the deep feelings of the people involved.

1. Identify three ideas that were important to Jan Scruggs in his campaign to build a memorial. What did you learn from his requirements?
2. Identify two ideas that influenced Maya Lin in the creation of her design. What did you learn about creative expression from her?

◆ Build Vocabulary

USING LATIN PLURAL FORMS

Some words in English, such as *criterion,* retain their Latin plural forms. Change *-on* to *-a* to form the plural of *criterion.* Change *-um* to *-a* to form the plural of other Latin words. On your paper, write the plural form of each of the words below. Refer to a dictionary if you need help.

1. medium   2. criterion   3. datum

SPELLING STRATEGY

Some word endings like *ant* and *ent* sound alike but are spelled differently. Because there is no rule about these spellings, it is best to memorize the correct spelling. On your paper, complete the following words with *ant* or *ent,* using a dictionary to help you.

1. The president's speech was eloqu_____?_____.
2. The registr_____?_____ looked forward to voting for the first time.
3. Her promin_____?_____ facial features were memorable.

USING THE WORD BANK

Match each Word Bank word in the left column with its definition on the right.

1. unanimous   **a.** without giving a name
2. criteria   **b.** vividly expressive
3. prominent   **c.** standards
4. anonymously   **d.** people who register
5. registrants   **e.** pleasing musical tones
6. eloquent   **f.** noticeable
7. harmonious   **g.** agreeing completely
8. conception   **h.** idea

◆ Literary Focus

BIOGRAPHICAL PROFILE

A **biographical profile** is a short biography. The author focuses on one or two important aspects of the subject's life.

1. (a) What does Ashabranner tell you about Maya Lin's childhood? (b) How does this information relate to her designing the memorial?
2. How do Maya Lin's studies in Europe affect her as an artist?
3. Why does Ashabranner use Maya Lin's own words to tell about her visit to the site of the memorial?

◆ Build Grammar Skills

PREPOSITIONAL PHRASES AS ADJECTIVES AND ADVERBS

A **prepositional phrase** is a group of words that begins with a preposition and ends with a noun or pronoun. Prepositional phrases function as adjectives or adverbs.

Adjective: The memorial could not make a political statement *about the war.* (Modifies *statement* and tells *what kind.*)

Adverb: This is very much a memorial . . . that could not have been achieved *in another time and place.* (Modifies *could have been achieved* and tells *when* and *where.*)

Practice Copy the following sentences. Underline each prepositional phrase, and draw an arrow to the word it modifies. Then, tell whether the phrase is acting as an adjective or an adverb.

1. American soldiers returned from the war.
2. The memorial stands between two monuments.
3. Announcement of the competition brought an astonishing response.
4. Designs were judged by a committee.
5. Maya Lin's design arrived near the deadline.

Writing Application Add two prepositional phrases to the following sentence. Tell whether they function as adjectives or adverbs.

The Vietnam Veterans Memorial is a symbol.

Build Your Portfolio

 Idea Bank

Writing

1. **Letter** Write a letter that Jan Scruggs might have written, asking Congress for funds to build the Vietnam Veterans Memorial.

2. **Journal Entry** Imagine that you visit the memorial and find the name of a friend or relative carved on the wall. Write a journal entry describing your feelings about the experience.

3. **Biographical Profile** Research Maya Lin's life. Write a short profile telling what she has done since designing the Vietnam Veterans Memorial.

Speaking and Listening

4. **Commencement Address** Pretend that you are Maya Lin. Deliver an address to a high-school graduating class, advising the class members about finding their own creative voices.

5. **Oral History** Interview several people who lived through the Vietnam War era. Find out what they thought about the war, how their views may have changed, and what they think about the importance of the Vietnam Veterans Memorial. Share an oral summary of your interviews with the class. **[Social Studies Link; Media Link]**

Projects

6. **Memorial Budget** Design your own memorial for a person or group you admire. Draw the design to "scale." For instance, one inch might represent ten feet. Decide on the materials you would use, and find out how much they cost. Then, calculate the total cost of your monument. **[Math Link; Art Link]**

7. **Multimedia Presentation [Group Activity]** With a group of classmates, create a multimedia presentation about the Vietnam era. Try to capture the sensitivies of the political turmoil and discord of the times. **[Social Studies Link; Media Link]**

 Writing Mini-Lesson

Tourist Brochure for a Memorial

A good tourist brochure for a memorial enriches the visitors' trip. It presents background, history, and facts in a way that helps visitors understand why the memorial is important. Write your own brochure that gives information about a memorial.

Writing Skills Focus: Persuasive Details

Besides giving information, a tourist brochure uses **persuasive details** to emphasize the importance of a particular place. Look at this description of the Vietnam Veterans Memorial:

Model From the Selection

This memorial . . . becomes a place of quiet reflection, and a tribute to those who served their nation in difficult times. All who come here can find it a place of healing.

Persuasive details such as *quiet reflection* and *place of healing* make you see why the memorial is important and special.

Prewriting Research why, when, and how your memorial was built. Visit the memorial, or study photographs of it. Then, make an outline, organizing your information into different topics.

Drafting Write a separate, catchy heading for each topic in your outline. Under each heading, use persuasive details to describe the memorial, its setting, and why it is an important place to visit.

> ◆ **Grammar Application**
> Use prepositional phrases as both adjectives and adverbs in your tourist brochure.

Revising If you were a visitor to the memorial, would this brochure be helpful? Do the headings draw you in? Add persuasive details to make your brochure more interesting.

Persuasive Essay

Writing Process Workshop

In this section, a young narrator convinces you that she is the fastest runner in her neighborhood, three poets help you to see the subjects of their poems as heroes, and Benjamin Franklin influences Thomas Jefferson by telling him a story. In all of these selections, the writers use persuasion. Persuasion is a type of writing that attempts to convince an audience to think or act in a certain way.

Lead the way by writing a **persuasive essay** that influences your audience to agree with your position or to take a certain action. The following skills, introduced in this section's Writing Mini-Lessons, will help you.

Writing Skills Focus

▶ **Provide relevant background** to help your readers understand your topic and to convince them that your arguments are sound. (See p. 301.)

▶ **Appeal to your audience** by addressing their concerns, stirring their emotions, or making them think. (See p. 319.)

▶ **Include persuasive details** to hook your audience and make them want to see things your way. (See p. 333.)

Notice how Toni Cade Bambara uses these skills in this passage from "Raymond's Run."

MODEL FROM LITERATURE

from "Raymond's Run" by Toni Cade Bambara

So as far as everyone's concerned, I'm the fastest ① and that goes for Gretchen, too, who has put out the tale that she is going to win the first-place medal this year. Ridiculous. ② In the second place, she's got short legs. In the third place, she's got freckles. In the first place, no one can beat me and that's all there is to it. ③

① The narrator provides relevant background—she is considered the fastest runner in town.

② The narrator's friendly, casual tone will appeal to her audience.

③ These details support the narrator's claim that she will win the race.

Prewriting

Choose a Topic Think of an issue that is important to you. For inspiration, check national and local news stories or ask friends and family members about topics that concern them. Jot down all the ideas you get, and choose the one you like best.

Know Your Audience In order to appeal to your audience, you have to know who they are. Is your persuasive essay directed toward your classmates? Your neighbors? An elected official? Knowing your audience will help you choose the writing style and details that will be most effective. Create an audience profile to help focus your writing:

Audience Profile

My Readers: eighth-grade teachers and the principal at my school

Language: I will use friendly but polite language, good grammar, a respectful tone.

Audience's Knowledge

About My Topic: I am suggesting a class trip to the Vietnam Veterans Memorial. My audience is familiar with my topic, but they may not realize how many students are interested in visiting the memorial.

Audience's Interests: My audience wants class trips to be interesting, educational, affordable, and safe.

Conduct Research If you know your topic well, you should be able to provide good support for your position. To develop the strongest argument possible, however, conduct research for additional background information and persuasive details.

Drafting

Write a Strong Introduction The introduction is the first thing your readers will see. Compare these introductions to see how powerful language can hook an audience right from the start:

Weak Introduction: The Vietnam Veterans Memorial would be a great place to visit on the eighth-grade class trip.

Strong Introduction: It's moving. It's historically important. It's a place no visitor will ever forget. The Vietnam Veterans Memorial should be the destination of this year's eighth-grade trip.

Consider Opposing Arguments Some members of your audience may disagree with your point of view—at least at first. Consider opposing arguments that readers might have, and address them in your essay. You may want to conduct additional research to strengthen your argument further.

APPLYING LANGUAGE SKILLS: Placing Adverbs

Adverbs that modify verbs can often be placed in more than one position in a sentence without changing the meaning.

Example: We visited the memorial <u>yesterday</u>.

Example: <u>Yesterday</u>, we visited the memorial.

Adverbs that modify adjectives or other adverbs come right before the word they modify and cannot be moved.

Example: I am <u>very</u> interested in U.S. history.

Practice On your paper, place the indicated adverbs in these sentences.

1. We return to Washington, D.C. [frequently]
2. I was moved by the monument. [very]
3. The trip passed quickly. [rather]

Writing Application As you draft, place adverbs effectively—next to the words they modify—or vary placement to give variety to your sentences.

Writer's Solution Connection Language Lab

For more practice with adverbs, complete the lesson on Using Modifiers in the Using Modifiers unit.

APPLYING LANGUAGE SKILLS:
Commas in a Series

Use commas to separate words, phrases, or clauses in a series.

Series of Words: Visitors leave flowers, letters, mementos, and candles as tributes.

Series of Phrases: We drove to the store, to the bank, and to the library.

Practice: On your paper, insert commas correctly.

1. We walked to the Washington Monument then we visited the Vietnam Memorial and finally we climbed the Lincoln Memorial.
2. Annie met visitors from Japan Indonesia Cambodia England Scotland and Hungary.
3. The parks were filled with thoughtful tourists determined joggers and playful toddlers.

Writing Application Review your essay, and correct any mistakes with commas in a series.

Writer's Solution Connection
Writing Lab

For help revising your persuasive essay, use the Revision Checker for sentence openers in the Self-Revision section of the Persuasion tutorial.

Revising

Use a Checklist Go back to the Writing Skills Focus on page 334, and use the items as a checklist to evaluate and revise your essay.

▶ Have I appealed to my audience?
Are the language and tone appropriate for my audience? Have I appealed to their interests?

▶ Do I provide relevant background?
Do I tell my audience what they need to know in order to fully understand my argument? Have I avoided telling my readers things they already know? What language and details can I add that will make my essay more appropriate for my audience?

▶ Have I used persuasive details?
Do I need to add facts, statistics, examples, reasons, or other evidence? How can I strengthen my evidence?

REVISION MODEL

A trip to the Vietnam Veterans Memorial would be good. ① a valuable educational experience

② Of twenty students polled, fourteen said they Many students want to visit the memorial. ③ The memorial was designed by Maya Ying Lin, who at the time was a college student at Yale.

① This detail will appeal to the intended audience of teachers and the school principal.

② This statistic provides background information and also helps to strengthen the writer's persuasive argument.

③ To provide relevant background, this sentence was added.

Publishing and Presenting

Speech Share your opinion by delivering a persuasive speech. You can present your speech "live" or prerecorded on videotape or audiotape. Here are some tips:

▶ Practice several times on your own.
▶ Mark places in your essay that you want to emphasize.
▶ Speak slowly and clearly.
▶ Allow your voice to rise and fall naturally.
▶ Speak loudly enough to be heard.
▶ Look at your audience or at the camera.
▶ Try looking in a mirror or, if possible, ask a friend to serve as your audience.

Real-World Reading Skills Workshop

Evaluating Persuasive Techniques

Strategies for Success

Persuasive techniques are the methods used by advertisers to try to convince you to buy products. These techniques work by making claims such as these:

- ▶ This product will make you feel smarter, more attractive, stronger, faster, cleaner, or more popular than you are now.
- ▶ Without this product, you will be less popular, attractive, intelligent, athletic, acceptable, or happy than you could be.
- ▶ You are smart to buy this product.
- ▶ You are foolish not to buy this product.

Find the Real Message Determine what is being sold in an advertisement—sneakers, shampoo, cereal. Almost everything else in the advertisement is a persuasive technique.

Identify Your Response People often respond because of how they *feel* rather than what they *think*. An advertisement can make you feel excited or curious. Before you know it, you smile to yourself and say, "I'll buy SuperStar Shampoo." Recognize your emotional response to an advertisement.

Identify Reality Remember that most of the people in advertisements are models or actors using persuasive techniques to sell products. Real athletes practice long hours and have great coaches. Real *A* students study hard. Before you believe all the claims in an advertisement, conduct a "reality check."

Make an Informed Decision Consider the product—not what is being said about it. Think about yourself and what you want and need. Base your decision on how well you and the product match.

Apply the Strategies

Read the advertisement below that appeared in the *Middle School News,* and analyze the persuasive techniques employed in it.

Hey, Math Students—
Go to the head of class!

Feeling bad about low grades in math? Now your troubles are over. The **Techtronix 2000** calculator is all you need to breeze through your homework and ace your next test.

Get the 10% discount for all Jefferson Middle School students. Quantities are limited, so HURRY!

1. What persuasive claims does this advertisement make?
2. What is the real message?
3. How might this advertisement make you feel? Explain.
4. How does "reality" match the picture painted by this advertisement? Explain.
5. Would you buy this product? Why or why not?

✔ *Here are other situations in which evaluating persuasive techniques is important:*
- ▶ *Reading an editorial*
- ▶ *Reading a request for a donation*
- ▶ *Reading the text of a political speech*

A **preposition** is a word that relates a noun or a pronoun to another word in the sentence. It often shows relationships of time (*after, before*) or space (*over, under*). Here are some common prepositions:

etc., predominate —pre·pon'der·a'tion n. prep·o·si·tion (prep'ə zish'ən) n. [ME preposiciou (< L praepositus, pp. of praeponere < prae-, before see PRE- & POSITION): transl. of Gr prothesis, PRO languages, a relation or function word, as English etc., that connects a lexical word, usually a nou syntactic construction, to another element of th verb (Ex.: he went to the store), to a noun (Ex.: music), or to an adj

Common Prepositions

about	behind	from	over
above	below	in	since
across	beneath	inside	through
after	beside	into	till
against	between	like	to
along	beyond	near	toward
among	by	of	under
around	down	off	until
as	during	on	up
at	except	out	upon
before	for	outside	with

A **prepositional phrase** is a group of words that begins with a preposition and ends with a noun or pronoun, called the object of the preposition. Prepositional phrases can act as adjectives or adverbs.

Adjective: Frietchie displayed the flag *outside her window.*
Adverb: Squeaky practiced *before the race.*

Practice 1 Copy these sentences, underlining each prepositional phrase once and each object of the preposition twice. Draw an arrow from the prepositional phrase to the word it modifies. Then, tell whether the prepositional phrase acts as an adjective or an adverb.

1. Squeaky stood near Gretchen in the line.

2. Revere saw a lamp in the window.

3. Elizabeth Blackwell graduated at the top of her class.

4. Jefferson spoke to Benjamin Franklin about the Declaration of Independence.

5. The memorial stands between two monuments in Washington, D.C.

Practice 2 Write a paragraph about someone who has led the way. Include at least three of the following prepositional phrases.

according to historians	from the beginning
like no other	before anyone else
during this time	with others
until the end	for everyone

Grammar in Writing

✔ *In most instances, it is better not to end a sentence with a preposition:*

Incorrect: A preposition is not a word you should end a sentence **with.**

Certain expressions, however, sound better when you break this rule:

Awkward: About what are you talking?

Better: What are you talking **about?**

Sometimes you can rewrite a sentence to avoid this situation:

Reworded sentence: What are you discussing?

When someone skillfully presents an idea—whether in a classroom report or in a political speech—it can be a powerful experience for the audience. Remember these tips the next time you give an oral presentation:

Write It Out A few people can deliver a presentation "off the cuff," without preparation, but most people must write out their ideas first. Prepare for an oral presentation by putting your ideas on paper. To present your ideas persuasively, state your major points early and repeat them at least once in the middle and again in the summary. Use strong, colorful words to catch your audience's attention. Using a rhetorical question (in which you ask a question you answer yourself) is another good technique. Allow your sense of humor and personality to show; you will communicate better with your audience.

Practice You don't have to memorize your speech, but practice it several times to become comfortable giving it. Listen to yourself, and change the tone, volume, and pace of your voice to provide variety. Speak loudly and clearly. Stress important points with your voice and with gestures. Stand straight and tall, and hold your arms in a relaxed manner. Watch yourself in a mirror as you practice. Before you make your presentation, ask a friend to critique your delivery—your voice, stance, and movements.

Apply the Strategies

Take turns with a partner role-playing and critiquing the following situations. Then, present one to the rest of your class, and ask them for feedback.

1. You want to join an after-school club that focuses on a hobby or interest of yours. Deliver a brief presentation in which you explain why you'd be an asset to the club.

2. You're a television newscaster delivering a report on an issue of local concern in your community.

3. You're the captain of the school team. Tomorrow is the game with your arch rival, and your best player is out with an injury. Talk to your teammates to convince them they can win without the star.

Tips for Presenting Persuasively
▶ Be confident about your speech and the way you deliver it.
▶ Stand straight and tall with your arms relaxed.
▶ Establish eye contact with your audience.
▶ Take your time.
▶ Smile. If you aren't having fun speaking, pretend you are. Soon, you'll convince yourself and your audience.

What's Behind the

Words

Vocabulary Adventures With Richard Lederer

Vocabulary From Government and Politics

From the ancient Greeks and Romans, we have inherited our system of democracy. From those same people, we have also gained many fascinating and colorful words that describe our form of government.

Government by the People

The word *politics* itself issues from the Greek word *polites*, which means "citizen." We also discover people in the word *democracy*, made from two Greek word parts—*demos*, "common people," and *kratos*, "rule by."

In a democracy, we have elections to pick out the candidates we prefer for office. In Latin, *e* means "out" and *lectus*, "pick" or "choose."

Before elections, candidates conduct campaigns. The first campaigns were carried out on battlefields, and *campaign* derives from the Latin *campus*, or "field." A military campaign is a series of operations mounted to achieve a particular wartime goal. A political campaign is an all-out effort to secure the election of a candidate to office.

Glowing Candidates

The word *candidate* has a shining history. When he went to the Forum in ancient Roman times, a candidate for office wore a bleached white toga to symbolize his humility, honesty, and purity of motive. The original Latin word, *candidarus*, meant "one who wears white," from the belief that white was the color of purity.

The Ship of State

President derives from the Latin *praesidio*, "to preside; sit in front of; protect." Presidents preside over our government and are sometimes likened to a captain steering the ship of state. That metaphor turns out to be quite accurate. The Greek word *kybernao* meant "to direct a ship." The Romans borrowed the word as *guberno*, and, ultimately, it crossed the Channel to England as *governor*, originally designating a steersman.

ACTIVITY 1 Research and report on the origins of these terms relating to politics and government:
1. capital/capitol
2. congress
3. conservative
4. legislator
5. liberal
6. senator

ACTIVITY 2 In ancient Rome, an *augur* was a kind of fortuneteller who made predictions based on the way that birds were flying. The augurs would tell a general whether to do battle, and the general would take the advice seriously. From that custom, we get the word *inauguration*, a ceremony that marks the start of the term of a president or other official.

Now that you know the story behind *inaugurate* and *inauguration*, find out the origins of two other animal-related terms in politics:
1. dark horse
2. lame duck

Extended Reading Opportunities

Central to our society is the belief that all are entitled to justice. The following novels explore the quest for fairness and understanding in a world filled with injustices.

Suggested Titles

The House of Dies Drear
Virginia Hamilton

The house of Dies Drear is not just a new home for the Small family, but an important part of the nation's history. The house, a stop on the Underground Railroad, was built by the abolitionist Dies Drear. Thirteen-year-old Thomas Small finds the house full of mystery. He encounters secret passageways, finds bizarre symbols left by an intruder, and flees in fear from an old man living in the forest. The novel traces Thomas and his family's steps in solving the mystery surrounding their new home.

The Pearl
John Steinbeck

The inability to see what is truly valuable in life when one's vision is clouded by the promise of material possessions is the focus of this novel. When he finds a magnificent pearl, the poverty-stricken Kino believes that he has found good fortune that will enable him to provide for his family. His wife, Juana, immediately sees how the pearl might change their lives and begs Kino for her sake and for the welfare of their son to throw it back into the ocean. Kino refuses, and the tragic events that follow change their lives forever.

my brother Sam is dead
James Lincoln Collier and Christopher Collier

Ten-year-old Tim Meeker lives in Redding Ridge, Connecticut, during the Revolutionary War. Tim's father is a British loyalist, while Tim's sixteen-year-old brother Sam has run off to join the Patriots in their fight for freedom. Throughout the novel, Tim struggles to understand both sides and to respect both his father's and his brother's beliefs. Through Tim's eyes, we are able to see the sacrifices made by ordinary people during the war.

Other Possibilities

The Slave Dancer	Paula Fox
April Morning	Howard Fast
Children of the River	Linda Crew
Farewell to Manzanar	Jeanne W. Houston and James D. Houston

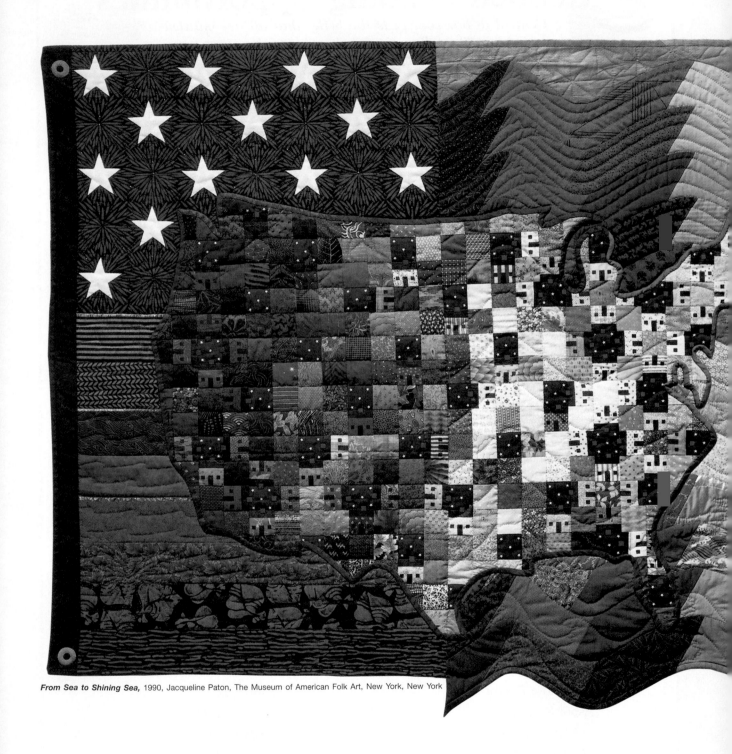

From Sea to Shining Sea, 1990, Jacqueline Paton, The Museum of American Folk Art, New York, New York

From Sea to Shining Sea

Some people describe the United States as a melting pot, in which people from all cultures blend to become American. Others prefer the image of the United States as a mosaic, in which people retain their original cultural heritage and pride, while sharing the values and beliefs that unite all Americans. No matter whether you choose to celebrate Americans' likenesses or differences, there's no disputing the fact that the United States is a rich nation—both in its people and in its geography and resources. The selections in this unit explore what it means to live in this vast and diverse nation.

Guide for Reading

Meet the Author:

Carl Sandburg (1878–1967)

Born in Galesburg, Illinois, Carl Sandburg became one of the best-known American poets. He often wrote about the lives of ordinary citizens, and his tone was generally upbeat.

A Man of Many Talents Besides being a poet, Sandburg was also a journalist, an author of children's books, and a historian. He won the Pulitzer Prize in 1940 for his six-volume biography of Abraham Lincoln, and he won it again in 1950 for his *Complete Poems*.

THE STORY BEHIND THE POEM

Sandburg's epic poem "The People, Yes" was published in 1936. At that time, the United States was experiencing the Great Depression, a time of economic struggle that began in 1929 and continued until World War II. Like many of Sandburg's other poems, "The People, Yes" celebrates the common people and their courage in facing hard times. Sandburg said of Americans during the Depression, "The people will live on, the people so peculiar in renewal and comeback."

◆ LITERATURE AND YOUR LIFE

CONNECT YOUR EXPERIENCE

Campfires seem to inspire the storyteller in us all. Often, the stories told around a campfire blend reality and fantasy; the listener happily puts reality aside and waits eagerly to find out what will happen. Think about some stories you've told or heard around a campfire or in a similar setting. In "The People, Yes," Carl Sandburg celebrates the tradition of tall tales and legends like those told around a campfire.

THEMATIC FOCUS: From Sea to Shining Sea

"The People, Yes" celebrates the American landscape and people. What characteristics does Sandburg emphasize?

◆ Background for Understanding

CULTURE

In this section of "The People, Yes," Carl Sandburg summarizes the story lines of many different yarns. A yarn is a long, made-up story filled with exaggeration. By describing characteristics or actions that the listener knows are impossible but that are fun to imagine, the teller of a yarn creates humor. Yarns became especially popular during America's pioneer days. People amused each other with yarns that reflected the accomplishments and obstacles faced as they settled an unknown land.

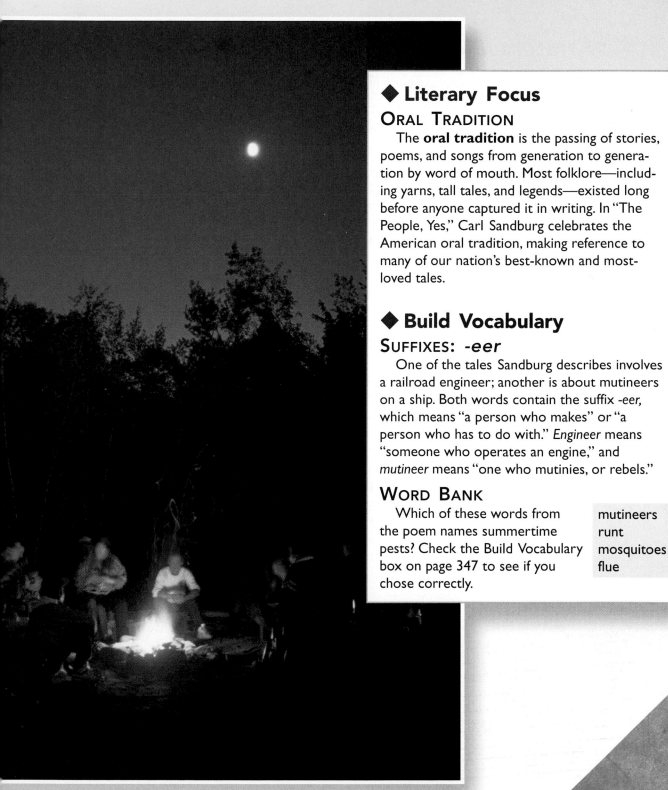

◆ *from* The People, Yes ◆

◆ Literary Focus

ORAL TRADITION

The **oral tradition** is the passing of stories, poems, and songs from generation to generation by word of mouth. Most folklore—including yarns, tall tales, and legends—existed long before anyone captured it in writing. In "The People, Yes," Carl Sandburg celebrates the American oral tradition, making reference to many of our nation's best-known and most-loved tales.

◆ Build Vocabulary

SUFFIXES: *-eer*

One of the tales Sandburg describes involves a railroad engineer; another is about mutineers on a ship. Both words contain the suffix *-eer,* which means "a person who makes" or "a person who has to do with." *Engineer* means "someone who operates an engine," and *mutineer* means "one who mutinies, or rebels."

WORD BANK

Which of these words from the poem names summertime pests? Check the Build Vocabulary box on page 347 to see if you chose correctly.

mutineers
runt
mosquitoes
flue

Guide for Reading ◆ 345

Reading for Success

Interactive Reading Strategies

Interactive computer games are fun because you take a real role in the proceedings. Interactive reading is similar: When you participate in your reading, the experience becomes fuller, richer, and more fun. Use these reading strategies to help you interact with your reading:

Envision what the writer is saying.

Use the details a writer provides, along with your own imagination and experience, to picture in your mind the people, places, objects, and events the writer describes. To help you do so, be on the lookout for sensory details—details that capture sights, sounds, tastes, smells, or physical sensations.

Use your prior knowledge.

Draw from your own knowledge and experience as you read. For example, you might use what you've learned about history to help you understand a story with a historical setting. Similarly, your knowledge of geography might help you appreciate the magnitude of one of the amazing accomplishments described in Sandburg's poem.

Passage:	My Knowledge:
Of the man who drove a swarm of bees across the Rocky Mountains . . .	The Rocky Mountain range is the tallest in the continental United States.

Clarify.

It's not unusual to come across confusing passages or words in your reading. Take time to clarify the details or information through the following strategies:

▶ Reread the passage slowly and carefully.
▶ Draw on prior knowledge to help you puzzle out the confusing section.
▶ Read ahead to see whether information there will clarify the confusion.

Respond.

Allow yourself to respond to what's happening or being described. Question the characters' actions, react to settings, and experience suspense or joy as the story, essay, or poem unfolds.

As you read this section from "The People, Yes," look at the notes in the boxes on each page. The notes demonstrate how to apply these strategies to a work of literature.

from THE PEOPLE, YES

Carl Sandburg

They have yarns
Of a skyscraper so tall they had to put hinges
On the two top stories so to let the moon go by,
Of one corn crop in Missouri when the roots
5   Went so deep and drew off so much water
The Mississippi riverbed that year was dry,
Of pancakes so thin they had only one side,
Of "a fog so thick we shingled the barn and six feet
    out on the fog,"
Of Pecos Pete straddling a cyclone in Texas and
    riding it to the west coast where "it rained out
    under him,"
10   Of the man who drove a swarm of bees across
    the Rocky Mountains and the Desert "and didn't
    lose a bee,"
Of a mountain railroad curve where the engineer
    in his cab can touch the caboose and spit in the
    conductor's eye,
Of the boy who climbed a cornstalk growing so fast
    he would have starved to death if they hadn't
    shot biscuits up to him,
Of the old man's whiskers: "When
    the wind was with him his whiskers
    arrived a day before he did,"
Of the hen laying a square egg and
    cackling, "Ouch!" and of hens laying
    eggs with the dates printed on them,
15   Of the ship captain's shadow: it froze to the deck
    one cold winter night,
Of mutineers on that same ship put to chipping
    rust with rubber hammers,
Of the sheep counter who was fast
    and accurate: "I just count their feet
    and divide by four,"
Of the man so tall he must climb a
    ladder to shave himself,
Of the runt so teeny-weeny it takes
two men and a boy to see him,
20   Of mosquitoes: one can kill a dog, two of them
    a man,
Of a cyclone that sucked cookstoves out of
    the kitchen, up the chimney flue, and on to
    the next town,

> To enjoy the humor in this passage, **envision** the wind blowing the old man's whiskers.

> To **clarify** the meaning of this passage, **reread** it or use your **prior knowledge** of division.

Paul Bunyan, Rockwell Kent

▲ **Critical Viewing** Which aspects of this illustration of Paul Bunyan are realistic? Which aspects are exaggerated? [Interpret]

◆ **Build Vocabulary**

mutineers (myo͞ot´ ən irz´) *n.*: People on a ship who revolt against their officers

runt (runt) *n.*: The smallest animal in a litter

mosquitoes (mə skēt´ ōz) *n.*: Insects having two wings, the females of which extract blood from animals and people

flue (flo͞o) *n.*: The pipe in a chimney that leads the smoke outside

Of the same cyclone picking up wagontracks in
    Nebraska and dropping them over in the
    Dakotas,
Of the hook-and-eye snake[1] unlocking itself
    into forty pieces, each piece two inches long,
    then in nine seconds flat snapping itself
    together again,

1. hook-and-eye snake: Here, a snake that is fastened together with metal hooks.

    Of the watch swallowed by the cow—when they butchered her
      a year later the watch was running and had the correct time,
25   Of horned snakes, hoop snakes that roll themselves where
      they want to go, and rattlesnakes carrying bells instead of
      rattles on their tails,
    Of the herd of cattle in California getting lost in a giant
      redwood tree that had hollowed out,
    Of the man who killed a snake by putting its tail in its mouth
      so it swallowed itself,
    Of railroad trains whizzing along so fast they reach the station
      before the whistle,

    Of pigs so thin the farmer had to tie knots in
      their tails to keep them from crawling through
      the cracks in their pens,
30   Of Paul Bunyan's big blue ox, Babe, measuring between the
      eyes forty-two ax-handles and a plug of Star tobacco exactly,
    Of John Henry's hammer and the curve of its swing and his
      singing of it as "a rainbow round my shoulder."

Guide for Responding

◆ LITERATURE AND YOUR LIFE

Reader's Response Which of the subjects in the tall tales that Sandburg mentions would you like to hear more about? Why?

Thematic Focus In what way does this poem reveal the character of the people of the United States?

☑ Check Your Comprehension

1. How would you describe the subject matter of "The People, Yes"?
2. Identify two yarns that involve exaggerated heights and two yarns that involve fantastic speed.

◆ Critical Thinking

INTERPRET

1. What characteristics do the people, animals, and things in these yarns share? **[Connect]**
2. What does John Henry mean when he describes the swing of his hammer as "a rainbow round my shoulder"? **[Interpret]**
3. What do the yarns suggest about the people who told them? **[Infer]**

APPLY

4. Why do you think people take pleasure in spinning yarns? **[Speculate]**

EXTEND

5. Why do you think most of these yarns are set in the Midwest and West? **[Social Studies Link]**

Guide for Responding (continued)

◆ Reading for Success

INTERACTIVE READING STRATEGIES

Review the reading strategies and the notes that show how to interact with your reading. Then, answer these questions:

1. Name one detail from the selection that you clarified.
2. How does your prior knowledge of trains help you understand the passage about the mountain railroad curve?
3. To which passage did you have the strongest response? Why?

◆ Build Vocabulary

USING THE SUFFIX -eer

The suffix -eer can be added to words to form nouns like *engineer*. Add the suffix -eer to these words. Then, use each of the words you created in a sentence.

1. ballad   **2.** musket   **3.** profit

SPELLING STRATEGY

Follow these rules to make plurals of nouns that end in *o*:

• For most nouns ending in an *o* that follows a vowel, add -*s*:

    radio + -s = radios   rodeo + -s = rodeos

• For most nouns ending in an *o* that follows a consonant, add -*es*:

    mosquito + -es = mosquitoes

• To form plurals of musical terms, add -*s*:

    piano + -s = pianos   solo + -s = solos

On your paper, write the plurals of the following:

1. potato   **2.** studio   **3.** zero   **4.** concerto

USING THE WORD BANK

On your paper, write the word from the Word Bank that best completes each statement.

1. A chimney ____?____ can become clogged.
2. The bites of some ____?____ can cause disease.
3. The puppy was the ____?____ of the litter.
4. ____?____ are people who disobey a captain's orders.

◆ Literary Focus

ORAL TRADITION

In the **oral tradition,** stories are passed from one generation to another by word of mouth. In "The People, Yes," Carl Sandburg summarizes stories from the American oral tradition, many of which are based on real events, like settling the frontier or encountering strange new animals.

1. In the yarn about corn crops, would it make a difference if the storyteller substituted the Missouri River for the Mississippi? Explain.
2. In the yarn about cyclones, what elements do you think are true? Which are invented?
3. Find two yarns that reveal the dangers of nature. Find two that reveal the need for hard work.

◆ Build Grammar Skills

SUBORDINATING CONJUNCTIONS

A conjunction connects words or groups of words. A **subordinating conjunction** connects two ideas by making one dependent on the other.

> *Although* the mountain lion was strong, it was not as strong as Paul Bunyan.

Common Subordinating Conjunctions:
after, although, as, because, before, if, since, when, where, whenever, wherever, while, unless, until

Practice Rewrite these sentences, underlining the subordinating conjunctions.

1. The boy would have starved to death if they hadn't shot biscuits up to him.
2. The cattle kept running until they reached California.
3. The horse couldn't keep up with Bill although it tried.
4. The herd got lost because the tree was hollow.
5. People stared whenever they saw Babe.

Writing Application On your paper, join each pair of sentences with a subordinating conjunction.

1. The snake hissed. It heard the wind.
2. He played the guitar. The rabbit fell asleep.
3. He pulled on his boots. He waded into the river.

Build Your Portfolio

 ## Idea Bank

Writing

1. **Personal Response** Write a journal entry in which you share your reactions to this poem—what you liked and disliked about it. Use details from the poem to support your responses.

2. **Yarn** Choose a passage from "The People, Yes" that presents a situation that you find especially interesting. Then, use your imagination to develop a complete yarn that tells a story based on the details Sandburg describes.

3. **Essay** Write a brief essay in which you explain what Sandburg's poem suggests about the United States and its people. Use details from the poem for support.

Speaking and Listening

4. **Memorized Reading** Memorize a passage from the poem, and recite it to the class using gestures and inflections suitable to the poem. You may wish to work with a classmate, with each of you memorizing parts of the poem. **[Performing Arts Link]**

5. **Group Story [Group Activity]** Sit in a circle with two classmates and tape-record a tall tale that you create. One person should begin the tale, and the next should add to it. The last person should complete the story. Play the recording for the class. **[Media Link]**

Projects

6. **Drawing or Painting** Use one or more images from the poem as an inspiration for a drawing or painting. In your artwork, convey the folk quality of a tall tale, yarn, or legend. **[Art Link]**

7. **Collection of Folk Tales [Group Activity]** With a group, brainstorm for tall tales like those told of Paul Bunyan and John Henry. Each group member can locate copies of the tall tales and photocopy them. Collect the tales in a book, and display it for the class to read.

 ## Writing Mini-Lesson

Profile of a Legendary Figure

If a legendary figure like Pecos Pete or John Henry were alive today, you'd probably read profiles about him or her in magazines. A profile is an article that offers a close-up look at an interesting personality. It usually includes biographical information and interesting stories about the person's life.

Write a profile of a legendary figure—either a real person, such as Michael Jordan, or a fictional character, such as John Henry.

Writing Skills Focus:
Precise Language

Use **precise language** to create a vivid picture of your subject for your readers. Carl Sandburg includes precise language in this description of Pecos Pete:

Model From the Poem
Of Pecos Pete straddling a cyclone in Texas and riding it to the west coast where "it rained out under him."

Prewriting To find out about a fictional subject's background, read stories and poems about him or her. If it's a real person, jot down information about his or her life. Then, focus your profile by deciding on one aspect of the person's life to cover.

Drafting First, introduce your subject to your readers. In the body, include anecdotes, quotations, and details about what makes your person legendary. End with a summary statement that reinforces the focus of the profile.

> ◆ **Grammar Application**
> Use subordinating conjunctions to join sentences in which one idea is dependent on the other.

Revising As you revise, replace general statements and descriptions with precise language that presents a vivid portrait of your subject.

PART 1

A Land of Promise

July Hay, 1942, Thomas Hart Benton, The Metropolitan Museum of Art, New York, NY/© T. H. Benton and R. P. Benton Testamentary Trusts/Licensed by VAGA, New York, NY.

Guide for Reading

Meet the Author:

John Steinbeck (1902–1968)

When John Steinbeck received the Nobel Prize for Literature in 1962, it capped a long, successful career in which he established himself as one of our nation's best-loved and most highly regarded writers.

Voice of the Working Class Steinbeck grew up in the Salinas Valley of California, where he became aware of the hard lives of migrant farm workers. After college, he spent five years drifting and writing; he even joined a hobo camp to study the lives of its people. His Pulitzer Prize-winning novel *The Grapes of Wrath* and the novels *Of Mice and Men* and *The Pearl* express sympathy for poor people who are exploited by society.

THE STORY BEHIND THE STORY

Although he had been acclaimed as one of the foremost writers of America's heartland, Steinbeck worried that he had lost touch with the country and its people. He decided to reestablish his ties by driving east to west—from Maine to California—along a northern route. He returned to New York along the southern route, passing through the Mohave Desert, Texas, and the Deep South. Steinbeck published an account of his travels entitled *Travels with Charley,* in 1962. The book's subtitle was "In Search of America."

◆ LITERATURE AND YOUR LIFE

CONNECT YOUR EXPERIENCE

Think for a moment of trips you've taken—to another country, state, or region. Did the people you meet have attitudes, beliefs, or ways of speaking different from your own? In *Travels with Charley,* John Steinbeck sets out to meet people all across the United States and learns about their different views of life in the process.

THEMATIC FOCUS: A Land of Promise

As you follow Steinbeck on his journey, ask yourself what qualities make the United States "a land of promise" for people from all regions of the land.

◆ Background for Understanding

GEOGRAPHY

As Steinbeck travels through the western United States, he finds himself in the Badlands of North Dakota. Located in the western parts of both North and South Dakota, the Badlands are a rugged region of fantastically shaped rock formations separated by valleys. In that barren landscape, there is little vegetation to prevent the erosion of the soft sedimentary rocks. The elevation of the Badlands is between 2,000 and 5,000 feet.

◆ Build Vocabulary

SUFFIXES: -ic

The suffix *-ic* means "like" or "having to do with." The word *diagnostic,* therefore, means "having to do with a diagnosis"—the study of facts.

WORD BANK

Which word from the story do you think might mean "the act of inquiring"? Check the Build Vocabulary box on page 356 to see if you chose correctly.

diagnostic
peripatetic
rigorous
maneuver
inquiry
inexplicable
celestial

from Travels with Charley

◆ Literary Focus

TRAVEL ESSAY

An essay is a short nonfiction work about a particular subject. A **travel essay** focuses on a trip or journey that someone actually made. In it, the writer may include factual information as well as descriptions that reveal how a place looks, sounds, or feels. It is, however, the writer's personal impressions and reflections that make the essay unique.

◆ Reading Strategy

CLARIFY DETAILS

When you don't completely understand a passage in a travel essay or other piece of writing, take time to stop and **clarify** what is not clear. Sometimes, this may simply involve pausing to think about the meaning of a detail. Other times, it may be necessary to reread a portion of the text or read ahead to piece together the meaning of something. Sometimes, it may even be necessary to go outside the text to find out what something means. Fill out a chart like the one below to clarify details as you read.

Detail to Clarify	Meaning of Detail	Strategy Used: Pause, Read Ahead, Read Back, Use Other Source

from Travels with Charley

John Steinbeck

My plan was clear, concise, and reasonable, I think. For many years I have traveled in many parts of the world. In America I live in New York, or dip into Chicago or San Francisco. But New York is no more America than Paris is France or London is England. Thus I discovered that I did not know my own country. I, an American writer, writing about America, was working from memory, and the memory is at best a faulty, warpy reservoir. I had not heard the speech of America, smelled the grass and trees and sewage, seen its hills and water, its color and quality of light. I knew the changes only from books and newspapers. But more than this, I had not felt the country for twenty-five years. In short, I was writing of something I did not know about, and it seems to me that in a so-called writer this is criminal. My memories were distorted by twenty-five intervening years.

Once I traveled about in an old bakery wagon, double-doored rattler with a mattress on its floor. I stopped where people stopped or gathered, I listened and looked and felt, and in the process had a picture of my country the accuracy of which was impaired only by my own shortcomings.

So it was that I determined to look again, to try to rediscover this monster land. Otherwise, in writing, I could not tell the small <u>diagnostic</u> truths which are the foundations of the larger truth. One sharp difficulty presented itself. In the intervening twenty-five years my name had become reasonably well known. And it has been my experience that when people have heard of you, favorably or not, they change; they become, through shyness or the other qualities that publicity inspires, something they are not under ordinary

◀ **Critical Viewing** Put yourself in the traveler's place. What feeling do you experience as you approach the mountains? **[Relate]**

◆ **Build Vocabulary**

diagnostic (dī′ əg näs′ tik) *adj.*: Providing a distinguishing sign or characteristic as evidence

circumstances. This being so, my trip demanded that I leave my name and my identity at home. I had to be peripatetic eyes and ears, a kind of moving gelatin plate.[1] I could not sign hotel registers, meet people I knew, interview others, or even ask searching questions. Furthermore, two or more people disturb the ecologic complex of an area. I had to go alone and I had to be self-contained, a kind of casual turtle carrying his house on his back.

With all this in mind I wrote to the head office of a great corporation which manufactures trucks. I specified my purpose and my needs. I wanted a three-quarter-ton pick-up truck, capable of going anywhere under possibly rigorous conditions, and on this truck I wanted a little house built like the cabin of a small boat. A trailer is difficult to maneuver on mountain roads, is impossible and often illegal to park, and is subject to many restrictions. In due time, specifications came through, for a tough, fast, comfortable vehicle, mounting a camper top—a little house with double bed, a four-burner stove, a heater, refrigerator and lights operating on butane, a chemical toilet, closet space, storage space, windows screened against insects—exactly what I wanted. It was delivered in the summer to my little fishing place at Sag Harbor near the end of Long Island. Although I didn't want to start before Labor Day, when the nation settles back to normal living, I did want to get used to my

turtle shell, to equip it and learn it. It arrived in August, a beautiful thing, powerful and yet lithe. It was almost as easy to handle as a passenger car. And because my planned trip had aroused some satiric remarks among my friends, I named it Rocinante, which you will remember was the name of Don Quixote's[2] horse.

◆ **Reading Strategy**
What strategy might you use to figure out the meaning of "turtle shell" in this passage?

Since I made no secret of my project, a number of controversies arose among my friends and advisers. (A projected journey spawns advisers in schools.) I was told that since my photograph was as widely distributed as my publisher could make it, I would find it impossible to move about without being recognized. Let me say in advance that in over ten thousand miles, in thirty-four states, I was not recognized even once. I believe that people identify things only in context. Even those people who might have known me against a background I am supposed to have, in no case identified me in Rocinante.

I was advised that the name Rocinante painted on the side of my truck in sixteenth-century Spanish script would cause curiosity and inquiry in some places. I do not know how many people recognized the name, but surely no one ever asked about it.

Next, I was told that a stranger's purpose in moving about the country might cause inquiry or even suspicion. For this reason I racked a shotgun, two rifles, and a couple of fishing rods in my truck, for it is my experience that if a man is going hunting or fishing his purpose is understood and even applauded. Actually, my hunting days are over. I no longer kill or catch anything I cannot get into a frying pan; I am too old for sport killing. This stage setting turned out to be unnecessary.

---

1. **gelatin plate:** Sensitive glass plate used to reproduce pictures.

2. **Don Quixote** (dän´ kē hōt´ ē): Hero of an early 17th-century satirical romance by Cervantes, who tries in a chivalrous but unrealistic way to rescue the oppressed and fight evil.

◆ **Build Vocabulary**

peripatetic (per´ i pə tet´ ik) *adj.*: Moving from place to place; walking about

rigorous (rig´ ər əs) *adj.*: Very strict or harsh

maneuver (mə n o͞o´ vər) *v.*: To manage; lead; control

inquiry (in´ kwə rē) *n.*: An investigation or examination; questioning

inexplicable (in eks´ pli kə bəl) *adj.*: That cannot be explained or understood

It was said that my New York license plates would arouse interest and perhaps questions, since they were the only outward identifying marks I had. And so they did—perhaps twenty or thirty times in the whole trip. But such contacts followed an invariable pattern, somewhat as follows:

Local man: "New York, huh?"

Me: "Yep."

Local man: "I was there in nineteen thirty-eight—or was it thirty-nine? Alice, was it thirty-eight or thirty-nine we went to New York?"

Alice: "It was thirty-six. I remember because it was the year Alfred died."

Local man: "Anyway, I hated it. Wouldn't live there if you paid me."

There was some genuine worry about my traveling alone, open to attack, robbery, assault. It is well known that our roads are dangerous. And here I admit I had senseless qualms. It is some years since I have been alone, nameless, friendless, without any of the safety one gets from family, friends, and accomplices. There is no reality in the danger. It's just a very lonely, helpless feeling at first—a kind of desolate feeling. For this reason I took one companion on my journey—an old French gentleman poodle known as Charley. Actually his name is Charles le Chien.[3] He was born in Bercy on the outskirts of Paris and trained in France, and while he knows a little poodle-English, he responds quickly only to commands in French. Otherwise he has to translate, and that slows him down. He is a very big poodle, of a color called *bleu,* and he is blue when he is clean. Charley is a born diplomat. He prefers negotiation to fighting, and properly so, since he is very bad at fighting. Only once in his ten years has he been in trouble—when he met a dog who refused to negotiate. Charley lost a piece of his right ear that time. But he is a good watch dog—has a roar like a lion, designed to conceal from night-wandering strangers the fact that he couldn't bite his way out of a *cornet de papier.*[4] He is a good friend and traveling companion, and would rather travel about than anything he can imagine. If he occurs at length in this account, it is because he contributed much to the trip. A dog, particularly an exotic like Charley, is a bond between strangers. Many conversations en route began with "What degree of a dog is that?"

The techniques of opening conversation are universal. I knew long ago and rediscovered that the best way to attract attention, help, and conversation is to be lost.

* * *

The night was loaded with omens. The grieving sky turned the little water to a dangerous metal and then the wind got up—not the gusty, rabbity wind of the seacoasts I know but a great bursting sweep of wind with nothing to inhibit it for a thousand miles in any direction. Because it was a wind strange to me, and therefore mysterious, it set up mysterious responses in me. In terms of reason, it was strange only because I found it so. But a goodly part of our experience which we find inexplicable must be like that. To my certain knowledge, many people conceal experiences for fear of ridicule. How many people have seen or heard or felt something which so outraged their sense of what should be that the whole thing was brushed quickly away like dirt under a rug?

For myself, I try to keep the line open even for things I can't understand or explain, but it is difficult in this frightened time. At this moment in North Dakota I had a reluctance to drive on that amounted to fear. At the same

---

3. **Charles le Chien** (shärl′ lə shē un′): French for "Charles the dog."

4. *cornet de papier* (kôr nā′ də pá pyā′): French for "paper bag."

time, Charley wanted to go—in fact, made such a commotion about going that I tried to reason with him.

"Listen to me, dog. I have a strong impulse to stay amounting to <u>celestial</u> command. If I should overcome it and go and a great snow should close in on us, I would recognize it as a warning disregarded. If we stay and a big snow should come I would be certain I had a pipeline to prophecy."

Charley sneezed and paced restlessly. "All right, *mon cur*,[5] let's take your side of it. You want to go on. Suppose we do, and in the night a tree should crash down right where we are presently standing. It would be you who have the attention of the gods. And there is always that chance. I could tell you many stories about faithful animals who saved their masters, but I think you are just bored and I'm not going to flatter you." Charley leveled at me his most cynical eye. I think he is neither a romantic nor a mystic. "I know what you mean. If we go, and no tree crashes down, or stay and no snow falls—what then? I'll tell you what then. We forget the whole episode and the field of prophecy is in no way injured. I vote to stay. You vote to go. But being nearer the pinnacle of creation than you, and also president, I cast the deciding vote."

We stayed and it didn't snow and no tree fell, so naturally we forgot the whole thing and are wide open for more mystic feelings when they come. And in the early morning swept clean of clouds and telescopically clear, we crunched around on the thick white ground cover of frost and got under way. The caravan of the arts was dark but the dog barked as we ground up to the highway.

Someone must have told me about the Missouri River at Bismarck, North Dakota, or I must have read about it. In either case, I hadn't paid attention. I came on it in amazement. Here is where the map should fold. Here is the boundary between east and west. On the Bismarck side it is eastern landscape, eastern grass, with the look and smell of eastern America. Across the Missouri on the Mandan side, it is pure west, with brown grass and water scorings and small outcrops. The two sides of the river might well be a thousand miles apart. As I was not prepared for the Missouri boundary, so I was not prepared for the Bad Lands. They deserve this name. They are like the work of an evil child. Such a place the Fallen Angels might have built as a spite to Heaven, dry and sharp, desolate and dangerous, and for me filled with foreboding. A sense comes from it that it does not like or welcome humans. But humans being what they are, and I being human, I turned off the highway on a shaley road and headed in among the buttes, but with a shyness as though I crashed a party. The road surface tore viciously at my tires and made Rocinante's overloaded springs cry with anguish. What a place for a colony of troglodytes, or better, of trolls. And here's an odd thing. Just as I felt unwanted in this land, so do I feel a reluctance in writing about it.

Presently I saw a man leaning on a two-strand barbed-wire fence, the wires fixed not to posts but to crooked tree limbs stuck in the

---

5. *mon cur* (mōn kʉr´): French slang for "my dear mutt."

◆ **Build Vocabulary**

celestial (sə les´ chəl) *adj.*: Of heaven; divine

▲ **Critical Viewing** Why is the name "Badlands" appropriate for the region pictured here? **[Analyze]**

ground. The man wore a dark hat, and jeans and long jacket washed palest blue with lighter places at knees and elbows. His pale eyes were frosted with sun glare and his lips scaly as snakeskin. A .22 rifle leaned against the fence beside him and on the ground lay a little heap of fur and feathers—rabbits and small birds. I pulled up to speak to him, saw his eyes wash over Rocinante, sweep up the details, and then retire into their sockets. And I found I had nothing to say to him. The "Looks like an early winter," or "Any good fishing hereabouts?" didn't seem to apply. And so we simply brooded at each other.

"Afternoon!"

"Yes, sir," he said.

"Any place nearby where I can buy some eggs?"

"Not real close by 'less you want to go as far as Galva or up to Beach."[6]

"I was set for some scratch-hen eggs."

"Powdered," he said. "My Mrs. gets powdered."

"Lived here long?"

"Yep."

I waited for him to ask something or to say something so we could go on, but he didn't. And as the silence continued, it became more and more impossible to think of something to say. I made one more try. "Does it get very cold here winters?"

"Fairly."

"You talk too much."

He grinned. "That's what my Mrs. says."

"So long," I said, and put the car in gear and moved along. And in my rear-view mirror I couldn't see that he looked after me. He may not be a typical Badlander, but he's one of the few I caught.

A little farther along I stopped at a small house, a section of war-surplus barracks, it looked, but painted white with yellow trim, and with the dying vestiges of a garden, frosted-down geraniums and a few clusters of chrysanthemums, little button things yellow and red-brown. I walked up the path with the certainty that I was being regarded from behind the white window curtains. An old woman answered my knock and gave me the drink of water I asked for and nearly talked my arm off. She was hungry to talk, frantic to talk, about her relatives, her friends, and how she wasn't used to this. For she was not a native and she didn't rightly belong here. Her native clime was a land of milk and honey and had its share of apes and ivory and peacocks. Her voice rattled on as though she was terrified of the silence that would settle when I was gone. As she talked it came to me that she was afraid of this place and, further, that so was I. I felt I wouldn't like to have the night catch me here.

I went into a state of flight, running to get away from the unearthly landscape. And then the late afternoon changed everything. As the sun angled, the buttes and coulees, the cliffs and sculptured hills and ravines lost their burned and dreadful look and glowed with yellow and rich browns and a hundred variations of red and silver gray, all picked out by streaks of coal black. It was so beautiful that I

---

6. **Galva . . . Beach:** Cities in western North Dakota near the border of Montana.

from *Travels with Charley* ◆ 359

stopped near a thicket of dwarfed and wind-warped cedars and junipers, and once stopped I was caught, trapped in color and dazzled by the clarity of the light. Against the descending sun the battlements were dark and clean-lined, while to the east, where the uninhibited light poured slantwise, the strange landscape shouted with color. And the night, far from being frightful, was lovely beyond thought, for the stars were close, and although there was no moon the starlight made a silver glow in the sky. The air cut the nostrils with dry frost. And for pure pleasure I collected a pile of dry dead cedar branches and built a small fire just to smell the perfume of the burning wood and to hear the excited crackle of the branches. My fire made a dome of yellow light over me, and nearby I heard a screech owl hunting and a barking of coyotes, not howling but the short chuckling bark of the dark of the moon. This is one of the few places I have ever seen where the night was friendlier than the day. And I can easily see how people are driven back to the Bad Lands.

Before I slept I spread a map on my bed, a Charley-tromped map. Beach was not far away, and that would be the end of North Dakota. And coming up would be Montana, where I had never been. That night was so cold that I put on my insulated underwear for pajamas, and when Charley had done his duties and had his biscuits and consumed his usual gallon of water and finally curled up in his place under the bed, I dug out an extra blanket and covered him—all except the tip of his nose—and he sighed and wriggled and gave a great groan of pure ecstatic comfort. And I thought how every safe generality I gathered in my travels was canceled by another. In the night the Bad Lands had become Good Lands. I can't explain it. That's how it was.

*G*uide for Responding

◆ LITERATURE AND YOUR LIFE

Reader's Response Would you have liked to join Steinbeck on his travels? Explain.

Thematic Focus Do you think Steinbeck succeeds in rediscovering the people of the United States? Explain.

Journal Writing In your journal, jot down places you'd like to visit someday. Also, mention why each destination interests you.

☑ Check Your Comprehension

1. For what purpose does Steinbeck make his trip?
2. Who is Charley, and why does he go along on the journey?
3. What causes the author's impressions of the Badlands to change?

◆ Critical Thinking

INTERPRET

1. What does Steinbeck mean by saying that he "had not felt the country for twenty-five years"? **[Interpret]**
2. What is the author's attitude when he is writing about people? When he describes the landscape? **[Compare and Contrast]**
3. What does Steinbeck's decision to stay overnight in the Badlands reveal about his character? **[Draw Conclusions]**

EVALUATE

4. Do you agree with Steinbeck that traveling around the country is the best way to learn about it? Explain. **[Evaluate]**

EXTEND

5. What qualities does a person need to become a good travel writer? **[Career Link]**

from ROAD TRIP USA

by Jamie Jensen

Mount Rushmore and Carhenge

Two of the nation's most distinctive outdoor sculptures stand along US-385 within a manageable drive from US-20. One is perhaps the best-known artwork in the U.S., the giant presidential memorial at Mount Rushmore. Roughly 100 miles north from Chadron, at the far eastern side of the beautiful Black Hills, Mount Rushmore is graced by the 60-foot heads of four U.S. Presidents—Washington, Jefferson, Lincoln, and Teddy Roosevelt—carved into a granite peak. It's equal parts impressive monument and kitschy Americana, and one of those places you really have to see to believe.

Another newer, less famous monument to America sits in a flat field along US-385 outside the town of Alliance, 62 miles south of Chadron. Built in 1987 as part of a local family reunion, Carhenge is a giant-sized replica of the famous Druidical ruin, Stonehenge; this one, however, is built entirely out of three dozen late-model American cars, stacked on top of one another to form a semi-circular temple.

1. What kind of information is revealed in this travel article?
2. Which travel destination—Mt. Rushmore or Carhenge—is more traditional? Which is more offbeat? Why might Jensen have chosen to include both types of tourist sites within one article?
3. Would John Steinbeck have enjoyed visiting these sites? Why or why not?

Guide for Responding (continued)

◆ Reading Strategy

CLARIFY DETAILS

Clarifying details, or checking your understanding, will help ensure that you get the most out of what you read. To clarify details, you can draw upon your prior knowledge, find clues within the text, and consult outside sources.

1. Identify two descriptive details about the physical landscape in the Badlands that might need clarification. How could you clarify them?
2. Charley the poodle understands French. Where would you look to find out what *le chien* means?
3. In what part of North Dakota is the Missouri River located? How would you clarify that detail?

◆ Build Vocabulary

USING THE SUFFIX -*ic*

The suffix -*ic,* as in *diagnostic,* means "like" or "having to do with." It can be added to nouns to form adjectives, such as *patriotic.* Define each of the following words, incorporating the definition of -*ic* into each answer.

1. fantastic　　2. sarcastic　　3. photographic

SPELLING STRATEGY

The *kw* sound is spelled *qu* when it occurs at the beginning or in the middle of a word, as in **qu**iet, in**qu**iry, and **qu**est. Replace the phonetic spellings with the actual spellings of these words.

1. (kwiz)　　2. (ri kwest´)　　3. (ʉrth´ kwāk´)

USING THE WORD BANK

In your notebook, write the letter of the word or words closest in meaning to the first word.

1. peripatetic: (a) located at, (b) walking from place to place, (c) formed by
2. celestial: (a) earthly, (b) clearly, (c) heavenly
3. diagnostic: (a) test, (b) related to finding the cause of, (c) related to finding the direction of
4. inexplicable: (a) unusual, (b) intentional, (c) not explainable
5. inquiry: (a) insight, (b) quietness, (c) search
6. maneuver: (a) jostle, (b) manage skillfully, (c) figure out
7. rigorous: (a) righteous, (b) straight, (c) strict

◆ Literary Focus

TRAVEL ESSAY

In **travel essays,** writers often focus on people and experiences as well as on places. Unlike standard travel guides, travel essays usually contain extended descriptions of characters and even dialogue, bringing to life the people as well as the scenery.

1. In what way does the dialogue between Steinbeck and the man he meets in the Badlands give you a taste of the region?
2. Does Steinbeck's description of his emotional reaction to the Badlands give you a deeper understanding of the landscape? Why or why not?

◆ Build Grammar Skills

COORDINATING CONJUNCTIONS

A conjunction connects single words or groups of words. **Coordinating conjunctions,** such as *and, but, or, nor, for, yet,* and *so,* link words or groups of words of equal rank, such as two or more nouns, phrases, or even entire sentences.

Connecting Nouns: . . . my friends *and* advisors

Connecting Verbs: How many people have seen *or* heard *or* felt something . . .

Connecting Sentences: Otherwise, he has to translate, *and* that slows him down.

Practice Copy the following sentences, and circle the coordinating conjunction in each. Then, underline the words or groups of words connected by the conjunction.

1. I had to go alone, and I had to be self-contained.
2. I specified my purpose and my needs.
3. A stranger's purpose in moving about the country might cause inquiry or even suspicion.
4. I think that he is neither a romantic nor a mystic.
5. The caravan of the arts was dark, but the dog barked as we ground up the highway.

Writing Application Write sentences that use the following coordinating conjunctions:

1. A sentence about Charley using *and*
2. A sentence about Steinbeck using *or*
3. A sentence about the Badlands using *but*

Build Your Portfolio

 ## Idea Bank

Writing

1. **Charley's Journal** Write a journal entry describing the Badlands from Charley's point of view.

2. **Guidebook Description** Write a description of the Badlands to be included in a guidebook for tourists. Tell what a visitor might expect to see. Also, make suggestions about how long a visitor might want to stay and what supplies or equipment might be useful for traveling in the area.

3. **Essay** Steinbeck once said, "To my certain knowledge, many people conceal experiences for fear of ridicule." Write an essay in which you explain how this selection might have been different if Steinbeck had been one of those people.

Speaking and Listening

4. **Radio Commentary** Rework the passage describing the Badlands to make it appropriate for a radio broadcast. Record your reworked version, and play the recording for your classmates. **[Media Link]**

5. **Panel Discussion [Group Activity]** With a small group, hold a panel discussion about the benefits of traveling. You may discuss whether learning about places through television and movies is an adequate substitute for firsthand experience. **[Social Studies Link]**

Projects

6. **Map** Create a map of North Dakota's Badlands. Label the places that Steinbeck mentions in his essay. Post your completed map in the classroom. **[Geography Link]**

7. **Documentary Script [Group Activity]** With a partner, write a documentary (true-life) film script based on *Travels with Charley*. In your script, specify the sights you want the camera to film, the order of the shots, and what the narrator will say. **[Media Link]**

 ## Writing Mini-Lesson

Travel Journal Entry

Like John Steinbeck, many people write about places they visit. Capture the essence of a place you've visited and your experience of it by writing an entry in a travel journal.

Writing Skills Focus: Use Supporting Details

Supporting details give information about your main ideas. Use supporting details to help bring your travel entry to life for readers. John Steinbeck uses supporting details that help describe his experience in the Badlands:

Model From the Story
The air cut the nostrils with dry frost.

Prewriting First, decide on a topic by searching your memory for interesting places you've visited and choosing one about which to write. Then, list supporting details you can include to describe the place and your experience of it.

Drafting Begin your travel entry by introducing your subject and revealing your overall impression of it. Then, follow with a description of your journey, including things that happened and people you met. Conclude with a summary of your experience.

Revising Review your draft, looking for places where supporting details can be added to make your description more vivid. Consider adding dialogue to bring to life the people you met. Proofread for errors in spelling, grammar, and punctuation.

> ◆ **Grammar Application**
> Unless you're using short sentences for dramatic effect, consider joining two or three short sentences with coordinating conjunctions.

Guide for Reading

Meet the Authors:

Emma Lazarus (1849–1887)

Born in New York City, Emma Lazarus began writing poetry in her teens. Enraged by the Russian massacre of Jews in 1882, she changed the focus of her writing to meet her new purpose: to defend and glorify the Jewish people. She is most famous for her sonnet "The New Colossus" (1883), the last lines of which are inscribed below the Statue of Liberty.

Joseph Bruchac (1942–   )

Joseph Bruchac is the son of an Abenaki Indian mother and a Czechoslovakian father. He grew up in the foothills of New York's Adirondacks. In addition to juggling careers as a writer, storyteller, editor, and lecturer, he is an avid gardener and holds a black belt in Pentjak Silat, the martial art of Indonesia.

Mario Cuomo (1932–   )

Mario Cuomo was the governor of New York from 1983 to 1995. He was widely regarded as one of the Democratic party's foremost thinkers. His main concern is that rich and poor Americans should work together to solve the country's problems.

Alice Walker (1944–   )

One of today's best-known and most highly regarded writers, Alice Walker produces fiction, poetry, and essays that focus mainly on social injustice. She received the Pulitzer Prize for her novel *The Color Purple* (1982), which was made into a movie in 1985.

◆ LITERATURE AND YOUR LIFE

CONNECT YOUR EXPERIENCE

Unless you are a Native American, you or your ancestors came from a culture that is based outside the United States. The selections you're about to read give voice to the hopes and dreams that prompted millions of people—possibly including your ancestors—to leave their native lands and come to America to forge a new life.

THEMATIC FOCUS: A Land of Promise

How do the visions of America in these selections compare with your own vision?

◆ Background for Understanding

HISTORY

The photograph opposite was taken at Ellis Island, the chief immigration station of the eastern United States from 1892 to 1954. Between 1892 and 1924, more than 12,000,000 immigrants entered the United States through Ellis Island, hoping to find a better life. Three of these selections are about immigrants coming through Ellis Island.

◆ Build Vocabulary

RELATED WORDS: FORMS OF *migrate*

The word *immigrate* includes the root *migrate*, which means "to move from one place to another." Other words related to *migrate* include *immigration, emigrate, migrant,* and *migratory*.

WORD BANK

Which word from the selections means "of or belonging to ancestors"? Check the Build Vocabulary box on page 369 to see if you chose correctly.

immigrate
apprehension
immersed
ancestral
colossal
conscience
literally

The New Colossus ◆ Ellis Island
◆ Achieving the American Dream ◆
Choice: A Tribute to Dr. Martin Luther King, Jr.

◆ Literary Focus
EPITHET
An **epithet** is a phrase used to point out a characteristic of a person or thing. For example, the "Milky Way" is an epithet for our galaxy, the "Big Apple" is a popular epithet for New York City, and "Honest Abe" is an epithet for Abraham Lincoln. Look for epithets in these selections, and note how they shape your impression of the people and things they describe.

◆ Reading Strategy
SUMMARIZE
When you read a group of selections such as these with related themes, or when you read a longer piece, it's helpful to pause every now and then to **summarize.** When you summarize, you restate in your own words the main points and key details of a piece or a section of a piece.

As you read these selections, summarize each section by filling out a chart like the one below.

Title	Section	Summary
"The New Colossus"	lines 10–14	Welcome to all immigrants.

THE NEW COLOSSUS
Emma Lazarus

Not like the brazen giant of Greek fame,[1]
With conquering limbs astride from land to land;
Here at our sea-washed, sunset gates shall stand
A mighty woman with a torch, whose flame
5   Is the imprisoned lightning, and her name
Mother of Exiles. From her beacon-hand
Glows world-wide welcome; her mild eyes command
The air-bridged harbor that twin cities frame.
"Keep, ancient lands, your storied pomp!" cries she
10   With silent lips. "Give me your tired, your poor,
Your huddled masses yearning to breathe free,
The wretched refuse of your teeming shore.
Send these, the homeless, tempest-tost[2] to me,
I lift my lamp beside the golden door!"

1. brazen giant of Greek fame: The Colossus of Rhodes, one of the Seven Wonders of the World, is a huge bronze statue built at the harbor of Rhodes in commemoration of the siege of Rhodes (305–304 B.C.).
2. tempest-tost (tem´ pist tôst): Here, having suffered a turbulent ocean journey.

▲ **Critical Viewing** In what ways does the Statue of Liberty seem like a welcoming figure? [**Analyze**]

ELLIS ISLAND

Joseph Bruchac

Beyond the red brick of Ellis Island
where the two Slovak children
who became my grandparents
waited the long days of quarantine,[1]
5   after leaving the sickness,
the old Empires of Europe,
a Circle Line ship slips easily
on its way to the island
of the tall woman, green
10 as dreams of forests and meadows
waiting for those who'd worked
a thousand years
yet never owned their own.

Like millions of others,
15 I too come to this island,
nine decades the answerer
of dreams.

Yet only one part of my blood loves
    that memory.
Another voice speaks
20 of native lands
within this nation.
Lands invaded
when the earth became owned.
Lands of those who followed
25 the changing Moon,
knowledge of the seasons
in their veins.

---

1. **quarantine** (kwôr´ ən tēn) n.: Period, originally 40 days, during which an arriving vessel suspected of carrying contagious disease is detained in port in strict isolation to prevent any diseases from spreading.

◇ Guide for Responding

◆ LITERATURE AND YOUR LIFE

Reader's Response Which symbol of the United States do you find more moving—the Statue of Liberty or Ellis Island? Explain.

Thematic Focus Which poem has a more optimistic vision of immigrants fulfilling their dreams? Explain.

☑ Check Your Comprehension

1. In "The New Colossus," who is the "mighty woman with a torch," called the "Mother of Exiles"?
2. What does the Colossus "say"?
3. In "Ellis Island," where does the speaker say his grandparents came from?
4. What is "the island of the tall woman" in lines 8 and 9?

◆ Critical Thinking

INTERPRET

1. According to Emma Lazarus's poem, what is the difference between the old Colossus "of Greek fame" and the new Colossus, the Statue of Liberty? **[Compare and Contrast]**
2. What is the attitude of the Colossus toward the immigrants? **[Infer]**
3. What does the speaker in "Ellis Island" mean by the phrase "native lands within this nation"? **[Interpret]**
4. In "Ellis Island," the attitude of the immigrants is different from that of the Native Americans concerning land ownership. Explain the difference. **[Compare and Contrast]**

APPLY

5. Why might people from other countries have viewed the United States as "a land of promise"? **[Apply]**

Achieving the American Dream
Mario Cuomo

In the Provincia di Salerno[1] just outside the Italian city of Naples, a laborer named Andrea Cuomo asked Immaculata Giordano to marry him. The young woman accepted under one condition: that the couple immigrate to the far-off land of her dreams—America. Andrea Cuomo agreed, and after marrying, the Cuomos made the long voyage to New York Harbor in the late 1920s. The young couple left the life, the language, the land, the family, and the friends they knew, arriving in Lady Liberty's shadow with no money, unable to speak English, and without any education. They were filled with both hope and apprehension.

All that my parents brought to their new home was their burning desire to climb out of poverty on the strength of their labor. They believed that hard work would bring them and their children better lives and help them achieve the American Dream.

At first, my father went to work in Jersey City, New Jersey, as a ditchdigger. After Momma and Poppa had three children, Poppa realized he needed to earn more to support his growing family. So he opened a small Italian American grocery store in South Jamaica, in the New York City borough of Queens.

By the time I was born in 1932, the store was open 24 hours a day, and it seemed as if Momma and Poppa were working there all the time. I can still see them waiting on customers and stocking shelves. And I can still smell and see and almost taste the food that brought in the customers: the provolone, the Genoa salami, the prosciutto,[2] the fresh bread, the

---

2. **prosciutto** (prə shoot′ ō) *n.*: Spicy Italian ham.

▲ **Critical Viewing** Do the facial expressions of the Cuomos pictured here reveal their determination to prosper in the United States? Why or why not? **[Deduce]**

---

1. **Provincia di Salerno** (prō vin′ sē ə dē sə lär′ nō): Region surrounding Salerno, a seaport in southern Italy.

fruits and vegetables. Our store gave our neighbors a delicious taste of Italy in New York.

My parents lacked the education to help us much with our schoolwork. But they taught us every single day, just by being who they were, about the values of family, hard work, honesty, and caring about others. These were not just Italian values, or American ones, but universal values that everyone can embrace.

From my earliest days, I felt <u>immersed</u> in the culture and traditions of my parents' homeland. I grew up speaking Italian. I heard story after story from my parents and relatives about life in the Old Country.

Though not an immigrant myself, I saw the hardships Italian immigrants had to endure. I saw their struggle to make themselves understood in an alien language, their struggle to rise out of poverty, and their struggle to overcome the prejudices of people who felt superior because they or their ancestors had arrived earlier on this nation's shores.

As an Italian American, I grew up believing that America is the greatest country on earth, and thankful that I was born here. But at the same time, I have always been intensely proud that I am the son of Italian immigrants and

that my Italian heritage helped make me the man I am.

The beauty of America is that I don't have to deny my past to affirm my present. No one does. We can love this nation like a parent and still embrace our <u>ancestral</u> home like cherished grandparents.

I like to tell the story of Andrea and Immaculata Cuomo because it tells us what America is about. Their story is the story not just of my parents, or of Italian immigrants at the beginning of this century, but of all immigrants. Our nation is renewed and strengthened by the infusion[3] of new Americans from around the world.

---

3. **infusion** (in fyoo´ zhən) *n.*: Addition.

◆ Build Vocabulary

immigrate (im´ ə grāt) *v.*: Come into a foreign country to make a new home

apprehension (ap´ rə hen´ shən) *n.*: Fear; anxiety that something bad will happen

immersed (i mʉrst´) *adj.*: Deeply involved in

ancestral (an ses´ trəl) *adj.*: Of or inherited from one's forefathers or ancestors

Guide for Responding

◆ LITERATURE AND YOUR LIFE

Reader's Response What is your reaction to hearing about the experiences of Cuomo's parents? Why?

Thematic Focus Would you say that Cuomo's parents fulfilled the "American Dream"? Explain.

☑ Check Your Comprehension

1. Why do Cuomo's parents move to the United States?
2. How do his parents make a living once they arrive in the United States?

◆ Critical Thinking

INTERPRET

1. What does Cuomo mean when he says that "I don't have to deny my past to affirm my present"? **[Analyze]**
2. Based on what he says about his own parents, what character traits do you think Mario Cuomo values? **[Deduce]**
3. (a) What is "the American Dream"? (b) How do Mario Cuomo's parents achieve it? **[Infer]**

APPLY

4. In what ways can Mario Cuomo's parents, as described in "Achieving the American Dream," be role models for everyone—not just for immigrants? **[Generalize]**

Choice:
A Tribute to
Dr. Martin Luther King, Jr.

Alice Walker

This address was made in 1972 at a Jackson, Mississippi, restaurant that refused to serve people of color until forced to do so by the Civil Rights Movement a few years before.

My great-great-great-grandmother walked as a slave from Virginia to Eatonton, Georgia—which passes for the Walker ancestral home—with two babies on her hips. She lived to be a hundred and twenty-five years old and my own father knew her as a boy. (It is in memory of this walk that I choose to keep and to embrace my "maiden" name, Walker.)

There is a cemetery near our family church where she is buried; but because her marker was made of wood and rotted years ago, it is impossible to tell exactly where her body lies. In the same cemetery are most of my mother's people, who have lived in Georgia for so long nobody even remembers when they came. And all of my great-aunts and -uncles are there, and my grandfather and grandmother, and, very recently, my own father.

If it is true that land does not belong to anyone until they have buried a body in it, then the land of my birthplace belongs to me,

dozens of times over. Yet the history of my family, like that of all black Southerners, is a history of dispossession. We loved the land and worked the land, but we never owned it; and even if we bought land, as my great-grandfather did after the Civil War, it was always in danger of being taken away, as his was, during the period following Reconstruction.[1]

My father inherited nothing of material value from his father, and when I came of age in the early sixties I awoke to the bitter knowledge that in order just to continue to love the land of my birth, I was expected to leave it. For black people—including my parents—had learned a long time ago that to stay willingly in a beloved but brutal place is to risk losing the love and being forced to acknowledge only the brutality.

It is a part of the black Southern sensibility that we treasure memories; for such a long

---

1. **Reconstruction:** Period following the American Civil War (1867–1877) when the South was rebuilt and reestablished as part of the Union.

▶ **Critical Viewing** Judging from the size of the crowd, what can you infer about Dr. Martin Luther King, Jr.? [Infer]

time, that is all of our homeland those of us who at one time or another were forced away from it have been allowed to have.

I watched my brothers, one by one, leave our home and leave the South. I watched my sisters do the same. This was not unusual; abandonment, except for memories, was the common thing, except for those who "could not do any better," or those whose strength or stubbornness was so <u>colossal</u> they took the risk that others could not bear.

In 1960, my mother bought a television set, and each day after school I watched Hamilton Holmes and Charlayne Hunter[2] as they struggled to integrate—fair-skinned as they were—the University of Georgia. And then, one day, there appeared the face of Dr. Martin Luther King, Jr. What a funny name, I thought. At the moment I first saw him, he was being handcuffed and shoved into a police truck. He had dared to claim his rights as a native son, and had been arrested. He displayed no fear, but seemed calm and serene, unaware of his own extraordinary courage. His whole body, like his <u>conscience</u>, was at peace.

At the moment I saw his resistance I knew I would never be able to live in this country without resisting everything that sought to disinherit me, and I would never be forced away from the land of my birth without a fight.

He was The One, The Hero, The One Fearless Person for whom we had waited. I hadn't even realized before that we *had* been waiting for Martin Luther King, Jr., but we had. And I knew it for sure when my mother added his name to the list of people she prayed for every night.

◆ **Literary Focus**
What epithets can you find in this paragraph? What impression do they convey?

I sometimes think that it was <u>literally</u> the prayers of people like my mother and father, who had bowed down in the struggle for such a long time, that kept Dr. King alive until five

years ago.[3] For years we went to bed praying for his life, and awoke with the question "Is the 'Lord' still here?"

The public acts of Dr. King you know. They are visible all around you. His voice you would recognize sooner than any other voice you have heard in this century—this in spite of the fact that certain municipal libraries, like the one in downtown Jackson, do not carry recordings of his speeches, and the librarians chuckle cruelly when asked why they do not.

You know, if you have read his books, that his is a complex and revolutionary philosophy that few people are capable of understanding fully or have the patience to embody in themselves. Which is our weakness, which is our loss.

And if you know anything about good Baptist preaching, you can imagine what you missed if you never had a chance to hear Martin Luther King, Jr., preach at Ebeneezer Baptist Church.

You know of the prizes and awards that he tended to think very little of. And you know of his concern for the disinherited: the American Indian, the Mexican-American, and the poor American white—for whom he cared much.

You know that this very room, in this very restaurant, was closed to people of color not more than five years ago. And that we eat here together tonight largely through his efforts and his blood. We accept the common pleasures of life, assuredly, in his name.

But add to all of these things the one thing that seems to me second to none in importance: He gave us back our heritage. He gave us back our homeland; the bones and dust of our

---

2. **Hamilton Holmes and Charlayne Hunter:** Hamilton Holmes and Charlayne Hunter made history in January 1961 by becoming the first two African Americans to attend the University of Georgia.

3. **until five years ago:** Dr. Martin Luther King, Jr. (b. 1929); U.S. clergyman and leader in the civil rights movement from the mid-1950's until his death by assassination on April 4, 1968.

◆ **Build Vocabulary**

colossal (kə läs′ əl) *adj.*: Astonishingly great; extraordinary

conscience (kän′ shəns) *n.*: Knowledge or sense of right and wrong; inner thoughts and feelings

literally (lit′ ər əl ē) *adv.*: Actually; in fact

ancestors, who may now sleep within our caring *and* our hearing. He gave us the blueness of the Georgia sky in autumn as in summer; the colors of the Southern winter as well as glimpses of the green of vacation-time spring. Those of our relatives we used to invite for a visit we now can ask to stay. . . . He gave us full-time use of our woods, and restored our memories to those of us who were forced to run away, as realities we might each day enjoy and leave for our children.

He gave us continuity of place, without which community is ephemeral. He gave us home.

1973

Beyond Literature

Social Studies Connection

March on Washington Until the 1960's, in many places African Americans were prevented from using public facilities, such as drinking fountains, restaurants, buses, and schools. On August 28, 1963, civil rights leader Martin Luther King, Jr., and more than 200,000 other people demonstrated to the world the importance of confronting and solving the racial problems of the United States. They peacefully gathered at the Lincoln Memorial to demand equal justice for all the citizens of the nation. The people were inspired by King's famous "I Have a Dream" speech, which emphasized his vision of a nation where all people would be free. The March on Washington had a strong effect on the country and led to the Civil Rights Act of 1964, which enforced desegregation and outlawed discrimination.

Cross-Curricular Activity
Martin Luther King, Jr., was awarded the Nobel Prize for Peace in 1964. Do some research on King, to achieve a better understanding of his career, his writings, and his important contributions to society. Share your findings with your class.

Guide for Responding

◆ LITERATURE AND YOUR LIFE

Reader's Response Would you have liked to be present when Walker delivered this address? Why or why not?

Thematic Focus How did Dr. Martin Luther King, Jr., help to ensure that America was a land of promise for all its citizens?

Journal Writing Jot down in your journal the names of some people you admire. Note their accomplishments and how they made the world a better place.

☑ Check Your Comprehension

1. Why does Walker say she kept her maiden name?
2. Whom does Walker describe as "The One, The Hero, The One Fearless Person"?
3. What does Alice Walker say is the greatest thing King did?

◆ Critical Thinking

INTERPRET
1. What does Walker mean when she says that the history of her family is one of dispossession? **[Interpret]**
2. Why did Walker and her brothers feel it necessary to leave the place of their birth? **[Analyze]**
3. With what qualities of King's was Walker impressed? **[Connect]**

APPLY
4. What might the atmosphere of the room have been like when Walker delivered this address? **[Speculate]**

COMPARE LITERARY WORKS
5. How does the black southern experience described by Alice Walker compare with that of the Italian immigrant experience described by Mario Cuomo? **[Compare and Contrast]**

Guide for Responding (continued)

◆ Reading Strategy

SUMMARIZE

Summarizing what you have read is a good way to check your understanding. A summary should restate in your own words the most important points of the original.

1. Summarize the first stanza, or group of lines, in "Ellis Island."
2. (a) List the main points of "Choice: A Tribute to Dr. Martin Luther King, Jr." (b) How can summarizing help you to identify the main points?

◆ Build Vocabulary

USING FORMS OF *migrate*

Remember that *migrate* means "to move from one place to another," and that this meaning is included in its related words. Copy these sentences on your paper. Complete them with one of these forms of *migrate: immigration, migrant,* or *migratory.*

1. The _____?_____ workers picked tomatoes.
2. Most countries control _____?_____.
3. What are the _____?_____ patterns of whales?

SPELLING STRATEGY

One way to master the spelling of a word is to remember smaller words within it. For example, if you remember that the word *loss* appears in the center of *colossal,* you will not be confused about which consonants are doubled.

Identify a smaller word in each word that might help you spell it.

1. balloon	3. piece	5. together
2. early	4. principal	6. glossy

USING THE WORD BANK

Match each Word Bank word with the word or phrase closest in meaning.

1. immigrate	a. inner voice
2. apprehension	b. dipped
3. immersed	c. inherited from ancestors
4. ancestral	d. huge
5. colossal	e. fear
6. conscience	f. actually
7. literally	g. move into a country

◆ Literary Focus

EPITHET

An **epithet** is a phrase that captures an essential quality of a person or thing. For example, an epithet often applied to the Statue of Liberty is "The Lady in the Harbor." Epithets help to make writing and speech colorful and memorable.

1. (a) What are two epithets for the Statue of Liberty in "The New Colossus"? (b) In "Achieving the American Dream," what epithet describes the Statue of Liberty?
2. (a) In "Choice: A Tribute . . .," what three epithets describe Dr. King? (b) On what qualities or characteristics do these epithets focus?

◆ Build Grammar Skills

CORRELATIVE CONJUNCTIONS

Correlative conjunctions, like all conjunctions, are used to join words or series of words. Unlike other conjunctions, correlative conjunctions always appear in pairs. The most commonly used correlative conjunctions are *both . . . and, either . . . or, neither . . . nor,* and *not only . . . but also.*

This story is *not just* of my parents, *but* of all immigrants.

Practice Rewrite these pairs of sentences, and underline the correlative conjunctions.

1. Neither Andrea nor Immaculata knew what to expect when they set sail for the United States.
2. They were filled with both hope and apprehension.
3. These were not just Italian values, or American ones, but universal values that everyone can embrace.
4. To be an American either you have to be born here or you have to take a citizenship oath.
5. America is not only renewed by new Americans, but also strengthened by them.

Writing Application Write sentences about the following that contain correlative conjunctions.

1. A sentence about the Statue of Liberty
2. A sentence about Martin Luther King, Jr.

Build Your Portfolio

 Idea Bank

Writing

1. **Postcard** Put yourself in the place of one of the Slovak children described in "Ellis Island." Write a postcard to the folks back home telling them of your first impressions of the United States.

2. **Journal** Imagine that the Statue of Liberty has come to life. She remembers a typical day when immigrants came through Ellis Island. Write her journal entry for that day. **[Social Studies Link]**

3. **Essay** Write a brief essay in which you describe the qualities that you believe people must possess in order to leave their homeland to emigrate to the United States. If possible, quote lines from one or more selections.

Speaking and Listening

4. **Address** "Choice: A Tribute to Dr. Martin Luther King, Jr.," is an address, or speech, originally given by Alice Walker. Rehearse and deliver this address to your class.

5. **Dramatization [Group Activity]** With a partner, act out a scene between a person who wants to emigrate to the United States and a parent who wants that person to stay home. **[Performing Arts Link]**

Projects

6. **Multimedia Report** Report on the life of Dr. Martin Luther King, Jr. Gather photos, news clippings, and, if possible, video- and audiotapes. Write text to explain and connect the pieces you gather. Then, present the report to the class. **[Media Link; Social Studies Link]**

7. **Monument [Group Activity]** Work with a group to design and build a model of a monument to honor past and future immigrants. Also, plan where you would like your monument to be erected. Finally, work together to write a poem that will be placed on the monument. **[Art Link]**

 Writing Mini-Lesson

Tribute

A **tribute** is something, such as a gift or a service, that is given to show respect, affection, or gratitude. In Alice Walker's case, the tribute she gives to Dr. Martin Luther King, Jr., is in the form of a public address, or speech, in his honor. Like Alice Walker, write a tribute to someone to show your respect, admiration, or gratitude—or to show all three of those feelings.

Writing Skills Focus: Transitions

Your writing will flow more easily if you use **transitions**—words and groups of words that connect one idea to another.

Model From "Achieving the American Dream"

At first, my father went to work in Jersey City, New Jersey, as a ditchdigger. *After Momma and Poppa had three children,* Poppa realized he needed to earn more to support his growing family. *So* he opened a small Italian American grocery store. . . .

Prewriting Choose a person to whom you would like to pay tribute. Jot down admirable qualities that the person possesses, and note good deeds he or she has done. Then, decide on the organization that best fits the details you've gathered.

Drafting As you draft, refer to the notes you've taken to include all the details you planned to use. Use transitions to make connections among your ideas.

> ◆ **Grammar Application**
> As you write, use correlative conjunctions in places where they will help show connections.

Revising Look for places to add transitions to make the connections between ideas clearer. Also, add details wherever appropriate to strengthen the portrait of your subject.

CONNECTING LITERATURE TO SOCIAL STUDIES

A YOUNG NATION

The Man Without a Country *by Edward Everett Hale*

The United States in 1803

United States (1802)	← Lewis and Clark 1804–1806
Louisiana Purchase (1803)	← Pike 1805–1806
	⇠ Pike 1806–1807

THE NATION TAKES SHAPE Following the Revolutionary War, the United States went through a some-times difficult process of establishing itself as a nation. As the system of government was put in place, political leaders came into conflict about the balance of power between the central government and individual states. At the same time, the country was rapidly expanding—the Louisiana Purchase (1803) doubled the size of the United States—and differences between the northern and southern states began to take on increasing importance.

Aaron Burr "The Man Without a Country" is set during this turbulent time. The main character is tried for treason after aligning himself with Aaron Burr, a key political figure of the late 1700's and early 1800's, whose career ended in disgrace. A lawyer and career politician, Burr ran for President in 1800. He received the same number of votes as Thomas Jefferson, and the U.S. House of Representatives had to vote to break the tie, making Jefferson President and Burr Vice President. Alexander Hamilton, who was Secretary of the Treasury, cast one of the votes that defeated Burr in the House. He later opposed Burr in his bid for governor of New York. Following Burr's loss, Burr challenged Hamilton to a duel, fatally wounding Hamilton with one shot. Following that incident, Burr's career declined. He was accused of planning to invade Mexico to establish a separate government there. He was tried for treason in 1807 but was acquitted of the charges.

A Story With a Moral Edward Everett Hale was a strong supporter of patriotism. He wrote "The Man Without a Country" as a way of getting his views across. Although the story is fictional, Hale wove many historical facts into the story, giving it the flavor of a nonfiction piece.

The Man Without a Country

Edward Everett Hale

I suppose that very few casual readers of the *New York Herald* of August 13, 1863, observed, in an <u>obscure</u> corner, among the "Deaths," the announcement:

NOLAN. Died, on board U.S. Corvette *Levant*, Lat. 2° 11' S., Long. 131° W., on the 11th of May, PHILIP NOLAN.

Hundreds of readers would have paused at the announcement had it read thus: "Died, May 11, THE MAN WITHOUT A COUNTRY." For it was as "The Man Without a Country" that poor Philip Nolan had generally been known by the officers who had him in charge during some fifty years, as, indeed, by all the men who sailed under them.

There can now be no possible harm in telling this poor creature's story. Reason enough there has been till now for very strict secrecy, the secrecy of honor itself, among the gentlemen of the Navy who have had Nolan in charge. And certainly it speaks well for the profession and the personal honor of its members that to the press this man's story has been wholly unknown—and, I think, to the country at large also. This I do know, that no naval officer has mentioned Nolan in his report of a cruise.

But there is no need for secrecy any longer. Now the poor creature is dead, it seems to me worthwhile to tell a little of his story, by way of showing young Americans of today what it is to be "A Man Without a Country."

Philip Nolan was as fine a young officer as there was in the "Legion of the West," as the Western division of our army was then called.

◆ **Build Vocabulary**

obscure (äb skyo͞or´) *adj*: Hidden; not obvious

When Aaron Burr[1] made his first dashing expedition down to New Orleans in 1805, he met this gay, dashing, bright young fellow. Burr marked[2] him, talked to him, walked with him, took him a day or two's voyage in his flatboat,[3] and, in short, fascinated him. For the next year, barrack life was very tame to poor Nolan. He occasionally <u>availed</u> himself of the permission the great man had given him to write to him. Long, <u>stilted</u> letters the poor boy wrote and rewrote and copied. But never a line did he have in reply. The other boys in the garrison[4] sneered at him, because he lost the fun which they found in shooting or rowing while he was working away on these grand letters to his grand friend. But before long the young fellow had his revenge. For this time His Excellency, the Honorable Aaron Burr, appeared again under a very different aspect. There were rumors that he had an army behind him and an empire before him. At that time the youngsters all envied him. Burr had not been talking twenty minutes with the commander before he asked him to send for Lieutenant Nolan. Then, after a little talk, he asked Nolan if he could show him something of the great river and the plans for the new post. He asked Nolan to take him out in his skiff to show him a canebrake[5] or a cottonwood tree, as he said—really to win him over; and by the time the sail was over, Nolan was enlisted body and soul. From that time, though he did not yet know it, he lived as a man without a country.

What Burr meant to do I know no more than you. It is none of our business just now. Only, when the grand catastrophe came—Burr's great treason trial at Richmond—some of the lesser fry at Fort Adams[6] got up a string of court-martials on the officers there. One and another of the colonels and majors were tried, and, to fill out the list, little Nolan, against whom there was evidence enough that he was sick of the service, had been willing to be false to it, and would have obeyed any order to march anywhere had the order been signed "By command of His Exc. A. Burr." The courts dragged on. The big flies[7] escaped—rightly, for all I know. Nolan was proved guilty enough, yet you and I would never have heard of him but that, when the president of the court asked him at the close whether he wished to say anything to show that he had always been faithful to the United States, he cried

---

1. **Aaron Burr:** American political leader (1756–1836). Burr was U.S. Vice President from 1801 to 1805. He was believed to have plotted to build an empire in the Southwest.
2. **marked** *v.*: Here, paid attention to.
3. **flatboat** *n.*: Boat with a flat bottom.
4. **garrison** (gar´ ə sən) *n.*: Military post or station.
5. **canebrake** (kān´ brāk´) *n.*: Dense area of cane plants.
6. **Fort Adams:** Fort at which Nolan was stationed.
7. **big flies:** Burr and the other important men who may have been involved in his scheme.

▲ **Critical Viewing** This is a portrait of Aaron Burr. In it, is he depicted as a distinguished statesman or as a disgraced traitor? Explain. **[Make a Judgment]**

out, in a fit of frenzy:

"Damn the United States! I wish I may never hear of the United States again!"

I suppose he did not know how the words shocked old Colonel Morgan, who was holding the court. Half the officers who sat in it had served through the Revolution, and their lives had been risked for the very idea which he cursed in his madness. He, on his part, had grown up in the West of those days. He had been educated on a plantation where the finest company was a Spanish officer or a French merchant from Orleans. His education had been perfected in commercial expeditions to Vera Cruz, and I think he told me his father once hired an Englishman to be a private tutor for a winter on the plantation. He had spent half his youth with an older brother, hunting horses in Texas; and to him "United States" was scarcely a reality. I do not excuse Nolan; I only explain to the reader why he cursed his country and wished he might never hear her name again.

Connecting Literature to Social Studies What does Hale suggest about how the term "United States" changed in meaning between 1776 and 1863?

From that moment, September 23, 1807, till the day he died, May 11, 1863, he never heard her name again. For that half century and more he was a man without a country.

Old Morgan, as I said, was terribly shocked. If Nolan had compared George Washington to Benedict Arnold, or had cried, "God save King George," Morgan would not have felt worse. He called the court into his private room, and returned in fifteen minutes, with a face like a sheet, to say: "Prisoner, hear the sentence of the Court! The Court decides, subject to the approval of the President, that you never hear the name of the United States again."

Nolan laughed. But nobody else laughed. Old Morgan was too solemn, and the whole room was hushed dead as night for a minute. Even Nolan lost his swagger in a moment. Then Morgan added: "Mr. Marshal, take the prisoner to Orleans in an armed boat, and deliver him to the naval commander there."

The marshal gave his orders and the prisoner was taken out of court.

"Mr. Marshal," continued old Morgan, "see that no one mentions the United States to the prisoner. Mr. Marshal, make my respects to Lieutenant Mitchell at Orleans, and request him to order that no one shall mention the United States to the prisoner while he is on board ship. You will receive your written orders from the officer on duty here this evening. The court is adjourned."

Before the *Nautilus*[8] got round from New Orleans to the Northern Atlantic coast with the prisoner on board, the sentence had been approved, and he was a man without a country.

The plan then adopted was substantially the same which was necessarily followed ever after. The Secretary of the Navy was requested to put Nolan on board a government vessel bound on a long cruise, and to direct that he should be only so far confined there as to make it certain that he never saw or heard of the country. We had few long cruises then, and I do not know certainly what his first cruise was. But the commander to whom he was entrusted regulated the etiquette and the precautions of the affair, and according to his scheme they were carried out till Nolan died.

When I was second officer of the *Intrepid*, some thirty years after, I saw the original paper of instructions. I have been sorry ever since that I did not copy the whole of it. It ran, however, much in this way:

> Washington (with a date, which must have been late in 1807).

Sir:

You will receive from Lieutenant Neale the person of Philip Nolan, late a lieutenant in the United States Army.

This person on his trial by court-

---

8. *Nautilus*: Naval ship to which Nolan was assigned.

◆ **Build Vocabulary**

availed (ə vāld´) *v.*: Made use of

stilted (stil´ təd) *adj.*: Unnatural; very formal

swagger (swag´ ər) *n.*: Arrogance or boastfulness

martial expressed, with an oath, the wish that he might "never hear of the United States again."

The court sentenced him to have his wish fulfilled.

For the present, the execution of the order is entrusted by the President to this department.

You will take the prisoner on board your ship, and keep him there with such precautions as shall prevent his escape.

You will provide him with such quarters, rations, and clothing as would be proper for an officer of his late rank, if he were a passenger on your vessel on the business of his government.

The gentlemen on board will make any arrangements agreeable to themselves regarding his society. He is to be exposed to no indignity of any kind, nor is he ever unnecessarily to be reminded that he is a prisoner.

But under no circumstances is he ever to hear of his country or to see any information regarding it; and you will especially caution all the officers under your command to take care that this rule, in which his punishment is involved, shall not be broken.

It is the intention of the government that he shall never again see the country which he has disowned. Before the end of your cruise you will receive orders which will give effect to this intention.

> Respectfully yours,
> W. Southard,
> for the Secretary of the Navy.

The rule adopted on board the ships on which I have met "the man without a country" was, I think, transmitted from the beginning. No mess[9] liked to have him permanently, because his presence cut off all talk of home or of the prospect of return, of politics or letters, of peace or of war—cut off

more than half the talk men liked to have at sea. But it was always thought too hard that he should never meet the rest of us, except to touch hats, and we finally sank into one system. He was not permitted to talk with the men, unless an officer was by. With officers he had unrestrained intercourse, as far as they and he chose. But he grew shy, though he had favorites: I was one. Then the captain always asked him to dinner on Monday. Every mess in succession took up the invitation in its turn. According to the size of the ship, you had him at your mess more or less often at dinner. His breakfast he ate in his own stateroom. Whatever else he ate or drank, he ate or drank alone. Sometimes, when the marines or sailors had any special jollification,[10] they were permitted to invite "Plain Buttons," as they called him. Then Nolan was sent with some officer, and the men were forbidden to speak of home while he was there. I believe the theory was that the sight of his punishment did them good. They called him "Plain Buttons," because, while he always chose to wear a regulation army uniform, he was not permitted to wear the army button, for the reason that it bore either the initials or the insignia of the country he had disowned.

I remember, soon after I joined the Navy, I was on shore with some of the older officers from our ship and some of the gentlemen fell to talking about Nolan. Someone told of the

---

9. **mess** *n.*: Here, a group of people who routinely have their meals together.

10. **jollification** (jäl´ ə fi kā´ shən) *n.*: Merry-making.

system which was adopted from the first about his books and other reading. As he was almost never permitted to go on shore, even though the vessel lay in port for months, his time at the best hung heavy. Everybody

USS **Constitution** and HMS **Guerriere** (Aug. 19, 1812), Thomas Birch, U.S. Naval Academy Museum

▲ **Critical Viewing** What might Nolan's life have been like, spent aboard ships like this? [Speculate]

was permitted to lend him books, if they were not published in America and made no allusion to it. These were common enough in the old days. He had almost all the foreign papers that came into the ship, sooner or later; only somebody must go over them first, and cut out any advertisement or stray paragraph that referred to America. This was a little cruel sometimes, when the back of what was cut out might be innocent. Right in the midst of one of Napoleon's battles poor Nolan would

find a great hole, because on the back of the page of that paper there had been an advertisement of a packet[11] for New York, or a scrap from the President's message. This was the first time I ever heard of this plan. I remember it, because poor Phillips, who was of the party, told a story of something which happened at the Cape of Good Hope on Nolan's first voyage. They had touched at the Cape, paid their respects to the English Admiral and the fleet, and then Phillips had borrowed a lot of English books from an officer. Among them was *The Lay of the Last Minstrel*,[12] which they had all of them heard of, but which most of them had never seen. I think it could not have been published long. Well, nobody thought there could be any risk of anything national in that. So Nolan was permitted to join the circle one afternoon when a lot of them sat on deck reading aloud. In his turn, Nolan took the book and read to the others; and he read very well. Nobody in the circle knew a line of the poem, only it was all magic and chivalry, and was ten thousand years ago. Poor Nolan read steadily through the fifth canto,[13] stopped a minute and drank something, and then began, without a thought of what was coming:

> Breathes there the man, with soul so dead
> Who never to himself hath said,—

It seems impossible to us that anybody ever heard this for the first time; but all these fellows did then, and poor Nolan himself

---

11. **packet** *n.*: Boat that carries passengers, freight, and mail along a regular route.
12. ***The Lay of the Last Minstrel:*** Narrative poem by Sir Walter Scott, Scottish poet and novelist (1771–1832).
13. **canto** (kan´ tō) *n.*: A main division of certain long poems.

went on, still unconsciously or mechanically:

This is my own, my native land!

Then they all saw that something was to pay; but he expected to get through, I suppose, turned a little pale, but plunged on:

Whose heart hath ne'er within him
    burned,
As home his footsteps he hath turned
From wandering on a foreign strand?—
If such there breathe, go, mark him well,—

By this time the men were all beside themselves, wishing there was any way to make him turn over two pages; but he had not quite presence of mind for that; he gagged a little, colored crimson, and staggered on:

For him no minstrel raptures swell;
High though his titles, proud his name,
Boundless his wealth as wish can claim,
Despite these titles, power, and pelf,[14]
The wretch, concentered all in self,—

and here the poor fellow choked, could not go on, but started up, swung the book into the sea, vanished into his stateroom, "And by Jove," said Phillips, "we did not see him for two months again. And I had to make up some beggarly story to that English surgeon why I did not return his Walter Scott to him."

That story shows about the time when Nolan's braggadocio[15] must have broken down. At first, they said, he took a very high tone, considered his imprisonment a mere farce, affected to enjoy the voyage, and all that; but Phillips said that after he came out of his stateroom he never was the same man again. He never read aloud again, unless it was the Bible or Shakespeare, or something else he was sure of. But it was not that merely. He never entered in with the other young men exactly as a companion again. He was always shy afterwards, when I knew him—very seldom spoke unless he was spoken to, except to a very few friends.

Generally he had the nervous, tired look of a heart-wounded man.

When Captain Shaw was coming home, rather to the surprise of everybody they made one of the Windward Islands, and lay off and on for nearly a week. The boys said the officers were sick of salt-junk,[16] and meant to have turtle-soup before they came home. But

▲ **Critical Viewing** What details in this drawing reveal that these men are prisoners? [Connect]

after several days the *Warren* came to the same rendezvous;[17] they exchanged signals; she told them she was outward bound, perhaps to the Mediterranean, and took poor Nolan and his traps[18] on the boat to try his second cruise. He looked very blank when he was told to get ready to join her. He had known enough of the signs of the sky to know that till that moment he was going

---

14. **pelf** *n.*: Ill-gotten wealth.
15. **braggadocio** (brag´ ə dō´ shē ō) *n.*: Here, pretense of bravery; Nolan acts as if he does not mind his imprisonment.

16. **salt-junk** *n.*: Hard salted meat.
17. **rendezvous** (rän´ dā vōō) *n.*: Meeting place.
18. **traps** *n.*: Here, bags or luggage.

"home." But this was a distinct evidence of something he had not thought of, perhaps— that there was no going home for him, even to a prison. And this was the first of some twenty such transfers, which brought him sooner or later into half our best vessels, but which kept him all his life at least some hundred miles from the country he had hoped he might never

Prisoners, from Iconographic Encyclopedia, drawn by G. Heck, eng. by Henry Winkles, Collection of The New-York Historical Society

hear of again.

It may have been on that second cruise— it was once when he was up the Mediter- ranean—that Mrs. Graff, the celebrated Southern beauty of those days, danced with him. The ship had been lying a long time in the Bay of Naples, and the officers were very intimate in the English fleet, and there had been great festivities, and our men thought they must give a great ball on board the ship. They wanted to use Nolan's stateroom for something, and they hated to do it without asking him to the ball; so the captain said they might ask him, if they would be respon- sible that he did not talk with the wrong

people, "who would give him intelligence."[19] So the dance went on. For ladies they had the family of the American consul, one or two travelers who had adventured so far, and a nice bevy of English girls and matrons.

Well, different officers relieved each other in standing and talking with Nolan in a friendly way, so as to be sure that nobody else spoke to him. The dancing went on with spirit, and after a while even the fellows who took this honorary guard of Nolan ceased to fear any trouble.

As the dancing went on, Nolan and our fellows all got at ease—so much so, that it seemed quite natural for him to bow to that splendid Mrs. Graff, and say, "I hope you have not forgotten me, Miss Rutledge. Shall I have the honor of dancing?"

He did it so quickly, that Fellows, who was with him, could not hinder him. She laughed and said, "I am not Miss Rutledge any longer, Mr. Nolan; but I will dance all the same." She nodded to Fellows, as if to say he must leave Mr. Nolan to her, and led him off to the place where the dance was forming.

> **Connecting Literature to Social Studies**
> Why would a song called "The Old Thirteen" be some- thing that could not be mentioned in front of Nolan?

Nolan thought he had got his chance. He had known her at Philadelphia, and at other places had met her. He began with her travels, and Europe, and then he said boldly—a little pale, she said, as she told me the story years after— "And what do you hear from home, Mrs. Graff?"

And that splendid creature looked through him. How she must have looked through him!

"Home! Mr. Nolan! I thought you were the man who never wanted to hear of home again!"—and she walked directly up the deck to her husband, and left poor Nolan alone. He did not dance again.

A happier story than either of these I have told is of the war.[20] That came along soon after. I have heard this affair told in three or four ways—and, indeed, it may have

---

19. **intelligence** *n.*: Here, news about his country.
20. **the war:** The War of 1812 between the United States and Great Britain.

The Man Without a Country ◆ 383

happened more than once. In one of the great frigate[21] duels with the English, in which the navy was really baptized, it happened that a round-shot[22] from the enemy entered one of our ports[23] square, and took right down the officer of the gun himself, and almost every man of the gun's crew. Now you may say what you choose about courage, but that is not a nice thing to see. But, as the men who were not killed picked themselves up, and as they and the surgeon's people were carrying off the bodies, there appeared Nolan in his shirt sleeves, with the rammer in his hand,

Connecting Literature to Social Studies
From the details in this paragraph, what can you learn about the War of 1812?

and, just as if he had been the officer, told them off with authority—who should go to the cockpit with the wounded men, who should stay with him—perfectly cheery, and with that way which makes men feel sure all is right and is going to be right. And he finished loading the gun with his own hands, aimed it, and bade the men fire. And there he stayed, captain of that gun, keeping those fellows in spirits, till the enemy struck[24]—sitting on the carriage while the gun was cooling, though he was exposed all the time—showing them easier ways to handle heavy shot—making the raw hands laugh at their own blunders—and when the gun cooled again, getting it loaded and fired twice as often as any other gun on the ship. The captain walked forward by way of encouraging the men, and Nolan touched his hat and said, "I am showing them how we do this in the artillery, sir."

And this is the part of the story where all the legends agree; the commodore said, "I see you do, and I thank you, sir; and I shall never forget this day, sir, and you never shall, sir."

And after the whole thing was over, and the commodore had the Englishman's

sword[25] in the midst of the state and ceremony of the quarter-deck, he said, "Where is Mr. Nolan? Ask Mr. Nolan to come here."

And when Nolan came, he said, "Mr. Nolan, we are all very grateful to you today; you are one of us today; you will be named in the dispatches."

And then the old man took off his own sword of ceremony, gave it to Nolan, and made him put it on. The man told me this who saw it. Nolan cried like a baby, and well he might. He had not worn a sword since that infernal day at Fort Adams. But always afterwards on occasions of ceremony, he wore that quaint old French sword of the commodore's.

The captain did mention him in the dispatches. It was always said he asked that Nolan might be pardoned. He wrote a special letter to the Secretary of War, but nothing ever came of it.

All that was nearly fifty years ago. If Nolan was thirty then, he must have been near eighty when he died. He looked sixty when he was forty. But he never seemed to me to change a hair afterwards. As I imagine his life, from what I have seen and heard of it, he must have been in every sea, and yet almost never on land. Till he grew very old, he went aloft a great deal. He always kept up his exercise, and I never heard that he was ill. If any other man was ill, he was the kindest nurse in the world; and he knew more than half the surgeons do. Then if anybody was sick or

---

21. frigate (frig′ it) *n*.: Fast-sailing warship equipped with guns.
22. round-shot: Cannonball.
23. ports *n*.: Here, portholes or openings for cannons.
24. struck *v*.: Lowered their flag to admit defeat.

25. the Englishman's sword: A defeated commander would turn over his sword to the victor.

died, or if the captain wanted him to, on any other occasion, he was always ready to read prayers. I have said that he read beautifully.

My own acquaintance with Philip Nolan began six or eight years after the English war, on my first voyage after I was appointed a midshipman. From the time I joined, I thought Nolan was a sort of lay chaplain—a chaplain

Row of Cannon, from Iconographic Encyclopedia, drawn by G. Heck, eng. by Henry Winkles, Collection of The New-York Historical Society

▲ **Critical Viewing** Judging from the details in this etching, what type of ship is this? [Interpret]

with a blue coat. I never asked about him. Everything in the ship was strange to me. I knew it was green to ask questions, and I suppose I thought there was a "Plain Buttons" on every ship. We had him to dine in our mess once a week, and the caution was given that on that day nothing was to be said about home. But if they had told us not to say anything about the planet Mars or the Book of Deuteronomy,[26] I should not have asked why; there were a great many things which seemed to me to have as little reason. I first came to

26. **Book of Deuteronomy** (do͞ot′ ər än′ ə mē): Fifth book of the Bible.

understand anything about "The Man Without a Country" one day when we overhauled a dirty little schooner which had slaves[27] on board. An officer named Vaughan was sent to take charge of her, and after a few minutes, he sent back his boat to ask that someone might be sent to him who could speak Portuguese. None of the officers did; and just as the captain was sending forward to ask if any of the people could, Nolan stepped out and said he should be glad to interpret, if the captain wished, as he understood the language. The captain thanked him, fitted out another boat with him, and in this boat it was my luck to go.

When we got there, it was such a scene as you seldom see, and never want to. Nastiness beyond account, and chaos run loose in the midst of the nastiness. There were not a great many of the Negroes; but by way of making what there were understand that they were free, Vaughan had had their handcuffs and anklecuffs knocked off. The Negroes were, most of them, out of the hold and swarming all round the dirty deck, with a central throng surrounding Vaughan and addressing him in every dialect.

As we came on deck, Vaughan looked down from a hogshead,[28] which he had mounted in desperation, and said, "Is there anybody who can make these people understand something?"

Nolan said he could speak Portuguese, and one or two fine-looking Kroomen who had

27. **slaves:** In 1808, it became illegal to bring slaves into the United States. In 1842, the U.S. and Great Britain agreed to use ships to patrol the African coast, to prevent slaves from being taken.
28. **hogshead** (hôgz′ hed′) n.: Large barrel or cask.

◆ **Build Vocabulary**

blunders (blun′ dərs) n.: Foolish or careless mistakes

The Man Without a Country ◆ 385

worked for the Portuguese on the coast were dragged out.

"Tell them they are free," said Vaughan.

Nolan explained it in such Portuguese as the Kroomen could understand, and they in turn to such of the Negroes as could understand them. Then there was a yell of delight, clenching of fists, and leaping and dancing by way of celebration.

"Tell them," said Vaughan, well pleased, "that I will take them all to Cape Palmas."

Connecting Literature to Social Studies
How does this incident relate to the Civil War, which was going on when the story was published in 1863?

This did not answer so well. Cape Palmas was practically as far from the homes of most of them as New Orleans or Rio de Janeiro was; that is, they would be eternally separated from home there. And their interpreters, as we could understand, instantly said, "*Ah, non Palmas,*" and began to protest volubly. Vaughan was rather disappointed at this result of his liberality, and asked Nolan eagerly what they said. The drops stood on poor Nolan's white forehead, as he hushed the men down, and said, "He says, 'Not Palmas.' He says, 'Take us home; take us to our own country; take us to our own house; take us to our own children and our own women.' He says he has an old father and mother who will die if they do not see him. And this one says he left his people all sick, and paddled down to Fernando to beg the white doctor to come and help them, and that these devils caught him in the bay just in sight of home, and that he has never seen anybody from home since then. And this one says," choked out Nolan, "that he has not heard a word from his home in six months."

Vaughan always said he grew gray himself while Nolan struggled through this interpretation. I, who did not understand anything of the passion involved in it, saw that the very elements were melting with fervent heat and that something was to pay somewhere. Even the Negroes themselves stopped howling, as they saw Nolan's agony and Vaughan's

almost equal agony of sympathy. As quick as he could get words, Vaughan said, "Tell them yes, yes, yes; tell them they shall go to the Mountains of the Moon, if they will. If I sail the schooner through the Great White Desert, they shall go home!"

And after some fashion Nolan said so. And then they all fell to kissing him again.

Officer of the Watch on the Horseblock, Heck's Iconographic Encyclopedia, 1851, Collection of The New-York Historical Society

▲ **Critical Viewing** Would you say that the ship in this illustration was well-run? Why or why not? [Draw Conclusions]

But he could not stand it long; and getting Vaughan to say he might go back, he beckoned me down into our boat. As we started back he said to me, "Youngster, let that show you what it is to be without a family, without a home, and without a country. And if you are ever tempted to say a word or to do a thing that shall put a bar between you and your family, your home, and your country, pray God in His mercy to take you that instant home to His own heaven. Think of your home, boy; write and send, and talk about it. Let it be nearer and nearer to your thought the farther you have to travel from it, and rush back to it when you are free, as that poor slave is doing now. And for your country, boy" and the words rattled in his throat, "and for that flag," and he pointed to the ship, "never dream a dream but of serving her as she bids you, though the service carry you through a thousand hells. No matter what happens to you,

no matter who flatters you or who abuses you, never look at another flag, never let a night pass but you pray God to bless that flag. Remember, boy, that behind all these men you have to do with, behind officers, and government, and people even, there is the Country herself, your Country, and that you belong to her as you belong to your own mother. Stand by her, boy, as you would stand by your mother!"

I was frightened to death by his calm, hard passion; but I blundered out that I would, by all that was holy, and that I had never thought of doing anything else. He hardly seemed to hear me; but he did, almost in a whisper, say, "Oh, if anybody had said so to me when I was of your age!"

I think it was this half-confidence of his, which I never abused, that afterward made us great friends. He was very kind to me. Often he sat up, or even got up, at night, to walk the deck with me, when it was my watch. He explained to me a great deal of my mathematics, and I owe to him my taste for mathematics. He

lent me books and helped me about my reading. He never referred so directly to his story again; but from one and another officer I have learned, in thirty years, what I am telling.

After that cruise I never saw Nolan again. The other men tell me that in those fifteen years he aged very fast, but he was still the same gentle, uncomplaining, silent sufferer that he ever was, bearing as best he could his self-appointed punishment. And now it seems the dear old fellow is dead. He has found a home at last, and a country.

Since writing this, and while considering whether or not I would print it, as a warning to the young Nolans of today of what it is to throw away a country, I have received from Danforth, who is on board the *Levant,* a letter which gives an account of Nolan's last hours. It removes all my doubts about telling this story.

Here is the letter:

Dear Fred,

I try to find heart and life to tell you that it is all over with dear old Nolan. I have been with him on this voyage more than I ever was, and I can understand wholly now the way in which you used to speak of the dear old fellow. I could see that he was not strong, but I had no idea the end was so near. The doctor has been watching him very carefully, and yesterday morning came to me and told me that Nolan was not so well, and had not left his stateroom—a thing I never remember before. He had let the doctor come and see him as he lay there—the first time the doctor had been in the stateroom—and he said he should like to see me. Do you remember the mysteries we boys used to invent about his room in the old *Intrepid* days? Well, I went in, and there, to be sure, the poor fellow lay in his berth, smiling pleasantly as he gave me his hand, but looking very frail. I could not help a glance round, which showed me what a little shrine he had made of the box he was lying in. The Stars and Stripes were draped up above and around a picture of Washington and he had painted a majestic eagle, with lightning blazing from his beak and his foot just clasping the whole globe, which his wings overshadowed. The dear old boy saw my glance, and said, with a sad smile, "Here, you see I have a country!" And then he pointed to the foot of his bed, where I had not seen before a great map of the United States, as he had drawn it from memory, and which he had there to look upon as he lay. Quaint, queer old names were on it, in large letters: "Indiana Territory," "Mississippi Territory," and "Louisiana Territory," as I suppose our fathers learned such things: but the old fellow had patched in Texas, too: he had carried his western boundary all the way to the Pacific, but on that shore he had defined nothing.

"O Captain," he said, "I know I am dying. I cannot get home. Surely you will tell me something now?— Stop! stop! Do not speak till I say what I am sure you know, that there is not in this ship, that there is not in America a more loyal man than I. There cannot be a man who loves the old flag as I do, or prays for it as I do, or hopes for it as I do. There are thirty-four stars in it now, Danforth, though I do not know what their names are. There has never been one taken away. I know by that that there has never been any successful Burr. O Danforth, Danforth," he sighed out, "how like a wretched night's dream a boy's idea of personal fame or of separate sovereignty seems, when one looks back on it after such a life as mine! But tell me—tell me something—tell me

everything, Danforth, before I die!"

I swear to you that I felt like a monster that I had not told him everything before. "Mr. Nolan," said I, "I will tell you everything you ask about. Only, where shall I begin?"

Ship Plans, from Iconographic Encyclopedia, drawn by G. Heck, eng. by Henry Winkles, Collection of The New-York Historical Society

▲ **Critical Viewing** This diagram shows various parts and features of a ship. Why do you think so much effort was put into ship-building design in the 1800's? [Speculate]

Oh, the blessed smile that crept over his white face! He pressed my hand and said, "Bless you! Tell me their names," and he pointed to the stars on the flag. "The last I know is Ohio. My father lived in Kentucky. But I have guessed Michigan and Indiana and Mississippi—that was where Fort Adams was—they make twenty. But where are your other fourteen? You have not cut up any of the old ones, I hope?"

Well, that was not a bad text, and I told him the names in as good order as I could, and he bade me take down his beautiful map and draw them in as I best could with my pencil. He was wild with delight about Texas, told me how his cousin died there; he had marked a gold cross near where he supposed his grave was; and he had guessed at Texas. Then he was delighted as he saw California and Oregon;—that, he said, he had suspected partly, because he had never been permitted to land on that shore, though the ships were there so much. Then he asked whether Burr ever tried again—and he ground his teeth with the only passion he showed. But in a moment that was over. He asked about the old war—told me the story of his serving the gun the day we took the *Java*. Then he settled down more quietly, and very happily, to hear me tell in an hour the history of fifty years.

How I wished it had been somebody who knew something! But I did as well as I could. I told him of the English war. I told him about Fulton[29] and the steamboat beginning. I told him about old Scott,[30] and Jackson:[31] told him all I could think of about the Mississippi, and New Orleans, and Texas, and his own old Kentucky.

I tell you, it was a hard thing to condense the history of half a century into that talk with a sick man. And I do not now know what I told him—of emigration, and the means of it—of steamboats, and railroads, and telegraphs—of inventions, and books, and literature—of the colleges, and West Point, and the Naval School—but with the queerest interruptions that ever you heard. You see it was Robinson Crusoe asking all the accumulated questions of fifty-six years!

I remember he asked, all of a sudden, who was President now; and when I told him, he asked if Old Abe was General Benjamin Lincoln's son. He said he met old General Lincoln, when he was quite a boy himself, at some Indian treaty. I said no, that Old Abe was a Kentuckian like himself, but I could not tell him of what family; he had worked up from the ranks. "Good for him!" cried Nolan; "I am glad of that." Then I got talking about my visit to Washington. I told him about the Smithsonian, and the Capitol. I told him everything I could think of that would show the grandeur of his country and its prosperity.

And he drank it in and enjoyed it as I cannot tell you. He grew more and more silent, yet I never thought he was tired or faint. I gave him a glass of water, but he just wet his lips, and told me not to go away. Then he asked me to bring the Presbyterian Book of Public Prayer which lay there, and said, with a smile, that it would open at the right place—and so it did. There was his double red mark down the page; and I knelt down and read, and he repeated with me:

For ourselves and our country, O gracious God, we thank Thee, that, notwithstanding our manifold transgressions of Thy holy laws, Thou hast continued to us Thy marvelous kindness . . . and so to the end of that thanksgiving.

Then he turned to the end of the same book, and I read the words more familiar to me:

Most heartily we beseech Thee with Thy favor to behold and bless Thy servant, the President of the United States, and all others in authority.

---

29. Fulton: Robert Fulton (1765–1815), who invented the steamboat.
30. Scott: General Winfield Scott (1786–1866), who served in the War of 1812 and the Mexican War.
31. Jackson: Andrew Jackson (1767–1845), seventh President of the United States (1829–1837) and a general in the War of 1812.

"Danforth," said he, "I have repeated those prayers night and morning—it is now fifty-five years." And then he said he would go to sleep. He bent me down over him and kissed me; and he said, "Look in my Bible, Captain, when I am gone." And I went away.

But I had no thought it was the end. I thought he was tired and would sleep. I knew he was happy, and I wanted him to be alone.

But in an hour, when the doctor went in gently, he found Nolan had breathed his life away with a smile.

We looked in his Bible, and there was a slip of paper at the place where he had marked the text:

They desire a country, even a heavenly: where God is not ashamed to be called their God: for He hath prepared for them a city.[32]

On this slip of paper he had written:

Bury me in the sea; it has been my home, and I love it. But will not someone set up a stone for my memory at Fort Adams or at Orleans, that my disgrace may not be more than I ought to bear? Say on it:

In Memory of
PHILIP NOLAN,
*Lieutenant in the Army
of the United States.*
He loved his country as no other
man has loved her; but no man
deserved less at her hands.

---

32. They desire . . . a city: A passage from the Bible, Hebrews 11:16.

Guide for Responding

◆ LITERATURE AND YOUR LIFE

Reader's Response Did Nolan deserve the punishment he was given? Explain.

Thematic Focus In what way did the United States change during the years when Nolan was a prisoner?

Journal Writing Take on the character of Nolan and write a journal entry he might have written about his first week of exile.

☑ Check Your Comprehension

1. Who is the narrator of the story?
2. Why is Nolan brought to trial?
3. What rash words does Nolan utter when the judge asks him if he wishes to say anything?
4. What is Nolan's sentence?
5. What is Nolan's last wish?

◆ Critical Thinking

INTERPRET

1. How is it that Aaron Burr is able to win Nolan over so easily? **[Interpret]**
2. How does the narrator feel about Nolan's punishment? **[Draw Conclusions]**
3. How does Nolan change during the course of the story? **[Analyze]**

EVALUATE

4. Do you think the government should have pardoned Nolan years after the trial was over? Why or why not? **[Make a Judgment]**

APPLY

5. What epitaph, or gravestone inscription, would you write for Nolan? **[Relate]**

Meet the Author

Edward Everett Hale (1822–1909) was a clergyman, a teacher, and the author of several books. He was also a distant relative of Nathan Hale, one of the heroes of the American Revolution. Hale began writing stories when he was a boy. He later published his own newspaper.

After graduating from Harvard University and becoming a Unitarian minister, Hale continued writing short stories, essays, and novels. "The Man Without a Country" may be viewed as one of Hale's sermons, in which he passionately offers his views on patriotism.

CONNECTING LITERATURE TO SOCIAL STUDIES

Edward Everett Hale used historical facts to make "The Man Without a Country" realistic. He did his job well. When the story first appeared in a magazine in 1863, many readers believed it was true. In fact, decades after the story first appeared, it was still accepted as true by many people.

1. What details in the story might have led readers to believe it had really happened?
2. What can you learn about the United States Navy by reading this story?
3. What might have been the inspiration for this tale about traitors and patriotism?
4. What do the characters and events from the story tell you about "the young nation"?

 Idea Bank

Writing

1. **Letter** Write a letter from Philip Nolan to a friend or relative telling them about the sentence he has received.
2. **Newspaper Account** As a reporter present at Philip Nolan's trial, write a newspaper story describing the charges against Nolan and the sentence he received.
3. **Persuasive Essay** Write an essay either condemning Nolan's actions or excusing them. Use details from the story as support.

Speaking and Listening

4. **Conversation** Role-play a conversation between two sailors on one of the ships that kept Nolan imprisoned. Assume that the sailors know of his crimes and his sentence but are not clear about how the sentence is to be carried out. **[Performing Arts Link]**

5. **Oral Report** Choose a historical figure or event mentioned in the story to research for a report. Use an encyclopedia and other sources to find out about the person or event. Share your findings with the class in an oral report. **[Social Studies Link]**

Project

6. **Illustrated Scene** Do some research on the kind of ships on which Nolan was kept prisoner. Then, find out about the uniforms worn by members of the navy at the time the story takes place. Use this information to illustrate any scene from the story. Here are some scenes you might consider:
   • Nolan is sentenced.
   • Nolan talks to the people captured as slaves.
   • Nolan shows his stateroom to Danforth.
     [Art Link]

Further Reading, Listening, and Viewing

- Ken Burns and Dayton Duncan's documentary film *Lewis and Clarke: The Journey of the Corps of Discovery* gives an in-depth view of the expanding American frontier.
- Edward Everett Hale's *A New England Boyhood* tells of life in the early 1800's.
- Roger Brun's *Thomas Jefferson: World Leaders Past and Present* is about the third president of the United States, under whom Aaron Burr served as vice president.

Writing Process Workshop

You probably summarize things constantly—books, movies, television programs, sporting events. As a reader or a writer, you'll find summaries extremely useful. They present the most important elements of an item or event in a concise, detailed way. You can summarize stories, political or historical events, movies, plays, poems, or time periods. A summary doesn't attempt to capture the tone or style of the original piece—just what the piece is about. Write a summary of an article or a story you've recently read, or summarize a real-life event.

The following skills from this section's Writing Mini-Lessons will help you write your summary:

Writing Skills Focus

▶ **Use precise language** to make your summary accurate and exact. (See p. 350.)

▶ **Choose supporting details** to convey the main ideas of the original piece. (See p. 363.)

▶ **Use transitions** to make connections and relationships among the details clear and easy to follow. (See p. 375.)

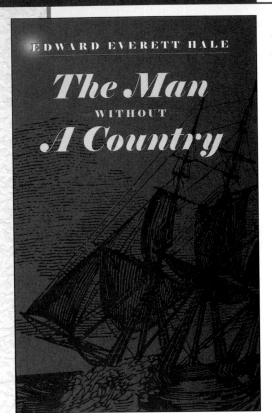

EDWARD EVERETT HALE

The Man
WITHOUT
A Country

MODEL FROM LITERATURE

On the death of Philip Nolan, who was known as "The Man Without a Country," the narrator decides that it is time to tell the exiled man's story. Nolan started out as a promising young officer stationed ① in New Orleans, but became infatuated with Aaron Burr's teachings and political schemes. ② When Burr was tried for treason, Nolan was court-martialed. At his trial, ③ he blurted out that he wished he would "never hear of the United States again." The outraged judge sentenced him to "have his wish fulfilled," and for the next fifty-six years, Nolan lived on U.S. government ships but was never again allowed to see, hear, or read about his country.

① Precise language like this gives the summary clarity.

② This detail is an important part of the original story.

③ Transitions like this one connect ideas.

Prewriting

Choose a Topic Summarize something you've seen, heard, or experienced that you'd like to share with a friend. Perhaps you've read a thriller, or seen an exciting movie or television documentary, or listened to a great concert that you want to tell your friends about. Any of those ideas would work, or you can use one of the topics in the box below.

> ### Topic Ideas
>
> - The last minutes of a significant ballgame
> - A lecture by a park ranger on wildlife
> - The biography of your personal hero

Choose Important Details Gather details for your summary. If you're writing a summary of a published work, reread the original, and jot down the most important details. If you're summarizing an event, re-create it in your mind. Then, write down the most exciting or significant details.

Use Precise Language Your summary should be to the point; each word should be exact and precise. To achieve that style, use specific nouns and active verbs.

> **Vague Noun:** He told the *man* to leave.
>
> **Specific Noun:** He told the *police officer* to leave.

Set Up a Chain of Events List the events to include in your summary, and organize the events chronologically. Use this chain of events as a model.

Drafting

Use an Introduction, Body, and Conclusion Give your summary an introduction, in which you reveal what you'll be summarizing; a body, which contains the essence of the summary; and a conclusion, in which you wrap up the summary with your personal views or insights.

Avoid Listing Events As you draft, don't simply list events. Instead, reweave the essential points in an interesting and entertaining way. Remember that this is a summary, not a list.

Use Transitions to Make Connections Transitional words offer guideposts to your reader; they connect your ideas. As you draft, include transitional words and phrases like *next, as a result,* and *surprisingly,* to keep your readers on track.

APPLYING LANGUAGE SKILLS: Verb Phrases With *Have*

When writing verb phrases or contractions containing the word *have,* avoid the common mistake of using the word *of* in place of *have.*

Incorrect:
He *should of* called first.

Correct:
He *should have* called first.

Correct:
He *should've* called first.

Practice Make contractions of each italicized verb phrase.

1. We *would have* traveled across the United States.
2. We *should have* checked the gas tank before we left.
3. We *could have* flown, but driving was cheaper and more fun.

Writing Application As you write your summary, be sure you write verb phrases and contractions containing *have* correctly.

Writer's Solution Connection Writing Lab

You may want to use the Cause-and-Effect Chain in the Exposition: Giving Information tutorial.

APPLYING LANGUAGE SKILLS:
Correcting Run-on Sentences

Run-on sentences occur when two or more sentences are written or punctuated as one. To correct, create separate sentences or combine the sentences with a conjunction.

Run-on: The whale watch was very exciting, we saw a mother and her two calves.

Correct: The whale watch was very exciting. We saw a mother and her two calves.

Correct: The whale watch was very exciting because we saw a mother and her two calves.

Practice On your paper, correct the run-on sentences.

1. We saw six whales we learned about ocean mammals.
2. Some kids got seasick I did not get sick.
3. A newborn whale weighs over five tons it drinks about 130 gallons of its mother's milk a day.

Writing Application Correct any run-on sentences you find in your draft.

Writer's Solution Connection Language Lab

For more practice correcting run-on sentences, complete the Run-on Sentences lesson in the Sentence Errors unit.

Revising

Use Transitions Review your draft. Have you clearly shown how major points are related to one another? Add transitions to make connections clear.

Time Order: *first, finally, next, then, after, when, following, while, during, meanwhile, immediately*

Logical Relationship: *therefore, consequently, for this reason, as a result of, since*

Concluding: *in short, to sum up, that is, therefore, in other words, in conclusion*

Review Writing Focus Points Review the Writing Skills Focus points on page 392, to make sure you've taken them into consideration in your summary.

Publishing and Presenting

Library Collect story summaries your classmates have written. Post them in the library for others to read.

Web Site Post your summary on a Web site that is dedicated to the topic of your summary.

REVISION MODEL

In this summary ^of "The Gift of the Magi," ① I'll ~~tell you about~~ [tells the story]

~~the story~~. Della is the girl in the story, and she's married to

Jim. ② ~~She is very friendly.~~ It's Christmas, and they don't have

enough money to buy each other presents. Della decides to

cut her ^hair and sell it to buy ~~this thing~~ for Jim's ^watch. [beautiful, long] [③ a chain] [pocket]

④ Meanwhile, Jim ~~does something with~~^ his watch to buy Della combs [⑤ pawns]

for her hair. It's ~~funny~~^ that they give up what they each [⑥ ironic]

treasured most for each other.

① Eliminate useless language; be concise.
② Delete unimportant details like this.
③ Include important details to make the meaning clear.
④ This time transition word connects ideas.
⑤ *Pawn* is more exact than *does something with*.
⑥ The exact word *ironic* conveys more than *funny* does.

Real-World Reading Skills Workshop

Strategies for Success

Identifying the main idea of an article will help you understand how the details work together to convey a single message. The main idea may be stated directly or implied. Use the following strategies to help you identify the main idea:

Check the Lead Sentence In an article, each paragraph may contain its own main idea, which is often stated in the lead sentence—or the first sentence—of the paragraph. As you read, you'll find details to support the main idea.

Look for Implied Main Ideas If the main idea is not directly stated, it will be implied. To identify implied main ideas, pause after you read each section and ask yourself these questions:

▶ What was that section about?
▶ Why did the writer include these details?
▶ How can I state the main idea of this section in one sentence?

Review the End of the Article The end of an article sometimes summarizes the main idea. If you find previously mentioned ideas repeated in this final paragraph, they are probably the main ideas of the article.

✔ *Here are situations in which finding the main idea is helpful:*
▶ *Reading a news story in a newspaper*
▶ *Reading a scientific article*
▶ *Reading an information sheet about a club*

Apply the Strategies

Read the article "Symbols of Freedom," and answer the questions that follow.

Symbols of Freedom

Ellis Island and the Statue of Liberty are two of the most important historical sites in our country. Ellis Island was used as an immigration center for over 60 years. More than 12 million people first entered the United States this way. These 12 million immigrants were greeted by the sight of the Statue of Liberty as they pulled into New York Harbor.

Imagine how breathtaking the sight of our Lady of Liberty must have been for those who risked everything to come to America. She represented to them the reasons they packed up their belongings, sold everything they had, and left their families. The opportunities that freedom entitled them to here could not be surpassed anywhere else on Earth!

1. In the first paragraph, is the main idea implied or stated directly? Explain.

2. Do any of the paragraphs have a lead sentence that states the main idea? If so, which one?

3. Use questions to determine the implied main idea of the second paragraph.

Conjunctions

Grammar Review

A **conjunction** joins words or groups of words. There are three types of conjunctions: **coordinating, correlative,** and **subordinating.**

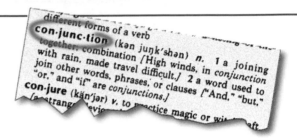

con·junc·tion (kən juŋk'shən) n. 1 a joining together; combination [High winds, in conjunction with rain, made travel difficult.] 2 a word used to join other words, phrases, or clauses ["And," "but," "or," and "if" are conjunctions.]
con·jure (kän'jər) v. to practice magic or witchcraft

Type	Examples	Use
Coordinating Conjunctions link words, phrases, or clauses that have the same function in a sentence (p. 362).	and, but, or, nor, for, yet, so	. . . I listened *and* felt *and* in the process had a picture of my country . . .
Correlative Conjunctions are used in pairs (p. 374). They link words, phrases, or clauses that have the same function.	both . . . and, either . . . or, neither . . . nor, not only . . . but also, whether . . . or	These were *not* just Italian values, or American, *but* universal values. . .
Subordinating Conjunctions connect two ideas by making one dependent on the other (p. 349).	after, although, as, because, before, if, since, when, where, while, unless, until	According to legend, *when* the weather was frigid, a ship captain and his daughter froze.

Practice 1 On your paper, write each conjunction. Then, label it as coordinating, correlative, or subordinating.

1. Not only was Sandburg a great poet, but he was also a journalist and historian.

2. Although yarns have always been told, they were especially popular during pioneer days.

3. Steinbeck and his dog Charley visited the Badlands of North Dakota.

4. "He displayed no fear, but seemed calm and serene. . . ."

5. "As an Italian American, I grew up believing that America is the greatest country on earth, and thankful that I was born here."

Practice 2 On your paper, join the sentences using the type of conjunction specified.

1. The sun went down. The Badlands were more comfortable. (subordinating)

2. Martin Luther King, Jr., did not approve of violence. King's followers did not approve of violence. (correlative)

3. The land of the United States belongs to all people. Many believe that it has not been divided fairly. (coordinating)

Grammar in Writing

✔ Decide on the relationship between or among ideas before choosing a conjunction.

✔ Avoid stringing together too many ideas or sentences with *and.*

PART 2 *An Album of Stories*

High Noon, New York, 1986, Chen Chi, The Butler Institute of American Art, Youngstown, Ohio

Guide for Reading

Meet the Authors:

J. Frank Dobie (1888–1964)

Texan J. Frank Dobie devoted himself to writing and teaching about the folklore and history of his native state. He described himself as "a historian of the longhorns, the mustangs, the coyote, and the other characters of the West." In 1964, President Johnson presented Dobie with the United States' highest civilian award, the Medal of Freedom, for his contributions to historic preservation and regional pride.

THE STORY BEHIND THE STORY

Dobie interviewed many Texans to gather stories for his collection *The Longhorns,* which tells amazing tales about these legendary Texas steers. "Sancho" is one of these tales. Dobie based the story of Sancho on a tale he heard from John Rigby, a trail boss on the Texas Range.

William Jay Smith (1918–   )

William Jay Smith wears many hats as a writer. The author of more than thirty books, he is a successful poet, critic, and translator. In his poetry, Smith vividly captures distinctively American settings. From 1968 to 1970, Smith served as Poet Laureate of the United States, sponsoring programs to promote reading and literature.

◆ LITERATURE AND YOUR LIFE

CONNECT YOUR EXPERIENCE

Homesickness strikes almost all of us at some point. Whether you're away for a night, for a week, or even for years, thoughts of home, with its comforting smells, sounds, and routines, sometimes overtake you. In "Sancho," you'll read about a very special animal who cures his homesickness in a unique and courageous way.

THEMATIC FOCUS: An Album of Stories

The story of "Sancho" was told to Dobie by someone who had heard the story. Ask yourself as you read: Why is "Sancho" worth telling over and over?

◆ Background for Understanding

SOCIAL STUDIES

"Sancho" takes place in the southwestern United States. Because most of the region is very dry, much of the vegetation is low to the ground and blooms only briefly. Dobie includes some of this unique vegetation in "Sancho." The spicy chiltipiquin peppers, the guajilla bush, and the fresh green mesquite bushes of spring play an important role in this story.

◆ Build Vocabulary

WORD ENDINGS: *-ent* AND *-ant*

The word endings *-ent* and *-ant* can be added to verbs to create adjectives. For example, *-ent,* added to the verb *persist,* which means "to refuse to give up," creates *persistent,* which means "in a stubborn way."

WORD BANK

Which word from the list means "an animal between one and two years old"? Check the Build Vocabulary box on page 401 to see if you chose correctly.

vigorous
yearling
persistent
accustomed

◆ Sancho ◆
The Closing of the Rodeo

Stampeded by Lightning, Frederic Remington

◆ Literary Focus

SETTING IN NONFICTION AND POETRY

As in a fictional short story, **setting** can play a key role in works of nonfiction that tell a story. For example, in "Sancho," the southwestern setting gives the piece its overall flavor and drives the events that occur. Similarly, in poetry, the setting can play a key role, especially in poems that tell a story or capture a moment in time.

◆ Reading Strategy

ENVISION SETTING

When you **envision a setting** while reading, picture it in your mind, like a movie. As you read details that describe setting in "Sancho" and "The Closing of the Rodeo," envision the time and place being described. You can use a sensory web like this one to help you use all of your senses as you envision a setting.

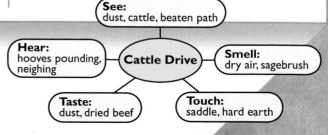

See: dust, cattle, beaten path

Hear: hooves pounding, neighing

Cattle Drive

Smell: dry air, sagebrush

Taste: dust, dried beef

Touch: saddle, hard earth

Sancho

J. Frank Dobie

The Wagon Boss, Charles M. Russell

A man by the name of Kerr had a little ranch on Esperanza Creek in Frio County, in the mesquite lands[1] south of San Antonio. He owned several good cow ponies, a few cattle, and a little bunch of goats that a dog guarded by day. At night they were shut up in a brush corral near the house. Three or four acres of land, fenced in with brush and poles, grew corn, watermelons and "kershaws"—except when the season was too drouthy.[2] A hand-dug well equipped with pulley wheel, rope and bucket furnished water for the establishment.

---

1. **mesquite** (mes kēt´) **lands** *n.*: Areas in which certain thorny trees and shrubs grow.
2. **drouthy** (drouth´ ē) *adj.*: Dried up due to drought— a lack of rain.

▲ **Critical Viewing** Based on the details in this painting, what can you tell about the job of herding cattle on a trail? **[Draw Conclusions]**

Kerr's wife was named María. They had no children. She was clean, thrifty, cheerful, always making pets of animals. She usually milked three or four cows and sometimes made cheese out of goat's milk.

Late in the winter of 1877, Kerr while riding over on the San Miguel found one of his cows dead in a bog-hole. Beside the cow was a mud-plastered little black-and-white paint bull calf less than a week old. It was too weak to run; perhaps other cattle had saved it from the coyotes. Kerr pitched his rope over its head, drew it up across the saddle in front of him, carried it home, and turned it over to María.

She had raised many dogie calves[3] and numerous colts captured from mustang mares. The first thing she did now was to pour milk from a bottle down the orphan's throat. With warm water she washed the caked mud off its body. But hand-raising a calf is no end of trouble. The next day Kerr rode around until he found a thrifty brown cow with a young calf. He drove them to the pen. By tying this cow's head up close to a post and hobbling her hind legs, Kerr and María forced her to let the orphan suckle. She did not give a cup of milk at this first sucking. Her calf was kept in the pen next day, and the poor thing bawled herself hoarse. María began feeding her some prickly pear[4] with the thorns singed off. After being tied up twice daily for a month, she adopted the orphan as a twin to her own offspring.

Now she was one of the household cows. Spring weeds came up plentifully and the guajilla brush put out in full leaf. When the brown cow came in about sundown and her two calves were released for their supper, it was a cheering sight to see them wiggle their tails while they guzzled milk.

The dogie was a <u>vigorous</u> little brute, and before long he was getting more milk than the brown cow's own calf. María called him Sancho, a Mexican name meaning "pet." She was especially fond of Sancho, and he grew to be especially fond of her.

She would give him the shucks wrapped around tamales. Then she began treating him to whole tamales, which are made of ground corn rolled around a core of chopped-up meat, this banana-shaped roll, done up in a shuck, then being steam-boiled. Sancho seemed not to mind the meat. As everybody who has eaten them knows, Mexican tamales are highly seasoned with pepper. Sancho seemed to like the seasoning.

In southern Texas the little chiltipiquin peppers,[5] red when ripe, grow wild in low, shaded places. Cattle never eat them, leaving them for the wild turkeys, mockingbirds and blue quail to pick off. Sometimes in the early fall wild turkeys used to gorge on them so avidly that their flesh became too peppery for human consumption. By eating tamales Sancho developed a taste for the little red peppers growing in the thickets along Esperanza Creek. In fact, he became a kind of chiltipiquin addict. He would hunt for the peppers.

Furthermore, the tamales gave him a tooth for corn in the ear. The summer after he became a <u>yearling</u> he began breaking through the brush fence that enclosed Kerr's corn patch. A forked stick had to be tied around his neck to prevent his getting through the fence. He had been branded and turned into a steer, but he was as strong as any young bull. Like many other pets, he was something of a nuisance. When he could not steal corn or was not humored with tamales, he was enormously contented with grass, mixed in summertime with the sweet mesquite beans. Now and then María gave him a lump of the brown *piloncillo* sugar,[6] from Mexico, that all the border country used.

Every night Sancho came to the ranch pen to sleep. His bed ground was near a certain mesquite tree just outside the gate. He spent hours every summer day in the shade of this mesquite. When it rained and other cattle drifted off, hunting fresh pasturage, Sancho stayed at home and drank at the well. He was strictly a home creature.

In the spring of 1880 Sancho was three years old and past, white of horn and as blocky of build as a long-legged Texas steer ever grew. Kerr's ranch lay in a big unfenced range grazed by the Shiner brothers. That spring they had a contract to deliver three herds of steers, each to number 2500 head, in Wyoming. Kerr was helping the Shiners

---

3. **dogie** (dō′ gē) **calves** *n.*: Motherless calves or strays.
4. **prickly pear**: A cactus plant with large flat oval stems, which bears pear-shaped fruit.
5. **chiltipiquin** (chil′ tē pē′ kwin) **peppers**: Peppers that are characterized by their hot and spicy flavor.

6. *piloncillo* (pē lōn′ sē yō) **sugar** *n.*: Unrefined sugar.

Cattle Stampede, Olaf C. Seltzer

▲ **Critical Viewing** What is the main impression conveyed in this painting of a cattle drive? **[Analyze]**

gather cattle, and, along with various other ranchers, sold them what steers he had.

Sancho was included. One day late in March the Shiner men road-branded him *7 Z* and put him in the first herd headed north. The other herds were to follow two or three days apart.

It was late in the afternoon when the "shaping up" of the herd was completed. It was watered and thrown out on open prairie ground to be bedded down. But Sancho had no disposition to lie down—there. He wanted to go back to that mesquite just outside the pen gate at the Kerr place on the Esperanza where he had without variation slept every night since he had been weaned. Perhaps he had in mind an evening tamale. He stood and roamed about on the south side of the herd. A dozen times during the night the men on guard had to drive him back. As reliefs were changed, word passed to keep an eye on that paint steer on the lower side.

When the herd started on next morning,

Sancho was at the tail end of it, often stopping and looking back. It took constant attention from one of the drag drivers to keep him moving. By the time the second night arrived, every hand in the outfit knew Sancho, by name and sight, as being the stubbornest and gentlest steer of the lot. About dark one of them pitched a loop over his horns and staked him to a bush. This saved bothering with his <u>persistent</u> efforts to walk off.

Daily when the herd was halted to graze, spreading out like a fan, the steers all eating their way northward, Sancho invariably pointed himself south. In his lazy way he grabbed many a mouthful of grass while the herd was moving. Finally, in some brush up on the Llano, after ten days of trailing, he dodged into freedom. On the second day following, one of the point men of the second Shiner herd saw him walking south, saw his *7 Z* road brand, rounded him in, and set him traveling north again. He became the chief drag animal of this herd. Somewhere north of the Colorado there was a run one night, and when morning came Sancho was missing. The other steers had held together; probably Sancho had not run at all. But he was picked up again, by the third Shiner herd coming on behind.

He took his <u>accustomed</u> place in the drag and continued to require special driving. He picked up in weight. He chewed his cud peacefully and slept soundly, but whenever he looked southward, which was often, he raised his head as if memory and expectation were stirring. The boys were all personally acquainted with him, and every night one of them would stake him.

One day the cattle balked and milled at a bank-full river. "Rope Old Sancho and lead him in," the boss ordered, "and we'll point the other cattle after him." Sancho led like a horse. The herd followed. As soon as he was released, he dropped back to the rear. After this, however, he was always led to the front when there was high water to cross.

By the time the herd got into No Man's Land, beyond Red River, the sand-hill plums and the low-running possum grapes were turning ripe. Pausing now and then to pick a little of the fruit, Sancho's driver saw the pet steer following his example.

Meantime the cattle were trailing, trailing, always north. For five hundred miles across Texas, counting the windings to find water and keep out of breaks, they had come. After getting into the Indian Territory, they snailed on across the Wichita, the South Canadian, the North Canadian, and the Cimarron. On into Kansas they trailed and across the Arkansas, around Dodge City, cowboy capital of the world, out of Kansas into Nebraska, over the wide, wide Platte, past the roaring cow town of Ogallala, up the North Platte, under the Black Hills, and then against the Big Horn Mountains. For two thousand miles, making ten or twelve miles a day, the Shiner herds trailed. They "walked with the grass." Slow, slow, they

moved. "Oh, it was a long and lonesome go"— as slow as the long drawn-out notes of "The Texas Lullaby," as slow as the night herder's song on a slow-walking horse:

> It's a whoop and a yea, get along my little
>   dogies,
> For camp is far away.
> It's a whoop and a yea and a-driving the
>   dogies,
> For Wyoming may be your new home.

When, finally, after listening for months, day and night, to the slow song of their motion, the "dogies" reached their "new home," Sancho was still halting every now and then to sniff southward for a whiff of the Mexican Gulf. The farther he got away from home, the less he seemed to like the change. He had never felt frost in September before. The Mexican peppers on the Esperanza were red ripe now.

The Wyoming outfit received the cattle. Then for a week the Texas men helped brand *C R* on their long sides before turning them loose on the new range. When Sancho's time came to be branded in the chute,[7] one of the Texans yelled out, "There goes my pet. Stamp that *C R* brand on him good and deep." Another one said, "The line riders had better watch for his tracks."

And now the Shiner men turned south, taking back with them their saddle horses and chuck wagons—and leaving Sancho behind. They made good time, but a blue norther was whistling at their backs when they turned the remuda[8] loose on the Frio River. After the "Cowboys' Christmas Ball" most of them settled down for a few weeks of winter sleep. They could rub tobacco juice in their eyes during the summer when they needed something in addition to night rides and runs to keep them awake.

Spring comes early down on the Esperanza. The mesquites were all in new leaf with that green so fresh and tender that the color seems to emanate into the sky. The bluebonnets and the pink phlox were sprinkling every hill and

---

◆ Build Vocabulary

persistent (pər sist´ ənt) *adj*.: Stubborn; persevering

accustomed (ə kus´ təmd) *adj*.: Customary; usual

7. **chute** (sho͞ot) *n*.: Narrow, high-walled device used to restrain cattle.
8. **remuda** (rə mo͞o´ də) *n*.: Group of extra saddle horses kept as a supply of remounts.

draw. The prickly pear was studded with waxy blossoms, and the glades were heavy with the perfume of white brush. It was a good season, and tallow weed and grass were coming together. It was time for the spring cow hunts and the putting up of herds for the annual drive north. The Shiners were at work.

"We were close to Kerr's cabin on Esperanza Creek," John Rigby told me, "when I looked across a pear flat and saw something that made me rub my eyes. I was riding with Joe Shiner, and we both stopped our horses."

"Do you see what I see?" John Rigby asked.

"Yes, but before I say, I'm going to read the brand," Joe Shiner answered.

They rode over. "You can hang me for a horse thief," John Rigby will tell, "if it wasn't that Sancho paint steer, four years old now, the Shiner *7 Z* road brand and the Wyoming *C R* range brand both showing on him as plain as boxcar letters."

The men rode on down to Kerr's.

"Yes," Kerr said, "Old Sancho got in about six weeks ago. His hoofs were worn mighty nigh down to the hair, but he wasn't lame. I thought María was going out of her senses, she was so glad to see him. She actually hugged him and she cried and then she begun feeding him hot tamales. She's made a batch of them nearly every day since, just to pet that steer. When she's not feeding him tamales, she's giving him *piloncillo*."

Sancho was slicking off and certainly did seem contented. He was coming up every night and sleeping at the gate, María said. She was nervous over the prospect of losing her pet, but Joe Shiner said that if that steer loved his home enough to walk back to it all the way from Wyoming, he wasn't going to drive him off again, even if he was putting up another herd for the *C R* owners.

As far as I can find out, Old Sancho lived right there on the Esperanza, now and then getting a tamale, tickling his palate with chili peppers in season, and generally staying fat on mesquite grass, until he died a natural death. He was one of the "walking Texas Longhorns."

*G*uide for Responding

◆ LITERATURE AND YOUR LIFE

Reader's Response Would you have enjoyed going on a cattle drive? Explain.

Thematic Focus What does the story of "Sancho" reveal about life in the United States?

Journal Writing In your journal, jot down your impressions of what it must have been like to go on a cattle drive.

☑ Check Your Comprehension

1. Why does María adopt Sancho as a pet?
2. What unusual traits does Sancho reveal while living on the ranch?
3. What finally happens to Sancho? Why does Joe Shiner agree to this decision?

◆ Critical Thinking

INTERPRET

1. How is Sancho different from other steer? **[Compare and Contrast]**
2. Find three examples of Sancho's humanlike personality. **[Connect]**
3. Dobie said that Sancho's story was the best range story he ever heard. Why do you think he liked the story so much? **[Interpret]**

EVALUATE

4. Why do you think writers often assign animals human characteristics? **[Assess]**

APPLY

5. Considering María's daily life, why would a pet be important to her? **[Hypothesize]**

The Closing of the Rodeo

William Jay Smith

The lariat[1] snaps; the cowboy rolls
    His pack, and mounts and rides away.
Back to the land the cowboy goes.

Plumes of smoke from the factory sway
5   In the setting sun. The curtain falls,
A train in the darkness pulls away.

Good-by, says the rain on the iron roofs.
    Good-by, say the barber poles.
Dark drum the vanishing horses' hooves.

---

1. **lariat** (lar′ ē it) *n.*: Rope used for tying or catching horses.

Beyond Literature

Science Connection

Animal Imprinting In "Sancho," a bull comes to regard himself as part of a human family. Certain newborn animals, like ducks and geese, have an instinct for "imprinting"—identifying as their mother the first thing they see. Although birds will almost always imprint on their mother, in the laboratory, birds can be imprinted on almost anything. Once a baby bird decides who its "mother" is, it will follow "her"—even if the real mother appears.

Cross-Curricular Activity
Write a song about an animal who chooses some unlikely object as its mother.

Guide for Responding

◆ LITERATURE AND YOUR LIFE

Reader's Response Which image in the poem affects you most strongly?

Thematic Focus Why do you think Smith selected this topic for a poem?

☑ Check Your Comprehension
1. What event is described in the poem?
2. Where has the rodeo been?
3. Where does the cowboy go?

◆ Critical Thinking

INTERPRET
1. Will the rodeo come back to the town? **[Speculate]**
2. Personification is assigning human feelings to nonhuman things. How does Smith use this technique? **[Classify]**

COMPARE LITERARY WORKS
3. Do you think that J. Frank Dobie would have enjoyed reading "The Closing of the Rodeo"? Why or why not? **[Speculate]**

Guide for Responding (continued)

◆ Reading Strategy

ENVISION SETTING

When you **envision the setting** of a story or poem, you use your senses to put yourself in the time and place in which the events occur.

1. Describe two major settings presented in "Sancho." What details bring these settings to life?
2. If you were to make a short film to accompany a reading of "The Closing of the Rodeo," what images would you choose? Where would you film?

◆ Build Grammar Skills

SUBJECTS AND PREDICATES

The **subject** of a sentence tells who or what the sentence is about. The **predicate** tells what the subject is or does.

> $\overset{S}{\text{A man by the name of Kerr}} \mid \overset{P}{\text{had a little ranch}}$ on Esperanza Creek. . . .

The **simple subject** is the main noun or pronoun in the complete subject. The **simple predicate** is the verb or verb phrase in the predicate.

> $\overset{SS}{\text{The Wyoming outfit}} \mid \overset{SP}{\text{received the cattle.}}$

Practice Copy the following sentences on your paper. Underline each subject once and each predicate twice. Circle each simple subject and simple predicate.

1. The steer arrived in Wyoming after the long trek.
2. Late that night, I heard a loud noise.
3. One of the new arrivals had escaped.
4. Our moonlit chase continued for an hour.
5. Finally, we cornered the frightened animal.

Writing Application Complete each sentence by adding the element shown in parentheses.

1. The old steer _____?_____. (predicate)
2. _____?_____ arrived at our ranch. (subject)
3. Then, _____?_____ bought a steer. (simple subject)
4. He _____?_____ the steer home in an open truck. (simple predicate)

◆ Literary Focus

SETTING IN NONFICTION AND POETRY

A setting is the time and place in which a literary work takes place. In each of these works, the **setting** plays an important role. As in a short story, the setting can have a huge impact on the events described and the mood or atmosphere of the work.

1. (a) Identify the setting of "Sancho." (b) Describe three details that helped you to identify the setting.
2. (a) How would "Sancho" be different if it were set in a different place? (b) If it were set in modern times?
3. (a) Which details in "The Closing of the Rodeo" reveal its setting? (b) In what ways does the setting support the meaning of the poem?

◆ Build Vocabulary

USING THE WORD ENDINGS -ent AND -ant

The word endings -ent and -ant can be added to verbs to create adjectives. Change each of these verbs to an adjective by adding -ant or -ent. Use a dictionary to check which spelling to use.

1. resist 2. exist 3. defend 3. attend

SPELLING STRATEGY

Accustomed and *accept* begin with *acc,* which can have the sound of *ak* or *aks.* Rearrange the letters at the end of each sentence to make a word beginning with *acc* that completes the sentence.

1. It was difficult to _____?_____ all of the steers on the drive. (c a d m a o t m c o e)
2. The rancher _____?_____ the job reluctantly. (e c t a d e c p)
3. The steers were _____?_____ to living on a ranch. (a e s m c o d u t c)

USING THE WORD BANK

On your paper, match the Word Bank words in Column A with the words and phrases in Column B that are most nearly the same in meaning.

Column A	Column B
1. vigorous	a. strong and lively
2. yearling	b. young animal
3. persistent	c. without giving up
4. accustomed	d. used to

Build Your Portfolio

 ## Idea Bank

Writing

1. **Letter** Imagine that you are María in "Sancho." Then, write a letter to a friend describing Sancho's return.

2. **Character Profile** Write a character profile of Sancho in which you describe his main characteristics. Support your points with details from the selection.

3. **Persuasive Essay** "Sancho" is said to be a true story. In a brief persuasive essay, explain whether you believe the story to be true. Use story details to support your views.

Speaking and Listening

4. **Oral Presentation** Memorize "The Closing of the Rodeo" and practice reciting it. You may wish to use a tape recorder to record your practice and refine your delivery. When you are ready, present the poem to your class. **[Performing Arts Link]**

5. **Tour Guide Speech** Imagine that you are a tour guide at a Texas ranch. Prepare a brief introduction that you would provide to give visitors an idea of ranch life. You may want to research ranches and Texas livestock. Present your speech to the class, and answer questions at the end. **[Career Link]**

Projects

6. **Poster** Create a poster advertising the opening of a new rodeo. Include specific details that will attract customers. **[Art Link]**

7. **Historic Newspaper [Group Activity]** Work with a team to create a newspaper from 1880, the year in which Sancho returned home. Some team members should act as reporters who find stories from 1880 to write about, including Sancho's tale. Other team members can edit and lay out the newspaper. **[Social Studies Link]**

 ## Writing Mini-Lesson

Report

The settings of "Sancho" and "The Closing of the Rodeo" make a great start to a research project. Do research about cattle drives or rodeos, and write a report to share your findings with the class.

Writing Skills Focus: Elaborate With Factual Details

The key to a successful report is the careful choice of **factual details** that convey a complete and accurate picture of the subject. Notice the details italicized in this example:

Model

Cattle drives were *long* and *grueling journeys. Most drives began in Texas* and *ended in the Midwest,* covering sometimes as much as *2,000 miles* of rugged terrain. A drive commonly took more than *six months.*

Prewriting Choose your topic. Then, gather information about your topic from a variety of sources, including nonfiction books, historic journals, encyclopedias, and Web sites. Organize your notes into an outline before you begin to write.

Drafting Follow your outline or refer to your notes as you draft. Then, weave together the facts you've gathered during your research.

Revising Work with a classmate to evaluate your draft. Ask your partner to identify unclear or vague sentences, as well as statements that should be elaborated with additional facts.

> ◆ **Grammar Application**
> Make sure that each sentence has both a subject and a predicate. If a sentence is missing one part, you have a sentence error—a fragment.

Guide for Reading

Meet the Authors:

Jesse Stuart (1906–1984)

Poet and novelist Jesse Stuart grew up in rural surroundings in eastern Kentucky. After high school, he worked for a circus and a steel mill before attending college. He then became a teacher and school superintendent. Stuart is known for his children's books, including *The Red Mule.* Although he received many awards and honors in his lifetime, he was most proud of being a teacher. "First, last, always, I am a school teacher," he said. "I love the firing line of the classroom."

Gish Jen (1956–   )

The daughter of Chinese immigrants, Gish Jen grew up in Yonkers and Scarsdale, New York, communities that had very few Asian Americans. Jen began writing fiction as an undergraduate at Harvard. After teaching English in China, she entered the University of Iowa writing program, where she wrote "The White Umbrella." Her first novel, *Typical American,* was published in 1991, and her second, *Mona in the Promised Land,* in 1996. Both of these novels deal with the clash of cultures that Asian Americans face in the United States.

◆ LITERATURE AND YOUR LIFE

CONNECT YOUR EXPERIENCE

Some accomplishments are rewarded with trophies. Others are more personal, bringing only a smile to the face of the person who's achieved something. Think for a moment about something special you accomplished and how it made you feel. In the following stories, you'll learn of two young people who strive to succeed at different things.

THEMATIC FOCUS: An Album of Stories

As you read these stories, think about what they reveal about people's needs to achieve success.

◆ Background for Understanding

SCIENCE

In "A Ribbon for Baldy," the main character plants corn for his school science project. On a small farm like the one in the story, planting and harvesting were done by hand rather than by machines. To prepare for planting, the land is cleared to a depth of about eight inches, plowed, and fertilized. Corn seeds are planted in early spring, most often in long rows. The growing season is four to six months, so the narrator's corn, planted in April, would be ready to harvest in August.

◆ Build Vocabulary

WORD ROOTS: -cred-

The narrator of "The White Umbrella" tries to convince her piano teacher of "the credibility of [her] lie." The word *credibility* comes from the root -cred-, which means "believe." Understanding the meaning of the root will help you figure out that *credibility* means "believability."

WORD BANK

Which word from the list is an adverb? Check the Build Vocabulary box on page 416 to see if you chose correctly.

surveyed
envelop
bargain
discreet
credibility
constellation
anxiously
revelation

◆ Literary Focus

CHARACTER TRAITS

Character traits are the qualities that make up a character's personality. For example, a character may be generous, clever, or stubborn. Writers reveal characters' traits through their actions, dialogue, and other characters' descriptions of and reactions to them. In "A Ribbon for Baldy," for example, this statement reveals the main character's trait of determination: "Every day I thought about my project for the General Science class."

◆ Reading Strategy

PREDICT

Understanding a character's traits can help you make **predictions,** or educated guesses, about what will happen in a story. Your predictions may also be guided by your own experiences in similar situations or by hints that the author provides. Predicting gets you involved in a story. As you read these two stories, compare your predictions with the actual outcomes. Fill out a chart like the one below to record your predictions and the actual outcomes.

Prediction	Based on	Outcome
The girls will find out where their mother works. →	"For weeks we wondered what kind of work she was doing." →	

A Ribbon for Baldy

Jesse Stuart

The day Professor Herbert started talking about a project for each member of our General Science class, I was more excited than I had ever been. I wanted to have an outstanding project. I wanted it to be greater, to be more unusual than those of my classmates. I wanted to do something worthwhile, and something to make them respect me.

I'd made the best grade in my class in General Science. I'd made more yardage, more tackles and carried the football across the goal line more times than any player on my team. But making good grades and playing rugged football hadn't made them forget that I rode a mule to school, that I had worn my mother's shoes the first year and that I slipped away at the noon hour so no one would see me eat fat pork between slices of corn bread.

Every day I thought about my project for the General Science class. We had to have our project by the end of the school year and it was now January.

In the classroom, in study hall and when I did odd jobs on my father's 50 acres, I thought about my project. But it wouldn't come to me like an algebra problem or memorizing a poem. I couldn't think of a project that would help my father and mother to support us. One that would be good and useful.

"If you set your mind on something and keep on thinking about it, the idea will eventually come," Professor Herbert told us when Bascom Wythe complained about how hard it was to find a project.

One morning in February I left home in a white cloud that had settled over the deep valleys. I could not see an object ten feet in front of me in this mist. I crossed the pasture into the orchard and the mist began to thin. When I reached the ridge road, the light thin air was clear of mist. I looked over the sea of rolling white clouds. The tops of the dark winter hills jutted up like little islands.

I have to ride a mule, but not one of my classmates lives in a prettier place, I thought, as I surveyed my world. Look at Little Baldy! What a pretty island in the sea of clouds. A thin ribbon of cloud seemed to envelop cone-shaped Little Baldy from bottom to top like the new rope Pa had just bought for the windlass[1] over our well.

Then, like a flash—the idea for my project came to me. And what an idea it was! I'd not

---

1. **windlass** (wind´ ləs) *n*.: Device for raising and lowering a bucket on a rope.

tell anybody about it! I wouldn't even tell my father, but I knew he'd be for it. Little Baldy wrapped in the white coils of mist had given me the idea for it.

I was so happy I didn't care who laughed at me, what anyone said or who watched me eat fat meat on corn bread for my lunch. I had an idea and I knew it was a wonderful one.

"I've got something to talk over with you," I told Pa when I got home. "Look over there at that broom-sedge[2] and the scattered pines on Little Baldy. I'd like to burn the broom-sedge and briers and cut the pines and farm that this summer."

We stood in our barnlot and looked at Little Baldy.

"Yes, I've been thinkin' about clearin' that hill up someday," Pa said.

"Pa, I'll clear up all this south side and you clear up the other side," I said. "And I'll plow all of it and we'll get it in corn this year."

"Now this will be some undertakin'," he said. "I can't clear that land up and work six days a week on the railroad section. But if you will clear up the south side, I'll hire Bob Lavender to do the other side."

"That's a bargain," I said.

That night while the wind was still and the broom-sedge and leaves were dry, my father and I set fire all the way around the base. Next morning Little Baldy was a dark hill jutting high into February's cold, windy sky.

Pa hired Bob Lavender to clear one portion and I started working on the other. I worked early of mornings before I went to school. I hurried home and worked into the night.

Finn, my ten-year-old brother, was big enough to help me saw down the scattered

▲ **Critical Viewing** How much effort do you think it would take to plant and harvest a cornfield like this one? [Draw Conclusions]

◆ **Build Vocabulary**

surveyed (sŭr vād´) v.: Looked over in a careful way; examined; inspected

envelop (en vel´ əp) v.: To wrap up; cover completely

bargain (bär´ gən) n.: Something bought, offered, or sold at a price favorable to the buyer

---

2. **broom-sedge** (broom´ sej) n.: Coarse grass used in making brooms.

▲ **Critical Viewing** Which area of this terrain is cleared for planting? How can you tell? **[Deduce]**

pines with a crosscut.[3] With a handspike I started the logs rolling and they rolled to the base of Little Baldy.

By middle March, I had my side cleared. Bob Lavender had finished his too. We burned the brush and I was ready to start plowing.

By April 15th I had plowed all of Little Baldy. My grades in school had fallen off some. Bascom Wythe made the highest mark in General Science and he had always wanted to pass me in this subject. But I let him make the grades.

◆ **Reading Strategy**
Predict whether or not the boy's plan will succeed.

---

3. crosscut (krôs´ kut) *n.*: Saw that cuts across the grain of wood.

If my father had known what I was up to, he might not have let me do it. But he was going early to work on the railway section and he never got home until nearly dark. So when I laid Little Baldy off to plant him in corn, I started at the bottom and went around and around this high cone-shaped hill like a corkscrew. I was three days reaching the top. Then, with a hand planter, I planted the corn on moonlit nights.

When I showed my father what I'd done, he looked strangely at me. Then he said, "What made you do a thing like this? What's behind all of this?"

"I'm going to have the longest corn row in the world," I said. "How long do you think it is, Pa?"

"That row is over 20 miles," Pa said, laughing.

Finn and I measured the corn row with a rod pole and it was 23.5 miles long.

When it came time to report on our projects and I stood up in class and said I had a row of corn on our hill farm 23.5 miles long, everybody laughed. But when I told how I got the idea and how I had worked to accomplish my project, everybody was silent.

Professor Herbert and the General Science class hiked to my home on a Saturday in early May when the young corn was pretty and green in the long row. Two newspapermen from a neighboring town came too, and a photographer took pictures of Little Baldy and his ribbon of corn. He took pictures of me, of my home and parents and also of Professor Herbert and my classmates.

When the article and pictures were published, a few of my classmates got a little jealous of me but not one of them ever laughed at me again. And my father and mother were the proudest two parents any son could ever hope to have.

Beyond Literature

Science Connection

Corn Crops Corn is a type of grass similar to wheat, rice, oats, and barley. Most varieties of corn grow in rich, dry soil. The crops are planted when the soil temperature is about 55 degrees Fahrenheit—which occurs around April or May, although states with warmer climates, such as Texas, may plant earlier. Harvesting begins when the water content of a mature kernel has dropped to 28 percent. Corn production in the United States provides two fifths of the world's corn supply.

Cross-Curricular Activity

Look at various food products in your kitchen. Create a list of every product that lists corn as an ingredient. Compare your list with those of other students.

Guide for Responding

◆ LITERATURE AND YOUR LIFE

Reader's Response What did you admire about the boy in this story?

Thematic Focus To whom would you recommend this story? Why?

Journal Writing Describe any contests you've entered in a brief journal entry.

☑ Check Your Comprehension

1. What does the boy have to decide at the beginning of the story?
2. Who or what is Little Baldy?
3. What kinds of preparations does the boy have to make in order to begin his project?
4. Does the boy succeed in his project?

◆ Critical Thinking

INTERPRET

1. Why does the boy feel he has to win the respect of his classmates? **[Analyze]**
2. Why does the boy keep his project a secret from his father? **[Infer]**
3. When the boy explains his project to the class, why are they silent? **[Draw Conclusions]**

EVALUATE

4. Were the boy's efforts to complete the project worth it? **[Make a Judgment]**

APPLY

5. What do you think the boy might have done if weather conditions had ruined the corn he planted? **[Hypothesize]**

The White
Umbrella

Gish Jen

Girl in Car Window, Winson Trang. Courtesy of the artist

W hen I was twelve, my mother went to work without telling me or my little sister.

"Not that we need the second income." The lilt of her accent drifted from the kitchen up to the top of the stairs, where Mona and I were listening.

"No," said my father, in a barely audible voice. "Not like the Lee family."

The Lees were the only other Chinese family in town. I remembered how sorry my parents had felt for Mrs. Lee when she started waitressing downtown the year before; and so when my mother began coming home late, I didn't say anything, and tried to keep Mona from saying anything either.

"But why shouldn't I?" she argued. "Lots of people's mothers work."

"Those are American people," I said.

"So what do you think we are? I can do the pledge of allegiance with my eyes closed."

Nevertheless, she tried to be <u>discreet</u>; and if my mother wasn't home by 5:30, we would start cooking by ourselves, to make sure dinner would be on time. Mona would wash the vegetables and put on the rice; I would chop.

For weeks we wondered what kind of work she was doing. I imagined that she was selling perfume, testing dessert recipes for the local newspaper. Or maybe she was working for the florist. Now that she had learned to drive, she might be delivering boxes of roses to people.

"I don't think so," said Mona as we walked to our piano lesson after school. "She would've hit something by now."

A gust of wind littered the street with leaves.

▲ **Critical Viewing** What inferences might you make about this story based on the painting above? **[Infer]**

"Maybe we better hurry up," she went on, looking at the sky. "It's going to pour."

"But we're too early." Her lesson didn't begin until 4:00, mine until 4:30, so we usually tried to walk as slowly as we could. "And anyway, those aren't the kind of clouds that rain. Those are cumulus clouds."[1]

We arrived out of breath and wet.

"Oh, you poor, poor dears," said old Miss Crosman. "Why don't you call me the next time it's like this out? If your mother won't drive you, I can come pick you up."

"No, that's okay," I answered. Mona wrung her hair out on Miss Crosman's rug. "We just couldn't get the roof of our car to close, is all. We took it to the beach last summer and got sand in the mechanism." I pronounced this last word carefully, as if the credibility of my lie depended on its middle syllable. "It's never been the same." I thought for a second. "It's a convertible."

"Well then make yourselves at home." She exchanged looks with Eugenie Roberts, whose lesson we were interrupting. Eugenie smiled good-naturedly. "The towels are in the closet across from the bathroom."

Huddling at the end of Miss Crosman's nine-foot leatherette couch, Mona and I watched Eugenie play. She was a grade ahead of me and, according to school rumor, had a boyfriend in high school. I believed it. . . . She had auburn hair, blue eyes, and, I noted with a particular pang, a pure white folding umbrella.

"I can't see," whispered Mona.

"So clean your glasses."

"My glasses *are* clean. You're in the way."

I looked at her. "They look dirty to me."

"That's because *your* glasses are dirty."

Eugenie came bouncing to the end of her piece.

"Oh! Just stupendous!" Miss Crosman hugged her, then looked up as Eugenie's mother walked in. "Stupendous!" she said again. "Oh! Mrs. Roberts! Your daughter has a gift, a real gift. It's an honor to teach her."

Mrs. Roberts, radiant with pride, swept her daughter out of the room as if she were royalty, born to the piano bench. Watching the way Eugenie carried herself, I sat up, and concentrated so hard on sucking in my stomach that I did not realize until the Robertses were gone that Eugenie had left her umbrella. As Mona began to play, I jumped up and ran to the window, meaning to call to them—only to see their brake lights flash then fade at the stop sign at the corner. As if to allow them passage, the rain had let up; a quivering sun lit their way.

The umbrella glowed like a scepter on the blue carpet while Mona, slumping over the keyboard, managed to eke out[2] a fair rendition of a catfight. At the end of the piece, Miss Crosman asked her to stand up.

"Stay right there," she said, then came back a minute later with a towel to cover the bench. "You must be cold," she continued. "Shall I call your mother and have her bring over some dry clothes?"

"No," answered Mona. "She won't come because she . . ."

"She's too busy," I broke in from the back of the room.

"I see." Miss Crosman sighed and shook her head a little. "Your glasses are filthy, honey," she said to Mona. "Shall I clean them for you?"

Sisterly embarrassment seized me. Why hadn't Mona wiped her lenses when I told her to? As she resumed abuse of the piano, I stared at the umbrella. I wanted to open it, twirl it around by its slender silver handle; I wanted to dangle it from my wrist on the way to school the way the

◆ **Literary Focus**
What does this passage reveal about the narrator's character traits?

---

1. **cumulus** (kyōō' myōō ləs) **clouds** n.: Fluffy, white clouds that usually indicate fair weather.

◆ **Build Vocabulary**

discreet (di skrēt') *adj.*: Careful about what one says or does; prudent

credibility (kred' ə bil' ə tē) n.: Believability

other girls did. I wondered what Miss Crosman would say if I offered to bring it to Eugenie at school tomorrow. She would be impressed with my consideration for others; Eugenie would be pleased to have it back; and I would have possession of the umbrella for an entire night. I looked at it again, toying with the idea of asking for one for Christmas. I knew, however, how my mother would react.

"Things," she would say. "What's the matter with a raincoat? All you want is things, just like an American."

Sitting down for my lesson, I was careful to keep the towel under me and sit up straight.

"I'll bet you can't see a thing either," said Miss Crosman, reaching for my glasses. "And you can relax, you poor dear." She touched my chest, in an area where she never would have touched Eugenie Roberts. "This isn't a boot camp."[3]

When Miss Crosman finally allowed me to start playing I played extra well, as well as I possibly could. See, I told her with my fingers. You don't have to feel sorry for me.

"That was wonderful," said Miss Crosman. "Oh! Just wonderful."

An entire <u>constellation</u> rose in my heart.

"And guess what," I announced proudly. "I have a surprise for you."

Then I played a second piece for her, a much more difficult one that she had not assigned.

"Oh! That was stupendous," she said without hugging me. "Stupendous! You are a genius, young lady. If your mother had started you younger, you'd be playing like Eugenie Roberts by now!"

I looked at the keyboard, wishing that I had still a third, even more difficult piece to play for her. I wanted to tell her that I was the school spelling bee champion, that I wasn't ticklish, that I could do karate.

"My mother is a concert pianist," I said.

She looked at me for a long moment, then finally, without saying anything, hugged me. I didn't say anything about bringing the umbrella to Eugenie at school.

The steps were dry when Mona and I sat down to wait for my mother.

"Do you want to wait inside?" Miss Crosman looked <u>anxiously</u> at the sky.

"No," I said. "Our mother will be here any minute."

"In a while," said Mona.

"Any minute," I said again, even though my mother had been at least twenty minutes late every week since she started working.

According to the church clock across the street we had been waiting twenty-five minutes when Miss Crosman came out again.

"Shall I give you ladies a ride home?"

"No," I said. "Our mother is coming any minute."

"Shall I at least give her a call and remind her you're here? Maybe she forgot about you."

"I don't think she *forgot*," said Mona.

"Shall I give her a call anyway? Just to be safe?"

"I bet she already left," I said. "How could she forget about us?"

Miss Crosman went in to call.

"There's no answer," she said, coming back out.

"See, she's on her way," I said.

"Are you sure you wouldn't like to come in?"

"No," said Mona.

"Yes," I said. I pointed at my sister. "She meant yes too. She meant no, she wouldn't like to go in."

Miss Crosman looked at her watch. "It's 5:30 now, ladies. My pot roast will be coming

◆ **Literature and Your Life**

If you were in the narrator's position, would you have accepted a ride from Miss Crosman? Why or why not?

---

3. **boot camp:** Place where soldiers receive basic training and are disciplined severely.

◆ **Build Vocabulary**

constellation (kän′ stə lā′ shən) *n.*: Group of stars named after, and thought to resemble, an object, an animal, or a mythological character in outline

anxiously (aŋk′ shəs lē) *adv.*: In a worried way

out in fifteen minutes. Maybe you'd like to come in and have some then?"

"My mother's almost here," I said. "She's on her way."

We watched and watched the street. I tried to imagine what my mother was doing; I tried to imagine her writing messages in the sky, even though I knew she was afraid of planes. I watched as the branches of Miss Crosman's big willow tree started to sway; they had all been trimmed to exactly the same height off the ground, so that they looked beautiful, like hair in the wind.

It started to rain.

"Miss Crosman is coming out again," said Mona.

"Don't let her talk you into going inside," I whispered.

"Why not?"

"Because that would mean Mom isn't really coming any minute."

"But she isn't," said Mona. "She's *working.*"

"Shhh! Miss Crosman is going to hear you."

"She's working! She's working! She's working!"

I put my hand over her mouth, but she licked it, and so I was wiping my hand on my wet dress when the front door opened.

"We're getting even *wetter,* " said Mona right away. "Wetter and wetter."

"Shall we all go in?" Miss Crosman pulled Mona to her feet. "Before you young ladies catch pneumonia? You've been out here an hour already."

"We're *freezing.*" Mona looked up at Miss Crosman. "Do you have any hot chocolate? We're going to catch *pneumonia.*"

"I'm not going in," I said. "My mother's coming any minute."

"Come on," said Mona. "Use your *noggin.*"[4]

"Any minute."

"Come on, Mona," Miss Crosman opened the door. "Shall we get you inside first?"

"See you in the hospital," said Mona as she went in. "See you in the hospital with pneumonia."

I stared out into the empty street. The rain was pricking me all over; I was cold; I wanted to go inside. I wanted to be able to let myself go inside. If Miss Crosman came out again, I decided, I would go in.

She came out with a blanket and the white umbrella.

I could not believe that I was actually holding the umbrella, opening it. It sprang up by itself as if it were alive, as if that were what it wanted to do—as if it belonged in my hands, above my head. I stared up at the network of silver spokes, then spun the umbrella around and around and around. It was so clean and white that it seemed to glow, to illuminate everything around it.

"It's beautiful," I said.

Miss Crosman sat down next to me, on one end of the blanket. I moved the umbrella over so that it covered that too. I could feel the rain on my left shoulder and shivered. She put her arm around me.

"You poor, poor dear."

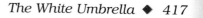

▲ **Critical Viewing** Are the girls in the photograph playing the piano in earnest or just having fun? Explain. [**Make a Judgment**]

4. **Use your *noggin*** (näg´ in): Informal expression for "use your head" or "think."

I knew that I was in store for another bolt of sympathy, and braced myself by staring up into the umbrella.

"You know, I very much wanted to have children when I was younger," she continued.

"You did?"

She stared at me a minute. Her face looked dry and crusty, like day-old frosting.

"I did. But then I never got married."

I twirled the umbrella around again.

"This is the most beautiful umbrella I have ever seen," I said. "Ever, in my whole life."

◆ **Reading Strategy**
Do you think the narrator will get to keep the umbrella? Why or why not?

"Do you have an umbrella?"

"No. But my mother's going to get me one just like this for Christmas."

"Is she? I tell you what. You don't have to wait until Christmas. You can have this one."

"But this one belongs to Eugenie Roberts," I protested. "I have to give it back to her tomorrow in school."

"Who told you it belongs to Eugenie? It's not Eugenie's. It's mine. And now I'm giving it to you, so it's yours."

"It is?"

She hugged me tighter. "That's right. It's all yours."

"It's mine?" I didn't know what to say. "Mine?" Suddenly I was jumping up and down in the rain. "It's beautiful! Oh! It's beautiful!" I laughed.

Miss Crosman laughed too, even though she was getting all wet.

"Thank you, Miss Crosman. Thank you very much. Thanks a zillion. It's beautiful. It's *stupendous!*"

"You're quite welcome," she said.

"Thank you," I said again, but that didn't seem like enough. Suddenly I knew just what she wanted to hear. "I wish you were my mother."

Right away I felt bad.

"You shouldn't say that," she said, but her face was opening into a huge smile as the lights of my mother's car cautiously turned the corner. I quickly collapsed the umbrella and put it up my skirt, holding onto it from the outside, through the material.

"Mona!" I shouted into the house. "Mona! Hurry up! Mom's here! I told you she was coming!"

Then I ran away from Miss Crosman, down to the curb. Mona came tearing up to my side as my mother neared the house. We both backed up a few feet, so that in case she went onto the curb, she wouldn't run us over.

"But why didn't you go inside with Mona?" my mother asked on the way home. She had taken off her own coat to put over me, and had the heat on high.

"She wasn't using her noggin," said Mona, next to me in the back seat.

"I should call next time," said my mother. "I just don't like to say where I am."

That was when she finally told us that she was working as a check-out clerk in the A&P. She was supposed to be on the day shift, but the other employees were unreliable, and her boss had promised her a promotion if she would stay until the evening shift filled in.

For a moment no one said anything. Even Mona seemed to find the revelation disappointing.

"A promotion already!" she said, finally.

I listened to the windshield wipers.

"You're so quiet." My mother looked at me in the rear view mirror. "What's the matter?"

"I wish you would quit," I said after a moment.

She sighed. "The Chinese have a saying: one beam cannot hold the roof up."

"But Eugenie Roberts's father supports their family."

She sighed once more. "Eugenie Roberts's father is Eugenie Roberts's father," she said.

As we entered the downtown area, Mona started leaning hard against me every time the car turned right, trying to push me over. Remembering what I had said to Miss Crosman, I tried to maneuver the umbrella under my leg so she wouldn't feel it.

"What's under your skirt?" Mona wanted to know as we came to a traffic light. My mother, watching us in the rear view mirror again, rolled slowly to a stop.

"What's the matter?" she asked.

"There's something under her skirt!" said Mona, pulling at me.

"Under her skirt?"

Meanwhile, a man crossing the street started to yell at us. "Who do you think you are, lady?" he said. "You're blocking the whole crosswalk."

We all froze. Other people walking by stopped to watch.

"Didn't you hear me?" he went on, starting to thump on the hood with his fist. "Don't you speak English?"

My mother began to back up, but the car behind us honked. Luckily, the light turned green right after that. She sighed in relief.

"What were you saying, Mona?" she asked.

We wouldn't have hit the car behind us that hard if he hadn't been moving too, but as it was our car bucked violently, throwing us all first back and then forward.

"Uh oh," said Mona when we stopped. "*Another* accident."

I was relieved to have attention diverted from the umbrella. Then I noticed my mother's head, tilted back onto the seat. Her eyes were closed.

"Mom!" I screamed. "Mom! Wake up!"

She opened her eyes. "Please don't yell," she said. "Enough people are going to yell already."

"I thought you were dead," I said, starting to cry. "I thought you were dead."

She turned around, looked at me intently, then put her hand to my forehead.

"Sick," she confirmed. "Some kind of sick is giving you crazy ideas."

As the man from the car behind us started tapping on the window, I moved the umbrella away from my leg. Then Mona and my mother were getting out of the car. I got out after them; and while everyone else was inspecting the damage we'd done, I threw the umbrella down a sewer.

◆ Build Vocabulary

revelation (rev´ ə lā´ shən) *n*: Something revealed; a disclosure of something not previously known or realized

Guide for Responding

◆ LITERATURE AND YOUR LIFE

Reader's Response Were you surprised when the narrator threw away the umbrella at the end of the story? Why or why not?

Thematic Focus What points does this story make about being an American?

Journal Writing Have you ever wanted something, like a white umbrella, that you thought would transform you? Jot down your thoughts in your journal.

☑ Check Your Comprehension

1. What excuse does the narrator give for arriving at the piano lesson soaking wet?

2. Why is the narrator's mother always late to pick up the sisters?

◆ Critical Thinking

INTERPRET

1. In what ways are the personalities of the sisters different? **[Compare and Contrast]**

2. What does the white umbrella represent to the narrator? **[Analyze]**

3. Why does the narrator have mixed feelings about going back into Miss Crossman's house to get out of the rain? **[Infer]**

4. Why does the narrator throw the umbrella away at the end of the story? **[Draw Conclusions]**

EVALUATE

5. Do you think that the narrator learned an important lesson that will change her behavior in the future? Explain. **[Evaluate]**

APPLY

6. The narrator believes that her mother's response to her desire for an umbrella will be "All you want is things, just like an American." The narrator disagrees. Choose either the narrator's or her mother's point of view to defend. **[Defend]**

Guide for Responding (continued)

◆ Reading Strategy

PREDICT

When you **predict,** you build on information the author gives you to determine what will happen next. Predicting helps keep you involved in a story, as you read on to see if your predictions came true.

1. When the narrator of "A Ribbon for Baldy" says, "Then, like a flash—the idea for my project came to me," what did you predict the project would be?

2. (a) What did you predict when the narrator in "The White Umbrella" said that her mother would pick them up "any minute"? (b) What led you to make that prediction?

◆ Build Vocabulary

USING THE WORD ROOT -cred-

The words below each contain the word root -cred-, meaning "believe." Rewrite the sentences, filling in the blank with the correct word from this list:

    a. incredibly   **b.** credit   **c.** credibility

1. She earned _____?_____ for taking piano lessons.
2. Planting miles of corn was _____?_____ difficult.
3. She told so many fibs that she didn't have much _____?_____ with her friends.

SPELLING STRATEGY

The *ksh* sound in *anxious* and in some other words is spelled *xi*. Write the following words, spelling the *sh* sound with the letters *xi*.

1. no__ous   3. obno__ous
2. comple__on   4. an__ously

USING THE WORD BANK

On your paper, write the word from the Word Bank that best completes each sentence.

1. The _____?_____ of Orion was visible in the sky.
2. He _____?_____ the land before building a fence.
3. They waited _____?_____ for their mom to arrive.
4. The story was so fantastic it had no _____?_____.
5. At dusk, the fog would _____?_____ the hilltop, making it invisible.
6. After his _____?_____, he solved the problem.
7. She was _____?_____, telling no one about her job.
8. At the sale, she got a _____?_____ on piano music.

◆ Literary Focus

CHARACTER TRAITS

Character traits are the qualities of a character's personality. These traits are revealed by a character's actions, words, and thoughts, as well as by what other characters say about him or her.

1. What does the first paragraph of "A Ribbon for Baldy" reveal about the narrator's character traits?
2. In "The White Umbrella," which sister is impatient? Which sister is accepting and calm?
3. Which character trait of the narrator's is revealed when she tells Miss Crosman, "my mother is a concert pianist"?

◆ Build Grammar Skills

COMPOUND SUBJECTS AND VERBS

Sentences may have more than one subject or verb. A **compound subject** is two or more subjects that have the same verb and are linked by a coordinating conjunction such as *and* or *or*:

Mona and I were listening.

A **compound verb** is two or more verbs that have the same subject and are linked by a coordinating conjunction such as *and* or *or*:

Mona *would wash* the vegetables and *put* on the rice.

Practice On your paper, underline each compound subject once and each compound verb twice.

1. We took it to the beach last summer and got sand in the mechanism.
2. Mona and I watched Eugenie play.
3. I could feel the rain on my left shoulder and shivered.
4. My father and I set fire all the way around the base.
5. I hurried home and worked into the night.

Writing Application Write a sentence about "The White Umbrella" that contains a compound subject. Then, write a sentence about "A Ribbon for Baldy" that contains a compound verb.

Build Your Portfolio

 ## Idea Bank

Writing

1. **Newspaper Article** Imagine that you are one of the students who visited the narrator's corn row with Professor Herbert's General Science class. Write an article for your school newspaper describing the boy's accomplishment.

2. **Diary Entry** Write a diary entry that Mona might have written on the night following the events in "The White Umbrella."

3. **Compare and Contrast** Write an essay in which you compare and contrast the personality traits of the main characters in "A Ribbon for Baldy" and "The White Umbrella." Use passages from both stories for support.

Speaking and Listening

4. **Dramatic Scene [Group Activity]** With several classmates, act out a scene from "The White Umbrella." As you write the script for your scene, show the character traits of each of the people you will portray. Present your scene to the class. **[Performing Arts Link]**

5. **Work Song** Write a song that the narrator in "A Ribbon for Baldy" might have made up and sung as he planted "the longest corn row in the world." When you have finished, sing the song for your class or make copies of the song lyrics to distribute to your classmates. **[Music Link]**

Projects

6. **History of the Piano** Write a short history of the piano. Give information about when it came into being and how it is played. Also, list famous composers of piano music. **[Music Link]**

7. **Kentucky Farm Report [Group Activity]** With a group, find out about the agriculture and livestock that are grown and raised in Kentucky. Present your findings in a report that might appear in a local magazine. Look for maps, photographs, and charts that you can include in your report. **[Social Studies Link; Science Link]**

 ## Writing Mini-Lesson

Recommendation

A recommendation is a written statement about someone's abilities or accomplishments. Recommendations are often written by teachers to call attention to the student's suitability for advancement. Imagine that you are a teacher of either the boy in "A Ribbon for Baldy" or the narrator in "The White Umbrella." Then, write a recommendation for that character, suggesting whether or not the pupil should advance a level.

Writing Skills Focus: Support Points

In your recommendation, give specific examples to **support** the statements you make. For example, if your character is a good student, give examples of his or her progress and accomplishments.

Prewriting Decide which character you will write about. Then, take notes about the qualities or accomplishments you will mention in your recommendation.

Drafting Begin your recommendation by stating who you are, your relationship to the student, and why you are recommending him or her. Continue by introducing each of your main points in a separate paragraph. End with a restatement of the main points of your recommendation.

Revising When you revise, make sure you have included at least two facts or details to support each point you make about the person. Check to see that the overall impression you give about the student is positive and supportive. Proofread to correct errors in grammar, spelling, and punctuation.

> ◆ **Grammar Application**
> Look for sentences in your draft that could be combined by making a compound subject or a compound verb.

Guide for Reading

Meet the Authors:

Robert Hayden (1913–1980)

Raised in a poor Detroit neighborhood, Robert Hayden became the first African American poet to be appointed as Consultant of Poetry to the Library of Congress. His poetry covers a wide range of subjects— from personal remembrances to celebrations of the history and achievements of African Americans.

Evelyn Tooley Hunt (1904–   )

In 1961, Evelyn Tooley Hunt won the Sidney Lanier Memorial Award for her first collection of poems, *Look Again, Adam.* Her poems demonstrate a keen interest in other cultures. "I like to write from the inside of some culture other than my own," she says. She is best known for her variations of haiku, a type of Asian poetry, which she writes under the pen name of Tao-Li.

Richard García (1941–   )

Richard García writes poetry for adults and children. He has published *Selected Poems* (1973) and a contemporary folk tale for children, *My Aunt Otilia's Spirits* (1978). García is the director of the Poets in Schools program in Marin, California. Born in San Francisco, he has also lived in Mexico and Israel.

◆ LITERATURE AND YOUR LIFE

CONNECT YOUR EXPERIENCE

Think for a moment about people and places you see every day and how they influence you. In two of the poems that follow, you'll meet very special people who have influenced the poets. In the third poem, you'll learn of a special place.

THEMATIC FOCUS: An Album of Stories

As you read, think about how these poems would fit into a scrapbook of someone's life.

◆ Background for Understanding

SOCIAL STUDIES

"Taught Me Purple" tells of a tenement in which the speaker and her mother lived. Tenements are buildings that provide housing for low-income families in urban environments. Conditions in many tenements are crowded and even dangerously substandard. They reflect one of the challenges of urban living—how to provide safe housing for millions of people living within a few square miles of one another.

◆ Build Vocabulary

WORD ROOTS: -chron-

The word root *-chron-* comes from the Greek word for time. Knowing this, you can figure out that *chronic* means "continuing for a long period of time."

WORD BANK

Which word from the list might be related to the noun *earthquake*? Check the Build Vocabulary box on page 427 to see if you chose correctly.

> banked
> chronic
> austere
> tenement
> molding
> quake

♦ **Those Winter Sundays** ♦
Taught Me Purple ♦ **The City Is So Big**

♦ Literary Focus

WORD CHOICE

Because poems tend to be brief, **word choice**—the specific decisions a poet makes about which words to use to present each idea and detail—is especially important. As you read poetry, pay careful attention to the words chosen by the poet. For example, in "Those Winter Sundays," Robert Hayden describes the cold as "blueblack." His choice of the word *blueblack* makes you both see and feel the cold. Blue is a color you associate with cold (people are said to turn blue from too much exposure to the cold), and black is the color of the cold night sky.

♦ Reading Strategy

RESPOND

Whenever you read a poem or other work of literature, you **respond** to it in a personal way. The work might please you, or you might connect it with an experience the writer is presenting, or you might totally disagree with the writer's view of something. You respond the way you do because you bring your own experiences and memories to everything you read.

Use a chart like the one below to record your responses to these poems.

Those Winter Sundays

Lines	Response
Lines 1–5	I felt cold and shivery. I felt sorry for his father.

Those Winter Sundays

Robert Hayden

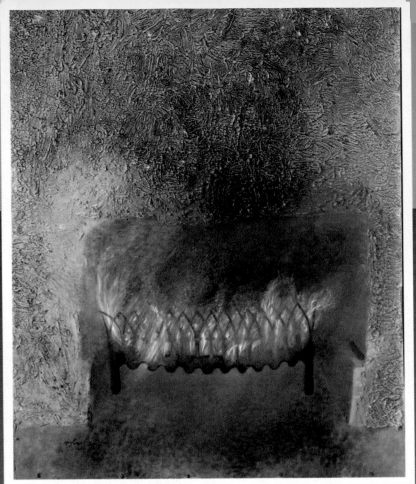

Sundays too my father got up early
and put his clothes on in the blueblack cold,
then with cracked hands that ached
from labor in the weekday weather made
5 banked fires blaze. No one ever thanked him.

I'd wake and hear the cold splintering, breaking.
When the rooms were warm, he'd call,
and slowly I would rise and dress,
fearing the chronic angers of that house,

10 Speaking indifferently to him,
who had driven out the cold
and polished my good shoes as well.
What did I know, what did I know
of love's austere and lonely offices?

▲ **Critical Viewing** Would you say that this fire has been banked? Explain. [**Make a Judgment**]

◆ **Build Vocabulary**

banked (baŋt) *adj.*: Adjusted to burn slowly and long

chronic (krän´ ik) *adj.*: Continuing indefinitely; perpetual; constant

austere (ô stir´) *adj.*: Showing strict self-discipline; severe

Taught Me Purple

Evelyn Tooley Hunt

My mother taught me purple
    Although she never wore it.
Wash-gray was her circle,
    The <u>tenement</u> her orbit.

5   My mother taught me golden
    And held me up to see it,
Above the broken <u>molding</u>,
    Beyond the filthy street.

My mother reached for beauty
10   And for its lack she died,
Who knew so much of duty
    She could not teach me pride.

◆ **Build Vocabulary**

tenement (ten´ ə mənt) *n.*: Here, a rundown apartment building

molding (mōl´ diŋ) *n.*: Ornamental woodwork that projects from the walls of a room

Guide for Responding

◆ LITERATURE AND YOUR LIFE

Reader's Response In what way are the father and mother in these poems admirable?

Thematic Focus What story about growing up would you like to tell in a poem?

☑ Check Your Comprehension

1. In "Those Winter Sundays," what did the speaker's father do on Sunday mornings?
2. How did the speaker respond to his father at the time?
3. What two things does the speaker in "Taught Me Purple" say her mother taught her?
4. What causes the speaker's mother's death?

◆ Critical Thinking

INTERPRET

1. In "Those Winter Sundays," what does the speaker mean when he says he could "hear the cold splintering, breaking"? **[Interpret]**
2. How have the speaker's feelings about his father changed since he was young? **[Infer]**
3. How does the speaker of "Taught Me Purple" feel about her mother? **[Infer]**
4. Why couldn't the mother teach her daughter pride? **[Draw Conclusions]**

COMPARE LITERARY WORKS

5. What are the similarities and differences in the feelings the two speakers describe? **[Compare]**

THE CITY IS SO
BIG

Richard García

The city is so big
Its bridges <u>quake</u> with fear
I know, I have seen at night

The lights sliding from house to house
5 And trains pass with windows shining
Like a smile full of teeth

I have seen machines eating houses
And stairways walk all by themselves
And elevator doors opening and closing
10 And people disappear.

◀ **Critical Viewing** What images from the poem does this photograph of New York City convey or suggest? **[Apply]**

◆ **Build Vocabulary**

quake (kwāk) *v.*: To tremble or shake; to shudder or shiver, as from fear or cold

Guide for Responding

◆ LITERATURE AND YOUR LIFE

Reader's Response Would you like to visit the city described in the poem? Why or why not?

Thematic Focus To whom might you recommend this poem? Why?

Journal Writing In your journal, jot down your impressions of a city—either one in which you live or one that you have visited. How do your impressions compare with García's?

☑ Check Your Comprehension

1. What is the setting of this poem?
2. What has the speaker seen the bridges doing?
3. What do the passing trains resemble?

◆ Critical Thinking

INTERPRET

1. Describe the mood or overall atmosphere of this poem. Find five details that help create this mood. **[Analyze]**
2. Explain how each of the events described in the final four lines of the poem is possible. **[Interpret]**
3. How does the title of the poem relate to its main theme or message? **[Connect]**

APPLY

4. This poem presents one side of living in a big city. Discuss with your classmates the pros and cons of city living. **[Relate]**

EVALUATE

5. How well has García captured the essence of a big city? Use details from the poem to support your opinion. **[Evaluate]**

Guide for Responding (continued)

◆ Reading Strategy

RESPOND

When you **respond** to a poem, you bring your own feelings and reactions to it.

1. In "Those Winter Sundays," the speaker says that "No one ever thanked" his father. How did you respond to this information?
2. Do you know anyone who is like the mother in "Taught Me Purple"? Explain.
3. What words would you use to describe your response to "The City Is So Big"?

◆ Build Vocabulary

USING THE WORD ROOT -chron-

The word root -chron- comes from the Greek word for time. Apply that information to suggest a meaning for each of the words below. Then, use a dictionary to check your definitions.

1. chronicle   2. chronological   3. chronometer

SPELLING STRATEGY

Some words, like tenement and cemetery, are spelled with three e's. To remember how to spell these words, think of the three e's in the word remember! Find the misspelled word in each sentence, and write it correctly on your paper.

1. I found the poet's age in a refirence book.
2. There is an elament of suspense in her poetry.
3. Her work clearly declares independance.

USING THE WORD BANK

Write the word from the Word Bank that best completes each sentence.

1. The ____?____ was built to house the poor.
2. The room was so bare that it looked ____?____ and forbidding.
3. The ____?____ problem with the heat kept the rooms from ever getting warm enough.
4. A ____?____ fire will burn through the night.
5. When the radiator came on, the pipes would quiver and the floors would ____?____.
6. The ____?____ around the door is decorative.

◆ Literary Focus

WORD CHOICE

Word choice is especially important in poetry. In fact, poets often labor over a single word. Sometimes they come up with unusual word choices to surprise readers and lead them to view things in new ways. For example, in "Taught Me Purple," the poet writes that the tenement was "her orbit." The word orbit draws the reader's attention to the mother's narrowly defined life.

1. What does Hayden mean by "the chronic angers of that house" in "Those Winter Sundays"?
2. Hayden uses the adjectives austere and lonely in the final line of his poem. What similar words might he have considered instead of these words? How would the choice of one of these other words have affected the poem's meaning?
3. What word appears at the beginning of four lines in "The City Is So Big"? Why might García have chosen to repeat that word?

◆ Build Grammar Skills

INVERTED SENTENCES

In most English sentences, the subject comes first, followed by the verb. Poets sometimes **invert** this order, placing the verb or some part of the predicate before the subject. For example, Evelyn Tooley Hunt writes:

> Wash-gray was her circle, . . .

In standard English, you would say "Her circle was wash-gray." Poets may invert sentences to create a particular rhythm, a rhyme, or a poetic sound.

Practice Identify the subject and the verb in each sentence. Then, label each as standard or inverted.

1. Bounding down the street went my father.
2. There on the corner was my mother.
3. My parents walked in the park.
4. The snow gently fell outside my window.
5. There are no clouds in the sky today.

Writing Application Write three sentences in standard order. Then, rewrite the sentences, inverting the subject and verb order.

Build Your Portfolio

 Idea Bank

Writing

1. **Book Jacket** Create a book title and jacket description for a collection of poems that includes "Those Winter Sundays," "Taught Me Purple," and "The City Is So Big." Describe the collection in a way that will attract readers. Mention each of the poems you've just read.

2. **Word Analysis** Find a word in one of the poems that is critical to the poem's overall meaning. Then, write a brief essay in which you discuss why the writer chose this word and how the word relates to the poem's message.

3. **Comparison of Poems** Compare and contrast "Those Winter Sundays" and "Taught Me Purple" in a brief essay. Use passages from the poems to support your points.

Speaking and Listening

4. **Choral Reading [Group Activity]** Prepare a choral reading of one of the poems with a group of classmates. Choose lines to read together and lines to read individually. Make sure everyone in your group has a specified role.

5. **Telephone Conversation [Group Activity]** With a partner, improvise for the class a telephone conversation between the speaker of "Taught Me Purple" and the speaker of "Those Winter Sundays." **[Performing Arts Link]**

Projects

6. **Poetry Display** Find more poems written by Hayden, Hunt, and García. Photocopy them, and create a colorful display that includes not only the poems but also related photographs and illustrations.

7. **City Life Magazine [Group Activity]** With a group, create a magazine that describes city life. Group members can contribute and edit articles, select illustrations, and write headlines. Display a copy of your magazine in your classroom or school library. **[Social Studies Link]**

 Writing Mini-Lesson

Response to Poems

When you respond to literature, you react on a personal level to what you've read. Choose two of the poems from this section, and share how they affected you by writing a response to them.

Writing Skills Focus: Compare-and-Contrast Organization

Use **comparison-and-contrast organization** in your response to the two poems. You might decide to write about one poem first and then write about the other poem, or you might discuss similarities in your responses in one paragraph and differences in the next paragraph.

Model

I had different reactions to the last lines of each poem. The final line of "Those Winter Sundays" made me feel regret and sympathy, and the final line of "The City Is So Big" made me feel tense and frightened.

Prewriting Reread the poems about which you're writing, and jot down notes about your response to each. List how your responses to the two poems are similar and different.

Drafting Organize your notes to compare and contrast your responses. As you draft, support the points you make by citing passages from the poems.

◆ **Grammar Application**

If inverted sentences appear in the poems, you may want to describe your response to their effect.

Revising Check your notes to see whether you have included all of your points in your essay. Review your organization to be sure that it's consistent and that your ideas are clearly presented.

Consumer Report

Writing Process Workshop

If Sancho were a person and not a steer, he would probably offer some great advice on what goes into excellent southwestern food. Whenever you need advice on purchasing a product, it's helpful to turn to a consumer report that will reveal the strengths and weaknesses of different products and the advantages of using one over another. A consumer report is objective; it presents facts, statistical data, product ratings, and recommendations. Write your own consumer report about a product that interests you.

The skills introduced in this section's Writing Mini-Lessons will help you write your consumer report.

Writing Skills Focus

▶ In your consumer report, **elaborate with factual details.** (See p. 407.)

▶ **Use supporting points** to back up your recommendations. (See p. 421.)

▶ **Use a comparison-and-contrast organization** to develop your consumer report. (See p. 429.)

MODEL

① The stick umbrella is easy to use and opens when a push button is pressed. ② Because of its size and strength, it offers protection from rain and wind without turning inside out. Prices vary from about $15 to $80 and above for a high-fashion design.

① Folding umbrellas ② are smaller; the smallest is about 8 inches long. They do not offer as much protection as the stick umbrella, and they are not as durable. Since they are so inexpensive— from $6 to $30—and easy to carry, many people keep them handy for protection from a sudden shower.

All in all, I recommend the folding umbrella. ③ For the difference in price and the ease of use, it's worth it.

① The writer uses a comparison-and-contrast organization to develop her consumer report.

② Factual details about umbrella size, strength, and cost are used to elaborate.

③ These supporting points back up the writer's recommendation.

Prewriting

Choose a Topic Television and magazine advertisements are great sources for products to use in your report. If those fail you, consider the ideas in the box below:

> ### Topic Ideas
> - A big purchase your family has made
> - Popular food products and their nutritional claims
> - Personal products that target the teen market

Limit Your Items A consumer report should focus only on a few items within one topic: three different brands of in-line skates, for example, rather than all in-line skates. Choose a category, such as *best known* or *least known* or a certain price range, to help you limit the items you're comparing.

Elaborate With Factual Details As you research the products you plan to discuss in your consumer report, write down factual details that will help you present your findings in an objective, unbiased way.

Use a Venn Diagram Use a Venn diagram like the one below to gather and organize details according to similarities and differences among the products in your report.

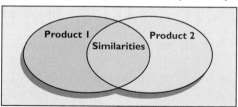

Use Comparison-and-Contrast Organization You can develop your paragraphs subject by subject or point by point. In other words, you can completely cover one item and then the next, or you can cover the cost of both, durability of both, and so on.

Drafting

Review Your Notes Before you begin drafting your consumer report, review your notes to keep fresh in your mind the points you'll be discussing and the order in which you plan to discuss them.

Write the Body First Write the body of your consumer report first. Then, create an introduction that leads into it and a conclusion in which you make your recommendation.

DRAFTING/REVISING

APPLYING LANGUAGE SKILLS: Using Precise Adjectives

Adjectives are words that point out, describe, and limit; *collie* dog, *white* dog, *six* dogs. Precise, exact adjectives present a clear picture to readers.

Vague Adjectives:
There were *some* people on the *old* boat.

Precise Adjectives:
There were *four tired, frightened* people on the *dilapidated* boat.

Notice how the precise adjectives *four, tired, frightened,* and *dilapidated* paint a much clearer picture than *some* and *old.*

Practice Replace the vague adjectives or add precise ones to these sentences:

1. They got into the car.
2. The boys went on a trip.
3. After seeing the show, they had some dinner.
4. The dog chased the cat.
5. Last year, I donated books to the flea market.

Writing Application As you edit your consumer report, include precise adjectives.

Writer's Solution Connection
Writing Lab

For help using precise adjectives, use the Revision Checker in the Revising section of the Description tutorial.

EDITING/PROOFREADING

APPLYING LANGUAGE SKILLS:
Avoiding Jargon

Jargon is a specialized language used by people in a certain group, such as actors, lawyers, bicyclists, or football fans. Jargon often confuses and excludes others. In your writing, use straightforward language that all readers will understand.

Jargon:
There was road rash on Pete's legs and arms.

Specific Language:
Pete's arms and legs were covered with cuts and scratches.

Practice Replace the jargon (defined in parentheses) in these sentences.

1. Tiara said, "I want the *411* on her." (information)
2. The editor asked her friend, "Will you *eyeball* this for me?" (look at)
3. "I'll write out a *scrip* for you this evening," the doctor assured him. (prescription)

Writing Application Check your draft to eliminate any jargon.

Writer's Solution Connection
Language Lab

For more practice using formal and informal language, complete the lesson in Formal and Informal English Idioms.

Revising

Add or Delete Details Look over your draft. If your point lacks support, add factual details. If you've included opinions, you may want to delete them to keep your report objective.

Improve Your Word Choice and Language Review your report to find vague adjectives and/or jargon. Replace them with precise, straightforward statements and descriptions.

Review Your Organization Make sure you maintained a subject-by-subject or a point-by-point organization as you developed your comparison-and-contrast consumer report.

REVISION MODEL

Both Jackson Airlines and Air Delight fly the same route from Calgary to Branston. Jackson flies small commuter jets and old DC9s. The basic flight costs about $150, and they serve ① coffee, soft drinks, and peanuts. food and drink. ② ~~Air Delight serves honey-coated cashews.~~ Their on-time record is ~~good.~~ ③ 82 percent. They don't post their accident record.

The basic flight on Air Delight costs more, but they use newer planes. Air Delight has an 88 percent on-time record and had only one minor accident in the last six years. ④ I'd recommend ~~It's hard~~ Air Delight based on its on-time record. ~~to tell which is better.~~

① These factual details were added to present a clear picture.
② The sentence about Air Delight was eliminated because it weakens the organization of the paper.
③ This detail supports the writer's point.
④ The recommendation was reworded to be more specific.

Publishing and Presenting

On Line Share your consumer reports either through e-mail or on your school's Web page.

Bulletin Board Post your consumer report in an area where interested individuals can read it. For example, a report on running shoes might be posted in the gym.

Real-World Reading Skills Workshop

Strategies for Success

Writers don't always tell you everything directly. You have to make inferences to arrive at ideas authors suggest but don't say. You make inferences by considering the details a writer includes or doesn't include. Making a series of inferences will help you draw conclusions about what you read.

Read Between the Lines Look beyond the literal meaning of the words to understand a writer's attitude or purpose for writing.

Example Passage: For those who like salmon, this entree is quite interesting.

Possible Inference: The writer doesn't like salmon, so his or her opinion may be biased.

Question One way to make inferences is to question the text. Ask the following as you read:

▶ Why did the writer include these details?
▶ Why did the writer exclude information?

Draw Conclusions Using the inferences you have made about a writer's choice of details, draw conclusions about what you read.

> ✔ Here are other situations in which making inferences is helpful:
> ▶ Reading a menu
> ▶ Reading an editorial
> ▶ Reading a news article
> ▶ Reading a poster

Apply the Strategies

Read the passage from a sports article. Then, make inferences about the text to answer the questions that follow:

Indoor Rock Climbing

A new sport is sweeping the nation: indoor rock climbing. The equipment—shoes, helmet, harness—are usually provided at the clubs at a low daily rental charge. Club memberships are also usually available, but if you'd like to test out the sport first, entrance fees average about $6 per day. Lessons range from $25 to $35 an hour.

Most indoor climbing clubs offer walls to challenge various levels of climber—from beginner to expert. Some walls are restricted: You have to take a test to prove that you have the ability to climb it safely.

Most rock-climbing clubs offer special deals for birthday parties and school outings. Parents, however, are required by law to sign a release form permitting children under the age of 17 to climb.

---

1. Is this an established sport, or might it be a fad?

2. What can you infer about the overall cost of participating in this sport?

3. Is this sport challenging—one you can grow in? How can you tell?

4. What might you infer about this sport, knowing that parents are required by law to sign a release form for minors?

Grammar Review

sen·tence (sen'təns) **n.** 1 a group of words that is used to tell, ask, command, or exclaim something, usually having a subject and a predicate: a sentence begins with a capital letter and ends with a period, question mark, or exclamation point

A sentence is a group of words that expresses a complete thought. Every sentence consists of two parts: the subject and the predicate. The **subject** states whom or what the sentence is about. The **predicate** tells what the subject is or does.

subject   predicate

Every night Sancho | came to the ranch pen to sleep.

Simple Subject and Simple Predicate Each complete subject and predicate contains a simple subject and a simple predicate. **The simple subject** is the main noun or pronoun in the complete subject, and the **simple predicate** is the verb or verb phrase in the predicate.

simple   simple
subject   predicate

Every night *Sancho* | *came* to the ranch pen to sleep.

Compound Subject and Compound Verb Some sentences may have more than one subject or verb. A **compound subject** is two or more subjects that have the same verb and are linked by a coordinating conjunction, such as *and* or *or*. A **compound verb** is two or more verbs that have the same subject and are linked by a coordinating conjunction, such as *and* or *or*.

Compound Subject: The *bluebonnets and pink phlox* were sprinkling every hill. . . .

Compound Verb: We *stood* in our barnlot *and looked* at Little Baldy.

Inverted Order In standard sentences, the subject comes before the verb. Writers sometimes **invert** this order, placing the verb or some part of the predicate before the subject.

subject   verb

Standard: The *herd* of cattle *moved* slowly.

verb   subject

Inverted: Slowly *moved* the *herd* of cattle.

Practice 1 Copy each sentence into your notebook. Underline the complete subject once and the complete predicate twice. Then, circle the simple subject and simple verb, and label those that are compound. Finally, identify each sentence as standard or inverted.

1. Mona and I watched Eugenie play.

2. Next morning Little Baldy was a dark hill jutting high into February's cold, windy sky.

3. Wash-gray was her circle . . .

4. He stood and roamed about on the south side of the herd.

5. Dark drum the vanishing horses' hooves.

Practice 2 Retell a story that has been told and retold about a family member. As you write, use two sentences with compound subjects, two with compound verbs, and two in inverted order.

Grammar in Writing

✔ *Avoid wordiness and repetition by combining sentences to use compound subjects and verbs.*

Repetitive: Mona took piano lessons. I also took piano lessons.

Revised: Mona and I took piano lessons.

Talking with friends, calling for help, ordering a pizza, carrying on business—for all these reasons and more, the telephone is an essential part of our lives. Your telephone transaction will go smoothly if you use good sense and good manners.

Get Off to a Good Start When you're making a personal or professional call, begin by introducing yourself and stating your purpose. "Hello, my name is Carolyn Keller. I'm calling in response to your advertisement for a baby sitter." "Hi, Mrs. Fagan, this is Darren. Is Dan at home?"

When calling for information or to order a product, it is not necessary to introduce yourself. If you're ordering something, you will be asked for personal information at the appropriate time.

Speak Clearly If your listeners keep asking you to repeat yourself, it's a good sign that you need to speak more clearly. Speak slowly and distinctly. Remember that the person on the other end of the phone is relying completely on your voice to receive information.

Say It Again Repeating information ensures that you have heard the other person correctly. When you are receiving phone numbers, addresses, directions, name spellings, or the date and time of appointments, repeat them to verify their accuracy.

Manners Count Be courteous when communicating on the phone. Say "please" and "thank you" when asking for and receiving information. End your call on a good note by saying "thank you." Confirm any future contact. "Thanks for calling, Scott. I'll speak with you again on Tuesday."

Apply the Strategies

Role-play the following telephone conversations with a classmate:

1. You see an injured dog on the street in front of your house. Call a veterinarian for help.

2. You want to apply for a baby-sitting job you saw advertised in Sunday's paper.

3. Call your father at work and leave a message for him to pick you up at 5:30 at Pat Kelly's house at 206 Waverly Ave.

4. You have to find out if your sister is visiting her friend Eliza or her friend Rachel and tell her to come home early.

Tips for Telephone Conversations

▶ Speak loudly and clearly.
▶ Greet your listener pleasantly.
▶ Identify yourself and your purpose for calling.
▶ Repeat important information.

What's Behind the Words

Vocabulary Adventures With Richard Lederer

Newspaper and Magazine Vocabulary

The United States is a newspaper nation. Because our country was the first great modern democracy, the free press was born here. Today, about one fifth of the newspapers around the globe are printed in our land.

America Reads the Newspaper

Americans are great newspaper readers. Because of our high literacy rate, about 20 percent of the world's news readers live here, even though we have only 6 or 7 percent of the Earth's population. Nearly 90 percent of American homes have newspapers in them, and four of five adults read a newspaper regularly.

Journalistic Words

Journalism—the writing, editing, and publishing of news—is borrowed from the French *journal*, "a daily record." Words dealing with newspapers and magazines have interesting origins:

advertisement: In Latin, *advertere* meant "to turn toward." The later French word, *advertir,* meant "to tell about or warn." An *advertisen* in early English was a notice about something, similar to the meaning of the word *advertisement* today.

article: In Latin, *articulus* was the word for "joint" or "knuckle." Articles were joined together to create a whole work.

cartoon: From the Latin *charta,* "a piece of paper," descends the Italian word *cartone,* meaning "pasteboard." The first cartoons were drawn on such large pieces of heavy paper.

column: Through the Greek *kolōnós* ("hill") to the Latin *columna* ("pillar or post"), the word *column* has taken on the additional meaning of "the vertical part of a page."

editor: This word is a combination of the Latin *e* ("out") and *dere* ("to give"). The meaning became "one who gives out, who publishes."

reporter: This word is a combination of Latin word parts, and you can figure out their meanings. *Re-*, as in *rework* and *repeat,* means "again." *Port* (from the Latin *portare*), as in *transport* and *porter,* means "to carry." In time, *reporter* came to mean "one who carries the news."

ACTIVITY 1 Define and show an example of the following parts of a newspaper:

1. banner
2. byline
3. headline
4. editorial
5. classified section
6. masthead
7. nameplate
8. review
9. opinion article
10. feature article

ACTIVITY 2 Headline writers must say a lot in a small space. They need to know many short words to replace the longer ones used in the stories themselves. These shortcuts are called headline words. What longer words do the following headline verbs replace?

1. bar
2. curb
3. nab
4. OK
5. quiz
6. seek
7. top
8. up
9. urge
10. vow

ACTIVITY 3 Newspapers are full of lines, including *bylines, deadlines,* and *headlines.* Report on the meanings and origins of these three words.

Extended Reading Opportunities

A land as vast as the United States poses all kinds of challenges. The following novels describe some of the challenges that humans and animals must overcome to live harmoniously with nature.

Suggested Titles

The Call of the Wild
Jack London

This novel follows the trail of Buck, a domestic dog who is kidnapped to be trained as a sled dog during the Alaskan Gold Rush. Buck reverts back to his primitive nature and undertakes a journey in which he abandons the safety of his domestic world for that of the wild. He becomes a hero when he is transformed into the legendary "Ghost Dog" of the Klondike.

Where the Lilies Bloom
Vera and Bill Cleaver

The saga of the Luther family is set in the Trial Valley between two fictional peaks of the Smoky Mountains on the Tennessee border of western North Carolina. The members of the Luther family are sharecroppers on land belonging to Kiser Pease and his sister. The story vividly describes the will of the Luther children to overcome their poverty, meet the challenges of nature, and find comfort in each other—all under the direction of fourteen-year-old Mary Call Luther.

The Yearling
Marjorie Kinnan Rawlings

The characters of this story focus on their daily struggle to earn a living in an isolated and harsh environment. Set in northcentral Florida in the years following the Civil War, the book follows the life of Jody Baxter, a boy on the verge of adulthood. Life on the farm becomes less grim for Jody when he adopts a fawn and names her Flag. Jody is then forced to make a painful decision, which helps him cross the border into manhood.

Other Possibilities

A Day No Pigs Would Die	Robert Newton Peck
Prairie Songs	Pamela Conrad
When the Legends Die	Hal Borland
Little Women	Louisa May Alcott

Les Memoires d'un saint, (The Memories of a Saint), 1960, René Magritte, The Menil Collection

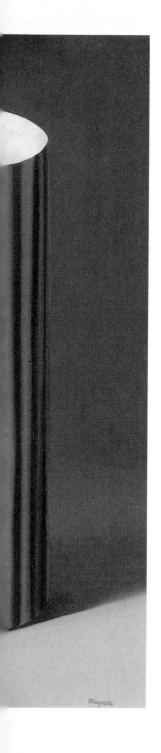

Magritte

Extraordinary Occurrences

Life is full of surprises, big and small. For example, on a "typical" day, you might be surprised by the strange behavior of birds, a spooky deserted mansion, or a frightening apparition that turned out to be nothing more than headlights through a window. As you read the selections in this unit, be prepared to encounter some extraordinary occurrences of all kinds.

Guide for Reading

Meet the Author:

Annie Dillard (1945–   )

An intense, creative writer, Annie Dillard spends as many as sixteen hours a day choosing and refining her words. Inspired partly by Henry David Thoreau's *Life on Walden Pond,* she spent four seasons living in a remote area. There, she kept a journal in which she recorded her observations of nature and humanity. She edited the journal material to create *Pilgrim at Tinker Creek,* which won the 1974 Pulitzer Prize for general nonfiction.

Early Fame Dillard was not always comfortable with the attention gained by winning this prestigious prize at the age of twenty-nine. Somewhat suspicious of the literary world and its influences, she moved to a small, isolated island in Puget Sound. Later, she relocated to Connecticut, where she is currently a professor and writer in residence at Wesleyan University. She also tours the country as a speaker and reader.

THE STORY BEHIND THE STORY

"Lights in the Night" is from *An American Childhood,* Dillard's memoir about growing up. In it, she describes how her parents fostered her eagerness to explore the world. She also discusses the importance of books in her early life, emphasizing the relationship between reading and life.

◆ LITERATURE AND YOUR LIFE

CONNECT YOUR EXPERIENCE

A shadowy figure in the back of the closet, an odd noise coming from downstairs, a feeling that you're being watched—these are all common experiences, especially in childhood, when you're most impressionable. Annie Dillard, a celebrated author, shares an eerie childhood episode in "Lights in the Night," a passage from *An American Childhood.*

THEMATIC FOCUS: Extraordinary Occurrences

As you read this true account, look for an ordinary explanation behind what appears to be an extraordinary occurrence.

◆ Background for Understanding

SCIENCE

In "Lights in the Night," Annie Dillard tells of the mysterious appearance of moving lights in her childhood bedroom at night.

Light has unique properties. It is a form of electromagnetic radiation, and it travels in waves. Light waves are affected by objects. Some objects block light. For example, when you are outside in sunlight, your body blocks the light waves from the sun and creates a shadow. Some objects, such as a mirror, reflect, or bounce, rays of light in another direction. Other objects refract, or bend, light waves. For example, a prism bends light waves and creates a rainbow of color.

◆ Lights in the Night ◆

◆ Literary Focus

VIGNETTE

Writers sometimes describe carefully observed events in their lives in vignettes. A **vignette** is a sketch or brief narrative of a memorable scene. You might think of a vignette as a close-up inspection of an event or feeling. It contains enough details to provide you with a complete understanding and vivid feeling for the incident being described. In "Lights in the Night," look for details and insights that characterize the piece as a vignette.

◆ Build Vocabulary

WORD ROOTS: *-lum-*

English words that come from the Latin root *-lum-* include the meaning "light." Something that is *luminous* reflects or produces a steady, glowing light.

WORD BANK

Look over these words from the selection. Which word might mean "long and narrow"? How did you guess? Check the Build Vocabulary box on page 446 to see if you chose correctly.

luminous
ascent
membrane
contiguous
conceivably
coincidental
elongate

Reading for Success

Strategies for Reading Critically

Whenever you read a work that contains an author's ideas or opinions, it is wise to read the work critically. When you read critically, you examine and question the author's ideas, statements, and message. You also evaluate information the author includes as support and form a judgment about the content and quality of the work. Use the following strategies to help you read critically:

Recognize the author's purpose.

An author's purpose is his or her reason for writing. An author's purpose may be obvious; for instance, a how-to essay is probably written to teach. Sometimes, however, an author's purpose is more subtle; for example, a how-to essay might also try to persuade you to buy a certain product.

Make inferences.

To make an inference, you use details from a literary work to arrive at a conclusion. In other words, you make an educated guess about characters, events, or an author's message, based on the details given.

> **Detail:** All night long she slept smoothly in a series of pleasant and serene, if artificial-looking, positions . . .
>
> **Inference:** The author is slightly jealous of her baby sister.

Understand the author's bias.

Bias is a strong feeling for or against something. An author's experience and background may sometimes bias his or her writing. For example, the attitude toward war of a victim of war will almost certainly differ from a career soldier's attitude toward war.

Evaluate the author's message.

An author's message is the main point or idea that he or she wants to convey to the reader. Evaluating involves making a critical judgment. Evaluate or judge the author's message according to how well it's presented and supported. You may also evaluate its originality and timeliness.

As you read "Lights in the Night," look at the notes and ideas in the boxes. The notes demonstrate how to apply these strategies to a work of literature.

Lights in the Night

from An American Childhood
Annie Dillard

When I was five, growing up in Pittsburgh in 1950, I would not go to bed willingly because something came into my room. This was a private matter between me and it. If I spoke of it, it would kill me.

Who could breathe as this thing searched for me over the very corners of the room? Who could ever breathe freely again? I lay in the dark.

My sister Amy, two years old, was asleep in the other bed. What did she know? She was innocent of evil. Even at two she composed herself attractively for sleep. She folded the top sheet tidily under her prettily outstretched arm; she laid her perfect head

▲ **Critical Viewing** Which word best describes this photograph of lights in the night: threatening, comforting, or useful? Explain. **[Interpret]**

lightly on an unwrinkled pillow, where her thick curls spread evenly in rays like petals. All night long she slept smoothly in a series of pleasant and serene, if artificial-looking, positions, a faint smile on her closed lips, as if she were posing for an ad for sheets. There was no messiness in her, no roughness for things to cling to, only a charming and charmed innocence that seemed then to protect her, an innocence I needed but couldn't muster. Since Amy was asleep, furthermore, and since when I needed someone most I was afraid to stir enough to wake her, she was useless.

I lay alone and was almost asleep when the thing entered the room by flattening itself against the open door and sliding in. It was a transparent, <u>luminous</u> oblong. I could see the door whiten at its touch; I could see the blue wall turn pale where it raced over it, and see the maple headboard of Amy's bed glow. It was a swift spirit; it was an awareness. It made noise. It had two joined parts, a head and a tail, like a Chinese dragon. It found the door, wall, and headboard; and it swiped them, charging them with its luminous glance. After its fleet, searching passage, things looked the same, but weren't.

I dared not blink or breathe; I tried to hush my whooping blood. If it found another awareness, it would destroy it.

> The **author's purpose** may be to keep the reader in suspense.

Every night before it got to me it gave up. It hit my wall's corner and couldn't get past. It shrank completely into itself and vanished like a cobra down a hole. I heard the rising roar it made when it died or left. I still couldn't breathe. I knew—it was the worst fact I knew, a very hard fact—that it could return again alive that same night.

Sometimes it came back, sometimes it didn't. Most often, restless, it came back. The light stripe slipped in the door, ran searching over Amy's wall, stopped, stretched lunatic at the first corner, raced wailing toward my wall, and vanished into the second corner with a cry. So I wouldn't go to bed.

It was a passing car whose windshield reflected the corner streetlight outside. I figured it out one night.

Figuring it out was as memorable as the oblong itself. Figuring it out was a long and forced <u>ascent</u> to the very rim of being, to the <u>membrane</u> of skin that both separates and connects the inner life and the

> Here, you can **infer** that the author enjoys intellectual activity.

▶ **Critical Viewing** Why might a light like this, casting shadows in a room at night, have caused the narrator anxiety? **[Relate]**

outer world. I climbed deliberately from the depths like a diver who releases the monster in his arms and hauls himself hand over hand up an anchor chain till he meets the ocean's sparkling membrane and bursts through it; he sights the sunlit, becalmed hull of his boat, which had bulked so ominously from below.

I recognized the noise it made when it left. That is, the noise it made called to mind, at last, my daytime sensations when a car passed—the sight and noise together. A car came roaring down hushed Edgerton Avenue in front of our house, stopped at the corner stop sign, and passed on shrieking as its engine shifted up the gears. What, precisely, came into the bedroom? A reflection from the car's oblong windshield. Why did it travel in two parts? The window sash split the light and cast a shadow.

Night after night I labored up the same long chain of reasoning, as night after night the thing burst into the room where I lay awake and Amy slept prettily and my loud heart thrashed and I froze.

There was a world outside my window and <u>contiguous</u> to it. If I was so all-fired bright, as my parents, who had patently no basis for comparison, seemed to think, why did I have to keep learning this same thing over and over? For I had learned it a summer ago, when men with jackhammers broke up Edgerton Avenue. I had watched them from the yard; the street came up in jagged slabs like floes. When I lay to nap, I listened. One restless afternoon I connected the new noise in my

◆ **Build Vocabulary**

luminous (lōō′ mə nəs) *adj.*: Giving off light; shining; bright

ascent (ə sent′) *n.*: The act of rising or climbing

membrane (mem′ brān) *n.*: A thin, soft sheet or layer serving as a covering

contiguous (kən tig′ yōō əs) *adj.*: In physical contact; near or next to

In this passage, the **author's message** is revealed: The outside and inside worlds are connected.

bedroom with the jack-hammer men I had been seeing outside. I understood abruptly that these worlds met, the outside and the inside.

I traveled the route in my mind: You walked downstairs from here, and outside from downstairs. "Outside," then, was conceivably just beyond my windows. It was the same world I reached by going out the front or the back door. I forced my imagination yet again over this route.

The world did not have me in mind; it had no mind. It was a coincidental collection of things and people, of items, and I myself was one such item—a child walking up the sidewalk, whom anyone could see or ignore. The things in the world did not necessarily cause my overwhelming feelings; the feelings were inside me, beneath my skin, behind my ribs, within my skull. They were even, to some extent, under my control.

I could be connected to the outer world by reason, if I chose, or I could yield to what

amounted to a narrative fiction, to a tale of terror whispered to me by the blood in my ears, a show in light projected on the room's blue walls. As time passed, I learned to amuse myself in bed in the darkened room by entering the fiction deliberately and replacing it by reason deliberately.

Here the author speaks of her own **bias**—her preference for playing make-believe.

When the low roar drew nigh and the oblong slid in the door, I threw my own switches for pleasure. It's coming after me; it's a car outside. It's after me. It's a car. It raced over the wall, lighting it blue wherever it ran; it bumped over Amy's maple headboard in a rush, paused, slithered elongate over the corner, shrank, flew my way, and vanished into itself with a wail. It was a car.

◆ **Build Vocabulary**

conceivably (kən sē′ və blē) *adv.*: Possibly

coincidental (kō in′ sə dent′ əl) *adj.*: Occurring at the same time or place

elongate (i lôn′ gāt) *adj.*: Long and narrow

Guide for Responding

◆ LITERATURE AND YOUR LIFE

Reader's Response Do you find Dillard's childhood fears understandable? Explain.

Thematic Focus How does Dillard make the ordinary event of a car passing in the street seem extraordinary?

Journal Writing Write a journal entry that Dillard might have written when she first saw the mysterious lights in the night.

☑ Check Your Comprehension

1. What did Dillard see in her room each night when she was five?
2. How did she feel about the event?
3. What did she finally figure out was the source of the event?

◆ Critical Thinking

INTERPRET

1. Why doesn't Dillard's sister, Amy, react to the event in the same way? **[Compare and Contrast]**
2. Why doesn't Dillard confide her fears to her parents? **[Draw Conclusions]**
3. What realization does Dillard come to after understanding the source of the mystery? **[Analyze]**
4. After she figures out the mystery, Dillard sometimes pretends that she does not know the solution. Why? **[Infer]**

EXTEND

5. Why do many writers draw on childhood experiences? Explain. **[Career Link]**

Guide for Responding (continued)

◆ Reading for Success

STRATEGIES FOR READING CRITICALLY

Review the strategies and the notes showing how to read critically. Then, answer the following questions:

1. (a) What is one inference you made about the author's personality? (b) Give details from the story to support your inference.
2. (a) What is Dillard's purpose in writing "Lights in the Night"? (b) How do you know?
3. (a) What details from the story led you to identify the author's message? (b) Give your evaluation of the message.

◆ Build Vocabulary

USING THE WORD ROOT -lum-

The word root -lum- in luminous comes from a Latin word meaning "light." You will find -lum- in the words that follow. Predict the meaning of each word. Then, use a dictionary to check your definitions.

1. luminescence   2. illuminate   3. luminary

SPELLING STRATEGY

When deciding whether to spell the long e sound ie or ei in a word like conceivable, remember this helpful rule: Use i before e except after c.

Find the spelling error or errors in each sentence, and rewrite the sentences correctly on your paper.

1. The child was deceived by the fictional feind.
2. She will receive a peice of cake.
3. She perceived a feild of roses in her dream.

USING THE WORD BANK

Decide how each word pair is related. On your paper, write synonyms for words similar in meaning and antonyms for words having opposite meanings.

1. luminous, dark
2. ascent, rise
3. membrane, layer
4. contiguous, separated
5. conceivably, impossibly
6. coincidental, intentional
7. elongate, narrow

◆ Literary Focus

VIGNETTE

Annie Dillard describes a vivid childhood memory in a short **vignette,** a sketch or brief narrative of a memorable scene. She carefully chooses words and images that bring the episode to life for the reader.

1. How does the opening line of Dillard's story grab a reader's interest?
2. Describe three details Dillard uses to describe the nightly event.
3. What does Dillard find most memorable about this event from her childhood?

◆ Build Grammar Skills

DIRECT OBJECTS

A **direct object** is a noun or a pronoun that receives the action of a verb. You can determine if a word is a direct object by asking whom or what following an action verb. For example, in this sentence, the direct object answers the question: "She heard what?"

I heard the rising *roar* it made when it died or left.

In the following example, the direct objects answer the questions "Split what?" and "Cast what?"

The window sash split the *light* and cast a *shadow.*

Practice Write these passages on your paper, and underline the direct object(s) in each.

1. She folded the top sheet tidily. . . .
2. She laid her perfect head lightly on an unwrinkled pillow. . . .
3. It found the door, wall, and headboard; . . .
4. It hit my wall's corner and couldn't get past.
5. I traveled the route in my mind: . . .

Writing Application On your paper, write sentences according to the following directions.

1. Write a sentence about light containing the direct object *wall.*
2. Write a sentence about Dillard containing the direct object *book.*

Build Your Portfolio

 ## Idea Bank

Writing

1. **Annotated List** Write a list of at least three common childhood fears, and describe how you might help a child overcome each of the fears.

2. **Letter** Imagine that you are Annie Dillard. Write a letter to your best friend, in which you describe the night you finally figured out the source of the mysterious light.

3. **Summary** Write a short summary of this story that might appear on the back of the book's jacket. Grab the interest of the reader without giving away too much of the story.

Speaking and Listening

4. **Oral Interpretation** Read the final two paragraphs of "Lights in the Night" aloud. Use your voice to project the excitement Dillard feels when she pretends that the light is a mysterious force. Indicate the feelings of tension and release by varying your tone and pitch.

5. **Role Play [Group Activity]** With two classmates, re-create a scene in which five-year-old Annie tells her parents about her fears. Show how her parents react to the frightened child's news. **[Performing Arts Link]**

Projects

6. **Diagram and Caption** Create a diagram or series of diagrams showing how reflected light created the illusion in Annie Dillard's bedroom. Write a detailed caption explaining the path of the light and the resulting image. **[Science Link]**

7. **Research Report [Group Activity]** With a group of classmates, find out more about the qualities of light. Write a report that includes charts and illustrations to show light's various properties. You may also want to research and report on the speed at which light travels. **[Science Link]**

 ## Writing Mini-Lesson

Childhood Remembrance

Your own childhood is a rich source of inspiration for writing. Almost any memory can become the subject of an interesting story—so long as it interests you to begin with. When you choose a particularly vivid memory, your enthusiasm will come through in your writing. Write a short remembrance explaining why a childhood memory is important to you.

Writing Skills Focus: Identify Your Purpose

Before you begin writing, **identify the purpose** of your remembrance. How do you want your audience to feel? Do you want them to laugh or to cry? Your purpose will guide your choice of details and words. Notice how Dillard amuses the reader with her re-creation of a child's overly serious attitude.

Model From the Story
This was a private matter between me and it. If I spoke of it, it would kill me.

Prewriting Make a list of memories, and choose the memory that interests you most. Then, use a cluster diagram to generate details and words for your remembrance. Decide on your purpose for writing, and select details that will help you achieve your purpose.

Drafting Put yourself in the time and place of the memory, and begin drafting.

Revising Read your remembrance aloud to a partner, and ask for feedback. Does your partner recognize your purpose? Incorporate changes that will help you to achieve your goal.

> ◆ **Grammar Application**
> In your draft, circle each direct object and underline the verb it completes.

Part 1

The Extraordinary in the Ordinary

Spring, ©1922, Georgia O'Keeffe, Frances Lehman Loeb Art Center, Vassar College, Poughkeepsie, New York

Guide for Reading

Meet the Authors:

Mark Twain (1835–1910)

Mark Twain wrote books that have become American classics, such as *The Adventures of Tom Sawyer* and *The Adventures of Huckleberry Finn*. Many of Twain's short stories and yarns are prized for his humorous, sometimes outrageous, style.

A Frequent Traveler
Although Twain was born near Hannibal, Missouri, and is most often associated with his books that center on the Mississippi River, his days as a reporter took him all across the country. "What Stumped the Blue Jays" combines Twain's humor with one of his favorite settings—the West. [For more on Mark Twain, see page 106.]

Diane Ackerman (1948–   )

A native of Waukegan, Illinois, nature writer Diane Ackerman studied psychology, physiology, and English in college, eventually earning two master's degrees and a Ph.D. at Cornell University. She has published five books of poems and five books of nonfiction, including *A Natural History of the Senses*. Her literary skills and scientific training enable her to describe the natural world in a captivating way.

◆ LITERATURE AND YOUR LIFE

CONNECT YOUR EXPERIENCE

Observing the natural world can be a source of pleasure and, often, surprise. Even if you don't think of yourself as a nature-lover, you have probably observed remarkable things in nature, such as birds migrating or mosquitoes swarming on a summer night. In the following selections, you'll read about two of nature's wonders—blues jays and the color changes of leaves in the fall.

THEMATIC FOCUS: The Extraordinary in the Ordinary

Which fascinates you more—the behavior of blue jays or the seasonal changes that autumn brings?

◆ Background for Understanding

SCIENCE

With their blue-gray crests and large size (about a foot long), blue jays are easy to spot. Their diet consists largely of nuts and seeds, although they sometimes steal eggs from other birds' nests. They are also easy to hear. Their voices are loud and harsh, like those of their relatives the crows and the magpies. Some people describe the sound blue jays make as a shriek.

◆ Build Vocabulary

WORD ROOTS: -grat-

The word *gratification* contains the root -grat-, which means "pleasing" or "satisfying." Knowing the meaning of -grat- will help you figure out that *gratification* is "the condition of being pleased or satisfied."

WORD BANK

Which word from the list means "single" or "unique"? Check the Build Vocabulary box on page 457 to see if you chose correctly.

gratification
countenance
singular
guffawed
macabre
camouflage
predisposed
capricious

◆ What Stumped the Blue Jays ◆
Why Leaves Turn Color in the Fall

◆ Literary Focus

OBSERVATION

An **observation** is a writer's eyewitness account of an event that he or she has studied over a period of time. The writer re-creates the event for the reader with precise details and vivid language. Ackerman's essay about why leaves turn color is an example of an observation.

◆ Reading Strategy

RECOGNIZE THE AUTHOR'S PURPOSE

An **author's purpose** is his or her reason for writing. Most authors have a broad purpose, such as to teach or to convince you of something. Sometimes, in addition to a broad purpose, an author will have a more specific purpose, such as to create suspense or to provoke laughter. As you read, use a chart like the one below to determine the author's purpose or purposes.

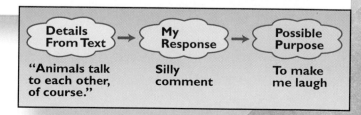

Details From Text	My Response	Possible Purpose
"Animals talk to each other, of course."	Silly comment	To make me laugh

What Stumped the

BLUE JAYS

Mark Twain

Animals talk to each other, of course. There can be no question about that; but I suppose there are very few people who can understand them. I never knew but one man who could. I knew he could, however, because he told me so himself. He was a middle-aged, simple-hearted miner who had lived in a lonely corner of California, among the woods and mountains, a good many years, and had studied the ways of his only neighbors, the beasts and the birds, until he believed he could accurately translate any remark which they made. This was Jim Baker. According to Jim Baker, some animals have only a limited education, and use only very simple words, and scarcely ever a comparison or a flowery figure; whereas, certain other animals have a large vocabulary, a fine command of language and a ready and fluent delivery; consequently these latter talk a great deal; they like it; they are conscious of their talent, and enjoy "showing off." Baker said, that after long and careful observation, he had come to the conclusion that the blue jays were the best talkers he had found among birds and beasts. Said he:—

"There's more *to* a blue jay than any other creature. He has got more moods, and more different kinds of feelings than any other creature; and mind you, whatever a blue jay feels, he can put into language. And no mere commonplace language, either, but rattling, out-and-out book-talk—and bristling with

metaphor, too—just bristling! And as for command of language—why *you* never see a blue jay get stuck for a word. No man ever did. They just boil out of him! And another thing: I've noticed a good deal, and there's no bird, or cow, or anything that uses as good grammar as a blue jay. You may say a cat uses good grammar. Well, a cat does—but you let a cat get excited once; you let a cat get to pulling fur with another cat on a shed, nights, and you'll hear grammar that will give you the lockjaw. Ignorant people think it's the *noise* which fighting cats make that is so aggravating, but it ain't so; it's the sickening grammar they use. Now I've never heard a jay use bad grammar but very seldom; and when they do, they are as ashamed as a human; they shut right down and leave.

"When I first begun to understand jay language correctly, there was a little incident happened here. Seven years ago, the last man in this region but me, moved away. There stands his house,—been empty ever since; a log house, with a plank roof—just one big room, and no more; no ceiling—nothing between the rafters and the floor. Well, one Sunday morning I was sitting out here in front of my cabin, with my cat, taking the sun, and looking at the blue hills, and listening to the leaves rustling so lonely in the trees, and thinking of the home away yonder in the States, and I hadn't heard from in thirteen years, when a blue jay lit on that house, with an acorn in his mouth, and says, 'Hello, I reckon I've struck something.' When he spoke, the acorn dropped out of his mouth and rolled

◀ **Critical Viewing** Based on this photograph, what "personality" might a blue jay have? [Draw Conclusions]

What Stumped the Blue Jays ◆ 453

down the roof, of course, but he didn't care; his mind was all on the thing he had struck. It was a knothole in the roof. He cocked his head to one side, shut one eye and put the other one to the hole, like a 'possum looking down a jug; then he glanced up with his bright eyes, gave a wink or two with his wings—which signifies <u>gratification</u>, you understand,—and says, 'It looks like a hole, it's located like a hole,—blamed if I don't believe it *is* a hole!'

"Then he cocked his head down and took another look; he glances up perfectly joyful,

▲ **Critical Viewing** What features does this log house have in common with the log house described on page 453? [Compare and Contrast]

this time; winks his wings and his tail both, and says, 'O, no, this ain't no fat thing, I reckon! If I ain't in luck!—why it's a perfectly elegant hole!' So he flew down and got that acorn, and fetched it up and dropped it in, and was just tilting his head back, with the heavenliest smile on his face, when all of a sudden he was paralyzed into a listening attitude and that smile faded gradually out of his <u>countenance</u> like breath off'n a razor, and the queerest look of surprise took its place. Then he says, 'Why, I didn't hear it fall!' He cocked his eye at the hole again, and took a long look; raised up and shook his head; stepped around to the other side of the hole and took another look from that side; shook his head again. He studied a while, then he just went into the *de-tails*—walked round and round the hole and spied into it from every point of the compass. No use. Now he took a thinking attitude on the comb of the roof and scratched the back of his head with his right foot a minute, and finally says, 'Well, it's too many for *me*, that's certain; must be a mighty long hole; however, I ain't got no time to fool around here, I got to 'tend to business; I reckon it's all right—chance it, anyway.'

"So he flew off and fetched another acorn and dropped it in, and tried to flirt his eye to the hole quick enough to see what become of it, but he was too late. He held his eye there as much as a minute; then he raised up and sighed, and says, 'Consound it, I don't seem to understand this thing, no way; however, I'll tackle her again.' He fetched another acorn, and done his level best to see what become of it, but he couldn't. He says, 'Well, *I* never struck no such a hole as this, before; I'm of the opinion it's a totally new kind of a hole.' Then he begun to get mad. He held in for a spell, walking up and down the comb

◆ **Build Vocabulary**

gratification (grat′ ə fi kā′ shən) *n.*: Satisfaction

countenance (koun′ tə nəns) *n.*: The look on a person's face that shows his or her nature or feeling

of the roof and shaking his head and muttering to himself; but his feelings got the upper hand of him, presently, and he broke loose and cussed himself black in the face. I never see a bird take on so about a little thing. When he got through he walks to the hole and looks in again for half a minute; then he says, 'Well, you're a long hole, and a deep hole, and a mighty <u>singular</u> hole altogether— but I've started in to fill you, if it takes a hundred years!'

"And with that, away he went. You never see a bird work so since you was born. He laid into his work, and the way he hove acorns into that hole for about two hours and a half was one of the most exciting and astonishing spectacles I ever struck. He never stopped to take a look any more—he just hove 'em in and went for more. Well at last he could hardly flop his wings, he was so tuckered out. He comes a drooping down, once more, sweating like an ice-pitcher, drops his acorn in and says, 'Now I guess I've got the bulge on you by this time!' So he bent down for a look. If you'll believe me, when his head come up again he was just pale with rage. He says, 'I've shoveled acorns enough in there to keep the family thirty years, and if I can see a sign of one of 'em I wish I may land in a museum with a belly full of sawdust in two minutes!'

"He just had strength enough to crawl up on to the comb and lean his back agin the chimbly, and then he collected his impressions and begun to free his mind.

"Another jay was going by, and stops to inquire what was up. The sufferer told him the whole circumstance, and says, 'Now yonder's the hole, and if you don't believe me, go and look for yourself.' So this fellow went and looked, and comes back and says, 'How many did you say you put in there?' 'Not any less than two tons,' says the sufferer. The other jay went and looked again. He couldn't seem to make it out, so he raised a yell, and three more jays come. They all examined the hole, they all made the sufferer tell it over again, then they all discussed it, and got off as many leather-headed opinions about it as an average crowd of humans could have done.

"They called in more jays; then more and more, till pretty soon this whole region 'peared to have a blue flush about it. There must have been five thousand of them; and such another jawing and disputing and ripping and cussing, you never heard. Every jay in the whole lot put his eye to the hole and delivered a more chuckle-headed opinion about the mystery than the jay that went there before him. They examined the house all over, too. The door was standing half open, and at last one old jay happened to go and light on it and look in. Of course that knocked the mystery galley-west in a second. There lay the acorns, scattered all over the floor. He flopped his wings and raised a whoop. 'Come here!' he says, 'Come here, everybody; hang'd if this fool hasn't been trying to fill up a house with acorns!' They all came a-swooping down like a blue cloud, and as each fellow lit on the door and took a glance, the whole absurdity of the contract that that first jay had tackled hit him home and he fell over backwards suffocating with laughter, and the next jay took his place and done the same.

◆ **Literature and Your Life**

Have you ever seen a huge flock of birds like the one described here? If so, describe the experience.

"Well, sir, they roosted around here on the house-top and the trees for an hour, and guffawed over that thing like human beings. It ain't any use to tell me a blue jay hasn't got a sense of humor, because I know better. And memory, too. They brought jays here from all over the United States to look down that hole, every summer for three years. Other birds, too. And they could all see the point, except an owl that come from Nova Scotia to visit the Yosemite and he took this thing in on his way back. He said he couldn't see anything funny in it. But then he was a good deal disappointed about Yosemite too."

◆ **Build Vocabulary**

singular (siŋ´ gyə lər) *adj.*: Unique; exceptional; extraordinary

guffawed (gə fôd´) *v.*: Laughed in a loud and coarse manner

Beyond Literature

Science Connection

Birds Vertebrates (animals with back-bones) are divided into eight classes. Birds form the class Aves. Within Aves, birds are classified into twenty-eight orders, based largely on internal features. Blue jays are members of the order Passeriformes, which are perching birds. Within this order are about 60 families, including broadbill, man-akin, and all songbirds. The blue jay is a member of the songbird family.

Cross-Curricular Activity
Research bird orders, and create a wall chart that includes illustrations and descriptions of various bird orders and families.

Guide for Responding

◆ **LITERATURE AND YOUR LIFE**

Reader's Response Would you have liked to witness the scene described in the story? Why or why not?

Thematic Focus Which aspects of blue jay behavior do you most appreciate?

☑ **Check Your Comprehension**

1. Who tells the story?
2. According to him, what is so special about blue Jays?
3. Why can't the blue jay hear the nut when it drops?
4. Why are all the blue jays laughing at the end of the story?

◆ **Critical Thinking**

INTERPRET
1. Why does Jim Baker admire blue jays? Give examples to support your opinion. **[Infer]**
2. What facts about blue jays are probably true? **[Distinguish]**
3. What human characteristics does Twain give to blue jays? **[Analyze]**
4. Why do the blue jays keep coming back for years to look at the hole in the roof? **[Draw Conclusions]**

APPLY
5. What message for readers might Twain hint at by including the passage about the owl at the end of the story? **[Speculate]**
6. Tales such as "What Stumped the Blue Jays" were often told on the American frontier to counteract loneliness, to entertain others, and to enliven a hardworking existence. What forms of entertainment today serve the same purpose? **[Relate]**

WHY LEAVES
TURN COLOR IN THE FALL
Diane Ackerman

The stealth of autumn catches one unaware. Was that a goldfinch perching in the early September woods, or just the first turning leaf? A red-winged blackbird or a sugar maple closing up shop for the winter? Keen-eyed as leopards, we stand still and squint hard, looking for signs of movement. Early-morning frost sits heavily on the grass, and turns barbed wire into a string of stars. On a distant hill, a small square of yellow appears to be a lighted stage. At last the truth dawns on us: Fall is staggering in, right on schedule, with its baggage of chilly nights, macabre holidays, and spectacular, heart-stoppingly beautiful leaves. Soon the leaves will start cringing on the trees, and roll up in clenched fists before they actually fall off. Dry seedpods will rattle like tiny gourds. But first there will be weeks of gushing color so bright, so pastel, so confettilike, that people will travel up and down the East Coast just to stare at it—a whole season of leaves.

Where do the colors come from? Sunlight rules most living things with its golden edicts.[1] When the days begin to shorten, soon after the summer solstice on June 21, a tree reconsiders its leaves. All summer it feeds them so they can process sunlight, but in the dog days of summer the tree begins pulling nutrients back into its trunk and roots, pares down, and gradually chokes off its leaves. A corky layer of cells forms at the leaves' slender petioles,[2] then scars over. Undernourished, the leaves stop producing the pigment chlorophyll,[3] and photosynthesis[4] ceases. Animals can migrate, hibernate, or store food to prepare for winter. But where can a tree go? It survives by dropping its leaves, and by the end of autumn only a few fragile threads of fluid-carrying xylem[5] hold leaves to their stems.

A turning leaf stays partly green at first, then reveals splotches of yellow and red as the chlorophyll gradually breaks down. Dark green seems to stay longest in the veins, outlining and defining them. During the summer, chlorophyll dissolves in the heat and light, but it is also being steadily replaced. In the fall, on the other hand, no new pigment is produced, and so we notice the other colors that were always there, right in the leaf, although chlorophyll's shocking green hid them from view. With their camouflage gone, we see these colors for the first time all year, and marvel, but they were always there, hidden

---

1. **edicts** (ē´ dikts´) *n*.: Authority; order.

2. **petioles** (pet´ ē ōlz´) *n*.: Stalks of leaves.
3. **chlorophyll** (klôr´ ə fil´) *n*.: Green pigment found in cellplants. It is essential for the photosynthetic process.
4. **photosynthesis** (fōt´ ō sin´ thə sis) *n*.: The production of organic substances; the transformation of radiant or light energy into chemical form.
5. **xylem** (zī´ ləm) *n*.: Woody tissue of a plant that carries water and minerals in the stems, roots, and leaves, giving support to softer tissues.

like a vivid secret beneath the hot glowing greens of summer.

The most spectacular range of fall foliage occurs in the northeastern United States and in eastern China, where the leaves are robustly colored thanks in part to a rich climate. European maples don't achieve the same flaming reds as their American relatives, which thrive on cold nights and sunny days. In Europe, the warm, humid weather turns the leaves brown or mildly yellow. Anthocyanin, the pigment that gives apples their red and turns leaves red or red-violet, is produced by sugars that remain in the leaf after the supply of nutrients dwindles. Unlike the carotenoids, which color carrots, squash, and corn, and turn leaves orange and yellow, anthocyanin varies from year to year, depending on the temperature and amount of sunlight. The fiercest colors occur in years when the fall sunlight is strongest and the nights are cool and dry (a state of grace scientists find vexing to forecast). This is also why leaves appear dizzyingly bright and clear on a sunny fall day: The anthocyanin flashes like a marquee.

Not all leaves turn the same color. Elms, weeping willows, and the ancient ginkgo all grow radiant yellow, along with hickories, aspens, bottlebrush buckeyes, cottonweeds, and tall, keening poplars. Basswood turns bronze, birches bright gold. Water-loving maples put on a symphonic display of scarlets. Sumacs turn red, too, as do flowering dogwoods, black gums, and sweet gums. Though some oaks yellow, most turn a pinkish brown. The farmlands also change color, as tepees of cornstalks and bales of shredded-wheat-textured hay stand drying in the fields. In some spots, one slope of a hill may be green and the other already in bright color, because the hillside facing south gets more sun and heat than the northern one.

◆ **Literary Focus**
What vivid details does the author observe?

An odd feature of the colors is that they don't seem to have any special purpose. We are predisposed to respond to their beauty, of course. They shimmer with the colors of sunset, spring flowers, the tawny[6] buff of a colt's pretty rump, the shuddering pink of a blush. Animals and flowers color for a reason—adaptation to their environment—but there is no adaptive reason for leaves to color so beautifully in the fall any more than there is for the sky or ocean to be blue. It's just one of the haphazard marvels the planet bestows every year. We find the sizzling colors thrilling, and in a sense they dupe us. Colored like living things, they signal death and disintegration. In time, they will become fragile and, like the body, return to dust. They are as we hope our own fate will be when we die; not to vanish, just to sublime from one beautiful state into another. Though leaves lose their green life, they bloom with urgent colors, as the woods grow mummified day by day, and Nature becomes more carnal, mute, and radiant.

We call the season "fall," from the Old English *feallan*, to fall, which leads back through time to the Indo-European *phol*, which also means to fall. So the word and the idea are both extremely ancient, and haven't really changed since the first of our kind needed a name for fall's leafy abundance. As we say the word, we're reminded of that other Fall, in the Garden of Eden, when fig leaves never withered and scales fell from our eyes. Fall is the time when leaves fall from the trees, just as spring is when flowers spring up, summer is when we simmer, and winter is when we whine from the cold.

Children love to play in piles of leaves, hurling them into the air like confetti, leaping into

---

6. **tawny** (tô´ nē) *adj.*: Brownish-yellow; tan.

◆ **Build Vocabulary**

macabre (mə käb´ rə) *adj.*: Gruesome; grim and horrible

camouflage (kam´ ə fläzh´) *n.*: Disguise or concealment

predisposed (prē´ dis pōzd´) *adj.*: Inclined; willing

▲ **Critical Viewing** Why might people "travel up and down the East Coast" to stare at this scenery? **[Connect]**

soft unruly mattresses of them. For children, leaf fall is just one of the odder figments of Nature, like hailstones or snowflakes. Walk down a lane overhung with trees in the never-never land of autumn, and you will forget about time and death, lost in the sheer delicious spill of color. . . .

◆ Build Vocabulary

capricious (kə prē´ shəs) *adj.*: Tending to change abruptly and without apparent reason

But how do the colored leaves fall? As a leaf ages, the growth hormone, auxin, fades, and cells at the base of the petiole divide. Two or three rows of small cells, lying at right angles to the axis of the petiole, react with water, then come apart, leaving the petioles hanging on by only a few threads of xylem. A light breeze, and the leaves are airborne. They glide and swoop, rocking in invisible cradles. They are all

◆ **Reading Strategy**
This passage suggests the author's purpose for writing. What might it be?

wing and may flutter from yard to yard on small whirlwinds or updrafts, swiveling as they go. Firmly tethered to earth, we love to see things rise up and fly—soap bubbles, balloons, birds, fall leaves. They remind us that the end of a season is capricious, as is the end of life. We especially like the way leaves rock, careen, and swoop as they fall. Everyone knows the motion. Pilots sometimes do a maneuver called a "falling leaf," in which the plane loses altitude quickly and on purpose, by slipping first to the right, then to the left. The machine weighs a ton or more, but in one pilot's mind it is a weightless thing, a falling leaf. She has seen the motion before, in the Vermont woods where she played as a child. Below her the trees radiate gold, copper, and red. Leaves are falling, although she can't see them fall, as she falls, swooping down for a closer view.

At last the leaves leave. But first they turn color and thrill us for weeks on end. Then they crunch and crackle underfoot. The *shush*, as children drag their small feet through leaves heaped along the curb. Dark, slimy mats of leaves cling to one's heels after a rain. A damp, stuccolike mortar of semidecayed leaves protects the tender shoots with a roof until spring, and makes a rich humus. An occasional bulge or ripple in the leafy mounds signals a shrew or a field mouse tunneling out of sight. Sometimes one finds in fossil stones the imprint of a leaf, long since disintegrated, whose outlines remind us how detailed, vibrant, and alive are the things of this earth that perish.

◆Guide for Responding

◆ LITERATURE AND YOUR LIFE

Reader's Response Which interested you more—the science details or the author's descriptions and language?

Thematic Focus Does a scientific explanation diminish the wonder of the color changes of the leaves in autumn? Explain.

Art Make a drawing or painting of an autumn scene that you've observed in your region of the country.

☑ Check Your Comprehension

1. When do leaves change color?
2. According to the author, in what two countries are the changing colors of the leaves most spectacular?
3. How does undernourishment affect leaves?
4. Why do leaves fall off trees?

◆ Critical Thinking

INTERPRET

1. What connection does Ackerman make between being a nature writer and a leopard? **[Connect]**
2. Do you think Ackerman's scientific knowledge about leaves comes from observation or research? Explain. **[Speculate]**
3. Do the coloring and falling of leaves have a larger meaning for Ackerman, or is she just writing a nature story? Explain. **[Draw Conclusions]**

APPLY

4. What appeal would this essay have for people who have never witnessed seasonal changes? **[Generalize]**

COMPARE LITERARY WORKS

5. How well did Twain and Ackerman achieve their purposes for writing? Explain. **[Evaluate]**

Guide for Responding (continued)

◆ Reading Strategy

RECOGNIZE THE AUTHOR'S PURPOSE

An **author's purpose** may be to inform, entertain, or persuade. In these selections, the writing style and content help reveal the authors' purposes. For example, the serious style of Ackerman's essay supports her purpose of informing the reader.

1. (a) What is the purpose of Twain's story? (b) What story details support your conclusion?
2. Describe two ways in which Ackerman fulfills her purpose of informing the reader.

◆ Build Vocabulary

USING THE WORD ROOT -grat-

The root -grat- in *gratification* means "pleasing" or "satisfying." On your paper, write the following sentences, filling in the blank with the appropriate word containing -grat- from this list:

    gratitude   ungrateful   gratified

1. Jim Baker was ____?____ that the blue jays used correct grammar.
2. The blue jay was filled with ____?____ for having discovered such a wonderful hole.
3. Only the owl was ____?____ for the privilege of viewing the site of the historic house.

SPELLING STRATEGY

The *er* sound at the end of *singular* is spelled *ar.* Sometimes, this sound at the end of a word may be spelled *er* (manner) or *or* (actor). Learn the following words that end in *ar.* On your paper, write a sentence using each of these words.

1. muscular **2.** popular **3.** circular **4.** calendar

USING THE WORD BANK

On your paper, write the word whose meaning is closest to that of the Word Bank word.

1. camouflage: (a) costume, (b) forest, (c) disguise
2. countenance: (a) look, (b) composure, (c) stature
3. predisposed: (a) wasted, (b) receptive, (c) changed
4. guffawed: (a) groped, (b) laughed, (c) smiled
5. capricious: (a) changeable, (b) easy, (c) flimsy
6. macabre: (a) sad, (b) grim, (c) mediocre
7. gratification: (a) honor, (b) satisfaction, (c) tip
8. singular: (a) alone, (b) chosen, (c) unique

◆ Literary Focus

OBSERVATION

In an **observation,** a writer gives details about an event that he or she has witnessed firsthand. Writers use precise words and vivid language to make readers feel that they are "in the picture."

1. Although Twain's story is told by a fictional narrator, what clues in the story point toward Twain's familiarity with blue jay behavior?
2. Give two examples of vivid language Ackerman uses to share her observations about leaves.
3. How does Ackerman use comparisons to help you understand the scientific facts in her story? Give an example.

◆ Build Grammar Skills

INDIRECT OBJECTS

An **indirect object** is a noun or pronoun that answers *to whom, for whom, to what,* or *for what* after an action verb. All sentences with an indirect object also have a direct object:

          I.O.   D.O.

The leaves showed *her* their <u>colors</u>. (Showed colors to whom? *her*)

          I.O.   D.O.

Ackerman offers *readers* scientific <u>information</u>. (Offered information to whom? *readers*)

Practice In your notebook, identify the indirect object and the direct object in each sentence.

1. The colors give the trees a festive look.
2. Autumn's foliage sends us a message.
3. Ackerman gives readers insights.
4. She brings people fresh insights about the seasons.
5. Fall offers lovers of beauty a unique opportunity.

Writing Application In your notebook, copy the sentences, and insert an indirect object between each action verb and direct object.

1. The bird-watcher gave ____?____ her binoculars.
2. Motels offer ____?____ special foliage season rates.
3. The scientist showed ____?____ examples of seasonal changes.

Build Your Portfolio

Idea Bank

Writing

1. **Descriptive Letter** Imagine that you are in the northeastern United States during fall foliage season. Write a letter to a friend that includes your observations of the changing leaves.

2. **Editor's Foreword** As the editor of an anthology of nature stories, write the foreword to the book, explaining why you included "What Stumped the Blue Jays" and "Why Leaves Turn Color in the Fall." Describe the unique qualities of each story.

3. **Science Magazine** As a writer for a science magazine, revise Twain's story to make it an article suited for your readers. **[Science Link]**

Speaking and Listening

4. **Oral Interpretation** In "What Stumped the Blue Jays" you can hear the blue jay's frantic effort to fill the hole. Read this story passage aloud, beginning with "Then he cocked his head down and took another look." Perform your reading for the class. **[Performing Arts Link]**

5. **Author's Chat [Group Activity]** In a group of three, stage a televised author's chat show with invited guests Mark Twain and Diane Ackerman. One of you will be the host and the others will be the guests. **[Performing Arts Link]**

Projects

6. **Research** Use various resources to find out about distinctive bird calls or songs and what they communicate. Share your findings with classmates by imitating the sounds and telling what you have learned about the birds. **[Science Link]**

7. **Botanical Drawing** Research trees and the distinguishing shapes and colors of their leaves. Then, make a botanical drawing of two or more kinds of leaves. On your completed drawing, identify the type of tree the leaf is from, and label its parts. **[Art Link]**

Writing Mini-Lesson

Observational Essay

Diane Ackerman's observations are more scientific than those presented in "What Stumped the Blue Jays," but both authors give sharp details about nature. Choose a natural event that interests you, observe it, and then share your observations in an essay for your classmates.

Writing Skills Focus: Writing to the Audience

When you write, choose details and a tone or attitude that will appeal to your **audience.** In the following example, Ackerman uses colorful language to appeal to the senses of her readers, who are the general public.

Model From the Essay
The fiercest colors occur in years when the fall sunlight is strongest and the nights are cool and dry. . . . This is also why leaves appear dizzyingly bright and clear on a sunny fall day.

Prewriting Choose a subject that you can observe firsthand. Make detailed notes as you observe your subject. Organize your notes so that you can follow them as you write.

Drafting Introduce the subject of your essay, and follow with a detailed description of your observations. Keep your audience in mind, and find ways to connect with your audience's own experiences.

Revising Review your essay to be sure you've included details appropriate for your audience. Rearrange any details that disrupt the organizational flow. Proofread carefully for errors.

> ◆ **Grammar Application**
> You may be able to replace a prepositional phrase beginning with *to* or *for* with an indirect object. **Phrase:** The dog brought the bone to me. **Indirect Object:** The dog brought me the bone.

Guide for Reading

Meet the Authors:

May Swenson (1919–1989)

May Swenson was born and educated in Utah. After completing college, she moved to New York City, where she worked as an editor and as a university lecturer. Swenson believed that poetry is based on the desire to see things as they are, rather than as they appear. In "Southbound on the Freeway," however, she portrays how our culture might appear to visiting aliens. [For more on May Swenson, see page 814.]

Mark Van Doren (1894–1972)

Mark Van Doren is best known as the winner of the 1940 Pulitzer Prize for Poetry for his *Collected Poems 1922–38.* An English professor at Columbia University, he also wrote critical studies of major writers, including William Shakespeare, Henry David Thoreau, and Nathaniel Hawthorne. Among his collections of poetry are *Spring Thunder and Other Poems* and *A Winter Diary and Other Poems.*

Victor Hernández Cruz (1949–)

Known as a "Nuyorican poet" (for "New York Puerto Rican"), Victor Hernández Cruz began publishing his poetry in the San Francisco Bay Area in the 1970's. His poetry often reads like music, in which the syllables act as chords and notes, producing catchy rhythms.

◆ LITERATURE AND YOUR LIFE

CONNECT YOUR EXPERIENCE

Is the glass half full or half empty? Is a test an obstacle or a chance to show what you know? Your answers to these questions reveal something about your perceptions—how you view the world. In the following poems, the perceptions of the speakers change ordinary people, places, and things into extraordinary ones.

THEMATIC FOCUS: The Extraordinary in the Ordinary

As you read these poems, look for unusual perceptions that make them unique.

◆ Background for Understanding

SOCIAL STUDIES

"Southbound on the Freeway" contains an unusual viewpoint about cars. Little more than a hundred years ago, cars as we know them did not exist. Yet today, much of our culture is based on cars. Because of cars, highways crisscross the country and the economy is based on oil. Collectors restore old cars, and mechanics maintain new ones. Try to imagine life without cars. How would your daily life change?

◆ Build Vocabulary

PREFIXES: *trans-*

In "Southbound on the Freeway," May Swenson uses the word *transparent.* The prefix *trans-,* which means "through" or "across," is a key to the meaning of *transparent,* which means "clear enough to see through."

WORD BANK

Which word from the list relates to the tropics and suggests heat and humidity? Check the Build Vocabulary box on page 469 to see if you chose correctly.

| transparent |
| galore |
| tropical |
| romp |

Southbound on the Freeway ◆ The Story-Teller
◆ Los New Yorks ◆

◆ Literary Focus

FREE VERSE

Free verse is "free" of the traditional structures of poetry. It may contain irregular rhythms and varied line lengths. If it uses rhymes, they are loose and also irregular. Free verse poetry sounds more like conversational speech than other types of poetry.

A poem written in free verse may be long or short, and it may or may not have stanzas. Sometimes, however, as in "Southbound on the Freeway," the stanzas are regular. In general, the lines in free verse flow according to the poet's thoughts, ideas, and images.

◆ Reading Strategy

UNDERSTAND THE AUTHOR'S BIAS

Writers may, intentionally or not, present ideas through their own bias—their own likes and dislikes and particular viewpoint. **Understanding the author's bias** helps you understand his or her world. For example, if you know that Victor Hernández Cruz has a Puerto Rican heritage, you can understand that he is biased toward a tropical environment:

> I present you the tall skyscrapers/as merely huge palm trees with lights . . .

As you read these selections, fill out a chart like the one below.

Poet	Passage	Bias
Swenson	The creatures of this star/are made of metal and glass.	She may feel that cars have taken over the Earth.

SOUTHBOUND ON THE FREEWAY

May Swenson

A tourist came in from Orbitville,
parked in the air, and said:

The creatures of this star
are made of metal and glass.

5 Through the <u>transparent</u> parts
you can see their guts.

Their feet are round and roll
on diagrams—or long

measuring tapes—dark
10 with white lines.

They have four eyes.
The two in the back are red.

Sometimes you can see a five-eyed
one, with a red eye turning

15 on the top of his head.
He must be special—

the others respect him,
and go slow,

when he passes, winding
20 among them from behind.

They all hiss as they glide,
like inches, down the marked

tapes. Those soft shapes,
shadowy inside

25 the hard bodies—are they
their guts or their brains?

◆ **Build Vocabulary**

transparent (trans par´ ənt) *adj.*:
Capable of being seen through;
clear

▶ **Critical Viewing** Judging from
the painting, why might an
alien mistake cars for Earth's
inhabitants? **[Infer]**

Where to? What For? #3, Nancie B. Warner, Courtesy of the artist

THE STORY-TELLER

Mark Van Doren

He talked, and as he talked
Wallpaper came alive;
Suddenly ghosts walked,
And four doors were five;

5   Calendars ran backward,
And maps had mouths;
Ships went tackward[1]
In a great drowse;[2]

Trains climbed trees,
10 And soon dripped down
Like honey of bees
On the cold brick town.

He had wakened a worm
In the world's brain,
15 And nothing stood firm
Until day again.

Inspiration, Daniel Nevins

1. **tackward** (tak´ wərd)
adv.: Against the wind.
2. **drowse** (drouz) *n.*:
Sluggishness; doze.

▲ **Critical Viewing** Does this painting capture the magical quality of the story-teller? Why or why not? **[Evaluate]**

Guide for Responding

◆ LITERATURE AND YOUR LIFE

Reader's Response Which images in "The Story-Teller" appealed to you most? Why?

Thematic Focus Which poem do you find more extraordinary? Explain.

☑ Check Your Comprehension

1. Who is the speaker in "Southbound on the Freeway"?
2. In "Southbound on the Freeway," what is the tourist describing?
3. Name seven magical things that the story-teller can do.
4. According to "The Story-Teller," when will things be back to normal?

◆ Critical Thinking

INTERPRET

1. Compare and contrast the different kinds of creatures described in "Southbound on the Freeway." **[Compare and Contrast]**
2. How would you answer the tourist's question? **[Interpret]**
3. (a) In "The Story-Teller," what is the "worm" referred to in line 13? (b) What is the "world's brain" in line 14? **[Interpret]**
4. What is the message or theme of "The Story-Teller"? **[Analyze]**

APPLY

5. How might the tourist in "Southbound on the Freeway" "see" a drive-through window at a fast-food restaurant? **[Relate]**

Los New Yorks

Victor Hernández Cruz

New York City—Bird's Eye View, 1920, Joaquin Torres-Garcia, Yale University Art Gallery

▲ **Critical Viewing** Do you have the feeling that in the world of this painting "Everything will pass you by"? Explain. **[Assess]**

In the news that sails through the air
Like the shaking seeds of maracas[1]
I find you out

Suena[2]

5   You don't have to move here
Just stand on the corner
Everything will pass you by
Like a merry-go-round the red
bricks will swing past your eyes
10 They will melt
So   old
will move out by themselves

Suena

I present you the tall skyscrapers
15 as merely huge palm trees with lights

Suena

The roaring of the trains is a fast
guaguanco[3]
dance of the ages

20 Suena

Snow falls
Coconut chips galore
Take the train to Caguas[4]
and the bus is only ten cents
25 to Aguas Buenas[5]

---

1. maracas (mə rä′ kəs) *n.*: Percussion instruments consisting of a rattle with loose pebbles in it, which are shaken.
2. Suena (swā′ nə): Spanish for "It echoes."

3. guaguanco (gwə gwän′ kō): Rumba, a dance with a complex rhythm.
4. Caguas (kä′ gwäs): City in the east-central region of Puerto Rico.
5. Aguas Buenas (ä′ gwäs bwā′ nəs): City in Puerto Rico, northwest of Caguas.

Suena

A tropical wave settled here
And it is pulling the sun
with a romp
30   No one knows what to do

Suena

I am going home now
I am settled there with my fruits
Everything tastes good today
35   Even the ones that are grown here
Taste like they're from outer space
Walk y Suena[6]
Do it strange
Los New Yorks.

---

6.   **y suena** (ē swā´ nə): Spanish for "With the rhythm of the echoes."

◆ Build Vocabulary

galore (gə lôr´) *adj.*: In abundance; plentiful

tropical (träp´ ə kəl) *adj.*: Very hot; sultry

romp (rämp) *n.*: Lively play or frolic

Beyond Literature

Social Studies Connection

Puerto Rico   In "Los New Yorks," Victor Hernández Cruz compares the tropical atmosphere of Puerto Rico, a commonwealth of the United States, with metropolitan New York. Puerto Rico is an island located about 1,000 miles southeast of Florida. It has a pleasant climate, largely influenced by the warm waters of the Caribbean. Most of the region's land is mountainous, but a walk along the coast provides picturesque views of beaches and rows of flourishing palm trees, which provide the meat and sweet milk of the coconut.

Cross-Curricular Activity
Do further research on the climate and geography of Puerto Rico. Combine your findings into a multimedia report to present to your class.

Guide for Responding

◆ LITERATURE AND YOUR LIFE

Reader's Response   Based on the details in this poem, would you like to visit "Los New Yorks"? Explain.

Thematic Focus   What is extraordinary about New York? What about New York is ordinary?

Sketch   Draw a sketch of New York based on the description provided in "Los New Yorks."

☑ **Check Your Comprehension**

1. Where is the speaker?
2. What two places is the speaker comparing?

◆ Critical Thinking

INTERPRET

1. What evidence is there that the speaker has strong memories of another place? **[Support]**
2. When the speaker says that he is going home, where is he going? **[Draw Conclusions]**
3. What effect does the repetition of the Spanish word *suena* have on the poem? **[Interpret]**

COMPARE LITERARY WORKS

4. Compare the rhythms, rhymes, and stanza lengths of "The Story-Teller," "Southbound on the Freeway," and "Los New Yorks." How does each style contribute to the feel and effect of the poem? **[Compare and Contrast]**

Guide for Responding (continued)

◆ Reading Strategy

UNDERSTAND THE AUTHOR'S BIAS

If you **understand the author's bias,** you recognize his or her tendency to be for or against something.

1. What is May Swenson's attitude toward cars and their importance in our lives?
2. How does Mark Van Doren feel about the art of storytelling?
3. What does "Los New Yorks" reveal about Victor Hernández Cruz's bias concerning New York?

◆ Build Vocabulary

USING THE PREFIX trans-

The prefix trans- in transparent means "through" or "across." Determine the meaning of the following words with the prefix trans-. Then, on your paper, complete the sentences with one of these words: transatlantic, transcontinental, transform, transplant.

1. Soon the ugly duckling will _____?_____ into a graceful swan.
2. We took a _____?_____ road trip.
3. Should we _____?_____ this tree in the back yard?
4. Our _____?_____ cruise took more than a week.

SPELLING STRATEGY

The ending cal usually indicates an adjective; cle is always a noun ending.

On your paper, write the word in each pair that is spelled correctly.

1. tropical, tropicle
2. icical, icicle
3. bicycal, bicycle
4. medical, medicle
5. historical, historicle
6. musical, musicle

USING THE WORD BANK

On your paper, write the letter of the definition that matches the numbered word from the Word Bank.

1. galore
2. romp
3. transparent
4. tropical

a. hot and humid
b. may be seen through
c. noisy play
d. in great amounts

◆ Literary Focus

FREE VERSE

Poetry that has irregular rhythms, rhymes, and stanzas is called **free verse.** You will notice that "Southbound on the Freeway" and "Los New Yorks," which are written in free verse, sound more like everyday speech than "The Story-Teller" does.

1. Explain why "The Story-Teller" does not fit the definition of free verse.
2. How do the stanzas of "Los New Yorks" illustrate free verse form?
3. What does a poet accomplish by using free verse rather than traditional forms?

◆ Build Grammar Skills

PREDICATE ADJECTIVES

A **predicate adjective** is an adjective that comes after a linking verb and refers to the subject, describing it.

Their feet are *round.* . . . (The adjective *round* describes the subject *feet.*)

He must be *special.* . . . (The adjective *special* describes the subject *he.*)

Practice Write these sentences on your paper, and underline the predicate adjective in each. Circle the subject to which it refers.

1. The storyteller is almost magical.
2. The aliens were strange.
3. The bricks are red.
4. The palm trees seem huge.
5. The fruit tastes good.

Writing Application On your paper, write a sentence that uses the idea in each phrase. Make the adjective in each phrase a predicate adjective in the sentence.

1. talkative storyteller
2. red eyes
3. special creature
4. shadowy shapes
5. tall skyscrapers
6. sweet peaches

Build Your Portfolio

 Idea Bank

Writing

1. **Travel Advertisement** Imagine that you are a travel agent from Orbitville. You are trying to interest tourists on your planet in travel to Earth. Write a travel advertisement, telling them what they might find if they make the trip. **[Career Link]**

2. **City Poem** The speaker in "Los New Yorks" describes New York City. Write your own description of a major city in the form of a free verse poem. **[Social Studies Link]**

3. **Analysis** Write a paper in which you analyze the images in one of these poems. Describe the poet's choice of words, the originality of the images, and their overall effectiveness. Cite lines from the poem to support your ideas.

Speaking and Listening

4. **Talk-Show Appearance [Group Activity]** With a partner, act out an episode of a talk show on Orbitville for the class. One of you is the host, and the other has just returned from a trip to Earth. **[Media Link]**

5. **Storyteller** Perform a story for your class. You may make up a story or tell one you know. Try to make your storytelling a magical experience, like the one described in Van Doren's poem. **[Performing Arts Link]**

Projects

6. **Multimedia Report** Put together a multimedia report on New York City. Gather photos, magazine and newspaper clippings, and, if possible, souvenirs and videotapes. Write your text, and present the report to the class. **[Social Studies Link]**

7. **Painting** Bring "Southbound on the Freeway" to life in a painting. Show Earthlings as seen by the poem's speaker. Display your painting for the class. **[Art Link]**

 Writing Mini-Lesson

Poem About a Person or Place

In these poems, you get the poet's attitude toward a person, place, or thing. To create their unique attitudes, the poets chose words to create very specific images. Write a poem about a person or place, and bring it to life through your word choice.

Writing Skills Focus: Using Appropriate Tone

Decide on your attitude toward your subject. Your attitude will help you develop an **appropriate tone,** which is achieved through word choice. In this example, the tone is somewhat distanced and unemotional, like that of a reporter.

Model From "Southbound on the Freeway"

> The creatures of this star
> are made of metal and glass.
>
> Through the transparent parts
> you can see their guts.

Prewriting Choose a subject for your poem. Decide on a tone, and choose details to use in your poem. Also, decide whether you will use free verse or a more traditional form that will require rhyme and specific line and stanza breaks.

Drafting Begin drafting. If you're writing free verse, break stanzas when you change a thought. If you're writing within a traditional poetic form, follow the appropriate structure and rhyme scheme.

◆ **Grammar Application**
Make your predicate adjectives, like all adjectives, vivid and precise.

Revising Look for places where more precise words will make your subject more vivid. Replace words and phrases that do not contribute to the tone you've chosen. Proofread your poem to correct errors.

Guide for Reading

Meet the Author:

Sir Arthur Conan Doyle (1859–1930)

Born in Edinburgh, Scotland, Doyle took up writing mystery stories in his early twenties. Although he had studied medicine, one of his professors said that Doyle was often more accurate in guessing the occupations of his patients than in diagnosing their illnesses. In 1887, he published the first Sherlock Holmes story, "A Study in Scarlet." Doyle went on to write fifty-six stories and four novels about Holmes.

The Detective That Would Not Die Doyle sometimes felt that his other writing was overlooked because of the success of his Sherlock Holmes stories. By 1893, he was so fed up with the character that he wrote "The Final Problem," in which Holmes dies. But public demand for more of Sherlock Holmes was so overwhelming that Doyle gave in and wrote "The Hound of the Baskervilles" in 1901 and in later years wrote other Holmes tales.

THE STORY BEHIND THE STORY

At the time Doyle wrote this mystery, Britain governed India. According to critic Michael Atkinson, Doyle became interested in Indian philosophy and encountered this statement: "[Y]ou see a rope and think it is a snake. As soon as you realize that the rope is a rope, your false perception of a snake ceases." Doyle then played with this idea, and it formed the backbone of the mystery in "The Adventure of the Speckled Band."

◆ LITERATURE AND YOUR LIFE

CONNECT YOUR EXPERIENCE

Who's your favorite fictional detective? Jessica Fletcher? Nancy Drew? One of the most beloved fictional detectives of all time is Sherlock Holmes, pictured at right. You'll read one of his most baffling cases in "The Adventure of the Speckled Band."

THEMATIC FOCUS: The Extraordinary in the Ordinary

As you read, ask: "What small and seemingly unimportant clues lead Holmes to surprising conclusions?

◆ Background for Understanding

LITERATURE

The mastermind detective Sherlock Holmes is known for his deductive reasoning: He analyzes evidence and draws specific conclusions. In one story, he notes that "when you have eliminated the impossible, whatever remains, *however improbable,* must be the truth." Created more than a hundred years ago, Holmes is as popular as ever, appearing in countless television series, films, and plays. Fan clubs devoted to the great detective thrive around the world and on the Internet.

◆ Build Vocabulary

RELATED WORDS: FORMS OF *convulse*

In this story, the limbs of a poisoning victim become dreadfully *convulsed.* The word *convulse* means "to shake violently." Related forms of the word include *convulsed, convulsion,* and *convulsive.*

WORD BANK

Which word from the list has a prefix meaning "many"? Check the Build Vocabulary box on page 477 to see if you chose correctly.

defray
manifold
morose
convulsed
imperturbably
reverie
tangible

◆ The Adventure of the Speckled Band ◆

◆ Literary Focus

MYSTERY STORY

A **mystery story** is a fictional tale that tells how a puzzling mystery is solved. The leading character in a mystery is often a detective or sleuth who matches wits with someone who has committed a crime. The conflict of the story usually lies in the criminal's attempts to avoid discovery and the detective's attempts to uncover the clues that will solve the mystery.

In "The Adventure of the Speckled Band," Sherlock Holmes uses his powers of deduction to identify and catch the criminal.

◆ Reading Strategy

IDENTIFY THE EVIDENCE

Mystery writers know that readers enjoy "playing detective" as they read, trying to guess the solution to the mystery. To solve the mystery, **identify the evidence,** or proof, from which to draw conclusions about who committed the crime. Keep in mind, however, that some details are intentionally included to mislead the reader.

As you read this mystery, keep an evidence chart like the one below. Like Holmes, use your powers of observation and logical reasoning to make predictions and solve the mystery.

Evidence	**Prediction**
A whistle was heard.	The whistle is an important clue.

THE ADVENTURE of the SPECKLED BAND

Sir Arthur Conan Doyle

On glancing over my notes of the seventy odd cases in which I have during the last eight years studied the methods of my friend Sherlock Holmes, I find many tragic, some comic, a large number merely strange, but none commonplace; for, working as he did rather for the love of his art than for the acquirement of wealth, he refused to associate himself with any investigation which did not tend towards the unusual, and even the fantastic. Of all these varied cases, however, I cannot recall any which presented more singular features than that which was associated with the well-known Surrey family of the Roylotts of Stoke Moran. The events in question occurred in the early days of my association with Holmes when we were sharing rooms as bachelors in Baker Street. It is possible that I might have placed them upon record before but a promise of secrecy was made at the time, from which I have only been freed during the last month by the untimely death of the lady to whom the pledge was given. It is perhaps as well that the facts should now come to light, for I have reasons to know that there are widespread rumors as to the death of Dr. Grimesby Roylott which tend to make the matter even more terrible than the truth.

It was early in April in the year 1883 that I woke one morning to find Sherlock Holmes standing, fully dressed, by the side of my bed. He was a late riser, as a rule, and as the clock on the mantelpiece showed me that it was only a quarter past seven, I blinked up at him in some surprise, and perhaps just a little resentment, for I was myself regular in my habits.

"Very sorry to wake you up, Watson," said he, "but it's the common lot this morning. Mrs. Hudson has been awakened, she retorted upon me, and I on you."

"What is it, then—a fire?"

"No; a client. It seems that a young lady has arrived in a considerable state of excitement who insists upon seeing me. She is waiting now in the sitting room. Now, when young ladies wander about the metropolis at this hour of the morning, and get sleepy people up out of their beds, I presume that it is something very pressing which they have to communicate. Should it prove to be an interesting case, you would, I am sure, wish to follow it from the outset. I thought, at any rate, that I should call you and give you the chance."

"My dear fellow, I would not miss it for anything."

I had no keener pleasure than in following Holmes in his professional investigations, and in admiring the rapid deductions, as swift as intuitions, and yet always founded on a logical basis, with which he unraveled the problems which were submitted to him. I rapidly threw on my clothes and was ready in a few minutes to accompany my friend down to the sitting room. A lady dressed in black and heavily veiled, who had been sitting in the window, rose as we entered.

"Good morning, madam," said Holmes cheerily. "My name is Sherlock Holmes. This is my intimate friend and associate, Dr. Watson, before whom you can speak as freely as before myself. Ha! I am glad to see that Mrs. Hudson has had the good sense to light the fire. Pray draw up to it, and I shall order you a cup of hot coffee, for I observe that you are shivering."

"It is not cold which makes me shiver," said the woman in a low voice,

◆ **Literature and Your Life**

Does this introduction to Sherlock Holmes fit the picture you have of him through film and television portrayals?

changing her seat as requested.

"What, then?"

"It is fear, Mr. Holmes. It is terror." She raised her veil as she spoke, and we could see that she was indeed in a pitiable state of agitation, her face all drawn and gray, with restless, frightened eyes, like those of some hunted animal. Her features and figure were those of a woman of thirty, but her hair was shot with premature gray, and her expression was weary and haggard. Sherlock Holmes ran her over with one of his quick, all-comprehensive glances.

"You must not fear," said he soothingly, bending forward and patting her forearm.

"We shall soon set matters right, I have no doubt. You have come in by train this morning, I see."

"You know me, then?"

"No, but I observe the second half of a return ticket in the palm of your left glove. You must have started early, and yet you had a good drive in a dogcart[1] along heavy roads, before you reached the station."

▲ **Critical Viewing** What can you tell about the characters of Helen Stoner, Holmes, and Watson based on this illustration? [Infer]

The lady gave a violent start and stared in bewilderment at my companion.

"There is no mystery, my dear madam," said he, smiling. "The left arm of your jacket is spattered with mud in no less than seven places. The marks are perfectly fresh. There is no vehicle save a dogcart which throws up mud in that way, and then only when you sit on the left-hand side of the driver."

"Whatever your reasons may be, you are perfectly correct," said she. "I started from home before six, reached Leatherhead at twenty past, and came in by the

---

1. **dogcart:** Small horse-drawn carriage with seats arranged back-to-back.

first train to Waterloo. Sir, I can stand this strain no longer; I shall go mad if it continues. I have no one to turn to—none, save only one, who cares for me, and he, poor fellow, can be of little aid. I have heard of you, Mr. Holmes. I have heard of you from Mrs. Farintosh, whom you helped in the hour of her sore need. It was from her that I had your address. Oh, sir, do you not think that you could help me, too, and at least throw a little light through the dense darkness which surrounds me? At present it is out of my power to reward you for your service, but in a month or six weeks I shall be married, with the control of my own income, and then at least you shall not find me ungrateful."

Holmes turned to his desk and, unlocking it, drew out a small case book, which he consulted.

"Farintosh," said he. "Ah yes, I recall the case; it was concerned with an opal tiara. I think it was before your time, Watson. I can only say, madam, that I shall be happy to devote the same care to your case as I did to that of your friend. As to reward, my profession is its own reward; but you are at liberty to defray whatever expenses I may be put to, at the time which suits you best. And now I beg that you will lay before us everything that may help us in forming an opinion upon the matter."

"Alas!" replied our visitor, "the very horror of my situation lies in the fact that my fears are so vague, and my suspicions depend so entirely upon small points, which might seem trivial to another, that even he to whom of all others I have a right to look for help and advice looks upon all that I tell him about it as fancy. He does not say so, but I can read it from his soothing answers and averted eyes. But I have heard, Mr. Holmes, that you can see deeply into the manifold wickedness of the human heart. You may advise me how to walk amid the dangers which encompass me."

"I am all attention, madam."

"My name is Helen Stoner, and I am living with my stepfather, who is the last survivor of one of the oldest Saxon families in England: the Roylotts of Stoke Moran, on the western border of Surrey."

Holmes nodded his head. "The name is familiar to me," said he.

"The family was at one time among the richest in England, and the estates extended over the borders into Berkshire in the north, and Hampshire in the west. In the last century, however, four successive heirs were of a dissolute and wasteful disposition, and the family ruin was eventually completed by a gambler in the days of the Regency. Nothing was left save a few acres of ground, and the two-hundred-year-old house, which is itself crushed under a heavy mortgage. The last squire dragged out his existence there, living the horrible life of an aristocratic pauper; but his only son, my stepfather, seeing that he must adapt himself to the new conditions, obtained an advance from a relative, which enabled him to take a medical degree and went out to Calcutta, where, by his professional skill and his force of character, he established a large practice. In a fit of anger, however, caused by some robberies which had been perpetrated in the house, he beat his native butler to death and narrowly escaped a capital sentence. As it was, he suffered a long term of imprisonment and afterwards returned to England a morose and disappointed man.

"When Dr. Roylott was in India he married my mother, Mrs. Stoner, the young widow of Major-General Stoner, of the Bengal Artillery. My sister Julia and I were twins, and we were only two years old at the time of my mother's remarriage. She had a considerable sum of money—not less than £1000 a year[2]—and this she bequeathed to Dr. Roylott entirely while we resided with him, with a provision that a certain annual sum should be allowed to

---

2. £1000: One thousand pounds; £ is the symbol for pound or pounds, the British unit of money.

each of us in the event of our marriage. Shortly after our return to England my mother died—she was killed eight years ago in a railway accident near Crewe. Dr. Roylott then abandoned his attempts to establish himself in practice in London and took us to live with him in the old ancestral house at Stoke Moran. The money which my mother had left was enough for all our wants, and there seemed to be no obstacle to our happiness.

"But a terrible change came over our stepfather about this time. Instead of making friends and exchanging visits with our neighbors, who had at first been overjoyed to see a Roylott of Stoke Moran back in the old family seat, he shut himself up in his house and seldom came out save to indulge in ferocious quarrels with whoever might cross his path. Violence of temper approaching to mania has been hereditary in the men of the family, and in my stepfather's case it had, I believe, been intensified by his long residence in the tropics. A series of disgraceful brawls took place, two of which ended in the police court, until at last he became the terror of the village, and the folks would fly at his approach, for he is a man of immense strength, and absolutely uncontrollable in his anger.

"Last week he hurled the local blacksmith over a parapet into a stream, and it was only by paying over all the money which I could gather together that I was able to avert another public exposure. He had no friends at all save the wandering gypsies, and he would give these vagabonds leave to encamp upon the few acres of bramble-covered land which represent

▲ **Critical Viewing** Which event in Roylott's life does this illustration depict? **[Connect]**

the family estate, and would accept in return the hospitality of their tents, wandering away with them sometimes for weeks on end. He has a passion also for Indian animals, which are sent over to him by a correspondent, and he has at this moment a cheetah and a baboon, which wander freely over his grounds and are feared by the villagers almost as much as is their master.

◆ Build Vocabulary

defray (di frā´) v.: To pay or furnish the money for

manifold (man´ ə fōld´) adj.: Many and varied

morose (mə rōs´) adj.: Gloomy; ill-tempered; sullen

"You can imagine from what I say that my poor sister Julia and I had no great pleasure in our lives. No servant would stay with us, and for a long time we did all the work of the house. She was but thirty at the time of her death, and yet her hair had already begun to whiten, even as mine has."

"Your sister is dead, then?"

"She died just two years ago, and it is of her death that I wish to speak to you. You can understand that, living the life which I have described, we were little likely to see anyone of our own age and position. We had, however, an aunt, my mother's maiden sister, Miss Honoria Westphail, who lives near Harrow, and we were occasionally allowed to pay short visits at this lady's house. Julia went there at Christmas two years ago, and met there a major in the Marines, to whom she became engaged. My stepfather learned of the engagement when my sister returned and offered no objection to the marriage; but within a fortnight of the day which had been fixed for the wedding, the terrible event occurred which has deprived me of my only companion."

Sherlock Holmes had been leaning back in his chair with his eyes closed and his head sunk in a cushion, but he half opened his lids now and glanced across at his visitor.

"Pray be precise as to details," said he.

"It is easy for me to be so, for every event of that dreadful time is seared into my memory. The manor house is, as I have already said, very old, and only one wing is now inhabited. The bedrooms in this wing are on the ground floor, the sitting rooms being in the central block of the buildings. Of these bedrooms the first is Dr. Roylott's, the second my sister's, and the third my own. There is no communication between them, but they all open out into the same corridor. Do I make myself plain?"

"Perfectly so."

"The windows of the three rooms open out upon the lawn. That fatal night Dr. Roylott had gone to his room early, though we knew that he had not retired to rest, for my sister was troubled by the smell of the strong Indian cigars which it was his custom to smoke. She left her room, therefore, and came into mine, where she sat for some time, chatting about her approaching wedding. At eleven o'clock she rose to leave me, but she paused at the door and looked back.

"'Tell me, Helen,' said she, 'have you ever heard anyone whistle in the dead of the night?'

"'Never,' said I.

"'I suppose that you could not possibly whistle, yourself, in your sleep?'

"'Certainly not. But why?'

"'Because during the last few nights I have always, about three in the morning, heard a low, clear whistle. I am a light sleeper, and it has awakened me. I cannot tell where it came from—perhaps from the next room, perhaps from the lawn. I thought that I would just ask you whether you had heard it.'

"'No, I have not. It must be the gypsies in the plantation.'

"'Very likely. And yet if it were on the lawn, I wonder that you did not hear it also.'

"'Ah, but I sleep more heavily than you.'

"'Well, it is of no great consequence, at any rate.' She smiled back at me, closed my door, and a few moments later I heard her key turn in the lock."

"Indeed," said Holmes. "Was it your custom always to lock yourselves in at night?"

"Always."

"And why?"

"I think that I mentioned to you that the doctor kept a cheetah and a baboon. We had no feeling of security unless our doors were locked."

"Quite so. Pray proceed with your statement."

"I could not sleep that night. A vague feeling of impending misfortune impressed me. My sister and I, you will recollect, were twins, and you know how subtle are the links which bind two souls which are so closely allied. It was a wild night. The wind was howling outside, and the rain was beating and splashing against the windows. Suddenly, amid all the hubbub of the gale, there burst forth the wild scream of a terrified woman. I knew that it was my sister's voice. I sprang from my bed, wrapped a shawl round me, and rushed into the corridor. As I opened my door I seemed to hear a low whistle, such as my sister described, and a few moments later a clanging sound, as if a mass of metal had fallen. As I ran down the passage, my sister's door was unlocked, and revolved slowly upon its hinges. I stared at it horror-stricken, not knowing what was about to issue from it. By the light of the corridor lamp I saw my sister appear at the opening, her face blanched with terror, her hands groping for help, her whole figure swaying to and fro like that of a drunkard. I ran to her and threw my arms round her, but at that moment her knees seemed to give way and she fell to the ground. She writhed as one who is in terrible pain, and her limbs were dreadfully <u>convulsed</u>. At first I thought that she had not recognized me, but as I bent over her she suddenly shrieked out in a voice which I shall never forget, 'Oh, Helen! It was the band! The speckled band!' There was something else which she would fain have said, and she stabbed with her finger into the air in the direction of the doctor's room, but a fresh convulsion

▲ **Critical Viewing** How well does this illustration convey Julia Stoner's face, "blanched with terror"? **[Evaluate]**

seized her and choked her words. I rushed out, calling loudly for my stepfather, and I met him hastening from his room in his dressing gown. When he reached my sister's side she was unconscious, and though he poured brandy down her throat and sent for medical aid from the village, all efforts were in vain, for she slowly sank and died without having recovered her consciousness. Such was the dreadful end of my beloved sister."

"One moment," said Holmes; "are you sure about this whistle and metallic sound? Could you swear to it?"

"That was what the county coroner asked me at the inquiry. It is my strong impression that I heard it, and yet, among the crash of the gale and the creaking of an old house, I may possibly have been deceived."

"Was your sister dressed?"

"No, she was in her nightdress. In her right hand was found the charred stump of a match, and in her left a matchbox."

"Showing that she had struck a light and looked about her when the alarm took place. That is important. And what conclusions did the coroner come to?"

"He investigated the case with great care, for Dr. Roylott's conduct had long been notorious in the county, but he was unable to find any satisfactory cause of

◆ **Build Vocabulary**

convulsed (kən vulst´) *adj.*: Taken over by violent, involuntary spasms

death. My evidence showed that the door had been fastened upon the inner side, and the windows were blocked by old-fashioned shutters with broad iron bars, which were secured every night. The walls were carefully sounded, and were shown to be quite solid all round, and the flooring was also thoroughly examined, with the same result. The chimney is wide, but is barred up by four large staples. It is certain, therefore, that my sister was quite alone when she met her end. Besides, there were no marks of any violence upon her."

♦ **Literary Focus**
What character would you say is the primary suspect in the death of Julia Stoner?

"How about poison?"

"The doctors examined her for it, but without success."

"What do you think that this unfortunate lady died of, then?"

"It is my belief that she died of pure fear and nervous shock, though what it was that frightened her I cannot imagine."

"Were there gypsies in the plantation at the time?"

"Yes, there are nearly always some there."

"Ah, and what did you gather from this allusion to a band—a speckled band?"

"Sometimes I have thought that it was merely the wild talk of delirium, sometimes that it may have referred to some band of people, perhaps to these very gypsies in the plantation. I do not know whether the spotted handkerchiefs which so many of them wear over their heads might have suggested the strange adjective which she used."

Holmes shook his head like a man who is far from being satisfied.

"These are very deep waters," said he; "pray go on with your narrative."

"Two years have passed since then, and my life has been until lately lonelier than ever. A month ago, however, a dear friend, whom I have known for many years, has done me the honor to ask my hand in marriage. His name is Armitage—Percy Armitage—the second son of Mr.

Armitage, of Crane Water, near Reading. My stepfather has offered no opposition to the match, and we are to be married in the course of the spring. Two days ago some repairs were started in the west wing of the building, and my bedroom wall has been pierced, so that I have had to move into the chamber in which my sister died, and to sleep in the very bed in which she slept. Imagine, then, my thrill of terror when last night, as I lay awake, thinking over her terrible fate, I suddenly heard in the silence of the night the low whistle which had been the herald of her own death. I sprang up and lit the lamp, but nothing was to be seen in the room. I was too shaken to go to bed again, however, so I dressed, and as soon as it was daylight I slipped down, got a dogcart at the Crown Inn, which is opposite, and drove to Leatherhead, from whence I have come on this morning with the one object of seeing you and asking your advice."

"You have done wisely," said my friend. "But have you told me all?"

"Yes, all."

"Miss Roylott, you have not. You are screening your stepfather."

"Why, what do you mean?"

For answer Holmes pushed back the frill of black lace which fringed the hand that lay upon our visitor's knee. Five little livid spots, the marks of four fingers and a thumb, were printed upon the white wrist.

"You have been cruelly used," said Holmes.

The lady colored deeply and covered over her injured wrist. "He is a hard man," she said, "and perhaps he hardly knows his own strength."

There was a long silence, during which Holmes leaned his chin upon his hands and stared into the crackling fire.

"This is a very deep business," he said at last. "There are a thousand details which I should desire to know before I decide upon our course of action. Yet we have not a moment to lose. If we were to come to Stoke Moran today, would it be possible for us to

▲ **Critical Viewing** Which figure in the illustration is Dr. Roylott? How do you know? [Deduce]

look over these rooms without the knowledge of your stepfather?"

"As it happens, he spoke of coming into town today upon some most important business. It is probable that he will be away all day and that there would be nothing to disturb you. We have a housekeeper now, but I could easily get her out of the way."

"Excellent. You are not averse to this trip, Watson?"

"By no means."

"Then we shall both come. What are you going to do yourself?"

"I have one or two things which I would wish to do now that I am in town. But I shall return by the twelve o'clock train, so as to be there in time for your coming."

"And you may expect us early in the afternoon. I have myself some small business matters to attend to. Will you not wait and breakfast?"

"No, I must go. My heart is lightened already since I have confided my trouble to you. I shall look forward to seeing you again this afternoon." She dropped her thick black veil over her face and glided from the room.

"And what do you think of it all, Watson?" asked Sherlock Holmes, leaning back in his chair.

"It seems to me to be a most dark and sinister business."

"Dark enough and sinister enough."

"Yet if the lady is correct in saying that the flooring and walls are sound, and that the door, window, and chimney are impassable, then her sister must have been undoubtedly alone when she met her mysterious end."

"What becomes, then, of these nocturnal whistles, and what of the very peculiar words of the dying woman?"

"I cannot think."

"When you combine the ideas of whistles at night, the presence of a band of gypsies who are on intimate terms with this old doctor, the fact that we have every reason to believe that the doctor has an interest in preventing his stepdaughter's marriage, the dying allusion to a band, and, finally, the fact that Miss Helen Stoner heard a metallic clang, which might have been caused by one of those metal bars that secured the shutters, falling back into its place, I think that there is good ground to think that the mystery may be cleared along those lines."

"But what, then, did the gypsies do?"

"I cannot imagine."

"I see many objections to any such theory."

"And so do I. It is precisely for that reason that we are going to Stoke Moran this day. I want to see whether the objections are fatal, or if they may be explained away. But what in the name of the devil!"

The ejaculation had been drawn from my companion by the fact that our door had been suddenly dashed open, and that a huge man had framed himself in the aperture. His costume was a peculiar mixture of the professional and of the agricultural, having a black top hat, a long frock coat, and a pair of high gaiters,[3] with a hunting crop swinging in his hand. So tall was he that his hat actually brushed the crossbar of the doorway, and his breadth seemed to span it across from side to side. A large face, seared with a thousand wrinkles, burned yellow with the sun, and marked with every evil passion, was turned from one to the other of us, while his deep-set, bile-shot eyes, and his high, thin, fleshless nose, gave him somewhat the resemblance to a fierce old bird of prey.

"Which of you is Holmes?" asked this apparition.

"My name, sir; but you have the advantage of me," said my companion quietly.

"I am Dr. Grimesby Roylott, of Stoke Moran."

"Indeed, Doctor," said Holmes blandly. "Pray take a seat."

"I will do nothing of the kind. My stepdaughter has been here. I have traced her. What has she been saying to you?"

"It is a little cold for the time of the year," said Holmes.

"What has she been saying to you?" screamed the old man furiously.

---

3. **gaiters** (gāt´ ərz) *n.*: Cloth or leather coverings for the ankles and calves of legs.

♦ **Build Vocabulary**

imperturbably (im´ pər tʉr´ bə blē) *adv.*: Unexcitedly; impassively

"But I have heard that the crocuses promise well," continued my companion imperturbably.

"Ha! You put me off, do you?" said our new visitor, taking a step forward and shaking his hunting crop. "I know you, you scoundrel! I have heard of you before. You are Holmes, the meddler."

My friend smiled.

"Holmes, the busybody!"

His smile broadened.

"Holmes, the Scotland Yard Jack-in-office!"

Holmes chuckled heartily. "Your conversation is most entertaining," said he. "When you go out close the door, for there is a decided draft."

"I will go when I have said my say. Don't you dare to meddle with my affairs. I know that Miss Stoner has been here. I traced her! I am a dangerous man to fall foul of! See here." He stepped swiftly forward, seized the poker, and bent it into a curve with his huge brown hands.

"See that you keep yourself out of my grip," he snarled, and hurling the twisted poker into the fireplace he strode out of the room.

"He seems a very amiable person," said Holmes, laughing. "I am not quite so bulky, but if he had remained I might have shown him that my grip was not much more feeble than his own." As he spoke he picked up the steel poker and, with a sudden effort, straightened it out again.

"Fancy his having the insolence to confound me with[4] the official detective force! This incident gives zest to our investigation, however, and I only trust that our little friend will not suffer from her imprudence in allowing this brute to trace her. And now, Watson, we shall order breakfast, and afterwards I shall walk down to Doctors' Commons, where I hope to get some data which may help us in this matter."

It was nearly one o'clock when Sherlock Holmes returned from his excursion. He

---

4. **confound . . . with:** Mistake me for.

held in his hand a sheet of blue paper, scrawled over with notes and figures.

"I have seen the will of the deceased wife," said he. "To determine its exact meaning I have been obliged to work out the present prices of the investments with which it is concerned. The total income, which at the time of the wife's death was little short of £1100, is now, through the fall in agricultural prices, not more than £750. Each daughter can claim an income of £250, in case of marriage. It is evident, therefore, that if both girls had married, this beauty would have had a mere pittance,[5] while even one of them would cripple him to a very serious extent. My morning's work has not been wasted, since it has proved that he has the very strongest motives for standing in the way of anything of the sort. And now, Watson, this is too serious for dawdling, especially as the old man is aware that we are interesting ourselves in his affairs; so if you are ready, we shall call a cab and drive to Waterloo. I should be very much obliged if you would slip your revolver into your pocket. An Eley's No. 2 is an excellent argument with gentlemen who can twist steel pokers into knots. That and a toothbrush are, I think, all that we need."

At Waterloo we were fortunate in catching a train for Leatherhead, where we hired a trap at the station inn and drove for four or five miles through the lovely Surrey lanes. It was a perfect day, with a bright sun and a few fleecy clouds in the heavens. The trees and wayside hedges were just throwing out their first green shoots, and the air was full of the pleasant smell of the moist earth. To me at least there was a strange contrast between the sweet promise of the spring and this sinister quest upon which we were engaged. My companion sat in the front of the trap, his arms folded, his hat pulled down over his eyes, and his chin sunk upon his breast, buried in the deepest thought. Suddenly, however, he started, tapped me on the shoulder, and pointed over the meadows.

"Look there!" said he.

A heavily timbered park stretched up in a gentle slope, thickening into a grove at the highest point. From amid the branches there jutted out the gray gables and high rooftop of a very old mansion.

"Stoke Moran?" said he.

"Yes, sir, that be the house of Dr. Grimesby Roylott," remarked the driver.

"There is some building going on there," said Holmes; "that is where we are going."

"There's the village," said the driver, pointing to a cluster of roofs some distance to the left; "but if you want to get to the house, you'll find it shorter to get over this stile, and so by the footpath over the fields. There it is, where the lady is walking."

"And the lady, I fancy, is Miss Stoner," observed Holmes, shading his eyes. "Yes, I think we had better do as you suggest."

We got off, paid our fare, and the trap rattled back on its way to Leatherhead.

"I thought it as well," said Holmes as we climbed the stile, "that this fellow should think we had come here as architects, or on some definite business. It may stop his gossip. Good afternoon, Miss Stoner. You see that we have been as good as our word."

Our client of the morning had hurried forward to meet us with a face which spoke her joy. "I have been waiting so eagerly for you," she cried, shaking hands with us warmly. "All has turned out splendidly. Dr. Roylott has gone to town, and it is unlikely that he will be back before evening."

"We have had the pleasure of making the doctor's acquaintance," said Holmes, and in a few words he sketched out what had occurred. Miss Stoner turned white to the lips as she listened.

"Good heavens!" she cried, "he has followed me, then."

"So it appears."

"He is so cunning that I never know

---

5. **pittance** (pit′ əns) *n*.: Small or barely sufficient allowance of money.

when I am safe from him. What will he say when he returns?"

"He must guard himself, for he may find that there is someone more cunning than himself upon his track. You must lock yourself up from him tonight. If he is violent, we shall take you away to your aunt's at Harrow. Now, we must make the best use of our time, so kindly take us at once to the rooms which we are to examine."

The building was of gray, lichen-blotched[6] stone, with a high central portion and two curving wings, like the claws of a crab, thrown out on each side. In one of these wings the windows were broken and blocked with wooden boards, while the roof was partly caved in, a picture of ruin. The central portion was in little better repair, but the right-hand block was comparatively modern, and the blinds in the windows, with the blue smoke curling up from the chimneys, showed that this was where the family resided. Some scaffolding had been erected against the end wall, and the stonework had been broken into, but there were no signs of any workmen at the moment of our visit. Holmes walked slowly up and down the ill-trimmed lawn and examined with deep attention the outsides of the windows.

"This, I take it, belongs to the room in which you used to sleep, the center one to your sister's, and the one next to the main building to Dr. Roylott's chamber?"

"Exactly so. But I am now sleeping in the middle one."

"Pending the alterations, as I understand. By the way, there does not seem to

▲ **Critical Viewing** Judging from the gestures and facial expressions in this illustration, what seems to be happening? [Draw Conclusions]

be any very pressing need for repairs at that end wall."

"There were none. I believe that it was an excuse to move me from my room."

"Ah! that is suggestive. Now, on the other side of this narrow wing runs the corridor from which these three rooms open. There are windows in it, of course?"

"Yes, but very small ones. Too narrow for anyone to pass through."

"As you both locked your doors at night, your rooms were unapproachable from that side. Now, would you have the kindness to go into your room and bar your shutters?"

---

6. **lichen-blotched** (līˊ kən blächt) *adj.*: Covered with patches of fungus.

Miss Stoner did so, and Holmes, after a careful examination through the open window, endeavored in every way to force the shutter open, but without success. There was no slit through which a knife could be passed to raise the bar. Then with his lens he tested the hinges, but they were of solid iron, built firmly into the massive masonry. "Hum!" said he, scratching his chin in some perplexity. "My theory certainly presents some difficulties. No one could pass through these shutters if they were bolted. Well, we shall see if the inside throws any light upon the matter."

A small side door led into the white-washed corridor from which the three bedrooms opened. Holmes refused to examine the third chamber, so we passed at once to the second, that in which Miss Stoner was now sleeping, and in which her sister had met with her fate. It was a homely little room, with a low ceiling and a gaping fireplace, after the fashion of old country houses. A brown chest of drawers stood in one corner, a narrow white-counterpaned bed in another, and a dressing table on the left-hand side of the window. These articles, with two small wickerwork chairs, made up all the furniture in the room save for a square of Wilton carpet in the center. The boards round and the paneling of the walls were of brown, worm-eaten oak, so old and discolored that it may have dated from the original building of the house. Holmes drew one of the chairs into a corner and sat silent, while his eyes traveled round and round and up and down, taking in every detail of the apartment.

"Where does that bell communicate with?" he asked at last, pointing to a thick bell-rope which hung down beside the bed, the tassel actually lying upon the pillow.

"It goes to the housekeeper's room."

"It looks newer than the other things?"

"Yes, it was only put there a couple of years ago."

"Your sister asked for it, I suppose?"

"No, I never heard of her using it. We used always to get what we wanted for ourselves."

"Indeed, it seemed unnecessary to put so nice a bell-pull there. You will excuse me for a few minutes while I satisfy myself as to this floor." He threw himself down upon his face with his lens in his hand and crawled swiftly backward and forward, examining minutely the cracks between the boards. Then he did the same with the woodwork with which the chamber was paneled. Finally he walked over to the bed and spent some time in staring at it and in running his eye up and down the wall. Finally he took the bell-rope in his hand and gave it a brisk tug.

"Why, it's a dummy," said he.

"Won't it ring?"

"No, it is not even attached to a wire. This is very interesting. You can see now that it is fastened to a hook just above where the little opening for the ventilator is."

"How very absurd! I never noticed that before!"

"Very strange!" muttered Holmes, pulling at the rope. "There are one or two very singular points about this room. For example, what a fool a builder must be to open a ventilator into another room, when, with the same trouble, he might have communicated with the outside air!"

"That is also quite modern," said the lady.

"Done about the same time as the bell-rope?" remarked Holmes.

"Yes, there were several little changes carried out about that time."

"They seem to have been of a most interesting character—dummy bell-ropes, and ventilators which do not ventilate. With your permission, Miss Stoner, we shall now carry our researches into the inner apartment."

Dr. Grimesby Roylott's chamber was larger than that of his stepdaughter, but was as plainly furnished. A camp bed, a small wooden shelf full of books, mostly of a technical character, an armchair beside the bed, a plain wooden chair against the wall, a round table, and a large iron safe were the principal things which met the eye. Holmes walked slowly round and examined each and all of them with the keenest interest.

"What's in here?" he asked, tapping the safe.

"My stepfather's business papers."

"Oh! you have seen inside, then?"

"Only once, some years ago. I remember that it was full of papers."

"There isn't a cat in it, for example?"

"No. What a strange idea!"

"Well, look at this!" He took up a small saucer of milk which stood on the top of it.

"No; we don't keep a cat. But there is a cheetah and a baboon."

◆ **Reading Strategy**
Do you think the saucer of milk is an important piece of evidence? What conclusion might you draw from its presence?

"Ah, yes, of course! Well, a cheetah is just a big cat, and yet a saucer of milk does not go very far in satisfying its wants, I daresay. There is one point which I should wish to determine." He squatted down in front of the wooden chair and examined the seat of it with the greatest attention.

"Thank you. That is quite settled," said he, rising and putting his lens in his pocket. "Hello! Here is something interesting!"

The object which had caught his eye was a small dog lash hung on one corner of the bed. The lash, however, was curled upon itself and tied so as to make a loop of whipcord.

"What do you make of that, Watson?"

"It's a common enough lash. But I don't know why it should be tied."

"That is not quite so common, is it? Ah, me! it's a wicked world, and when a clever man turns his brains to crime it is the worst of all. I think that I have seen enough now, Miss Stoner, and with your permission we shall walk out upon the lawn."

I had never seen my friend's face so grim or his brow so dark as it was when we turned from the scene of this investigation. We had walked several times up and down the lawn, neither Miss Stoner nor myself liking to break in upon his thoughts before he roused himself from his <u>reverie</u>.

"It is very essential, Miss Stoner," said he, "that you should absolutely follow my advice in every respect."

"I shall most certainly do so."

"The matter is too serious for any hesitation. Your life may depend upon your compliance."[7]

"I assure you that I am in your hands."

"In the first place, both my friend and I must spend the night in your room."

Both Miss Stoner and I gazed at him in astonishment.

"Yes, it must be so. Let me explain. I believe that that is the village inn over there?"

"Yes, that is the Crown."

"Very good. Your windows would be visible from there?"

"Certainly."

"You must confine yourself to your room, on pretense of a headache, when your stepfather comes back. Then when you hear him retire for the night, you must open the shutters of your window, undo the hasp,[8] put your lamp there as a signal to us, and then withdraw quietly with everything which you are likely to want into the room which you used to occupy. I have no doubt that, in spite of the repairs, you could manage there for one night."

"Oh, yes, easily."

"The rest you will leave in our hands."

"But what will you do?"

"We shall spend the night in your room, and we shall investigate the cause of this noise which has disturbed you."

"I believe, Mr. Holmes, that you have already made up your mind," said Miss

---

7. **compliance** (kəm plīˊ əns) *n.*: Agreement to a request.
8. **hasp** *n.*: Hinged metal fastening of a window.

Stoner, laying her hand upon my companion's sleeve.

"Perhaps I have."

"Then, for pity's sake, tell me what was the cause of my sister's death."

"I should prefer to have clearer proofs before I speak."

"You can at least tell me whether my own thought is correct, and if she died from some sudden fright."

"No, I do not think so. I think that there was probably some more <u>tangible</u> cause. And now, Miss Stoner, we must leave you, for if Dr. Roylott returned and saw us our journey would be in vain. Goodbye, and be brave, for if you will do what I have told you, you may rest assured that we shall soon drive away the dangers that threaten you."

Sherlock Holmes and I had no difficulty in engaging a bedroom and sitting room at the Crown Inn. They were on the upper floor, and from our window we could command a view of the avenue gate, and of the inhabited wing of Stoke Moran Manor House. At dusk we saw Dr. Grimesby Roylott drive past, his huge form looming up beside the little figure of the lad who drove him. The boy had some slight difficulty in undoing the heavy iron gates, and we heard the hoarse roar of the doctor's voice and saw the fury with which he shook his clinched fists at him. The trap drove on, and a few minutes later we saw a sudden light spring up among the trees as the lamp was lit in one of the sitting rooms.

"Do you know, Watson," said Holmes as we sat together in the gathering darkness, "I have really some scruples as to taking you tonight. There is a distinct element of danger."

"Can I be of assistance?"

"Your presence might be invaluable."

"Then I shall certainly come."

"It is very kind of you."

"You speak of danger. You have evidently seen more in these rooms than was visible to me."

"No, but I fancy that I may have deduced a little more. I imagine that you saw all that I did."

"I saw nothing remarkable save the bell-rope, and what purpose that could answer I confess is more than I can imagine."

"You saw the ventilator, too?"

"Yes, but I do not think that it is such a very unusual thing to have a small opening between two rooms. It was so small that a rat could hardly pass through."

"I knew that we should find a ventilator before ever we came to Stoke Moran."

"My dear Holmes!"

"Oh, yes, I did. You remember in her statement she said that her sister could smell Dr. Roylott's cigar. Now, of course that suggested at once that there must be a communication between the two rooms. It could only be a small one, or it would have been remarked upon at the coroner's inquiry. I deduced a ventilator."

"But what harm can there be in that?"

"Well, there is at least a curious coincidence of dates. A ventilator is made, a cord is hung, and a lady who sleeps in the bed dies. Does not that strike you?"

"I cannot as yet see any connection."

"Did you observe anything very peculiar about that bed?"

"No."

"It was clamped to the floor. Did you ever see a bed fastened like that before?"

"I cannot say that I have."

"The lady could not move her bed. It must always be in the same relative position to the ventilator and to the rope—or so we may call it, since it was clearly never meant for a bell-pull."

"Holmes," I cried, "I seem to see dimly what you are hinting at. We are only just in time to prevent some subtle and horrible crime."

◆ Build Vocabulary

reverie (rev´ ər ē) *n.*: Daydream

tangible (tan´ jə bəl) *adj.*: Having form and substance; that can be touched or felt by touch

"Subtle enough and horrible enough. When a doctor does go wrong he is the first of criminals. He has nerve and he has knowledge. Palmer and Pritchard were among the heads of their profession. This man strikes even deeper, but I think, Watson, that we shall be able to strike deeper still. But we shall have horrors enough before the night is over; for goodness' sake let us have a quiet pipe and turn our minds for a few hours to something more cheerful."

About nine o'clock the light among the trees was extinguished, and all was dark in the direction of the Manor House. Two hours passed slowly away, and then, suddenly, just at the stroke of eleven, a single bright light shone out right in front of us.

"That is our signal," said Holmes, springing to his feet; "it comes from the middle window."

As we passed out he exchanged a few words with the landlord, explaining that we were going on a late visit to an acquaintance, and that it was possible that we might spend the night there. A moment later we were out on the dark road, a chill wind blowing in our faces, and one yellow light twinkling in front of us through the gloom to guide us on our somber errand.

There was little difficulty in entering the grounds; for unrepaired breaches gaped in the old park wall. Making our way among the trees, we reached the lawn, crossed it, and were about to enter through the window when out from a clump of laurel bushes there darted what seemed to be a hideous and distorted child, who threw itself upon the grass with writhing limbs and then ran swiftly across the lawn into the darkness.

"My God!" I whispered; "did you see it?"

Holmes was for the moment as startled as I. His hand closed like a vise upon my wrist in his agitation. Then he broke into a low laugh and put his lips to my ear.

"It is a nice household," he murmured. "That is the baboon."

I had forgotten the strange pets which the doctor affected. There was a cheetah, too; perhaps we might find it upon our shoulders at any moment. I confess that I felt easier in my mind when, after following Holmes's example and slipping off my shoes, I found myself inside the bedroom. My companion noiselessly closed the shutters, moved the lamp onto the table, and cast his eyes round the room. All was as we had seen it in the daytime. Then creeping up to me and making a trumpet of his hand, he whispered into my ear again so gently that it was all that I could do to distinguish the words:

"The least sound would be fatal to our plans."

I nodded to show that I had heard.

"We must sit without light. He would see it through the ventilator."

I nodded again.

"Do not go asleep; your very life may depend upon it. Have your pistol ready in case we should need it. I will sit on the side of the bed, and you in that chair."

I took out my revolver and laid it on the corner of the table.

Holmes had brought up a long thin cane, and this he placed upon the bed beside him. By it he laid the box of matches and the stump of a candle. Then he turned down the lamp, and we were left in darkness.

How shall I ever forget that dreadful vigil? I could not hear a sound, not even the drawing of a breath, and yet I knew that my companion sat open-eyed, within a few feet of me, in the same state of nervous tension in which I was myself. The shutters cut off the least ray of light, and we waited in absolute darkness. From outside came the occasional cry of a night bird, and once at our very window a long-drawn catlike whine, which told us that the cheetah was indeed at liberty. Far away we could hear the deep tones of the parish clock, which boomed out every quarter of an hour. How long they seemed, those quarters! Twelve struck, and one

▲ **Critical Viewing** Does this illustration effectively bring to life the story's climax? Why or why not? [Make a Judgment]

"You see it, Watson?" he yelled. "You see it?"

But I saw nothing. At the moment when Holmes struck the light I heard a low, clear whistle, but the sudden glare flashing into my weary eyes made it impossible for me to tell what it was at which my friend lashed so savagely. I could, however, see that his face was deadly pale and filled with horror and loathing.

He had ceased to strike and was gazing up at the ventilator when suddenly there broke from the silence of the night the most horrible cry to which I have ever listened. It swelled up louder and louder, a hoarse yell of pain and fear and anger all mingled in the one dreadful shriek. They say that away down in the village, and even in the distant parsonage, that cry raised the sleepers from their beds. It struck cold to our hearts, and I stood gazing at Holmes, and he at me, until the last echoes of it had died away into the silence from which it rose.

"What can it mean?" I gasped.

"It means that it is all over," Holmes answered. "And perhaps, after all, it is for the best. Take your pistol, and we will enter Dr. Roylott's room."

With a grave face he lit the lamp and led the way down the corridor. Twice he struck at the chamber door without any reply from within. Then he turned the handle and entered, I at his heels, with the cocked pistol in my hand.

It was a singular sight which met our eyes. On the table stood a dark lantern with the shutter half open, throwing a brilliant beam of light upon the iron safe, the door of which was ajar. Beside this table, on the wooden chair, sat Dr. Grimesby Roylott, clad in a long gray dressing gown, his bare ankles protruding beneath, and his feet thrust into red

and two and three, and still we sat waiting silently for whatever might befall.

Suddenly there was the momentary gleam of a light up in the direction of the ventilator, which vanished immediately, but was succeeded by a strong smell of burning oil and heated metal. Someone in the next room had lit a dark lantern.[9] I heard a gentle sound of movement, and then all was silent once more, though the smell grew stronger. For half an hour I sat with straining ears. Then suddenly another sound became audible—a very gentle, soothing sound, like that of a small jet of steam escaping continually from a kettle. The instant that we heard it, Holmes sprang from the bed, struck a match, and lashed furiously with his cane at the bell-pull.

9. **dark lantern:** Lantern with a shutter that can hide the light.

heelless Turkish slippers. Across his lap lay the short stock with the long lash which we had noticed during the day. His chin was cocked upward and his eyes were fixed in a dreadful, rigid stare at the corner of the ceiling. Round his brow he had a peculiar yellow band, with brownish speckles, which seemed to be bound tightly round his head. As we entered he made neither sound nor motion.

"The band! the speckled band!" whispered Holmes.

I took a step forward. In an instant his strange headgear began to move, and there reared itself from among his hair the squat diamond-shaped head and puffed neck of a loathsome serpent.

"It is a swamp adder!" cried Holmes; "the deadliest snake in India. He has died within ten seconds of being bitten. Violence does, in truth, recoil upon the violent, and the schemer falls into the pit which he digs for another. Let us thrust this creature back into its den, and we can then remove Miss Stoner to some place of shelter and let the county police know what has happened."

As he spoke he drew the dog whip swiftly from the dead man's lap, and throwing the noose round the reptile's neck he drew it from its horrid perch and, carrying it at arm's length, threw it into the iron safe, which he closed upon it.

Such are the true facts of the death of Dr. Grimesby Roylott, of Stoke Moran. It is not necessary that I should prolong a narrative which has already run to too great a length by telling how we broke the sad news to the terrified girl, how we conveyed her by the morning train to the care of her good aunt at Harrow, of how the slow process of official inquiry came to the conclusion that the doctor met his fate while indiscreetly playing with a dangerous pet. The little which I had yet to learn of the case was told me by Sherlock Holmes as we traveled back next day.

"I had," said he, "come to an entirely erroneous conclusion which shows, my dear Watson, how dangerous it always is to reason from insufficient data. The presence of the gypsies, and the use of the word *band*, which was used by the poor girl, no doubt to explain the appearance which she had caught a hurried glimpse of by the light of her match, were sufficient to put me upon an entirely wrong scent. I can only claim the merit that I instantly reconsidered my position when, however, it became clear to me that whatever danger threatened an occupant of the room could not come either from the window or the door. My attention was speedily drawn, as I have already remarked to you, to this ventilator, and to the bell-rope which hung down to the bed. The discovery that this was a dummy, and that the bed was clamped to the floor, instantly gave rise to the suspicion that the rope was there as a bridge for something passing through the hole and coming to the bed. The idea of a snake instantly occurred to me, and when I coupled it with my knowledge that the doctor was furnished with a supply of creatures from India, I felt that I was probably on the right track. The idea of using a form of poison which could not possibly be discovered by any chemical test was just such a one as would occur to a clever and ruthless man who had had an Eastern training. The rapidity with which such a poison would take effect would also, from his point of view, be an advantage. It would be a sharp-eyed coroner, indeed, who could distinguish the two little dark punctures which would show where the poison fangs had done their work. Then I thought of the whistle. Of course he must recall the snake before the morning light revealed it to the victim. He had trained it, probably by the use of the milk which we saw, to return to him when summoned. He would put it through this ventilator at the hour that he

◆ Literary Focus
Mysteries often end with a wrap-up. Notice how Holmes leads you step by step through his reasoning process.

thought best, with the certainty that it would crawl down the rope and land on the bed. It might or might not bite the occupant, perhaps she might escape every night for a week, but sooner or later she must fall a victim.

"I had come to these conclusions before ever I had entered his room. An inspection of his chair showed me that he had been in the habit of standing on it, which of course would be necessary in order that he should reach the ventilator. The sight of the safe, the saucer of milk, and the loop of whipcord were enough to finally dispel any doubts which may have remained. The metallic clang heard by Miss Stoner was obviously caused by her stepfather hastily closing the door of his safe upon its terrible occupant. Having once made up my mind, you know the steps which I took in order to put the matter to the proof. I heard the creature hiss as I have no doubt that you did also, and I instantly lit the light and attacked it."

"With the result of driving it through the ventilator."

"And also with the result of causing it to turn upon its master at the other side. Some of the blows of my cane came home and roused its snakish temper, so that it flew upon the first person it saw. In this way I am no doubt indirectly responsible for Dr. Grimesby Roylott's death, and I cannot say that it is likely to weigh very heavily upon my conscience."

Guide for Responding

◆ LITERATURE AND YOUR LIFE

Reader's Response Would you have liked to be Sherlock Holmes's partner? Why or why not?

Thematic Focus In what ways is Holmes ordinary? In what ways is he extraordinary?

Journal Writing Write a journal entry from Watson's point of view about working on this case with Holmes.

☑ Check Your Comprehension

1. Why does Helen Stoner come to see Holmes?
2. What two sounds did Helen hear after she was awakened by her sister's scream? What did her sister then say?
3. Why does Dr. Roylott pay a visit to Holmes?
4. How do Holmes and Watson spend the night at Stoke Moran?
5. What is the speckled band?

◆ Critical Thinking

INTERPRET

1. Name three ways in which Helen's situation when she comes to Holmes is similar to Julia's just before Julia's death. **[Compare and Contrast]**
2. What is Dr. Roylott's motive for the crimes? **[Infer]**
3. How does Dr. Roylott's plan backfire? **[Analyze]**
4. What do you think would have happened if Helen had not consulted Holmes? **[Speculate]**

EXTEND

5. Sherlock Holmes uses his powers of observation well. Name three ways to improve your own powers of observation. **[Relate]**

APPLY

6. How would you test an applicant who wants to enter a school for detectives? What tests could you invent that would determine whether someone has the necessary natural skills? **[Career Link]**

Guide for Responding (continued)

◆ Reading Strategy

IDENTIFY EVIDENCE

Holmes solved the mystery of the speckled band by analyzing all pieces of **evidence** and drawing a conclusion. Did you recognize the evidence as it was revealed? Review your clue chart as you answer these questions.

1. Explain the significance of each of these clues: the dummy bell-rope, the ventilator, and the bed anchored to the floor in Julia's room.
2. How did background information about Dr. Roylott help Holmes solve the mystery?
3. (a) What had Holmes thought was the significance of Julia's last words? (b) In what way could her words be considered a misleading clue?

◆ Build Vocabulary

USING FORMS OF *convulse*

Convulse means "shake violently." Write the form of *convulse* that best completes each sentence.

convulse   convulsions   convulsive

1. The victim's arm made one _____?_____ twitch.
2. The frightening _____?_____ will stop when the poison takes effect.
3. Some poisons cause their victims to _____?_____.

SPELLING STRATEGY

The *er* sound can be spelled *ur* and *er*. Notice that *perturb* includes both spellings of the sound. Rewrite each sentence, correcting any misspellings.

1. She reterned after cerfew.
2. Do these clues purtain to this murdur case?
3. The culprit hid undur the certain.

USING THE WORD BANK

On your paper, match the Word Bank words in Column A with their synonyms in Column B.

Column A	Column B
1. defray	a. gloomy
2. manifold	b. calmly
3. morose	c. daydream
4. convulsed	d. solid
5. imperturbably	e. numerous
6. reverie	f. pay
7. tangible	g. twitched

◆ Literary Focus

MYSTERY STORY

A **mystery story** usually contains a conflict between a detective and someone who has committed a crime. The detective uses evidence to discover the criminal; the criminal tries to remain undiscovered. The conflict is resolved when the detective proves the identity of the criminal.

1. Who commits the crime in "The Adventure of the Speckled Band"?
2. In what ways does the criminal display cleverness?
3. How does Holmes outwit the criminal?
4. What role does Watson play in the story?
5. Do you think a mystery would be satisfying if it included all of the clues but left the solution up to the reader?

◆ Build Grammar Skills

PREDICATE NOUNS

A **predicate noun** appears after a linking verb and renames, identifies, or explains the subject of the sentence.

My name is *Sherlock Holmes,* . . . (*Sherlock Holmes* is a predicate noun that renames the subject, *name*.)

He seems a very amiable *person. (Person* is a predicate noun that identifies the subject, *he*.)

Practice On your paper, write the subject and predicate noun in each sentence.

1. He was a late riser, as a rule. . . .
2. "Which of you is Holmes?" asked this apparition.
3. I am a dangerous man to fall foul of!
4. . . . my profession is its own reward; . . .
5. It was a singular sight which met our eyes.

Writing Application On your paper, write a sentence with a linking verb and predicate noun that renames each subject below.

1. Holmes   3. Roylott
2. Helen   4. snake

Build Your Portfolio

 ## Idea Bank

Writing

1. Advertisement Write an advertisement for his services that Sherlock Holmes might have placed in a newspaper or magazine. Include appropriate drawings, as well as detailed descriptions of the services he offers.

2. Action Plan Choose a modern mystery, such as an unsolved crime described in a newspaper article, and write an action plan describing the steps you think Sherlock Holmes would take to find a solution.

3. Personal Essay Write a personal essay describing how you used logic or observation to solve a problem.

Speaking and Listening

4. Talk Show [Group Activity] Imagine that Holmes, Watson, and Helen Stoner are guests on a talk show, where they describe how Dr. Roylott was captured. With classmates, take the parts of the characters and the talk-show host, and improvise the discussion for your class.

5. Radio Play [Group Activity] With a group, create a radio drama based on "The Adventure of the Speckled Band." Plan the dialogue, sound effects, and narration. Cast the parts, choose a director, and select sound engineers to produce the effects. Record your drama, and play it for the class. **[Performing Arts Link]**

Projects

6. Classroom Mystery [Group Activity] Work with a team to create a mystery for others to solve. Invent a crime, and leave at least three clues that point to the culprit. Challenge your classmates to solve the mystery.

7. Collage Research the time period and place in which Sherlock Holmes "lived." Then, create a collage that brings that time and place to life. Display your work for the class. **[Art Link]**

 ## Writing Mini-Lesson

Letter of Recommendation

A letter of recommendation is written by a client or customer to speak favorably of someone's services. For example, satisfied homeowners might write a letter of recommendation for the builder of their home. The builder could show the letter to prospective customers. Imagine that you are a client of Sherlock Holmes, such as Helen Stoner. Write a letter recommending Holmes's services.

Writing Skills Focus: Support Your Points

Support your recommendation by giving specific examples to illustrate the point you are making.

Model

Holmes's powers of observation are amazing. Within minutes of my arrival, he had deduced that I traveled by train and then dogcart. He drew these correct conclusions simply by looking at me carefully.

Prewriting Choose a character from whose point of view you will write. You can choose Helen Stoner or make up another character who has used Holmes's services. Make a list of Holmes's qualities you want to emphasize in your letter.

Drafting Begin your letter with a general opening, such as "To Whom It May Concern." Then, draft your recommendation. Support your points with precise details.

> ◆ **Grammar Application**
>
> Use predicate nouns in some of your statements about Sherlock Holmes. For example: Mr. Holmes is a highly analytical detective.

Revising Ask a partner whether your letter is effective. You may need to add support for the points you've made.

Although Sherlock Holmes is a fictional character, his crime-solving procedures are still in use today. Over the years, detectives' tools have become more sophisticated, but basic observational skills—like Holmes's— are still all-important, as you'll see in the article that follows.

CRIME-SOLVING PROCEDURES
for the MODERN DETECTIVE

This information was adapted from the workbook of the California Commission on Peace Officer Standards and Training for the "Forensic Technology for Law Enforcement" Telecourse presented on May 13, 1993.

* * *

The purpose of crime scene investigation is to help establish what happened (crime scene reconstruction) and to identify the responsible person. This is done by carefully documenting the conditions at a crime scene and recognizing all relevant physical evidence. The ability to recognize and properly collect physical evidence is oftentimes critical to both solving and prosecuting violent crimes. It is no exaggeration to say that in the majority of cases, the law enforcement officer who protects and searches a crime scene plays a critical role in determining whether physical evidence will be used in solving or prosecuting violent crimes.

Despite Hollywood's portrayal, crime scene investigation is a difficult and time-consuming job. There is no substitute for a careful and thoughtful approach. An investigator must not leap to an immediate conclusion as to what happened based upon limited information but must generate several different theories of the crime,

keeping the ones that are not eliminated by incoming information at the scene. Reasonable inferences[1] about what happened are produced from the scene appearance and information from witnesses. These theories will help guide the investigator to document specific conditions and recognize valuable evidence.

Documenting crime scene conditions can include immediately recording transient[2] details such as lighting (on/off), drapes (open/closed), weather, or furniture moved by medical teams. Certain evidence such as shoeprints or gunshot residue is fragile and if not collected immediately can easily be destroyed or lost. The scope of the investigation also extends to considerations of arguments which might be generated in this case and documenting conditions which would support or refute these arguments.

In addition, it is important to be able to recognize what should be present at a scene but is not (victim's vehicle/wallet) and objects which appear to be out of

---

1. **inferences**: Conclusions arrived at through reason.
2. **transient** (tran´ sē ənt) *adj.*: Temporary.

place (ski mask) and might have been left by the assailant. It is also important to determine the full extent of a crime scene. A crime scene is not merely the immediate area where a body is located or where an assailant concentrated his activities but can also encompass a vehicle and access/escape routes.

Although there are common items which are frequently collected as evidence (fingerprints, shoeprints, or bloodstains), literally any object can be physical evidence. Anything which can be used to connect a victim to a suspect or a suspect to a victim or crime scene is relevant physical evidence. Using the "shopping list" approach (collecting bloodstains, hairs, or shoeprints) will probably not result in recognizing the best evidence. For example, collecting bloodstains under a victim's body or shoeprints from emergency personnel will rarely answer important questions. Conversely, a single matchstick (usually not mentioned as physical evidence) recovered on the floor near a victim's body can be excellent physical evidence since it can be directly tied to a matchbook found in a suspect's pocket.

Since a weapon or burglar tool is easily recognized as significant physical evidence, it is frequently destroyed by the perpetrator.[3] Sometimes the only remaining evidence is microscopic evidence consisting of hairs, fibers, or other small traces the assailant unknowingly leaves behind or takes with him. Although this evidence is effectively collected when the clothing of the victim or suspect is taken, protocols (involving tape lifts) should be in place so as not to lose this fragile evidence.

---

3. **perpetrator** (pʉr′ pə trāt ər) *n*.: One who commits a crime.

1. According to the article, what is the basic purpose of a crime-scene investigation?
2. Which common items are often collected as evidence?
3. In what ways does the modern detective resemble Sherlock Holmes?

Writing Process Workshop

In this section, we found Sherlock Holmes conducting business as usual in "The Adventure of the Speckled Band." Although Holmes conducts his business in person, often business transactions are conducted through letters. Whenever you write to get information or advice, to express satisfaction or dissatisfaction with a product, or to propose an idea, you are writing a business letter.

Write a business letter to obtain information about a product or service or to seek the advice of a professional. The following skills, introduced in this section's Writing Mini-Lessons, will help you.

Writing Skills Focus

▶ Your **purpose** will guide you in your choice of details. (See p. 448.)

▶ The level of language and the information that you include should be appropriate for your **audience.** (See p. 463.)

▶ **Use an appropriate tone.** Clarify your attitude toward the subject of your letter. (See p. 471.)

▶ **Support your points** with specific facts and examples. (See p. 493.)

Notice how these skills are used in the following model:

WRITING MODEL

To Whom It May Concern:

    I am writing to inquire about the behavior of blue jays. ① I know that as an expert for the Audubon Society, you can provide me with information about their nesting habits. ② I have several blue jays living in my yard, and I am interested in whether or not they will return next spring. ③

① This letter begins with a statement of purpose. The formal word *inquire* gives the letter a serious tone.

② The writer directly addresses her audience. She knows that an expert will be able to answer her questions.

③ These specific details support the writer's interest in the nesting habits of blue jays.

Prewriting

Choose a Topic Think of a product or a service that you are curious about. Write a letter requesting information or asking for an expert's advice. You may want to use one of the following ideas:

> ### Topic Ideas
> - Football camp
> - Dance lessons
> - Value of a classic comic book

Identify Your Audience Knowing your audience will help you determine what information you need to include in your letter. For example, if you are writing to a computer expert about a problem, chances are you need not include much background. If you are writing to a complaint department, you will have to include detailed information about your problem.

Drafting

Keep to a Format A business letter must follow an appropriate format. Follow this model as you prepare your business letter:

Heading: *(the address of the writer)*

_____

_____

_____

Date:_____

Inside Address: *(the address of the recipient)*

_____

_____

Salutation: *(to whom the letter is addressed)*

_____:

Body: *(the main part of the letter)*

_____

_____

Closing: _____,

Signature: _____

DRAFTING/REVISING

APPLYING LANGUAGE SKILLS: Using Informal and Formal English

Informal English is the language of everyday speech. Formal English is the standard language of written communication, formal speeches, and presentations. Use formal English in your business letter.

Informal English:
- Allows contractions
- Accepts some slang
- May contain incomplete sentences

Formal English:
- Does not allow contractions
- Does not accept slang
- Adheres to grammatical standards

Informal English:
Can you give me a break on the next CD I buy?

Formal English:
Can you discount the price of the next CD I purchase?

Writing Application As you draft your business letter, use complete sentences, a formal tone, and avoid slang.

Writer's Solution Connection
Writing Lab

For more help with choosing the right words, use the Audience Profile in the Writer's Toolkit.

APPLYING LANGUAGE SKILLS:
Correctly Writing Company Names

Find out the exact name of the company to which you are writing, so that you can write it accurately. Pay attention to details of spelling, abbreviations, and completeness. For example, notice the variety among these companies' names:

Acme Lamprey Co.

International Business Machines, Inc.

Simon & Schuster, Inc.

Practice Use a telephone book to check and correct the company names in these sentences.

1. If you want telephone service, call A, T, and T.
2. Do you ever shop at KMart?
3. Ups can deliver your package the next day.

Writing Application In addition to checking company names, verify the title of the person with whom you're corresponding.

Writer's Solution Connection
Language Lab

For more practice with capitalization, complete the Proper Nouns lesson in the Capitalization unit.

Revising

Use a Checklist Use the following checklist and tips to help you revise your letter:

▶ **Have you stated your purpose?** Did you include a statement of purpose? If not, include a sentence that clearly lets the reader know why you are writing.

▶ **Did you write to the audience?** If your audience is an expert on rare comic books, you may not have to provide as much information as you might for a clerk in a comic-book store. Review your letter, and either add or delete information, depending on your audience.

▶ **Is the tone of the letter appropriate?** Did you choose words that reflect your attitude: serious, dissatisfied, interested? If not, add words that are more descriptive of your tone.

▶ **Did you support your points?** Did you include specific, concrete facts and examples that support your purpose? For example, if you are dissatisfied with a product, provide concrete examples that will enable your audience to understand your problem.

REVISION MODEL

---

① I am writing to find out how to identify blue jays' nests.
I have noticed that the blue jays' nests are not as tidy as
                                                    ② very loose and
other birds' nests. but instead are loose. They use many

twigs. Some blue jays' nests appear in shrubs. Could you
                                        ③ interesting
please send me information about those crazy birds?

① The writer adds a statement of purpose.
② This sentence was deleted because an expert on blue jays would already know.
③ The word *interesting* replaces the word *crazy* to maintain a formal tone for a business letter.

Publishing and Presenting

E-Mail Instead of sending your business letter through the mail, send it through e-mail. Use the Internet, or check the packaging of a product to find the address. Using e-mail often provides you with a faster reply.

Real-World Reading Skills Workshop

Reading Product Labels

Strategies for Success

To make an informed decision about any purchase—food, clothes, games, software—you must read and understand the information printed on the packaging.

Identify the Types of Information Identify the kinds of information you are reading—ingredients, care instructions, safety warnings, nutritional information, or directions for use. Classifying information will help you focus your reading.

Read Carefully To use information on product labels to your advantage, read carefully, applying these strategies:

▶ Study the order of ingredients listed on food products; it appears in order of greatest volume.

▶ Use headings and labels to understand chart data.

▶ Consider how required care—"hand wash only," for example—might influence your use of this product.

▶ Note addresses or phone numbers for assistance or questions.

▶ Check for warnings about who should not use the product. The label might offer important information about side effects as well. For example, many cold medications warn about drowsiness or slowed reaction times.

Apply the Strategies

Your health teacher has assigned you to find a nutritious cookie for a class party. Examine

this label and decide whether this product meets your criteria—can be eaten by everyone, contains small amounts of sugar and fat, and has vitamins and minerals.

1. (a) What is the serving size? (b) How many calories are in one cookie? (c) How much sugar is in one cookie?

2. Are there any vitamins or minerals in the cookie?

3. Could students who are allergic to nuts eat these cookies? Where can you find that information?

4. In your opinion, would these cookies be a nutritious choice?

✔ **Here are other situations in which it is important to read labels:**
▶ Care labels for clothing
▶ Allergy notations on health and beauty aids
▶ Warnings on medications

Julia's Cookies

Nutrition Facts
Serving Size: 1 cookie (23g)
Servings Per Container: about 15

Amount Per Serving	
Calories 110	Calories from fat 40

	% Daily Value **
Total Fat 4.5g	7%
Saturated Fat 1g	5%
Cholesterol 0mg	0%
Sodium 55mg	2%
Total Carbohydrates 16g	5%
Dietary Fiber 0g	
Sugars 9g	
Protein 1g	

Vitamin A 0%	•	Vitamin C 0%
Calcium 0%	•	Iron 4%

* Percent Daily Values are based on a 2,000 calorie diet. Your daily values may be higher or lower depending on your calorie needs:

		Calories:	2,000	2,500
Total Fat	Less than		65g	80g
Sat. Fat	Less than		20g	25g
Cholesterol	Less than		300mg	300mg
Sodium	Less than		2,400mg	2,400mg
Total Carbohydrates			300g	375g
Dietary Fiber			25g	30g

Calories per gram:
Fat 9 • Carbohydrate 4 • Protein 4

INGREDIENTS: ENRICHED FLOUR (WHEAT FLOUR, NIACIN, REDUCED IRON, THIAMINE MONONITRATE, RIBOFLAVIN, FOLIC ACID), VEGETABLE OIL, SHORTENING [PARTIALLY HYDROGENATED SOYBEAN AND COTTONSEED OILS, BHA AND BHT (AS PRESERVATIVES)], POWDERED SUGAR, SUGAR, COCOA (PROCESSED WITH ALKALI), CHOCOLATE LIQUOR, CORN STARCH, LEAVENING (SODIUM BICARBONATE, AMMONIUM BICARBONATE, SODIUM ACID PYROPHOSPHATE, MONOCALCIUM PHOSPHATE, CALCIUM SULFATE), SALT, SOYBEAN LECITHIN (AN EMULSIFIER), CARAMEL COLOR, ARTIFICIAL FLAVOR.

MAY CONTAIN TRACES OF PEANUTS AND/OR NUTS.

PACKED FOR JULIA'S COOKIES
CEDAR GROVE, NJ 07009
© 1999

Complements

*G*rammar *R*eview

A **complement** is a word or a group of words that completes the meaning of a verb. There are four kinds of complements:

A **direct object** receives the action of the verb or shows the result of the action. It answers the questions *whom* or *what*. (See p. 447.)

  A.V.   D.O.
I ordered you a *cup* of cocoa.

An **indirect object** follows an action verb and tells *to whom* or *what* or *for whom* or *what* the action of the verb is performed. (See p. 462.)

  A.V.   I.O.
I ordered *you* a cup of cocoa.

A **predicate noun** is a noun that follows a linking verb and renames the subject. (See p. 492.)

  L.V.   P.N.
"I am *Dr. Grimesby Roylott,* of Stoke Moran."

A **predicate adjective** is an adjective that follows a linking verb and describes the subject. (See p. 470.)

      L.V.   P.A.
"The marks are perfectly *fresh.*"

Some verbs, such as those that relate to the senses—*sound, look, taste, feel, smell, appear*—or those that express a condition or placement—*remain, grow, seem, stay, become*—can function either as linking verbs or action verbs. Notice the differences in these two sentences:

          L.V.   P.A.
The blue jay's song *sounds* delightful.

       A.V.   D.O.
The captain *sounded* the horn that signaled the boats to return to the dock.

com·ple·ment (käm′plə mənt) *n.* **1** something that completes a whole or makes perfect *[The sharp cheese was a delicious complement to the apple pie.]* **2** the word or words that complete a predicate *[In "We made her our captain," "our captain" is a complement.]*

Practice 1 Copy the following sentences into your notebook. Then, underline verbs and label the complements.

1. "I recognized the noise. . . ."

2. "My sister Amy, two years old, was asleep . . ."

3. "Everything tastes good today."

4. "I present you the tall skyscrapers/as merely huge palm trees with lights."

5. "It is terror."

Practice 2 Use the following subjects and verbs to create sentences that include the type of complement indicated.

1. Subject: trees **Verb:** are (predicate adjective)

2. Subject: Holmes **Verb:** gave (indirect object, direct object)

3. Subject: noise **Verb:** was (predicate noun)

4. Subject: blue jay **Verb:** dropped (direct object)

5. Subject: shadow **Verb:** grew (predicate adjective)

Grammar in Writing

✔ *When writing a sentence with a predicate noun or a predicate adjective, choose the most exact noun or precise adjective to complete your thought.*

PART 2 *Strange Doings*

The Blank Signature (Carte Blanche), 1965, René Magritte, National Gallery of Art, Washington, D.C.

Guide for Reading

Meet the Authors:

Gary Paulsen (1939–)

Gary Paulsen has won three Newbery Honor awards—for his books *Hatchet, Dog Song,* and *The Winter Room*. With his more than sixty books in print around the world, it is astonishing to learn that the books were all written within a ten-year period.

Sylvia Plath (1932–1963)

Sylvia Plath was born in Boston. She developed an early interest in writing and published her first poems at the age of seventeen. Her *Collected Poems* won the Pulitzer Prize for Poetry in 1982.

Arna Bontemps (1902–1973)

Born in Louisiana and educated at the University of Chicago, Arna Bontemps was a college professor for more than twenty years. In addition to teaching, Bontemps had a career as an editor, writer, librarian, and literary critic.

Theodore Roethke (1908–1963)

The son of a florist, young Theodore Roethke loved to play in and around the family greenhouse, where he developed a kinship with nature that he never lost. Roethke's poetry earned him the Bollingen Prize, the Pulitzer Prize, and the National Book Award.

◆ LITERATURE AND YOUR LIFE

CONNECT YOUR EXPERIENCE

A flower bed of pansies seems like faces looking up at you. A sunset reminds you that the world can be a beautiful place. A meal in a restaurant makes you think of a vacation taken last year. Everyday objects and occurrences often inspire thoughts that, on the surface, may appear unrelated.

THEMATIC FOCUS: Strange Doings

The essay and poems that follow present everyday objects in an unusual light. What is strange or haunting about the way the writers describe them?

◆ Background for Understanding

SCIENCE

Roethke's poem "The Bat" describes the behavior of a bat. Though bats fly, they are not birds. A bat is a mammal, meaning that the young are born live, not hatched, and get milk from their mothers. Using a process called echolocation, bats can fly around in the dark without bumping into obstacles. As they fly, they emit high-pitched cries that humans can't hear. These sounds are reflected by all obstacles in the bat's path, echoing back to its sensitive ears. The bat responds to the signal and avoids the obstacles.

◆ Build Vocabulary

PREFIXES: *a-*

Amiss, which means "wrongly placed" contains the prefix *a-*, which can mean "on" or "in." Other words containing this prefix include *asleep, amid,* and *ashore*.

WORD BANK

Which word from the list describes how someone might whisper to another? Check the Build Vocabulary box on page 508 to see if you guessed correctly.

| diffused |
| discreetly |
| acquire |
| amiss |

A Glow in the Dark ◆ Mushrooms
Southern Mansion ◆ The Bat

◆ Literary Focus

TONE

The **tone** of a literary work is the writer's attitude toward the subject and the audience. Tone can often be described in a single word, such as *formal, informal, serious,* or *humorous.* Tone is revealed in the writer's choice of subject, choice of words, and even sentence structure. For example, in these lines from "Mushrooms," the poet's word choice and style create a mysterious tone:

> We are shelves, we are / Tables, we are
> meek, / We are edible.

◆ Reading Strategy

MAKE INFERENCES

In most literary works, writers do not tell you everything directly; instead, they imply, or hint at, meanings or ideas. Therefore, you may have to **make inferences,** or use clues from the text, to determine the writer's message or a line's meaning. For example, in "A Glow in the Dark," you can infer from Paulsen's actions that he is an experienced dog-sledder.

As you read, fill out a chart like the one below to help you to make inferences.

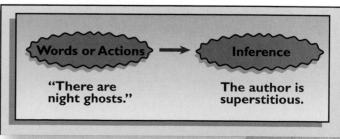

Words or Actions ➔ Inference

"There are night ghosts." — The author is superstitious.

A Glow in the Dark
from Woodsong
Gary Paulsen

There are night ghosts. Some people say that we can understand all things if we can know them, but there came a dark night in the fall when I thought that was wrong, and so did the dogs.

We had been running all morning and were tired; some of the dogs were young and could not sustain a long run. So we stopped in the middle of the afternoon when they seemed to want to rest. I made a fire, set up a gentle, peaceful camp, and went to sleep for four hours.

It hadn't snowed yet so we had been running with a three-wheel cart, which meant we had to run on logging roads and open areas. I had been hard pressed to find new country to run in to keep the young dogs from becoming bored and this logging trail was one we hadn't run. It had been rough going, with a lot of ruts and mud and the cart was a mess so I spent some time fixing it after I awakened, carving off the dried mud. The end result was we didn't get going again until close to one in the morning. This did not pose a problem except that as soon as I hooked the dogs up and got them lined out—I was running an eight-dog team—my head lamp went out. I replaced the bulb and tried a new battery, but that didn't help—the internal wiring was bad. I thought briefly of sleeping again until daylight but the dogs were slamming into the harnesses, screaming to run, so I shrugged and

▶ **Critical Viewing** If you came upon this sight while alone in a dark forest, how would you react? [Relate]

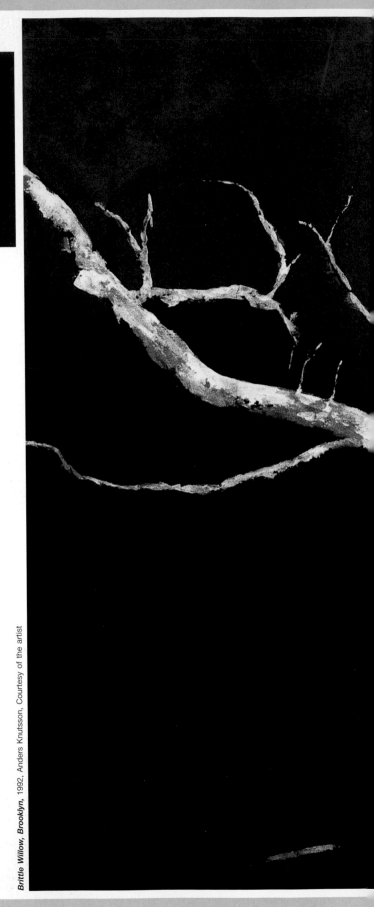

jumped on the rig and untied it. Certainly, I thought, running without a head lamp would not be the worst thing I had ever done.

Immediately we blew into the darkness and the ride was madness. Without a lamp I could

▲ **Critical Viewing** Why might dog-sledding be popular with naturalists like Paulsen? **[Speculate]**

not tell when the rig was going to hit a rut or a puddle. It was cloudy and fairly warm—close to fifty—and had rained the night before. Without the moon or even starlight I had no idea where the puddles were until they splashed me—largely in the face—so I was soon dripping wet. Coupled with that, tree limbs I couldn't see hit at me as we passed, almost tearing me off the back of the rig. Inside an hour I wasn't sure if I was up, down, or sideways.

And the dogs stopped.

They weren't tired, not even a little, judging by the way they had been ripping through the night, but they stopped dead.

◆ **Literary Focus**
What is the author's tone? How can you tell?

I had just taken a limb in the face and was temporarily blinded. All I knew was that they had stopped suddenly and that I had to jam down on the brakes to keep from running over them. It took me a couple of seconds to clear my eyes and when I did, I saw the light.

In the first seconds I thought it was another person coming toward me. The light had an eerie green-yellow glow. It was quite bright and filled a whole part of the dark night ahead, down the trail. It seemed to be moving. I was in deep woods and couldn't think what a person would be doing there—there are no other teams where I train—but I was glad to see the light.

At first.

Then I realized the light was strange. It glowed and ebbed and seemed to fill too much space to be a regular light source. It was low to the ground, and wide.

I was still not frightened, and would probably not have become frightened except that the dogs suddenly started to sing.

I have already talked about some of their songs. Rain songs and first-snow songs and meat songs and come-back-and-stay-with-us songs and even puppy-training songs, but I had heard this song only once, when an old dog had died in the kennel. It was a death song.

And that frightened me.

They all sat. I could see them quite well in the glow from the light—the soft glow, the green glow, the ghost glow. It crept into my thinking without my knowing it: the ghost glow. Against my wishes I started thinking of all the things in my life that had scared me.

Ghosts and goblins and dark nights and snakes under the bed and sounds I didn't know and bodies I had found and graveyards under covered pale moons and death, death, death . . .

And they sang and sang. The cold song in the strange light. For a time I could do nothing but stand on the back of the wheeled rig and stare at the light with old, dusty terror.

But curiosity was stronger. My legs moved without my wanting them to move and my body followed them, alongside the team in the dark, holding to each dog like a security blanket until I reached the next one, moving closer to the light until I was at the front and there were no more dogs to hold.

The light had gotten brighter, seemed to pulse and flood back and forth, but I still could not see the source. I took another step, then another, trying to look around the corner, deeply feeling the distance from the dogs, the aloneness.

Two more steps, then one more, leaning to see around the corner and at last I saw it and when I did it was worse.

It was a form. Not human. A large, standing form glowing in the dark. The light came from within it, a cold-glowing green light with yellow edges that <u>diffused</u> the shape, making it change and grow as I watched.

I felt my heart slam up into my throat.

I couldn't move. I stared at the upright form and was sure it was a ghost, a being from the dead sent for me. I could not move and might not have ever moved except that the dogs had followed me, pulling the rig quietly until they were around my legs, peering ahead, and I looked down at them and had to laugh.

They were caught in the green light, curved around my legs staring at the standing form, ears cocked and heads turned sideways while they studied it. I took another short step forward and they all followed me, then another, and they stayed with me until we were right next to the form.

It was a stump.

A six-foot-tall, old rotten stump with the bark knocked off, glowing in the dark with a bright green glow. Impossible. I stood there with the dogs around my legs, smelling the stump and touching it with their noses. I found out later that it glowed because it had sucked phosphorus[1] from the ground up into the wood and held the light from day all night.

But that was later. There in the night I did not know this. Touching the stump, and feeling the cold light, I could not quite get rid of the fear until a black-and-white dog named Fonzie came up, smelled the stump, snorted, and relieved himself on it.

So much for ghosts.

---

1. **phosphorus** (fäs´ fə rəs) *n.*: Substance that gives off light after exposure to radiant energy.

◆ **Build Vocabulary**

diffused (di fyo͞ozd´) *v.*: Spread out widely into different directions

Guide for Responding

◆ **LITERATURE AND YOUR LIFE**

Reader's Response What would you have thought you were seeing if you saw the "green-yellow glow"?

Thematic Focus In what way is the story about a "strange doing"?

☑ **Check Your Comprehension**

1. Describe where and why Paulsen and the dogs are running.
2. Why did the dogs stop suddenly when they were running through the night?
3. What did the author think he saw? What did he actually see?

◆ **Critical Thinking**

INTERPRET
1. How would you describe the author's personality? Give examples. **[Analyze]**
2. How does Paulsen show respect for the dogs? How do the dogs show they trust Paulsen? **[Connect]**
3. Why isn't the company of dogs enough to make Paulsen feel less alone in the story? **[Interpret]**

APPLY
4. Would you call Paulsen courageous? Explain. **[Make a Judgment]**

MUSHROOMS

SYLVIA PLATH

Overnight, very
Whitely, discreetly,
Very quietly

Our toes, our noses
5   Take hold on the loam,[1]
Acquire the air.

Nobody sees us,
Stops us, betrays us;
The small grains make room.

10   Soft fists insist on
Heaving the needles,
The leafy bedding.

Even the paving.
Our hammers, our rams,
15   Earless and eyeless,

---

1. loam (lōm) *n.*: Any rich, dark soil.

▲ **Critical Viewing** What different stages of growth can you observe in the mushrooms on these pages? **[Classify]**

◆ **Build Vocabulary**

discreetly (dis krēt′ lē) *adv.*: Carefully; silently

acquire (ə kwīr′) *v.*: To get; come to have as one's own

Perfectly voiceless,
Widen the crannies,
Shoulder through holes. We

Diet on water,
20 On crumbs of shadow,
Bland-mannered, asking
Little or nothing.
So many of us!
So many of us!

25 We are shelves, we are
Tables, we are meek,
We are edible,

Nudgers and shovers
In spite of ourselves.
30 Our kind multiplies:

We shall by morning
Inherit the earth.
Our foot's in the door.

Beyond Literature

Science Connection

Mushrooms In "Mushrooms," Sylvia Plath depicts mushrooms as a silent army that constantly multiply and will one day "inherit the earth." Mushrooms are a type of fungus that grows in arcs or rings. When a spore from a mushroom falls on a suitable spot on the ground, it produces tiny strands that grow out in all directions and eventually emerge as stalks and caps of mushrooms. As long as nourishment, adequate temperature, and moisture are provided, mushrooms can live and multiply for hundreds of years.

Cross-Curricular Activity

Many mushrooms are edible, but there are more than seventy kinds of mushrooms that are poisonous and sometimes fatal. Do research about mushrooms, and create an illustrated poster of poisonous mushrooms. List the regions in which each type of poisonous mushroom is commonly found.

Guide for Responding

◆ LITERATURE AND YOUR LIFE

Reader's Response Have your ideas about mushrooms changed since reading this poem? Why or why not?

Thematic Focus What is strange about what the mushrooms are doing and how they see themselves?

☑ Check Your Comprehension

1. What are the mushrooms doing at night?
2. How do the mushrooms overcome the obstacles in their way?
3. Why does no one notice what the mushrooms are doing?

◆ Critical Thinking

INTERPRET

1. What seems to be the goal or purpose of the mushrooms? **[Infer]**
2. What demands, if any, do the mushrooms make on their surroundings? **[Interpret]**
3. What quality of the mushrooms will enable them to "Inherit the earth"? **[Deduce]**

APPLY

4. "Blessed are the meek: for they shall inherit the earth" is a well-known quotation. How does it apply to "Mushrooms"? **[Apply]**

Southern Mansion

Arna Bontemps

Poplars[1] are standing there still as death
And ghosts of dead men
Meet their ladies walking
Two by two beneath the shade
5 And standing on the marble steps.

There is a sound of music echoing
Through the open door
And in the field there is
Another sound tinkling in the cotton:
10 Chains of bondmen[2] dragging on the ground.

The years go back with an iron clank,
A hand is on the gate,
A dry leaf trembles on the wall.
Ghosts are walking.
15 They have broken roses down
And poplars stand there still as death.

▲ **Critical Viewing** Does this southern mansion appear to be deserted or inhabited? How can you tell? **[Deduce]**

---

1. **Poplars** (päp´ lərz) *n.*: Trees of the willow family, with soft wood and flowers.
2. **bondmen** (bänd´ mən) *n.*: Slaves.

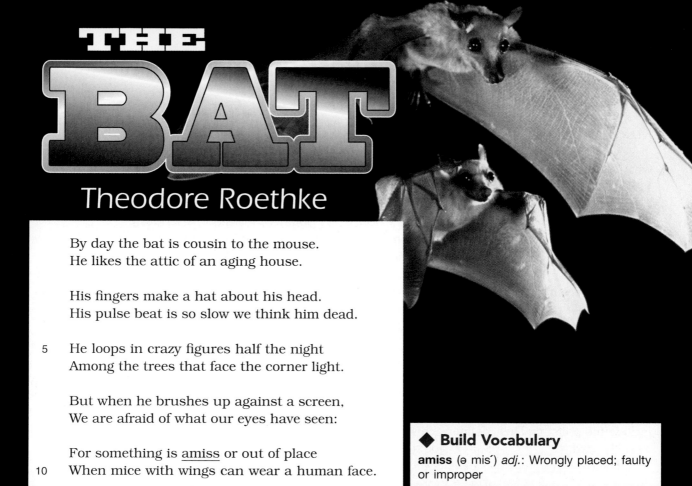

THE BAT

Theodore Roethke

By day the bat is cousin to the mouse.
He likes the attic of an aging house.

His fingers make a hat about his head.
His pulse beat is so slow we think him dead.

5   He loops in crazy figures half the night
Among the trees that face the corner light.

But when he brushes up against a screen,
We are afraid of what our eyes have seen:

For something is <u>amiss</u> or out of place
10   When mice with wings can wear a human face.

◆ **Build Vocabulary**
amiss (ə mis´) *adj.*: Wrongly placed; faulty or improper

Guide for Responding

◆ LITERATURE AND YOUR LIFE

Reader's Response With which poet would you rather have a conversation? Why?

Thematic Focus What is strange and extraordinary about the scene Arna Bontemps describes in "Southern Mansion"?

☑ Check Your Comprehension

1. In "Southern Mansion," who are the people mentioned in the poem?
2. What two sounds are mentioned in "Southern Mansion"?
3. In "The Bat," Roethke compares the bat to two other creatures. Name them.

◆ Critical Thinking

INTERPRET

1. What is the effect of the repetition of line 1 at the end of "Southern Mansion"? **[Interpret]**
2. What do the "roses" in the last stanza of "Southern Mansion" represent? **[Interpret]**
3. Compare the daytime and nighttime activities of the bat in "The Bat." **[Compare and Contrast]**
4. What details in line 10 make the picture that Roethke paints so strange? **[Interpret]**

COMPARE LITERARY WORKS

5. In these poems, living things that are normally not threatening to humans are presented in a frightening way. Identify the language each poet uses to accomplish this effect. **[Connect]**

Guide for Responding (continued)

◆ Reading Strategy

MAKE INFERENCES

When you **make inferences,** you look beyond what the words state to what they imply.

1. Paulsen says that he "replaced the bulb and tried a new battery" when his headlamp blew out. What can you infer about him from this action?
2. What can you infer from these lines from "Mushrooms": "We / Diet on water, / On crumbs of shadow"?
3. In "Southern Mansion," what inference can you make about the speaker's attitude toward slavery in the South?

◆ Build Vocabulary

USING THE PREFIX a-

The prefix a-, as in amiss, means "on" or "in." On your paper, complete these word equations that include the prefix a-. Then, define each word.

1. a- + board = ____?____   3. a- + side = ____?____
   definition: ____?____   definition: ____?____
2. a- + fire = ____?____   4. a- + shore = ____?____
   definition: ____?____   definition: ____?____

SPELLING STRATEGY

The sound ak can be spelled acq, as in acquire, or aq, as in aqua. Words having to do with water are usually spelled with aq.

On your paper, complete the following words by adding acq or aq in the blank.

1. ___?___uisition   4. ___?___uamarine
2. ___?___uainted   5. ___?___uit
3. ___?___uarium   6. ___?___ualung

USING THE WORD BANK

On your paper, complete each sentence with a word from the Word Bank.

1. We knew something was ____?____ when the cat raced across the room.
2. We disposed of the broken lamp ____?____ to avoid upsetting Mom.
3. We must ____?____ a new lamp immediately.
4. The filter ____?____ the ray of light, scattering it around the room.

◆ Literary Focus

TONE

The **tone** of a literary work is the attitude the writer has toward the subject and toward the audience. For example, when Arna Bontemps uses the phrase "still as death," you know the tone of "Southern Mansion" is serious.

1. How would you describe the tone of "A Glow in the Dark"? Explain.
2. The tone in "The Bat" seems to change. Explain the difference in tone between the first three stanzas and the last two stanzas.

◆ Build Grammar Skills

APPOSITIVE PHRASES

An appositive is a noun or pronoun placed near another noun or pronoun to explain or identify it. An **appositive phrase** includes the appositive and its modifiers and complements. Appositive phrases are often set off by commas or dashes.

> I could see them quite well in the glow from the light—*the soft glow, the green glow, the ghost glow.* (The italicized words all further identify the first noun *glow.*)

Practice On your paper, write the appositive phrases in each of the following.

1. The light came from within it, a cold-glowing green light with yellow edges. . . .
2. The dogs' song—a death song—echoed eerily.
3. We are edible, / Nudgers and shovers / In spite of ourselves.
4. The mansion, a crumbling ruin, was outside Savannah.
5. A bat's screech, a noise undetectable by humans, helps it navigate in darkness.

Writing Application Write sentences, using appositive phrases to further describe each noun below:

1. sled dogs   4. mansion
2. tree trunk   5. bat
3. mushrooms   6. mice

Build Your Portfolio

Idea Bank

Writing

1. **List** Make a list of supplies that would be necessary to have with you while dog-sledding in the wilderness.

2. **News Story** Imagine that the mushrooms described in "Mushrooms" have taken over a large area. Write the newspaper story that might cover that event. Include the five W's: *who, what, when, where,* and *why.* **[Media Link]**

3. **Essay** Choose one of the pieces in this group. Write an essay in which you explain how the tone of the work contributes to its meaning.

Speaking and Listening

4. **Monologue** Imagine that you are walking on the grounds described in "Southern Mansion." You can be in the present time, or you can be in the time when the mansion was new. What thoughts go through your head? Write, rehearse, and perform a monologue on this subject for the class. **[Social Studies Link]**

5. **Oral Presentation** Prepare a presentation on bats, giving information about their method of navigation, their habitats, and their diet. Present the information to your classmates. **[Science Link]**

Projects

6. **Science Article [Group Activity]** With a partner, prepare a science article about mushrooms. Include information about the different types of mushrooms, methods of growing and collecting them, how to distinguish edible mushrooms from poisonous ones, and recipes that use mushrooms. Add photos and art to your written text, and display your article in the classroom. **[Science Link]**

7. **Story Illustration** Create a series of drawings that brings to life Gary Paulsen's experience in "A Glow in the Dark." **[Art Link]**

Writing Mini-Lesson

I-Search Paper

The selections in this group cover a variety of topics—from dog-sledding and phosphorescent trees to bats and mushrooms. Choose a topic from these selections that interests you, and prepare an I-Search paper, a self-directed research project. Publish your findings in written form.

Writing Skills Focus: State Your Main Points Clearly

Your writing will make more sense if you **state your main points clearly.**

Model
Vague: Bats have a special ability to navigate in darkness.

Clear: To navigate in darkness, bats use echolocation, which operates like sonar in a submarine.

Prewriting Decide on a topic for your I-Search, and gather information. Carefully note details as you find them. Also, jot down the source from which they came.

Drafting Begin your I-Search paper with an introduction, in which you reveal the subject you've researched. Develop your findings in the body of the paper, and summarize your findings in the conclusion. Be sure to state clearly the points you're making.

> ◆ **Grammar Application**
> As you write, use appositive phrases to insert additional information about nouns or pronouns in your sentences.

Revising Rephrase unclear or vague passages to make them more clear. Add details where necessary, and delete details that are beside the point. Proofread carefully for errors in grammar, spelling, and punctuation.

CONNECTING LITERATURE TO SOCIAL STUDIES

THE CIVIL WAR: FAMILIES TORN APART

A Horseman in the Sky by Ambrose Bierce

A SHADOW FALLS A family is eating a meal when suddenly a shadow falls across the table. The shadow divides the family in half, brother from brother and parent from child. This image doesn't come from a science-fiction story. It symbolizes what happened to real families during the Civil War—and to the fictional family in "A Horseman in the Sky."

Choosing Sides in the Civil War

*West Virginia separated from Virginia in 1861 and was admitted to the Union in 1863.

- ☐ Union states
- ☐ Confederate states
- ☐ Border states that stayed in the Union
- ☐ States that joined the Confederacy after April 1861

A Divided Country A symbolic shadow fell across the U.S. map when war broke out between the northern and southern states in 1861. An issue dividing the industrialized North and the agricultural South was slavery. The South believed its economy depended on slaves, but many in the North opposed slavery. In some cases, this dispute between states divided families.

A War Between Brothers One of the shadowed and divided households was that of the Terrills of Virginia. When Virginia seceded from the Union, James Terrill joined the Confederate army. His brother William, a West Point officer, decided to fight for the Union. William's father angrily told him, "Your name shall be stricken from the family records."

"God Alone Knows" Both Terrills fought bravely, both were made generals, and both died in combat. In its grief, the Terrill family carved these words on the monument it created for the fallen brothers: "God Alone Knows Which Was Right." Like the Terrills, the Virginia family in this story by Ambrose Bierce is shadowed by division and death.

A Horseman in the Sky

Ambrose Bierce

One sunny afternoon in the autumn of the year 1861[1] a soldier lay in a clump of laurel by the side of a road in western Virginia. He lay at full length upon his stomach, his feet resting upon the toes, his head upon the left forearm. His extended right hand loosely grasped his rifle. But for the somewhat methodical disposition of his limbs and a slight rhythmic movement of the cartridge-box at the back of his belt he might have been thought to be dead. He was asleep at his post of duty. But if detected he would be dead shortly afterward, death being the just and legal penalty of his crime.

> **Connecting Literature to Social Studies**
> What clues reveal that the story is set during the Civil War and on Confederate soil?

The clump of laurel in which the criminal lay was in the angle of a road which after ascending southward a steep acclivity[2] to that point turned sharply to the west, running along the summit for perhaps one hundred yards. There it turned southward again and went zigzagging downward through the forest. At the salient of that second angle[3] was a large flat rock, jutting out northward, overlooking the deep valley from which the road ascended. The rock capped a high cliff; a stone dropped from its outer edge would have fallen sheer downward one thousand feet to the tops of the pines. The angle where the soldier lay was on another spur of the same cliff. Had he been awake he would have commanded a view, not only of the short arm of the road and the jutting rock, but of the entire profile of the cliff below it. It might well have made him giddy to look.

The country was wooded everywhere except at the bottom of the valley to the northward, where there was a small natural meadow, through which flowed a stream scarcely visible from the valley's rim. This open ground looked hardly larger than an ordinary door-yard, but was really several acres in extent. Its green was more vivid than that of the inclosing forest. Away beyond it rose a line of giant cliffs similar to those upon which we are supposed to stand in our survey of the savage scene, and through which the road had somehow made its climb to the summit. The configuration of the valley, indeed, was such that from this point of observation it seemed entirely shut in, and one could but have wondered how the road which found a way out of it had found a way into it, and

---

1. **1861:** Marks the beginning of the American Civil War (1861–1865) between the North (the Union) and the South (the Confederacy).
2. **acclivity** (ə kliv´ ə tē) *n.*: Upward slope of the ground.
3. **salient** (sāl´ lē ənt) **of that second angle:** Referring to the point where the summit projects or points outward.

◆ **Build Vocabulary**

configuration (kən fig´ yo͞o rā´ shən) *n.*: Structure; arrangement

Album of Virginia "Rockfish Gap and Mountain House," Edward Beyer, The Library of Virginia

▲ **Critical Viewing** Why would countryside like this be ideal for advancing troops in secret? [Infer]

whence came and whither went the waters of the stream that parted the meadow more than a thousand feet below.

No country is so wild and difficult but men will make it a theater of war; concealed in the forest at the bottom of that military rat-trap, in which half a hundred men in possession of the exits might have starved an army to submission, lay five regiments of Federal infantry.[4] They had marched all the previous day and night and were resting. At nightfall they would take to the road again, climb to the place where their unfaithful <u>sentinel</u> now slept, and descending the other slope of the ridge fall upon a camp of the enemy at about midnight. Their hope was to surprise it, for the road led to the rear of it. In case of failure, their position would be perilous in the extreme; and fail they surely would should accident or vigilance apprise the enemy of the movement.

The sleeping sentinel in the clump of laurel was a young Virginian named Carter Druse. He was the son of wealthy parents, an only child, and had known such ease and cultivation and high living as wealth and taste were able to command in the mountain country of western Virginia. His home was but a few miles from where he now lay. One morning he had risen from the breakfast-table and said, quietly but gravely: "Father, a Union regiment has arrived at Grafton. I am going to join it."

The father lifted his leonine[5] head, looked at the son a moment in silence, and replied: "Well, go, sir, and whatever may occur do what you conceive to be your duty. Virginia, to which you are a

> **Connecting Literature to Social Studies**
> What word in the father's speech suggests the bitterness of this family division?

traitor, must get on without you. Should we both live to the end of the war, we will speak further of the matter. Your mother, as the physician has informed you, is in a most

---

4. Federal infantry: Foot-soldiers of the Federal Union, or the North.

5. leonine (lē´ ə nīn´) *adj.*: Characteristic of, or like a lion.

critical condition; at the best she cannot be with us longer than a few weeks, but that time is precious. It would be better not to disturb her."

So Carter Druse, bowing reverently to his father, who returned the salute with a stately courtesy that masked a breaking heart, left the home of his childhood to go soldiering. By conscience and courage, by deeds of devotion and daring, he soon commended himself to his fellows and his officers; and it was to these qualities and to some knowledge of the country that he owed his selection for his present perilous duty at the extreme outpost. Nevertheless, fatigue had been stronger than resolution and he had fallen asleep. What good or bad angel came in a dream to rouse him from his state of crime, who shall say? Without a movement, without a sound, in the profound silence and the <u>languor</u> of the late afternoon, some invisible messenger of fate touched with unsealing finger the eyes of his consciousness—whispered into the ear of his spirit the mysterious awakening word which no human lips ever have spoken, no human memory ever has recalled. He quietly raised his forehead from his arm and looked between the masking stems of the laurels, instinctively closing his right hand about the stock of his rifle.

His first feeling was a keen artistic delight. On a colossal pedestal, the cliff,—motionless at the extreme edge of the capping rock and sharply outlined against the sky,—was an <u>equestrian</u> statue of impressive dignity. The figure of the man sat the figure of the horse, straight and soldierly, but with the repose of a Grecian god carved in the marble which limits the suggestion of activity. The gray costume harmonized with its aerial background; the metal of accoutrement and caparison[6] was softened and subdued by the shadow; the animal's skin had no points of high light.

6. **accoutrement** (ə kōō' trə mənt) **and caparison** (kə par' i sən): The clothing or dress of the man and the ornamented covering of the horse.

A carbine[7] strikingly foreshortened lay across the pommel of the saddle, kept in place by the right hand grasping it at the "grip"; the left hand, holding the bridle rein, was invisible. In silhouette against the sky the profile of the horse was cut with the sharpness of a cameo; it looked across the heights of air to the confronting cliffs beyond. The face of the rider, turned slightly away, showed only an outline of temple and beard; he was looking downward to the bottom of the valley. Magnified by its lift against the sky and by the soldier's testifying sense of the formidableness of a near enemy the group appeared of heroic, almost colossal, size.

For an instant Druse had a strange, half-defined feeling that he had slept to the end of the war and was looking upon a noble work of art reared upon that <u>eminence</u> to commemorate the deeds of an heroic past of which he had been an inglorious part. The feeling was dispelled by a slight movement of the group: the horse, without moving its feet, had drawn its body slightly backward from the verge; the man remained immobile as before. Broad awake and keenly alive to the significance of the situation, Druse now brought the butt of his rifle against his cheek by cautiously pushing the barrel forward through the bushes, cocked the piece, and glancing through the sights covered a vital spot of the horseman's breast. A touch upon the trigger and all would have been well with Carter Druse. At that instant the horseman turned his head and looked in the direction of his concealed foeman—seemed to look into his

7. **carbine** (cär' bīn') n.: Rifle with a short barrel.

◆ Build Vocabulary

sentinel (sen' ti nəl) n.: Guard

languor (laŋ' gər) n.: Listlessness; indifference

equestrian (ē kwes' trē ən) adj.: On horseback, or so represented

eminence (em' i nəns) n.: High or lofty place

very face, into his eyes, into his brave, compassionate heart.

Is it then so terrible to kill an enemy in war—an enemy who has surprised a secret vital to the safety of one's self and comrades—an enemy more formidable for his knowledge than all his army for its numbers? Carter Druse grew pale; he shook in every limb, turned faint, and saw the statuesque group before him as black figures, rising, falling, moving unsteadily in arcs of circles in a fiery sky. His hand fell away from his weapon, his head slowly dropped until his face rested on the leaves in which he lay. This courageous gentleman and hardy soldier was near swooning from intensity of emotion.

It was not for long; in another moment his face was raised from earth, his hands resumed their places on the rifle, his forefinger sought the trigger; mind, heart, and eyes were clear, conscience and reason sound. He could not hope to capture that enemy; to alarm him would but send him dashing to his camp with his fatal news. The duty of the soldier was plain: the man

▲ **Critical Viewing** What does this illustration reveal about warfare during the Civil War? **[Deduce]**

must be shot dead from ambush—without warning, without a moment's spiritual preparation, with never so much as an unspoken prayer, he must be sent to his account. But no—there is a hope; he may have discovered nothing—perhaps he is but admiring the sublimity of the landscape. If permitted, he may turn and ride carelessly away in the direction whence he came. Surely it will be possible to judge at the instant of his withdrawing whether he knows. It may well be that his fixity of attention—Druse turned his head and looked through the deeps of air downward, as from the surface to the bottom of a translucent sea. He saw creeping across the green meadow a sinuous line of figures of men and horses—some foolish commander was permitting the soldiers of his escort to water their beasts in the open, in plain view from a dozen summits!

Druse withdrew his eyes from the valley

and fixed them again upon the group of man and horse in the sky, and again it was through the sights of his rifle. But this time his aim was at the horse. In his memory, as if they were a divine <u>mandate</u>, rang the words of his father at their parting: "Whatever may occur, do what you conceive to be your duty." He was calm now. His teeth were firmly but not rigidly closed; his nerves were as tranquil as a sleeping babe's—not a tremor affected any muscle of his body; his breathing, until suspended in the act of taking aim, was regular and slow. Duty had conquered; the spirit had said to the body: "Peace, be still." He fired.

An officer of the Federal force, who in a spirit of adventure or in quest of knowledge had left the hidden *bivouac*[8] in the valley, and with aimless feet, had made his way to the lower edge of a small open space near the foot of the cliff, was considering what he had to gain by pushing his exploration further. At a distance of a quarter-mile before him, but apparently at a stone's throw, rose from its fringe of pines the gigantic face of rock, towering to so great a height above him that it made him giddy to look up to where its edge cut a sharp, rugged line against the sky. At some distance to his right it presented a clean, vertical profile against a background of blue sky to a point half the way down, and of distant hills, hardly less blue, thence to the tops of the trees at its base. Lifting his eyes to the dizzy altitude of its summit the officer saw an astonishing sight—a man on horseback riding down into the valley through the air!

Straight upright sat the rider, in military fashion, with a firm seat in the saddle, a strong clutch upon the rein to hold his charger from too <u>impetuous</u> a plunge. From his bare head his long hair streamed upward, waving like a plume. His hands were concealed in the cloud of the horse's lifted mane. The animal's body was as level as if every

---

8. **bivouac** (biv´ wak´) *n.*: Temporary encampment.

hoof-stroke encountered the resistant earth. Its motions were those of a wild gallop, but even as the officer looked they ceased, with all the legs thrown sharply forward as in the act of alighting from a leap. But this was a flight!

Filled with amazement and terror by this apparition of a horseman in the sky—half believing himself the chosen scribe of some new Apocalypse,[9] the officer was overcome by the intensity of his emotions; his legs failed him and he fell. Almost at the same instant he heard a crashing sound in the trees—a sound that died without an echo—and all was still.

The officer rose to his feet, trembling. The familiar sensation of an abraded shin recalled his dazed faculties. Pulling himself together he ran rapidly obliquely away from the cliff to a point distant from its foot; thereabout he expected to find his man; and thereabout he naturally failed. In the fleeting instant of his vision his imagination had been so wrought upon by the apparent grace and ease and intention of the marvelous performance that it did not occur to him that the line of march of aerial cavalry is directly downward, and that he could find the objects of his search at the very foot of the cliff. A half-hour later he returned to camp.

This officer was a wise man; he knew better than to tell an incredible truth. He said nothing of what he had seen. But when the commander asked him if in his scout he had learned anything of advantage to the expedition he answered:

---

9. **Apocalypse** (ə päk´ ə lips´): A disclosure regarded as prophetic; revelation.

◆ Build Vocabulary

sublimity (sə blim´ ə tē) *n.*: The state or quality of being majestic; noble

mandate (man´ dāt´) *n.*: Order or command

impetuous (im pech´ o͞o əs) *adj.*: Moving with great force or violence

"Yes, sir; there is no road leading down into this valley from the southward."

The commander, knowing better, smiled.

After firing his shot, Private Carter Druse reloaded his rifle and resumed his watch. Ten minutes had hardly passed when a Federal sergeant crept cautiously to him on his hands and knees. Druse neither turned his head nor looked at him, but lay without motion or sign of recognition.

"Did you fire?" the sergeant whispered.

"Yes."

"At what?"

"A horse. It was standing on yonder rock—pretty far out. You see it is no longer there. It went over the cliff."

The man's face was white, but he showed no other sign of emotion. Having answered, he turned away his eyes and said no more. The sergeant did not understand.

"See here, Druse," he said, after a moment's silence, "it's no use making a mystery. I order you to report. Was there anybody on the horse?"

"Yes."

"Well?"

"My father."

The sergeant rose to his feet and walked away. "Good God!" he said.

> **Connecting Literature to Social Studies**
> How does the tragedy of the Druse family dramatize the nation's experience in the Civil War?

Meet the Author

Ambrose Bierce (1842–1914?) served as a Union officer in the Civil War. This experience helped determine the bleak view of the world he expressed in his writing.

After the Civil War, Bierce settled in San Francisco as a journalist. His bitter but lively writing, together with his personal charm, won him great popularity. In 1891, he published *Tales of Soldiers and Civilians,* from which this story comes.

Despite his literary success, Bierce's life was tragic. His marriage ended in divorce, and his two sons died at an early age. In 1913, he traveled to Mexico and never returned. The circumstances of his death are still a mystery.

Guide for Responding

◆ LITERATURE AND YOUR LIFE

Reader's Response What would you have said to Druse if he had told you what he had done?

Thematic Focus In what way is this story ordinary and extraordinary?

Role Play With a classmate, reenact the scene between Carter and his father at the breakfast table.

☑ Check Your Comprehension

1. Briefly describe the time and place in which the story is set.
2. What disagreement did Druse and his father have at the breakfast table?
3. How does Druse's decision produce a remarkable sight?
4. What is the surprise at the end of the story?

◆ Critical Thinking

INTERPRET

1. Why is the description of the landscape so important to understanding Druse's decision about whether to shoot? **[Connect]**
2. What is strange or unexpected about the fact that Druse is a "criminal" for sleeping but a good soldier for killing his father? **[Analyze]**
3. How do the title of the story and the image it describes suggest a total devotion to duty? **[Draw Conclusions]**

APPLY

4. E. M. Forster wrote that he'd rather betray his country than his friend. What do you think Forster would have said about Carter Druse? Explain. **[Apply]**

CONNECTING LITERATURE TO SOCIAL STUDIES

Abraham Lincoln said, "A house divided against itself cannot stand." He was referring to a divided country—part based on slavery and part free. Here's how the two sides looked in 1861:

Category	North	South
Railroad track	21,847 miles	8,947 miles
Factories	119,500	20,600
Population	22,340,000	9,103,000 (3,954,000 slaves)

Bierce puts a human face on these numbers. His story shows how the nation's divided house, and the war it led to, affects a single household.

Also, as the true story of the Terrills indicates, Bierce's fictional family is based on reality.

Besides focusing on a single household, Bierce zooms in on a moment of truth: A son who is a Union soldier must decide whether to kill his Confederate father in order to protect Union soldiers. The son's ordeal reflects the nation's.

1. What does the story suggest about the cost of duty and of victory in a civil war?
2. In what way does the sergeant's "Good God!" sum up the horror of Druse's choice and of the whole war?
3. Does the chart at left suggest which side might win the war? Explain.

Idea Bank

Writing

1. **Diary Entry** As Carter Druse, write a diary entry for the day described in "A Horseman in the Sky."
2. **Prequel** Write an introductory episode to the story, explaining what led to the division in the Druse family. Be sure that the facts you make up are consistent with the ones in the story.
3. **Reflective Essay** Write an essay expressing your thoughts on the conflict that Carter Druse faces and the way in which he resolves it. Support your points with your own experience and insights from stories you've read or viewed.

Speaking and Listening

4. **Retelling** As the federal officer who saw the horseman fall, tell your best friend about this remarkable sight.
5. **Debate [Group Activity]** With several classmates, debate the pros and cons of this resolution: Druse was right to follow his military duty.

Project

6. **Multimedia Presentation [Group Activity]** With a partner, give a presentation on families divided by the Civil War. Weave together excerpts from letters and diaries, photographs, film clips, and recordings of Civil War songs.

Further Reading, Listening, and Viewing

- *War Between Brothers* (New York: Time-Life Books, 1996) is a fascinating illustrated account of the Civil War.
- *In the Midst of Life: Tales of Soldiers and Civilians* (New York: Boni, 1924) is the book by Ambrose Bierce that contains "A Horseman in the Sky" and other Civil War stories.
- *The Civil War* (1990), directed by Ken Burns, is an award-winning documentary about the American Civil War.
- Irene Hunt's *Across Five Aprils* is a young-adult novel about a divided family.

Writing Process Workshop

If writer Gary Paulsen had a how-to guide for identifying the mysteries of nature, he may not have been so terrified by the mysterious green glow of the tree stump. How-to guides or essays provide instructions for accomplishing a specific task or meeting a goal, such as putting together a bicycle or identifying a natural event.

Write a how-to essay about a subject on which you are an expert. The following skills will help you.

Writing Skills Focus

▶ **State your main points clearly** so your readers know exactly what they must do to accomplish the task. (See p. 513.)

▶ **Elaborate** to provide necessary details and explanations for each step of instruction.

▶ **Use transitions** to show the relationships between ideas.

Read the following how-to guide on how to evaluate a work of abstract art:

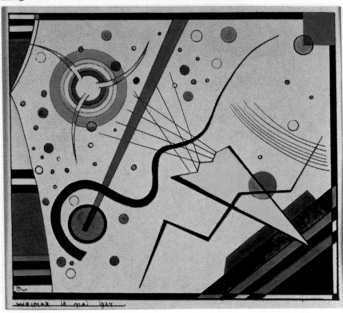

Variation IV, Wassily Kandinsky, Russian Bauhaus Archive

WRITING MODEL

Evaluating Abstract Art

When evaluating abstract art, follow this formula: First, give it a gut reaction. ① Decide if you like it and why. ② Then, think it over. Look at the title and the work to try to determine the artist's purpose for creating the work. After you have appreciated the work personally and objectively, you can evaluate it. ③ Decide whether the artist accomplishes what you believe was his or her purpose. Also, ask yourself whether the work has long-standing appeal or is a work only "today's" audience would appreciate.

① The writer's first instruction is stated clearly.

② This detail elaborates by explaining a gut reaction.

③ The transitional word after lets you know when this step should be completed.

Prewriting

Choose a Topic For your how-to essay, pick a subject about which you know a great deal. Here are more suggestions:

Topic Ideas

- Playing a sport or game
- Taking care of a pet
- Preparing food
- Getting used to a new school

Develop Details by Anticipating Questions Jot down some questions that readers might ask, and gather information that will answer them. For example, if you are explaining how to play the guitar, provide answers to questions like these:

▶ What kind of guitar is best for a beginner?
▶ Do you need anything besides a guitar to start?
▶ Where do you get sheet music?

Create an Organizer Use a graphic organizer like the following to map out the steps of the procedure you are describing:

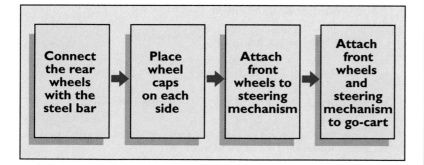

Drafting

State Your Main Points Clearly Too much descriptive detail can cause readers to miss the main point. Before adding details, clearly state instructions in order. Present the most important information first. Then, add any supporting information.

Use Transitions Use words that indicate cause-and-effect relationships—*since, therefore, as a result, because, for that reason, due to, consequently, so,* and *for*. As you draft your paper, use these words to show relationships among ideas, such as steps in programming a VCR or the importance of preheating the oven before starting a recipe.

APPLYING LANGUAGE SKILLS: Using Transitions to Indicate Time

Transitions help your reader connect ideas. Here are some transitions that indicate a time relationship:

after, as soon as, at last, at the same time, before, during, earlier, eventually, finally, first, later, meanwhile, next, now, second, soon, then

Practice Copy each sentence below into your notebook. Then, fill in the blanks with an appropriate time transition.

1. Preheat the oven to 450°. _____?_____, grease and flour a 9" round pan.
2. _____?_____ mixing the ingredients, pour them into a dish.
3. One hour will pass _____?_____ the edges will turn brown.
4. _____?_____, let it cool.
5. _____?_____, enjoy the soufflé!

Writing Application As you write your essay, add transitions to show the order in which steps must be followed.

Writer's Solution Connection
Writing Lab

For more help, use the Transitions Word Bin in the Drafting section of the Exposition: Making Connections tutorial.

EDITING/PROOFREADING

APPLYING LANGUAGE SKILLS: Using Commas After Introductory Transitions

Transitions are used to signal relationships between sentences. When a transition begins a sentence, it is usually set off from the rest of the sentence by a comma:

<u>First</u>, make sure you have matches and newspapers.

<u>Meanwhile</u>, gather dry pinecones, twigs, and bark.

Practice Copy the following sentences into your notebook. Set off introductory transitions with commas.

1. First gather the materials you need.
2. After that find one mushroom near your house.
3. Then check your field guide.
4. Now identify whether the mushroom is poisonous.
5. Next repeat steps two through four.

Writing Application Insert commas following transitions in your how-to essay.

Writer's Solution Connection Language Lab

For more about commas, see the Commas lesson in the Punctuation unit.

Create Visual Aids Create graphs, diagrams, and charts to convey complex information in an easy-to-understand form. For example, diagrams can sometimes convey assembly instructions better than a bulleted list.

Revising

Do a Test Run Ask a classmate to use your instructions to accomplish the task. Your classmate should use these questions for reviewing your directions:

- ▶ Are the steps clearly stated?
- ▶ Does background information help in understanding the task or does it cause confusion?
- ▶ Are relationships among ideas indicated by transitional words?

REVISION MODEL

My favorite cookies are chocolate chip. Here is my recipe:

① *2 c. flour, 2 T. baking soda, 2 sticks of butter, 2 eggs, 1 T. of vanilla, 2 c. of sugar, 3/4 c. of chocolate chips*

~~Gather flower and baking soda and put them to the side.~~

~~Then get butter, eggs, 1 tablespoon of vanilla, two cups~~

~~of sugar, and chocolate chips.~~

② *First,* *then*

1. Soften the butter and whip it.

③ *to prevent cookies from sticking.*

2. Grease a cookie sheet.

3. Mix butter, sugar, and eggs. Beat until smooth.

① The writer replaced his list of ingredients with a precise list of ingredients and measurements.

② Adding the transitions *first* and *then* indicates the order in which the steps must be completed.

③ The writer elaborated with this detail to let readers know why this step is important.

Publishing and Presenting

Classroom Turn your essay into a 5- to 10-minute talk. Demonstrate your instructions for your class.

School Create a step-by-step poster that illustrates your how-to essay. Post your work in school.

Fair Organize a fair at which class members can teach one another the procedures they have written about. Ask classmates to distribute copies at the fair.

Real-World Reading Skills Workshop

Strategies for Success

Whether you are installing a new computer game or putting together a bicycle, you'll be more successful if you read the directions. The owner's manual that comes with new products includes detailed directions and important information that will help you put together and use a product correctly.

Skim the Manual Get acquainted with the organization of the manual. Review the table of contents to see what topics are covered in the manual—what the product does and how information is organized. Read the introduction for a general overview of the product.

Check the Manual for Parts Before you completely unpack the shipping crate or box, find the list of parts you should have for assembling the item. Check off the parts one by one as you unpack them. Sometimes special tools or connections are necessary. Make sure you have those before you proceed.

Read Specific Sections Carefully Your preview will help you determine what parts of the manual you want to read. You will probably read through most of the beginning sections of the manual, but you can put off reading the supplementary material until a later time.

Read to Solve Problems Keep the manual for reference in case you have a problem with the product. A troubleshooting section, providing solutions for common problems, is included in most manuals. You can use the index to locate specific details that pertain to your problem.

Apply the Strategies

You recently purchased a computer program that makes greeting cards. You would like to start preparing cards for the upcoming holiday.

Use the manual's table of contents, shown below, to answer the following questions:

1. Where would you find information on installing the program?
2. Describe the information found in each of the four sections.
3. Which section would you use if you wanted the time and day to be displayed on your screen?
4. Which section would you read first? Why?

Keller's Holiday Cardmaker

Introduction 1

I. Getting Started
   Installation 3
   Main Menu 6

II. Graphics
   Finding Graphics 10
   Choosing Graphics 15
   Saving Graphics 20

III. Cardmaker
   Choosing a Style 25
   Importing Graphics 28

IV. Customizing Holiday Cardmaker
   Display Preferences 30
   Print Preferences 33

Troubleshooting 35
Index 38

✔ *Here are other situations in which you should read the manuals:*
- ▶ *Using a new word-processing program*
- ▶ *Assembling a bicycle*
- ▶ *Setting up an audio system*

Real-World Reading Skills Workshop ◆ 525

Grammar Review

A **phrase** is a group of words that usually serves as a single part of speech and does not contain a subject or a verb. Two types of phrases are participial phrases and appositive phrases.

phrase (frāz) *n.* 1 a group of words that is not a complete sentence, but that gives a single idea, usually as a separate part of a sentence ["Drinking fresh milk," "with meals," and "to be healthy" are phrases.]

Participial Phrases A **participial phrase** functions as an adjective. It contains a participle, a verb form ending in *-ing* or *-ed,* and all the participle's modifiers and complements.

"Even Tommy Wright, *wedged between his parents in the front seat,* was subdued."

The participial phrase, *wedged between his parents in the front seat,* modifies Tommy Wright.

Appositive Phrases An **appositive phrase** contains an appositive, a noun or pronoun placed near another noun or pronoun to explain or identify it, and all its modifiers and complements. Appositive phrases are often set off by commas or dashes.

Gary Paulsen, a nature writer, creates suspense in "A Glow in the Dark."

The appositive phrase "a nature writer" identifies the sentence's subject, Gary Paulsen.

Practice 1 Copy these passages into your notebook. Underline and label any participial or appositive phrases.

1. "A large, standing form glowing in the dark"

2. "Touching the stump, and feeling the cold light, I could not quite get rid of the fear until a black and white dog named Fonzie came up. . . ."

3. Fonzie, a dog that ran with the pack, confronted the glowing stump.

4. Some mushrooms, a fungus, are highly prized by chefs.

5. Bats often fly at night, circling in the sky and looking for prey.

Practice 2 In your notebook, combine each pair of sentences into one sentence that includes the type of phrase indicated.

1. The mushrooms covered the ground. The mushrooms are a kind of fungus. (appositive phrase)

2. The abandoned mansion was swaying in the strong wind. It looked unstable. (participial phrase)

3. The tree stump was glowing with a green tint. The stump frightened the dogs. (participial phrase)

4. The bat likes the attic of an aging house. The bat is a cousin to the mouse. (appositive)

5. The ancient house was hidden by overgrown trees. It was crumbling from decay. (participial phrase)

Grammar in Writing

✔ *Use appositive phrases to insert additional information into sentences.*

✔ *To vary your sentence beginnings, start some sentences with participial phrases.*

Speaking, Listening, and Viewing Workshop

Delivering a Speech

Now that you have chosen a topic, completed your research, and written a final draft of your speech, it is time to deliver it in a way that will accomplish your purpose. Whether your purpose is to inform young children about safety rules or to persuade your classmates to vote for you in an upcoming school election, you must capture the attention of your audience and hold it. The way you deliver information is just as important as what you have to say.

Engage Your Audience Capture the attention of your audience by beginning with a humorous story, a thought-provoking question, or a firm statement of belief that relates to your topic.

Tips for Delivering a Speech

✔ *If you want to make a good impression and seem like a professional, follow these strategies:*

▶ *Look directly at your audience.*
▶ *Use appropriate gestures and tone of voice.*
▶ *Speak loudly and clearly.*

Look at Your Audience To keep your audience's attention, maintain eye contact. If you simply read from your notes, your audience won't feel that you are speaking to them and may lose interest. Practice your speech so you are comfortable looking up from your notes.

Keep Your Audience's Attention Using your voice emphatically to show enthusiasm about your topic will help keep the attention of your audience. Don't stand stiffly or appear to be simply reading your speech. Instead, use gestures to emphasize important points—raising your hand, tapping the lectern, or pointing to a chart or graph.

Apply the Strategies

Prepare and deliver speeches for the following situations. Then, invite your classmates to share feedback on your effectiveness.

1. Your school is having a Club Fair. You have been chosen by your club, The Ecology Crowd, to give a speech describing the purpose of the club, what you do, and how often you meet.

2. As a member of the student council, you have been asked to introduce the new principal to the student body. You have met the principal and really like her, and you want to communicate that to the student body.

3. You do volunteer work at an animal shelter. Give a brief talk to classmates. Explain the benefits of your work, and try to get others to volunteer.

What's Behind the
Words

Vocabulary Adventures With Richard Lederer

Mystery and Detective Vocabulary

With his short story "The Murders in the Rue Morgue," in 1841, American author Edgar Allan Poe launched the literary genre of the mystery story. The mystery of the word *mystery* takes us back to the Greek *mysterion,* a secret religious ceremony in which one was "to have closed eyes and lips." Later, the word came to mean anything that was not understood.

Making a Case for Detectives

Poe's detective, named Monsieur C. Auguste Dupin, became a model for many other private investigators, including Sherlock Holmes. Detectives derive their title from the Latin *detectus,* "uncover" (*de,* "from," and *tegere,* "to cover"). The detective's mission is to uncover a villain, a plot, or a dastardly deed.

A detective is sometimes called a sleuth. The word *sleuth* is a shortening of *sleuthhound,* a Scottish bloodhound noted for its dogged pursuit of game, suspects, and fugitives.

Detectives are also known as private eyes. The famous Pinkerton Detective Agency had the motto "We never sleep." The motto was printed on cards, posters, and stationery over a drawing of an open eye, and their detectives became known as private eyes.

Threading Your Way Through Clues

Detectives uncover clues to *deduce* (Latin *deducere,* "lead from") the solutions to mysteries. *Clue* is a native English word, but its origin lies in Greek mythology. The Minotaur, a dreaded monster that was half man and half bull, prowled a labyrinth, on the island of Crete. The hero Theseus offered to enter the

maze and kill the beast. Ariadne, daughter of the King of Crete, was in love with Theseus and gave him a thread—in Middle English, a *clewe*—to guide him out of the labyrinth after he had slain the monster. From this story, the word *clewe,* now *clue,* came to mean anything that guides us through a perplexing situation, such as a crime.

ACTIVITY 1 You can be a word detective by using *context* (Latin *contextere,* "to weave together") as a powerful clue to learning new words. When you meet an unknown word, you can infer its meaning from its context by taking account of the surrounding words and the situation being taught or written about. From their contexts on this page, infer the meanings of the words *genre, dastardly, labyrinth,* and *perplexing.*

ACTIVITY 2 Word detectives dig down to the roots of words. They know that words are often related to each other by roots—basic units of language that convey important meanings. As an exercise in root detection, examine each three-word cluster, and then deduce the meaning of each root:

1. autobiography, autograph, automatic
   auto = _____?_____
2. chronic, chronology, synchronize
   chron = _____?_____
3. contradict, dictionary, predict
   dict = _____?_____
4. microphone, phonics, telephone
   phon = _____?_____
5. extract, intractable, tractor
   tract = _____?_____

Extended Reading Opportunities

The world is full of unusual and extraordinary occurrences that bewilder and fascinate. The following novels explore amazing worlds of mystery and fantasy.

Suggested Titles

The Man Who Was Poe
Avi

Young Edmund finds himself alone in the city. His mother is gone, his father is missing, and his twin sister has disappeared. Edmund is being followed by a mysterious stranger who turns out to be Edgar Allan Poe. Poe offers to help Edmund solve the mystery surrounding the disappearance of his family in exchange for the boy's help with his own mission. The thriller follows their adventures through the shadowy city of Providence, Rhode Island, in 1848.

Twenty Thousand Leagues Under the Sea
Jules Verne

A ship hunting a deadly sea-monster is destroyed in an explosion, and a French scientist, his sidekick, and a Canadian harpoonist are the only survivors. They are then swallowed up by a technological monster—a submarine. The men take part in an underwater odyssey commanded by the madman Captain Nemo. The novel, written in 1870, lays the foundation for much of today's science fiction in its accurate prediction of twentieth-century technological advances.

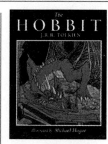

The Hobbit
J.R.R. Tolkien

Bilbo Baggins, a middle-aged hobbit, is about to have the adventure of his life. With a wizard named Gandalf and thirteen dwarves, Bilbo is headed for Lonely Mountain to confront a dragon that is hoarding treasure. The novel, although set in a world of fantasy, echoes much of the history of the Middle Ages, with knights, warfare, castles, and armies. Having confronted evil and overcome hardship, Bilbo returns from his quest a hero.

Other Possibilities

The Lord of the Rings	J.R.R. Tolkein
Canyons	Gary Paulsen
Invitation to the Game	Monica Hughes

Mrs. Cushman's House, 1942, N.C. Wyeth, New Britain Museum of American Art, Connecticut

Short Stories

Short stories take you on a quick trip to other worlds and into other people's lives. Within the pages of a short story, you may encounter anything—from deadly cobras to absent-minded professors to deranged criminals. Despite their varied content, almost all short stories have the following elements in common:

- **Plot:** the sequence of events that catches your interest and takes you through the story.

- **Characters:** the people, animals, or other beings that take part in the story's action.

- **Setting:** the time and place in which the story takes place.

- **Theme:** the message about life that the story conveys.

This unit highlights the elements of the short story while it shows the power and variety of the form.

*G*uide for Reading

Meet the Author:

Mona Gardner (1900–1982)

Mona Gardner was born in Seattle, Washington, and graduated from California's Stanford University.

Asian Interests Being a West Coast resident may have given Gardner a special interest in Asia, which lies across the Pacific. One of her best-known works, for example, is the historical novel *Hong Kong* (1958). This novel tells about the founding of the Chinese city of Hong Kong.

Writing Career In her long writing career, Gardner contributed stories and articles to such well-known magazines as *The New Yorker, The Atlantic,* and *The Saturday Evening Post.*

THE STORY BEHIND THE STORY

"The Dinner Party" was first published in *The Saturday Review* on January 31, 1942. The story is set in India, which was then a British colony. Most of the guests at the story's dinner party are British officials who control India on behalf of Britain.

◆ LITERATURE AND YOUR LIFE

CONNECT YOUR EXPERIENCE

Life is full of surprises. In "The Dinner Party," a cobra, a deadly snake, intrudes upon an elegant dinner party like the one shown in the painting. Think about unexpected things that have happened in your life. How did you handle the surprise?

THEMATIC FOCUS: Conflicts and Challenges

Think about the different types of challenges people face as you read "The Dinner Party."

◆ Background for Understanding

SCIENCE

In this story, you'll meet with a snake native to India that invades a dinner party. The Indian cobra, which averages 5.5 feet in length and displays a neck "hood" as a warning, kills a few thousand people every year. (Cobra venom is fatal to humans in one out of ten cases.) These deaths usually result from a cobra's twilight visit to a house in search of rats.

◆ Build Vocabulary

WORD ROOTS: -spir-

The word root -spir-, from a Latin word meaning "breath," breathes its life into a whole family of words. In this story, for instance, a young girl is described as *spirited,* which means "filled with life; lively."

WORD BANK

Which of these words from the list describes someone who studies nature? Check the Build Vocabulary box on page 535 to see if you chose correctly.

naturalist
spirited
arresting
sobers

◆ The Dinner Party ◆

Dinner at Haddo House, Alfred Edward Emslie, National Portrait Gallery, London

◆ Literary Focus

PLOT

A story's **plot** is a sequence of events in which each event results from a previous one and causes the next. The plot centers on a **conflict,** a struggle between opposing forces. This struggle, explained in the **exposition,** builds in the **rising action** and reaches its point of greatest tension at the **climax.** Afterward, in the **falling action,** the conflict is **resolved.**

As you read "The Dinner Party," use this chart to follow the roller-coaster ride of its plot:

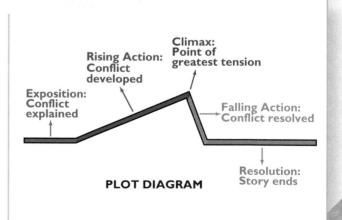

PLOT DIAGRAM

Reading for Success

Strategies for Reading Fiction

Reading fiction isn't like reading a how-to article. You need to pack a few extra things in your reading kit besides your brain—for example, your feeling for other people, your imagination, and your willingness to enter and live in a made-up world. Following are strategies for reading fiction, which will help you as you explore the new worlds revealed in these short stories.

Identify with a character or situation.
Enter into the characters' lives, sharing their thoughts and feelings, and rooting for or against them. Relate their experiences and the events that occur to situations you have experienced.

Predict what will happen.
▶ When story characters make broad statements, predict whether or not those statements will prove true.
▶ As story events unfold, predict what will happen.

Ask questions about plot, characters, and theme.
Your questions are worth asking. Question what is happening in a story. Ask why characters do what they do or why the author includes certain details. Here's a sample question:

Passage	Question
. . . a spirited discussion springs up between a young girl and a colonel.	Why does the author bring up this discussion?

Make inferences about what you read.
Writers don't always tell you everything directly. You have to make inferences to arrive at ideas that writers suggest but don't say. Inferences are conclusions based on evidence or the details that the writer includes.

Passage	Inference
The American scientist does not join in the argument, but sits watching the faces of the other guests.	The American is a thoughtful person.

As you read "The Dinner Party," look at the notes along the sides of the pages. The notes demonstrate how to apply these strategies to a work of literature.

The DINNER Party

Mona Gardner

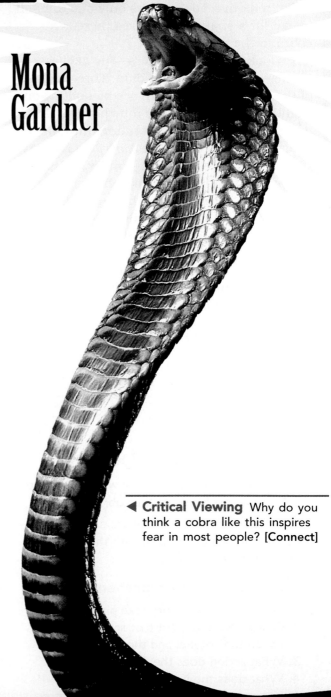

The country is India. A large dinner party is being given in an up-country station by a colonial official and his wife. The guests are army officers and government attachés and their wives, and an American naturalist.

At one side of the long table a spirited discussion springs up between a young girl and a colonel. The girl insists women have long outgrown the jumping-on-a-chair-at-sight-of-a-mouse era, that they are not as fluttery as their grandmothers. The

> **Identify** with one side or the other in this argument.

colonel says they are, explaining that women haven't the actual nerve control of men. The other men at the table agree with him.

"A woman's unfailing reaction in any crisis,"

> You can **predict** that a woman will prove the colonal wrong.

the colonel says, "is to scream. And while a man may feel like it, yet he has that ounce more of control than a woman has. And that last ounce is what counts!"

The American scientist does not join in the argument, but sits watching the faces of the other guests. As he looks, he sees a strange expression come over the face of the hostess.

◆ **Build Vocabulary**

naturalist (nach´ ər əl ist) *n.*: One who studies nature

spirited (spir´ it id) *adj.*: Lively; energetic

◀ **Critical Viewing** Why do you think a cobra like this inspires fear in most people? [**Connect**]

She is staring straight ahead, the muscles of her face contracting slightly. With a small gesture she summons the native boy standing behind her chair. She whispers to him. The boy's eyes widen: he turns quickly and leaves the room. No one else sees this, nor the boy when he puts a bowl of milk on the verandah[1] outside the glass doors.

The American comes to with a start. In India, milk in a bowl means only one thing. It is bait for a snake. He realizes there is a cobra in the room.

He looks up at the rafters—the likeliest place—and sees they are bare. Three corners of the room, which he can see by shifting only slightly, are empty. In the fourth corner a group of servants stand, waiting until the next course can be served. The American realizes there is only one place left—under the table.

His first impulse is to jump back and warn the others. But he knows the commotion will frighten the cobra and it will strike. He speaks quickly, the quality of his voice so <u>arresting</u> that it <u>sobers</u> everyone.

"I want to know just what control everyone at this table has. I will count three hundred—that's five minutes—and not one of you is to

---

1. **verandah** (və ran´ də) *n.*: Open porch.

move a single muscle. The persons who move will forfeit 50 rupees.[2] Now! Ready!"

Ask yourself why the American suddenly begins a game.

The 20 people sit like stone images while he counts. He is saying ". . . two hundred and eighty . . ." when, out of the corner of his eye, he sees the cobra emerge and make for the bowl of milk. Four or five screams ring out as he jumps to slam shut the verandah doors.

"You certainly were right, Colonel!" the host says. "A man has just shown us an example of real control."

You can **infer** that the host has not seen what the American has.

"Just a minute," the American says, turning to his hostess, "there's one thing I'd like to know. Mrs. Wynnes, how did you know that cobra was in the room?"

A faint smile lights up the woman's face as she replies. "Because it was lying across my foot."

---

2. **rupees** (rōō´ pēs) *n.*: Basic monetary unit of India.

◆ **Build Vocabulary**

arresting (ə rest´ iŋ) *adj.*: Attracting attention; striking

sobers (sō´ bərz) *v.*: Calms; sedates

Guide for Responding

◆ **LITERATURE AND YOUR LIFE**

Reader's Response How would you have solved the "problem" of the cobra?

Thematic Focus In what ways did the hostess and the American deal with the conflict presented by the cobra?

☑ **Check Your Comprehension**

1. Where does the story take place?
2. Explain the argument that springs up between the colonel and the young woman.
3. What action does the American take?
4. What does the hostess reveal at the end?

◆ **Critical Thinking**

INTERPRET

1. Why does the American have everyone play at sitting still without telling them why? **[Infer]**
2. What is the host assuming when he makes his remark about the colonel's being right? **[Infer]**
3. In what way is the final sentence of the story a response to the colonel's argument? **[Connect]**

APPLY

4. How have attitudes toward women changed since the time of this story? **[Relate]**

536 ◆ *Short Stories*

Guide for Responding (continued)

◆ Reading for Success

STRATEGIES FOR READING FICTION

Review the strategies and the notes showing how to read fiction. Then, answer these questions about your experience with the story.

1. With which character did you most identify? Why?
2. Note a prediction you made, explain what you based it on, and tell whether it proved accurate.
3. Tell how you answered a question you asked while reading.
4. Explain how you made an inference based on a passage.

◆ Build Vocabulary

USING THE WORD ROOT -spir-

Spirited contains the word root *-spir-*, meaning "breath." Fill in each blank with a *-spir-* word.

perspire   spirited   inspire

The naturalist wanted to ____?____ the guests to sit still and hardly ____?____. When the danger was over, their conversation became very ____?____.

SPELLING STRATEGY

In a two-syllable word, if the first syllable has a long vowel sound, the consonant that follows is not doubled:

sobers   (long *o*, followed by single *b*)

On your paper, choose the correct spelling.

1. I'll see you (later, latter).
2. This is your (final, finnal) notice.
3. The (motor, mottor) wouldn't start.
4. I couldn't read the (label, labbel).

USING THE WORD BANK

On your paper, write sentences using the words from the Word Bank as directed.

1. Describe an outdoor scene using the word *naturalist*.
2. Describe an argument using the word *spirited*.
3. Describe a strange sight using the word *arresting*.
4. Describe a newscast using the word *sobers*.

◆ Literary Focus

PLOT

A real dinner party might consist of a series of unrelated conversations and small happenings. However, the story entitled "The Dinner Party" contains a tightly woven **plot** in which one event flows out of another and all the events are related.

1. Summarize the plot, showing how one event flows from another.
2. Diagram the story on your paper, showing the exposition, rising action, climax, and falling action (see p. 533).

◆ Build Grammar Skills

CLAUSES

A **clause** is a group of words with its own subject and verb:

    S   V

The country is India

An **independent clause** (main clause) has a subject and a verb and can stand by itself as a complete sentence. A **subordinate clause** has a subject and a verb but cannot stand by itself as a complete sentence.

Independent Clause	Subordinate Clause
S V	S V

The 20 people sit like stone images|while he counts.

Practice On your paper, identify the independent clause and the subordinate clause, if any, in each sentence. Also, identify the subject and verb in each clause.

1. The persons who move will forfeit 50 rupees.
2. The American comes to with a start.
3. The corners of the room, which he can see, are empty.
4. As he jumps up to shut the door, screams ring out.
5. A smile lights up her face as she replies.

Writing Application On your paper, write three sentences. Each sentence should contain a main clause and a subordinate clause.

Build Your Portfolio

 ## Idea Bank

Writing

1. **Research Plan** Jot down two questions that you have after reading "The Dinner Party." Then, explain how you will go about answering these questions. Name specific sources that you'd use to investigate the answers to your questions.

2. **Diary Entry** Take on the role of the colonel in the story. From his point of view, write a diary entry recording his thoughts and feelings about the dinner party.

3. **Sequel** Write a sequel to "The Dinner Party." In it, explore how two or more of the characters reacted to the evening's remarkable events. In your sequel, stay true to the characters as described in the original version.

Speaking and Listening

4. **Scene [Group Activity]** With several class-mates, rewrite "The Dinner Party" in script form. Assign parts, and rehearse the dialogue you create. Present your scene for your class-mates. **[Performing Arts Link]**

5. **Dinner Speech** As the naturalist, speak to the group around the dinner table. Summarize the evening's events, and explain how they relate to the colonel's statement about women. **[Performing Arts Link]**

Projects

6. **Reality Check** Learn about the habits and be-havior of the Indian cobra. Then, use what you've learned to determine whether or not the events of the story could really have occurred. Report your findings to the class. **[Science Link]**

7. **Film Treatment [Group Activity]** With a few classmates, write a memo showing how you would turn this story into a film. Indicate passages where you might insert extra dialogue, include ideas for camera shots, and suggest actors to play the main roles. **[Media Link]**

 ## Writing Mini-Lesson

Interior Monologue

Perhaps you wondered what the hostess was thinking during the story. Write an interior mono-logue—a speech revealing a character's inner thoughts—that captures the flow of ideas, feelings, and images in the hostess's mind. You may include a few incomplete sentences to give the monologue the flavor of real thought. Be sure your writing is clear enough for readers to follow.

Writing Skills Focus: Use Details to Reveal Character

Use details that reveal the personality of the hostess. These details are the words that she uses and the thoughts and feelings that she expresses in reaction to events. To express the hostess's frustration with her husband at the end of the story, you might write this:

Model
. . . He doesn't see. Doesn't understand how brave I've been.

Prewriting Outline the events of the plot. Then, beside each item in the outline, jot down the host-ess's reactions to it.

Drafting Refer to your annotated outline as you write. However, if you have a new inspiration about her reactions to events, don't hesitate to include it.

> ◆ **Grammar Application**
> Write some sentences containing both inde-pendent and subordinate clauses. Put the more important idea in the independent clause and less important ideas in subordinate clauses.

Revising As you read your draft, follow the plot outline to be sure that the character is reacting to events in the right sequence. Also, be sure that her reactions are in keeping with her personality.

Part 1 *Plot and Character*

Fisherman's Family, B.J.O. Nordfeldt, Amon Carter Museum, Fort Worth, Texas

Guide for Reading

Meet the Author:
Edgar Allan Poe (1809–1849)

If Poe's stories and poems deal with sorrow, crime, and horror, it's because his own life was so troubled. He was born in Boston, Massachusetts, to a family of impover-ished traveling actors. While Poe was still a young child, his father deserted the family. Shortly afterward, his mother died.

A Family Rift Poe was raised, but never formally adopted, by Mr. and Mrs. John Allan of Richmond, Virginia. As he grew up, Poe quarreled with his adoptive father. Often their disputes focused on Poe's spending and his increasing debts.

Famed, but Poor Poe achieved early recognition when his story "MS. found in a bottle" won a literary contest in 1833. His stories and poems continued to at-tract notice, but they did not gain him financial success. In 1849, two years after the death of his wife, Virginia, Poe died penniless and alone.

THE STORY BEHIND THE STORY

While reading an 1830 pamphlet about a real murder, Poe found many of the details he used in "The Tell-Tale Heart." Here are passages from this pamphlet: "Deep sleep had fallen on the destined victim. . . . A healthful old man . . . The assassin enters, and beholds his victim before him. . . ."

◆ LITERATURE AND YOUR LIFE
CONNECT YOUR EXPERIENCE

You're lying in bed, trying to fall asleep, but a leaky faucet won't stop dripping. It's not a loud noise, really, but it seems to become louder and louder, filling the house. Anxiously, you wait for every drop. This common experience shows that, at times, your imagination may exaggerate what you hear or see. In this story, Poe uses this type of experience to create terror.

THEMATIC FOCUS: Strange Doings

How does Poe's choice of a storyteller make this tale even stranger and more frightening?

◆ Background for Understanding
LITERATURE

Poe's great contribution to American literature was to make the short story into an art form. He believed that in a brief story, a writer could create a "unity of effect." By this he meant that every element—from sentence rhythm to a character's personality—would help create a single impression. In "The Tell-Tale Heart" and many of his stories, that impression is one of horror.

◆ Build Vocabulary
WORD ROOTS: -found-

The word root -found- means "bottom." When the narrator of this story suggests that an old man isn't "profound" enough to understand a killer's deceptions, he means the old man is not "able to get to the bottom of things."

WORD BANK

Which word from the list means "ability of a sage" or "wisdom"? Check the Build Vocabulary box on page 543 to see if you chose correctly.

acute
dissimulation
profound
sagacity
crevice
gesticulations
derision

◆ The Tell-Tale Heart ◆

M.C. Escher "Self-Portrait" © 1998 Cordon Art B.V. Baarn–Holland

◆ Literary Focus

SUSPENSE IN A PLOT

Suspense is a feeling of uncertainty about the outcome of events, which keeps you interested in a story's plot. Writers create suspense by hinting at an outcome or by delaying an event that you know is coming. In other words, suspense is a kind of game that writers play with you, showing you some things and hiding others.

To follow Poe's game of suspense in "The Tell-Tale Heart," take notice of the details the narrator gives you and those he holds back.

◆ Reading Strategy

PREDICT

You'll enjoy the suspense in a plot if you continually **predict** what will happen next. This kind of guessing is what involves you in the story. It's not important to be right every time, but it is important to keep predicting and to base your predictions on details found in the story.

Use a diagram like the one below to play the "suspense game" with Poe:

Author's Clue	My Prediction
➡️	
Proved ☐ True ☐ False	

The Tell-Tale Heart

EDGAR ALLAN POE

True!—nervous—very, very dreadfully nervous I had been and am; but why *will* you say that I am mad? The disease had sharpened my senses—not destroyed—not dulled them. Above all was the sense of hearing <u>acute</u>. I heard all things in the heaven and in the earth. I heard many things in hell. How, then, am I mad? Hearken![1] and observe how healthily—how calmly I can tell you the whole story.

It is impossible to say how first the idea entered my brain; but once conceived, it haunted me day and night. Object there was none. Passion there was none. I loved the old man. He had never wronged me. He had never given me insult. For his gold I had no desire. I think it was his eye! yes, it was this! One of his eyes resembled that of a vulture— a pale blue eye, with a film over it. Whenever it fell upon me, my blood ran cold; and so by degrees—very gradually—I made up my mind to take the life of the old man, and thus rid myself of the eye forever.

Now this is the point. You fancy me mad. Madmen know nothing. But you should have seen *me*. You should have seen how wisely I proceeded—with what caution— with what foresight—with what <u>dissimulation</u> I went to work! I was never kinder to the old man than during the whole week before I killed him. And every night, about midnight, I turned the latch of his door and opened it—oh, so gently! And then, when I had made an opening sufficient for my head, I put in a dark lantern, all closed, closed, so that no light shone out, and then I thrust in my head. Oh, you would have laughed to see how cunningly I thrust it in! I moved it slowly—very, very slowly, so that I might not disturb the old man's sleep. It took me an

---

1. **Hearken** (här´ kən) *v.*: Listen.

◆ **Literary Focus**
How do you think Poe will keep you in suspense about a murder that you know already has occurred?

A scene from "The Tell-Tale Heart," a U.P.A. short based on the Edgar Allan Poe story distributed by Columbia Pictures

hour to place my whole head within the opening so far that I could see him as he lay upon his bed. Ha!—would a madman have been so wise as this? And then, when my head was well in the room, I undid the lantern cautiously—oh, so cautiously—cautiously (for the hinges creaked)—I undid it just so much that a single thin ray fell upon the vulture eye. And this I did for seven long nights—every night just at midnight—but I found the eye always closed; and so it was impossible to do the work; for it was not the old man who vexed me, but his evil eye. And every morning, when the day broke, I went boldly into the chamber, and spoke courageously to him, calling him by name in a hearty tone, and inquiring how he had passed the night. So you see he would have been a very profound old man, indeed, to suspect that every night, just at twelve, I looked in upon him while he slept.

Upon the eighth night I was more than usually cautious in opening the door. A watch's minute hand moves more quickly than did

▲ **Critical Viewing** Does the man in this drawing seem to have a "vulture eye," as described in the beginning of the story? Explain. **[Connect]**

mine. Never, before that night, had I *felt* the extent of my own powers—of my sagacity. I could scarcely contain my feelings of triumph. To think that there I was, opening the door, little by little, and he not even to dream of my secret deeds or thoughts. I fairly chuckled at the idea; and perhaps he heard me; for he moved on the bed suddenly, as if startled. Now you may think that I drew back—but no. His room was as black as pitch with the thick

◆ **Build Vocabulary**

acute (ə kyo͞ot´) *adj.*: Sensitive

dissimulation (di sim´ yə lā´ shən) *n.*: Hiding of one's feelings or purposes

profound (prō found´) *adj.*: Intellectually deep; getting to the bottom of the matter

sagacity (sə gas´ ə tē) *n.*: High intelligence and sound judgment

darkness (for the shutters were close fastened, through fear of robbers), and so I knew that he could not see the opening of the door, and I kept pushing it on steadily, steadily.

I had my head in, and was about to open the lantern, when my thumb slipped upon the tin fastening, and the old man sprang up in the bed, crying out—"Who's there?"

I kept quite still and said nothing. For a whole hour I did not move a muscle, and in the meantime I did not hear him lie down. He was still sitting up in the bed, listening;—just as I have done, night after night, hearkening to the deathwatches[2] in the wall.

Presently I heard a slight groan, and I knew it was the groan of mortal terror. It was not a groan of pain or of grief—oh, no!—it was the low stifled sound that arises from the bottom of the soul when overcharged with awe. I knew the sound well. Many a night, just at midnight, when all the world slept, it has welled up from my own bosom, deepening, with its dreadful echo, the terrors that distracted me. I say I knew it well. I knew what the old man felt, and pitied him, although I chuckled at heart. I knew that he had been lying awake ever since the first slight noise, when he had turned in the bed. His fears had been ever since growing upon him. He had been trying to fancy them causeless, but could not. He had been saying to himself— "It is nothing but the wind in the chimney— it is only a mouse crossing the floor," or "it is merely a cricket which has made a single chirp." Yes, he has been trying to comfort himself with these suppositions: but he had found all in vain. *All in vain;* because Death, in approaching him, had stalked with his black shadow before him, and enveloped the victim. And it was the mournful influence of the unperceived shadow that caused him to feel—although he neither saw nor heard—to *feel* the presence of my head within the room.

---

2. **deathwatches** (deth´ woch´ əz) *n.*: Wood-boring beetles whose heads make a tapping sound superstitiously regarded as an omen of death.

When I had waited a long time, very patiently, without hearing him lie down, I resolved to open a little—a very, very little crevice in the lantern. So I opened it—you cannot imagine how stealthily, stealthily— until, at length, a single dim ray, like the thread of the spider, shot from out the crevice and fell upon the vulture eye.

It was open—wide, wide open—and I grew furious as I gazed upon it. I saw it with perfect distinctness—all a dull blue, with a hideous veil over it that chilled the very marrow in my bones; but I could see nothing else of the old man's face or person for I had directed the ray as if by instinct, precisely upon the spot.

And now—have I not told you that what you mistake for madness is but overacuteness of the senses?—now, I say, there came to my ears a low, dull, quick sound, such as a watch makes when enveloped in cotton. I knew *that* sound well, too. It was the beating of the old man's heart. It increased my fury, as the beating of a drum stimulates the soldier into courage.

But even yet I refrained and kept still. I scarcely breathed. I held the lantern motionless. I tried how steadily I could maintain the ray upon the eye. Meantime the hellish tattoo of the heart increased. It grew quicker and quicker, and louder and louder every instant. The old man's terror *must* have been extreme! It grew louder, I say, louder every moment!—do you mark me well? I have told you that I am nervous: so I am. And now at the dead hour of the night, amid the dreadful silence of that old house, so strange a noise as this excited me to uncontrollable terror. Yet, for some minutes longer I refrained and stood still. But the beating grew

◆ **Build Vocabulary**
crevice (krev´ is) *n.*: A narrow opening

louder, louder! I thought the heart must burst. And now a new anxiety seized me—the sound would be heard by a neighbor! The old man's hour had come! With a loud yell, I threw open the lantern and leaped into the room. He shrieked once —once only. In an instant I dragged him to the floor, and pulled the heavy bed over him. I then smiled gaily, to find the deed so far done. But, for many minutes, the heart beat on with a muffled sound. This, however, did not vex me; it would not be heard through the wall. At length it ceased. The old man was dead. I removed the bed and examined the corpse. Yes, he was stone, stone dead. I placed my hand upon the heart and held it there many minutes. There was no pulsation. He was stone dead. His eye would trouble me no more.

If still you think me mad, you will think so no longer when I describe the wise precautions I took for the concealment of the body. The night waned, and I worked hastily, but in silence. First of all I dismembered the corpse. I cut off the head and the arms and the legs.

I then took up three planks from the flooring of the chamber, and deposited all between the scantlings.[3] I then replaced the boards so cleverly, so cunningly, that no human eye—not even *his* —could have detected anything wrong. There was nothing to wash out—no stain of any kind— no blood-spot whatever. I had been too wary for that. A tub had caught all—ha! ha!

When I had made an end of these labors, it was four o'clock—still dark as midnight. As the bell sounded the hour, there came a knocking at the street door. I went down to open it with a light heart—for what had I *now* to fear? There entered three men, who introduced themselves, with perfect suavity, as officers of the police. A shriek had been heard by a neighbor during the

---

3. **scantlings** (skant´ liŋz) *n.*: Small beams or timbers.

▶ Critical Viewing This drawing depicts the two policemen sent to search the house. What do they know or what can they infer about the situation to make them cautious? [Assess]

A scene from "The Tell-Tale Heart," a U.P.A. short based on the Edgar Allan Poe story distributed by Columbia Pictures

night; suspicion of foul play had been aroused; information had been lodged at the police office, and they (the officers) had been deputed to search the premises.

◆ **Reading Strategy**
Will the police officers discover the crime? Explain.

I smiled—for *what* had I to fear? I bade the gentlemen welcome. The shriek, I said, was my own in a dream. The old man, I mentioned, was absent in the country. I took my visitors all over the house. I bade them search—search *well.* I led them, at length, to *his* chamber. I showed them his treasures, secure, undisturbed. In the enthusiasm of my confidence, I brought chairs into the room, and desired them *here* to rest from their fatigues, while I myself, in the wild audacity of my perfect triumph, placed my own seat upon the very spot beneath which reposed the corpse of the victim.

The officers were satisfied. My *manner* had convinced them. I was singularly at ease.

▲ **Critical Viewing** What point in the story does this drawing illustrate? [**Connect**]

They sat, and while I answered cheerily, they chatted of familiar things. But, ere long, I felt myself getting pale and wished them gone. My head ached, and I fancied a ringing in my ears: but still they sat and still chatted. The ringing became more distinct:—it continued and became more distinct: I talked more freely to get rid of the feeling: but it continued and gained definitiveness—until, at length, I found that the noise was *not* within my ears.

No doubt I now grew *very* pale—but I talked more fluently, and with a heightened voice. Yet the sound increased—and what could I do? It was a *low, dull, quick sound*—

◆ **Build Vocabulary**

gesticulations (jes tik′ yōō lā′ shənz) *n.*: Energetic hand or arm movements

derision (di rizh′ ən) *n.*: Contempt; ridicule

much such a sound as a watch makes when enveloped in cotton. I gasped for breath—and yet the officers heard it not. I talked more quickly—more vehemently; but the noise steadily increased. I arose and argued about trifles, in a high key and with violent gesticulations; but the noise steadily increased. Why *would* they not be gone? I paced the floor to and fro with heavy strides, as if excited to fury by the observations of the men—but the noise steadily increased. Oh! what *could* I do? I foamed—I raved—I swore! I swung the chair upon which I had been sitting, and grated it upon the boards, but the noise arose over all, and continually increased. It grew louder—louder—*louder!* And still the men chatted pleasantly, and smiled.

Was it possible they heard not?— no, no! They heard!—they suspected!— they *knew!* —they were making a mockery of my horror!—this I thought, and this I think. But anything was better than this agony! Anything was more tolerable than this derision! I could bear those hypocritical smiles no longer! I felt that I must scream or die!—and now again! hark! louder! louder! louder! *louder!*—

"Villains!" I shrieked, "dissemble[4] no more! I admit the deed!—tear up the planks!—here, here!—it is the beating of his hideous heart!"

---

4. **dissemble** (di sem´ bəl) *v.*: Conceal under a false appearance; to conceal the truth of one's true feelings or motives.

Guide for Responding

◆ LITERATURE AND YOUR LIFE

Reader's Response What are your thoughts about the narrator of this story?

Thematic Focus Would this tale seem less strange if it were told by a police officer? Explain.

Tableau Think of a scene between the old man and the narrator that best conveys the effect of the story. Then, "pose" with a partner to create a tableau of this scene. Don't speak. Convey feelings through body language and facial expression.

☑ Check Your Comprehension

1. Why does the narrator kill the old man?
2. Summarize the steps of his plan.
3. Why do the police arrive?
4. What sound drives the narrator to confess to the crime?

◆ Critical Thinking

INTERPRET
1. In what way is the narrator careful about the means he uses and careless about whether his act is justified? **[Analyze]**
2. Do you think that the narrator feels guilty for his crime? Why or why not? **[Interpret]**
3. At the end, do you think anyone but the narrator hears the beating of the old man's heart? Explain. **[Infer]**

EVALUATE
4. Do the narrator's cleverness and carefulness prove he isn't "mad"? Explain. **[Make a Judgment]**

APPLY
5. Why do you think people like to read tales of terror, such as this one? **[Speculate]**

Guide for Responding (continued)

◆ Reading Strategy

PREDICT

When you **predict,** you use information the author provides to guess what will happen.

1. When the narrator says that he "made up his mind to take the life of the old man," did you predict he really would kill him? Why or why not?
2. Give one of your predictions and the evidence on which it was based.
3. Was there an event you didn't predict? Explain.

◆ Build Vocabulary

USING THE WORD ROOT -found-

Profound contains the word root *-found-,* meaning "bottom." Show how each *-found-* word relates to starting from, or getting to, the "bottom."

1. Poe laid the *foundation* for the detective story.
2. He was *profound* in his knowledge of tales.
3. Critics regard him as one of the *founders* of American literature.

SPELLING STRATEGY

The *zhun* sound at the end of a word, as in *derision,* is usually spelled *sion.* On your paper, fill in each blank with a word ending in a *zhun* sound.

1. The noun form of the adjective *precise:*
   _____?_____
2. The noun form of the verb *revise:* _____?_____
3. The noun form of the verb *collide:* _____?_____

USING THE WORD BANK

On your paper, write the letter of the word or words opposite in meaning to the Word Bank word.

1. acute: (a) pretty, (b) dull, (c) crooked
2. dissimulation: (a) honesty, (b) frown, (c) imitation
3. profound: (a) lost, (b) unfounded, (c) shallow
4. sagacity: (a) wisdom, (b) stiffness, (c) stupidity
5. crevice: (a) wide opening, (b) small opening, (c) deep hole
6. gesticulations: (a) food, (b) graceful gestures, (c) cramps
7. derision: (a) praise, (b) mockery, (c) revision

◆ Literary Focus

SUSPENSE IN A PLOT

Poe creates **suspense,** a feeling of uncertainty, by having his narrator confess his crime right away but then give a slow, detailed account of the crime. He forces you to experience, instant by instant, every detail of the murder. Also, he leaves you wondering about the sanity of the narrator and whether or not he'll be caught.

1. Cite a passage from the story that shows how Poe creates suspense by slowing the action to a crawl.
2. How does not knowing the police officers' real thoughts increase the suspense at the story's end?

◆ Build Grammar Skills

ADVERB CLAUSES

An **adverb clause** is a subordinate clause that functions as an adverb; that is, it modifies a verb, an adjective, or another adverb and answers the questions *when, where, how, why, to what extent,* or *under what conditions.* Adverb clauses begin with subordinating conjunctions like *after, as, although, because, if, since, when, unless,* and *until.* In this example, the adverb clause is italicized:

> *As the bell sounded the hour,* there came a knocking at the street door. (The adverb clause modifies *came* and answers the question *when.*)

Practice On your paper, identify the adverb clause in each sentence. Then, tell what question it answers.

1. When the day broke, I went boldly into the chamber.
2. I could see him as he lay upon his bed.
3. He had been lying awake since the first slight noise.
4. When I had made an end of these labors, it was four o'clock.
5. The police suspected the narrator because he acted strangely.

Writing Application Write three sentences about the narrator's trial for murder, using an adverb clause in each.

Build Your Portfolio

 Idea Bank

Writing

1. **Prediction** Write a prediction explaining what happens to the narrator of the story after he confesses to the crime.

2. **Police Report** As one of the officers who interviewed the narrator, write a police report on the arrest. Include what the narrator said and did and when you realized he was the murderer. Also, note the time and place of the arrest, the charge, and the police precinct to which you took the accused.

3. **Comparative Essay** In an essay, compare and contrast the techniques Poe uses to create suspense with those used by filmmakers: suspenseful music, camera shots that slowly explore a dangerous environment, and sudden close-ups. **[Media Link]**

Speaking and Listening

4. **News Interview [Group Activity]** With a classmate, stage an interview between the narrator, awaiting trial for murder, and a reporter for a newspaper. **[Career Link; Performing Arts Link]**

5. **Opening Argument** The narrator is being tried for murder. As his attorney, address the jury (your classmates) at the beginning of the trial and introduce your case—not guilty by reason of insanity. **[Career Link; Performing Arts Link]**

Projects

6. **Movie Review** View a film version of a Poe story—for example, *The Fall of the House of Usher* (1960) or *The Masque of the Red Death* (1964). In a report to the class, compare the story to the film version and give the film a thumbs-up or a thumbs-down. **[Media Link]**

7. **Literary Panel [Group Activity]** With several classmates, stage a panel discussion on Poe for the class. Each panelist should research and present a different aspect of this author: his life, his poetry, his tales of horror, and his influence on other writers.

 Writing Mini-Lesson

Suspenseful Anecdote

Poe involves you in his tale by keeping you guessing until the end. You use the same device when you tell an anecdote—a brief story about a remarkable or humorous event you've experienced. Write down such an anecdote as if you were telling it to a friend in a personal letter.

Writing Skills Focus: Create Suspense

Hook the reader by **creating suspense,** a feeling of uncertainty about the outcome. Here are two strategies to heighten suspense:

- Tease the reader with hints that suggest, but don't give away, the final outcome. For example, introduce an idea that seems important to the outcome, but don't let readers know for sure.

- Tell what will happen, but keep the reader wondering *how* and *when* it will happen. Poe uses this approach in his slow-motion account of the murderer's movements.

Prewriting Choose an event you've experienced that is remarkable or funny and that has a clear beginning, middle, and end. Create suspense by hiding, and hinting at, the ending or by revealing it and keeping the *when* and *how* uncertain.

Drafting Write as if you were playing a teasing game with your friend: Give some details and hold back others.

◆ **Grammar Application**

Use adverb clauses to give information about *when, how, why,* and *to what extent.*

Revising Have several classmates read your suspenseful anecdote. If it doesn't keep them on the edge of their seats, include some details that hint at the outcome, so your readers will experience suspense.

CONNECTING LITERATURE TO SOCIAL STUDIES

THE CIVIL WAR: BATTLES

An Episode of War *by Stephen Crane*

CIVIL WAR BATTLES In 1861, six southern states seceded from the United States and formed the Confederate States of America. When the Confederates fired on Fort Sumter, a U.S. Army post, Union soldiers defended the fort, and the country found itself in a Civil War. Fighting during the Civil War took place in three major areas: the East, the West, and at sea. The Union planned an offensive strategy: They would blockade southern ports, stop the South from using the Mississippi to move supplies, and capture the Confederate government headquartered in Richmond, Virginia. The South originally planned to stay at home and fight a defensive war. Northerners, they believed, would quickly tire of fighting.

Destruction in the Civil War

The fighting, it turns out, did not end quickly: The Civil War raged from 1861–1865. One million Americans died in the conflict—more than in any other war the country has ever fought. It has been called the first modern war because land mines and other modern weapons were used. When the war was over, most Americans remembered the destruction with horror; very few thought of it as a heroic period in American history.

Stephen Crane's War Stories

Although Stephen Crane was not born until five years after the Civil War ended, he wrote stories about the war that were known for their realism. In "An Episode of War," Crane takes you to the battlefield's edge and vividly depicts the unexpected, severe wounding of an army lieutenant.

The Civil War in the East, 1861–1863

PENNSYLVANIA

Gettysburg

LEE 1863

Potomac R.

— MEADE 1863

Antietam

Harpers Ferry

McCLELLAN 1862

WEST VIRGINIA

MARYLAND

Washington, D.C.

Bull Run

Shenandoah R.

Chancellorsville

Fredericksburg

York R.

VIRGINIA

LEE 1862

James R.

Seven Days

Richmond

CHESAPEAKE BAY

McCLELLAN 1862

Monitor versus Merrimack

N W E S

—— Union troops	—— Confederate troops
☆ Union victories	☆ Confederate victories

An Episode of War

Stephen Crane

◀ **Critical Viewing** How does this photograph correspond to Crane's description of the wounded lieutenant's being helped by his men? [Connect]

The lieutenant's rubber blanket lay on the ground, and upon it he had poured the company's supply of coffee. Corporals and other representatives of the grimy and hot-throated men who lined the breast-work[1] had come for each squad's portion.

The lieutenant was frowning and serious at this task of division. His lips pursed as he drew with his sword various crevices in the heap, until brown squares of coffee, astoundingly equal in size, appeared on the blanket. He was on the verge of a great triumph in mathematics, and the corporals were thronging forward, each to reap a little square, when suddenly the lieutenant cried out and looked quickly at a man near him as if he suspected it was a case of personal assault. The others cried out also when they saw blood upon the lieutenant's sleeve.

He had winced like a man stung, swayed dangerously, and then straightened. The sound of his hoarse breathing was plainly audible. He looked sadly, mystically, over the breast-work at the green face of a wood, where now were many little puffs of white smoke. During this moment the men about him gazed statuelike and silent, astonished and awed by this catastrophe which happened when catastrophes were not expected—when they had leisure to observe it.

As the lieutenant stared at the wood, they too swung their heads, so that for another instant all hands, still silent, contemplated the distant forest as if their minds were fixed upon the mystery of a bullet's journey.

The officer had, of course, been compelled to take his sword into his left hand. He did not hold it by the hilt. He gripped it at the middle of the blade, awkwardly. Turning his eyes from the hostile wood, he looked at the sword as he held it there, and seemed puzzled as to what to do with it, where to put it. In short, this weapon had of a sudden become a strange thing to him. He looked at it in a kind of stupefaction, as if he had been endowed with a trident, a sceptre, or a spade.[2]

---

1. **breast-work:** Low wall put up quickly as a defense in battle.

2. **a trident, a sceptre, or a spade** (trīd′ ənt; sep′ tər): Symbols of royal authority.

Finally he tried to sheathe it. To sheathe a sword held by the left hand, at the middle of the blade, in a scabbard hung at the left hip, is a feat worthy of a sawdust ring.[3] This wounded officer engaged in a desperate struggle with the sword and the wobbling scabbard, and during the time of it breathed like a wrestler.

But at this instant the men, the spectators, awoke from their stone-like poses and crowded forward sympathetically. The orderly-sergeant took the sword and tenderly placed it in the scabbard. At the time, he leaned nervously backward, and did not allow even his finger to brush the body of the lieutenant.

▲ **Critical Viewing** This is an actual photograph of a temporary Civil War hospital. What quality of treatment do you think the soldiers received there? On what details do you base your answer? **[Assess]**

A wound gives strange dignity to him who bears it. Well men shy from his new and terrible majesty. It is as if the wounded man's hand is upon the curtain which hangs before the revelations of all existence—the meaning of ants, potentates,[4] wars, cities, sunshine, snow, a feather dropped from a bird's wing; and the power of it sheds radiance upon a bloody form, and makes the other men understand sometimes that they are little. His comrades look at him with large eyes thoughtfully. Moreover, they fear vaguely

that the weight of a finger upon him might send him headlong, precipitate the tragedy, hurl him at once into the dim, grey unknown. And so the orderly-sergeant, while sheathing the sword, leaned nervously backward.

There were others who proffered assistance. One timidly presented his shoulder and asked the lieutenant if he cared to lean upon it, but the latter waved him away mournfully. He wore the look of one who knows he is the victim of a terrible disease and understands his helplessness. He again stared over the breast-work at the forest, and then, turning, went slowly rearward. He held his right wrist tenderly in his left hand as if the wounded arm was made of very brittle glass.

And the men in silence stared at the wood, then at the departing lieutenant; then at the wood, then at the lieutenant.

As the wounded officer passed from the line of battle, he was enabled to see many things which as a participant in the fight were unknown to him. He saw a general on a black horse gazing over the lines of blue infantry at the green woods which veiled his problems. An aide galloped furiously, dragged his horse suddenly to a halt, saluted, and presented a paper. It was, for a wonder, precisely like a historical painting.

To the rear of the general and his staff a group, composed of a bugler, two or three orderlies, and the bearer of the corps

---

3. **sawdust ring:** Ring in which circus acts are performed.
4. **potentates** (pōt′ ən tāts): *n.:* Rulers; powerful people.

standard,[5] all upon maniacal horses, were working like slaves to hold their ground, preserve their respectful interval, while the shells boomed in the air about them, and caused their chargers to make furious quivering leaps.

A battery, a tumultuous and shining mass, was swirling toward the right. The wild thud of hoofs, the cries of the riders shouting blame and praise, menace and encouragement, and, last, the roar of the wheels, the slant of the glistening guns, brought the lieutenant to an intent pause. The battery swept in curves that stirred the heart; it made halts as dramatic as the crash of a wave on the rocks, and when it fled onward this <u>aggregation</u> of wheels, levers, motors had a beautiful unity, as if it were a missile. The sound of it was a war-chorus that reached into the depths of man's emotion.

The lieutenant, still holding his arm as if it were of glass, stood watching this battery until all detail of it was lost, save the figures of the riders, which rose and fell and waved lashes over the black mass.

Later, he turned his eyes toward the battle, where the shooting sometimes crackled like bush-fires, sometimes sputtered with exasperating irregularity, and sometimes reverberated like the thunder. He saw the smoke rolling upward and saw crowds of men who ran and cheered, or stood and blazed away at the <u>inscrutable</u> distance.

He came upon some stragglers, and they told him how to find the field hospital. They described its exact location. In fact, these men, no longer having part in the battle, knew more of it than others. They told the performance of every corps, every division, the opinion of every general. The lieutenant, carrying his wounded arm rearward, looked upon them with wonder.

---

5. **corps standard** (kôr): Flag or banner representing a military unit.

At the roadside a brigade was making coffee and buzzing with talk like a girls' boarding-school. Several officers came out to him and inquired concerning things of which he knew nothing. One, seeing his arm, began to scold. "Why, man, that's no way to do. You want to fix that thing." He appropriated the lieutenant and the lieutenant's wound. He cut the sleeve and laid bare the arm, every nerve of which softly fluttered under his touch. He bound his handkerchief over the wound, scolding away in the meantime. His tone allowed one to think that he was in the habit of being wounded every day. The lieutenant hung his head, feeling, in this presence, that he did not know how to be correctly wounded.

The low white tents of the hospital were grouped around an old schoolhouse. There was here a singular commotion. In the foreground two ambulances interlocked wheels in the deep mud. The drivers were tossing the blame of it back and forth, gesticulating and berating, while from the ambulances, both crammed with wounded, there came an occasional groan. An interminable crowd of bandaged men were coming and going. Great numbers sat under the trees nursing heads or arms or legs. There was a dispute of some kind raging on the steps of the schoolhouse. Sitting with his back against a tree a man with a face as grey as a new army blanket was serenely smoking a corncob pipe. The lieutenant wished to rush forward and inform him that he was dying.

A busy surgeon was passing near the

◆ Build Vocabulary

precipitate (prē sip′ ə tāt′) v.: Cause to happen before expected or desired

aggregation (ag′ grə gā′ shən) n.: Group or mass of distinct objects or individuals

inscrutable (in skrōōt′ ə bəl) adj.: Impossible to see or understand

Connecting Literature to Social Studies
What does this incident suggest about the kind of medical care Civil War soldiers received?

lieutenant. "Good-morning," he said, with a friendly smile. Then he caught sight of the lieutenant's arm, and his face at once changed. "Well, let's have a look at it." He seemed possessed suddenly of a great contempt for the lieutenant. This wound evidently placed the latter on a very low social plane. The doctor cried out impatiently, "What mutton-head had tied it up that way anyhow?" The lieutenant answered, "Oh, a man."

When the wound was disclosed the doctor fingered it disdainfully. "Humph," he said. "You come along with me and I'll 'tend to you." His voice contained the same scorn as if he were saying: "You will have to go to jail."

The lieutenant had been very meek, but now his face flushed, and he looked into the doctor's eyes. "I guess I won't have it amputated," he said.

"Nonsense, man! Nonsense! Nonsense!" cried the doctor. "Come along, now. I won't amputate it. Come along. Don't be a baby."

"Let go of me," said the lieutenant, holding back wrathfully, his glance fixed upon the door of the old schoolhouse, as sinister to him as the portals of death.

And this is the story of how the lieutenant lost his arm. When he reached home, his sisters, his mother, his wife, sobbed for a long time at the sight of the flat sleeve. "Oh, well," he said, standing shamefaced amid these tears, "I don't suppose it matters so much as all that."

◆ LITERATURE AND YOUR LIFE

Reader's Response Think of a time when you or someone you know was seriously hurt. Did people treat you or the other person differently because of what had happened?

Thematic Focus Would you describe the lieutenant as a hero? Why or why not?

☑ Check Your Comprehension

1. Who gets wounded? Where is he wounded?
2. What makes the soldiers act differently toward the lieutenant after he has been shot?
3. How does the surgeon react when the lieutenant asks if his arm will have to be amputated?

◆ Critical Thinking

INTERPRET
1. Compare and contrast the lieutenant's and the other soldiers' reactions to the wound. **[Compare and Contrast]**
2. How do the lieutenant's last words in the story relate to his earlier attitude toward his wound? **[Compare and Contrast]**
3. What details in the story suggest Crane's attitude that war is ugly and impersonal? **[Support]**

APPLY
4. Imagine a veteran from the Union army and a veteran from the Confederate army as readers of this story. Would their reactions to the story be similar or different? Explain your reasoning. **[Speculate]**

Meet the Author

Stephen Crane (1871–1900)
The son of a minister, Crane grew up in New Jersey and attended Syracuse University. After playing baseball in college, Crane seriously considered becoming a shortstop in the newly formed National League. He decided instead that he wanted to be a writer. He became internationally famous as a writer of stories so realistic that they seemed to be true. His novel *The Red Badge of Courage* is considered one of the best war novels ever written by an American.

CONNECTING LITERATURE TO SOCIAL STUDIES

"An Episode of War" vividly captures an incident that changes a soldier's life forever. The character's experience was one shared by thousands of real soldiers who fought in the Civil War. Through his brief account of one soldier's experience, Stephen Crane brings to life the tragic impact that the Civil War had on those who were caught up in the conflict. He finds, however, that the realities of war are very different from what he encountered in books.

1. Why do you think Crane did not give names to any of his characters in this story?
2. Why doesn't Crane specify whether the soldiers in the story are in the Union or the Confederate army?
3. How do you learn about the conditions of the Civil War by reading this story?
4. How do the lieutenant's final words relate to the point Crane is making about war?

Idea Bank

Writing

1. **Journal Entry** Imagine that you were one of the corporals waiting for a supply of coffee when the lieutenant was shot. Write an entry in your journal describing the incident.
2. **Official Report** As the surgeon who examined the lieutenant's wound, write a report of your examination for the records you keep of your daily activities.
3. **Essay** Write an essay to explain the main message, or theme, that Crane conveys in "An Episode of War." Support your idea with details from the story.

Speaking and Listening

4. **Role Play [Group Activity]** Role-play a conversation between two of the corporals who were near the lieutenant when he was shot.

Projects

5. **Report** Using various sources, find information about the daily lives of soldiers in either or both of the armies in the Civil War. Report to the class on what you learn.
6. **Drawings [Group Activity]** Form teams to create drawings of Civil War soldiers. Use encyclopedias, books of photographs taken by Mathew Brady, and the pictures that accompany "An Episode of War" as guides.

Further Reading, Listening, and Viewing

- Stephen Crane's novel *The Red Badge of Courage* is a realistic account of the experiences of a young soldier during the Civil War.
- *Behind the Lines: A Sourcebook on the Civil War* by C. Carter Smith is an illustrated history of the Civil War.
- Ken Burns's *The Civil War* is an award-winning documentary film on the Civil War.

Guide for Reading

Meet the Authors:

Isaac Bashevis Singer (1904–1991)

Isaac Bashevis Singer came from a family of Jewish religious leaders in Poland. He grew up in Warsaw, Poland's capital, and received a Jewish education. However, Singer decided to become a writer instead of a religious leader.

A Rediscovered Home In 1935, Singer left his home and moved to the United States. However, he rediscovered his lost home in the many Yiddish stories he wrote about Poland's Jews. Translated from Yiddish into English and other languages, these stories won him the Nobel Prize for Literature in 1978.

Naomi Shihab Nye (1952–   )

A poet and fiction writer, Naomi Shihab Nye is concerned with "paying attention to the world." Perhaps her travels and the richness of her heritage inspired her to "pay attention." She grew up in St. Louis as the daughter of a Palestinian father and an American mother. However, she has also lived in Jerusalem and Texas. The poems in *The Words Under the Words* (1995) and the story "Hamadi" show that her imagination is well traveled too.

◆ Literature and Your Life

Connect Your Experience

In today's busy world, people tend to rush through their daily routines. They race from home to school or the office, back home, through dinner, and out again to various social functions. However, these stories hint that sometimes it's the people who march to their own drummer—who are "outside" the norm—who find wisdom and peace.

Thematic Focus: Appreciating Others

As you read these stories, look for ways in which the story characters display their individuality.

◆ Background for Understanding

Literature

Both these stories use a type of character from folk tales known as the wise fool. This character is a fool because he may forget his address, speak strangely, or wear unfashionable clothes. Yet this "fool" turns out to be wiser than the characters who seem to know where they're going.

◆ Build Vocabulary

Word Roots: -chol-

People once believed that health depended on the balance of bodily fluids. One of these, bile (*chole* in Greek), was thought to make people feel low. Words with the root *-chol-* still relate to a problem in physical or mental health. For example, the word *melancholy* in "Hamadi" means "sad."

Word Bank

Which of these words from the stories is associated with a lot of noisy demons? Check the Build Vocabulary box on page 560 to see if you chose correctly.

forsaken
pandemonium
brittle
lavish
refugees
melancholy

The Day I Got Lost ◆ Hamadi

Transfer to the #6, Kathy Ruttenberg, Gallery Henoch

◆ Literary Focus

CHARACTERIZATION

The characters you meet in stories can be so memorable that they become friends for life. The process by which authors create memorable characters is called **characterization.** Authors use **direct characterization** when they tell you what a character is like. They use **indirect characterization** when they reveal a character's personality through his or her appearance, words, actions, and effects on others.

◆ Reading Strategy

IDENTIFY WITH A CHARACTER

If you want to fully understand literary characters, you must read with your heart as well as your head. When you **identify** with a character, you experience that character's joys and sorrows as if they were your own. You may also compare the situations in which characters find themselves with similar situations from your own life.

As you read each story, identify with a character by creating an organizer like the one below:

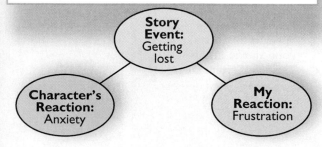

The Day I Got Lost

Isaac Bashevis Singer

▶ **Critical Viewing**
Explain the ways a person might get lost in a setting like the one shown in the painting. **[Summarize]**

Windows, 1951, Charles Sheeler, Collection, Hirschl & Adler Galleries

It is easy to recognize me. See a man in the street wearing a too long coat, too large shoes, a crumpled hat with a wide brim, spectacles with one lens missing, and carrying an umbrella though the sun is shining, and that man will be me, Professor Shlemiel.[1] There are other unmistakable clues to my identity. My pockets are always bulging with newspapers, magazines, and just papers. I carry an overstuffed briefcase, and I'm forever making mistakes. I've been living in New York City for over forty years, yet whenever I want to go uptown, I find myself walking downtown, and when I want to go east, I go west. I'm always late and I never recognize anybody.

I'm always misplacing things. A hundred times a day I ask myself, Where is my pen? Where is my money? Where is my handkerchief? Where is my address book? I am what is known as an absentminded professor.

◆ **Literary Focus**
In this paragraph, what does the narrator tell you directly about himself?

For many years I have been teaching philosophy in the same university, and I still have difficulty in locating my classrooms. Elevators play strange tricks on me. I want to go to the top floor and I land in the basement. Hardly a day passes when an elevator door doesn't close on me. Elevator doors are my worst enemies.

In addition to my constant blundering and losing things, I'm forgetful. I enter a coffee shop, hang up my coat, and leave without it. By the time I remember to go back for it, I've forgotten where I've been. I lose hats, books, umbrellas, rubbers, and above all manuscripts. Sometimes I even forget my own address. One evening I took a taxi because I was in a hurry to get home. The taxi driver said, "Where to?" And I could not remember where I lived.

"Home!" I said.

"Where is home?" he asked in astonishment.

"I don't remember," I replied.

"What is your name?"

"Professor Shlemiel."

"Professor," the driver said, "I'll get you to a telephone booth. Look in the telephone book and you'll find your address."

He drove me to the nearest drugstore with a telephone booth in it, but he refused to wait. I was about to enter the store when I realized I had left my briefcase behind. I ran after the taxi, shouting, "My briefcase, my briefcase!" But the taxi was already out of earshot.

In the drugstore, I found a telephone book, but when I looked under S, I saw to my horror that though there were a number of Shlemiels listed, I was not among them. At that moment I recalled that several months before, Mrs. Shlemiel had decided that we should have an unlisted telephone number. The reason was that my students thought nothing of calling me in the middle of the night and waking me up. It also happened quite frequently that someone wanted to call another Shlemiel and got me by mistake. That was all very well—but how was I going to get home?

I usually had some letters addressed to me in my breast pocket. But just that day I had decided to clean out my pockets. It was my birthday and my wife had invited friends in for the evening. She had baked a huge cake and decorated it with birthday candles. I could see my friends sitting in our living room, waiting to wish me a happy birthday. And here I stood in

---

1. **Shlemiel** (shlə mēl'): Version of the slang word *schlemiel*, an ineffectual, bungling person.

▲ **Critical Viewing** Does the man in the photograph look confused and absent-minded? Explain. **[Assess]**

some drugstore, for the life of me not able to remember where I lived.

Then I recalled the telephone number of a friend of mine, Dr. Motherhead, and I decided to call him for help. I dialed and a young girl's voice answered.

"Is Dr. Motherhead at home?"

"No," she replied.

"Is his wife at home?"

"They're both out," the girl said.

"Perhaps you can tell me where they can be reached?" I said.

"I'm only the babysitter, but I think they went to a party at Professor Shlemiel's. Would you like to leave a message?" she said. "Who shall I say called, please?"

"Professor Shlemiel," I said.

"They left for your house about an hour ago," the girl said.

"Can you tell me where they went?" I asked.

"I've just told you," she said. "They went to your house."

◆ **Reading Strategy**
Identify with Professor Shlemiel. How do you think he feels at this moment?

"But where do I live?"

"You must be kidding!" the girl said, and hung up.

I tried to call a number of friends (those whose telephone numbers I happened to think of), but wherever I called, I got the same reply: "They've gone to a party at Professor Shlemiel's."

As I stood in the street wondering what to do, it began to rain. "Where's my umbrella?" I said to myself. And I knew the answer at once. I'd left it—somewhere. I got under a nearby canopy. It was now raining cats and dogs. It lightninged and thundered. All day it had been sunny and warm, but now that I was lost and my umbrella was lost, it had to storm. And it looked as if it would go on for the rest of the night.

To distract myself, I began to ponder the ancient philosophical problem. A mother chicken lays an egg, I thought to myself, and when it hatches, there is a chicken. That's how it has always been. Every chicken comes from an egg and every egg comes from a chicken. But was there a chicken first? Or an

egg first? No philosopher has ever been able to solve this eternal question. Just the same, there must be an answer. Perhaps I, Shlemiel, am destined to stumble on it.

It continued to pour buckets. My feet were getting wet and I was chilled. I began to sneeze and I wanted to wipe my nose, but my handkerchief, too, was gone.

At that moment I saw a big black dog. He was standing in the rain getting soaked and looking at me with sad eyes. I knew immediately what the trouble was. The dog was lost. He, too, had forgotten his address. I felt a great love for that innocent animal. I called to him and he came running to me. I talked to him as if he were human. "Fellow, we're in the same boat," I said. "I'm a man shlemiel and you're a dog shlemiel. Perhaps it's also your birthday, and there's a party for you, too. And here you stand shivering and <u>forsaken</u> in the rain, while your loving master is searching for you everywhere. You're probably just as hungry as I am."

I patted the dog on his wet head and he wagged his tail. "Whatever happens to me will happen to you," I said. "I'll keep you with me until we both find our homes. If we don't find your master, you'll stay with me. Give me your paw," I said. The dog lifted his right paw. There was no question that he understood.

A taxi drove by and splattered us both. Suddenly it stopped and I heard someone shouting, "Shlemiel! Shlemiel!" I looked up and saw the taxi door open, and the head of a friend of mine appeared. "Shlemiel," he called. "What are you doing here? Who are you waiting for?"

"Where are you going?" I asked.

"To your house, of course. I'm sorry I'm late, but I was detained. Anyhow, better late than never. But why aren't you at home? And whose dog is that?"

"Only God could have sent you!" I exclaimed. "What a night! I've forgotten my

◆ **Build Vocabulary**

forsaken (fər sā´ kən) *adj.*: Abandoned; desolate

pandemonium (pan´ də mō´ nē əm) *n.*: A scene of wild disorder

address, I've left my briefcase in a taxi, I've lost my umbrella, and I don't know where my rubbers are."

"Shlemiel," my friend said, "if there was ever an absentminded professor, you're it!"

When I rang the bell of my apartment, my wife opened the door. "Shlemiel!" she shrieked. "Everybody is waiting for you. Where have you been? Where is your briefcase? Your umbrella? Your rubbers? And who is this dog?"

Our friends surrounded me. "Where have you been?" they cried. "We were so worried. We thought surely something had happened to you!"

"Who is this dog?" my wife kept repeating.

"I don't know," I said finally. "I found him in the street. Let's just call him Bow Wow for the time being."

"Bow Wow, indeed!" my wife scolded. "You know our cat hates dogs. And what about the parakeets? He'll scare them to death."

"He's a quiet dog," I said. "He'll make friends with the cat. I'm sure he loves parakeets. I could not leave him shivering in the rain. He's a good soul."

The moment I said this the dog let out a bloodcurdling howl. The cat ran into the room. When she saw the dog, she arched her back and spat at him, ready to scratch out his eyes. The parakeets in their cage began flapping their wings and screeching. Everybody started talking at once. There was pandemonium.

Would you like to know how it all ended?

Bow Wow still lives with us. He and the cat are great friends. The parakeets have learned to ride on his back as if he were a horse. As for my wife, she loves Bow Wow even more than I do. Whenever I take the dog out, she says, "Now, don't forget your address, both of you."

I never did find my briefcase, or my umbrella, or my rubbers. Like many philosophers before me, I've given up trying to solve the riddle of which came first, the chicken or the egg. Instead, I've started writing a book called *The Memoirs of Shlemiel*. If I don't forget the manuscript in a taxi, or a restaurant, or on a bench in the park, you may read them someday. In the meantime, here is a sample chapter.

*G*uide for Responding

◆ LITERATURE AND YOUR LIFE

Reader's Response Have you ever known anyone who was a little like Professor Shlemiel? Explain.

Thematic Focus What good qualities does the professor exhibit?

☑ Check Your Comprehension

1. Tell how the professor tries to find out his own address.
2. Why can't he get in touch with anyone he knows?
3. How does the professor get home, and what does he bring with him?

◆ Critical Thinking

INTERPRET

1. How does the professor's behavior illustrate the meaning of his name—"a bungler or incompetent person"? **[Support]**
2. How are the professor and the dog alike? **[Connect]**
3. How does the professor seem to be rewarded for his kindness to the dog? **[Interpret]**
4. In what way is the professor a fool who stumbles into wisdom? **[Draw Conclusions]**

EVALUATE

5. Could a person really be as absent-minded as Professor Shlemiel? Why or why not? **[Assess]**

Hamadi

Naomi Shihab Nye

Susan didn't really feel interested in Saleh Hamadi until she was a freshman in high school carrying a thousand questions around. Why this way? Why not another way? Who said so and why can't I say something else? Those <u>brittle</u> women at school in the counselor's office treated the world as if it were a yardstick and they had tight hold of both ends.

Sometimes Susan felt polite with them, sorting attendance cards during her free period, listening to them gab about fingernail polish and television. And other times she felt she could run out of the building yelling. That's when she daydreamed about Saleh Hamadi, who had nothing to do with any of it. Maybe she thought of him as escape, the way she used to think about the Sphinx at Giza[1] when she was younger. She would picture the golden Sphinx sitting quietly in the desert with sand blowing around its face, never changing its expression. She would think of its wry, slightly crooked mouth and how her grandmother looked a little like that as she waited

1. **Sphinx** (sfiŋks) **at Giza** (gē′ zə): Huge statue with the head of a man and the body of a lion, located near Cario in northern Egypt.

◆ **Literary Focus**

Why is this an example of direct characterization?

◆ **Build Vocabulary**

brittle (brit′ əl) *adj.*: Stiff and unbending in manner; lacking warmth

▲ **Critical Viewing** Based on the details in this photograph, would you say the man pictured grew up in the United States? Why or why not? [Draw Conclusions]

for her bread to bake in the old village north of Jerusalem. Susan's family had lived in Jerusalem for three years before she was ten and drove out to see her grandmother every weekend. They would find her patting fresh dough between her hands, or pressing cakes of dough onto the black rocks in the *taboon,* the rounded old oven outdoors. Sometimes she moved her lips as she worked. Was she praying? Singing a secret song? Susan had never seen her grandmother rushing.

Now that she was fourteen, she took long walks in America with her father down by the drainage ditch at the end of their street. Pecan trees shaded the path. She tried to get him to tell stories about his childhood in Palestine. She didn't want him to forget anything. She helped her American mother complete tedious kitchen tasks without complaining—rolling grape leaves around their lemony rice stuffing, scrubbing carrots for the roaring juicer. Some evenings when the soft Texas twilight pulled them all outside, she thought of her far-away grandmother and said, "Let's go see Saleh Hamadi. Wouldn't he like some of that cheese pie Mom made?" And they would wrap a slice of pie and drive downtown. Somehow he felt like a good substitute for a grandmother, even though he was a man.

Usually Hamadi was wearing a white shirt, shiny black tie, and a jacket that reminded Susan of the earth's surface just above the treeline on a mountain—thin, somehow purified. He would raise his hands high before giving advice.

"It is good to drink a tall glass of water every morning upon arising!" If anyone doubted this, he would shake his head. "Oh Susan, Susan, Susan," he would say.

He did not like to sit down, but he wanted everyone else to sit down. He made Susan sit on the wobbly chair beside the desk and he

made her father or mother sit in the saggy center of the bed. He told them people should eat six small meals a day.

They visited him on the sixth floor of the Traveler's Hotel, where he had lived so long nobody could remember him ever traveling. Susan's father used to remind him of the apartments available over the Victory Cleaners, next to the park with the fizzy pink fountain, but Hamadi would shake his head, pinching kisses at his spartan room. "A white handkerchief spread across a tabletop, my two extra shoes lined by the wall, this spells 'home' to me, this says 'mi casa.' What more do I need?"

Hamadi liked to use Spanish words. They made him feel expansive, worldly. He'd learned them when he worked at the fruits and vegetables warehouse on Zarzamora Street, marking off crates of apples and avocados on a long white pad. Occasionally he would speak Arabic, his own first language, with Susan's father and uncles, but he said it made him feel too sad, as if his mother might step into the room at any minute, her arms laden with fresh mint leaves.

He had come to the United States on a boat when he was eighteen years old and he had never been married. "I married books," he said. "I married the wide horizon."

"What is he to us?" Susan used to ask her father. "He's not a relative, right? How did we meet him to begin with?"

Susan's father couldn't remember. "I think we just drifted together. Maybe we met at your uncle Hani's house. Maybe that old Maronite priest who used to cry after every service introduced us. The priest once shared an apartment with Kahlil Gibran[2] in New York—so he said. And Saleh always says he stayed

> "It is good to drink a tall glass of water every morning upon arising!"

---

2. **Kahlil Gibran** (kä lēl´ ji brän´): Lebanese novelist, poet, and artist who lived from 1883 to 1931; his most famous book is *The Prophet.*

with Gibran when he first got off the boat. I'll bet that popular guy Gibran has had a lot of roommates he doesn't even know about."

"Susan said, "Dad, he's dead."

"I know, I know," her father said.

Later Susan said, "Mr. Hamadi, did you really meet Kahlil Gibran? He's one of my favorite writers." Hamadi walked slowly to the window of his room and stared out. There wasn't much to look at down on the street—a bedraggled[3] flower shop, a boarded-up tavern with a hand-lettered sign tacked to the front, GONE TO FIND JESUS. Susan's father said the owners had really gone to Alabama.

Hamadi spoke patiently. "Yes, I met brother Gibran. And I meet him in my heart every day. When I was a young man—shocked by all the visions of the new world—the tall buildings—the wild traffic—the young people without shame—the proud mailboxes in their blue uniforms—I met him. And he has stayed with me every day of my life."

"But did you really meet him, like in person, or just in a book?"

He turned dramatically. "Make no such distinctions, my friend. Or your life will be a pod with only dried-up beans inside. Believe anything can happen."

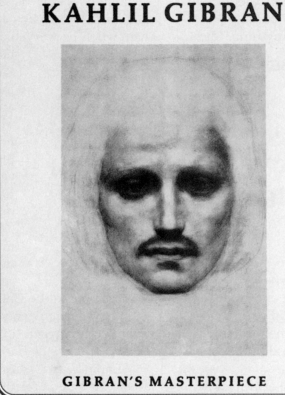

THE PROPHET

KAHLIL GIBRAN

GIBRAN'S MASTERPIECE

Susan's father looked irritated, but Susan smiled. "I do," she said. "I believe that. I want fat beans. If I imagine something, it's true, too. Just a different kind of true."

Susan's father was twiddling with the knobs on the old-fashioned sink. "Don't they even give you hot water here? You don't mean to tell me you've been living without hot water?"

On Hamadi's rickety desk lay a row of different "Love" stamps issued by the post office.

"You must write a lot of letters," Susan said.

"No, no, I'm just focusing on that word," Hamadi said. "I particularly like the globe in the shape of a heart," he added.

"Why don't you take a trip back to his village in Lebanon?" Susan's father asked. "Maybe you still have relatives living there."

Hamadi looked pained. "'Remembrance is a form of meeting,' my brother Gibran says, and I do believe I meet with my cousins every day."

"But aren't you curious? You've been gone so long! Wouldn't you like to find out what has happened to everybody and everything you knew as a boy?" Susan's father traveled back to Jerusalem once every year to see his family.

▲ **Critical Viewing** Would you like to read *The Prophet*, judging by its cover? Why or why not? **[Make a Judgment]**

---

3. **bedraggled** (bē drag′ əld) *adj.*: Limp and dirty, as if dragged through mud.

"I would not. In fact, I already know. It is there and it is not there. Would you like to share an orange with me?"

His long fingers, tenderly peeling. Once when Susan was younger, he'd given her a lavish ribbon off a holiday fruit basket and expected her to wear it on her head. In the car, Susan's father said, "Riddles. He talks in riddles. I don't know why I have patience with him." Susan stared at the people talking and laughing in the next car. She did not even exist in their world.

Susan carried *The Prophet* around on top of her English textbook and her Texas history. She and her friend Tracy read it out loud to one another at lunch. Tracy was a junior—they'd met at the literary magazine meeting where Susan, the only freshman on the staff, got assigned to do proofreading. They never ate in the cafeteria; they sat outside at picnic tables with sack lunches, whole wheat crackers and fresh peaches. Both of them had given up meat.

Tracy's eyes looked steamy. "You know that place where Gibran says, 'Hate is a dead thing. Who of you would be a tomb?'"

Susan nodded. Tracy continued. "Well, I hate someone. I'm trying not to, but I can't help it. I hate Debbie for liking Eddie and it's driving me nuts."

"Why shouldn't Debbie like Eddie?" Susan said. "*You* do."

Tracy put her head down on her arms. A gang of cheerleaders walked by giggling. One of them flicked her finger in greeting.

"In fact, we *all* like Eddie," Susan said. "Remember, here in this book—wait and I'll find it—where Gibran says that loving teaches us the secrets of our hearts and that's the way we connect to all of Life's heart? You're not talking about liking or loving, you're talking about owning."

Tracy looked glum. "Sometimes you remind me of a minister."

Susan said, "Well, just talk to me someday when *I'm* depressed."

Susan didn't want a boyfriend. Everyone who had boyfriends or girlfriends all seemed to have troubles. Susan told people she had a boyfriend far away, on a farm in Missouri, but the truth was, boys still seemed like cousins to her. Or brothers. Or even girls.

A squirrel sat in the crook of a tree, eyeing their sandwiches. When the end-of-lunch bell blared, Susan and Tracy jumped—it always seemed too soon. Squirrels were lucky; they didn't have to go to school.

Susan's father said her idea was ridiculous: to invite Saleh Hamadi to go Christmas caroling with the English Club. "His English is archaic,[4] for one thing, and he won't know any of the songs."

"How could you live in America for years and not know 'Joy to the World' or 'Away in a Manger'?"

"Listen, I grew up right down the road from 'Oh Little Town of Bethlehem' and I still don't know a single verse."

"I want him. We need him. It's boring being with the same bunch of people all the time."

So they called Saleh and he said he would come—"thrilled" was the word he used. He wanted to ride the bus to their house, he didn't want anyone to pick him up. Her father muttered, "He'll probably forget to get off." Saleh thought "caroling" meant they were

> **"Everyone who had boyfriends or girlfriends all seemed to have troubles."**

---

4. **archaic** (är kā´ ik) *adj.*: Old-fashioned; out-of-date.

◆ **Build Vocabulary**

lavish (lav´ ish) *adj.*: Showy; more than enough

◆ **Reading Strategy**
If you were Susan, what would you be feeling toward your father right now? Why?

Hamadi ◆ 565

going out with a woman named Carol. He said, "Holiday spirit—I was just reading about it in the newspaper."

Susan said, "Dress warm."

Saleh replied, "Friend, my heart is warmed simply to hear your voice."

All that evening Susan felt light and bouncy. She decorated the coffee can they would use to collect donations to be sent to the children's hospital in Bethlehem. She had started doing this last year in middle school, when a singing group collected $100 and the hospital responded on exotic onion-skin stationery that they were "eternally grateful."

Her father shook his head. "You get something into your mind and it really takes over," he said. "Why do you like Hamadi so much all of a sudden? You could show half as much interest in your own uncles."

Susan laughed. Her uncles were dull. Her uncles shopped at the mall and watched TV. "Anyone who watches TV more than twelve minutes a week is uninteresting," she said.

Her father lifted an eyebrow.

"He's my surrogate grandmother," she said. "He says interesting things. He makes me think. Remember when I was little and he called me The Thinker? We have a connection." She added, "Listen, do you want to go too? It is not a big deal. And Mom has a *great* voice, why don't you both come?"

A minute later her mother was digging in the closet for neck scarves, and her father was digging in the drawer for flashlight batteries.

Saleh Hamadi arrived precisely on time, with flushed red cheeks and a sack of dates stuffed in his pocket. "We may need sustenance on our journey." Susan thought the older people seemed quite giddy as they drove down to the high school to meet the rest of the carolers. Strands of winking lights wrapped around their neighbors' drainpipes and trees. A giant Santa tipped his hat on Dr. Garcia's roof.

Her friends stood gathered in front of the school. Some were smoothing out song sheets that had been crammed in a drawer or cabinet for a whole year. Susan thought holidays were strange; they came, and you were supposed to

feel ready for them. What if you could make up your own holidays as you went along? She had read about a woman who used to have parties to celebrate the arrival of fresh asparagus in the local market. Susan's friends might make holidays called Eddie Looked at Me Today and Smiled.

Two people were alleluia-ing in harmony. Saleh Hamadi went around the group formally introducing himself to each person and shaking hands. A few people laughed behind their hands when his back was turned. He had stepped out of a painting, or a newscast, with his outdated long overcoat, his clunky old men's shoes and elegant manners.

Susan spoke more loudly than usual. "I'm honored to introduce you to one of my best friends, Mr. Hamadi."

"Good evening to you," he pronounced musically, bowing a bit from the waist.

What could you say back but "Good evening, sir." His old-fashioned manners were contagious.

They sang at three houses which never opened their doors. They sang "We Wish You a Merry Christmas" each time they moved on. Lisa had a fine, clear soprano. Tracy could find the alto harmony to any line. Cameron and Elliot had more enthusiasm than accuracy. Lily, Rita, and Jeannette laughed every time they said a wrong word and fumbled to find their places again. Susan loved to see how her mother knew every word of every verse without looking at the paper, and her father kept his hands in his pockets and seemed more interested in examining people's mailboxes or yard displays than in trying to sing. And Saleh Hamadi—what language was he singing in? He didn't even seem to be pronouncing words, but humming deeply from his throat. Was he saying, "Om?" Speaking Arabic? Once he caught her looking and whispered, "That was an Aramaic word that just drifted into my mouth—the true language of the Bible, you know, the language Jesus Christ himself spoke."

By the fourth block their voices felt tuned up and friendly people came outside to listen. Trays of cookies were passed around and dollar bills stuffed into the little can. Thank you, thank you. Out of the dark from down the block, Susan noticed Eddie sprinting toward them with his coat flapping, unbuttoned. She shot a glance at Tracy, who pretended not to notice. "Hey, guys!" shouted Eddie. "The first time in my life I'm late and everyone else is on time! You could at least have left a note about which way you were going." Someone slapped him on the back. Saleh Hamadi, whom he had never seen before, was the only one who managed a reply. "Welcome, welcome to our cheery group!"

Eddie looked mystified. "Who is this guy?"

Susan whispered, "My friend."

Eddie approached Tracy, who read her song sheet intently just then, and stuck his face over her shoulder to whisper, "Hi." Tracy stared straight ahead into the air and whispered "Hi" vaguely, glumly. Susan shook her head. Couldn't Tracy act more cheerful at least?

They were walking again. They passed a string of blinking reindeer and a wooden snowman holding a painted candle. Ridiculous!

Eddie fell into step beside Tracy, murmuring so Susan couldn't hear him anymore. Saleh Hamadi was flinging his arms up high as he strode. Was he power walking? Did he even know what power walking was? Between

▲ **Critical Viewing** Do the girls in the photograph seem to share qualities with Susan and Tracy? Explain. **[Compare and Contrast]**

houses, Susan's mother hummed obscure songs people never remembered: "What Child Is This?" and "The Friendly Beasts."

Lisa moved over to Eddie's other side. "I'm so *excited* about you and Debbie!" she said loudly. "Why didn't she come tonight?"

Eddie said, "She has a sore throat."

Tracy shrank up inside her coat.

Lisa chattered on. "James said we should make our reservations *now* for dinner at the

▲ Critical Viewing How would Saleh Hamadi fit in with this group of carolers? What might he say or do? [Speculate]

Tower after the Sweetheart Dance, can you believe it? In December, making a reservation for February? But otherwise it might get booked up!"

Saleh Hamadi tuned into this conversation with interest; the Tower was downtown, in his neighborhood. He said, "This sounds like significant preliminary planning! Maybe you can be an international advisor someday." Susan's mother bellowed, "Joy to the World!" and voices followed her, stretching for notes. Susan's father was gazing off into the sky. Maybe he thought about all the refugees in camps in Palestine far from doorbells and shutters. Maybe he thought about the horizon beyond Jerusalem when he was a boy, how it seemed to be inviting him, "Come over, come over." Well, he'd come all the way to the other side of the world, and now he was doomed to live in two places at once. To Susan, immigrants seemed bigger than other people, and

always slightly melancholy. They also seemed doubly interesting. Maybe someday Susan would meet one her own age.

Two thin streams of tears rolled down Tracy's face. Eddie had drifted to the other side of the group and was clowning with Cameron, doing a tap dance shuffle. "While fields and floods, rocks hills and plains, repeat the sounding joy, repeat the sounding joy . . ." Susan and Saleh Hamadi noticed her. Hamadi peered into Tracy's face, inquiring, "Why? Is it pain? Is it gratitude? We are such mysterious creatures, human beings!"

Tracy turned to him, pressing her face against the old wool of his coat, and wailed. The song ended. All eyes on Tracy, and this tall, courteous stranger who would never in a thousand years have felt comfortable stroking her hair. But he let her stand there, crying as Susan stepped up to stand firmly on the other side of Tracy, putting her arms around her friend. Hamadi said something Susan would remember years later, whenever she was sad herself, even after college, a creaky anthem sneaking back into her ear, "We go on. On and on. We don't stop where it hurts. We turn a corner. It is the reason why we are living. To turn a corner. Come, let's move."

Above them, in the heavens, stars lived out their lonely lives. People whispered, "What happened? What's wrong?" Half of them were already walking down the street.

◆ **Literature and Your Life**

What words of wisdom have you thought about long after you heard them said? Why?

◆ **Build Vocabulary**

refugees (ref´ yoo jēz´) *n.*: People who flee from their homes in a time of trouble

melancholy (mel´ ən käl´ ē) *adj.*: Sad; depressed

Beyond Literature

Social Studies Connection

Jerusalem Susan's father in "Hamadi" is originally from Jerusalem, an ancient city in the Middle East. "Jerusalem is a golden basin filled with scorpions," an Arab philosopher observed centuries ago. Today, Jerusalem is still a place of religious treasures and dangerous conflicts. This ancient city is a holy place to Jews, Christians, and Muslims. In the past, all three groups have fought for control of Jerusalem. During the Crusades, Christians conquered the city and controlled it for a time until the Muslims recaptured it. In modern times, Israel gained control of the city after several wars with Arab neighbors.

Cross-Curricular Activity
Research the Middle East, and draw a map showing current boundaries of its countries.

Guide for Responding

◆ LITERATURE AND YOUR LIFE

Reader's Response Would you like to know someone like Hamadi? Why or why not?

Thematic Focus In what ways is Hamadi a good friend?

☑ Check Your Comprehension

1. When does Susan first become interested in Hamadi?
2. Briefly describe Hamadi's background, where he lives now, and the type of things he says.
3. How do Susan and Tracy differ in the way they think about Eddie?
4. Why doesn't Susan want a boyfriend?
5. Summarize what occurs during the caroling.

◆ Critical Thinking

INTERPRET

1. Why do you think Susan feels Hamadi is a "surrogate grandmother"? **[Infer]**
2. What does Hamadi mean when he says, "I married the wide horizon"? **[Interpret]**
3. What does Susan see in Hamadi that her father and most of her friends don't? **[Analyze]**
4. Why do Hamadi's words and actions at the end of the story become so important to Susan? **[Draw Conclusions]**

COMPARE LITERARY WORKS

5. In what ways are Professor Shlemiel and Hamadi different and alike? **[Compare and Contrast]**

Guide for Responding (continued)

◆ Reading Strategy

IDENTIFY WITH A CHARACTER

By **identifying with characters,** you think and feel with them. In this way, you experience stories as a participant rather than as an onlooker.

1. In "The Day I Got Lost," how might the professor have felt as he finally rang the bell of his apartment?
2. What may have compelled Susan to put her arms around Tracy at the end of "Hamadi"?

◆ Build Vocabulary

USING THE WORD ROOT -chol-

Words with -chol-, as in melancholy, reflect an old medical idea about the bad effects of bile. On your paper, match each -chol- word in the first column with its meaning in the second column.

1. melancholy   **a.** a disease of the intestines
2. cholesterol   **b.** deep sadness
3. cholera   **c.** a fatty substance that can clog arteries

SPELLING STRATEGY

In final, unstressed syllables, the letters f, g, and t are usually followed by le rather than el:

     brittle   giggle   raffle

Determine which of the following words are misspelled. Write each misspelled word correctly on your paper.

1. rattel   2. tattle   3. baffel   4. haggle

USING THE WORD BANK

Answer each question yes or no. Then, explain your answer.

1. Might you see a forsaken dog wandering in the streets?
2. Can a scene of pandemonium make you hold your ears?
3. Are brittle people usually open to new ideas?
4. Might you be noticed if you wore something lavish?
5. Do refugees usually live in fancy houses?
6. Does loss often create a feeling of melancholy?

◆ Literary Focus

DIRECT AND INDIRECT CHARACTERIZATION

These authors tell you **directly** what characters are like. They also show you **indirectly** what characters are like through their words, actions, and effects on others. The professor himself tells the story in "The Day I Got Lost," and his self-descriptions are direct characterization. However, you learn of his kindness indirectly through his rescue of the dog.

1. Find another example of indirect characterization in "The Day I Got Lost." Explain what you learn.
2. Locate one example each of direct and indirect characterization in "Hamadi." Explain how they differ.

◆ Build Grammar Skills

ADJECTIVE CLAUSES

An **adjective clause** is a subordinate clause that functions as an adjective; that is, it modifies a noun or a pronoun. Adjective clauses usually begin with a relative pronoun that relates the clause to the word it modifies. Relative pronouns are *who, whom, which, that,* and *whose.*

Adjective Clause

Everyone *who had boyfriends or girlfriends* all seemed to have troubles. (The adjective clause modifies *everyone.*)

Practice Identify the adjective clause in each sentence and the noun or pronoun it modifies.

1. Anyone who watches TV more than twelve minutes a week is uninteresting.
2. She had read about a woman who used to have parties to celebrate the arrival of fresh asparagus.
3. They sang at three houses which never opened their doors.
4. Hamadi had a jacket that reminded her of the earth's surface.
5. That was an Aramaic word that just drifted into my mouth.

Writing Application Use three sentences to describe Shlemiel or Hamadi, and include an adjective clause in each.

Build Your Portfolio

 Idea Bank

Writing

1. **Missing-Person Bulletin** Professor Shlemiel is wandering around town again. Give the police a brief description that will help them locate him.

2. **Self-Portrait** As Shlemiel or Hamadi, create a written self-portrait. Include your outstanding traits, your likes and dislikes, and a description of your appearance.

3. **Episode** Write about another episode in the life of Professor Shlemiel or Hamadi. Be sure that your character is consistent with Singer's or Nye's. Also, use both direct and indirect characterization to portray the person.

Speaking and Listening

4. **Monologue** As Shlemiel or Hamadi, step out of your story and onto the stage. In a speech, tell an audience who you are and why you're special. **[Performing Arts Link]**

5. **Role Play [Group Activity]** With a partner, role-play a meeting between Shlemiel and Hamadi. As you make up your scene, keep in mind how each of these characters acts and speaks in his story. **[Performing Arts Link]**

Projects

6. **Report on Kahlil Gibran** In "Hamadi," Susan mentions and quotes from the Lebanese poet Kahlil Gibran. Read aloud to your classmates some of Gibran's poems from *The Prophet*. Also, tell them about Gibran's life. **[Literature Link]**

7. **Wise Fools and Tricksters** Find folk tales about wise fools and tricksters. Examples include the wise fool Djuha in the Arabic tradition and the trickster Anansi in African stories. Retell some of these stories to your class. Then, comment on the similarities and differences among the wise fools and tricksters. **[Social Studies Link; Literature Link]**

 Writing Mini-Lesson

Dialogue

One way in which Singer and Nye reveal character is through dialogue, a conversation between two or more people. Write a dialogue between two fictional characters. Use what they say to reveal their personalities indirectly. Also, reveal their personalities, and incorporate action into your dialogue by describing their gestures, actions, and expressions as they talk.

Writing Skills Focus: Create Realistic Dialogue

To **create realistic dialogue,** imitate the informal way in which people usually speak. This informality includes the use of sentence fragments. Here's an example from "Hamadi":

> ***Model From the Story***
> Eddie looked mystified. "Who is this guy?"
> Susan whispered, "My friend."

Prewriting Create the framework for your dialogue by inventing two characters and a situation that causes them to meet. Also, jot down a profile of each character. Then, think about how their personalities will influence their speech.

Drafting Refer to your Prewriting notes for ideas. As you write your dialogue, say it aloud to make sure it sounds realistic and natural. Remember that dialogue works by cause and effect—characters respond to what they've just heard.

◆ **Grammar Application**

In your dialogue, use adjective clauses to provide further information about nouns or pronouns.

Revising Have two classmates act out your dialogue. Whenever it sounds unrealistic, have the speaker improvise a more natural way of saying the same thing. Then, incorporate the improvisation into your dialogue.

Fictional Narrative

Writing Process Workshop

The Tell-Tale Heart, 1883, Odilon Redon, Santa Barbara Museum of Art

The tales of suspense, emotion, and achievement in this unit are all **fictional narratives.** The writers create events and characters that make you want to keep reading. A fictional narrative can be amusing, sad, or spine-chilling. It can be told by a character in the story or by an observer.

Although fictional narratives can be very different, they contain the same elements: They are made up, and they all have characters that face a conflict or a problem that is resolved by the end. Keeping these elements in mind, write your own fictional narrative.

The following skills, introduced in the Writing Mini-Lessons in this section, will help you plan and write your fictional narrative.

Writing Skills Focus

▶ **Create details that reveal character** and to make your plot believable. (See p. 538.)

▶ **Use suspense** to keep the reader guessing and to move the plot toward the climax and resolution. (See p. 549.)

▶ **Create realistic dialogue.** (See p. 571.)

MODEL FROM LITERATURE

from *"The Tell-Tale Heart"* by Edgar Allan Poe

I had my head in, and was about to open the lantern, when my thumb slipped upon the tin fastening, and the old man sprang up in the bed, crying out—"Who's there?" ①

I kept quite still and said nothing. For a whole hour, I did not move a muscle, ② and in the meantime I did not hear him lie down. He was still sitting up in the bed listening;—just as I have done, night after night, hearkening to the deathwatches in the wall. ③

① Poe uses realistic dialogue to portray the old man's fear.

② This detail reveals the main character's determination not to be seen or heard.

③ This final sentence creates suspense.

Prewriting

Choose an Idea Find an idea for a story by wondering *what if?* What if all the schools were suddenly closed? Where would kids go? Would they have to work? Use this questioning technique to come up with an idea, or try one of the following suggestions.

> ### Story Ideas
>
> - A teenager travels to another planet
> - A friendly bear cub appears in your yard
> - A contest
> - A championship game

Make a Timeline or Storyboard In simple terms, any narrative is a series of events. To plan your story's plot, simply list the events you will include as they will occur or—if you like to draw—create a storyboard that shows what events will occur.

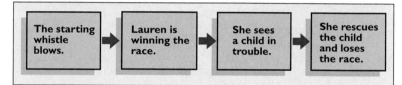

Drafting

Use Dialogue As you tell your story, incorporate dialogue. Instead of simply telling the events, let them unravel through conversation. Keep in mind that in ordinary speech, people often don't use complete sentences and may pause between thoughts. The use of contractions and even nonstandard English is also common in ordinary conversation.

Description: Lauren became emotional when she was given a "hero" award.

Dialogue: Award giver: "Lauren, we would like to present you with this award for unselfishness and bravery."

Lauren replied, with her voice cracking: "Tha-ank you. Winning a race," Lauren wiped away her tears, "could never be as important as helping someone else."

Build Suspense Let your story move toward one moment of high tension—the turning point. Include hints or clues to increase your readers' sense of curiosity or anxiety about the outcome of the events.

DRAFTING/REVISING

APPLYING LANGUAGE SKILLS: Varying Tag Words

Tag words are the phrases, such as *he said* or *she said*, in dialogue. They show who is speaking and how the words are being said. For example:

"Villains!" I shrieked, "dissemble no more!" (Edgar Allan Poe)

"Climb up here," I whispered to Brooke.

"You *like* pickled broccoli?" I teased.

Practice Copy the following sentences into your notebook, replacing the tag words with more descriptive ones.

1. "Lincoln!" I said, "Come here this instant!"
2. "I'm very sorry," Molly said.
3. My mother said, "Why is your hair green?"
4. "Hamadi," she said, "be careful!"
5. "There was a cobra lying on her foot," he said.

Writing Application As you write dialogue for your fictional narrative, use descriptive tag words to help readers understand how the speaker is feeling.

> ### Writer's Solution Connection Writing Lab
>
> For more help with story ideas, use the Storyboard Activity in the Narration tutorial.

APPLYING LANGUAGE SKILLS:
Consistency in Verb Tense

When writing a fictional narrative, use verbs in the same tense to express events occurring at the same time. If you shift tenses when no shift is necessary, your meaning will become unclear.

Unnecessary Shifts:

Edgar *pulled* back the curtain. He *screams*—and *shut* the window just in time.

Consistent Tense:

Edgar *pulls* back the curtain. He *screams*—and *shuts* the window just in time.

Practice Rewrite the following pairs of sentences so they are in the same tense.

1. The boys ran across the lot. They leave their bikes behind.
2. A full moon rises. The Big Dipper hung above our heads.
3. Lightning flashed. Thunder rumbled. Rain pelts our faces.

Writer's Solution Connection
Language Lab

For more help with consistent tense, see the Avoiding Shifts in Tense lesson in the Using Verbs unit.

Revising

Follow These Tips for Revising Use the following tips to help revise your narrative.

▶ **Characters** Give a boring character an endearing habit to make him or her more interesting.

▶ **Dialogue** Make sure that dialogue is realistic. The use of contractions and incomplete statements is acceptable in realistic dialogue. Read dialogue aloud to be sure that it sounds like natural speech.

▶ **Suspense** Examine plot events to ensure that they make sense and build suspense. Double-check your hints and clues to make sure they don't reveal too much before the climax.

REVISION MODEL

Normally, Quinn was not very frightened of strange noises ① , but this noise was moving.

② Having been an Eagle Scout, the wonders of the outdoors were not a mystery, but

He was completely unprepared for the large disc flying directly at his head. ③ "Help! He-e-e-lp!" he stammered as he attempted to defend himself.

① The writer adds this clause to create suspense and make the reader wonder what was moving toward Quinn.

② This detail provides more background about Quinn's personality. If he was fearful of the object, then it must have been especially frightening.

③ This dialogue reveals Quinn's feelings of fear.

Publishing and Presenting

Classroom Have classmates sit in a circle, and take turns telling or reading your stories. After each, ask listeners to tell what details in the story they liked or remembered most.

Magazines and Journals Submit your story for possible publication. Ask your librarian to help you find magazines for young people that accept unsolicited manuscripts, and send them your fictional narrative.

E-Mail Use e-mail to send your narrative to friends and family who live far away from you.

Real-World Reading Skills Workshop

Reading Novels and Other Extended Works

Strategies for Success

Reading a novel, a biography, or a full-length play differs from reading a short story or a poem. Reading an extended work can take several days or several weeks. Longer works usually involve more complex settings and characters than shorter works do. As a result, you need to approach longer works differently from shorter works.

Make a Plan Before beginning an extended work, establish a reading plan. Set goals for the amount you must read at each sitting, based on the time you have. Don't rush through the book, or you may miss important details.

Get an Overview Find out about the work before you begin reading. For a novel, scan the chapter titles to see how the book is divided. Titles of chapters or sections hint at the novel's plot and setting. For nonfiction, look at the table of contents to see how the book is divided. Also, preview any maps or illustrations that are included in the work.

Pause and Reflect Stop periodically to review what you have read. Reflecting on a chapter's main idea or a character's actions will help you better understand the rest of the work. Also, review any changes that have occurred. Has time passed? Has the setting changed? What major events have occurred? Jot down major changes in your journal. Then, refresh your memory by reviewing these details before reading new sections.

Appreciate Details A novelist or biographer has time and space to provide thorough descriptions. As you read, take time to enjoy descriptive passages. These details may help you better understand an upcoming twist in the plot or an action of the subject of a biography.

Apply the Strategies

Use the table of contents for the first part of *Shark Beneath the Reef* to answer the questions that follow.

1. Which chapters are the shortest? Which are the longest chapters?

2. About how many pages a day would you have to read in order to finish the first four chapters in three days?

3. What can you tell about the setting of the book from the listing of chapter titles? What can you tell about the plot?

✔ Here are some other extended works that you can read strategically:
▶ Biographies
▶ Autobiographies
▶ Full-length plays

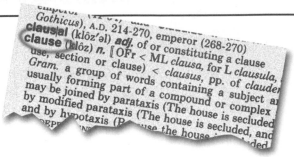

A **clause** is a group of words that contains a subject and a verb. There are two kinds of clauses—independent and subordinate. (See page 537.) An **independent clause** can stand alone as a complete sentence. A **subordinate clause** is dependent on an independent, or main, clause to express a complete thought. Subordinate clauses can act as adjectives or adverbs in a sentence.

An **adjective clause** begins with a relative pronoun and modifies a noun or a pronoun. It answers the questions *what kind* or *which one*. (See page 570.)

Relative Pronouns

that, which, who, whom, whose

Maybe that old Maronite priest *who used to cry after every service* introduced us.

An **adverb clause** begins with a subordinating conjunction and usually modifies a verb, an adjective, or an adverb in another clause. It answers the questions *when, where, how, why,* and *to what extent.* (See page 548.)

Common Subordinating Conjunctions

after, although, as, because, before, if, since, though, unless, until, when, where

When she saw the dog, she arched her back and spat at him, ready to scratch his eyes out.

Practice 1 Write each sentence in your notebook. Underline the independent clauses once and the subordinate clauses twice. Label the subordinate clauses as adjective or adverb. Tell what word each modifies.

1. Susan didn't really feel interested in Saleh Hamadi until she was a freshman in high school . . .

2. I swung the chair upon which I had been sitting. . . .

3. "And here you stand shivering and forsaken in the rain, while your loving master is searching for you everywhere."

4. I tried to call a number of friends, those whose telephone numbers I knew.

5. When all were sleeping, it came to me.

Practice 2 Combine the following pairs of sentences into one sentence. Make one of the clauses a subordinate clause as indicated.

1. Edgar Allan Poe wrote many tales of terror. He wrote "A Tell-Tale Heart." (adjective clause beginning with *who*)

2. Professor Shlemiel left his briefcase in the taxi. It might have contained his address. (adjective clause beginning with *which*)

3. The old man shrieked in terror. I entered the room. (adverb clause beginning with *when*)

4. The lady had screamed. This could have caused a cobra attack. (adverb clause beginning with *if*)

Grammar in Writing

✔ *A subordinate clause can never stand alone. A clause standing alone is a sentence error called a fragment.*

Setting and Theme

Moonwalk, 1987, Andy Warhol, ©1999 Andy Warhol Foundation for the Visual Arts/Ronald Feldman Fine Arts

Guide for Reading

Meet the Authors:

Paul Laurence Dunbar (1872–1906)

The first African American to support himself as an author, Dunbar wrote poems, novels, and short stories. He was born in Dayton, Ohio, the son of former slaves.

An Influential Poet
At an early age, Dunbar won recognition for his poetry. Written both in dialect and in standard English, his poems have continued to influence many writers. The title of Maya Angelou's autobiography, *I Know Why the Caged Bird Sings*, comes from Dunbar's poem "Sympathy."

THE STORY BEHIND THE STORY

Like Patsy Barnes, Dunbar was raised by a mother who "had come North from Kentucky." Patsy loves horses, and Dunbar was riding horses in Colorado when he wrote the story. He had moved there in 1899 for his health.

Yoshiko Uchida (1921–1992)

Uchida's twenty-seven children's books include *Picture Bride*, *Journey to Topaz*, and *Desert Exile*. In addition to works of fiction, she wrote books on Japanese American history and Japanese folklore. She said of her writing, "I hope to give young Asian Americans a sense of their past and to reinforce their self-esteem and self-knowledge."

◆ LITERATURE AND YOUR LIFE

CONNECT YOUR EXPERIENCE

You are rich in worlds. First, you have the everyday world in which you live. Then, you have the places that open out for you on television screens, movie screens, and the pages of books. These two stories will add to your wealth of worlds. They'll take you back in time a hundred years—to a thrilling horse race and to a ship sailing to California on a rough sea.

THEMATIC FOCUS: Conflicts and Challenges

The main characters in each of these stories take risks. In what ways do they display courage?

◆ Background for Understanding

SOCIAL STUDIES

"Tears of Autumn" takes place about a century ago, a time when most Japanese families arranged marriages for their children. An older relative or family friend would help set up these unions. Before reaching an agreement, each family had to be satisfied that the other was worthy. When the bride and groom lived far apart, they often exchanged pictures before meeting.

◆ Build Vocabulary

WORD ROOTS: *-flu-*

The root *-flu-*, meaning "flow," appears in words dealing with flow or movement. For example, the word *affluence* means "wealth." Wealth is a flow of goods to someone or something: *af-* ("to") + *-fluence* ("flow").

WORD BANK

Which word from the list means "one who practices diplomacy, the art of dealing with people"? Check the Build Vocabulary box on page 583 to see if you chose correctly.

compulsory
meager
obdurate
diplomatic
turbulent
affluence
degrading

The Finish of Patsy Barnes ◆ Tears of Autumn

The Jockey, Toulouse Lautrec

◆ Reading Strategy
Ask Questions

Because a story introduces you to a new world, you'll have questions as you read. To become more comfortable in a story's world, learn how to **ask questions** and answer them. Let yourself wonder about everything—from why a street has a certain name to what a puzzling sentence means. You can find the answers by rereading the passage, looking in a reference book for factual information, or simply reading the rest of the story to see how all the pieces fit together.

◆ Literary Focus
Setting

The picture on this page takes you into a world of horses and riders. In the same way, a story takes you into the world of its **setting,** the time and place of its action. The setting consists of *all* the details of a place and time—anything from a galloping horse to a rainstorm to a marriage ceremony.

Use a chart like the one below to capture the settings of these stories (some details have been filled in for you).

"The Finish of Patsy Barnes"			
Time	**Place**	**Weather Conditions**	**Attitudes and Beliefs**
Early 1900's	"Little Africa"; racetrack	Not mentioned	Prejudice

THE FINISH of PATSY BARNES

Paul Laurence Dunbar

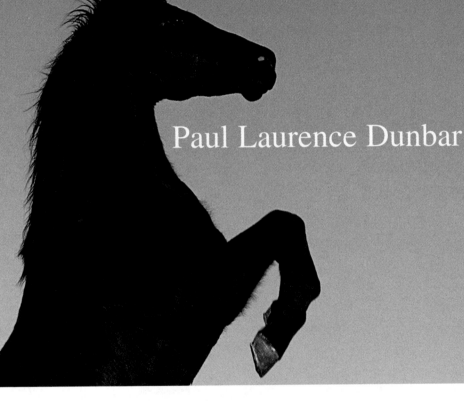

His name was Patsy Barnes, and he was a denizen of Little Africa.[1] In fact, he lived on Douglass Street. By all the laws governing the relations between people and their names, he should have been Irish—but he was not. He was colored, and very much so. That was the reason he lived on Douglass Street. The Negro has very strong within him the instinct of colonization and it was in

accordance with this that Patsy's mother had found her way to Little Africa when she had come North from Kentucky.

Patsy was incorrigible. Even into the confines of Little Africa had penetrated the truant officer and the terrible penalty of the

◆ **Literary Focus**
What do you learn about the setting from this first paragraph?

▲ **Critical Viewing** Would you approach the pictured horse with eagerness or caution? Explain. **[Make a Decision]**

compulsory education law. Time and time again had poor Eliza Barnes been brought up on account of the shortcomings of that son of hers. She was a hard-working, honest woman, and day by day bent over her tub, scrubbing away to keep Patsy in shoes and jackets, that would wear out so much faster than they could be bought. But she never murmured, for she loved the boy with a deep affection, though his misdeeds were a sore thorn in her side.

She wanted him to go to school. She wanted him to learn. She had the notion that he might become something better, something higher than she had been. But for him school had no charms; his school was the cool stalls in the big livery stable[2] near at hand; the arena of his pursuits its sawdust floor; the height of his ambition, to be a horseman. Either here or in the racing stables at the Fair-grounds he spent his truant hours. It was a school that taught much, and Patsy was as apt a pupil as he was a constant attendant. He learned strange things about horses, and fine, sonorous oaths that sounded eerie on his young lips, for he had only turned into his fourteenth year.

A man goes where he is appreciated; then could this slim black boy be blamed for doing the same thing? He was a great favorite with the horsemen, and picked up many a dime or nickel for dancing or singing, or even a quarter for warming up a horse for its owner. He was not to be blamed for this, for, first of all, he was born in Kentucky, and had spent the very days of his infancy about the paddocks[3] near Lexington, where his father had sacrificed his life on account of his love for horses. The little fellow had shed no tears when he looked at his father's bleeding body, bruised and broken by the fiery young two-year-old he was trying to subdue. Patsy did not sob or whimper, though his heart ached, for over all the feeling of his grief was a mad, burning desire to ride that horse.

His tears were shed, however, when, actu-ated by the idea that times would be easier up North, they moved to Dalesford. Then, when he learned that he must leave his old friends, the horses and their masters, whom he had known, he wept. The comparatively meager appointments of the Fair-grounds at Dalesford proved a poor compensation for all these. For the first few weeks Patsy had dreams of run-ning away—back to Kentucky and the horses and stables. Then after a while he settled him-self with heroic resolution to make the best of what he had, and with a mighty effort took up the burden of life away from his beloved home.

Eliza Barnes, older and more experienced though she was, took up her burden with a less cheerful philosophy than her son. She worked hard, and made a scanty livelihood, it is true, but she did not make the best of what she had. Her complainings were loud in the land, and her wailings for her old home smote the ears of any who would listen to her.

They had been living in Dalesford for a year nearly, when hard work and exposure brought the woman down to bed with pneumonia.[4] They were very poor—too poor even to call in a doctor, so there was nothing to do but to call in the city physician. Now this medical man had too frequent calls into Little Africa, and he did not like to go there. So he was very gruff when any of its denizens called him, and it was even said that he was careless of his patients.

Patsy's heart bled as he heard the doctor talking to his mother:

"Now, there can't be any foolishness about this," he said. "You've got to stay in bed and not get yourself damp."

"How long you think I got to lay hyeah, doctah?" she asked.

"I'm a doctor, not a fortune-teller," was the

---

2. livery (liv′ ər ē) **stable** *n.*: Place where horses are kept and fed.
3. paddocks (pad′ əks) *n.*: Enclosed areas near a stable in which horses are exercised.

4. pneumonia (no͞o mōn′ yə) *n.*: Inflammation of the lungs.

◆ Build Vocabulary

compulsory (kəm pul′ sə rē) *adj.*: Enforced; required
meager (mē′ gər) *adj.*: Lacking in some way; inadequate

Farm Boy, 1941, Charles Alston, Courtesy of Clark Atlanta University

▲ **Critical Viewing** Would you describe the boy in this painting as "obdurate"? Why or why not? [Draw Conclusions]

reply. "You'll lie there as long as the disease holds you."

"But I can't lay hyeah long, doctah, case I ain't got nuffin' to go on."

"Well, take your choice: the bed or the boneyard."

Eliza began to cry.

"You needn't sniffle," said the doctor; "I don't see what you people want to come up here for anyhow. Why don't you stay down South where you belong? You come up here and you're just a burden and a trouble to the city. The South deals with all of you better, both in poverty and crime."

◆ **Literary Focus**
People's attitudes are part of the setting. What prejudice does the doctor express?

He knew that these people did not understand him, but he wanted an outlet for the heat within him.

There was another angry being in the room, and that was Patsy. His eyes were full of tears that scorched him and would not fall. The memory of many beautiful and appropriate oaths came to him; but he dared not let his mother hear him swear. Oh! to have a stone—to be across the street from that man!

When the physician walked out, Patsy went to the bed, took his mother's hand, and bent over shame-facedly to kiss her. The little mark of affection comforted Eliza unspeakably. The mother-feeling overwhelmed her in one burst of tears. Then she dried her eyes and smiled at him.

"Honey," she said; "mammy ain' gwine lay hyeah long. She be all right putty soon."

"Nevah you min'," said Patsy with a choke in his voice. "I can do somep'n', an' we'll have an-othah doctah."

"La, listen at de chile; what kin you do?"

"I'm goin' down to McCarthy's stable and see if I kin git some horses to exercise."

A sad look came into Eliza's eyes as she said: "You'd bettah not go, Patsy; dem hosses'll kill you yit, des lak dey did yo' pappy."

But the boy, used to doing pretty much as he pleased, was <u>obdurate</u>, and even while she was talking, put on his ragged jacket and left the room.

Patsy was not wise enough to be <u>diplomatic</u>. He went right to the point with McCarthy, the liveryman.

The big red-faced fellow slapped him until he spun round and round. Then he said, "Ye little devil, ye, I've a mind to knock the whole head off o' ye. Ye want harses to exercise, do ye? Well git on that 'un, an' see what ye kin do with him."

The boy's honest desire to be helpful had tickled the big, generous Irishman's peculiar sense of humor, and from now on, instead of giving Patsy a horse to ride now and then as he had formerly done, he put into his charge all the animals that needed exercise.

It was with a king's pride that Patsy marched home with his first considerable earnings.

They were small yet, and would go for food rather than a doctor, but Eliza was inordinately proud, and it was this pride that gave her strength and the desire of life to carry her through the days approaching the crisis of her disease.

As Patsy saw his mother growing worse, saw her gasping for breath, heard the rattling as she drew in the little air that kept going her clogged lungs, felt the heat of her burning hands, and saw the pitiful appeal in her poor eyes, he became convinced that the city doctor was not helping her. She must have another. But the money?

That afternoon, after his work with McCarthy, found him at the Fair-grounds. The spring races were on, and he thought he might get a job warming up the horse of some independent jockey. He hung around the stables, listening to the talk of men he knew and some he had never seen before. Among the latter was a tall, lanky man, holding forth to a group of men.

"No, suh," he was saying to them generally, "I'm goin' to withdraw my hoss, because thaih ain't nobody to ride him as he ought to be rode. I haven't brought a jockey along with me, so I've got to depend on pick-ups. Now, the talent's set again my hoss, Black Boy, because he's been losin' regular, but that hoss has lost for the want of ridin', that's all."

The crowd looked in at the slim-legged, raw-boned horse, and walked away laughing.

"The fools!" muttered the stranger. "If I could ride myself I'd show 'em!"

Patsy was gazing into the stall at the horse.

"What are you doing thaih?" called the owner to him.

"Look hyeah, mistah," said Patsy, "ain't that a bluegrass hoss?"

"Of co'se it is, an' one o' the fastest that evah grazed."

"I'll ride that hoss, mistah."

"What do you know bout ridin'?"

"I used to gin'ally be' roun' Mistah Boone's paddock in Lexington, an'—"

"Aroun' Boone's paddock—what! Look here, if you can ride that hoss to a winnin' I'll give you more money than you ever seen before."

"I'll ride him."

Patsy's heart was beating very wildly beneath his jacket. That horse. He knew that glossy coat. He knew that raw-boned frame and those flashing nostrils. That black horse there owed something to the orphan he had made.

The horse was to ride in the race before the last. Somehow out of

◆ Reading Strategy
Why does the black horse owe something to Patsy?

odds and ends, his owner scraped together a suit and colors for Patsy. The colors were maroon and green, a curious combination. But then it was a curious horse, a curious rider, and a more curious combination that brought the two together.

Long before the time for the race Patsy went into the stall to become better acquainted with his horse. The animal turned its wild eyes upon him and neighed. He patted the long, slender head, and grinned as the horse stepped aside as gently as a lady.

"He sholy is full o' ginger," he said to the owner, whose name he had found to be Brackett.

"He'll show 'em a thing or two," laughed Brackett.

"His dam[5] was a fast one," said Patsy, unconsciously.

Brackett whirled on him in a flash. "What do you know about his dam?" he asked.

The boy would have retracted, but it was too late. Stammeringly he told the story of his

---

5. **dam** (dam) *n*.: Female parent of a four-legged animal.

◆ Build Vocabulary

obdurate (äb´ door it) *adj*.: Stubbornly persistent

diplomatic (dip´ lə mat´ ik) *adj*.: Tactful; showing skill in dealing with people

father's death and the horse's connection therewith.

"Well," said Bracket, "if you don't turn out a hoodoo,[6] you're a winner, sure. But I'll be blessed if this don't sound like a story! But I've heard that story before. The man I got Black Boy from, no matter how I got him, you're too young to understand the ins and outs of poker, told it to me."

When the bell sounded and Patsy went out to warm up, he felt as if he were riding on air. Some of the jockeys laughed at

his getup, but there was something in him—or under him, maybe—that made him scorn their derision. He saw a sea of faces about him, then saw no more. Only a shining white track loomed ahead of him, and a restless steed[7] was cantering with him around the curve. Then the bell called him back to the stand.

They did not get away at first, and back they trooped. A second trial was a failure. But at the third they were off in a line as straight as a chalk-mark. There were Essex and Firefly, Queen Bess and Mosquito, galloping away side by side, and Black Boy a neck ahead. Patsy knew the family reputation of his horse for endurance as well as fire, and began riding the race from the first. Black Boy came of blood that would not be passed, and to this his rider trusted. At the eighth the line was hardly broken, but as the quarter was reached Black

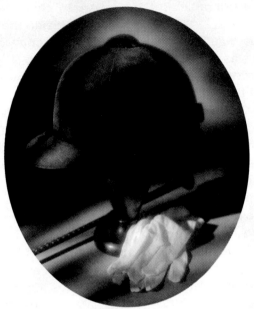

▲ **Critical Viewing** How would Patsy Barnes feel about these symbols of a jockey? [Infer]

Boy had forged a length ahead, and Mosquito was at his flank. Then, like a flash, Essex shot out ahead under whip and spur, his jockey standing straight in the stirrups.

The crowd in the stand screamed; but Patsy smiled as he lay low over his horse's neck. He saw that Essex had made his best spurt. His only fear was for Mosquito, who hugged and hugged his flank. They were nearing the three-quarter post, and he was tightening his grip on the black. Essex fell back; his spurt was over. The whip fell unheeded on his sides. The spurs dug him in vain.

Black Boy's breath touches the leader's ear. They are neck and neck—nose to nose. The black stallion passes him.

Another cheer from the stand, and again Patsy smiles as they turn into the stretch. Mosquito has gained a head. The colored boy flashes one glance at the horse and rider who are so surely gaining upon him, and his lips close in a grim line. They are half-way down the stretch, and Mosquito's head is at the stallion's neck.

For a single moment Patsy thinks of the sick woman at home and what that race will mean to her, and then his knees close against the horse's sides with a firmer dig. The spurs shoot deeper into the steaming flanks. Black Boy shall win; he must win. The horse that has taken away his father shall give him back his mother. The stallion leaps away like a flash, and goes under the wire—a length ahead.

Then the band thundered, and Patsy was off his horse, very warm and very happy, following his mount to the stable. There, a little later, Brackett found him. He rushed to him, and flung his arms around him.

"You little devil," he cried, "you rode like you

---

6. **hoodoo** (hōō′ dōō) *n.*: Here, someone or something that causes bad luck.
7. **steed** (stēd) *n.*: High-spirited riding horse.

were kin to that hoss! We've won! We've won!" And he began sticking banknotes[8] at the boy. At first Patsy's eyes bulged, and then he seized the money and got into his clothes.

"Goin' out to spend it?" asked Brackett.

"I'm goin' for a doctah fu' my mother," said Patsy, "she's sick."

"Don't let me lose sight of you."

"Oh, I'll see you again. So long," said the boy.

An hour later he walked into his mother's room with a very big doctor, the greatest the druggist could direct him to. The doctor left his medicines and his orders, but, when Patsy told his story, it was Eliza's pride that started her on the road to recovery. Patsy did not tell his horse's name.

---

8. **banknotes** (baŋk´ nōts) *n*.: Form of paper money.

Beyond ◆ *Literature*

Career Connection

Horse Trainer A horse trainer deals firmly but gently as he or she teaches a horse to respond to certain commands or situations. The trainer begins soon after the horse's birth, getting it used to being handled by humans. When the horse is a year old, the trainer slowly accustoms it to having a saddle on its back. Eventually, the horse is mounted and ridden for a few steps, then a few more, until it is used to having a rider. Once that is accomplished, the horse is taught to obey the signals used by riders and drivers. Finally, the trainer teaches the horse to fulfill the job or compete in the sport he's been trained to do.

Cross-Curricular Activity
Choosing Your Own Career Learn what it takes to become a horse trainer. Then, create a chart, showing the training and skills necessary to become successful at that career.

Guide for Responding

◆ LITERATURE AND YOUR LIFE

Reader's Response What do you think will happen to Patsy and his mother?

Thematic Focus What conflict inspires Patsy to take the risk of riding Black Boy?

Journal Writing In your journal, jot down a play-by-play description of Patsy's race.

☑ Check Your Comprehension

1. Instead of going to school, how does Patsy spend his time?
2. What happens to Patsy's mother that keeps her from working?
3. Why is Black Boy not a stranger to Patsy?
4. What does Patsy do with his earnings from the race?

◆ Critical Thinking

INTERPRET

1. What is similar about Patsy's reaction to his father's death and his reaction to the prejudiced doctor? **[Compare and Contrast]**
2. Explain the meaning of this statement: "That black horse there owed something to the orphan he had made." **[Interpret]**
3. How does Patsy show intelligence and judgment during the race? **[Support]**
4. In what way is Patsy's triumph a victory for both his father and mother? **[Infer]**

EVALUATE

5. Was Patsy's decision not to tell his mother the horse's name a good one? Why or why not? **[Make a Judgment]**

EXTEND

6. What does this story reveal about the problems African Americans faced when they moved from the South to the North? **[Social Studies Link]**

Tears of Autumn

Yoshiko Uchida

▲ **Critical Viewing** What kinds of emotions do you see on the faces of the newly arrived immigrants pictured here? **[Interpret]**

*H*ana Omiya stood at the railing of the small ship that shuddered toward America in a <u>turbulent</u> November sea. She shivered as she pulled the folds of her silk kimono close to her throat and tightened the wool shawl about her shoulders.

She was thin and small, her dark eyes shadowed in her pale face, her black hair piled high in a pompadour that seemed too heavy for so slight a woman. She clung to the moist rail and breathed the damp salt air deep into her lungs. Her body seemed leaden and lifeless, as though it were simply the vehicle transporting her soul to a strange new life, and she longed with childlike intensity to be home again in Oka Village.

She longed to see the bright persimmon dotting the barren trees beside the thatched roofs, to see the fields of golden rice stretching to the mountains where only last fall she had gathered plum white mushrooms, and to see once more the maple trees lacing their flaming colors through the green pine. If only she could see a familiar face, eat a meal without retching, walk on solid ground, and stretch out at night on a *tatami* mat[1] instead of in a hard narrow bunk. She thought now of seeking the warm shelter of her bunk but could

---

1. *tatami* (tə tä´ mē) **mat** *n.*: Floor mat woven of rice straw, traditionally used in Japanese homes.

not bear to face the relentless smell of fish that penetrated the lower decks.

Why did I ever leave Japan? she wondered bitterly. Why did I ever listen to my uncle? And yet she knew it was she herself who had begun the chain of events that placed her on this heaving ship. It was she who had first planted in her uncle's mind the thought that she would make a good wife for Taro Takeda, the lonely man who had gone to America to make his fortune in Oakland, California.

It all began one day when her uncle had come to visit her mother.

"I must find a nice young bride," he had said, startling Hana with this blunt talk of marriage in her presence. She blushed and was ready to leave the room when her uncle quickly added, "My good friend Takeda has a son in America. I must find someone willing to travel to that far land."

This last remark was intended to indicate to Hana and her mother that he didn't consider this a suitable prospect for Hana, who was the youngest daughter of what once had been a fine family. Her father, until his death fifteen years ago, had been the largest landholder of the village and one of its last samurai.[2] They had once had many servants and field hands, but now all that was changed. Their money was gone. Hana's three older sisters had made good marriages, and the eldest remained in their home with her husband to carry on the Omiya name and perpetuate the homestead. Her other sisters had married merchants in Osaka and Nagoya and were living comfortably.

◆ Literary Focus
What attitudes toward marriage are part of the setting of this story?

Now that Hana was twenty-one, finding a proper husband for her had taken on an urgency that produced an embarrassing secretive air over the entire matter. Usually, her mother didn't speak of it until they were lying side by side on their quilts at night. Then, under the protective cover of darkness, she would suggest one name and then another, hoping that Hana would indicate an interest in one of them.

Her uncle spoke freely of Taro Takeda only because he was so sure Hana would never consider him. "He is a conscientious, hard-working man who has been in the United States for almost ten years. He is thirty-one, operates a small shop, and rents some rooms above the shop where he lives." Her uncle rubbed his chin thoughtfully. "He could provide well for a wife," he added.

"Ah," Hana's mother said softly.

"You say he is successful in this business?" Hana's sister inquired.

"His father tells me he sells many things in his shop—clothing, stockings, needles, thread, and buttons—such things as that. He also sells bean paste, pickled radish, bean cake, and soy sauce. A wife of his would not go cold or hungry."

They all nodded, each of them picturing this merchant in varying degrees of success and <u>affluence</u>. There were many Japanese emigrating to America these days, and Hana had heard of the picture brides who went with nothing more than an exchange of photographs to bind them to a strange man.

◆ **Build Vocabulary**
turbulent (tur´ byŌŌ lənt) adj.: Full of commotion; wild
affluence (af´ lŌŌ əns) n.: Wealth; abundance

---

2. **samurai** (sam´ ə rī´) n.: Japanese army officer or member of the military class.

"Taro San[3] is lonely," her uncle continued. "I want to find for him a fine young woman who is strong and brave enough to cross the ocean alone."

"It would certainly be a different kind of life," Hana's sister ventured, and for a moment, Hana thought she glimpsed a longing ordinarily concealed behind her quiet, obedient face. In that same instant, Hana knew she wanted more for herself than her sisters had in their proper, arranged, and loveless marriages. She wanted to escape the smothering strictures of life in her village. She certainly was not going to marry a farmer and spend her life working beside him planting, weeding, and harvesting in the rice paddies until her back became bent from too many years of stooping and her skin was turned to brown leather by the sun and wind. Neither did she particularly relish the idea of marrying a merchant in a big city as her two sisters had done. Since her mother objected to her going to Tokyo to seek employment as a teacher, perhaps she would consent to a flight to America for what seemed a proper and respectable marriage.

Almost before she realized what she was doing, she spoke to her uncle. "Oji San, perhaps I should go to America to make this lonely man a good wife."

"You, Hana Chan?"[4] Her uncle observed her with startled curiosity. "You would go all alone to a foreign land so far away from your mother and family?"

"I would not allow it." Her mother spoke fiercely. Hana was her youngest and she had lavished upon her the attention and latitude that often befall the last child. How could she permit her to travel so far, even to marry the son of Takeda who was known to her brother?

But now, a notion that had seemed quite impossible a moment before was lodged in his receptive mind, and Hana's uncle grasped it with the pleasure that comes from an unexpected discovery.

"You know," he said looking at Hana, "it might be a very good life in America."

Hana felt a faint fluttering in her heart. Perhaps this lonely man in America was her means of escaping both the village and the encirclement of her family.

Her uncle spoke with increasing enthusiasm of sending Hana to become Taro's wife. And the husband of Hana's sister, who was head of their household, spoke with equal eagerness. Although he never said so, Hana guessed he would be pleased to be rid of her, the spirited younger sister who stirred up his placid life with what he considered radical ideas about life and the role of women. He often claimed

---

3. **San** (sän): Japanese term added to names, indicating respect.

4. **Chan** (chän): Japanese term added to children's names.

that Hana had too much schooling for a girl. She had graduated from Women's High School in Kyoto, which gave her five more years of schooling than her older sister.

"It has addled her brain—all that learning from those books," he said when he tired of arguing with Hana.

A man's word carried much weight for Hana's mother. Pressed by the two men, she consulted her other daughters and their husbands. She discussed the matter carefully with her brother and asked the village priest. Finally, she agreed to an exchange of family histories and an investigation was begun into Taro Takeda's family, his education, and his health, so they would be assured there was no insanity or tuberculosis or police records concealed in his family's past. Soon Hana's uncle was devoting his energies entirely to serving as go-between for Hana's mother and Taro Takeda's father.

◆ **Literary Focus**
For a Japanese family living at this time, what was necessary before a marriage could be approved?

When at last an agreement to the marriage was almost reached, Taro wrote his first letter to Hana. It was brief and proper and gave no more clue to his character than the stiff formal portrait taken at his graduation from middle school. Hana's uncle had given her the picture with apologies from his parents, because it was the only photo they had of him and it was not a flattering likeness.

Hana hid the letter and photograph in the sleeve of her kimono and took them to the outhouse to study in private. Squinting in the dim light and trying to ignore the foul odor, she read and reread Taro's letter, trying to find the real man somewhere in the sparse unbending prose.

By the time he sent her money for her steamship tickets, she had received ten more letters, but none revealed much more of the man than the first. In none did he disclose his loneliness or his need, but Hana understood this. In fact, she would have recoiled from a man who bared his intimate thoughts to her so soon. After all, they would have a lifetime together to get to know one another.

So it was that Hana had left her family and sailed alone to America with a small hope trembling inside of her. Tomorrow, at last, the ship would dock in San Francisco and she would meet face to face the man she was soon to marry. Hana was overcome with excitement at the thought of being in America, and terrified of the meeting about to take place. What would she say to Taro Takeda when they first met, and for all the days and years after?

Hana wondered about the flat above the shop. Perhaps it would be luxuriously furnished with the finest of brocades and lacquers,[5] and perhaps there would be a servant, although he had not mentioned it. She worried whether she would be able to manage on the meager English she had learned at Women's High School. The overwhelming anxiety for the day to come and the violent rolling of the ship were more than Hana could bear. Shuddering in the face of the wind, she leaned over the railing and became violently and wretchedly ill.

By five the next morning, Hana was up and dressed in her finest purple silk kimono and coat. She could not eat the bean soup and rice that appeared for breakfast and took only a few bites of the yellow pickled radish. Her bags, which had scarcely been touched since she boarded the ship, were easily packed, for all they contained were her kimonos and some of her favorite books. The large willow basket, tightly secured by a rope, remained under the bunk, untouched since her uncle had placed it there.

She had not befriended the other women in her cabin, for they had lain in their bunks for most of the voyage, too sick to be company to anyone. Each morning Hana had fled the closeness of the sleeping quarters and spent most of the day huddled in a corner of the deck, listening to the lonely songs of some Russians also traveling to an alien land.

As the ship approached land, Hana hurried up to the deck to look out at the gray expanse

---

5. **brocades** (brō′ kādz′) **and lacquers** (lak′ ərz) n.: Brocades are rich cloths with raised designs; lacquers are highly polished, decorative pieces of wood.

Enoshima. Island at left with cluster of buildings among trees. Fuji in distance at right, c. 1823. (detail), Katsusika Hokusai, The Newark Museum

of ocean and sky, eager for a first glimpse of her new homeland.

"We won't be docking until almost noon," one of the deckhands told her.

Hana nodded, "I can wait," she answered, but the last hours seemed the longest.

When she set foot on American soil at last, it was not in the city of San Francisco as she had expected, but on Angel Island, where all third-class passengers were taken. She spent two miserable days and nights waiting, as the immigrants were questioned by officials, examined for trachoma[6] and tuberculosis, and tested for hookworm.[7] It was a bewildering, <u>degrading</u> beginning, and Hana was sick with anxiety, wondering if she would ever be released.

On the third day, a Japanese messenger from San Francisco appeared with a letter for her from Taro. He had written it the day of her arrival, but it had not reached her for two days.

Taro welcomed her to America, and told her that the bearer of the letter would inform Taro

▲ **Critical Viewing** This painting depicts a Japanese village like the one Hana left. Why would her arrival at Angel Island cause her confusion and worry? [**Infer**]

when she was to be released so he could be at the pier to meet her.

The letter eased her anxiety for a while, but as soon as she was released and boarded the launch for San Francisco, new fears rose up to smother her with a feeling almost of dread.

The early morning mist had become a light chilling rain, and on the pier black umbrellas bobbed here and there, making the task of recognition even harder. Hana searched desperately for a face that resembled the photo she had studied so long and hard. Suppose he hadn't come. What would she do then?

Hana took a deep breath, lifted her head and walked slowly from the launch. The moment she was on the pier, a man in a black coat, wearing a derby and carrying an umbrella, came quickly to her side. He was of slight build, not much taller than she, and his

---

6. **trachoma** (trə kō′ mə) *n*.: Contagious infection of the eyes.
7. **hookworm** (hŏŏk′ wurm′) *n*.: Disease caused by hookworms, small worms that attach themselves to the intestines.

◆ **Build Vocabulary**

degrading (dē grād′ iŋ) *adj*.: Insulting; dishonorable

face was sallow and pale. He bowed stiffly and murmured, "You have had a long trip, Miss Omiya. I hope you are well."

Hana caught her breath. "You are Takeda San?" she asked.

He removed his hat and Hana was further startled to see that he was already turning bald.

"You are Takeda San?" she asked again. He looked older than thirty-one.

"I am afraid I no longer resemble the early photo my parents gave you. I am sorry."

Hana had not meant to begin like this. It was not going well.

"No, no," she said quickly. "It is just that I . . . that is, I am terribly nervous. . . ." Hana stopped abruptly, too flustered to go on.

"I understand," Taro said gently. "You will feel better when you meet my friends and have some tea. Mr. and Mrs. Toda are expecting you in Oakland. You will be staying with them until . . ." He couldn't bring himself to mention the marriage just yet and Hana was grateful he hadn't.

He quickly made arrangements to have her baggage sent to Oakland, then led her carefully along the rain-slick pier toward the streetcar that would take them to the ferry.

Hana shuddered at the sight of another boat, and as they climbed to its upper deck she felt a queasy tightening of her stomach.

"I hope it will not rock too much," she said anxiously. "Is it many hours to your city?"

Taro laughed for the first time since their meeting, revealing the gold fillings of his teeth. "Oakland is just across the bay," he explained. "We will be there in twenty minutes."

Raising a hand to cover her mouth, Hana laughed with him and suddenly felt better. I am in America now, she thought, and this is the man I came to marry. Then she sat down carefully beside Taro, so no part of their clothing touched.

Guide for Responding

◆ LITERATURE AND YOUR LIFE

Reader's Response If you were Hana, would you feel you had made a mistake in coming to the United States?

Thematic Focus What is courageous about Hana's journey?

Journal Writing As Hana, write a brief diary entry to record your first impressions of Taro.

☑ Check Your Comprehension

1. What problems at home make Hana willing to go to the United States?
2. Why does her mother change her mind about the marriage?
3. What keeps Hana from befriending the other women on the ship?
4. Summarize what happens when she meets Taro.

◆ Critical Thinking

INTERPRET

1. How does a phrase like "the small ship that shuddered" reflect Hana's feelings about her voyage? **[Connect]**
2. In what way does the description of her life in Japan reveal that she is "spirited"? **[Support]**
3. What does Taro's behavior toward Hana suggest about his personality? **[Infer]**
4. What does the end of the story suggest about Hana's future happiness? Explain. **[Draw Conclusions]**

EXTEND

5. What do you think ended the custom of arranged marriages in modern societies? **[Social Studies Link]**

COMPARE LITERARY WORKS

6. In which of these stories does the main character face greater obstacles? Why? **[Compare and Contrast]**

Guide for Responding (continued)

◆ Reading Strategy

ASK QUESTIONS

By **asking questions** and answering them, you come to a more thorough understanding of the fictional worlds in "The Finish of Patsy Barnes" and "Tears of Autumn."

1. For each story, jot down a question you asked about a passage or phrase. Then, explain how you answered it or found the answer.
2. Identify a question you have about either of these stories that is still unanswered. Explain how you will answer it.

◆ Build Vocabulary

USING THE WORD ROOT -flu-

Explain how each of these -flu- words relates to the idea of flowing or movement. Use a dictionary if you need help.

1. influence
2. fluent
3. affluence
4. fluid

SPELLING STRATEGY

The long e sound in words such as *meager, peas,* and *league* is spelled *ea* rather than *ee.*

On your paper, write the answers to the following clues. Each answer is a word containing the *ea* spelling of the long e sound:

1. What you do as you look at the words on a page: _____?_____.
2. What you do as you get in front and show the way: _____?_____.

USING THE WORD BANK

On your paper, match each Word Bank word in the first column with the word or phrase closest in meaning in the second column.

1. compulsory   a. stubborn
2. meager   b. disturbed and wild
3. obdurate   c. wealth
4. diplomatic   d. required
5. turbulent   e. making one feel worthless
6. affluence   f. scanty; skimpy
7. degrading   g. polite in dealing with people

◆ Literary Focus

SETTING

The **setting** of these stories—where and when they take place—affects what happens in them. If Patsy Barnes hadn't grown up around horses, he wouldn't have learned how to ride. Also, if the city to which he moved didn't have a racetrack, he might have had no way to earn money.

1. Tell where and when each story takes place.
2. Attitudes are also part of the setting. Show how the doctor's prejudice influences Patsy.
3. Explain how a detail from the setting—including a belief or custom—influences Hana in "Tears of Autumn."

◆ Build Grammar Skills

SIMPLE AND COMPOUND SENTENCES

A **simple sentence** is one independent clause, and a **compound sentence** is two or more independent clauses joined by a coordinating conjunction or a semicolon.

Simple Sentence: Patsy was incorrigible.

Compound Sentence: His name was Patsy Barnes, and he was a denizen of Little Africa.

Practice On your paper, indicate which sentences are simple and which are compound. Underline each independent clause.

1. She wanted him to go to school.
2. The little mark of affection comforted Eliza unspeakably.
3. The boy would have retracted, but it was too late.
4. He knew that raw-boned frame and those flashing nostrils.
5. They were nearing the three-quarter post, and he was tightening his grip on the black.

Writing Application Choose one of these stories, and write a prediction about what will become of its main character. Use two simple and three compound sentences.

Build Your Portfolio

 ## Idea Bank

Writing

1. **Description** Find a passage in one of these stories that describes the setting. Then, write a paragraph of your own, continuing the description. Be sure that the details you make up are in keeping with the ones the author uses.

2. **Personal Letter** Write a letter home as Hana, telling about your first week in the United States. As an alternative, write as Patsy to a friend in Kentucky, telling him about the race.

3. **Critical Review** Write a review of either story, exploring in detail the use of setting within it. Use details from the story to support your views.

Speaking and Listening

4. **Monologue** Write a monologue—a speech revealing a character's inner thoughts—for Hana or Patsy. Rehearse your monologue, and perform it for the class. Tape-record your performance if possible. **[Performing Arts Link]**

5. **Sportscast** Reread the account of the race in "The Finish of Patsy Barnes." Then, adapt it as a script for a radio broadcast, and read it aloud to the class. **[Media Link]**

Projects

6. **Museum Display [Group Activity]** With a few classmates, create a museum display on immigration. Using history books and Web sites, research the emigration of African Americans from the South to the North or the emigration of Japanese to California. In a display, show what you've learned. **[Art Link; Social Studies Link]**

7. **Set Design** Design a set for a play based on one of these stories. Figure out how to suggest the story's setting on a stage. Sketch out your ideas, including notes on the set's dimensions and building materials. **[Art Link]**

 ## Writing Mini-Lesson

Comparison and Contrast

It's natural to compare these stories, which are set at about the same time. For example, both Patsy and Hana have to fight prejudice and take risks. Write a comparison-and-contrast essay about the stories, showing how they're alike and different.

**Writing Skills Focus:
Clear and Logical Organization**

Readers will follow your comparison more easily if it has a **clear and logical organization.** There are two basic types of organization that work well for a comparison-and-contrast paper. In subject-by-subject organization, you discuss one story first and then the next. In point-by-point organization, you discuss each point of comparison in turn.

Prewriting Decide which element of the stories you will compare and contrast—for example, the risks that the main characters take or the prejudices they face. Then, jot down ways in which this element is similar and different in both stories.

Drafting Choose a clear and logical organization, like one of those suggested in the Writing Skills Focus. Refer to your notes about similarities and differences as you write.

◆ **Grammar Application**

For variety, use both simple and compound sentences in your essay.

Revising Check that your organization is consistent. For example, if you included ideas about Hana in a paragraph devoted to Patsy, move these ideas to where they belong. If you forgot a summary, stating your conclusion, add it now.

uide for Reading

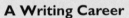

Meet the Authors:

Saki (H. H. Munro) (1870–1916)

Long before today's celebrities started using single names, H. H. Munro became famous under the pen name of Saki. Born to British parents in Burma (Myanmar), Saki was sent to England to be raised by two aunts after his mother died.

A Writing Career Plagued by illness for most of his life, Saki was unable to follow his father in a career as a Burmese police-man. However, Saki made his name as a witty newspaper writer in London. He also became famous for his humorous short stories, which often had surprise endings.

A Soldier's End Saki's own life ended with a surprise twist. After surviving all the illnesses in his life, he died a soldier in World War I.

Virginia Driving Hawk Sneve
(1933–   )

Virginia Driving Hawk Sneve (snā vē) grew up on the Sioux Reserva-tion in South Dakota. A writer and teacher, she has won many awards for her fiction. In novels like *Jimmy Yellow Hawk* and *High Elk's Treasure,* she draws on her inti-mate knowledge of Sioux life. Her Sioux heritage also plays an important role in "The Medicine Bag."

◆ LITERATURE AND YOUR LIFE
CONNECT YOUR EXPERIENCE

You've probably received gifts from older friends and family members. Some you can touch—for example, a ring passed down from a great-grandparent. Other gifts, just as valuable, touch your heart but cannot be physi-cally touched—for example, a wise or funny story.

These two stories deal with the gifts that adults give to young people, in a casual way or with great ceremony.

THEMATIC FOCUS: Appreciating Others

In what ways do the characters in these stories earn the gratitude of others?

◆ Background for Understanding
SOCIAL STUDIES

In "The Medicine Bag," you'll read about a young boy who receives his grandfather's medicine bag. For Native American groups living on the Great Plains, medicine bags were sacred gifts. A personal medicine bag would contain symbolic items that were suggested to an indi-vidual by a supernatural power. A tribal medicine bundle would contain items given to the group in ancient times.

◆ Build Vocabulary
SUFFIXES: -less

The suffix *-less* means "without." In "The Story-Teller," Saki writes that children moved *listlessly.* The word part *list-* means "to wish or desire," and *-less,* which acts as a "minus sign," changes the meaning to "without desire."

WORD BANK

Which of these words from the list describes someone who is not married? Check the Build Vocabulary box on page 597 to see if you chose correctly.

| bachelor |
| resolute |
| listlessly |
| authentic |
| procession |

The Story-Teller
◆ The Medicine Bag ◆

Story Teller, Velino "Shije" Herrera, National Museum of American Art, Washington, D.C.

◆ Literary Focus

THEME

The **theme** of a story—its insight into life—is a gift of meaning that the author gives you. Usually, you can sum up a story's theme in a sentence or two about people or life. Sometimes, an author hands you the gift of meaning and **states the theme** directly in the story. Other times, an author **implies the theme,** asking you to figure it out for yourself.

In each of these stories, the author implies the theme.

◆ Reading Strategy

MAKE INFERENCES

You must **make inferences,** reach conclusions based on evidence, to figure out an implied theme as you read. The evidence you use may include the way in which events develop, the contrasts between characters, and the changes in a character. Reflecting on these details, you decide what message they suggest about life and human relationships.

Use a flowchart like the one below to make inferences about these stories:

Detail	Reflection	Inference
The bachelor's frown turns to a scowl.	He is not happy.	The bachelor is annoyed with the children.

The Story-Teller
Saki

Stirling Station, 1887, William Kennedy, Collection of Andrew McIntosh Patrick, UK

▲ **Critical Viewing** Basing your answer on the details in this painting, describe what rail travel was like in the early 1900's in England. **[Draw Conclusions]**

It was a hot afternoon, and the railway carriage was correspondingly sultry, and the next stop was at Templecombe, nearly an hour ahead. The occupants of the carriage were a small girl, and a smaller girl, and a small boy. An aunt belonging to the children occupied one corner seat, and the further corner seat on the opposite side was occupied by a <u>bachelor</u> who was a stranger to their party, but the small girls and the small boy emphatically occupied the compartment. Both the aunt and the children were conversational in a limited, persistent way, reminding one of the attentions of a housefly that refused to be discouraged. Most of the aunt's remarks seemed to begin with "Don't," and nearly all of the children's remarks began with "Why?" The bachelor said nothing out loud.

"Don't, Cyril, don't," exclaimed the aunt, as the small boy began smacking the cushions of the seat, producing a cloud of dust at each blow.

"Come and look out of the window," she added.

The child moved reluctantly to the window. "Why are those sheep being driven out of that field?" he asked.

"I expect they are being driven to another field where there is more grass," said the aunt weakly.

"But there is lots of grass in that field," protested the boy; "there's nothing else but grass there. Aunt, there's lots of grass in that field."

"Perhaps the grass in the other field is better," suggested the aunt fatuously.[1]

"Why is it better?" came the swift, inevitable question.

"Oh, look at those cows!" exclaimed the aunt. Nearly every field along the line had contained cows or bullocks, but she spoke as

though she were drawing attention to a rarity.

"Why is the grass in the other field better?" persisted Cyril.

The frown on the bachelor's face was deepening to a scowl. He was a hard, unsympathetic man, the aunt decided in her mind. She was utterly unable to come to any satisfactory decision about the grass in the other field.

The smaller girl created a diversion by beginning to recite "On the Road to Mandalay."[2] She only knew the first line, but she put her limited knowledge to the fullest possible use. She repeated the line over and over again in a dreamy but <u>resolute</u> and very audible voice; it seemed to the bachelor as though someone had had a bet with her that she could not repeat the line aloud two thousand times without stopping. Whoever it was who had made the wager was likely to lose his bet.

"Come over here and listen to a story," said the aunt, when the bachelor had looked twice at her and once at the communication cord.

The children moved <u>listlessly</u> toward the aunt's end of the carriage. Evidently her reputation as a story-teller did not rank high in their estimation.

In a low, confidential voice, interrupted at frequent intervals by loud, petulant[3] questions

---

2. **"On the Road to Mandalay":** Poem by Rudyard Kipling.
3. **petulant** (pech' oo lənt) *adj.*: Impatient.

◆ **Build Vocabulary**

bachelor (bach' ə lər) *n.*: A man who has not married

resolute (rez' ə loot') *adj.*: Fixed in purpose; resolved

listlessly (list' lis lē) *adv.*: Without interest; spiritlessly

---

1. **fatuously** (fach' oo wəs lē) *adv.*: In a foolish way.

from her listeners, she began an unenterprising and deplorably uninteresting story about a little girl who was good, and made friends with everyone on account of her goodness, and was finally saved from a mad bull by a number of rescuers who admired her moral character.

"Wouldn't they have saved her if she hadn't been good?" demanded the bigger of the small girls. It was exactly the question that the bachelor had wanted to ask.

"Well, yes," admitted the aunt lamely, "but I don't think they would have run quite so fast to her help if they had not liked her so much."

"It's the stupidest story I've ever heard," said the bigger of the small girls, with immense conviction.

"I didn't listen after the first bit, it was so stupid," said Cyril.

The smaller girl made no actual comment on the story, but she had long ago recommenced a murmured repetition of her favorite line.

"You don't seem to be a success as a story-teller," said the bachelor suddenly from his corner.

The aunt bristled in instant defense at this unexpected attack.

"It's a very difficult thing to tell stories that children can both understand and appreciate," she said stiffly.

"I don't agree with you," said the bachelor.

"Perhaps *you* would like to tell them a story," was the aunt's retort.

"Tell us a story," demanded the bigger of the small girls.

"Once upon a time," began the bachelor, "there was a little girl called Bertha, who was extraordinarily good."

The children's momentarily aroused interest began at once to flicker; all stories seemed dreadfully alike, no matter who told them.

"She did all that she was told, she was always truthful, she kept her clothes clean, ate milk puddings as though they were jam tarts, learned her lessons perfectly, and was polite in her manners."

"Was she pretty?" asked the bigger of the small girls.

"Not as pretty as any of you." said the bachelor, "but she was horribly good."

There was a wave of reaction in favor of the story; the word horrible in connection with goodness was a novelty that commended itself. It seemed to introduce a ring of truth that was absent from the aunt's tales of infant life.

"She was so good," continued the bachelor, "that she won several medals for goodness, which she always wore, pinned on to her dress. There was a medal for obedience, another medal for punctuality, and a third for good behavior. They were large metal medals and they clinked against one another as she walked. No other child in town where she lived had as many as three medals, so everybody knew that she must be an extra good child."

"Horribly good," quoted Cyril.

"Everybody talked about her goodness, and the Prince of the country got to hear about it, and he said that as she was so very good she might be allowed once a week to walk in his park, which was just outside the town. It was a beautiful park, and no children were ever allowed in it, so it was a great honor for Bertha to be allowed to go there."

"Were there any sheep in the park?" demanded Cyril.

"No," said the bachelor, "there were no sheep."

"Why weren't there any sheep?" came the inevitable question arising out of that answer.

The aunt permitted herself a smile, which might almost have been described as a grin.

"There were no sheep in the park," said the bachelor, "because the Prince's mother had once had a dream that her son would either be killed by a sheep or else by a clock falling on him. For that reason the Prince never kept a sheep in his park or a clock in his palace."

The aunt suppressed a gasp of admiration.

"Was the Prince killed by a sheep or by a clock?" asked Cyril.

"He is still alive, so we can't tell whether the dream will come true," said the bachelor unconcernedly; "anyway, there were no sheep in the park, but there were lots of little pigs running all over the place."

"What color were they?"

"Black with white faces, white with black spots, black all over, gray with white patches, and some were white all over."

The story-teller paused to let a full idea of the park's treasures sink into the children's imaginations; then he resumed:

"Bertha was rather sorry to find that there were no flowers in the park. She had promised her aunts, with tears in her eyes, that she would not pick any of the kind Prince's flowers, and she had meant to keep her promise, so of course it made her feel silly to find that there were no flowers to pick."

"Why weren't there any flowers?"

"Because the pigs had eaten them all," said the bachelor promptly. "The gardeners had told the Prince that you couldn't have pigs and flowers, so he decided to have pigs and no flowers."

There was a murmur of approval at the excellence of the Prince's decision; so many people would have decided the other way.

"There were lots of other delightful things in the park. There were ponds with gold and blue and green fish in them, and trees with beautiful parrots that said clever things at a moment's notice, and hummingbirds that hummed all the popular tunes of the day. Bertha walked up and down and enjoyed herself immensely, and thought to herself: 'If I were not so extraordinarily good, I should not have been allowed to come into this beautiful park and enjoy all that there is to be seen in it,' and her three medals clinked against one another as she walked and helped to remind her how very good she really was. Just then an enormous wolf came prowling into the park to see if it could catch a fat little pig for its supper."

"What color was it?" asked the children, amid an immediate quickening of interest.

"Mud color all over, with a black tongue and pale gray eyes that gleamed with unspeakable ferocity. The first thing that it saw in the park was Bertha; her pinafore[4] was so spotlessly white and clean that it could be seen from a great distance. Bertha saw the wolf and saw that it was stealing toward her, and she began to wish that she had never been allowed to come into the park. She ran as hard as she could, and the wolf came after her with huge leaps and bounds. She managed to reach a shrubbery of myrtle bushes, and she hid herself in one of the thickest of the bushes. The wolf came sniffing among the branches, its black tongue lolling out of its mouth and its pale gray eyes glaring with rage. Bertha was terribly frightened, and thought to herself: 'If I had not been so extraordinarily good, I should have been safe in the town at this moment.' However, the scent of the myrtle was so strong that the wolf could not sniff out where Bertha was hiding, and the bushes were so thick that he might have hunted about in them for a long time without catching sight of her, so he thought he might as well go off and catch a little pig instead. Bertha was trembling very much at having the wolf prowling and sniffing so near her, and as she trembled the medal for obedience clinked against the medals for good conduct and punctuality. The wolf was just moving away when he heard the sound of the medals clinking and stopped to listen; they clinked again in a bush quite near him. He dashed into the bush, his pale gray eyes gleaming with ferocity and triumph, and dragged Bertha out and devoured her to the last morsel. All that was left of her were her shoes, bits of clothing, and the three medals for goodness."

"Were any of the little pigs killed?"

---

4. **pinafore** (pin´ ə fôr´) *n.*: An apronlike garment worn over a dress.

"No, they all escaped."

"The story began badly," said the smaller of the small girls, "but it had a beautiful ending."

"It is the most beautiful story that I ever heard," said the bigger of the small girls, with immense decision.

"It is the *only* beautiful story I have ever heard," said Cyril.

A dissentient[5] opinion came from the aunt.

"A most improper story to tell to young children! You have undermined the effect of years of careful teaching."

"At any rate," said the bachelor, collecting his belongings preparatory to leaving the carriage, "I kept them quiet for ten minutes, which was more than you were able to do."

"Unhappy woman!" he observed to himself as he walked down the platform of Templecombe station; "for the next six months or so those children will assail her in public with demands for an improper story!"

> ◆ **Literary Focus**
> What does the contrast between the two stories suggest about this story's theme?

---

5. **dissentient** (di sen´ shənt) *adj.*: Differing from the majority.

Guide for Responding

◆ LITERATURE AND YOUR LIFE

Reader's Response Did you like the bachelor's story? Why or why not?

Thematic Focus In addition to quieting the children, what message or moral does the bachelor's story teach them?

Story Guidelines [Group Activity] With several classmates, use the bachelor's tale to list some guidelines for children's stories. Jot down the qualities that make such stories effective.

☑ Check Your Comprehension

1. Describe the children's behavior at the start of the trip.
2. Why does the aunt decide to tell them a story?
3. How do the children react to her story?
4. (a) Summarize the story that the bachelor tells the children. (b) What is he able to accomplish that the aunt could not?

◆ Critical Thinking

INTERPRET

1. Why are the children unsatisfied by the aunt's answers to their questions? **[Infer]**
2. What makes the aunt's story "deplorably uninteresting"? **[Analyze]**
3. Why do you think the children like the use of the word "horribly" and the ending of the bachelor's story? **[Interpret]**
4. In general, what makes the bachelor's story more effective than the aunt's? **[Draw Conclusions]**
5. Are stories like the one the bachelor tells helpful to children? Why or why not? **[Evaluate]**

APPLY

6. Why do you think adults tell children stories that teach moral lessons? **[Speculate]**

CONNECTIONS TO TODAY'S WORLD

Saki's storyteller continues an age-old tradition: enthralling an audience through the magic of words and ideas. To this day, storytelling continues to be an important part of life, and it can take many forms— from a friend recounting a true-life event to a formal storytelling presentation, complete with costumes and props. The following article contains some storytelling tips that will help you to capture and hold the interest of your audience successfully.

How to Tell a Good Story
Chris Granstorm

Whether you're a grandmother with a lapful of youngsters, or a new parent tucking the kids into bed, whether you're telling stories about your own life, or spinning yarns about life in outer space, you'll need the same techniques for performing the story.

1. Select a story that's appropriate for you and your audience. Younger audiences like more action; older students and adults will enjoy more complex characters and humor.

2. Take time to memorize your story, and to practice it. But don't recite it verbatim. Allow it to develop itself each time you tell it. Visualize the scenes as you learn it and retell it. Stories with repetitive phrases are easier to remember. Practice telling the story to anyone who will listen.

3. Try to assure a favorable storytelling environment. Select a quiet location where your listeners can sit comfortably in a semicircle close to you.

4. Vary the pitch, tone and rhythm of your story. (You can learn this by watching good storytellers.) Except with young children, keep your gestures to a minimum—enrich the story with your eyes and facial expressions instead. Build to a climax, and when you get to the end, stop. Don't trail off.

5. Your voice can help listeners keep track of your characters, and it can convey moods and emotions. You can whisper, yell, moan, sigh and laugh. You can also select a different tone for each character. This is perhaps the most effective technique, but don't do it unless you're good at it.

6. Make eye contact. Look at your listeners directly. If you have a large crowd, pick a few faces around the audience, and beam the story to them.

7. Go slowly. Take your time and move gradually through the material. Vary the cadence of your voice, allow dramatic pauses. And, if you lose track of your place momentarily, don't get flustered, just take your time. You'll remember.

8. Use body language. Move around. Act out the scenes a little. But don't distract your audience. Find a comfortable level of theatrics.

---

1. Of these tips, which do you imagine the storyteller in Saki's story has mastered? Explain.

2. If you were to tell a story to very young children, would you use a lot of gestures? Why or why not?

3. Which of the tips listed come to you naturally? Which would you have to work on?

The Story-Teller ◆ 601

The Medicine Bag

Virginia Driving Hawk Sneve

My kid sister Cheryl and I always bragged about our Sioux[1] grandpa, Joe Iron Shell. Our friends, who had always lived in the city and only knew about Indians from movies and TV, were impressed by our stories. Maybe we exaggerated and made Grandpa and the reservation sound glamorous, but when we'd return home to Iowa after our yearly summer visit to Grandpa, we always had some exciting tale to tell.

We always had some <u>authentic</u> Sioux article to show our listeners. One year Cheryl had new moccasins[2] that Grandpa had made. On another visit he gave me a small, round, flat, rawhide drum that was decorated with a painting of a warrior riding a horse. He taught me a real Sioux chant to sing while I beat the drum with a leather-covered stick that had a feather on the end. Man that really made an impression.

We never showed our friends Grandpa's picture. Not that we were ashamed of him, but because we knew that the glamorous tales we told didn't go with the real thing. Our friends would have laughed at the picture because Grandpa wasn't tall and stately like TV Indians. His hair wasn't in braids but hung in stringy, gray strands on his neck, and he was old. He was our great-grandfather, and he didn't live in a tepee,[3] but all by himself in a part log, part tar-paper shack on the Rosebud Reservation[4]

---

1. Sioux (so͞o) *n.*: Native American tribes of the northern plains of the United States and nearby southern Canada.
2. moccasins (mäk´ ə sənz) *n.*: Heelless slippers of soft, flexible leather.
3. tepee (tē´ pē) *n.*: Cone-shaped tent of animal skins; used by the Plains Indians.

▲ **Critical Viewing** Do you think the medicine bag pictured was manufactured or handmade? How can you tell? **[Infer]**

◆ **Reading Strategy**
What inferences can you make about the narrator based on his conflicting attitudes toward his great-grandfather?

in South Dakota. So when Grandpa came to visit us, I was so ashamed and embarrassed I could've died.

There are a lot of yippy poodles and other fancy little dogs in our neighborhood, but they usually barked singly at the mailman from the safety of their own yards. Now it sounded as if a whole pack of mutts were barking together in one place.

I got up and walked to the curb to see what the commotion was. About a block away I saw a crowd of little kids yelling, with the dogs yipping and growling around someone who was walking down the middle of the street.

I watched the group as it slowly came closer and saw that in the center of the strange procession was a man wearing a tall black hat. He'd pause now and then to peer at something in his hand and then at the houses on either side of the street. I felt cold and hot at the same time as I recognized the man. "Oh, no!" I whispered. "It's Grandpa!"

I stood on the curb, unable to move even though I wanted to run and hide. Then I got mad when I saw how the yippy dogs were growling and nipping at the old man's baggy pant legs and how wearily he poked them away with his cane. "Stupid mutts," I said as I ran to rescue Grandpa.

When I kicked and hollered at the dogs to get away, they put their tails between their legs and scattered. The kids ran to the curb where they watched me and the old man.

"Grandpa," I said and felt pretty dumb when my voice cracked. I reached for his beat-up old tin suitcase, which was tied shut with a rope. But he set it down right in the street and shook my hand.

"*Hau, Takoza,* Grandchild," he greeted me formally in Sioux.

All I could do was stand there with the whole neighborhood watching and shake the hand of the leather-brown old man. I saw how his gray hair straggled from under his big black hat, which had a drooping feather in its crown. His rumpled black suit hung like a sack over his stooped frame. As he shook my hand, his coat fell open to expose a bright red satin shirt with a beaded bolo tie[5] under the collar. His get-up wasn't out of place on the reservation, but it sure was here, and I wanted to sink right through the pavement.

"Hi," I muttered with my head down. I tried to pull my hand away when I felt his bony hand trembling, and looked up to see fatigue in his face. I felt like crying. I couldn't think of anything to say so I picked up Grandpa's suitcase, took his arm, and guided him up the driveway to our house.

Mom was standing on the steps. I don't know how long she'd been watching, but her hand was over her mouth and she looked as if she couldn't believe what she saw. Then she ran to us.

---

4. Rosebud Reservation: Small Indian reservation in southcentral South Dakota.

5. bolo (bō′ lō) **tie** *n.*: String tie held together with a decorated sliding device.

◆ **Build Vocabulary**
authentic (ô then′ tik) *adj.*: Genuine; real
procession (prō sesh′ ən) *n.*: A group of people or things moving forward

"Grandpa," she gasped. "How in the world did you get here?"

She checked her move to embrace Grandpa and I remembered that such a display of affection is unseemly to the Sioux and would embarrass him.

"*Hau*, Marie," he said as he shook Mom's hand. She smiled and took his other arm.

As we supported him up the steps, the door banged open and Cheryl came bursting out of the house. She was all smiles and was so obviously glad to see Grandpa that I was ashamed of how I felt.

"Grandpa!" she yelled happily. "You came to see us!"

Grandpa smiled, and Mom and I let go of him as he stretched out his arms to my ten-year-old sister, who was still young enough to be hugged.

"*Wicincala*, little girl," he greeted her and then collapsed.

He had fainted. Mom and I carried him into her sewing room, where we had a spare bed.

After we had Grandpa on the bed, Mom stood there helplessly patting his shoulder.

"Shouldn't we call the doctor, Mom?" I suggested, since she didn't seem to know what to do.

"Yes," she agreed with a sigh. "You make Grandpa comfortable, Martin."

I reluctantly moved to the bed. I knew Grandpa wouldn't want to have Mom undress him, but I didn't want to, either. He was so skinny and frail that his coat slipped off easily. When I loosened his tie and opened his shirt collar, I felt a small leather pouch that hung from a thong[6] around his neck. I left it alone and moved to remove his boots. The scuffed old cowboy boots were tight, and he moaned as I put pressure on his legs to jerk them off.

---

6. **thong** *n.*: Narrow strip of leather.

I put the boots on the floor and saw why they fit so tight. Each one was stuffed with money. I looked at the bills that lined the boots and started to ask about them, but Grandpa's eyes were closed again.

Mom came back with a basin of water. "The doctor thinks Grandpa is suffering from heat exhaustion," she explained as she bathed Grandpa's face. Mom gave a big sigh, "*Oh, hinh*, Martin. How do you suppose he got here?"

We found out after the doctor's visit. Grandpa was angrily sitting up in bed while Mom tried to feed him some soup.

"Tonight you let Marie feed you, Grandpa," spoke my dad, who had gotten home from work just as the doctor was leaving. "You're not really sick," he said as he gently pushed Grandpa back against the pillows. "The doctor said you just got too tired and hot after your long trip."

Grandpa relaxed, and between sips of soup, he told us of his journey. Soon after our visit to him, Grandpa decided that he would like to see where his only living descendants lived and what our home was like. Besides, he admitted sheepishly, he was lonesome after we left.

I knew that everybody felt as guilty as I did—especially Mom. Mom was all Grandpa had left. So even after she married my dad, who's a white man and teaches in the college in our city, and after Cheryl and I were born, Mom made sure that every summer we spent a week with Grandpa.

I never thought that Grandpa would be lonely after our visits, and none of us noticed how old and weak he had become. But Grandpa knew, and so he came to us. He had ridden on buses for two and a half days. When he arrived in the city, tired and stiff from sitting for so long, he set out, walking, to find us.

He had stopped to rest on the steps of

some building downtown, and a policeman found him. The cop, according to Grandpa, was a good man who took him to the bus stop and waited until the bus came and told the driver to let Grandpa out at Bell View Drive. After Grandpa got off the bus, he started walking again. But he couldn't see the house numbers on the other side when he walked on the sidewalk, so he walked in the middle of the street. That's when all the little kids and dogs followed him.

I knew everybody felt as bad as I did. Yet I was so proud of this eighty-six-year-old man, who had never been away from the reservation, having the courage to travel so far alone.

"You found the money in my boots?" he asked Mom.

"Martin did," she answered, and roused herself to scold. "Grandpa, you shouldn't have carried so much money. What if someone had stolen it from you?"

Grandpa laughed. "I would've known if anyone tried to take the boots off my feet. The money is what I've saved for a long time—a hundred dollars—for my funeral. But you take it now to buy groceries so that I won't be a burden to you while I am here."

"That won't be necessary, Grandpa," Dad said. "We are honored to have you with us, and you will never be a burden. I am only sorry that we never thought to bring you home with us this summer and spare you the discomfort of a long trip."

Grandpa was pleased. "Thank you," he answered. "But do not feel bad that you didn't bring me with you, for I would not have come then. It was not time." He said this in such a way that no one could argue with him. To Grandpa and the Sioux, he once told me, a thing would be done when it was the right time to do it, and that's the way it was.

"Also," Grandpa went on, looking at me, "I have come because it is soon time for Martin to have the medicine bag."

"I have come because it is soon time for Martin to have the medicine bag."

We all knew what that meant. Grandpa thought he was going to die, and he had to follow the tradition of his family to pass the medicine bag, along with its history, to the oldest male child.

"Even though the boy," he said still looking at me, "bears a white man's name, the medicine bag will be his."

I didn't know what to say. I had the same hot and cold feeling that I had when I first saw Grandpa in the street. The medicine bag was the dirty leather pouch I had found around his neck. "I could never wear such a thing," I almost said aloud. I thought of having my friends see it in gym class or at the swimming pool and could imagine the smart things they would say. But I just swallowed hard and took a step toward the bed. I knew I would have to take it.

But Grandpa was tired. "Not now, Martin," he said, waving his hand in dismissal. "It is not time. Now I will sleep."

So that's how Grandpa came to be with us for two months. My friends kept asking to come see the old man, but I put them off. I told myself that I didn't want them laughing at Grandpa. But even as I made excuses, I knew it wasn't Grandpa that I was afraid they'd laugh at.

Nothing bothered Cheryl about bringing her friends to see Grandpa. Every day after school started, there'd be a crew of giggling little girls or round-eyed little boys crowded around the old man on the patio, where he'd gotten in the habit of sitting every afternoon.

Grandpa would smile in his gentle way and patiently answer their questions, or he'd tell them stories of brave warriors, ghosts, animals; and the kids listened in awed silence. Those little guys thought Grandpa was great.

◆ Literary Focus
What does Martin's reaction to the medicine bag reveal about his attitude toward his Sioux heritage?

Finally, one day after school, my friends came home with me because nothing I said stopped them. "We're going to see the great Indian of Bell View Drive," said Hank, who was supposed to be my best friend. "My brother has seen him three times so he oughta be well enough to see us."

When we got to my house, Grandpa was sitting on the patio. He had on his red shirt, but today he also wore a fringed leather vest that was decorated with beads. Instead of his usual cowboy boots, he had solidly beaded moccasins on his feet that stuck out of his black trousers. Of course, he had his old black hat on—he was seldom without it. But it had been brushed, and the feather in the beaded head-band was proudly erect, its tip a brighter white. His hair lay in silver strands over the red shirt collar.

I stared just as my friends did, and I heard one of them murmur, "Wow!"

Grandpa looked up, and, when his eyes met mine, they twinkled as if he were laughing inside. He nodded to me, and my face got all hot. I could tell that he had known all along I was afraid he'd embarrass me in front of my friends.

"*Hau, hoksilas,* boys," he greeted and held out his hand.

My buddies passed in a single file and shook his hand as I introduced them. They were so polite I almost laughed. "How, there, Grandpa," and even a "How-do-you-do, sir."

"You look fine, Grandpa," I said as the guys sat on the lawn chairs or on the patio floor.

"*Hanh,* yes," he agreed. "When I woke up this morning, it seemed the right time to dress in the good clothes. I knew that my grandson would be bringing his friends."

"You guys want some lemonade or something?" I offered. No one answered. They were listening to Grandpa as he started telling how he'd killed the deer from which his vest was made.

Grandpa did most of the talking while my friends were there. I was so proud of him and amazed at how respect-fully quiet my buddies were. Mom had to chase them home at supper time. As they left, they shook Grandpa's hand again and said to me,

"Martin, he's really great!"

"Yeah, man! Don't blame you for keeping him to yourself."

"Can we come back?"

But after they left, Mom said, "No more visitors for a while, Martin. Grandpa won't admit it, but his strength hasn't returned. He likes having company, but it tires him."

That evening Grandpa called me to his room before he

went to sleep. "Tomorrow," he said, "when you come home, it will be time to give you the medicine bag."

I felt a hard squeeze from where my heart is supposed to be and was scared, but I answered, "OK, Grandpa."

All night I had weird dreams about thunder and lightning on a high hill. From a distance I heard the slow beat of a drum. When I woke up in the morning, I felt as if I hadn't slept at all. At school it seemed as if the day would never end and, when it finally did, I ran home.

Grandpa was in his room, sitting on the bed.

▲ **Critical Viewing** How does this scene fit the image of a vision quest as described on page 608? Explain. [**Connect**]

The shades were down, and the place was dim and cool. I sat on the floor in front of Grandpa, but he didn't even look at me. After what seemed a long time he spoke.

"I sent your mother and sister away. What you will hear today is only for a man's ears. What you will receive is only for a man's hands." He fell silent, and I felt shivers down my back.

"My father in his early manhood," Grandpa

began, "made a vision quest[7] to find a spirit guide for his life. You cannot understand how it was in that time, when the great Teton Sioux were first made to stay on the reservation. There was a strong need for guidance from *Wakantanka*,[8] the Great Spirit. But too many of the young men were filled with despair and hatred. They thought it was hopeless to search for a vision when the glorious life was gone and only the hated confines of a reservation lay ahead. But my father held to the old ways.

"He carefully prepared for his quest with a purifying sweat bath, and then he went alone to a high butte top[9] to fast and pray. After three days he received his sacred dream—in which he found, after long searching, the white man's iron. He did not understand his vision of finding something belonging to the white people, for in that time they were the enemy. When he came down from the butte to cleanse himself at the stream below, he found the remains of a campfire and the broken shell of an iron kettle. This was a sign that reinforced his dream. He took a piece of the iron for his medicine bag, which he had made of elk skin years before, to prepare for his quest.

"He returned to his village, where he told his dream to the wise old men of the tribe. They gave him the name *Iron Shell*, but neither did they understand the meaning of the dream. The first Iron Shell kept the piece of iron with him at all times and believed it gave him protection from the evils of those unhappy days.

"Then a terrible thing happened to Iron Shell. He and several other young men were taken from their homes by the soldiers and sent far away to a white man's boarding school. He was angry and lonesome for his parents and the young girl he had wed before he was taken away. At first Iron Shell resisted the teacher's attempts to change him, and he did not try to learn. One day it was his turn to work in the school's blacksmith shop. As he walked into the place, he knew that his medicine had brought him there to learn and work with the white man's iron.

"Iron Shell became a blacksmith and worked at the trade when he returned to the reservation. All of his life he treasured the medicine bag. When he was old, and I was a man, he gave it to me, for no one made the vision quest any more."

Grandpa quit talking, and I stared in disbelief as he covered his face with his hands. His shoulders were shaking with quiet sobs, and I looked away until he began to speak again.

"I kept the bag until my son, your mother's father, was a man and had to leave us to fight in the war across the ocean. I gave him the bag, for I believed it would protect him in battle, but he did not take it with him. He was afraid that he would lose it. He died in a faraway place."

Again Grandpa was still, and I felt his grief around me.

"My son," he went on after clearing his throat, "had only a daughter, and it is not proper for her to know of these things."

He unbuttoned his shirt, pulled out the leather pouch, and lifted it over his head. He held it in his hand, turning it over and over as if memorizing how it looked.

"In the bag," he said as he opened it and removed two objects, "is the broken shell of the iron kettle, a pebble from the butte, and a piece of the sacred sage."[10] He held the pouch upside down and dust drifted down.

"After the bag is yours you must put a piece of prairie sage within and never open it again until you pass it on to your son." He replaced the pebble and the piece of iron, and tied the bag.

I stood up, somehow knowing I should. Grandpa slowly rose from the bed and stood

---

7. vision quest: A search for a revelation that would aid understanding.

8. Wakantanka (wä′ kən tank′ ə) *n.*: The Sioux religion's most important spirit—the creator of the world.

9. butte (byo͞ot) **top** *n.*: Top of a steep hill standing alone in a plain.

10. sage: (sāj) *n.*: Plant belonging to the mint family.

upright in front of me holding the bag before my face. I closed my eyes and waited for him to slip it over my head. But he spoke.

"No, you need not wear it." He placed the soft leather bag in my right hand and closed my other hand over it. "It would not be right to wear it in this time and place where no one will understand. Put it safely away until you are again on the reservation. Wear it then, when you replace the sacred sage."

Grandpa turned and sat again on the bed. Wearily he leaned his head against the pillow. "Go," he said. "I will sleep now."

"Thank you, Grandpa," I said softly and left with the bag in my hands.

Beyond Literature

Cultural Connection

The Sioux Grandpa Joe lived on a Sioux reservation. The Sioux used to live throughout the northern plains of North America, and they were famous for their bravery and fighting ability.

Tension developed and increased between the Sioux and the United States in the mid-1800's. The two main reasons for this friction were settlers' slaughtering of the buffalo and gold prospectors' violating the sacred Black Hills. The United States decided to settle the conflict by forcing the Sioux onto reservations. Many Sioux decided to fight, led by the famous chiefs Sitting Bull and Crazy Horse. They were eventually defeated, but not before inflicting a major defeat on the United States Army by killing the celebrated Civil War hero George Custer and his troops at Little Big Horn.

Cross-Curricular Activity
Research the Battle of Little Big Horn, and create an illustrated map showing the opposing forces and areas of battle. Post your map in the classroom.

That night Mom and Dad took Grandpa to the hospital. Two weeks later I stood alone on the lonely prairie of the reservation and put the sacred sage in my medicine bag.

Guide for Responding

◆ LITERATURE AND YOUR LIFE

Reader's Response What items do you own that have a special meaning for you? Explain.

Thematic Focus In what way does Martin come to appreciate his grandfather?

☑ Check Your Comprehension

1. Describe how each family member welcomes Grandpa.
2. What three reasons for coming does Grandpa give?
3. How does Martin's attitude toward the medicine bag change after his friends visit Grandpa?
4. What does Martin do at the very end of the story?

◆ Critical Thinking

INTERPRET
1. What causes Martin to feel ashamed when his Grandpa suddenly appears? **[Analyze]**
2. How do the events of the story support Grandpa's idea that things will be done when it's "the right time"? **[Support]**
3. In what way does the Sioux heritage Martin brags about differ at first from the Sioux heritage Grandpa describes to him? **[Compare and Contrast]**
4. What does Martin's final action in the story reveal about his relationship to his heritage? **[Draw Conclusions]**

COMPARE LITERARY WORKS
5. In what way do both the bachelor in "The Story-Teller" and Grandpa in "The Medicine Bag" influence the lives of others? **[Compare and Contrast]**

Guide for Responding (continued)

◆ Reading Strategy

MAKE INFERENCES

Making inferences involves formulating ideas based on evidence. Making inferences while you read helps you build toward an understanding of the theme. For example, you may have inferred that Martin's "glamorous tales" about his Sioux heritage in "The Medicine Bag" show his insecurity.

1. In "The Story-Teller," what does the term "horribly good" suggest about the bachelor's knowledge of children?
2. How does Grandpa's success with Martin's friends relate to Martin's agreement to receive the medicine bag?

◆ Build Vocabulary

USING THE SUFFIX -less

The suffix -less in listless means "without." Explain how adding the suffix -less to each of these good qualities turns them into negative ones:

1. care   2. faith   3. help   4. mind   5. rest

SPELLING STRATEGY

When a noun refers to a person or thing that does something, spell the final ur sound or:

direct + or = director   confess + or = confessor

On your paper, write the noun that corresponds to each verb:

1. collect   3. connect   5. process
2. direct   4. calculate

USING THE WORD BANK

On your paper, fill in each blank with a suitable word from the Word Bank.

1. Despite problems, Grandpa is ____?____ in locating his family.
2. The children approached ____?____ to hear the boring story.
3. The ____?____ had never met a woman he wanted to marry.
4. The museum displayed an ____?____ medicine bag.
5. The ____?____ consisted of three kids, a dog, and Grandpa.

◆ Literary Focus

THEME

Some stories have **themes**—insights into life—that are **stated** directly. However, these two stories have **implied** themes, so you must figure out the author's message. In "The Story-Teller," the contrast between the aunt's dull story and the bachelor's lively tale leads you to the theme.

1. State the theme of "The Story-Teller" by completing this sentence in your notebook: The contrast between the stories shows that children _____?_____.
2. Reflecting on Martin's change of heart in "The Medicine Bag," state an insight about the importance of heritage.

◆ Build Grammar Skills

COMPLEX SENTENCES

A **complex sentence** contains one independent clause and one or more subordinate clauses. Here is an example of a complex sentence from "The Medicine Bag":

┌──── **independent clause** ────┐
One year Cheryl had new moccasins

┌── **subordinate clause** ──┐
that Grandpa had made.

Practice On your paper, identify the independent and subordinate clauses in the following complex sentences.

1. "Wouldn't they have saved her if she hadn't been good?"
2. "It is a very difficult thing to tell stories that children can both understand and appreciate."
3. "I kept them quiet for ten minutes, which was more than you were able to do."
4. Our friends would have laughed at the picture because Grandpa wasn't tall and stately like TV Indians.
5. Mom and I carried him into her sewing room, where we had a spare bed.

Writing Application Using five complex sentences, describe a gift you have received from an older friend or family member.

Build Your Portfolio

 ## Idea Bank

Writing

1. **List** Write a list of items you'd like to put in your own medicine bag.

2. **Compare and Contrast** Compare and contrast the aunt's ideas about the upbringing of children with the bachelor's. Use details from "The Story-Teller" to support your points.

3. **Analysis and Evaluation** In a brief essay, analyze the importance of the title for either story. Make inferences about why the author chose it and how it relates to the theme. Then, after considering alternative titles, decide whether the original is the best choice.

Speaking and Listening

4. **Storytelling** Like the bachelor in "The Story-Teller," write a story that is sure to interest young children. Practice reading your story aloud, and then tell it to your classmates. **[Performing Arts Link]**

5. **DJ's Rap** Brainstorm for a group of songs that deal with a similar theme—for example, the trials and tribulations of love. Then, play the songs for the class, introducing each one with a speech that links it to the other songs. **[Music Link; Career Link]**

Projects

6. **Space Capsule [Group Activity]** A space capsule is like a medicine bag for our planet. With two classmates, choose five items that convey the theme of friendship to include in a capsule aimed at a distant star. Write a brief explanation to go with each item. **[Science Link]**

7. **Travel Itinerary** Using travel guides and other resources, create a one-week automobile tour of Sioux sites in South Dakota. Indicate mileage, travel time, and hotels or motels. Also, summarize the historical importance of each site on the tour. **[Social Studies Link]**

 ## Writing Mini-Lesson

Book Jacket

Like the tale of Bertha in "The Story-Teller," a book jacket tries to be lively and engaging. It gives you a taste of the plot, characters, setting, and theme of a story—just enough to make you want to buy it. Write a book jacket for one of these stories that will have readers reaching for their wallets.

Writing Skills Focus: Supporting Details

Make your book jacket engaging by providing **supporting details** from the story—brief quotations, summaries, or descriptions. This passage from the jacket of Amy Tan's *The Kitchen God's Wife* entices you with a summary of the plot and details of the characters and setting:

Model of Real-World Writing
"Thus begins an unfolding of secrets that takes mother and daughter back to a small island outside Shanghai in the 1920s. . . ."

Prewriting Decide how much of the story's plot you can summarize without giving away the ending. Also, review the story for details that will illustrate the characters, setting, and theme in a lively way.

Drafting Imagine that you're facing the customer, trying to sell the book. Give a partial summary of the plot, breaking off at a suspenseful point. Also, use details from the story to support what you say about plot, characters, setting, or theme.

> ◆ **Grammar Application**
>
> When you use complex sentences in your book jacket, put a main idea in the independent clause and a less important idea in the subordinate clause.

Revising Have a few classmates read your book jacket. If it doesn't interest them in the story, use livelier details to support your descriptions of the story's elements.

Literary Analysis

Writing Process Workshop

Have you ever discussed a book with a friend and traded opinions on the best and worst parts of it? If you have, you were doing a literary analysis. A literary analysis is a response to a work of literature in which you closely examine the work by taking it apart and discussing its various elements.

Write a literary analysis of one of the short stories in this section. Use the following skills, introduced in the Writing Mini-lessons in this section, to help you:

Writing Skills Focus

▶ **Use supporting details** to back up your ideas about the work. Use quotations and specific examples from the literature. (See p. 611.)

▶ **Use a clear organization.** Include an introduction, body, and conclusion. Organize details in a logical way, such as from the least important to the most important or vice versa. (See p. 593.)

▶ **Be accurate** when referring to titles, author's names, dates, or when using exact quotations.

The following excerpt from a student's literary analysis shows these skills:

MODEL FROM LITERATURE

"The Finish of Patsy Barnes" by Paul Laurence Dunbar

"The Finish of Patsy Barnes" by Paul Laurence Dunbar illustrates a young boy's determination to help a sick parent. ① He plans to win enough money racing a horse to get a good doctor for his mother. The determination is evident in Dunbar's description of Patsy's motivation: "For a single moment Patsy thinks of the sick woman at home and what that race will mean to her, and then his knees close against the horse's sides with a firmer dig." ② Barnes wins the race and helps his mother, but the real story lies in the many incidents that lead up to the race. First, ... ③

① The title and author are spelled and punctuated correctly.

② A quotation supports the writer's analysis of the author's purpose.

③ The writer plans to organize the paper by listing the events that lead to the climax of the story. The transition word *first* indicates that he will explain events in order.

Prewriting

Focus Your Topic Explore your reactions to the work you've chosen. You won't be able to include everything you think and feel about the work, so concentrate on one of its literary elements, such as setting, character, plot, or theme.

Interview Yourself Answer the following questions about the story you've chosen to analyze:

▶ What were the most enjoyable and interesting parts of the story? Why?

▶ What was especially memorable about the story? Explain.

▶ Which characters came to life in an especially vivid way? How did the writer achieve this effect?

▶ What was unique about the setting?

▶ Would you recommend this book to others?

Use your answers to provide content for your paper.

Gather Supporting Details Make a list of the key points you are going to address in your literary analysis. Then, find specific examples from the short story that support each point. For example:

Tears of Autumn

Key Point: The author uses vivid descriptions of the settings; she includes details that help you visualize the places Hana describes.

Supporting Example: "She longed to see the bright persimmon dotting the barren trees beside the thatched roofs, to see the fields of golden rice stretching to the mountains where only last fall she had gathered plum white mushrooms, and to see once more the maple trees lacing their flaming colors through the green pine."

Drafting

Grab Your Readers Write an introduction that grabs your readers' attention. Use a quotation from the story, a startling fact, or a thought-provoking question to begin your paper.

Include Key Points The body of your paper includes the key points that you have already listed. Choose a logical organization for your points, such as order of importance. Incorporate quotations from the story to support your points.

Summarize Complete your analysis with a brief summary of your main points. Restate your main idea, and make a final compelling point.

APPLYING LANGUAGE SKILLS: Avoiding Wordiness

Clean up your writing by getting rid of words that aren't necessary to the meaning:

Wordy: Although Patsy Barnes has never been a jockey who rode a horse before, he rides the black stallion named Black Boy in a race and even wins.

Clean: Although Patsy has never been a jockey, he rides Black Boy and wins.

Practice Rewrite these sentences to eliminate wordiness:

1. Patsy's mother needs a good doctor who can take care of her because she is sick with pneumonia and can't really get out of bed.
2. Patsy is a stubborn boy who won't listen to his mother when she tells him not to go to the racetrack.
3. Mr. Brackett, the owner of the horse that wins the race, is very happy when Patsy wins the race.

Writing Application In your paper, create sentences that are clear and concise.

Writer's Solution Connection Language Lab

For practice eliminating unnecessary words, complete the lesson Eliminating Unnecessary Words.

Applying LANGUAGE SKILLS: Writing Titles Correctly

Different titles are punctuated differently. In general, if a work is short, its title goes in quotation marks. If a work is long, its title is underlined or written in italics.

Underline or italicize a novel or full-length play:
Black Beauty or Black Beauty

Enclose a short story, poem, or essay in quotation marks:
"January"

Practice Copy the following sentences, punctuating the titles correctly.

1. The novel "War and Peace" has over 1,000 pages!
2. The short story <u>The Tell-Tale Heart</u> scared me.
3. Is <u>The Bat</u> a poem about baseball?

Writing Application In your literary analysis, punctuate titles correctly.

Writer's Solution Connection Writing Lab

To check whether your organization is clear and logical, use the Revision Checker for Unity and Coherence in the Revising and Editing section of the Response to Literature tutorial.

Revising

Use a Checklist Use the following checklist to help you revise your literary analysis.

▶ Are there enough supporting details to make key points understandable? *If not, find additional examples from the story to support points you are making about the work of literature.*

▶ Does the analysis have a clear introduction, body, and conclusion? *Make sure that you state your main idea in your introduction, discuss it in the body, and refer to it in your conclusion.*

▶ Are details organized in a logical way? *If not, reorganize them in a way that will help your readers follow your points, such as order of importance.*

▶ Do you refer to titles and use quotations accurately? *Double-check against the text all quotations taken from the story. Also, make sure you have punctuated titles correctly.*

REVISION MODEL

① Imagine reading an action story and not knowing where it took place or the time period in which it occurred?
A story is incomplete without a description of the setting.

② "
The settings in Tears of Autumn by Yoshiko Uchida help
"
the reader visualize the scenes that the main character,

③ Uchida uses such phrases as "plum white mushrooms" and "maple trees lacing their flaming colors through the green pine" to help us visualize the scenes.
Hana, describes.

① The writer adds to the introduction to grab the readers' attention.
② A short-story title must be enclosed in quotation marks.
③ These quotations from the story support the writer's point that Uchida describes settings beautifully.

Publishing and Presenting

Classroom Use a camcorder to tape a 20-minute program that analyzes several stories, poems, and essays for a young audience. With several classmates, take turns reading your analyses in front of the camera. Share your program with other students.

Library Combine your essays into a class literary magazine, and give the magazine a table of contents and an introduction. Display it in your school library.

Real-World Reading Skills Workshop

Recognizing Bias

Strategies for Success

Short stories, poems, and personal essays are shaped by the writer's personal beliefs and opinions. Other types of writing, such as news articles or informative articles in a magazine, are meant to be objective but sometimes show a bias—a leaning toward a certain position. Use the following strategies to help you recognize bias:

Look for Loaded Words Writers often use words loaded with emotional meanings. For example, calling someone *self-confident* gives a positive slant to a person's actions. The same actions could be described as *arrogant* or *conceited*, which have negative connotations. Words like these might reflect the writer's bias.

Be Aware of Stereotypes Stereotypes unfairly suggest that all members of a group are exactly the same. A stereotype creates a label that ignores each person's individual differences. Statements like "all teenagers watch too much television" are misleading and show a bias against teenagers.

Examine Slanted Arguments A slanted argument promotes only one side of an issue and omits information that goes against that side. For example, a candidate for student government might tell students that he has attended every student government meeting in the last three months—but leave out that he had missed all the previous meetings. This misinformation is biased. It may lead people to believe an untruth.

Apply the Strategies

Read this article from the *Marston News,* and answer the questions that follow.

New Leash Law in Marston

Proponents of a stricter leash law have finally scared the town leaders into accepting a new leash law. Citing the many individuals (seven reported cases) who have been mauled by crazed dogs, these people have gotten their way. Dogs can no longer be off their leashes any place in Marston, including the back field at Cold Creek Park, for years an accepted and safe place for dogs to run. Now all these dangerous tiny toy poodles and Chihuahuas will be controlled.

1. What words in this article have negative meanings?
2. Has the writer used stereotypes to describe anyone in the article? Explain.
3. Point out the writer's slanted arguments.
4. Do you think the writer of this news article has a bias? If so, describe it.

✔ *Watch for bias in these places:*
► Editorials
► Letters to the editor
► Regular feature columns in the newspaper
► Petitions

Sentence Structure Grammar Review

Sentences can be classified according to the number and kinds of clauses they contain. Sentences are either simple, compound, or complex.

Simple Sentences Simple sentences consist of one independent clause. (See page 592.) A simple sentence may have a compound subject or a compound verb, as well as modifiers and complements, but it does not contain a subordinate clause.

   S   V   V

"She clung to the moist rail and breathed the damp salt air deep into her lungs."

Compound Sentences A compound sentence contains two or more independent clauses. The independent clauses are joined by a comma and a coordinating conjunction (*and, but, for, nor, or, so, yet*) or sometimes by a semicolon. Compound sentences do not contain subordinate clauses:

        S   V   S V

His name was Patsy Barnes, and he was a denizen of Little Africa.

Complex Sentences A complex sentence contains one independent clause and one or more subordinate clauses. (See page 610.)

Independent Clause	Subordinate Clause
S V	S V
It all began one day	when her uncle had come

to visit her mother.

Practice 1 In your notebook, identify the following sentences as simple, compound, or complex.

1. Her uncle spoke freely of Taro Takedao only because he was so sure Hana . . .

2. A man's word carried much weight for Hana's mother.

3. In none did he disclose his loneliness or his need, but Hana understood this.

4. The horse that has taken away his father shall give him back his mother.

5. We are honored to have you with us, and you will never be a burden.

Practice 2 Combine the following pairs of sentences into one sentence as indicated.

1. There are a lot of yippy little dogs in our neighborhood. They usually bark at the mailman from the safety of their own yards. (compound sentence)

2. Bertha was sad. There were no flowers in the park. (complex sentence using the subordinating conjunction *because*)

3. Cheryl and her brother adored their grandfather. He was a Sioux Indian. (complex sentence using the relative pronoun *who*)

4. An agreement to the marriage was almost reached. Taro wrote his first letter to Hana. (complex sentence using the subordinating conjunction *when*)

Grammar in Writing

✔ *Do not join independent clauses with a comma. If you do, you create a run-on sentence—an error to be avoided. If you use a comma between independent clauses, you must also use a coordinating conjunction.*

Speaking, Listening, and Viewing Workshop

Conducting interviews is a great way to gather information. Whether you use the telephone or meet person to person, interviewing provides you with firsthand information about your subject.

Plan Your Questions Before you begin, research your topic so you can ask appropriate questions. List specific things you want to find out in the interview. Ask questions that cannot be answered with a simple yes or no but that require elaboration or explanation.

Prepare for Responses As an interviewer, you must be ready to record information quickly. If you conduct an interview in person, ask your subject for permission to tape-record the interview. If you are not using a tape recorder, jot down key words and phrases that will help you remember the entire answer later. If you missed part of an answer, politely ask the speaker to repeat it.

Apply the Strategies

Practice interviewing strategies by doing the following activities:

1. Ask a peer about his or her last vacation. Before interviewing, find out where he or she visited and gather information about the vacation spot. Then, develop questions that will get firsthand descriptions and opinions of the vacation spot.

2. Interview an older family member about a period of history that he or she experienced. Research that period of time, and construct intelligent questions before the interview.

3. Conduct a telephone interview about a product or service that interests you. Before getting on the phone, have a list of questions ready, along with a pen and paper to jot down notes.

Strategies for Interviewing

✔ *To conduct a successful interview, follow these strategies:*

► *For an in-person interview, dress appropriately and arrive promptly.*

► *Be respectful when the speaker is answering your questions. Pay attention, and do not interrupt.*

► *Be polite. Begin and end the interview by thanking the person for his or her time.*

What's Behind the Words

Vocabulary Adventures With Richard Lederer

Phobia Words

Do you have a pet fear? No? Think again. Does your stomach want to scream when it and you arrive at the zenith of a Ferris wheel? Does your head retract turtlelike into your body when lightning flashes and thunder cracks? Does a snake send your mind into a spin cycle?

Fearsome Phobias

Excessive fears are called phobias. In ancient Greek mythology, Phobos was the son of the god of war. The names of our deepest dreads generally include the Greek root *phobia,* meaning "fear" or "hatred." The two most common human phobias are *acrophobia,* a fear of heights, and *claustrophobia,* a fear of enclosed spaces. By giving names to these terrors, you may be taking the first step in overcoming them.

What's Your Phobia?

The charts below list some of people's most persistent fears, along with the names we have assigned to them.

Fears of Animals	
1. bees	apiphobia
2. cats	ailurophobia
3. dogs	cynophobia
4. sharks	galeophobia
5. spiders	arachnophobia

Fears of Nature	
1. comets	cometophobia
2. darkness	nyctophobia
3. fire	pyrophobia
4. the sea	thalassophobia
5. water	hydrophobia

Fearless About Phobias

Enough people fear the number thirteen that many buildings pretend not to have a thirteenth floor. Still, we assign this dread a name—*triskaidekaphobia,* from *tris,* "three," *kai,* "and," *deka,* "ten," and *phobia,* "fear." Incredible as it may seem, there is even a label for the fear of getting peanut butter stuck to the roof of the mouth. It's called *arachibutyrophobia.*

When President Franklin Delano Roosevelt said, in his 1933 inaugural address, "The only thing we have to fear is fear itself," he was warning us against *phobophobia,* the fear of being afraid. Now that you know that all your phobias have names, you may experience less fear about your fears—and about fear itself.

ACTIVITY 1 Here's a quiz about other psychological fears. Match each fear in the left column with its corresponding phobia in the right column.

1. fear of numbers   **a.** agoraphobia
2. fear of spirits or goblins   **b.** bogyphobia
3. fear of open spaces   **c.** chronophobia
4. fear of speaking in public   **d.** numerophobia
5. fear of time   **e.** phonophobia
6. fear of strangers   **f.** xenophobia

ACTIVITY 2 Make up three original phobias and a name for each. Example: *malohumorophobia,* a fear of bad jokes.

Extended Reading Opportunities

Throughout time, people have told stories in an attempt to share the human experience. While Poe's collection of short stories explores the darker side of humanity, the other collections celebrate the diversity of the American experience.

Suggested Titles

18 Best Stories by Edgar Allan Poe
Vincent Price and Chandler Brossard, Editors

Poe's most terrifying and hair-raising stories can be found in this collection. Introduced by co-editor and master of movie horror Vincent Price, the reader begins a journey into the most bone-chilling and suspenseful stories ever written. The collection includes his best-loved tales, among them, "The Black Cat," "The Masque of the Red Death," "The Murders in the Rue Morgue," "The Tell-Tale Heart," and "The Cask of Amontillado."

America Street
Anne Mazer, Editor

America's diversity is celebrated in this collection of fourteen short stories by renowned authors. Story themes range from Lesley Namioka's "The All-American Slurp," a comical story of an Asian family's introduction to American table manners, to Francisco Jimenez's sober account of a migrant child laborer in "The Circuit." The stories are unified in their depiction of common themes and experiences across cultures.

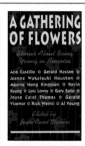

A Gathering of Flowers: Stories About Being Young in America
Joyce Carol Thomas, Editor

Focusing on the rich cultural heritage of America, Thomas collects eleven stories by such distinguished authors as Maxine Hong Kingston and Gary Soto. The settings of these stories range from rural Oklahoma to a Chicago Latino barrio to a Chippewa Indian reservation. As the reader explores these different places, he or she experiences the fantasies, fables, and stories that address what it means to be young and American.

Other Possibilities

100 Selected Stories	O. Henry
Sixteen: Short Stories by Outstanding Young Adult Writers	Donald Gallo, Editor
El Bronx Remembered	Nicholasa Mohr

Still Life #31, 1963, Tom Wesselmann, Frederick P. Weisman Art Foundation, ©Tom Wesselmann/Licensed by VAGA, New York, NY

Nonfiction

Nonfiction writing tells about real people, events, places, and objects. Nonfiction falls into several categories, which you'll encounter in this unit:

- An **autobiography** is the writer's own story of his or her life.

- A **biography** is the story of someone's life written by another person.

- An **essay** is a short nonfiction work about a particular subject. A **reflective essay** shares the writer's inner thoughts and feelings. A **narrative essay** tells a story about an actual event. A **descriptive essay** brings to life an event, a person, or a thing. An **expository essay** explains something about a subject. A **persuasive essay** attempts to convince the reader to think or act in a certain way.

- A **speech** is an oral presentation of facts and insights.

Guide for Reading

Meet the Author:

Bruce Brooks (1950–   )

"I have an affinity for independence, for loners, for smart people who are watchers," says Bruce Brooks. It's not surprising, then, that Brooks displays these characteristics as he studies the nest-building techniques of wasps in "Animal Craftsmen."

Honors and Awards

Brooks has shown his versatility as a writer. His first novel, *The Moves Make the Man,* was a Newbery Honor book. More recently, his novel *What Hearts* also won a Newbery Honor. His first nonfiction book, *On the Wing,* was an American Library Association Best Book for young adults.

THE STORY BEHIND THE STORY

Bruce Brooks hadn't originally planned to introduce his book on animal architecture with "Animal Craftsmen." When he finished the book, however, he realized that he needed to tell the reader why he had chosen this topic in the first place. "It seemed that I had forgotten to begin with a beginning," he says. "So I went back to the incident that had started my interest, and I simply told that story, hoping my readers would get a similar sense of starting up."

◆ LITERATURE AND YOUR LIFE

CONNECT YOUR EXPERIENCE

As you walk down the street, out in the park, or in your back yard, you discover something miraculous. You wonder how that flower can bloom in a concrete crack, or you speculate about a tiny nest resting in the branch of a tree. You're not alone in your feelings of awe and amazement. The wonders of nature have intrigued many people, including Bruce Brooks.

THEMATIC FOCUS: Respecting Nature

As you read this essay, look for evidence of Brooks's awe and respect for the world around him.

◆ Background for Understanding

SCIENCE

In "Animal Craftsmen," Bruce Brooks marvels at the skill of mud wasps as they build their incredible nests. Your experience with wasps, like most people's, is probably limited: Many people avoid wasps for fear of being stung. Yet wasps play an important role in the ecology of their territory and provide a beneficial service to humans. Once the mud wasp's nest is built, the female paralyzes spiders or insects with a sting and places them alongside eggs that she has laid. This provides food for the developing wasps and rids an area of insects that would otherwise damage crops or trees.

◆ Animal Craftsmen ◆

◆ Literary Focus

REFLECTIVE ESSAY

In this reflective essay, Bruce Brooks expresses his appreciation of animals' skills at designing and engineering their homes. A **reflective essay** is a work of nonfiction that communicates a writer's thoughts about a topic of personal interest. In presenting his or her thoughts, the writer may re-create and evaluate personal experiences to make a point.

◆ Build Vocabulary

RELATED WORDS: FORMS OF *habitable*

In "Animal Craftsmen," mud wasps make a hive *habitable,* which means "fit to be lived in." Words related to *habitable* include *habitat,* meaning "native environment," *inhabitant,* meaning "resident," and *inhabit,* meaning "to live in."

WORD BANK

Which word from the list shares a root with the verb *sympathy?* Check the Build Vocabulary box on page 627 to see if you chose correctly.

subtle
infusion
habitable
empathy

Reading for Success

Strategies for Reading Nonfiction

Nonfiction is prose that presents and explains ideas or tells about real people, places, things, and events. Your school books, newspapers, magazines, encyclopedias, and certain information on the Internet are all examples of nonfiction. So are biographies, autobiographies, and essays. Although the writing is nonfiction, that doesn't mean that you should accept everything the writer tells you. Instead, judge the facts for yourself, and form your own opinions. The following strategies will help you read nonfiction effectively:

Set a purpose for reading.

Before you begin, set a goal for reading a work of nonfiction. Your goal may be to find facts, to analyze a writer's theory, to understand an opinion, or simply to be entertained. Keep your purpose in mind, and look for details in your reading that support that purpose.

Identify the author's main points.

Ask yourself what the author wants you to learn or think as a result of reading his or her nonfiction work. These main points are the most important ideas in the piece. Bruce Brooks makes the following point early in "Animal Craftsmen."

> I *did* find something under the eaves—something very strange.

As he continues the essay, Brooks makes points about the strange and extraordinary "homes" that animals build for themselves.

Understand the author's purpose.

Authors of nonfiction have a reason, or a purpose, for writing. Their details and information support their purpose. They also adopt a tone, or attitude, toward their topic and the reader that indicates their purpose.

▶ Consider the details that the author includes or does not include. Also, consider the author's tone: Is it friendly? Warning? Serious? Think about what the choices of details and tone reveal about the writer's beliefs and purpose for writing.

▶ Once you recognize the author's purpose, decide whether you will accept the writer's ideas or whether you should question them.

As you read "Animal Craftsmen" by Bruce Brooks, notice the notes along the sides. The notes demonstrate how to apply these strategies to your reading.

Animal Craftsmen

Bruce Brooks

One evening, when I was about five, I climbed up a ladder on the outside of a rickety old tobacco barn at sunset. The barn was part of a small farm near the home of a country relative my mother and I visited periodically; though we did not really know the farm's family, I was allowed to roam, poke around, and conduct sudden studies of anything small and harmless. On this evening, as on most of my jaunts, I was not looking for anything; I was simply climbing with an open mind. But as I balanced on the next-to-the-top rung and inhaled the spicy stink of the tobacco drying inside, I *did* find something under the eaves[1] —something very strange.

> Your **purpose for reading** may be to learn about the "animal craftsmen" of the essay's title.

It appeared to be a kind of gray paper sphere, suspended from the dark planks by a thin stalk, like an apple made of ashes hanging on its stem. I studied it closely in the clear light. I saw that the bottom was a little ragged, and open. I could not tell if it had been torn, or if it had been made that way on purpose—for it was clear to me, as I studied it, that this thing had been *made*. This was no fruit or fungus.[2] Its shape, rough but trim; its intricately[3] colored surface with <u>subtle</u> swirls of gray and tan; and most of all the uncanny adhesiveness with which the perfectly tapered stem stuck against the rotten old pine boards—all of these features gave evidence of some intentional design. The troubling thing was figuring out who had designed it, and why.

I assumed the designer was a human being: someone from the farm, someone wise and skilled in a craft that had so far escaped my curiosity. Even when I saw wasps entering and leaving the thing (during a vigil I kept every evening for two weeks), it did not occur to me that the wasps might have fashioned it for themselves. I assumed it was a man-made "wasp house" placed there expressly for the purpose of attracting a family of wasps, much as the "martin hotel," a giant birdhouse on a pole near the farmhouse, was maintained to shelter migrant[4] purple martins who returned every spring. I didn't ask myself why anyone would want to give wasps a bivouac;[5] it seemed no more odd than attracting birds.

> From this paragraph and what you have already read, you know that at least part of the **author's purpose** is to explain his discovery.

As I grew less wary of the wasps (and they grew less wary of me), and as my confidence on the ladder improved, I moved to the upper rung and peered through the sphere's bottom. I could see that the paper swirled in layers around some secret center the wasps inhabited, and I marveled at the delicate hands of the craftsman who had devised such tiny apertures[6] for their protection.

I left the area in the late summer, and in my

---

1. **eaves** (ēvz) *n.*: Lower edges of a roof.
2. **fungus** (fuŋ´ gəs) *n.*: Growth caused by parasites living on organisms.
3. **intricately** (in´ tri kit lē) *adv.*: In a complex, highly detailed way.

◆ **Build Vocabulary**

subtle (sut´ əl) *adj.*: Delicate; fine

---

4. **migrant** (mī´ grənt) *adj.*: Moving from one region to another with the changing seasons.
5. **bivouac** (biv´ wak´) *n.*: Temporary shelter.
6. **apertures** (ap´ ər chərz) *n.*: Openings.

imagination I took the strange structure with me. I envisioned unwrapping it, and in the middle finding—what? A tiny room full of bits of wool for sleeping, and countless manufactured pellets of scientifically determined wasp food? A glowing blue jewel that drew the wasps at twilight, and gave them a cool infusion of energy as they clung to it overnight? My most definite idea was that the wasps lived in a small block of fine cedar the craftsman had drilled full of holes, into which they slipped snugly, rather like the bunks aboard submarines in World War II movies.

As it turned out, I got the chance to discover that my idea of the cedar block had not been wrong by much. We visited our relative again in the winter. We arrived at night, but first thing in the morning I made straight for the farm and its barn. The shadows under the eaves were too dense to let me spot the sphere from far off. I stepped on the bottom rung of the ladder—slick with frost—and climbed carefully up. My hands and feet kept slipping, so my eyes stayed on the rung ahead, and it was not until I was secure at the top that I could look up. The sphere was gone.

I was crushed. That object had fascinated me like nothing I had come across in my life; I had even grown to love wasps because of it. I sagged on the ladder and watched my breath

eddy[7] around the blank eaves. I'm afraid I pitied myself more than the apparently homeless wasps.

But then something snapped me out of my sense of loss: I recalled that I had watched the farmer taking in the purple martin hotel every November, after the birds left. From its spruce appearance when he brought it out in March, it was clear he had cleaned it and repainted it and kept it out of the weather. Of course he would do the same thing for *this* house, which was even more fragile. I had never mentioned the wasp dwelling to anyone, but now I decided I would go to the farm, introduce myself, and inquire about it. Perhaps I would even be permitted to handle it, or, best of all, learn how to make one myself.

I scrambled down the ladder, leaping from the third rung and landing in the frosty salad of tobacco leaves and windswept grass that collected at the foot of the barn wall. I looked down and saw that my left boot had, by no more than an inch, just missed crushing the very thing I was rushing off to seek. There, lying dry and separate on the leaves, was the wasp house.

I looked up. Yes. I was standing directly beneath the spot where the sphere had hung—it was a straight fall. I picked up the wasp house, gave it a shake to see if any insects were inside, and, discovering none, took it home.

My awe of the craftsman grew as I unwrapped the layers of the nest. Such beautiful paper! It was much tougher than any I had encountered, and it held a curve (something my experimental paper airplanes never did), but it was very light, too. The secret at the center of the swirl turned out to be a neatly made fan of tiny cells, all of the same size and shape, reminding me of the heart of a sunflower that had lost its seeds to birds. The fan hung from the sphere's ceiling by a stem the thickness of a pencil lead.

---

7. eddy (edˊ ē) *v.*: Move in a circular motion.

◀ **Critical Viewing** In what way does this wasps' nest look like "an apple made of ashes hanging on its stem"? **[Connect]**

The rest of the story is a little embarrassing. More impressed than ever, I decided to pay homage to the creator of this <u>habitable</u> sculpture. I went boldly to the farmhouse. The farmer's wife answered my knock. I showed her the nest and asked to speak with the person in the house who had made it. She blinked and frowned. I had to repeat my question twice before she understood what I believed my mission to be; then, with a gentle laugh, she dispelled my illusion about an ingenious old papersmith fond of wasps. The nest, she explained, had been made entirely by the insects themselves, and wasn't that amazing?

Well, of course it was. It still is. I needn't have been so embarrassed—the structures

> Brooks presents a **main point** here: Ordinary animals that we take for granted can do extraordinary things.

that animals build, and the sense of design they display, *should* always astound us. On my way home from the farmhouse, in my own defense I kept thinking, "But *I* couldn't build anything like this! Nobody could!"

The most natural thing in the world for us to do, when we are confronted with a piece of animal architecture, is to figure out if we could possibly make it or live in it. Who hasn't peered into the dark end of a mysterious hole in the woods and thought, "It must be pretty weird to live in there!" or looked up at a hawk's nest atop a huge sycamore and shuddered at the thought of waking up every morning with nothing but a few twigs preventing a hundred-foot fall. How, we wonder, do those twigs stay together, and withstand the wind so high?

> Another **main point** is that people tend to find similarities between animal behavior and human behavior.

It is a human tendency always to regard animals first in terms of ourselves. Seeing the defensive courage of a mother bear whose cubs are threatened, or the cooperative determination of a string of ants dismantling a stray chunk of cake, we naturally use our own behavior as reference for our <u>empathy</u>. We put ourselves in the same situation and express the animal's action in

▲ **Critical Viewing** What about this spiderweb do you find "awesome"? Explain. **[Evaluate]**

feelings—and words—that apply to the way people do things.

Sometimes this is useful. But sometimes it is misleading. Attributing human-like intentions to an animal can keep us from looking at the *animal's* sense of itself in its surroundings—its immediate and future needs, its physical and mental capabilities, its genetic[8] instincts. Most animals, for example, use their five senses in ways that human beings cannot possibly understand or express. How can a forty-two-year-old nearsighted biologist have any real idea what a two-week-old barn owl sees in the dark? How can a sixteen-year-old who lives in the Arizona desert identify with

8. **genetic** (jə net´ ik) *adj.*: Inherited biologically.

◆ Build Vocabulary

infusion (in fy$\overline{oo}$´ zhən) *n.*: The act of putting one thing into another

habitable (hab´ ə tə bəl) *adj.*: Fit to live in

empathy (em´ pə thē) *n.*: Ability to share another's emotions, thoughts, or feelings

the muscular jumps improvised by a waterfall-leaping salmon in Alaska? There's nothing wrong with trying to empathize with an animal, but we shouldn't forget that ultimately animals live *animal* lives.

Animal structures let us have it both ways—we can be struck with a strange wonder, and we can empathize right away, too. Seeing a vast spiderweb, taut and glistening between two bushes, it's easy to think, "I have no idea how that is done; the engineering is awesome." But it is just as easy to imagine climbing across the bright strands, springing from one to the next as if the web were a new Epcot attraction, the Invisible Flying Flexible Space Orb. That a clear artifact of an animal's wits and agility[9] stands right there in front of us—that we can touch it, look at it from different angles, sometimes take it home—inspires our imagination as only a strange reality can. We needn't move into a molehill to experience a life of darkness and digging; our creative wonder takes us down there in a second, without even getting our hands dirty.

_____

9. **agility** (ə jil′ ə tē) *n.*: Ability to move quickly and easily.

But what if we discover some of the mechanics of how the web is made? Once we see how the spider works (or the humming bird, or the bee), is the engineering no longer awesome? This would be too bad: we don't want to lose our sense of wonder just because we gain understanding.

And we certainly do *not* lose it. In fact, seeing how an animal makes its nest or egg case or food storage vaults has the effect of increasing our amazement. The builder's energy, concentration, and athletic adroitness are qualities we can readily admire and envy. Even more startling is the recognition that the animal is working from a precise design in its head, a design that is exactly replicated time after time. This knowledge of architecture—knowing where to build, what materials to use, how to put them together—remains one of the most intriguing mysteries of animal behavior. And the more *we* develop that same knowledge, the more we appreciate the instincts and intelligence of the animals.

> Brooks indicates his **purpose:** He wants you to understand that animal behavior is mysterious and deserving of appreciation.

Guide for Responding

◆ LITERATURE AND YOUR LIFE

Reader's Response Do you agree with the author that animal behavior and nature itself are fascinating? Explain.

Thematic Focus What aspects of nature inspire your respect? Explain.

Natural Art Sketch something from nature that you find extraordinary.

☑ Check Your Comprehension

1. As the child in the essay, what assumptions does Brooks make about the nest he finds?
2. What does Brooks discover as he unwraps layers of the wasps' nest?
3 According to Brooks, what are two natural reactions to seeing animal structures?

◆ Critical Thinking

INTERPRET

1. What evidence in the essay indicates that as a child, Brooks showed a tendency to regard animals in human terms? **[Analyze]**
2. What do you learn about Brooks when he says, "Perhaps I would even be permitted to handle [the nest], or, best of all, learn how to make one myself." **[Infer]**
3. What is the theme or central message of the essay? **[Interpret]**

EVALUATE

4. Brooks states that it is not necessary to move into a molehill to experience a life underground. Do you agree? Why or why not? **[Evaluate]**

Guide for Responding (continued)

◆ Reading for Success

STRATEGIES FOR READING NONFICTION

Review the reading strategies and the notes showing how to read nonfiction. Then, apply the strategies to answer the following:

1. What purpose did you set when you began reading this essay? Explain how you fulfilled your purpose.
2. (a) State the author's purpose for writing "Animal Craftsmen." (b) How does his attitude reflect his purpose?
3. List the author's main points, and explain how they support his purpose.

◆ Build Vocabulary

USING FORMS OF *habitable*

The word *habitable* means "suitable for living in." Write the following sentences, completing each with one of these words related to *habitable*:

    habitat   inhabit   inhabitant

1. The starlings ____?____ a bird house.
2. The polar bear's ____?____ is very cold.
3. The wasp was an ____?____ of the hive.

SPELLING STRATEGY

The *b* in *subtle* is silent. Several other common English words contain a silent *b*. On your paper, answer each clue with a word that contains a silent *b*.

1. This person fixes water-supply pipes.
2. You use this to untangle your hair.
3. This is another word for a tree bough.

USING THE WORD BANK

On your paper, match the Word Bank word in Column A with the word or phrase closest in meaning in Column B.

Column A	Column B
1. subtle	a. shared feeling
2. infusion	b. injection
3. habitable	c. livable
4. empathy	d. delicate

◆ Literary Focus

REFLECTIVE ESSAY

The goal of a **reflective essay** is to present a writer's ideas about a topic of personal interest. In a reflective essay, a writer may share how his or her life has been affected by his or her experience. In "Animal Craftsmen," Brooks recalls how a childhood experience—finding a wasps' nest—fascinated him and led to a lifelong love of nature's wonders.

1. List two statements in which Brooks shares his thoughts, feelings, and opinions.
2. Explain how Brooks uses the tale of the nest to lead to a broader subject.
3. In what way was Brooks's life changed by the experience described in the essay?

◆ Build Grammar Skills

SUBJECTIVE CASE PRONOUNS

Personal pronouns change form based on their grammatical use in a sentence. This form is called its *case*. When a pronoun is a subject or a predicate pronoun (following a linking verb), use the **subjective case.** These are the subjective case pronouns: *I, we, you, he, she, it, they.*

Subject: *I* climbed up a ladder.
Predicate Pronoun: It was *I* who discovered the nest.

Practice On your paper, identify the subjective case pronoun in each sentence.

1. I was not looking for anything.
2. We visited our relative again in the winter.
3. It was he who unwrapped the wasps' nest.
4. She blinked and frowned.
5. It seems they built the nests themselves.

Writing Application On your paper, use each of the following pronouns in a sentence according to the instructions in parentheses.

1. They (as a subject)
2. She (as a predicate pronoun)
3. I (as a predicate pronoun)
4. He (as a subject)
5. They (as a predicate pronoun)

Build Your Portfolio

 Idea Bank

Writing

1. **Fan Letter** Compose a fan letter to the builders of the wasps' nest, telling how much you admire their work. Use the correct form for a friendly letter.

2. **Nature Poem** Think about something in nature that fascinates you. Then, write a poem in which you convey its appearance and essence.

3. **Essay** Write an essay about "Animal Craftsmen," explaining what you learn about the author from reading about his childhood experience.

Speaking and Listening

4. **Discussion [Group Activity]** As a class, discuss examples of animal instinct and animal intelligence that seem to be similar to that of humans. Cite personal observations and experiences as examples. Create a chart, listing your examples.

5. **Dramatic Reading** Prepare and present a dramatic reading of a section of "Animal Craftsmen." Consider turning some of the narrative into dialogue or adding a narrator or other characters. **[Performing Arts Link]**

Projects

6. **Animal Poster** Choose an animal that interests you. Research its habits and behavior, paying special attention to any humanlike actions or exceptional skills. Present your findings on a poster entitled, "The Extraordinary _____?_____." **[Science Link]**

7. **Mud Wasps' Nest** Brooks becomes fascinated with a mud wasps' nest in "Animal Craftsmen." Research the type of nest that mud wasps build. Then, draw a diagram of the nest, labeling its parts. One diagram should show the interior of the nest. **[Science Link; Art Link]**

 Writing Mini-Lesson

Article for the School Newspaper

In "Animal Craftsmen," Brooks chose the form of a reflective essay to describe the amazing ability of animals to engineer and build their habitats. Using the form of a newspaper article—another type of nonfiction—write an article for your school paper about a scientific discovery or an extraordinary animal.

Writing Focus: Appropriate Tone

In your article, create an **appropriate tone,** or attitude, toward your subject and audience by choosing your words carefully. Notice how Brooks created a tone of wonder in these lines:

Model From the Essay

It appeared to be a kind of gray paper sphere, suspended from the dark planks by a thin stalk, like an apple made of ashes hanging on its stem.

Prewriting Research your subject, and jot down notes. With your audience and subject in mind, decide on the appropriate tone for your article.

Drafting Use your notes to draft your newspaper article. In the first paragraph, introduce your subject and hook your readers' interest. Then, develop your main points in the body of the article. Conclude by restating your main points and summing up your ideas.

Revising Reread your article, revising your word choice, where necessary, to create a consistent tone. Delete any unnecessary details.

◆ **Grammar Application**

You may want to replace some proper nouns with subjective case pronouns in your article.

Personal Accounts and Biographies

Portrait of Joseph Roulin, 1889, Vincent Van Gogh, Museum of Modern Art, New York, NY

Guide for Reading

Meet the Authors:

Eudora Welty (1909–   )

Eudora Welty was born and raised in Jackson, Mississippi, and this environment formed the backdrop for most of her writing. Her childhood was a happy one. Her parents filled their home with books and encouraged their children to learn.

Writing Inspiration
Following college in New York, Welty traveled around Mississippi, reporting, interviewing, and taking photographs. Her desire to become a writer grew out of this experience. In 1973, she was awarded a Pulitzer Prize for her novel *The Optimist's Daughter.*

Lionel G. García (1935–   )

Lionel García chronicles the world of people of Mexican ancestry living in the United States. García was born in San Diego, Texas. As a child, he lived with his grandfather, who was a goat herder. As an adult, he became a veterinarian.

Pets and Writing
García trained himself to write at night after his day's work as a veterinarian was done. His novels and short stories tell of the joys and sorrows of people struggling to survive in a difficult world. "A writer's job is to present people as they are," he says, "usually to the surprise of the reader."

◆ LITERATURE AND YOUR LIFE

CONNECT YOUR EXPERIENCE

In many ways, childhood is the most important time of your life. The things you learn, the beliefs you form, even the games you play influence your life in profound ways. In these selections, you'll learn about childhood events of two writers, Eudora Welty and Lionel García.

THEMATIC FOCUS: Living Each Day

As you read, look for ways in which a "typical day" can generate enlightenment and joy.

◆ Background for Understanding

SPORTS

In "Baseball," you'll read about an informal version of the popular game. Here are a few terms you're likely to hear when you watch a baseball game:

Strike Zone: Area from batter's armpits to knees and over home plate
Ball: A pitch outside the strike zone
Strike: When a batter swings at a pitch and misses or lets a ball go by that's within the strike zone
Count: Number of balls and strikes a batter has
Double Play: A play in which two outs are made

◆ Build Vocabulary

WORD ROOTS: -vis-

Eudora Welty describes the risen moon in the *visible* sky. The word root -*vis*- means "to see"; *visible* means "able to be seen."

WORD BANK

Which word from the list has to do with a stellar, or starry, arrangement? Check the Build Vocabulary box on page 634 to see if you chose correctly.

visible
reigning
respectively
constellations
eclipses
devices
evaded

◆ Literary Focus

AUTOBIOGRAPHY

An **autobiography** is the story of a writer's own life, told by the writer. Usually, the writer of an autobiography uses the first-person pronoun "I" to write about his or her experiences. In an autobiography, you meet people and learn of events through the eyes of the author. In both "One Writer's Beginnings" and "Baseball," the authors recount vivid memories of childhood events that helped shape the direction of their lives.

◆ Reading Strategy

UNDERSTAND THE AUTHOR'S PURPOSE

Authors write for a reason. They may aim to teach or to convince you about something, or they may aim to make you laugh, or cry, or think. A good way to **understand the author's purpose** is to ask yourself, "Why is he or she telling me this?" When you know the author's purpose, you can read accordingly— to learn, to be entertained, or to be alert for an attempt to persuade you of something. As you read, fill in a chart like the one below to help you determine the author's purpose.

Text From Story	How It Affects Me	Possible Purpose
"Learning stamps you with its moments."	It makes me stop and think.	To teach

from One Writer's Beginnings

Eudora Welty

Learning stamps you with its moments. Childhood's learning is made up of moments. It isn't steady. It's a pulse.

In a children's art class, we sat in a ring on kindergarten chairs and drew three daffodils that had just been picked out of the yard; and while I was drawing, my sharpened yellow pencil and the cup of the yellow daffodil gave off whiffs just alike. That the pencil doing the drawing should give off the same smell as the flower it drew seemed part of the art lesson—as shouldn't it be? Children, like animals, use all their senses to discover the world. Then artists come along and discover it the same way, all over again. Here and there, it's the same world. Or now and then we'll hear from an artist who's never lost it.

◆ **Literary Focus**
How can you tell that this is the writer's own story?

In my sensory[1] education I include my physical awareness of the *word.* Of a certain word, that is; the connection it has with what it stands for. At around age six, perhaps, I was standing by myself in our front yard waiting for supper, just at that hour in a late summer day when the sun is already below the horizon and the risen full moon in the visible sky stops being chalky and begins to take on light. There

---

1. **sensory** (sen′ sər ē) *adj.*: Appealing to the senses of sight, hearing, smell, taste, and touch.

◆ **Build Vocabulary**

visible (viz′ ə bəl) *adj.*: Able to be seen

reigning (rān′ iŋ) *adj.*: Ruling

respectively (ri spek′ tiv lē) *adv.*: In the order named

constellations (kän′ stə lā′ shəns) *n.*: Collections of stars

eclipses (i klips′ əz) *n.*: Here, lunar eclipses: when the moon is obscured by the Earth's shadow

▲ **Critical Viewing** Why has the moon, especially as seen here, been an object of fascination throughout the centuries? **[Infer]**

comes the moment, and I saw it then, when the moon goes from flat to round. For the first time it met my eyes as a globe. The word "moon" came into my mouth as though fed to me out of a silver spoon. Held in my mouth the moon became a word. It had the roundness of a Concord grape Grandpa took off his vine and gave me to suck out of its skin and swallow whole, in Ohio.

This love did not prevent me from living for years in foolish error about the moon. The new moon just appearing in the west was the rising moon to me. The new should be rising. And in early childhood the sun and moon, those opposite reigning powers, I just as easily assumed rose in east and west respectively in their opposite sides of the sky, and like partners in a reel[2] they advanced, sun from the east, moon from the west, crossed over (when I wasn't looking) and went down on the other side. My father couldn't have known I believed that when bending behind me and guiding my

shoulder, he positioned me at our telescope in the front yard and, with careful adjustment of the focus, brought the moon close to me.

The night sky over my childhood Jackson was velvety black. I could see the full constellations in it and call their names; when I could read, I knew their myths. Though I was always waked for eclipses and indeed carried to the window as an infant in arms and shown Halley's Comet[3] in my sleep, and though I'd been taught at our diningroom table about the solar system and knew the earth revolved around the sun, and our moon around us, I never found out the moon didn't come up in the west until I was a writer and Herschel Brickell, the literary critic, told me after I misplaced it in a story. He said valuable words to me about my new profession: "Always be sure you get your moon in the right part of the sky."

---

2. **reel** (rēl) *n.*: Lively Scottish dance.

3. **Halley's Comet:** Famous comet that reappears every 75 years.

*G*uide for Responding

◆ LITERATURE AND YOUR LIFE

Reader's Response Do you agree with Welty that "rising" is an appropriate image for new things, such as the new moon? Explain.

Thematic Focus In what way was Welty's day "typical"? Why did it become so memorable?

Journal Writing Jot down some childhood beliefs you once held that proved to be false.

☑ Check Your Comprehension

1. According to Welty, how are children and animals alike?
2. What did Welty realize about the moon while waiting in her front yard for supper?
3. What error does Welty believe about the moon's movement?

◆ Critical Thinking

INTERPRET

1. What does Welty mean when she says, "Learning stamps you with its moments"? **[Analyze]**
2. Compare Welty's way of learning about the moon with her father's way of teaching her. **[Compare and Contrast]**
3. What does Welty believe about the role the senses play in the development of a writer? **[Infer]**

EXTEND

4. The last sentence of the story is, "Always be sure you get your moon in the right part of the sky." Identify three professions, besides writing, for which this would be good advice. Explain why. **[Career Link]**

BASEBALL

Lionel G. García

W e loved to play baseball. We would take the old mesquite[1] stick and the old ball across the street to the parochial[2] school grounds to play a game. Father Zavala enjoyed watching us. We could hear him laugh mightily from the screened porch at the rear of the rectory[3] where he sat.

The way we played baseball was to rotate positions after every out. First base, the only base we used, was located where one would normally find second base.

This made the batter have to run past the pitcher and a long way to first baseman, increasing the odds of getting thrown out. The pitcher stood in line with the batter, and with first base, and could stand as close or as far from the batter as he or she wanted. Aside from the pitcher, the batter and the first baseman, we had a catcher. All the rest of us would stand in the outfield. After an out, the catcher would come up to bat. The pitcher

---

1. **mesquite** (mes´ kēt´): Thorny shrub of North America.
2. **parochial** (pə rō´ kē əl) *adj.*: Supported by a church.
3. **rectory** (rek´ tər ē) *n.*: Residence for priests.

◀ **Critical Viewing** What does it feel like to learn a new skill or game? [Relate]

took the position of catcher, and the first baseman moved up to be the pitcher. Those in the
outfield were left to their own <u>devices</u>. I don't
remember ever getting to bat.

There was one exception to the rotation
scheme. I don't know who thought of this, but
whoever caught the ball on the fly would go directly to be the batter. This was not a popular
thing to do. You could expect to have the ball
thrown at you on the next pitch.

There was no set distance for first base.

◆ Literary Focus
What does this
passage reveal
about García's
background?

First base was wherever
Matías or Juan or Cota
tossed a stone. They were
the law. The distance
could be long or short depending on how soon we
thought we were going to be called in to eat.
The size of the stone marking the base mat-
tered more than the distance from home plate
to first base. If we hadn't been called in to eat

▲ Critical Viewing How do young players adapt
the game of baseball to their own neighborhood
or circumstances? **[Generalize]**

by dusk, first base was hard to find. Sometimes someone would kick the stone farther
away and arguments erupted.

When the batter hit the ball in the air and
it was caught that was an out. So far so
good. But if the ball hit the ground, the fielder
had two choices. One, in keeping with the
standard rules of the game, the ball could be
thrown to the first baseman and, if caught
before the batter arrived at the base, that
was an out. But the second, more interesting
option allowed the fielder, ball in hand, to
take off running after the batter. When close

◆ Build Vocabulary
devices (di vīs´ ez) *n.*: Technique or means for
working things out

▲ **Critical Viewing** How can you tell that these children are enjoying the game of baseball? **[Support]**

enough, the fielder would throw the ball at the batter. If the batter was hit before reaching first base, the batter was out. But if the batter <u>evaded</u> being hit with the ball, he or she could either run to first base or run back to home plate. All the while, everyone was chasing the batter, picking up the ball and throwing it at him or her. To complicate matters, on the way to home plate the batter had the choice of running anywhere possible to avoid getting hit. For example, the batter could run to hide behind the hackberry trees[4] at the parochial school grounds, going from tree to tree until he or she could make it safely back to home plate. Many a time we would wind up playing the game past Father Zavala and in front of the rectory half a block away. Or we could be seen running after the batter several blocks

---

4. **hackberry trees:** Fruit-bearing trees of the elm family.

◆ **Build Vocabulary**

evaded (ē vād′ əd) *v.*: Avoided

down the street toward town, trying to hit the batter with the ball. One time we wound up all the way across town before we cornered Juan against a fence, held him down, and hit him with the ball. Afterwards, we all fell laughing in a pile on top of each other, exhausted from the run through town.

The old codgers, the old shiftless men who spent their day talking at the street corners, never caught on to what we were doing. They would halt their idle conversation just long enough to watch us run by them, hollering and throwing the old ball at the batter.

It was the only kind of baseball game Father Zavala had ever seen. What a wonderful game it must have been for him to see us hit the ball, run to a rock, then run for our lives down the street. He loved the game, shouting from the screened porch at us, pushing us on. And then all of a sudden we were gone, running after the batter. What a game! In what enormous stadium would it be played to allow

◆ **Reading Strategy**
What is the author's purpose in providing this information?

such freedom over such an expanse of ground.

My uncle Adolfo, who had pitched for the Yankees and the Cardinals in the majors, had given us the ball several years before. Once when he returned for a visit, he saw us playing from across the street and walked over to ask us what we were doing.

"Playing baseball," we answered as though we thought he should know better. After all, he was the professional baseball player.

He walked away shaking his head. "What a waste of a good ball," we heard him say, marveling at our ignorance.

Beyond Literature

Sports Connection

Little League Baseball In "Baseball," Lionel García describes the street version of a baseball game he and his friends played when they were children. The game became a fond memory.

Many people have fond memories of baseball games they played in Little League. In 1939, in Williamsport, Pennsylvania, the international baseball organization for Little League began its long career of adapting America's "favorite" pastime for boys aged eight to twelve. In 1974, the league began admitting girls of the same age. The game is played on a field two thirds the size of a professional baseball diamond, and games last six innings instead of the customary nine. Each Little League consists of four to twelve teams that play a fifteen-game season climaxing with the Little League World Series.

Cross-Curricular Activity

Major league baseball is composed of two leagues, the American League and the National League, which each contain a number of teams grouped into various divisions. Research to find out how many divisions there are in each league, how many teams are in each division, and how this grouping is determined. Share your findings with your classmates.

Guide for Responding

◆ LITERATURE AND YOUR LIFE

Reader's Response Do you think Lionel García and his friends would have had more fun playing baseball by the standard rules?

Thematic Focus In what ways does reflecting on his childhood give García insights into his adult life?

Rule Book Using the rules described in the story, create a baseball rule book.

☑ **Check Your Comprehension**

1. How many bases did García and his friends use when they played ball?
2. How was the distance from home plate to first base determined?
3. Why would García and his friends have needed an enormous stadium to play their version of baseball?
4. (a) What did Father Zavala know about baseball? (b) What did Uncle Adolfo know about baseball?

◆ Critical Thinking

INTERPRET

1. What do you learn about the circumstances of García's childhood from his account of playing baseball? **[Infer]**
2. When García's uncle Adolfo sees the way Lionel and his friends play, he says they are wasting a good ball. Compare his attitude toward baseball with the attitude of the children. **[Compare and Contrast]**
3. García doesn't mention anyone winning or losing. Why do you think this is so? **[Speculate]**
4. García and his friends thought they were playing baseball. If they had found out how real baseball is played, do you think they would have changed their game? Explain your answer. **[Speculate]**

COMPARE LITERARY WORKS

5. What basic idea do both Welty and García convey to readers? Explain. **[Compare and Contrast]**

Guide for Responding (continued)

◆ Reading Strategy

UNDERSTAND THE AUTHOR'S PURPOSE

These writers tell about episodes in their lives. Their **purposes** may be to teach you, charm you, convince you, or impress you. As they share what they value in life, you can relate their experiences to your own.

1. Welty describes how the word *moon* and the actual moon became one and the same in her mind. Why does she tell about this experience?
2. (a) What is García's purpose in writing "Baseball"? (b) How do you know?

◆ Build Vocabulary

USING THE WORD ROOT -*vis*-

The word root -*vis*- in *visible* means "to see." On your paper, replace each word or phrase in parentheses with a word containing -*vis*-.

1. The moon is usually (not able to be seen) during the day.
2. A pitcher needs good (eyesight).

SPELLING STRATEGY

Apply this useful rule when spelling *reigning*: Place *i* before *e* except after *c* or when sounded like *a* as in *neighbor* and *weigh*. Copy the following sentences. Fill in the blanks with *ie* or *ei*.

1. Welty rec_?_ved advice from a literary critic.
2. García and his fr_?_nds were the r_?_gning champions.

USING THE WORD BANK

On your paper, label each statement true or false. Then, explain your responses.

1. The important thing about first base was that it be *visible*.
2. Welty's *reigning* passion was for words.
3. Welty assumed that the sun and the moon rose in the west and the east, *respectively*.
4. Welty's approach to the *constellations* was largely literary.
5. *Eclipses* occur when the moon falls within the Earth's shadow.
6. Educationally, Welty was left to her own *devices*.
7. The boys tried to *evade* the ball.

◆ Literary Focus

AUTOBIOGRAPHY

An **autobiography** is more than a factual account of the writer's life. It includes thoughts, feelings, and memories of incidents that only the writer could know. By revealing these things, the writer shares his or her life with the reader.

1. Identify two memories that Welty shares with readers. Explain why these memories are important to her.
2. By describing a game of baseball, García shares the world of his childhood. How could this account differ if it were told by an outside narrator instead of by García himself?

◆ Build Grammar Skills

OBJECTIVE CASE PRONOUNS

Personal pronouns change form according to their use in a sentence. When the pronoun is a direct object, an indirect object, or an object of a preposition, use the **objective case.** Objective case pronouns are *me, you, him, her, it, us,* and *them.*

Direct Object: We could hear *him* laugh.
Indirect Object: He gave *me* a baseball bat.
Object of a Preposition: All the rest of *us* would stand in the outfield . . .

Practice Copy the following sentences. Underline the objective case pronouns. Write D.O. (direct object), I.O. (indirect object), and O.P. (object of a preposition) over each underlined pronoun.

1. Learning stamps you with its moments.
2. Grandpa gave me a grape from his vine.
3. Everyone was chasing the batter, picking up the ball and throwing it at him or her.
4. My uncle Adolfo had given us the ball several years before.
5. He hit the baseball over the building.

Writing Application Write three sentences, using objective case pronouns. Use the pronouns in the following situations: direct object, indirect object, and object of a preposition.

Build Your Portfolio

 ## Idea Bank

Writing

1. **Glossary** Put together a complete glossary of baseball terms that could be used to help someone read "Baseball."

2. **Autobiography** Using García's "Baseball" as a model, write an autobiographical account of one of your favorite childhood games or activities.

3. **Report** Eudora Welty had the mistaken idea that the sun and the moon rose at opposite sides of the sky and passed each other on their daily journey. Find out the real movements of the sun and moon, and write a report on your findings. **[Science Link]**

Speaking and Listening

4. **Sports Radio** Imagine that you are a radio sportscaster covering a baseball game played by Lionel García and his friends. Present a play-by-play commentary on the game to your class. **[Media Link]**

5. **Monologue** Rewrite Welty's story as a monologue. Rehearse and deliver your monologue for the class. In your performance, try to capture the young girl's sense of wonder and awe. **[Performing Arts Link]**

Projects

6. **Plan for a Baseball Field [Group Activity]** With a partner, create a diagram of a playing field for García's version of baseball. Label the various parts of the field and the positions of the players.

7. **Moon Chart** During her childhood, Eudora Welty made a magical discovery about the moon. Make your own "discovery" of the moon by researching and observing its appearance in the night sky. Then, create a moon chart in which you illustrate the various stages of the moon during its monthly cycle. Post your completed chart in the classroom. **[Science Link]**

 ## Writing Mini-Lesson

Rule Book

Every board or computer game you play comes with a set of rules. Organizations or clubs, such as Scouts and 4-H, have rules, too. Write a short rule book for a real or an imaginary game or club. If you like, you can write a baseball rule book that Lionel García and his friends might have used or a rule book for an astronomy club that Eudora Welty might have joined.

Writing Skills Focus: Clarity

Rules have to be clear. Otherwise, people will argue about them. To achieve **clarity,** you first need to understand the rules yourself, then write them in short declarative sentences and organize them in a logical way.

Model From "Baseball"

After an out, the catcher would come up to bat. The pitcher took the position of the catcher, and the first baseman moved up to be the pitcher.

Prewriting Study the rules for a game you like to play or a club to which you belong. Notice how the rules are organized and presented. Then, make a list of all the rules you want to include in your rule book.

Drafting Decide which rules a newcomer would need to know first. Organize the rules in a logical way, and write them in short declarative sentences. You may want to number the rules or present them in outline form.

Revising Give your rule book to a classmate to read. Ask if he or she is able to understand the rules and if your writing is clear. Revise to answer any questions your classmate may have.

> ◆ **Grammar Application**
> Underline objective case pronouns you've used in your rule book.

CONNECTING LITERATURE TO SOCIAL STUDIES
THE SUFFRAGIST MOVEMENT

The United States vs. Susan B. Anthony *by Margaret Truman*

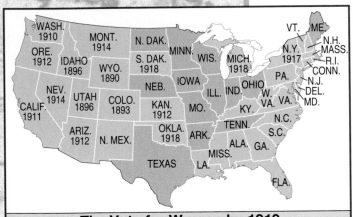

The Vote for Women by 1919

☐ Equal suffrage (date effective)   ☐ Partial suffrage
☐ No statewide suffrage

In 1920, American women gained the right to vote. Before 1920, some states allowed women to vote in certain types of elections—for example, presidential or primary elections only. This map shows the years in which states with equal rights prior to 1920 granted women the right to vote.

WOMAN SUFFRAGE *Suffrage* means "the right to vote." For more than half its history, the United States did not extend that right to women. In the early 1800's, more educational opportunities for women became available and women began to participate more openly in political reform movements. During the 1830's, women began organizing, speaking, and marching in hopes of winning the right to vote.

The Suffragist Movements By the year 1869, two major women's suffrage movements had formed. The American Woman Suffragist movement, led by Lucy Stone and her husband, Henry Blackwell, worked to win voting rights for women state by state. It was considered more conservative than the National Woman Suffrage Association, which was led by Elizabeth Cady Stanton and Susan B. Anthony. This group's main goal was to amend the United States Constitution to give women the right to vote.

The two movements joined forces in 1890 to form the American Woman Suffrage Association. In the early 1900's, the movement received a boost from dynamic new leaders Carrie Chapman Catt and Maud Wood Park. These women organized rallies and gathered support for their cause among middle-class women. It was not until 1920, however, that the Nineteenth Amendment to the Constitution was ratified, giving all women in the United States the right to vote.

Susan B. Anthony Of all the people who spoke and demonstrated for women's rights, one of the most famous is Susan B. Anthony (1820–1906). She gave speeches, organized marches, and edited a magazine called *The Revolution.* This essay by Margaret Truman shows how this memorable, dynamic woman helped change the course of history.

from
The United States vs. Susan B. Anthony

Margaret Truman

Susan B. Anthony was a stern and single-minded woman. Like most crusaders for causes—especially unpopular causes—she had little time for fun and games. But I have a sneaky feeling that behind her severe manner and <u>unremitting</u> devotion to duty, she may actually have had a sense of humor. Let me tell you about my favorite episode in Susan B. Anthony's career, and perhaps you'll agree.

It began on Friday morning, November 1, 1872. Susan was reading the morning paper at her home in Rochester. There, at the top of the editorial page of the *Democrat and Chronicle*, was an exhortation[1] to the city's residents:

Now register! Today and tomorrow are the only remaining opportunities. If you were not permitted to vote, you would fight for the right, undergo all privations for it, face death for it. You have it now at the cost of five minutes' time to be spent in seeking your place of registration and having your name entered. And yet, on election day, less than a week hence, hundreds of you are likely to lose your votes because you have not thought it worth while to give the five minutes. Today and tomorrow are your only opportunities. Register now!

Connecting Literature to Social Studies
Why might this editorial have been offensive to many women in 1872?

Susan B. Anthony read the editorial again. Just as she thought, it said nothing about being addressed to men only. With a gleam in her eye, she put down the paper and summoned her sister Guelma, with whom she lived. The two women donned their hats and cloaks and went off to call on two other Anthony sisters who lived nearby. Together, the four women headed for the barber shop on West Street, where voters from the Eighth Ward were being registered.

For some time, Susan B. Anthony had been looking for an opportunity to test the Fourteenth Amendment to the Constitution

---

1. **exhortation** (eg´ zôr tā´ shən) *n.*: Plea, sermon, or warning.

◆ **Build Vocabulary**

unremitting (un ri mit´ iŋ) *adj.*: Not stopping; persistent

as a weapon to win the vote for women. Adopted in 1870, the amendment had been designed to protect the civil rights—especially the voting rights—of recently freed slaves. It stated that:

> All persons born or naturalized in the United States, and subject to the jurisdiction thereof, are citizens of the United States and of the State wherein they reside. No State shall make or enforce any law which shall <u>abridge</u> the privileges or immunities[2] of citizens of the United States, nor shall any State deprive any person of life, liberty, or property without due process of law, nor deny to any person within its jurisdiction the equal protection of the laws.

The amendment did not say that "persons" meant only males, nor did it spell out "the privileges or immunities of citizens." Susan B. Anthony felt perfectly justified in concluding that the right to vote was among the privileges of citizenship and that it extended to women as well as men. I'm sure she must have also seen the humor of outwitting the supposedly superior males who wrote the Amendment.

It was bad enough for a bunch of women to barge into one sacred male precinct—the barber shop—but to insist on being admitted to another holy of holies—the voting booth—was absolutely outrageous. Moustaches twitched, throats were cleared, a whispered conference was held in the corner.

Susan had brought along a copy of the Fourteenth Amendment. She read it aloud, carefully pointing out to the men in charge of registration that the document failed to state that the privilege of voting extended only to males.

Only one man in the barber shop had the nerve to refuse the Anthony sisters the right to register. The rest buckled under Susan's determined <u>oratory</u> and allowed them to sign the huge, leather-bound voter registration book. If the men in the barber shop

thought they were getting rid of a little band of crackpots the easy way, they were wrong. Susan urged all her followers in Rochester to register. The next day, a dozen women invaded the Eighth Ward barber shop, and another thirty-five appeared at registration sites elsewhere in the city. The *Democrat and Chronicle*, which had <u>inadvertently</u> prompted the registrations, expressed no editorial opinion on the phenomenon, but its rival, the *Union and Advertiser*, denounced the women. If they were allowed to vote, the paper declared, the poll inspectors "should be prosecuted to the full extent of the law."

The following Tuesday, November 5, was Election Day. Most of the poll inspectors in Rochester had read the editorial in the *Union and Advertiser* and were too <u>intimidated</u> to allow any of the women who had registered to vote. Only in the Eighth Ward did the males weaken. Maybe the inspectors were *Democrat and Chronicle* readers, or perhaps they were more afraid of Susan B. Anthony than they were of the law. Whatever the reason, when Susan and her sisters showed up at the polls shortly after 7 A.M., there was only a minimum of fuss. A couple of inspectors were hesitant about letting the women vote, but when Susan assured them that she would pay all their legal expenses if they were prosecuted, the men relented, and one by one, the women took their ballots and stepped into the voting booth. There were no insults or sneers, no rude remarks. They marked their ballots, dropped them into the ballot box, and returned to their homes.

Susan B. Anthony's feat quickly became the talk of the country. She was applauded

> **Connecting Literature to Social Studies**
> Why would the men have thought the Anthony sisters were "crackpots"?

◆ Build Vocabulary

abridge (ə brij´) v.: Reduce in scope; shorten; lessen

oratory (ôr´ ə tôr´ ē) n.: Skill or eloquence in public speaking

inadvertently (in´ ad vʉrt´ ənt lē) adv.: Unintentionally

intimidated (in tim´ ə dāt´ əd) v.: Made afraid through threats and violence

---

2. **immunities** (im myōōn´ i tēs) n.: Freedom from public services or duties.

in some circles, vilified[3] in others. But the day of reckoning was not long in arriving. On November 28, Deputy U.S. Marshall E. J. Keeney appeared at her door with a warrant for her arrest. She had violated Section 19 of the Enforcement Act of the Fourteenth Amendment, which held that anyone who voted illegally was to be arrested and tried on criminal charges.

Susan B. Anthony was a great believer in planning ahead. The day after she registered, she decided to get a legal opinion on whether or not she should attempt to vote. A number of lawyers turned her away, but she finally found one who agreed to consider the case. He was Henry R. Selden, a former judge of the Court of Appeals, now a partner in one of Rochester's most prestigious law firms.

On the Monday before Election Day, Henry Selden informed his new client that he agreed with her interpretation of the Fourteenth Amendment and that in his opinion, she had every right to cast her ballot. The U.S. Commissioner of Elections in Rochester, William C. Storrs, did not concur.

E. J. Keeney, the marshal dispatched to arrest Susan B. Anthony, was not at all happy with his assignment. He nervously twirled his tall felt hat while waiting for her to come to the front door. When she finally appeared, he blushed and stammered, shifted uncomfortably from one foot to the other, and finally blurted out, "The Commissioner wishes to arrest you."

Susan couldn't help being amused at Keeney's embarrassment. "Is this your usual method of serving a warrant?" she asked calmly. With that, the marshal recovered his official dignity, presented her with the warrant, and told her that he had come to escort her to the office of the Commissioner of Elections.

When Susan asked if she could change into a more suitable dress, the marshal saw his opportunity to escape. "Of course," he said, turning to leave. "Just come down to the Commissioner's office whenever you're ready."

I'll do no such thing," Susan informed him curtly. "You were sent here to arrest me and take me to court. It's your duty to do so."

Keeney had no choice but to wait while his prisoner when upstairs and put on a more appropriate outfit. When she returned, she thrust out her wrists and said, "Don't you want to handcuff me, too?"

"I assure you, madam," Marshal Keeney muttered, "it isn't at all necessary."

With the U.S. Marshal at her side, Susan was brought before the Federal Commissioner of Elections, William C. Storrs. Her arrest was recorded, and she was ordered to appear the next day for a hearing. It was conducted by U.S. District Attorney Richard Crowley and his assistant, John E. Pound.

Susan answered District Attorney Crowley's questions politely. She said that she thought the Fourteenth Amendment gave her the right to vote. She admitted that she had consulted an attorney on the question but said that she would have voted even if he had not advised her to do so. When Crowley asked if she had voted deliberately to test the law, she said, "Yes, sir. I have

> W hen she returned, she thrust out her wrists and said, "Don't you want to handcuff me, too?"

Connecting Literature to Social Studies
Why would Anthony insist on being taken in, instead of going in alone?

3. **vilified** (vil′ ə fid′) v.: Spoken of in abusive or slanderous language; defamed.

been determined for three years to vote the first time I happened to be at home for the required thirty days before an election."

The District Attorney's next step was to convene a grand jury to draw up a bill of indictment.[4] He and his assistant fell to wrangling over a suitable trial date. Susan interrupted them. "I have lecture dates that will take me to central Ohio," she said. "I won't be available until December 10."

"But you're supposed to be in custody until the hearing," Crowley informed her.

"Is that so?" said Susan coolly. "I didn't know that."

The District Attorney backed down without an argument and scheduled the grand jury session for December 23.

Sixteen women had voted in Rochester. All sixteen were arrested and taken before the grand jury, but Susan alone was brought to trial. The District Attorney had decided to single her out as a test case. The three poll inspectors who had allowed the women to vote were also arrested. The grand jury indicted them too, set bail at five hundred dollars each, and ordered their trial set for the summer term of the U.S. District Court.

Susan Anthony's case now involved nineteen other men and women. All of them—including Susan—were liable to go to prison if they were found guilty and the judge

was in a sentencing mood. Prison in the 1870s was a very unpleasant place. There were no minimum security setups where a benevolent government allowed corrupt politicians, crooked labor leaders, and political agitators to rest and rehabilitate, as we do today. Prison meant a cold cell, wretched food, the company of thieves and murderers.

For a while it looked as if Susan might be behind bars even before her trial. She refused to post a bond for her five-hundred dollar bail. Henry Selden paid the money for her. "I could not see a lady I respected put in jail." he said.

It must be agonizing to sweat out the weeks before a trial. There is time to look ahead and brood about the possibility of an unfavorable verdict and time to look back, perhaps with regret, at the decision that placed you in the hands of the law. But Susan B. Anthony had no regrets. Nor did she appear to have any anxieties about her trial. She had already proven her fortitude by devoting twenty years of her life to fighting for the right to vote. If she won her case, the struggle would be over. But even if she lost, Susan was not ready to give up the fight. . . .

The trial of *The United States* vs. *Susan B. Anthony* opened on the afternoon of June 17, 1873, with the tolling of the Canandaigua Courthouse bell. The presiding justice was

---

4. **bill of indictment:** A formal written accusation.

▲ **Critical Viewing** District Attorney Richard Crowley conducted the inquiry to indict Susan B. Anthony. He also "backed down" about keeping her in custody. What kind of person do you think he was? [Assess]

Ward Hunt, a prim, pale man, who owed his judgeship to the good offices of Senator Roscoe Conkling, the Republican boss of New York State. Conkling was a fierce foe of woman suffrage, and Hunt, who had no wish to offend his powerful patron, had written his decision before the trial started.

District Attorney Crowley opened the arguments for the prosecution. They didn't make much sense at the time, and in retrospect, they sound nothing short of ridiculous. The district attorney mentioned that Susan B. Anthony was a woman and therefore she had no right to vote. His principal witness was an inspector of elections for the Eighth Ward, who swore that on November 5 he had seen Miss Anthony put her ballot in the ballot box. To back up his testimony, the inspector produced the voter registration book with Susan B. Anthony's signature in it.

Henry Selden's reply for the defense was equally simple. He contended that Susan Anthony had registered and voted in good faith, believing that it was her constitutional right to do so. When he attempted to call his client to the stand, however, District Attorney Crowley announced that she was not competent to testify in her own behalf. Judge Hunt agreed, and the only thing Henry Selden could do was read excerpts from the testimony Susan had given at her previous hearings when presumably she was no less incompetent than she was right now.

Henry Selden tried to make up for this gross injustice by making his closing argument a dramatic, three-hour speech on behalf of woman suffrage. District Attorney Crowley replied with a two-hour rehash of the original charge.

By the afternoon of June 18, the case of *The United States* vs. *Susan B. Anthony* was ready to go to the jury. It was impossible to predict what their verdict might be, so Judge Hunt, determined to make it the verdict he and Roscoe Conkling wanted, took matters into his own hands. "Gentlemen of the jury," he said, "I direct that you find the defendant guilty."

Henry Selden leaped to his feet. "I object, your honor," he thundered. "The court has no power to direct the jury in a criminal case."

Judge Hunt ignored him. "Take the verdict, Mr. Clerk," he said.

The clerk of the court must have been another Conkling man. "Gentlemen of the jury," he intoned as if the whole proceeding was perfectly normal, "hearken to the verdict as the court hath recorded it. You say you find the defendant guilty of the offense charged. So say you all."

The twelve jurymen looked stunned. They had not even met to discuss the case, much

▲ **Critical Viewing** What character traits of Susan B. Anthony are evident in this photograph? [Analyze]

◆ **Build Vocabulary**

retrospect (re´ trə spekt´) n.: Hindsight

◀ **Critical Viewing**
What might it have been like to attend a woman's suffrage meeting, such as this one? **[Speculate]**

A meeting of the National Woman's Suffrage Association in the 1870's, with Susan B. Anthony and Elizabeth Cady Stanton on the platform

less agree on a verdict. When Henry Selden asked if the clerk could at least poll the jury, Judge Hunt rapped his gavel sharply and declared, "That cannot be allowed. Gentlemen of the jury, you are discharged."

An enraged Henry Selden lost no time in introducing a motion for a new trial on the grounds that his client had been denied the right to a jury verdict. Judge Hunt denied the motion. He turned to Susan B. Anthony and said, "The prisoner will stand up. Has the prisoner anything to say why sentence shall not be pronounced?"

Thus far in the trial, Susan B. Anthony had remained silent. Now, she rose to her feet and said slowly, "Yes, Your Honor, I have many things to say."

Without further preliminaries, she launched into a scathing denunciation of Judge Hunt's conduct of her trial. ". . . In your ordered verdict of guilty," she said, "you have trampled underfoot every vital principle of our government. My natural rights, my civil rights, my political rights, are all alike ignored. Robbed of the fundamental privilege of citizenship, I am degraded from the status of a citizen to that of a subject; and not only myself individually, but all of my sex, are, by your honor's verdict, doomed to political subjection under this so-called Republican government."

Judge Hunt reached for his gavel, but Susan B. Anthony refused to be silent.

"May it please your honor," she continued. "Your denial of my citizen's right to vote is the denial of my right to a trial by a jury of my peers as an offender against law, therefore, the denial of my sacred rights to life, liberty, property, and—"

"The court cannot allow the prisoner to go on," Judge Hunt cried out.

Susan ignored him and continued her impassioned tirade against the court. Hunt frantically rapped his gavel and ordered her to sit down and be quiet. But Susan, who must have been taking delight in his <u>consternation</u>, kept on talking. She deplored the fact that she had been denied the right to a fair trial. Even if she had been given such a trial, she insisted, it would not have been by her peers. Jury, judges, and lawyers were not her equals, but her superiors, because they

◆ **Build Vocabulary**

consternation (kän′ stər nā′ shən) *n.*: Great shock that makes one feel helpless or bewildered

futile (fyoo̅t′ əl) *adj.*: Ineffective

could vote and she could not. Susan was adamant about the fact that she had been denied the justice guaranteed in the Constitution to every citizen of the United States.

Judge Hunt was sufficiently cowed by now to try to defend himself. "The prisoner has been tried according to the established forms of law," he sputtered.

"Yes, Your Honor," retorted Susan, overlooking his blatant lie, "but by forms of law all made by men, interpreted by men, administered by men, in favor of men, and against women; and hence your honor's ordered verdict of guilty, against a United States citizen for the exercise of that citizen's right to vote, simply because that citizen was a woman and not a man. But yesterday, the same manmade forms of law declared it a crime punishable with a one-thousand-dollar fine and six months imprisonment, for you, or me, or any of us, to give a cup of cold water, a crust of bread, or a night's shelter to a panting fugitive while he was tracking his way to Canada. And every man or woman in whose veins coursed a drop of human sympathy violated that wicked law, reckless of consequences, and was justified in so doing. As, then, the slaves who got their freedom must take it over, or under, or through the unjust forms of law, precisely so now must women, to get their right to a voice in this government, take it, and I have taken mine and mean to take it at every opportunity."

Judge Hunt flailed his gavel and gave the by now <u>futile</u> order for the prisoner to sit down and be quiet. Susan kept right on talking.

"When I was brought before your honor for trial," she said, "I hoped for a broad and liberal interpretation of the Constitution and its recent Amendments. One that would declare all United States citizens under its protection. But failing to get this justice—failing, even, to get a trial by a jury *not* of my peers—

I ask not leniency at your hands—but to take the full rigors of the law."

With that Susan finally obeyed Judge Hunt's orders and sat down. Now he had to reverse himself and order her to stand up so he could impose sentence. As soon as he pronounced the sentence—a fine of one hundred dollars plus the costs of prosecuting the trial—Susan spoke up again. "May it please your honor," she said, "I shall never pay a dollar of your unjust penalty. All the stock in trade I possess is a ten-thousand-dollar debt, incurred by publishing my paper—*The Revolution*—four years ago, the sole object of which was to educate all women to do precisely as I have done, rebel against your manmade, unjust, unconstitutional forms of law, that tax, fine, imprison, and hang women, while they deny them the right of representation in the government; and I shall work on with might and main to pay every dollar of that honest debt, but not a penny shall go to this unjust claim. And I shall earnestly and persistently continue to urge all women to the practical recognition of the old Revolutionary maxim, that 'Resistance to tyranny is obedience to God.'"

Judge Hunt must have had strict orders not only to see that the defendant was convicted, but to do everything he could to prevent the case from going on to a higher court. He allowed Susan to walk out of the courtroom without imposing a prison sentence in lieu of[5] her unpaid fine. If he had sent her to prison, she could have been released on a writ of habeas corpus[6] and would have

---

5. **in lieu (lōō) of:** In place of.
6. **writ of habeas corpus** (hā′ bē əs kôr′ pəs): Legal document requiring that a detained person be brought before a court to decide the lawfulness of the imprisonment.

▲ **Critical Viewing** What accomplishments of Susan B. Anthony made her worthy of appearing on U.S. currency? **[Connect]**

had the right to appeal. As it was, the case was closed.

Although she was disappointed that her case would not go to the Supreme Court as she had originally hoped, Susan knew that she had struck an important blow for woman's suffrage. Henry Selden's arguments and her own speech at the end of the trial were widely publicized, and Judge Hunt's conduct of the trial stood as proof that women were treated unjustly before the law.

Susan did not forget the election inspectors who had allowed her to cast her ballot. The men were fined twenty-five dollars each and sent to jail when they refused to pay. In all, they spent about a week behind bars before Susan, through the influence of friends in Washington, obtained presidential pardons for each of them. In the meantime, her followers, who included some of the best cooks in Rochester, saw to it that the men were supplied with delicious hot meals and home-baked pies.

True to her promise, Susan paid the legal expenses for the three inspectors. With the help of contributions from sympathetic admirers, she paid the costs of her own trial. But she never paid that one-hundred-dollar fine. Susan B. Anthony was a woman of her word as well as a woman of courage.

Guide for Responding

◆ LITERATURE AND YOUR LIFE

Reader's Response Was Anthony justified in using the wording of the Fourteenth Amendment to support her actions? Explain.

Thematic Focus In what ways can Susan B. Anthony be considered a hero? Explain.

☑ Check Your Comprehension

1. Summarize the editorial that led Anthony to register to vote.
2. What missing feature of the Fourteenth Amendment did Anthony use as support for her right to register?
3. Why did the district attorney agree to postpone Anthony's trial until late December?

◆ Critical Thinking

INTERPRET

1. How was the behavior of Marshal Keeney similar to and different from the behavior of the men in the barber shop? **[Compare and Contrast]**
2. Why did Anthony have trouble finding a lawyer who would defend her in court? **[Infer]**
3. What do you think the author means when she says, "I have a sneaky feeling that . . . she may actually have had a sense of humor"? **[Interpret]**

APPLY

4. What other situations do you know in which a person publicly violated a law he or she considered unjust? **[Relate]**

Meet the Author

Margaret Truman (1924–) spent a good part of her life being known as the daughter of President Harry Truman (1945–1953). She has since become known as the author of more than twenty books. Truman has written a dozen murder mysteries, all of them set in Washington, D.C. She has also written books about each of her parents and about life in the White House. *First Ladies* is a series of essays about wives of American presidents.

CONNECTING LITERATURE TO SOCIAL STUDIES

In the nineteenth century, many Americans believed that a woman could not be as intelligent as a man, that a woman could not handle business affairs the way a man could, and that a "normal" woman wanted nothing more than to stay at home, raise children, and care for a husband. As a result of these beliefs, the idea of allowing women to vote was outrageous to many people. Susan B. Anthony and others decided to show how foolish these beliefs were. It took more than a century for women's groups to win the right to vote for all American women.

1. Think about the society of Susan B. Anthony's time. Explain whether or not her methods of raising the issue of woman suffrage were effective.
2. List other actions Anthony might have taken. Would they have been more effective or less effective? Explain.
3. For what other rights have Americans publicly fought? How have their methods been similar to those Anthony used?

 Idea Bank

Writing

1. **Journal Entry** Write an entry that Anthony might have put into her journal after her first visit to the barber shop.
2. **Dialogue** Write a dialogue between two men who were in the barber shop when the Anthony sisters made their demand.
3. **Editorial** Write an editorial for a Rochester newspaper, either praising or condemning the Anthony sisters for trying to register to vote.

Speaking and Listening

4. **Legal Arguments [Group Activity]** With a classmate, role-play parts in the hearing before the Federal Commissioner of Elections. Decide who will be U.S. District Attorney Crowley and who will be Henry R. Selden, Anthony's defense attorney. Then, present your arguments to the class.

Project

5. **Timeline of the Woman Suffrage Movement** Do research to learn about the struggle to win voting rights for women in the United States. Create a timeline showing significant events on the road to the approval of the Nineteenth Amendment. **[Social Studies Link]**

Further Reading, Listening, and Viewing

- Margaret Truman's book *Women of Courage* (1976) contains the full story of the 1872 incident described in this essay, along with stories of other women who brought about changes.
- Susan Clinton's *The Story of Susan B. Anthony* (1986) is a biography of Susan B. Anthony.
- Kate Connell's *They Shall Be Heard* is a biography of Susan B. Anthony and Elizabeth Cady Stanton.
- The Susan B. Anthony House online at http://www.susanbanthonyhouse.org/ contains an interactive tour through this historic site.

Guide for Reading

Meet the Authors:

Stephen Longstreet (1907–   )

Stephen Longstreet has written screenplays, novels, art criticism, television scripts, and detective stories. In addition to being a writer, he is an experienced artist who has studied painting in Paris, Rome, London, and Berlin. While living in Europe in the 1920's, Longstreet met such famous artists as Marc Chagall, Henri Matisse, and Pablo Picasso.

John Hersey (1914–1993)

John Hersey was born in Tientsin, China, where his parents were missionaries. After his early education in China, he attended Yale, as well as Clare College in Cambridge, England. He was an assistant to the famous author Sinclair Lewis and then worked as a journalist for several New York magazines.

THE STORY BEHIND THE STORY

"Not to Go With the Others" tells of the escape of Frantizek Zaremski from a Nazi prison camp during World War II. Hersey describes meeting Zaremski a few days after his escape: "The skin of his face was drawn tight over the bones and cartilage, and the hair on his head, which had been shaved by the Nazis, was just beginning to grow back. . . . More than once, as he told his story, he covered his eyes with his free hand, and I thought he might faint."

◆ LITERATURE AND YOUR LIFE

CONNECT YOUR EXPERIENCE

You may admire people for many different reasons. Some have exceptional talent; some have great courage; some inspire strong emotional connections. You will meet two people in these biographies—Katsushika Hokusai and Frantizek Zaremski—who are likely to fit your definition of admirable.

THEMATIC FOCUS: Heroes

Both Hokusai and Zaremski are heroes in different ways. What makes each a hero?

◆ Background for Understanding

HISTORY

In "Not to Go With the Others," Frantizek Zaremski is put in a Gestapo prison during World War II. The Gestapo was a German military police force. Its mission was to eliminate all enemies of Nazi Germany, including Jews, Catholics, political opponents, Gypsies, and the mentally ill. The Gestapo operated outside the law. Its officers had the power to imprison people without trials. Many Gestapo prisoners were tortured, sent to concentration camps, or executed.

◆ Build Vocabulary

PREFIXES: *en-*

Longstreet describes one of Hokusai's pictures as "great waves engulfing fishermen." The prefix *en-* in *engulf* means "cover with." *Engulf* means "to swallow up" or "to cover completely."

WORD BANK

Which word from the list is related to the verb *pretend*? Check the Build Vocabulary box on page 657 to see if you chose correctly.

apprenticed
engulfing
mania
feigned
ensued
dispatched
pretense
immersed

Hokusai: The Old Man Mad About Drawing
◆ Not to Go With the Others ◆

VII, Fuji in clear weather. One of the "Thirty-six Views of Fuji," Hokusai, British Museum

◆ Literary Focus

BIOGRAPHY

Both "Hokusai: The Old Man Mad About Drawing" and "Not to Go With the Others" are biographies. A **biography** is a form of nonfiction in which a writer tells about the life of another person. Most biographies are written about famous or admirable people. Although biographies are nonfiction, many share the elements of narrative writing—settings, interesting characters and dialogue, and a theme or message.

Main Point of Selection:

Paragraph 4 – Main Point:

Paragraph 3 – Main Point:

Paragraph 2 – Main Point:

Paragraph 1 – Main Point:
Hokusai had a unique personality.

◆ Reading Strategy

IDENTIFY THE AUTHOR'S MAIN POINTS

To **identify the author's main points,** ask yourself what he or she wants you to discover or think as you read. These main points are the most important ideas. In many cases, you'll find a main point in each paragraph, as well as in the introduction and conclusion to an essay. Often, you can piece together the main points of individual paragraphs to determine the main point of the work as a whole. To help you, fill in a chart like the one at left as you read:

Hokusai: The Old Man Mad About Drawing

Stephen Longstreet

▶ **Critical Viewing**
What do you appreciate most about this drawing by Hokusai—its colors, sense of movement, style, or lines? [Assess]

The Great Wave of Kangawa, Katsushika Hokusai, The Metropolitan Museum of Art, New York, NY

Of all the great artists of Japan, the one Westerners probably like and understand best is Katsushika Hokusai. He was a restless, unpredictable man who lived in as many as a hundred different houses and changed his name at least thirty times. For a very great artist, he acted at times like P.T. Barnum[1] or a Hollywood producer with his curiosity and drive for novelty.

Hokusai was born in 1760 outside the city of Edo[2] in the province of Shimofusa. He was apprenticed early in life to a mirror maker and then worked in a lending library, where he was fascinated by the woodcut illustrations of the piled-up books. At eighteen he became a pupil of Shunsho, a great artist known mainly for his prints of actors. Hokusai was soon signing his name as Shunro, and for the next fifteen years he, too, made actor prints, as well as illustrations for popular novels. By 1795 he was calling himself Sori and had begun working with the European copper etchings which had become popular in Japan. Every time Hokusai changed his name, he changed his style. He drew, he designed fine surimino (greeting prints), he experimented with pure landscape.

Hokusai never stayed long with a period or style, but was always off and running to something new. A great show-off, he painted with his fingers, toothpicks, a bottle, an eggshell; he worked left-handed, from the bottom up, and from left to right. Once he painted two sparrows on a grain of rice. Commissioned by a shogun (a military ruler in 18th century Japan) to decorate a door of the Temple of Dempo-ji, he tore it off its hinges, laid it in the courtyard, and painted wavy blue lines on it to represent running water, then dipped the feet of a live rooster in red seal ink and chased the bird over the painted door. When the shogun came to see the finished job, he at once saw the river Tatsuta and the falling red maple leaves of autumn. Another time Hokusai used a large broom dipped into a vat of ink to draw the full-length figure of a god, over a hundred feet long, on the floor of a courtyard.

When he was fifty-four, Hokusai began to

---

1. **P. T. Barnum:** Phineas Taylor Barnum (1810–1891); U.S. showman and circus operator.
2. **Edo** (ē′ dō): Former name of Tokyo.

issue books of his sketches, which he called *The Manga.* He found everything worth sketching: radish grinders, pancake women, street processions, jugglers, and wrestlers. And he was already over sixty when he began his great series, *Thirty-six Views of Fuji,* a remarkable set of woodcut prints that tell the story of the countryside around Edo: people at play or work, great waves engulfing fishermen, silks drying in the sun, lightning playing on great mountains, and always, somewhere, the ash-tipped top of Fuji.

Hokusai did thirty thousand pictures during a full and long life. When he was seventy-five he wrote:

From the age of six I had a mania for drawing the shapes of things. When I was fifty I had published a universe of designs. But all I have done before the age of seventy is not worth bothering with. At seventy-five I have learned something of the pattern of nature, of animals, of plants, of trees, birds, fish, and insects. When I am eighty you will see real progress. At ninety I shall have cut my way deeply into the mystery of life itself. At a hundred I shall be a marvelous artist. At a hundred and ten everything I create, a dot, a line, will jump to life as never before. To all of you who are going to live as long as I do, I promise to keep my word. I am writing this in my old age. I used to call myself Hokusai, but today I sign myself "The Old Man Mad About Drawing."

He didn't reach a hundred and ten, but he nearly reached ninety. On the day of his death, in 1849, he was cheerfully at work on a new drawing.

◆ **Build Vocabulary**

apprenticed (ə pren´ tist) *v.*: Contracted to learn a trade under a skilled worker

engulfing (en gulf´ iŋ) *v.*: Flowing over and swallowing

mania (mā´ nē ə) *n.*: Uncontrollable enthusiasm

Guide for Responding

◆ LITERATURE AND YOUR LIFE

Reader's Response What do you admire most about Hokusai? Explain.

Thematic Focus In what way can Hokusai be considered a hero?

☑ Check Your Comprehension

1. Where and when was Hokusai born?
2. What kind of work did he do when he was a young man?
3. Name five styles of art that Hokusai produced.
4. How many pictures and illustrations did Hokusai create during his lifetime?
5. What was Hokusai doing the day that he died?
6. How long did Hokusai live?

◆ Critical Thinking

INTERPRET

1. What does the first paragraph tell you about Hokusai? What kind of person was he? **[Analyze]**
2. Why might Hokusai be considered a man ahead of his time? **[Speculate]**
3. What did Hokusai mean when he said, "At a hundred I shall be a marvelous artist"? **[Interpret]**

EVALUATE

4. Would Hokusai fit into the art world today? Explain. **[Make a Judgment]**

APPLY

5. Hokusai lived a very long and productive life. How would a present-day senior citizen feel after reading this essay? **[Hypothesize]**

Not to Go With the Others

John Hersey

The Watchtower, 1942, Savielly Schleifer, Musée d'Histoire Contemporaine, Paris, France

▲ **Critical Viewing** What do the colors in this painting convey about conditions within the prison camp? **[Analyze]**

In the third year of the war, Frantizek Zaremski was arrested by the invaders on a charge of spreading underground literature—specifically, for carrying about his person a poem a friend from Gdynia[1] had given him, which began: *Sleep, beloved Hitler, planes will come by night . . .*

After he had spent six weeks of a three-year sentence for this crime in the Gestapo[2] prison at Inowroczon, Zaremski was sent to Kalice[3] to do carpentry. By bad luck, at the time when his term expired, the Russians had broken through at the Vistula, and his captors, instead of releasing him, took him, in their general panic, to the transfer camp for Polish political prisoners at Rodogoszcz,[4] where he was placed in Hall Number Four with nine hundred men. Altogether there were between two and three thousand men and women—no Jews, only "Aryan"[5] Poles suspected or convicted of political activity—in the prison.

---

1. **Gdynia** (gə din´ ē ə): A city in the northern region of Poland.
2. **Gestapo** (gə stä´ pō): The secret police force of the German Nazi state, notorious for its terrorism and brutality.
3. **Inowroczon** (ē nəv rô´ zôn´) **. . . Kalice** (kä´ lish): Cities in the central region of Poland.

4. **Rodogoszcz** (rô dô gôzh´): A suburb of the city of Lódź.
5. **"Aryan"** (âr´ ē ən): In Naziism, people of northern European descent who were said to possess racially superior traits and capacities for government, social organization, and civilization, while the non-Aryan peoples, such as the Jews, were seen as being inferior.

Late in the evening of Wednesday, January 17, 1945, three days before Lódź was to fall to the Russians, all the prisoners were gathered on the third and fourth floors of the main building, even those who were sick, and there they all lay down on wooden bunks and floors to try to sleep. At about two in the morning guards came and ordered the inmates to get up for roll call.

They divided the prisoners into groups of about twenty each and lined up the groups in pairs. Zaremski was in the second group. SS[6] men led it down concrete stairs in a brick-walled stairwell at one end of the building and halted it on a landing of the stairway, near a door opening into a large loft on the second floor. The first group had apparently been led down to the ground floor.

Someone gave an order that the prisoners should run in pairs into the loft as fast as they could. When the first pairs of Zaremski's group ran in, SS men with their backs to the wall inside the room began to shoot at them from behind. Zaremski's turn came. He ran in terror. A bullet burned through his trouser leg. Another grazed his thigh. He fell down and <u>feigned</u> death.

Others, from Zaremski's and later groups, ran into the hall and were shot and fell dead or wounded on top of Zaremski and those who had gone first. At one time Zaremski heard the Polish national anthem being sung somewhere.

Finally the running and shooting ended, and there <u>ensued</u> some shooting on the upper floors, perhaps of people who had refused to run downstairs.

SS men with flashlights waded among the bodies, shining lights in the faces of the prostrate victims. Any wounded who moaned or moved, or any whose eyes reacted when the shafts of light hit their faces, were <u>dispatched</u> with pistol shots. Somehow Zaremski passed the test of <u>pretense</u>.

---

6. **SS:** Abbreviation of the German *Schutzstaffel,* meaning "protective rank." They were a quasi-military unit of the Nazi party used as a special police force.

As dawn began to break, Zaremski heard the iron doors of the main building being locked, and he heard some sort of grenades or bombs being thrown into the lowest hall and exploding there; they seemed to him to make only smoke, but they may have been incendiaries.[7] Later, in any case, the ground floor began to burn. Perhaps benzine or petrol[8] had been poured around. Zaremski was still lying among the bodies of others.

There were several who were still alive, and they began jumping out of the burning building, some from windows on the upper stories. A few broke through a skylight to the roof, tied blankets from the prisoners' bunks into long ropes and let themselves down outside. Zaremski, now scurrying about the building, held back to see what would happen. Those who jumped or climbed down were shot at at leisure in the camp enclosure by SS men in the turrets on the walls, and Zaremski decided to try to stay inside.

On the fourth floor, at the top of the reinforced concrete staircase, in the bricked stairwell at the end of the building, Zaremski found the plant's water tank, and for a time he and others poured water over the wounded lying on the wooden floors in the main rooms. Later Zaremski took all his clothes off, soaked them in the tank, and put them back on. He lay down and kept pouring water over himself. He put a soaked blanket around his head.

The tank was a tall one, separated from the main room by the stairwell's brick wall, and

---

7. **incendiaries** (in sen′ dē er′ ēz): Bombs made with a chemical substance that cause a large fire when exploded.
8. **benzine** (ben′ zēn′) **. . . petrol** (pet′ rəl): Clear, poisonous, highly flammable liquid fuels.

◆ **Build Vocabulary**

feigned (fānd) *v.*: Imitated; pretended

ensued (en sōōd′) *v.*: Came afterward; followed immediately

dispatched (di spacht′) *v.*: Put an end to; killed

pretense (prē tens′) *n.*: False showing; pretending

when the fire began to eat through the wooden floor of the fourth story and the heat in the stairwell grew unbearable, Zaremski climbed up and got right into the water in the tank. He stayed immersed there all day long. Every few minutes he could hear shots from the wall turrets. He heard floors of the main halls fall and heard the side walls collapse. The staircase shell and the concrete stairs remained standing.

It was evening before the shooting and the fire died down. When he felt sure both had ended, Zaremski pulled himself out of the tank and lay awhile on the cement floor beside it. Then, his strength somewhat restored, he made his way down the stairs, and on the way he found six others who were wounded but could walk.

The seven went outside. Dusk. All quiet. They thought the Germans had left, and they wanted to climb the wall and escape. The first three climbed up and dropped away in apparent safety, but then the lights flashed on in the turrets and bursts of firing broke out. Three of the remaining four decided to take their chances at climbing out after total darkness; they did not know whether the first three had been killed or

had escaped. Only Zaremski decided to stay.

The three climbed, but this time the lights came sooner, and the guards killed all three while they were still scaling the wall.

Zaremski crept into the camp's storehouse in a separate building. Finding some damp blankets, he wrapped them around himself and climbed into a big box, where he stayed all night. Once during the night he heard steps outside the building, and in the early morning he heard walking again. This time the footsteps approached the storeroom door. The door opened. The steps entered. Through the cracks of the box Zaremski sensed that the beam of a flashlight was probing the room. Zaremski could hear box tops opening and slamming and a foot kicking barrels. He held the lid of his box from the inside. Steps came near, a hand tried the lid, but Zaremski held tight, and the searcher must have decided the box was locked or nailed down. The footsteps went away.

Later two others came at different times and inspected the room, but neither tried

The Unattainable, Henri Pieck, by courtesy of Karrie Pieck, Holland, and Ineke Pieck, England

▲ **Critical Viewing** What might the prisoner depicted in this painting be longing for? [Speculate]

◆ **Literary Focus**
What fact about Zaremski's life may have given the author the idea for the title of this biography?

◆ **Build Vocabulary**
immersed (im murst´) v.: Plunged into; submerged

Zaremski's box; the third hunter locked the door from the outside.

Much later Zaremski heard a car start and drive away.

Much later still—some time on the nineteenth of January in the year of victory—Zaremski heard the Polish language being spoken, even by the voices of women and children. He jumped out of the box and broke the window of the storehouse and climbed out to his countrymen.

Beyond Literature

Social Studies Connection

Axis vs. Allies World War II (1939–1945) directly involved nearly every country in the world, with fighting raging over four continents. It started when the three main Axis countries—Japan, Germany, and Italy—invaded their weaker neighbors to gain land and natural resources. The opponents of the Axis—the Allies—consisted of fifty countries, including the United States, Great Britain, and the Soviet Union. These countries fought against the nine countries comprising the Axis. The war lasted for several years, and there was a time when it looked as if the Axis might win. By the war's end, more than seventy million people had served in the armies of either side and more than seventeen million soldiers died. Civilian casualties, including the Jewish Holocaust, brought the total death figure to between twenty-five and thirty million people.

Cross-Curricular Activity
Interviewing Speak with a person old enough to remember World War II. Ask him or her what it was like to live through that period. Record the interview and your reactions to it, and share it with the rest of the class.

Guide for Responding

◆ LITERATURE AND YOUR LIFE

Reader's Response Zaremski was able to think clearly in an extremely challenging and dangerous situation. What would you have done if you had been in his position?

Thematic Focus What challenges did Zaremski face and overcome?

Journal Writing Jot down in your journal qualities or characteristics that are useful during crisis situations.

☑ Check Your Comprehension

1. For what crime was Zaremski arrested?
2. What happened to Zaremski after his term of imprisonment expired?
3. What did the SS men do to the prisoners who were running into the loft?
4. How did Zaremski save himself from the fire?
5. After the fire died out, where did Zaremski hide from the Nazi soldiers?

◆ Critical Thinking

INTERPRET
1. Why do you think the Nazis did not release the political prisoners from Rodogoszcz when the Russians were advancing? **[Infer]**
2. What would have happened to Zaremski if he had not pretended to be dead? **[Draw Conclusions]**
3. Instead of climbing the prison walls to escape, Zaremski held back. How did he know it was safer to stay? **[Infer]**

EVALUATE
4. Zaremski was the only prisoner to survive the Nazi slaughter. What characteristics did he have that enabled him to live? **[Assess]**

COMPARE LITERARY WORKS
5. In what way do both Hokusai and Zaremski triumph? Explain. **[Compare and Contrast]**

Guide for Responding (continued)

◆ Reading Strategy

IDENTIFY THE AUTHOR'S MAIN POINTS

To discover the **main points** in a nonfiction work, ask yourself what the author wants you to learn or think as a result of reading.

1. What is the main point Longstreet makes about Hokusai?
2. List three examples from "Not to Go With the Others" that support Hersey's main point that Zaremski was a man of great courage.

◆ Build Vocabulary Skills

USING THE PREFIX *en-*

The prefix *en-* has several meanings. They include "in or into," "cover with," and "cause to be." Using these *en-* words, complete the sentences that follow.

      enrich   enjoy   enclosed

1. The people were _____?_____ in a room.
2. Following his escape, Zaremski could _____?_____ his freedom.
3. Stories like this _____?_____ our lives.

SPELLING STRATEGY

In some words, the letter *g* is silent—often when the *g* comes before an *n,* such as in the words *feigned* and *design*. Practice spelling words with a silent *g* by unscrambling the words in parentheses.

1. A small insect (tagn)
2. What a dog does to a bone (gawn)
3. To quit a job (sireng)
4. To rule (ernig)

USING THE WORD BANK

Match the Word Bank word in Column A with its definition or synonym in Column B.

Column A	Column B
1. apprenticed	a. pretended
2. engulfing	b. deception
3. mania	c. put to death
4. feigned	d. trained
5. ensued	e. excessive enthusiasm
6. dispatched	f. swallowing up
7. pretense	g. followed
8. immersed	h. submerged

◆ Literary Focus

BIOGRAPHY

A **biography** is an account of a person's life, written by another person. It often focuses on the individual's achievements and explains the difficulties that the subject had to overcome.

1. What do you think Longstreet wants you to know about Hokusai?
2. Find two details from "Hokusai: The Old Man Mad About Drawing" that help create a strong impression about its subject.
3. For what reasons do you think Hokusai and Zaremski are good subjects for biographies?

◆ Build Grammar Skills

USING *who* AND *whom*

Many people have problems deciding when to use *whom* instead of *who*. *Who* is in the subjective case; use it for the subject of a sentence or a clause. *Whom* is the objective case; use it for a direct object, an indirect object, or an object of a preposition.

Subject: To all of you *who* are going to live as long as I do, I promise . . .

Direct Object: Hokusai was an artist *whom* others imitated. [Others imitated *whom*.]

Object of a Preposition: At *whom* were the shots directed?

Practice On your paper, complete the following sentences with *who* or *whom*.

1. The guards, _____?_____ led the prisoners to the loft, were silent.
2. From _____?_____ did Hokusai learn to draw?
3. To _____?_____ did the prisoner explain the escape plans?
4. _____?_____ asked for a woodcut of Mt. Fuji?
5. The man _____?_____ the Nazis pursued.

Writing Application Write a short description of Hokusai or Zaremski, using *who* and *whom* at least once each.

Build Your Portfolio

 ## Idea Bank

Writing

1. **Advice Letters** Write a letter asking advice about how to overcome an obstacle. Then, write the response that either Hokusai or Zaremski might offer.

2. **Casting Memo** Write a memo suggesting actors to play parts in a movie about Zaremski's life. Give reasons for your choices.

3. **Biography** Write a short biography about a person you admire. Stress the individual's admirable accomplishments and the challenges he or she faced. Include direct quotations whenever possible.

Speaking and Listening

4. **Radio Play [Group Activity]** With a group of classmates, adapt "Not to Go With the Others" as a radio play. Rehearse first; then perform or record the play for the class. **[Performing Arts Link]**

5. **Dialogue [Group Activity]** With a classmate, write and perform a dialogue that Hokusai and Zaremski might have about the importance of not giving up. Perform the dialogue for the class. **[Performing Arts Link]**

Projects

6. **Holocaust Exhibit** Research information about the concentration camps and political prisons run by the Nazis. Collect copies of paintings, photographs, and first-person accounts of the Holocaust. Prepare an exhibit about the Holocaust for your classmates. **[Social Studies Link]**

7. **Art Catalog** Research the life and works of Hokusai. Then, create an art catalog in which you give a brief biography of the artist and his works. Include photocopies of some of Hokusai's most famous drawings in your catalog. **[Art Link]**

 ## Writing Mini-Lesson

Testimonial

A testimonial is a short speech that expresses appreciation or gratitude for an individual. Testimonials are usually given at dinners or meetings that honor the subject of the speech. Certainly, both Hokusai and Zaremski would be worthy subjects for this kind of praise. Choose a person you admire, and write a testimonial to him or her.

Writing Skills Focus: Support With Examples

A testimonial contains main points supported by **examples** that illustrate why the subject is admirable. Notice how Longstreet supports a main point—that Hokusai was unpredictable and forever changing—with these examples:

Model From "Hokusai: . . ."

A great show-off, he painted with his fingers, toothpicks, a bottle, an eggshell; he worked left-handed, from the bottom up, and from left to right.

Prewriting Brainstorm for examples, details, facts and incidents that show your individual in the most positive light. Group your notes according to the points they make about the person. Organize your ideas in an outline.

Drafting Draft your testimonial, emphasizing your points and supporting them with examples. Include transitions to make your thoughts flow smoothly.

Revising Read your testimonial aloud to a partner. Ask whether or not you have included enough examples to show why your individual is admirable, and revise accordingly. Proofread your draft for errors in grammar.

> ◆ **Grammar Application**
> Be sure that you have used the correct forms of *who* and *whom* in your testimonial.

Writing Process Workshop

The writers in this section share important information with others. One way they could bring their information to a larger audience is through public-service announcements. A **public-service announcement** is a message intended to educate, advise, or persuade the public about an issue of public concern. It involves words plus visuals or sound, depending on whether the announcement appears in print, on radio, or on television.

Write a public-service announcement. Use the following writing skills, introduced in this section's Writing Mini-Lessons, to help you make your point:

Writing Skills Focus

▶ **Choose an appropriate tone** for your subject and audience. (See p. 630.)

▶ **Strive for clarity** to ensure that you get your points across. (See p. 641.)

▶ **Support your points.** Examples, reasons, and statistics will help you persuade, advise, educate, or inform. (See p. 661.)

The following excerpt is from a public-service announcement encouraging those who have the right to vote to use it.

WRITING MODEL

If you enjoy your freedom, then exercise your right to vote! ① In this country, we are entitled to choose our leaders, yet each November, millions don't bother to show up at the voting booths. In fact, almost half the eligible voters don't vote in a presidential election. ② Make sure you are not one of those people. Don't throw away your precious right to vote. ③

① The purpose behind this public-service announcement is clearly stated.

② This startling statistic supports the writer's point.

③ The writer uses a forceful tone to try to persuade readers to vote.

Prewriting

State Your Purpose First, you must have something to say. What is your purpose in calling people to action? To inspire change? To get people to think about something seriously? Here are a few suggestions:

Topic Ideas

- Persuade your audience to take care of their environment
- Advise people on saving or spending money wisely
- Educate teenagers on maintaining good health
- Inform parents of issues that concern teenagers

Define Your Audience Who will hear or read your announcement? Before you begin, define your "target audience" very specifically. These questions may help:

▶ How old is your audience?
▶ What do they care about?
▶ What gender are they?
▶ Where do they live?
▶ What do they have in common?
▶ What do they already know about the topic?

Review your answers to these questions. Then, choose information that would appeal to this audience.

Choose Strong Examples Gather information or examples that will illustrate the points you are making. Statistics are often a strong way of supporting your points.

Drafting

State Your Message With Clarity Because a public-service announcement is usually brief, you must be clear about your message. Don't try to say too much, or your message may become unfocused.

Use Examples That Support Work in examples that support your main points. If your examples don't directly support your subject, people will be confused by your message.

Use an Appropriate Tone Choose words that communicate your attitude toward your subject and audience. For example, if you are scolding people for not voting, use a stern tone to let them know how serious the issue is.

APPLYING LANGUAGE SKILLS: Using Appositives

An **appositive** is a noun phrase, usually set off by commas, that further identifies or defines the noun it follows:

Women's suffrage, the right to vote, was denied nationwide until 1920.

In a public-service announcement, you may identify or define something or someone using an appositive.

Practice Copy these sentences into your notebook. Combine them so one of the sentences becomes an appositive phrase.

1. Heart disease affects us all. Heart disease is the leading cause of death.

2. Clean water is everyone's business. Clean water is our most basic need.

3. Walking is a great exercise. Walking is a lot of fun.

Writing Application As you write your public-service announcement, include at least one appositive and punctuate it correctly.

Writer's Solution Connection Language Lab

For help punctuating appositives, complete the lesson on Commas in the Punctuation unit.

Applying Language Skills:
Using *Who, That,* and *Which* Correctly

Who, that, and *which* are relative pronouns. They introduce clauses that add information about a person or thing. Use *that* and *which* to refer to things. Use *who* or *whom* to refer to people.

- The computer is a tool *that* changed the world.
- Baseball, *which* is played all over the world, began in the United States.
- She is a woman *who* changed the world.

Practice As you copy these sentences into your notebook, correct the use of *who, that,* and *which* as necessary.

1. Voting is a right who should be exercised.
2. My father is a man that always votes.
3. The United States is a country which depends on public opinion.

Writing Application As you write your public-service announcement, use *who, that,* and *which* correctly.

Writer's Solution
Writing Lab

For more help with revising, use the Self-Evaluation Checklist in the Revising section of the Persuasion tutorial.

Revising

Use a Checklist Use the Writing Skills Focus list on p. 662 as a checklist for your self-revision.

Ask a Listener Share your announcement with a partner. Read your draft to your partner, and ask these questions:
- Does my opening grab your attention?
- Are my words strong?
- Is my purpose clear?
- Is there enough information?
- Have I used an appropriate tone?
- Does the announcement hold your interest until the end?

If your partner answers no to any of these questions, make revisions that will enable your partner to answer yes.

REVISION MODEL

People all over the world are struggling for simple human rights. ① , such as the right to vote. In April 1994, South Africans had to stand in line for days to vote, and they did. ② The polls had to stay open for four days to accommodate everyone who wanted to vote. In the United States, more than half the people eligible to vote do not do so. They let others make the choice for them. ③ Don't be one of those people!

① For clarity, the writer adds the specific human right that is the subject of this announcement.
② The writer adds this information to strengthen her argument that voting is a precious right.
③ The writer ends with a forceful tone.

Publishing and Presenting

School Turn your announcement into a colorful, eye-catching poster. Choose a visual that makes sense and stands out. Display your poster somewhere in your school.

Radio Get permission to read your announcement over your school's public address system, or send it to a local radio station. If appropriate, include music or sound effects to help make your point.

Strategies for Success

Every time you turn on the radio or the television or pick up a newspaper or a magazine, you encounter advertisements. Advertisers try to persuade you to buy, do, or believe something. Whatever forms these ads take, you need to decide how to respond to them.

Recognize Persuasion As you evaluate an advertisement, remember that its purpose is to persuade you. When deciding how to respond to an advertisement, try to make an informed decision. Do not simply go with your "gut reaction."

Evaluate the Message In order to make an informed decision, first examine the writer's statements. Evaluate them by answering questions like these:

▶ Are the statements true?
▶ Do the statements contain facts, or are they statements of the writer's opinions?
▶ To what feelings or beliefs is the advertisement appealing?

Make a Decision After evaluating the ad, decide whether or not you accept the advertiser's claims. If you accept them, you will probably make the purchase or do what the advertiser wishes. If not, you will probably not make a purchase. With either choice, you will have made an informed decision.

Apply the Strategies

You are looking for a special gift for your mother, an avid baseball fan. Evaluate the claims of this advertisement before deciding whether to make a purchase.

EVERY BASEBALL FAN MUST HAVE THE SOUVENIR PRINTING PLATES OF MCGWIRE'S RECORD HOME RUNS! ! !

If you love baseball, you'll have to have these beautiful metal souvenir plates from home-run history! These copies of the *Sun's* front pages capture the special moment forever. They will look perfect on the den wall, and you will be the envy of every baseball fan.

To order call 1-XXX-BASEBALL.
Don't Delay! Limited Offer!
(Plates cost $10.00 each plus $3.00 postage and handling.)

1. What is the writer's purpose? How do you know?

2. What does this advertisement claim the product will do?

3. What statements are written to persuade you to make a purchase?

4. Would you buy a printing plate as a gift for your mother?

✔ Here are some forms of advertising that are important to evaluate:
▶ Infomercials on television
▶ Ads for cosmetics
▶ Flyers

Pronoun Case Case is the form of a personal pronoun that shows its use in a sentence. To use pronouns correctly, you must know when to use the subjective case and when to use the objective case. (See pp. 629 and 640.)

case¹ (kās) **n. 1** Grammar the form of a noun, pronoun, or adjective that shows how it is related to the other words around it (Example: in "He hit me," the subject he is in the nominative case and the object me is in the objective case)

Singular		Plural	
Subjective	**Objective**	**Subjective**	**Objective**
I, you, he, she, it	me, you, him, her, it	we, you, they	us, you, them

Use the subjective case when the pronoun is a subject or a subject complement:

Subject of a Verb: ". . . *I* climbed up a ladder . . ."

Subject Complement (Predicate pronoun): The first people in the barn were *she* and *I*.

Use the objective case when the pronoun is a direct object, an indirect object, or an object of the preposition:

Direct Object: "But then something snapped *me* out of my sense of loss. . . ."

Indirect Object: Susan B. Anthony's fight gave *us* the right to vote.

Object of a Preposition: For *whom* did she vote?

Who and **Whom** You can use the forms of *who* either as interrogative or relative pronouns. *Who* is the subjective form; *whom* is the objective form. (See p. 660.)

Subject: *Who* can believe that wasps could create such an amazing piece of architecture?

Direct Object: I wondered about the man *whom* I had met earlier.

Object of a Preposition:
With *whom* did Susan B. Anthony live?

Practice Choose the correct pronoun to complete the following sentences:

1. (We, Us) believe that everyone should explore nature.

2. We found (they, them) in the tree.

3. His uncle gave (he, him) a baseball.

4. That is (he, him) up at bat.

5. Caroline and (I, me) are thankful to (she, her) for defending our rights.

6. (Who, whom) hasn't wondered about the mysteries of nature?

7. To (who, whom) did you give your notes?

Grammar in Writing

✔ *To determine which pronoun case to use in a compound structure, say the sentence to yourself without the other part of the compound construction.*

My mother took Melinda and _____?_____ to see Hokusai's paintings.

Say: My mother took *me* to see Hokusai's paintings.

Correct: My mother took Melinda and *me* to see Hokusai's paintings.

PART 2 *Essays and Speeches*

Guide for Reading

Meet the Authors:

James Herriot (1916–1995)

Born in Scotland, James Herriot wrote many memorable true stories about his fifty years as a veterinarian. The incidents Herriot describes, such as the one in "Debbie," have filled more than ten books and inspired a popular television series. Although he didn't start writing until he was fifty, he found a natural talent for describing the people and animals that made his career memorable. As Herriot told one interviewer, "I think it was the fact that I liked it so much that made the writing just come out of me automatically."

Anaïs Nin (1903–1977)

A native of France, Anaïs Nin grew up in the United States. At age eleven, she began the writing that continued throughout her life. Although she wrote novels and short stories, Nin was best known for her six diaries spanning sixty years. "Forest Fire," from the fifth diary, illustrates how Nin looked at life "as an adventure and a tale."

Virginia Shea

A widely published journalist, Virginia Shea's writing has appeared in newspapers and journals. After attending Princeton, she moved to Sunnyvale, California, with her husband and four cats. Inspired by the booming computer industry there, Shea became an expert on Internet manners and skills. Recognizing her insights into the do's and don'ts of on-line communication, the San Jose *Mercury News* declared Shea the "network manners guru."

◆ LITERATURE AND YOUR LIFE

CONNECT YOUR EXPERIENCE

In the course of daily life—on the bus, in a store, or at a school game—you probably observe funny, interesting, or frightening things that you relate to your family and friends. In the following essays, James Herriot, Anaïs Nin, and Virginia Shea share their observations of the world around them.

THEMATIC FOCUS: Living Each Day

Look for the surprises of everyday life as you read the essays that follow.

◆ Background for Understanding

SCIENCE

Anaïs Nin writes about a raging forest fire she witnesses while living in California. In addition to time-tested firefighting strategies like the ones Nin describes, today's firefighters use the latest technology to combat wildfires. Once a forest fire breaks out, airplanes and helicopters are often used to gather data and spray fire retardants. In NASA's Firefly system, airplanes fly an infrared scanner over a fire in progress. The information is relayed to a satellite and then to firefighters on the ground so that they can attack the fire efficiently.

◆ Build Vocabulary

WORD ROOTS: -vac-

The word *evacuees* contains the word root -vac-, which means "empty." An *evacuee* is someone who is removed from a place, leaving that place empty.

WORD BANK

Which word from the list means "things one is deprived of"? Check the Build Vocabulary box on page 673 to see if you chose correctly.

privations
evacuees
tenacious
dissolution
ravaging
implemented
encompasses

Debbie ◆ Forest Fire
◆ How to Be Polite Online ◆

◆ Literary Focus

ESSAY

An **essay** is a short nonfiction work about a particular subject. A **narrative essay,** like "Debbie," tells a true story about real people. You learn about them the same way you learn about characters in fiction—through their actions, words, and thoughts. In a **descriptive essay,** such as "Forest Fire," the author describes events and feelings by including images and details that show how things look, sound, smell, taste, or feel. An **expository essay,** like "How to Be Polite Online," presents information, explains a process, or discusses ideas.

◆ Reading Strategy

SET A PURPOSE FOR READING

When reading nonfiction, you may become bewildered by the amount of factual information you encounter. A good way to focus your reading is to **set a purpose** before you read. Read the first paragraph of an essay, and then stop to set a purpose for reading the rest.

A KWL chart like the one below, set up for "How to Be Polite Online," can help you focus your purpose. A KWL chart can show what you **K**now about the subject, what you **W**ant to know, and what you **L**earn from your reading.

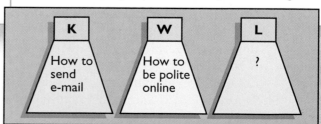

K	W	L
How to send e-mail	How to be polite online	?

Debbie James Herriot

Autumn Leaves, 1994, Ditz, Private Collection

I first saw her one autumn day when I was called to see one of Mrs. Ainsworth's dogs, and I looked in some surprise at the furry black creature sitting before the fire.

"I didn't know you had a cat," I said.

The lady smiled. "We haven't, this is Debbie."

"Debbie?"

"Yes, at least that's what we call her. She's a stray. Comes here two or three times a week and we give her some food. I don't know where she lives but I believe she spends a lot of her time around one of the farms along the road."

"Do you ever get the feeling that she wants to stay with you?"

"No." Mrs. Ainsworth shook her head. "She's a timid little thing. Just creeps in, has some food then flits away. There's something so appealing about her but she doesn't seem to want to let me or anybody into her life."

I looked again at the little cat. "But she isn't just having food today."

"That's right. It's a funny thing but every now and again she slips through here into the lounge and sits by the fire for a few minutes. It's as though she was giving herself a treat."

"Yes . . . I see what you mean." There was no doubt there was something unusual in the attitude of the little animal. She was sitting bolt upright on the thick rug which lay before the fireplace in which the coals glowed and flamed. She made no effort to curl up or wash herself or do anything other than gaze quietly ahead. And there was something in the dusty black of her coat, the half-wild scrawny look of her, that gave me a clue. This was a special event in her life, a rare and wonderful thing; she was lapping up a comfort undreamed of in her daily existence.

As I watched she turned, crept soundlessly from the room and was gone.

"That's always the way with Debbie," Mrs. Ainsworth laughed. "She never stays more than ten minutes or so, then she's off."

Mrs. Ainsworth was a plumpish, pleasant-faced woman in her forties and the kind of client veterinary surgeons dream of; well off, generous, and the owner of three cosseted[1] Basset hounds. And it only needed the habitually mournful expression of one of the dogs to deepen a little and I was round there posthaste.[2] Today one of the Bassets had raised its paw and scratched its ear a couple of times and that was enough to send its mistress scurrying to the phone in great alarm.

So my visits to the Ainsworth home were frequent but undemanding, and I had ample opportunity to look out for the little cat that had intrigued me. On one occasion I spotted her nibbling daintily from a saucer at the kitchen door. As I watched she turned and almost floated on light footsteps into the hall then through the lounge door.

The three Bassets were already in residence, draped snoring on the fireside rug, but they seemed to be used to Debbie because two of them sniffed her in a bored manner and the third merely cocked a sleepy eye at her before flopping back on the rich pile.

Debbie sat among them in her usual posture; upright, intent, gazing absorbedly into the glowing coals. This time I tried to make friends with her. I approached her carefully but she leaned away as I stretched out my hand. However, by patient wheedling[3] and soft talk I managed to touch her and gently stroked her cheek with one finger. There was a moment when she responded by putting her head on one side and rubbing back against

my hand but soon she was ready to leave. Once outside the house she darted quickly along the road then through a gap in a hedge and the last I saw was the little black figure flitting over the rain-swept grass of a field.

"I wonder where she goes," I murmured half to myself.

Mrs. Ainsworth appeared at my elbow. "That's something we've never been able to find out."

It must have been nearly three months before I heard from Mrs. Ainsworth, and in fact I had begun to wonder at the Bassets' long symptomless run when she came on the phone.

It was Christmas morning and she was apologetic. "Mr. Herriot, I'm so sorry to bother you today of all days. I should think you want a rest at Christmas like anybody else." But her natural politeness could not hide the distress in her voice.

"Please don't worry about that," I said. "Which one is it this time?"

"It's not one of the dogs. It's . . . Debbie."

"Debbie? She's at your house now?"

"Yes. . . but there's something wrong. Please come quickly."

Driving through the marketplace I thought again that Darrowby on Christmas Day was like Dickens come to life; the empty square with the snow thick on the cobbles and hanging from the eaves of the fretted[4] lines of roofs; the shops closed and the colored lights of the Christmas trees winking at the windows of the clustering houses, warmly inviting against the cold white bulk of the fells[5] behind.

Mrs. Ainsworth's home was lavishly decorated with tinsel and holly, rows of drinks stood on the sideboard and the rich aroma of turkey and sage and onion stuffing wafted[6] from the kitchen. But her eyes were full of pain as she led me through to the lounge.

Debbie was there all right, but this time everything was different. She wasn't sitting upright in her usual position; she was

---

1. **cosseted** (käs´ it əd) *adj.*: Pampered; indulged.
2. **posthaste** (pōst´ hāst´) *adv.*: With great speed.
3. **wheedling** (hwēd´ liŋ) *v.*: Gentle, constant persuading.
4. **fretted** (fret´ əd) *adj.*: Decoratively arranged.
5. **fells** *n.*: Rocky or barren hills.
6. **wafted** (waf´ təd) *v.*: Moved lightly through the air.

stretched quite motionless on her side, and huddled close to her lay a tiny black kitten.

I looked down in bewilderment. "What's happened here?"

◆ **Literary Focus**
What does Mrs. Ainsworth's story reveal about Debbie's personality?

"It's the strangest thing," Mrs. Ainsworth replied. "I haven't seen her for several weeks then she came in about two hours ago—sort of staggered into the kitchen, and she was carrying the kitten in her mouth. She took it through to the lounge and laid it on the rug and at first I was amused. But I could see all was not well because she sat as she usually does, but for a long time—over an hour—then she lay down like this and she hasn't moved."

I knelt on the rug and passed my hand over Debbie's neck and ribs. She was thinner than ever, her fur dirty and mudcaked. She did not resist as I gently opened her mouth. The tongue and mucous membranes were abnormally pale and the lips ice-cold against my fingers. When I pulled down her eyelid and saw the dead white conjunctiva[7] a knell[8] sounded in my mind.

I palpated[9] the abdomen with a grim certainty as to what I would find and there was no surprise, only a dull sadness as my fingers closed around a hard lobulated[10] mass deep among the viscera.[11] Massive lymphosarcoma.[12] Terminal and hopeless. I put my stethoscope on her heart and listened to the increasingly faint, rapid beat then I straightened up and sat on the rug looking sightlessly into the fireplace, feeling the warmth of the flames on my face.

Mrs. Ainsworth's voice seemed to come from afar. "Is she ill, Mr. Herriot?"

I hesitated. "Yes . . . yes, I'm afraid so. She has a malignant growth." I stood up. "There's absolutely nothing I can do. I'm sorry."

---

7. **conjunctiva** (kän´ jəŋk tī´ və) *n.*: Lining of the inner surface of the eyelids.
8. **knell** (nel) *n.*: Sound of a bell slowly ringing, as for a funeral.
9. **palpated** (pal´ pāt ed) *v.*: Examined by touching.
10. **lobulated** (läb´ yoo lā´ ted) *adj.*: Subdivided.
11. **viscera** (vis´ ər ə) *n.*: Internal organs.
12. **lymphosarcoma** (lim´ fō sär kō´ mə) *n.*: Malignant tumor in the tissue.

"Oh!" Her hand went to her mouth and she looked at me wide-eyed. When at last she spoke her voice trembled. "Well, you must put her to sleep immediately. It's the only thing to do. We can't let her suffer."

"Mrs. Ainsworth," I said. "There's no need. She's dying now—in a coma—far beyond suffering."

She turned quickly away from me and was very still as she fought with her emotions. Then she gave up the struggle and dropped on her knees beside Debbie.

"Oh, poor little thing!" she sobbed and stroked the cat's head again and again as the tears fell unchecked on the matted fur. "What she must have come through. I feel I ought to have done more for her."

For a few moments I was silent, feeling her sorrow, so discordant among the bright seasonal colors of this festive room. Then I spoke gently.

"Nobody could have done more than you," I said. "Nobody could have been kinder."

"But I'd have kept her here—in comfort. It must have been terrible out there in the cold when she was so desperately ill—I daren't think about it. And having kittens, too—I . . . I wonder how many she did have?"

I shrugged. "I don't suppose we'll ever know. Maybe just this one. It happens sometimes. And she brought it to you, didn't she?"

"Yes . . . that's right . . . she did . . . she did." Mrs. Ainsworth reached out and lifted the bedraggled black morsel. She smoothed her finger along the muddy fur and the tiny mouth opened in a soundless miaow. "Isn't it strange? She was dying and she brought her kitten here. And on Christmas Day."

I bent and put my hand on Debbie's heart. There was no beat.

I looked up. "I'm afraid she's gone." I lifted the small body, almost feather light, wrapped it in the sheet which had been spread on the rug and took it out to the car.

When I came back Mrs. Ainsworth was still stroking the kitten. The tears had dried on her cheeks and she was brighteyed as she looked at me.

"I've never had a cat before," she said.

◆ **Reading Strategy**
Did you satisfy your purpose for reading? If so, set a new purpose before you finish the essay.

I smiled. "Well, it looks as though you've got one now."

And she certainly had. That kitten grew rapidly into a sleek handsome cat with a boisterous nature which earned him the name of Buster. In every way he was the opposite to his timid little mother. Not for him the <u>privations</u> of the

▲ **Critical Viewing** In what ways might an energetic kitten stir up the life of Basset hounds like these? [Speculate]

secret outdoor life; he stalked the rich carpets of the Ainsworth home like a king and the ornate collar he always wore added something more to his presence.

On my visits I watched his development with delight but the occasion which stays in my mind was the following Christmas Day, a year from his arrival.

I was out on my rounds as usual. I can't remember when I haven't had to work on Christmas Day because the animals have never got

◆ **Build Vocabulary**

privations (prī vā´ shənz) *n.*: Deprivation or lack of common comforts

round to recognizing it as a holiday; but with the passage of the years the vague resentment I used to feel has been replaced by philosophical acceptance. After all, as I tramped around the hillside barns in the frosty air I was working up a better appetite for my turkey than all the millions lying in bed or slumped by the fire.

I was on my way home, bathed in a rosy glow. I heard the cry as I was passing Mrs. Ainsworth's house.

"Merry Christmas, Mr. Herriot!" She was letting a visitor out of the front door and she waved at me gaily. "Come in and have a drink to warm you up."

I didn't need warming up but I pulled in to the curb without hesitation. In the house there was all the festive cheer of last year and the same glorious whiff of sage and onion which set my gastric[13] juices surging. But there was not the sorrow; there was Buster.

He was darting up to each of the dogs in turn, ears pricked, eyes blazing with devilment, dabbing a paw at them then streaking away.

Mrs. Ainsworth laughed. "You know, he plagues the life out of them. Gives them no peace."

She was right. To the Bassets, Buster's arrival was rather like the intrusion of an irreverent outsider into an exclusive London club. For a long time they had led a life of measured grace; regular sedate walks with their mistress, superb food in ample quantities and long snoring sessions on the rugs and armchairs. Their days followed one upon another in unruffled calm. And then came Buster.

He was dancing up to the youngest dog

---

13. **gastric** (gas´ trik) *adj.*: Of the stomach.

again, sideways this time, head on one side, goading him. When he started boxing with both paws it was too much even for the Basset. He dropped his dignity and rolled over with the cat in a brief wrestling match.

"I want to show you something." Mrs. Ainsworth lifted a hard rubber ball from the sideboard and went out to the garden, followed by Buster. She threw the ball across the lawn and the cat bounded after it over the frosted grass, the muscles rippling under the black sheen of his coat. He seized the ball in his teeth, brought it back to his mistress, dropped it at her feet and waited expectantly. She threw it and he brought it back again.

I gasped incredulously. A feline retriever!

The Bassets looked on disdainfully. Nothing would ever have induced them to chase a ball, but Buster did it again and again as though he would never tire of it.

Mrs. Ainsworth turned to me. "Have you ever seen anything like that?"

"No," I replied. "I never have. He is a most remarkable cat."

She snatched Buster from his play and we went back into the house where she held him close to her face, laughing as the big cat purred and arched himself ecstatically against her cheek.

Looking at him, a picture of health and contentment, my mind went back to his mother. Was it too much to think that that dying little creature with the last of her strength had carried her kitten to the only haven of comfort and warmth she had ever known in the hope that it would be cared for there? Maybe it was.

But it seemed I wasn't the only one with such fancies. Mrs. Ainsworth turned to me and though she was smiling her eyes were wistful.

"Debbie would be pleased," she said.

I nodded. "Yes, she would . . . It was just a year ago today she brought him, wasn't it?"

"That's right." She hugged Buster to her again. "The best Christmas present I ever had."

*G*uide for Responding

◆ LITERATURE AND YOUR LIFE

Reader's Response How would you react if Debbie had left you her newborn kitten?

Thematic Focus Describe the ways in which Buster is a welcome surprise.

Group Activity Work with a team to create a pamphlet of advice for new pet owners.

☑ Check Your Comprehension

1. Describe Debbie and her life.
2. Describe how Buster came to live with Mrs. Ainsworth.
3. How did the Ainsworth household change after Buster arrived?
4. What thoughts do Herriot and Mrs. Ainsworth share at the end of the essay?

◆ Critical Thinking

INTERPRET

1. Why did Debbie never stay with Mrs. Ainsworth for long? **[Infer]**
2. Why might she have chosen to bring Buster to Mrs. Ainsworth's home? **[Speculate]**
3. How is Buster different from his mother? **[Compare and Contrast]**

APPLY

4. Mrs. Ainsworth receives an unexpected reward for her kindness to Debbie. Why are unexpected rewards sometimes more valued than expected ones? **[Generalize]**

EXTEND

5. What qualities and training do you think it takes to be a successful veterinarian? **[Career Link]**

Forest Fire

Anaïs Nin

A man rushed in to announce he had seen smoke on Monrovia Peak.[1] As I looked out of the window I saw the two mountains facing the house on fire. The entire rim burning wildly in the night. The flames, driven by hot Santa Ana winds[2] from the desert, were as tall as the tallest trees, the sky already tinted coral, and the crackling noise of burning trees, the ashes and the smoke were already increasing. The fire raced along, sometimes descending behind the mountain where I could only see the glow, sometimes descending toward us. I thought of the foresters in danger. I made coffee for the weary men who came down occasionally with horses they had led out, or with old people from the isolated cabins. They were covered with soot from their battle with the flames.

At six o'clock the fire was on our left side and rushing toward Mount Wilson. <u>Evacuees</u> from the cabins began to arrive and had to be given blankets and hot coffee. The streets were blocked with fire engines readying to fight the fire if it touched the houses. Policemen and firemen and guards turned away the sightseers. Some were relatives concerned over the fate of the foresters, or the pack station family. The policemen lighted flares, which gave the scene a theatrical, tragic air. The red lights on

▲ **Critical Viewing** Why are forest fires such dangerous occurrences? Refer to details in the photograph in your response. **[Deduce]**

the police cars twinkled alarmingly. More fire engines arrived. Ashes fell, and the roar of the fire was now like thunder.

We were told to ready ourselves for evacuation. I packed the diaries. The saddest spectacle, beside that of the men fighting the fire as they would a war, were the animals, rabbits, coyotes, mountain lions, deer, driven by the fire to the edge of the mountain, taking a look at the crowd of people and panicking, choosing rather to rush back into the fire.

The fire now was like a ring around Sierra Madre,[3] every mountain was burning. People living at the foot of the mountain were packing

---

3. **Sierra** (sē er´ ə) **Madre** (mä´ drā): Mountain range.

◆ **Build Vocabulary**

evacuees (ē vak´ yōō ēz´) *n.*: People who leave a place, especially because of danger

---

1. **Monrovia** (mən rō´ vē ə) **Peak**: Mountain in southwest California.
2. **Santa** (san´ tə) **Ana** (an´ ə) **winds**: Hot desert winds from the east or northeast in southern California.

their cars. I rushed next door to the Campion children, who had been left with a baby-sitter, and got them into the car. It was impossible to save all the horses. We parked the car on the field below us. I called up the Campions, who were out for the evening, and reassured them. The baby-sitter dressed the children warmly. I made more coffee. I answered frantic telephone calls.

All night the fire engines sprayed water over the houses. But the fire grew immense, angry, and rushing at a speed I could not believe. It would rush along and suddenly leap over a road, a trail, like a monster, devouring all in its path. The firefighters cut breaks in the heavy brush, but when the wind was strong enough, the fire leaped across them. At dawn one arm of the fire reached the back of our houses but was finally contained.

But high above and all around, the fire was burning, more vivid than the sun, throwing spirals of smoke in the air like the smoke from a volcano. Thirty-three cabins burned, and twelve thousand acres of forest still burning endangered countless homes below the fire. The fire was burning to the back of us now, and a rain of ashes began to fall and continued for days. The smell of the burn in the air, acid and pungent and <u>tenacious</u>. The dragon tongues of flames devouring, the flames leaping, the roar of destruction and <u>dissolution</u>, the eyes of the panicked animals, caught between fire and human beings, between two forms of death. They chose the fire. It was as if the fire had come from the bowels of the earth, like that of a fiery volcano, it was so powerful, so swift, and so <u>ravaging</u>. I saw trees become skeletons in one minute, I saw trees fall, I saw bushes turned to ashes in a second, I saw weary,

ash-covered men, looking like men returned from war, some with burns, others overcome by smoke.

The men were rushing from one spot to another watching for recrudescence.[4] Some started backfiring up the mountain so that the ascending flames could counteract the descending ones.

As the flames reached the cities below, hundreds of roofs burst into flame at once. There was no water pressure because all the fire hydrants were turned on at the same time, and the fire departments were helpless to save more than a few of the burning homes.

The blaring loudspeakers of passing police cars warned us to prepare to evacuate in case the wind changed and drove the fire in our direction. What did I wish to save? I thought only of the diaries. I appeared on the porch carrying a huge stack of diary volumes, preparing to pack them in the car. A reporter for the Pasadena *Star News* was taking pictures of the evacuation. He came up, very annoyed with me. "Hey, lady, next time could you bring out something more important than all those old papers? Carry some clothes on the next trip. We gotta

◆ **Build Vocabulary**

tenacious (tə nā´ shəs) *adj.*: Holding on firmly

dissolution (dis´ ə loo´ shən) *n.*: The act of breaking down and crumbling

ravaging (rav´ ij iŋ) *adj.*: Severely damaging

4. **recrudescence** (rē´ kroo des´ əns) *n.*: Fresh outbreak of something that has been inactive.

◀ **Critical Viewing** What details in this photograph show the fire as being "immense" and "angry"? [Interpret]

mountains cannot hold the rains and slide down bringing rocks and mud. One of the rangers must now take photographs and movies of the disaster. He asks if I will help by holding an umbrella over the cameras. I put on my raincoat and he lends me hip boots which look to me like seven-league boots.

We drive a little way up the road. At the third curve it is impassable. A river is rushing across the road. The ranger takes pictures while I hold the umbrella over the camera. It is terrifying to see the muddied waters and rocks, the mountain disintegrating. When we are ready to return, the road before us is covered by large rocks but the ranger pushes on as if the truck were a jeep and forces it through. The edge of the road is being carried away.

I am laughing and scared too. The ranger is at ease in nature, and without fear. It is a wild moment of danger. It is easy to love nature in its peaceful and consoling moments, but one must love it in its furies too, in its despairs and wildness, especially when the damage is caused by us.

have human interest in these pictures!"

A week later, the danger was over.

Gray ashy days.

In Sierra Madre, following the fire, the January rains brought floods. People are sandbagging their homes. At four A.M. the streets are covered with mud. The bare, burnt, naked

*G*uide *for Responding*

◆ LITERATURE AND YOUR LIFE

Reader's Response What would you try to save if you were caught in a fire?

Thematic Focus In what ways does life go on during the fire? In what ways is life disrupted?

☑ Check Your Comprehension

1. Describe the setting—the time and place— of the forest fire.
2. What does Nin rescue from the fire?
3. What natural disaster occurred after the fire?

◆ Critical Thinking

INTERPRET

1. How are the fire and mudslides related? **[Connect]**
2. What is the effect of Nin's use of figurative language, such as "the dragon tongues of flames"? **[Interpret]**
3. What conclusion does Nin draw from observing these disasters? **[Draw Conclusions]**

COMPARE LITERARY WORKS

4. Compare and contrast the messages or themes within "Debbie" and "Forest Fire." **[Compare and Contrast]**

How to Be Polite Online

from Netiquette

Virginia Shea

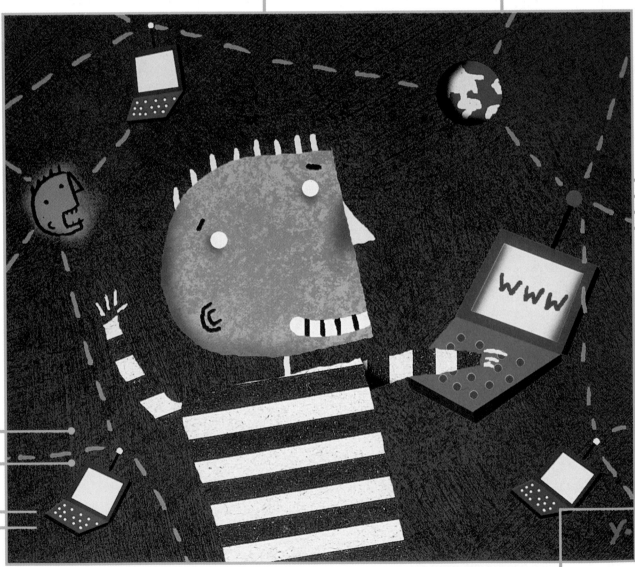

Untitled, James Yang

▲ **Critical Viewing** What does this painting seem to say about the relationship between people and technology? **[Infer]**

The truth is that computer networking is still in its infancy. Probably nothing illustrates this more clearly than the "ASCII[1] jail": 90% of network communications are still limited to plain old ASCII text—that is, the characters of the alphabet, the numerals 0 through 9, and the most basic punctuation marks. It's bad enough that multimedia communications have not been <u>implemented</u> in most of cyberspace.[2] Most of the time you can't even put a word in bold or italics!

Because people cannot see or hear you in cyberspace, you need to pay close attention to the style of your electronic communications if you hope to make a good impression there. The *style* of electronic communications <u>encompasses</u> everything about your correspondence except its content, from your use of network conventions like "smileys" and "sigs" to the number of characters per line in your email messages.

Style considerations are influenced by several of the rules of Netiquette, especially Rule 4, Respect other people's time, and Rule 5, Make yourself look good online. It doesn't matter how brilliant your messages are if they're formatted in such a way that no one can read them.

Tone of voice online

The fact that most network interactions are limited to written words can be the source of misunderstandings. Fortunately, clever network users have had years to deal with this. They've created a shorthand to help communicate the tone that you'd otherwise get from the other person's voice, facial expressions, and gestures. These shorthand expressions are known as smileys or emoticons.

◆ **Literature and Your Life**
What expressions and gestures do you often use when conversing with others?

They're easy to figure out once you get the hang of it. Just remember that they're all sideways faces.

See Table 1 for a list of the most commonly used emoticons. There are whole books about smileys for those who are interested, including the enjoyable *Smiley Dictionary* by Seth Godin.

People also use abbreviations to express emotional states or to qualify what they're saying. See Table 2 for a list of common abbreviations.

The "FLAME ON/FLAME OFF" notifier

When you really want to run off at the keyboard—but you want your readers to know that you know that you're not expressing yourself in your usual measured, reasoned manner—you need to let them know that you know that you're flaming.[3] So before you begin your rant, simply

---

1. **ASCII:** Abbreviation of American Standard Code for Information Interchange, a standard computer code used to assist the interchange of information among various types of data-processing equipment.
2. **cyberspace:** Global communication performed through the use of computer technology.

3. **flaming:** Slang for "ranting."

◆ **Build Vocabulary**
implemented (im´ plə mənt´ əd) *v.:* Put into effect
encompasses (en kum´ pəs´ səz) *v.:* Contains; includes

enter the words FLAME ON. Then rant away. When you're done, write FLAME OFF and resume normal discourse.

Looking good online

One of the neat things about computers is that they let us use all kinds of special effects in our docu- ments that we didn't even dream of back in the days of typewriters (if you're old enough to remember those days). But when you're communicating online, in most cases it's back to the typewriter as far as effects go. Even if your mail system lets you use boldface, italics, and tabs, there's no guarantee that your correspon- dent's system will understand them. At worst, your communication will turn into unreadable gibberish.

What to do?

- Forget about boldface, italics, tabs, and font changes. Never use any effect you couldn't get on an old-fashioned typewriter. In fact, you can't even use all of those. Underlining won't work, for example. Nor can you use the old "required backspace" trick to put a diacritical mark[4] (a tilde or an accent mark, for example) over another character.

- Most systems won't read the diacritical marks anyway, so just leave them out. If you feel an accent mark is ab- solutely necessary, type an apostrophe *after* the letter the accent would have gone over.

- Use only ASCII characters. This in- cludes all 26 letters of the alphabet

◆ **Literary Focus**
Why might a writer use tables in an expository essay?

Table 1: Emoticons	
:-)	Smile; laugh; "I'm joking"
:-(	Frown; sadness; "Bummer"
:)	Variant of :-) or "Have a nice day"
:(	Variant of :-(
;-)	Wink; denotes a pun or sly joke
:-O	Yelling or screaming; or completely shocked
:-()	Can't (or won't) stop talking
:-D	Big, delighted grin
:-P	Sticking out your tongue
:-] or :-)	Sarcastic smile
%-)	Confused but happy
%-(	Confused and unhappy
:'-(	Crying
:'-)	Crying happy tears
:-I	Can't decide how to feel; no feelings either way
:-\	Mixed but mostly happy
:-/	Mixed but mostly sad
*	Kiss
{ } or [ ]	Hug
{{{*** }}}	Hugs and kisses

Table 2: Abbreviations	
BTW	By the way
IMHO	In my humble opinion
IMNSHO	In my not so humble opinion
IOW	In other words
IRL	In real life
ITRW	In the real world
LOL	Laughing out loud
OTF	On the floor (laughing)
ROTFL	Rolling on the floor laughing
WRT	With regard to
YMMV	Your mileage may vary
<g> or <G>	Grin
<bg>	Big grin

(upper and lower case), the numerals 0 through 9, and most commonly used punctuation marks. For any publishing mavens out there, however, it excludes em dashes ("—"), en dashes ("–"), and bullets.

- Limit your line length to 80 characters, or better yet, 60 characters.

  Otherwise, your lines may break in weird places and your readers

  will have to wade through notes that look like this.

  Believe me,

  it gets annoying after a very short while.

- NEVER TYPE YOUR NOTES IN ALL CAPS, LIKE THIS. It's rude—like shouting constantly. And, like constant shouting, it makes people stop listening. All caps may be used, IN MODERATION, for emphasis.

- To indicate *italics*, you may *surround the material to be italicized with asterisks.*

Guide for Responding

◆ LITERATURE AND YOUR LIFE

Reader's Response Which of the emoticons do you find most clever? Why?

Thematic Focus In what ways does communicating on-line provide a newness to everyday life?

Group Activity Design your own emoticons, or smileys. Display the new emoticons, and have classmates guess their meanings.

☑ Check Your Comprehension

1. What does "the *style* of electronic communications" include?
2. What is "flaming"?
3. What formatting recommendations does Shea make?
4. Why does Shea discourage the reader from typing in all caps?

◆ Critical Thinking

INTERPRET

1. Which of Shea's rules of Netiquette do you think is most important? Why? **[Support]**
2. Which of the emoticons do you think would be understood by someone who didn't have Shea's reference chart? **[Infer]**
3. How is writing online similar to and different from handwriting a note? **[Compare and Contrast]**

APPLY

4. People didn't use emoticons when they wrote with typewriters. Why do you think emoticons became popular in computer communications? **[Generalize]**

EVALUATE

5. Is electronic mail appropriate for all occasions? In what situation might a traditional letter be a better choice? **[Assess]**

Guide for Responding (continued)

◆ Reading Strategy

SET A PURPOSE FOR READING

Setting a purpose helps you to focus your reading. Your purpose makes it easier to identify and remember important information.

1. (a) What was your purpose for reading each essay? (b) Was each purpose met?
2. Did you shift or extend your purpose while reading any of the essays? If so, explain how and why.
3. When do you think it is helpful to change a purpose you have set for reading?

◆ Build Vocabulary

USING THE WORD ROOT -vac-

The Latin root -vac-, as in *evacuees,* means "empty." Complete each sentence with the most appropriate word containing the word root -vac-.

vacuum   evacuate   vacant

1. After the forest fire, the town was ___?___.
2. The suction of the backdraft left a ___?___ inside the room.
3. We were forced to ___?___ when the fire reached our property line.

SPELLING STRATEGY

The *j* sound can be spelled with a *g,* as in the word *ravaging.* Rewrite these sentences, correcting misspelled words.

1. The averaje pet owner should not keep an endanjered species as a pet.
2. Some ajing animals become savaje when ill.
3. Only an experienced surjeon can operate on an animal's dijestive system.

USING THE WORD BANK

On your paper, write the letter of the word most opposite in meaning to the Word Bank word.

1. privations: (a) riches, (b) limits, (c) public
2. evacuees: (a) helpers, (b) fears, (c) inhabitants
3. tenacious: (a) wild, (b) brilliant, (c) weak
4. dissolution: (a) height, (b) growth, (c) visible
5. ravaging: (a) harmless, (b) evil, (c) sharp
6. implemented: (a) held, (b) spoken, (c) unused
7. encompasses: (a) believes, (b) refers, (c) omits

◆ Literary Focus

ESSAY

Authors write **essays** to communicate information and ideas about the real world. A **narrative essay** tells about a true event. A **descriptive essay** presents a detailed view of an incident or experience. An **expository essay** provides the reader with information, explanations, or instruction.

1. (a) Which character do you think is most fully drawn in Herriot's essay? (b) Tell how Herriot brought this character to life.
2. (a) Find three different images Nin uses to describe the fire. (b) Explain the effectiveness of each image.
3. Give three examples of ways that "How to Be Polite Online" informs the reader.

◆ Build Grammar Skills

PRONOUN AND ANTECEDENT AGREEMENT

A personal pronoun must **agree** with its antecedent in gender (masculine, feminine, or neither) and number (singular or plural).

Buster did it again and again as though *he* would never tire of it. (The pronoun *he* agrees with the singular masculine antecedent *Buster.*)

Practice On your paper, write the pronoun and antecedent in each example. Then, identify the gender and number of each pair.

1. The Bassets were used to Debbie and sniffed her in a bored way. . . .
2. Mrs. Ainsworth threw the ball across the lawn, and the cat bounded after it.
3. A man rushed in to announce he had seen smoke on Monrovia Peak.
4. I rushed next door to the Campion children . . . and got them into the car.
5. Most systems won't read the diacritical marks anyway, so just leave them out.

Writing Application Write sentences with pronouns that agree with the antecedents below:

1. Mrs. Ainsworth   3. firefighters
2. Buster   4. computer

Build Your Portfolio

 ## Idea Bank

Writing

1. **Computer Checklist** Write a list of hints to help others use a computer. Use ideas from "How to Be Polite Online" as well as your own experience.

2. **Essay** Choose an interesting location, and watch the area for at least thirty minutes. Write a descriptive essay to share your observations and insights.

3. **Analysis** In a brief paper, describe the ways in which "Debbie" is like a fictional short story. Then, describe the ways in which it is nonfiction.

Speaking and Listening

4. **Role Play** Imagine that you are a reporter interviewing people who survived the Santa Ana forest fire. Write a list of questions about the fire, and then conduct interviews with your classmates, who should pose as survivors.

5. **Oral Interpretation** Read one of the essays aloud, as if you were performing for a radio audience. Practice your delivery before reading the essay for the class. **[Media Link]**

Projects

6. **Survey and Analysis [Group Activity]** With a partner, conduct a survey about people's attitudes toward their pets. Write survey questions that can be statistically analyzed. For example, ask people to rate favorite pets on a scale from 1 to 10. Then, work together to graph and interpret your data. Compile the results in a report to share with the class. **[Math Link]**

7. **Firefighting Report** Visit your local fire department, and request an interview with a firefighter or with the fire chief. Ask questions about the educational requirements and the training necessary to become a firefighter. Also, ask about careers related to fire safety and prevention. Present your findings to the class. **[Career Link]**

 ## Writing Mini-Lesson

Interview

True stories make some of the most interesting reading. One of the best ways to get firsthand information about an exciting event is to interview someone who was there. Plan and conduct an interview with someone in your community who witnessed an exciting event.

Writing Skills Focus: Using Quotation Marks

When quoting people—whether from interviews or from their writing—always **use quotation marks** around their exact words.

Model

Although she enjoys the fame she has gained, it hasn't gone to her head. "My patients are cats and dogs," she says. "They really aren't impressed by a piece of paper."

Prewriting Choose an interview subject. Then, prepare a list of questions. If possible, bring a tape recorder to the interview. After the interview, evaluate your information and decide which information you want to include.

Drafting Write about your interview, sharing both your subject's experiences as well as your insights into his or her personality. Use quotation marks to indicate your subject's exact words.

Revising Reread your draft, and review your notes. Add interesting or relevant details that you left out. Be sure you've used quotation marks correctly.

> ◆ **Grammar Application**
> Check to be sure that your pronouns agree with their antecedents.

Guide for Reading

Meet the Authors:

Robert MacNeil (1931–   )

Born in Montreal, Canada, Robert MacNeil worked on a children's show for the Canadian Broadcasting System early in his career. After becoming a broadcast journalist, MacNeil went to public television to host his own news analysis program, which grew into the highly regarded *MacNeil/Lehrer NewsHour*. His show differed from other news programs by offering more in-depth reports on important issues.

Martin Luther King, Jr. (1929–1968)

The grandson and son of Baptist ministers, Rev. Dr. Martin Luther King, Jr., followed the family tradition and became a clergyman and an activist. King's first well-publicized venture into civil rights occurred in 1953. After Rosa Parks refused to give up her bus seat to a white person as required by the law, King led a boycott of buses in Montgomery, Alabama.

"I Have a Dream" Ten years later, King led a civil rights march in Washington, D.C. There, he delivered his famous "I Have a Dream" speech. In the spring of 1968, King was shot and killed in Memphis, Tennessee, where he had gone to support striking city workers.

◆ LITERATURE AND YOUR LIFE

CONNECT YOUR EXPERIENCE

For how many hours a day is the television on in your home? In "The Trouble with Television," you'll learn what one highly regarded journalist thinks about the amount of time some people spend watching television.

THEMATIC FOCUS: Facing Hard Questions

In the essay and speech in this group, MacNeil and King put hard questions before the American public. What are the answers?

◆ Background for Understanding

MATH

According to Robert MacNeil, Americans watch too much television. The A. C. Nielson Co., which keeps statistics about television, stated that in 1996, the average American watched more than four hours of television every day. That's over two months of nonstop TV watching per year! In a sixty-five-year life, that person will have spent nine years glued to the tube. To figure how many hours a year you watch television, multiply the number of hours you watch per day by seven, and then multiply that number by fifty-two.

◆ Build Vocabulary

PREFIXES: *anti-*

In "The American Dream," King speaks of the *antithesis* of democracy. The prefix *anti-* means "opposed to" or "opposite." Combined with *thesis,* "a statement supported by argument," *antithesis* refers to a statement that is the opposite of another.

WORD BANK

Which word from the list describes something as empty, or void? Check the Build Vocabulary box on page 690 to see if you chose correctly.

diverts
usurps
august
pervading
antithesis
paradoxes
devoid

The Trouble with Television ◆ The American Dream

◆ Literary Focus
PERSUASIVE ESSAY

In a **persuasive essay,** a writer presents his or her views in order to convince you to accept those views or to act in a certain way. Because you may not share the opinion, the writer offers strong arguments, or reasons, to support his or her position or to propel you to act.

Use a graphic organizer like the one below to identify each writer's opinions and arguments.

MacNeil's Opinion:

Supporting Arguments:

◆ Reading Strategy
IDENTIFY PERSUASIVE TECHNIQUES

Writers like MacNeil and King use **persuasive techniques.** These techniques include supporting points with facts, statistics, and quotations; using words that have strong emotional impact; appealing to the masses by quoting popular movies and books; repeating key ideas or beliefs; and using slogans or chants that can stir an audience to action. Notice MacNeil's and King's use of these techniques in their essays.

The Trouble with TELEVISION

Robert MacNeil

It is difficult to escape the influence of television. If you fit the statistical averages, by the age of 20 you will have been exposed to at least 20,000 hours of television. You can add 10,000 hours for each decade you have lived after the age of 20. The only things Americans do more than watch television are work and sleep.

Calculate for a moment what could be done with even a part of those hours. Five thousand hours, I am told, are what a typical college undergraduate spends working on a bachelor's degree. In 10,000 hours you could have learned enough to become an astronomer or engineer. You could have learned several languages fluently. If it appealed to you, you could be reading Homer[1] in the original Greek or Dostoevski[2] in Russian. If it didn't, you could have walked around the world and written a book about it.

The trouble with television is that it discourages concentration. Almost anything

▲ **Critical Viewing** What effect does watching television seem to be having on this girl? **[Make a Judgment]**

interesting and rewarding in life requires some constructive, consistently applied effort. The dullest, the least gifted of us can achieve things that seem miraculous to those who never concentrate on anything. But television encourages us to apply no effort. It sells us instant gratification. It <u>diverts</u> us only to divert, to make the time pass without pain.

Television's variety becomes a narcotic,[3] not a stimulus.[4] Its serial, kaleidoscopic[5] exposures force us to follow its lead. The viewer is on a perpetual guided tour: thirty minutes at the museum, thirty at the cathedral, then back on the bus to the next attraction—except on television, typically, the spans allotted are on the order of minutes or seconds, and the chosen delights are more often car crashes and people killing one another. In short, a lot

---

1. **Homer** (hō′ mər): Greek epic poet of the eighth century B.C.
2. **Dostoevski** (dôs′ tô yef′ skē): Fyodor (fyô′ dôr) Dostoevski (1821–1881); Russian novelist.

3. **narcotic** (när kät′ ik) *n.*: Something that has a soothing effect.
4. **stimulus** (stim′ yə ləs) *n.*: Something that rouses to action.
5. **kaleidoscopic** (kə lī′ də skäp′ ik) *adj.*: Constantly changing.

◄ **Critical Viewing** How does this photograph support MacNeil's statement that "television encourages us to apply no effort"? [**Analyze**]

of television <u>usurps</u> one of the most precious of all human <u>gifts</u>, the ability to focus your attention yourself, rather than just passively surrender it.

Capturing your attention—and holding it—is the prime motive of most television programming and enhances its role as a profitable advertising vehicle. Programmers live in constant fear of losing anyone's attention—anyone's. The surest way to avoid doing so is to keep everything brief, not to strain the attention of anyone but instead to provide constant stimulation through variety, novelty, action and movement. Quite simply, television operates on the appeal to the short attention span.

It is simply the easiest way out. But it has come to be regarded as a given, as inherent[6] in the medium[7] itself: as an imperative, as though General Sarnoff, or one of the other <u>august</u> pioneers of video, had bequeathed to us tablets of stone commanding that nothing in television shall ever require more than a few moments' concentration.

In its place that is fine. Who can quarrel with a medium that so brilliantly packages escapist entertainment as a mass-marketing tool? But I see its values now <u>pervading</u> this nation and its life. It has become fashionable to think that, like fast food, fast ideas are the

way to get to a fast-moving, impatient public.

In the case of news, this practice, in my view, results in inefficient communication. I question how much of television's nightly news effort is really absorbable and understandable.

Much of it is what has been aptly described as "machine gunning with scraps." I think its technique fights coherence.[8] I think it tends to make things ultimately boring and dismissable (unless they are accompanied by horrifying pictures) because almost anything is boring and dismissable if you know almost nothing about it.

I believe that TV's appeal to the short attention span is not only inefficient communication but decivilizing as well. Consider the casual assumptions that television tends to cultivate: that complexity must be avoided, that visual stimulation is a substitute for thought, that verbal precision is an anachronism.[9] It may be old-fashioned, but I was taught that thought is words, arranged in grammatically precise ways.

There is a crisis of literacy in this country. One study estimates that some 30 million adult Americans are "functionally illiterate" and cannot read or write well enough to answer a want ad or understand the instructions on a medicine bottle.

---

6. inherent (in hir′ ənt) *adj.*: Natural.
7. medium (mē′ dē əm) *n.*: Means of communication.

8. coherence (kō hir′ əns) *n.*: The quality of being connected in an intelligible way.
9. anachronism (ə nak′ rə niz′ əm) *n.*: Anything that seems to be out of its proper place in history.

◆ **Build Vocabulary**

diverts (dī vʉrts′) *v.*: Distracts
usurps (yо̄о̄ sʉrps′) *v.*: Takes over
august (ô gust′) *adj.*: Honored
pervading (pər vād′ iŋ) *v.*: Spreading throughout

Literacy may not be an inalienable human right, but it is one that the highly literate Founding Fathers might not have found unreasonable or even unattainable. We are not only not attaining it as a nation, statistically speaking, but we are falling further and further short of attaining it. And, while I would not be so simplistic as to suggest that television is the cause, I believe it contributes and is an influence.

Everything about this nation—the structure of the society, its forms of family organization, its economy, its place in the world—has become more complex, not less. Yet its dominating communications instrument, its principal form of national linkage, is one that sells neat resolutions to human problems that usually have no neat resolutions. It is all symbolized in my mind by the hugely successful art form that television has made central to the culture, the thirty-second commercial: the tiny drama of the earnest housewife who finds happiness in choosing the right toothpaste.

When before in human history has so much humanity collectively surrendered so much of its leisure to one toy, one mass diversion? When before has virtually an entire nation surrendered itself wholesale to a medium for selling?

Some years ago Yale University law professor Charles L. Black, Jr. wrote: ". . . forced feeding on trivial fare is not itself a trivial matter." I think this society is being force fed with trivial fare, and I fear that the effects on our habits of mind, our language, our tolerance for effort, and our appetite for complexity are only dimly perceived. If I am wrong, we will have done no harm to look at the issue skeptically and critically, to consider how we should be resisting it. I hope you will join with me in doing so.

◆ **Reading Strategy**
What persuasive techniques does MacNeil use in this paragraph?

Guide for Responding

◆ LITERATURE AND YOUR LIFE

Reader's Response Is television a waste of time or a valuable source of information? Explain.

Thematic Focus What hard question does MacNeil present?

Television Log For one week, keep a log of the programs you watch on television and what you learn from each.

☑ Check Your Comprehension

1. When the average viewer reaches the age of twenty, how many hours of television has he or she watched?
2. According to MacNeil, what is the major trouble with television?
3. To what growing crisis in the United States does MacNeil believe television contributes?

◆ Critical Thinking

INTERPRET

1. MacNeil writes that much of television news is "'machine gunning with scraps.'" Explain what he means. **[Interpret]**
2. What do you think MacNeil wants people to do instead of watching television? Explain. **[Draw Conclusions]**
3. If MacNeil were the president of a television network, what changes in the programming might he make? **[Speculate]**

EVALUATE

4. Are MacNeil's arguments justified? Explain. **[Evaluate]**

APPLY

5. (a) How do you think television could be improved? (b) In what ways is it a valuable tool for society? **[Generalize]**

The American Dream

MARTIN LUTHER KING, JR.

▲ **Critical Viewing** What qualities of King does this portrait emphasize? [Interpret]

*A*merica is essentially a dream, a dream as yet unfulfilled. It is a dream of a land where men of all races, of all nationalities and of all creeds can live together as brothers. The substance of the dream is expressed in these sublime words, words lifted to cosmic proportions: "We hold these truths to be self-evident, that all men are created equal, that they are endowed by their Creator with certain unalienable rights, that among these are life, liberty, and pursuit of happiness."[1] This is the dream.

One of the first things we notice in this dream is an amazing universalism. It does not say some men, but it says all men. It does not say all white men, but it says all men, which includes black men. It does not say all Gentiles, but it says all men, which includes Jews. It does not say all Protestants, but it says all men, which includes Catholics.

And there is another thing we see in this dream that ultimately distinguishes democracy and our form of government from all of the totalitarian regimes[2] that emerge in history. It says that each individual has certain basic rights that are neither conferred by nor derived from the state. To discover where they came from it is necessary to move back behind the dim mist of eternity, for they are God-given. Very seldom if ever in the history of the world has a sociopolitical document expressed in such profoundly eloquent and unequivocal language the dignity and the worth of human personality. The American dream reminds us that every man is heir to the legacy of worthiness.

Ever since the Founding Fathers of our nation dreamed this noble dream, America has been something of a schizophrenic[3] personality, tragically divided against herself. On the one hand we have proudly professed the principles of democracy, and on the other hand we have sadly practiced the very antithesis of those principles. Indeed slavery and segregation have been strange paradoxes in a nation founded on the principle that all men are created equal. This is what the Swedish sociologist, Gunnar Myrdal, referred to as the American dilemma.

But the shape of the world today does not permit us the luxury of an anemic democracy. The price America must pay for the continued exploitation of the Negro and other minority groups is the price of its own destruction. The hour is late; the clock of destiny is ticking out. It is trite, but urgently true, that if America is to remain a first-class nation she can no longer have second-class citizens. Now, more than ever before, America is challenged to bring her noble dream into reality, and those who are working to implement the American dream are the true saviors of democracy.

Now may I suggest some of the things we must do if we are to make the American dream a reality. First I think all of us must develop a world perspective if we are to survive. The American dream will not become a reality devoid of the larger dream of a world of brotherhood and peace and good will. The world in which we live is a world of geographical oneness and we are challenged now to make it spiritually one.

Man's specific genius and technological ingenuity has dwarfed distance and placed time in chains. Jet planes have compressed into minutes distances that once took days and months to cover. It is not common for a preacher to be quoting Bob Hope, but I think he has aptly described this jet age in which we live. If, on taking off on a nonstop flight from Los Angeles to New York City, you develop hiccups, he said, you will hic in Los Angeles and

---

1. **"We hold these . . . pursuit of happiness":** From the Declaration of Independence, which declares the American colonies free and independent of Great Britain.
2. **totalitarian** (tō tal′ ə ter′ ē ən) **regimes:** Governments or states in which one political party or group maintains complete control under a dictatorship.
3. **schizophrenic** (skit′ se fren′ ik) *adj.*: Characterized by a separation between the thought processes and emotions.

cup in New York City. That is really *moving*. If you take a flight from Tokyo, Japan, on Sunday morning, you will arrive in Seattle, Washington, on the preceding Saturday night. When your friends meet you at the airport and ask you when you left Tokyo, you will have to say, "I left tomorrow." This is the kind of world in which we live. Now this is a bit humorous but I am trying to laugh a basic fact into all of us: the world in which we live has become a single neighborhood.

Through our scientific genius we have made of this world a neighborhood; now through our moral and spiritual development we must make of it a brotherhood. In a real sense, we must all learn to live together as brothers, or we will all perish together as fools. We must come to see that no individual can live alone; no nation can live alone. We must all live together; we must all be concerned about each other.

Beyond Literature

Social Studies Connection

The Nobel Prize Dr. Martin Luther King, Jr., was awarded the Nobel Peace Prize in 1964. The Prize is named after the Swedish chemist Alfred Bernhard Nobel (1883–1896), who upon his death left the bulk of his fortune to establish a prize that would be annually awarded to those who have made the greatest contributions in the fields of physics, chemistry, medicine, literature, the promotion of peace, and, in 1968, economics. The first prizes were presented on December 10, 1901, five years after the death of Nobel.

Cross-Curricular Activity
Make a timeline, beginning with the year you were born, listing all the Nobel Prize winners in the field of study that you find most exciting. Share this project with your class.

Guide for Responding

◆ LITERATURE AND YOUR LIFE

Reader's Response What is your "American Dream"?

Thematic Focus What hard question does King want America to address?

Journal Writing Jot down ideas for an inspirational speech you'd like to give.

☑ Check Your Comprehension

1. According to King, what historic document reveals "the American dream"?
2. What does King think will happen if the United States continues to exploit minority groups?
3. King talks about the impact of rapid travel on the world. What does he say has been a result of this ability to travel?

◆ Critical Thinking

INTERPRET
1. What is the significance of the lines King recites from the Declaration of Independence? **[Interpret]**
2. Explain what King means when he speaks of the "American dilemma." **[Infer]**
3. According to King, what is the difference between a neighborhood and a brotherhood? **[Analyze]**

EVALUATE
4. (a) What does King think must be done if the American dream is to become a reality? (b) Do you agree? Explain. **[Assess]**

COMPARE LITERARY WORKS
5. Of these two persuasive selections, which do you find more appropriate for today's audience? Explain. **[Make a Judgment]**

Guide for Responding (continued)

◆ Reading Strategy

IDENTIFY PERSUASIVE TECHNIQUES

To convince readers or listeners to think or act in a certain way, writers use **persuasive techniques.** These include supporting evidence, persuasive language, references to popular culture, repetition, and slogans.

1. Which types of persuasive techniques does MacNeil use most throughout "The Trouble with Television"? Explain.
2. What technique is King employing when he quotes Bob Hope?
3. Find an example of repetition in the final paragraph of King's speech.

◆ Build Vocabulary

USING THE PREFIX *anti-*

The prefix *anti-*, as in *antithesis,* means "opposed to" or "against." Combine the following words with the prefix *anti-*, and define the new word:

1. slavery   2. climax   3. terrorism   4. freeze

SPELLING STRATEGY

The *oy* sound is spelled differently, depending on its location in a word. If the *oy* sound is in the middle of a word, it is spelled *oi*, as in the word *devoid*. At the end of a word, it is spelled *oy* as in *toy*. Choose the correct spelling of the *oy* word:

1. annoi, annoy   2. avoid, avoyd   3. coil, coyl

USING THE WORD BANK

Match each Word Bank word in Column A with the word or phrase closest in meaning in Column B:

Column A	Column B
1. diverts	a. spreading throughout
2. usurps	b. seizes power
3. august	c empty
4. pervading	d. distracts
5. antithesis	e. something opposite of
6. paradoxes	f. seemingly contradictory statements
7. devoid	g. honored

◆ Literary Focus

PERSUASIVE ESSAY

A **persuasive essay** is a short piece of nonfiction in which the writer strives to make readers act or think in a certain way.

1. (a) List three points MacNeil makes that warn against watching television. (b) Explain why each point is or is not effective.
2. In what ways is "The American Dream" an example of persuasive writing?

◆ Build Grammar Skills

PRONOUN AGREEMENT WITH INDEFINITE SUBJECTS

Pronouns must agree with their antecedents in both number and gender, even when the antecedent is indefinite.

Some antecedents may be masculine or feminine. When referring to such antecedents, use both the masculine and the feminine singular forms:

Each *person* must do what *he or she* (not *they*) thinks is right.

If the antecedent is *anybody, anyone, everybody, everyone, neither, nobody, no one, someone,* or *somebody,* use a singular pronoun to refer to it: Everyone can help in *his or her* own way.

Practice On your paper, identify the pronoun and its antecedent:

1. Not one of the programs reached (its, their) audience.
2. Nobody volunteered to give up (their, his or her) favorite television show.
3. Many spend (their, his or her) time watching television.
4. Give each person (their, his or her) civil rights.
5. Several volunteered (their, his or her) time.

Writing Application On your paper, write corrected versions of the following sentences:

1. Neither of these writers wrote their essays in a narrative style.
2. Each of the men had their own message to communicate.

Build Your Portfolio

 ## Idea Bank

Writing

1. **List** Make a list of television programs that you or your family watch regularly. You may also list the hours each family member spends watching television during an average week.

2. **Business Letter** Write to a television network or producer offering suggestions about programming that would make television a more worthwhile experience. Use correct business letter form.

3. **News Analysis** News commentators often review or critique political speeches after they're delivered. Write an analysis of King's speech, identifying its message and overall effectiveness.

Speaking and Listening

4. **Speech** Martin Luther King, Jr., was a powerful speaker. Practice reading "The American Dream" aloud until you can give an inspiring rendition. Then, present it to your classmates. **[Performing Arts Link]**

5. **Dialogue [Group Activity]** With a partner, role-play a conversation between King and MacNeil in which they discuss ways to improve American life. **[Social Studies Link]**

Projects

6. **Civil Rights Exhibit** Research the history of the civil rights movement, using the library and other reference materials. Create a multimedia exhibit that shows a chronological progression in the battle for civil rights. **[Media Link; Social Studies Link]**

7. **Multimedia Presentation** Learn about some aspect of television—how satellites work, how broadcasting stations send and receive television signals, or how your television set works. Then, develop a multimedia presentation, complete with diagrams and charts, to present to the class. **[Media Link; Science Link]**

 ## Writing Mini-Lesson

Persuasive Speech

A persuasive speech like Martin Luther King's "The American Dream" can inspire an audience to think in a particular way or to perform some action. Prepare a persuasive speech about how your school, community, or nation can be made better.

Writing Skills Focus: Strong Beginning and Ending

Effective speeches have **strong beginnings and endings.** Choose one of the following to begin your speech: a startling fact or surprising statistic, a quotation, a question, or an anecdote. MacNeil used the first method:

Model From the Essay
If you fit the statistical averages, by the age of 20 you will have been exposed to at least 20,000 hours of television.

Prewriting Choose a subject about which you feel strongly. Then, gather all the facts and supporting details you need to persuade your listeners. Organize your main ideas and supporting details in outline form.

Drafting From your outline, draft your speech, creating a strong beginning and ending. Use powerful words that you can stress when you deliver your speech.

Revising Read your speech to a classmate, and ask for feedback. If your beginning and ending are not effective, revise them to provide more impact. Also, proofread to correct any errors in grammar.

> ◆ **Grammar Application**
> If you have used pronouns to refer to indefinite antecedents, check that your pronouns agree in number and gender.

"The American Dream" is an idea that has inspired many political figures and writers. The following speech was given by General Colin Powell at the National Volunteer Summit in Philadelphia, Pennsylvania, on June 1, 1997. In the speech, he shares his vision for what America can become through volunteerism.

from

Sharing the American Dream

Colin Powell

Over 200 years ago, a group of volunteers gathered on this sacred spot to found a new nation. In perfect words, they voiced their dreams and aspirations of an imperfect world. They pledged their lives, their fortune and their sacred honor to secure inalienable rights given by God for life, liberty and pursuit of happiness—pledged that they would provide them to all who would inhabit this new nation.

They look down on us today in spirit, with pride for all we have done to keep faith with their ideals and their sacrifices. Yet, despite all we have done, this is still an imperfect world. We still live in an imperfect society. Despite more than two centuries of moral and material progress, despite all our efforts to achieve a more perfect union, there are still Americans who are not sharing in the American Dream. There are still Americans who wonder: is the journey there for them, is the dream there for them, or, whether it is, at best, a dream deferred.

The great American poet, Langston Hughes, talked about a dream deferred, and he said, "What happens to a dream deferred? Does it dry up like a raisin in the sun, or fester like a sore and then run? Does it stink like rotten meat or crust and sugar over like a syrupy sweet? Maybe it just sags, like a heavy load. Or, does it explode?" . . .

So today, we gather here today to pledge that the dream must no longer be deferred and it will never, as long as we can do anything about it, become a dream denied. That is why we are here, my friends. We gather here to pledge that those of us who are more fortunate will not forsake those who are less fortunate. We are a compassionate and caring people. We are a generous people. We will reach down, we will reach back, we will reach across to help our brothers and sisters who are in need.

Above all, we pledge to reach out to the most vulnerable members of the American family, our children. As you've heard, up to 15 million young Americans today are at risk. . . .

In terms of numbers the task may seem staggering. But if we look at the simple needs that these children have, then the task is manageable, the goal is

▲ **Critical Viewing** In what ways are Powell and the volunteers in this photograph helping others to achieve "the American dream"? **[Connect]**

alliance. It is an alliance between government and corporate America and nonprofit America, between our institutions of faith, but especially between individual Americans.

You heard the governors and the mayors, and you'll hear more in a little minute that says the real answer is for each and every one of us, not just here in Philadelphia, but across this land—for each and every one of us to reach out and touch someone in need.

All of us can spare 30 minutes a week or an hour a week. All of us can give an extra dollar. All of us can touch someone who doesn't look like us, who doesn't speak like us, who may not dress like us, but needs us in their lives. And that's what we all have to do to keep this going.

And so there's a spirit of Philadelphia here today. There's a spirit of Philadelphia that we saw yesterday in Germantown. There is a spirit of Philadelphia that will leave Philadelphia tomorrow afternoon and spread across this whole nation—30 governors will go back and spread it; over 100 mayors will go back and spread it, and hundreds of others, leaders around this country who are watching will go back and spread it. Corporate America will spread it, nonprofits will spread it. And each and every one of us will spread it because it has to be done, we have no choice. We cannot leave these children behind if we are going to meet the dreams of our founding fathers.

And so let us all join in this great crusade. Let us make sure that no child in America is left behind, no child in America has their dream deferred or denied. We can do it. We can do it because we are Americans.

achievable. We know what they need. They need an adult caring person in their life, a safe place to learn and grow, a healthy start, marketable skills and an opportunity to serve so that early in their lives they learn the virtue of service so that they can reach out then and touch another young American in need.

These are basic needs that we commit ourselves today, we promise today. We are making America's promise today to provide to those children in need. This is a grand

1. To what group of people does Powell refer in his opening paragraph?
2. What is Powell's pledge?
3. According to Powell, what do the children of the United States need?
4. What action does Powell urge citizens to take?
5. In what ways is Powell's speech similar to King's? How does it differ?

Research Paper

Writing Process Workshop

A report based on information you've researched—such as animal behavior or the effects of television—is called a research paper. A research paper consists of an introduction that states your main idea, a body that offers information with evidence from your research, and a conclusion that sums up the main points of the paper. The body of your paper includes citations that give credit to the sources of the information and ideas you've used in your paper.

Write a research paper on a topic that interests you. These writing skills, covered in the Writing Mini-Lessons in this part, will help you:

Writing Skills Focus

▶ **Use quotation marks** around information you take directly from a source. You must acknowledge information and ideas that are not your own. (See p. 683.)

▶ **Write a strong beginning** to hook your readers and **a strong ending** to leave a lasting impression. (See p. 693.)

▶ **Maintain a clear organization** with an introduction, a body, and a conclusion.

Anaïs Nin's essay about forest fires prompted one student to write a research paper about the career of firefighting:

WRITING MODEL

Although firefighting looks exciting, it's a dangerous occupation. The chance of a firefighter's being killed on the job is thirteen times as high as it is for other workers. ① "Every week in the United States, an average of one firefighter is killed and four hundred others are injured." (Dean, p. 103) ② The physical act of fighting fires occurs in four steps—protection of uninvolved buildings and areas, confinement of a fire, ventilation of a building, and extinguishment of a fire. ③

① The writer begins strongly with a startling fact.

② Quotation marks indicate that these words come from an outside source, noted in parentheses.

③ The writer ends the introduction with a statement of the main idea that will be explored in the body of the paper.

Prewriting

Choose a Topic Choose a topic that interests you. Browsing through a library can stimulate some ideas. Flipping through a news magazine or looking through your journal can generate more. Possible topics include historical figures, historical events, scientific occurrences, music, art, and sports.

Write a Main Idea Statement Write a statement of your main idea or the point you plan to make in the body of your paper. Refer to this statement as you draft.

Use a Variety of Sources Use different kinds of sources. In addition to print sources (encyclopedias, nonfiction books, and articles), you might talk to an expert or watch a documentary on your subject. Use up-to-date resources.

Take Careful Notes Be accurate when researching your paper. Assign each source a number, and use that number to identify all notes taken from the source. Use the following tips when taking notes:

Source Cards	Note Cards
• Create one card for each source, and give it a number.	• Enter only one item of information on each card.
• Include title, author, date and place of publication, etc.	• Include the page number and number of source.
	• When copying exact words, use quotation marks.

Drafting

Maintain a Clear Organization

▶ **Introduction** Start your paper by grabbing your readers' attention. Use a lively quotation, a fascinating statistic, an intriguing question, an interesting anecdote, or a vivid description to hook your readers. Then, include a statement of the main idea of your paper.

▶ **Body** In the main part of your paper, explore and develop your main idea. Incorporate quotations from your research to support the points you are making.

▶ **Strong Conclusion** End with a thought-provoking question or a strong statement of fact. Leave your reader with a strong impression about your topic.

APPLYING LANGUAGE SKILLS: Varying Sentence Structure

Vary your sentence structure to make your writing more interesting. Use simple, compound, and complex sentences:

Simple:
Many fires occur because of carelessness.

Compound:
Many fires are accidentally started at campsites, and the fires sometimes destroy entire forests.

Complex:
Although rangers remind campers to extinguish campfires, many still leave behind live embers.

Practice Rewrite this paragraph to vary sentence style and length:

Chemicals help fight forest fires. Borate or bentonite is usually used. The chemicals penetrate heavy foliage. They make trees resist fire longer than water alone.

Writing Application As you draft your paper, vary the structure of your sentences.

Writer's Solution Connection Language Lab

For additional practice, complete the lesson on Varying Sentence Structure.

APPLYING LANGUAGE SKILLS: Citing Your Sources

List your sources in alphabetical order in a bibliography at the end of your paper. Follow these examples:

Book:

Ragan, Bridget. *Firefighting in America.* New York: Acme Publishing, 1998.

Article:

Lin, Sam. "Fighting Fires from the Air," *Real People*, June 1997, p. 52.

Interview:

Moore, Robert. Personal Interview, Portland, Maine, April 12, 1998.

Internet:

Smoke Jumpers: http://eagle.online.discovery.com

When you use quotations from these sources within your paper, cite the author's last name and add the page number of the work in parentheses.

"Steam fire engines were used in the great fire of Chicago." (Holmes, p. 19.)

Writing Application Use the proper format to cite sources in your research paper.

Writer's Solution Connection Writing Lab

For help with revising, use the Self-Evaluation Checklist in the Revising section of the Reports tutorial.

Revising

Use a Checklist Use the following checklist to help you revise your research paper:

▶ Does your paper have a strong beginning?
  If not, add a startling quotation or fact, an anecdote, or a thought-provoking question.

▶ Did you quote accurately and use quotation marks to indicate material from other sources?
  Check that quotations are exact, and enclose them in quotation marks.

▶ Did you use a logical organization?
  Begin with an introduction that states your main idea, explore the subtopics of your main idea in the body, and end the paper with a conclusion.

▶ Do you end strongly?
  Use your conclusion to summarize the main points of the paper. Ending with a thought-provoking question can leave a lasting impression on your readers.

REVISION MODEL

① Firefighting is as systematic as using a computer.

The four steps of firefighting are protection of uninvolved

buildings and areas, confinement of a fire, ventilation of a

② Although a firefighter uses a system, this job is much more dangerous than working at a computer.

building, and extinguishment of a fire. B. Ramelli sums up

③ "

the importance of a firefighter's job. Daily, the firefighter

dons heavy gear and faces nature's fury. Yet how often do

we stop to thank the men and women who have placed our

"

protection above their own lives?

① The writer adds this statement to lead the reader to a conclusion about firefighting.

② The writer adds this sentence to introduce the quotation. Using this quotation leaves a lasting impression.

③ The writer added quotation marks around the words that were not his own.

Publishing and Presenting

▶ **Home** Present your report orally to your family and friends. Include at least one visual aid to make your presentation more appealing.

▶ **Library** Place a copy of your finished report in your school library.

Real-World Reading Skills Workshop

Evaluating Sources of Information

Strategies for Success

As you read for information, you will encounter magazines, encyclopedias, and Web sites that contain interesting information. Before using this information, you should evaluate whether or not it is credible and relevant to your needs. Use the following guidelines for evaluating sources:

Evaluate the Author Relying on the information of experts in each field is usually a good idea. Look at bibliographical information to find out whether an author is an expert or has firsthand experience in the topic being covered.

Check the Publication Date In the fields of science, technology, and politics, changes happen quickly. Use the most current sources. Information in older sources might be outdated. Check for the most recent date on the copyright page. If your topic requires current information, choose sources that have been published very recently.

Check the Web Site The Internet carries a huge amount of information—some reliable and some not reliable. Note who publishes the Web site: The United States government or *National Geographic,* for example, are reliable. If the site ends in **.edu,** it is an educational source, and its information is likely correct.

Apply the Strategies

Suppose your assignment is a paper on Dubrovnik, a city in Croatia, which declared its independence from Yugoslavia in 1991. You have found the sources shown in the left column. Answer the following questions about these sources.

1. Which encyclopedia is the better choice? Why?
2. Which of the Web sites is designed for educational purposes? How do you know that?
3. Of the three Web sites, which two would you use? Why?
4. The book on Yugoslavia probably has information on Dubrovnik. Would you use it? Why or why not?

Sources for Assignment

- **The Encyclopedia Britannica,** Vol. D, © 1960
- **The World Book,** Vol. D, © 1998
- www.FUN FACTS@pqr.letsbuy.com
- www.nationalgeographic.com
- www.smithsonianmag.si.edu (click on Dubrovnik)
- **Yugoslavia,** by Breshniv Kovacs, © 1968 by Prentice Hall

✔ *Here are other situations in which it's important to evaluate sources of information:*
  ▶ *Reading a political pamphlet*
  ▶ *Reading a newspaper editorial*
  ▶ *Investigating a rumor*

Grammar Review

ante·ced·ent (an'ta sēd"nt) 4 *Gram.* the word, phrase, or clause to which a pronoun refers /"man" is the *antecedent* of "who" in "the man who spoke"/ 5 *Logic* the part of a conditional proposition that

A pronoun usually refers to another noun or pronoun, called its **antecedent.** A personal pronoun must agree with its antecedent in number (singular or plural) and gender (masculine, feminine, or neither). (See p. 682.)

Use a **singular pronoun** to refer to a **singular antecedent:**

A *man* rushed in to announce *he* had seen smoke on Monrovia Peak. (The singular masculine pronoun *he* refers to the singular masculine noun *man*.)

Use a **plural pronoun** to refer to a **plural antecedent:**

The three *Bassets* were already in residence, draped snoring on the fireside rug, but *they* seemed to be used to Debbie. . . . (The plural pronoun *they* refers to the plural noun *Bassets*.)

Indefinite Pronouns Sometimes an antecedent may be an **indefinite pronoun.** Some indefinite pronouns are singular, some are plural, and some can be either:

Singular		Plural	Singular or Plural
another	much	both	all
anybody	neither	few	any
each	no one	many	more
either	nothing	others	most
everyone	other	several	none
everything	something		some
little			

Singular: *Neither* of the women brought *her* pets to the picnic.

Plural: *Both* of the foresters struggled to keep *their* feet on the sliding mud.

Either:
Singular: Take *all* of the food and eat *it*.

Plural: *All* of the dogs were checked by *their* veterinarians.

Agreement in Gender Some antecedents may be either masculine or feminine. When referring to such antecedents, use both the masculine and the feminine forms:

The *person* who lost *his* or *her* notebook will be looking for it.

Practice 1 Copy the following sentences into your notebook, completing them with a pronoun that agrees with its antecedent:

1. Mrs. Ainsworth answered the door and I showed _____?_____ the cat.

2. "People living at the foot of the mountain were packing _____?_____ cars."

3. Each student turned off _____?_____ television set for a week.

Practice 2 Copy the following sentences into your notebook, correcting any errors in pronoun and antecedent agreement:

1. Everyone packed their bags and left as quickly as possible.

2. Both the spectators and the reporters expressed his or her desire to help.

Grammar in Writing

✔ Sometimes using *his* or *her* to refer to an indefinite antecedent is awkward and confusing. When that is the case, rewrite the sentence with a plural antecedent and pronoun.

Awkward: Each student will copy the sentences into his or her notebook.

Plural: Students will copy the sentences into their notebooks.

Are you easily persuaded? Do you ever wonder why you agreed to do something that you didn't really want to do or bought a useless item because someone convinced you to buy it? Like many people, you've probably been persuaded to do things you wish you hadn't. As a responsible listener, you should resist easy persuasion. Evaluate *what* is said as well as *how* it is said.

Listen for Loaded Language Don't be misled or trapped by language that plays on your emotions. Listen for the following devices:

Flattery: "Those sunglasses were *made* for you!"

Empty Promises: "With Perfecto, all your blemishes will disappear."

Threats: "Your grades will suffer without EZSpellCheck."

Compromise You need to keep your best interests in mind when someone is trying to persuade you. For example, a friend wants you to go rollerblading in the park, but you recently hurt your knee and would rather go to a movie. Think about how you would respond.

Friend: "I really want to go skating; your knee won't hurt. You were walking around on it all day today."

You: "I'm sorry, but I can't risk hurting it again so soon. How about going to a movie today, and as soon as I'm feeling better, we'll go skating."

Apply the Strategies

Role-play the following situations with a partner. Work out a conversation that shows how you would resist persuasion.

1. You've agreed to baby sit for your little brother on Saturday night. Your friend Max wants you to baby sit for his little brother so he can go out that same Saturday night. How does he try to persuade you? How do you resist?

2. You've gone to buy simple swimming goggles at $5.95 a pair. A new sales-person, the best diver on the high-school swim team, tries to convince you that you really need the $12.50 pair. What does she say? What do you say?

Tips for Resisting Persuasion

✔ *If you want to resist persuasion and make responsible decisions, follow these guidelines:*

▶ Ignore loaded words that trigger emotions.
▶ Be on the lookout for empty promises.
▶ Ask yourself what is *really* being said.

What's Behind the
Words
Vocabulary Adventures With Richard Lederer

Sportspeak

Because sports occupy such a prominent place in American life and imagination, athletic expressions fill up our everyday speech and writing. The sporty metaphors that make our English language so athletic are vivid reminders of the games that we, as a people, watch and play.

Horsing Around With Politics

Take the language of politics. American political life is filled with horse racing and track metaphors that shape our thinking about campaigns and elections. Some candidates are *dark horses* *champing at the bit* to make a *stretch run.* Others are *front-runners* whose *track records* give them the *inside track* on the nomination. Still others are *shoo-ins* who take the whole thing *in stride.* In some campaigns, the *pacesetters* stumble, trying to *clear the initial hurdles,* and those *back in the pack* give them a good *run for the money.* Then, the contest turns into *a real horse race*—a marathon that may go right *down to the wire.*

Politics and Boxing

When candidates enter a political race, they *throw their hat in the ring.* This popular expression, dating back to the nineteenth century, springs from the custom of throwing a hat in a boxing ring to signal acceptance of a fighter's challenge. *Straight from the shoulder,* boxing metaphors *pull no punches* in our language.

ACTIVITY 1 Find out the origins of the following expressions from racing:
1. dark horse
2. champing at the bit
3. shoo-in

ACTIVITY 2 Explain the popular usage of the following expressions from boxing:
1. throw in the towel
2. beat someone to the punch
3. come out swinging
4. saved by the bell
5. a low blow

ACTIVITY 3 Okay, sports fans, how many sports and games can you find hidden in the following game plan:

When the situation is up for grabs and your opponent is tossing in a red herring, you must knuckle down, hold the line, call the shots, hit the bull's-eye, get the ball rolling, take the bull by the horns with no holds barred, keep one jump ahead, and put the ball in the other guy's court. Otherwise, you may end up jumping the gun; not up to par; down and out; out in left field; behind the eight ball; coming a cropper; taking the bait hook, line, and sinker; and facing a sticky wicket.

ACTIVITY 4 Research the origins of five of the phrases you identified in Activity 3.

Extended Reading Opportunities

True stories—biographies, histories, essays, and articles—let us see the world around us more clearly. The following works of nonfiction will help you better understand our world.

Suggested Titles

Nonfiction Readings Across the Curriculum

This collection of nonfiction works includes essays, speeches, memoirs, book introductions, and excerpts from biographies and auto-biographies. The collection includes nonfiction works related to the major subject areas: language arts, science, social studies, math, physical education, music, and art. You are guaranteed to find a work about your favorite academic subject.

Lincoln: A Photobiography
Russell Freedman

Recipient of the Newbery Medal, the Jefferson Cup Award, and the Golden Kite Honor Book Award, this comprehensive work provides insight into the life of one of the nation's most fascinating presidents. Freedman uses drawings and photos to tell the story of an ambitious but modest man who came from humble beginnings. The inter-esting facts of Lincoln's boy-hood and manhood, as well as his presidency, are sure to hold your attention.

Now Is Your Time! The African-American Struggle for Freedom
Walter Dean Myers

This compelling history of African Americans is unified with the accounts of outstand-ing lives, such as Ibrahima, unconquerable African prince; James Forten, entrepreneur; and Ida B. Wells. Myers also describes the many contribu-tions that African Americans have made to the United States—black soldiers fighting in the Civil War, the landmark decision of *Plessy* vs. *Ferguson,* and the civil rights movement.

Other Possibilities

Puppies, Dogs, and Blue Northers   Gary Paulsen

Ishi, Last of His Tribe   Theodora Kroebler

A Photohistory of American Women in Sports:
    Winning Ways   Sue Macy

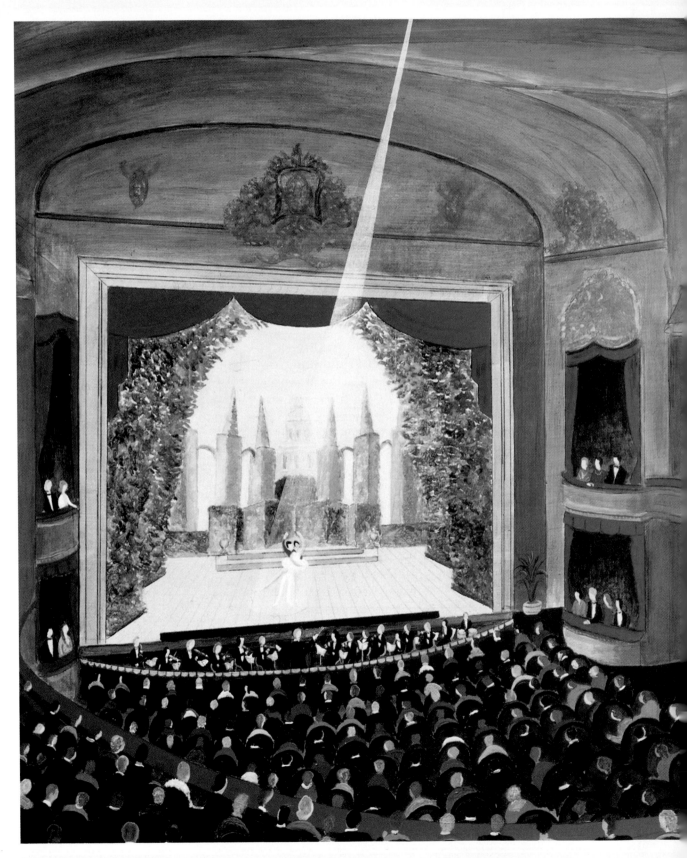

First Night, Mark Baring, Private Collection

Drama

Drama is a form of literature that is meant to be performed on a stage. When you read a drama, you should picture in your mind how it would appear and sound to an audience. As you read the dramas in this unit, notice the following elements, which can help bring the dramas to life in your mind:

- **Stage Directions:** These notes convey information to the cast, crew, and readers of the drama about sound effects, actions, sets, and line readings.

- **Dialogue:** In drama, much of what you learn about the characters, setting, and events is revealed through dialogue—conversations among the characters.

- **Characters:** Dramatic characters are brought to life by their dialogue and actions onstage.

- **Plot:** Most dramas contain a plot in which events unfold, rise to a climax, and are resolved.

- **Theme:** A theme is the central message the playwright conveys to the audience.

Reading for Success

Strategies for Reading Drama

Although dramas have existed for thousands of years, they have remained basically the same: Actors assume roles and interact with one another. Dramas share many elements with other forms of literature: most contain a plot, build to a climax, and reveal themes. Some dramas are written entirely in poetry!

The one thing, however, that distinguishes dramas from other types of literature is that they are meant to be performed. The written script is merely a blueprint, or guide, that allows the actors and you, the reader, to understand the playwright's vision.

When you read a drama, apply the following strategies to interact with the text:

Envision the setting, action, and characters.

Use your senses to envision the setting, action, and characters.

▶ Use information in the stage directions to picture in your mind the time and place of the drama's action.

▶ Use the stage directions to understand the characters' attitudes and to picture their physical actions.

▶ Try to imagine the dialogue being spoken. You may even find it helpful to read passages aloud.

Summarize.

Most dramas are broken into acts and scenes. As you finish each scene and act, summarize what has happened. Take note of how characters change and how the action progresses during the course of the play.

Passage	Summary
Act 1, Scene 1	Mr. Frank and Miep return to the attic in which the Frank family hid. They find Anne's diary.

Be aware of historical context.

If a drama was written long ago, or if the drama takes place during a specific time period, be aware of the historical context in which it was written. For example, when you read *The Diary of Anne Frank,* it's necessary to know that Anne Frank's family is Jewish and that the Nazis persecuted Jews during World War II. This context enables you to understand the tension and fear in the play.

Apply these strategies as you read the dramas in this unit. They will help you to read the dramas more effectively.

Modern Drama

Theater poster for the 1996 season for the McCarter Theatre in Princeton, New Jersey, Wiktor Sadowski

Guide for Reading

Meet the Authors:

Frances Goodrich (1890–1984) and Albert Hackett (1900–1995)

Frances Goodrich and Albert Hackett spent two years writing the drama *The Diary of Anne Frank*, which is based on the world-renowned *The Diary of a Young Girl* by Anne Frank. Their play won a Pulitzer Prize, the Drama Critics Circle award, and the Tony award for best play of the 1955–1956 season.

From Acting to Writing

Goodrich and Hackett began working together in 1927 and were married in 1931. Both had been actors. Hackett had worked in both vaudeville and silent films. Goodrich had been a stage actor who had appeared on Broadway. The couple ended their writing careers in 1962, after writing the script for the screenplay of *The Diary of Anne Frank*.

◆ LITERATURE AND YOUR LIFE

CONNECT YOUR EXPERIENCE

Can you imagine what it would be like if all your plans for life—school, career, raising a family—were cut short, and you had to change your life radically? In this drama, you'll learn of a young girl who has to put aside all her plans when she is forced into hiding with her family because of a war.

THEMATIC FOCUS: Heroes

As you read, note the heroic qualities that the young girl and her family display as they try to cope with their terrifying situation.

◆ Build Vocabulary

PREFIXES: *un-* AND *in-*

The prefix *un-* and its variation *in-* mean "not" or "without." When these prefixes are joined to a word, the meaning of the word is the opposite. For example, *insufferable* means "*not* able to be suffered or tolerated."

WORD BANK

Which word from the list describes a person who believes in fate? Check the Build Vocabulary box on page 737 to see if you chose correctly.

conspicuous
mercurial
leisure
unabashed
insufferable
meticulous
fatalist
ostentatiously

The Diary of Anne Frank ◆

◆ Background for Understanding

HISTORY: WORLD WAR II AND THE HOLOCAUST

Hitler and the Nazis In 1933, Adolf Hitler and the National Socialist (Nazi) party seized power in Germany. The Nazis claimed that Germans were superior to non-Germans. They blamed Jews and other minorities for all of Germany's troubles—from its defeat in World War I to the severe economic depression of the 1920's. To punish Jews for these imagined sins, the Nazis denied them the right to own property, attend schools, and serve in the professions.

The Start of World War II In foreign affairs, Hitler worked for a "Greater Germany" by occupying Austria and seizing Czechoslovakia. Then, after signing a secret treaty with the Soviet Union, he invaded Poland on September 1, 1939. Two days later, Britain and France declared war on Germany. However, they could not prevent Hitler's forces from conquering much of Europe, including Belgium and France.

The Defeat of Hitler Two events in 1941 foreshadowed Hitler's downfall. In June of that year, Hitler staged a surprise invasion of the Soviet Union, his former ally. Eventually, however, German troops would suffer great losses in this campaign. The second key development of that year was the entry of the United States into the war. American military and industrial might was important in defeating Germany. It was not until May 1945, however, that Germany surrendered to the Allies.

◆ Background for Understanding (continued)

The Holocaust Meanwhile, during World War II, everywhere the German army went, Jews and other peoples were persecuted. The name that has been given to these events is the Holocaust, which comes from a Greek word meaning "burnt whole."

Jews were made to wear yellow stars on their clothing and were sent to ghettos—crowded, closed-off neighborhoods in cities. There, many died of starvation and disease. Those who survived were eventually transported in freight cars to special prisons known as concentration camps, where most died within a few months. Then, the Nazis thought of an even more efficient way to destroy the Jews: camps where people were gassed to death in special rooms almost as soon as they arrived.

The number of people killed by the Nazis is staggering. An estimated three million Jews died in concentration camps. Another three million were either shot or died in the ghettos of starvation and disease. By the end of the war, some six million Jews had perished, three fourths of Europe's Jewish population.

Persecution of Other Peoples Another group that nearly disappeared during the Holocaust was Europe's Gypsies. Many Gypsies had lived for centuries in Germany, but along with the Jews, they were targeted for destruction as a so-called foreign race. It is estimated that during the Holocaust, a half million Gypsies died, 80 percent of the European Gypsy population.

Millions of other people died as well, especially in Eastern Europe. In addition to losing three million Jews, Poland lost another three million citizens through slave labor, starvation, and murder. The Soviet Union lost at least seven million people—not counting the millions of prisoners of war who never returned home.

THE STORY BEHIND THE PLAY The Diary of Anne Frank is based on a real diary written by a young girl during the Holocaust. Anne Frank was born to a Jewish family in Frankfurt, Germany, on June 12, 1929. She had a normal, happy childhood until the Nazis took power in 1933.

That year, Anne's family left their home in Germany to escape persecution, moving to the Netherlands. In Amsterdam, Mr. Frank reestablished his business, and Mrs. Frank set up their new household. Anne and her older sister, Margot, attended school and made new friends.

In 1940, the German army invaded the Netherlands. Unfortunately, the Dutch army was unable to withstand the German army, and in May 1940, the Netherlands fell under German control. It wasn't long before Jews there were subjected to Nazi discrimination and abuse.

Even as late as 1942, however, the Frank family and many other European Jews were unaware of the dangers they faced. Most simply thought they would be temporarily imprisoned by the Nazis. To avoid this fate, the Frank family hid in the attic of a warehouse and office building that had been part of Mr. Frank's business in Amsterdam.

On her thirteenth birthday, Anne had received a diary as a gift. When her family went into hiding, she began to write regularly in this diary. The play you are about to read is based on this diary, which Mr. Frank recovered when he returned to the secret attic after the war.

◆ The Diary of Anne Frank, Act I ◆

◆ Literary Focus

STAGING

Staging is a term that refers to the techniques that bring a drama to life. These techniques include scenery, costumes, lighting, and sound effects, as well as actors' movements and characters' motives. This information appears in the script within brackets. Directors use these stage directions to help them produce the drama. Readers use the information to help them to visualize the characters and action onstage.

As you read, create a chart like the one below for each scene.

◆ Reading Strategy

BE AWARE OF HISTORICAL CONTEXT

As you read any type of literature that takes place in the past, be aware of the **historical context** in which it takes place. Historical context includes the political forces, cultural beliefs and attitudes, and events of the time that affect the action and characters. For example, the characters in *The Diary of Anne Frank* lived during World War II in Holland, which had been taken over by the Nazis. Knowing the history of the Holocaust helps you to understand why the Frank family, who were Jewish, acted as they did.

Act I	Scenery	Lighting	Sound	Costumes	Actors' Movements
Scene 1:	3 small attic rooms	Dim— windows painted over	Church bells	Mr. Frank: worn and tattered suit	Mr. Frank walks slowly, as if ill.

The Diary of Anne Frank

Frances Goodrich and Albert Hackett

CHARACTERS

MR. FRANK

MIEP

MRS. VAN DAAN

MR. VAN DAAN

PETER VAN DAAN

MRS. FRANK

MARGOT FRANK

ANNE FRANK

MR. KRALER

MR. DUSSEL

ACT I

Scene 1

[*The scene remains the same throughout the play. It is the top floor of a warehouse and office building in Amsterdam, Holland. The sharply peaked roof of the building is outlined against a sea of other rooftops, stretching away into the distance. Nearby is the belfry[1] of a church tower, the Westertoren, whose carillon[2] rings out the hours. Occasionally faint sounds float up from below: the voices of children playing in the street, the tramp of marching feet, a boat whistle from the canal.*

The three rooms of the top floor and a small attic space above are exposed to our view. The largest of the rooms is in the center, with two small rooms, slightly raised, on either side. On the right is a bathroom, out of sight. A narrow steep flight of stairs at the back leads up to the attic. The rooms are sparsely furnished with a few chairs, cots, a table or two. The windows are painted over, or covered with makeshift blackout curtains.[3] In the main room there is a sink, a gas ring for cooking and a woodburning stove for warmth.

---

1. **belfry** (bel´ frē) *n.*: The part of a tower that holds the bells.
2. **carillon** (kar´ ə län´) *n.*: A set of stationary bells, each producing one note of the scale.
3. **blackout curtains:** Draperies that conceal all lights that might otherwise be visible to enemy air raiders at night.

The room on the left is hardly more than a closet. There is a skylight in the sloping ceiling. Directly under this room is a small steep stairwell, with steps leading down to a door. This is the only entrance from the building below. When the door is opened we see that it has been concealed on the outer side by a bookcase attached to it.

The curtain rises on an empty stage. It is late afternoon, November 1945.

The rooms are dusty, the curtains in rags. Chairs and tables are overturned.

The door at the foot of the small stairwell swings open. MR. FRANK *comes up the steps into view. He is a gentle, cultured European in his middle years. There is still a trace of a German accent in his speech.*

He stands looking slowly around, making a supreme effort at self-control. He is weak, ill. His clothes are threadbare.

After a second he drops his rucksack[4] on the couch and moves slowly about. He opens the door to one of the smaller rooms, and then abruptly closes it again, turning away. He goes to the window at the back, looking off at the Westertoren as its carillon strikes the hour of six, then he moves restlessly on.

From the street below we hear the sound of a barrel organ[5] and children's voices at play. There is a many-colored scarf hanging from a nail. MR. FRANK *takes it, putting it around his neck. As he starts back for his rucksack, his eye is caught by something lying on the floor. It is a woman's white glove. He holds it in his hand and suddenly all of his self-control is gone. He breaks down, crying.*

We hear footsteps on the stairs. MIEP GIES *comes up, looking for* MR. FRANK. MIEP *is a Dutch girl of about twenty-two. She wears a coat and hat, ready to go home. She is pregnant. Her attitude toward* MR. FRANK *is protective, compassionate.*]

MIEP. Are you all right, Mr. Frank?

MR. FRANK. [*Quickly controlling himself*] Yes, Miep, yes.

---

4. **rucksack** (ruk´ sak´) *n.*: Knapsack or backpack.
5. **barrel organ** *n.*: Mechanical musical instrument played by turning a crank.

▲ **Critical Viewing** This photograph captures the Frank family out for a walk with friends. How would you describe their mood, judging from their expressions? [**Connect**]

MIEP. Everyone in the office has gone home . . . It's after six. [*Then pleading*] Don't stay up here, Mr. Frank. What's the use of torturing yourself like this?

MR. FRANK. I've come to say good-bye . . . I'm leaving here, Miep.

MIEP. What do you mean? Where are you going? Where?

MR. FRANK. I don't know yet. I haven't decided.

MIEP. Mr. Frank, you can't leave here! This is your home! Amsterdam is your home. Your business is here, waiting for you . . . You're needed here . . . Now that the war is over, there are things that . . .

MR. FRANK. I can't stay in Amsterdam, Miep. It has too many memories for me. Everywhere there's something . . . the house we lived in . . . the school . . . that street organ playing out there . . . I'm not the person you used to know, Miep. I'm a bitter old man. [*Breaking off*] Forgive me. I shouldn't speak to you like this . . . after all that you did for us . . . the suffering . . .

MIEP. No. No. It wasn't suffering. You can't say we suffered. [*As she speaks, she straightens a chair which is overturned.*]

MR. FRANK. I know what you went through, you and Mr. Kraler. I'll remember it as long as I live. [*He gives one last look around.*] Come, Miep. [*He starts for the steps, then remembers his rucksack, going back to get it.*]

MIEP. [*Hurrying up to a cupboard*] Mr. Frank, did you see? There are some of your papers here. [*She brings a bundle of papers to him.*] We found them in a heap of rubbish on the floor after . . . after you left.

MR. FRANK. Burn them. [*He opens his rucksack to put the glove in it.*]

MIEP. But, Mr. Frank, there are letters, notes . . .

MR. FRANK. Burn them. All of them.

MIEP. Burn this? [*She hands him a paper-bound notebook.*]

MR. FRANK. [*quietly*] Anne's diary. [*He opens the diary and begins to read.*] "Monday, the sixth of July, nineteen forty-two." [*To* MIEP] Nineteen forty-two. Is it possible, Miep? . . . Only three years ago. [*As he continues his reading, he sits down on the couch.*] "Dear Diary, since you and I are going to be great friends, I will start by telling you about myself. My name is Anne Frank. I am thirteen years old. I was born in Germany the twelfth of June, nineteen twenty-nine. As my family is Jewish, we emigrated to Holland when Hitler came to power."

> ◆ **Reading Strategy**
> Why was the rise of Hitler as a political figure a concern for the Frank family?

[*As* MR. FRANK *reads on, another voice joins his, as if coming from the air. It is* ANNE'S VOICE.]

MR. FRANK and **ANNE.** "My father started a business, importing spice and herbs. Things went well for us until nineteen forty. Then the war came, and the Dutch capitulation,[6] followed by the arrival of the Germans. Then things got very bad for the Jews."

[MR. FRANK'S VOICE *dies out.* ANNE'S VOICE *continues alone. The lights dim slowly to darkness. The curtain falls on the scene.*]

ANNE'S VOICE. You could not do this and you could not do that. They forced Father out of his business. We had to wear yellow stars.[7] I had to turn in my bike. I couldn't go to a Dutch school any more. I couldn't go to the movies, or ride in an automobile, or even on a streetcar, and a million other things. But somehow we children still managed to have fun. Yesterday Father told me we were going into hiding. Where, he wouldn't say. At five

---

6. **capitulation** (kə pich′ ə lā′ shən) *n.*: Surrender.
7. **yellow stars:** Stars of David, which are six-pointed stars that are symbols of Judaism. The Nazis ordered all Jews to wear them sewn to their clothing so that Jews could be easily identified.

◆ **Build Vocabulary**

conspicuous (kən spik′ yōō əs) *adj.*: Noticeable

---

o'clock this morning Mother woke me and told me to hurry and get dressed. I was to put on as many clothes as I could. It would look too suspicious if we walked along carrying suitcases. It wasn't until we were on our way that I learned where we were going. Our hiding place was to be upstairs in the building where Father used to have his business. Three other people were coming in with us . . . the Van Daans and their son Peter . . . Father knew the Van Daans but we had never met them . . .

[*During the last lines the curtain rises on the scene. The lights dim on.* ANNE'S VOICE *fades out.*]

Scene 2

[*It is early morning, July 1942. The rooms are bare, as before, but they are now clean and orderly.*

MR. VAN DAAN, *a tall, portly[8] man in his late forties, is in the main room, pacing up and down, nervously smoking a cigarette. His clothes and overcoat are expensive and well cut.*

MRS. VAN DAAN *sits on the couch, clutching her possessions, a hatbox, bags, etc. She is a pretty woman in her early forties. She wears a fur coat over her other clothes.*

PETER VAN DAAN *is standing at the window of the room on the right, looking down at the street below. He is a shy, awkward boy of sixteen. He wears a cap, a raincoat, and long Dutch trousers, like "plus fours."[9] At his feet is a black case, a carrier for his cat.*

The yellow Star of David is conspicuous *on all of their clothes.*]

MRS. VAN DAAN. [*Rising, nervous, excited*] Something's happened to them! I know it!

MR. VAN DAAN. Now, Kerli!

MRS. VAN DAAN. Mr. Frank said they'd be here at seven o'clock. He said . . .

MR. VAN DAAN. They have two miles to walk. You can't expect . . .

MRS. VAN DAAN. They've been picked up. That's what's happened. They've been taken . . .

---

8. **portly** (pôrt′ lē) *adj.*: Large, heavy, and dignified.
9. **plus fours** *n.*: Loose knickers worn for active sports.

[MR. VAN DAAN *indicates that he hears someone coming.*]

MR. VAN DAAN. You see?

[PETER *takes up his carrier and his schoolbag, etc., and goes into the main room as* MR. FRANK *comes up the stairwell from below.* MR. FRANK *looks much younger now. His movements are brisk, his manner confident. He wears an overcoat and carries his hat and a small cardboard box. He crosses to the* VAN DAANS, *shaking hands with each of them.*]

MR. FRANK. Mrs. Van Daan, Mr. Van Daan, Peter. [*Then, in explanation of their lateness*] There were too many of the Green Police[10] on the streets . . . we had to take the long way around.

[*Up the steps come* MARGOT FRANK, MRS. FRANK, MIEP *(not pregnant now) and* MR. KRALER. *All of them carry bags, packages, and so forth. The Star of David is conspicuous on all of the* FRANKS' *clothing.* MARGOT *is eighteen, beautiful, quiet, shy.* MRS. FRANK *is a young mother, gently bred, reserved. She, like* MR. FRANK, *has a slight German accent.* MR. KRALER *is a Dutchman, dependable, kindly.*

  As MR. KRALER *and* MIEP *go upstage to put down their parcels,* MRS. FRANK *turns back to call* ANNE.]

MRS. FRANK. Anne?

[ANNE *comes running up the stairs. She is thirteen, quick in her movements, interested in everything,* mercurial *in her emotions. She wears a cape, long wool socks and carries a schoolbag.*]

MR. FRANK. [*Introducing them*] My wife, Edith. Mr. and Mrs. Van Daan . . . their son, Peter . . . my daughters, Margot and Anne.

[MRS. FRANK *hurries over, shaking hands with them.*]

[ANNE *gives a polite little curtsy as she shakes* MR. VAN DAAN'*s hand. Then she immediately starts off on a tour of investigation of her new home, going upstairs to the attic room.*

---

10. Green Police: Nazi police, who wore green uniforms.

MIEP *and* MR. KRALER *are putting the various things they have brought on the shelves.*]

MR. KRALER. I'm sorry there is still so much confusion.

MR. FRANK. Please. Don't think of it. After all, we'll have plenty of leisure to arrange everything ourselves.

MIEP. [*To* MRS. FRANK] We put the stores of food you sent in here. Your drugs are here . . . soap, linen here.

MRS. FRANK. Thank you, Miep.

MIEP. I made up the beds . . . the way Mr. Frank and Mr. Kraler said. [*She starts out.*] Forgive me. I have to hurry. I've got to go to the other side of town to get some ration books[11] for you.

MRS. VAN DAAN. Ration books? If they see our names on ration books, they'll know we're here.

MR. KRALER. There isn't anything . . .

MIEP. Don't worry. Your names won't be on them. [*As she hurries out*] I'll be up later.

MR. FRANK. Thank you, Miep.

MRS. FRANK. [*To* MR. KRALER] It's illegal, then, the ration books? We've never done anything illegal.

MR. FRANK. We won't be living here exactly according to regulations.

[*As* MR. KRALER *reassures* MRS. FRANK, *he takes various small things, such as matches, soap, etc., from his pockets, handing them to her.*]

MR. KRALER. This isn't the black market,[12] Mrs. Frank. This is what we call the white market . . . helping all of the hundreds

---

11. ration books (rash´ ən books) *n.:* Books of stamps given to ensure the even distribution of scarce items, especially in wartime. Stamps as well as money must be given to obtain an item that is scarce.

12. black market: Illegal way of buying scarce items without ration stamps.

◆ **Build Vocabulary**

mercurial (mər kyo͞or´ ē əl) *adj.:* Quick or changeable in behavior

leisure (lezh´ ər) *n.:* Free and unoccupied time

and hundreds who are hiding out in Amsterdam.

[*The carillon is heard playing the quarter-hour before eight.* MR. KRALER *looks at his watch.* ANNE *stops at the window as she comes down the stairs.*]

ANNE. It's the Westertoren!

MR. KRALER. I must go. I must be out of here and downstairs in the office before the workmen get here. [*He starts for the stairs leading out.*] Miep or I, or both of us, will be up each day to bring you food and news and find out what your needs are. Tomorrow I'll get you a better bolt for the door at the foot of the stairs. It needs a bolt that you can throw yourself and open only at our signal. [*To* MR. FRANK] Oh . . . You'll tell them about the noise?

MR. FRANK. I'll tell them.

MR. KRALER. Good-bye then for the moment. I'll come up again, after the workmen leave.

MR. FRANK. Good-bye, Mr. Kraler.

MRS. FRANK. [*Shaking his hand*] How can we thank you?

[*The others murmur their good-byes.*]

MR. KRALER. I never thought I'd live to see the day when a man like Mr. Frank would have to go into hiding. When you think—

[*He breaks off, going out.* MR. FRANK *follows him down the steps, bolting the door after him. In the interval before he returns,* PETER *goes over to* MARGOT, *shaking hands with her. As* MR. FRANK *comes back up the steps,* MRS. FRANK *questions him anxiously.*]

MRS. FRANK. What did he mean, about the noise?

MR. FRANK. First let us take off some of these clothes.

▶ **Critical Viewing** The photograph shows the front view of the building in which the Franks hid. Why was this location a good one for hiding? [**Assess**]

[*They all start to take off garment after garment. On each of their coats, sweaters, blouses, suits, dresses, is another yellow Star of David.* MR. *and* MRS. FRANK *are underdressed quite simply. The others wear several things, sweaters, extra dresses, bathrobes, aprons, nightgowns, etc.*]

MR. VAN DAAN. It's a wonder we weren't arrested, walking along the streets . . . Petronella with a fur coat in July . . . and that cat of Peter's crying all the way.

ANNE. A cat?

[*Finally, as they have all removed their surplus clothes, they look to* MR. FRANK, *waiting for him to speak.*]

MR. FRANK. Now. About the noise. While the men are in the building below, we must have complete quiet. Every sound can be heard down there, not only in the work-rooms, but in the offices too. The men come at about eight-thirty, and leave at about five-thirty. So, to be perfectly safe, from eight in the morning until six in the evening we must move only when it is necessary, and then in stockinged feet. We must not speak above a whisper. We must not run any water. We cannot use the sink, or even, forgive me, the w.c.[13] The pipes go down through the workrooms. It would be heard. No trash . . .

[MR. FRANK *stops abruptly as he hears the sound of marching feet from the street below. Everyone is motionless, paralyzed with fear.* MR. FRANK *goes quietly into the room on the right to look down out of the window.* ANNE *runs after him, peering out with him. The tramping feet pass without stopping. The tension is relieved.* MR. FRANK, *followed by* ANNE, *returns to the main room and resumes his instructions to the group.*]

. . . No trash must ever be thrown out which might reveal that someone is living up here . . . not even a potato paring. We must burn everything in the stove at night. This is the way we must live until it is over, if we are to survive.

[*There is silence for a second.*]

MRS. FRANK. Until it is over.

MR. FRANK. [*Reassuringly*] After six we can move about . . . we can talk and laugh and have our supper and read and play games . . . just as we would at home. [*He looks at his watch.*] And now I think it would be wise if we all went to our rooms, and were settled before eight o'clock. Mrs. Van Daan, you and your husband will be up-stairs. I regret that there's no place up there for Peter. But he will be here, near us. This will be our common room, where we'll meet to talk and eat and read, like one family.

MR. VAN DAAN. And where do you and Mrs. Frank sleep?

MR. FRANK. This room is also our bedroom.

[*Together*]
{
MRS. VAN DAAN. That isn't right. We'll sleep here and you take the room upstairs.

MR. VAN DAAN. It's your place.
}

MR. FRANK. Please. I've thought this out for weeks. It's the best arrangement. The only arrangement.

MRS. VAN DAAN. [*To* MR. FRANK] Never, never can we thank you. [*Then to* MRS. FRANK] I don't know what would have happened to us, if it hadn't been for Mr. Frank.

MR. FRANK. You don't know how your husband helped me when I came to this country . . . knowing no one . . . not able to speak the language. I can never repay him for that. [*Going to* VAN DAAN] May I help you with your things?

MR. VAN DAAN. No. No. [*To* MRS. VAN DAAN] Come along, *liefje.*[14]

MRS. VAN DAAN. You'll be all right, Peter? You're not afraid?

PETER. [*Embarrassed*] Please, Mother.

---

13. w.c.: Water closet; bathroom.

14. *liefje* (lēf´ hyə): Dutch for "little love."

[*They start up the stairs to the attic room above.* MR. FRANK *turns to* MRS. FRANK.]

MR. FRANK. You too must have some rest, Edith. You didn't close your eyes last night. Nor you, Margot.

ANNE. I slept, Father. Wasn't that funny? I knew it was the last night in my own bed, and yet I slept soundly.

MR. FRANK. I'm glad, Anne. Now you'll be able to help me straighten things in here. [*To* MRS. FRANK *and* MARGOT] Come with me . . . You and Margot rest in this room for the time being.

[*He picks up their clothes, starting for the room on the right.*]

MRS. FRANK. You're sure . . . ? I could help . . . And Anne hasn't had her milk . . .

MR. FRANK. I'll give it to her. [*To* ANNE *and* PETER] Anne, Peter . . . it's best that you take off your shoes now, before you forget.

[*He leads the way to the room, followed by* MARGOT.]

MRS. FRANK. You're sure you're not tired, Anne?

ANNE. I feel fine. I'm going to help Father.

MRS. FRANK. Peter, I'm glad you are to be with us.

PETER. Yes, Mrs. Frank.

[MRS. FRANK *goes to join* MR. FRANK *and* MARGOT.]

[*During the following scene* MR. FRANK *helps* MARGOT *and* MRS. FRANK *to hang up their clothes. Then he persuades them both to lie down and rest. The* VAN DAANS *in their room above settle themselves. In the main room* ANNE *and* PETER *remove their shoes.* PETER *takes his cat out of the carrier.*]

ANNE. What's your cat's name?

PETER. Mouschi.

ANNE. Mouschi! Mouschi! Mouschi! [*She picks up the cat, walking away with it. To* PETER] I love cats. I have one . . . a darling little cat.

But they made me leave her behind. I left some food and a note for the neighbors to take care of her . . . I'm going to miss her terribly. What is yours? A him or a her?

PETER. He's a tom. He doesn't like strangers. [*He takes the cat from her, putting it back in its carrier.*]

ANNE. [*Unabashed*] Then I'll have to stop being a stranger, won't I? Where did you go to school?

PETER. Jewish Secondary.

ANNE. But that's where Margot and I go! I never saw you around.

PETER. I used to see you . . . sometimes . . .

ANNE. You did?

PETER. . . . In the school yard. You were always in the middle of a bunch of kids. [*He takes a penknife from his pocket.*]

ANNE. Why didn't you ever come over?

PETER. I'm sort of a lone wolf. [*He starts to rip off his Star of David.*]

ANNE. What are you doing?

PETER. Taking it off.

ANNE. But you can't do that. They'll arrest you if you go out without your star.

[*He tosses his knife on the table.*]

PETER. Who's going out?

ANNE. Why, of course! You're right! Of course we don't need them any more. [*She picks up his knife and starts to take her star off.*] I wonder what our friends will think when we don't show up today?

PETER. I didn't have any dates with anyone.

ANNE. Oh, I did. I had a date with Jopie to go and play ping-pong at her house. Do you know Jopie de Waal?

PETER. No.

ANNE. Jopie's my best friend. I wonder what she'll think when she telephones and there's

◆ **Build Vocabulary**
unabashed (un ə basht´) *adj.:* Unashamed

no answer? . . . Probably she'll go over to the house . . . I wonder what she'll think . . . we left everything as if we'd suddenly been called away . . . breakfast dishes in the sink . . . beds not made . . . [*As she pulls off her star, the cloth underneath shows clearly the color and form of the star.*] Look! It's still there!

[PETER *goes over to the stove with his star.*]

What're you going to do with yours?

PETER. Burn it.

ANNE. [*She starts to throw hers in, and cannot.*] It's funny, I can't throw mine away. I don't know why.

PETER. You can't throw . . . ? Something they branded you with . . . ? That they made you wear so they could spit on you?

ANNE. I know. I know. But after all, it is the Star of David, isn't it?

[*In the bedroom, right,* MARGOT *and* MRS. FRANK *are lying down.* MR. FRANK *starts quietly out.*]

PETER. Maybe it's different for a girl.

[MR. FRANK *comes into the main room.*]

MR. FRANK. Forgive me, Peter. Now let me see. We must find a bed for your cat. [*He goes to a cupboard.*] I'm glad you brought your cat. Anne was feeling so badly about hers. [*Getting a used small washtub*] Here we are. Will it be comfortable in that?

PETER. [*Gathering up his things*] Thanks.

MR. FRANK. [*Opening the door of the room on the left*] And here is your room. But I warn you, Peter, you can't grow any more. Not an inch, or you'll have to sleep with your feet out of the skylight. Are you hungry?

PETER. No.

MR. FRANK. We have some bread and butter.

PETER. No, thank you.

MR. FRANK. You can have it for luncheon then. And tonight we will have a real supper . . . our first supper together.

PETER. Thanks. Thanks. [*He goes into his room. During the following scene he arranges his possessions in his new room.*]

MR. FRANK. That's a nice boy, Peter.

ANNE. He's awfully shy, isn't he?

MR. FRANK. You'll like him, I know.

ANNE. I certainly hope so, since he's the only boy I'm likely to see for months and months.

[MR. FRANK *sits down, taking off his shoes.*]

MR. FRANK. Annele,[15] there's a box there. Will you open it?

[*He indicates a carton on the couch.* ANNE brings it to the center table. In the street below there is the sound of children playing.*]

ANNE. [*As she opens the carton*] You know the way I'm going to think of it here? I'm going to think of it as a boarding house. A very peculiar summer boarding house, like the one that we—[*She breaks off as she pulls out some photographs.*] Father! My movie stars! I was wondering where they were! I was looking for them this morning . . . and Queen Wilhelmina![16] How wonderful!

MR. FRANK. There's something more. Go on. Look further. [*He goes over to the sink, pouring a glass of milk from a thermos bottle.*]

ANNE. [*Pulling out a pasteboard-bound book*] A diary! [*She throws her arms around her

---

▲ **Critical Viewing** Why do you think Jews were forced to wear yellow stars like this one? [**Infer**]

---

15. **Annele** (än´ ə lə): Nickname for *Anne*.
16. **Queen Wilhelmina** (wil´ hel mē´ nə): Queen of the Netherlands from 1890 to 1948.

father.] I've never had a diary. And I've always longed for one. [*She looks around the room.*] Pencil, pencil, pencil, pencil. [*She starts down the stairs.*] I'm going down to the office to get a pencil.

MR. FRANK. Anne! No! [*He goes after her, catching her by the arm and pulling her back.*]

ANNE. [*Startled*] But there's no one in the building now.

MR. FRANK. It doesn't matter. I don't want you ever to go beyond that door.

ANNE. [*Sobered*] Never . . . ? Not even at nighttime, when everyone is gone? Or on Sundays? Can't I go down to listen to the radio?

MR. FRANK. Never. I am sorry, Anneke.[17] It isn't safe. No, you must never go beyond that door.

[*For the first time* ANNE *realizes what "going into hiding" means.*]

ANNE. I see.

MR. FRANK. It'll be hard, I know. But always remember this, Anneke. There are no walls, there are no bolts, no locks that anyone can put on your mind. Miep will bring us books. We will read history, poetry, mythology. [*He gives her the glass of milk.*] Here's your milk. [*With his arm about her, they go over to the couch, sitting down side by side.*] As a matter of fact, between us, Anne, being here has certain advantages for you. For instance, you remember the battle you had with your mother the other day on the subject of overshoes? You said you'd rather die than wear overshoes? But in the end you had to wear them? Well now, you see, for as long as we are here you will never have to wear overshoes! Isn't that good? And the coat that you inherited from Margot, you won't have to wear that any more. And the piano! You won't have to practice on the piano. I tell you, this is going to be a fine life for you!

[ANNE*'s panic is gone.* PETER *appears in the doorway of his room, with a saucer in his hand. He is carrying his cat.*]

---

17. **Anneke** (än´ ə kə): Nickname for "Anne."

PETER. I . . . I . . . I thought I'd better get some water for Mouschi before . . .

MR. FRANK. Of course.

[*As he starts toward the sink the carillon begins to chime the hour of eight. He tiptoes to the window at the back and looks down at the street below. He turns to* PETER, *indicating in pantomime that it is too late.* PETER *starts back for his room. He steps on a creaking board. The three of them are frozen for a minute in fear. As* PETER *starts away again,* ANNE *tiptoes over to him and pours some of the milk from her glass into the saucer for the cat.* PETER *squats on the floor, putting the milk before the cat.* MR. FRANK *gives* ANNE *his fountain pen, and then goes into the room at the right. For a second* ANNE *watches the cat, then she goes over to the center table, and opens her diary.*

In the room at the right, MRS. FRANK *has sat up quickly at the sound of the carillon.* MR. FRANK *comes in and sits down beside her on the settee, his arm comfortingly around her.*

Upstairs, in the attic room, MR. *and* MRS. VAN DAAN *have hung their clothes in the closet and are now seated on the iron bed.* MRS. VAN DAAN *leans back exhausted.* MR. VAN DAAN *fans her with a newspaper.*

ANNE *starts to write in her diary. The lights dim out, the curtain falls.*

In the darkness ANNE'S VOICE *comes to us again, faintly at first, and then with growing strength.*]

ANNE'S VOICE. I expect I should be describing what it feels like to go into hiding. But I really don't know yet myself. I only know it's funny never to be able to go outdoors . . . never to breathe fresh air . . . never to run and shout and jump. It's the silence in the nights that frightens me most. Every time I hear a creak in the house, or a step on the street outside, I'm sure they're coming for us. The days aren't so bad. At least we know that Miep and Mr. Kraler are down there below us in the office. Our protectors, we call them. I asked Father what would happen to them if the Nazis found out they were hiding us. Pim said that they would suffer the same fate that we would . . . Imagine!

They know this, and yet when they come up here, they're always cheerful and gay as if there were nothing in the world to bother them . . . Friday, the twenty-first of August, nineteen forty-two. Today I'm going to tell you our general news. Mother is unbearable. She insists on treating me like a baby, which I loathe. Otherwise things are going better. The weather is . . .

[As ANNE'S VOICE *is fading out, the curtain rises on the scene.*]

Scene 3

[*It is a little after six o'clock in the evening, two months later.*

MARGOT *is in the bedroom at the right, studying.* MR. VAN DAAN *is lying down in the attic room above.*

The rest of the "family" is in the main room. ANNE *and* PETER *sit opposite each other at the center table, where they have been doing their lessons.* MRS. FRANK *is on the couch.* MRS. VAN DAAN *is seated with her fur coat, on which she has been sewing, in her lap. None of them are wearing their shoes.*

Their eyes are on MR. FRANK, *waiting for him to give them the signal which will release them from their day-long quiet.* MR. FRANK, *his shoes in his hand, stands looking down out of the window at the back, watching to be sure that all of the workmen have left the building below.*

After a few seconds of motionless silence, MR. FRANK *turns from the window.*]

MR. FRANK. [*Quietly, to the group*] It's safe now. The last workman has left.

[*There is an immediate stir of relief.*]

ANNE. [*Her pent-up energy explodes.*] WHEE!

MR. FRANK. [*Startled, amused*] Anne!

MRS. VAN DAAN. I'm first for the w.c.

[*She hurries off to the bathroom.* MRS. FRANK *puts on her shoes and starts up to the sink to prepare supper.* ANNE *sneaks* PETER'S *shoes from under the table and hides them behind her back.* MR. FRANK *goes in to* MARGOT'S *room.*]

MR. FRANK. [*To* MARGOT] Six o'clock. School's over.

[MARGOT *gets up, stretching.* MR. FRANK *sits down*

to put on his shoes. In the main room PETER *tries to find his.*]

PETER. [*To* ANNE] Have you seen my shoes?

ANNE. [*Innocently*] Your shoes?

PETER. You've taken them, haven't you?

ANNE. I don't know what you're talking about.

PETER. You're going to be sorry!

ANNE. Am I?

[PETER *goes after her.* ANNE, *with his shoes in her hand, runs from him, dodging behind her mother.*]

MRS. FRANK. [*Protesting*] Anne, dear!

PETER. Wait till I get you!

ANNE. I'm waiting!

[PETER *makes a lunge for her. They both fall to the floor.* PETER *pins her down, wrestling with her to get the shoes.*]

Don't! Don't! Peter, stop it. Ouch!

MRS. FRANK. Anne! . . . Peter!

[*Suddenly* PETER *becomes self-conscious. He grabs his shoes roughly and starts for his room.*]

ANNE. [*Following him*] Peter, where are you going? Come dance with me.

PETER. I tell you I don't know how.

ANNE. I'll teach you.

PETER. I'm going to give Mouschi his dinner.

ANNE. Can I watch?

PETER. He doesn't like people around while he eats.

ANNE. Peter, please.

PETER. No! [*He goes into his room.* ANNE *slams his door after him.*]

MRS. FRANK. Anne, dear, I think you shouldn't play like that with Peter. It's not dignified.

ANNE. Who cares if it's dignified? I don't want to be dignified.

[MR. FRANK *and* MARGOT *come from the room on the right.* MARGOT *goes to help her mother.* MR. FRANK *starts for the center table to correct* MARGOT'S *school papers.*]

MRS. FRANK. [*To* ANNE] You complain that I

don't treat you like a grownup. But when I do, you resent it.

ANNE. I only want some fun . . . someone to laugh and clown with . . . After you've sat still all day and hardly moved, you've got to have some fun. I don't know what's the matter with that boy.

MR. FRANK. He isn't used to girls. Give him a little time.

ANNE. Time? Isn't two months time? I could cry. [*Catching hold of* MARGOT] Come on, Margot . . . dance with me. Come on, please.

MARGOT. I have to help with supper.

ANNE. You know we're going to forget how to dance . . . When we get out we won't remember a thing.

[*She starts to sing and dance by herself.* MR. FRANK *takes her in his arms, waltzing with her.* MRS. VAN DAAN *comes in from the bathroom.*]

MRS. VAN DAAN. Next? [*She looks around as she starts putting on her shoes.*] Where's Peter?

ANNE. [*As they are dancing*] Where would he be!

MRS. VAN DAAN. He hasn't finished his lessons, has he? His father'll kill him if he catches him in there with that cat and his work not done.

[MR. FRANK *and* ANNE *finish their dance. They bow to each other with extravagant formality.*]

Anne, get him out of there, will you?

ANNE. [*At* PETER's *door*] Peter? Peter?

PETER. [*Opening the door a crack*] What is it?

ANNE. Your mother says to come out.

PETER. I'm giving Mouschi his dinner.

MRS. VAN DAAN. You know what your father says. [*She sits on the couch, sewing on the lining of her fur coat.*]

PETER. For heaven's sake, I haven't even looked at him since lunch.

MRS. VAN DAAN. I'm just telling you, that's all.

ANNE. I'll feed him.

PETER. I don't want you in there.

MRS. VAN DAAN. Peter!

PETER. [*To* ANNE] Then give him his dinner and come right out, you hear?

[*He comes back to the table.* ANNE *shuts the door of* PETER's *room after her and disappears behind the curtain covering his closet.*]

MRS. VAN DAAN. [*To* PETER] Now is that any way to talk to your little girl friend?

PETER. Mother . . . for heaven's sake . . . will you please stop saying that?

MRS. VAN DAAN. Look at him blush! Look at him!

PETER. Please! I'm not . . . anyway . . . let me alone, will you?

MRS. VAN DAAN. He acts like it was something to be ashamed of. It's nothing to be ashamed of, to have a little girl friend.

PETER. You're crazy. She's only thirteen.

MRS. VAN DAAN. So what? And you're sixteen. Just perfect. Your father's ten years older than I am. [*To* MR. FRANK] I warn you, Mr. Frank, if this war lasts much longer, we're going to be related and then . . .

MR. FRANK. *Mazeltov!*[18]

MRS. FRANK. [*Deliberately changing the conversation*] I wonder where Miep is. She's usually so prompt.

[*Suddenly everything else is forgotten as they hear the sound of an automobile coming to a screeching stop in the street below. They are tense, motionless in their terror. The car starts away. A wave of relief sweeps over them. They pick up their occupations again.* ANNE *flings open the door of* PETER's *room, making a dramatic entrance. She is dressed in* PETER's *clothes.* PETER *looks at her in fury. The others are amused.*]

ANNE. Good evening, everyone. Forgive me if I don't stay. [*She jumps up on a chair.*] I have a friend waiting for me in there. My friend

---

18. *Mazeltov* (mä′ zəl tōv′): "Good luck" in Hebrew and Yiddish.

Tom. Tom Cat. Some people say that we look alike. But Tom has the most beautiful whiskers, and I have only a little fuzz. I am hoping . . . in time . . .

PETER. All right, Mrs. Quack Quack!

ANNE. [*Outraged—jumping down*] Peter!

PETER. I heard about you . . . How you talked so much in class they called you Mrs. Quack Quack. How Mr. Smitter made you write a composition . . . "'Quack, Quack,' said Mrs. Quack Quack."

ANNE. Well, go on. Tell them the rest. How it was so good he read it out loud to the class and then read it to all his other classes!

PETER. Quack! Quack! Quack . . . Quack . . . Quack . . .

[ANNE *pulls off the coat and trousers.*]

ANNE. You are the most intolerable, <u>insufferable</u> boy I've ever met!

[*She throws the clothes down the stairwell.* PETER *goes down after them.*]

PETER. Quack, Quack, Quack!

MRS. VAN DAAN. [*To* ANNE] That's right, Anneke! Give it to him!

ANNE. With all the boys in the world . . . Why I had to get locked up with one like you! . . .

PETER. Quack, Quack, Quack, and from now on stay out of my room!

[*As* PETER *passes her,* ANNE *puts out her foot, tripping him. He picks himself up, and goes on into his room.*]

MRS. FRANK. [*Quietly*] Anne, dear . . . your hair. [*She feels* ANNE'*s forehead.*] You're warm. Are you feeling all right?

ANNE. Please, Mother. [*She goes over to the center table, slipping into her shoes.*]

MRS. FRANK. [*Following her*] You haven't a fever, have you?

ANNE. [*Pulling away*] No. No.

MRS. FRANK. You know we can't call a doctor here, ever. There's only one thing to do . . . watch carefully. Prevent an illness before it comes. Let me see your tongue.

ANNE. Mother, this is perfectly absurd.

MRS. FRANK. Anne, dear, don't be such a baby. Let me see your tongue. [*As* ANNE *refuses,* MRS. FRANK *appeals to* MR. FRANK] Otto . . . ?

MR. FRANK. You hear your mother, Anne.

[ANNE *flicks out her tongue for a second, then turns away.*]

MRS. FRANK. Come on—open up! [*As* ANNE *opens her mouth very wide*] You seem all right . . . but perhaps an aspirin . . .

MRS. VAN DAAN. For heaven's sake, don't give that child any pills. I waited for fifteen minutes this morning for her to come out of the w.c.

ANNE. I was washing my hair!

MR. FRANK. I think there's nothing the matter with our Anne that a ride on her bike, or a visit with her friend Jopie de Waal wouldn't cure. Isn't that so, Anne?

[MR. VAN DAAN *comes down into the room. From outside we hear faint sounds of bombers going over and a burst of ack-ack.*][19]

MR. VAN DAAN. Miep not come yet?

MRS. VAN DAAN. The workmen just left, a little while ago.

MR. VAN DAAN. What's for dinner tonight?

MRS. VAN DAAN. Beans.

MR. VAN DAAN. Not again!

MRS. VAN DAAN. Poor Putti! I know. But what can we do? That's all that Miep brought us.

[MR. VAN DAAN *starts to pace, his hands behind his back.* ANNE *follows behind him, imitating him.*]

ANNE. We are now in what is known as the "bean cycle." Beans boiled, beans en casserole, beans with strings, beans without strings . . .

[PETER *has come out of his room. He slides into his place at the table, becoming immediately absorbed in his studies.*]

MR. VAN DAAN. [*To* PETER] I saw you . . . in there, playing with your cat.

---

19. ack-ack (ak′ ak′) *n.*: Slang for an antiaircraft gun's fire.

MRS. VAN DAAN. He just went in for a second, putting his coat away. He's been out here all the time, doing his lessons.

MR. FRANK. [*Looking up from the papers*] Anne, you got an excellent in your history paper today . . . and very good in Latin.

ANNE. [*Sitting beside him*] How about algebra?

MR. FRANK. I'll have to make a confession. Up until now I've managed to stay ahead of you in algebra. Today you caught up with me. We'll leave it to Margot to correct.

ANNE. Isn't algebra *vile*, Pim!

MR. FRANK. Vile!

MARGOT. [*To* MR. FRANK] How did I do?

ANNE. [*Getting up*] Excellent, excellent, excellent, excellent!

MR. FRANK. [*To* MARGOT] You should have used the subjunctive[20] here . . .

MARGOT. Should I? . . . I thought . . . look here . . . I didn't use it here . . .

[*The two become absorbed in the papers.*]

ANNE. Mrs. Van Daan, may I try on your coat?

MRS. FRANK. No, Anne.

MRS. VAN DAAN. [*Giving it to* ANNE] It's all right . . . but careful with it.
[ANNE *puts it on and struts with it.*]
My father gave me that the year before he died. He always bought the best that money could buy.

ANNE. Mrs. Van Daan, did you have a lot of boy friends before you were married?

MRS. FRANK. Anne, that's a personal question. It's not courteous to ask personal questions.

MRS. VAN DAAN. Oh I don't mind. [*To* ANNE] Our house was always swarming with boys. When I was a girl we had . . .

MR. VAN DAAN. Oh, no. Not again!

MRS. VAN DAAN. [*Good-humored*] Shut up!

---

20. **subjunctive** (səb junk´ tiv) *n.*: A particular form of a verb.

◆ **Build Vocabulary**

insufferable (in suf´ ər ə bəl) *adj.*: Unbearable

[*Without a pause, to* ANNE, MR. VAN DAAN *mimics* MRS. VAN DAAN, *speaking the first few words in unison with her.*]

One summer we had a big house in Hilversum. The boys came buzzing round like bees around a jam pot. And when I was sixteen! . . . We were wearing our skirts very short those days and I had good-looking legs. [*She pulls up her skirt, going to* MR. FRANK.] I still have 'em. I may not be as pretty as I used to be, but I still have my legs. How about it, Mr. Frank?

MR. VAN DAAN. All right. All right. We see them.

MRS. VAN DAAN. I'm not asking you. I'm asking Mr. Frank.

PETER. Mother, for heaven's sake.

MRS. VAN DAAN. Oh, I embarrass you, do I? Well, I just hope the girl you marry has as good. [*Then to* ANNE] My father used to worry about me, with so many boys hanging round. He told me, if any of them gets fresh, you say to him . . . "Remember, Mr. So-and-So, remember I'm a lady."

ANNE. "Remember, Mr. So-and-So, remember I'm a lady." [*She gives* MRS. VAN DAAN *her coat.*]

MR. VAN DAAN. Look at you, talking that way in front of her! Don't you know she puts it all down in that diary?

MRS. VAN DAAN. So, if she does? I'm only telling the truth!

[ANNE *stretches out, putting her ear to the floor, listening to what is going on below. The sound of the bombers fades away.*]

MRS. FRANK. [*Setting the table*] Would you mind, Peter, if I moved you over to the couch?

ANNE. [*Listening*] Miep must have the radio on.

[PETER *picks up his papers, going over to the couch beside* MRS. VAN DAAN.]

MR. VAN DAAN. [*Accusingly, to* PETER] Haven't you finished yet?

PETER. No.

MR. VAN DAAN. You ought to be ashamed of yourself.

PETER. All right. All right. I'm a dunce. I'm a hopeless case. Why do I go on?

MRS. VAN DAAN. You're not hopeless. Don't talk that way. It's just that you haven't anyone to help you, like the girls have. [*To* MR. FRANK] Maybe you could help him, Mr. Frank?

MR. FRANK. I'm sure that his father . . . ?

MR. VAN DAAN. Not me. I can't do anything with him. He won't listen to me. You go ahead . . . if you want.

MR. FRANK. [*Going to* PETER] What about it, Peter? Shall we make our school coeducational?

MRS. VAN DAAN. [*Kissing* MR. FRANK] You're an angel, Mr. Frank. An angel. I don't know why I didn't meet you before I met that one there. Here, sit down, Mr. Frank . . . [*She forces him down on the couch beside* PETER.] Now, Peter, you listen to Mr. Frank.

MR. FRANK. It might be better for us to go into Peter's room.

[PETER *jumps up eagerly, leading the way.*]

MRS. VAN DAAN. That's right. You go in there, Peter. You listen to Mr. Frank. Mr. Frank is a highly educated man.

[*As* MR. FRANK *is about to follow* PETER *into his room,* MRS. FRANK *stops him and wipes the lipstick from his lips. Then she closes the door after them.*]

ANNE. [*On the floor, listening*] Shh! I can hear a man's voice talking.

MR. VAN DAAN. [*To* ANNE] Isn't it bad enough here without your sprawling all over the place?

[ANNE *sits up.*]

MRS. VAN DAAN. [*To* MR. VAN DAAN] If you didn't smoke so much, you wouldn't be so bad-tempered.

MR. VAN DAAN. Am I smoking? Do you see me smoking?

MRS. VAN DAAN. Don't tell me you've used up all those cigarettes.

MR. VAN DAAN. One package. Miep only brought me one package.

MRS. VAN DAAN. It's a filthy habit anyway. It's a good time to break yourself.

MR. VAN DAAN. Oh, stop it, please.

MRS. VAN DAAN. You're smoking up all our money. You know that, don't you?

MR. VAN DAAN. Will you shut up?

[*During this,* MRS. FRANK *and* MARGOT *have studiously kept their eyes down. But* ANNE, *seated on the floor, has been following the discussion interestedly.* MR. VAN DAAN *turns to see her staring up at him.*]

And what are you staring at?

ANNE. I never heard grownups quarrel before. I thought only children quarreled.

MR. VAN DAAN. This isn't a quarrel! It's a discussion. And I never heard children so rude before.

ANNE. [*Rising, indignantly*] I, rude!

MR. VAN DAAN. Yes!

MRS. FRANK. [*Quickly*] Anne, will you get me my knitting?

[ANNE *goes to get it.*]

I must remember, when Miep comes, to ask her to bring me some more wool.

MARGOT. [*Going to her room*] I need some hairpins and some soap. I made a list. [*She goes into her bedroom to get the list.*]

MRS. FRANK. [*To* ANNE] Have you some library books for Miep when she comes?

ANNE. It's a wonder that Miep has a life of her own, the way we make her run errands for us. Please, Miep, get me some starch. Please take my hair out and have it cut. Tell me all the latest news, Miep. [*She goes over, kneeling on the couch beside* MRS. VAN DAAN] Did you know she was engaged? His name is Dirk, and Miep's afraid the Nazis will ship him off to Germany to work in one of their war plants. That's what they're doing with some of the young Dutchmen . . . they pick them up off the streets—

MR. VAN DAAN. [*Interrupting*] Don't you ever get tired of talking? Suppose you try keeping still for five minutes. Just five minutes.

[*He starts to pace again. Again* ANNE *follows him, mimicking him.* MRS. FRANK *jumps up and takes her by the arm up to the sink, and gives her a glass of milk.*]

MRS. FRANK. Come here, Anne. It's time for your glass of milk.

MR. VAN DAAN. Talk, talk, talk. I never heard such a child. Where is my . . . ? Every evening it's the same talk, talk, talk. [*He looks around.*] Where is my . . . ?

MRS. VAN DAAN. What're you looking for?

MR. VAN DAAN. My pipe. Have you seen my pipe?

MRS. VAN DAAN. What good's a pipe? You haven't got any tobacco.

MR. VAN DAAN. At least I'll have something to hold in my mouth! [*Opening* MARGOT*'s bedroom door*] Margot, have you seen my pipe?

MARGOT. It was on the table last night.

[ANNE *puts her glass of milk on the table and picks up his pipe, hiding it behind her back.*]

MR. VAN DAAN. I know. I know. Anne, did you see my pipe? . . . Anne!

MRS. FRANK. Anne, Mr. Van Daan is speaking to you.

ANNE. Am I allowed to talk now?

MR. VAN DAAN. You're the most aggravating . . . The trouble with you is, you've been spoiled. What you need is a good old-fashioned spanking.

ANNE. [*Mimicking* MRS. VAN DAAN] "Remember, Mr. So-and-So, remember I'm a lady." [*She thrusts the pipe into his mouth, then picks up her glass of milk.*]

MR. VAN DAAN. [*Restraining himself with difficulty*] Why aren't you nice and quiet like your sister Margot? Why do you have to show off all the time? Let me give you a little advice, young lady. Men don't like that kind of thing in a girl. You know that? A man likes a girl who'll listen to him once in a while . . . a domestic girl, who'll keep her house shining for her husband . . . who loves to cook and sew and . . .

ANNE. I'd cut my throat first! I'd open my veins! I'm going to be remarkable! I'm going to Paris . . .

MR. VAN DAAN. [*Scoffingly*] Paris!

ANNE. . . . to study music and art.

▲ **Critical Viewing** What kind of personality would you say Mrs. Frank had, based on details in this photograph? [**Infer**]

MR. VAN DAAN. Yeah! Yeah!

ANNE. I'm going to be a famous dancer or singer . . . or something wonderful.

[*She makes a wide gesture, spilling the glass of milk on the fur coat in* MRS. VAN DAAN*'s lap.* MARGOT *rushes quickly over with a towel.* ANNE *tries to brush the milk off with her skirt.*]

MRS. VAN DAAN. Now look what you've done . . . you clumsy little fool! My beautiful fur coat my father gave me . . .

ANNE. I'm so sorry.

MRS. VAN DAAN. What do you care? It isn't yours . . . So go on, ruin it! Do you know what that coat cost? Do you? And now look at it! Look at it!

ANNE. I'm very, very sorry.

MRS. VAN DAAN. I could kill you for this. I could just kill you!

[MRS. VAN DAAN *goes up the stairs, clutching the coat.* MR. VAN DAAN *starts after her.*]

MR. VAN DAAN. Petronella . . . *Liefje! Liefje!* . . . Come back . . . the supper . . . come back!

MRS. FRANK. Anne, you must not behave in that way.

ANNE. It was an accident. Anyone can have an accident.

MRS. FRANK. I don't mean that. I mean the answering back. You must not answer back. They are our guests. We must always show the greatest courtesy to them. We're all living under terrible tension.

[*She stops as* MARGOT *indicates that* VAN DAAN *can hear. When he is gone, she continues.*]

That's why we must control ourselves . . . You don't hear Margot getting into arguments with them, do you? Watch Margot. She's always courteous with them. Never familiar. She keeps her distance. And they respect her for it. Try to be like Margot.

ANNE. And have them walk all over me, the way they do her? No, thanks!

MRS. FRANK. I'm not afraid that anyone is going to walk all over you, Anne. I'm afraid for other people, that you'll walk on them. I don't know what happens to you, Anne. You are wild, self-willed. If I had ever talked to my mother as you talk to me . . .

ANNE. Things have changed. People aren't like that any more. "Yes, Mother." "No, Mother." "Anything you say, Mother." I've got to fight things out for myself! Make something of myself!

MRS. FRANK. It isn't necessary to fight to do it. Margot doesn't fight, and isn't she . . . ?

ANNE. [*Violently rebellious*] Margot! Margot! Margot! That's all I hear from everyone . . . how wonderful Margot is . . . "Why aren't you like Margot?"

MARGOT. [*Protesting*] Oh, come on, Anne, don't be so . . .

ANNE. [*Paying no attention*] Everything she does is right, and everything I do is wrong! I'm the goat around here! . . . You're all against me! . . . And you worst of all!

[*She rushes off into her room and throws herself down on the settee, stifling her sobs.* MRS. FRANK *sighs and starts toward the stove.*]

MRS. FRANK. [*To* MARGOT] Let's put the soup on the stove . . . if there's anyone who cares to eat. Margot, will you take the bread out?

[MARGOT *gets the bread from the cupboard.*]

I don't know how we can go on living this way . . . I can't say a word to Anne . . . she flies at me . . .

MARGOT. You know Anne. In half an hour she'll be out here, laughing and joking.

MRS. FRANK. And . . . [*She makes a motion upwards, indicating the* VAN DAANS.] . . . I told your father it wouldn't work . . . but no . . . no . . . he had to ask them, he said . . . he owed it to him, he said . . . Well, he knows now that I was right! These quarrels! . . . This bickering!

MARGOT. [*With a warning look*] Shush. Shush.

[*The buzzer for the door sounds.* MRS. FRANK *gasps, startled.*]

MRS. FRANK. Every time I hear that sound, my heart stops!

MARGOT. [*Starting for* PETER*'s door*] It's Miep. [*She knocks at the door.*] Father?

[MR. FRANK *comes quickly from* PETER*'s room.*]

MR. FRANK. Thank you, Margot. [*As he goes down the steps to open the outer door*] Has everyone his list?

MARGOT. I'll get my books. [*Giving her mother a list*] Here's your list.

[MARGOT *goes into her and* ANNE*'s bedroom on the right.* ANNE *sits up, hiding her tears, as* MARGOT *comes in.*]

Miep's here.

[MARGOT *picks up her books and goes back.* ANNE *hurries over to the mirror, smoothing her hair.*]

MR. VAN DAAN. [*Coming down the stairs*] Is it Miep?

MARGOT. Yes. Father's gone down to let her in.

MR. VAN DAAN. At last I'll have some cigarettes!

MRS. FRANK. [*To* MR. VAN DAAN] I can't tell you how unhappy I am about Mrs. Van Daan's coat. Anne should never have touched it.

MR. VAN DAAN. She'll be all right.

MRS. FRANK. Is there anything I can do?

MR. VAN DAAN. Don't worry.

[*He turns to meet* MIEP. *But it is not* MIEP *who comes up the steps. It is* MR. KRALER, *followed by* MR. FRANK. *Their faces are grave.* ANNE *comes from the bedroom.* PETER *comes from his room.*]

MRS. FRANK. Mr. Kraler!

MR. VAN DAAN. How are you, Mr. Kraler?

MARGOT. This is a surprise.

MRS. FRANK. When Mr. Kraler comes, the sun begins to shine.

MR. VAN DAAN. Miep is coming?

MR. KRALER. Not tonight.

[KRALER *goes to* MARGOT *and* MRS. FRANK *and* ANNE, *shaking hands with them.*]

MRS. FRANK. Wouldn't you like a cup of coffee? . . . Or, better still, will you have supper with us?

MR. FRANK. Mr. Kraler has something to talk over with us. Something has happened, he says, which demands an immediate decision.

MRS. FRANK. [*Fearful*] What is it?

[MR. KRALER *sits down on the couch. As he talks he takes bread, cabbages, milk, etc., from his briefcase, giving them to* MARGOT *and* ANNE *to put away.*]

MR. KRALER. Usually, when I come up here, I try to bring you some bit of good news. What's the use of telling you the bad news when there's nothing that you can do about it? But today something has happened . . . Dirk . . . Miep's Dirk, you know, came to me just now. He tells me that he has a Jewish friend living near him. A dentist. He says he's in trouble. He begged me, could I do anything for this man? Could I find him a hiding place? . . . So I've come to you . . . I know it's a terrible thing to ask of you, living as you are, but would you take him in with you?

MR. FRANK. Of course we will.

MR. KRALER. [*Rising*] It'll be just for a night or two . . . until I find some other place. This happened so suddenly that I didn't know where to turn.

MR. FRANK. Where is he?

MR. KRALER. Downstairs in the office.

MR. FRANK. Good. Bring him up.

MR. KRALER. His name is Dussel . . . Jan Dussel.

MR. FRANK. Dussel . . . I think I know him.

MR. KRALER. I'll get him.

[*He goes quickly down the steps and out.* MR. FRANK *suddenly becomes conscious of the others.*]

MR. FRANK. Forgive me. I spoke without consulting you. But I knew you'd feel as I do.

MR. VAN DAAN. There's no reason for you to consult anyone. This is your place. You have a right to do exactly as you please. The only thing I feel . . . there's so little food as it is . . . and to take in another person . . .

[PETER *turns away, ashamed of his father.*]

MR. FRANK. We can stretch the food a little. It's only for a few days.

MR. VAN DAAN. You want to make a bet?

MRS. FRANK. I think it's fine to have him. But, Otto, where are you going to put him? Where?

PETER. He can have my bed. I can sleep on the floor. I wouldn't mind.

MR. FRANK. That's good of you, Peter. But your room's too small . . . even for *you.*

ANNE. I have a much better idea. I'll come in here with you and Mother, and Margot can take Peter's room and Peter can go in our room with Mr. Dussel.

MARGOT. That's right. We could do that.

MR. FRANK. No, Margot. You mustn't sleep in that room . . . neither you nor Anne. Mouschi has caught some rats in there. Peter's brave. He doesn't mind.

ANNE. Then how about *this?* I'll come in here with you and Mother, and Mr. Dussel can have my bed.

MRS. FRANK. No. No. *No!* Margot will come in here with us and he can have her bed. It's the only way. Margot, bring your things in here. Help her, Anne.

[MARGOT *hurries into her room to get her things.*]

ANNE. [*To her mother*] Why Margot? Why can't I come in here?

MRS. FRANK. Because it wouldn't be proper for Margot to sleep with a . . . Please, Anne. Don't argue. Please.

[ANNE *starts slowly away.*]

MR. FRANK. [*To* ANNE] You don't mind sharing your room with Mr. Dussel, do you, Anne?

ANNE. No. No, of course not.

MR. FRANK. Good.

[ANNE *goes off into her bedroom, helping* MARGOT. MR. FRANK *starts to search in the cupboards.*]

Where's the cognac?

MRS. FRANK. It's there. But, Otto, I was saving it in case of illness.

MR. FRANK. I think we couldn't find a better time to use it. Peter, will you get five glasses for me?

[PETER *goes for the glasses.* MARGOT *comes out of her bedroom, carrying her possessions, which she hangs behind a curtain in the main room.* MR. FRANK *finds the cognac and pours it into the*

five glasses that PETER *brings him.* MR. VAN DAAN *stands looking on sourly.* MRS. VAN DAAN *comes downstairs and looks around at all the bustle.*]

MRS. VAN DAAN. What's happening? What's going on?

MR. VAN DAAN. Someone's moving in with us.

MRS. VAN DAAN. In here? You're joking.

MARGOT. It's only for a night or two . . . until Mr. Kraler finds him another place.

MR. VAN DAAN. Yeah! Yeah!

[MR. FRANK *hurries over as* MR. KRALER *and* DUSSEL *come up.* DUSSEL *is a man in his late fifties,* <u>meticulous</u>, *finicky . . . bewildered now. He wears a raincoat. He carries a briefcase, stuffed full, and a small medicine case.*]

MR. FRANK. Come in, Mr. Dussel.

MR. KRALER. This is Mr. Frank.

DUSSEL. Mr. Otto Frank?

MR. FRANK. Yes. Let me take your things. [*He takes the hat and briefcase, but* DUSSEL *clings to his medicine case.*] This is my wife Edith . . . Mr. and Mrs. Van Daan . . . their son, Peter . . . and my daughters, Margot and Anne.

[DUSSEL *shakes hands with everyone.*]

MR. KRALER. Thank you, Mr. Frank. Thank you all. Mr. Dussel, I leave you in good hands. Oh . . . Dirk's coat.

[DUSSEL *hurriedly takes off the raincoat, giving it to* MR. KRALER. *Underneath is his white dentist's jacket, with a yellow Star of David on it.*]

DUSSEL. [*To* MR. KRALER] What can I say to thank you . . . ?

MRS. FRANK. [*To* DUSSEL] Mr. Kraler and Miep . . . They're our life line. Without them we couldn't live.

MR. KRALER. Please. Please. You make us seem very heroic. It isn't that at all. We simply don't like the Nazis. [*To* MR. FRANK, *who offers him a drink*] No, thanks. [*Then going on*] We don't like their methods. We don't like . . .

MR. FRANK. [*Smiling*] I know. I know. "No one's going to tell us Dutchmen what to do with our Jews!"

MR. KRALER. [*To* DUSSEL] Pay no attention to Mr.

Frank. I'll be up tomorrow to see that they're treating you right. [*To* MR. FRANK] Don't trouble to come down again. Peter will bolt the door after me, won't you, Peter?

PETER. Yes, sir.

MR. FRANK. Thank you, Peter. I'll do it.

MR. KRALER. Good night. Good night.

GROUP. Good night, Mr. Kraler. We'll see you tomorrow, etc., etc.

[MR. KRALER *goes out with* MR. FRANK. MRS. FRANK *gives each one of the "grownups" a glass of cognac.*]

MRS. FRANK. Please, Mr. Dussel, sit down.

[MR. DUSSEL *sinks into a chair.* MRS. FRANK *gives him a glass of cognac.*]

DUSSEL. I'm dreaming. I know it. I can't believe my eyes. Mr. Otto Frank here! [*To* MRS. FRANK] You're not in Switzerland then? A woman told me . . . She said she'd gone to your house . . . the door was open, everything was in disorder, dishes in the sink. She said she found a piece of paper in the wastebasket with an address scribbled on it . . . an address in Zurich. She said you must have escaped to Zurich.

ANNE. Father put that there purposely . . . just so people would think that very thing!

DUSSEL. And you've been *here* all the time?

MRS. FRANK. All the time . . . ever since July.

[ANNE *speaks to her father as he comes back.*]

ANNE. It worked, Pim . . . the address you left! Mr. Dussel says that people believe we escaped to Switzerland.

MR. FRANK. I'm glad. . . . And now let's have a little drink to welcome Mr. Dussel.

[*Before they can drink,* MR. DUSSEL *bolts his drink.* MR. FRANK *smiles and raises his glass.*]

To Mr. Dussel. Welcome. We're very honored to have you with us.

MRS. FRANK. To Mr. Dussel, welcome.

◆ Build Vocabulary

meticulous (mə tik′ yoo ləs) *adj.:* Extremely careful about details

[*The* VAN DAANS *murmur a welcome. The "grownups" drink.*]

MRS. VAN DAAN. Um. That was good.

MR. VAN DAAN. Did Mr. Kraler warn you that you won't get much to eat here? You can imagine . . . three ration books among the seven of us . . . and now you make eight.

[PETER *walks away, humiliated. Outside a street organ is heard dimly.*]

DUSSEL. [*Rising*] Mr. Van Daan, you don't realize what is happening outside that you should warn me of a thing like that. You don't realize what's going on . . .

[*As* MR. VAN DAAN *starts his characteristic pacing,* DUSSEL *turns to speak to the others.*]

Right here in Amsterdam every day hundreds of Jews disappear . . . They surround a block and search house by house. Children come home from school to find their parents gone. Hundreds are being deported . . . people that you and I know . . . the Hallensteins . . . the Wessels . . .

MRS. FRANK. [*In tears*] Oh, no. No!

DUSSEL. They get their call-up notice . . . come to the Jewish theater on such and such a day and hour . . . bring only what you can carry in a rucksack. And if you refuse the call-up notice, then they come and drag you from your home and ship you off to Mauthausen.[21] The death camp!

MRS. FRANK. We didn't know that things had got so much worse.

DUSSEL. Forgive me for speaking so.

ANNE. [*Coming to* DUSSEL] Do you know the de Waals? . . . What's become of them? Their daughter Jopie and I are in the same class. Jopie's my best friend.

DUSSEL. They are gone.

ANNE. Gone?

DUSSEL. With all the others.

ANNE. Oh, no. Not Jopie!

---

21. Mauthausen (mou tou′ zən): Village in Austria that was the site of a Nazi concentration camp.

[*She turns away, in tears.* MRS. FRANK *motions to* MARGOT *to comfort her.* MARGOT *goes to* ANNE, *putting her arms comfortingly around her.*]

MRS. VAN DAAN. There were some people called Wagner. They lived near us . . . ?

MR. FRANK. [*Interrupting, with a glance at* ANNE] I think we should put this off until later. We all have many questions we want to ask . . . But I'm sure that Mr. Dussel would like to get settled before supper.

DUSSEL. Thank you. I would. I brought very little with me.

MR. FRANK. [*Giving him his hat and briefcase*] I'm sorry we can't give you a room alone. But I hope you won't be too uncomfortable. We've had to make strict rules here . . . a schedule of hours . . . We'll tell you after supper. Anne, would you like to take Mr. Dussel to his room?

ANNE. [*Controlling her tears*] If you'll come with me, Mr. Dussel? [*She starts for her room.*]

DUSSEL. [*Shaking hands with each in turn*] Forgive me if I haven't really expressed my gratitude to all of you. This has been such a shock to me. I'd always thought of myself as Dutch. I was born in Holland. My father was born in Holland, and my grandfather. And now . . . after all these years . . . [*He breaks off.*] If you'll excuse me.

[DUSSEL *gives a little bow and hurries off after* ANNE. MR. FRANK *and the others are subdued.*]

ANNE. [*Turning on the light*] Well, here we are.

[DUSSEL *looks around the room. In the main room* MARGOT *speaks to her mother.*]

MARGOT. The news sounds pretty bad, doesn't it? It's so different from what Mr. Kraler tells us. Mr. Kraler says things are improving.

MR. VAN DAAN. I like it better the way Kraler tells it.

[*They resume their occupations, quietly.* PETER *goes off into his room. In* ANNE'*s room,* ANNE *turns to* DUSSEL.]

ANNE. You're going to share the room with me.

DUSSEL. I'm a man who's always lived alone. I haven't had to adjust myself to others. I

hope you'll bear with me until I learn.

ANNE. Let me help you. [*She takes his briefcase.*] Do you always live all alone? Have you no family at all?

DUSSEL. No one. [*He opens his medicine case and spreads his bottles on the dressing table.*]

ANNE. How dreadful. You must be terribly lonely.

DUSSEL. I'm used to it.

ANNE. I don't think I could ever get used to it. Didn't you even have a pet? A cat, or a dog?

DUSSEL. I have an allergy for fur-bearing animals. They give me asthma.

ANNE. Oh, dear. Peter has a cat.

DUSSEL. Here? He has it here?

ANNE. Yes. But we hardly ever see it. He keeps it in his room all the time. I'm sure it will be all right.

DUSSEL. Let us hope so. [*He takes some pills to fortify himself.*]

ANNE. That's Margot's bed, where you're going to sleep. I sleep on the sofa there. [*Indicating the clothes hooks on the wall*] We cleared these off for your things. [*She goes over to the window.*] The best part about this room . . . you can look down and see a bit of the street and the canal. There's a houseboat . . . you can see the end of it . . . a bargeman lives there with his family . . . They have a baby and he's just beginning to walk and I'm so afraid he's going to fall into the canal some day. I watch him. . . .

DUSSEL. [*Interrupting*] Your father spoke of a schedule.

ANNE. [*Coming away from the window*] Oh, yes. It's mostly about the times we have to be quiet. And times for the w.c. You can use it now if you like.

DUSSEL. [*Stiffly*] No, thank you.

ANNE. I suppose you think it's awful, my talking about a thing like that. But you don't know how important it can get to be, especially when you're frightened . . . About this room, the way Margot and I did . . . she

▲ **Critical Viewing** This photograph shows the block of Amsterdam in which the Franks hid. The inset shows the building they lived in close up. Why do you think the Franks chose to remain in Amsterdam, in hiding, rather than flee to Switzerland? **[Draw Conclusions]**

had it to herself in the afternoons for studying, reading . . . lessons, you know . . . and I took the mornings. Would that be all right with you?

DUSSEL. I'm not at my best in the morning.

ANNE. You stay here in the mornings then. I'll take the room in the afternoons.

DUSSEL. Tell me, when you're in here, what happens to me? Where am I spending my time? In there, with all the people?

ANNE. Yes.

DUSSEL. I see. I see.

ANNE. We have supper at half past six.

DUSSEL. [*Going over to the sofa*] Then, if you don't mind . . . I like to lie down quietly for ten minutes before eating. I find it helps the digestion.

ANNE. Of course. I hope I'm not going to be too much of a bother to you. I seem to be able to get everyone's back up.

[DUSSEL *lies down on the sofa, curled up, his back to her.*]

DUSSEL. I always get along very well with children. My patients all bring their children to me, because they know I get on well with them. So don't you worry about that.

[ANNE *leans over him, taking his hand and shaking it gratefully.*]

ANNE. Thank you. Thank you, Mr. Dussel.

[*The lights dim to darkness. The curtain falls on the scene.* ANNE'S VOICE *comes to us faintly at first, and then with increasing power.*]

ANNE'S VOICE. . . . And yesterday I finished Cissy Van Marxvelt's latest book. I think she is a first-class writer. I shall definitely let my children read her. Monday the twenty-first of September, nineteen forty-two. Mr. Dussel and I had another battle yesterday. Yes, Mr. Dussel! According to him, nothing, I repeat . . . nothing, is right about me . . . my appearance, my character, my manners. While he was going on at me I thought . . . sometime I'll give you such a smack that you'll fly right up to the ceiling! Why is it that every grownup thinks he knows the way to bring up children? Particularly the grownups that never had any. I keep wishing that Peter was a girl instead of a boy. Then I would have someone to talk to. Margot's a darling, but she takes everything too seriously. To pause for a moment on the subject of Mrs. Van Daan. I must tell you that her attempts to flirt with father are getting her nowhere. Pim, thank goodness, won't play.

[*As she is saying the last lines, the curtain rises on the darkened scene.* ANNE'S VOICE *fades out.*]

Scene 4

[*It is the middle of the night, several months later. The stage is dark except for a little light which comes through the skylight in* PETER'*s room.*

Everyone is in bed. MR. *and* MRS. FRANK *lie on the couch in the main room, which has been pulled out to serve as a makeshift double bed.*

MARGOT *is sleeping on a mattress on the floor in the main room, behind a curtain stretched across for privacy. The others are all in their accustomed rooms.*

From outside we hear two drunken soldiers singing "Lili Marlene." A girl's high giggle is heard. The sound of running feet is heard coming closer and then fading in the distance. Throughout the scene there is the distant sound of airplanes passing overhead.

A match suddenly flares up in the attic. We dimly see MR. VAN DAAN. *He is getting his bearings. He comes quickly down the stairs, and goes to the cupboard where the food is stored. Again the match flares up, and is as quickly blown out. The dim figure is seen to steal back up the stairs.*

There is quiet for a second or two, broken only by the sound of airplanes, and running feet on the street below.

Suddenly, out of the silence and the dark, we hear ANNE *scream.*]

ANNE. [*Screaming*] No! No! Don't . . . don't take me!

[*She moans, tossing and crying in her sleep. The other people wake, terrified.* DUSSEL *sits up in bed, furious.*]

> **◆ Reading Strategy**
> Why is it so dangerous for everyone when Anne screams in her sleep?

DUSSEL. Shush! Anne! Shush!

ANNE. [*Still in her nightmare*] Save me! Save me!

[*She screams and screams.* DUSSEL *gets out of bed, going over to her, trying to wake her.*]

DUSSEL. Quiet! Quiet! You want someone to hear?

[*In the main room* MRS. FRANK *grabs a shawl and pulls it around her. She rushes in to* ANNE, *taking her in her arms.* MR. FRANK *hurriedly gets up, putting on his overcoat.* MARGOT *sits up, terrified.* PETER'*s light goes on in his room.*]

MRS. FRANK. [*To* ANNE, *in her room*] Hush, darling, hush. It's all right. It's all right. [*Over her shoulder to* DUSSEL] Will you be kind enough to turn on the light, Mr. Dussel? [*Back to* ANNE] It's nothing, my darling. It was just a dream.

[DUSSEL *turns on the light in the bedroom.* MRS. FRANK *holds* ANNE *in her arms. Gradually* ANNE *comes out of her nightmare still trembling with horror.* MR. FRANK *comes into the room, and goes quickly to the window, looking out to be sure that no one outside has heard* ANNE'*s screams.* MRS. FRANK *holds* ANNE, *talking softly to her. In the main room* MARGOT *stands on a chair, turning on the center hanging lamp. A light goes on in the* VAN DAANS' *room overhead.* PETER *puts his robe on, coming out of his room.*]

DUSSEL. [*To* MRS. FRANK, *blowing his nose*] Something must be done about that child, Mrs. Frank. Yelling like that! Who knows but there's somebody on the streets? She's endangering all our lives.

MRS. FRANK. Anne, darling.

DUSSEL. Every night she twists and turns. I don't sleep. I spend half my night shushing her. And now it's nightmares!

[MARGOT *comes to the door of* ANNE'*s room, followed by* PETER. MR. FRANK *goes to them, indicating that everything is all right.* PETER *takes* MARGOT *back.*]

MRS. FRANK. [*To* ANNE] You're here, safe, you see? Nothing has happened. [*To* DUSSEL] Please, Mr. Dussel, go back to bed. She'll be herself in a minute or two. Won't you, Anne?

DUSSEL. [*Picking up a book and a pillow*] Thank you, but I'm going to the w.c. The one place where there's peace!

[*He stalks out.* MR. VAN DAAN, *in underwear and trousers, comes down the stairs.*]

MR. VAN DAAN. [*To* DUSSEL] What is it? What happened?

DUSSEL. A nightmare. She was having a nightmare!

MR. VAN DAAN. I thought someone was murdering her.

DUSSEL. Unfortunately, no.

[*He goes into the bathroom.* MR. VAN DAAN *goes back up the stairs.* MR. FRANK, *in the main room, sends* PETER *back to his own bedroom.*]

MR. FRANK. Thank you, Peter. Go back to bed.

[PETER *goes back to his room.* MR. FRANK *follows him, turning out the light and looking out the window. Then he goes back to the main room, and gets up on a chair, turning out the center hanging lamp.*]

MRS. FRANK. [*To* ANNE] Would you like some water? [ANNE *shakes her head.*] Was it a very bad dream? Perhaps if you told me . . . ?

ANNE. I'd rather not talk about it.

MRS. FRANK. Poor darling. Try to sleep then. I'll sit right here beside you until you fall asleep. [*She brings a stool over, sitting there.*]

ANNE. You don't have to.

MRS. FRANK. But I'd like to stay with you . . . very much. Really.

ANNE. I'd rather you didn't.

MRS. FRANK. Good night, then.

[*She leans down to kiss* ANNE. ANNE *throws her arm up over her face, turning away.* MRS. FRANK, *hiding her hurt, kisses* ANNE'*s arm.*]

You'll be all right? There's nothing that you want?

ANNE. Will you please ask Father to come.

MRS. FRANK. [*After a second*] Of course, Anne dear.

[*She hurries out into the other room.* MR. FRANK *comes to her as she comes in.*]

Sie verlangt nach Dir! [22]

MR. FRANK. [*Sensing her hurt*] Edith, *Liebe, schau . . .*[23]

MRS. FRANK. *Es macht nichts! Ich danke dem lieben Herrgott, dass sie sich wenigstens an Dich wendet, wenn sie Trost braucht! Geh hinein, Otto, sie ist ganz hysterisch vor Angst.*[24] [*As* MR. FRANK *hesitates*] *Geh zu ihr.*[25]

[*He looks at her for a second and then goes to get a cup of water for* ANNE. MRS. FRANK *sinks down on the bed, her face in her hands, trying to keep from sobbing aloud.* MARGOT *comes over to her, putting her arms around her.*]

She wants nothing of me. She pulled away when I leaned down to kiss her.

MARGOT. It's a phase . . . You heard Father . . . Most girls go through it . . . they turn to their fathers at this age . . . they give all their love to their fathers.

MRS. FRANK. You weren't like this. You didn't shut me out.

MARGOT. She'll get over it . . .

[*She smooths the bed for* MRS. FRANK *and sits beside her a moment as* MRS. FRANK *lies down. In* ANNE'*s room* MR. FRANK *comes in, sitting down*

---

22. Sie verlangt nach Dir (sē fer´ laŋt´ näk dir): German for "She is asking for you."
23. Liebe, schau (lē´ bə shou): German for "Dear, look."
24. Es macht . . . vor Angst (es mäkt nichts ich dän´ kə dəm lē´ bən här´ gôt däs sē sich ven´ ig stəns än dish ven´ dət ven sē träst broukt gē hē nīn ät´ tō sē ist gänz hi stə rik fär äŋst): German for "It's all right. I thank dear God that at least she turns to you when she needs comfort. Go in, Otto, she is hysterical because of fear."
25. Geh zu ihr (gē tsōō ēr): German for "Go to her."

by ANNE. ANNE *flings her arms around him, clinging to him. In the distance we hear the sound of ack-ack.*]

ANNE. Oh, Pim. I dreamed that they came to get us! The Green Police! They broke down the door and grabbed me and started to drag me out the way they did Jopie.

MR. FRANK. I want you to take this pill.

ANNE. What is it?

MR. FRANK. Something to quiet you.

[*She takes it and drinks the water. In the main room* MARGOT *turns out the light and goes back to her bed.*]

MR. FRANK. [*To* ANNE] Do you want me to read to you for a while?

ANNE. No. Just sit with me for a minute. Was I awful? Did I yell terribly loud? Do you think anyone outside could have heard?

MR. FRANK. No. No. Lie quietly now. Try to sleep.

ANNE. I'm a terrible coward. I'm so disappointed in myself. I think I've conquered my fear . . . I think I'm really grown-up . . . and then something happens . . . and I run to you like a baby . . . I love you, Father. I don't love anyone but you.

MR. FRANK. [*Reproachfully*] Annele!

ANNE. It's true. I've been thinking about it for a long time. You're the only one I love.

MR. FRANK. It's fine to hear you tell me that you love me. But I'd be happier if you said you loved your mother as well . . . She needs your help so much . . . your love . . .

ANNE. We have nothing in common. She doesn't understand me. Whenever I try to explain my views on life to her she asks me if I'm constipated.

MR. FRANK. You hurt her very much just now. She's crying. She's in there crying.

ANNE. I can't help it. I only told the truth. I didn't want her here . . . [*Then, with sudden change*] Oh, Pim, I was horrible, wasn't I? And the worst of it is, I can stand off and look at myself doing it and know it's cruel and yet I can't stop doing it. What's the matter with me? Tell me. Don't say it's just a phase! Help me.

MR. FRANK. There is so little that we parents can do to help our children. We can only try to set a good example . . . point the way. The rest you must do yourself. You must build your own character.

ANNE. I'm trying. Really I am. Every night I think back over all of the things I did that day that were wrong . . . like putting the wet mop in Mr. Dussel's bed . . . and this thing now with Mother. I say to myself, that was wrong. I make up my mind, I'm never going to do that again. Never! Of course I may do something worse . . . but at least I'll never do *that* again! . . . I have a nicer side, Father . . . a sweeter, nicer side. But I'm scared to show it. I'm afraid that people are going to laugh at me if I'm serious. So the mean Anne comes to the outside and the good Anne stays on the inside, and I keep on trying to switch them around and have the good Anne outside and the bad Anne inside and be what I'd like to be . . . and might be . . . if only . . . only . . .

[*She is asleep.* MR. FRANK *watches her for a moment and then turns off the light, and starts out. The lights dim out. The curtain falls on the scene.* ANNE*'s voice is heard dimly at first, and then with growing strength.*]

ANNE'S VOICE. . . . The air raids are getting worse. They come over day and night. The noise is terrifying. Pim says it should be music to our ears. The more planes, the sooner will come the end of the war. Mrs. Van Daan pretends to be a <u>fatalist</u>. What will be, will be. But when the planes come over, who is the most frightened? No one else but Petronella! . . . Monday, the ninth of November, nineteen forty-two. Wonderful news! The Allies have landed in Africa. Pim says that we can look for an early finish to the war. Just for fun he asked each of us what was the first thing we wanted to do when we got out of here. Mrs. Van Daan longs to be home with her own things, her needle-point chairs, the Beckstein piano her father gave her . . . the best that money could buy. Peter would like to go to a movie. Mr. Dussel wants to get back to his dentist's drill. He's afraid he is losing his touch. For myself, there are so many things . . . to ride a bike again . . . to laugh till my belly aches . . . to have new clothes from the skin out . . . to have a hot tub filled to overflowing and wallow in it for hours . . . to be back in school with my friends . . .

[*As the last lines are being said, the curtain rises on the scene. The lights dim on as* ANNE*'s* VOICE *fades away.*]

Scene 5

[*It is the first night of the Hanukkah*[26] *celebration.* MR. FRANK *is standing at the head of the table on which is the Menorah.*[27] *He lights the Shamos,*[28] *or servant candle, and holds it as he says the blessing. Seated listening is all of the "family," dressed in their best. The men wear hats,* PETER *wears his cap.*]

MR. FRANK. [*Reading from a prayer book*] "Praised be Thou, oh Lord our God, Ruler of the universe, who has sanctified us with Thy commandments and bidden us kindle the Hanukkah lights. Praised be Thou, oh Lord our God, Ruler of the universe, who has wrought wondrous deliverances for our fathers in days of old. Praised be Thou, oh Lord our God, Ruler of the universe, that Thou has given us life and sustenance and brought us to this happy season." [MR. FRANK *lights the one candle of the Menorah as he continues.*] "We kindle this Hanukkah light to celebrate the great and wonderful deeds wrought through the zeal with which God filled the hearts of the heroic Maccabees, two thousand years ago. They fought against indifference, against tyranny and oppression, and they restored our Temple to us. May these lights remind us that we should ever look to God, whence cometh our help." Amen.

---

26. **Hanukkah** (khä´ nʊ kä´) *n.*: Jewish celebration that lasts eight days.
27. **menorah** (mə nō´ rə) *n.*: A candle holder with nine candles, used during Hanukkah.
28. **shamos** (shä´ məs) *n.*: The candle used to light the others in a menorah.

ALL. Amen.

[MR. FRANK *hands* MRS. FRANK *the prayer book.*]

MRS. FRANK. [*Reading*] "I lift up mine eyes unto the mountains, from whence cometh my help. My help cometh from the Lord who made heaven and earth. He will not suffer thy foot to be moved. He that keepeth thee will not slumber. He that keepeth Israel doth neither slumber nor sleep. The Lord is thy keeper. The Lord is thy shade upon thy right hand. The sun shall not smite thee by day, nor the moon by night. The Lord shall keep thee from all evil. He shall keep thy soul. The Lord shall guard thy going out and thy coming in, from this time forth and forevermore." Amen.

ALL. Amen.

[MRS. FRANK *puts down the prayer book and goes to get the food and wine.* MARGOT *helps her.* MR. FRANK *takes the men's hats and puts them aside.*]

DUSSEL. [*Rising*] That was very moving.

ANNE. [*Pulling him back*] It isn't over yet!

MRS. VAN DAAN. Sit down! Sit down!

ANNE. There's a lot more, songs and presents.

DUSSEL. Presents?

MRS. FRANK. Not this year, unfortunately.

MRS. VAN DAAN. But always on Hanukkah everyone gives presents . . . everyone!

DUSSEL. Like our St. Nicholas' Day.[29]

[*There is a chorus of "no's" from the group.*]

MRS. VAN DAAN. No! Not like St. Nicholas! What kind of a Jew are you that you don't know Hanukkah?

MRS. FRANK. [*As she brings the food*] I remember particularly the candles . . . First one, as we have tonight. Then the

---

29. **St. Nicholas' Day:** December 6, the day Christian children in Holland receive gifts.

◆ **Build Vocabulary**

fatalist (fā´ tə list) *n.*: One who believes that all events are determined by fate and cannot be changed

◀ Critical Viewing What evidence in this photograph of Anne Frank can you find that reveals Anne's exuberant personality? [Connect]

second night you light two candles, the next night three . . . and so on until you have eight candles burning. When there are eight candles it is truly beautiful.

MRS. VAN DAAN. And the potato pancakes.

MR. VAN DAAN. Don't talk about them!

MRS. VAN DAAN. I make the best *latkes* you ever tasted!

MRS. FRANK. Invite us all next year . . . in your own home.

MR. FRANK. God willing!

MRS. VAN DAAN. God willing.

MARGOT. What I remember best is the presents we used to get when we were little . . . eight days of presents . . . and each day they got better and better.

MRS. FRANK. [*Sitting down*] We are all here, alive. That is present enough.

ANNE. No, it isn't. I've got something . . . [*She rushes into her room, hurriedly puts on a little hat improvised from the lamp shade, grabs a satchel bulging with parcels and comes running back.*]

MRS. FRANK. What is it?

ANNE. Presents!

MRS. VAN DAAN. Presents!

DUSSEL. Look!

MR. VAN DAAN. What's she got on her head?

PETER. A lamp shade!

ANNE. [*She picks out one at random.*] This is for Margot. [*She hands it to* MARGOT, *pulling her to her feet.*] Read it out loud.

MARGOT. [*Reading*]
"You have never lost your temper.
You never will, I fear,
You are so good.
But if you should,
Put all your cross words here."

[*She tears open the package.*] A new crossword puzzle book! Where did you get it?

ANNE. It isn't new. It's one that you've done. But I rubbed it all out, and if you wait a little and forget, you can do it all over again.

MARGOT. [*Sitting*] It's wonderful, Anne. Thank you. You'd never know it wasn't new.

[*From outside we hear the sound of a streetcar passing.*]

ANNE. [*With another gift*] Mrs. Van Daan.

MRS. VAN DAAN. [*Taking it*] This is awful . . . I haven't anything for anyone . . . I never thought . . .

MR. FRANK. This is all Anne's idea.

MRS. VAN DAAN. [*Holding up a bottle*] What is it?

ANNE. It's hair shampoo. I took all the odds and ends of soap and mixed them with the last of my toilet water.

MRS. VAN DAAN. Oh, Anneke!

ANNE. I wanted to write a poem for all of them, but I didn't have time. [*Offering a large box to* MR. VAN DAAN] Yours, Mr. Van Daan, is *really* something . . . something you want more than anything. [*As she waits for him to open it*] Look! Cigarettes!

MR. VAN DAAN. Cigarettes!

ANNE. Two of them! Pim found some old pipe tobacco in the pocket lining of his coat . . . and we made them . . . or rather, Pim did.

MRS. VAN DAAN. Let me see . . . Well, look at that! Light it, Putti! Light it.

[MR. VAN DAAN *hesitates.*]

ANNE. It's tobacco, really it is! There's a little fluff in it, but not much.

[*Everyone watches intently as* MR. VAN DAAN *cautiously lights it. The cigarette flares up. Everyone laughs.*]

PETER. It works!

MRS. VAN DAAN. Look at him.

MR. VAN DAAN. [*Spluttering*] Thank you, Anne. Thank you.

[ANNE *rushes back to her satchel for another present.*]

ANNE. [*Handing her mother a piece of paper*] For Mother, Hanukkah greeting.

[*She pulls her mother to her feet.*]

MRS. FRANK. [*She reads*] "Here's an I.O.U. that I promise to pay. Ten hours of doing whatever you say. Signed, Anne Frank." [MRS. FRANK, *touched, takes* ANNE *in her arms, holding her close.*]

DUSSEL. [*To* ANNE] Ten hours of doing what you're told? *Anything* you're told?

ANNE. That's right.

DUSSEL. You wouldn't want to sell that, Mrs. Frank?

MRS. FRANK. Never! This is the most precious gift I've ever had!

[*She sits, showing her present to the others.* ANNE *hurries back to the satchel and pulls out a scarf, the scarf that* MR. FRANK *found in the first scene.*]

ANNE. [*Offering it to her father*] For Pim.

MR. FRANK. Anneke . . . I wasn't supposed to have a present! [*He takes it, unfolding it and showing it to the others.*]

ANNE. It's a muffler . . . to put round your neck . . . like an ascot, you know. I made it myself out of odds and ends . . . I knitted it in the dark each night, after I'd gone to bed. I'm afraid it looks better in the dark!

MR. FRANK. [*Putting it on*] It's fine. It fits me perfectly. Thank you, Annele.

[ANNE *hands* PETER *a ball of paper with a string attached to it.*]

ANNE. That's for Mouschi.

PETER. [*Rising to bow*] On behalf of Mouschi, I thank you.

ANNE. [*Hesitant, handing him a gift*] And . . . this is yours . . . from Mrs. Quack Quack. [*As he holds it gingerly in his hands*] Well . . . open it . . . Aren't you going to open it?

PETER. I'm scared to. I know something's going to jump out and hit me.

ANNE. No. It's nothing like that, really.

MRS. VAN DAAN. [*As he is opening it*] What is it, Peter? Go on. Show it.

ANNE. [*Excitedly*] It's a safety razor!

DUSSEL. A what?

ANNE. A razor!

MRS. VAN DAAN. [*Looking at it*] You didn't make that out of odds and ends.

ANNE. [*To* PETER] Miep got it for me. It's not new. It's second-hand. But you really do need a razor now.

DUSSEL. For what?

ANNE. Look on his upper lip . . . you can see the beginning of a mustache.

DUSSEL. He wants to get rid of that? Put a little milk on it and let the cat lick it off.

PETER. [*Starting for his room*] Think you're funny, don't you.

DUSSEL. Look! He can't wait! He's going in to try it!

PETER. I'm going to give Mouschi his present!

[*He goes into his room, slamming the door behind him.*]

MR. VAN DAAN. [*Disgustedly*] Mouschi, Mouschi, Mouschi.

[*In the distance we hear a dog persistently barking.* ANNE *brings a gift to* DUSSEL.]

ANNE. And last but never least, my roommate, Mr. Dussel.

DUSSEL. For me? You have something for me?

[*He opens the small box she gives him.*]

ANNE. I made them myself.

DUSSEL. [*Puzzled*] Capsules! Two capsules!

ANNE. They're ear-plugs!

DUSSEL. Ear-plugs?

ANNE. To put in your ears so you won't hear me when I thrash around at night. I saw them advertised in a magazine. They're not real ones . . . I made them out of cotton and candle wax. Try them . . . See if they don't work . . . see if you can hear me talk . . .

DUSSEL. [*Putting them in his ears*] Wait now until I get them in . . . so.

ANNE. Are you ready?

DUSSEL. Huh?

ANNE. Are you ready?

DUSSEL. Oh! They've gone inside! I can't get them out! [*They laugh as* MR. DUSSEL *jumps about, trying to shake the plugs out of his ears. Finally he gets them out. Putting them away*] Thank you, Anne! Thank you!

[*Together*]
{
MR. VAN DAAN. A real Hanukkah!

MRS. VAN DAAN. Wasn't it cute of her?

MRS. FRANK. I don't know when she did it.

MARGOT. I love my present.
}

ANNE. [*Sitting at the table*] And now let's have the song, Father . . . please . . . [*To* DUSSEL] Have you heard the Hanukkah song, Mr. Dussel? The song is the whole thing! [*She sings.*] "Oh, Hanukkah! Oh, Hanukkah! The sweet celebration . . ."

MR. FRANK. [*Quieting her*] I'm afraid, Anne, we shouldn't sing that song tonight. [*To* DUSSEL] It's a song of jubilation, of rejoicing. One is apt to become too enthusiastic.

ANNE. Oh, please, please. Let's sing the song. I promise not to shout!

MR. FRANK. Very well. But quietly now . . . I'll keep an eye on you and when . . .

[*As* ANNE *starts to sing, she is interrupted by*

◆ **Build Vocabulary**

ostentatiously (äs´ tən tā´ shəs lē) *adv.*: In a showy way

DUSSEL, *who is snorting and wheezing.*]

DUSSEL. [*Pointing to* PETER] You . . . You!

[PETER *is coming from his bedroom, ostentatiously holding a bulge in his coat as if he were holding his cat, and dangling* ANNE*'s present before it.*]

How many times . . . I told you . . . Out! Out!

MR. VAN DAAN. [*Going to* PETER] What's the matter with you? Haven't you any sense? Get that cat out of here.

PETER. [*Innocently*] Cat?

MR. VAN DAAN. You heard me. Get it out of here!

PETER. I have no cat. [*Delighted with his joke, he opens his coat and pulls out a bath towel. The group at the table laugh, enjoying the joke.*]

DUSSEL. [*Still wheezing*] It doesn't need to be the cat . . . his clothes are enough . . . when he comes out of that room . . .

MR. VAN DAAN. Don't worry. You won't be bothered any more. We're getting rid of it.

DUSSEL. At last you listen to me. [*He goes off into his bedroom.*]

MR. VAN DAAN. [*Calling after him*] I'm not doing it for you. That's all in your mind . . . all of it! [*He starts back to his place at the table.*] I'm doing it because I'm sick of seeing that cat eat all our food.

PETER. That's not true! I only give him bones . . . scraps . . .

MR. VAN DAAN. Don't tell me! He gets fatter every day! Damn cat looks better than any of us. Out he goes tonight!

PETER. No! No!

ANNE. Mr. Van Daan, you can't do that! That's Peter's cat. Peter loves that cat.

MRS. FRANK. [*Quietly*] Anne.

PETER. [*To* MR. VAN DAAN] If he goes, I go.

MR. VAN DAAN. Go! Go!

MRS. VAN DAAN. You're not going and the cat's not going! Now please . . . this is Hanukkah . . . Hanukkah . . . this is the time to celebrate . . . What's the matter with all of you? Come on, Anne. Let's have the song.

ANNE. [*Singing*]

"Oh, Hanukkah! Oh, Hanukkah! The sweet celebration."

MR. FRANK. [*Rising*] I think we should first blow out the candle . . . then we'll have something for tomorrow night.

MARGOT. But, Father, you're supposed to let it burn itself out.

MR. FRANK. I'm sure that God understands shortages. [*Before blowing it out*] "Praised be Thou, oh Lord our God, who hast sustained us and permitted us to celebrate this joyous festival."

[*He is about to blow out the candle when suddenly there is a crash of something falling below. They all freeze in horror, motionless. For a few seconds there is complete silence.* MR. FRANK *slips off his shoes. The others noiselessly follow his example.* MR. FRANK *turns out a light near him. He motions to* PETER *to turn off the center lamp.* PETER *tries to reach it, realizes he cannot and gets up on a chair. Just as he is touching the lamp he loses his balance. The chair goes out from under him. He falls. The iron lamp shade crashes to the floor. There is a sound of feet below, running down the stairs.*]

MR. VAN DAAN. [*Under his breath*] Oh, oh!

[*The only light left comes from the Hanukkah candle.* DUSSEL *comes from his room.* MR. FRANK *creeps over to the stairwell and stands listening. The dog is heard barking excitedly.*]

Do you hear anything?

MR. FRANK. [*In a whisper*] No. I think they've gone.

MRS. VAN DAAN. It's the Green Police. They've found us.

MR. FRANK. If they had, they wouldn't have left. They'd be up here by now.

MRS. VAN DAAN. I know it's the Green Police. They've gone to get help. That's all. They'll be back!

MRS. VAN DAAN. Or it may have been the Gestapo,[30] looking for papers . . .

MR. FRANK. [*Interrupting*] Or a thief, looking for money.

MRS. VAN DAAN. We've got to do something . . . Quick! Quick! Before they come back.

MR. VAN DAAN. There isn't anything to do. Just wait.

[MR. FRANK *holds up his hand for them to be quiet. He is listening intently. There is complete silence as they all strain to hear any sound from below. Suddenly* ANNE *begins to sway. With a low cry she falls to the floor in a faint.* MRS. FRANK *goes to her quickly, sitting beside her on the floor and taking her in her arms.*]

MRS. FRANK. Get some water, please! Get some water!

[MARGOT *starts for the sink.*]

MR. VAN DAAN. [*Grabbing* MARGOT] No! No! No one's going to run water!

MR. FRANK. If they've found us, they've found us. Get the water. [MARGOT *starts again for the sink.* MR. FRANK, *getting a flashlight*] I'm going down.

[MARGOT *rushes to him, clinging to him.* ANNE *struggles to consciousness.*]

MARGOT. No, Father, no! There may be someone there, waiting . . . It may be a trap!

MR. FRANK. This is Saturday. There is no way for us to know what has happened until Miep or Mr. Kraler comes on Monday morning. We cannot live with this uncertainty.

MARGOT. Don't go, Father!

MRS. FRANK. Hush, darling, hush.

[MR. FRANK *slips quietly out, down the steps and out through the door below.*]

Margot! Stay close to me.

[MARGOT *goes to her mother.*]

MR. VAN DAAN. Shush! Shush!

[MRS. FRANK *whispers to* MARGOT *to get the water.* MARGOT *goes for it.*]

---

30. Gestapo (gə stä′ pō) *n.:* The secret police force of the German Nazi state, known for its terrorism and atrocities.

MRS. VAN DAAN. Putti, where's our money? Get our money. I hear you can buy the Green Police off, so much a head. Go upstairs quick! Get the money!

MR. VAN DAAN. Keep still!

MRS. VAN DAAN. [*Kneeling before him, pleading*] Do you want to be dragged off to a concentration camp? Are you going to stand there and wait for them to come up and get you? Do something, I tell you!

MR. VAN DAAN. [*Pushing her aside*] Will you keep still!

[*He goes over to the stairwell to listen.* PETER *goes to his mother, helping her up onto the sofa. There is a second of silence, then* ANNE *can stand it no longer.*]

ANNE. Someone go after Father! Make Father come back!

PETER. [*Starting for the door*] I'll go.

MR. VAN DAAN. Haven't you done enough?

[*He pushes* PETER *roughly away. In his anger against his father* PETER *grabs a chair as if to hit him with it, then puts it down, burying his face in his hands.* MRS. FRANK *begins to pray softly.*]

ANNE. Please, please, Mr. Van Daan. Get Father.

MR. VAN DAAN. Quiet! Quiet!

[ANNE *is shocked into silence.* MRS. FRANK *pulls her closer, holding her protectively in her arms.*]

MRS. FRANK. [*Softly, praying*] "I lift up mine eyes unto the mountains, from whence cometh my help. My help cometh from the Lord who made heaven and earth. He will not suffer thy foot to be moved . . . He that keepeth thee will not slumber . . ."

[*She stops as she hears someone coming. They all watch the door tensely.* MR. FRANK *comes quietly in.* ANNE *rushes to him, holding him tight.*]

MR. FRANK. It was a thief. That noise must have scared him away.

MRS. VAN DAAN. Thank goodness!

MR. FRANK. He took the cash box. And the radio. He ran away in such a hurry that he didn't stop to shut the street door. It was swinging wide open. [*A breath of relief sweeps over them.*] I think it would be good to have some light.

MARGOT. Are you sure it's all right?

MR. FRANK. The danger has passed.

[MARGOT *goes to light the small lamp.*]

Don't be so terrified, Anne. We're safe.

DUSSEL. Who says the danger has passed? Don't you realize we are in greater danger than ever?

MR. FRANK. Mr. Dussel, will you be still!

[MR. FRANK *takes* ANNE *back to the table, making her sit down with him, trying to calm her.*]

DUSSEL. [*Pointing to* PETER] Thanks to this clumsy fool, there's someone now who knows we're up here! Someone now knows we're up here, hiding!

MRS. VAN DAAN. [*Going to* DUSSEL] Someone knows we're here, yes. But who is the someone? A thief! A thief! You think a thief is going to go to the Green Police and say . . . I was robbing a place the other night and I heard a noise up over my head? You think a thief is going to do that?

DUSSEL. Yes. I think he will.

MRS. VAN DAAN. [*Hysterically*] You're crazy!

[*She stumbles back to her seat at the table.* PETER *follows protectively, pushing* DUSSEL *aside.*]

DUSSEL. I think some day he'll be caught and then he'll make a bargain with the Green Police . . . if they'll let him off, he'll tell them where some Jews are hiding!

[*He goes off into the bedroom. There is a second of appalled silence.*]

MR. VAN DAAN. He's right.

ANNE. Father, let's get out of here! We can't stay here now . . . Let's go . . .

MR. VAN DAAN. Go! Where?

MRS. FRANK. [*Sinking into her chair at the table*] Yes. Where?

MR. FRANK. [*Rising, to them all*] Have we lost all faith? All courage? A moment ago we thought that they'd come for us. We were

sure it was the end. But it wasn't the end. We're alive, safe.

[MR. VAN DAAN *goes to the table and sits.* MR. FRANK *prays.*]

"We thank Thee, oh Lord our God, that in Thy infinite mercy Thou hast again seen fit to spare us." [*He blows out the candle, then turns to* ANNE.] Come on, Anne. The song! Let's have the song!

[*He starts to sing.* ANNE *finally starts falteringly to sing, as* MR. FRANK *urges her on. Her voice is hardly audible at first.*]

ANNE. [*Singing*] "Oh, Hanukkah! Oh, Hanukkah! The sweet . . . celebration . . ."

[*As she goes on singing, the others gradually join in, their voices still shaking with fear.* MRS. VAN DAAN *sobs as she sings.*]

GROUP. "Around the feast . . . we . . . gather
In complete . . . jubilation . . .
Happiest of sea . . . sons
Now is here.
Many are the reasons for good cheer."

[DUSSEL *comes from the bedroom. He comes over to the table, standing beside* MARGOT, *listening to them as they sing.*]

"Together/We'll weather/Whatever tomorrow may bring."

[*As they sing on with growing courage, the lights start to dim.*]

"So hear us rejoicing/And merrily voicing/The Hanukkah song that we sing./Hoy!"

[*The lights are out. The curtain starts slowly to fall.*]

"Hear us rejoicing/And merrily voicing/The Hanukkah song that we sing."

[*They are still singing, as the curtain falls.*]

Beyond Literature

Social Studies Connection

Broadway Theaters Goodrich and Hackett's award-winning play first appeared on the Broadway stage in 1955. The Broadway theater district consists of the thirty-five or so theaters located in a small section of New York City between Sixth and Eighth avenues. Broadway gained its status as an important theater district in the mid-nineteenth century, attracting various staging companies through its central location and fashionable reputation. The term "Broadway" also refers to the size, scale, and type of production. A Broadway show is a large-scaled project with a tremendous budget whose purpose is to showcase commercial entertainment. An Off-Broadway show is usually produced on a smaller budget, in a smaller theater, and the content is generally more experimental.

Cross-Curricular Activity
In the 1927–1928 season, there were 280 new productions on Broadway—a record number. There are significantly fewer productions in these times. Do some research to find out the current number of Broadway productions and how many years each has been running.

Guide for Responding

◆ LITERATURE AND YOUR LIFE

Reader's Response The families live by strict rules in order to prevent discovery. Which of these rules would be hardest for you to follow? Why?

Thematic Focus Would you describe Miep as a hero? Explain.

Journal Writing In your journal, write down the activities that you could, or could not, continue if you had to live silently with eight other people in a three-room attic.

☑ Check Your Comprehension

1. How does going into hiding affect Anne at first?
2. When does Anne realize what going into hiding really means?
3. In what ways do the families try to live their lives normally? Which events remind them that their lives are not normal?
4. What are Anne's hopes for her future?
5. What special meaning does Hanukkah have for the families?

◆ Critical Thinking

INTERPRET
1. (a) How are Margot and Anne different? (b) How does the difference between the two sisters account for their relationship with Mrs. Frank? **[Compare and Contrast]**
2. What do Anne's dreams at night reveal? **[Analyze Cause and Effect]**
3. (a) What do Anne's Hanukkah presents reveal about her? (b) How do you think the presents affect her family? **[Deduce]**
4. Describe the feeling at the end of Act I. What event causes this feeling? **[Interpret]**

APPLY
5. Anne's father tells her, "There are no walls, there are no bolts, no locks that anyone can put on your mind." How does Anne prove that this is true? **[Generalize]**

Guide for Responding (continued)

◆ Reading Strategy

BE AWARE OF HISTORICAL CONTEXT

When you know the **historical context** of a story, you can more fully understand why characters act and think as they do.

1. List three details from Act I that place *The Diary of Anne Frank* into its historical context.
2. What outside force determines which characters can come and go from the attic?
3. Could the events in this play have taken place at a different time in history? Why or why not?

◆ Build Vocabulary

USING THE PREFIXES *un-* AND *in-*

The prefixes *un-* and *in-* create opposite meanings of the words to which they are added. On your paper, complete the second sentence by adding *un-* or *in-* to the word in italics in the first sentence.

1. Before the war, the Frank family felt *secure*. After the war began, they felt _____?_____.
2. Anne's lack of freedom was *bearable* when she forgot about the past. It was _____?_____ if she remembered all the fun she used to have.

SPELLING STRATEGY

Most words with *ie* or *ei* combinations follow the rule, "Put *i* before *e* except after *c* or when sounded like *a* as in *neighbor* and *weigh*." A few words that do not follow this rule include *either, leisure, seize, height, weird,* and *their*. On your paper, alphabetize the *ei* words that do not follow the rule.

USING THE WORD BANK

On your paper, replace each word or phrase in italics with the Word Bank word closest in meaning.

1. He was a *person who believed that there was nothing one could do to change one's destiny*.
2. Her temper was so *changeable* people never knew what she would do next.
3. She dressed *in a showy manner*.
4. He was *not shy* about telling his secrets.
5. Her handwriting was *extremely careful*.
6. The heat in the room became *unbearable*.
7. The yellow star made her *very visible*.
8. Her busy schedule allowed for no *rest* time.

◆ Literary Focus

STAGING

Throughout *The Diary of Anne Frank,* **staging**—the scenery, lighting, sounds, costumes, and stage directions—helps bring the drama vividly to life.

1. Explain why the scenery is crucial in conveying the Franks' situation.
2. Why is the staging information about costumes and actors' movements helpful for the reader?

◆ Build Grammar Skills

SUBJECT AND VERB AGREEMENT

A **verb** must agree with its **subject** in number (singular or plural). Verbs change form to **agree** with their subjects. Notice that the singular form of the verb ends in *s*, but the plural form does not:

Singular: The *scene remains* the same. . . .
Plural: The *lights dim* slowly to darkness.

Practice On your paper, write the form of the verb in parentheses that agrees with the subject.

1. The curtain (fall, falls) on the scene.
2. There is complete silence as they all (strain, strains) to hear any sound from below.
3. Mrs. Frank (begin, begins) to pray softly.
4. Anne and Peter (remove, removes) their shoes.
5. A narrow flight of stairs (lead, leads) up to the attic.

Idea Bank

Writing

1. **Letter** Imagine that you are Anne or Peter. Write a letter to a friend about what life in hiding is like.
2. **Program Notes** To introduce each of the play's characters, write several sentences that could be included in the audience's program notes.

Speaking and Listening

3. **Reading [Group Activity]** With a small group, tape-record a dramatic reading of the last half of Act I, Scene 5, to play for the class.

CONNECTIONS TO TODAY'S WORLD

The Diary of Anne Frank was first produced on Broadway in 1955. Since then, the play has been produced time and again, touching countless audiences through the years. Below are pages from a Playbill that gives information about a 1998 production.

Anne Frank . . . *on Broadway*

PLAYBILL®

THE MUSIC BOX

THE DIARY OF ANNE FRANK

NATALIE PORTMAN

GEORGE HEARN   LINDA LAVIN
HARRIS YULIN   AUSTIN PENDLETON

THE DIARY OF
Anne Frank

A PLAY BY
FRANCES GOODRICH AND ALBERT HACKETT
NEWLY ADAPTED BY
WENDY KESSELMAN
ALSO STARRING
SOPHIE HAYDEN

PHILIP GOODWIN   JESSICA WALLING

WHO'S WHO IN

NATALIE PORTMAN (*Anne Frank*). *The Diary of Anne Frank* marks Natalie's Broadway debut. She made her feature film debut in Luc Besson's *The Professional*. Other films include Ted Demme's *Beautiful Girls* and Michael Mann's *Heat*, as well as last year's Woody Allen musical, *Everyone Says I Love You*, and Tim Burton's *Mars Attacks!*. She will next be seen on the big screen in the first prequel to George Lucas' *Star Wars* series. Born in Jerusalem and raised on the East Coast, Natalie is a high school student. She would like to dedicate her performance to children who are victims of war.

GEORGE HEARN (*Otto Frank*) last appeared on Broadway in *Sunset Boulevard*, winning his second Tony Award for his per...

1. What detail in Portman's biography reveals her sympathy toward Anne Frank?
2. Would you expect this production to remain true to the original drama? Why or why not?

Guide for Reading, Act II

◆ Review and Anticipate

In Act I, Anne Frank's family, along with the Van Daans and Mr. Dussel, are hiding from the Nazis in the attic of a house in Amsterdam. As Act I closes, they are keeping up their courage and celebrating the Jewish holiday Hanukkah. Just as they begin the ceremony, they are frightened by a thief in the building. At first, they think the thief is a member of the Green Police. How does this scare hint at what might occur in Act II?

◆ Literary Focus

CHARACTERIZATION AND THEME IN DRAMA

Playwrights reveal characters' personalities through **characterization**—what characters say, their actions, and what others say about them. Observing the growth and changes in characters in the course of a drama can lead you to understand the theme of the work.

The **theme** of a literary work is the general message about life that it communicates. As the characters struggle with their situation, they reveal how humans can behave in difficult circumstances.

◆ Reading Strategy

ENVISION

When you see a live performance of a drama, the characters are brought to life by the actors who portray them. It takes a little more work to bring the characters to life when you read a drama. However, you can do so by envisioning, or picturing in your mind, the characters, setting, and action. Use the stage directions to help you do this. Look carefully for details that describe how the characters and setting look, and rely on your imagination to fill in any gaps.

◆ Build Vocabulary

RELATED WORDS: FORMS OF *effect*

The word *effect* means "result." You can use your knowledge of the prefix *in-*, meaning "not," to help you figure out that *ineffectually* means "without results" or "uselessly."

WORD BANK

Which word on the list means "secretly"? Check the Build Vocabulary Box on page 761 to see if you chose correctly.

inarticulate
apprehension
intuition
sarcastic
indignant
stealthily
ineffectually

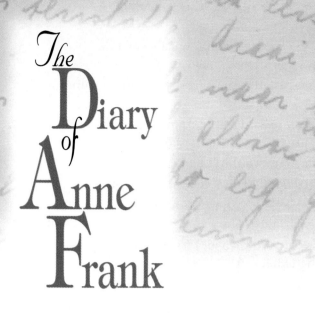

The Diary of Anne Frank

ACT II

Scene 1

[*In the darkness we hear* ANNE'S VOICE, *again reading from the diary.*]

ANNE'S VOICE. Saturday, the first of January, nineteen forty-four. Another new year has begun and we find ourselves still in our hiding place. We have been here now for one year, five months and twenty-five days. It seems that our life is at a standstill.

[*The curtain rises on the scene. It is late afternoon. Everyone is bundled up against the cold. In the main room* MRS. FRANK *is taking down the laundry which is hung across the back.* MR. FRANK *sits in the chair down left, reading.* MARGOT *is lying on the couch with a blanket over her and the many-colored knitted scarf around her throat.* ANNE *is seated at the center table, writing in her diary.* PETER, MR. *and* MRS. VAN DAAN *and* DUSSEL *are all in their own rooms, reading or lying down.*

As the lights dim on, ANNE'S VOICE *continues, without a break.*]

ANNE'S VOICE. We are all a little thinner. The Van Daans' "discussions" are as violent as ever. Mother still does not understand me.

◄ **Critical Viewing** Behind the bookcase is the staircase leading to the attic in which the Franks hid. How does this photograph of the setting contribute to your understanding of the suspense and tension in the play? [**Relate**]

But then I don't understand her either. There is one great change, however. A change in myself. I read somewhere that girls of my age don't feel quite certain of themselves. . . .

[*We hear the chimes and then a hymn being played on the carillon outside. The buzzer of the door below suddenly sounds. Everyone is startled.* MR. FRANK *tiptoes cautiously to the top of the steps and listens. Again the buzzer sounds, in* MIEP's *V-for-Victory signal.*][1]

MR. FRANK. It's Miep!

[*He goes quickly down the steps to unbolt the door.* MRS. FRANK *calls upstairs to the* VAN DAANS *and then to* PETER.]

MRS. FRANK. Wake up, everyone! Miep is here!

[ANNE *quickly puts her diary away.* MARGOT *sits up, pulling the blanket around her shoulders.* MR. DUSSEL *sits on the edge of his bed, listening, disgruntled.* MIEP *comes up the steps, followed by* MR. KRALER. *They bring flowers, books, newspapers, etc.* ANNE *rushes to* MIEP, *throwing her arms affectionately around her.*]

Miep . . . and Mr. Kraler . . . What a delightful surprise!

MR. KRALER. We came to bring you New Year's greetings.

MRS. FRANK. You shouldn't . . . you should have at least one day to yourselves. [*She goes quickly to the stove and brings down teacups and tea for all of them.*]

ANNE. Don't say that, it's so wonderful to see them! [*Sniffing at* MIEP's *coat*] I can smell the wind and the cold on your clothes.

MIEP. [*Giving her the flowers*] There you are. [*Then to* MARGOT, *feeling her forehead*] How are you, Margot? . . . Feeling any better?

MARGOT. I'm all right.

ANNE. We filled her full of every kind of pill so she won't cough and make a noise.[*She runs into her room to put the flowers in water.* MR. *and* MRS. VAN DAAN *come from upstairs. Outside there is the sound of a band playing.*]

---

1. **V-for-Victory signal:** Three short rings and one long one (the letter *V* in Morse code).

MRS. VAN DAAN. Well, hello, Miep. Mr. Kraler.

MR. KRALER. [*Giving a bouquet of flowers to* MRS. VAN DAAN] With my hope for peace in the New Year.

PETER. [*Anxiously*] Miep, have you seen Mouschi? Have you seen him anywhere around?

MIEP. I'm sorry, Peter. I asked everyone in the neighborhood had they seen a gray cat. But they said no.

[MRS. FRANK *gives* MIEP *a cup of tea.* MR. FRANK *comes up the steps, carrying a small cake on a plate.*]

MR. FRANK. Look what Miep's brought for us!

MRS. FRANK. [*Taking it*] A cake!

MR. VAN DAAN. A cake! [*He pinches* MIEP's *cheeks gaily and hurries up to the cupboard.*] I'll get some plates.

[DUSSEL, *in his room, hastily puts a coat on and starts out to join the others.*]

MRS. FRANK. Thank you, Miepia. You shouldn't have done it. You must have used all of your sugar ration for weeks. [*Giving it to* MRS. VAN DAAN] It's beautiful, isn't it?

MRS. VAN DAAN. It's been ages since I even saw a cake. Not since you brought us one last year. [*Without looking at the cake, to* MIEP] Remember? Don't you remember, you gave us one on New Year's Day? Just this time last year? I'll never forget it because you had "Peace in nineteen forty-three" on it. [*She looks at the cake and reads*] "Peace in nineteen forty-four!"

MIEP. Well, it has to come sometime, you know. [*As* DUSSEL *comes from his room*] Hello, Mr. Dussel.

MR. KRALER. How are you?

MR. VAN DAAN. [*Bringing plates and a knife*] Here's the knife, *liefje*. Now, how many of us are there?

MIEP. None for me, thank you.

MR. FRANK. Oh, please. You must.

MIEP. I couldn't.

MR. VAN DAAN. Good! That leaves one . . . two . . . three . . . seven of us.

DUSSEL. Eight! Eight! It's the same number as it always is!

MR. VAN DAAN. I left Margot out. I take it for granted Margot won't eat any.

ANNE. Why wouldn't she!

MRS. FRANK. I think it won't harm her.

MR. VAN DAAN. All right! All right! I just didn't want her to start coughing again, that's all.

DUSSEL. And please, Mrs. Frank should cut the cake.

[*Together*]

> **MR. VAN DAAN.** What's the difference?
>
> **MRS. VAN DAAN.** It's not Mrs. Frank's cake, is it, Miep? It's for all of us.

DUSSEL. Mrs. Frank divides things better.

[*Together*]

> **MRS. VAN DAAN.** [*Going to* DUSSEL] What are you trying to say?
>
> **MR. VAN DAAN.** Oh, come on! Stop wasting time!

MRS. VAN DAAN. [*To* DUSSEL] Don't I always give everybody exactly the same? Don't I?

MR. VAN DAAN. Forget it, Kerli.

MRS. VAN DAAN. No. I want an answer! Don't I?

DUSSEL. Yes. Yes. Everybody gets exactly the same . . . except Mr. Van Daan always gets a little bit more.

[VAN DAAN *advances on* DUSSEL, *the knife still in his hand.*]

MR. VAN DAAN. That's a lie!

[DUSSEL *retreats before the onslaught of the* VAN DAANS.]

MR. FRANK. Please, please! [*Then to* MIEP] You see what a little sugar cake does to us? It goes right to our heads!

◆ **Build Vocabulary**

inarticulate (in′ är tik′ yə lit) *adj.*: Speechless or unable to express oneself

MR. VAN DAAN. [*Handing* MRS. FRANK *the knife*] Here you are, Mrs. Frank.

MRS. FRANK. Thank you. [*Then to* MIEP *as she goes to the table to cut the cake*] Are you sure you won't have some?

MIEP. [*Drinking her tea*] No, really, I have to go in a minute.

[*The sound of the band fades out in the distance.*]

PETER. [*To* MIEP] Maybe Mouschi went back to our house . . . they say that cats . . . Do you ever get over there . . . ? I mean . . . do you suppose you could . . . ?

MIEP. I'll try, Peter. The first minute I get I'll try. But I'm afraid, with him gone a week . . .

DUSSEL. Make up your mind, already someone has had a nice big dinner from that cat!

[PETER *is furious,* inarticulate. *He starts toward* DUSSEL *as if to hit him.* MR. FRANK *stops him.* MRS. FRANK *speaks quickly to ease the situation.*]

MRS. FRANK. [*To* MIEP] This is delicious, Miep!

MRS. VAN DAAN. [*Eating hers*] Delicious!

MR. VAN DAAN. [*Finishing it in one gulp*] Dirk's in luck to get a girl who can bake like this!

MIEP. [*Putting down her empty teacup*] I have to run. Dirk's taking me to a party tonight.

ANNE. How heavenly! Remember now what everyone is wearing, and what you have to eat and everything, so you can tell us tomorrow.

MIEP. I'll give you a full report! Good-bye, everyone!

MR. VAN DAAN. [*To* MIEP] Just a minute. There's something I'd like you to do for me.

[*He hurries off up the stairs to his room.*]

MRS. VAN DAAN. [*Sharply*] Putti, where are you going? [*She rushes up the stairs after him, calling hysterically.*] What do you want? Putti, what are you going to do?

MIEP. [*To* PETER] What's wrong?

PETER. [*His sympathy is with his mother.*] Father says he's going to sell her fur coat. She's crazy about that old fur coat.

DUSSEL. Is it possible? Is it possible that anyone is so silly as to worry about a fur coat in times like this?

PETER. It's none of your darn business . . . and if you say one more thing . . . I'll, I'll take you and I'll . . . I mean it . . . I'll . . .

[*There is a piercing scream from* MRS. VAN DAAN *above. She grabs at the fur coat as* MR. VAN DAAN *is starting downstairs with it.*]

MRS. VAN DAAN. No! No! No! Don't you dare take that! You hear? It's mine!

[*Downstairs* PETER *turns away, embarrassed, miserable.*]

My father gave me that! You didn't give it to me. You have no right. Let go of it . . . you hear?

[MR. VAN DAAN *pulls the coat from her hands and hurries downstairs.* MRS. VAN DAAN *sinks to the floor, sobbing. As* MR. VAN DAAN *comes into the main room the others look away, embarrassed for him.*]

MR. VAN DAAN. [*To* MR. KRALER] Just a little—discussion over the advisability of selling this coat. As I have often reminded Mrs. Van Daan, it's very selfish of her to keep it when people outside are in such desperate need of clothing . . . [*He gives the coat to* MIEP.] So if you will please to sell it for us? It should fetch a good price. And by the way, will you get me cigarettes. I don't care what kind they are . . . get all you can.

MIEP. It's terribly difficult to get them, Mr. Van Daan. But I'll try. Good-bye.

[*She goes.* MR. FRANK *follows her down the steps to bolt the door after her.* MRS. FRANK *gives* MR. KRALER *a cup of tea.*]

MRS. FRANK. Are you sure you won't have some cake, Mr. Kraler?

MR. KRALER. I'd better not.

MR. VAN DAAN. You're still feeling badly? What does your doctor say?

MR. KRALER. I haven't been to him.

MRS. FRANK. Now, Mr. Kraler! . . .

MR. KRALER. [*Sitting at the table*] Oh, I tried. But you can't get near a doctor these days . . . they're so busy. After weeks I finally managed to get one on the telephone. I told him I'd like an appointment . . . I wasn't feeling very well. You know what he answers . . . over the telephone . . . Stick out your tongue! [*They laugh. He turns to* MR. FRANK *as* MR. FRANK *comes back.*] I have some contracts here . . . I wonder if you'd look over them with me . . .

MR. FRANK. [*Putting out his hand*] Of course.

MR. KRALER. [*He rises*] If we could go down-stairs . . . [MR. FRANK *starts ahead;* MR. KRALER *speaks to the others.*] Will you forgive us? I won't keep him but a minute. [*He starts to follow* MR. FRANK *down the steps.*]

MARGOT. [*With sudden foreboding*] What's happened? Something's happened! Hasn't it, Mr. Kraler?

[MR. KRALER *stops and comes back, trying to reassure* MARGOT *with a pretense of casualness.*]

MR. KRALER. No, really. I want your father's advice . . .

MARGOT. Something's gone wrong! I know it!

MR. FRANK. [*Coming back, to* MR. KRALER] If it's something that concerns us here, it's better that we all hear it.

MR. KRALER. [*Turning to him, quietly*] But . . . the children . . . ?

MR. FRANK. What they'd imagine would be worse than any reality.

[*As* MR. KRALER *speaks, they all listen with intense apprehension.* MRS. VAN DAAN *comes down the stairs and sits on the bottom step.*]

MR. KRALER. It's a man in the storeroom . . . I don't know whether or not you remember him . . . Carl, about fifty, heavy-set, near-sighted . . . He came with us just before you left.

MR. FRANK. He was from Utrecht?

◆ **Build Vocabulary**

apprehension (ap′ rə hen′ shən) *n*.: A fearful feeling about the future; dread

MR. KRALER. That's the man. A couple of weeks ago, when I was in the storeroom, he closed the door and asked me . . . how's Mr. Frank? What do you hear from Mr. Frank? I told him I only knew there was a rumor that you were in Switzerland. He said he'd heard that rumor too, but he thought I might know something more. I didn't pay any attention to it . . . but then a thing happened yesterday . . . He'd brought some invoices to the office for me to sign. As I was going through them, I looked up. He was standing staring at the bookcase . . . your bookcase. He said he thought he remembered a door there . . . Wasn't there a door there that used to go up to the loft? Then he told me he wanted more money. Twenty guilders[2] more a week.

MR. VAN DAAN. Blackmail!

MR. FRANK. Twenty guilders? Very modest blackmail.

MR. VAN DAAN. That's just the beginning.

DUSSEL. [*Coming to* MR. FRANK] You know what I think? He was the thief who was down there that night. That's how he knows we're here.

MR. FRANK. [*To* MR. KRALER] How was it left? What did you tell him?

MR. KRALER. I said I had to think about it. What shall I do? Pay him the money? . . . Take a chance on firing him . . . or what? I don't know.

DUSSEL. [*Frantic*] Don't fire him! Pay him what he asks . . . keep him here where you can have your eye on him.

MR. FRANK. Is it so much that he's asking? What are they paying nowadays?

MR. KRALER. He could get it in a war plant. But this isn't a war plant. Mind you, I don't know if he really knows . . . or if he doesn't know.

MR. FRANK. Offer him half. Then we'll soon find out if it's blackmail or not.

DUSSEL. And if it is? We've got to pay it, haven't we?

◆ **Literary Focus**

In what ways do the characters of Mr. Frank and Dussel differ?

---

2. **guilders** (gil′ dərz) *n*.: Monetary units of the Netherlands.

Anything he asks we've got to pay!

MR. FRANK. Let's decide that when the time comes.

MR. KRALER. This may be all my imagination. You get to a point, these days, where you suspect everyone and everything. Again and again . . . on some simple look or word, I've found myself . . .

[*The telephone rings in the office below.*]

MRS. VAN DAAN. [*Hurrying to* MR. KRALER] There's the telephone! What does that mean, the telephone ringing on a holiday?

MR. KRALER. That's my wife. I told her I had to go over some papers in my office . . . to call me there when she got out of church. [*He starts out.*] I'll offer him half then. Good-bye . . . we'll hope for the best!

[*The group calls their good-byes halfheartedly.* MR. FRANK *follows* MR. KRALER *to bolt the door below. During the following scene,* MR. FRANK *comes back up and stands listening, disturbed.*]

DUSSEL. [*To* MR. VAN DAAN] You can thank your son for this . . . smashing the light! I tell you, it's just a question of time now.

[*He goes to the window at the back and stands looking out.*]

MARGOT. Sometimes I wish the end would come . . . whatever it is.

MRS. FRANK. [*Shocked*] Margot!

[ANNE *goes to* MARGOT, *sitting beside her on the couch with her arms around her.*]

MARGOT. Then at least we'd know where we were.

MRS. FRANK. You should be ashamed of yourself! Talking that way! Think how lucky we are! Think of the thousands dying in the war, every day. Think of the people in concentration camps.

ANNE. [*Interrupting*] What's the good of that? What's the good of thinking of misery when you're already miserable? That's stupid!

MRS. FRANK. Anne!

[*As* ANNE *goes on raging at her mother,* MRS. FRANK *tries to break in, in an effort to quiet her.*]

ANNE. We're young, Margot and Peter and I! You grownups have had your chance! But look at us . . . If we begin thinking of all the horror in the world, we're lost! We're trying to hold onto some kind of ideals . . . when everything . . . ideals, hopes . . . everything, are being destroyed! It isn't our fault that the world is in such a mess! We weren't around when all this started! So don't try to take it out on us! [*She rushes off to her room, slamming the door after her. She picks up a brush from the chest and hurls it to the floor. Then she sits on the settee, trying to control her anger.*]

MR. VAN DAAN. She talks as if we started the war! Did we start the war?

[*He spots* ANNE's *cake. As he starts to take it,* PETER *anticipates him.*]

PETER. She left her cake.

[*He starts for* ANNE's *room with the cake. There is silence in the main room.* MRS. VAN DAAN *goes up to her room, followed by* VAN DAAN. DUSSEL *stays looking out the window.* MR. FRANK *brings* MRS. FRANK *her cake.*

◆ **Reading Strategy**
How do you envision the scene described in this stage direction?

She eats it slowly, without relish. MR. FRANK *takes his cake to* MARGOT *and sits quietly on the sofa beside her.* PETER *stands in the doorway of* ANNE's *darkened room, looking at her, then makes a little movement to let her know he is there.* ANNE *sits up, quickly, trying to hide the signs of her tears.* PETER *holds out the cake to her.*]

You left this.

ANNE. [*Dully*] Thanks.

[PETER *starts to go out, then comes back.*]

PETER. I thought you were fine just now. You know just how to talk to them. You know just how to say it. I'm no good . . . I never can think . . . especially when I'm mad . . . That Dussel . . . when he said that about Mouschi . . . someone eating him . . . all I could think is . . . I wanted to hit him. I wanted to give him such a . . . a . . . that he'd . . . That's what I used to do when there was an argument at school . . . That's the way I . . . but here . . . And an old man like that . . . it wouldn't be so good.

ANNE. You're making a big mistake about me. I do it all wrong. I say too much. I go too far. I hurt people's feelings . . .

[DUSSEL *leaves the window, going to his room.*]

PETER. I think you're just fine . . . What I want to say . . . if it wasn't for you around here, I don't know. What I mean . . .

[PETER *is interrupted by* DUSSEL*'s turning on the light.* DUSSEL *stands in the doorway, startled to see* PETER. PETER *advances toward him forbiddingly.* DUSSEL *backs out of the room.* PETER *closes the door on him.*]

ANNE. Do you mean it, Peter? Do you really mean it?

PETER. I said it, didn't I?

ANNE. Thank you, Peter!

[*In the main room* MR. *and* MRS. FRANK *collect the dishes and take them to the sink, washing them.* MARGOT *lies down again on the couch.* DUSSEL, *lost, wanders into* PETER*'s room and takes up a book, starting to read.*]

PETER. [*Looking at the photographs on the wall*] You've got quite a collection.

ANNE. Wouldn't you like some in your room? I could give you some. Heaven knows you spend enough time in there . . . doing heaven knows what . . .

PETER. It's easier. A fight starts, or an argument . . . I duck in there.

ANNE. You're lucky, having a room to go to. His lordship is always here . . . I hardly ever get a minute alone. When they start in on me, I can't duck away. I have to stand there and take it.

PETER. You gave some of it back just now.

ANNE. I get so mad. They've formed their opinions . . . about everything . . . but we . . . we're still trying to find out . . . We have problems here that no other people our age have ever had. And just as you think you've solved them, something comes along and bang! You have to start all over again.

PETER. At least you've got someone you can talk to.

ANNE. Not really. Mother . . . I never discuss anything serious with her. She doesn't understand. Father's all right. We can talk about everything . . . everything but one thing. Mother. He simply won't talk about her. I don't think you can be really intimate with anyone if he holds something back, do you?

PETER. I think your father's fine.

ANNE. Oh, he is, Peter! He is! He's the only one who's ever given me the feeling that I have any sense. But anyway, nothing can take the place of school and play and friends of your own age . . . or near your age . . . can it?

PETER. I suppose you miss your friends and all.

ANNE. It isn't just . . .
[*She breaks off, staring up at him for a second.*] Isn't it funny, you and I? Here we've been seeing each other every minute for almost a year and a half, and this is the first time we've ever really talked. It helps a lot to

have someone to talk to, don't you think? It helps you to let off steam.

PETER. [*Going to the door*] Well, any time you want to let off steam, you can come into my room.

ANNE. [*Following him*] I can get up an awful lot

▲ **Critical Viewing** This photograph shows a wall in Anne Frank's room. In what ways does Anne's room resemble a typical teenager's room today? [Relate]

of steam. You'll have to be careful how you say that.

PETER. It's all right with me.

ANNE. Do you mean it?

PETER. I said it, didn't I?

[*He goes out.* ANNE *stands in her doorway looking after him. As* PETER *gets to his door he stands for a minute looking back at her. Then he goes into his room.* DUSSEL *rises as he comes in, and quickly passes him, going out. He starts across for his room.* ANNE *sees him coming, and pulls her door shut.* DUSSEL *turns back toward* PETER's *room.* PETER *pulls his door shut.* DUSSEL *stands there, bewildered, forlorn.*

The scene slowly dims out. The curtain falls on the scene. ANNE'S VOICE *comes over in the darkness . . . faintly at first, and then with growing strength.*]

ANNE'S VOICE. We've had bad news. The people from whom Miep got our ration books have been arrested. So we have had to cut down on our food. Our stomachs are so empty that they rumble and make strange noises, all in different keys. Mr. Van Daan's is deep and low, like a bass fiddle. Mine is high, whistling like a flute. As we all sit around waiting for supper, it's like an orchestra tuning up. It only needs Toscanini[3] to raise his baton and we'd be off in the Ride of the Valkyries.[4] Monday, the sixth of March, nineteen forty-four. Mr. Kraler is in the hospital. It seems he has ulcers. Pim says we are his ulcers. Miep has to run the business and us too. The Americans have landed on the southern tip of Italy. Father looks for a quick finish to the war. Mr. Dussel is waiting every day for the warehouse man to demand more money. Have I been skipping too much from one subject to another? I can't help it. I feel that spring is coming. I feel it in my whole body and soul. I feel utterly confused. I am longing . . . so longing . . . for everything . . . for friends . . . for someone to talk to . . . someone who understands . . . someone young, who feels as I do . . .

---

3. **Toscanini** (täs′ kə nē′ nē): Arturo Toscanini, a famous Italian American orchestra conductor.
4. **Ride of the Valkyries** (val′ kir′ ēz): A stirring selection from an opera by Richard Wagner, a German composer.

[*As these last lines are being said, the curtain rises on the scene. The lights dim on.* ANNE'S VOICE *fades out.*]

Scene 2

[*It is evening, after supper. From outside we hear the sound of children playing. The "grownups," with the exception of* MR. VAN DAAN, *are all in the main room.* MRS. FRANK *is doing some mending,* MRS. VAN DAAN *is reading a fashion magazine.* MR. FRANK *is going over business accounts.* DUSSEL, *in his dentist's jacket, is pacing up and down, impatient to get into his bedroom.* MR. VAN DAAN *is upstairs working on a piece of embroidery in an embroidery frame.*

In his room PETER *is sitting before the mirror, smoothing his hair. As the scene goes on, he puts on his tie, brushes his coat and puts it on, preparing himself meticulously for a visit from* ANNE. *On his wall are now hung some of* ANNE's *motion picture stars.*

In her room ANNE *too is getting dressed. She stands before the mirror in her slip, trying various ways of dressing her hair.* MARGOT *is seated on the sofa, hemming a skirt for* ANNE *to wear.*

In the main room DUSSEL *can stand it no longer. He comes over, rapping sharply on the door of his and* ANNE's *bedroom.*]

ANNE. [*Calling to him*] No, no, Mr. Dussel! I am not dressed yet.

[DUSSEL *walks away, furious, sitting down and burying his head in his hands.* ANNE *turns to* MARGOT.]

How is that? How does that look?

MARGOT. [*Glancing at her briefly*] Fine.

ANNE. You didn't even look.

MARGOT. Of course I did. It's fine.

ANNE. Margot, tell me, am I terribly ugly?

MARGOT. Oh, stop fishing.

ANNE. No. No. Tell me.

MARGOT. Of course you're not. You've got nice eyes . . . and a lot of animation, and . . .

ANNE. A little vague, aren't you?

[*Outside,* MRS. FRANK, *feeling sorry for* DUSSEL, *comes over, knocking at the girls' door.*]

MRS. FRANK. [*Outside*] May I come in?

MARGOT. Come in, Mother.

MRS. FRANK. [*Shutting the door behind her*] Mr. Dussel's impatient to get in here.

ANNE. Heavens, he takes the room for himself the entire day.

MRS. FRANK. [*Gently*] Anne, dear, you're not going in again tonight to see Peter?

ANNE. [*Dignified*] That is my intention.

MRS. FRANK. But you've already spent a great deal of time in there today.

ANNE. I was in there exactly twice. Once to get the dictionary, and then three-quarters of an hour before supper.

MRS. FRANK. Aren't you afraid you're disturbing him?

ANNE. Mother, I have some <u>intuition</u>.

MRS. FRANK. Then may I ask you this much, Anne. Please don't shut the door when you go in.

ANNE. You sound like Mrs. Van Daan! [*She picks up her blouse, putting it on.*]

MRS. FRANK. No. No. I don't mean to suggest anything wrong. I only wish that you wouldn't expose yourself to criticism . . . that you wouldn't give Mrs. Van Daan the opportunity to be unpleasant.

ANNE. Mrs. Van Daan doesn't need an opportunity to be unpleasant!

MRS. FRANK. Everyone's on edge, worried about Mr. Kraler. This is one more thing . . .

ANNE. I'm sorry, Mother. I'm going to Peter's room. I'm not going to let Petronella Van Daan spoil our friendship.

[*MRS. FRANK hesitates for a second, then goes out, closing the door after her. She gets a pack of playing cards and sits at the center table, playing solitaire. In* ANNE's *room* MARGOT *hands the finished skirt to* ANNE. *As* ANNE *is putting it on,* MARGOT *takes off her high-heeled shoes*

◆ **Build Vocabulary**

intuition (in´ tōō wish´ ən) *n.*: Ability to know immediately, without reasoning

and stuffs paper in the toes so that ANNE *can wear them.*]

MARGOT. [*To* ANNE] Why don't you two talk in the main room? It'd save a lot of trouble. It's hard on Mother, having to listen to those remarks from Mrs. Van Daan and not say a word.

ANNE. Why doesn't she say a word? I think it's ridiculous to take it and take it.

MARGOT. You don't understand Mother at all, do you? She can't talk back. She's not like you. It's just not in her nature to fight back.

ANNE. Anyway . . . the only one I worry about is you. I feel awfully guilty about you. [*She sits on the stool near* MARGOT, *putting on* MARGOT's *high-heeled shoes.*]

MARGOT. What about?

ANNE. I mean, every time I go into Peter's room, I have a feeling I may be hurting you. [MARGOT *shakes her head.*] I know if it were me, I'd be wild. I'd be desperately jealous, if it were me.

MARGOT. Well, I'm not.

ANNE. You don't feel badly? Really? Truly? You're not jealous?

MARGOT. Of course I'm jealous . . . jealous that you've got something to get up in the morning for . . . But jealous of you and Peter? No.

[ANNE *goes back to the mirror.*]

ANNE. Maybe there's nothing to be jealous of. Maybe he doesn't really like me. Maybe I'm just taking the place of his cat . . . [*She picks up a pair of short white gloves, putting them on.*] Wouldn't you like to come in with us?

MARGOT. I have a book.

[*The sound of the children playing outside fades out. In the main room* DUSSEL *can stand it no longer. He jumps up, going to the bedroom door and knocking sharply.*]

DUSSEL. Will you please let me in my room!

ANNE. Just a minute, dear, dear Mr. Dussel. [*She picks up her mother's pink stole and adjusts it elegantly over her shoulders, then* *gives a last look in the mirror.*] Well, here I go . . . to run the gauntlet.[5]

[*She starts out, followed by* MARGOT.]

DUSSEL. [*As she appears—sarcastic*] Thank you so much.

[DUSSEL *goes into his room.* ANNE *goes toward* PETER's *room, passing* MRS. VAN DAAN *and her parents at the center table.*]

MRS. VAN DAAN. My God, look at her!

[ANNE *pays no attention. She knocks at* PETER's *door.*]

I don't know what good it is to have a son. I never see him. He wouldn't care if I killed myself.

[PETER *opens the door and stands aside for* ANNE *to come in.*]

Just a minute, Anne. [*She goes to them at the door.*] I'd like to say a few words to my son. Do you mind?

[PETER *and* ANNE *stand waiting.*]

Peter, I don't want you staying up till all hours tonight. You've got to have your sleep. You're a growing boy. You hear?

MRS. FRANK. Anne won't stay late. She's going to bed promptly at nine. Aren't you, Anne?

ANNE. Yes, Mother . . . [*To* MRS. VAN DAAN] May we go now?

MRS. VAN DAAN. Are you asking me? I didn't know I had anything to say about it.

MRS. FRANK. Listen for the chimes, Anne dear.

[*The two young people go off into* PETER's *room, shutting the door after them.*]

MRS. VAN DAAN. [*To* MRS. FRANK] In my day it was the boys who called on the girls. Not the girls on the boys.

MRS. FRANK. You know how young people like to feel that they have secrets. Peter's room is the only place where they can talk.

MRS. VAN DAAN. Talk! That's not what they called it when I was young.

---

5. **to run the gauntlet** (gônt' lit): Formerly, to pass between two rows of men who struck at the offender with clubs as he passed; here, a series of troubles or difficulties.

[MRS. VAN DAAN *goes off to the bathroom.* MARGOT *settles down to read her book.* MR. FRANK *puts his papers away and brings a chess game to the center table. He and* MRS. FRANK *start to play. In* PETER's *room,* ANNE *speaks to* PETER, *indignant, humiliated.*]

ANNE. Aren't they awful? Aren't they impossible? Treating us as if we were still in the nursery.

[*She sits on the cot.* PETER *gets a bottle of pop and two glasses.*]

PETER. Don't let it bother you. It doesn't bother me.

ANNE. I suppose you can't really blame them . . . they think back to what *they* were like at our age. They don't realize how much more advanced we are . . . When you think what wonderful discussions we've had! . . . Oh, I forgot. I was going to bring you some more pictures.

PETER. Oh, these are fine, thanks.

ANNE. Don't you want some more? Miep just brought me some new ones.

PETER. Maybe later. [*He gives her a glass of pop and, taking some for himself, sits down facing her.*]

ANNE. [*Looking up at one of the photographs*] I remember when I got that . . . I won it. I bet Jopie that I could eat five ice-cream cones. We'd all been playing ping-pong . . . We used to have heavenly times . . . we'd finish up with ice cream at the Delphi, or the Oasis, where Jews were allowed . . . there'd always be a lot of boys . . . we'd laugh and joke . . . I'd like to go back to it for a few days or a week. But after that I know I'd be bored to

◆ **Literature and Your Life**

Have you ever collected or traded pictures from magazines with friends? Explain.

◆ **Build Vocabulary**

sarcastic (sär kas´ tik) *adj.:* Speaking with sharp mockery intended to hurt another

indignant (in dig´ nənt) *adj.:* Filled with anger over some meanness or injustice

death. I think more seriously about life now. I want to be a journalist . . . or something. I love to write. What do you want to do?

PETER. I thought I might go off some place . . . work on a farm or something . . . some job that doesn't take much brains.

ANNE. You shouldn't talk that way. You've got the most awful inferiority complex.

PETER. I know I'm not smart.

ANNE. That isn't true. You're much better than I am in dozens of things . . . arithmetic and algebra and . . . well, you're a million times better than I am in algebra. [*With sudden directness*] You like Margot, don't you? Right from the start you liked her, liked her much better than me.

PETER. [*Uncomfortably*] Oh, I don't know.

[*In the main room* MRS. VAN DAAN *comes from the bathroom and goes over to the sink, polishing a coffee pot.*]

ANNE. It's all right. Everyone feels that way. Margot's so good. She's sweet and bright and beautiful and I'm not.

PETER. I wouldn't say that.

ANNE. Oh, no, I'm not. I know that. I know quite well that I'm not a beauty. I never have been and never shall be.

PETER. I don't agree at all. I think you're pretty.

ANNE. That's not true!

PETER. And another thing. You've changed . . . from at first, I mean.

ANNE. I have?

PETER. I used to think you were awful noisy.

ANNE. And what do you think now, Peter? How have I changed?

PETER. Well . . . er . . . you're . . . quieter.

[*In his room* DUSSEL *takes his pajamas and toilet articles and goes into the bathroom to change.*]

ANNE. I'm glad you don't just hate me.

PETER. I never said that.

ANNE. I bet when you get out of here you'll never think of me again.

PETER. That's crazy.

ANNE. When you get back with all of your friends, you're going to say . . . now what did I ever see in that Mrs. Quack Quack.

PETER. I haven't got any friends.

ANNE. Oh, Peter, of course you have. Everyone has friends.

PETER. Not me. I don't want any. I get along all right without them.

ANNE. Does that mean you can get along without me? I think of myself as your friend.

PETER. No. If they were all like you, it'd be different.

[*He takes the glasses and the bottle and puts them away. There is a second's silence and then* ANNE *speaks, hesitantly, shyly.*]

ANNE. Peter, did you ever kiss a girl?

PETER. Yes. Once.

ANNE. [*To cover her feelings*] That picture's crooked.

[PETER *goes over, straightening the photograph.*]

Was she pretty?

PETER. Huh?

ANNE. The girl that you kissed.

PETER. I don't know. I was blindfolded. [*He comes back and sits down again.*] It was at a party. One of those kissing games.

ANNE. [*Relieved*] Oh. I don't suppose that really counts, does it?

PETER. It didn't with me.

ANNE. I've been kissed twice. Once a man I'd never seen before kissed me on the cheek when he picked me up off the ice and I was crying. And the other was Mr. Koophuis, a friend of Father's who kissed my hand. You wouldn't say those counted, would you?

PETER. I wouldn't say so.

ANNE. I know almost for certain that Margot would never kiss anyone unless she was engaged to them. And I'm sure too that Mother never touched a man before Pim. But I don't know . . . things are so different now . . . What do you think? Do you think a girl

PETER. I suppose it'd depend on the girl. Some girls, anything they do's wrong. But others . . . well . . . it wouldn't necessarily be wrong with them.

[*The carillon starts to strike nine o'clock.*]

I've always thought that when two people . . .

ANNE. Nine o'clock. I have to go.

PETER. That's right.

ANNE. [*Without moving*] Good night.

[*There is a second's pause, then* PETER *gets up and moves toward the door.*]

PETER. You won't let them stop you coming?

ANNE. No. [*She rises and starts for the door.*] Sometimes I might bring my diary. There are so many things in it that I want to talk over with you. There's a lot about you.

PETER. What kind of thing?

ANNE. I wouldn't want you to see some of it. I thought you were a nothing, just the way you thought about me.

PETER. Did you change your mind, the way I changed my mind about you?

ANNE. Well . . . You'll see . . .

[*For a second* ANNE *stands looking up at* PETER, *longing for him to kiss her. As he makes no move she turns away. Then suddenly* PETER *grabs her awkwardly in his arms, kissing her on the cheek.* ANNE *walks out dazed. She stands for a minute, her back to the people in the main room. As she regains her poise she goes to her mother and father and* MARGOT, *silently kissing them. They murmur their good nights to her. As she is about to open her bedroom door, she catches sight of* MRS. VAN DAAN. *She goes quickly*

▲ **Critical Viewing** Does this photograph of Peter Van Daan seem to capture his personality? Explain. [Assess]

shouldn't kiss anyone except if she's engaged or something? It's so hard to try to think what to do, when here we are with the whole world falling around our ears and you think . . . well . . . you don't know what's going to happen tomorrow and . . . What do you think?

to her, taking her face in her hands and kissing her first on one cheek and then on the other. Then she hurries off into her room. MRS. VAN DAAN *looks after her, and then looks over at* PETER'*s room. Her suspicions are confirmed.*]

MRS. VAN DAAN. [*She knows.*] Ah hah!

[*The lights dim out. The curtain falls on the scene. In the darkness* ANNE'S VOICE *comes faintly at first and then with growing strength.*]

ANNE'S VOICE. By this time we all know each other so well that if anyone starts to tell a story, the rest can finish it for him. We're having to cut down still further on our meals. What makes it worse, the rats have been at work again. They've carried off some of our precious food. Even Mr. Dussel wishes now that Mouschi was here. Thursday, the twentieth of April, nineteen forty-four. Invasion fever is mounting every day. Miep tells us that people outside talk of nothing else. For myself, life has become much more pleasant. I often go to Peter's room after supper. Oh, don't think I'm in love, because I'm not. But it does make life more bearable to have someone with whom you can exchange views. No more tonight. P.S. . . . I must be honest. I must confess that I actually live for the next meeting. Is there anything lovelier than to sit under the skylight and feel the sun on your cheeks and have a darling boy in your arms? I admit now that I'm glad the Van Daans had a son and not a daughter. I've outgrown another dress. That's the third. I'm having to wear Margot's clothes after all. I'm working hard on my French and am now reading *La Belle Nivernaise.*[6]

[*As she is saying the last lines—the curtain rises on the scene. The lights dim on, as* ANNE'S VOICE *fades out.*]

Scene 3

[*It is night, a few weeks later. Everyone is in bed. There is complete quiet. In the* VAN DAANS' *room a match flares up for a moment and then*

is quickly put out. MR. VAN DAAN, *in bare feet, dressed in underwear and trousers, is dimly seen coming* stealthily *down the stairs and into the main room, where* MR. *and* MRS. FRANK *and* MARGOT *are sleeping. He goes to the food safe and again lights a match. Then he cautiously opens the safe, taking out a half-loaf of bread. As he closes the safe, it creaks. He stands rigid.* MRS. FRANK *sits up in bed. She sees him.*]

MRS. FRANK. [*Screaming*] Otto! Otto! *Komme schnell!*[7]

[*The rest of the people wake, hurriedly getting up.*]

MR. FRANK. *Was ist los? Was ist passiert?*[8]

[DUSSEL, *followed by* ANNE, *comes from his room.*]

MRS. FRANK. [*As she rushes over to* MR. VAN DAAN] *Er stiehlt das Essen!*[9]

DUSSEL. [*Grabbing* MR. VAN DAAN] You! You! Give me that.

MRS. VAN DAAN. [*Coming down the stairs*] Putti . . . Putti . . . what is it?

DUSSEL. [*His hands on* VAN DAAN'*s neck*] You dirty thief . . . stealing food . . . you good-for-nothing . . .

MR. FRANK. Mr. Dussel! Oh! Help me, Peter!

[PETER *comes over, trying, with* MR. FRANK, *to separate the two struggling men.*]

PETER. Let him go! Let go!

[DUSSEL *drops* MR. VAN DAAN, *pushing him away. He shows them the end of a loaf of bread that he has taken from* VAN DAAN.]

DUSSEL. You greedy, selfish . . . !

[MARGOT *turns on the lights.*]

MRS. VAN DAAN. Putti . . . what is it?

[*All of* MRS. FRANK'*s gentleness, her self-control,*

---

7. Komme schnell! (käm´ ə shnel): German for "Come quick!"
8. Was ist los? Was ist passiert? (väs ist los väs ist päs´ ērt): German for "What's the matter? What happened?"
9. Er stiehlt das Essen! (er stēlt däs es´ ən): German for "He steals food!"

◆ **Build Vocabulary**

stealthily (stel´ thi lē) *adv.*: In a secretive or sneaky way

---

6. La Belle Nivernaise: A story by Alphonse Daudet, a French author.

is gone. She is outraged, in a frenzy of indignation.]

MRS. FRANK. The bread! He was stealing the bread!

DUSSEL. It was you, and all the time we thought it was the rats!

MR. FRANK. Mr. Van Daan, how could you!

MR. VAN DAAN. I'm hungry.

MRS. FRANK. We're all of us hungry! I see the children getting thinner and thinner. Your own son Peter . . . I've heard him moan in his sleep, he's so hungry. And you come in the night and steal food that should go to them . . . to the children!

MRS. VAN DAAN. [*Going to* MR. VAN DAAN *protectively*] He needs more food than the rest of us. He's used to more. He's a big man.

[MR. VAN DAAN *breaks away, going over and sitting on the couch.*]

MRS. FRANK. [*Turning on* MRS. VAN DAAN] And you . . . you're worse than he is! You're a mother, and yet you sacrifice your child to this man . . . this . . . this . . .

MR. FRANK. Edith! Edith!

[MARGOT *picks up the pink woolen stole, putting it over her mother's shoulders.*]

MRS. FRANK. [*Paying no attention, going on to* MRS. VAN DAAN] Don't think I haven't seen you! Always saving the choicest bits for him! I've watched you day after day and I've held my tongue. But not any longer! Not after this! Now I want him to go! I want him to get out of here!

[*Together*]
{
MR. FRANK. Edith!

MR. VAN DAAN. Get out of here?

MRS. VAN DAAN. What do you mean?
}

MRS. FRANK. Just that! Take your things and get out!

MR. FRANK. [*To* MRS. FRANK] You're speaking in anger. You cannot mean what you are saying.

MRS. FRANK. I mean exactly that!

[MRS. VAN DAAN *takes a cover from the* FRANKS' *bed, pulling it about her.*]

MR. FRANK. For two long years we have lived here, side by side. We have respected each other's rights . . . we have managed to live in peace. Are we now going to throw it all away? I know this will never happen again, will it, Mr. Van Daan?

MR. VAN DAAN. No. No.

MRS. FRANK. He steals once! He'll steal again!

[MR. VAN DAAN, *holding his stomach, starts for the bathroom.* ANNE *puts her arms around him, helping him up the step.*]

MR. FRANK. Edith, please. Let us be calm. We'll all go to our rooms . . . and afterwards we'll sit down quietly and talk this out . . . we'll find some way . . .

MRS. FRANK. No! No! No more talk! I want them to leave!

MRS. VAN DAAN. You'd put us out, on the streets?

MRS. FRANK. There are other hiding places.

MRS. VAN DAAN. A cellar . . . a closet. I know. And we have no money left even to pay for that.

MRS. FRANK. I'll give you money. Out of my own pocket I'll give it gladly. [*She gets her purse from a shelf and comes back with it.*]

MRS. VAN DAAN. Mr. Frank, you told Putti you'd never forget what he'd done for you when you came to Amsterdam. You said you could never repay him, that you . . .

MRS. FRANK. [*Counting out money*] If my husband had any obligation to you, he's paid it, over and over.

MR. FRANK. Edith, I've never seen you like this before. I don't know you.

MRS. FRANK. I should have spoken out long ago.

DUSSEL. You can't be nice to some people.

MRS. VAN DAAN. [*Turning on* DUSSEL] There would have been plenty for all of us, if *you* hadn't come in here!

MR. FRANK. We don't need the Nazis to destroy us. We're destroying ourselves.

[*He sits down, with his head in his hands.* MRS. FRANK *goes to* MRS. VAN DAAN.]

MRS. FRANK. [*Giving* MRS. VAN DAAN *some money*] Give this to Miep. She'll find you a place.

ANNE. Mother, you're not putting *Peter* out. Peter hasn't done anything.

MRS. FRANK. He'll stay, of course. When I say I must protect the children, I mean Peter too.

[PETER *rises from the steps where he has been sitting.*]

PETER. I'd have to go if Father goes.

[MR. VAN DAAN *comes from the bathroom.* MRS. VAN DAAN *hurries to him and takes him to the couch. Then she gets water from the sink to bathe his face.*]

MRS. FRANK. [*While this is going on*] He's no father to you . . . that man! He doesn't know what it is to be a father!

PETER. [*Starting for his room*] I wouldn't feel right. I couldn't stay.

MRS. FRANK. Very well, then. I'm sorry.

ANNE. [*Rushing over to* PETER] No, Peter! No!

[PETER *goes into his room, closing the door after him.* ANNE *turns back to her mother, crying.*]

I don't care about the food. They can have mine! I don't want it! Only don't send them away. It'll be daylight soon. They'll be caught . . .

MARGOT. [*Putting her arms comfortingly around* ANNE] Please, Mother!

MRS. FRANK. They're not going now. They'll stay here until Miep finds them a place. [*To* MRS. VAN DAAN] But one thing I insist on! He must never come down here again! He must never come to this room where the food is stored! We'll divide what we have . . . an equal share for each!

[DUSSEL *hurries over to get a sack of potatoes from the food safe.* MRS. FRANK *goes on, to* MRS. VAN DAAN]

You can cook it here and take it up to him.

[DUSSEL *brings the sack of potatoes back to the center table.*]

MARGOT. Oh, no. No. We haven't sunk so far

that we're going to fight over a handful of rotten potatoes.

DUSSEL. [*Dividing the potatoes into piles*] Mrs. Frank, Mr. Frank, Margot, Anne, Peter, Mrs. Van Daan, Mr. Van Daan, myself . . . Mrs. Frank . . .

[*The buzzer sounds in* MIEP'S *signal.*]

MR. FRANK. It's Miep! [*He hurries over, getting his overcoat and putting it on.*]

MARGOT. At this hour?

MRS. FRANK. It is trouble.

MR. FRANK. [*As he starts down to unbolt the door*] I beg you, don't let her see a thing like this!

MR. DUSSEL. [*Counting without stopping*] . . . Anne, Peter, Mrs. Van Daan, Mr. Van Daan, myself . . .

MARGOT. [*To* DUSSEL] Stop it! Stop it!

DUSSEL. . . . Mr. Frank, Margot, Anne, Peter, Mrs. Van Daan, Mr. Van Daan, myself, Mrs. Frank . . .

MRS. VAN DAAN. You're keeping the big ones for yourself! All the big ones . . . Look at the size of that! . . . And that! . . .

[DUSSEL *continues on with his dividing.* PETER, *with his shirt and trousers on, comes from his room.*]

MARGOT. Stop it! Stop it!

[*We hear* MIEP'S *excited voice speaking to* MR. FRANK *below.*]

MIEP. Mr. Frank . . . the most wonderful news! . . . The invasion has begun!

MR. FRANK. Go on, tell them! Tell them!

[MIEP *comes running up the steps ahead of* MR. FRANK. *She has a man's raincoat on over her nightclothes and a bunch of orange-colored flowers in her hand.*]

MIEP. Did you hear that, everybody? Did you hear what I said? The invasion has begun! The invasion!

[*They all stare at* MIEP, *unable to grasp what she is telling them.* PETER *is the first to recover his wits.*]

PETER. Where?

MRS. VAN DAAN. When? When, Miep?

MIEP. It began early this morning . . .

[*As she talks on, the realization of what she has said begins to dawn on them. Everyone goes crazy. A wild demonstration takes place.* MRS. FRANK *hugs* MR. VAN DAAN.]

MRS. FRANK. Oh, Mr. Van Daan, did you hear that?

[DUSSEL *embraces* MRS. VAN DAAN. PETER *grabs a frying pan and parades around the room, beating on it, singing the Dutch National Anthem.* ANNE *and* MARGOT *follow him, singing, weaving in and out among the excited grown-ups.* MARGOT *breaks away to take the flowers from* MIEP *and distribute them to everyone. While this pandemonium is going on* MRS. FRANK *tries to make herself heard above the excitement.*]

MRS. FRANK. [*To* MIEP] How do you know?

MIEP. The radio . . . The B.B.C.![10] They said they landed on the coast of Normandy![11]

PETER. The British?

MIEP. British, Americans, French, Dutch, Poles, Norwegians . . . all of them! More than four thousand ships! Churchill spoke, and General Eisenhower! D-Day they call it!

MR. FRANK. Thank God, it's come!

MRS. VAN DAAN. At last!

MIEP. [*Starting out*] I'm going to tell Mr. Kraler. This'll be better than any blood transfusion.

MR. FRANK. [*Stopping her*] What part of Normandy did they land, did they say?

MIEP. Normandy . . . that's all I know now . . . I'll be up the minute I hear some more! [*She goes hurriedly out.*]

MR. FRANK. [*To* MRS. FRANK] What did I tell you? What did I tell you?

[MRS. FRANK *indicates that he has forgotten to bolt the door after* MIEP. *He hurries down the steps.* MR. VAN DAAN, *sitting on the couch, suddenly breaks into a convulsive[12] sob. Everybody looks at him, bewildered.*]

MRS. VAN DAAN. [*Hurrying to him*] Putti! Putti! What is it? What happened?

MR. VAN DAAN. Please, I'm so ashamed.

[MR. FRANK *comes back up the steps.*]

DUSSEL. Oh!

MRS. VAN DAAN. Don't, Putti.

MARGOT. It doesn't matter now!

MR. FRANK. [*Going to* MR. VAN DAAN] Didn't you hear what Miep said? The invasion has come! We're going to be liberated! This is a time to celebrate! [*He embraces* MRS. FRANK *and then hurries to the cupboard and gets the cognac and a glass.*]

MR. VAN DAAN. To steal bread from children!

MRS. FRANK. We've all done things that we're ashamed of.

ANNE. Look at me, the way I've treated Mother . . . so mean and horrid to her.

MRS. FRANK. No, Anneke, no.

[ANNE *runs to her mother, putting her arms around her.*]

ANNE. Oh, Mother, I was. I was awful.

MR. VAN DAAN. Not like me. No one is as bad as me!

DUSSEL. [*To* MR. VAN DAAN] Stop it now! Let's be happy!

MR. FRANK. [*Giving* MR. VAN DAAN *a glass of cognac*] Here! Here! *Schnapps! L'chaim!*[13]

[VAN DAAN *takes the cognac. They all watch him. He gives them a feeble smile.* ANNE *puts up her fingers in a V-for-Victory sign. As* VAN DAAN *gives an answering V-sign, they are startled to hear a loud sob from behind them. It is* MRS. FRANK, *stricken with remorse. She is sitting on the other side of the room.*]

MRS. FRANK. [*Through her sobs*] When I think of the terrible things I said . . .

[MR. FRANK, ANNE *and* MARGOT *hurry to her, trying to comfort her.* MR. VAN DAAN *brings her his glass of cognac.*]

MR. VAN DAAN. No! No! You were right!

---

10. **B.B.C.:** British Broadcasting Corporation.
11. **Normandy** (nôr′mən dē): A region in northwest France, on the English Channel.
12. **convulsive** (kən vul′ siv) *adj.*: Having an involuntary contraction or spasm of the muscles; shuddering.

13. *Schnapps! L'chaim!* (shnäps lə khä′ yim): German for "a drink," and a Hebrew toast meaning "To life."

MRS. FRANK. That I should speak that way to you! . . . Our friends! . . . Our guests! [*She starts to cry again.*]

DUSSEL. Stop it, you're spoiling the whole invasion!

[*As they are comforting her, the lights dim out. The curtain falls.*]

ANNE'S VOICE. [*Faintly at first and then with growing strength*] We're all in much better spirits these days.

◆ **Literary Focus**
What does this passage reveal about Anne's character?

There's still excellent news of the invasion. The best part about it is that I have a feeling that friends are coming. Who knows? Maybe I'll be back in school by fall. Ha, ha! The joke is on us! The warehouse man doesn't know a thing and we are paying him all that money! . . . Wednesday, the second of July, nineteen forty-four. The invasion seems temporarily to be bogged down. Mr. Kraler has to have an operation, which looks bad. The Gestapo have found the radio that was stolen. Mr. Dussel says they'll trace it back and back to the thief, and then, it's just a matter of time till they get to us. Everyone is low. Even poor Pim can't raise their spirits. I have often been downcast myself . . . but never in despair. I can shake off everything if I write. But . . . and that is the great question . . . will I ever be able to write well? I want to so much. I want to go on living even after my death. Another birthday has gone by, so now I am fifteen. Already I know what I want. I have a goal, an opinion.

[*As this is being said—the curtain rises on the scene, the lights dim on, and* ANNE'S VOICE *fades out.*]

Scene 4

[*It is an afternoon a few weeks later . . . Everyone but* MARGOT *is in the main room. There is a sense of great tension.*

Both MRS. FRANK *and* MR. VAN DAAN *are nervously pacing back and forth,* DUSSEL *is*

▲ **Critical Viewing** This is a page of Anne Frank's diary. Judging from its appearance, was Anne a careful writer or a careless one? Explain. [**Deduce**]

standing at the window, looking down fixedly at the street below. PETER *is at the center table, trying to do his lessons.* ANNE *sits opposite him, writing in her diary.* MRS. VAN DAAN *is seated on the couch, her eyes on* MR. FRANK *as he sits reading.*

The sound of a telephone ringing comes from the office below. They all are rigid, listening tensely. DUSSEL *rushes down to* MR. FRANK.]

DUSSEL. There it goes again, the telephone! Mr. Frank, do you hear?

MR. FRANK. [*Quietly*] Yes. I hear.

DUSSEL. [*Pleading, insistent*] But this is the third time, Mr. Frank! The third time in quick succession! It's a signal! I tell you it's Miep, trying to get us! For some reason she can't come to us and she's trying to warn us of something!

MR. FRANK. Please. Please.

MR. VAN DAAN. [*To* DUSSEL] You're wasting your breath.

DUSSEL. Something has happened, Mr. Frank. For three days now Miep hasn't been to see us! And today not a man has come to work. There hasn't been a sound in the building!

MRS. FRANK. Perhaps it's Sunday. We may have lost track of the days.

MR. VAN DAAN. [*To* ANNE] You with the diary there. What day is it?

DUSSEL. [*Going to* MRS. FRANK] I don't lose track of the days! I know exactly what day it is! It's Friday, the fourth of August. Friday, and not a man at work. [*He rushes back to* MR. FRANK, *pleading with him, almost in tears.*] I tell you Mr. Kraler's dead. That's the only explanation. He's dead and they've closed down the building, and Miep's trying to tell us!

MR. FRANK. She'd never telephone us.

DUSSEL. [*Frantic*] Mr. Frank, answer that! I beg you, answer it!

MR. FRANK. No.

MR. VAN DAAN. Just pick it up and listen. You don't have to speak. Just listen and see if it's Miep.

DUSSEL. [*Speaking at the same time*] Please . . . I ask you.

MR. FRANK. No. I've told you, no. I'll do nothing that might let anyone know we're in the building.

PETER. Mr. Frank's right.

MR. VAN DAAN. There's no need to tell us what side you're on.

MR. FRANK. If we wait patiently, quietly, I believe that help will come.

[*There is silence for a minute as they all listen to the telephone ringing.*]

DUSSEL. I'm going down.

◆ **Build Vocabulary**

ineffectually (in´ e fek´ chōō ə lē) *adv.*: Without producing the desired effect

[*He rushes down the steps.* MR. FRANK *tries* <u>ineffectually</u> *to hold him.* DUSSEL *runs to the lower door, unbolting it. The telephone stops ringing.* DUSSEL *bolts the door and comes slowly back up the steps.*]

Too late.

[MR. FRANK *goes to* MARGOT *in* ANNE's *bedroom.*]

MR. VAN DAAN. So we just wait here until we die.

MRS. VAN DAAN. [*Hysterically*] I can't stand it! I'll kill myself! I'll kill myself!

MR. VAN DAAN. Stop it!

[*In the distance, a German military band is heard playing a Viennese waltz.*]

MRS. VAN DAAN. I think you'd be glad if I did! I think you want me to die!

MR. VAN DAAN. Whose fault is it we're here?

[MRS. VAN DAAN *starts for her room. He follows, talking at her.*]

We could've been safe somewhere . . . in America or Switzerland. But no! No! You wouldn't leave when I wanted to. You couldn't leave your things. You couldn't leave your precious furniture.

MRS. VAN DAAN. Don't touch me!

[*She hurries up the stairs, followed by* MR. VAN DAAN. PETER, *unable to bear it, goes to his room.* ANNE *looks after him, deeply concerned.* DUSSEL *returns to his post at the window.* MR. FRANK *comes back into the main room and takes a book, trying to read.* MRS. FRANK *sits near the sink, starting to peel some potatoes.* ANNE *quietly goes to* PETER's *room, closing the door after her.* PETER *is lying face down on the cot.* ANNE *leans over him, holding him in her arms, trying to bring him out of his despair.*]

ANNE. Look, Peter, the sky. [*She looks up through the skylight.*] What a lovely, lovely day! Aren't the clouds beautiful? You know what I do when it seems as if I couldn't stand being cooped up for one more minute? I *think* myself out. I think myself on a walk in the park where I used to go with Pim. Where the jonquils and the crocus and the violets grow down the slopes. You know the

DEUTSCHE BUNDESPOST

60

ANNE FRANK · 12.6.1929 · 31.3.1945

1979

▲ **Critical Viewing** In what ways is Anne Frank deserving of being honored on a postage stamp? [Connect]

most wonderful part about *thinking* yourself out? You can have it any way you like. You can have roses and violets and chrysanthemums all blooming at the same time . . . It's funny . . . I used to take it all for granted . . . and now I've gone crazy about everything to do with nature. Haven't you?

PETER. I've just gone crazy. I think if something doesn't happen soon . . . if we don't get out of here . . . I can't stand much more of it!

ANNE. [*Softly*] I wish you had a religion, Peter.

PETER. No, thanks! Not me!

ANNE. Oh, I don't mean you have to be Orthodox[14] . . . or believe in heaven and hell and purgatory[15] and things . . . I just mean some religion . . . it doesn't matter what. Just to believe in something! When I think of all

---

14. **Orthodox** (ôr´ thə däks´) *adj.*: Strictly observing the rites and traditions of Judaism.
15. **purgatory** (pur´gə tôr´ ē) *n.*: A state or place of temporary punishment.

that's out there . . . the trees . . . and flowers . . . and seagulls . . . when I think of the dearness of you, Peter . . . and the goodness of the people we know . . . Mr. Kraler, Miep, Dirk, the vegetable man, all risking their lives for us every day . . . When I think of these good things, I'm not afraid any more . . . I find myself, and God, and I . . .

◆ **Literary Focus**
What do you learn about the play's theme in this passage?

[PETER *interrupts, getting up and walking away.*]

PETER. That's fine! But when I begin to think, I get mad! Look at us, hiding out for two years. Not able to move! Caught here like . . . waiting for them to come and get us . . . and all for what?

ANNE. We're not the only people that've had to suffer. There've always been people that've had to . . . sometimes one race . . . sometimes another . . . and yet . . .

PETER. That doesn't make me feel any better!

ANNE. [*Going to him*] I know it's terrible, trying to have any faith . . . when people are doing such horrible . . . But you know what I sometimes think? I think the world may be going through a phase, the way I was with Mother. It'll pass, maybe not for hundreds of years, but some day . . . I still believe, in spite of everything, that people are really good at heart.

PETER. I want to see something now . . . Not a thousand years from now! [*He goes over, sitting down again on the cot.*]

ANNE. But, Peter, if you'd only look at it as part of a great pattern . . . that we're just a little minute in the life . . . [*She breaks off.*] Listen to us, going at each other like a couple of stupid grownups! Look at the sky now. Isn't it lovely?

[*She holds out her hand to him.* PETER *takes it and rises, standing with her at the window looking out, his arms around her.*]

Some day, when we're outside again, I'm going to . . .

[*She breaks off as she hears the sound of a car, its brakes squealing as it comes to a sudden stop. The people in the other rooms also become aware of the sound. They listen tensely. Another car roars up to a screeching stop.* ANNE *and* PETER *come from* PETER'*s room.* MR. *and* MRS. VAN DAAN *creep down the stairs.* DUSSEL *comes out from his room. Everyone is listening, hardly breathing. A doorbell clangs again and again in the building below.* MR. FRANK *starts quietly down the steps to the door.* DUSSEL *and* PETER *follow him. The others stand rigid, waiting, terrified.*]

In a few seconds DUSSEL *comes stumbling back up the steps. He shakes off* PETER'*s help and goes to his room.* MR. FRANK *bolts the door below, and comes slowly back up the steps. Their eyes are all on him as he stands there for a minute. They realize that what they feared has happened.* MRS. VAN DAAN *starts to whimper.* MR. VAN DAAN *puts her gently in a chair, and then hurries off up the stairs to their room to collect their things.* PETER *goes to comfort his mother. There is a sound of violent pounding on a door below.*]

MR. FRANK. [*Quietly*] For the past two years we have lived in fear. Now we can live in hope.

[*The pounding below becomes more insistent. There are muffled sounds of voices, shouting commands.*]

MEN'S VOICES. *Auf machen! Da drinnen! Auf machen! Schnell! Schnell! Schnell!*[16] *etc., etc.*

[*The street door below is forced open. We hear the heavy tread of footsteps coming up.* MR. FRANK *gets two school bags from the shelves, and gives one to* ANNE *and the other to* MARGOT. *He goes to get a bag for* MRS. FRANK. *The sound of feet coming up grows louder.* PETER *comes to* ANNE, *kissing her good-bye, then he goes to his room to collect his things. The buzzer of their door starts to ring.* MR. FRANK *brings* MRS. FRANK *a bag. They stand together, waiting. We hear the thud of gun butts on the door, trying to break it down.*]

---

16. ***Auf machen! . . . Schnell!*** (ouf mäk´ ən dä drĭ´ nən ouf mäk´ ən shnel shnel shnel): German for "Open up, you in there, open up, quick, quick, quick."

ANNE *stands, holding her school satchel, looking over at her father and mother with a soft, reassuring smile. She is no longer a child, but a woman with courage to meet whatever lies ahead.*

The lights dim out. The curtain falls on the scene. We hear a mighty crash as the door is shattered. After a second ANNE'S VOICE *is heard.*]

ANNE'S VOICE. And so it seems our stay here is over. They are waiting for us now. They've allowed us five minutes to get our things. We can each take a bag and whatever it will hold of clothing. Nothing else. So, dear Diary, that means I must leave you behind. Good-bye for a while. P.S. Please, please, Miep, or Mr. Kraler, or anyone else. If you should find this diary, will you please keep it safe for me, because some day I hope . . .

[*Her voice stops abruptly. There is silence. After a second the curtain rises.*]

Scene 5

[*It is again the afternoon in November, 1945. The rooms are as we saw them in the first scene.* MR. KRALER *has joined* MIEP *and* MR. FRANK. *There are coffee cups on the table. We see a great change in* MR. FRANK. *He is calm now. His bitterness is gone. He slowly turns a few pages of the diary. They are blank.*]

MR. FRANK. No more. [*He closes the diary and puts it down on the couch beside him.*]

MIEP. I'd gone to the country to find food. When I got back the block was surrounded by police . . .

MR. KRALER. We made it our business to learn how they knew. It was the thief . . . the thief who told them.

[MIEP *goes up to the gas burner, bringing back a pot of coffee.*]

MR. FRANK. [*After a pause*] It seems strange to say this, that anyone could be happy in a concentration camp. But Anne was happy in the camp in Holland where they first took us. After two years of being shut up in these rooms, she could be out . . . out in the sunshine and the fresh air that she loved.

MIEP. [*Offering the coffee to* MR. FRANK] A little more?

MR. FRANK. [*Holding out his cup to her*] The news of the war was good. The British and Americans were sweeping through France. We felt sure that they would get to us in time. In September we were told that we were to be shipped to Poland . . . The men to one camp. The women to another. I was sent to Auschwitz.[17] They went to Belsen.[18] In January we were freed, the few of us who were left. The war wasn't yet over, so it took us a long time to get home. We'd be sent here and there behind the lines where we'd be safe. Each time our train would stop . . . at a siding, or a crossing . . . we'd all get out and go from group to group . . . Where were you? Were you at Belsen? At Buchenwald?[19] At Mauthausen? Is it possible that you knew my wife? Did you ever see my husband? My son? My daughter? That's how I found out about my wife's death . . . of Margot, the Van Daans . . . Dussel. But Anne . . . I still hoped . . . Yesterday I went to Rotterdam. I'd heard of a woman there . . . She'd been in Belsen with Anne . . . I know now.

[*He picks up the diary again, and turns the pages back to find a certain passage. As he finds it we hear* ANNE'S VOICE.]

ANNE'S VOICE. In spite of everything, I still believe that people are really good at heart. [MR. FRANK *slowly closes the diary.*]

MR. FRANK. She puts me to shame.

[*They are silent.*]

---

17. Auschwitz (oush′ vits): Nazi concentration camp in Poland notorious as an extermination center.
18. Belsen (bel′ zən): Village in Germany that with the village of Bergen was the site of Bergen-Belsen, a Nazi concentration camp and extermination center.
19. Buchenwald (bōō′ kən wôld′): Notorious Nazi concentration camp and extermination center in central Germany.

Guide for Responding

◆ LITERATURE AND YOUR LIFE

Reader's Response What do you like best about Anne Frank? In what way was she an ordinary teenager?

Thematic Focus What did the world learn from Anne Frank's diary?

Journal Writing Jot down in your journal your reactions to the drama's ending.

☑ Check Your Comprehension

1. When does Act II take place?
2. How does the relationship between Anne and Peter change during Act II?
3. Why does Mrs. Frank want to make the Van Daans leave the attic?
4. What happens to the families at the end of the play?

◆ Critical Thinking

INTERPRET

1. In Act I, Anne explains to her father that she worries about the bad things she does and that she is afraid people will laugh at her if she is serious. How do we know that a year later, in Act II, she has changed? **[Support]**
2. In what way does Anne's friendship with Peter help her live through a difficult time? **[Infer]**
3. How can Anne believe that "in spite of everything, . . . people are really good at heart"? **[Draw Conclusions]**
4. Scene 5 occurs several years after Scene 4 closes. Explain what Mr. Frank might mean by his last line: "She puts me to shame." **[Interpret]**

APPLY

5. How might Anne's speech on page 754 beginning "I get so mad" express the attitudes of other young people toward their parents' generation? **[Relate]**

EVALUATE

6. Does the fact the Anne Frank was a real person make this play more meaningful for you? Explain. **[Assess]**

Guide for Responding (continued)

◆ Reading Strategy

ENVISION

As you read a play, the stage directions and your imagination enable you to **envision** the characters, setting, and action. View the play in your mind just as you would on the stage.

1. (a) Which details at the beginning of Act II, Scene 2 call to mind visual images? (b) Which details appeal to your sense of hearing?
2. Describe Mr. Frank's actions throughout Act II, Scene 5.

◆ Build Vocabulary

USING FORMS OF *effect*

Knowing that the word *effect* means "result," define the following words. Then, copy the sentences on your paper. Complete each sentence by writing the correct word.

effective   effectiveness   ineffective

1. The fever remained because the medicine was _____?_____.
2. She learned her lessons well because her method of studying was _____?_____.
3. The _____?_____ of the play was proved by the audience's enthusiastic applause.

SPELLING STRATEGY

The *choo* sound is sometimes spelled *tu* when the sound occurs in the middle of a word, as in *ineffectual* and *situation*. Unscramble the letters in parentheses to find a word that contains the *choo* sound spelled *tu* that answers each clue. Write the words on your paper.

1. a great amount of money (routfen)
2. something that is real (ltacua)

USING THE WORD BANK

Write the word from the Word Bank that is closest in meaning to the following:

1. fear
2. secretly
3. unintelligible
4. cutting; mocking
5. hunch; inner knowledge
6. resentful
7. uselessly

◆ Literary Focus

CHARACTERIZATION AND THEME IN DRAMA

You learn about the personalities of dramatic characters through **characterization**—what a character says and does, as well as what others say about the characters. Often, a character's thoughts and actions will lead you to the **theme** of the drama, the insight into life revealed by the work.

1. What do you learn about Anne's personality through dialogue?
2. What do the changes in the characters reveal about people's ability to deal with a crisis?
3. What does the play reveal about the nature of hope and courage?

◆ Build Grammar Skills

VERB AGREEMENT WITH INDEFINITE PRONOUNS

A verb must agree with its subject in number. One type of subject that can cause confusion is an **indefinite pronoun,** a pronoun that does not refer to any particular person, place, or thing. The following indefinite pronouns are always singular and, therefore, always take a singular verb: *anybody, anyone, everybody, everyone, nobody, somebody, someone.* The following indefinite pronouns are always plural: *both, few, many, others, several.*

Everyone is bundled up. . . . (The singular pronoun *everyone* requires a singular verb form.)

Practice Copy the following sentences, choosing the correct form of the verb to agree with the indefinite pronoun subject.

1. Someone (make, makes) a noise downstairs.
2. Everyone (is, are) on edge, worried about Mr. Kraler.
3. Few (know, knows) about the Franks' place of hiding.
4. Is it possible that anyone (is, are) so silly as to worry . . .
5. Many (is, are) touched by Anne Frank's story.

Writing Application Write a brief review of this play. Use the indefinite pronouns *everyone, someone,* and *anyone* in your paragraph, making sure the subjects and verbs agree.

Build Your Portfolio

 ## Idea Bank

Writing

1. **Timeline** Make a timeline of the major events in the play. Write a few sentences that explain what occurs at each of the important points.

2. **Diary Entry** Imagine that you are Miep. Write a diary entry about helping to hide the people in the attic.

3. **Essay** Write an essay telling what important lessons the play offers that people today can apply to their daily lives. Support your points with passages from the play.

Speaking and Listening

4. **Scene [Group Activity]** With classmates, choose a scene from *The Diary of Anne Frank* to perform for the class. Rehearse the scene, and have it videotaped as you perform it. **[Performing Arts Link]**

5. **Dramatic Monologue** Imagine that you are Anne Frank on the day of the fight over the cake. Use passages from the play to help you write and perform a monologue—a dramatic speech—expressing her feelings about the arguments taking place in the attic. **[Performing Arts Link]**

Projects

6. **Book Club** From the library, get a copy of Anne Frank's *The Diary of a Young Girl.* With a group of classmates, hold several book club meetings for the purpose of discussing the diary. Take meeting notes that detail the group's responses. **[Literature Link]**

7. **Holocaust Research [Group Activity]** Working with a group, research information about the Holocaust that occurred during World War II. Find articles, books, maps, and Web sites that will help you. You may wish to write to the National Holocaust Museum in Washington, D.C., for free materials. Present your findings to the class. **[Social Studies Link]**

Writing Mini-Lesson

Scene With Dialogue

The words that the characters speak in a drama are called **dialogue.** In *The Diary of Anne Frank,* the dialogue reveals characters' personalities and advances the action of the play. Write a dramatic scene that develops a conflict through dialogue.

Writing Skills Focus: Script Format

The **format** of a play script—the way it appears on the page—makes it easier for everyone working on a play to do his or her job. Actors find their lines by looking for the name of their character printed in boldface. Stage directions, which tell about the actors' actions and give important information about the setting, are written in brackets and printed in italics.

Model From the Play

MR. FRANK. Good-bye, Mr. Kraler.

MRS. FRANK. [*Shaking his hand*] How can we thank you?

Prewriting Decide on the subject of your scene, and jot down notes about the characters, the conflict they face, and the setting.

Drafting Draft the scene, introducing the characters and conflict. Weave stage directions into the script. Let your characters reveal themselves through dialogue.

Revising Review your script for correct script format. Then, review your dialogue to make sure it's realistic and that it furthers the audience's knowledge of the characters or furthers the play's action.

> ◆ **Grammar Application**
>
> If you use any indefinite pronouns, be sure you have used the correct verb form to agree with them.

CONNECTING LITERATURE TO SOCIAL STUDIES

THE COLD WAR

from *A Walk in the Woods* by Lee Blessing

THE COLD WAR During World War II, the United States and the Soviet Union were allies. After the war, however, tension developed between the two countries over governmental philosophies and practices. Before long, the two countries were threatening each other with nuclear weapons that could kill millions of people.

Nuclear Weapons The atomic bomb was developed during World War II. The first atomic bomb was dropped on Hiroshima, Japan, in August 1945. The destruction was horrifying. After the war, the Soviet Union announced that it, too, had developed an atomic bomb. This was the beginning of the "arms race," as each country tried to make more bombs than its enemy.

Opposing Alliances Countries in Europe aligned themselves with either the Soviet Union or the United States. The map on this page shows which countries were part of the North Atlantic Treaty Organization (NATO), aligned with the United States; which were part of the Warsaw Pact, aligned with the Soviet Union; and which were unaligned.

The Cold War in Europe

NATO, 1955   Warsaw Pact, 1955   Nonaligned nations   Areas added to the Soviet Union after World War II

A Timely Play When *A Walk in the Woods* was first produced, in 1987, the Cold War had been going on for decades, and the arms race was still raging. The two characters in the play represent the governments of the Soviet Union and the United States. They have been meeting off and on for years to try to negotiate an arms reduction treaty, which would lessen the threat of a nuclear war.

from
A Walk in the Woods

Lee Blessing

HONEYMAN. Why did your government delay so long? What was it about the proposal you objected to? . . .

* * *

BOTVINNIK. Nothing. We liked the whole proposal.

HONEYMAN. I don't understand. You liked it?

BOTVINNIK. Very much.

HONEYMAN. Then why did you delay so long?

BOTVINNIK. Because your proposal was . . . too good.

HONEYMAN. Too good?

BOTVINNIK. It could have led to real arms reductions. Serious ones.

HONEYMAN. Don't you want that?

BOTVINNIK. Of course. But . . . also we are afraid of it.

HONEYMAN. Why? It's a treaty. We've made treaties before.

BOTVINNIK. Look at those treaties, John. They aren't treaties—they're blueprints. We determine what weapons we'll build in the next few years, then agree to let each other build them. We get rid of small systems so that we can keep bigger ones. We trade obsolete technology for state-of-the-art, we take weapons out of Europe so we can put up new ones in space. Then we say to the world, "See? We are capable of restraint. Here is a small step forward." It is laughable.

HONEYMAN. But it is a step forward. Every treaty is. Each time we come—stumbling—to some sort of agreement, even if it's self-serving, even if it's flawed . . . that's progress.

BOTVINNIK. It is not progress to take a step and slide back three. Every ten years we wake up and say, "It is time to take the first step." But meanwhile we have spent a decade creating bargaining chips—new weapons built expressly so they can be bargained away later. And what is the result? We build and get rid of bargaining chips. Nothing more. The real arsenals remain untouched. In fact, they grow.

HONEYMAN. You're right. Each year, each month, each day someone is proposing a new weapons system. Someone is securing a grant for more research, dreaming up a new technology that will do God-knows-what destruction—to our economies, if nothing else. How, knowing that, can we let any opportunity slip through our fingers? Especially this opportunity, this treaty, these comprehensive reductions. These *real* reductions.

BOTVINNIK. I know, I know. But we have problems with reductions such as these.

HONEYMAN. What are they?

BOTVINNIK. We don't trust you.

HONEYMAN. You don't trust us?

> **Connecting Literature to Social Studies**
> What role does "trust" play in negotiations between nations?

BOTVINNIK. Do you trust *us*?

HONEYMAN. Yes. Well—we try to. But whether we trust each other or not, the proposal has provisions. It has safeguards.

BOTVINNIK. We don't trust the safeguards.

HONEYMAN. There are checks on the safe-guards. Verifications.

BOTVINNIK. We don't trust them.

HONEYMAN. Andrey . . .

BOTVINNIK. Even if there were checks on the checks on the checks, we wouldn't trust them.

HONEYMAN. Why not?

BOTVINNIK. Because we don't trust *you*. Who knows what you are making right now that lies outside this proposal?

HONEYMAN. We're not making any . . .

BOTVINNIK. Multiple warheads, Star Wars—these things came *after* treaties were signed, not before.

HONEYMAN. We can control new technologies. Together.

BOTVINNIK. Can we? How can you be sure of what's going on in your own country right now? Do you think they tell you everything? Face it, John—you can't even completely trust *your* side. And you want to trust ours?

HONEYMAN. We *can* work . . .

BOTVINNIK. Suppose we sign an agreement, and the next day you—or we—suddenly unveil a new weapon. What happens? Immediately, a new arms race.

HONEYMAN. Even if you're right—you're not, but even if you were . . .

BOTVINNIK. I am right. I am always right. And how do we appear to the rest of the world? As two warmongers who can't keep a treaty. If, however, we have never agreed to a treaty, then when a new technology comes along, we are simply two nations who are trying to make a treaty, but who must remain prepared for war. It creates a much better impression.

HONEYMAN. Looking for peace, and purposely never finding it?

BOTVINNIK. [*Taking out his eyedrops, applying them.*] It is better for everyone. Broken treaties make people too nervous, yes?

HONEYMAN. So this makes your job and my job—what? Sort of a nuclear night light? Providing no real hope, just . . .

BOTVINNIK. The appearance. Yes.

HONEYMAN. This is what you truly think is preferable?

BOTVINNIK. Not I. My leaders. Your leaders.

HONEYMAN. How long do you—do they—think this is supposed to go on?

BOTVINNIK. [*Shrugging, putting away his eyedrops.*] Until the world ends.

Meet the Author

Lee Blessing (1949–   ) has been writing plays since he was in college. *A Walk in the Woods* was first performed at Yale University. In 1987, it became the first of Blessing's plays to be produced on Broadway.

Guide for Responding

◆ LITERATURE AND YOUR LIFE

Reader's Response Is Botvinnik's pessimistic view of his job justified? Explain.

Thematic Focus What kind of conflicts and challenges did diplomats like Botvinnik and Honeyman face during the Cold War?

☑ Check Your Comprehension

1. What fault did the Soviets find with the treaty proposal?
2. What reason does Botvinnik give for not trusting any promises made by Americans?

◆ Critical Thinking

INTERPRET

1. What is each man's goal in the ongoing negotiations? **[Compare and Contrast]**
2. What feature would a plan need in order to satisfy Botvinnik and his superiors? **[Deduce]**
3. What do you think Botvinnik means by the last line? **[Interpret]**

EVALUATE

4. How well does Blessing convey the personalities of the two characters? **[Assess]**

EXTEND

5. What sort of relationship do the United States and Russia (formerly a part of the Soviet Union) share today? **[Social Studies Link]**

CONNECTING LITERATURE TO SOCIAL STUDIES

This play provides a "behind-the-scenes" look at how governments work. At the same time, it puts a human face on those diplomats who negotiate with their counterparts in "enemy" countries. Lastly, *A Walk in the Woods* is full of ironic humor, as the efforts of Botvinnik and Honeyman to create a workable treaty are defeated time and time again.

1. Why might the Soviet government be "afraid" of arms reductions?
2. Why doesn't Botvinnik feel the treaties are useful?
3. Why does neither government trust the other?
4. Why do you think it was important for it to "appear" as if the United States and the Soviet Union were working toward a treaty?

Idea Bank

Writing

1. **Description** Based on this scene, write a description of either Honeyman or Botvinnik.
2. **Reporter's Questions** Imagine that Botvinnik and Honeyman will hold a press conference after their walk in the woods. As a reporter, write a series of questions you might ask either or both of them.
3. **Official Report** Write a summary of the conversation that either Botvinnik or Honeyman might submit to his superiors about the progress they've made.

Speaking and Listening

4. **Dramatic Reading [Group Activity]** With a partner, rehearse this scene and perform it for the class. Videotape the performance, and view it afterwards. **[Performing Arts Link]**

Project

5. **Maps** Since the time of the Cold War, the Soviet Union has disbanded. Do research and create a map that shows the Soviet Union as it was in 1980. Then, create a map showing the nations of the former Soviet Union today.

Further Reading, Listening, and Viewing

- Lee Blessing's *A Walk in the Woods* is the full-length play from which this excerpt was taken.
- Victoria Sherrow's *Joseph McCarthy and the Cold War* shows how the Cold War sparked a "witch hunt" for communists.
- *The Cold War* is a television documentary originally aired in 1998.

Video Script

Writing Process Workshop

Plays are written to be performed on stage. When you read a play, you are reading the script that actors and directors use to create a performance. Some performances are done for film rather than for a live audience. Actors in those performances use a video script. A video script includes dialogue and instructions to actors, but it is meant to be performed in front of a camera. Write a one-scene video script of an eventful day in your life. In addition to dialogue, include the directions for actors' movements, sound, lighting, and camera angles.

The following skills will help you write a video script:

Writing Skills Focus

▶ **Use a script format.** To show that a character is speaking, write the character's name followed by a colon or period. Write directions for lights, sound, camera angles, and actors' movements in italics, if you are writing with a computer, and enclose them in brackets. (See p. 771.)

▶ **Use realistic dialogue** to create believable characters.

The following excerpt from *The Diary of Anne Frank* shows some features found in video scripts.

MODEL FROM LITERATURE

from *The Diary of Anne Frank*

MR. FRANK. ① [*Quietly*] Anne's diary. [*He opens the diary and begins to read.*] "Monday, the sixth of July, nineteen forty-two." [*To* MIEP] Nineteen forty-two. Is it possible, Miep? . . . Only three years ago. ② [*As he continues his reading, he sits down on the couch.*] ③ "Dear Diary, since you and I are going to be great friends, I will start by telling you about myself. My name is Anne Frank. I am thirteen years old. . . ."

① The character's name precedes the words he speaks.

② Mr. Frank's remarks reveal his shock that so many terrible things have happened in just three years.

③ Directions appear in italics and brackets.

Prewriting

Choose the Scene For your scene, choose a day in your life that was memorable. It could be a winning game, a day trip taken with your family, the program where you won an award, the first time you went to a large city, and so on. Write down answers to *who, when,* and *where.* You can fictionalize events and add new characters to make the scene interesting.

Develop Each Character In a dramatic scene, you reveal the personalities of characters through their dialogue and actions, as well as through the comments and behavior of other characters. Fill out a chart like the one below for each character, choosing details that help you imagine how your characters will look, sound, and act.

CHARACTER'S NAME: _____	
Male or female:	Age:
Hair and eyes:	Physical type:
Clothes:	Personality:
Favorite foods:	Favorite activities:
What he/she wants:	What he/she dislikes:

Use this information to guide you in writing appropriate dialogue and coming up with actions and events that would be performed by a person with these characteristics. For example, a character's heroism can be revealed to the audience when he or she helps an elderly person or takes responsibility for a mistake. A character's personality can also be revealed when other characters discuss the heroic or brave act.

Drafting

Create Realistic Dialogue Review the format of dialogue in *The Diary of Anne Frank* and *A Walk in the Woods.* Use it as a model for formatting your dialogue. As you develop your dialogue, keep in mind how people actually speak. Conversational language may include slang, contractions, and incomplete sentences.

Include Stage and Camera Directions Provide instructions that describe the actors' delivery, settings, costumes, and movements. Also, include directions that indicate camera shots, such as INT for an interior shot (filmed indoors) and EXT for an exterior shot (filmed outdoors).

DRAFTING/REVISING

APPLYING LANGUAGE SKILLS: Using Pronouns Correctly

Directions in a video script often include pronouns. Personal pronouns have different forms, or cases, that reflect how they are used in a sentence.

Subjective case:
[He *answers the phone. It is* she.]

Objective Case:
[*The phone call is for* him. *He then gives* her *the phone. The caller tells* her *about the meeting.*]

Practice On your paper, write the following stage directions, choosing the correct pronoun.

[EXT. VERONA PARK. *Sean runs across the field to (she, her). (She, Her) then turns to pick (he, him) up. After (he, him) kisses (she, her), the little boy and his mother leave holding hands.*]

Writing Application As you write your video script, make sure that all your personal pronouns are in the correct case.

Writer's Solution Connection Writing Lab

For help with a topic, use the Inspirations Browser in the Creative Writing tutorial.

Applying Language Skills: Avoiding Double Negatives

In math, two negatives make a positive. In writing, if you want to express a negative idea, use only one negative word.

Negative Words: *not, never, no, none, nothing, nowhere*

Contractions including *not* are also negative, such as *didn't, wouldn't, don't,* and *can't.*

Double Negative:

I *don't* want *no* popcorn.

Revised:

I *don't* want *any* popcorn.

Practice Write the following sentences, correcting the double negatives.

1. The detective couldn't find no proof.
2. You shouldn't go nowhere in this storm.
3. I don't want to hear none of your excuses.

Writing Application As you write, avoid double negatives unless you want to show a character speaking in non-standard English.

Writer's Solution Connection
Language Lab

For more practice identifying and correcting double negatives, complete the Using Modifiers lesson, in the Using Modifiers unit.

Revising

Read It Aloud When you have completed your draft, read the dialogue aloud. Then, ask yourself whether it sounds realistic. Does this sound like something this character would say? If the dialogue sounds too stiff, revise it to include aspects of everyday speech, such as contractions or incomplete sentences. If your dialogue does not sound appropriate to your characters, review your character chart. Then, choose words that indicate your character's personality.

Make a Test Run Ask a few classmates to act out your scene. If they are confused by camera directions or perform the scene differently than you intended, revise the problem areas to clearly and concisely communicate your vision.

REVISION MODEL

① [INT. LIVING ROOM.]

② I'm
LARA. ~~I am~~ so excited about going to see *Phantom of the*
        How did you ever get these tickets?
Opera.
③ [Winks and smiles]
GARY. I have my ways.

① The writer adds this camera direction so that the crew will know where to shoot the scene.
② The writer changes *I am* to the contraction *I'm* to make the dialogue sound more conversational.
③ This stage direction, which appears in italics in brackets, helps reveal Gary's good-natured personality.

Publishing and Presenting

Videotape Share your work with an audience by capturing it on videotape. Follow these suggestions to record your production:

▶ Use the directions to guide actors, set designers, and camera operators.
▶ Have your cast rehearse the scene. Plan and practice where actors will stand, how they will move, and where the camera will be in each scene. Run through the action a few times before filming.
▶ Don't take technology for granted. Make sure that the camera operator is skilled in using the equipment.

Real-World Reading Skills Workshop

Strategies for Success

Illustrations, photographs, maps, charts, and graphs are types of visuals that support the written text of the article, story, poem, play, or chapter in which they appear. Learn to use visuals to improve your reading performance:

Preview the Visuals Before reading, examine the visuals. Ask yourself:

▶ What information do they provide?
▶ How do they relate to the title of the work?
▶ Does information in the captions explain the visuals?
▶ What mood does a piece of art set?

Previewing the visuals will help you understand what you are about to read.

Make the Connections Think of visuals as extensions of the text rather than something separate. As you read, refer to the visuals, and make connections between what you are reading and the visual information. After you have finished reading, ask yourself: What do the visuals add to what I have read?

A visual can add humor, set a mood, give background on a period of history, provide statistical information, give the geographical location, or illustrate something in the text.

Apply the Strategies

Examine the visuals on the page at right from an American history textbook. Then, answer the questions that follow.

> ✔ Here are other texts in which
> visual clues might provide
> additional information:
> ▶ Cookbooks
> ▶ Instruction manuals
> ▶ Magazine articles

A Search for Peace and Prosperity 10

(1919–1928)

Flag Day by Childe Hassam

Chapter Outline   Readings, page 503

1 The Rocky Road to Peacetime

2 The Politics of Normalcy

3 Calvin Coolidge and the Business of America

When the World War ended on November 11, 1918, Americans jubilantly looked forward to better times. After a period of fighting abroad and new government regulations at home, many yearned for calmer, more familiar times. Instead, they entered a decade of startling, bewildering change. The 1920s opened with labor unrest, social turmoil, and widespread panic about the possible effect of the Russian Revolution on the United States.

In such turbulent times, voters turned to politicians who promised calm and a return to prewar order. Business became the symbol of that order. Americans seemed worn out by crusades for peace abroad and reform at home. Many were far more concerned with gaining a bigger share of the "good life" for themselves.

Yet while newspapers wrote of rich movie stars and fancy new cars, many Americans struggled just to earn enough to eat. The prosperity of the Roaring Twenties masked underlying economic problems.

Politics of "normalcy"

1918	1920	1922	1924	1926	1928
1919 Labor unrest; Red Scare begins	**1920** Warren G. Harding elected President	**1923** Calvin Coolidge succeeds Harding	**1924** Immigration Act passed	**1926** Revenue Act passed	**1928** Coolidge vetoes McNary-Haugen bill

196

1. What does the painting suggest about the outcome of American involvement in World War I? What mood does it set?

2. How does the timeline support the chapter outline?

3. Which presidents were in office during the time period the chapter covers?

4. What important acts were passed between 1918 and 1928?

5. Why might a writer provide these visuals with the written text?

Grammar Review

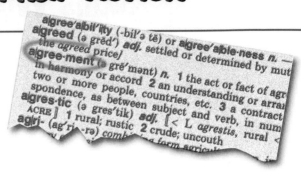

The **verb** in a sentence or clause must **agree** with its subject in number (singular or plural). Verbs in the present tense change form to agree with a singular or plural subject. (See p. 745.) Notice how the verbs change in the following examples to agree with a singular or a plural subject:

Singular: "The *curtain falls* on the scene."

Plural: "The *curtains fall* on the scene"

Verbs that end in *-s* or *-es* agree with singular subjects. Verbs that do not end with *-s* or *-es* agree with plural subjects.

A **subject** may be an indefinite pronoun, which is a pronoun that does not refer to any particular person, place, or thing. Some indefinite pronouns are always singular, some are always plural, and some can be either. The verb in a sentence must agree in number with the number of the indefinite pronoun. (See p. 770.) The following chart lists the indefinite pronouns that are singular, plural, or either:

Singular:	another, anybody, anyone, each, either, everybody, everyone, everything, much, neither, nobody, no one, nothing, one, somebody, something "*Everyone watches* intently. . . ."
Plural:	both, few, many, others, several *Both* of the men *remain* quiet.
Singular or Plural:	all, any, more, most, none, some **Singular:** *Most* of the day *is spent* studying. **Plural:** *Most* of the children *miss* their "old life."

Practice 1 Write the following sentences, choosing the verb that agrees with the subject.

1. Mr. Frank (look, looks) around the rooms where they hid.

2. Anne's diary (record, records) the days spent in hiding.

3. The police (search, searches) house by house.

4. Margot and Anne (dance, dances) to the music.

5. The ration cards (fall, falls) to the ground.

Practice 2 Write the following sentences, choosing the verb that agrees with the subject.

1. Neither of the two cats (like, likes) Mr. Dussel.

2. Most of the food (was, were) eaten.

3. Someone (know, knows) we're up here, hiding!

4. Each of the girls (listen, listens) for noises.

5. Others (seem, seems) too frightened to live silently in an attic.

Grammar in Writing

✔ *To make verbs agree, identify the subject and the verb of the sentence. Be sure the verb agrees with the subject, not with another word in the sentence.*

PART 2 *Scenes and Soliloquies*

The Singer Faure as Hamlet, Edouard Manet, Kunsthalle, Hamburg, Germany/A.K.G., Berlin

Guide for Reading

Meet the Author:

William Shakespeare (1564–1616)

Widely regarded as one of the best writers of all time, William Shakespeare wrote plays and poems that are among the best in the English language. They endure through the years because of his insight into human nature, his ability to lighten the tragic with the humorous, and his portrayal of kings and scoundrels with equal understanding.

A Life in the Theater Shakespeare was a part owner of the Lord Chamberlain's Men of London, a theater company that built and then performed in the Globe theater, located on the south bank of the Thames River. He sometimes performed in the plays, but it was as a playwright that he became famous. His thirty-seven plays continue to be performed throughout the world.

THE STORY BEHIND THE PLAYS

In *A Midsummer Night's Dream,* Shakespeare added new inventions to tales that would have been familiar to his audiences. The lovesick quartet, who serve as the play's main characters, may have been inspired by Geoffrey Chaucer's "Knight's Tale" from *The Canterbury Tales.*

The Life and Death of King Richard III is based loosely on the reign of this king of England.

Much Ado About Nothing is a romantic comedy whose plot echoes Edmund Spenser's *Faerie Queene,* Book II, Canto 4.

◆ LITERATURE AND YOUR LIFE

CONNECT YOUR EXPERIENCE

In recent years, Shakespeare's *Romeo and Juliet, Hamlet,* and *Much Ado About Nothing* have been made into major motion pictures, inspiring a new generation of fans. If you were to make a movie based on a Shakespearean tale, how would you attract a modern audience?

THEMATIC FOCUS: Relationships

As you read these scenes from Shakespeare's plays, look for his insights into human relationships.

◆ Background for Understanding

CULTURE

Shakespeare's plays were performed in open-air theaters in London. The most famous theater was the Globe, a three-tiered circle of seats surrounding a central area called the pit. The audience stood in the pit or sat on benches in the gallery. The arrangement was somewhat like a modern stadium, only much smaller.

Plays were staged with very little scenery, and, because they were performed in daylight, no lighting was used. To provide this kind of information for the audience, playwrights revealed the place, time of day, and weather conditions through dialogue.

◆ Build Vocabulary

SUFFIX: -ous

The suffix *-ous* means "full of." When *-ous* is added to the noun *office,* meaning "an important position, job, or duty," it creates the word *officious,* an adjective meaning "excessively full of the sense of one's office."

WORD BANK

Which word means "enemies"? Check the Build Vocabulary box on page 793 to see if you chose correctly.

apprehension
confederacy
officious
discourse
censured
adversaries

from A Midsummer Night's Dream
◆ *from* Much Ado About Nothing ◆
from The Life and Death of King Richard III

◆ Literary Focus

SCENES AND SOLILOQUIES

Like most plays, Shakespeare's plays are divided into acts and scenes. A **scene** is a unified series of action that takes place between two or more characters. The scenes linked together tell the story of the drama.

A **soliloquy** is a speech that reveals the inner thoughts of a character. Soliloquies can be delivered either directly to the audience or as internal monologues, as though the character were speaking to himself or herself. The speeches from *Much Ado About Nothing* and *The Life and Death of King Richard III* are both soliloquies.

◆ Reading Strategy

SUMMARIZE

When you **summarize** a soliloquy or a scene, you tell its key ideas or events in your own words. Summarizing passages and scenes of a Shakespeare play will help you keep track of what's happening.

Practice this technique as you read the following sections from Shakespeare's plays. Keep a chart like the one below to summarize.

Shakespeare's Version	Summary
A Midsummer Night's Dream: Act III, scene ii, lines 1–7	Hermia asks Lysander why he's left her.

from

A Midsummer Night's Dream

William Shakespeare

In this lighthearted comedy, fairies place a spell on four young people, and succeed in transferring the love of Lysander and Demetrius for Hermia to Helena, her friend. In the following scene, the mixed-up lovers meet in a nearby forest, and express their feelings of love, anger, and confusion.

▲ **Critical Viewing**
Judging from the characters' expressions, what is happening in this scene? **[Infer]**

from *Act III, scene ii.* *Another part of the wood.*

[*Enter* HERMIA.]

HERMIA. Dark night, that from the eye his function takes,
The ear more quick of <u>apprehension</u> makes;
Wherein it doth impair the seeing sense,

It pays the hearing double recompense.[1]

5   Thou art not by mine eye, Lysander, found;
    Mine ear, I thank it, brought me to thy sound.
    But why unkindly didst thou leave me so?

LYSANDER. Why should he stay, whom love doth press to go?

HERMIA. What love could press Lysander from my side?

10 **LYSANDER.** Lysander's love, that would not let him bide,[2]
    Fair Helena, who more engilds[3] the night
    Than all yon fiery oes[4] and eyes of light.
    Why seek'st thou me? Could not this make thee know,
    The hate I bare thee made me leave thee so?

15 **HERMIA.** You speak not as you think: it cannot be.

    HELENA.   Lo, she is one of this confederacy!
    Now I perceive they have conjoined all three
    To fashion this false sport, in spite of me.
    Injurious Hermia! Most ungrateful maid!
20 Have you conspired, have you with these contrived
    To bait me with this foul derision?
    Is all the counsel[5] that we two have shared,
    The sisters' vows, the hours that we have spent,
    When we have chid[6] the hasty-footed time
25 For parting us—O, is all forgot?
    All school days friendship, childhood innocence?
    We, Hermia, like two artificial gods,
    Have with our needles created both one flower,
    Both on one sampler,[7] sitting on one cushion,
30 Both warbling of one song, both in one key;
    As if our hands, our sides, voices, and minds
    Had been incorporate.[8] So we grew together,
    Like to a double cherry, seeming parted,
    But yet an union in partition;[9]
35 Two lovely berries moulded on one stem;
    So, with two seeming bodies, but one heart;
    Two of the first, like coats in heraldry,
    Due but to one, and crownèd with one crest.[10]
    And will you rent our ancient love asunder,
40 To join with men in scorning your poor friend?
    It is not friendly, 'tis not maidenly.
    Our sex, as well as I, may chide you for it,
    Though I alone do feel the injury.

    HERMIA. I am amazèd at your passionate words.
45 I scorn you not. It seems that you scorn me.

    HELENA. Have you not sent Lysander, as in scorn,
    To follow me and praise my eyes and face?
    And made your other love, Demetrius
    (Who even but now did spurn me with his foot),

1. **recompense** (rek´ əm pens´): Something given in return for something lost.

2. **bide:** Remain.

3. **engilds:** Brightens ornately.

4. **oes** (ōz): Any of the celestial spheres, such as the sun, moon, and other stars.

◆ **Reading Strategy**
Summarize lines 16–44?

5. **counsel:** Discussion.

6. **chid:** Scolded; reprimanded.

7. **sampler:** Work of embroidery.

8. **incorporate** (in kôr´ pər it): One body.

9. **partition:** Separation.

10. **Two of . . . one crest:** Helena imagines a shield on which the coat of arms appears twice but which has a single crest; Helena and Hermia have two bodies but a single heart.

◆ **Build Vocabulary**

apprehension (ap´ rə hen´ shən) n.: Mental grasp; perception or understanding

confederacy (kən fed´ ər ə sē) n.: Conspiracy

50   To call me goddess, nymph, divine and rare,
      Precious, celestial? Wherefore speaks he this
      To her he hates? And wherefore doth Lysander
      Deny your love, so rich within his soul,
      And tender me (forsooth)[11] affection,
55   But by your setting on, by your consent?
      What though I be not so in grace as you,
      So hung upon with love, so fortunate,
      But miserable most, to love unloved?
      This you should pity rather than despise.

60 **HERMIA.** I understand not what you mean by this.

   HELENA. Ay, do! Persever,[12] counterfeit sad looks,
      Make mouths[13] upon me when I turn my back;
      Wink each at other; hold the sweet jest up.
      This sport, well carried, shall be chronicled.

11. **forsooth**
(fôr sooth´): In truth.

12. **persever** (pʉr´ sə
vir´): Continue in some
effort.
13. **Make mouths:**
Make mocking faces.

◀ Critical Viewing
Which characters are
depicted in each of
these photographs?
How can you tell?
[Deduce]

65   If you have any pity, grace, or manners,
      You would not make me such an argument.[14]
      But fare ye well. 'Tis partly my own fault,
      Which death or absence soon shall remedy.

   LYSANDER. Stay, gentle Helena; hear my excuse:
70   My love, my life, my soul, fair Helena!

   HELENA. O excellent!

   HERMIA.   Sweet, do not scorn her so.

   DEMETRIUS. If she cannot entreat, I can compel.

   LYSANDER. Thou canst compel no more than she entreat.
75   Thy threats have no more strength than her weak prayers.
      Helen, I love thee; by my life I do!
      I swear by that which I will lose for thee,
      To prove him false that says I love thee not.

   DEMETRIUS. I say I love thee more than he can do.

14. **argument:**
Subject of scorn and
ridicule.

80 **LYSANDER.** If thou say so, withdraw and prove it too.

DEMETRIUS. Quick, come!

HERMIA.   Lysander, whereto tends all this?

LYSANDER. Away, you Ethiope![15]

DEMETRIUS.   No, no; he'll

85   Seem to break loose; take on as you would follow,[16]
    But yet come not: you are a tame man, go!

LYSANDER. Hang off, thou cat, thou burr! Vile thing, let loose,
    Or I will shake thee from me like a serpent!

HERMIA. Why are you grown so rude! What change is this,

90   Sweet love?

LYSANDER.   Thy love! Out, tawny Tartar,[17] out!
    Out, loathèd med'cine! O hated potion, hence!

HERMIA. Do you not jest?

HELENA.   Yes, sooth;[18] and so do you.

95 **LYSANDER.** Demetrius, I will keep my word with thee.

DEMETRIUS. I would I had your bond; for I perceive
    A weak bond holds you. I'll not trust your word.

LYSANDER. What, should I hurt her, strike her, kill her dead?
    Although I hate her, I'll not harm her so.

100 **HERMIA.** What, can you do me greater harm than hate?
    Hate me! wherefore? O me! What news, my love!
    Am not I Hermia? Are not you Lysander?
    I am as fair now as I was erewhile.[19]
    Since night[20] you loved me; yet since night you left me.

105   Why, then, you left me—O, the gods forbid!—
    In earnest, shall I say?

LYSANDER.   Ay, by my life!
    And never did desire to see thee more.
    Therefore be out of hope, of question, of doubt;

110   Be certain, nothing truer. 'Tis no jest
    That I do hate thee, and love Helena.

HERMIA. O me! You juggler! You canker blossom!
    You thief of love! What, have you come by night
    And stol'n my love's heart from him?

115 **HELENA.**   Fine, i' faith!
    Have you no modesty, no maiden shame,
    No touch of bashfulness? What, will you tear
    Impatient answers from my gentle tongue?
    Fie, fie! You counterfeit, you puppet, you!

120 **HERMIA.** Puppet? Why so? Ay, that way goes the game.
    Now I perceive that she hath made compare[21]
    Between our statures; she hath urged her height,
    And with her personage, her tall personage,

15. Ethiope
(ē′ thē ōp′): Here,
a brunette.
**16. take on as you
would follow:** Act as
if you (Hermia) will
pursue him (Lysander).

17. Tartar (tär′ tər):
Irritable person.

18. sooth: Truly.

19. erewhile (er′
hwīl′): A short time
ago.
20. Since night:
Since the beginning of
this night.

21. compare:
Comparison.

Her height, forsooth, she hath prevailed with him.
125 And are you grown so high in his esteem,
Because I am so dwarfish and so low?
How low am I, thou painted maypole? Speak!
How low am I? I am not yet so low
But that my nails can reach unto thine eyes.

130 **HELENA.** I pray you, though you mock me, gentlemen,
Let her not hurt me. I was not curst;[22]
I have no gift at all in shrewishness;[23]
I am a right maid[24] for my cowardice.
Let her not strike me. You perhaps may think,
135 Because she's something lower than myself,
That I can match her.

HERMIA. Lower! Hark, again!

HELENA. Good Hermia, do not be so bitter with me.
I evermore did love you, Hermia,
140 Did ever keep your counsels, never wronged you;
Save that, in love unto Demetrius,
I told him of your stealth unto this wood.
He followed you; for love I followed him.
But he hath chid me hence, and threatened me
145 To strike me, spurn me, nay, to kill me too.
And now, so you will let me quiet go,
To Athens will I bear my folly back,
And follow you no further. Let me go.
You see how simple and how fond[25] I am.

150 **HERMIA.** Why, get you gone. Who is't that hinders you?

HELENA. A foolish heart, that I leave here behind.

HERMIA. What! with Lysander?

HELENA. With Demetrius.

LYSANDER. Be not afraid. She shall not harm thee, Helena.

155 **DEMETRIUS.** No sir, she shall not, though you take her part.

HELENA. O, when she's angry, she is keen and shrewd![26]
She was a vixen[27] when she went to school;
And though she be but little, she is fierce.

HERMIA. "Little" again! Nothing but "low" and "little"!
160 Why will you suffer her to flout[28] me thus?
Let me come to her.

LYSANDER. Get you gone, you dwarf;
You minimus,[29] of hind'ring knotgrass[30] made;
You bead, you acorn!

165 **DEMETRIUS.** You are too <u>officious</u>
In her behalf that scorns your services.
Let her alone. Speak not of Helena;

22. **curst:** Quarrelsome.
23. **shrewishness** (shrōō′ ish nəs′): Having a scolding, evil temperament.
24. **right maid:** Young virtuous woman.

◆ **Literature and Your Life**
If you were in Hermia's place, would you forgive Helena at this point? Why or why not?

25. **fond:** Foolish.

26. **keen and shrewd:** Sharp-tongued and overbearing.
27. **vixen:** Malicious woman.
28. **flout** (flout): Show scorn and contempt for; to mock.

29. **minimus** (min′ ə mus): Smallest thing.
30. **knotgrass:** A weed that allegedly stunted one's growth.

Take not her part; for if thou dost intend
Never so little show of love to her,
170   Thou shalt aby³¹ it.

LYSANDER.   Now she holds me not.
Now follow, if thou dar'st, to try whose right,
Or thine or mine, is most in Helena.

DEMETRIUS.   Follow! Nay, I'll go with thee, cheek by jowl.³²

[*Exeunt* LYSANDER *and* DEMETRIUS.]

175 HERMIA.   You, mistress, all this coil is 'long of you:³³
Nay, go not back.

HELENA.   I will not trust you, I,
Nor longer stay in your curst company.
Your hands than mine are quicker for a fray,³⁴
180   My legs are longer though, to run away.

HERMIA.   I am amazed, and know not what to say.

[*Exeunt* HELENA *and* HERMIA.]

31. aby (ə bī´): Pay for.
32. cheek by jowl:
Close together.

**33. all this coil is
'long of you:** All this
turmoil is brought
about by you.

34. fray: Fight; brawl.

◆ **Build Vocabulary**

officious (ə fish´ əs) *adj.*: Overly
eager to serve; excessively obliging

Guide for Responding

◆ LITERATURE AND YOUR LIFE

Reader's Response Which parts of the
scene did you find funny? Did you find any
parts sad or moving?

Thematic Focus In what ways do the
relationships among the four people become
confused?

☑ Check Your Comprehension

1. Why is Hermia surprised by Lysander's actions?
2. What do Lysander and Demetrius have in
common?
3. (a) How do Helena and Hermia feel about
each other at the beginning of the scene?
(b) How do their feelings change by the
scene's end?

◆ Critical Thinking

INTERPRET
1. How does Helena describe her childhood with
Hermia? **[Interpret]**
2. How does this description contrast with later
events in the scene? **[Compare and Contrast]**
3. (a) Which characters are given more focus in
this scene: the women or the men? (b) Why
do you think Shakespeare wrote the scene
with this emphasis? **[Draw Conclusions]**

EVALUATE
4. Whom would you rather have as a friend—
Helena or Hermia? Why? **[Make a Judgment]**

APPLY
5. What advice would you give Hermia and
Helena to help them resolve their conflict?
[Solve]

from # Much Ado About Nothing

William Shakespeare

▶ **Critical Viewing** What do the characters' facial expressions and posture reveal about their relationship? [Draw Conclusions]

Benedick and Beatrice have for years had a barbed friendship, trading insults and witticisms whenever they meet. Benedick, who rejoices in being single, reveals his attitude toward love in this soliloquy.

from *Act II, scene iii.* *Leonato's garden.*

BENEDICK. . . . I do much wonder
that one man, seeing how much another man is a
fool when he dedicates his behaviors to love, will,
after he hath laughed at such shallow follies in
5 others, become the argument[1] of his own scorn by
falling in love; and such a man is Claudio. I have
known when there was no music with him but the
drum and the fife;[2] and now had he rather hear the
tabor and the pipe.[3] I have known when he would
10 have walked ten mile afoot to see a good armor; and
now will he lie ten nights awake carving the fashion
of a new doublet.[4] He was wont[5] to speak plain and
to the purpose, like an honest man and a soldier;
and now is he turned orthography;[6] his words are
15 a very fantastical banquet—just so many strange
dishes. May I be so converted and see with these
eyes? I cannot tell; I think not. I will not be sworn[7]
but love may transform me to an oyster;[8] but I'll take

1. **argument:** Subject matter.
2. **drum and the fife:** Instruments associated with war.
3. **tabor** (tā´ bər) **and the pipe:** Music associated with dancing.
4. **doublet** (dub´ lit): A close-fitting jacket.
5. **wont:** Accustomed.
6. **turned orthography** (ôr thäg´ rə fē): Begun speaking in an affected manner.
7. **sworn:** Bound by an oath.
8. **oyster:** Someone who can be taken advantage of.

20 my oath on it, till he have made an oyster of me he
shall never make me such a fool. One woman is fair,
yet I am well; another is wise, yet I am well; another
virtuous, yet I am well. But till all graces be in one
woman, one woman shall not come in my grace.
25 Rich she shall be, that's certain; wise, or I'll none;
virtuous, or I'll never cheapen[9] her; fair, or I'll never
look on her; mild, or come not near me; noble, or
not I for an angel; of good <u>discourse</u>, an excellent
musician, and her hair shall be of what color it
please God. Ha, the Prince and Monsieur Love!
30 [*Retiring*] I will hide me in the arbor. . . .[10]

*Benedick's friends play a trick on him, causing him
to think that Beatrice is secretly in love with him. In this
soliloquy, Benedick shows another side of himself, one
that welcomes Beatrice's love.*

BENEDICK. . . . [*Advancing*] This can be no trick; the con–
ference was sadly borne.[11] They have the truth of
this from Hero. They seem to pity the lady; it seems
her affections have their full bent.[12] Love me? Why,
35 it must be requited.[13] I hear how I am <u>censured</u>. They
say I will bear myself proudly if I perceive the love
come from her. They say too that she will rather die
than give any sign of affection. I did never think to
marry; I must not seem proud. Happy are they that
40 hear their detractions and can put them to mending.
They say the lady is fair—'tis a truth, I can bear
them witness; and virtuous—'tis so, I cannot reprove[14]
it; and wise, but for loving me; by my troth,[15] it is
no addition to her wit, nor no great argument of her
45 folly; for I will be horribly in love with her. I may
chance have some odd quirks and remnants of wit
broken on me because I have railed so long against
marriage; but doth not the appetite alter? A man
loves the meat in his youth that he cannot endure
50 in his age. Shall quips and sentences[16] and these
paper bullets of the brain awe a man from the
career of his humor?[17] No, the world must be peo–
pled. When I said I would die a bachelor, I did not
think I should live till I were married. . . .

9. **cheapen:** Bargain for (court her against other suitors).

10. **arbor:** Garden.

11. **sadly borne:** Seriously carried out.
12. **affections have their full bent:** Emotions are tightly stretched (like a bent bow).
13. **requited** (ri kwit′ əd): Returned.

14. **reprove:** Refute; disprove.
15. **troth** (trôth): Faithfulness; loyalty.
16. **sentences:** Maxims or moral sayings.
17. **humor:** Disposition; temperament.

◆ **Build Vocabulary**

discourse (dis′ kôrs) *n.*: Reasoning or rationality

censured (sen′ shərd) *v.*: Condemned as wrong; criticized

from

The Life and Death of King Richard III

William Shakespeare

▶ **Critical Viewing** Does the king in the photograph appear to be "discontented"? Explain. **[Make a Judgment]**

This soliloquy is one of Shakespeare's most famous. In it, you are introduced to Richard, Duke of Gloucester, King Edward's brother, who has recently triumphed in battle along with his brothers in the Wars of the Roses. Richard is an unhappy man who resents his place in life and begins plotting to seize the throne of England for himself.

Act I, scene i. *London. A street.*

[*Enter* RICHARD, DUKE OF GLOUCESTER, *alone.*]

    RICHARD. Now is the winter of our discontent
      Made glorious summer by this sun[1] of York;
      And all the clouds that loured[2] upon our house
      In the deep bosom of the ocean buried.
5   Now are our brows bound with victorious wreaths,
      Our bruisèd arms hung up for monuments,
      Our stern alarums chang'd to merry meetings,
      Our dreadful marches to delightful measures.
      Grim-visaged War hath smooth'd his wrinkled front,[3]
10   And now, instead of mounting barbèd steeds
      To fright the souls of fearful <u>adversaries</u>,
      He capers[4] nimbly in a lady's chamber
      To the lascivious[5] pleasing of a lute.
      But I, that am not shaped for sportive tricks
15   Nor made to court an amorous looking glass;
      I, that am rudely stamped, and want[6] love's majesty
      To strut before a wanton[7] ambling nymph;
      I, that am curtailed[8] of this fair proportion,
      Cheated of feature[9] by dissembling Nature,

1. **sun:** (1) Emblem of King Edward. (2) Son.
2. **loured** (lou´ərd): Lowered.

3. **front:** Forehead.
4. **capers** (kā´pərz): Skips or jumps about in a playful way.

5. **lascivious** (lə siv´ ē əs): Unrestrained.
6. **want:** Lack.
7. **wanton:** Unreserved; playful.
8. **curtailed:** Reduced; cut short.
9. **feature:** Good shape and pleasing appearance.

20　　Deformed, unfinished, sent before my time
　　　Into this breathing world scarce half made up,
　　　And that so lamely and unfashionable
　　　That dogs bark at me as I halt by them;
　　　Why, I, in this weak piping time[10] of peace,
25　　Have no delight to pass away the time,
　　　Unless to spy my shadow in the sun
　　　And descant[11] on mine own deformity.
　　　And therefore, since I cannot prove a lover
　　　To entertain these fair well-spoken days,
30　　I am determinèd to prove a villain
　　　And hate the idle pleasures of these days.
　　　Plots have I laid, inductions[12] dangerous,
　　　By drunken prophecies, libels, and dreams,
　　　To set my brother Clarence and the King
35　　In deadly hate the one against the other;
　　　And if King Edward be as true and just
　　　As I am subtle, false, and treacherous,
　　　This day should Clarence closely be mewed up[13]
　　　About a prophecy which says that G
40　　Of Edward's heirs the murderer shall be.
　　　Dive, thoughts, down to my soul. . . .

10. piping time: Of a pleasing and simple time where shepherds play flutes; idyllic; pastoral.
11. descant (des kant´): Comment.

12. inductions: First steps.
13. mewed up: Confined or caged in prison.

◆ **Build Vocabulary**
adversaries (ad´ vər ser´ ēz) *n.*: Enemies; opponents

Guide for Responding

◆ LITERATURE AND YOUR LIFE

Reader's Response Do you find Benedick or Richard III more likeable? Explain.

Thematic Focus What kind of relationship does Richard III have with his relatives?

☑ Check Your Comprehension

1. In *Much Ado About Nothing,* why does Benedick say he scorns Claudio?
2. How does Benedick describe the perfect woman in the first soliloquy?
3. Why do the dogs bark at Richard?
4. Whom does Richard plan to set against each other? Why?
5. (a) In the second soliloquy, whom does Benedick believe to be in love with him? (b) How does he feel about that?

◆ Critical Thinking

INTERPRET
1. Whom does Benedick view as "oysters" in *Much Ado About Nothing*? **[Connect]**
2. Describe the ways in which Benedick has changed from the first to the second soliloquy. **[Compare and Contrast]**
3. In lines 5 through 13, what does Richard III reveal about the setting of the play? **[Interpret]**
4. What comparison does Richard make between himself and King Edward? **[Compare and Contrast]**

COMPARE LITERARY WORKS
5. Which soliloquy do you think would be more effective if read in an aggressive tone? Why? **[Speculate]**

Guide for Responding (continued)

◆ Reading Strategy

SUMMARIZE

Summarizing is retelling key events and ideas in your own words. Summarizing can help you focus on a play's main events.

1. Imagine that you were summarizing the lovers' quarrel from *A Midsummer Night's Dream* to an audience of fifth graders. Which events would you emphasize?
2. How would you summarize Richard III's soliloquy?
3. (a) Summarize the first soliloquy of Benedick in *Much Ado About Nothing*. (b) Summarize the second soliloquy. (c) How do they differ?

◆ Build Vocabulary

USING THE SUFFIX -ous

The suffix *-ous*, meaning "full of," creates an adjective from a noun. On your paper, define these adjectives containing the suffix *-ous*.

1. ridiculous
2. virtuous
3. pompous
4. victorious

SPELLING STRATEGY

The *shus* sound can be spelled *cious,* as in *officious*. On your paper, correct the misspelled word in each sentence.

1. King Richard III was a malishous man.
2. *Much Ado About Nothing* was especially delishous.

USING THE WORD BANK

On your paper, write the letter of the word or phrase closest in meaning to the Word Bank word.

1. apprehension: (a) understanding, (b) catch, (c) arrest
2. confederacy: (a) union, (b) friendship, (c) antigovernment
3. officious: (a) correct, (b) overly eager, (c) vain
4. discourse: (a) silence, (b) conversation, (c) track
5. censured: (a) disapproved, (b) counted, (c) estimated
6. adversaries: (a) sayings, (b) opponents, (c) camels

◆ Literary Focus

SCENES AND SOLILOQUIES

Scenes are divisions of plays that show action and dialogue between characters. **Soliloquies** are speeches that reveal a character's inner thoughts. The sequence of scenes moves the dramatic action of a play forward. Soliloquies can indicate important plot turning points by drawing attention to a character's feelings and motives for action.

1. (a) What do you learn about the characters in the scene from *A Midsummer Night's Dream*? (b) What action occurs?
2. (a) What do you learn about Benedick in the first soliloquy from *Much Ado About Nothing*? (b) What do you learn about him in the second soliloquy?
3. Richard's soliloquy opens *The Life and Death of King Richard III*. Why do you think Shakespeare chose to start the play with a soliloquy?

◆ Build Grammar Skills

SUBJECT AND VERB AGREEMENT IN INVERTED SENTENCES

In an **inverted sentence,** the subject follows the verb. Most sentences beginning with *here* and *there* are inverted. When a sentence is inverted, identify the subject and make the verb agree with it.

Singular Verb and Subject: Now *is the winter* of our discontent / Made glorious summer . . .
Plural Verb and Subject: Happy *are they* that hear their detractions. . . .

Practice Identify the subjects and verbs in the following inverted passages. Tell whether the subject and verb are singular or plural.

1. Now are our brows bound . . .
2. Wherefore speaks he this to her he hates?
3. And wherefore doth Lysander deny your love . . .
4. Plots have I laid, inductions dangerous . . .
5. Here are comedies to keep you amused.

Writing Application Write *is* or *are* to complete each inverted sentence.

1. Here _____?_____ a few more lines for your play.
2. There _____?_____ an exciting scene in Act II.
3. Now, _____?_____ we ready to begin rehearsal?

Build Your Portfolio

 Idea Bank

Writing

1. **Summary** Choose one of Shakespeare's soliloquies, and write a summary in your own words. Include the main ideas in your retelling.

2. **Casting Advice** Choose one of these scenes or soliloquies and cast the parts with famous actors. In a note to the play's director, give reasons why you think each actor will suit his or her role so well.

3. **Comparison-and-Contrast Essay** In an essay, compare and contrast either Helena and Hermia or Demetrius and Lysander from *A Midsummer Night's Dream*. Use details from the play to support your points.

Speaking and Listening

4. **Shakespeare Recitation** Memorize 5 to 10 lines from one of the plays. Choose lines that you like and would like to study closely. Practice saying them aloud. When you are ready, recite your lines for the class. **[Performing Arts Link]**

5. **Radio Drama [Group Activity]** With a group, rehearse and tape-record one of the Shakespearean scenes or soliloquies for a radio show. Play the finished product for the class. **[Media Link]**

Projects

6. **Comic Book [Group Activity]** Create a comic book based on one of these selections. You may wish to use some of the original Shakespearean lines in your character's speech balloons. Divide the jobs required to create your comic. You might need a writer, an artist, an editor, and a layout director. Hold team meetings to keep your project on course. **[Art Link]**

7. **Historical Soliloquy** *The Life and Death of King Richard III* is about an English king. Choose a well-known political figure of the twentieth century, and write a soliloquy for that character to begin a play about his or her life. **[History Link]**

 Writing Mini-Lesson

Biographical Report

Knowing about an author's life can help you appreciate his or her writing. Even though William Shakespeare lived more than 400 years ago, much is known about his life. Write a biographical report about Shakespeare to help others come to appreciate his accomplishments.

Writing Skills Focus: Narrowing Your Topic

The topic of Shakespeare is too large for a brief biographical report. Choose a **narrower topic** that is manageable and interesting. For example, instead of writing about Shakespeare's entire life, you might write about one part of it, such as his childhood.

Model

Although no written evidence of Shakespeare's boyhood exists, it is likely that he attended the Stratford Grammar School. As part of his schooling there, he would have learned Latin and other subjects.

Prewriting Research Shakespeare's life using various sources. Jot down ideas for specific topics you might write about. Choose one, and gather information for your report.

Drafting Begin your report with a sentence that tells what aspect of Shakespeare's life your report will discuss. Develop the body of your report by arranging details in a logical order.

Revising Read your report aloud to a team of classmates. Ask them to identify sections that could be written more clearly or could be elaborated. Follow their suggestions for revision.

◆ **Grammar Application**

Make sure that your subjects and verbs agree, even in sentences in which the verb comes before the subject.

Critical Review

Writing Process Workshop

We often determine whether to read a book or go to a movie based on other people's evaluations. Critical reviews provide this type of evaluation. As a writer of a critical evaluation, it's important to give specific reasons to support your opinions.

Write a critical review of your favorite book, play, or movie. The following writing skills will help you:

Writing Skills Focus

▶ **Narrow your topic** to focus on a specific aspect of your topic. (See p. 795.)

▶ **Be accurate** with titles, authors, dates, and other vital information so your evaluation seems credible.

▶ **Support** your opinions with passages from the work.

After reading the scenes and soliloquies from Shakespeare's plays, one writer wrote a critical review of a scene from *The Life and Death of King Richard III:*

WRITING MODEL

I am amazed that the issues that Shakespeare writes about are as relevant today as they were in his time. ① For example, in *The Life and Death of King Richard III,* ② Shakespeare shows how Richard, an evil man, is caught up in wanting more. Because he feels slighted, he is "determined to prove a villain." ③ Like Richard, many people today are unable to appreciate what they have and want more at any cost.

① In this sentence, the writer gives her purpose for writing about the soliloquy. She feels its topic is still relevant.

② The writer uses the complete and accurate title of the play.

③ This quotation from the play supports the writer's point.

Prewriting

Choose a Topic Think about a book you read or a play or movie you saw that has had a lasting impression. A topic that you feel strongly about will make the best subject for your critical review.

Clarify Your Opinions Once you've chosen your topic, collect your thoughts about it. Create a chart like the one below. List what you liked about the selection and what you didn't like about it.

What I Liked	What I Disliked
_____	_____
_____	_____
_____	_____

Look at Some Models Look in a newspaper for models of reviews. In a big-city Sunday newspaper, for example, you should be able to find reviews of plays and books. Notice what points they focus on, what language they use to indicate positive or negative opinions, and how they use details to support opinions.

Identify Your Purpose Review your list of likes and dislikes. Decide whether you will or will not recommend the work to others.

Collect Supporting Details Jot down your opinions about various aspects of the book, play, or movie you have chosen. Finally, list specific details that support each opinion.

Drafting

Follow a Format Using your Prewriting notes and lists, draft your evaluation. Start with a paragraph that states your general opinion. Then, elaborate on your opinion of the work, providing examples and details for support. End with a recommendation to the readers.

Use Descriptive Language Choose words that convey your positive or negative evaluations. Look at the following examples:

Negative Language	Positive Language
unfocused, awful, confusing, vague, boring	imaginative, hilarious, original, expressive, stimulating

Get the Facts Right Check your facts to make sure they're accurate. Be sure to capitalize and punctuate titles correctly, spell names correctly, quote lines exactly, and enclose quotations in quotation marks.

DRAFTING/REVISING

APPLYING LANGUAGE SKILLS: Direct and Indirect Quotations

Direct quotations represent a person's exact spoken or written words. Enclose them in quotation marks, and give credit to the owner of the words. **Indirect quotations** report the general meaning of what a person says. They don't require quotation marks.

Direct: The goal of Richard's plan is "To set my brother Clarence and the King/ In deadly hate the one against the other."

Indirect: Shakespeare describes the goal of Richard's plan as getting his brother Clarence and the King to hate each other.

Practice On your paper, cite the following two ways: as a direct quotation and as an indirect quotation.

Dr. Fried said "Shakespeare is a writer for all time."

Writing Application In your critical review, use direct quotations when the speaker's words are especially powerful. Use indirect quotations to summarize information.

Writer's Solution Connection Language Lab

For more practice, complete the Quotation Marks lesson in the Punctuation unit.

APPLYING LANGUAGE SKILLS: Using *good* and *well* Correctly

Good (like *bad*) is an adjective. It cannot be used as an adverb after an action verb. It can, however, be used as a predicate adjective (after a linking verb). *Well* (like *badly*) is an adverb. It should be used after an action verb.

Incorrect:
The band played *good.*

Correct:
The band played *well.* (adverb describing *played*)

Correct:
It was a *good* movie. (adjective describing *movie*)

Practice Rewrite the following sentences, choosing *good* or *well.*
1. *Hamlet* is written (good, well).
2. They performed (good, well).
3. The food at the restaurant was cooked (good, well).

Writing Application *Good* and *well* convey a positive attitude. Use them correctly in your critical review.

Writer's Solution Connection
Writing Lab

To add precise words to your review, use the Descriptive Word Bin in the Revising section of the Description tutorial.

Revising

Use a Checklist Use the following checklist to help you revise your critical review.

▶ Have you clearly expressed your opinion of the work? *Ask a friend to read your paper and state your opinion. If what your friend gets out of your paper is different from what you meant to convey, add language and details that make your opinion clear.*

▶ Does your language express the appropriate degree of praise or disappointment? *List words in your paper that convey your feelings. Then, decide whether you have enough and whether they are strong enough. If not, add more or stronger words.*

▶ Is your information accurate? *Check all quotations, titles, and references to Shakespeare to make sure they are spelled and punctuated correctly.*

REVISION MODEL

① from *The Life and Death of King Richard III*
The soliloquy ∧ provides a chilling look into Richard's mind. ② In it, he contemplates his reasons for committing an evil deed. Satisfied that he is justified in his evil desire, he devises a

③ well-crafted
treacherous plan. This ∧ soliloquy helps the reader determine

his or her own feelings toward Richard.

① For accuracy, the writer adds the full title of the play.
② This point was added to support the writer's point.
③ The writer adds positive language to indicate her feelings about the soliloquy.

Publishing and Presenting

Library With classmates, create a class magazine of critical reviews. Post the magazine in the school library.

Talk Show Television and radio talk shows often include critical reviews. With a partner, imagine that you are a guest and a host. Using a question-and-answer format, the host should quiz the guest about his or her critical evaluation. If you can, videotape your talk show.

Real-World Reading Skills Workshop

Strategies for Success

Have you ever watched a movie and become so absorbed with some unimportant detail that you missed important dialogue? The same thing can happen in reading. It is also important to stay focused on the details that will help you follow and understand what you are reading. Don't be distracted by unimportant and unrelated details.

Set Your Purpose First, determine your purpose for reading. You may be reading to find facts for a report, to get information about a club you want to join, or to be entertained. Setting your purpose before you read will enable you to focus on details that will help you accomplish your goal.

Look for Key Points As you read, determine which information is central, or key, to understanding. For example, if you are reading a mystery in which a gem is stolen, the movements and whereabouts of *all* the characters are very important. If you are reading a biography about a man who solves mysteries, the only movements and whereabouts that are important are those of the man.

> ✔ *Here are other texts in which it's important to distinguish between important and unimportant information:*
> ▶ Newspaper articles
> ▶ Textbooks
> ▶ Magazine articles
> ▶ Camp brochures

RARE BEAUTIES MAY SOON BE GONE

Many people know of endangered animal species—such as the gray wolf, the bald eagle, and the white leopard—but few know about endangered plant species. Actually, there are now almost 700 plants listed as endangered, or threatened. Hawaii is home to 263 of them! Most plants are endangered because their habitat is being destroyed by new construction and the elimination of open spaces. Aside from losing the beauty of the plants, scientists worry about losing the possibility of their life-saving medical properties.

Endangered Wildflowers

Northern wild monkshood
Large-flowered fiddleneck
Western prairie fringed orchid
Silversword
Rough-leaf loosestrife
Addison's leatherflower

Apply the Strategies

Scan the article above. Then, answer the following questions:

1. What might be your purpose for reading this article?
2. Just by skimming this article, tell what it's about.
3. List three key points.
4. Which sentence could be deleted from this article without changing its meaning?
5. How does the special boxed section help you determine what's important in this article?

Subject and Verb Agreement

Grammar Review

The subject and verb of a sentence must **agree** in number (singular or plural). (See p. 794.) In most sentences, the subject comes before the verb. Sometimes, however, the normal word order of the sentence is inverted, and the subject comes after the verb. Even though the subject comes after the verb, the verb must still agree with the subject in number:

                V

"Moving across the stage were two

  S

actors."

Sentences beginning with *here* or *there* are almost always in inverted word order.

      V   S

Here are Shakespeare's most famous lines.

Many questions are also in inverted word order:

        V   S

"Wherefore speaks he this to her he hates?"

Practice 1 On your paper, write the following sentences with the correct verb. Then, underline the subject.

1. Beyond London (is, are) someone who knows of Richard's plot.

2. Here (come, comes) the two lovers, Beatrice and Benedick.

3. What (make, makes) Lysander profess his love to her?

4. How wickedly (do, does) Richard plan against the King!

5. There (is, are) many Shakespearean plays and sonnets to read.

Practice 2

Rewrite the following sentences, making the change indicated in parentheses and any other changes necessary.

1. Where is my book? (Change *book* to *books.*)

2. Here comes Hermia. (Change *Hermia* to *Hermia and Helena.*)

3. What is the meaning of Benedick's statement? (change *meaning* to *meanings.*)

4. There are flowers growing along the fence. (Change *flowers* to *a flower.*)

5. There seems no plan crueler than Richard's. (Change *plan* to *plans.*)

Grammar in Writing

✔ *Be careful not to use the contractions there's (there is), here's (here is), and where's (where is), which contain the singular verb is with plural subjects.*

Incorrect: Here's the plays of Shakespeare.

Correct: Here are the plays of Shakespeare.

Speaking, Listening, and Viewing Workshop

Debates are conducted in Congress, as well as in middle schools, high schools, and universities. A debate is a formal argument in which two people or teams prepare and present arguments on opposing sides of an issue. The issue or question is a stated proposition, such as: "Should all students be required to take swimming?" The debaters either *defend* or *attack* the stated proposition.

Know the Rules In most debates, the affirmative side argues first. Then, the opposing side presents its arguments. Each side has an opportunity for rebuttal, in which they may challenge or question the other side's arguments. Each speech is timed. At the conclusion, a judge or panel decides the winner.

Be Prepared To prepare for a debate, decide whether you are "for" (affirmative) or "against" (negative) the proposition. Then, prepare your argument—the points you will make to prove your side of the proposition. If necessary, do research to find information to support your argument. In your opening, include the points that most strongly support your position. Also, acknowledge any weaknesses that your argument may have. By dealing with possible weaknesses, you can make them sound insignificant, and your opponent cannot use them against you. Your research can provide background knowledge that will help you defend your points.

After you have presented your argument, be prepared to defend your position. Think of any possible points your opponent might make, and practice how you will respond. Speak loudly, clearly, and directly to your audience.

Apply the Strategies

With a classmate, practice debating one of the following propositions:

1. Students should wear uniforms to school.

2. The privilege of voting should be revoked if not used in two consecutive presidential elections.

3. School should be in session twelve months a year.

4. Television programs should be censored.

Debating Tips

▶ Prepare a strong factual opening.
▶ Speak loudly and clearly.
▶ Be prepared to refute your opponent's points and to defend your own.

What's Behind the Words

Vocabulary Adventures With Richard Lederer

Movie Vocabulary

For more than a century, people around the globe have drawn many of their hopes and dreams and their images of life from the cinema. *Cinema* itself is a word that was coined from the Greek *kinematos,* or "motion," to describe the movies.

Movie is a shortening of *moving* or *motion picture.* Movies don't really "move" at all. What we see is a series of still pictures flashed on the screen one after the other. They seem to move because each is just a little different from the one before, and we see each image for just a fraction of a second.

The Language of Film

Most words having to do with movies existed long before the motion picture was invented. Many of them have old and fascinating origins:

In Latin, *camera* meant "chamber" or "room." Our picture-taking camera gets its name from the small dark "room" inside that holds the film.

Our word *film* comes from the Old English *filmen,* or "thin skin." The idea of a thin coating is expressed in "a film of dust on the furniture." Modern camera film is coated with a thin skin of light-sensitive chemicals.

A Flourishing Root

Film stars work from a movie *script.* The Latin roots *script* and *scribe* mean "write." These roots flourish in words such as *ascribe, conscript, describe, inscribe, manuscript, nondescript, postscript, prescribe, proscribe, scribble, scripture,* and *transcribe.*

Film and stage actors also *rehearse.* The origins of the word *rehearse* differ greatly from its meaning today. The root of *rehearse* grows out of the Old French *hercer,* "to harrow; to cultivate the soil for farming." The Middle English *rehersen* meant "to harrow over again," that is, to go over the same ground. This idea of a repeated action is seen in our modern use of the word. When actors rehearse a film script, they go over the same lines many times.

Chasing a Phrase

An expression that is quite popular these days is *cut to the chase.* Here, the reference is to the movies. The idea is that we should get past the boring stuff, such as a mushy love scene, and cut to the chase scene for more excitement. Since its birth in the movies, *cut to the chase* has broadened to mean "stop wasting time and get to the point!"

ACTIVITY 1 Look up and explain the following film terms:

1. actor	5. director	9. producer
2. angle	6. dissolve	10. projector
3. credits	7. frame	11. screen
4. cut	8. pan(orama)	12. shot

ACTIVITY 2 Discover the meanings of three specialized movie terms that you see in the credits that follow the movie:

1. gaffer   2. best boy   3. key grip

Extended Reading Opportunities

Envisioning the action of a play will help you bring the drama to life. Following are just a few possibilities for extending your exploration of drama.

Suggested Titles

Tales From Shakespeare
Charles Lamb and Mary Lamb

This book provides an excellent introduction to the exciting plots and beautiful language of Shakespeare's plays. This brother-and-sister team turn the plays into short narratives that make the stories of Shakespeare's plays understandable to a young audience. Written in 1807, it is as easy to read today as it was when it was written. Before tackling the plays of Shakespeare, use this book to familiarize yourself with the plots, settings, and characters of his works.

Nothing But The Truth
Ronn Smith

This play is based on a novel by Avi. When ninth-grader Philip Malloy hums along with a tape of "The Star-Spangled Banner" during homeroom, he is told he is breaking school rules. What happens next stirs a national controversy. Now everyone has a different story and no one except the reader knows the truth. As you read, you will be amazed at how the versions of what happened continue to change until no one seems to know the truth.

Let Me Hear You Whisper
Paul Zindel

A new cleaning lady is hired at a laboratory. The supervisor instructs her not to touch anything—especially a dolphin that the scientists have been unsuccessful in getting to speak. Helen is happy to mind her own business, but when the dolphin decides to speak to her, she feels compelled to become involved. After a confrontation with her supervisor and the scientists, she makes a bold protest against the misuse of animals.

Other Possibilities

It's a Wonderful Life	Frances Goodrich
Invasion of the Body Snatchers	Al LaValley
I Remember Mama	John Van Druten

Man at the Edge of Paradise, 1994, Adam Straus, Courtesy Nohra Haime Gallery

Poetry

In poetry, language is used in special ways to create vivid, memorable, and sometimes musical impressions. Poems may capture a single moment in time, take you into a world of make-believe, or tell the story of a person's life. As you explore the poems in this unit, you will encounter the following terms:

- **Lyric poetry** is poetry that expresses vivid thoughts and feelings.

- **Narrative poetry** tells a story.

- **Poetic form** refers to the structure of a poem—its stanzas and its pattern of rhymes and rhythms.

- **Sound devices** are such elements as *rhyme, rhythm, alliteration,* and *onomatopoeia* that give poems a musical quality.

- **Figurative language** refers to the use of figures of speech—such as *simile, metaphor,* and *personification*—which present a fresh and unusual way of looking at things.

Guide for Reading

Meet the Author:
Robert P. Tristram Coffin
(1892–1955)

Robert P. Tristram Coffin grew up on a farm in Brunswick, Maine. He attended Bowdoin College and Oxford University, where he was a Rhodes scholar. After serving in World War I, he became a professor at Wells College. Later, he returned to his alma mater, Bowdoin, where he was a professor of English from 1934 until his death.

Literature and Art Coffin published thirty-seven books of poetry, prose, essays, and biographies during his lifetime. He won the Pulitzer Prize in Poetry in 1936 for his book *Strange Holiness*. Besides all these accomplishments, Coffin was an artist who created etchings and sketches. His artistic imagination served his poetry well, as is shown in the poem "The Secret Heart."

◆ LITERATURE AND YOUR LIFE

CONNECT YOUR EXPERIENCE

How would you complete the sentence, "I'll never forget . . . ?" Our minds hold thousands of memories, but some stand out as vividly as if they happened only yesterday. These memories are almost like short films that we can run before our eyes at will, with all their colors, smells, and characters. In this poem, Robert Coffin describes such a memory.

THEMATIC FOCUS: **Appreciating Others**

How might evidence of a father's unspoken love for his child form a cherished memory?

◆ Background for Understanding

CULTURE

"The Secret Heart" contains an unusual image of a heart. Traditionally, the heart is used to symbolize love. For instance, valentines and other love tokens are often decorated with hearts, and Cupid, the Roman god of love, is often depicted shooting his arrow through a heart. Further examples of the heart as a symbol of love include the phrases "dear to my heart," "sweetheart," and "heartache."

◆ The Secret Heart ◆

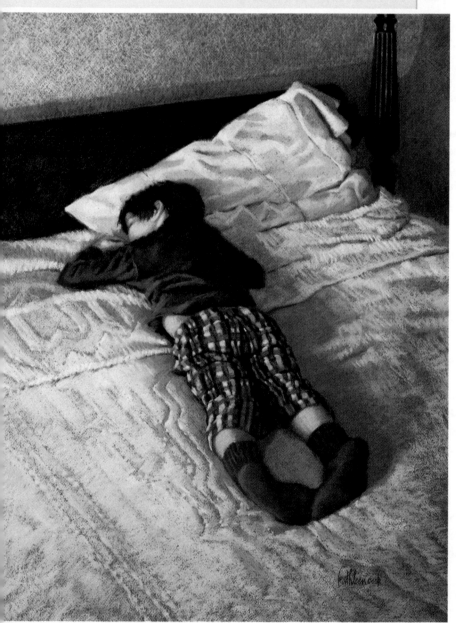

Nap in the Afternoon, Kathleen Cook, Courtesy of the artist

◆ Literary Focus

SYMBOLS

A **symbol** is an object, person, or idea that stands for something beyond itself. For example, the heart is a universal symbol of love and affection. Writers use symbols as a kind of poetic shorthand in order to make a point, create a mood, or reinforce a theme. Depending on the subject of a poem or story, practically anything may serve as a symbol—an egg may represent a beginning, a horse may stand for nature, or a grandmother may represent history.

◆ Build Vocabulary

WORD ROOTS: -semble-

In "The Secret Heart," you will read: "His two hands were curved apart / In the semblance of a heart." *Semblance* includes the word root *-semble-*, which means "to seem or appear." *Semblance* means "appearance" or "likeness."

WORD BANK

Kindling means "small twigs used to start a fire." Use the definition to help you guess at the meaning of *kindled*. See the Build Vocabulary box on page 810 to see if you guessed correctly.

kindled
semblance

Reading for Success

Strategies for Reading Poetry

Poetry is unlike other types of literature. Poets use language imaginatively to create images, tell stories, explore feelings and experiences, and suggest meanings. They choose and combine words carefully to enable you to see your world in a new and fresh way. They may also use rhythm and rhyme to create musical effects in a poem. To appreciate and enjoy poetry fully, use the following reading strategies:

Read the lines according to punctuation.

Punctuation marks are like traffic signals to the reader of poetry. They tell you when to pause, for how long to pause, and when to stop. Look for sentences or complete thoughts in a poem. If there is no punctuation mark at the end of a line, read on without pausing or stopping.

For example, the first line of "The Secret Heart" contains no end punctuation. Therefore, you would read on without pausing until you get to the period at the end of the second line: "Across the years he could recall / His father one way best of all."

Identify the speaker.

The speaker in poetry is the voice that the poet creates to communicate his or her message. Sometimes the speaker is identified; sometimes the speaker is a nameless voice; and sometimes the speaker is the poet him- or herself.

Use your senses.

Poetry is full of images that appeal to your senses of sight, hearing, taste, smell, and touch. Identify those images as you read, and pause to experience and appreciate their appeal.

Paraphrase the lines.

When reading poetry, periodically pause to restate in your own words the poet's ideas. Paraphrasing in this way ensures that you understand the basic meaning of the poem.

Lines From Poem:	Paraphrase:
In the stillest hour of the night The boy awakened to a light.	A light woke the boy in the middle of the night.

As you read "The Secret Heart," look at the notes along the sides of the pages. They will demonstrate how to apply these strategies to a poem.

The SECRET HEART

Robert P. Tristram Coffin

Across the years he could recall
His father one way best of all.

In the stillest hour of night
The boy awakened to a light.

5   Half in dreams, he saw his sire[1]
With his great hands full of fire.

The man had struck a match to see
If his son slept peacefully.

---

1. **sire** (sīr) *n.*: Father.

> At this point, you realize that the **speaker** of the poem is not a character in the poem.

▲ **Critical Viewing** What sort of mood do the colors in this photograph evoke? Explain. **[Interpret]**

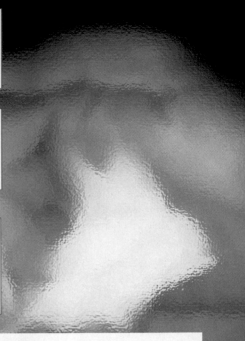

He held his palms each side the spark
10 His love had <u>kindled</u> in the dark.

His two hands were curved apart
In the <u>semblance</u> of a heart.

He wore, it seemed to his small son,
A bare heart on his hidden one.

15 A heart that gave out such a glow
No son awake could bear to know.

It showed a look upon a face
Too tender for the day to trace.

One instant, it lit all about,
20 And then the secret heart went out.

But it shone long enough for one
To know that hands held up the sun.

> You might **para-phrase** these lines as, "He cupped his hands around the flame of the match."

> **Use the punctuation** to aid your understanding. Pause at the commas, and stop at the period.

> This image in line 18, which describes the father's facial expression, appeals to your **sense** of sight.

◆ Build Vocabulary

kindled (kin´ dəld) v.: Stirred up; awakened
semblance (sem´ bləns) n.: Look or appearance

◇ Guide for Responding

◆ LITERATURE AND YOUR LIFE

Reader's Response Should the father have been less secretive about his love? Why or why not?

Thematic Focus Why does the son come to appreciate his father?

Sketch Capture the essence of this poem in a drawing or a sketch.

☑ Check Your Comprehension

1. Whose point of view is reflected in the poem?
2. What event is recalled in the poem?
3. What is the real cause of the "glowing heart"?
4. What does the boy discover about his father?

◆ Critical Thinking

INTERPRET

1. The son is "half in dreams" when he sees his father. How might being half asleep affect the boy's impressions? **[Infer]**
2. What is the difference between "a bare heart" and "his hidden one" in line 14? What does each one mean? **[Draw Conclusions]**
3. Give two meanings of what Coffin means by "the secret heart." **[Interpret]**

EVALUATE

4. Do you think Coffin succeeds in creating a strong central image in "The Secret Heart"? Explain. **[Assess]**

APPLY

5. Coffin implies that the love between father and son was not expressed the same way during the daytime. Do you think this bothered the son? Explain. **[Speculate]**

Guide for Responding (continued)

◆ Reading for Success

STRATEGIES FOR READING POETRY

Review the reading strategies and the notes showing how to read poetry. Then, apply those strategies to answer the following questions:

1. Where would you pause when reading lines 19 and 20? Where would you stop?
2. Is the poem's speaker identified? Explain.
3. To which sense does this poem appeal most? Give two examples.
4. How would you paraphrase lines 15 and 16?

◆ Build Vocabulary

USING THE WORD ROOT -semble-

The word root -semble- means "to seem" or "to appear." Complete each sentence with one of these words containing -semble-:

resemblance   resembling   resemble

1. When he cupped his hands around the burning match, he made a shape _____?_____ a fiery heart.
2. The _____?_____ between the twin boys was almost startling.
3. The child hoped that he would _____?_____ his father when he grew up.

SPELLING STRATEGY

Most English words that end in the *uhl* sound are spelled *le*, as in the word *resemble*. The *uhl* sound occurs most often in an unaccented syllable:

apple   candle   mingle   trouble

Some common exceptions to the *le* spelling are *nickel* and *panel*. On your paper, write the word that matches the definition and ends in *le*.

1. a silly type of laugh
2. a squirming movement
3. not complicated

WORD BANK

On a piece of paper, complete each sentence with the correct word from the Word Bank.

1. The boy's drawing had the _____?_____ of a boat, but he had added some odd details.
2. The description of the villain _____?_____ the young boy's interest in the story.

◆ Literary Focus

SYMBOLS

A **symbol** is anything that stands for or represents something else. An object that serves as a symbol has its own meaning, but it also represents an idea or a quality. For example, a dawn is a dawn, but as a symbol, *dawn* may mean a new start or a discovery.

1. (a) What is the main symbol of "The Secret Heart"? (b) How do you know it's a symbol?
2. What words in the poem reinforce the meaning of the symbol?

◆ Build Grammar Skills

COMPARISON OF MODIFIERS

Adjectives modify or describe nouns or pronouns. Adverbs modify verbs, adjectives, or other adverbs. Both adjectives and adverbs have different forms, which can be used to compare people, places, and things.

The comparative form of adjectives and adverbs compares two items. The superlative form compares more than two items.

Positive	Comparative	Superlative
fast	faster	fastest
speedy	speedier	speediest
sadly	more sadly	most sadly

Practice On your paper, underline each modifier, and indicate whether it is comparative or superlative. Then, circle the word that it modifies.

1. In the stillest hour of the night . . .
2. His father loved him more dearly than anything else.
3. The boy was happier than he had been before.
4. It was his most cherished memory.
5. Of the two, it is the harder poem.

Writing Application Write each sentence, using the correct form of the modifier.

1. The guidebook never mentioned the _____?_____ part of the two-week trip. (exciting)
2. She was _____?_____ than her friend Yolanda. (healthy)

The Secret Heart ◆ 811

Build Your Portfolio

 ## Idea Bank

Writing

1. **List** Make a list of memories that would be suitable for sharing in a poem.

2. **Poem** Write a poem about a child's memory. Include vivid details that will show the "picture" of the memory.

3. **Essay** Write an essay to explain how Robert P. Tristram Coffin used symbols in "The Secret Heart." Support your ideas with examples from the poem.

Speaking and Listening

4. **Love Song** Write a song about love using the word *heart*. You may want to write a rap, a ballad, or a pop song. Read or perform the song for your class. **[Performing Arts Link]**

5. **Poetry Reading [Group Activity]** With a partner, rehearse and perform "The Secret Heart" for your classmates. You may want to alternate lines or divide the poem in half, with each of you reading one section. **[Performing Arts Link]**

Projects

6. **Salute to the Poet [Group Activity]** With a partner, find more poems by Robert P. Tristram Coffin. Choose your five favorites, and create a classroom display that includes photocopies of the poems and original artwork you create to accompany each. **[Literature Link; Art Link]**

7. **Musical Archives [Group Activity]** Love is one of the most popular subjects in song, and the heart as a symbol is used in love songs very often. With a small group of classmates, find songs about love. Then, collect the lyrics for five songs that include the word *heart*. Next, make a display that includes lyric sheets and lists the lyricist and performing artist. If possible, play some of the songs for your classmates. **[Music Link]**

 ## Writing Mini-Lesson

Explanation of a Symbol

"The Secret Heart" contains a symbol of a heart, which stands for the love of a father for his son. Choose a familiar symbol, such as a dove, a flag, a heart, a turtle, the peace sign, or a lion. Then, write an explanation that reveals what the symbol means.

Writing Skills Focus: Give Reasons

As you write your explanation, **give reasons** or information to justify your conclusions about the meaning of a symbol. A reason may be a fact, an opinion, a situation, or an example. For example, in an explanation of the heart symbol, you could include the following lines as an example:

Model From the Poem
He wore, it seemed to his small son,
A bare heart on his hidden one.

Prewriting Start by choosing a symbol. Then, try out several definitions of its meaning. List some reasons why the symbol is recognized as standing for another idea. If necessary, do some research to find examples of how that symbol has been used in literature.

Drafting Begin your paper by identifying the symbol you plan to explain. Give your explanation, and organize your reasons in logical order in the body. For example, you might list facts and examples in one paragraph and include your opinions in a separate paragraph.

Revising Read your explanation to a partner, and ask for feedback. Make revisions according to his or her comments. Also, check that you've given enough reasons to support your ideas. Proofread carefully to correct errors in grammar, punctuation, and spelling.

> ◆ **Grammar Application**
>
> If you've used comparisons in your explanation, check to be sure you've chosen the correct form of the modifying words.

Types of Poetry

Birds of the Bagaduce, 1939, Marsden Hartley, The Butler Institute of American Art, Youngstown, Ohio

Guide for Reading

Meet the Authors:

Henry Wadsworth Longfellow
(1807–1882)

Longfellow was the most popular poet of his time. When he entered a room, people stood up and gentlemen took off their hats. He published his first poem when he was thirteen. At fifteen, he entered Bowdoin College, where he excelled as a student. His poem *The Song of Hiawatha* sold over a million copies in his lifetime. [For more on Longfellow, see page 304.]

THE STORY BEHIND THE POEM

Longfellow's journal entry of December 17, 1839, tells of his horror on reading about a schooner called the *Hesperus*, which had been wrecked off Norman's Reef near Gloucester, Massachusetts. Twenty bodies were washed ashore, one of them tied to a piece of the wreckage. A few weeks later, Longfellow wrote this poem.

May Swenson (1919–1989)

May Swenson was born in Ogden, Utah, and later attended Utah State University. After working for a while as a newspaper reporter, she moved to New York City, where she worked as an editor and as a college lecturer. Her poems were published in such magazines as *The New Yorker*, *Harper's*, and *The Nation*. [For more on May Swenson, see page 464.]

◆ LITERATURE AND YOUR LIFE

CONNECT YOUR EXPERIENCE

Certain moments in time seem to be etched forever on our memories. Whether the memories are horrific or sweetly nostalgic, they form part of who we are. "The Wreck of the Hesperus" was inspired by a real-life disaster at sea, and "The Centaur" was inspired by memories of a child's play.

THEMATIC FOCUS: Respecting Nature

In "The Wreck of the Hesperus," look for the poet's message about respecting the forces of nature.

◆ Background for Understanding

LITERATURE

In Longfellow's day, the fireside was the focal point of the home. During the long, cold, dark evenings, most families sat around the fire, knitting, reading, and talking. During this era, four poets—Longfellow, Oliver Wendell Holmes, James Russell Lowell, and John Greenleaf Whitter—came to be known as the Fireside Poets. They emerged as literary giants whose poems were read time and time again by countless families around the fireside.

◆ Build Vocabulary

SUFFIXES: -ful

The skipper of the *Hesperus* "laughed a scornful laugh." Knowing that the suffix *-ful* means "full of" or "having the qualities of," you can figure out that *scornful* means "full of scorn or contempt."

WORD BANK

Which word names waves that break as they reach the shore? Check the Build Vocabulary box on page 818 to see if you chose correctly.

scornful
gale
breakers
cinched
canter
negligent

The Wreck of the Hesperus
◆ The Centaur ◆

◆ Literary Focus
NARRATIVE POETRY

A poem that tells a story is called a **narrative poem.** Like short stories, narrative poems have a plot, setting, characters, dialogue, and a theme. Unlike stories, however, narrative poems rely on rhyme and rhythm and are broken into stanzas rather than paragraphs. Such a poem can be simple or complex, long or short. It can be based on a true story or a fictional story.

As you read these narrative poems, keep track of story events by filling in a plot diagram such as this one:

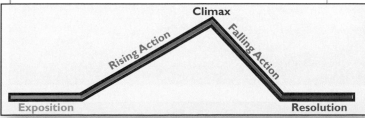

◆ Reading Strategy
READ LINES ACCORDING TO PUNCTUATION

Just as a driver follows road signs that tell when to stop, slow down, or go, so too does the reader of a poem follow "signs." In poetry, these signs are the punctuation marks. **Read lines of poetry according to punctuation.** If there is no mark of punctuation at the end of a line of poetry, keep going until you get to a punctuation mark. A comma tells you to slow down; a period tells you to stop. Exclamation marks, question marks, and dashes give you other signals to help in your reading.

The Lookout — "All's Well," Winslow Homer, Courtesy, Museum of Fine Arts, Boston, MA

The Wreck of the Hesperus

Henry Wadsworth Longfellow

It was the schooner[1] Hesperus,
    That sailed the wintry sea;
And the skipper had taken his little daughter,
    To bear him company.

5   Blue were her eyes as the fairy-flax,[2]
    Her cheeks like the dawn of day,
And her bosom white as the hawthorn buds
    That ope in the month of May.

The skipper he stood beside the helm,
10   His pipe was in his mouth,
And he watched how the veering flaw[3] did blow
    The smoke now West, now South.

Then up and spake an old sailor,
    Had sailed to the Spanish Main,[4]
15   "I pray thee, put into yonder port,
    For I fear a hurricane.

"Last night the moon had a golden ring,
    And tonight no moon we see!"
The skipper he blew a whiff from his pipe,
20   And a <u>scornful</u> laugh laughed he.

Colder and colder blew the wind,
    A <u>gale</u> from the Northeast,
The snow fell hissing in the brine,
    And the billows frothed like yeast.

25   Down came the storm, and smote amain,[5]
    The vessel in its strength;
She shuddered and paused, like a frighted steed,
    Then leaped her cable's length.

1. **schooner** (sko͞on′ ər) *n.*: Ship with two or more masts.

2. **fairy-flax:** Slender plant with delicate blue flowers.

3. **veering flaw:** Gust of wind that changes direction.
4. **Spanish Main:** Coastal region bordering the Caribbean Sea.
5. **smote** (smōt) **amain** (ə mān′): Struck with great, vigorous force.

◀ **Critical Viewing** What details in this painting convey the roughness of the sea? [Connect]

◆ **Build Vocabulary**
scornful (skôrn′ fəl) *adj.*: Full of contempt or disdain
gale (gāl) *n.*: Strong wind

"Come hither! come hither! my little daughter,
  And do not tremble so;
For I can weather the roughest gale,
  That ever wind did blow."

He wrapped her warm in his seaman's coat
  Against the stinging blast;
He cut a rope from a broken spar,[6]
  And bound her to the mast.

"O father! I hear the church-bells ring,
  O say, what may it be?"
"'Tis a fog-bell on a rock-bound coast!—"
  And he steered for the open sea.

"O father! I hear the sound of guns,
  O say, what may it be?"
"Some ship in distress, that cannot live
  In such an angry sea!"

"O father! I see a gleaming light,
  O say, what may it be?"
But the father answered never a word,
  A frozen corpse was he.

Lashed to the helm, all stiff and stark,
  With his face turned to the skies,
The lantern gleamed through the gleaming snow
  On his fixed and glassy eyes.

Then the maiden clasped her hands and prayed
  That savèd she might be;
And she thought of Christ, who stilled the wave,
  On the Lake of Galilee.[7]

And fast through the midnight dark and drear
  Through the whistling sleet and snow,
Like a sheeted ghost, the vessel swept
  Towards the reef of Norman's Woe.

And ever the fitful gusts between
  A sound came from the land;
It was the sound of the trampling surf,
  On the rocks and the hard sea-sand.

The breakers were right beneath her bows,
  She drifted a dreary wreck,
And a whooping billow swept the crew
  Like icicles from her deck.

6. spar (spär) *n.*:
Pole supporting the
sail of a ship.

7. Lake of Galilee
(gal´ ə lē´): Lake in
northeastern Israel.

◆ **Build Vocabulary**

breakers (brāk´ ərz) *n.*: Waves
that break into foam

She struck where the white and fleecy waves
    Looked soft as carded[8] wool,
70 But the cruel rocks, they gored[9] her side
    Like the horns of an angry bull.

Her rattling shrouds,[10] all sheathed in ice,
    With the masts went by the board;
75 Like a vessel of glass, she stove[11] and sank,
    Ho! ho! the breakers roared!

At daybreak, on the bleak sea-beach,
    A fisherman stood aghast,[12]
To see the form of a maiden fair,
80   Lashed close to a drifting mast.

The salt sea was frozen on her breast,
    The salt tears in her eyes;
And he saw her hair, like the brown sea-weed,
    On the billows fall and rise.

85 Such was the wreck of the Hesperus,
    In the midnight and the snow!
Christ save us all from a death like this,
    On the reef of Norman's Woe!

8. **carded:** Combed.
9. **gored:** Pierced.

10. **shrouds:** Ropes or wires stretched from the ship's side to the mast.
11. **stove:** Broke.

12. **aghast** (ə gäst′) *adj.*: In horror; terrified.

Guide for Responding

◆ LITERATURE AND YOUR LIFE

Reader's Response What would you say to the skipper about his decision not to listen to the old sailor's advice?

Thematic Focus What does this poem have to say about the power of nature?

☑ Check Your Comprehension

1. What warning does the old sailor give?
2. Why does the skipper head for the open sea instead of toward land?
3. What finally happens to the schooner?
4. What happens to everyone on board, including the skipper's daughter?

◆ Critical Thinking

INTERPRET

1. What character trait in the skipper leads to the shipwreck? **[Infer]**
2. Compare and contrast the attitudes of the skipper and the old sailor about the sea and its dangers. **[Compare and Contrast]**
3. Why do you think the old sailor is afraid of what might happen? **[Deduce]**
4. (a) What is the message or theme of this poem? (b) How do you know? **[Interpret]**

APPLY

5. What lesson about the relationship between human beings and nature can you draw from this poem? **[Generalize]**

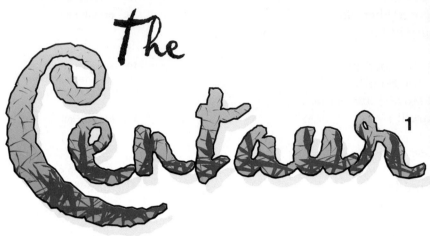

The Centaur[1]

May Swenson

The summer that I was ten—
Can it be there was only one
summer that I was ten? It must

have been a long one then—
5   each day I'd go out to choose
a fresh horse from my stable

which was a willow grove
down by the old canal.
I'd go on my two bare feet.

10   But when, with my brother's jack-knife,
I had cut me a long limber horse
with a good thick knob for a head,

and peeled him slick and clean
except a few leaves for the tail,
15   and <u>cinched</u> my brother's belt

around his head for a rein,
I'd straddle and <u>canter</u> him fast
up the grass bank to the path,

1. **Centaur** (sen´ tôr´):
Mythological creature
with a man's head,
trunk, and arms, and a
horse's body and legs.

◆ **Build Vocabulary**

cinched (sincht) *v.*: Bound firmly; tightly
fastened

canter (kan´ tər) *v.*: Ride at a smooth,
gentle pace

trot along in the lovely dust
20 that talcumed[2] over his hoofs,
hiding my toes, and turning

his feet to swift half–moons.
The willow knob with the strap
jouncing between my thighs

25 was the pommel[3] and yet the poll[4]
of my nickering pony's head.
My head and my neck were mine,

yet they were shaped like a horse.
My hair flopped to the side
30 like the mane of a horse in the wind.

My forelock swung in my eyes,
my neck arched and I snorted.
I shied and skittered and reared,

stopped and raised my knees,
35 pawed at the ground and quivered.
My teeth bared as we wheeled

2. **talcumed** (tal´ kəmd´)
v.: Blew like fine powder.

3. **pommel** (päm´ əl) *n.*:
The rounded knob on the
front part of a saddle.
4. **poll:** Head or mane (the
long hair growing from the
top of a horse).

▲ **Critical Viewing** How do the actions
of the girl in the photograph compare
with the actions of the poem's speaker?
[Compare and Contrast]

and swished through the dust again.
I was the horse and the rider,
and the leather I slapped to his rump

40 spanked my own behind.
Doubled, my two hoofs beat—
a gallop along the bank,

the wind twanged in my mane,
my mouth squared to the bit.
45 And yet I sat on my steed

quiet, <u>negligent</u> riding,
my toes standing the stirrups,
my thighs hugging his ribs.

At a walk we drew up to the porch.
50 I tethered him to a paling.[5]
Dismounting, I smoothed my skirt

5. **paling** (pāl´ iŋ) *n.*: Fence.

◆ **Build Vocabulary**

negligent (neg´ lə jənt) *adj.*: Without care or attention; indifferent

Horse in the Countryside, 1910, Franz Marc, Museum Folkwang Essen, Essen, Germany

▲ **Critical Viewing** How does this painting reflect the magic of the speaker's imaginary world? **[Interpret]**

and entered the dusky hall.
My feet on the clean linoleum
left ghostly toes in the hall.

55   *Where have you been?* said my mother.
Been riding, I said from the sink,
and filled me a glass of water.

What's that in your pocket? she said.
Just my knife. It weighted my pocket
60   and stretched my dress awry.

Go tie back your hair, said my mother,
and *Why is your mouth all green?*
*Rob Roy, he pulled some clover
as we crossed the field,* I told her.

Beyond Literature

Humanities Connection

The Centaur The speaker in this poem imagines herself to be a Centaur. This mythical creature of Greek origin generally is represented as having the upper body and head of a man attached to the lower half and hindlegs of a horse. Centaurs were thought to inhabit the mountains and forests of Thessaly and Arcadia. In Greek mythology, they are chiefly known for conducting countless battles with their neighbors, the Lapiths, which resulted from the Centaurs' attempts to abduct the princess of that kingdom. In later Greek times, they were often depicted as drawing the chariot of Dionysus or being ridden by Eros, the god of love. Centaurs are typically regarded as being wild, lawless, and vulgar characters, with little control of their animal instincts.

Cross-Curricular Activity
Draw your own version of a mythological creature that is part human and part beast. In a caption to the drawing, name your creature and describe its characteristics.

Guide for Responding

◆ LITERATURE AND YOUR LIFE

Reader's Response If you could have a conversation with the narrator in "The Centaur," what would you want to talk about? Why?

Thematic Focus In what way does the natural world enhance the speaker's life?

Journal Writing Rewrite "The Centaur" as if it were a diary entry written by the speaker.

☑ Check Your Comprehension

1. The speaker says she got a fresh horse from her stable. What was the "stable"?
2. Describe the speaker's horse.
3. What does the speaker use for reins?
4. Why is the speaker's mouth green at the end of the poem?

◆ Critical Thinking

INTERPRET

1. What kind of relationship do you think the narrator in "The Centaur" has with her brother? Explain. **[Speculate]**
2. According to the speaker, how are she and a real horse alike? **[Connect]**
3. How does the speaker's mother think a ten-year-old girl should behave? **[Infer]**

EVALUATE

4. Do you think "The Centaur" is an appropriate title for this poem? Why? **[Evaluate]**

COMPARE LITERARY WORKS

5. "The Wreck of the Hesperus" and "The Centaur" are both examples of narrative poetry, yet they are very different from each other. Contrast the formats and themes of the poems. **[Compare and Contrast]**

Guide for Responding (continued)

◆ Reading Strategy

READ LINES ACCORDING TO PUNCTUATION

When you **read according to punctuation,** you use the commas, dashes, quotation marks, semicolons, and end marks in these poems as guides to pauses, breaks, changes of tone, and stops.

1. Explain where you would pause, change tone, and stop in lines 13–16 of "The Wreck of the Hesperus."
2. Begin at line 10 of "The Centaur," and count the lines until you come to a full stop. How many lines is it? Explain how you know to stop there.

◆ Build Vocabulary

USING THE SUFFIX -ful

The suffix -ful, as in scornful, can mean "full of" or "having the qualities of." On your paper, complete each sentence with the most appropriate word from this list: beautiful, cheerful, fearful, successful, peaceful.

1. Work hard, and you'll be _____?_____.
2. Don't be _____?_____; the dog won't bite.
3. The painting of the sunset was _____?_____.
4. The tune she whistled was quite _____?_____.
5. The sleeping baby had a _____?_____ look.

SPELLING STRATEGY

When you write words with the suffix -ful, do not double the final l.

On your paper, complete the following words by adding -ful.

1. master_____?_____   4. play_____?_____
2. event_____?_____   5. use_____?_____
3. joy_____?_____   6. hope_____?_____

USING THE WORD BANK

On your paper, write the letter of the word that is closest in meaning to the Word Bank word.

1. breakers: (a) lights, (b) repairs, (c) waves
2. canter: (a) scold, (b) run, (c) crawl
3. cinched: (a) tied, (b) cut, (c) cheated
4. gale: (a) valley, (b) wind, (c) innocence
5. negligent: (a) careless, (b) fast, (c) slow
6. scornful: (a) respectful, (b) sneering, (c) lucky

◆ Literary Focus

NARRATIVE POETRY

Like a work of fiction, **narrative poetry** has certain elements that you can count on. Those elements are character, plot, setting, and theme. If a poem has a story with a beginning, a middle, and an end, you can be sure it is narrative poetry.

1. What are the plot highlights of "The Wreck of the Hesperus"?
2. In "The Wreck of the Hesperus," what theme or message is revealed?
3. (a) What happens in "The Centaur"? (b) Who is the main character? (c) How is dialogue indicated?

◆ Build Grammar Skills

COMPARISONS WITH more AND most

With longer adjectives and adverbs, you make comparisons by adding more or most. If you are comparing two things, use more. If you are comparing three or more things, use most.

Comparative: Of the two poems, which is more interesting? (comparing two poems)

Superlative: It was the most dangerous storm in years. (comparing all the storms ever)

Practice On your paper, write more or most to complete each sentence.

1. Of the two nights, this is _____?_____ ominous.
2. He is the _____?_____ fearful sailor ever.
3. This is the _____?_____ useful type of wood for carving.
4. This daughter is _____?_____ adventurous than the other.
5. She thinks that the centaur is the _____?_____ fascinating mythological figure.

Writing Application Write a paragraph about a fierce storm like the one in "The Wreck of the Hesperus." In the paragraph, use more or most with the following adjectives: ferocious, frigid, frightened, and dangerous. Be sure to use the comparative and superlative forms correctly.

Build Your Portfolio

 ## Idea Bank

Writing

1. **Continue the Poem** Write another stanza (grouping of lines) for "The Centaur," continuing the story.

2. **News Story** Imagine that there was a survivor of the shipwreck in "The Wreck of the Hesperus." Write the newspaper story that might have resulted from an interview with the survivor. Don't forget to reveal the five W's: *who, what, when, where,* and *why.* **[Media Link]**

3. **Character Study** Why is the skipper of the *Hesperus* so determined to sail? Write a character sketch in which you describe the skipper's personality and reasons for his actions. Use details from the poem to support your points.

Speaking and Listening

4. **"Fireside" Reading** Perform for the class "The Wreck of the Hesperus" as it may have been read by a family member sitting by the fireside on a cold New England night. If you like, ask a classmate to work with you, and divide up the reading of the poem. **[Performing Arts Link]**

5. **Anecdotes [Group Activity]** With a group of classmates, prepare anecdotes that tell of something that happened to you the summer you were ten. Rehearse your anecdotes before presenting them to the class. Tape-record your presentation to review afterward. **[Performing Arts Link]**

Projects

6. **Weather Report** Find out about the weather conditions that may have caused the fierce storm that sank the *Hesperus.* Prepare a chart that reveals the information you find. **[Science Link]**

7. **Mythical Creatures Poster** Create a poster about mythical creatures, such as centaurs, unicorns, sphinxes, and phoenixes. Include drawings and captions describing each creature and its characteristics. **[Art Link]**

 ## Writing Mini-Lesson

Response to a Poem

When you finish reading a poem, you have a certain response to it. You might say to yourself, "I really enjoyed the rhyme and rhythm in that poem," or you might say, "I could really picture what the poet was describing in that poem." Capture your response to either "The Wreck of the Hesperus" or "The Centaur" in written form.

Writing Skills Focus: Support Points

Your response will have greater impact if you **support your points** with examples from the poem. For example, if you enjoyed the vivid descriptions in a poem, you would quote the lines that were especially effective.

Model

The visual images in the lines "Lashed to the helm, all stiff and stark, / With his face turned to the skies, . . ." impressed me the most.

Prewriting Decide whether or not you like the poem, and jot down the poem's strengths or weaknesses. For example, you could comment on the use of language, vivid descriptions, memorable characters, and rhyme scheme (if any).

Drafting Open your response with a general statement about your reaction to the poem. In the body, develop your opening statement with examples that support your opinion.

> ◆ **Grammar Application**
> As you write, use comparisons with *more* and *most* if they will help you make your points.

Revising Look for places where you could use more examples to support your points. Then, proofread your writing to correct errors in grammar, punctuation, and spelling.

Guide for Reading

Meet the Authors:

Langston Hughes (1902–1967)

Langston Hughes wrote poems, stories, plays, essays, histories, and songs. As a songwriter, he wrote the lyrics for Kurt Weill's music for *Street Scene*, a successful 1947 Broadway musical. [For more on Langston Hughes, see pages 88 and 184.]

William Shakespeare (1564–1616)

Probably the most famous author in English literature, William Shakespeare was born in Stratford-on-Avon, a small town in England. In addition to writing thirty-seven plays, he also wrote poems and songs. [For more on William Shakespeare, see page 782.]

E. E. Cummings (1894–1962)

Best known for the playful, experimental nature of his poetry, E. E. Cummings once said that poetry is "the only thing that matters." In his poems, he celebrates families, parents, children, and fun.

Robert Frost (1874–1963)

Although identified with New England, Robert Frost was born in San Francisco. He is recognized as one of the best-known American poets, winning the Pulitzer Prize four times. [For more on Robert Frost, see page 32.]

◆ LITERATURE AND YOUR LIFE

CONNECT YOUR EXPERIENCE

The beauty of the world can sometimes take your breath away. You can be walking along, having an ordinary day, when suddenly a flock of birds, a field of flowers, or the moon awakens you to the wonders around you. These poems celebrate such moments in the lives of the poets.

THEMATIC FOCUS: Respecting Nature

In what ways does the world around them inspire these poets?

◆ Background for Understanding

SCIENCE

Poets frequently refer to the light of the moon. The moon, however, does not shine with its own light: It reflects the light of the sun. From Earth, the moon appears to change throughout the month, although it does not. We always see the same side of the moon, but the amount of illumination on that side varies, depending on the moon's position in relation to the Earth and the sun. When Robert Frost speaks of the "new moon," he refers to the moon seen as a thin crescent with the hollow side on the left. At this stage, the moon's dark side is toward the Earth, making the moon appear almost invisible.

◆ Build Vocabulary

WORD ROOTS: *-lus-*

The word root *-lus-* comes from a Latin word that means "to light." The word *luster,* which contains this root, means "shine."

WORD BANK

Which word on the list means "faking"? Check the Build Vocabulary box on page 828 to see if you chose correctly.

roam
keen
feigning
breadth
luster

Harlem Night Song
◆ Blow, Blow, Thou Winter Wind ◆
love is a place ◆ The Freedom of the Moon

◆ Literary Focus
LYRIC POETRY

   Lyric poetry expresses the poet's thoughts and feelings, creating a mood through vivid images, descriptive words, and the musical quality of the lines. In lyric poetry, you can almost "see" or "hear" the images the poet presents. Lyric poems may be made up of regular stanzas, like "Blow, Blow, Thou Winter Wind," or they may have uneven stanzas, like "Harlem Night Song."

   Keep track of your favorite images from these poems by completing a chart like this one:

Poem	Image
"Harlem Night Song"	A band is playing.

◆ Reading Strategy
IDENTIFY THE SPEAKER

   The **speaker** in a poem is the imaginary voice assumed by the poet. Sometimes the speaker is the poet; sometimes the speaker is a character created by the poet. When a poet uses the pronoun "I," it does not necessarily mean that the speaker represents the poet. The "I" could be an imaginary character, such as another person, an animal, or an inanimate object.

HARLEM NIGHT SONG

Langston Hughes

Come,
Let us <u>roam</u> the night together
Singing.

I love you.

5   Across
The Harlem[1] roof-tops
Moon is shining.
Night sky is blue.
Stars are great drops
10   Of golden dew.

Down the street
A band is playing.

I love you.

Come,
15   Let us roam the night together
Singing.

---

1. Harlem (här´ ləm) *n.*: Section of New York City in the northern part of Manhattan.

Relics, Martin Lewis, Philadelphia Museum of Art, Philadelphia, PA

▲ **Critical Viewing** In what ways has the artist captured the spirit of the night in this drawing? [Interpret]

◆ Build Vocabulary

roam (rōm) *v.*: Go aimlessly; wander

keen (kēn) *adj.*: Having a sharp cutting edge

feigning (fān´ iŋ) *v.*: Pretending

Blow, Blow, Thou Winter Wind

William Shakespeare

Blow, blow, thou winter wind.
Thou art not so unkind
   As man's ingratitude.
Thy tooth is not so <u>keen</u>,
5 Because thou art not seen,
   Although thy breath be rude.[1]
Heigh-ho! Sing, heigh-ho! unto the green holly.
Most friendship is <u>feigning</u>, most loving mere folly.
  Then, heigh-ho, the holly!
10   This life is most jolly.

   Freeze, freeze, thou bitter sky,
That dost not bite so nigh
   As benefits forgot.
Though thou the waters warp,[2]
15 Thy sting is not so sharp
   As friend remembered not.
Heigh-ho! Sing, heigh-ho! unto the green holly.
Most friendship is feigning, most loving mere folly.
  Then, heigh-ho, the holly!
20   This life is most jolly.

---

1. **rude** *adj.*: Rough; harsh.
2. **warp** *v.*: Freeze.

◆ Guide for Responding

◆ LITERATURE AND YOUR LIFE

Reader's Response Do you share the view toward friendship expressed by the speaker in "Blow, Blow, Thou Winter Wind"? Explain.

Thematic Focus Explain how each poem celebrates the physical world.

☑ Check Your Comprehension

1. (a) To whom is the speaker of "Harlem Night Song" speaking? (b) What does the speaker want the listener to do?
2. (a) In "Blow, Blow, Thou Winter Wind," what does the speaker say is more unkind than the winter wind? (b) What is sharper than the sting of the bitter sky?

◆ Critical Thinking

INTERPRET

1. In "Harlem Night Song," why does the speaker feel so full of life? **[Infer]**
2. Explain what "Blow, Blow, Thou Winter Wind" suggests about the harshness of nature compared to the pain of human relationships. **[Interpret]**

COMPARE LITERARY WORKS

3. Compare and contrast the attitudes toward love and friendship of the speakers in "Harlem Night Song" and in "Blow, Blow, Thou Winter Wind." **[Compare and Contrast]**

love is a place

E.E. Cummings

The Nest, 1893, Constant Montald, Musées Royaux des Beaux-Arts de Belgique, Bruxelles-Koninklijke Musea voor Schone Kunsten van Belgie, Brussels, Belgium

▲ **Critical Viewing** In what ways does this painting bring to life the phrase "brightness of peace"? [Interpret]

love is a place
& through this place of
love move
(with brightness of peace)
5   all places

yes is a world
& in this world of
yes live
(skillfully curled)
10   all worlds

The Freedom of the Moon

Robert Frost

I've tried the new moon tilted in the air
Above a hazy tree-and-farmhouse cluster
As you might try a jewel in your hair.
I've tried it fine with little <u>breadth</u> of <u>luster</u>,
5   Alone, or in one ornament combining
With one first-water star almost as shining.

I put it shining anywhere I please.
By walking slowly on some evening later,
I've pulled it from a crate of crooked trees
10   And brought it over glossy water, greater,
And dropped it in, and seen the image wallow,
The color run, all sorts of wonder follow.

◆ Build Vocabulary

breadth (bredth) *n.*: Width
luster (lus´ tər) *n.*: Brightness; radiance

▲ **Critical Viewing** Which line from the poem does this photograph best illustrate? **[Make a Judgment]**

Guide for Responding

◆ LITERATURE AND YOUR LIFE

Reader's Response Are you inspired by the moon, as the speaker is in "The Freedom of the Moon"? Why or why not?

Thematic Focus In what ways do both Frost and Cummings celebrate nature?

Sketch Sketch the moon as described in the second stanza of Frost's poem.

☑ Check Your Comprehension

1. (a) In "love is a place," what does the speaker say moves through the place of love? (b) Where does the speaker say all worlds live?
2. With what activity is the speaker in "The Freedom of the Moon" occupied?

◆ Critical Thinking

INTERPRET

1. In "love is a place," what do you think the speaker means when he describes "all worlds" in the "world of yes" as being "skillfully curled"? **[Interpret]**
2. "First-water" describes gems of the highest luster. Explain its meaning as used in "The Freedom of the Moon." **[Connect]**
3. How does alliteration—repetition of beginning consonant sounds—in "The Freedom of the Moon" add to the poem's effect? **[Analyze]**

COMPARING LITERARY WORKS

4. Which speaker seems more satisfied with the world as it is—the one in "love is a place" or the one in "The Freedom of the Moon"? Explain. **[Assess]**

Guide for Responding (continued)

◆ Reading Strategy

IDENTIFY THE SPEAKER

When you read poetry, be aware of the **speaker,** the character or voice assumed by the poet. Even if the poet uses the pronoun "I," that doesn't always mean that the speaker is the poet.

1. (a) In "Harlem Night Song," what can you infer about the speaker's attitude concerning what is worthwhile in life? (b) What makes you think so?
2. (a) In "Blow, Blow, Thou Winter Wind," what does the speaker value in life? (b) How do you know?
3. How would you describe the speaker of "The Freedom of the Moon"?

◆ Build Vocabulary

USING THE WORD ROOT -lus-

The word root -lus-, as in *luster,* means "light." On your paper, complete each sentence with the correct word from this list:

illustrate: to make clear by giving an example
illustrious: brilliantly outstanding
lustrous: reflecting light evenly without sparkle

1. Our ____?____ guest of honor will now speak.
2. Let me ____?____ what I mean.
3. The opal in her ring was ____?____.

SPELLING STRATEGY

When choosing between *ei* and *ie,* follow this rule: Put *i* before *e* except after *c* or when sounded like *ay* as in *neighbor* and *weigh.*

On your paper, complete the following words by adding *ei* or *ie.*

1. sl_?_gh
2. c_?_ling
3. fr_?_nd
4. n_?_ce
5. rec_?_ve
6. b_?_ge

USING THE WORD BANK

On your paper, write the Word Bank word that best completes each sentence.

1. ____?____ sleep, the child kept her eyes closed.
2. We toured the length and ____?____ of the country by train.
3. David has a ____?____ interest in science.
4. This conditioner will restore the ____?____ in your hair.
5. Be careful when you ____?____ the streets at night.

◆ Literary Focus

LYRIC POETRY

To determine whether a poem is a **lyric poem,** ask yourself these questions: Is it a personal expression of feeling? Is it emotional? Is it musical? Does it create a single impression on the reader? If you can answer yes to all these questions, it is an example of lyric poetry.

1. What is the emotion expressed by the speaker in "Harlem Night Song"?
2. Give three examples of lines with musical quality in "Blow, Blow, Thou Winter Wind."
3. What might be two favorite words of the speaker of "love is a place"?
4. With what single impression does "The Freedom of the Moon" leave you?

◆ Build Grammar Skills

IRREGULAR COMPARISONS OF MODIFIERS

Some modifiers have **irregular forms for comparisons:**

Positive	Comparative	Superlative
bad	worse	worst
good	better	best
well	better	best
little	less	least
many, much	more	most

Practice Write these sentences, underlining the modifiers and labeling them as comparative or superlative.

1. Most friendship is feigning, most loving mere folly.
2. Winter is the least friendly season.
3. More stars are visible tonight.
4. Give me less war and more peace.
5. The moon looked better over the water.

Writing Application To each sentence, add a second part, in which you use a different form of comparison of the italicized modifier.

1. You can see the moon *well* tonight.
2. I saw *many* colors reflected in the water.
3. She felt *good* today.
4. It's a *bad* season for skiing.
5. The wind stings a *little.*

Build Your Portfolio

 Idea Bank

Writing

1. Invitation The speaker in "Harlem Night Song" invites the listener to join him on a walk through the night. Write your own invitation to someone, asking him or her to join you for an outing.

2. Paraphrase Shakespeare's "Blow, Blow, Thou Winter Wind" was written about four hundred years ago. Write a line-by-line paraphrase—restatement in your own words—to put the poem's essence in modern English.

3. Essay Write an essay on "The Freedom of the Moon." In it, examine Frost's use of rhyme and repetition. Also, explore the images he creates, and comment on their effectiveness.

Speaking and Listening

4. Monologue The speaker of "Blow, Blow, Thou Winter Wind" speaks to the wind as if it were a person. Write and perform for the class a monologue, which is a dramatic speech in which the speaker addresses some force of nature.

5. Discussion [Group Activity] Suppose that the speaker of "Harlem Night Song" and the speaker of "The Freedom of the Moon" are discussing the best night scenes. One likes the country; the other likes the city. With a classmate, stage for the class the discussion they might have. **[Performing Arts Link]**

Projects

6. Music of the 1920's [Group Activity] With a small group, research the music that might have been playing "down the street" in "Harlem Night Song." Prepare a presentation for the class about music in Harlem in the 1920's. Play recordings of the songs, and include information about the composers and performers. **[Music Link]**

7. Constellations Poster Two of these poems mention stars. Create a poster about constellations—configurations of stars. Include captions that tell about each one. **[Science Link]**

 Writing Mini-Lesson

Retelling of a Poem in Prose

Poems contain highly charged, emotional language that is unlike ordinary, conversational language. Choose one poem from this grouping to retell in prose—in ordinary language. In your retelling, capture the original essence of the poem.

Writing Skills Focus: Use an Appropriate Tone

When you write a prose retelling of a poem, it is important to **use an appropriate tone.** Once you figure out what the tone of the poem is—serious, playful, ironic, bitter—you should use that same tone in the prose retelling.

Model Based on "The Freedom of the Moon"

Original: I've tried the new moon tilted in the air / Above a hazy tree-and-farmhouse cluster / As you might try a jewel in your hair.

Prose Retelling: While walking by a farmhouse that had trees near it, I saw the new moon. It seemed like a jewel that you might fasten in your hair. . . .

Prewriting Paraphrase the poem you want to retell. You may have to look up some words in a dictionary to make sure you understand their exact meaning. Also, pinpoint the tone of the poem, and plan how you'll capture that tone in the retelling.

Drafting Rewrite the poem as prose. You will find that it takes more words to tell the same thing in prose than it does in poetry.

Revising Check your retelling against the original to be sure you've included all the poet's ideas. Replace words wherever the tone does not match that of the poem.

> ◆ **Grammar Application**
> If you used irregular modifiers in your retelling, be sure you've used the correct form.

Guide for Reading

Meet the Authors:

John Updike (1932–   )

Best known as a Pulitzer Prize-winning novelist, John Updike is also an essayist, poet, and editor. Updike's quartet of novels—*Rabbit Run, Rabbit Redux, Rabbit Is Rich,* and *Rabbit at Rest*—is considered to be one of the great chronicles of modern life.

Matsuo Bashō (1644–1694)

Japanese poet Matsuo Bashō is widely regarded as the greatest of haiku poets. He began writing poetry at age nine, and at the age of thirty, he founded a school for the study of haiku.

Moritake (1452–1540)

A priest as well as a poet, Moritake is considered one of the leading Japanese poets of the sixteenth century.

Julio Noboa Polanco (1949–   )

Bilingual poet Julio Noboa Polanco was an eighth-grader at the time he wrote "Identity." Of "Identity," the poet says, "The whole poem is essentially a search for my individuality—finding myself as a person, as opposed to being one of the crowd."

Maxine Kumin (1925–   )

In addition to poetry, Maxine Kumin has written novels, essays, and children's books. In Kumin's poems, the reader hears the music of nature and is sometimes given a warm glimpse of Kumin's family and her New Hampshire farm.

◆ LITERATURE AND YOUR LIFE

CONNECT YOUR EXPERIENCE

When was the last time you saw or experienced a bitterly cold day, flowers, lightning, a magnificent weed, or a swimming competition? These sights and experiences inspired the poems that follow.

THEMATIC FOCUS: Respecting Nature

How does the environment contribute to the subject matter of these poems?

◆ Background for Understanding

SCIENCE

In "January," Updike mentions the shortness of the winter days, which is caused by the twenty-four-hour rotation of the Earth on its axis. The part of the Earth facing the sun has day. However, the Earth's axis is permanently tilted about twenty-three degrees off-center. So, as the Earth travels on its 365-day orbit around the sun, the part that is tilted toward the sun has the longer days. The Northern Hemisphere tilts away from the sun in winter and receives fewer hours of sunlight then than it does in summer.

◆ Build Vocabulary

RELATED WORDS: FORMS OF *fertile*

In "Identity," Polanco writes that he'd rather be unseen than grow in a "fertile" valley. The adjective *fertile* means "rich or productive." Knowing the definition of *fertile* will help you understand the meaning of related words, such as *fertilizer* and *fertilization*.

WORD BANK

Which word from the poems means "done in a sly or cunning way"? Check the Build Vocabulary box on page 840 to see if you chose correctly.

harnessed
abyss
shunned
fertile
catapults
cunningly
extravagance
nurtures

January ◆ Two Haiku ◆ Identity
◆ 400-Meter Free Style ◆

View to Orchard, Winter, Cerney House, Charles Neal

◆ Literary Focus
POETIC FORM

Poetic form is the structure of a poem. Updike's "January" is a lyric poem that captures a single image. This particular poem contains four stanzas of four lines each. The Japanese **haiku** is a form that consists of three lines of verse whose subject is nature. The first and third lines have five syllables each. The second line has seven syllables. Polanco's "Identity" is written in **free verse,** which means that the poet created its line breaks and stanzas where he wanted them. Kumin's poem is an example of **concrete poetry,** which uses the shape of the poem on the page to symbolize an idea or image within the poem.

◆ Reading Strategy
PARAPHRASE LINES

When you **paraphrase,** you restate in your own words what someone else has written. You can paraphrase lines of a poem to express the thought or image in your own words. The following example shows how paraphrasing helps you to identify the basic meaning of a line.

Original Text
The days are short,
The sun a spark
Hung thin between
The dark and dark.

Paraphrase
The sun shines only briefly between dawn and dusk on short winter days.

JANUARY
John Updike

The Magpie, 1869, Claude Monet, Musée d'Orsay, Paris, France

The days are short,
  The sun a spark
Hung thin between
  The dark and dark.

5 Fat snowy footsteps
  Track the floor,
And parkas pile up
  Near the door.

The river is
10 A frozen place
Held still beneath
  The trees' black lace.

The sky is low.
  The wind is gray.
15 The radiator
  Purrs all day.

▲ **Critical Viewing** Compare and contrast the artist's concept of winter with Updike's. **[Compare and Contrast]**

Two Haiku

The lightning flashes!
And slashing through the darkness,
A night-heron's[1] screech.

Bashō

5 The falling flower
I saw drift back to the branch
Was a butterfly.

Moritake

---

1. **night-heron** (nīt′ her′ ən) *n.*: A large wading bird with a long neck and long legs that is active at night.

▶ **Critical Viewing** Bashō's haiku has images of sight and sound. To what senses does this painting of herons appeal? **[Extend]**

Herons and Reeds, Japanese, Asian Art Museum of San Francisco, CA

Guide for Responding

◆ LITERATURE AND YOUR LIFE

Reader's Response Which image in "January" best conveys to you the essence of that month? Why?

Thematic Focus Describe the ways in which these poets celebrate the wonders of nature.

☑ Check Your Comprehension

1. (a) In "January," how does Updike describe the sun? (b) What sound fills the air at the end of the poem?
2. (a) What is the subject in the haiku by Bashō? (b) What is the subject in the haiku by Moritake?

◆ Critical Thinking

INTERPRET

1. Explain the image "dark and dark" in line 4 of "January." **[Interpret]**
2. In "January," why do the trees appear to be made of lace? **[Interpret]**
3. How does the image in Bashō's haiku change by the third line? **[Interpret]**
4. To what does Moritake compare the falling flower? **[Connect]**

APPLY

5. Updike uses the color gray to describe wind in winter. What colors do you associate with the other seasons? Explain. **[Relate]**

Identity

Julio Noboa Polanco

Seashore at Palavas, 1854, Gustave Courbet, Musée Fabre, Montpellier, France

Let them be as flowers,
always watered, fed, guarded, admired,
but <u>harnessed</u> to a pot of dirt.

I'd rather be a tall, ugly weed,
5   clinging on cliffs, like an eagle
wind-wavering above high, jagged rocks.

To have broken through the surface
   of stone,
to live, to feel exposed to the madness
of the vast, eternal sky.
10 To be swayed by the breezes of an
   ancient sea,
carrying my soul, my seed, beyond
   the mountains of time
or into the <u>abyss</u> of the bizarre.

I'd rather be unseen, and if
then <u>shunned</u> by everyone,
15 than to be a pleasant-smelling flower,
growing in clusters in the <u>fertile</u> valley,
where they're praised, handled, and
   plucked
by greedy, human hands.

I'd rather smell of musty, green stench
20 than of sweet, fragrant lilac.
If I could stand alone, strong and free,
I'd rather be a tall, ugly weed.

▲ **Critical Viewing** What qualities do the speaker of the poem and the subject of the painting share? **[Compare and Contrast]**

◆ **Build Vocabulary**

harnessed (här´ nist) *v.*: Tied; bound

abyss (ə bis´) *n.*: Great depth

shunned (shund) *v.*: Avoided

fertile (fur´ təl) *adj.*: Rich; fruitful

catapults (kat´ ə pults´) *v.*: Launches; leaps

400-Meter Free Style

Maxine Kumin

The gun full swing the swimmer catapults and cracks
s
i
x

▼ **Critical Viewing** What words would you choose to describe the swimmer pictured here? **[Interpret]**

feet away onto that perfect glass he catches at
  a
  n
  d
throws behind him scoop[1] after scoop cunningly moving
                t
                 h
                  e
water back to move him forward. Thrift is his wonderful
  s
  e
  c

5   ret; he has schooled out all extravagance. No muscle
                          r
                          i
                          p
ples without compensation wrist cock[2] to heel snap to
  h
  i
  s
mobile mouth that siphons[3] in the air that nurtures
                        h
                        i
                        m
at half an inch above sea level so to speak.
  T
  h
  e
astonishing whites of the soles of his feet rise
                        a
                        n
                        d

10 salute us on the turns. He flips, converts, and is gone
  a
  l
  l
in one. We watch him for signs. His arms are steady at
                        t
                        h
                        e
catch, his cadent[4] feet tick in the stretch, they know
  t
  h
  e

1. **scoop** (sko͞op) *n.*: The amount taken up; in this case, with a cupped hand.

2. **wrist cock:** The tilted position of the wrist.

3. **siphons** (sī´ fənz) *v.*: Draws; pulls.

4. **cadent** (kā´ dənt) *adj.*: Rhythmic beating.

◆ **Build Vocabulary**

cunningly (kun´ iŋ lē) *adv.*: Skillfully

extravagance (ik strav´ ə gəns) *n.*: Wastefulness

nurtures (nʉr´ chərz) *v.*: Nourishes

lesson well. Lungs know, too; he does not list[5] for
        a
        i
        r

he drives along on little sips carefully expended
 b
u
t

15   that plum[6] red heart pumps hard cries hurt how soon
        i
        t
        s

near one more and makes its final surge   TIME 4:25:9

5. list (list) *v*.: Tilt to one side.

6. plum (plum) *adj*.: Here, first class.

Guide for Responding

◆ LITERATURE AND YOUR LIFE

Reader's Response How does the shape of "400-Meter Free Style" affect your reading?

Thematic Focus In what way does Kumin's poem celebrate the swimming environment?

☑ Check Your Comprehension

1. According to the speaker in "Identity," what benefits and drawbacks do flowers have?
2. In "400-Meter Free Style," what pattern do the poem's lines make?

◆ Critical Thinking

INTERPRET

1. (a) What is the speaker really choosing between in "Identity?" **[Interpret]**
2. How can you tell that Maxine Kumin admires the swimmer? **[Infer]**
3. Why did Kumin end "400-Meter Free Style" with the swimmer's racing time? **[Interpret]**

COMPARE LITERARY WORKS

4. Describe the similarities between the swimmer and the speaker in these poems.
[Compare and Contrast]

Beyond Literature

Sports Connection

Freestyle Swimming In "400-Meter Free Style," Maxine Kumin depicts the body movements of a swimmer in competition. The stroke described in the poem is the free style, or crawl. It is the fastest of all strokes used in swimming competition and is executed through alternate arm movements, timed so that one arm will start pulling water just before the other has finished giving continuous motion to the swimmer.

Other kinds of strokes most often used in competitive swimming are the breaststroke, the butterfly, and the backstroke.

Cross-Curricular Activity
Do some research to learn how to perform each of the swimming strokes mentioned above. Then, create a how-to manual, illustrating each.

Guide for Responding (continued)

◆ Reading Strategy

PARAPHRASE LINES

When you **paraphrase** lines of a poem, you express the meaning of the lines in your own words. Paraphrasing lines helps you understand the key ideas, which in turn will help you discover the meaning of the whole poem.

1. Paraphrase lines 1–4 of "January."
2. (a) Paraphrase lines 13–18 of "Identity." (b) How does your paraphrase enable you to understand the meaning of that passage?
3. Explain why paraphrasing a poem like "400-Meter Free Style" is especially useful.

◆ Build Vocabulary

USING FORMS OF *fertile*

On your paper, complete the following sentences with the appropriate form of the word *fertile*.

1. Every farmer or gardener seeks the best _____?_____ for the crops they cultivate.
2. On a large farm, _____?_____ is a big expense.

SPELLING STRATEGY

Some words spell the short sound of *i* with the letter *y*, as in *abyss*, *lynch*, and *myth*.

On your paper, choose the correct spelling of the word in each sentence. Check a dictionary if you are unsure how to spell a word.

1. Bashō's poem is (tipical, typical) of haiku.
2. How the rules for writing a haiku came to be is a (mystery, mistery) to me.

USING THE WORD BANK

On your paper, fill in the blanks with the appropriate Word Bank word or form of the word.

1. Because of our _____?_____, our once _____?_____ farmland is now barren.
2. We used _____?_____ to get us out of the _____?_____.
3. The _____?_____ business woman _____?_____ won back her clients.
4. The horse was _____?_____ to a post.
5. A healthy diet _____?_____ growing children.

◆ Literary Focus

POETIC FORM

Poetic form is the structure of a poem. It is the framework on which the poem is built. Some forms, like haiku, have strict rules. Other forms, like concrete poetry and lyric poetry, have more general rules. Free verse has no rules about the number of lines or rhythmic pattern; however, most free-verse poets attempt to capture the rhythms of speech using everyday language.

1. How can you tell whether a poem is a haiku?
2. Why is free verse an appropriate form for "Identity"?
3. Explain how "400-Meter Free Style" illustrates its subject.

◆ Build Grammar Skills

COORDINATE ADJECTIVES

Adjectives that modify the same noun separately and equally are **coordinate.**

Example: wind-wavering above *high, jagged* rocks

Use a comma to separate coordinate adjectives. To test whether two adjectives are coordinate, switch the order of the adjectives. If the new order still makes sense, the adjectives are coordinate. Do not use a comma between adjectives whose order cannot be reversed.

Practice Write the following passages on your paper. Punctuate the coordinate adjectives correctly.

1. I'd rather be a tall ugly weed . . .
2. to feel exposed to the madness/of a vast eternal sky, . . .
3. The stubborn unsightly weeds grew wild.
4. Polanco is an effective creative poet.
5. His vivid colorful word choice is memorable.

Writing Application On your paper, write coordinate adjectives for the following sentences.

1. The _____?_____ snowflakes fell all night.
2. Shoveling the _____?_____ snow took all day.
3. The garden will burst with _____?_____ flowers.
4. The _____?_____ smells of herbs will fill the air.

Build Your Portfolio

 Idea Bank

Writing

1. **Glossary** Write glossary entries in which you define and give examples of various poetic forms.

2. **Concrete Poem** Write a concrete poem using an image, such as a key, that you could illustrate with word placement and line breaks.

3. **Essay** Free verse has no strict form, but it does attempt to capture the rhythms and sounds of everyday speech. Write an essay in which you examine how effectively "Identity" meets these criteria. Use details from the poem to support your points.

Speaking and Listening

4. **Rebuttal** In "Identity," Polanco argues that it's better to be ugly but free than to be beautiful and pampered. Take the opposing view, and deliver a short speech to the class in which you support your views.

5. **Dramatic Reading** Choose one of the poems in this section to read aloud. Practice reading it, paying attention to its rhythms but avoiding a singsong effect. Then, read the poem to the class. Tape-record your presentation to listen to afterward. **[Performing Arts Link]**

Projects

6. **Multimedia Presentation [Group Activity]** With a small group of classmates, conduct research to learn more about the Japanese haiku and how it fits into Japanese culture. Collect information about Japanese music, art, and architecture, and explain how haiku fits into Japanese society's views of art and beauty. Present your findings to the class. **[Social Studies Link]**

7. **Glossary of Terms** "400-Meter Free Style" is full of swimming terms. Choose a sport you admire, and create a glossary in which you define terms that are used in that sport. **[Sports Link]**

 Writing Mini-Lesson

Description of Yourself With a Comparison

Making a comparison is a way of describing something. In "Identity," Julio Polanco gives his reasons for preferring to be like a weed. Write a description of yourself that includes insights into your personality, appearance, or beliefs. Choose an idea, object, or even another person, to which you can compare yourself as you write your description.

Writing Skills Focus: Elaborate With Supporting Details

Once you present an idea, **elaborate** with vivid, precise details that give the reader a full-color picture rather than a sketch. In the following example, Polanco elaborates on why he would rather be a weed than a flower by comparing a weed to an eagle:

> **Model From the Poem**
> I'd rather be a tall, ugly weed,
> clinging on cliffs, like an eagle

Prewriting Decide on the main comparison you will make in your description of yourself. Then, create a list of details that are related to the description of yourself or to the comparison.

Drafting Give your self-description a memorable beginning. As you write, include comparisons that describe you.

Revising Revise by further elaborating with supporting details. Check to be sure that your comparison contains no errors in spelling, grammar, or punctuation.

> ◆ **Grammar Application**
> Look for places where you have used coordinate adjectives. Make sure you've used a comma to separate them.

CONNECTING LITERATURE TO SOCIAL STUDIES
THE VIETNAM WAR
Wahbegan *by Jim Northrup*

TWO NATIONS COLLIDE Following Vietnam's independence from France, an agreement was signed at Geneva, Switzerland, in 1954 that divided Vietnam into two nations. Communist-led North Vietnam received aid from the Soviet Union, and South Vietnam was supported by the United States. During the next few years, the aggressive activities of the Viet Cong—North Vietnamese guerrillas—and pro-Communist rebels in South Vietnam led the United States to take a stand. The result was the Vietnam War.

The Challenge of War From 1961 to 1973, more than a half million American soldiers fought in Vietnam. The troops would patrol the steamy jungles of a countryside in search of the Viet Cong, who could be hiding anywhere. No matter how carefully soldiers kept watch, they were often ambushed. In conditions that proved to be so uncertain and dangerous, it was difficult to win clear victories.

An Unpleasant Return In the United States, disapproval about United States' participation in the war rose steadily. Politicians and citizens questioned the success and legitimacy of the war effort, and by 1973, almost all American troops had been withdrawn. Since many people had been against the war, Vietnam veterans were not honored as veterans of other wars had been. In addition, many veterans suffered mentally from the memory of their traumatic experiences in the war and would reexperience these events in nightmares and daytime hallucinations.

In "Wahbegan," the poet describes the tragic, emotionally numbing effects that the Vietnam War had on a veteran.

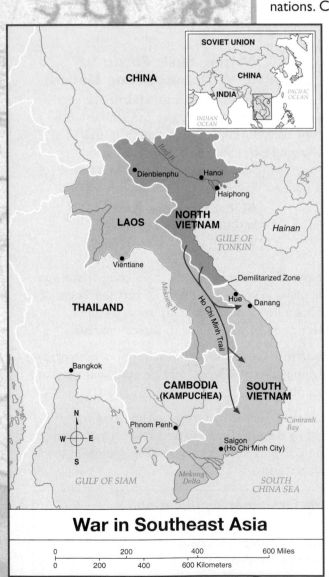

War in Southeast Asia

| 0 | 200 | 400 | 600 Miles |
| 0 | 200 | 400 | 600 Kilometers |

Wahbegan[1]

Jim Northrup

Didja ever hear a sound
smell something
taste something
that brought you back
5 to Vietnam, instantly?
Didja ever wonder
when it would end?
It ended for my brother.

---

1. **Wahbegan:** Ojibwe name.

▲ **Critical Viewing** What can you infer about
this soldier from the details in the photograph?
[Infer]

He died in the war
10 but didn't fall down
for fifteen tortured years.
His flashbacks[2] are over,
another <u>casualty</u> whose name
will never be on the Wall.[3]
15 Some can find peace
only in death.
The sound of his
family crying hurt.
The smell of the flowers
20 didn't comfort us.
The bitter taste
in my mouth
still sours me.
How about a memorial
25 for those who made it
through the war
but still died
before their time?

---

2. **flashbacks:** Past incidents recurring in the mind.
3. **Wall:** Vietnam Veterans Memorial, which is inscribed with the names of all Americans who died or who remained classified as missing in action in the Vietnam War.

◆ **Build Vocabulary**

casualty (kazh´ o͞o əl tē) *n.*: Loss resulting from some unfortunate or unseen happening

Guide for Responding

◆ **LITERATURE AND YOUR LIFE**

Reader's Response Why might veterans of war have difficulty coping with postwar living?

Thematic Focus What does the poem suggest about the conflicts and challenges faced by those in combat?

☑ **Check Your Comprehension**

1. What three senses does the poet say could bring a man back to Vietnam?
2. How many years of the man's life are said to be "tortured"?
3. What scent provided no comfort?

◆ **Critical Thinking**

INTERPRET
1. How does the repetition of the senses of sound, smell, and taste add meaning to the poem? **[Interpret]**
2. Explain the message or main idea of the poem. **[Analyze]**
3. What do you think is the cause of the man's "flashbacks"? **[Infer]**
4. Why do some "find peace only in death"? **[Draw Conclusions]**

APPLY
5. What perspective can be gained from this poem by someone who has never experienced war? **[Relate]**

Meet the Author

Jim Northrup (1943–   ) is a Native American short-story writer, poet, and syndicated columnist who presents in his writings the rich and singular lives of Native Americans. For six years, he served in the Marine Corps and made a tour of duty through Vietnam. In poems such as "Wahbegan," he relates the experience of Vietnam and its aftermath. With his wife and family, he currently lives the traditional life of the Chippewa on the Fond du Lac Reservation in northern Minnesota.

CONNECTING LITERATURE TO SOCIAL STUDIES

In "Wahbegan," Northrup gives insights into the life of a war veteran. He describes how the veteran's experience of the war has resulted in flashbacks that cripple him emotionally. The United States has tried to eliminate the stress of war on its armed forces through such practices as frequent troop rotations, regular hot meals, increased rest and recreation, and the use of psychiatric techniques. Also, many studies have been done to determine whether the stressful conditions and hardships of battle have lasting harmful consequences.

1. Which lines of the poem tell you that the man has suffered since the war?
2. Why would the poet suggest that a memorial be built for those who made it through the war?
3. What evidence does the poem give to suggest that war does have lasting consequences?

 Idea Bank

Writing

1. **Letter Home** Imagine that you are a soldier in the Vietnam War. Write a letter home describing the conditions there.
2. **Response to a Poem** What is the poem's central idea? What images and details does Northrup use to express this idea effectively? Explain.
3. **Persuasive Essay** Write an essay either in favor of or against the building of a memorial or some other kind of public display honoring those who fought and lived through the Vietnam War.

Speaking and Listening

4. **Discussion** With a group of classmates, discuss under what conditions, if any, war is justified. Share your conclusions with classmates.

Projects

5. **Art** Make an illustrated map of Vietnam during the war, and outline the different regions, plains, and rivers in which the soldiers patrolled and fought.
6. **Encyclopedia Entry** With a group of students, do some research on the Ho Chi Minh Trail. What purpose did it serve throughout the Vietnam War? Report your findings to the class.

Further Reading, Listening, and Viewing

- Frederick Porter and Walter Dean Myers's book *A Place Called Heartbreak: A Story of Vietnam* describes the ordeal of Major Fred Cherry, who was shot down in combat over Vietnam.
- "Goodnight Saigon" is a song by Billy Joel about the Vietnam War.
- *In Country* is a motion picture based on a novel by Bobbie Ann Mason about a young girl's coming to terms with her father's death in Vietnam.
- Barry Denenberg's book *Voices from Vietnam* contains personal narratives of people who experienced the war firsthand—from presidents and generals to soldiers, nurses, and Vietnamese citizens.

Comparison-and-Contrast Essay

Writing Process Workshop

While reading the poems in this section, you probably noticed the similarities and differences in form, rhyme, and subject.

A **comparison-and-contrast essay** is a brief written exploration of the similarities and differences between two or more things. Using the Writing Skills introduced in this section's Writing Mini-Lessons, compare and contrast two poems.

Writing Skills Focus

▶ **Give reasons** for your choice of poems. Also, give reasons for your ideas and evaluations. (See p. 812.)

▶ **Support your points** by using examples from both poems. (See p. 825.)

▶ **Choose an appropriate tone.** For a formal comparison-and-contrast essay, an objective or neutral tone is most effective. (See p. 833.)

▶ **Elaborate with supporting details** to make your points clear. (See p. 843.)

One writer who loves sports and enjoyed "400-Meter Free Style" found another sports poem to compare and contrast with "400-Meter Free Style." Here is the introductory paragraph to his essay:

WRITING MODEL

Maxine Kumin's "400-Meter Free Style" and Edwin Hoey's "Foul Shot" are both concrete poems about sports—swimming and basketball. ① Both poets describe an athletic event but in very different ways. ② While Kumin's poem uses form to express its meaning, Hoey's poem depends more on the words. The words in Kumin's poem stretch across the page, resembling the stroke of a swimmer. ③

① The writer gives the reasons for choosing these two poems.

② The tone of the essay is formal. The writer shows no preference for either poem.

③ Here, the writer provides a supporting detail to elaborate on the differences in form.

Prewriting

Choose the Poems Choose two poems to examine in your comparison-and-contrast essay. Following are some ideas about types of poems to compare:

> ### Topic Ideas
> - Two poems by the same poet
> - Two poems about the same subject
> - Two poems that have the same form (for example, a sonnet or a haiku)

Organize Details Before you begin writing, use a Venn diagram like the one below to help organize your details. Write the similarities in the space where the circles overlap, and write the differences in the outer sections of the circles.

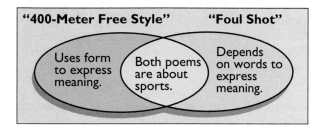

"400-Meter Free Style"   "Foul Shot"

Uses form to express meaning. | Both poems are about sports. | Depends on words to express meaning.

Locate Passages Locate passages from the poems you're comparing to use as support for your ideas. Make sure you copy the passages accurately.

Drafting

Choose an Organization There are two basic ways to organize a comparison-and-contrast essay: the point-by-point method and the subject-by-subject method. Choose the one that works best for your subject and ideas.

POINT BY POINT	SUBJECT BY SUBJECT
• Moves back and forth between the two subjects	• Covers one subject completely, then the other subject completely
• Each paragraph is about a different point of comparison as it applies to both subjects.	• Each paragraph is all about one subject.

Use a Consistent Tone The tone of your essay should be consistent throughout. To achieve an objective tone, avoid words with positive or negative connotations. Use long straightforward sentences. They often lend a more serious, objective tone than short sentences do. Stick to the facts, and steer clear of opinions.

DRAFTING/REVISING

APPLYING LANGUAGE SKILLS: Varying Sentence Beginnings

Effective writers vary their sentence beginnings to make their work lively and interesting.

Subject: *The flower in the meadow gently swayed in the wind.*

Adverb: *Gently, the flower in the meadow swayed in the wind.*

Prepositional Phrase: *In the meadow, the flower gently swayed in the wind.*

Practice Rewrite this paragraph, shifting a part of each sentence to the beginning to add variety:

The poem about nature with unusual examples of figurative language conveys an important message. The poet obviously spent a lot of time choosing words that convey a specific mood. The poem stands up well when you compare it against others of its kind.

Writing Application As you write your comparison-and-contrast essay, vary your sentence beginnings.

Writer's Solution Connection Writing Lab

For help organizing your essay, see the Organizing section of the Exposition: Making Connections tutorial.

APPLYING LANGUAGE SKILLS: Avoiding Double Comparisons

A double comparison is an error caused by using both *-er* or *-est* and *more* or *most* to form the comparative and superlative degrees. It can also be caused by adding any of these endings or words to an irregular modifier:

Incorrect: It was *the most happiest* day of my life.

Correct: It was *the happiest* day of my life.

Incorrect: It was *more better* than I thought it could be.

Correct: It was *better* than I thought it could be.

Practice On your paper, correct any double comparisons:

1. The poems of Robert Frost are more better than mine.
2. Writing poetry is the most pleasantest hobby.
3. Shakespeare's poems are more harder to read than Robert Frost's.

Writing Application As you write your essay, avoid double comparisons.

Writer's Solution Connection Language Lab

For more help, complete the Problems With Modifiers lesson in the Using Modifiers unit.

Revising

Use a Checklist Refer to the Writing Skills Focus points on page 848 as you revise your comparison-and-contrast essay.

Write Clear Paragraphs Review your paragraphs. Make sure each paragraph has a clear, distinct purpose and a good topic sentence.

Be Specific Replace any vague, general words with concrete, specific ones. As with any expository writing, the more specific your examples and support, the better your essay will be.

Ask a Peer Read your essay aloud to a peer. Ask the following, and revise accordingly:

▶ Is my conclusion clear?
▶ Are any sections of the essay confusing?
▶ Is the tone consistent throughout?
▶ Should I add supporting points?

REVISION MODEL

① *had striking similarities in form and content.*
The two haiku I read ~~were alike.~~ They were both about

② *For example, Bashō's is about a night-heron's cry,* ③ *"The lightning and Moritake's is about a butterfly.* flashes! . . ."

nature. Bashō's begins ~~with a reference to lightning.~~ ~~I liked~~

④ *Both poems were satisfying because they manage to capture vivid images in nature in three short lines.*
~~both poems.~~

① This sentence was revised to make it more formal and to provide a reason for the essay.

② This line was added to support the first sentence.

③ Citing a passage from the work is stronger than referring to a passage.

④ This line was changed to match the tone of the essay and to support the writer's idea.

Publishing and Presenting

Classroom Hold a special "Pairs of Poems" session in which pairs of students read pairs of poems and lead the class in discussions about their similarities and differences. Use ideas from your essay to guide the discussion. How many of your points do your classmates observe?

Library Print out or copy the two poems you've chosen. Display them on a poster along with your essay. Include illustrations or drawings to make your display visually appealing. Ask a librarian if you can hang your poster in the poetry section of your school library.

Real-World Reading Skills Workshop

Strategies for Success

When reading about people with backgrounds different from your own, you may make interesting discoveries about the way people all over the world live. For example, when reading a story about another culture, you notice that a teenager bows her head when speaking with her elders. You learn that not looking an elder in the eye is a sign of respect in her culture. A person's culture is his or her ideas, traditions, and way of life.

Identify Cultural Characteristics When you read about another culture, notice the characteristics of that culture. Pay attention to the way people interact with each other, their clothing, modes of transportation, food, education, celebration of holidays, and aspects of daily life. Make a list of these characteristics.

Make Connections Make connections as you read to learn about different cultures. For example, a boy in the novel you are reading lives on an island and goes fishing with his father every day after school. You do your homework every day after school. From your reading, you learn that the father supports his family by fishing. By making connections, you can understand why it is important for the boy to fish everyday and finish his homework later.

Explore Common Elements All cultures share common elements. Respect the distinctions between cultures, and look for similarities. Although approaches may be different, the experiences and emotions are similar. You may not bow to your elders, but you treat them with respect; you may not fish with your father every day, but you help your parents in other ways.

Apply the Strategies

Read this brief description of *Dogsong* by Gary Paulsen, and answer the following questions:

1. What do you learn about the Inuits?
2. What common experience does this description suggest?
3. How does this passage increase your understanding of the Inuit culture?

Come, see my dogs.
With them I ran,
ran north to the sea.
I stand by the sea and I sing.
I sing of my hunts
and of Oogruk.

This is the "Dogsong" of Russel Suskitt, a fourteen-year-old Inuit who undertakes the demanding journey of his ancestors. Unhappy with the modern life of his village—the awful sounds of the snow-machines and the cramped "boxed" government houses of the village, he follows the stories of the old shaman Oogruk to take the dog team and sled and travel to the sea—across ice floes, tundra, and mountains—to find himself and his own "song." Russel discovers the pride of his people and the strength of human and dog working together as a team.

✔ *Here are other types of reading through which you can extend your cultural understanding:*
► **News and specialty magazines**
► **Novels**
► **Newspapers**
► **Nonfiction**

Correct Use of Modifiers

Grammar Review

modi·fy (mäd'ə fī') *vt.* **-fied·, -fy'ing** [ME *modifien* < MFr < L *modificare*, to limit, regulate < *modus*, measure (see MODE) + *facere*, to make: see DO!] 1 *Gram.* to limit the meaning of; qualify ["old" modifies "man" in "old man"] 2 *Linguis.* to change the form of a morpheme to indicate grammatical relations or derivation —*vi.* to be modified —SYN. CHANGE —**mod'i·fi'able** *adj.*

Adjectives and adverbs are modifiers—they describe or limit the meaning of another word. Most adjectives and adverbs change form to show degrees of comparison. The three degrees of comparison are the positive, comparative, and superlative (see p. 811).

The **positive** degree is the basic form of an adjective or an adverb. It is used when no comparison is being made:

The **comparative** degree is used when two things are being compared. For most one- and two-syllable modifiers, the comparative degree is formed by adding -er. For longer words, use *more* with the positive form:

The **superlative** degree is used when more than two things are being compared. For most one- and two-syllable modifiers, the superlative degree is formed by adding -est. For longer words, use *most* with the positive form:

Positive	Comparative	Superlative
small	smaller	smallest
distant	more distant	most distant
eagerly	more eagerly	most eagerly

Irregular Comparisons Some adjectives and adverbs are irregular in form (see p. 832). Memorize the comparative and superlative forms of these modifiers.

Positive	Comparative	Superlative
bad, badly	worse	worst
little	less	least
good, well	better	best
many, much	more	most

Coordinate Adjectives When you use more than one adjective to modify the same noun separately and equally, the adjectives are coordinate (see p. 842). Use commas to separate coordinate adjectives: "I'd rather smell of *musty, green* stench/ than of *sweet, fragrant* lilac."

Practice 1 Write each sentence, using the correct form of the modifier given.

1. The train moved _____?_____ than the horses that ran alongside it. (fast)
2. The sky was full of gray clouds. The _____?_____ clouds seemed to hover over the ship. (dark)
3. Langston Hughes's poetry is _____?_____ to read than Shakespeare's poetry. (easy)
4. Swimming is a _____?_____ sport than volleyball. (competitive)
5. The _____?_____ poem I have ever read is "The Wreck of the Hesperus." (good)

Practice 2 Write the following paragraph, punctuating any coordinate adjectives:

The vivid interesting poems in this section represent different types of poetry. The storylike suspenseful elements of the narrative poem are evident in "The Wreck of the Hesperus." Lyric poems, such as the musical rhythmic "Blow, Blow, Thou Winter Wind," are meant to be read aloud.

Grammar in Writing

✔ *Avoid double comparisons, which use -er or -est as well as more or most.*

Incorrect: The poem was *more funnier* than the one we read last week.

Correct: The poem was *funnier* than the one we read last week.

PART 2 *Elements of Poetry*

Black Hat on a Yellow Chair, 1952, Fernand Leger, University of Iowa Museum of Art, Iowa City, IA

Guide for Reading

Meet the Authors:

Walter de la Mare (1873–1956)

For years, this British poet worked in the statistics department of a big oil company. At night, however, his imagination roamed freely as he wrote poems about the magic and mystery of life. These poems, found in books like *The Listeners,* delight children and adults alike. [For more on Walter de la Mare, see page 32.]

Shel Silverstein (1932–   )

Silverstein is a poet, a writer of children's books, a cartoonist, a folk singer, and a composer. The critic William Cole has called Silverstein's poems "tender, funny, sentimental, philosophical, and ridiculous in turn . . ."

Wendy Rose (1948–   )

The work of this award-winning poet reflects her Native American ancestry. However, she wants readers to view her poems not only as Native American but as human.

Emily Dickinson (1830–1886)

Dickinson led a quiet life in Amherst, Massachusetts. She published only a few poems in her lifetime. However, she secretly wrote the 1,775 lyric poems that made her one of the founders of American poetry. Sparkling with thought and feeling, these poems show how active her inner life really was. [For more on Emily Dickinson, see page 192.]

◆ LITERATURE AND YOUR LIFE

CONNECT YOUR EXPERIENCE

Sometimes, with a friend or a family member, you just need to share a look or a single word. Then, both of you nod or burst into laughter. You don't need to spell things out because you share a secret language. As these poems show, poetry is also a kind of secret language. It begins with a child's wisdom, speaks in the rhythm of a heartbeat, and offers words to save a breaking heart.

THEMATIC FOCUS: Relationships

How does each of these poems speak to you as a friend, telling you something secret or surprising?

◆ Background for Understanding

CULTURE

In Native American cultures, as Wendy Rose reveals in "Drum Song," poetry and dance were accompanied by drums. These instruments usually consisted of a hide stretched on a frame. Drums came in all shapes and sizes—from the small water drum of the Iroquois to the large Great Plains drum that was beaten by four men together.

◆ Build Vocabulary

WORD PAIRS

Because some words occur in pairs, as opposites, it's useful to learn them together. The word *vertical,* from "Drum Song" is part of such a pair: vertical/horizontal. *Vertical* means "upright," while *horizontal* means "flat."

WORD BANK

Which word from these poems is related to the word *vertex,* a mathematical term meaning "the highest point of a triangle"? Check the Build Vocabulary box on page 858 to see if you chose correctly.

> vertical
> burrow
> gourds

Silver ◆ Forgotten Language ◆ Drum Song
◆ If I can stop one Heart from breaking ◆

Egrets in Summer, 1940–45, N.C. Wyeth, Courtesy of Metropolitan Life Insurance Company, New York, NY

◆ Literary Focus

SOUND DEVICES

Poets use **sound devices** to create musical effects in poems. The most familiar of these devices is **rhyme,** identical sounds at the ends of words: "...*sees* / ... *trees*" ("Silver"). Another device is **repetition,** repeated words or grammatical structures: "Once I... / Once I... ("Forgotten Language"). Still another is **alliteration,** repeated vowel sounds at the beginning of words or stressed syllables near each other: "*b*ush to *b*urrow" ("Drum Song").

Read the poems aloud to hear these sound devices. Also, think about the effect of these devices on each poem.

◆ Reading Strategy

MAKE INFERENCES

To get at the sense of a poem, you can **make inferences,** or reach conclusions based on evidence in the poems. First, notice details like sound devices, pictures the poem creates, and the thoughts or feelings it expresses. Then, compare these details, and think about what meanings they suggest.

Use a chart like the one below to record your inferences (a sample is filled in):

Detail	Inference
The poet repeats sentences beginning with "Once I ..."	Repetition of the word *once* as in "Once upon a time" calls to mind a fairy tale or a situation that is magical.

Silver

Walter de la Mare

Slowly, silently, now the moon
Walks the night in her silver shoon;[1]
This way, and that, she peers, and sees
Silver fruit upon silver trees;
5 One by one the casements catch
Her beams beneath the silvery thatch;
Couched in his kennel, like a log,
With paws of silver sleeps the dog;
From their shadowy coat the white breasts peep
10 Of doves in a silver-feathered sleep;
A harvest mouse goes scampering by,
With silver claws, and silver eye;
And moveless fish in the water gleam,
By silver reeds in a silver stream.

---

1. **shoon** (sho̅o̅n) *n.*: Old-fashioned word for "shoes."

▼ **Critical Viewing** What mood
does this silvery scene evoke?
[Analyze]

Forgotten Language

Shel Silverstein

Once I spoke the language of the flowers,
Once I understood each word the caterpillar said,
Once I smiled in secret at the gossip of the starlings,[1]
And shared a conversation with the housefly
    in my bed.
5   Once I heard and answered all the questions
    of the crickets,
And joined the crying of each falling dying
    flake of snow,
Once I spoke the language of the flowers . . .
    How did it go?
    How did it go?

---

1. starlings (stär´ linz) *n.*: Dark-colored birds with a short tail,
long wings, and a sharp, pointed bill.

Guide for Responding

◆ LITERATURE AND YOUR LIFE

Reader's Response Describe a time when something in nature "spoke" to you.

Thematic Focus Do you think it's possible to remember the "Forgotten Language" that Silverstein describes? Why or why not?

☑ Check Your Comprehension

1. What kind of night does De la Mare describe in "Silver"?
2. (a) Name the only creature that moves in "Silver." (b) What are the other animals doing?
3. Name six things from nature that speak a "Forgotten Language" in Silverstein's poem.
4. What does he ask at the end of "Forgotten Language"?

◆ Critical Thinking

INTERPRET

1. Describe the effects of the moon's walk in "Silver." **[Analyze Cause and Effect]**
2. Which details in "Silver" contribute to the poem's sense of magic? Explain. **[Support]**
3. When do you think Silverstein understood the "Forgotten Language" he describes? Explain. **[Infer]**
4. How does the language to which Silverstein refers differ from a language like English or Spanish? **[Draw Conclusions]**

COMPARE LITERARY WORKS

5. Does "Silver" use the "Forgotten Language" Silverstein mentions? Explain. **[Connect]**

DRUM SONG
Wendy Rose

Listen. Turtle
    your flat round feet
    of four claws each
    go slow, go steady,
5   from rock to water
    to land to rock to
water.

Listen. Woodpecker
    you lift your red head
10   on wind, perch
    on <u>vertical</u> earth
    of tree bark and
branch.

Listen. Snowhare[1]
15   your belly drags,
    your whiskers dance
    bush to <u>burrow</u>
    your eyes turn up
    to where owls
20 hunt.

Listen. Women
    your tongues melt,
    your seeds are planted
    mesa[2] to mesa a shake
25   of <u>gourds</u>,
    a line of mountains
    with blankets
    on their
hips.

Crawling Turtle II, Barry Wilson

---

1. Snowhare (snō´ her) *n.*: Snoeshoe hare, a large rabbitlike animal whose color changes from brown in summer to white in winter and whose broad feet resemble snowshoes.

2. mesa (mā´ sə) *n.*: Small, high plateau with steep sides.

▲ **Critical Viewing** What physical characteristics of the turtle allow it to go from "land to rock to water"? [**Connect**]

◆ **Build Vocabulary**

vertical (vʉr´ ti kəl) *adj.*: Straight up and down; upright

burrow (bʉr´ ō) *n.*: Passage or hole for shelter

gourds (gôrdz) *n.*: Dried, hollowed-out shell of fruits such as melons and pumpkins

If I can stop one Heart from breaking

Emily Dickinson

If I can stop one Heart from breaking
I shall not live in vain
If I can ease one Life the Aching
Or cool one Pain

5 Or help one fainting Robin
Unto his Nest again
I shall not live in Vain.

Guide for Responding

◆ LITERATURE AND YOUR LIFE

Reader's Response What makes you feel that you haven't lived "in vain"?

Thematic Focus In what way can performing or hearing "Drum Song" help you better understand the natural world?

Journal Writing Jot down ways in which you could help others, as Dickinson does with her poetry.

☑ Check Your Comprehension

1. (a) What is each of the animals in "Drum Song" doing? (b) What are the women in the last stanza doing?
2. In "If I can stop one Heart . . . ," what four things will keep the speaker from living in vain?

◆ Critical Thinking

INTERPRET

1. In "Drum Song," to whom is the word *listen* addressed in each stanza? Explain. **[Infer]**
2. Find details that support this description of "Drum Song": It tells how living things go about their business, and the drum is like the pulse of daily rhythms. **[Support]**
3. Judging by "If I can stop one Heart . . . ," what do you think Dickinson wanted poetry to do? Explain. **[Draw Conclusions]**

COMPARE LITERARY WORKS

4. If a drum goes best with "Drum Song," what instrument would you use with "If I can stop one Heart . . ."? Why? **[Compare and Contrast]**

Guide for Responding (continued)

◆ Reading Strategy

MAKE INFERENCES

Making inferences—using evidence to reach conclusions—helps you appreciate these poems. For example, the repetition of the ending question in "Forgotten Language" hints at its importance. Further thought reveals that the lines pose a dual question: *What was that language?* and *How did it vanish?*

1. What can you infer about De la Mare's attitude toward the moon in "Silver"? What evidence helped you make your inference?
2. What can you infer about the speaker of "Forgotten Language" from the line: "Once I heard and answered all the questions of the crickets"?
3. What inference can you make about women's place in the world, according to "Drum Song"?

◆ Build Vocabulary

USING WORD PAIRS

Some words with opposite or complementary meanings are often used in pairs, like *vertical* and *horizontal*. On your paper, use your knowledge of word pairs to fill in the blanks.

1. If *convex* means "curving outward," *concave* means ____?____.
2. If *longitude* is "a measure of east-west distance using lines drawn through the Earth's poles and at right angles to the equator," *latitude* is ____?____.

SPELLING STRATEGY

The long *o* sound in words may be spelled *ow*, as in *low* and *burrow*. On your paper, write these sentences, filling in the blanks with the correct spelling for the long *o* sound.

1. Look at the furr_ _s on the poet's forehead.
2. He feels sorr_ _ because he's forgotten a magical language.

USING THE WORD BANK

On your paper, answer each question true or false. Then, explain your answer.

1. To cross a street, you'd go in a *vertical* direction.
2. Animals that like to *burrow* can be found in the ground.
3. You might use *gourds* to carry water in a desert.

◆ Literary Focus

SOUND DEVICES

In these poems and others, **sound devices** that add to the music of the poems also add to the meaning. Think about what "Silver" would lose without its **rhymes**—chiming sounds at the ends of lines. Imagine "Drum Song" without the drumming **repetition** of "Listen" or "Forgotten Language" without whispering **alliteration** like "smiled in secret."

1. Within these poems, find another example of each sound device.
2. (a) Which sound device is more apparent in "Drum Song"? (b) How does use of the sound device enhance the poem's meaning?

◆ Build Grammar Skills

CORRECT USE OF ADJECTIVES AND ADVERBS

Don't confuse the use of **adjectives** and **adverbs.** Adjectives modify nouns, and adverbs modify verbs, adjectives, and other adverbs. A common mistake is the use of an adjective, rather than an adverb, to modify a verb. In "Silver," for example, using the adjectives *slow* and *silent* to modify "Walks" would be an error: "Slowly, silently, now the moon / Walks . . ." However, expressions like "go slow" in "Drum Song" are generally acceptable in informal speech.

Practice On your paper, write the correct modifier for each sentence. Then, explain your choice.

1. The snowhare drags its belly (awkward, awkwardly).
2. I spoke the language of flowers really (good, well).
3. The doves in their nests were sleeping (deep, deeply).
4. She spoke a (softly, soft) word to him to calm his heart.
5. I joined the (sad, sadly) crying of each falling flake.

Writing Application Write five sentences about a moonlit night in which you correctly use these adjectives and adverbs: *bright, brightly; silent, silently; quiet, quietly.*

Build Your Portfolio

 ## Idea Bank

Writing

1. **Stanza of Poetry** Choose an animal that is familiar to you, and write a stanza of poetry about it. Imitate the form of the stanzas in "Drum Song." Also, use alliteration and repetition to make your stanza sound musical.

2. **Public-Service Announcement** Write a public-service announcement in which you encourage people to volunteer their time helping others. You may want to model your announcement on Dickinson's "If I can stop one Heart from breaking."

3. **Inference About an Author** Using details from "Silver," make inferences about the ideas and feelings that De la Mare associates with the moon. Consider such details as rhythm, sound devices, and pictures created by the words.

Speaking and Listening

4. **Reading** Choose one of these poems to read aloud. Note on a copy of the poem where you will pause, stop, or stress repeated words. Don't pause at the ends of lines where there is no punctuation. **[Performing Arts Link]**

5. **Poem With Drums** Recite Wendy Rose's "Drum Song" and use a drum to accompany your reading. Tape-record your performance to listen to afterward. **[Music Link]**

Projects

6. **Sound Devices in Speeches [Group Activity]** With a few classmates, point out the use of sound devices in famous American political speeches. Use live readings, recordings, and video clips to demonstrate examples. **[Social Studies Link]**

7. **Report on Animal Communication** Using inference, summarize Silverstein's ideas about animal communication in "Forgotten Language." Then, compare and contrast his ideas with scientists' views on the subject. **[Science Link]**

 ## Writing Mini-Lesson

Song Lyrics

Shel Silverstein is a songwriter as well as a poet, so you can imagine hearing his "Forgotten Language" set to music. Using his poems and your favorite songs as a source of inspiration, write your own song lyrics. Write in any style that feels comfortable—rock, folk, rap, or romantic ballad.

Writing Skills Focus: Use Effective Repetition

As you know, song lyrics use **effective repetition.** A catchy phrase or verse, called a refrain, usually appears after every verse of the song. In fact, when you start to memorize the lyrics of a song, the refrain is often what you recall first. In adapting "Forgotten Language" as a song, Silverstein might use the last two lines as a refrain, repeating them after each verse:

Model From the Poem
How did it go?
How did it go?

Prewriting Jot down some of the thoughts and feelings that you'd like to express in your song lyrics. Think about which ideas you'd like to emphasize through repetition.

Drafting Refer to your prewriting notes as you draft the song lyrics. The phrase or verse you repeat—the refrain—should sum up the main thoughts and feelings you'd like to convey. Also, use devices like alliteration to make the refrain memorable.

Revising Read your lyrics to a classmate. If he or she doesn't find the refrain memorable, spice it up with alliteration, rhyme, or rhythms.

> ◆ **Grammar Application**
> Be sure that you haven't used an adjective to modify a verb, an adverb, or another adjective.

Guide for Reading

Meet the Authors:

M. Scott Momaday (1934–)

A Kiowa Indian, N. Scott Momaday is known for his poetry, his essays, and his Pulitzer Prize-winning novel, *House Made of Dawn* (1968).

Momaday says that "New World" was inspired by: ". . . the realization of himself in the New World, [where] the Indian has assumed a deep ethical regard for the earth and sky, a reverence for the natural world . . ."

William Stafford (1914–1993)

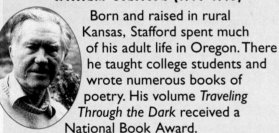

Born and raised in rural Kansas, Stafford spent much of his adult life in Oregon. There he taught college students and wrote numerous books of poetry. His volume *Traveling Through the Dark* received a National Book Award.

José Garcia Villa (1914–)

Garcia Villa came to the United States from the Philippines in 1930. He has published several volumes of poetry and was honored by the Poetry Society of America in 1959.

Alice Walker (1944–)

Walker's parents were farmers in rural Georgia, and she was the youngest of their eight children. Her family life inspired the poem "For My Sister Molly . . ." Family stories about her great-grandmother inspired her novel *The Color Purple*. That book won a Pulitzer Prize and was adapted as a feature film starring Whoopi Goldberg.

◆ LITERATURE AND YOUR LIFE

CONNECT YOUR EXPERIENCE

In your purse or wallet, you may carry around photos with a special meaning for you. They may show people who have touched your life or places where you feel at home. The images are out of sight but always near. These poems are also like wallets or purses. They hold images of people, places, or ideas that the poets want to save and keep close.

THEMATIC FOCUS: Relationships

In what way do these poems reveal insights about relationships?

◆ Background for Understanding

SCIENCE

Both "New World" and "One Time" deal with the passage of a day. The Earth's rotation around its axis creates day and night. This rotation exposes a region to the sun, producing daylight. Then, the Earth is turned away from the sun, producing night. A single day results from a complete spin of the Earth—which takes not twenty-four hours, but twenty-three hours, fifty-six minutes, and four seconds!

◆ Build Vocabulary

WORD ROOTS: -cede

To describe rotation or any movement, you might use a word with the root -cede, which means "to go." In "New World," for example, you'll read that "Meadows/recede . . ." *Recede* means "to move back": re- ("back") + -cede ("go").

WORD BANK

Which of these words from the poem is a noun? Check the Build Vocabulary box on page 867 to see if you chose correctly.

glistens
borne
low
hover
recede
luminance

New World ◆ One Time ◆ Lyric 17
For My Sister Molly Who in the Fifties

◆ Literary Focus

IMAGERY

Scientists use models to help you visualize the Earth's rotation and other phenomena. In a different way, poets help you see a scene by using **imagery,** language that appeals to your senses. Often an image is a visual description of color, shape, or movement. However, it can also appeal to senses other than sight.

Find images by looking for words that speak to your senses. In "New World," for example, you will find this image, which speaks to your sense of sight: "the earth/*glitters*/with leaves."

◆ Reading Strategy

USE YOUR SENSES

It's not enough to find the words that create an image. That would be reading with your mind alone, and poets want you to **use your senses** to experience imagery. They want you to call on your own sense memories to see, hear, taste, smell, and touch what the words are describing.

Use a chart like the one below to bring your senses into play as you read (one example is done for you):

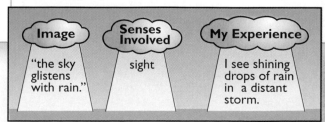

Image	Senses Involved	My Experience
"the sky glistens with rain."	sight	I see shining drops of rain in a distant storm.

New World

N. Scott Momaday

1.

First Man,
behold:
the earth
glitters
5   with leaves;
the sky
glistens
with rain.
Pollen[1]
10   is borne
on winds
that low
and lean
upon
15   mountains.
Cedars
blacken
the slopes—
and pines.

Wallowa Lake, Harley, Abby Aldrich Rockefeller Folk Art Center, Williamsburg, VA

1. pollen (päl´ ən) *n.:* Yellow, powderlike male cells formed in the stamen of a flower.

▲ **Critical Viewing** What aspects of this painting convey the idea of a "new world"? **[Interpret]**

Jack's Fireplace, Jack Palance

2.

20   At dawn
eagles
hie[2] and
hover
above
25   the plain
where light
gathers
in pools.
Grasses
30   shimmer
and shine.
Shadows
withdraw
and lie
35   away
like smoke.

2. hie (hī) *v.:* Hurry or hasten.

◄ **Critical Viewing** Which stanza of the poem does this painting best illustrate? Explain. **[Connect]**

3.

At noon
turtles
enter
40 slowly
into
the warm
dark loam.[3]
Bees hold
45 the swarm.
Meadows
<u>recede</u>
through planes
of heat
50 and pure
distance.

4.

At dusk
the gray
foxes
55 stiffen
in cold;
blackbirds
are fixed
in the
60 branches.
Rivers
follow
the moon,
the long
65 white track
of the
full moon.

---

3. loam (lōm) *n.:*
Rich, dark soil.

◆ Build Vocabulary

glistens (glis´ ənz) *v.:* Shines; sparkles

borne (bôrn) *v.:* Carried

low (lō) *v.:* Make the typical sound that a cow makes; moo

hover (huv´ ər) *v.:* Flutter in the air

recede (ri sēd´) *v.:* Move away

◆ Guide for Responding

◆ LITERATURE AND YOUR LIFE

Reader's Response How is the world you live in different from and similar to the one described in the poem?

Thematic Focus In what ways are different aspects of nature interrelated?

Sketch Using pencil or pen, quickly sketch one of the images from "New World."

☑ Check Your Comprehension

1. Whom does Momaday address at the start of the poem?
2. What are the main features in the landscape that Momaday describes?
3. Summarize the progression of time in the poem.

◆ Critical Thinking

INTERPRET

1. Who is "First Man"? **[Infer]**
2. What do you think Momaday wants "First Man" to feel as he beholds his world? Why? **[Infer]**
3. What meaning or meanings does the title of the poem suggest? Explain. **[Connect]**
4. How is the poem's title related to its central message? **[Draw Conclusions]**

EVALUATE

5. Would this poem work better with long lines? Why or why not? **[Assess]**

APPLY

6. In what way is the world new every day? **[Speculate]**

One Time

William Stafford

When evening had flowed between houses
and paused on the schoolground, I met
Hilary's blind little sister following
the gray smooth railing still warm from the
    sun
5   with her hand; and she stood by the edge
holding her face upward waiting
while the last light found her cheek
and her hair, and then on over the trees.

You could hear the great sprinkler arm
10 of water find and then leave the pavement,
and pigeons telling each other their dreams
or the dreams they would have. We were
deep in the well of shadow by then, and I
held out my hand, saying, "Tina, it's me—
15 Hilary says I should tell you it's dark,
and, oh, Tina, it is. Together now—"

And I reached, our hands touched,
and we found our way home.

▲ Critical Viewing Do the children in this photograph seem to share a relationship like the one described in the poem? Explain. [Assess]

Beyond Literature

Science Connection

Braille The girl in "One Time" is blind, and the poem's speaker helps guide her home at sundown. The lives of the blind, however, are not wholly dependent on others, partly because of Louis Braille. Braille (1809–1852) was a Frenchman who became blind at the age of three. At the age of fifteen, he developed a system of writing for the blind.

Braille is a code of small, raised dots that are read by touch. Various arrangements of six dots stand for letters, numbers, and punctuation. Although Braille was developed in 1824, it is still widely used today.

Cross-Curricular Activity
Research the Braille system, and create a chart showing the arrangements of dots and what they stand for. Then, spell out your name and address using Braille.

Lyric 17

José Garcia Villa

First, a poem must be magical,
Then musical as a sea-gull.
It must be a brightness moving
And hold secret a bird's flowering.
5   It must be slender as a bell,
And it must hold fire as well.
It must have the wisdom of bows
And it must kneel like a rose.
It must be able to hear
10 The <u>luminance</u> of dove and deer.
It must be able to hide
What it seeks, like a bride.
And over all I would like to hover
God, smiling from the poem's cover.

◆ **Build Vocabulary**

luminance (lo̅o̅´ mə nəns) *n.*: Brightness; brilliance

Guide for Responding

◆ Literature and Your Life

Reader's Response In answer to "Lyric 17," tell what you think "a poem must be."

Thematic Focus In what way is the relationship described in "One Time" special?

Journal Writing Thinking of "One Time," describe a quiet but meaningful moment that you once experienced.

☑ Check Your Comprehension

1. (a) Who takes part in the moment described in "One Time"? (b) At what time of day does this moment take place?
2. Briefly describe what happens in the poem.
3. According to "Lyric 17," what are three of the qualities a poem must have?

◆ Critical Thinking

INTERPRET

1. Find a detail in "One Time" that creates a sense of mystery. Then, explain your choice. **[Support]**
2. What makes the moment described in "One Time" so memorable? Explain. **[Analyze]**
3. In what ways does "Lyric 17" make poetry seem mysterious? Explain. **[Connect]**

EVALUATE

4. Is "Lyric 17" effective as a definition of poetry? Why or why not? **[Evaluate]**

COMPARE LITERARY WORKS

5. Compare and contrast the descriptions of dusk in "One Time" and stanza 4 of "New World." **[Compare and Contrast]**

For My Sister Molly Who in the Fifties
Alice Walker

For my Sister Molly Who in the Fifties
Once made a fairy rooster from
Mashed potatoes
Whose eyes I forget
5   But green onions were his tail
And his two legs were carrot sticks
A tomato slice his crown.
Who came home on vacation
When the sun was hot
10 and cooked
and cleaned
And minded least of all
The children's questions
A million or more
15 Pouring in on her
Who had been to school
And knew (and told us too) that certain
Words were no longer good
And taught me not to say us for we
20 No matter what "Sonny said" up the
road.

FOR MY SISTER MOLLY WHO IN THE FIFTIES
Knew Hamlet well and read into the night
And coached me in my songs of Africa
25 A continent I never knew
But learned to love
Because "they" she said could carry
A tune
And spoke in accents never heard
30 In Eatonton.[1]
Who read from *Prose and Poetry*
And loved to read "Sam McGee from
   Tennessee"
On nights the fire was burning low
And Christmas wrapped in angel hair[2]
35 And I for one prayed for snow.

---

1. **Eatonton** (ēt′ ən tən): Town in Georgia.
2. **angel hair:** Fine, white, filmy Christmas tree decoration.

▲ **Critical Viewing** How would you describe the relationship between the girls in the photograph? **[Infer]**

WHO IN THE FIFTIES
Knew all the written things that made
Us laugh and stories by
The hour   Waking up the story buds
40   Like fruit. Who walked among the flowers
And brought them inside the house
And smelled as good as they
And looked as bright.
Who made dresses, braided
45   Hair. Moved chairs about
Hung things from walls
Ordered baths
Frowned on wasp bites
And seemed to know the endings
50   Of all the tales
I had forgot.

Guide for Responding

◆ LITERATURE AND YOUR LIFE

Reader's Response Have you looked up to someone the way the speaker looked up to her sister? Explain.

Thematic Focus How would you describe the relationship between the speaker and her sister?

Personality Profile Using the poem as evidence, jot down a brief profile of Molly.

☑ Check Your Comprehension

1. How does Molly help take care of the house?
2. Name three ways in which Molly takes physical care of the younger children.
3. List three things that the speaker learned from Molly.

◆ Critical Thinking

INTERPRET

1. What do you think is the difference in age between the speaker and Molly? Explain. **[Infer]**
2. (a) How does Molly reveal her creative spirit? (b) How does Molly awaken the creative spirit in the children? **[Analyze]**
3. In what ways does Molly bring home the world to her little sister? **[Support]**

EVALUATE

4. Is the speaker successful in expressing her appreciation for her sister? Why or why not? **[Make a Judgment]**

COMPARE LITERARY WORKS

5. In what way is "For My Sister Molly . . ." a poem of many moments while "One Time" is a poem of a single moment? **[Compare and Contrast]**

Guide for Responding (continued)

◆ Reading Strategy

USE YOUR SENSES

By using **your senses,** you saw, heard, touched, tasted, and smelled what these poems described. Reading "New World," for example, you heard the winds "low" like cows and saw "Grasses/shimmer."

Tell how the sense listed next to each poem helped you experience one description in it:

1. "New World"—touch
2. "One Time"—hearing
3. "Lyric 17"—sight
4. "For My Sister Molly Who . . ."—smell

◆ Build Vocabulary

USING THE WORD ROOT -cede

Sometimes the root -cede- is spelled -ceed. Match the -cede or -ceed ("to go") words in the first column with their meanings in the second column:

1. recede   **a.** to go apart
2. secede   **b.** to go forward
3. proceed   **c.** to go back

SPELLING STRATEGY

Only three words ending in the *seed* sound are spelled *ceed: exceed, succeed,* and *proceed.* In all other words, this ending sound is spelled *cede.* On your paper, identify and correct the misspelled words:

1. secede   3. recede   5. succede
2. preceed   4. exceed

USING THE WORD BANK

On your paper, write a sentence that is a response to each direction:

1. Use the word *glistens* to describe a lake.
2. Describe a flying kite using the word *borne.*
3. Use the word *low* in a description of barnyard sounds.
4. Paint a word picture of a hawk using the word *hover.*
5. Using the word *recede,* describe a glacier's movement.
6. Use the word *luminance* to compare a flashlight and a firefly.

◆ Literary Focus

IMAGERY

In addition to giving you ideas to think about and emotions to feel, each of these poems gives you a world to experience. It does this by using **imagery,** or language that appeals to your senses. "New World," for example, has sensory words like "*shimmer*/and *shine*," which help you see an image.

As in many poems, the imagery of "New World" also supports the theme. Momaday wants you to feel the wonder of nature, so he uses images that capture the beauty of the natural world.

1. Identify two images in each of these poems. Then, explain why they are images.
2. Choose a poem other than "New World," and show how its imagery supports its message or overall feeling.

◆ Build Grammar Skills

PRONOUNS IN COMPARISONS WITH *than* OR *as*

In some **comparisons using *than* or *as,*** one or more words are implied rather than stated. If you mentally supply the missing words, you can easily select the pronoun form to use. Here's an example from "For My Sister Molly . . .":

> And smelled as good as *they* [smelled]
> (*They* is the correct pronoun, not *them*.)

Practice On your paper, fill in the missing word or words for each comparison. Then, choose the right pronoun form.

1. Hilary's sister sensed the light as well as (him, he).
2. No one loved the evening better than (they, them).
3. Who defines poetry better than (he, him)?
4. No one learned grammar as well as (us, we).
5. Her sister looked as bright as (they, them).

Writing Application Use three *than* or *as* comparisons with pronouns to discuss the performances of athletes. Be sure you choose the correct form of each pronoun.

Build Your Portfolio

 Idea Bank

Writing

1. **Description** Support Momaday's theme about the wonder of nature with an image of your own. Appealing to one or more senses, describe a scene from the natural world.

2. **License-Plate Proposal** Suggest an image to appear on the automobile license plates of your state. Describe your image, and explain why it suggests the values or beauty of your region. **[Career Link]**

3. **Essay** Choose one of the poems in this section, and write an essay in which you explore its imagery. Give examples from the work to support your views.

Speaking and Listening

4. **Choral Reading [Group Activity]** With several classmates, give a group reading of "New World" or one of the other poems. Divide the poem into sections, and have one or more readers perform each section. **[Performing Arts Link]**

5. **Tribute** Publicly thank someone who has positively influenced your life with an oral tribute. Deliver the tribute to your classmates. Tape-record your tribute to analyze afterward.

Projects

6. **Presentation** Research events in space that create morning, noon, and night. Make a model or poster that illustrates the process. Then, present your findings to the class. **[Science Link; Career Link]**

7. **Captioned Picture** Illustrate an image from one of these poems with a collage, oil painting, or watercolor. Use the words of the poem's image as a caption for your illustration. Display your finished picture in the classroom. **[Art Link]**

 Writing Mini-Lesson

Free-Verse Poem

Except for "Lyric 17," the poems in this group are in free verse. They are unrhymed and do not make use of regular rhythms. Imitate them by writing your own free-verse poem. Use line lengths and rhythms that seem right for the subject you choose. Also, focus on creating a single, vivid image.

Writing Skills Focus: Dominant Image

By using a **dominant image** that runs through your whole poem, you can create a powerful effect. In "One Time," for instance, the disappearing light of day is such an image:

Model From the Poem

"When evening had flowed between houses . . ."

"while the last light found her cheek . . ."

"deep in the well of shadow . . ."

Prewriting Write about something you can experience or imagine experiencing. Then, freewrite about your subject, letting the lines break wherever you like. Scan your freewriting to find a dominant image you'll use.

Drafting Let your prewriting notes suggest the best line lengths and rhythms for your subject. Momaday, for example, uses short lines to stress each word. Also, focus on your dominant image throughout the poem.

Revising Have several classmates read your poem, and ask them to describe the dominant image. If they get it wrong, add sensory language throughout the poem to help you better convey that image.

> ◆ **Grammar Application**
>
> In comparisons with *than* or *as,* be sure you have used the right form of the pronoun.

The Wind Beneath My Wings

Larry Henley and Jeff Silbar

It must have been cold there in my shadow,
To never have sunlight on your face.
You were content to let me shine, that's your way,
You always walked a step behind.
5   So, I was the one with all the glory,
While you were the one with all the strength.
A beautiful face without a name for so long,
A beautiful smile to hide the pain.

Did you ever know that you're my hero,
10 And everything I would like to be?
I can fly higher than an eagle,
'Cause you are the wind beneath my wings.

It might have appeared to go unnoticed,
But I've got it all here in my heart.
15 I want you to know I know the truth,
Of course I know it,
I would be nothing without you.

Did you ever know that you're my hero,
And everything I would like to be?
20 I can fly higher than an eagle,
'Cause you are the wind beneath my wings.

Fly, fly, fly away,
You let me fly so high.
Oh, fly, fly,
25 So high against the sky,
So high I almost touch the sky.
Thank you, thank you, thank God for you,
The wind beneath my wings.

---

1. Explain the meaning of the phrase "wind beneath my wings."
2. Name three things the speaker appreciates about her "hero."
3. In what ways are "For My Sister Molly . . ." and "The Wind Beneath My Wings" similar and different?

Guide for Reading

Meet the Authors:

Edwin Arlington Robinson (1869–1935)

Robinson was raised in Gardiner, Maine. This small town served as the model for Tilbury Town, the fictional setting of his finest poems. Many of his poems grew out of his childhood observations of Gardiner and focus on people's inner struggles.

Philip Larkin (1922–1985)

Larkin was a British poet whose clear-eyed, honest writing won him international fame. His poetry speaks of everyday realities, sometimes discouragingly, but is quietly haunted by realities beyond everyday life. In "Solar," he focuses on one of these greater realities: the sun.

Donald Justice (1925–   )

Donald Justice was awarded the Pulitzer Prize for his *Selected Poems* and the Bollingen Prize for his lifetime achievement in poetry.

THE STORY BEHIND THE POEM

Justice's poem was inspired by this traditional story set in southwestern Asia: A servant meets Death, a female, in the marketplace of Baghdad. Believing that Death has threatened him, the servant flees to the city of Samarra. The servant's employer asks Death why she threatened his servant. Death explains that she didn't threaten the servant: She was surprised to see him in Baghdad because she knew she had an appointment with him that night in Samarra!

◆ LITERATURE AND YOUR LIFE

CONNECT YOUR EXPERIENCE

A movie *star*, a *jackknifed* tractor-trailer, a *bookworm*: These phrases are so common that you're often unaware they are comparisons. However, you can't miss the unusual and lively comparisons in these poems.

THEMATIC FOCUS: Respecting Nature

As you read, notice how the natural world inspires these poets.

◆ Background for Understanding

SCIENCE

In "Solar," Larkin uses a poetic language of comparison to describe the sun. Scientifically speaking, our sun is classified as a yellow star. It is 93 million miles from Earth. Basically a ball of gases, the sun provides the heat and light necessary to sustain life on Earth.

◆ Build Vocabulary

COMMONLY CONFUSED WORDS: *continuously* AND *continually*

Larkin writes in "Solar" that the sun is "Continuously exploding." Don't confuse *continuously*, which means "without interruption," with *continually*, which means "occurring again and again."

WORD BANK

Which of these words from the poems comes from the old word *becen*, meaning "a beacon or sign"? Check the Build Vocabulary Box on page 879 to see if you chose correctly.

hovers
legions
unrecompensed
continuously
scythe
beckoned
gestures

The Dark Hills ◆ Solar
◆ Incident in a Rose Garden ◆

◆ Literary Focus
FIGURATIVE LANGUAGE

Based on comparisons, **figurative language** is an imaginative use of words that goes beyond dictionary meanings. A **simile** is a comparison of two apparently unlike items that uses the words *like* or *as*. A **metaphor** is a description of one item as if it were another, without using *like* or *as*. **Personification** is a description of something nonhuman as if it were human.

Use a chart like the one below to identify the figures of speech as you read:

◆ Reading Strategy
RESPOND

Poetry will sleep on a page unless you **respond** to it, bringing your own experience to the words. Use your memory and senses to picture what the poet describes. Feel the beat of the rhythm, just as you do when you listen to a song.

When reading these poems, focus your response on the figurative language. Picture the items being compared. No matter how different they are, search for the hidden similarities that the poet has found.

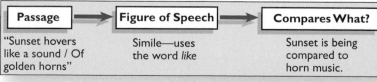

Passage	→	Figure of Speech	→	Compares What?
"Sunset hovers like a sound / Of golden horns"		Simile—uses the word *like*		Sunset is being compared to horn music.

THE DARK HILLS

Edwin Arlington Robinson

Dark hills at evening in the west,
Where sunset <u>hovers</u> like a sound
Of golden horns that sang to rest
Old bones of warriors under ground,
5   Far now from all the bannered ways
Where flash the <u>legions</u> of the sun,
You fade—as if the last of days
Were fading, and all wars were done.

▼ **Critical Viewing** Are the dark hills in this painting
inviting or forbidding? Explain. [**Assess**]

Red Hills, Lake George, 1927, Georgia O'Keeffe, The Phillips Collection, Washington, DC

SOLAR[1]

PHILIP LARKIN

Suspended lion face
Spilling at the centre[2]
Of an unfurnished sky
How still you stand,
5 And how unaided
Single stalkless flower
You pour unrecompensed.

The eye sees you
Simplified by distance
10 Into an origin,
Your petalled head of flames
Continuously exploding.
Heat is the echo of your
Gold.

15 Coined there among
Lonely horizontals
You exist openly.
Our needs hourly
Climb and return like angels.
20 Unclosing like a hand,
You give for ever.

---

1. **solar:** Of or having to do with the sun.
2. **centre:** British spelling of *center*.

Guide for Responding

◆ LITERATURE AND YOUR LIFE

Reader's Response Briefly describe a time when you saw the sun in a fresh way—whether at dawn, midday, or sunset.

Thematic Focus Describe the element of nature common to both these poems.

Monologue Write and deliver a brief speech the sun might make in response to "Solar."

☑ Check Your Comprehension

1. To what does Robinson compare the sunset in "The Dark Hills"?
2. List three things to which Larkin compares the sun in "Solar."

Critical Thinking

INTERPRET

1. Find two phrases in "The Dark Hills" that help you experience the sunset. Explain. **[Analyze]**
2. What overall feeling do the details in "The Dark Hills" create? Why? **[Interpret]**
3. Does Larkin organize "Solar" as a story or as a series of descriptions? Explain. **[Analyze]**
4. How do the last four lines of "Solar" reveal Larkin's attitude toward the sun? **[Infer]**

COMPARE LITERARY WORKS

5. In what way do these two poems communicate opposite moods? **[Compare and Contrast]**

Incident in a Rose Garden

Donald Justice

China Roses, Broadway, Alfred William Parsons, Christopher Wood Gallery, London, UK

◀ **Critical View-
ing** Why would
a figure like
Death be so
startling to
encounter in a
setting such as
this? [Connect]

	Gardener:	Sir, I encountered Death Just now among our roses. Thin as a <u>scythe</u> he stood there.
5		I knew him by his pictures. He had his black coat on, Black gloves, a broad black hat.
		I think he would have spoken. Seeing his mouth stood open. Big it was, with white teeth.
10		As soon as he <u>beckoned</u>, I ran. I ran until I found you. Sir, I am quitting my job.
15		I want to see my sons Once more before I die. I want to see California.
	Master:	Sir, you must be that stranger Who threatened my gardener. This is my property, sir.
20	Death:	I welcome only friends here. Sir, I knew your father. And we were friends at the end.
		As for your gardener, I did not threaten him. Old men mistake my <u>gestures</u>.
25		I only meant to ask him To show me to his master. I take it you are he?

◆ Build Vocabulary

scythe (sīth) *n.*: Long tool with a single-edged blade used in cutting tall grass

beckoned (bek´ ənd) *v.*: Summoned by a silent motion; called

gestures (jes´ chərz) *n.*: Movements used to convey an idea, emotion, or intention

Guide for Responding

◆ LITERATURE AND YOUR LIFE

Reader's Response Do you find this poem amusing or alarming? Explain.

Thematic Focus What message about nature does this poem convey?

Journal Writing As the Gardener, write a diary entry describing your encounter with Death.

☑ Check Your Comprehension

1. Describe Death as he appears in the poem.
2. What does Death do to make the Gardener run away?
3. Paraphrase what the Master says to Death.
4. Whom does Death really want?

◆ Critical Thinking

1. In what way do lines 25–27 give you a surprising view of the Gardener's flight? **[Connect]**
2. What does Death mean when he tells the Master, "I knew your father. / And we were friends at the end"? **[Interpret]**
3. Why do you think old men "mistake" Death's "gestures"? **[Interpret]**
4. What do you think Death wants from the Master? **[Infer]**
5. The Master is full of pride. What lesson does he learn? **[Draw Conclusions]**

APPLY

6. Is there a lesson about life that you can take from this poem? Explain. **[Apply]**

COMPARE LITERARY WORKS

7. Compare "Incident . . ." with the traditional story that inspired it (see The Story Behind the Poem, p. 874). **[Compare and Contrast]**

Guide for Responding (continued)

◆ Reading Strategy

RESPOND

You **responded** to the figurative language in these poems by thinking about the comparisons the poets made. For example, you may have responded to Larkin's comparison of the sun to a "lion face."

1. Which image or phrase in "The Dark Hills" provoked the strongest response in you? Explain.

2. How did you respond to the image of Death in a rose garden? Would your response have been different if Death had appeared in a more sinister setting? Why or why not?

◆ Build Vocabulary

USING COMMONLY CONFUSED WORDS

Note these commonly confused words: *continuously* ("without interruption") and *continually* ("frequently repeated"); *beside* ("next to") and *besides* ("in addition to"); and *imply* ("suggest") and *infer* ("deduce"). On your paper, correct any misused italicized words, and explain your changes:

The Gardener *implies* from the stranger's behavior that danger threatens. Death then stands *besides* the Master, saying that old men *continually* mistake his gestures.

SPELLING STRATEGY

The *uh* sound is sometimes spelled with an *o* rather than a *u*, as in *hovers* and *other*. Working on your own paper, correct any of the following words that are misspelled.

1. of   2. luvers   3. bruther   4. abuve   5. mother

USING THE WORD BANK

On your paper, answer each question:

1. What's the difference between *hovers* and *soars*?
2. What's the difference between *legions* and *several*?
3. What's the difference between *unrecompensed* and *paid*?
4. What's the difference between *continuously* and *continually*?
5. What's the difference between *scythe* and *ax*?
6. What's the difference between *beckoned* and *dismissed*?

◆ Literary Focus

FIGURATIVE LANGUAGE

These poets enable you to see the world in a fresh way by using **figurative language,** such as **simile** (comparison with *like* or *as*), **metaphor** (comparison without *like* or *as*), and **personification** (giving human qualities to the nonhuman). If "The Dark Hills" didn't use comparisons to describe a sunset, you'd think only of a day's end. Through simile ("sunset hovers like a sound") and metaphor ("legions of the sun"), the poem suggests the end of "all wars."

1. Show how "Solar" uses metaphor and simile to suggest that the sun is living and giving.

2. Without personification, could "Incident in a Rose Garden" effectively convey its message about death? Explain.

◆ Build Grammar Skills

CORRECT USE OF *like* AND *as*

Like and **as** are sometimes confused. *Like* is a preposition introducing a prepositional phrase. *As* may be a preposition, but *as* (or *as if* or *as though*) is also a subordinating conjunction in a clause with a noun and a verb. Don't use *like* as a conjunction.

Like: Where sunset hovers *like* a sound/Of golden horns . . . (prepositional phrase: like a sound)

As: You fade—*as if* [not *like*] the last of days/Were fading . . . (subordinating conjunction)

Practice On your paper, choose *like* or a form of *as* for each sentence. Then, explain your choice.

1. (Like, As) Larkin, I feel strongly about the sun.
2. The Master acts (like, as if) he doesn't recognize Death.
3. Robinson's poem is itself (as, like) a horn melody.
4. Larkin addresses the sun (like, as though) it were a person.
5. (Like, As) I was telling you, Robinson is a great poet.

Writing Application On your paper, write a description of the moon using two sentences with *like* and two with *as*.

Build Your Portfolio

 ## Idea Bank

Writing

1. Personification Create a cartoon character based on the personification of a natural phenomenon, like a hurricane. Describe what the character would look like, wear, and carry. Also, think of an appropriate name for the character.

2. Report on Hidden Figures of Speech Find five similes or metaphors that are hidden in common words and phrases, like *skyscraper*. Then, explain how each of your choices is a simile, metaphor, or personification.

3. Figurative Definition Write a definition of a word or a concept, like justice, using similes and metaphors rather than synonyms.

Speaking and Listening

4. Readers Theatre [Group Activity] With a few classmates, give a dramatic reading of "Incident in a Rose Garden." You can remain seated, but you should read your parts with expression. **[Performing Arts Link]**

5. Oral Interpretation Read one of these poems aloud for the class. Remember to pause briefly for commas and longer for end marks. Don't automatically stop at the ends of lines where there is no punctuation. **[Performing Arts Link]**

Projects

6. Presentation and Discussion Describe a natural phenomenon using both scientific terms and figures of speech. Then, present both descriptions to the class, and invite questions from the class. **[Science Link]**

7. Personification in Art Find paintings in which Death is personified, as in Albert Pinkham Ryder's *The Race Track* or *Death on a Pale Horse*. Display copies of these for the class, and write captions comparing the personifications. **[Art Link]**

 ## Writing Mini-Lesson

Dialogue

"Incident in a Rose Garden" is a dialogue in the form of a poem. Write your own dialogue, using two or more characters. Imitate "Incident in a Rose Garden" by making your dialogue into a complete scene in which characters face and solve a problem. You can have your characters speak in prose rather than poetry. However, they should sometimes use figurative language.

Writing Skills Focus:
Use Figurative Language

When characters use **figurative language,** they add to the drama and interest of what they're saying. For example, the Gardener in "Incident . . ." uses a simile, a comparison with *like* or *as*, to describe Death:

Model From the Poem
Sir, I encountered Death/Just now among our roses./*Thin* as a *scythe* he stood there.

Prewriting Invent two or three characters, and give them a problem to solve. Plan how the problem will build to a climax and be resolved.

Drafting Have the characters engage with each other to solve the problem you have given them. Step into the shoes of each character as you write his or her words. The more you identify with the characters and get excited with them, the more naturally they'll "speak" in figurative language.

Revising Be sure that your dialogue introduces and resolves a problem. Also, check that your characters use some figurative language—metaphors as well as similes.

◆ **Grammar Application**
Check your dialogue to be sure you've used *like* and *as* correctly.

Poem

Writing Process Workshop

As you can see from this unit, just about anything can become a poet's subject: memories, sports, sounds, or love. Now it's time to try your hand at writing a poem. Choose a moment of your own experience that was important to you—something that was especially fun, exciting, sad, frustrating, or beautiful. You might write a lyric poem or a narrative poem. It might rhyme or it might not. The important part is that no one else could have written it—just you.

Use these Writing Skills, covered in the Writing Mini-Lessons in this part, to help you:

Writing Skills Focus

▶ **Use repetition** of a key word, phrase, or line for emphasis and rhythm. (See p. 861.)

▶ **Create a dominant image** that guides your writing and your readers' reading. (See p. 871.)

▶ **Use figurative language** to give your poem interest and variety. (See p. 881.)

One young poet wrote this lyric poem after a weekend camping trip:

MODEL

Northern Lights

Someone took a paint box ① and a black
   velvet night,
Blended pinks and turquoise until she got
   it right.
She brushed and she studied and stood
   back very far,
Then threw glitter—and each piece
   became a star. ②
She watercolored streaks of yellow, gold,
   and red,
Then put away her paint box ③ and
   snuggled back in bed.

① The image of a painter painting dominates this poem.

② The metaphor "each piece became a star" provides an interesting comparison.

③ Repeating *paint box* emphasizes the dominant image and brings the poem full circle.

Prewriting

Choose a Topic Choose a subject or a topic for your poem. You may want to choose a topic that is unique and meaningful, startling, frightening, hilarious, or lovely. Here are a few suggestions to spark your imagination:

> ### Topic Ideas
> - A person's face
> - An animal you've loved
> - A delicious food
> - A machine you think is cool

Make a Sensory Chart Don't just rely on your sense of sight. Include sounds (and sound words), tastes—even smells. Appeal to the sense of touch. Make your poem as rich as the experience itself.

Decide on a Dominant Image What is the main idea you want to convey? For example, is your dog funny, sad, clumsy, old, crazy, or lazy? Is he your best friend or a big pest? Once you settle on a dominant impression, make the details of your poem contribute to it.

Drafting

Use Figurative Language Compare the subject of your poem to various things, people, or places. To create a simile, connect the image with *like* or *as*. To create a metaphor, describe your subject as if it were the thing to which you're comparing it. Other forms of figurative language include personification—investing your subject with humanlike qualities—and hyperbole—greatly exaggerating your subject's qualities or abilities.

Repeat for Effect If you've got a great line—or a great word—repeat it for emphasis and rhythm.

Make Every Word Count Since poems are short, take the time to make every word ring with truth. For example, in the model poem about the Northern Lights, the poet chose *turquoise* instead of just *blue, brushed* and *watercolored* instead of just *painted,* and *threw* instead of just *put.* Use a dictionary or thesaurus to discover wonderfully rich words.

APPLYING LANGUAGE SKILLS: Avoiding Clichés

A cliché is an expression that is overused. Avoid clichés in your writing. Instead, rephrase your ideas or create new, fresh comparisons.

Cliché: As happy as a clam

New comparison: As happy as a playful puppy

Newly phrased: Radiating happiness

Cliché: Raining cats and dogs

Newly phrased: Wall to wall rain

Personification: The rain viciously pelted the houses.

Practice Rewrite these clichés to convey original ideas:

1. Quiet as a mouse
2. A deafening silence
3. Like a ton of bricks
4. Bubbling over with enthusiasm
5. Mother Nature

Writing Application Avoid using clichés in your poetry. Rephrase or create new comparisons.

Writer's Solution Connection Language Lab

For help with figurative language, complete the lessons on Simile and Metaphor in the Choosing Words unit.

APPLYING LANGUAGE SKILLS: Choosing the Correct Homophone

Words that sound alike but have different meanings and spellings are called homophones. Check to be sure that you've selected the correct homophone in your writing.

Examples:

to, two, too

their, they're, there

threw, through

so, sew, sow

Practice On your paper, write the correct homophone for each passage.

1. (To, Too, Two) children wanted to go, (to, too, two).
2. (They're, Their) doing (they're, their) homework now.
3. How can I (bare, bear) life without you?
4. (Who's, Whose) papers are these?
5. (Night, knight) fell over the town.

Writing Application In your poem, be sure you've chosen the correct homophones.

Writer's Solution Connection Writing Lab

For help revising, use the Proofreading Checklist for Poetry in the Creative Writing tutorial.

Revising

Use a Checklist Use the Writing Skills Focus points on page 882 as a revision checklist. An effective poem usually contains these elements.

Read It Aloud Read your poem aloud to yourself or to a peer. Consider adding repetition to emphasize ideas. Be sure the figurative language you've used is fresh and original; if not, delete it. Lastly, delete or revise details that do not support the dominant image you've created.

Keep It Short The delete key can be the poet's best friend. If some lines in your poem are weak or not really working, don't be afraid to cross them out. Your poem will be better for it.

REVISION MODEL

① It is Twilight

② Like a purple cloud

Soft purple hazy

End of day

Sleeping

③ dwindling dwindling

Dwindling fading ebbing

Night

① To make the image more dominant, the writer deleted "It is."
② This simile lends interest to the poem.
③ Repetition makes this line more memorable and to the point.

Publishing and Presenting

Classroom Collect poems into a class anthology in which everyone contributes one poem. Together, choose a title. Have volunteers design a cover, create a table of contents, and even write a brief introduction. If possible, make sure each contributor gets one copy to keep.

Podium With classmates, hold a poetry reading in your class or school. Take turns reading your poetry.

Real-World Reading Skills Workshop

Strategies for Success

Occasionally you have to read something that appears difficult, such as a technical manual or a research article. The sentence structure and vocabulary can look overwhelming. The following strategies can help you break down difficult texts so that you can get what you need from them:

Preview the Selection First, get an overall sense of the work. Note its title, which provides you with clues to its content. Then, look at the organization of the piece, its length, its chapters or sections, and its use of study questions. If there are subtitles, read them for clues to the content.

Break It Into Sections Tackle only one section at a time. Use captions, highlighted words, footnotes, and sidenotes. These aids offer additional information to help you understand the text. Next, go through the text sentence by sentence. If a sentence is long, break it into parts where commas appear. Read the text once for general meaning. Then, go back and reread those parts you didn't understand fully.

Decipher the Vocabulary As you read, note any words that are unfamiliar. Try to figure out a word's meaning from its context—how it's used in the passage. If this doesn't work, look up the word in a dictionary before rereading.

✔ Here are situations in which you might use these strategies for breaking down difficult texts:
▶ Reading Shakespearean plays and sonnets
▶ Reading school texts
▶ Reading a contract

Apply the Strategies

Answer the following questions about the passage below. Use the strategies from this lesson to help you.

1. Scan the passage, and break it into sections.

2. Use context clues to determine the meaning of *pedagogy, valor, amaranthine.*

3. What is *Crispin Crispian?* How do you know?

4. What is the general meaning of Prince Hal's speech?

The Use of Shakespeare's Speeches in Military Leadership

For many years, Shakespeare's speeches have been part of the pedagogy of military academies as examples of inspiration, leadership, and valor.

The Inspirational Speech

Prince Hal inspires his men with his own bravery and promises them not only unending, amaranthine glory but brotherhood with him—their noble and extraordinary king and leader:

This story shall the good man teach his son:
And Crispin Crispian[1] shall ne'er go by,
From this day to the ending of the world,
But we in it shall be remembered—
We few, we happy few, we band of brothers.

Henry V: 4.3

1. The feast day of St. Crispin, October 25.

Grammar Review

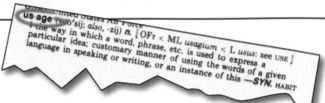

us·age (yōo'sij; also, -zij) *n.* [OFr < ML *usagium* < L *usus:* see USE] 1 the way in which a word, phrase, etc. is used to express a particular idea; customary manner of using the words of a given language in speaking or writing, or an instance of this —**SYN.** HABIT

Correct Use of Adjectives and Adverbs
Do not confuse the use of adjectives and adverbs (see p. 860). Use adjectives to modify nouns and pronouns; use adverbs to modify verbs, adjectives, and adverbs. A common mistake is to use an adjective instead of an adverb to modify a verb.

Incorrect: The turtle addressed in "Drum Song" probably didn't move very *quick.* (adjective)

Correct: The turtle addressed in "Drum Song" probably didn't move very *quickly.* (adverb modifying the verb *move*)

Pronouns in Comparisons Sometimes it is difficult to know which pronouns to use in a comparison using *than* or *as* (see p. 870). In these comparisons, one or more words are implied instead of stated. In order to select the correct pronoun, mentally fill in the missing words, and use the pronoun you would use if the comparison were complete.

Incorrect: Molly was a better sister than *her.*

Correct: Molly was a better sister than *she* [was].

When you supply the missing words, you can see that you need a pronoun in the subjective case to complete the comparison.

Correct Use of *Like* and *As* The word *like* is commonly misused (see p. 880). *Like* is a preposition that introduces a prepositional phrase. *As* can be used as a preposition and as a subordinating conjunction (or *as if* or *as though*) that introduces a subordinate clause. Do not use *like* to begin a subordinate clause.

Incorrect: If she can stop one heart from breaking, she will feel *like* she did not live in vain.

Correct: If she can stop one heart from breaking, she will feel *as if* she did not live in vain.

Practice 1 Choose the adjective or adverb to complete these sentences correctly:

1. The language of the flowers was (delicate, delicately).

2. The moon rose (slow, slowly) in the night.

3. The animals described in "Drum Song" are all (real, really) small.

4. The Robin did not move (quick, quickly) enough to catch the worm.

5. Molly took care of her siblings very (careful, carefully).

Practice 2 Write the following sentences in your notebook. Complete each sentence with the correct word in parentheses.

1. My brother is a better poet than (he, him).

2. It seemed (like, as if) night came quickly after school ended.

3. The gardener was more frightened by the visitor than (he, him).

4. No one is as bold as (she, her).

Grammar in Writing

✔ *When deciding between* like *or* as, *look for a subject and a verb following the word. If both appear, then the subordinating conjunction* as *is needed.* Like *is never a conjunction.*

Television offers you all kinds of variety. You can view drama and comedy programs, commercials, newscasts, news bulletins, public-service announcements, advertisements, and infomercials. Whatever kinds of programs you watch, look for the messages in them, and evaluate the messages before you accept them.

Identify the Purpose Identify the message of a program and the goal of the program. The purpose of an advertisement or infomercial is to get you to make a purchase or to take some action. The claims made about a product or a service or a candidate include only information that the advertiser wants you to know. For example, a toothpaste might claim "Dentists recommend this toothpaste." What you are not told is that only fifty dentists recommend it. Listen carefully, and question claims made by advertisers. Ask yourself, "Are they telling me everything?"

Consider the Source With advertisements, it's easy to figure out the purpose of the message. With news reports, it is often difficult to know what is fact and what is opinion or what is simply a guess. Objective news programs, such as nightly news reports, are better sources for factual information. Television "magazines" may include reporting that entertains more than it informs, and it can be misleading. To keep an audience's interest, they may make assumptions about people and report those assumptions as fact. Before accepting a television message as fact, evaluate the source.

Consider Bias Bias is the tendency to think in a certain way. As you watch television programs, consider whether the information is being presented in a one-sided way or whether it takes into account all points of view.

Apply the Strategies

Complete one or both of the following activities.

1. Watch a television "magazine" show, and write a report in which you critically evaluate its messages.

2. Tape a commercial or infomercial. With your class, determine its purpose, question its claims, and evaluate its message.

Tips for Viewing TV Messages Critically

▶ Be aware of the kind of program you're watching and its purpose.
▶ Listen for bias.
▶ Remember that there is often another point of view to a public-service announcement or a station editorial.
▶ Infomercials are designed to sell something.

What's Behind the Words

Vocabulary Adventures With Richard Lederer

Analogies

An analogy, derived from the Greek *analogia,* "relation," is a relationship between one idea and another. When you take analogies tests, you will usually be asked to demonstrate your under-standing of how one word relates to another.

Typically, you will be given one pair of words that are capitalized and four or five other uncapitalized pairs. You must identify the relationship between the two capitalized terms and then find another pair of words with the same relationship. Often, colons are used to suggest "is to," as shown in the following examples:

EAGER:LAZY:: (a) angry:mad, (b) enthusi-astic:bored, (c) energetic:vigorous, (d) intelligent:curious (e) brilliant:genius.

DAWN:DAY:: (a) star:heavens, (b) curtain:play, (c) beginning:end, (d) moon:night, (e) birth:life

Making Connections

When you encounter analogies tests, try to find the exact connection between the capitalized words. Before examining the choices for the answer, state the relationship as clearly as you can in a sentence, as "EAGER is the opposite of LAZY" and "DAWN is the beginning of DAY."

Such a statement will be a powerful aid in your arriving at a correct answer: "EAGER is the opposite of LAZY, and *enthusiastic* is the opposite of *bored*"; "DAWN is the beginning of DAY, and *birth* is the beginning of *life*."

The Most Common Relationships

Practice recognizing the most common relationships used in analogies:

Relationship	Examples
synonyms	rich:wealthy; mammoth:colossal
antonyms	pleasure:pain; patience:intolerance
part of the whole	tree:woods; song:repertoire
one of a group	pear:fruit; giraffe:animal
characteristic of	light:feather; hard:diamond
degree of intensity	warm:boiling; breeze:gale
lack of	food:starvation; generosity:miser
purpose of	school:learning; sandbox:play
sign of	applause:approval; blush:shyness

From a study of related words, you will become more accurate in recognizing shades of meaning.

ACTIVITY 1. State clearly the relationship between each of the following pairs:

1. clumsy:awkward
2. lead:heavy
3. bear:den
4. human being:mammal
5. incision:scar
6. automobile:travel

ACTIVITY 2. Choose the pair that shows the same relationship as the first pair.

1. KITTEN:CAT:: (a) modem:computer, (b) gosling:goose, (c) cat:lion
2. CARROT:VEGETABLE:: (a) cheddar:cheese, (b) car:automobile, (c) crayon:pen
3. HAPPY:SAD:: (a) noisy:loud, (b) high:low, (c) smart:intelligent

Extended Reading Opportunities

The musical language of poetry, along with form and theme, can present a rewarding reading experience. Following are a few possibilities for further exploration of poetry.

Suggested Titles

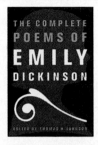

101 Great American Poems
The American Poetry & Literacy Project

This collection of poetry was assembled by the American Poetry & Literacy Project. Its aim is to provide poetry to the American public free of charge. Collections like this one are distributed free at hospitals, train stations, libraries, and other public places. This collection of well-loved works from various classic poets provides an opportunity to appreciate the magical and musical language of poetry.

Poem-Making: Ways to Begin Writing Poetry
Myra Cohn Livingston

This book is an excellent handbook for the budding poet. Basing the work on the formal terminology of poetic techniques, Livingston makes the mechanics of writing a poem understandable. She invites young people to "make the image, the thought, even the sound, come alive" and to enjoy the experience of writing a poem.

The Complete Poems of Emily Dickinson
Thomas H. Johnson, Editor

All 1,775 of Dickinson's poems are available in this collection exactly as she first wrote them. The brief poems express her ideas on nature and life. The comprehensive collection includes poems from her youth to the end of her career—even valentines she wrote during the 1850's. The editor also includes an introduction that outlines Dickinson's career.

Other Possibilities

American Sports Poems	R. R. Knudson
101 Famous Poems	Roy J. Cook, Editor
Poetry After Lunch: Poems to Read Aloud	Joyce Armstrong Carroll and Edward E. Wilson

Woodcutter, 1891, Winslow Homer, Private Collection

The American Folk Tradition

The American folk tradition is a rich collection of literature that grew out of the oral tradition. These stories amaze, explain, teach, and amuse the reader of today just as they did the listener of generations ago. Following are the types of folk literature you'll encounter in this unit:

- **Myths** are ancient tales that explain or summarize the beliefs of a culture.

- **Folk Tales** are stories of a region that are passed down through the generations to teach a lesson or to entertain.

- **Tall Tales,** written in the language of the common people, often tell of life on the American frontier and contain larger-than-life characters who take part in or witness fantastic events.

Guide for Reading

Meet the Author:

Rosemary Carr Benét (1898–1962)

Many of Rosemary Carr Benét's poems were inspired by historical events and legends. She often wrote poems with her husband, Stephen Vincent Benét. Their close friends called them "the last of the romantics" because of their close bond and love of poetry.

Poetry for Young People After their children were born, the Benéts started to write poetry for young people. In 1933, they published *A Book of Americans,* a collection of verses that expand on United States history and American personalities.

THE STORY BEHIND THE STORY

Johnny Appleseed (1774–1845) was a frontiersman whose real name was John Chapman. Born in Leominster, Massachusetts, Chapman's life was so extraordinary that he became a folk hero. In stories about him, which blend truth and fantasy, he collected apple seeds from Pennsylvania cider mills and planted them in fertile spots throughout Ohio, Indiana, and Illinois. He received no pay for his work, but he was often given a meal or a cast-off piece of clothing by those who appreciated his efforts.

◆ LITERATURE AND YOUR LIFE

CONNECT YOUR EXPERIENCE

Perhaps you've planted or tended flowers in your home or garden; perhaps you've grown sea monkeys or tended newborn kittens. Think about the rewards that come from watching something grow and thrive. In "Johnny Appleseed," you'll learn of a special person who devoted his life to planting apple trees.

THEMATIC FOCUS: Heroes

Johnny Appleseed is an unusual folk hero. As you read about him in this poem, look for the qualities that make him heroic.

◆ Background for Understanding

GEOGRAPHY

Johnny Appleseed is a folk hero who planted apple trees throughout the midwestern United States. Apples have been grown in many regions of the world since the earliest human cultures flourished. They are mentioned in the earliest writings of China, Babylon, and Egypt. Charred apples have been discovered in the mud of prehistoric cave homes. They even show up in some early stone carvings.

Today, China is the world's largest producer of apples, followed by the United States, France, Italy, and Turkey. In the United States, the Pacific Northwest produces the most apples, led by Washington State. California, New York, Michigan, and Virginia are also major apple producers. Three varieties make up about two thirds of all apples grown in the United States: Delicious, Golden Delicious, and Granny Smith.

◆ Johnny Appleseed ◆

John Chapman, known as Johnny Appleseed (1775–1845)

◆ Literary Focus

ORAL TRADITION

The **oral tradition** is the passing of stories, beliefs, and customs from generation to generation by word of mouth. Many folk stories and tales were originally sung as ballads. Only after years of being heard, remembered, and loved were they written down.

Modern writers often return to the powerful and engaging stories kept alive by the oral tradition. Rosemary Carr Benét's poem was inspired by the vibrant body of American folk tales and songs about Johnny Appleseed.

◆ Build Vocabulary

RELATED WORDS: FORMS OF *encumber*

The verb *encumber* means "to weigh down." Words related to encumber include *cumbersome, encumbrance,* and *unencumbered.*

WORD BANK

Which word from the poem might mean "having a healthy red color"? Check the Build Vocabulary box on page 895 to see if you chose correctly.

gnarled
ruddy
encumber
tendril
stalking
lair

Reading for Success

Strategies for Reading Folk Literature

Folk literature is older than recorded history: Its tales, stories, legends, and myths have been passed down for many generations. Because these tales were told orally, they often contain repetition (making them easier to remember) and dialect (specialized vocabulary and grammar of a region). As you read the folk literature in this unit, use the following strategies to guide your reading:

Understand the cultural context.

You will better understand the action and characters of a story if you know the culture from which it comes. For example, a southwestern tale—a *cuento*—would reveal different beliefs or customs from a Native American tale or a pioneer tale. Look at the following example based on "Johnny Appleseed."

> **Poem Passage:** For fifty years over/Of harvest and dew,/He planted his apples/Where no apples grew.
>
> **Cultural Context:** The pioneers admired rugged individualism.

Recognize the storyteller's purpose.

Folk literature often amuses the reader at the same time that it teaches a lesson or conveys a message. Storytellers often used folk tales to transmit beliefs or values. Some tales serve to explain scientific mysteries or natural occurrences. As you read, consider what message the story might be conveying to listeners.
▶ Examine the details of the tale for clues to the storyteller's purpose.
▶ Look for a stated message or moral near the story's end.

Predict.

Folk literature is predictable. Good characters and deeds are rewarded; bad characters are either banished or reformed. This pattern makes it easy for you to predict the instructional message.

> **Story Event:** Chicoria makes a bet with someone.
>
> **What I Know:** Chicoria is the "good" character.
>
> **Prediction:** He will probably win the bet.

As you read "Johnny Appleseed," look at the notes in the boxes. The notes demonstrate how to apply these strategies to your reading.

Johnny Appleseed

Rosemary Carr Benét

John Chapman, known as Johnny Appleseed (1775–1845)

▲ **Critical Viewing** What does Johnny Appleseed appear to be doing in this illustration? Support your answer. **[Deduce]**

◆ **Build Vocabulary**

gnarled (närld) *adj.*: Knotty and twisted, as the trunk of an old tree

ruddy (rud′ ē) *adj.*: Having a healthy red color

encumber (in kum′ bər) *v.*: Weigh down

tendril (ten′ drəl) *n.*: Thin shoot from a plant

Of Jonathan Chapman
Two things are known,
That he loved apples,
That he walked alone.

5   At seventy-odd
He was gnarled as could be,
But ruddy and sound
As a good apple tree.

> You can recognize that the **story-teller's purpose** is to tell of Jonathan Chapman.

For fifty years over
10 Of harvest and dew,
He planted his apples
Where no apples grew.

The winds of the prairie
Might blow through his rags,
15 But he carried his seeds
In the best deerskin bags.

From old Ashtabula
To frontier Fort Wayne,
He planted and pruned
20 And he planted again.

He had not a hat
To encumber his head.
He wore a tin pan
On his white hair instead.

25 He nested with owl,
And with bear-cub and possum,
And knew all his orchards
Root, tendril and blossom.

A fine old man,
30 As ripe as a pippin,[1]
His heart still light,
And his step still skipping.

The stalking Indian,
The beast in its lair
35 Did no hurt
While he was there.

For they could tell,
As wild things can,
That Jonathan
    Chapman
40 Was God's own man.

Why did he do it?
We do not know.
He wished that apples
Might root and grow.

45 He has no statue.
He has no tomb.
He has his apple trees
Still in bloom.

Consider, consider,
50 Think well upon
The marvelous story
Of Appleseed John.

---

1. **pippin** (pip´ in) *n.*: A type of apple.

> When you put this poem in **cultural context**, you'll realize that at the time this poem was written, many people of European ancestry misunderstood Native Americans.

> You can **predict** that Chapman will be remembered, despite the lack of memorials.

◆ Build Vocabulary

stalking (stôk´ iŋ) *adj.*: Secretly approaching

lair (ler) *n.*: Den of a wild animal

Guide for Responding

◆ LITERATURE AND YOUR LIFE

Reader's Response Would the work of Johnny Appleseed be appreciated today? Why or why not?

Thematic Focus What heroic qualities does Johnny Appleseed display?

Journal Writing What modern figures remind you of Johnny Appleseed? Jot down a list in your journal.

☑ Check Your Comprehension

1. By what name is Jonathan Chapman better known?
2. List three physical details that Benét uses to describe Chapman.
3. Describe Chapman's life on the frontier.

◆ Critical Thinking

INTERPRET

1. What is Chapman's most important possession? **[Infer]**
2. How does Chapman feel about nature? **[Infer]**
3. How would you describe the speaker's attitude toward the person who became known as Johnny Appleseed? **[Analyze]**

APPLY

4. What areas in today's world would benefit from having someone provide help in growing food? Explain what those areas most need. **[Relate]**

EXTEND

5. How might a scientist in a laboratory today carry on Johnny Appleseed's legacy? **[Science Link]**

Guide for Responding (continued)

◆ Reading for Success

STRATEGIES FOR READING FOLK LITERATURE

Review the reading strategies and the notes showing how to read folk literature. Then, apply the strategies to answer the following:

1. How does knowing about prairie life help you to understand "Johnny Appleseed"?
2. What is the storyteller's purpose in telling "Johnny Appleseed"? What details helped you to identify the purpose?

◆ Build Vocabulary

USING FORMS OF encumber

The verb *encumber* means "to weigh down." Related words convey a similar meaning. Complete the following sentences with these related words: *cumbersome, unencumbered, encumbrance*. Then state each sentence in your own words.

1. The heavy bags of grass seed are ____?____.
2. A weighty ____?____ can make it hard to walk.
3. When his sack of seed was empty, Johnny felt ____?____.

SPELLING STRATEGY

Words containing the letter combinations of *ai* and *ia* are often mistakenly or carelessly misspelled. For example, *lair* and *liar* are often confused, as are *trail* and *trial*. Rewrite the following sentences, correcting any misspelled words.

1. The liar of the wolf was deep inside a cave.
2. The trial led through the prairie to an orchard.

USING THE WORD BANK

On your paper, write the Word Bank word that completes each sentence.

1. Stay away from the ____?____ of a bear family.
2. She watered the knotty and ____?____ old tree.
3. After planting the seedlings, her face was glowing and ____?____.
4. A young ____?____ from the tree wrapped around stones and clay.
5. A ____?____ cat hid in the branches.
6. In a short time, the bushels of apples will ____?____ the orchard's fruit pickers.

◆ Literary Focus

ORAL TRADITION

The **oral tradition** is the passing of songs, stories, and poems from generation to generation by word of mouth. Songs, myths, legends, and tall tales are all products of the oral tradition.

1. Why do you think Benét chose a poetic form for her retelling of a legend about a folk hero?
2. In a song, a catchy melody or memorable phrase is called a "hook" because it catches a listener's attention. (a) Does Benét's poem include any hooks? (b) How can a strong hook help a song or poem become part of the oral tradition?

◆ Build Grammar Skills

UNNECESSARY COMMAS

Commas are supposed to help readers, not confuse them. **Unnecessary commas** can cause confusion. One place where a comma is unnecessary is before a coordinating conjunction that links words or groups that are *not* independent clauses. Notice that Rosemary Carr Benét does not use a comma when she joins two adjectives or two verbs:

> But ruddy and sound/as a good apple tree.
> (*Not:* ruddy, and sound)
>
> He wished that apples might root and grow.
> (*Not:* might root, and grow)

Practice Copy the following sentences, leaving out unnecessary commas.

1. In song, and story, Johnny Appleseed planted healthy, and robust apples.
2. For more than fifty years, he planted, and pruned his trees.
3. Many ballads describe, and praise his gentle, and heroic deeds.
4. In addition to seeding apples, Chapman also sowed herbs, and other plants.
5. Tales describe his life in vivid, and sharp details, although some are certainly exaggerated.

Writing Application Use each of the following phrases in a sentence. Avoid unnecessary commas.

1. apples and pears
2. slowly and steadily

Build Your Portfolio

 ## Idea Bank

Writing

1. **Epitaph** Write a three- or four-line epitaph—an inscription for a gravestone—that might have been carved on John Chapman's memorial. Your epitaph can be written in prose or in verse.

2. **Folk Ballad** Write a poem about a modern folk hero. Use Rosemary Carr Benét's rhyming pattern, and give your poem a strong beat.

3. **Essay** Write an essay in which you tell what made Johnny Appleseed a folk hero. Use details from the poem and other sources to support your ideas.

Speaking and Listening

4. **Interview** Imagine what would happen if Johnny Appleseed were suddenly transported to the present day. How would he react to modern life in your community? Role-play an interview between a local news commentator and the newly modernized folk hero. **[Performing Arts Link]**

5. **Musical Setting** Set "Johnny Appleseed" to music. Choose a simple, catchy tune that's easy to sing. If you play an instrument, create an instrumental accompaniment. Teach the song to your class, and sing it together. **[Music Link]**

Projects

6. **Apple Poster [Group Activity]** With a group of classmates, create a poster illustrating various types of apples. Include information that lists differences between varieties, regions in which they are grown, and popular recipes. Display your poster in the classroom. **[Science Link]**

7. **How-to Booklet** Work with a team to create a how-to booklet for growing apples. Research how and where to plant trees, kinds of fertilizer to use, and methods of harvesting. Your finished brochure can include diagrams, articles, and sources of additional information. **[Science Link]**

 ## Writing Mini-Lesson

Legendary Story

Modern writers often retell stories of legendary characters to bring them to life for contemporary readers. Choose a favorite legendary tale, and write your own version.

Writing Skills Focus: Show, Don't Tell

One of the best pieces of advice you'll hear about writing is **"show, don't tell."** This means that you should avoid simply *telling* readers what a character is like; instead, *show* the character doing something that reveals what the character is like. For example, Benét doesn't just tell readers that Chapman loved nature; instead, she shows him in action.

Model From the Poem

> For fifty years over
> Of harvest and dew,
> He planted his apples
> Where no apples grew.

Prewriting Choose a legendary tale you'd like to retell. Make a story map to jot down the basic story elements. Think about story details you want to emphasize in your version.

Drafting Write the story events chronologically. Don't worry about including every little detail in your first draft. It's more important to get the main events clearly stated.

Revising Apply the rule "show, don't tell." Look for spots where you've *told* the reader directly about a character. Replace those sentences with scenes that show the character in action.

> ◆ **Grammar Application**
> Check your writing to eliminate unnecessary commas.

PART 1 *A Sampling of Stories*

His Hair Flows Like a River, T. C. Cannon, Philbrook Museum of Art, Tulsa, Oklahoma

Guide for Reading

Meet the Authors:

Richard Erdoes (1912–   )
Alfonso Ortiz (1939–   )

For their book *American Indian Myths and Legends*, Richard Erdoes and Alfonso Ortiz collected many stories over a period of twenty-five years. Some of the stories in that book "were jotted down at powwows, around campfires, even inside a moving car."

Richard Erdoes (top) was born in Frankfurt, Germany.

Alfonso Ortiz (bottom)was born in San Juan, a Tewa pueblo in New Mexico.

Mourning Dove (1884?–1936)

Mourning Dove is the pen name of Christine Quintasket. While earning her living as a migrant worker, Quintasket became a writer and political activist. Always interested in the stories she had heard all her life from relatives and visitors, she collected and recorded the folklore of her people to preserve it for posterity. This story is from her collection *Coyote Stories*, originally published in 1933.

◆ LITERATURE AND YOUR LIFE

CONNECT YOUR EXPERIENCE

Imagine if you didn't understand or couldn't explain why things are as they are. Every people since the beginning of time has created stories to explain the world around them. The stories in this section are creation myths invented by Native Americans.

THEMATIC FOCUS: Respecting Nature

As you read these myths, notice how they explain and highlight the wonders of nature.

◆ Background for Understanding

SCIENCE

Coyote is a common character in many Native American stories. The coyote is a smaller cousin of the wolf. Its habitat is most of North America. Usually a solitary animal, it has been known to hunt in pairs and sometimes in an odd partnership with the badger. The Coyote of Native American tales is a combination of godlike, human, and animal characteristics. He symbolizes the balance of qualities within us all, including wisdom and foolishness, generosity and greed, honesty and deception.

◆ Build Vocabulary

SUFFIXES: *-ify*

The suffix *-ify*, meaning "to make," changes a noun or adjective into a verb. It appears in the Word Bank word *purify*, which means "to make pure."

WORD BANK

Which word from the list means "to awaken" or "to stir or rouse"? Check the Build Vocabulary box on page 906 to see if you chose correctly.

shriveled
pursuit
arouse
purify

◆ Coyote Steals the Sun and Moon ◆
The Spirit Chief Names the Animal People

Sunset in Memoriam (detail), 1946, Woody (Woodrow Wilson) Crumbo, Philbrook Museum of Art, Tulsa, Oklahoma

◆ Literary Focus

MYTH

A **myth** is an ancient tale having its roots in the beliefs of a particular group or nation. Just as science and history teach and explain about the world, mythology develops certain common themes, such as creation, the origin of the universe, the meaning of existence and death, and natural occurrences. Myths often tell about the adventures of great heroes who possess special powers.

◆ Reading Strategy

UNDERSTAND THE CULTURAL CONTEXT

As you read, look for details within the myth to help you **understand the cultural context** of the story. For example, in these works, details about animal behavior, the weather, and the change of seasons may lead you to understand that, like all peoples of centuries ago, the culture originating these tales was agricultural, depending on aspects of nature for survival.

As you read, keep track of the details that reveal the cultural context. You might want to use a chart like the one below to help you.

Detail	What It Shows
Coyote steals the sun and moon	
The Spirit Chief names the Animal People	

Coyote Steals the Sun and Moon

Zuñi Myth

Retold by Richard Erdoes and Alfonso Ortiz

Cosmic Canine, John Nieto, Courtesy of the artist

Coyote is a bad hunter who never kills anything. Once he watched Eagle hunting rabbits, catching one after another—more rabbits than he could eat. Coyote thought, "I'll team up with Eagle so I can have enough meat." Coyote is always up to something.

"Friend," Coyote said to Eagle, "we should hunt together. Two can catch more than one."

"Why not?" Eagle said, and so they began to hunt in partnership. Eagle caught many rabbits, but all Coyote caught was some little bugs.

At this time the world was still dark; the sun and moon had not yet been put in the sky. "Friend," Coyote said to Eagle, "no wonder I can't catch anything; I can't see. Do you know where we can get some light?"

"You're right, friend, there should be some light," Eagle said. "I think there's a little toward the west. Let's try and find it."

And so they went looking for the sun and moon. They came to a big river, which Eagle flew over. Coyote swam, and swallowed so much water that he almost drowned. He crawled out with his fur full of mud, and Eagle asked, "Why don't you fly like me?"

"You have wings; I just have hair," Coyote said. "I can't fly without feathers."

At last they came to a pueblo,[1] where the Kachinas[2] happened to be dancing. The people invited Eagle and Coyote to sit down and have something to eat while they watched the sacred dances. Seeing the power of the Kachinas, Eagle said, "I believe these are the people who have light."

Coyote, who had been looking all around, pointed out two boxes, one large and one small, that the people opened whenever they wanted light. To produce a lot of light, they opened the lid of the big box, which contained the sun. For less light they opened the small box, which held the moon.

---

1. **pueblo** (pweb´ lō): Native American village in the southwestern United States.
2. **Kachinas** (kə chē´ nəz): Masked dancers who imitate gods or the spirits of their ancestors.

◄ **Critical Viewing** Why might the artist have chosen to depict Coyote as multicolored? [Infer]

Coyote nudged Eagle. "Friend, did you see that? They have all the light we need in the big box. Let's steal it."

"You always want to steal and rob. I say we should just borrow it."

"They won't lend it to us."

"You may be right," said Eagle. "Let's wait till they finish dancing and then steal it."

After a while the Kachinas went home to sleep, and Eagle scooped up the large box and flew off. Coyote ran along trying to keep up, panting, his tongue hanging out. Soon he yelled up to Eagle, "Ho, friend, let me carry the box a little way."

"No, no," said Eagle, "you never do anything right."

He flew on, and Coyote ran after him. After a while Coyote shouted again: "Friend, you're my chief, and it's not right for you to carry the box; people will call me lazy. Let me have it."

"No, no, you always mess everything up." And Eagle flew on and Coyote ran along.

So it went for a stretch, and then Coyote started again. "Ho, friend, it isn't right for you to do this. What will people think of you and me?"

"I don't care what people think. I'm going to carry this box."

Again Eagle flew on and again Coyote ran after him. Finally Coyote begged for the fourth time: "Let me carry it. You're the chief, and I'm just Coyote. Let me carry it."

Eagle couldn't stand any more pestering. Also, Coyote had asked him four times, and if someone asks four times, you'd better give him what he wants. Eagle said, "Since you won't let up on me, go ahead and carry the box for a while. But promise not to open it."

"Oh, sure, oh yes, I promise." They went on as before, but now Coyote had the box. Soon Eagle was far ahead, and Coyote lagged behind a hill where Eagle couldn't see him. "I wonder what the light looks like, inside there," he said to himself. "Why shouldn't I take a peek? Probably there's something extra in the box, something good that Eagle wants to keep to himself."

And Coyote opened the lid. Now, not only was the sun inside, but the moon also. Eagle had put them both together, thinking that it would be easier to carry one box than two.

As soon as Coyote opened the lid, the moon escaped, flying high into the sky. At once all the plants shriveled up and turned brown. Just as quickly, all the leaves fell off the trees,

◆ **Literary Focus**
What event in nature does this story explain?

and it was winter. Trying to catch the moon and put it back in the box, Coyote ran in pursuit as it skipped away from him. Meanwhile the sun flew out and rose into the sky. It drifted far away, and the peaches, squashes, and melons shriveled up with cold.

Eagle turned and flew back to see what had delayed Coyote. "You fool! Look what you've done!" he said. "You let the sun and moon escape, and now it's cold." Indeed, it began to snow, and Coyote shivered. "Now your teeth are chattering," Eagle said, "and it's your fault that cold has come into the world."

It's true. If it weren't for Coyote's curiosity and mischief making, we wouldn't have winter; we could enjoy summer all the time.

◆ **Build Vocabulary**

shriveled (shriv´ əld) v.: Dried up; withered

pursuit (pər sōōt´) n.: Following in order to overtake and capture

Beyond Literature

Cultural Connection

Coyote the Trickster Tales of tricks and pranks and those who play them on others have amused people from the dawn of time to the present day. Among Native Americans, the greatest trickster is Coyote. The character of Coyote the Trickster had the form of a coyote but exhibited human qualities. Tales of Coyote's exploits have been told from Alaska to the southern deserts and from coast to coast. These stories tell of Coyote's cleverness and foolishness, his ability to cheat his enemies, and his never-ending appetite. They also tell of those who manage to play tricks on Coyote.

Cross-Curricular Activity
Report Use a variety of sources to learn about coyotes—where they live, what they eat, how long they live, and so on. Reveal your findings in a report.

Guide for Responding

◆ LITERATURE AND YOUR LIFE

Reader's Response What advice would you like to give to Eagle?

Thematic Focus In what way does "Coyote Steals the Sun and Moon" caution the reader to respect nature?

☑ Check Your Comprehension

1. (a) Why does Coyote want to team up with Eagle? (b) What do they decide to search for?
2. Where do Coyote and Eagle find what they have been searching for?
3. (a) Why does Eagle finally let Coyote carry the box? (b) What happens once Coyote gets it?

◆ Critical Thinking

INTERPRET

1. Contrast the characters of Eagle and Coyote in terms of their appearance, their abilities, and their attitudes. **[Compare and Contrast]**
2. What can you tell about Coyote from the fact that he pesters Eagle until he gets the box? **[Infer]**
3. Which details in this story are based on fact, and which ones are invented? **[Distinguish]**

EXTEND

4. This story offers one explanation for why we have summer and winter. What are the scientific reasons? **[Science Link]**

The Spirit Chief Names the Animal People
Mourning Dove

Hah-ah' Eel-me'-whem, the great Spirit Chief,[1] called the Animal People together. They came from all parts of the world. Then the Spirit Chief told them there was to be a change, that a new kind of people was coming to live on the earth.

"All of you *Chip-chap-tiqulk*—Animal People—must have names," the Spirit Chief said. "Some of you have names now, some of you haven't. But tomorrow all will have names that shall be kept by you and your descendants forever. In the morning, as the first light of day shows in the sky, come to my lodge and choose your names. The first to come may choose any name that he or she wants. The next person may take any other name. That is the way it will go until all the names are taken. And to each person I will give work to do."

That talk made the Animal People very excited. Each wanted a proud name and the power to rule some tribe or some part of the world, and everyone determined to get up early and hurry to the Spirit Chief's lodge.

Sin-ka-lip'—Coyote—boasted that no one would be ahead of him. He walked among the people and told them that he would be the first. Coyote did not like his name; he wanted another. Nobody respected his name, Imitator, but it fitted him. He was called *Sin-ka-lip'* because he liked to imitate people. He thought that he could do anything that other persons

Thunder Knives, 1957, Pablita Velarde, Museum of Indian Arts & Culture/Laboratory of Anthropology Collections, Museum of New Mexico, Santa Fe, NM

▲ **Critical Viewing** What animals can you identify in this painting? **[Connect]**

did, and he pretended to know everything. He would ask a question, and when the answer was given he would say:

"I knew that before. I did not have to be told."

Such smart talk did not make friends for Coyote. Nor did he make friends by the foolish things he did and the rude tricks he played on people.

"I shall have my choice of the three biggest names," he boasted. "Those names are: *Kee-lau-naw,* the Mountain Person—Grizzly Bear, who will rule the four-footed people; *Milka-noups*—Eagle, who will rule the birds; and *En-tee-tee-ueh,* the Good Swimmer—Salmon. Salmon will be the chief of all the fish that the New People use for food."

Coyote's twin brother, Fox, who at the next sun took the name *Why-ay'-looh*—Soft Fur, laughed. "Do not be so sure, *Sin-ka-lip'*," said Fox. "Maybe you will have to keep the name you have. People despise that name. No one wants it."

"I am tired of that name," Coyote said in an angry voice. "Let someone else carry it. Let some old person take it—someone who cannot win in war. I am going to be a great warrior. My smart brother, I will make you beg of me when I am called Grizzly Bear, Eagle, or Salmon."

"Your strong words mean nothing," scoffed Fox. "Better go to your *swool'-hu* (tepee) and get some sleep, or you will not wake up in time to choose any name."

---

1. **Spirit Chief:** Many Native American groups believe in a Spirit Chief, an all-powerful god.

Coyote stalked off to his tepee. He told himself that he would not sleep any that night; he would stay wide awake. He entered the lodge, and his three sons called as if with one voice:

"Le-ee'-oo!" ("Father!")

They were hungry, but Coyote had brought them nothing to eat. Their mother, who after the naming day was known as *Pul'-laqu-whu*—Mole, the Mound Digger—sat on her foot at one side of the doorway. Mole was a good woman, always loyal to her husband in spite of his mean ways, his mischief-making, and his foolishness. She never was jealous, never talked back, never replied to his words of abuse. She looked up and said:

"Have you no food for the children? They are starving. I can find no roots to dig."

"Eh-ha!" Coyote grunted. "I am no common person to be addressed in that manner. I am going to be a great chief tomorrow. Did you know that? I will have a new name. I will be Grizzly Bear. Then I can devour my enemies with ease. And I shall need you no longer. You are growing too old and homely to be the wife of a great warrior and chief."

Mole said nothing. She turned to her corner of the lodge and collected a few old bones, which she put into a *klek'-chin* (cooking-basket). With two sticks she lifted hot stones from the fire and dropped them into the basket. Soon the water boiled, and there was weak soup for the hungry children.

"Gather plenty of wood for the fire," Coyote ordered. "I am going to sit up all night."

Mole obeyed. Then she and the children went to bed.

Coyote sat watching the fire. Half of the night passed. He got sleepy. His eyes grew heavy. So he picked up two little sticks and braced his eyelids apart. "Now I can stay awake," he thought, but before long he was fast asleep, although his eyes were wide open.

The sun was high in the sky when Coyote awoke. But for Mole he would not have wakened then. Mole called him. She called him

> **◆ Reading Strategy**
> What does Mole's action tell about how the people cooked their food?

after she returned with her name from the Spirit Chief's lodge. Mole loved her husband. She did not want him to have a big name and be a powerful chief. For then, she feared, he would leave her. That was why she did not <u>arouse</u> him at daybreak. Of this she said nothing.

Only half-awake and thinking it was early morning, Coyote jumped at the sound of Mole's voice and ran to the lodge of the Spirit Chief. None of the other *Chip-chap-tiqulk* were there. Coyote laughed. Blinking his sleepy eyes, he walked into the lodge. "I am going to be *Kee-lau-naw*, " he announced in a strong voice. "That shall be my name."

"The name Grizzly Bear was taken at dawn," the Spirit Chief answered.

"Then I shall be *Milka-noups*," said Coyote, and his voice was not so loud.

"Eagle flew away at sunup," the other replied.

"Well, I shall be called *En-tee-tee-ueh*," Coyote said in a voice that was not loud at all.

"The name Salmon also has been taken," explained the Spirit Chief. "All the names except your own have been taken. No one wished to steal your name."

Poor Coyote's knees grew weak. He sank down beside the fire that blazed in the great tepee, and the heart of *Hah-ah' Eel-me'-whem* was touched.

"Sin-ka-lip'," said that Person, "you must keep your name. It is a good name for you. You slept long because I wanted you to be the last one here. I have important work for you, much for you to do before the New People come. You are to be chief of all the tribes.

"Many bad creatures inhabit the earth. They bother and kill people, and the tribes cannot increase as I wish. These *En-alt-na Skil-ten*—People-Devouring Monsters—cannot keep on like that. They must be stopped. It is for you to conquer them. For doing that, for all the good things you do, you will be honored and

◆ Build Vocabulary

arouse (ə rouz´) *v*.: Awaken, as from sleep
purify (pyoor´ ə fī) *v*.: To rid of impurities

praised by the people that are here now and that come afterward. But, for the foolish and mean things you do, you will be laughed at and despised. That you cannot help. It is your way.

"To make your work easier, I give you *squas-tenk'*. It is your own special magic power. No one else ever shall have it. When you are in danger, whenever you need help, call to your power. It will do much for you, and with it you can change yourself into any form, into anything you wish.

"To your twin brother, *Why-ay'-looh,* and to others I have given *shoo'-mesh.*[2] It is strong power. With that power Fox can restore your life should you be killed. Your bones may be scattered but, if there is one hair of your body left, Fox can make you live again. Others of the people can do the same with their *shoo'-mesh.* Now, go, *Sin-ka-lip'!* Do well the work laid for your trail!"

Well, Coyote was a chief after all, and he felt good again. After that day his eyes were different. They grew slant from being propped open that night while he sat by his fire. The New People, the Indians, got their slightly slant eyes from Coyote.

After Coyote had gone, the Spirit Chief thought it would be nice for the Animal People and the coming New People to have the benefit of the spiritual sweat-house.[3] But all of the Animal People had names, and there was no one to take the name of Sweathouse—*Quil'-sten,* the Warmer. So the wife of the Spirit Chief took the name. She wanted the people to have the sweat-house, for she pitied them. She wanted them to have a place to go to purify themselves, a place where they could pray for strength and good luck and strong medicine-power, and where they could fight sickness and get relief from their troubles.

The ribs, the frame poles, of the sweathouse represent the wife of *Hah-ah, Eel-me'-whem.* As she is a spirit, she cannot be seen, but she always is near. Songs to her are sung by the present generation. She hears them. She hears what her people say, and in her heart there is love and pity.

---

2. **shoo'-mesh** (shoo´ mesh) *n.*: Medicine, or strong magic power, provided by the Spirit Chief.

3. **sweat-house:** A mound-shaped lodge where bathers cleanse themselves physically and spiritually.

*G*uide for Responding

◆ LITERATURE AND YOUR LIFE

Reader's Response Did you want Coyote to get a new name? Why or why not?

Thematic Focus What aspect of nature does this story explain?

☑ Check Your Comprehension

1. Why does the Spirit Chief convene a council of the Animal People?
2. Why does Coyote want to change his name?
3. What happens to prevent Coyote from getting a new name?
4. What physical characteristic of Coyote is passed on to the New People, the Indians?

◆ Critical Thinking

INTERPRET

1. Why does Coyote want to be named Grizzly Bear, Eagle, or Salmon? **[Connect]**
2. How does Coyote's behavior lead to his misfortune? **[Interpret]**
3. Why does the Spirit Chief give Fox powers to restore Coyote's life? **[Draw Conclusions]**

COMPARE LITERARY WORKS

4. In "The Spirit Chief Names the Animal People," Coyote is given a very important job: to conquer the People-Devouring Monsters. Based on what you learn about Coyote in "Coyote Steals the Sun and Moon," do you think Coyote will succeed at this? **[Assess]**

Guide for Responding (continued)

◆ Reading Strategy

UNDERSTAND THE CULTURAL CONTEXT

When reading myths, it is useful to **understand the cultural context** from which they came. For example, if you know that a myth is Native American in origin, you would understand the importance of animals in main character roles.

1. In "Coyote Steals the Sun and Moon," the snows of winter come when Coyote loses the sun, and this occurrence causes great suffering. What does this tell you about the people's way of life?
2. The importance of the sweat-house is explained in "The Spirit Chief Names the Animal People." What does this explanation reveal about the culture?

◆ Build Vocabulary

USING THE SUFFIX -ify

The suffix -ify, which means "to make," changes a noun or an adjective to a verb. Sometimes the noun or adjective form changes slightly when -ify is added. On your paper, write a definition for the following words:

1. solidify   2. intensify   3. mystify

SPELLING STRATEGY

When adding -ify to words ending in e or y, drop the e or y:

pure + -ify = purify   glory + -ify = glorify

Add -ify to the following words. Write the new words on your paper.

1. simple   2. beauty   3. code

USING THE WORD BANK

On your paper, write the letter of the definition that matches each Word Bank word.

1. shriveled   **a.** to make clean
2. pursuit   **b.** dried up
3. arouse   **c.** awaken
4. purify   **d.** chase

◆ Literary Focus

MYTH

A **myth** is a story handed down through the generations by word of mouth. Myths often explain something about nature. These explanations often involve an interaction between gods, humans, and forces of nature.

1. (a) What forces of nature are explained in "Coyote Steals the Sun and Moon"? (b) Summarize the explanations.
2. What human physical characteristic is explained in "The Spirit Chief Names the Animal People"?

◆ Build Grammar Skills

COMMAS IN COMPOUND SENTENCES

These stories have many examples of compound sentences, which contain two independent clauses joined by a coordinating conjunction (*and, but, or,* or *nor*). Use a **comma** in a compound sentence before the coordinating conjunction. Notice the comma before *and* in this example of a compound sentence:

independent   coordinating   independent
  clause   conjunction   clause
[He flew on,] and [Coyote ran after him.]

Practice On your paper, write these compound sentences, placing commas correctly.

1. After a while, the Kachinas went home to sleep and Eagle scooped up the large box and flew off.
2. You're the chief and I'm just Coyote.
3. They went on as before but now Coyote had the box.
4. They were hungry but Coyote had brought them nothing to eat.
5. Soon the water boiled and there was weak soup for the hungry children.

Writing Application. On your paper, write each pair of sentences as a compound sentence. Place commas correctly.

1. The Kachinas left. Eagle took the box.
2. Eagle flew on. Coyote ran after him.
3. Coyote's sons were hungry. Coyote had brought them nothing to eat.

Build Your Portfolio

 Idea Bank

Writing

1. **Letter** Take the part of Mole in "The Spirit Chief Names the Animal People," and think about how you'd feel about Coyote's treatment of you. Write a letter to your best friend, telling how you feel and what you plan to do.

2. **Newspaper Story** Write a newspaper story based on the day the Spirit Chief named the animals. **[Media Link]**

3. **Essay** Write an essay in which you identify the theme or message of "Coyote Steals the Sun and Moon." Explain whether or not it is effectively presented. Use details from the story to support your ideas. **[Literature Link]**

Speaking and Listening

4. **Coyote's Trial [Group Activity]** Imagine that the Kachinas are taking Coyote and Eagle to court for the crime of stealing the sun and the moon. With a group, assume the roles of judge, prosecuting attorney, defense attorney, witnesses, Coyote, Eagle, and the jury. Act out the trial for the class.

5. **Dramatic Reading** "The Spirit Chief Names the Animal People" was originally told orally. Read the story dramatically, and tape-record your performance. Play the finished tape for the class. **[Performing Arts Link]**

Projects

6. **Multimedia Report [Group Activity]** Work with a group of classmates to create a multimedia presentation about Zuñi culture—past or present. Include photographs, recordings, and drawings of artifacts. **[Social Studies Link]**

7. **Collection of Story Summaries [Group Activity]** With a group, find and read more stories about Coyote. Write the title and a summary of each on an index card. Put the cards in a box labeled "Coyote Stories," and make them available for others to read. **[Literature Link]**

 Writing Mini-Lesson

Report on an Animal

Many animals are mentioned in these myths—coyotes, eagles, and foxes, to name a few. Choose one animal that holds special interest for you, and write a report on it.

Writing Skills Focus: Give Visual Support

Give visual support to help your readers understand what you are saying. Among the types of visual support you can use are maps, graphs, pictures, diagrams, and charts.

Model

Coyote	
Length	approx. 4 ft., including tail
Height	approx. 2 ft.
Weight	from 25 to 30 lbs.

Prewriting Conduct research on your animal before creating your visual aids. You could create a timeline of the animal's life span, a chart giving physical statistics, or a diagram of the animal's anatomy. You can also photocopy appropriate maps, photographs, and illustrations.

Drafting Using the information gathered in your research, write a draft of your report. Place visual aids where they'll be most effective.

> ◆ **Grammar Application**
> For variety, use some compound sentences. Be sure that you use a comma before the coordinating conjunction.

Revising Look for places where visual aids will make the information clearer. Be sure the data in your report is accurate and provable. Proofread your report to correct errors in grammar, spelling, and punctuation.

$\mathcal{G}$uide for Reading

Meet the Authors:

José Griego y Maestas

José Griego y Maestas received a master's degree from the University of New Mexico. An expert in bilingual education, he became the director of the Guadalupe Historic Foundation in Santa Fe, New Mexico.

Rudolfo A. Anaya (1937–)

New Mexico resident Rudolfo Anaya, an acclaimed writer of short stories and novels that evoke the culture of the Hispanic people, translated the folk tales collected by José Griego y Maestas into English.

Jackie Torrence (1944–)

Widely known to audiences as "the Story Lady," Jackie Torrence has written several collections of folk tales and stories for children, including *The Accidental Angel, My Grandmother's Treasure,* and *Classic Children's Tales.* A popular and entertaining reader, Torrence has recorded many of her stories on compact disks.

Zora Neale Hurston (1901–1960)

Zora Neale Hurston was the first American to collect and publish African American folklore. She re-created and interpreted the folk tales that she had heard while growing up in Eatonville, Florida, and used the local dialect in her tales. She also wrote novels, short stories, and magazine articles.

◆ LITERATURE AND YOUR LIFE

CONNECT YOUR EXPERIENCE

Folk tales often provide insights into human nature. In observing how characters think or act in certain situations, these folk tales point out how they *should* act. As you read these folk tales, decide which of their lessons you could apply to your own life.

THEMATIC FOCUS: **Relationships**

What do these folk tales teach you about relationships?

◆ Background for Understanding

SCIENCE

In "Why the Waves Have Whitecaps," you'll find a folk explanation for what causes whitecaps—waves with white-foam tops. Scientifically, this is what really happens: Wind pushes the water, making waves on the water's surface. As the wave nears the shore, where the water is shallower, the height of the wave increases. When the wind has driven the wave to its highest possible point, the crest of the wave breaks up into water droplets. The droplets reflect light and appear to be white. People call these waves either *whitecaps* or *breakers.*

◆ Build Vocabulary

SYNONYMS

Synonyms are words that have nearly the same meaning. In "Chicoria," the author uses the word *haughty,* meaning "full of disdainful pride" to describe a rancher. You may be more familiar with its synonyms: *conceited, arrogant, snobbish, egotistical.*

WORD BANK

Which word from the list means "inspiring pity"? Check the Build Vocabulary box on page 917 to see if you chose correctly.

cordially
haughty
commenced
pitiful

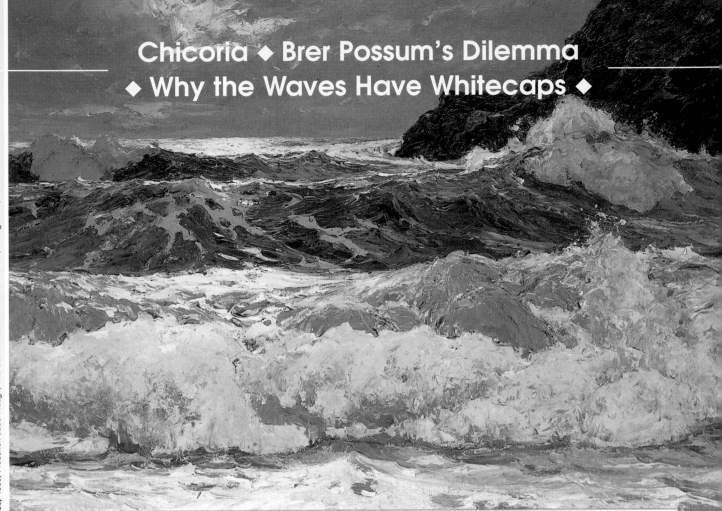

Chicoria ◆ Brer Possum's Dilemma
◆ Why the Waves Have Whitecaps ◆

◆ Literary Focus

FOLK TALE

Folk tales were composed orally and passed by word of mouth from generation to generation. Many folk tales have been collected and written down for all to enjoy. These stories often express a belief or a custom of the culture that creates them. Folk tales usually entertain, explain something in nature, or teach a lesson. Look for the lessons in the New Mexican tale "Chicoria" and the African American tales "Brer Possum's Dilemma" and "Why the Waves Have Whitecaps."

◆ Reading Strategy

RECOGNIZE THE STORYTELLER'S PURPOSE

It is storytellers who carry on the oral tradition. Storytellers want to entertain their audience, of course, but they have an additional purpose: They must communicate the message of the tale they are telling. For example, they may instruct listeners about why things are as they are or about how to behave.

Fill in a chart like the one below to help you **recognize the storyteller's purpose.**

Chicoria		
Purpose		**Details From the Tale**
to entertain		Chicoria makes a bet.
to teach		
to model behavior		
to explain		

CHICORIA¹

Adapted in Spanish by José Griego y Maestas
Retold in English by Rudolfo A. Anaya

Invitation to the Dance (el convite), Theodore Gentilz, The Daughters of the Republic of Texas Library, San Antonio, Texas

▲ **Critical Viewing** Are the men on horseback welcomed or feared? Explain. **[Draw Conclusions]**

1. **Chicoria** (chē kō′ rē ä)

There were once many big ranches in California, and many New Mexicans went to work there. One day one of the big ranch owners asked his workers if there were any poets in New Mexico.

"Of course, we have many fine poets," they replied. "We have old Vilmas,[2] Chicoria, Cinfuegos,[3] to say nothing of the poets of Cebolleta[4] and the Black Poet."

"Well, when you return next season, why don't you bring one of your poets to compete with Gracia[5]—here none can compare with him!"

When the harvest was done the New Mexicans returned home. The following season when they returned to California they took with them the poet Chicoria, knowing well that in spinning a rhyme or in weaving wit there was no *Californio*[6] who could beat him.

As soon as the rancher found out that the workers had brought Chicoria with them, he sent his servants to invite his good neighbor and friend to come and hear the new poet. Meanwhile, the cooks set about preparing a big meal. When the maids began to dish up the plates of food, Chicoria turned to one of the servers and said, "Ah, my friends, it looks like they are going to feed us well tonight!"

The servant was surprised. "No, my friend," he explained, "the food is for *them.* We don't eat at the master's table. It is not permitted. We eat in the kitchen."

"Well, I'll bet I can sit down and eat with them," Chicoria boasted.

"If you beg or if you ask, perhaps, but if you don't ask they won't invite you," replied the servant.

"I never beg," the New Mexican answered.

"The master will invite me of his own accord, and I'll bet you twenty-dollars he will!"

So they made a twenty-dollar bet and they instructed the serving maid to watch if this self-confident New Mexican had to ask the master for a place at the table. Then the maid took Chicoria into the dining room. Chicoria greeted the rancher cordially, but the rancher appeared haughty and did not invite Chicoria to sit with him and his guest at the table. Instead, he asked that a chair be brought and placed by the wall where Chicoria was to sit. The rich ranchers began to eat without inviting Chicoria.

So it is just as the servant predicted, Chicoria thought. The poor are not invited to share the rich man's food!

Then the master spoke: "Tell us about the country where you live. What are some of the customs of New Mexico?"

"Well, in New Mexico when a family sits down to eat each member uses one spoon for each biteful of food," Chicoria said with a twinkle in his eyes.

The ranchers were amazed that the New Mexicans ate in that manner, but what Chicoria hadn't told them was that each spoon was a piece of tortilla:[7] one fold and it became a spoon with which to scoop up the meal.

"Furthermore," he continued, "our goats are not like yours."

"How are they different?" the rancher asked.

"Here your nannies[8] give birth to two kids, in New Mexico they give birth to three!"

"What a strange thing!" the master said.

---

7. **tortilla** (tôr tē´ yə) *n.:* Thin, round pancake of cornmeal or flour.
8. **nannies** (nan´ ēz) *n.:* Female goats.

---

2. **Vilmas** (vēl´ mäs)
3. **Cinfuegos** (sin fwä´ gōs)
4. **Cebolleta** (sā bō´ yā tä)
5. **Gracia** (grä´ sē ä)
6. *Californio* (kä lē fôr´ nyō) *n.:* Spanish for "person from California."

◆ **Build Vocabulary**

cordially (kôr´ jəl lē) *adv.:* Warm and friendly
haughty (hôt´ ē) *adj.:* Proud of oneself and scornful of others

"But tell us, how can the female nurse three kids?"

"Well, they do it exactly as you're doing it now: While two of them are eating the third one looks on."

The rancher then realized his lack of manners and took Chicoria's hint. He apologized and invited his New Mexico guest to dine at the table. After dinner, Chicoria sang and recited his poetry, putting Gracia to shame. And he won his bet as well.

Beyond Literature

Social Studies Connection

The Mexican-American War "Chicoria" subtly portrays the relationship and history of the states of California and New Mexico, both of which were the territory of the independent Republic of Mexico until 1848. The first American settlers traveled by wagon to these areas during the early 1800's. During the next few decades, the relationship between the United States and Mexico deteriorated over boundary disputes. After many failed negotiations, the countries severed all ties with each other. Hostilities increased between the two countries and provoked the Mexican-American War, which began in 1846. The war was marked by a series of United States victories and ended in 1848 with the signing of the treaty of Guadelupe. According to the treaty, Mexico ceded, among other land, the territory now included in the states of California and New Mexico. California became the thirty-first state in 1850, and New Mexico became the forty-seventh state in 1912.

Cross-Curricular Activity
The central conflict of the Mexican-American War was the disagreement over which territories were claimed by which country and how far these territories expanded. Do research, and draw a map showing the territory under dispute between the United States and Mexico during this war.

Guide for Responding

◆ LITERATURE AND YOUR LIFE

Reader's Response Whom did you think would win the bet—the servants or Chicoria?

Thematic Focus What did you learn about relationships from reading this tale?

Journal Writing Jot down other ways in which Chicoria might have taught the rancher a lesson.

☑ Check Your Comprehension

1. Who is Chicoria?
2. Why do the New Mexicans bring Chicoria to California?
3. What bet does Chicoria make with the servants on the ranch?
4. How does Chicoria win the bet?

◆ Critical Thinking

INTERPRET
1. Why does Chicoria assume that he will eat at the rancher's table? **[Analyze]**
2. Chicoria states that "I never beg," and then makes a bet with the servants. What does this show about his character? **[Interpret]**
3. What determines who sits with the rancher at dinner and who does not? **[Connect]**
4. How does Chicoria's story about the goats mirror the situation in the dining room? **[Compare and Contrast]**

EVALUATE
5. Explain why telling the story about the goats was a good way to get the rancher to invite Chicoria to the table. **[Evaluate]**

APPLY
6. What might have happened if Chicoria had been so insulted that he started a confrontation with the rancher? **[Speculate]**

BRER POSSUM'S DILEMMA

JACKIE TORRENCE

Back in the days when the animals could talk, there lived ol' Brer[1] Possum. He was a fine feller. Why, he never liked to see no critters[2] in trouble. He was always helpin' out, a-doin' somethin' for others.

Ever' night, ol' Brer Possum climbed into a persimmon tree, hung by his tail, and slept all night long. And each mornin', he climbed outa the tree and walked down the road to sun 'imself.

One mornin', as he walked, he come to a big hole in the middle of the road. Now, ol' Brer Possum was kind and gentle, but he was also nosy, so he went over to the hole and looked in. All at once, he stepped back, 'cause layin'

---

1. Brer (brʉr): Dialect for "brother," used before a name.
2. critters: Dialect for "creatures"; animals.

in the bottom of that hole was ol' Brer Snake with a brick on his back.

Brer Possum said to 'imself, "I best git on outa here, 'cause ol' Brer Snake is mean and evil and lowdown, and if I git to stayin' around 'im, he jist might git to bitin' me."

So Brer Possum went on down the road.

But Brer Snake had seen Brer Possum, and he <u>commenced</u> to callin' for 'im.

◆ **Build Vocabulary**

commenced (kə menst´) *v.*: Started; began

◀ **Critical Viewing** What human characteristics does the snake exhibit in this illustration? **[Interpret]**

"Help me, Brer Possum."

Brer Possum stopped and turned around. He said to 'imself, "That's ol' Brer Snake a-callin' me. What do you reckon he wants?"

Well, ol' Brer Possum was kindhearted, so he went back down the road to the hole, stood at the edge, and looked down at Brer Snake.

"Was that you a-callin' me? What do you want?"

Brer Snake looked up and said, "I've been down here in this hole for a mighty long time with this brick on my back. Won't you help git it offa me?"

Brer Possum thought.

◆ Reading Strategy

Why does the story-teller point out the contrast between the characters of Brer Possum and Brer Snake at the begin-ning of the story?

"Now listen here, Brer Snake. I knows you. You's mean and evil and lowdown, and if'n I was to git down in that hole and git to liftin' that brick offa your back, you wouldn't do nothin' but bite me."

Ol' Brer Snake just hissed.

"Maybe not. Maybe not. Maaaaaaaybe not."

Brer Possum said, "I ain't sure 'bout you at all. I jist don't know. You're a-goin' to have to let me think about it."

So ol' Brer Possum thought—he thought high, and he thought low—and jist as he was thinkin', he looked up into a tree and saw a dead limb a-hangin' down. He climbed into the tree, broke off the limb, and with that ol' stick, pushed that brick offa Brer Snake's back. Then he took off down the road.

Brer Possum thought he was away from ol' Brer Snake when all at once he heard somethin'.

"Help me, Brer Possum."

Brer Possum said, "Oh, no, that's him agin."

But bein' so kindhearted, Brer Possum turned around, went back to the hole, and stood at the edge.

"Brer Snake, was that you a-callin' me? What do you want now?"

Ol' Brer Snake looked up outa the hole and hissed.

"I've been down here for a mighty long time, and I've gotten a little weak, and the sides of this ol' hole are too slick for me to climb. Do you think you can lift me outa here?"

Brer Possum thought.

"Now, you jist wait a minute. If'n I was to git down into that hole and lift you outa there, you wouldn't do nothin' but bite me."

Brer Snake hissed.

"Maybe not. Maybe not. Maaaaaaaybe not."

Brer Possum said, "I jist don't know. You're a-goin' to have to give me time to think about this."

So ol' Brer Possum thought.

And as he thought, he jist happened to look down there in that hole and see that ol' dead limb. So he pushed the limb underneath ol' Brer Snake and he lifted 'im outa the hole, way up into the air, and throwed 'im into the high grass.

Brer Possum took off a-runnin' down the road.

Well, he thought he was away from ol' Brer Snake when all at once he heard somethin'.

"Help me, Brer Possum."

Brer Possum thought, "That's him agin."

But bein' so kindhearted, he turned around, went back to the hole, and stood there a-lookin' for Brer Snake. Brer Snake crawled outa the high grass just as slow as he could, stretched 'imself out across the road, rared up,[3] and looked at ol' Brer Possum.

Then he hissed. "I've been down there in that ol' hole for a mighty long time, and I've gotten a little cold 'cause the sun didn't shine. Do you think you could put me in your pocket and git me warm?"

Brer Possum said, "Now you listen here, Brer Snake. I knows you. You's mean and evil and lowdown, and if'n I put you in my pocket you wouldn't do nothin' but bite me."

Brer Snake hissed.

"Maybe not. Maybe not. Maaaaaaaybe not."

"No sireee. Brer Snake. I knows you. I jist ain't a-goin' to do it."

---

3. **rared up:** Dialect for "reared up."

But jist as Brer Possum was talkin' to Brer Snake, he happened to git a real good look at 'im. He was a-layin' there lookin' so <u>pitiful</u>, and Brer Possum's great big heart began to feel sorry for ol' Brer Snake.

"All right," said Brer Possum. "You must be cold. So jist this once I'm a-goin' to put you in my pocket."

So ol' Brer Snake coiled up jist as little as he could, and Brer Possum picked 'im up and put 'im in his pocket.

Brer Snake laid quiet and still—so quiet and still that Brer Possum even forgot that he was a-carryin' 'im around. But all of a sudden, Brer Snake commenced to crawlin' out, and he turned and faced Brer Possum and hissed.

"I'm a-goin' to bite you."

But Brer Possum said, "Now wait a minute. Why are you a-goin' to bite me? I done took that brick offa your back, I got you outa that hole, and I put you in my pocket to git you warm. Why are you a-goin' to bite me?"

Brer Snake hissed.

"You knowed I was a snake before you put me in you pocket."

And when you're mindin' your own business and you spot trouble, don't never trouble trouble 'til trouble troubles you.

◆ **Literary Focus**
How does stating the message of the tale contribute to the humor of this story?

◆ **Build Vocabulary**

pitiful (pit´ i fəl) *adj.*: Deserving compassion or sympathy

*G*uide for Responding

◆ LITERATURE AND YOUR LIFE

Reader's Response Is Brer Snake to be blamed for his behavior? Why or why not?

Thematic Focus What does this tale reveal about the relationship between opossums and snakes?

Journal Writing If you were to defend Brer Snake's actions in a courtroom, what would you say? Jot down your ideas in your journal.

☑ Check Your Comprehension

1. What is Brer Possum's dilemma?
2. What does Brer Possum do every time Brer Snake asks for help?
3. Why does Brer Possum keep helping Brer Snake?
4. Why does Brer Snake bite Brer Possum?

◆ Critical Thinking

INTERPRET
1. In what ways are Brer Possum and Brer Snake different? **[Compare and Contrast]**
2. Why might Brer Possum think it was safe to put Brer Snake in his pocket even though he says the snake is mean and evil? **[Deduce]**
3. Is Brer Possum meant to look foolish or simply big-hearted? Explain. **[Infer]**

APPLY
4. How does the action of Brer Snake reveal the difficulty of changing an animal's or a person's basic nature? **[Relate]**

EXTEND
5. What do you know about opossum behavior that suits the character of Brer Possum in the story? **[Science Link]**

Why the Waves Have WHITECAPS

ZORA NEALE HURSTON

Wind and Geometry, 1978, David True, Courtesy of the artist

De wind is a woman, and de water is a woman too. They useter[1] talk together a whole heap. Mrs. Wind useter go set down by de ocean and talk and patch and crochet.

They was jus' like all lady people. They loved to talk about their chillun, and brag on 'em.

Mrs. Water useter say, "Look at *my* chillun! Ah[2] got de biggest and de littlest in de world.

All kinds of chillun. Every color in de world, and every shape!"

De wind lady bragged louder than de water woman:

"Oh, but Ah got mo' different chilluns than anybody in de world. They flies, they walks, they swims, they sings, they talks, they cries. They got all de colors from de sun. Lawd, my

---

1. **useter** (yo͞o′ stə) *v.*: Dialect for "used to."
2. **Ah** *pron.*: Dialect for "I."

▲ **Critical Viewing** In this painting, which force would you say is stronger—the wind or the water? Explain. **[Make a Judgment]**

chillun sho is a pleasure. 'Tain't nobody got no babies like mine."

Mrs. Water got tired of hearin' 'bout Mrs. Wind's chillun so she got so she hated 'em.

One day a whole passle[3] of her chillun come to Mrs. Wind and says: "Mama, wese thirsty. Kin we go git us a cool drink of water?"

She says, "Yeah chillun. Run on over to Mrs. Water and hurry right back soon."

When them chillun went to squinch they thirst Mrs. Water grabbed 'em all and drowned 'em.

When her chillun didn't come home, de wind woman got worried. So she went on

down to de water and ast for her babies.

"Good evenin' Mis' Water, you see my chillun today?"

De water woman tole her, "No-oo-oo."

Mrs. Wind knew her chillun had come down to Mrs. Water's house, so she passed over de ocean callin' her chillun, and every time she call de white feathers would come up on top of de water. And dat's how come we got white caps on waves. It's de feathers comin' up when de wind woman calls her lost babies.

When you see a storm on de water, it's de wind and de water fightin' over dem chillun.

◆ Reading Strategy
What is the story-teller's purpose in this tale?

---

3. **passle** *n.*: Dialect for "parcel."

*G*uide *for Responding*

◆ LITERATURE AND YOUR LIFE

Reader's Response What did you enjoy most about "Why the Waves Have Whitecaps"?

Thematic Focus How would you describe the relationship between Mrs. Wind and Mrs. Water?

Role Play With a classmate, role-play the scene between Mrs. Wind and Mrs. Water.

☑ Check Your Comprehension

1. Who are the main characters in this tale?
2. What do the characters brag about?
3. Why are the children drowned?
4. According to this tale, what are the white-caps on the waves?

◆ Critical Thinking

INTERPRET

1. In what ways are Mrs. Wind's and Mrs. Water's activities like those of ordinary women? **[Analyze]**
2. What negative human traits are shown by Mrs. Water and Mrs. Wind? **[Compare and Contrast]**
3. What is the moral of this story? **[Draw Conclusions]**

EXTEND

4. In what sense are whitecaps truly the result of a "dialogue" between wind and water? **[Science Link]**

COMPARE LITERARY WORKS

5. What do "Chicoria," "Brer Possum's Dilemma," and "Why the Waves Have Whitecaps" have in common? **[Connect]**

Guide for Responding (continued)

◆ Reading Strategy

RECOGNIZE THE STORYTELLER'S PURPOSE

Storytellers have a **purpose** in sharing folk tales. They pass on beliefs, customs, and instruction.

1. (a) What is the storyteller's purpose in "Chicoria"? (b) At what point do you recognize this purpose?
2. In "Brer Possum's Dilemma," the storyteller directly states the message. What is the message?
3. What does the title "Why the Waves Have Whitecaps" reveal about the storyteller's purpose?

◆ Build Vocabulary

USING SYNONYMS

Synonyms are words with the same basic meaning but different connotations—associations or slight variations in meaning. On your paper, choose the synonym that fits best in each sentence.

1. The lady of the manor was _____?_____. (snobbish, haughty)
2. The _____?_____ man shunned people he considered lower class. (haughty, snobbish)

SPELLING STRATEGY

One way to spell the *aw* sound is *au*, as in *haughty* and the words *caught, taught,* and *taut.* The *aw* sound can also be spelled *ou, o, a,* or *aw,* like *thought, toss, tall,* and *dawn.* Consult your dictionary, if necessary, to find the correct spelling.

On your paper, write the correct spelling of each of these misspelled words:

1. oudience   2. soght   3. lauss   4. hawghty

USING THE WORD BANK

On your paper, write the word from the Word Bank that best completes each sentence.

The entertainment _____?_____ with a parade of magnificently clothed riders. In contrast, my own plain clothes and old horse seemed _____?_____. The king and queen's _____?_____ appearance was in keeping with the stately procession, although they waved _____?_____ at the passersby.

◆ Literary Focus

FOLK TALES

Part of the oral tradition, **folk tales** were passed on for many generations before finally being written down. Folk tales often use humor to engage listeners while they pass on cultural information, explain mysteries of nature, or teach a lesson.

1. What can you learn about life in the Southwest by reading "Chicoria"?
2. In "Brer Possum's Dilemma," how do words like *a-callin'* and *a-lookin'* indicate that this tale came from the oral tradition?
3. (a) In what ways does "Why the Waves Have Whitecaps" teach a lesson? (b) In what ways does it explain a natural occurrence?

◆ Build Grammar Skills

COMMAS IN A SERIES

Writers use **commas** to separate three or more words, phrases, or elements in a series. Include a comma before the final conjunction. The following example has a series of three phrases:

Ever' night, ol' Brer Possum *climbed into a persimmon tree, hung by his tail,* and *slept all night long.*

Practice On your paper, copy the sentences, adding commas in the series.

1. The waves can talk sing and cry.
2. When Mrs. Water got angry, she grabbed the children drowned them and lied to Mrs. Wind.
3. Mrs. Water had children of every color all shapes and different sizes.
4. The women used to chat sew brag and crochet.
5. The wind never found her children her happiness or her peace of mind.

Writing Application Write the following sentences, adding another item to create a series, and placing commas where they are needed.

1. When Chicoria began telling his fantastic tale, the servants and the rancher listened.
2. Brer Snake is mean and evil.
3. Folk tales amuse and teach their listeners.

Build Your Portfolio

 ## Idea Bank

Writing

1. **List** Create a list of details from "Chicoria" that reveal its cultural setting.

2. **Retelling** Update "Chicoria" by writing a modern version of the tale. Maintain the lesson taught in the original tale.

3. **Essay** Could Brer Snake have overcome his natural inclinations and refrained from biting Brer Possum? In a brief essay, examine the characters of Brer Possum and Brer Snake, and come to a conclusion about their natures. Use details from the story to support your points.

Speaking and Listening

4. **Skit [Group Activity]** With a group of classmates, present a skit based on one of the folk tales in this group. First, prepare a written script that includes dialogue and stage notes. Then, create costumes. Finally, perform your skit for your class. **[Performing Arts Link]**

5. **Oral Tale [Group Activity]** Without ever writing it down, make up a new folk tale. After the tale is firm in your mind, practice telling it aloud. Then, tell your tale to a classmate. Have your classmate tell your tale to the class. Finally, discuss the subtle changes that occurred from one telling to the next.

Projects

6. **Folk-Tale Collection [Group Activity]** With a small group of classmates, find folk tales from different parts of the world. Compile a collection of folk tales to share with the class. **[Literature Link]**

7. **Illustration of a Story** Choose a story from this group to illustrate. Use paints, pastels, or whatever art materials you prefer. Display your artwork for the class. **[Art Link]**

 ## Writing Mini-Lesson

Persuasive Advertisement

A persuasive advertisement attempts to convince you to accept an idea or buy a product. In order to be convincing, the ad makes claims about or offers reasons why the product or idea is important or superior to another one. Write an advertisement that persuades your audience to buy a copy of one of the stories in this group.

Writing Skills Focus: Use an Effective Format

Advertisements are not written in paragraph form because they aim to capture readers' attention quickly and easily. **Use an effective format,** like bulleted lists, numbered lists, and boldface headings, to make your ideas stand out.

Model
"A Thrilling Read!" *New Britain Daily Journal*

- Adventure
- Romance
- Suspense

Prewriting Choose the story you will advertise. Write catchy phrases you could use as headlines, and list the details you will include in your ad.

Drafting As you draft, include the persuasive details you thought of while prewriting. Experiment with different formats. When you find a format you like, such as a bulleted list, make another draft that keeps to that format.

Revising Make sure you have a strong opening line and that you include details that will persuade your audience to buy the story. Then, check to make sure that your format is clear and effective.

> ◆ **Grammar Application**
> Insert commas between words or phrases in a series of three or more.

CONNECTING LITERATURE TO SOCIAL STUDIES

THE SPACE AGE: PUSHING THE FRONTIER

from **The Right Stuff** *by Tom Wolfe*

Shepard's Flight
Altitude: 116.5 statute miles
Duration: 15 min., 12 sec.
Distance: 303 statute miles
Velocity: 5,134 m.p.h.

THE FRONTIER IN AMERICAN HISTORY

Throughout most of American history, there was a far-off land that was unsettled or unexplored. This area was known as "the frontier." In the minds of many people, the frontier was what made the United States different from most European countries. Americans—at least in their imaginations—could embark on adventure by heading for the frontier.

The New Frontier By the middle of the twentieth century, virtually all large tracts of land in the United States had been developed and populated. Many people felt they no longer had an unexplored place to dream about. When John F. Kennedy was elected President in 1960, he began using the term "The New Frontier." He said Americans needed to think of ways to replace the frontier that no longer existed. As one replacement, Kennedy suggested Americans begin thinking about exploring the last frontier—the moon.

"The Right Stuff" One of the biggest news topics of the 1960's was the preparation for a trip to the moon. Tom Wolfe later wrote a book about the former test pilots who were selected and the rigorous training they underwent for the trip into space. It was a difficult and very dangerous job, requiring levels of ability and courage that few people had. The outstanding qualifications needed to be an astronaut were known as "the right stuff." Wolfe used this expression as the title of his book about these men.

The following excerpt from *The Right Stuff* tells how Alan Shepard was elevated to hero status following a groundbreaking rocket flight.

from THE RIGHT STUFF

Tom Wolfe

Glenn[1] and the others now watched from the sidelines as Al Shepard[2] was hoisted out of their midst and installed as a national hero on the order of a Lindbergh.[3] That was the way it looked. As soon as his technical debriefings[4] had been completed, Shepard was flown straight from Grand Bahama Island to Washington. The next day the six also-rans[5] joined him there. They stood by as President Kennedy gave Al the Distinguished Service Medal in a ceremony in the Rose Garden of the White House. Then they followed in his wake as Al sat up on the back of an open limousine waving to the crowds along Constitution Avenue. Tens of thousands of people had turned out to watch the motorcade, even though it had been arranged with barely twenty-four hours' notice. They were screaming to Al, reaching out,

> **Connecting Literature to Social Studies**
> Why would the spectators feel gratitude toward Shepard?

---

1. **Glenn:** John Herschel Glenn, Jr. (b. 1921); First American to orbit the Earth (1962).
2. **Shepard:** Alan B. Shepard, Jr. (1923–1998); on May 5, 1961, he became the first U.S. astronaut to travel in space.
3. **Lindbergh** (lind´ bərg): Charles Augustus Lindbergh (1902–1974); U.S. navigator who made the first nonstop flight from New York to Paris in 1927.
4. **debriefings:** Information given concerning a flight or mission just completed.
5. **also-rans:** Nonwinners in a race, competition, or election.

▲ **Critical Viewing** This photograph captures Alan Shepard being honored in a parade. What evidence shows that he had become a hero of the people? **[Connect]**

crying, awash with awe and gratitude. It took the motorcade half an hour to travel the one mile from the White House to the Capitol. Al sometimes seemed to have transistors in his solar plexus.[6] But not now; now he seemed truly moved. They adored him. He was on . . . the Pope's balcony . . . Thirty minutes of it . . . The next day New York City gave Al a ticker-tape parade up Broadway. There was Al on the back ledge of the limousine, with all that paper snow and confetti coming down, just the way you used to see it in the Movietone News in the theaters. Al's hometown, Derry, New Hampshire, which was not much more than a village, gave Al a parade, and it drew the biggest crowd the state had ever seen. Army, Navy, Marine, Air Force, and National Guard troops from all over New England marched down Main Street, and <u>aerobatic</u> teams of jet fighters flew overhead. The politicians thought New Hampshire was entering Metro Heaven and came close to renaming Derry "Spacetown U.S.A." before they got hold of themselves. In the town of Deerfield, Illinois, a new school was named for Al, overnight, just like that. Then Al started getting tons of greeting cards in the mail, cards saying "Congratulations to Alan Shepard, Our First Man in Space!" That was already printed on the cards, along with NASA's address. All the buyers had to do was sign them and mail them. The card companies were cranking these things out. Al was that much of a hero.

---

6. **seemed to have transistors in his solar plexus:** Showed little or no emotion.

◆ Build Vocabulary

aerobatic (er′ ə bat′ ik) *adj.*: Performing loops, rolls, etc., with an airplane; stuntlike

---

Guide for Responding

◆ LITERATURE AND YOUR LIFE

Reader's Response Do you think the crowd overreacted to Shepard's accomplishment? Explain.

Thematic Focus What does this selection suggest about heroism and how heroes are made?

☑ Check Your Comprehension

1. What did the other astronauts do while Shepard was being honored by President Kennedy and the crowds of people?
2. How was Shepard's reaction to the crowds different from his usual reaction to things?
3. How did the town of Deerfield, Illinois, honor Alan Shepard?

◆ Critical Thinking

INTERPRET

1. Wolfe refers to "Glenn and the others," the astronauts who were not chosen to take that first flight into space. What phrases does he use to suggest that they were not happy with their situation? **[Infer]**
2. As the days pass, does the public become more appreciative or less appreciative of Shepard? Explain. **[Analyze]**
3. Wolfe continually refers to Shepard as "Al." What can you conclude about Wolfe's attitude toward Shepard from this reference? **[Draw Conclusions]**

APPLY

4. In what other situations have you seen one or more people treated as Alan Shepard was treated after his flight? How do their accomplishments compare with Shepard's? **[Relate]**

Meet the Author

Tom Wolfe (1931–) began his career as a reporter for the *Washington Post* in 1959 and then worked for the *New York Herald Tribune* in 1962. His first collection of articles, published in 1965, was entitled *The Kandy-Kolored Tangerine-Flake Streamline Baby.* He has since published eight books of nonfiction and three novels. He is best known for his style of humorously criticizing some of the more foolish things that Americans do.

CONNECTING LITERATURE TO SOCIAL STUDIES

In *The Right Stuff*, Tom Wolfe shows that the work done by test pilots and astronauts was both difficult and dangerous. But he also shows that the American people were more than ready to celebrate new American heroes. This need for heroes was perhaps due to political unrest during the Vietnam War and the ever-present threat of Soviet aggression during the Cold War.

1. What qualities and achievements do Alan Shepard and Charles Lindbergh share?
2. List the details in the selection that make Alan Shepard seem like a heroic figure.
3. According to Tom Wolfe, is Shepard truly deserving of the adoration of the public? Why or why not?

 Idea Bank

Writing

1. **Journal Entry** Write an entry that Alan Shepard might have put into his journal after the events described in the selection.
2. **News Article** Write a newspaper article describing the parade honoring Shepard. You may want to "interview" parade watchers and get their reactions to Shepard's accomplishments.
3. **Essay** In an essay, describe the qualities that an astronaut must have in order to be successful. You may also want to include information about the training and education necessary to qualify for the job.

Speaking and Listening

4. **Dialogue [Group Activity]** With a classmate, pretend you are at one of the parades given for Alan Shepard. Discuss your feelings about

what he accomplished. **[Performing Arts Link]**
5. **Speech** Write a speech for Alan Shepard to make at one of the parades honoring him. Deliver the speech to your class.

Projects

6. **Report** Use an encyclopedia and other sources to learn about the accomplishments of Alan Shepard and other early astronauts. Report to the class on what you learn.
7. **Illustration** Use reference works to learn about the rocket ship that Shepard rode on his first flight into space. Create a detailed illustration of the ship, and place it on the classroom bulletin board. **[Art Link; Science Link]**

Further Reading, Listening, and Viewing

- *The Right Stuff*, a feature film based on Tom Wolfe's book, tells the story of the group of pilots selected to be trained as astronauts for America's first flight to the moon.
- Paul Westman's *Alan Shepard, The First American in Space* (1979) covers the life of Shepard from his boyhood in New England to his walk on the moon.
- Carolyn Blacknall's *Sally Ride* (1984) is a biography of the first American woman in space.

Multimedia Presentation

Writing Process Workshop

Storytellers and writers have brought folk tales to life for centuries through their dynamic presentations of the tales. In the contemporary age, you have other resources for creating a dynamic presentation. You can create a multimedia presentation, which supplies information through a variety of media, such as written materials, slides, videos, music, audio, maps, charts, graphs, photos, drawings, and fine art reproductions.

Create a multimedia presentation of or about folk tales. The following skills from this section's Writing Mini-Lessons will help you make an interesting multimedia presentation:

Writing Skills Focus

▶ Use vivid descriptions to **show, not just tell,** information. (See p. 898.)

▶ **Use visual support** to portray a character, event, or description. (See p. 909.)

▶ **Use an effective format.** Choose a method of presenting that is manageable and suits your audience. (See p. 921.)

After reading "Coyote Steals the Sun and Moon," one student created a multimedia presentation about the Zuñi.

MODEL FROM LITERATURE

"Coyote Steals the Sun and Moon" comes from the Zuñi culture. The Zuñi live in New Mexico on the Arizona border. [Show map of southwestern United States.] ① Zuñi Pueblo—a village including modern and traditional dwellings, mostly made of adobe bricks and wood— ② is still home to many of the Zuñi people. This is what a pueblo looks like. [Show picture of pueblo.] ③

① A map of the southwestern United States visually supports the writer's point.

② This description of a pueblo helps the audience visualize it.

③ Directions placed in brackets remind the presenter when to introduce the media.

Prewriting

Choose a Topic For your topic, you may want to use one of the folk tales in this unit, find a new folk tale (see p. 963 for Extended Reading Opportunities), or write about the culture or history related to a folk tale. You may decide, however, to use one of the topic ideas suggested below:

Other Topic Ideas

- Cyclones and tornadoes
- Transcontinental railroads of the 1800's
- Heroes of our time

Find Multimedia Support Visual aids and other types of media will significantly enliven your presentation. Indicate how the media will enhance your audience's understanding of the folk tale. For instance, your written report may indicate when readers should press Play. If you are giving an oral presentation, explain why you are showing a visual.

- ▶ **Maps** can clarify historical or geographical information.
- ▶ **Graphs and charts** can make complicated information easier to understand.
- ▶ **Pictures or drawings** illustrate objects, scenes, and other details.
- ▶ **Audio and video** provide visual and auditory support for your points.

Plan Your Organization Make an outline of the organization for your presentation. On the outline, note the points during which you plan to present audio and visual aspects of your presentation.

    I. **Cyclones**

        A. [Show photograph of cyclone]

            1. [Post chart of statistics]

Drafting

Show, Don't Tell Use visual support to back up your vivid descriptions. When incorporating media, make sure you introduce the pieces and explain why you are using them.

Use an Effective Format As you draft, use an effective format to make the information within your multimedia presentation easy to find. You may want to use bulleted lists, numbered lists, boldface, italics, and other visual clues to call out important information.

DRAFTING/REVISING

APPLYING LANGUAGE SKILLS: Creating Unity

When every detail in a piece of writing supports one idea, that writing has **unity.** In a multimedia presentation, all the media used should relate to the main point. Use the following strategies to achieve unity:

- **Identify your main idea,** and choose details that support it.
- **Delete ideas** that are unrelated to the main point.

Practice Identify the main idea, and eliminate any details that do not belong.

In 1977, a spacecraft named *Voyager 2* was launched on a mission to the outer edge of the solar system. The solar system, as you know, has nine planets. Using radio signals, *Voyager 2* sent back thousands of photographs. *Voyager 2* has provided crucial clues to the origins of our solar system. It has also given humans a vivid sense of the vastness of space.

Writing Application In your presentation, create unity by deleting details that do not support your main point.

Writer's Solution Connection Writing Lab

For help finding sources, see the instruction on library resources in the Prewriting section of the Reports tutorial.

APPLYING LANGUAGE SKILLS: Using Commas in Compound Sentences

A **compound sentence** combines two or more independent clauses with a comma and a coordinating conjunction (*and, or, but, for, nor, yet, so*). Following are examples:

Cleopatra was born in 69 B.C., **and** she died in 30 B.C.

Cleopatra was not beautiful, **but** she attracted some of the greatest Romans of her time.

Practice Write these sentences with correct punctuation:

1. This Zuñi girl is learning French but she already speaks three languages.
2. The Zuñi raise corn and wheat and they engage in sheep herding on a large scale.
3. You could watch the masked dancers or you could attend a Zuñi feast.

Writing Application As you write your multimedia presentation, use commas in compound sentences correctly.

Writer's Solution Connection Language Lab

For more help with commas, complete the Commas lesson in the Punctuation unit.

Revising

Use a Checklist Use the following checklist to help you evaluate and revise your presentation:

▶ Do my descriptions show, not just tell, information? *Read descriptive passages to a partner. Ask him or her to describe what type of visual picture the description gives. If he or she comes up with a picture that doesn't resemble your description, revise by deleting or adding descriptive details to create the impression you want.*

▶ Did I use appropriate visual support? *Review your choice of visuals. Ask yourself whether they really support your points. If a visual is not strong support, don't use it. It will only confuse your audience.*

▶ Did I use an effective format? *Review your placement of media to make sure they clearly support the points they accompany. Make sure media are manageable. If you have to use audio, television, and several pictures one after another, it might distract your audience. Spread the media throughout your presentation.*

REVISION MODEL

Cyclone Bill invented the Fourth of July. The holiday ① [Press cassette for audio of fireworks]

celebrated with fireworks and picnics angered the cyclone. ② [Play video of cyclone]

As you can see, the ② twisting and turning cyclone is dangerous, but Pecos Bill

[Show drawing of Bill] was not afraid.

① Since this presentation will be read by the teacher, the writer made the format more effective by including directions for using the media.

② The writer included the video of the cyclone because not everyone knows what one is and how powerful it is.

③ The writer adds these words to make his description more vivid.

Publishing and Presenting

Live Audience Find a live audience who will appreciate your presentation: an elementary-school class, a local organization, or a group or club in your school. Encourage questions following your presentation.

Internet Publish your work on a site devoted to your topic.

Real-World Reading Skills Workshop

Strategies for Success

By working with the text and the layout—or overall design—of a page, editors and designers create pages that are attractive and easy to use. To make different sections of text stand out, they use some of these features:

- ▶ Heads in different colors or fonts
- ▶ Text in **bold** or *italic* typeface
- ▶ Bulleted/or numbered lists
- ▶ Boxed sections

Learn to take advantage of the structure of text on a page.

Scan the Headings Often the main topics of a chapter or an article are printed in larger or darker headings. If you scan these headings, you can gain an overview of the entire article before you read it. The overview will provide a context for the information in the article.

Determine Text Functions As you read, you'll soon find a pattern in the use of headings and **boldface** and *italic* type. Usually, headings of the same size and style indicate equal importance; for example, a large heading would be the main topic and four equally smaller subheads would indicate supporting sections. **Boldface** is often used to draw attention to important terms. *Italics* are often used for glossary or vocabulary terms.

Look for Set-off Items Significant terms, related concepts, formulas, dates, and summaries may be set apart in a box, a sidebar, or with special shading.

Apply the Strategies

Use the headings and text structure in the article at left to answer the following questions.

1. Scan the headings and provide an overview of this article.

2. Locate three technical terms. How are they printed?

3. Why is the information on summer protection presented in a box?

THE SUN'S EFFECT ON THE SKIN

The largest and most visible organ of your body, the skin is greatly affected by the sun.

THE ROLE OF MELANIN

Melanin is the dark, protective coloring in the skin. The amount of melanin determines whether a person tans or burns in the sun. . . .

SEVERE SUN BURN

Sunburn can be a serious problem, causing fever, chills, and first- and second-degree burn damage to the skin.

Sun blisters are one defense the body raises against serious burns. . . .

THE WORK OF SWEAT

Without the sweat glands in the skin, the body would overheat and expire. Sweat glands produce about a pint of sweat daily, but in the hot summer, they can produce up to four pints.

> **Summer Protection Plan**
> * Always wear sunscreen outdoors
> * Wear a hat when the sun is highest
> * Wear sunglasses
> * Drink plenty of water
> * If you begin to burn, get out of the sun

> ✔ Use headings and text structure to read the following texts more efficiently:
> - ▶ Newspaper feature articles
> - ▶ Textbooks
> - ▶ Long encyclopedia entries
> - ▶ World Wide Web pages

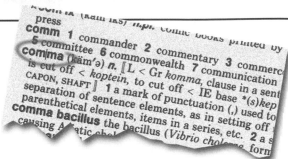

Commas are used to create pauses in sentences that help readers follow ideas.

Commas in Compound Sentences A comma is used in a compound sentence to separate two independent clauses that are joined by a comma and a coordinating conjunction (*and, but, for, nor, or, so,* and *yet*). (See p. 908.) An independent clause has a subject and a verb and expresses a complete thought. In the following example, the comma before the conjunction *but* separates independent clauses:

Nobody respected his name, Imitator, *but* it fit him.

Commas in a Series When listing three or more items in a series, use commas to separate them. The items may be words, phrases, or other elements. Include a comma before the conjunction preceding the final item. In the following example, commas separate the three things that Chicoria did:

Chicoria *sang, recited poetry,* and *put Gracia to shame.*

Unnecessary Commas Using unnecessary commas can mislead the reader. (See p. 897.) A comma is not necessary before a coordinating conjunction when it links words or groups of words that are *not* independent clauses.

Unnecessary: Of Johnny Appleseed, two things are known: he loved apples, *and* walking alone.

Correct: Of Johnny Appleseed, two things are known: he loved apples *and* walking alone.

Practice 1 In your notebook, write these sentences, adding commas where necessary and eliminating unnecessary commas:

1. "They bother and kill people and the tribes cannot increase as I wish."

2. They fly, and walk, and sing and cry.

3. "Well, Coyote was a chief after all and he felt good again."

4. For fifty years, Johnny Appleseed planted nurtured and harvested apple trees.

5. He lived with owl, and bear-cub, and possum.

Practice 2 Revise the following sentences according to the directions in parentheses. Place commas correctly.

1. The master will invite me of his own accord. I'll sit at the master's table. (Make compound sentence)

2. You can beg or ask but they won't invite you. (Add one item to make a series)

3. Chicoria greeted the rancher. The rancher replied haughtily. (Make a compound sentence)

4. Johnny Appleseed wished trees would root and blossom. (Add one item to make a series)

5. Coyote is often a troublemaker. Other animals distrusted him because he stole a box and the sun. (Make compound sentence, and add one item to make a series)

Grammar in Writing

✔ *Be careful not to write run-on sentences when you are writing compound sentences. A run-on sentence is one that omits the comma and conjunction between two independent clauses or has only a comma between the two clauses.*

PART 2 *Tales of American Heroes*

The Giant, 1923, N.C. Wyeth, Brandywine River Museum, Chadds Ford, PA

Guide for Reading

Meet the Authors:

Adrien Stoutenburg (1916–1982)

A poet, biographer, and writer, Adrien Stoutenburg wrote close to forty books. In addition to writing, Stoutenburg worked as a librarian and a political reporter. "Hammerman" was taken from her book *American Tall Tales.*

Carl Sandburg (1878–1976)

Carl Sandburg is best known for his poetry, but he was also a journalist, an author of children's books, and a historian. Sandburg received two Pulitzer Prizes—one in 1940 for his biography of Abraham Lincoln and one in 1950 for his *Complete Poems.* [For more on Carl Sandburg, see page 344.]

Harold W. Felton (1902–)

Harold William Felton practiced law and worked for the Internal Revenue Service, yet he became increasingly interested in the legends and folklore of the United States. He has published collections of stories about folk heroes and the cowboys of the West.

Davy Crockett (1786–1836)

Davy Crockett was a celebrated frontiersman, soldier in the United States Army, and Tennessee congressman. His tall tales strongly influenced the comic tradition and legendary history of the western frontier. He fought at the Alamo for Texan independence and was killed there by Mexican troops.

◆ LITERATURE AND YOUR LIFE

CONNECT YOUR EXPERIENCE

Think about people from real life and fiction who perform heroic deeds that amaze and surprise you. The tales in this group are about several such larger-than-life heroes.

THEMATIC FOCUS: Heroes

What qualities and actions elevate these characters to folk-hero status?

◆ Background for Understanding

SOCIAL STUDIES

John Henry was an actual person who was employed by the Chesapeake and Ohio Railroad. Railroad companies boomed during the 1870's. The Central Pacific Railroad began building tracks west from Omaha, Nebraska, and the Union Pacific Railroad began building tracks east from Sacramento, California. The tracks met and joined to create the first transcontinental railroad. By the end of the decade, more than 70,000 miles of railroad track crisscrossed the United States.

◆ Build Vocabulary

RELATED WORDS: FORMS OF *skeptic*

Skeptic is a noun meaning "a person who questions matters that are generally accepted." Words related to *skeptic* include the adjective *skeptical* and the adverb *skeptically.*

WORD BANK

Which word from the selections means "unexplainable"? Check the Build Vocabulary box on page 949 to see if you chose correctly.

> hefted
> granite
> commotion
> usurped
> invincible
> futile
> inexplicable
> skeptics

Hammerman ◆ John Henry
◆ Paul Bunyan of the North Woods ◆
Pecos Bill: The Cyclone ◆ Davy Crockett's Dream

Hammer in His Hand, Palmer C. Hayden, Museum of African American Art, Los Angeles, CA

◆ Literary Focus

TALL TALE

A **tall tale** is a humorous story that recounts exaggerated events in a matter-of-fact way, using the everyday speech of the common people. Tall tales are often associated with life on the American frontier. They are considered to be part of the oral tradition because they have been handed down from generation to generation by word of mouth.

◆ Reading Strategy

PREDICT

Tall tales, like other folk tales, develop in predictable patterns. You can **predict** that the characters will perform exaggerated or even impossible feats. Once you learn the character's traits, you can predict the kinds of events that will occur. For example, John Henry is known for his strength, so you can predict that he will perform some amazing feat of strength.

Use a chart like the one below to predict the kinds of events the stories will tell.

Character	Trait	Prediction
John Henry	Strength	

HAMMERMAN
Adrien Stoutenburg

People down South still tell stories about John Henry, how strong he was, and how he could whirl a big sledge[1] so lightning-fast you could hear thunder behind it. They even say he was born with a hammer in his hand. John Henry himself said it, but he probably didn't mean it exactly as it sounded.

The story seems to be that when John Henry was a baby, the first thing he reached out for was a hammer, which was hung nearby on the cabin wall.

John Henry's father put his arm around his wife's shoulder. "He's going to grow up to be a steel-driving man. I can see it plain as rows of cotton running uphill."

As John Henry grew a bit older, he practiced swinging the hammer, not hitting at things, but just enjoying the feel of it whooshing against the air. When he was old enough to talk, he told everyone, "I was born with a hammer in my hand."

John Henry was still a boy when the Civil War started, but he was a big, hard-muscled boy, and he could outwork and outplay all the other boys on the plantation.

"You're going to be a mighty man, John Henry," his father told him.

"A man ain't nothing but a man," young John Henry said. "And I'm a natural man, born to swing a hammer in my hand."

At night, lying on a straw bed on the floor, John Henry listened to a far-off train whistling through the darkness. Railroad tracks had been laid to carry trainloads of Southern soldiers to fight against the armies of the North. The trains had a lonesome, longing sound that made John Henry want to go wherever they were going.

When the war ended, a man from the North came to John Henry where he was working in the field. He said, "The slaves are free now. You can pack up and go wherever you want, young fellow."

"I'm craving to go where the trains go," said John Henry.

The man shook his head. "There are too many young fellows trailing the trains around now. You better settle down to doing what you know, like handling a cotton hook or driving a mule team."

John Henry thought to himself, there's a big hammer waiting for me somewhere, because I know I'm a steel-driving man. All I have to do is

---

1. **sledge** (slej) *n.*: Heavy hammer, usually swung with both hands.

hunt 'til I find it.

That night, he told his folks about a dream he had had.

"I dreamed I was working on a railroad somewhere," he said, "a big, new railroad called the C.& O., and I had a mighty hammer in my hand. Every time I swung it, it made a whirling flash around my shoulder. And every time my hammer hit a spike,[2] the sky lit up from the sparks."

"I believe it," his father said. "You were born to drive steel."

"That ain't all of the dream," John Henry said. "I dreamed that the railroad was going to be the end of me and I'd die with the hammer in my hand."

The next morning, John Henry bundled up some food in a red bandanna handkerchief, told his parents good-bye, and set off into the world. He walked until he heard the clang-clang of hammers in the distance. He followed the sound to a place where gangs of men were building a railroad. John Henry watched the men driving steel spikes down into the crossties[3] to hold the rails in place. Three men would stand around a spike, then each, in turn, would swing a long hammer.

John Henry on the Right, Steam Drill on the Left, Palmer Hayden, Collection of The Museum of African American Art, Los Angeles, CA

▲ **Critical Viewing** What story event does this painting illustrate? Point out the details that reflect details in the story. **[Connect]**

◆ **Reading Strategy**
Do you predict John Henry's dream will come true? Why or why not?

John Henry's heart beat in rhythm with the falling hammers. His fingers ached for the feel of a hammer in his own hands. He walked over to the foreman.

"I'm a natural steel-driving man," he said. "And I'm looking for a job."

"How much steel-driving have you done?" the foreman asked.

"I was born knowing how," John Henry said.

The foreman shook his head. "That ain't good enough, boy. I can't take any chances. Steel-driving's dangerous work, and you might hit somebody."

"I wouldn't hit anybody," John Henry said, "because I can drive one of those spikes all by myself."

The foreman said sharply, "The one kind of man I don't need in this outfit is a bragger. Stop wasting my time."

John Henry didn't move. He got a stubborn look around his jaw. "You loan me a hammer, mister, and if somebody will hold the spike for me, I'll prove what I can do."

The three men who had just finished driving in a spike looked toward him and laughed. One of them said, "Anybody who would hold a spike for a greenhorn[4] don't want to live long."

"I'll hold it," a fourth man said.

John Henry saw that the speaker was a small, dark-skinned fellow about his own age.

The foreman asked the small man, "D'you aim to get yourself killed, Li'l Willie?"

Li'l Willie didn't answer. He knelt and set a

2. **spike** (spīk) *n.:* Long, thick metal nail used for splitting rock.
3. **crossties** (krôs´ tīz) *n.:* Beams laid crosswise under railroad tracks to support them.

4. **greenhorn** (grēn´ hôrn) *n.:* Inexperienced person; a beginner.

spike down through the rail on the crosstie. "Come on, big boy," he said.

John Henry picked up one of the sheepnose hammers lying in the cinders. He <u>hefted</u> it and decided it was too light. He picked up a larger one which weighed twelve pounds. The handle was lean and limber and greased with tallow[5] to make it smooth.

Everyone was quiet, watching, as he stepped over to the spike.

John Henry swung the hammer over his shoulder so far that the hammer head hung down against the back of his knees. He felt a thrill run through his arms and chest.

"Tap it down gentle, first," said Li'l Willie.

But John Henry had already started to swing. He brought the hammer flashing down, banging the spike squarely on the head. Before the other men could draw a breath of surprise, the hammer flashed again, whirring through the air like a giant hummingbird. One more swing, and the spike was down, its steel head smoking from the force of the blow.

The foreman blinked, swallowed, and blinked again. "Man," he told John Henry, "you're hired!"

That's the way John Henry started steel driving. From then on, Li'l Willie was always with him, setting the spikes, or placing the drills[6] that John Henry drove with his hammer. There wasn't another steel-driving man in the world who could touch John Henry for speed and power. He could hammer every which way, up or down or sidewise. He could drive for ten hours at a stretch and never miss a stroke.

After he'd been at the work for a few years, he started using a twenty-pound hammer in each hand. It took six men, working fast, to carry fresh drills to him. People would come for miles around to watch John Henry.

Whenever John Henry worked, he sang. Li'l Willie sang with him, chanting the rhythm of the clanging hammer strokes.

Those were happy days for John Henry. One of the happiest days came when he met a black-eyed, curly-haired girl called Polly Ann. And, on the day that Polly Ann said she would marry him, John Henry almost burst his throat with singing.

Every now and then, John Henry would remember the strange dream he had had years before, about the C. & O. Railroad and dying with a hammer in his hand. One night, he had the dream again. The next morning, when he went to work, the steel gang gathered round him, hopping with excitement.

"The Chesapeake and Ohio Railroad wants men to drive a tunnel through a mountain in West Virginia!" they said.

"The C. & O. wants the best hammermen there are!" they said. "And they'll pay twice as much as anybody else."

Li'l Willie looked at John Henry. "If they want the best, John Henry, they're goin' to need you."

John Henry looked back at his friend. "They're going to need you, too, Li'l Willie. I ain't going without you." He stood a minute, looking at the sky. There was a black thundercloud way off, with sunlight flashing behind it. John Henry felt a small chill between his shoulder blades. He shook himself, put his hammer on his shoulder, and said, "Let's go, Willie!"

When they reached Summers County where the Big Bend Tunnel was to be built, John Henry sized up the mountain standing in the way. It was almost solid rock.

"Looks soft," said John Henry. "Hold a drill up there, Li'l Willie."

Li'l Willie did. John Henry took a seventy-pound hammer and drove the drill in with one mountain-cracking stroke. Then he settled down to working the regular way, pounding in the drills with four or five strokes of a twenty-pound sledge. He worked so fast that his helpers had to keep buckets of water ready to pour on his hammers so they wouldn't catch fire.

---

5. **tallow** (tal´ ō) *n.*: Solid fat obtained from sheep or cattle.
6. **drills** (drilz) *n.*: Pointed tools used for making holes in hard substances.

Polly Ann, who had come along to West Virginia, sat and watched and cheered him on. She sang along with him, clapping her hands to the rhythm of his hammer, and the sound echoed around the mountains. The songs blended with the rumble of dynamite where the blasting crews were at work. For every time John Henry drilled a hole in the mountain's face, other men poked dynamite and black powder into the hole and then lighted a fuse to blow the rock apart.

It's Wrote on the Rock, Palmer C. Hayden, Museum of African American Art, Los Angeles, CA

▲ **Critical Viewing** What do the couple in this painting appear to be doing? Support your answer. **[Infer]**

One day the tunnel boss Cap'n Tommy Walters was standing watching John Henry, when a stranger in city clothes walked up to him.

"Howdy, Cap'n Tommy," said the stranger. "I'd like to talk to you about a steam engine[7] I've got for sale. My engine can drive a drill through rock so fast that not even a crew of your best men can keep up with it."

"I don't need any machine," Cap'n Tommy said proudly. "My man John Henry can out-drill any machine ever built."

"I'll place a bet with you, Cap'n," said the salesman. "You race your man against my machine for a full day. If he wins, I'll give you the steam engine free."

Cap'n Tommy thought it over. "That sounds fair enough, but I'll have to talk to John Henry first." He told John Henry what the stranger had said. "Are you willing to race a steam drill?" Cap'n Tommy asked.

John Henry ran his big hands over the handle of his hammer, feeling the strength in the wood and in his own great muscles.

"A man's a man," he said, "but a machine ain't nothing but a machine. I'll beat that steam drill, or I'll die with my hammer in my hand!"

"All right, then," said Cap'n Tommy. "We'll set a day for the contest."

Polly Ann looked worried when John Henry told her what he had promised to do.

"Don't you worry, honey," John Henry said. It was the end of the workday, with the sunset burning across the mountain, and the sky shining like copper. He tapped his chest. "I've got a man's heart in here. All a machine has is a metal engine." He smiled and picked Polly Ann up in his arms, as if she were no heavier than a blade of grass.

On the morning of the contest, the slopes around the tunnel were crowded with people. At one side stood the steam engine, its gears and valves and mechanical drill gleaming. Its operators rushed around, giving it final spurts of grease and oil and shoving fresh pine knots into the fire that fed the steam boiler.

---

7. **steam engine:** Here, a machine that drives a drill by means of steam power.

John Henry stood leaning on his hammer, as still as the mountain rock, his shoulders shining like hard coal in the rising sun.

"How do you feel, John Henry?" asked Li'l Willie. Li'l Willie's hands trembled a bit as he held the drill ready.

"I feel like a bird ready to bust out of a nest egg," John Henry said. "I feel like a rooster ready to crow. I feel pride hammering at my heart, and I can hardly wait to get started against that machine." He sucked in the mountain air. "I feel powerful free, Li'l Willie."

Cap'n Tommy held up the starting gun. For a second everything was as silent as the dust in a drill hole. Then the gun barked, making a yelp that bounced against mountain and sky.

John Henry swung his hammer, and it rang against the drill.

At the same time, the steam engine gave a roar and a hiss. Steam whistled through its escape valve. Its drill crashed down, gnawing into the granite.

John Henry paid no attention to anything except his hammer, nor to any sound except the steady pumping of his heart. At the end of an hour, he paused long enough to ask, "How are we doing, Li'l Willie?"

Willie licked his lips. His face was pale with rock dust and with fear. "The machine's ahead, John Henry."

John Henry tossed his smoking hammer aside and called to another helper, "Bring me two hammers! I'm only getting warmed up."

He began swinging a hammer in each hand. Sparks flew so fast and hot they singed his face. The hammers heated up until they glowed like torches.

"How're we doing now, Li'l Willie?" John Henry asked at the end of another hour.

Li'l Willie grinned. "The machine's drill busted. They have to take time to fix up a new one. You're almost even now, John Henry! How're you feeling?"

"I'm feeling like sunrise," John Henry took time to say before he flashed one of his hammers down against the drill. "Clean out the hole, Willie, and we'll drive right down to China."

Above the clash of his hammers, he heard the chug and hiss of the steam engine starting up again and the whine of its rotary drill biting into rock. The sound hurt John Henry's ears.

"Sing me a song, Li'l Willie!" he gasped. "Sing me a natural song for my hammers to sing along with."

Li'l Willie sang, and John Henry kept his hammers going in time. Hour after hour, he kept driving, sweat sliding from his forehead and chest.

The sun rolled past noon and toward the west.

"How're you feeling, John Henry?" Li'l Willie asked.

"I ain't tired yet," said John Henry and stood back, gasping, while Willie put a freshly sharpened drill into the rock wall. "Only, I have a kind of roaring in my ears."

"That's only the steam engine," Li'l Willie said, but he wet his lips again. "You're gaining on it, John Henry. I reckon you're at least two inches ahead."

John Henry coughed and slung his hammer back. "I'll beat it by a mile, before the sun sets."

At the end of another hour, Li'l Willie called out, his eyes sparkling, "You're going to win, John Henry, if you can keep on drivin'!"

John Henry ground his teeth together and tried not to hear the roar in his ears or the racing thunder of his heart. "I'll go until I drop," he gasped. "I'm a steel-driving man and I'm bound to win, because a machine ain't nothing but a machine."

The sun slid lower. The shadows of the crowd grew long and purple.

"John Henry can't keep it up," someone said.

"The machine can't keep it up," another said.

Polly Ann twisted her hands together and waited for Cap'n Tommy to fire the gun to mark the end of the contest.

"Who's winning?" a voice cried.

"Wait and see," another voice answered.

There were only ten minutes left.

"How're you feeling, John Henry?" Li'l Willie whispered, sweat dripping down his own face.

John Henry didn't answer. He just kept slamming his hammers against the drill, his mouth open.

Li'l Willie tried to go on singing. "Flash that hammer—uh! Wham that drill—uh!" he croaked.

Out beside the railroad tracks, Polly beat her hands together in time, until they were numb.

The sun flared an instant, then died behind the mountain. Cap'n Tommy's gun cracked. The judges ran forward to measure the depth of the holes drilled by the steam engine and by John Henry. At last, the judges came walking back and said something to Cap'n Tommy before they turned to announce their findings to the crowd.

Cap'n Tommy walked over to John Henry, who stood leaning against the face of the mountain.

"John Henry," he said, "you beat that steam engine by four feet!" He held out his hand and smiled.

John Henry heard a distant cheering. He held his own hand out, and then he staggered. He fell and lay on his back, staring up at the mountain and the sky, and then he saw Polly Ann and Li'l Willie leaning over him.

"Oh, how do you feel, John Henry?" Polly Ann asked.

"I feel a bit tuckered out," said John Henry.

"Do you want me to sing to you?" Li'l Willie asked.

"I got a song in my own heart, thank you, Li'l Willie," John Henry said. He raised up on his elbow and looked at all the people and the last sunset light gleaming like the edge of a golden trumpet. "I was a steel-driving man," he said, and lay back and closed his eyes forever.

Down South, and in the North, too, people still talk about John Henry and how he beat the steam engine at the Big Bend Tunnel. They say, if John Henry were alive today, he could beat almost every other kind of machine, too.

Maybe so. At least, John Henry would die trying.

Guide for Responding

◆ LITERATURE AND YOUR LIFE

Reader's Response Describe your reactions as you read about the contest between John Henry and the steam engine. Who did you think would win and why?

Thematic Focus What does "Hammerman" reveal about people's resistance to technology?

Journal Writing What modern hero reminds you of John Henry? Write your response in your journal.

☑ Check Your Comprehension

1. According to legend, what did John Henry have in his hand when he was born?
2. Describe John Henry's dream.
3. (a) Against what does John Henry compete? (b) Who wins the contest?

◆ Critical Thinking

INTERPRET

1. How does the prophetic dream contribute to John Henry's status as a hero? **[Connect]**
2. Why is Li'l Willie willing to hold the spike for John Henry even though the others refuse? **[Interpret]**
3. (a) What does John Henry believe his purpose in life to be? (b) Why is it important to him that he follow this purpose even when others disapprove? **[Speculate]**

EVALUATE

4. (a) Do you think that John Henry would have won the contest if the machine had not temporarily broken down? (b) What would be the effect of this story if John Henry had lost? **[Modify]**

JOHN HENRY

Traditional

Big Bend Tunnel, Palmer Hayden, Collection of The Museum of African American Art, Los Angeles, CA

▲ **Critical Viewing** What message does this painting convey? **[Analyze]**

John Henry was a lil baby,
Sittin' on his mama's knee,
Said: 'The Big Bend Tunnel on the C. & O. road
Gonna cause the death of me,
5   Lawd, Lawd, gonna cause the death of me.'

Cap'n says to John Henry,
'Gonna bring me a steam drill 'round,
Gonna take that steam drill out on the job,
Gonna whop that steel on down,
10   Lawd, Lawd, gonna whop that steel on down.'

John Henry tol' his cap'n,
Lightnin' was in his eye:
'Cap'n, bet yo' las, red cent on me,
Fo' I'll beat it to the bottom or I'll die,
15   Lawd, Lawd, I'll beat it to the bottom or I'll die.'

Sun shine hot an' burnin',
Wer'n't no breeze a-tall,
Sweat ran down like water down a hill,
That day John Henry let his hammer fall,
20 Lawd, Lawd, that day John Henry let his hammer fall.

John Henry went to the tunnel,
An' they put him in the lead to drive,
The rock so tall an' John Henry so small,
That he lied down his hammer an' he cried,
25 Lawd, Lawd, that he lied down his hammer an' he cried.

John Henry started on the right hand,
The steam drill started on the lef'—
'Before I'd let this steam drill beat me down,
I'd hammer my fool self to death,
30 Lawd, Lawd, I'd hammer my fool self to death.'

John Henry had a lil woman,
Her name were Polly Ann,
John Henry took sick an' had to go to bed,
Polly Ann drove steel like a man,
35 Lawd, Lawd, Polly Ann drove steel like a man.

John Henry said to his shaker,[1]
'Shaker, why don' you sing?
I'm throwin' twelve poun's from my hips on down,
Jes' listen to the col' steel ring,
40 Lawd, Lawd, jes' listen to the col' steel ring.'

Oh, the captain said to John Henry,
'I b'lieve this mountain's sinkin' in.'
John Henry said to his captain, oh my!
'Ain' nothin' but my hammer suckin' win',
45 Lawd, Lawd, ain' nothin' but my hammer suckin' win'.'

John Henry tol' his shaker,
'Shaker, you better pray,
For, if I miss this six-foot steel,
Tomorrow'll be yo' buryin' day,
50 Lawd, Lawd, tomorrow'll be yo' buryin' day.'

John Henry tol' his captain,
'Look yonder what I see—
Yo' drill's done broke an' yo' hole's done choke,
An' you cain' drive steel like me,
55 Lawd, Lawd, an' you cain' drive steel like me.'

1. **shaker** (shā′ kər)
n.: Person who sets the spikes and places the drills for a steel-driver to hammer.

He Layed Down His Hammer and Cried, 1944–47, Palmer C. Hayden, Museum of African American Art, Los Angeles, CA

◀ **Critical Viewing** Does this painting depict John Henry as a superhero or as a man? Explain. **[Evaluate]**

The man that invented the steam drill,
Thought he was mighty fine.
John Henry drove his fifteen feet,
An' the steam drill only made nine,
60   Lawd, Lawd, an' the steam drill only made nine.

The hammer that John Henry swung,
It weighed over nine pound;
He broke a rib in his lef'-han' side,
An' his intrels[2] fell on the groun',
65   Lawd, Lawd, an' his intrels fell on the groun'.

All the womens in the Wes',
When they heared of John Henry's death,
Stood in the rain, flagged the eas'-boun' train,
Goin' where John Henry fell dead,
70   Lawd, Lawd, goin' where John Henry fell dead.

2. intrels (en´ trālz) *n.*: Entrails; inner organs.

John Henry's lil mother,
She was all dressed in red,
She jumped in bed, covered up her head,
Said she didn' know her son was dead,
75 Lawd, Lawd, didn' know her son was
    dead.

Dey took John Henry to the graveyard,
An' they buried him in the san',
An' every locomotive come roarin' by,
Says, 'There lays a steel-drivin' man,
80 Lawd, Lawd, there lays a steel-drivin'
    man.'

Beyond Literature

Science Connection

Development of the Locomotive
Although the first reported locomotive, or steam-driven vehicle, was built in the late seventeenth century, it was not until 1823, when George Stephenson constructed the first railway system and locomotive built for both freight and passengers, that the railroad era really began. The steam locomotive became the dominant form of railway transportation for more than a century. At the turn of the century, however, the steam locomotive began to be replaced by the electric locomotive and the improved diesel-electric locomotive, in part because they were powered by cheap electricity instead of expensive coal and produced no hazardous smoke or fumes.

Today, high-speed electrified trains travel on major routes at speeds over 100 miles per hour. Magnetically levitated trains (ma-glev) in Europe and Japan travel at speeds approaching 200 miles per hour.

Cross-Curricular Activity
Learn more about maglev technology, and create a diagram showing how these trains operate.

Guide for Responding

◆ LITERATURE AND YOUR LIFE

Reader's Response Do you admire John Henry's decision to challenge the steam engine in a drilling match? Explain.

Thematic Focus Did John Henry display heroism or foolishness? Explain.

Journal Writing Jot down in your journal other instances in which a human pitted his or her strength against that of a machine.

☑ Check Your Comprehension

1. At what stage in his life does John Henry predict his own death?
2. What tribute do the people in the trains give John Henry when they pass by his grave?

◆ Critical Thinking

INTERPRET
1. In the first few stanzas, how do descriptions of nature intensify the drama of the contest? **[Analyze]**
2. How important is it to John Henry to beat the steam engine? Explain. **[Infer]**
3. (a) Why do you think people pay tribute to John Henry? (b) What do their tributes tell you about his character? **[Speculate]**
4. What qualities of John Henry make him a folk hero? **[Interpret]**

EVALUATE
5. Do you think the tribute to John Henry in lines 78–80 accurately sums up his character? **[Make a Judgment]**

COMPARE LITERARY WORKS
6. "John Henry" is a ballad, a sentimental song that tells a story in short stanzas with the repetition of lines, while "Hammerman" is written in prose. (a) Which form do you find more enjoyable to read? (b) Which one is more effective in relating the tale of John Henry? **[Evaluate]**

PAUL BUNYAN OF THE NORTH WOODS

Carl Sandburg

Who made Paul Bunyan, who gave him birth as a myth, who joked him into life as the Master Lumberjack, who fashioned him forth as an apparition[1] easing the hours of men amid axes and trees, saws and lumber? The people, the bookless people, they made Paul and had him alive long before he got into the books for those who read. He grew up in shanties, around the hot stoves of winter, among socks and mittens drying, in the smell of tobacco smoke and the roar of laughter mocking the outside weather. And some of Paul came overseas in wooden bunks below decks in sailing vessels. And some of Paul is old as the hills, young as the alphabet.

Paul Bunyan Carrying a Tree on His Shoulder and an Ax in His Hand

▲ **Critical Viewing** What impression of Paul Bunyan does this illustration convey? [Summarize]

The Pacific Ocean froze over in the winter of the Blue Snow and Paul Bunyan had long teams of oxen hauling regular white snow over from China. This was the winter Paul gave a party to the Seven Axmen. Paul fixed a <u>granite</u> floor sunk two hundred feet deep for them to dance on. Still, it tipped and tilted as the dance went on. And because the Seven Axmen refused to take off their hobnailed boots, the sparks from the nails of their dancing feet lit up the place so that Paul didn't light the kerosene lamps. No women being on the Big Onion river at that time the Seven Axmen had to dance with each other, the one left over in each set taking Paul as a partner. The <u>commotion</u> of the dancing that night brought on an earthquake and the Big Onion river moved over three counties to the east.

One year when it rained from St. Patrick's Day till the Fourth of July, Paul Bunyan got disgusted because his celebration on the Fourth was spoiled. He dived into Lake Superior and swam to where a solid pillar of water was coming down. He dived under this pillar, swam up into it and climbed with

---

1. **apparition** (ap´ ə rish´ ən) *n.*: A strange figure appearing suddenly or in an extraordinary way.

powerful swimming strokes, was gone about an hour, came splashing down, and as the rain stopped, he explained, "I turned the darn thing off." This is told in the Big North Woods and on the Great Lakes, with many particulars.

Two mosquitoes lighted on one of Paul Bunyan's oxen, killed it, ate it, cleaned the bones, and sat on a grub shanty picking their teeth as Paul came along. Paul sent to Australia for two special bumblebees to kill these mosquitoes. But the bees and the mosquitoes intermarried; their children had stingers on both ends. And things kept getting worse till Paul brought a big boatload of sorghum[2] up from Louisiana and while all the bee-mosquitoes were eating at the sweet sorghum he floated them down to the Gulf of Mexico. They got so fat that it was easy to drown them all between New Orleans and Galveston.

Paul logged on the Little Gimlet in Oregon one winter. The cookstove at that camp covered an acre of ground. They fastened the side of a hog on each snowshoe and four men used to skate on the griddle while the cook flipped the pancakes. The eating table was three miles long; elevators carried the cakes to the ends of the table where boys on bicycles rode back and forth on a path down the center of the table dropping the cakes where called for.

Benny, the Little Blue Ox of Paul Bunyan, grew two feet every time Paul looked at him, when a youngster. The barn was gone one morning and they found it on Benny's back; he grew out of it in a night. One night he kept pawing and bellowing for more pancakes, till there were two hundred men at the cookshanty stove trying to keep him fed. About breakfast time Benny broke loose, tore down the cookshanty, ate all the pancakes piled up for the loggers' breakfast. And after that Benny made his mistake; he ate the red hot stove; and that finished him. This is only one of the hot-stove stories told in the North Woods.

◆ **Literary Focus**
Explain how the tone of this passage fits the tall-tale tradition.

◆ **Build Vocabulary**
granite (gran´ it) *adj.*: Made of granite, a very hard rock
commotion (kə mō´ shən) *n.*: Noisy movement

2. **sorghum** (sôr´ gəm) *n.*: Tropical grasses bearing flowers and seeds, grown for use as grain or syrup.

*G*uide for Responding

◆ LITERATURE AND YOUR LIFE

Reader's Response Which tall tale about Paul Bunyan is your favorite? Why?

Thematic Focus In what ways does Paul Bunyan display heroic qualities?

☑ Check Your Comprehension

1. What is Paul Bunyan's occupation?
2. What natural occurrence is caused by the dancing of the Axmen?
3. (a) What is the name of Paul Bunyan's Little Blue Ox? (b) How did the ox die?

◆ Critical Thinking

INTERPRET
1. What qualities and abilities are valued in this tale? **[Interpret]**
2. Interpret the following statement: "And some of Paul is old as the hills, young as the alphabet." **[Interpret]**
3. Explain how Bunyan combines cleverness with strength to achieve his purpose. **[Support]**

APPLY
4. What generalization can you make about folk tales based on your reading of "Paul Bunyan of the North Woods"? **[Generalize]**

Pecos Bill: THE CYCLONE

Harold W. Felton

One of Bill's greatest feats, if not the greatest feat of all time, occurred unexpectedly one Fourth of July. He had invented the Fourth of July some years before. It was a great day for the cowpunchers.[1] They had taken to it right off like the real Americans they were. But the celebration had always ended on a dismal note. Somehow it seemed to be spoiled by a cyclone.

Bill had never minded the cyclone much. The truth is he rather liked it. But the other celebrants ran into caves for safety. He invented cyclone cellars for them. He even named the cellars. He called them "'fraid holes." Pecos wouldn't even say the word "afraid." The cyclone was something like he was. It was big and strong too. He always stood by musing[2] pleasantly as he watched it.

The cyclone caused Bill some trouble, though. Usually it would destroy a few hundred miles of fence by blowing the postholes away. But it wasn't much trouble for him to fix it. All he had to do was to go and get the postholes and then take them back and put the fence posts in them. The holes were rarely ever blown more than twenty or thirty miles.

In one respect Bill even welcomed the cyclone, for it blew so hard it blew the earth away from his wells. The first time this happened, he thought the wells would be a total loss. There they were, sticking up several hundred feet out of the ground. As wells they were useless. But he found he could cut them up into lengths and sell them for postholes to farmers in Iowa and Nebraska. It was very profitable, especially after he invented a special posthole saw to cut them with. He didn't use that type of posthole himself. He got the prairie dogs to dig his for him. He simply caught a few gross[3] of prairie dogs and set them down at proper intervals. The prairie dog would dig a hole. Then Bill would put a post in it. The prairie dog would get disgusted and go down the row ahead of the others and dig another hole. Bill fenced all of Texas and parts of New Mexico and Arizona in this manner. He took a few contracts and fenced most of the Southern Pacific right of way too. That's the reason it is so crooked. He had trouble getting the prairie dogs to run a straight fence.

As for his wells, the badgers dug them. The system was the same as with the prairie dogs. The labor was cheap so it didn't make much difference if the cyclone did spoil some of the wells. The badgers were digging all of the time anyway. They didn't seem to care whether they dug wells or just badger holes.

One year he tried shipping the prairie dog holes up north, too, for postholes. It was not successful. They didn't keep in storage and they couldn't stand the handling in shipping. After they were installed they seemed to wear out quickly. Bill always thought the difference in climate had something to do with it.

It should be said that in those days there

---

1. **cowpunchers** (kou′ pun chərz) *n*.: Cowboys.
2. **musing** (myōōz′ ing) *adj*.: Thinking deeply.

3. **gross** (grōs) *n*.: Twelve dozen.

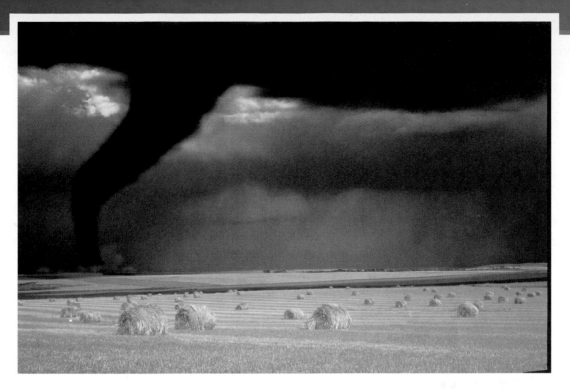

▲ **Critical Viewing** Does this cyclone seem capable of destroying "a few hundred miles of fence"? Explain. [**Assess**]

was only one cyclone. It was the first and original cyclone, bigger and more terrible by far than the small cyclones of today. It usually stayed by itself up north around Kansas and Oklahoma and didn't bother anyone much. But it was attracted by the noise of the Fourth of July celebration and without fail managed to put in an appearance before the close of the day.

On this particular Fourth of July, the celebration had gone off fine. The speeches were loud and long. The contests and games were hard fought. The high point of the day was Bill's exhibition with Widow Maker, which came right after he showed off Scat and Rat. People seemed never to tire of seeing them in action. The mountain lion was almost useless as a work animal after his accident, and the snake had grown old and somewhat infirm, and was troubled with rheumatism in his rattles. But they too enjoyed the Fourth of July and liked to make a public appearance. They relived the old days.

Widow Maker had put on a good show, bucking as no ordinary horse could ever buck. Then Bill undertook to show the gaits[4] he had taught the palomino.[5] Other mustangs[6] at that time had only two gaits. Walking and running. Only Widow Maker could pace. But now Bill had developed and taught him other gaits. Twenty-seven in all. Twenty-three forward and three reverse. He was very proud of the achievement. He showed off the slow gaits and the crowd was eager for more.

He showed the walk, trot, canter, lope, jog, slow rack, fast rack, single foot, pace, stepping pace, fox trot, running walk and the others now known. Both men and horses confuse the various gaits nowadays. Some of the gaits are now thought to be the same, such as the rack and the single foot. But with Widow Maker and Pecos Bill, each one was different. Each was precise and to be distinguished from the others. No one had ever imagined such a thing.

Then the cyclone came! All of the people except Bill ran into the 'fraid holes. Bill was

---

4. **gaits** (gāts) *n.*: Foot movements of a horse.
5. **palomino** (pal′ ə mē′ nō) *n.*: A light-tan or golden-brown horse with a cream-colored mane and tail.
6. **mustangs** (mus′ taŋz) *n.*: Wild horses.

annoyed. He stopped the performance. The remaining gaits were not shown. From that day to this horses have used no more than the gaits Widow Maker exhibited that day. It is unfortunate that the really fast gaits were not shown. If they were, horses might be much faster today than they are.

Bill glanced up at the cyclone and the quiet smile on his face faded into a frown. He saw the cyclone was angry. Very, very angry indeed.

The cyclone had always been the center of attention. Everywhere it went people would look up in wonder, fear and amazement. It had been the undisputed master of the country. It had observed Bill's rapid climb to fame and had seen the Fourth of July celebration grow. It had been keeping an eye on things all right.

In the beginning, the Fourth of July crowd had aroused its curiosity. It liked nothing more than to show its superiority and power by breaking the crowd up sometime during the day. But every year the crowd was larger. This preyed on the cyclone's mind. This year it did not come to watch. It deliberately came to spoil the celebration. Jealous of Bill and of his success, it resolved to do away with the whole institution of the Fourth of July once and for all. So much havoc and destruction would be wrought that there would never be another Independence Day Celebration. On that day, in future years, it would circle around the horizon leering[7] and gloating. At least, so it thought.

The cyclone was resolved, also, to do away with this bold fellow who did not hold it in awe and run for the 'fraid hole at its approach. For untold years it had been the most powerful thing in the land. And now, here was a mere man who threatened its position. More! Who had usurped its position!

When Bill looked at the horizon and saw the cyclone coming, he recognized the anger and rage. While a cyclone does not often smile, Bill had felt from the beginning that it was just a grouchy fellow who never had a pleasant word for anyone. But now, instead of merely an un-

pleasant character, Bill saw all the viciousness of which an angry cyclone is capable. He had no way of knowing that the cyclone saw its kingship tottering and was determined to stop this man who threatened its supremacy.

But Bill understood the violence of the onslaught even as the monster came into view. He knew he must meet it. The center of the cyclone was larger than ever before. The fact is, the cyclone had been training for this fight all winter and spring. It was in best form and at top weight. It headed straight for Bill intent on his destruction. In an instant it was upon him. Bill had sat quietly and silently on the great pacing mustang. But his mind was working rapidly. In the split second between his first sight of the monster and the time for action he had made his plans. Pecos Bill was ready! Ready and waiting!

Green clouds were dripping from the cyclone's jaws. Lightning flashed from its eyes as it swept down upon him. Its plan was to envelop Bill in one mighty grasp. Just as it was upon him, Bill turned Widow Maker to its left. This was a clever move for the cyclone was right-handed, and while it had been training hard to get its left in shape, that was not its best side. Bill gave rein to his mount. Widow Maker wheeled and turned on a dime which Pecos had, with great foresight[8] and accuracy, thrown to the ground to mark the exact spot for this maneuver. It was the first time that anyone had thought of turning on a dime. Then he urged the great horse forward. The cyclone, filled with surprise, lost its balance and rushed forward at an increased speed. It went so fast that it met itself coming back. This confused the cyclone, but it did not confuse Pecos Bill. He had expected that to happen. Widow Maker went into his twenty-first gait and edged up close to the whirlwind. Soon they were running neck and neck.

At the proper instant Bill grabbed the cyclone's ears, kicked himself free of the stirrups and pulled himself lightly on its back.

◆ **Literary Focus**
Find five examples of exaggeration in this paragraph.

---

7. **leering** (lir´ ing) *adj.*: Looking with malicious triumph.

8. **foresight** (fôr´ sīt) *n.*: The act of seeing beforehand.

Bill never used spurs on Widow Maker. Sometimes he wore them for show and because he liked the jingling sound they made. They made a nice accompaniment for his cowboy songs. But he had not been singing, so he had no spurs. He did not have his rattlesnake for a quirt.[9] Of course there was no bridle. It was man against monster! There he was! Pecos Bill astride a raging cyclone, slick heeled and without a saddle!

The cyclone was taken by surprise at this sudden turn of events. But it was undaunted. It was sure of itself. Months of training had given it a conviction that it was <u>invincible</u>. With a mighty heave, it twisted to its full height. Then it fell back suddenly, twisting and turning violently, so that before it came back to earth, it had turned around a thousand times. Surely no rider could ever withstand such an attack. No rider ever had. Little wonder. No one had ever ridden a cyclone before. But Pecos Bill did! He fanned the tornado's ears with his hat and dug his heels into the demon's flanks and yelled, "Yipee-ee!"

The people who had run for shelter began to come out. The audience further enraged the cyclone. It was bad enough to be disgraced by having a man astride it. It was unbearable not to have thrown him. To have all the people see the failure was too much! It got down flat on the ground and rolled over and over. Bill retained his seat throughout this ruse.[10] Evidence of this desperate but <u>futile</u> stratagem[11] remains today. The great Staked Plains, or as the Mexicans call it, *Llano Estacado* is the result. Its small, rugged mountains were covered with trees at the time. The rolling of the cyclone destroyed the mountains, the trees, and almost everything else in the area. The destruction was so complete, that part of the country is flat and treeless to this day. When the settlers came, there were no landmarks to guide them across the vast unmarked space, so they drove stakes in the ground to mark the trails. That is the reason it is called "Staked Plains." Here is an example of the proof of the events of history by careful and painstaking research. It is also an example of how seemingly <u>inexplicable</u> geographical facts can be explained.

It was far more dangerous for the rider when the cyclone shot straight up to the sky. Once there, the twister tried the same thing it had tried on the ground. It rolled on the sky. It was no use. Bill could not be unseated. He kept his place, and he didn't have a sky hook with him either.

As for Bill, he was having the time of his life, shouting at the top of his voice, kicking his opponent in the ribs and jabbing his thumb in its flanks. It responded and went on a wild bucking rampage over the entire West. It used all the bucking tricks known to the wildest broncos as well as those known only to cyclones. The wind howled furiously and beat against the fearless rider. The rain poured. The lightning flashed around his ears. The fight went on and on. Bill enjoyed himself immensely. In spite of the elements he easily kept his place. . . .

The raging cyclone saw this out of the corner of its eye. It knew then who the victor was. It was twisting far above the Rocky Mountains when the awful truth came to it. In a horrible heave it disintegrated! Small pieces of cyclone flew in all directions. Bill still kept his seat on the main central portion until that rained out from under him. Then he jumped to a nearby streak of lightning and slid down it toward earth. But it was raining so hard that the rain put out the lightning. When it fizzled out from under him, Bill dropped the rest of the way. He lit in what is now called Death Valley. He hit quite hard, as is apparent from the fact that he so compressed the place that it is still two hundred and seventy-six feet below sea level.

◆ **Build Vocabulary**

usurped (yo͞o sʉrpt′) *v.*: Took power or authority away from

invincible (in vin′ sə bəl) *adj.*: Unbeatable

futile (fyo͞ot′ əl) *adj.*: Useless; hopeless

inexplicable (in eks′ pli kə bəl) *adj.*: Unexplainable

---

9. **quirt** (kwurt) *n.*: Short-handled riding whip with a braided rawhide lash.
10. **ruse** (ro͞oz) *n.*: Trick.
11. **stratagem** (strat′ ə jəm) *n.*: Plan for defeating an opponent.

The Grand Canyon was washed out by the rain, though it must be understood that this happened after Paul Bunyan had given it a good start by carelessly dragging his ax behind him when he went west a short time before.

The cyclones and the hurricanes and the tornadoes nowadays are the small pieces that broke off of the big cyclone Pecos Bill rode. In fact, the rainstorms of the present day came into being in the same way. There are always <u>skeptics</u>, but even they will recognize the logic of the proof of this event. They will recall that even now it almost always rains on the Fourth of July. That is because the rainstorms of to-day still retain some of the characteristics of the giant cyclone that met its comeuppance at the hands of Pecos Bill.

Bill lay where he landed and looked up at the sky, but he could see no sign of the cy-clone. Then he laughed softly as he felt the warm sand of Death Valley on his back. . . .

It was a rough ride though, and Bill had re-sisted unusual tensions and pressures. When he got on the cyclone he had a twenty-dollar gold piece and a bowie knife[12] in his pocket. The tremendous force of the cyclone was such that when he finished the ride he found that his pocket contained a plugged nickel[13] and a little pearl-handled penknife. His two giant six-shooters were compressed and trans-formed into a small water pistol and a popgun.

It is a strange circumstance that lesser men have monuments raised in their honor. Death Valley is Bill's monument. Sort of a monument in reverse. Sunk in his honor, you might say. Perhaps that is as it should be. After all, Bill was different. He made his own monument. He made it with his hips, as is evident from the great depth of the valley. That is the hard way.

---

12. **bowie** (bō´ ē) **knife:** A strong, single-edged hunting knife named after James Bowie (1799–1836), a soldier.
13. **plugged nickel:** Fake nickel.

◆ Build Vocabulary

skeptics (skep´ tiks) *n.*: People who frequently doubt and question matters generally accepted

Guide for Responding

◆ LITERATURE AND YOUR LIFE

Reader's Response Which parts of the story did you find humorous? Explain.

Thematic Focus Describe the qualities of Pecos Bill that are heroic.

☑ Check Your Comprehension

1. Which two animals does Pecos Bill employ to help him dig holes?
2. (a) What is the name of Pecos Bill's horse? (b) Name some of the gaits, or foot move-ments, that Pecos Bill taught him.
3. Why is the cyclone angry with Pecos Bill?
4. What happens to the cyclone when it real-izes that Pecos Bill is the victor?

◆ Critical Thinking

INTERPRET

1. In what ways does the cyclone resemble Pecos Bill? **[Infer]**
2. What do you learn about the character of Pecos Bill from his refusal to join the others in the caves? **[Interpret]**
3. Explain the meaning of these sentences: "Death Valley is Bill's monument. Sort of a monument in reverse." **[Analyze]**
4. How does Pecos Bill's resolution never to say the word "afraid" explain why he is a folk hero? **[Draw Conclusions]**

COMPARE LITERARY WORKS

5. Who possesses greater qualities and abili-ties—Paul Bunyan or Pecos Bill? Explain. **[Make a Judgment]**

CONNECTIONS TO TODAY'S WORLD

John Henry, Pecos Bill, and Davy Crockett all possessed extraordinary abilities that made them folk heroes. The twentieth century has its own special folk hero: Superman. Following is a portion of a Web site dedicated to fans of Superman, the superhero.

Netscape: DC Comics

Netsite: http://www.dccomics.com/

TM

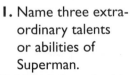

TM

Netscape: DC Comics

Netsite: http://www.dccomics.com/

Superman

• Super-strength, super-speed, super-invulnerability, and the power of flight. An arsenal of super-senses, including X-ray vision, telescopic vision, microscopic vision, heat vision, and super-hearing.

• He is especially vulnerable to Kryptonite radiation.

Real Name: Clark Kent, Kal-El
Occupation: Journalist, novelist
Base of Operations: Metropolis
Marital Status: Married
Height: 6'3"
Weight: 225 lbs.
Eyes: Blue
Hair: Black
First Appearance: Historical, ACTION COMICS #1 (JUNE, 1938); canonical, MAN OF STEEL #1 (June, 1986)

Though genetically an alien conceived on the late planet Krypton, Superman is an American by birth, born in a Kansas corn field. Living by the moral values instilled in him by his Earthly parents, Superman's high ideals are sometimes mistaken for naivete, his steadfast determination for unrealistic optimism, by those who cannot or will not understand him.

Through his deeds, Superman has become Earth's preeminent super hero. Time and again, through all adversity, he has proven himself a true hero, capable of whatever bravery and self-sacrifice is necessary to right a wrong or save a life.

Superman has actually been worshipped by some of his many admirers, but he is not a god. Though slow to anger, he does not suffer villains gladly. Superman is, at heart, a warm, compassionate, courageous man with powers and abilities far beyond those of mortal men. He has devoted his life to the promotion of truth, justice, and the great ideals of the American way.

---

1. Name three extraordinary talents or abilities of Superman.
2. Which hero in this section does Superman remind you of most? Why?

Davy Crockett's Dream

Davy Crockett

One day when it was so cold that I was afeard to open my mouth, lest I should freeze my tongue, I took my little dog named Grizzle and cut out for Salt River Bay to kill something for dinner. I got a good ways from home afore I knowed where I was, and as I had swetted some before I left the house my hat froze fast to my head, and I like to have put my neck out of joint in trying to pull it off. When I sneezed the icicles crackled all up and down the inside of my nose, like when you walk over a bog in winter time. The varmints was so scarce that I couldn't find one, and so when I come to an old log hut that had belonged to some squatter that had ben reformed out by the nabors, I stood my rifle up agin one of the door posts and went in. I kindled up a little fire and told Grizzle I was going to take a nap. I piled up a heap of chestnut burs for a pillow and straitened myself out on the ground, for I can curl closer than a

▲ Critical Viewing Does Davy Crockett, pictured here, look as if he might use "a heap of chestnut burs" for a pillow? Explain. [Assess]

rattlesnake and lay straiter than a log. I laid with the back of my head agin the hearth, and my eyes looking up chimney so that I could see when it was noon by the sun, for Mrs. Crockett was always rantankerous[1] when I staid out over the time. I got to sleep before Grizzle had done warming the eend of his nose, and I had swallowed so much cold wind that it laid hard on my stomach, and as I laid gulping and belching the wind went out of me and roared up chimney like a young whirlwind. So I had a pesky dream, and kinder thought, till I waked up, that I was floating down the Massassippy in a holler tree, and I hadn't room to stir my legs and arms no more than they were withed together with young saplings. While I was there and want able to help myself a feller called Oak Wing that lived about twenty miles

---

1. **rantankerous** (ran taŋ´ kər əs) *adj.*: Dialect for *cantankerous*, meaning "wildly and noisily upset."

off, and that I had give a most almighty licking once, cum and looked in with his blind

◆ **Literary Focus**
Explain how Crockett's use of language is appropriate for a tall tale.

eye that I had gouged out five years before, and I saw him looking in one end of the hollow log, and he axed me if I wanted to get out. I told him to tie a rope to one of my legs and draw me out as soon as God would let him and as much sooner as he was a mind to. But he said he wouldn't do it that way, he would ram me out with a pole. So he took a long pole and rammed it down agin my head as if he was ramming home the cattridge in a cannon. This didn't make me budge an inch, but it pounded my head down in between my shoulders till I look'd like a turcle with his head drawn in. This started my temper a trifle, and I ript and swore till the breath boiled out of the end of the log like the steam out of the funnel pipe of a steemboat. Jest then I woke up, and seed my wife pulling my leg, for it was enermost sundown and she had cum arter me. There was a long icicle hanging to her nose, and when she tried to kiss me, she run it right into my eye. I telled her my dreem, and sed I would have revenge on Oak Wing for pounding my head. She said it was all a dreem and that Oak was not to blame; but I had a very diffrent idea of the matter. So I went and talked to him, and telled him what he had done to me in a dreem, and it was settled that he should make me an apology in his next dreem, and that wood make us square,[2] for I don't like to be run upon when I'm asleep, any more than I do when I'm awake.

---

2. **square:** Even.

Guide for Responding

◆ LITERATURE AND YOUR LIFE

Reader's Response Do you think you would like Davy Crockett if you met him? Why or why not?

Thematic Focus Do you find Crockett heroic? Why or why not?

☑ Check Your Comprehension

1. Name three instances in which Davy Crockett exaggerates events.
2. Describe Davy Crockett's dream.
3. Where does Davy Crockett take his nap?
4. What is the arrangement made at the end of the tale between Davy Crockett and Oak Wing?

◆ Critical Thinking

INTERPRET

1. Describe ways in which exaggeration adds humor to this tale. **[Connect]**
2. How does the absurd and humorous settlement between Crockett and Oak Wing indicate that this is a tall tale? **[Draw Conclusions]**
3. (a) Do you think that Davy Crockett's descriptions are meant to be taken literally? (b) How does your answer explain Crockett's anger toward Oak Wing? **[Interpret]**

APPLY

4. (a) How does Crockett's dialect affect the narration of the tale? (b) How would the story be different if it had been written in standard English? **[Modify]**
5. What agreement would you suggest to Davy Crockett and Oak Wing to settle the conflict? **[Solve]**

COMPARE LITERARY WORKS

6. Characters in these tall tales generally achieve their goals through a combination of reason and strength. Find examples in the stories that illustrate this point. **[Analyze]**

Guide for Responding (continued)

◆ Reading Strategy

PREDICT

Because tall tales have very predictable patterns, you can easily **predict** the types of events that will occur once you discover the character's traits or qualities.

1. In "Hammerman," John Henry says that he would "die with a hammer in my hand." What did you predict based on that statement?
2. Which quality or trait of Pecos Bill helped you to predict what would happen?
3. When Davy Crockett says that he "piled up a heap of chestnut burs for a pillow," what might you predict about his future actions?

◆ Build Vocabulary

USING FORMS OF *skeptic*

Knowing that *skeptics* means "people who doubt what others accept as true," you can figure out the meaning of related words. Complete the sentences that follow with words related to *skeptic*:

skeptically   skeptical

1. Although several people assured her that bungee jumping was safe, she remained _____?_____.
2. Before signing the standard lease, the lawyer _____?_____ reviewed the contract again.

SPELLING STRATEGY

Most multi-syllable words with the *m* sound in the middle, like *commotion*, are spelled with two *m*s, not one. Practice this rule by correcting the spelling of the following words:

1. comitment   2. comander   3. accomodate

USING THE WORD BANK

On your paper, match the Word Bank word with its definition.

1. hefted   a. doubters
2. granite   b. useless
3. commotion   c. lifted or heaved
4. usurped   d. took power
5. invincible   e. unexplainable
6. futile   f. hard stone
7. inexplicable   g. unbeatable
8. skeptics   h. disturbance

◆ Literary Focus

TALL TALES

Tall tales are stories that are highly exaggerated. Because many tall tales originally were told by western pioneers, they often reveal aspects of the settling of the American West.

1. (a) Which elements of "Hammerman" are based on fact? (b) Which elements are exaggerated?
2. (a) What aspects of Peco Bill's character are believable? (b) What aspects are highly exaggerated?
3. What can you learn about frontier life from "Davy Crockett's Dream"?

◆ Build Grammar Skills

VARIETY IN SENTENCE BEGINNINGS

Writers use a **variety of sentence beginnings** to keep their stories interesting. Look at these possible ways to begin sentences:

Subject: *People down South* still tell stories about John Henry. . . .
Adverb: *The next morning,* John Henry bundled up some food. . . .
Adverb Clause: *As John Henry grew a bit older,* he practiced swinging the hammer. . . .
Prepositional Phrase: *At night,* . . . John Henry listened to a far-off train . . .

Practice On your paper, identify the type of sentence element that begins each of the following:

1. When the war ended, a man from the North came to John Henry. . . .
2. The cyclone caused Bill some trouble, though.
3. One year, he tried shipping the prairie dog holes up north. . . .
4. Usually it would destroy a few hundred miles of fence. . . .
5. In the beginning, the Fourth of July crowd had aroused its curiosity.

Writing Application Rewrite the following, varying the sentence beginnings to add variety:

Tall tales are full of exaggeration. Tall tales often tell about life on the American frontier. Cowboys on the frontier liked to tell tall tales at night by the campfire.

Build Your Portfolio

 Idea Bank

Writing

1. **Journal Entry** Imagine that you are one of the spectators watching the contest in "Hammerman" or watching Pecos Bill ride the cyclone. Write a journal entry describing the fantastic event and your reactions to it.

2. **Tall Tale** Write about a daily occurrence in your life, but make it a tall tale by exaggerating the events or your abilities.

3. **Analysis** Analyze the qualities of the tall tale character using examples from the stories. Write an essay outlining these qualities and how they account for the hero's actions.

Speaking and Listening

4. **Performance** "John Henry" is a ballad. Ballads are usually sung long before they are ever put into writing. Rehearse and recite this ballad for your classmates. You may wish to accompany yourself on the piano or the guitar if you are able to. **[Performing Arts Link]**

5. **Oral Storytelling** Continue the oral tradition by making up a tall tale and telling it to the class. Tape-record your recitation to evaluate it afterwards. **[Performing Arts Link]**

Projects

6. **Collage** Reread "Paul Bunyan of the North Woods," and draw pictures illustrating the adventures and merriment of Paul Bunyan and his friends. Then, combine your work into a collage, and display it for your classmates. **[Art Link]**

7. **Report [Group Activity]** In "Pecos Bill: The Cyclone," the hero is said to have caused many of the natural wonders in the United States. With a small group of classmates, research the scientific explanations of the origins of the Great Plains, Death Valley, and the Grand Canyon. Share your findings with the class. **[Science Link]**

 Writing Mini-Lesson

Nomination for Hero of the Year

Many of the characters in tall tales display heroic qualities: They seem to be larger than life, displaying amazing abilities of strength and courage. Choose a person, real or fictional, who exhibits heroic qualities, to nominate for hero of the year. In your nomination, explain why that person deserves the honor.

Writing Skills Focus: Use Only Important Details

Because an effective nomination is brief and to the point, **use only important details** within it.

Model

Sassie Betty displays all the qualities that a hero should have: She's kind, strong, generous, and selfless.

Prewriting Choose a candidate for hero of the year, and list all the positive qualities that your hero possesses. For each quality, list an important point that supports it.

Drafting Draft an introduction in which you present your nominee to the audience. Then, in the body, explain why your nominee deserves to be hero of the year. Conclude by summarizing your most important ideas.

Revising Read your nomination to a classmate, and ask whether or not your points are convincing. Delete any points that are unimportant, and add details where needed to support your views.

> ◆ **Grammar Application**
> Review your sentence beginnings. Vary them, where necessary, to avoid monotony and dullness in your writing.

Writing Process Workshop

The information superhighway—the Internet—is quickly becoming the fastest way to acquire information on any topic. One reason that the Internet is so popular is that anyone from anywhere in the world can share expertise through his or her own Web site. Web sites on the Internet contain a Home Page that provides information and often includes media as well as links to other sites. Each Web site has its own address.

Create a plan for your own Web page through which you can communicate your knowledge to the world. This workshop will help you design an **Internet Web page.** The following writing skills will help you get started:

Writing Skills Focus

▶ **Use only important details** on your Web Home Page. Too much text onscreen is difficult to read. (See p. 955.)

▶ **Include an explanation of your purpose.** Introduce your Web page by explaining why you created it.

▶ **Give visual support.** Drawings, photos, and videos that support the topic of your Web page can be included.

▶ **Choose an organization** that is visually appealing and easy to follow.

Following is a plan for a Web page on superheroes:

WRITING MODEL

The Mighty Heroes of the Comics

The superheroes of the comics have long been saving the world from doom. This page is dedicated to their selfless adventures. ① I chose three super-heroes—Xena, Superman, and Batman—to feature on this page. ② Click on each picture, and you will learn all I have learned about each superhero.
[Image of Xena, Warrior Princess]
[Image of Superman]
[Image of Batman] ③

① This sentence explains the writer's purpose for creating this Web page.

② Here, the writer explains the organization of the Home Page.

③ These visuals help support the content of the Web page.

Prewriting

Choose a Subject Create an informative Web page on a hobby or an interest that you have, or select one of the following topics:

> ### Topic Ideas
> - An animal
> - A favorite author
> - A sports player
> - Cultural traditions

Research the Links Browse the Internet for sites related to your topic. Then, choose those that best support your topic. You can use these links for your Web page.

Create a Plan Before writing the text, create a plan for the appearance of your page. Consider how many headings you want on a page, how many links, what will be highlighted as "hot text," and what type of media you will include.

The following chart shows the codes you'll need to format a page:

FORMATTING A PAGE	
HTML codes:	
`<title></title>`	Title
`<h1></h1>through<h5></h5>`	Heading sizes
`<center></center>`	Centers text
`<hr>`	Inserts rule (a straight line)
`<p></p>`	Paragraph
`<li>`	Bulleted list item
` `	Break between lines
`<img src="name of graphic file">`	Graphic or image tag
`<a href="address of Internet site"></a>`	Hyperlink

Drafting

Maintain a Consistent Purpose Introduce your Web page by stating your purpose. Make sure that all text, media, and links relate to that purpose.

Introduce Media When you place media on your site, introduce each piece by explaining what it is and why it is on your Web page.

DRAFTING/REVISING

APPLYING LANGUAGE SKILLS: Commonly Confused Words

The following are a few commonly confused word pairs:

accept, except: *Accept is a verb meaning "to receive" or "to agree with." Except is a preposition meaning "not including"; it is also sometimes a verb meaning "to leave out."*

affect, effect: *Affect is a verb meaning "to influence." Effect is a noun meaning "result" or a verb meaning "to bring about."*

than, then: *Than introduces the second part of a comparison. Then means "next" or "after that."*

Practice Choose the correct word to complete the sentence:

1. Harvey plays ball better ___?___ Abe does. (than, then)
2. The story had a strange ___?___ on the listeners. (affect, effect)
3. No one ___?___ Wilma is allowed to enter that room. (accept, except)

Writing Application As you write, refer to the above definitions to choose the correct word.

Writer's Solution Connection
Writing Lab

For help organizing your Web page, use the Outliner in the Organizing section of the Writer's Toolkit.

APPLYING LANGUAGE SKILLS:
Capitalization of Proper Nouns

Nouns are either common or proper. A common noun names any one of a class of people, places, or things. A proper noun names a specific person, place, or thing. Proper nouns are capitalized.

Common Nouns	Proper Nouns
computer	Macintosh, Compaq
city	Dallas, Honolulu
language	Danish, Spanish

Practice Write these sentences, capitalizing all proper nouns:

1. My favorite players are babe ruth and jackie robinson.

2. I've been to ballparks in houston, toronto, and cleveland.

3. Sometimes, it's chilly to watch baseball in april and october.

Writing Application As you revise your Internet Web page, make sure all proper nouns are capitalized.

Writer's Solution Connection
Language Lab

For more help with capitalization, see the Capitalization in Sentences lesson in the Capitalization unit.

Revising

Use a Checklist Review the Writing Skills Focus on page 956. Use the items as a checklist to evaluate and revise your Web page.

Check Links Make sure you have the correct addresses for links you have chosen for your Web page.

Get More Advice Here are some on-line resources for your Web author toolbox:

▶ A beginner's guide to HTML:
http://www.ncsa.uiuc.edu/General/Internet/WWW/HTML Primer.html

▶ A list of software that provides the HTML codes (HTML editors): info@classroom.net

▶ Free textures, clip art, and images:
http://www.itw.com:80/~imagesys/Ftpto:ftp.classroom.net

REVISION MODEL

① I designed this Web page so I could share my knowledge of comic books.

Comic books are a hobby and an obsession of mine.
② and the following text of Superman to learn more about his first comic book.
Click on this image.

① The writer added this statement to make clear his purpose for creating the Web page.

② This statement introduces the media and lets the reader know why it's there.

Publishing and Presenting

On-line To mount or launch your Web page onto the Internet so that other Internet users can visit it, you must copy the folder or directory onto a Web server. The server lets anyone connected to the Net access your pages with a Web browser. Once you've found a server, you can send your page to your host (the server you've chosen) via diskette, by e-mail, or by uploading it via ftp (file transfer protocol).

Visitors Ask visitors to your Web site to give you feedback. You might want to use their suggestions when you update your page.

Strategies for Success

Using the Internet means using Web pages. Each Web page contains information on a specific topic, as well as media and links to other pages. The following information will help you use a Web page effectively:

Click on the Highlighted Text The text that is highlighted is called hot text. It leads you to more information. When you click on a highlighted term, it will take you to another page that offers information about the topic.

Use the Links A link on a Web site is hot text that takes you directly to another Web site. Instead of locating a Web page by using an address, you can get there by clicking on the link provided by the Web sponsor—the person who created the Web site.

Evaluate the Web Site Don't get caught up in the colors and graphics of a Web site. Remember that you're after reliable information—for a school report or your personal life—and you want current, accurate facts. Check the site's sponsor: Government or education sites are usually the most reliable.

Guides exist that review and evaluate Web sites for their reliability. For practice, look up a Web site you have recently used in these two guides:

▶ **Argus Clearinghouse**
  http://www.clearinghouse.net/chhome.html
▶ **Mining Company**
  http://miningco.com

Superhero Central

Welcome to my collection of superhero trivia. I am a middle-school student at Rock Middle School Rock, SC. I am a lover of comic books and all superheroes.

Xena

Superman

Batman

Hercules

Other cool superhero sites:
http://www.thebat.com
http://www.histsupher.edu

Apply the Strategies

Using the Internet page above, answer the following questions:

1. Which words are hot text? What happens if you click on them?

2. Is there a list of links available? Where can you find them?

3. Would you consider this site a reliable source? Why or why not?

✔ Here are situations in which you may use an Internet Web page for information:
  ▶ Reading the daily news
  ▶ Finding weather reports for a vacation destination

To keep their writing interesting, writers **vary the beginnings of their sentences** (see p. 954). You need not always begin a sentence with the subject. Sometimes you can place other sentence elements at the beginning of the sentence.

The following chart shows different ways that you may begin a sentence:

phrase (frāz) *n.* **1** a group of words that is not a complete sentence, but that gives a single idea, usually as a separate part of a sentence ["Drinking fresh milk," "with meals," and "to be healthy" are phrases.]

Sentence Beginnings	Examples
Subject:	*John Henry's father put his arm around her shoulder.*
Adverb:	*Still, it tipped and tilted as the dance went on.*
Phrases: **Prepositional Phrases:**	*On the morning of the contest, the slopes around the tunnel were loaded with people.*
Participial Phrase:	*Lying in bed at night, young John Henry listened to far-off train whistles.*
Adverb Clause:	*As John Henry grew a bit older, he practiced swinging his hammer. . . . .*

Practice 1 Write the following sentences in your notebook. Then, underline each sentence beginning and identify what type it is.

1. At night, lying on a straw bed on the floor, John Henry listened to a far-off train whistling through the darkness.

2. Whenever John Henry worked, he sang.

3. The cookstove at that camp covered an acre of ground.

4. Usually, it would destroy a few hundred miles of fence by blowing the postholes away.

5. Raging toward the town, the cyclone twisted in the air a thousand times.

Practice 2 Write each of the following sentences using the type of sentence beginning specified.

1. The cyclone was strong and fierce, frightening most people. (participial phrase)

2. Everyone knew that Pecos Bill had defeated the cyclone when it disintegrated. (adverb clause)

3. Paul Bunyan, angered by the bad weather, stopped the rain. (participial phrase)

4. John Henry collapsed suddenly from exhaustion after the race. (adverb)

5. John Henry dreamed during the night of driving steel. (prepositional phrase)

Grammar in Writing

✔ *When you begin a sentence with an adverb, a phrase, or a clause, use a comma to separate it from the rest of the sentence.*

Speaking, Listening, and Viewing Workshop

Conducting business is a part of life. You need business skills to order items from a catalog, to open and/or use a savings account, to request product information, to find and keep a job, to return a defective item, to correct a mistake (yours or the business's), or to praise a job well done.

Always Be Courteous "Please" and "thank you" are part of a business vocabulary. Be polite and respectful—whether you are ordering an item, complaining about a defect or problem, or requesting information. Everyone likes and deserves to be treated with respect.

Be Direct and Specific Know exactly what you want and ask for it. If you are ordering an item, know your size and the item number. If you are returning something, decide whether you want a replacement or a refund.

Be Responsible; Do Your Math Check the prices of items you're buying. Check your change. Keep your receipts in case you want to exchange something. If you're offering services or looking for a job, have a fee or wage in mind.

Follow Up If someone has done something particularly nice for you, such as helping you get a job or training you in a helpful, cheerful way, thank him or her with a note or a call. If something you've ordered is late in coming, check on it. Complete the warranty application for your new items.

Apply the Strategies

With a partner, role-play these situations, following the strategies in this lesson. Switch roles with your partner.

1. You received a shirt as a gift, but you need it in a larger size. The sales clerk has asked you for a receipt, but you don't have it.

2. You ordered a three-dimensional puzzle from a catalog and the puzzle is missing several pieces. You did not lose them.

3. You are answering an ad for someone to water plants and bring in mail. You want to know the hours and the wages. Your parents want some information about the person for whom you'd be working.

Tips for Conducting Business

▶ Be polite and respectful.
▶ Be organized, direct, and specific.
▶ Follow up.

What's Behind the Words

Vocabulary Adventures With Richard Lederer

Regional Vocabulary

Midway through John Steinbeck's novel *The Grapes of Wrath*, young Ivy observes, "Ever'body says words different. Arkansas folks says 'em different, and Oklahomy folks says 'em different. And we seen a lady from Massachusetts, an' she said 'em differentest of all. Couldn't hardly make out what she was sayin'."

One aspect of our sprawling American language is that not all of us say the same word in the same way. Sometimes we don't even use the same name for the same object. These vocabulary and pronunciation differences create dialects, the form of speech used in a particular region.

Food for Thought

You probably enjoy eating a certain sandwich made with cold cuts, cheese, tomatoes, pickles, and onions stuffed into a long, hard-crusted Italian bread. That sandwich was invented in the Italian section of Philadelphia known as Hog Island. Some language experts claim that from *Hog Island* came the word *hoagie*. Others contend that *hoagie* arose because only a hog had the appetite or the technique to eat one properly.

In New England, the same sandwich is called a *grinder*—you need a good set of *grinders,* or teeth, to chew it. Around the United States, the *hoagie* or *grinder* is called at least a dozen other names—a *bomber, Cuban sandwich, Garibaldi, hero, Italian sandwich, rocket, sub, submarine, torpedo, wedge, wedgie,* and, in the deep South, a *poor-boy* (usually pronounced "poh-boy").

In Philadelphia, people wash their *hoagies* down with *soda.* In New England, they wash *grinders* down with *tonic. Soda* and *tonic* in other areas are known as *pop, soda pop,* a *soft drink,* or *Coke.*

All-American Dialects

Clear—Or is it clean? Or is it plumb?— across the nation, Americans sure do talk "different." Is that simple strip of grass between the street and the sidewalk a *berm, boulevard, boulevard strip, city strip, green belt, the parking, the parking strip, parkway, sidewalk plot, strip, swale, tree bank,* or *tree lawn*? Is the part of the highway that separates the northbound lanes from the southbound lanes the *centerline, center strip, mall, medial strip, median strip, medium strip,* or *neutral ground*? It depends where you live and to whom you're speaking.

Everyone—including you—speaks a dialect. *Dialect* isn't a label for careless, uneducated, incorrect speech or something to be avoided or cured. Each language is a great pie. Each slice of that pie is a dialect, and no single slice is the language. Be proud of your slice of the pie.

ACTIVITY With a partner, learn about the dialect of another region of the country. Make a list comparing the words you use for lining up for something (*on line, in line*), the sandwich you eat (*hoagie, sub, grinder, hero*), the soft drink (*soda* or *pop*) you prefer. Then, write a skit in which two characters from different regions have difficulty communicating because of language differences. Perform the skit for the class.

Extended Reading Opportunities

The people of the United States, with their diverse backgrounds, have contributed stories and songs to the national folk literature. This literature reveals something of the culture from which it originated. For further exploration of American folklore, consider the following.

Suggested Titles

From Sea to Shining Sea: A Treasury of American Folklore and Folk Songs
Amy Cohn, Editor

This anthology includes 140 folk songs and stories illustrated by award-winning artists. A collection for all ages, the book begins with Native American stories and ends with the folklore of this century. It includes such diverse material as classic tall tales to Abbott and Costello's famous skit "Who's on First?" Each piece includes an introduction and end-notes. The collection reflects the richness of American diversity.

Big Men, Big Country: A Collection of American Tall Tales
Paul Robert Walker and James Bernardin

This collection includes episodes of tall-tale heroes like the mythical Paul Bunyan, Pecos Bill, and New York City's Big Mose as well as real historical figures like Gib Morgan, John Darling, and Jim Bridger. Walker bases each tale on the earliest printed version of the story. A note at the end of each story gives information about the tale's origin and, for tales based on historical figures, it includes information on each man's life.

Native American Literature

This anthology includes Native American origin stories, legends, and songs. The works show Native American culture as the foundation for American literature. Following the trail of Coyote the trickster, we are led on a journey through the magical, beautiful world of America's first people.

Other Possibilities

Cut From the Same Cloth: American Women of Myth, Legend, and Tall Tale — Robert D. San Souci

Her Stories: African American Folktales, Fairy Tales, and True Tales — Virginia Hamilton

Come Go With Me: Old Timers From the Southern Mountains — Roy Edwin Thomas

GLOSSARY

abhorrence (əb hôr´ əns) *n.*: Loathing; disgust

abridge (ə brij´) *v.*: Reduce in scope; shorten; lessen

abyss (ə bis´) *n.*: Great depth

acquiescent (ak´ wē es´ ənt) *adj.*: Agreeing without protest

acute (ə kyōōt´) *adj.*: Sensitive

adversaries (ad´ vər ser´ ēz) *n.*: Enemies; opponents

aerobatic (er´ ə bat´ ik) *adj.*: Performing loops, rolls, etc., with an airplane; stuntlike

affluence (af´ lōō əns) *n.*: Wealth; abundance

aggregation (ag´ grə gā´ shən) *n.*: Group or mass of distinct objects or individuals

aghast (ə gast´) *adj.*: Feeling great horror or dismay

alienate (āl´ yən āt´) *v.*: To make unfriendly; estrange

amendments (ə mend´ mənts) *n.*: Corrections

amiss (ə mis´) *adj.*: Wrongly placed; faulty or improper

ancestral (an ses´ trəl) *adj.*: Of or inherited from one's forefathers or ancestors

anguish (aŋ´ gwish) *n.*: Great suffering from worry

anonymously (ə nän´ ə məs lē) *adv.*: With the name withheld or secret

antithesis (an tith´ ə sis) *n.*: Contrast or opposition of thought

apprehension (ap´ rə hen´ shən) *n.*: **1** Fear; anxiety that something bad will happen; mental grasp; **2** perception or understanding

apprenticed (ə pren´ tist) *v.*: Contracted to learn a trade under a skilled worker

arouse (ə rouz´) *v.*: Awaken, as from sleep

arresting (ə rest´ iŋ) *adj.*: Attracting attention; striking

ascent (ə sent´) *n.*: The act of climbing or rising

assent (a sent´) *v.*: Consent

assiduously (ə sij´ ōō wəs lē) *adv.*: Carefully and busily

august (ô gust´) *adj.*: Honored

austere (ô stir´) *adj.*: Showing strict self-discipline

authentic (ô then´ tik) *adj.*: Genuine; real

availed (ə vāld´) *v.*: Made use of

bafflement (baf´ əl mənt) *n.*: State of confusion or puzzlement

banked (baŋt) *adj.*: Adjusted to burn slowly and long

barren (bar´ ən) *adj.*: Sterile; empty

beckoned (bek´ ənd) *v.*: Summoned by a silent motion; called

bedraggled (bi drag´ əld) *adj.*: Dirty and wet

benediction (ben´ ə dik´ shən) *n.*: Blessing

benign (bi nīn´) *adj.*: Kindly

bitter (bit´ ər) *adj.*: Showing discomfort, sorrow, or pain

blunders (blun´ dərz) *n.*: Foolish or careless mistakes

borne (bôrn) *v.*: Carried

brandishing (bran´ dish iŋ) *v.*: Waving or exhibiting in a challenging way

breadth (bredth) *n.*: Width

breakers (brāk´ ərs) *n.*: Waves that break into foam

brisk (brisk) *adj.*: Quick in manner

brittle (brit´ əl) *adj.*: Stiff and unbending in manner; lacking warmth

broached (brōcht) *v.*: Started a discussion about a topic

burrow (bur´ ō) *n.*: Passage or hole for shelter

cajoling (kə jōl´ iŋ) *v.*: Coaxing or persuading gently

canter (kan´ tər) *v.*: Ride at a smooth, gentle pace

capricious (kə prē´ shəs) *adj.*: Tending to change abruptly and without apparent reason

catapults (kat´ ə pults´) *v.*: Launches; leaps

celestial (sə les´ chəl) *adj.*: Of heaven; divine

censured (sen´ shərd) *v.*: Condemned as wrong; criticized

chronic (krän´ ik) *adj.*: Continuing indefinitely; perpetual; constant

cinched (sincht) *v.*: Bound firmly; tightly fastened

coincidental (kō in´ sə dent´ əl) *adj.*: Occurring at the same time or place

colossal (kə läs´ əl) *adj.*: Astonishingly great; extraordinary

commenced (kə menst´) *v.*: Started; began

commotion (kə mō´ shən) *n.*: Noisy movement

compensate (käm´ pən sāt´) *v.*: To repay

competent (käm´ pə tənt) *adj.*: Well qualified and capable

compounded (käm pound´ əd) *adj.*: Mixed or combined

compulsory (kəm pul´ sə rē) *adj.*: Enforced; required

conceivably (kən sē´ və blē) *adv.*: Possibly

conception (kən sep´ shən) *n.*: An original idea, design, plan, etc.

confederacy (kən fed´ ər ə sē) *n.*: Conspiracy

configuration (kən fig´ yōō rā´ shən) *n.*: Structure; arrangement

conspicuous (kən spik´ yōō əs) *adj.*: Noticeable

consternation (kän´ stər nā´ shən) *n.*: Great shock that makes one feel helpless or bewildered

contiguous (kən tig´ yōō əs) *adj.*: In physical contact; near or next to

convulsed (kən vulst´) *adj.*: Taken over by violent, involuntary spasms

cordially (kôr´ jəl lē) *adv.*: Warm and friendly

couched (koucht) *v.*: Put into words; expressed

countenance (koun´ tə nəns) *n.*: The look on a person's face that shows his or her nature or feeling

credibility (kred´ ə bil´ ə tē) *n.*: Believability

crevice (krev´ is) *n.*: A narrow opening

criteria (krī tir´ ē ə) *n.*: Standards or tests by which something can be judged

cunningly (kun´ iŋ lē) *adv.*: Skillfully

defray (di frā´) *v.*: To pay or furnish the money for

degrading (dē grād´ iŋ) *adj.*: Insulting; dishonorable

deliberating (di lib´ ə rā tiŋ) *v.*: Thinking or considering very carefully and fully

derision (di rizh´ ən) *n.*: Contempt; ridicule

descended (dē send´ id) *v.*: Came down

descent (dē sent´) *n.*: The act of climbing down

devices (di vīs´ ez) *n.*: Ways of amusing yourself

devoid (di void´) *adj.*: Completely without; lacking

devoured (di vourd´) *v.*: Ate greedily

diffused (di fyōōsd´) *v.*: Spread out widely into different directions

diligent (dil´ ə jənt) *adj.*: Done with careful, steady effort; hardworking

diplomatic (dip´ lə mat´ ik) *adj.*: Tactful; showing skill in dealing with people

discerning (di surn´ iŋ) *adj.*: Having keen perception or judgment

discharged (dis chärjd´) *v.*: Relieved or released from something; fired

discourse (dis´ kôrs) *n.*: Reasoning or rationality

discreet (di skrēt´) *adj.*: Careful about what one says or does; prudent

discrepancies (di skrep´ ən sēz) *n.*: Differences; inconsistencies; lack of agreement

disheveled (di shev´ əld) *adj.*: Untidy; messy

dispatched (di spacht´) *v.*: Put an end to; killed

dissimulation (di sim´ yə lā´ shən) *n.*: Hiding of one's feelings or purposes

dissolution (dis´ ə lōō´ shən) *n.*: The act of breaking down and crumbling

diverged (dī vurjd´) *v.*: Branched off

diverts (dī vurts´) *v.*: Distracts

elongate (i lôŋ´ gāt) *adj.*: Long and narrow

eloquent (el´ ə kwənt) *adj.*: Fluent, forceful, and persuasive

elusive (i lōō´ siv) *adj.*: Hard to grasp or retain mentally

emancipated (i man´ sə pā´ təd) *v.*: Freed from the control or power of another

eminence (em´ i nəns) *n.*: High or lofty place

empathy (em´ pə thē) *n.*: Ability to share another's emotions, thoughts, or feelings

encompasses (en kum´ pəs´ sez) *v.*: Contains; includes

encumber (in kum´ bər) *v.*: Weigh down

engulfing (en gulf´ iŋ) *v.*: Flowing over and swallowing

ensued (en sōōd´) *v.*: Came afterward; followed immediately

envelop (en vel´ əp) *v.*: To wrap up; cover completely

equestrian (ē kwes´ trē ən) *adj.*: On horseback, or so represented

etiquette (et´ i kit) *n.*: Rules for behavior

evacuees (ē vak´ yōō ēz´) *n.*: People who leave a place, especially because of danger

evade (i vād´) *v.*: Escape; avoid

exertion (eg zur´ shən) *n.*: Energetic activity; effort

extravagance (ek strav´ ə gəns) *n.*: A spending of more than is necessary; wastefulness

exulting (eg zult´ iŋ) *v.*: Rejoicing

fastidious (fas tid´ ē əs) *adj.*: Refined in an oversensitive way, so as to be easily disgusted or displeased

fatalist (fā´ tə list) *n.*: One who believes that all events are determined by fate and cannot be changed

feigned (fānd) *v.*: Imitated; pretended

feigning (fān´ iŋ) *v.*: Pretending

fertile (fur´ təl) *adj.*: Rich; fruitful

fiscal (fis´ kəl) *adj.*: Having to do with finances

flue (flōō) *n.*: The pipe in a chimney that leads the smoke outside

forsaken (fər sā´ kən) *adj.*: Abandoned; desolate

friction (frik´ shən) *n.*: Rubbing of one object against another

fugitives (fyōō´ ji tivs´) *n.*: People fleeing

furrows (fur´ ōz) *n.*: Deep wrinkles

furtive (fur´ tiv) *adj.*: Sly or done in secret

futile (fyōōt´ əl) *adj.*: Ineffective; useless; hopeless

gale (gāl) *n.*: Strong wind

galore (gə lôr´) *adj.*: In abundance; plentiful

gesticulations (jes tik´ yōō lā´ shənz) *n.*: Energetic hand or arm movements

gestures (jes´ chərs) *n.*: Movements used to convey an idea, emotion, or intention

glistens (glis´ ənz) *v.*: Shines; sparkles

gnarled (närld) *adj.*: Knotty and twisted, as the trunk of an old tree

gratification (grat´ ə fi kā´ shən) *n.*: Satisfaction

guffawed (gə fôd´) *v.*: Laughed in a loud and coarse manner

guileless (gīl´ lis) *adj.*: Without deceit, slyness, or trickery

guttural (gut´ ər əl) *adj.*: Made in the back of the throat

habitable (hab´ ə tə bəl) *adj.*: Fit to live in

harnessed (här´ nist) *v.*: Tied; bound

haughty (hôt´ ē) *adj.*: Proud of oneself and scornful of others

heedless (hēd´ lis) *adj.*: Unmindfully careless

hefted (hef´ tid) *v.*: Lifted; tested the weight of

hemisphere (hem´ i sfir´) *n.*: Half of a sphere; dome

horde (hôrd) *n.*: Large, moving group

hover (huv´ ər) *v.*: Flutter in the air; linger

illiteracy (il lit´ ər ə sē) *n.*: Inability to read or write

immersed (im murst´) *adj.*: Deeply involved in

immersed (im murst´) *v.*: Plunged into; submerged

immigrate (im´ ə grāt) *v.*: Come into a foreign country to make a new home

imperturbably (im´ pər tur´ bə blē) *adv.*: Unexcitedly; impassively

impetuous (im pech´ ōō əs) *adj.*: Moving with great force or violence; done suddenly with little thought

implications (im´ pli kā´ shəns) *n.*: Possible conclusions

inadvertently (in´ ad vurt´ ənt lē) *adv.*: Unintentionally

inarticulate (in´ är tik´ yə lit) *adj.*: Speechless or unable to express oneself

incentive (in sent´ iv) n.: Something that stimulates one to action; encouragement

incredulously (in krej´ ͞oo ləs lē) adv.: With doubt or disbelief

indicative (in dik´ ə tiv) adj.: Giving a suggestion; showing

indignant (in dig´ nənt) adj.: Filled with anger over some meanness or injustice

indomitable (in däm´ it ə bəl) adj.: Not easily discouraged

indulgent (in dul´ jənt) adj.: Very mild and tolerant; not strict or critical

ineffectually (in´ e fek˝ ch͞oo ə lē) adv.: Without producing the desired effect

inferior (in fir´ ē ər) adj.: Lower in status, order, or rank

infinite (in´ fə nit) adj.: Extending beyond measure or comprehension

infuse (in fy͞ooz´) v.: Put into

infusion (in fy͞oo´ zhən) n.: The act of putting one thing into another

innumerable (i n͞oo´ mər ə bəl) adj.: Too many to be counted

inscription (in skrip´ shən) n.: Something written or engraved onto a surface

inscrutable (in skr͞oot´ ə bəl) adj.: Impossible to see or understand

insolently (in´ sə lənt lē) adv.: Boldly disrespectful in speech or behavior

insufferable (in suf´ ər ə bəl) adj.: Unbearable

intangible (in tan´ jə bəl) adj.: Not able to be touched or grasped

interaction (in´ tər ak˝ shən) n.: Actions that affect each other

intimate (in´ tə mət) adj.: Private or personal

intimation (in´ tə mā˝ shən) n.: Hint or suggestion

introspective (in´ trō spekt˝ iv) adj.: Inward looking; thoughtful

intuition (in´ t͞oo wish´ ən) n.: Ability to know immediately, without reasoning

invincible (in vin´ sə bəl) adj.: Unbeatable

ire (ir) n.: Anger; wrath

judicious (j͞oo dish´ əs) adj.: Showing sound judgment; wise and careful

kindled (kin´ dəld) v.: Stirred up; awakened

keen (kēn) adj.: Having a sharp cutting edge

lair (ler) n.: Den of a wild animal

languor (laŋ´ gər) n.: Listlessness; indifference

latching (lach´ iŋ) v.: Grasping or attaching oneself to

lavish (lav´ ish) adj.: Showy; more than enough

legions (lē´ jəns) n.: Large number; multitude

leisure (lezh´ ər) n.: Free and unoccupied time

lilting (lilt´ iŋ) adj.: Singing or speaking with a light, graceful rhythm

listlessly (list´ lis lē) adv.: Without interest; spiritlessly

literally (lit´ ər əl ē) adv.: Actually; in fact

loitering (loit´ ər iŋ) n.: Lingering in an aimless way

looming (l͞oom´ iŋ) adj.: Ominous and awe-inspiring

low (lō) v.: Make the typical sound that a cow makes; moo

luminous (l͞oo´ mə nəs) adj.: Giving off light; shining; bright

luster (lus´ tər) n.: Brightness; radiance

macabre (mə käb´ rə) adj.: Gruesome; grim and horrible

mandate (man´ dāt˝) n.: Order or command

mania (mā´ nē ə) n.: Uncontrollable enthusiasm

manifestly (man´ ə fest˝ lē) adv.: Clearly

manifold (man´ ə fōld˝) adj.: Many and varied

mantle (man´ təl) n.: Sleeveless coat or cape

meager (mē´ gər) adj.: Lacking in some way; inadequate

melancholy (mel´ ən käl ē) adj.: Sad; depressed

membrane (mem´ brān) n.: A thin, soft sheet or layer serving as a covering

mercurial (mər ky͞oor´ ē əl) adj.: Quick or changeable in behavior

meticulous (mə tik´ y͞oo ləs) adj.: Extremely careful about details

misinterpret (mis´ in tur´ prit) v.: To understand or explain incorrectly

mistrusted (mis´ trust´ əd) v.: Doubted

molding (mōl´ diŋ) n.: Ornamental woodwork that projects from the walls of a room

morose (mə rōs´) adj.: Gloomy; ill-tempered;

sullen

mutineers (my͞oot´ ən irz´) n.: People on a ship who revolt against their officers

mutinous (my͞oot´ ən əs) adj.: Rebellious

negligent (neg´ lə jənt) adj.: Without care or attention; indifferent

negotiation (ni gō´ shē ā˝ shen) n.: Discussion to reach an agreement

nurtures (nur´ chərz) v.: Nourishes

obdurate (äb´ d͞oor it) adj.: Stubbornly persistent

obscure (äb sky͞oor´) adj.: Hidden; not obvious

obscure (əb sky͞oor´) v.: Conceal or hide

officious (ə fish´ əs) adj.: Overly eager to serve; excessively obliging

oppressed (ə prest´) adj.: Kept down by cruel or unjust use of power

orators (ôr´ ət ərz) n.: Public speakers

oratory (ôr´ ə tôr˝ ē) n.: Skill or eloquence in public speaking

ostentatiously (äs´ tən tā˝ shəs lē) adv.: In a showy way

pandemonium (pan də mō´ nē əm) n.: A scene of wild disorder

paradoxes (par´ ə däks´ es) n.: Things that seem to be contradictory

peril (per´ əl) n.: Exposure to harm or injury; danger

peripatetic (per´ i pə tet˝ ik) adj.: Moving from place to place; walking about

persistent (pər sist´ ənt) adj.: Stubborn; persevering

pervading (pər vād´ iŋ) v.: Spreading throughout

pitiful (pit´ i fəl) adj.: Deserving compassion or sympathy

placidly (plas´ id lē) adv.: In a calm way

precipitate (prē sip´ ə tāt˝) v.: Cause to happen before expected or desired

predisposed (prē´ dis pōzd´) adj.: Inclined; willing

predominantly (pri däm´ ə nənt lē) adj.: Mainly; most noticeably

pretense (prē tens´) n.: False showing; pretending

pretext (prē´ tekst) n.: False reason or motive used to hide a real intention

prevail (prē vāl´) v.: Win; triumph

privations (pri vā´ shənz) n.: Deprivation or lack of common comforts

procession (prō sesh´ ən) n.: A group of people or things moving forward

procured (prō ky͞oord´) v.: Obtained by some effort

prodigy (präd´ ə jē) n.: A wonder; an unusually talented person

profound (prō found´) adj.: Intellectually deep; getting to the bottom of the matter

prominent (präm´ ə nənt) adj.: Widely and favorably known

psychology (sī käl´ ə jē) n.: Science dealing with the mind and with mental and emotional processes

purify (py͞oor´ ə fī˝) v.: To rid of impurities

pursuit (pər s͞oot´) n.: Following in order to overtake and capture

quake (kwāk) v.: To tremble or shake; to shudder or shiver, as from fear or cold

radial (rā´ dē əl) adj.: Branching out in all directions from a common center

ravaging (rav´ ij iŋ) adj.: Severely damaging

recede (re sēd´) v.: Move away; fade

refute (ri fy͞oot´) v.: Prove (an argument or statement) to be false by argument or evidence

registrants (rej´ is trənts) n.: People who register to participate in something

reigning (rān´ iŋ) adj.: Ruling

respectively (ri spek´ tiv lē) adv.: In the order named

retribution (re´ trə by͞oo˝ shən) n.: Punishment for wrongdoing

retrospect (re´ trə spekt´) n.: Hindsight

reverie (rev´ ər ē) n.: Daydream

rigorous (rig´ ər əs) adj.: Very strict or harsh

riveted (riv´ it əd) v.: Fastened or made firm

rivulets (riv´ y͞oo lits) n.: Little streams

roam (rōm) v.: Go aimlessly; wander

romp (rämp) v.: Lively play or frolic

ruddy (rud´ ē) adj.: Having a healthy red color

runt (runt) n.: The smallest animal in a litter

sagacity (sə gas´ ə tē) n.: High intelligence and sound judgment

sarcastic (sär kas´ tik) adj.: Speaking with sharp mockery intended to hurt another

sauntering (sän´ tər iŋ) v.: Walking slowly and confidently

scolded (skōld´ əd) v.: Criticized harshly

scornful (skôrn´ fəl) adj.: Full of contempt or disdain

semblance (sem´ bləns) n.: Look or appearance

sentinel (sen´ ti nəl) n.: Guard

shackles (shak´ əls) n.: Metal fastenings, usually a linked pair for the wrists or ankles of a prisoner

shriveled (shriv´ əld) v.: Dried up; withered

shunned (shund) v.: Avoided

signify (sig´ nə fī) v.: To show or make known, as by a sign, words, etc.

singular (siŋ´ gyə lər) adj.: Unique; exceptional; extraordinary

smoldering (smōl´ dər iŋ) adj.: Burning or smoking without flame

sobers (sō´ bərs) v.: Calms; sedates

somber (säm´ bər) adj.: Dark and gloomy

specter (spek´ tər) n.: Disturbing thoughts

spirited (spir´ it id) adj.: Lively; energetic

spontaneously (spän tā´ nē əs id) adv.: Resulting from a natural feeling

stalking (stôk´ iŋ) adj.: Secretly approaching

stalwart (stôl´ wərt) adj.: Resolute; firm; unyielding

stealthily (stel´ thi lē) adv.: In a secretive or sneaky way

stealthy (ste´ thē) adj.: Artfully sly and secretive

stilted (stil´ təd) adj.: Unnatural; very formal

stoic (stō´ ik) adj.: Calm and unbothered in spite of suffering

strictures (strik´ chərs) n.: Criticisms

strife (strīf) n.: Conflict

sturdy (stur´ dē) adj.: Firm; strong

sublimity (sə blim´ ə tē) n.: The state or quality of being majestic; noble

subtle (sut´ əl) adj.: Delicate; fine

supple (sup´ əl) adj.: Flexible and pliant

swarthy (swôr´ thē) adj.: Having a dark complexion

tangible (tan´ jə bəl) adj.: Having form and substance; that can be touched or felt by touch; that can be understood; definite; objective

taut (tôt) adj.: Tightly stretched

tenacious (tə nā´ shəs) adj.: Holding on firmly

tendril (ten´ drəl) n.: Thin shoot from a plant

tenement (ten´ ə mənt) n.: Here, a rundown apartment building

thoroughly (thur´ ō lē) adv.: Accurately and with regard to detail

timidly (tim´ id lē) adv.: In a shy manner

transparent (trans par´ ənt) adj.: Capable of being seen through; clear

tread (tred) n.: Step

tranquil (tran´ kwil) adj.: Quiet or motionless; peaceful

tropical (träp´ ə kəl) adj.: Very hot; sultry

turbulent (tur´ by͞oo lənt) adj.: Full of commotion; wild

unabashed (un ə basht´) adj.: Unashamed

unanimous (y͞oo nan´ ə məs) adj.: Agreeing completely; united in opinion

unfurled (un furld´) v.: Unfolded

unobtrusively (un´ əb tr͞oo´ siv lē) adv.: Without calling attention to oneself

unrecompensed (un rek´ əm penst´) v.: Unrewarded

unremitting (un ri mit´ iŋ) adj.: Not stopping; persistent

unwonted (un wän´ tid) adj.: Not usual

usurped (y͞oo surpt´) v.: Took power or authority away from

usurps (y͞oo surps´) v.: Takes over

vertical (vur´ ti kəl) adj.: Straight up and down; upright

vigorous (vig´ ər əs) adj.: Strong and energetic

virtuous (vur´ ch͞oo wəs) adj.: Moral; upright

voracious (vô rā´ shəs) adj.: Eager to devour large quantities of food

wan (wän) adj.: Pale

wizened (wiz´ ənd) v.: Shriveled or withered

worthily (wur´ thə lē) adv.: Having value

LITERARY TERMS HANDBOOK

ALLITERATION *Alliteration* is the repetition of initial consonant sounds. Writers use alliteration to draw attention to certain words or ideas, to imitate sounds, and to create musical effects. In the opening lines from "Silver," on page 856, notice how Walter de la Mare includes alliteration to create a sense of musical enchantment in the moonlit night:

> Slowly, silently, now the moon
> Walks the night in her silver shoon;

See *Repetition.*

ALLUSION An *allusion* is a reference to a well-known person, place, event, literary work, or work of art. Understanding what a writer is saying often depends on recognizing allusions. Walt Whitman's "O Captain! My Captain!" on page 266, contains allusions to the Civil War.

ANECDOTE An *anecdote* is a brief story about an interesting, amusing, or strange event. Writers tell anecdotes to entertain or to make a point. In "Animal Craftsmen," on page 625, Bruce Brooks relates an anecdote from his childhood.

ANTAGONIST An *antagonist* is a character or force in conflict with a main character, or protagonist. In "The Girl Who Hunted Rabbits," on page 49, both the Demon and the weather are antagonists to the young maiden.

See *Conflict* and *Protagonist.*

ATMOSPHERE See *Mood.*

AUTOBIOGRAPHY An *autobiography* is a form of nonfiction in which the writer tells the story of his or her own life. An autobiography may tell about the person's whole life or only a part of it. Lionel García tells about his childhood neighborhood and activities in "Baseball," on page 636.

See *Biography* and *Nonfiction.*

BALLAD A *ballad* is a songlike poem that tells a story, often one dealing with adventure and romance. Most ballads are written in four- to six-line stanzas and have regular rhythms and rhyme schemes. A ballad often features a refrain—a regularly repeated line or group of lines. "John Henry," on page 940, is an example of a *folk ballad.*

See *Oral Tradition* and *Refrain.*

BIOGRAPHY A *biography* is a form of nonfiction in which a writer tells the life story of another person. Most biographies are written about famous or admirable people. Although biographies are nonfiction, the most effective ones share the qualities of good narrative writing. Stephen Longstreet's "Hokusai: The Old Man Mad About Drawing," on page 654, is a biography.

See *Autobiography* and *Nonfiction.*

BLANK VERSE *Blank verse* is poetry written in unrhymed iambic pentameter lines. William Shakespeare wrote many of his plays in blank verse. The following example is from King Richard's soliloquy, on page 792:

> Now is the winter of our discontent
> Made glorious summer by this sun of York;
> And all the clouds that loured upon our house
> In the deep bosom of the ocean buried.

See *Meter.*

CHARACTER A *character* is a person or an animal that takes part in the action of a literary work. A *main,* or *major, character* is the most important character in a story, poem, or play. A *minor character* plays a lesser role but is necessary for the story to develop. In "Raymond's Run," on page 292, the major character, Squeaky, tells the story.

Characters are sometimes classified as flat or round. A *flat character* is one-sided and often stereotypical. A *round character,* on the other hand, is fully developed and exhibits many traits. Characters can also be classified as dynamic or static. A *dynamic character* is one who changes or grows during the course of the work. A *static character* is one who does not change.

See *Characterization, Hero/Heroine,* and *Motivation.*

CHARACTERIZATION *Characterization* is the process by which authors create memorable characters. Authors use two major methods of characterization—*direct* and *indirect.* When using *direct characterization,* an author tells what a character is like. In "The Day I Got Lost," on page 558, Isaac Bashevis Singer directly tells about Professor Shlemiel—what he looks like and what he does.

When using *indirect characterization,* a writer reveals a character's personality through his or her appearance, words, actions, and effects on others. Sometimes the writer describes what other participants in the story say and think about the character. The reader then draws his or her own conclusions.

See *Character* and *Motivation.*

CLIMAX See *Conflict* and *Plot.*

CONCRETE POEM A *concrete poem* is one with a shape that suggests its subject. The poet arranges the letters, punctuation, and lines to create an image, or picture, on the page. Maxine Kumin's poem "400-Meter Free Style," on page 839, is an example of a concrete poem.

CONFLICT A *conflict* is a struggle between opposing forces. Conflict is one of the most important elements of stories, novels, and plays because it causes the action. Conflict can be external or internal. *External conflict* may be between two characters and may be caused by a difference in ideas or personalities. In "Cub Pilot on the Mississippi," on page 109, Mark Twain describes the conflict between himself and the steamboat pilot. Another type of external conflict may take place between a character and some force in nature. For example, in "Up the Slide," on page 154, the conflict is between a character and the cold, icy Yukon. An *internal conflict* takes place within the mind of a character, as in "A Retrieved Reformation," on page 252.
See *Plot.*

DESCRIPTION A *description* is a portrait, in words, of a person, place, or object. Descriptive writing uses images that appeal to the five senses—sight, hearing, touch, taste, and smell.
See *Image.*

DEVELOPMENT See *Plot.*

DIALECT *Dialect* is the form of a language spoken by people in a particular region or group. Dialects differ in pronunciation, grammar, and word choice.

Writers use dialect to make their characters seem realistic. For example, in Paul Laurence Dunbar's "The Finish of Patsy Barnes," on page 580, notice the dialect spoken by Patsy and his mother:

"Honey," she said; "mammy ain' gwine lay hyeah long. She be all right putty soon."

"Nevah you min'," said Patsy with a choke in his voice. "I can do somep'n', an' we'll have anothah doctah."

DIALOGUE A *dialogue* is a conversation between characters. In poems, novels, and short stories, dialogue is usually set off by quotation marks to indicate a speaker's exact words. In a play, dialogue follows the names of the characters, and no quotation marks are used. The following example is from *A Walk in the Woods,* on page 773.

HONEYMAN.	I don't understand. You liked it?
BOTVINNIK.	Very much.
HONEYMAN.	Then why did you delay so long?
BOTVINNIK.	Because your proposal was . . . too good.

See *Drama.*

DRAMA A *drama* is a story written to be performed. Although a drama is meant to be performed, one can also read the *script,* or written version, and imagine the action. The script of a drama is made up of dialogue and stage directions. The *dialogue* is the words spoken by the actors. The *stage directions,* usually printed in italics, tell how the actors should look, move, and speak. They also describe the setting, sound effects, and lighting.

Dramas are often divided into parts called *acts.* The acts are often divided into smaller parts called *scenes.*

DYNAMIC CHARACTER See *Character.*

ESSAY An *essay* is a short nonfiction work about a particular subject. Most essays have a single major focus and a clear introduction, body, and conclusion.

There are many types of essays. A *narrative essay,* like "Debbie," on page 670, tells a true story about real people. An *expository essay,* like "Netiquette," on page 678, presents information, discusses ideas, or explains a process. A *persuasive essay,* like "The Trouble with Television," on page 686, presents and supports an opinion with strong arguments, or reasons. A *descriptive essay,* such as "Forest Fire," on page 675, describes events and feelings by including images and details. A *reflective essay,* like "Animal Craftsmen," on page 625, communicates a writer's thoughts about a topic of personal interest.
See *Description, Exposition, Narration,* and *Persuasion.*

EXPOSITION *Exposition* is writing or speech that explains a process or presents information. This Literary Terms Handbook and the introductions to the selections in this text are both examples of exposition. In the plot of a story or drama, the exposition, or introduction, is the part of the work that introduces the characters, setting, and basic situation.
See *Plot.*

EXTENDED METAPHOR In an *extended metaphor,* as in a regular metaphor, a subject is spoken of, or written, as though it were something else. However, an extended metaphor differs from a regular metaphor in that several comparisons are made. In her poem "Mushrooms," on page 508, Sylvia Plath uses extended metaphors to creatively describe mushrooms.
See *Metaphor.*

FABLE A *fable* is a brief story or poem, usually with animal characters, that teaches a lesson, or moral. The moral is usually stated at the end of the fable.

The fable is an ancient literary form found in many cultures. The fables written by Aesop, a Greek slave who lived in the sixth century B.C., are still popular with children today. Many familiar expressions, such as "crying wolf," "sour grapes," and "crying over spilt milk," come from Aesop's fables.

See *Moral*.

FANTASY A *fantasy* is highly imaginative writing that contains elements not found in real life. Examples of fantasy include stories that involve supernatural elements, stories that resemble fairy tales, stories that deal with imaginary places and creatures, and science-fiction stories.

See *Science Fiction*.

FICTION *Fiction* is prose writing that tells about imaginary characters and events. Short stories and novels are works of fiction. Some writers base their fiction on actual events and people, adding invented characters, dialogue, settings, and plots. Other writers of fiction rely on imagination alone to provide their materials.

See *Narration, Nonfiction,* and *Prose*.

FIGURATIVE LANGUAGE *Figurative language* is writing or speech that is not meant to be taken literally. The many types of figurative language are known as *figures of speech*. Common figures of speech include metaphor, simile, and personification. Writers use figurative language to state ideas in vivid and imaginative ways.

See *Metaphor, Personification, Simile,* and *Symbol*.

FIGURE OF SPEECH See *Figurative Language*.

FLASHBACK A *flashback* is a scene within a story that interrupts the sequence of events to relate events that occurred in the past. "Christmas Day in the Morning," on page 64, contains flashback.

FLAT CHARACTER See *Character*.

FOLK TALE A *folk tale* is a story composed orally and then passed from person to person by word of mouth. Most folk tales are highly entertaining, with plots featuring heroes, adventure, magic, or romance. The folk tales in this text tell of legendary heroes such as Pecos Bill, Paul Bunyan, and Davy Crockett.

See *Fable, Legend, Myth,* and *Oral Tradition*.

FORESHADOWING *Foreshadowing* is the author's use of clues to hint at what might happen later in the story. Writers use foreshadowing to build their readers' expectations and to create suspense. In "Flowers for Algernon," on page 204, the death of Algernon foreshadows Charlie's fate.

FREE VERSE *Free verse* is poetry not written in a regular rhythmical pattern, or meter. Free verse poems may contain lines of any length or with any number of stresses, or beats. Julio Noboa Polanco's "Identity," on page 838, is an example of free verse.

See *Meter*.

GENRE A *genre* is a division or type of literature. Literature is commonly divided into three major genres: poetry, prose, and drama. Each major genre is in turn divided into lesser genres, as follows:

1. *Poetry:* lyric poetry, concrete poetry, dramatic poetry, narrative poetry, epic poetry
2. *Prose:* fiction (novels and short stories) and nonfiction (biography, autobiography, letters, essays, and reports)
3. *Drama:* serious drama and tragedy, comic drama, melodrama, and farce

See *Drama, Poetry,* and *Prose*.

HAIKU The *haiku* is a three-line Japanese verse form. The first and third lines of a haiku each have five syllables. The second line has seven syllables. A writer of haiku uses images to create a single, vivid picture, generally of a scene from nature. See the examples of haiku by Bashō and Moritake on page 837.

HERO/HEROINE A *hero* or *heroine* is a character whose actions are inspiring or noble. Often, heroes and heroines struggle mightily to overcome the obstacles and problems that stand in their way. Some examples of heroic characters are the title characters in "Paul Revere's Ride," "Barbara Frietchie," and "Elizabeth Blackwell." The most obvious examples of heroes and heroines are the larger-than-life characters in myths and legends, like John Henry and Pecos Bill.

The term *heroes* was originally used only for male characters, while heroic female characters were always called *heroines*. However, it is now acceptable to use the word *hero* to refer to females as well as to males.

HUBRIS *Hubris* is excessive pride, and it is often the downfall of literary characters.

IAMB See *Meter*.

IMAGE An *image* is a word or a phrase that appeals to one or more of the five senses. Writers use images to describe how their subjects look, sound, feel, taste, and smell. "This We Know," on page 196, includes images that appeal to the senses of sight, sound, and smell.

IRONY *Irony* is the general name given to literary techniques that involve surprising, interesting, or amusing contradictions. In *verbal irony*, words are used to suggest the opposite of their usual meanings. In *dramatic irony*, there is a contradiction between what a character thinks and what the reader or audience knows to be true. In *irony of situation*, an event occurs that directly contradicts the expectations of the characters, the reader, or the audience. For example, in "A Retrieved Reformation," on page 252, Jimmy Valentine has to resume safecracking in order to earn the respect of a policeman.

LEGEND A *legend* is a widely told story about the past, one that may or may not have a foundation in fact. Every culture has its own legends—its familiar, traditional stories. "The Girl Who Hunted Rabbits," on page 49, is a legend that originated with the Zuñi culture.

See *Oral Tradition.*

LYRIC POEM A *lyric poem* is a short, highly musical poem that expresses the observations and feelings of a single speaker. "Harlem Night Song," on page 828, is an example of a lyric poem.

MAIN CHARACTER See *Character.*

MEMOIR A *memoir* is a form of autobiographical writing that deals with the writer's memory of someone or of a significant event. Often, the writing is very personal, as in the excerpt from *I Know Why the Caged Bird Sings,* on page 24.

See *Autobiography.*

METAPHOR A *metaphor* is a figure of speech in which something is described as though it were something else. A metaphor, like a simile, works by pointing out a similarity between two unlike things. For example, in Robert Frost's "The Road Not Taken," on page 34, the diverging roads are a metaphor for the major choices that people must make in their lives.

See *Extended Metaphor* and *Simile.*

METER The *meter* of a poem is its rhythmical pattern. This pattern is determined by the number of stresses, or beats, in each line. To describe the meter of a poem, you must *scan* its lines. *Scanning* involves marking the stressed and unstressed syllables, as follows:

Most | friendship is | feigning, most | loving mere |

folly

Each stress is marked with a slanted line (´) and each unstressed syllable with a horseshoe symbol (˘). The stressed and unstressed syllables are then divided by vertical lines (|) into groups called feet. The following types of feet are common in English poetry:

1. *Iamb:* a foot with one unstressed syllable followed by one stressed syllable, as in the word "begin"
2. *Trochee:* a foot with one stressed syllable followed by one unstressed syllable, as in the word "people"
3. *Anapest:* a foot with two unstressed syllables followed by one stressed syllable, as in the phrase "on the sea"
4. *Dactyl:* a foot with one stressed syllable followed by two unstressed syllables, as in the word "happiness"
5. *Spondee:* a foot with two stressed syllables, as in the word "downtown"

Depending on the type of foot that is most common in them, lines of poetry are described as *iambic, trochaic, anapestic,* or *dactylic.*

Lines are also described in terms of the number of feet that occur in them, as follows:

1. *Monometer:* verse written in one-foot lines:
   First Man,
   behold:
   —N. Scott Momaday, "New World"

2. *Dimeter:* verse written in two-foot lines:
   The days | are short
   The sun | a spark
   Hung thin | between
   The dark | and dark.
   —John Updike, "January"

3. *Trimeter:* verse written in three-foot lines:
   My mother | taught me | purple
   Although | she never | wore it
   —Evelyn Tooley Hunt, "Taught Me Purple"

4. *Tetrameter:* verse written in four-foot lines:
   O Captain! | My Captain! | our fearful trip | is done,
   The ship has weathered | every rack, | the prize we sought | is won,
   —Walt Whitman, "O Captain! My Captain!"

5. *Pentameter:* verse written in five-foot lines:
   All things | within | this fad | ing world | hath end,
   Adver | sity | doth still | our joys | attend;
   No ties | so strong, | no friends | so dear | and sweet,
   But with | death's part | ing blow | is sure | to meet.
   —Anne Bradstreet,
   "Before the Birth of One of Her Children"

A six-foot line is called a *hexameter.* A seven-foot line is called a *heptameter.* A complete description of the meter of a line tells the kinds of feet each line contains, as well as how many feet of each kind. Thus, the lines from Anne Bradstreet's poem would be described as *iambic pentameter. Blank verse* is poetry written in unrhymed iambic pentameter. Poetry that does not have a regular meter is called *free verse.*

See *Blank Verse* and *Free Verse.*

MINOR CHARACTER See *Character.*

MOOD *Mood,* or *atmosphere,* is the feeling created in the reader by a literary work or passage. Writers use many devices to create mood, including images, dialogue, setting, and plot. Often, a writer creates a mood at the beginning of a work and then sustains this mood throughout. Sometimes, however, the mood of the work changes dramatically. For example, the mood of "The Finish of Patsy Barnes," on page 580, changes from one of tension and despair to one of success and hope as Patsy wins the race and then finds a caring doctor for his mother.

MORAL A *moral* is a lesson taught by a literary work. A fable usually ends with a moral that is directly stated. For example, the concluding words of "Brer Possum's Dilemma" are, "And when you're mindin' your own business and you spot trouble, don't never trouble trouble 'til trouble troubles you." A poem, novel, short story, or essay often suggests a moral that is not directly stated. The moral must be drawn by the reader, based on other elements in the work.

See *Fable*.

MOTIVATION A *motivation* is a reason that explains, or partially explains, a character's thoughts, feelings, actions, or speech. Writers try to make their characters' motivations, or motives, as clear as possible. If the motives of a main character are not clear, then the character will not be believable.

Characters are often motivated by needs, such as food and shelter. They are also motivated by feelings, such as fear, love, and pride. For example, in "The Adventure of the Speckled Band," on page 474, fear motivates Miss Stoner to seek the help of Sherlock Holmes.

MYTH A *myth* is a fictional tale that explains the actions of gods or heroes or the origins of elements of nature. Myths are part of the oral tradition. They are composed orally and then passed from generation to generation by word of mouth. Every ancient culture has its own mythology, or collection of myths. The Zuñi myth "Coyote Steals the Sun and Moon," on page 902, explains the origins of winter and gives insight into Zuñi beliefs.

See *Oral Tradition*.

NARRATION *Narration* is writing that tells a story. The act of telling a story is also called narration. Fictional works, such as novels and short stories, are examples of *narration*, as are poems that tell stories, such as "Elizabeth Blackwell," on page 314. Narration can also be found in many kinds of nonfiction, including autobiographies, biographies, and newspaper reports. A story told in fiction, nonfiction, poetry, or even in drama is called a narrative.

See *Narrative Poem* and *Narrator*.

NARRATIVE See *Narration*.

NARRATIVE POEM A *narrative poem* is a story told in verse. Narrative poems often have all the elements of short stories, including characters, conflict, and plot. An example of a narrative poem is John Greenleaf Whittier's "Barbara Frietchie," on page 311.

NARRATOR A *narrator* is a speaker or character who tells a story. A *third-person narrator* is one who stands outside the action and speaks about it. A *first-person narrator* is one who tells a story and participates in its action.

In some dramas, there is a separate character called "The Narrator" who introduces, comments on, and concludes the play.

See *Point of View*.

NONFICTION *Nonfiction* is prose writing that presents and explains ideas or that tells about real people, places, objects, or events. Autobiographies, biographies, essays, reports, letters, memos, and newspaper articles are all types of nonfiction.

See *Fiction*.

NOVEL A *novel* is a long work of fiction. Novels contain such elements as characters, plot, conflict, and setting. The writer of novels, or novelist, develops these elements in the story. A novel may have several themes, and in addition to its main plot, a novel may contain one or more subplots, or independent, related stories.

See *Fiction*.

ONOMATOPOEIA *Onomatopoeia* is the use of words that imitate sounds. *Crash, buzz, screech, hiss, neigh, jingle,* and *cluck* are examples of onomatopoeia. In the following line from Bashō's "The falling flower," on page 837, the word *screech* is an example of onomatopoeia: "A night-heron's screech."

ORAL TRADITION *Oral tradition* is the passing of songs, stories, and poems from generation to generation by word of mouth. Folk songs, folk tales, legends, and myths all come from the oral tradition. No one knows who first created these stories and poems. In the selection from "The People, Yes," on page 347, Carl Sandburg pulls together stories from the oral tradition.

See *Folk Tale, Legend,* and *Myth*.

PERSONIFICATION *Personification* is a type of figurative language in which a nonhuman subject is given human characteristics. In "Incident in a Rose Garden," on page 878, Donald Justice personifies death as a walking, talking, questioning being.

PERSUASION *Persuasion* is used in writing or in speech that attempts to convince the reader or listener to adopt a particular opinion or course of action. Newspaper editorials and letters to the editor use persuasion. So do advertisements and campaign speeches given by political candidates. Robert MacNeil's essay "The Trouble with Television," on page 686, is an example of a persuasive essay.

PLOT *Plot* is the sequence of events in which each event results from a previous one and causes the next. In most novels, dramas, short stories, and narrative poems, the plot involves both characters and a central conflict. The plot usually begins with an *exposition* that introduces the setting, the characters, and the basic situation. This is followed by the *rising action,* in which the central conflict is introduced and developed. The conflict then increases until it reaches a high point of interest or suspense, the *climax.* The climax is followed by the *falling action,* or end, of the central conflict. Any events that occur during the falling action make up the *resolution.*

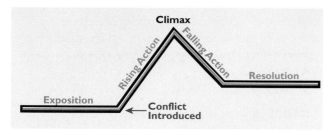

Some plots do not contain all of these elements. For example, some stories begin in the midst of a conflict and end with the resolution.

See *Conflict.*

POETRY *Poetry* is one of the three major types of literature, the others being prose and drama. Defining poetry more precisely isn't easy, for there is no single, unique characteristic that all poems share. Poems are often divided into lines and stanzas and often employ regular rhythmical patterns, or meters. However, some poems are written out just like prose, and some are written in free verse. Most poems make use of highly concise, musical, and emotionally charged language. Many also make use of imagery, figurative language, and special devices of sound such as rhyme.

Major types of poetry include *lyric poetry, narrative poetry,* and *concrete poetry.*

Other forms of poetry include *dramatic poetry,* in which characters speak in their own voices, and *epic poetry,* in which the poet tells a long, involved tale about gods or heroes.

See *Concrete Poem, Genre, Lyric Poem,* and *Narrative Poem.*

POINT OF VIEW *Point of view* is the perspective, or vantage point, from which a story is told. Three commonly used points of view are first person, omniscient third person, and limited third person.

First-person point of view is told by a character who uses the first-person pronoun "I." "Flowers for Algernon," on page 204, is told in the first person by the subject of the experiment.

"Charles," on page 14, is told from the *third-person limited point of view*—the point of view of the main character's mother. The narrator uses third-person pronouns such as "he" and "she" to refer to the characters.

In stories told from the *omniscient third-person point of view,* the narrator knows and tells about what each character feels and thinks. Jack London's "Up the Slide," on page 154, is written from the omniscient third-person point of view.

See *Narrator.*

PROSE *Prose* is the ordinary form of written language. Most writing that is not poetry, drama, or song is considered prose. Prose is one of the major genres of literature and occurs in two forms, fiction and nonfiction.

See *Fiction, Genre,* and *Nonfiction.*

PROTAGONIST The *protagonist* is the main character in a literary work. In "A Ribbon for Baldy," on page 410, the protagonist, or main character, is the boy who plants the corn and has the best science project.

See *Antagonist* and *Character.*

REFRAIN A *refrain* is a regularly repeated line or group of lines in a poem or a song. In the following passage from "Columbus," on page 144, the refrain has been italicized:

> Brave Adm'r'l, say but one good word:
> What shall we do when hope is gone?
> The words leapt like a leaping sword:
> *"Sail on! sail on! sail on! and on!"*

REPETITION *Repetition* is the use, more than once, of any element of language—a sound, word, phrase, clause, or sentence. Repetition is used in both prose and poetry. In prose fiction, a plot may be repeated, with variations, in a subplot; or a minor character may be similar to a major character in important ways. In poetry, repetition often involves the recurring use of certain words, images, structures, and devices. *Rhyme, alliteration,* and *rhythm* are all repetitions of sounds or sound patterns. A *refrain* is a repeated line or group of lines.

See *Alliteration, Meter, Plot, Rhyme,* and *Rhyme Scheme.*

RESOLUTION See *Plot.*

RHYME *Rhyme* is the repetition of sounds at the ends

of words. Poets use rhyme to lend a songlike quality to their verses and to emphasize certain words and ideas. Many traditional-style poems contain *end rhymes,* or rhyming words at the ends of lines. Alfred, Lord Tennyson, uses end rhyme in "Ring Out, Wild Bells," on page 92:

> Ring out, wild bells, to the wild *sky,*
> > The flying cloud, the frosty *light:*
> > The year is dying in the *night;*
> Ring out, wild bells, and let him *die.*

Another common device is the use of *internal rhymes,* or rhyming words within lines. Notice, for example, the internal rhymes in this passage of "Annabel Lee," by Edgar Allan Poe: "For the moon never *beams* without bringing me *dreams* / Of the beautiful Annabel Lee."
See *Rhyme Scheme.*

RHYME SCHEME A *rhyme scheme* is a regular pattern of rhyming words in a poem. The rhyme scheme of a poem is indicated by lowercase letters. Each rhyme is assigned a different letter, as follows, in the poem "Dark Hills," by Edwin Arlington Robinson:

Dark hills at evening in the west,	*a*
Where sunset hovers like a sound	*b*
Of golden horns that sang to rest	*a*
Old bones of warriors under ground,	*b*
Far now from all the bannered ways	*c*
Where flash the legions of the sun,	*d*
You fade—as if the last of days	*c*
Were fading, and all wars were done.	*d*

Thus, this poem has the rhyme scheme *ababcdcd.*

RHYTHM *Rhythm* is the pattern of beats, or stresses, in spoken or written language.
See *Meter.*

ROUND CHARACTER See *Character.*

SCIENCE FICTION *Science fiction* combines elements of fiction and fantasy with scientific fact. This type of writing is most effective when the writer creates a believable setting and characters, and balances new ideas with familiar details. "The Secret," on page 122, is a science-fiction story with elements that are "possible" and "impossible." Many science-fiction stories are set in the future.

SENSORY LANGUAGE *Sensory language* is writing or speech that appeals to one or more of the five senses.
See *Image.*

SETTING The *setting* of a literary work is the time and place of the action. The setting includes *all* the details of a place and time—the year, the time of day, even the weather. The place may be a specific country, state, region, community, neighborhood, building, institution, or home. Details such as dialect, clothing, customs, and modes of transportation are often used to establish setting.

In most stories, the setting serves as a backdrop—a context in which the characters interact. The setting of Ray Bradbury's "The Drummer Boy of Shiloh," on page 5, is an April night in 1862 during the Civil War, at a place named Shiloh near the Tennessee River, close to a church.

The setting of a story often helps to create a particular mood, or feeling. The mood of Ray Bradbury's story is one of nervous expectation—of fear mingled with resolve.
See *Mood.*

SHORT STORY A *short story* is a brief work of fiction. Like a novel, a short story presents a sequence of events, or plot. The plot usually deals with a central conflict faced by a main character, or protagonist. Like a lyric poem, a short story is concise and creates a single effect, or dominant impression, on its reader. The events in a short story usually communicate a message about life or human nature. This message, or central idea, is the story's theme.
See *Conflict, Plot,* and *Theme.*

SIMILE A *simile* is a figure of speech that uses *like* or *as* to make a direct comparison between two unlike ideas. Everyday speech often contains similes, such as "pale as a ghost," "good as gold," "spread like wildfire," and "clever as a fox."

Writers use similes to describe people, places, and things vividly. Poets, especially, create similes to point out new and interesting ways of viewing the world. José Garcia Villa's poem "Lyric 17," on page 867, contains several similes to describe poetry, such as "musical as a sea-gull," "slender as a bell," and "it must kneel like a rose."

SOLILOQUY A soliloquy is a long speech in a play or in a prose work made by a character who is alone. The character reveals his or her private thoughts and feelings to the audience or reader. In William Shakespeare's *Much Ado About Nothing,* Act II, scene iii, on page 790, Benedick speaks a soliloquy.

SPEAKER The *speaker* is the imaginary voice assumed by the writer of a poem. In other words, the speaker is the character who tells the poem. This character, or voice, is often not identified by name. In Robert Frost's poem "The Road Not Taken," on page 34, the speaker is contemplative, and even a bit sad, as he tells the poem.
See *Narrator.*

STAGE DIRECTIONS *Stage directions* are notes included in a drama to describe how the work is to be performed or staged. Stage directions are usually printed in italics and enclosed within parentheses or brackets. Some stage directions describe the movements and costumes, as well as the emotional states and ways of speaking of the characters. The following lines are from *The Diary of Anne Frank*:

ANNE. [*Screaming*] No! No! Don't . . . don't take me!
[*She moans, tossing and crying in her sleep. The other people wake, terrified.* DUSSEL *sits up in bed, furious.*]
DUSSEL. Shush! Anne! Shush!

See *Drama*.

STANZA A *stanza* is a formal division of lines in a poem, considered as a unit. Many poems are divided into stanzas that are separated by spaces. Stanzas often function just like paragraphs in prose. Each stanza states and develops a single main idea.

Stanzas are commonly named according to the number of lines found in them, as follows:

1. *Couplet:* two-line stanza
2. *Tercet:* three-line stanza
3. *Quatrain:* four-line stanza
4. *Cinquain:* five-line stanza
5. *Sestet:* six-line stanza
6. *Heptastich:* seven-line stanza
7. *Octave:* eight-line stanza

Evelyn Tooley Hunt's "Taught Me Purple" is written in quatrains:

My mother taught me purple
    Although she never wore it.
Wash-gray was her circle,
    The tenement her orbit.

Division into stanzas is common in traditional poetry and is often accompanied by rhyme. Notice, for example, that in the stanza above from "Taught Me Purple," the first and third lines and the second and fourth lines rhyme. That is, it follows the rhyme scheme *abab*. The remaining stanzas of the poem also have the rhyme scheme *abab*. However, some rhyming poems are not divided into stanzas, and some poems divided into stanzas do not contain rhyme.

STATIC CHARACTER See *Character*.

SURPRISE ENDING A *surprise ending* is a conclusion that is unexpected. Sometimes a surprise ending follows a false resolution. The reader thinks that the conflict has already been resolved but then is confronted with a new twist that changes the outcome of the plot. Often a surprise ending is *foreshadowed,* or subtly hinted at, in the course of the work. O. Henry's "A Retrieved Reformation," on page 252, contains a surprise ending for both the reader and the main character.

See *Foreshadowing* and *Plot*.

SUSPENSE *Suspense* is a feeling of anxious uncertainty about the outcome of events in a literary work. Writers create suspense by raising questions in the minds of their readers. For example, in "The Tell-Tale Heart," on page 542, Edgar Allan Poe uses the intensity of the narrator to create suspense.

SYMBOL A *symbol* is anything that stands for or represents something else. Symbols are common in everyday life. A dove with an olive branch in its beak is a symbol of peace, and a blindfolded woman holding a balanced scale is a symbol of justice.

TALL TALE Most *tall tales* come out of the oral tradition of the American frontier. They typically involve characters with highly exaggerated abilities and qualities. "Paul Bunyan of the North Woods," on page 944, and "Pecos Bill: The Cyclone," on page 946, are both examples of tall tales.

See *Legend, Myth,* and *Oral Tradition*.

THEME The *theme* of a literary work is its central message, concern, or purpose. A theme can usually be expressed as a generalization, or general statement, about people or life.

The theme may be stated directly by the writer, although it is more often presented indirectly. When the theme is stated indirectly, the reader must figure out the theme by looking carefully at what the work reveals about people or about life.

TONE The *tone* is the writer's attitude toward the readers and toward the subject, conveyed by the language and rhythm of the speaker. For example, the tone of Edgar Allan Poe's "The Tell-Tale Heart," on page 542, is frantic and sinister. In contrast, the tone of John Updike's poem "January," on page 836, is light and humorous.

See *Mood*.

WRITING HANDBOOK

THE WRITING PROCESS

The writing process can be roughly divided into a series of stages: prewriting, drafting, revising, editing, proofreading, and publishing. It is important to remember that the writing process is one that moves backward as well as forward. Even while you are moving forward in the creation of your composition, you may still return to a previous stage—to rethink or to rewrite.

Following are stages of the writing process, with key points to address during each stage.

Prewriting

In this stage, you plan out the work to be done. You prepare to write by exploring ideas, gathering information, and working out an organization plan. Following are the key steps to take at this stage:

Step 1: Analyze the writing situation. Before writing, analyze or study the parts of the writing assignment. To do this, ask yourself the following questions:

- *Topic (the subject you will be writing about):* What will you write about? Can you state your subject in a sentence? Is your subject too broad or too narrow?
- *Purpose (what you want your writing to accomplish):* Do you want your writing to explain? To describe? To persuade? To tell a story? To entertain? What do you want your audience to learn or to understand?
- *Audience (the people who will read or listen to your writing):* Who is your audience? What might they already know about your subject? What basic facts will you have to provide for them?

Step 2: Gather ideas and information. After thinking about the writing situation, you may find that you need more information. If so, you must decide how to gather this information. On the other hand, you may find that you already have too much information—that your topic is too broad. If this is the case, then you must decide how to narrow your topic. If you have the right amount of information but don't know how to present it clearly, you will have to choose a way to organize your information.

There are many ways to gather information, to narrow a topic, and to organize ideas. Following are some ways:

- *Brainstorm:* Discuss the topic with a group of people. Try to generate as many ideas as possible. Not all of your ideas will be useful or suitable. You'll need to evaluate them later.
- *Consult other people about your topic:* Speaking with others may suggest an idea or approach you did not think about.
- *Make a list of questions about your topic:* Begin your questions with words like *who, what, where, when, why,* and *how.* Then, find answers to your questions.
- *Do research:* Your topic may require you to go to other sources to find information. Read relevant books, pamphlets, newspapers, magazines, and reference works.

Step 3: Organize your notes. Once you have gathered enough information, organize it. Sort your ideas and notes; decide which points are most important. You can make an outline to show the order of ideas, or you can use some other organizing plan.

There are many ways to organize and develop your material. Careful organization will make your writing easy to read and understand. The following are common methods of organizing information:

- *Time Order or Chronological Order:* Events are organized in order of occurrence (from earliest to latest, for example).
- *Spatial Order:* Details are organized by position in space (from left to right, for example).
- *Degree Order:* This order is organization by size, amount, or intensity (from coldest to warmest, for example).
- *Priority Order:* This is organization by importance, value, usefulness, or familiarity (from worst to best, for example).

Drafting

Drafting follows prewriting and is the second stage in the writing process. Working from your prewriting notes and your outline or plan, you develop and present your ideas in sentences and paragraphs. The following are important points to remember about drafting:

- Write your rough draft in whichever way works best for you. Some writers like to develop each paragraph carefully and thoughtfully, writing very slowly, correcting and polishing as they write. Others prefer to write their rough drafts very quickly—putting down all their ideas without stopping to evaluate them.
- Do not try to make your rough draft perfect. Concentrate on getting your ideas on paper. Once this is done, you can make improvements in the revision and proofreading stages.
- Keep your audience and purpose in mind as you write. This will help you determine what you say and how you say it.
- Don't be afraid to set aside earlier ideas if later ones work better. Some of the best ideas are those that were not planned at the beginning. After you have written one draft, you might review it and realize that

you need to add more information, to change your purpose, or to narrow your focus.

Most papers, regardless of the topic, are developed with an introduction, a body, and a conclusion. Here are tips for developing these parts of a paper:

Introduction In the introduction to a paper, you want to engage your readers' attention and let them know the purpose of your paper. You may use the following strategies in your introduction:

- State your main idea.
- Use an anecdote.
- Startle your readers.
- Take a stand.
- Quote someone.

Body of the paper In the body of your paper, you present your information and make your points. Your organization is an important factor in leading readers through your ideas. Your elaboration on your main ideas is also important. Elaboration is the development of ideas to make your written work precise and complete. You can use the following to elaborate your main ideas:

- Facts and statistics
- Sensory details
- Explanation and definition
- Anecdotes
- Examples
- Quotations

Conclusion The ending of your paper is the final impression you leave with your readers. It should give readers the sense that you have pulled everything together. Following are some effective ways to end your paper:

- Summarize and restate.
- State an opinion.
- Tell an anecdote.
- Ask a question.
- Call for action.

Revising

Once you have a draft, you can look at it critically or have others review it. This is the time to make changes on many levels. Revising is the process of reworking what you have written to make it as good as it can be. You may change some details so that your ideas flow smoothly and are clearly supported. You may discover that some details don't work, and you'll need to discard them. Two strategies may help you start the revising process:

- Read your work aloud. This is an excellent way to catch any ideas or details that have been left out and to notice errors in logic.
- Ask someone else to read your work. Choose someone who can point out how to improve it.

How do you know what to look for and what to change? Here is a checklist of major writing issues. If the answer to any of these questions is no, then that is an area that needs revision.

1. Does the writing achieve my purpose?
2. Does the paper have unity—a single focus, with all details and information contributing to that focus?
3. Is the arrangement of information clear and logical?
4. Have I elaborated enough to give my audience adequate information?

Editing

When you edit, you refine your language to express your ideas in the most effective way possible.

- Replace dull language with vivid, precise words.
- Cut or change unnecessary repetition.
- Cut empty words and phrases, (those that do not add anything to the writing).
- Check passive voice; active voice is more effective.
- Replace wordy expressions with shorter, more precise ones.

Proofreading

When you have completed your final draft, proofread it to make it accurate for the reader. You may do this on your own or with the help of a partner. Refer to a dictionary, writing textbook, or style handbook as necessary.

- Correct errors in grammar and usage.
- Correct errors in punctuation and capitalization.
- Correct errors in spelling.

Publishing and Presenting

These are some of the many ways in which you can share your work:

- Share your writing in a small group by reading it aloud or by passing it around for others to read.
- Read your work aloud to the class.
- Display your work on a classroom bulletin board.
- Save your writing in a folder for later publication. At the end of the year, choose the best pieces from your folder and bind them together. Share the collection with your relatives and friends.
- Submit your writing to the school literary magazine, or start a literary magazine for your school or class.
- Submit your writing to your school or community newspaper.
- Enter your writing in literary contests for student writers.
- Submit your writing to a magazine that publishes work by young people.

THE MODES OF WRITING

Expression

Expression is any writing that conveys your personal thoughts, feelings, or experiences. Some expressive writing is private, written only for you to read. Some is written to be shared with an audience—friends, family, or other interested readers. Through expressive writing, you can capture on paper what is most meaningful to you. Expressive writing takes many forms. Here are a few of them:

Anecdote An anecdote is a brief, entertaining account of one specific, true event. Most anecdotes contain an observation about life or human nature, often in a humorous way.

Personal Journal A journal, or diary, is a record of a

person's experiences and feelings over a period of time. Most personal journals are kept private because they are very personal, although some journals have been published to be read by the public.

Personal Letter Writing a personal letter is a good way to reveal your thoughts, attitudes, opinions, and experiences about many different subjects.

Personal Memoir In a memoir, you write about significant events from your past, including your thoughts and experiences about those experiences. A memoir can be brief and focus on a single event or it can describe a larger part of your life.

Description

Description is writing that creates a vivid picture for readers, draws readers into a scene, and makes readers feel as if they are meeting a character or experiencing an event firsthand. A description may stand on its own or be part of a longer work, such as a short story.

When you write a description, bring it to life with sensory details that tell you how your subject looks, smells, sounds, tastes, or feels. You'll want to choose your details carefully so that you create a single main impression of your subject. Here are a few types of description:

Remembrance When you write a remembrance, you use vivid, descriptive details to convey your impressions of people or places from your past. When writing a remembrance of a person, include details that capture both the person's personality and physical appearance.

Observation In an observation, you describe an event or occurrence that you have witnessed firsthand, often over an extended period of time. An observation may focus on an aspect of daily life or on a scientific phenomenon, such as a storm or a change of season.

Travelogue A travelogue is descriptive writing that takes the reader to the place being described. It is a record of a writer's journey. Travelogues often include information about a locale's climate, geography, foods, and tourist attractions, as well as your experiences.

Narration

Whenever writers tell any type of story, they are using *narration.* While there are many kinds of narration, most narratives share certain elements—characters, a setting, a sequence of events (or plot, in fiction), and, often, a theme. You might be asked to write one of these types of narration:

Personal Narrative A personal narrative is a story based on the writer's real-life experiences. In a personal narrative, past events are brought to life through dialogue, action, and description. The first-person point of view is used to tell a personal narrative.

Autobiographical Incident An autobiographical incident tells a true story about a specific event in the writer's life. It contains characters, a plot, and a theme, but it reveals more about the writer than it does about the other characters.

Firsthand Biography In a firsthand biography, you tell about the entire life, or a period in the life, of a person whom you know or knew personally. In firsthand biography, the writer usually plays a part, but he or she is not the main character. The writer's firsthand knowledge of the subject gives the reader an unusual perspective on the subject.

Short Story A short story is a brief fictional narrative with a beginning, in which we meet the characters; a middle, in which problems arise between characters; and an end, in which the problems are resolved. A short story usually has a theme, or message, to convey to the reader. In a short story, dialogue reveals the thoughts and feelings of the characters. Details help the reader understand the world in which the story takes place.

Exposition: Giving Information

Exposition to give information is writing that informs or explains. In this type of writing, include factual information to clarify or explain your topic. Here are some examples of exposition that give information:

Classification Classification is writing that puts a subject into a category or a class. Classification is used when you explain several parts of a single subject. In classification, you organize your information by grouping facts and examples into categories and then showing the similarities and/or differences among the various categories. For example, to classify types of motorcycles, break the topic down into categories of dirt bikes, street bikes, and a combination of dirt and street bikes.

Summary To write a summary of a true or fictional event, include the main characters in the event, the time period, and present the most important details as factually as possible. Avoid giving personal opinions and observations about the events.

How-to Composition A how-to composition, or a set of instructions, tells the reader how to do or to make something. In writing how-to instructions, it is important to anticipate and answer questions the reader may have about why a particular procedure or direction is included.

Exposition: Making Connections

Exposition can *make connections* for readers by comparing and contrasting two subjects, by examining a problem and its solution, or by connecting information to an opinion about something. Here are some types of exposition that makes connections:

Comparison-and-Contrast Essay A comparison-and-contrast essay explores the similarities and differences between two or more people, places, events, or ideas. When writing this type of essay, organize your point of comparison subject by subject or point by point.

Problem-and-Solution Essay A problem-and-solution essay focuses on a problem and offers one or more possible solutions to it. The solutions presented should be supported by facts and examples. When writing a problem-and-solution essay, first identify the problem. Then, present all possible solutions by describing the steps necessary to achieve the goal.

Persuasion

Persuasion is writing or speaking that attempts to convince people to agree with you about something or to urge them to take a certain kind of action. When used effectively, persuasive writing has the power to change people's lives. As a reader and a writer, you will find yourself engaged in many forms of persuasion. Here are a few:

Letter to the Editor A letter to the editor is a reader's response to an article or an editorial in a newspaper or magazine. When writing a letter to an editor, present clear, organized reasons to support your opinion.

Advertisement An advertisement tries to persuade people to buy something, accept an idea, vote for a candidate, or support a cause. When you write an advertisement, present your information in an appealing way to make your product or service seem desirable.

Persuasive Essay A persuasive essay is a short piece of writing that aims to convince an audience to take action or to accept a position on an issue. In writing a persuasive essay, you build an argument and support your opinions with a variety of evidence: facts, statistics, examples, and statements from experts. You also anticipate and develop counter-arguments to opposing opinions.

Persuasive Speech A persuasive speech is a persuasive essay that's presented orally instead of in writing. As a persuasive speaker, address the audience directly and with enthusiasm, use vivid language, repeat key points, and include facts and statistics to support your argument.

Reports

A *report* is any writing based on outside research. People write reports to present information and ideas, to share findings and research, and to explain subjects they have studied. To write reports, you will have to research, organize, and present information. The following are some types of reports:

Biographical Report A biographical report gives information about a person's life and achievements. When you write a biographical report, include the dates and details of the main events in the person's life, presenting the information in chronological order beginning with childhood.

I-Search Report An I-search report is a personal, in-depth exploration of a topic that especially interests you. In the report, you tell how you became interested in the topic, how you explored it, and what you learned.

Library Research Report A library research report can be about any topic for which information can be researched in the library. When you write a library research report, you put together information from books and other sources. You must credit source materials and authors in footnotes and bibliographies.

Creative Writing

Creative writing blends imagination, experience, ideas, and emotions. It allows you to present your own unique view of the world. Poems, plays, short stories, and dramas are examples of creative writing. Following are some types of creative writing:

Poem Writing a poem is a way to express thoughts and feelings about a subject. In writing poems, use figurative language and sensory images to create a strong impact. Also, consider using rhyme, rhythm, and repetition within your poem to create a musical quality.

Monologue A monologue is a dramatic speech written to be spoken by a single character to another character or directly to an audience. In writing a monologue, choose a subject and write the details from the point of view of your subject or from your own point of view.

Dialogue A dialogue is a conversation between characters in a drama. Use realistic language to develop characters, explain the setting, and advance the plot.

Short Video or Play Script A script for a video or stage play includes dialogue and stage directions. A video script also includes technical directions in capital letters for the camera person.

Response to Literature

In a *response to literature,* you express your thoughts and feelings about the work. Often, in so doing, you gain a better understanding of the work. Your response to literature can take many forms—oral or written, formal or informal. Following are a few examples:

Reader's Response Journal Entry Your reader's response journal is a record of your thoughts and feelings about works you have read. Use it to remind yourself of writers and works that you particularly liked or disliked or to provide a source of writing ideas.

Response to a Literary Work When you respond to a literary work, you analyze one or more of the following aspects: its theme, characters, setting, form, timeliness, and originality. Use details from the work in your response to support the point you make.

Critical Review When you write a review of a literary work, you offer an opinion of the work and give specific details and quotes from the book to support that opinion.

GRAMMAR AND MECHANICS HANDBOOK

Nouns A **noun** is the name of a person, place, or thing. A **common noun** names any one of a class of people, places, or things. A **proper noun** names a specific person, place, or thing.

Common Nouns	Proper Nouns
writer	Edgar Allan Poe
city	Fort Worth

Pronouns A **pronoun** is a word that stands for a noun or for a word that takes the place of a noun.

A **personal pronoun** refers to (1) the person speaking, (2) the person spoken to, or (3) the person, place, or thing spoken about.

	Singular	Plural
First Person	I, me, my, mine	we, us, our, ours
Second Person	you, your, yours	you, your, yours
Third Person	he, him, his, she, her, hers, it, its	they, them, their, theirs

He took them downstairs into the living room.
— "Christmas Day in the Morning," Buck, p. 68

A **demonstrative pronoun** directs attention to a specific person, place, or thing.

this lamp   *these* rugs   *that* chair   *those* tables

An **interrogative pronoun** is used to begin a question.

What did all of this mean to Andy?
— "Saving the Wetlands," Lewis, p. 280
Who is the author of "Space Oddity"?

An **indefinite pronoun** refers to a person, place, or thing, often without specifying which one.

Many of the students participated.
Everyone arrived early.

Verbs A **verb** is a word that expresses time while showing an action, a condition, or the fact that something exists.

An **action verb** indicates the action of someone or something.

I *loved* the old man.
— "The Tell-Tale Heart," Poe, p. 542

A **linking verb** connects the subject of a sentence with a noun or a pronoun that renames or describes the subject.

There *were* others who proffered assistance.
— "An Episode of War," Crane, p. 552

A **helping verb** can be added to another verb to make a single verb phrase.

They *had been* living in Dalesford for a year nearly, . . .
— "The Finish of Patsy Barnes," Dunbar, p. 581

Adjectives An **adjective** describes a noun or a pronoun or gives a noun or a pronoun a more specific meaning. Adjectives answer these questions:

What kind?	*big* cyclone, *pink* petunia
Which one?	*this* land, *those* people
How many?	*two* cats, *many* flies
How much?	*some* snow, *little* effort

The articles *the, a,* and *an* are adjectives. *An* is used before a word beginning with a vowel sound.

A noun may sometimes be used as an adjective.

family home   *science* fiction

Adverbs An **adverb** modifies a verb, an adjective, or another adverb. Adverbs answer the questions *where, when, in what way,* or *to what extent.*

He ran *outside.* (modifies verb *ran*)
She *never* wrote us. (modifies verb *wrote*)
Close the window *quickly.* (modifies verb *close*)
We were *very* sad. (modifies adjective *sad*)
They left *too* suddenly. (modifies adverb *suddenly*)

Prepositions A **preposition** relates a noun or a pronoun following it to another word in the sentence.

across the road	*near* the corner
except me	*during* the show
at school	*with* them

Conjunctions A **conjunction** connects other words or groups of words.

A **coordinating conjunction** connects similar kinds or groups of words.

lions *and* tigers   small *but* strong

Correlative conjunctions are used in pairs to connect similar words or groups of words.

both Jonah *and* Elias   *neither* they *nor* I

Interjections An **interjection** is a word that expresses feeling or emotion and functions independently of a sentence.

> *"Oh, no!"* I whispered.
> — "Medicine Bag," Sneve, p. 603

Sentences A **sentence** is a group of words with two main parts: a complete subject and a complete predicate. Together, these parts express a complete thought.

> The rest of the story is a little embarrassing.
> — "Animal Craftsmen," p. 627

A **fragment** is a group of words that does not contain a subject or a verb and does not express a complete thought.

> With the others.
> Left suddenly.

Subject-Verb Agreement To make a **subject** and a **verb agree,** make sure that both are singular or both are plural. Two or more singular subjects joined by *or* or *nor* must have a singular verb. When singular and plural subjects are joined by *or* or *nor,* the verb must agree with the closest subject.

> *He is* at the door.
> *They drive* home every day.
> *Jeff* or *Sam is* absent.
> Both *pets are* hungry.
> Either the *chairs* or the *table is* on sale.
> Neither the *tree* nor the *shrubs were* in bloom.

Phrases A **phrase** is a group of words, without a subject and a verb, that functions in a sentence as one part of speech.

A **prepositional phrase** is a group of words that includes a preposition and a noun or a pronoun that is the object of the preposition.

> near the town   with them
> inside our house   beneath the floor

An **adjective phrase** is a prepositional phrase that modifies a noun or a pronoun by telling *what kind* or *which one.*

> The left arm *of your jacket* is spattered with mud. . . .
> — *The Adventure of the Speckled Band,*
> Doyle, p. 475

An **adverb phrase** is a prepositional phrase that modifies a verb, an adjective, or an adverb by pointing out *where, when, in what way,* or *to what extent.*

The lady gave a violent start and stared in *bewilderment* at my companion.

> — "The Adventure of the Speckled Band,"
> Doyle, p. 475

An **appositive phrase** is a noun or a pronoun with modifiers that is placed next to a noun or a pronoun to add information and details.

> When Dr. Roylott was in India he married my mother, *Mrs. Stoner, the young widow of Major-General Stoner,* of the Bengal Artillery.
> — "The Adventure of the Speckled Band,"
> Doyle, p. 476

A **participial phrase** is a participle with its modifiers and complements. The entire phrase acts as an adjective.

> *Turning his eyes from the hostile wood,* he looked at the sword as he held it there. . . .
> — "An Episode of War," Crane, p. 551

An **infinitive phrase** is an infinitive with modifiers, complements, or a subject, all acting together as a single part of speech.

> I was about *to enter the store* when I realized I had left my briefcase behind.
> — "The Day I Got Lost," Singer, p. 559

Clauses A **clause** is a group of words with a subject and verb.

An **independent clause** can stand by itself as a complete sentence.

A **subordinate clause** has a subject and a verb, but it cannot stand by itself as a complete sentence; it can only be part of a sentence.

An **adjective clause** is a subordinate clause that modifies a noun or a pronoun by telling *what kind* or *which one.*

> He wore the look of one *who knows he is the victim of a terrible disease and understands his helplessness.*
> — "An Episode of War," Crane, p. 552

An **adverb clause** modifies a verb, an adjective, or an adverb by telling *where, when, in what way, to what extent, under what condition,* or *why.*

> As I stood in the street wondering what to do, it began to rain.
> — "The Day I Got Lost," Singer, p. 560

SUMMARY OF CAPITALIZATION AND PUNCTUATION

Capitalization

Capitalize the first word of a sentence.

The light had an eerie green-yellow glow.

> — *A Glow in the Dark*, Paulsen, p. 506

Capitalize all proper nouns and adjectives.

Amy Ling	Amazon River	Thanksgiving Day
Florida	October	Italian

Capitalize a person's title when it is followed by the person's name or when it is used in direct address.

Congressman Brooks Hays   Professor Shlemiel
King Edward

Capitalize titles showing family relationships when they refer to a specific person unless they are preceded by a possessive noun or a pronoun.

Uncle Charlie   my aunt   Susan's father

Capitalize the first word and all other key words in the titles of books, periodicals, poems, stories, plays, paintings, and other works of art.

The Diary of Anne Frank

"Drum Song"

Capitalize the first word and all nouns in letter salutations and the first word in letter closings.

Dear Fred,   Yours truly,

Punctuation

End Marks   Use a **period** to end a declarative sentence, an imperative sentence, and most abbreviations.

There are half a dozen meteor showers each year.

> — "Shooting Stars," Borland, p. 82

Take this book of poems and memorize one for me.

> — from *I Know Why the Caged Bird Sings*, Maya Angelou, p. 28

Use a **question mark** to end a direct question or an incomplete question in which the rest of the question is understood.

"Was I bothering *you* when I turned that corner?" asked the woman.

> — "Thank You, M'am," Hughes, p. 187

"You're sure . . . ?"

> — *The Diary of Anne Frank,* Goodrich and Hackett, p. 719

Use an **exclamation mark** after a statement showing strong emotion, an urgent imperative sentence, or an interjection expressing strong emotion.

When he heard these words, something in him woke: his father loved him!

> — "Christmas Day in the Morning," Buck, p. 67

"Hold up your foot!"

> — "Cub Pilot on the Mississippi," Twain, p. 111

Commas   Use a **comma** before the coordinating conjunction to separate two independent clauses in a compound sentence.

The door was standing half open, and at last one old jay happened to go and light on it and look in.

> — "What Stumped the Blue Jays," Twain, p. 456

Use commas to separate three or more words, phrases, or clauses in a series.

He twisted himself over on his stomach, thrust both hands out to one side, and pressed them heavily against the flying surface.

> — "Up the Slide," London, p. 157

Use commas to separate adjectives of equal rank. Do not use commas to separate adjectives that must stay in a specific order.

The clerks were pleased to be greeted by the good-looking, agreeable young man . . .

> — "A Retrieved Reformation," Henry, p. 255

Use a comma after an introductory word, phrase, or clause.

"Mom, you've got to take me to the library," Andy insisted.

> — "Saving the Wetlands," Lewis, p. 276

Even on this trip, she suddenly fell asleep in the woods.

> — "Harriet Tubman: Guide to Freedom" Petry, p. 137

Use commas to set off parenthetical and nonessential expressions.

Animals talk to teach other, of course.

> — "What Stumped the Blue Jays," Twain, p. 453

Use commas with places and dates made up of two or more parts.

Ray Bradbury was born in Waukegan, Illinois.

On May 17, 1954, after deliberating for nearly a year and a half, the Supreme Court made its ruling.

> — "Brown *vs.* Board of Education," Myers, p. 245

Use commas after items in addresses, after the salutation in a personal letter, after the closing in all letters, and in numbers of more than three digits.

Linden Lane, Durham, N.C.   My dear Cal,
Sincerely yours,   1,372,597

Use a comma to set off a direct quotation.

"All right, Charlie," he said, "you've seen these cards before, remember?"

> — "Flowers for Algernon," Keyes, p. 213

Semicolons Use a **semicolon** to join independent clauses that are not already joined by a conjunction.

But nature guards her greatest secrets well; to such places men must come to find them.

> — "The Secret," Clarke, p. 124

Use a semicolon to join independent clauses or items in a series that already contain commas.

I could see the door whiten at its touch; I could see the blue wall turn pale where it raced over it, and see the maple headboard of Amy's bed glow.

> — from "An American Childhood," Dillard, p. 444

Colons Use a **colon** before a list of items following an independent clause.

The following words are examples of onomatopoeia: *buzz, hiss, jingle,* and *cluck.*

Use a colon in numbers giving the time, in salutations in business letters, and in labels used to signal important ideas.

4:30 A.M.   Dear Dr. Strauss:
Danger: Landslide Area Ahead

Quotation Marks A **direct quotation** represents a person's exact speech or thoughts and is enclosed in quotation marks.

"Good morning, madam," said Holmes cheerily.

> — "The Adventure of the Speckled Band," Doyle, p. 475

An **indirect quotation** reports only the general meaning of what a person said or thought and does not require quotation marks.

He tells us that your land extends across the river and that you own almost twice as much as you thought.

> — "Gentleman of Río en Medio," Sedillo, p. 273

Always place a comma or a period inside the final quotation mark of a direct quotation.

He pressed my hand and said, "Bless you! Tell me their names," and he pointed to the stars on the flag.

> — "The Man Without a Country," Hale, p. 388

Place a question mark or an exclamation mark inside the final quotation mark if the end mark is part of the quotation; if it is not part of the quotation, place it outside the final quotation mark.

"Then we shall both come. What are you going to do yourself?"

> — "The Adventure of the Speckled Band," Doyle p. 481

Does the poem by Robert Frost start with the line, "Two roads diverged in a yellow wood"?

Underline or italicize the titles of long written works, movies, television and radio shows, lengthy works of music, paintings, and sculptures.

The Diary of Anne Frank   *Star Trek*   The Mona Lisa

Use quotation marks around the titles of short written works, episodes in a series, songs, and titles of works mentioned as parts of collections.

"The Road Not Taken"   "Something From the Sixties"
"Space Oddity"   "January"

Hyphens Use a **hyphen** with certain numbers, after certain prefixes, with two or more words used as one word, and with a compound modifier that comes before a noun.

fifty-four   self-employed
daughter-in-law   happy-go-lucky friend

Apostrophes Add an **apostrophe** and -s to show the possessive case of most singular nouns.

Simon's plays   the author's story
Hughes's poems

Add an apostrophe to show the possessive case of plural nouns ending in -s and -es.

the bats' squeaks   the Robertses' home

Add an apostrophe and -s to show the possessive case of plural nouns that do not end in -s or -es.

the women's hats   the mice's whiskers

Use an apostrophe in a contraction to indicate the position of the missing letter or letters.

"I would've known if anyone tried to take the boots off my feet."

— "Medicine Bag," Sneve, p. 605

GLOSSARY OF COMMON USAGE

accept, except
Accept is a verb that means "to receive" or "to agree to." *Except* is a preposition that means "other than" or "leaving out." Do not confuse these two words.

The dinner party *accepted* the challenge to sit still for five minutes.

Every person *except* Philip Nolan has a country.

affect, effect
Affect is normally a verb meaning "to influence" or "to bring about a change in." *Effect* is usually a noun meaning "result."

Rob's special Christmas gift deeply *affected* his father.

Shooting his father may have a lasting *effect* on Carter Druse.

among, between
Among is usually used with three or more items. *Between* is generally used with only two items.

"Charles" was *among* the stories I liked best.

There is tension *between* Squeaky and Gretchen in "Raymond's Run."

amount, number
Amount refers to a mass or a unit, whereas *number* refers to individual items that can be counted. Therefore, *amount* generally appears with singular nouns, and *number* appears with plural nouns.

To remain calm while in danger, Clay Dilham needed a huge *amount* of determination.

In "The White Umbrella," the narrator makes a *number* of excuses about her mother's activities.

bad, badly
Use the predicate adjective *bad* after linking verbs such

as *feel, look,* and *seem.* Use *badly* whenever an adverb is required.

Knowing how much his father loves him, Rob feels *bad* about getting him only a necktie for Christmas.

When the blue jay does not hear the acorn fall to the bottom of the hole, he is *badly* confused.

because of, due to
Use *due to* if it can logically replace the phrase *caused by.* In introductory phrases, however, *because of* is better usage than *due to.*

O. Henry's popularity was largely *due to* the intriguing endings of his stories.

Because of Philip Nolan's brashness, the judge gave him a unique sentence.

beside, besides
Do not confuse these two prepositions, which have different meanings. *Beside* means "at the side of" or "close to." *Besides* means "in addition to."

Martin sits *beside* his Grandfather's bed when it is time to receive the medicine bag.

No one *besides* me wrote a paper on Amy Ling's poem "Grandma."

can, may
The verb *can* generally refers to the ability to do something. The verb *may* generally refers to permission to do something.

The bachelor *may* tell a story if he believes he *can* captivate the children.

compare, contrast
The verb *compare* can involve both similarities and differences. The verb *contrast* always involves differences. Use *to* or *with* after *compare.* Use *with* after *contrast.*

Stan *compared* King Richard's soliloquy *with* Benedick's.

Joaquin Miller's tribute to Christopher Columbus *contrasts with* many people's opinions.

different from, different than
Different from is generally preferred over *different than.*

Similes are *different from* metaphors because similes use the words *like* or *as* to make comparisons.

farther, further
Use *farther* when you refer to distance. Use *further* when you mean "to a greater degree or extent" or "additional."

As he races *farther* down the track, Patsy knows his horse still has plenty of energy.

The singing of his dogs *further* unsettles the narrator in "A Glow in the Dark."

fewer, less

Use *fewer* for things that can be counted. Use *less* for amounts or quantities that cannot be counted.

Which animals have *fewer* legs: spiders or ladybugs?

The Sioux grandfather is *less* willing to let some of the customs die than are many of the younger Sioux.

good, well

Use the predicate adjective *good* after linking verbs such as *feel, look, smell, taste,* and *seem.* Use *well* whenever you need an adverb.

The narrator in "A Ribbon for Baldy" feels *good* about his science project idea.

Jack London describes the Yukon *well.*

hopefully

You should not loosely attach this adverb to a sentence, as in "*Hopefully,* the rain will stop by noon." Rewrite the sentence so *hopefully* modifies a specific verb. Other possible ways of revising such sentences include using the adjective *hopeful* or a phrase like "everyone *hopes* that."

Robert MacNeil writes *hopefully* that the American public will be skeptical about what they see and hear on television.

Laurie's parents were *hopeful* that Charles's mother would come to the PTA meeting.

its, it's

Do not confuse the possessive pronoun *its* with the contraction *it's,* standing for "it is" or "it has."

If a rattler thinks *it's* not seen, it will lie quietly without revealing *its* location.

lay, lie

Do not confuse these verbs. *Lay* is a transitive verb meaning "to set or put something down." Its principal parts are *lay, laying, laid, laid. Lie* is an intransitive verb meaning "to recline." Its principal parts are *lie, lying, lay, lain.*

The soldiers *lay* down their guns.

Debbie likes to *lie* down in front of the fireplace.

leave, let

Be careful not to confuse these verbs. *Leave* means

"to go away" or "to allow to remain." *Let* means "to permit."

Carter Druse *left* his parents to fight for the Union army in the war.

Clay Dilham did not *let* challenging circumstances defeat him.

like

Like is a preposition that usually means "similar to" or "in the same way as." *Like* should always be followed by an object. Do not use *like* before a subject and a verb. Use *as* or *that* instead.

A story *like* "The Tell-Tale Heart" by Edgar Allan Poe uses suspense to hold the reader's interest.

Jimmy Valentine's final meeting with Ben Price did not end *as* he expected.

loose, lose

Loose can be either an adjective (meaning "unattached") or a verb (meaning "to untie"). *Lose* is always a verb (meaning "to fail to keep, have, or win").

There is often only a *loose* connection between the speaker of a poem and the poem's author; sometimes there is no link whatsoever between the two.

Professor Shlemiel continually *loses* anything he has in his hands.

many, much

Use *many* to refer to a specific quantity. Use *much* for an indefinite amount or for an abstract concept.

Mark Twain wrote *many* humorous stories.

Maya Angelou has won *much* praise for her writing.

of, have

Do not use *of* in place of *have* after auxiliary verbs like *would, could, should, may, might,* or *must.*

Jimmy Valentine's heroic decision to open the safe and reveal himself *must have* distressed him greatly.

raise, rise

Raise is a transitive verb that usually takes a direct object. *Rise* is intransitive and never takes a direct object.

The purpose of Colin Powell's speech is to *raise* the consciousness of all Americans to help America's children at risk.

Squeaky listens for the starting gun, then *rises* from the ground and becomes weightless as she flies past the other runners.

set, sit

Do not confuse these verbs. *Set* is a transitive verb meaning "to put (something) in a certain place." Its principal parts are *set, setting, set, set. Sit* is an intransitive verb meaning "to be seated." Its principal parts are *sit, sitting, sat, sat.*

> The speaker *sets* the planks in the furnace.
>
> Every now and then, Debbie would *sit* by the fire for a few minutes.

than, then

The conjunction *than* is used to connect the two parts of a comparison. Do not confuse *than* with the adverb *then,* which usually refers to time.

> Gina liked "The Ninny" more *than* "The Governess."
>
> Mark Twain worked on a riverboat and *then* moved to California to search for gold.

that, which, who

Use the relative pronoun *that* to refer to things or people. Use *which* only for things and *who* only for people.

> The season *that* Langston Hughes describes is winter.
>
> Lyric poems, *which* express personal emotions, are often brief.
>
> One writer *who* has vividly captured the experiences of African Americans is Alice Walker.

their, there, they're

Do not confuse the spelling of these three words. *Their* is a possessive adjective and always modifies a noun. *There* is usually used either at the beginning of a sentence or as an adverb. *They're* is a contraction for "they are."

> Todd and his parents are very happy about *their* new pet.
>
> For most people, *there* are few creatures more terrifying than sharks.
>
> Tim and Nina are in the class production of *The Diary of Anne Frank,* and *they're* rehearsing right now in the auditorium.

to, too, two

Do not confuse the spelling of these words. *To* is a preposition that begins a prepositional phrase or an infinitive. *Too,* with two *o*'s, is an adverb and modifies adjectives and other adverbs. *Two* is a number.

> Mrs. Frank wants Anne *to* show courtesy *to* their guests.
>
> Josh thought that his paper on the Civil War was *too* short, so he added another paragraph.
>
> *Two* poems that Helen especially liked were Walt Whitman's "O Captain! My Captain!" and John Greenleaf Whittier's "Barbara Frietchie."

unique

Because *unique* means "one of a kind," you should not use it carelessly to mean "interesting" or "unusual." Avoid such illogical expressions as *most unique, very unique,* and *extremely unique.*

> Mark Twain's experiences in California gave him a *unique* insight into the gold-mining camps.

when, where, why

Do not use *when, where,* or *why* directly after a linking verb such as *is.* Reword the sentence.

> **Faulty:** Suspense is *when* an author increases the reader's tension.
>
> **Revised:** An author uses suspense to increase the reader's tension.
>
> **Faulty:** Holland is *where* the drama *The Diary of Anne Frank* takes place.
>
> **Revised:** *The Diary of Anne Frank* takes place in Holland.

who, whom

In formal writing, remember to use *who* only as a subject in clauses and sentences and *whom* only as an object.

> Amy Ling, *who* is Chinese American, writes about a meeting with her grandmother.
>
> Langston Hughes, *whom* we discussed yesterday, was a leader in an important cultural movement during the 1920's called the Harlem Renaissance.

Speaking, Listening, and Viewing Handbook

Communication is the way in which people convey their ideas and interact with one another. The literature in this book is written, which is one form of communication, but much of your personal communication is probably oral or visual. Oral communication involves both speaking and listening. Visual communication involves both conveying messages through physical expression or pictorial representations and interpreting images. Developing strong communication skills can benefit your school life and your life outside of school.

Many of the assignments accompanying the literature in this textbook involve speaking, listening, viewing, and representing. This handbook identifies some of the terminology related to the oral and visual communication you experience every day and the assignments you may do in conjunction with the literature in this book.

Communication

You use many different kinds of communication every day. When you communicate with your friends, your teachers, or your parents, or when you interact with a cashier in a store, you are communicating orally. In addition to ordinary conversation, oral communication includes class discussions, speeches, interviews, presentations, and debates. When you communicate face to face, you usually use more than your voice to get your message across. If you communicate by telephone, however, you must rely solely on your verbal skills. At times, you may use more visual communication than any other kind. For example, when you paint a picture, participate in a dance recital, or prepare a multimedia presentation, you use strategies of visual communication.

The following terms will give you a better understanding of the many elements that are a part of oral and visual communication:

BODY LANGUAGE refers to the use of facial expressions, eye contact, gestures, posture, and movement to communicate a feeling or an idea.

CONNOTATION is the set of associations a word calls to mind. The connotations of the words you choose influence the message you send. For example, most people respond more favorably to being described as "slim" rather than as "skinny." The connotation of *slim* is more appealing than that of *skinny*.

EYE CONTACT is direct visual contact with another person's eyes.

FEEDBACK is the set of verbal and nonverbal reactions that indicate to a speaker that a message has been received and understood.

GESTURES are the movements made with arms, hands, face, and fingers to communicate.

LISTENING is understanding and interpreting sound in a meaningful way. You listen differently for different purposes.

Listening for key information: For example, when a teacher gives an assignment, or when someone gives you directions to a place, you listen for key information.
Listening for main points: In a classroom exchange of ideas or information, or while watching a television documentary, you listen for main points.
Listening critically: When you evaluate a performance, a song, or a persuasive or political speech, you listen critically, questioning and judging the speaker's message.

MEDIUM is the material or technique used to present a visual image. Common media include paint, clay, and film.

NONVERBAL COMMUNICATION is communication without the use of words. People communicate nonverbally through gestures, facial expressions, posture, and body movements. Sign language is an entire language based on nonverbal communication.

VIEWING is observing, understanding, analyzing, and evaluating information presented through visual means. You might use the following questions to help you interpret what you view:
- What subject is presented?
- What is communicated about the subject?
- Which parts are factual? Which are opinion?
- What mood, attitude, or opinion is conveyed?
- What is your emotional response?

VOCAL DELIVERY is the way in which you present a message. Your vocal delivery involves all of the following elements:

Volume: the loudness or quietness of your voice
Pitch: the high or low quality of your voice
Rate: the speed at which you speak; also called pace
Stress: the amount of emphasis placed on different syllables in a word or on different words in a sentence

All of these elements individually, and the way in which they are combined, contribute to the meaning of a spoken message.

Speaking, Listening, and Viewing Situations

Here are some of the many types of situations in which you apply speaking, listening, and viewing skills:

AUDIENCE Your audience in any situation refers to the person or people to whom you direct your message. An audience can be a group of people sitting in a classroom or auditorium observing a performance or just one person to whom you address a question or a comment. When preparing for any speaking situation, it's useful to analyze your audience, learning what you can about their backgrounds, interests, and attitudes so that you can tailor your message to them.

CHARTS AND GRAPHS are visual representations of statistical information. For example, a pie chart might indicate how the average dollar is spent by government, and a bar graph might compare populations in cities over time.

DEBATE A debate is a formal public-speaking situation in which participants prepare and present arguments on opposing sides of a question, stated as a **proposition.**

The two sides in a debate are the *affirmative* (pro) and the *negative* (con). The affirmative side argues in favor of the proposition, while the negative side argues against it. The affirmative side begins the debate, since it is seeking a change in belief or policy. The opposing sides take turns presenting their arguments, and each side has an opportunity for *rebuttal,* in which they may challenge or question the other side's argument.

DOCUMENTARIES are nonfiction films that analyze news events or other focused subjects. You can watch a documentary for the information on its subject.

GROUP DISCUSSION results when three or more people meet to solve a common problem, arrive at a decision, or answer a question of mutual interest. Group discussion is one of the most widely used forms of interpersonal communication in modern society.

INTERVIEW An interview is a form of interaction in which one person, the interviewer, asks questions of another person, the interviewee. Interviews may take place for many purposes: to obtain information, to discover a person's suitability for a job or a college, or to inform the public of a notable person's opinions.

MAPS are visual representations of the Earth's surface. Maps may show political boundaries or physical features. They can also provide information on a variety of other topics. A map's title and its key identify the content of the map.

ORAL INTERPRETATION is the reading or speaking of a work of literature aloud for an audience. Oral interpretation involves giving expression to the ideas, meaning, or even the structure of a work of literature. The speaker interprets the work through his or her vocal delivery. **Storytelling,** in which a speaker reads or tells a story expressively, is a form of oral interpretation.

PANEL DISCUSSION is a group discussion on a topic of interest common to all members of a panel and to a listening audience. A panel is usually composed of four to six experts on a particular topic who are brought together to share information and opinions.

PANTOMIME is a form of nonverbal communication in which an idea or a story is communicated completely through the use of gesture, body language, and facial expressions, without any words at all.

POLITICAL CARTOONS are drawings that comment on important political or social issues. Often, these cartoons use humor to convey a message about their subject. Viewers use their own knowledge of events to evaluate the cartoonist's opinion.

READERS THEATRE is a dramatic reading of a work of literature in which participants take parts from a story or a play and read them aloud in expressive voices. Unlike a play, however, sets and costumes are not part of the performance, and the participants remain seated as they deliver their lines.

ROLE PLAY To role-play is to take the role of a person or character and, as that character, act out a given situation, speaking, acting, and responding in the manner of the character.

SPEECH A speech is a talk or an address given to an audience. A speech may be **impromptu**—delivered on the spur of the moment with no preparation—or formally prepared and delivered for a specific purpose or occasion.

- *Purposes:* The most common purposes of speeches are to persuade (for example, political speeches), to entertain, to explain, and to inform.
- *Occasions:* Different occasions call for different types of speeches. Speeches given on these occasions could be persuasive, entertaining, or informative, as appropriate. The following are common occasions for speeches:

Introduction: Introducing a speaker at a meeting
Presentation: Giving an award or acknowledging the contributions of someone
Acceptance: Accepting an award or a tribute
Keynote: Giving an inspirational address at a large meeting or convention
Commencement: Honoring the graduates of a school

Test Preparation Handbook

Contents
Test Preparation Workshops

Test Preparation Workshop 1

Reading Comprehension

Strategies for Success

The reading sections of standardized tests ask you to read a passage and answer questions about word meanings. Some questions require you to determine the meanings of words by using context clues, prefixes, and suffixes. Use the following strategies to help you answer this type of test question:

Use Context Clues The words or phrases near an unfamiliar word are context clues that can help you figure out the word's meaning. A context clue may be a synonym (word with the same meaning) or an antonym (word with the opposite meaning) for the unfamiliar word. Sometimes the passage contains a definition or an explanation of the unfamiliar word or a description with details or examples that can help you figure out the word's meaning. Even if the unfamiliar word is part of the technical vocabulary of people who share a particular activity or interest, context clues can help you determine its meaning. Look at this example:

> The town's first Amateur Scientists Night was a huge success. The most popular participant was a local **ornithologist,** who showed slides of birds he had studied all over the world.

The word **ornithologist** in this passage means—
- **A** worldwide traveler
- **B** person who studies birds
- **C** photographer
- **D** endangered species

The context tells you that the correct answer has to be an amateur scientist, so **A** and **C** are incorrect. **D** does not make sense because humans are not an endangered species. **B** is correct.

Use Prefixes and Suffixes Knowing the meanings of prefixes and suffixes—such as *circum-* (around), *pre-* (before), *re-* (again), *un-* (not), *-ful* (full of), *-ness* (condition of, state of), *-logy* (study of), and *-less* (without)—can help you determine the meanings of unfamiliar words. Look at this example:

> In a few hours we were able to **circumnavigate** the small island.

In this passage, **circumnavigate** means—
- **A** cross over
- **C** sail around
- **B** map
- **D** explore thoroughly

The prefix *circum-* means around. *Navigate* comes from the Latin word meaning "to sail." So the correct answer is **C**.

Apply the Strategies

Answer these test questions based on the passage.

> On her way home from work, Janice saw the sign in the storefront: Cooking Classes Start Tonight at 8 P.M. She imagined herself surprising her family with one **culinary** treat after another. Promptly at eight, she returned to the store, only to discover that **preregistration** was required.

1 In this passage, the word **culinary** means—
- **A** related to school
- **C** related to cooking
- **B** related to money
- **D** related to dessert

2 The word **preregistration** in this passage means—
- **A** wearing specialized clothing
- **B** bringing supplies
- **C** paying cash
- **D** signing up ahead of time

Test Preparation Workshop 2

Reading Comprehension — Following Written Directions

Strategies for Success

The reading sections of standardized tests require you to read a passage and answer multiple-choice questions about directions. Use the following strategies to help you answer test questions about directions:

Notice the Details In written directions, every detail is important. Read the question carefully and notice what detail you are being asked to recall. Then, skim the passage quickly to locate the specific detail. Look at the following example:

Follow these directions to make a melted cheese sandwich using only the sun for heat:

Find an empty shoebox, discard the cover, and cut off one of the long sides. On each short side, draw a diagonal line from the corner where the short and long sides are connected to the opposite corner. Next, cut along the two diagonal lines you have drawn until you have removed a triangle from each short side. Tape a piece of black construction paper to the bottom of the shoebox. Tape aluminum foil to the three sides. Tape plastic wrap tightly over the opening, leaving one corner loose. Place a thin slice of cheese on a piece of bread, and put the bread in the box. Finally, put the box outside in the sun. In a while, you will have a melted cheese sandwich.

With what do you cover the bottom of the shoebox?

A shiny black paper   **C** plastic wrap
B black construction paper   **D** aluminum foil

A is not mentioned in the passage. **C** covers the opening. **D** covers the three sides. **B** is correct.

Notice the Sequence of Steps Test questions about directions require you to understand the order in which steps should be taken. Words

such as *first, next, then, after, before, finally,* and *last* give you clues to the correct sequence of steps. Look at the following question based on the passage:

What should you do immediately before cutting a triangle from each short side?

A Line the bottom with black construction paper
B Cut off one long side
C Tape aluminum foil to three sides
D Draw a diagonal line on each short side

A and **C** are done after the triangles are cut off. **B** is done before the triangles are cut off but not immediately before. **D** is correct.

Apply the Strategies

Answer the questions based on this passage.

Everyone should know what to do in case of a burn. Here are the basic steps. First, put cool water on the burn. If you cannot apply running water to the burn, soak clean cloths in cool water and apply them. Keep adding cool water to the cloths. After you have cooled the burn for several minutes, cover it loosely with a clean dry cloth. This helps prevent infection. Get the burn victim medical attention as soon as possible. For minor burns that do not require medical attention, wash the burned area with soap and water, pat it dry gently, and apply antibiotic ointment.

1 What should be applied first to a burn?
   A clean dry cloths   **C** cool water
   B ice   **D** lukewarm water

2 For minor burns, what should you do after washing the burn?
   A Apply antibiotic ointment
   B Apply a loose bandage
   C Call a doctor
   D Check for infection

Test Preparation Workshop 3

Reading Comprehension

Identify Main Idea; Identify Best Summary

Strategies for Success

The reading sections of both national and Texas standardized tests require you to read a passage and answer multiple-choice questions about main ideas and summaries. Use the following strategies to help you answer such questions:

Identify the Main Idea Sometimes the main idea of a passage is stated in a topic sentence, which may appear anywhere in the passage. Sometimes the main idea is not stated directly but is implied, or suggested, by the details in the passage. Look at the following passage and find the answer choice that summarizes the author's message:

> The platypus lives in the lakes and streams of eastern Australia. It looks like a duck-billed seal and acts like a lizard. Being a mammal, the platypus is warm-blooded and has fur. However, it also has some characteristics of a reptile. For example, instead of bearing live young, it lays eggs. Like a lizard, its legs are attached to the side of its body rather than underneath it.

What is the main idea of this passage?

A The platypus lives in Australia.

B Although it is a mammal, the platypus shares some characteristics with reptiles.

C The platypus looks like a duck-billed seal.

D The platypus is a graceful swimmer.

A and **C** are details. **D** is not mentioned in the passage. **B** is the implied main idea of the passage.

Identify the Best Summary A summary briefly restates the most important information or ideas in a passage. A good summary describes the most important information of the passage as a whole, not just the beginning or end. Look at this question based on the passage above:

What is the best summary of this passage?

A The platypus is a mammal that shares characteristics with reptiles.

B The platypus is found in eastern Australia.

C The platypus, found in Australia, is a mammal who lays eggs and has legs attached to its sides like a reptile.

D Found in streams and lakes, the platypus is warm-blooded, fur-bearing, and egg-laying.

A states the main idea but is not a summary. **B** and **D** don't include all the important information. **C** is correct.

Apply the Strategies

Answer the questions based on this passage:

> On Saturday, at 7:30 A.M., students began gathering in the school parking lot. Many carried home-baked goodies. Others brought pails, soap, sponges, and clothes. The students had formed a committee to raise money for the Tiny Tots Preschool, which has been severely damaged in a fire. With the car wash and bake sale, they hoped to raise funds to replace most of the school's books. By one o'clock, the students were counting their hard-earned money.

1 What is the main idea of the passage?

A Students held a car wash and bake sale to benefit the Tiny Tots Preschool.

B The Tiny Tots Preschool had fire damage.

C Students like to help out in a crisis.

D The students worked hard to earn money.

2 What is the best summary of the passage?

A Students brought food and cleaning supplies to the car wash and bake sale.

B When a local preschool was damaged in a fire, students held a bake sale and car wash.

C Students counted their money.

D The Tiny Tots Preschool lost all of its books.

Test Preparation Workshop 4

Reading Comprehension | Analyzing Information and Making Judgments

Strategies for Success

The reading sections of both national and Texas standardized tests require you to read a passage and answer multiple-choice questions by analyzing information and making judgments. Use the following strategies to answer such questions:

Analyze Information Some test questions require you not only to locate information in a passage but also to apply it. You may have to put information in categories, compare and contrast things, or determine causes and effects. Think about what the question is asking you to do, and analyze the information you need in order to do it. Look at this example:

Mr. and Mrs. Alvarez had left the babysitter a list of instructions:
1. Feed the children at 5:30. Warm up the soup in the refrigerator.
2. They can watch half an hour of TV.
3. Be sure they brush their teeth and wash their faces and hands.
4. Read them a story of their choice.
5. They should be in bed by 8:00.

Martin fed the children on time. At 6:00, while cleaning up, he heard the TV. At 7:30, the children were still watching TV. Martin hurried them off to the bathroom and tucked them into bed. Then he started his homework.

Which of the guidelines did Martin not follow?

A 1 and 2   **C** 2 and 3
B 2 and 4   **D** 3 and 5

Comparing the list with the description of what Martin did, you see that he did 1, 3, and 5. He didn't do 2 and 4, so **B** is correct.

Make Judgments When you make judgments, you evaluate a thing or an action based on a standard. The first step is deciding what the standard is. The second step is asking yourself how the thing or action measures up to it. Look at the following question:

Martin would have been a better babysitter if he had—

A not brought his homework
B given the children supper earlier
C limited the children's TV viewing
D cleaned the house

The standard for a good babysitter is to follow the parents' instructions. Martin let the children watch TV one hour longer than the parents wanted, so **C** is correct.

Apply the Strategies

Answer the questions based on this passage:

Erica made a list of the features she wanted in a new binder:
1. zipper closure
2. inside pockets for ruler and calculator
3. inside pouch for pens and pencils
4. subject dividers
5. inside pocket for loose papers.

Then she saw this ad:

STUDY AID 3-RING BINDER

- Zips closed to keep paper from falling out
- Full-sized pockets inside back and front
- Inside pouch
- Available in a variety of colors
- Only $15.95!

---

1 Which of Erica's requirements is not mentioned in the ad?

A 2   **B** 3   **C** 4   **D** 5

2 Erica's list would be more helpful to her process of choosing a new binder if it specified—

A the brand she bought last year
B the price range she can afford
C the colors she likes

Test Preparation Workshop 5

Reading Comprehension
Interpreting Diagrams, Graphs, and Statistical Illustrations

Strategies for Success

The reading sections of both national and Texas standardized tests require you to read a passage and answer multiple-choice questions about visual aids. Use the following strategies to help you answer such questions:

Study the Key Diagrams, graphs, and statistical illustrations present information visually with a minimum of words. A key tells you what the visual symbols represent. Study the key to learn what each symbol stands for or what each axis of a graph measures.

Interpret the Visual Questions of this nature may ask you to locate information, to compare two items of information, or to make calculations using the information. Read the questions carefully. Look at this example:

As treasurer of Student Council, Tony prepared a bar graph to show how many boxes of greeting cards each class sold for the school fund-raiser. Here is his graph on the fourth day of the sale.

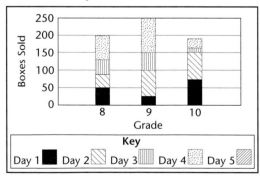

I How many boxes did the eighth grade sell on Day 2?
A 25 **B** 50 **C** 75 **D** 100

On Day I, eighth-graders sold 50. On Day 2 the number went from 50 to 75, so 25 were sold.

A is correct.

2 By Day 4, how many classes had sold 200 or more boxes of cards?
A 0 **B** I **C** 2 **D** 3

At the end of Day 4, the eighth grade had sold 200; the seventh grade had sold over 200; the sixth grade had sold fewer than 200. Since the question asks how may classes had sold 200 or more boxes, **C** is correct.

Apply the Strategies

Answer the questions based on the passage.

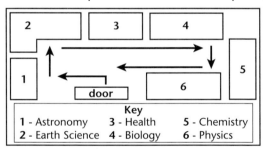

At the school science fair, Tanya, Alan, Dominic, and Gloria wanted to look at all four of their projects before looking at any other projects. Tanya's project was on the earth science table; Alan's was an astronomy project; Gloria did a physics experiment; and Dominic reported on a health issue.

I If the four students follow the suggested flow of traffic, whose project will they see first?
A Tanya's **C** Alan's
B Dominic's **D** Gloria's

2 After looking at Gloria's physics experiment, the friends wanted to look at all of the earth science projects. Which table did they pass on their way to the earth science table?
A health **C** biology
B chemistry **D** astronomy

Test Preparation Workshop 6

Reading Comprehension
Cause and Effect

Strategies for Success

The reading sections of both national and Texas standardized tests require you to read a passage and answer multiple-choice questions about cause-and-effect relationships. Use the following strategies to answer such questions:

Notice Cause-and-Effect Relationships A cause is an event or condition that makes something else happen. What happens is the effect or result. In the sentence, *Because we got lost, we were an hour late,* our getting lost is the cause, and our being late is the effect. One cause may have several effects, and one effect may have multiple causes. However, do not confuse time sequence with cause and effect. Even if one event follows another, the first event does not necessarily cause the second one.

Look for Signal Words Certain words or phrases in a passage may signal cause-and-effect relationships. These words and phrases include *because, why, the reason for, as a result of,* and *in order to.* When you see these words or phrases, read carefully. Consider this sentence: *As a result of poor playing, they lost the game.* The words that follow the phrase, *as a result of,* describe the cause, not the effect. Look at the following passage and questions:

> Tigers are an endangered species. In 1999 there were fewer than seven thousand of them living in the wild. These few are dying off fast as a result of illegal hunting and loss of habitat. When land is cleared to make room for a growing human population, tigers have less land on which to hunt and raise their young. To save wild tigers, governments need to protect tiger habitats and impose stricter hunting penalties.

1 What are two reasons that tigers are an endangered species?
  A hunting and limitations on development
  B loss of habitat and illegal hunting
  C new habitats and stricter hunting penalties
  D growing human population

The phrase "as a result of illegal hunting and loss of habitat" tells you that **B** is correct.

2 In order to prevent tigers from dying out, governments need to—
  A clear land   **C** protect habitats
  B encourage hunters   **D** place tigers in zoos

A and **B** are not causes that will have the effect of protecting tigers. **D** is not mentioned in the passage. **C** is correct.

Apply the Strategies

Answer the questions based on this passage.

> The extra half-hour of practice each day had paid off. Maya could hear the improvement in her violin playing. She was sure that her new-found confidence would result in her being more relaxed at the audition for Senior Orchestra. Just as she was about to raise her bow for the first note, she heard a ping. One of her strings had snapped. Maya's face fell. "Don't worry," smiled the director. "I always bring an extra set of strings to auditions. We'll have your violin restrung in a jiffy."

1 Maya's new confidence was a result of—
  A being more relaxed at the audition
  B getting a new string
  C extra practice each day
  D the director's friendly attitude

2 What caused Maya's face to fall?
  A the snap of her violin string
  B the director's comment
  C the sound of a wrong note
  D her lack of confidence

Test Preparation Workshop 7

Reading Comprehension — Fact and Opinion; Propaganda and Persuasive Language

Strategies for Success

The reading sections of standardized tests require you to read a passage and answer multiple-choice questions about fact and opinion, propaganda, and persuasive language. Use the following strategies to help you answer such questions:

Recognize Facts and Opinions A fact can be proven true by a reliable source, such as an unbiased book or an expert. An opinion is a statement of belief. A writer may use facts to support opinions, but that does not make the opinions true. Look at this example:

Bob Giles for Student Council President

Why vote for Bob?

✔ Bob was SC treasurer last year.
✔ Bob is captain of the football team.
✔ Bob is well liked by everyone.
● Bob's opponent has no school spirit.
● Bob's opponent is a one-issue candidate.
● Bob's opponent is new to the school.

Bob Giles will put this school on the map!

Which of the following is an OPINION?
  A Bob is captain of the football team.
  B His opponent has no school spirit.
  C His opponent is new to the school.
  D Bob was SC treasurer last year.

Research can prove that **A**, **C**, and **D** are true. **B** is an opinion.

Recognize Propaganda and Persuasive Language When writers want to influence you to think or act in a certain way, they often use words that appeal to your emotions rather than to your thinking. Propaganda is meant to influence the way you respond. Propaganda techniques include loaded words (words that appeal

to emotions), sweeping generalizations (statements too general to be meaningful), and empty promises (promises that cannot be kept). Look at this question based on the passage above:

Which of the following is a sweeping generalization?
  A Bob's opponent is a one-issue candidate.
  B Bob is captain of the football team.
  C Bob will put this school on the map.
  D Bob is well liked by everyone.

A is not a generalization. **B** is a fact. **C** is an empty promise. **D** is correct.

Apply the Strategies

Read the passage and answer the questions.

Dear Editor:
  I am writing to protest the new city law that dogs must be on leashes at all times. Everyone knows dogs deserve to run free. They can't enjoy running at a human's pace. I know the law is designed to keep dogs from annoying people and fighting with other dogs. However, my dog is obedient and has never been in a fight. The leash law is unfair to well-behaved dogs. It was passed by dog haters!
  A Dog Lover

1 Which of these statements is a FACT?
  A The leash law is unfair to well-behaved dogs.
  B My dog has never been in a fight.
  C Everyone knows dogs deserve to run free.
  D Dogs can't enjoy running at a human's pace.

2 Which statement is an example of propaganda?
  A The law is designed to keep dogs from annoying people.
  B I'm writing to protest the new city law.
  C My dog has never been in a fight.
  D It was passed by dog haters!

Test Preparation Workshop 8

Writing Skills Sentence Construction

Strategies for Success

The writing sections of standardized tests require you to read a passage and answer multiple-choice questions about sentence construction. Use the following strategies to help you answer such questions:

Recognize Incomplete Sentences and Run-on Sentences An incomplete sentence does not express a complete thought. Correct an incomplete sentence by making sure it has a subject and a verb. A run-on sentence is made up of two or more sentences without the proper punctuation between them. Correct a run-on sentence by adding the correct punctuation and, if necessary, a conjunction.

Combine Sentences Sometimes two short sentences sound better if they are combined. When you join two short sentences on a test, make sure that they are closely related in subject matter. Look at the following example:

> Over the years, numerous animals have spent time in the White House. (1) Abraham Lincoln rescued a turkey. It was supposed to be killed for Thanksgiving. It became a family pet. (2) Theodore Roosevelt's children had a pony. They once took it up in a service elevator.

Choose the best way to rewrite each underlined passage. If it needs no change, choose "Correct as is."

1 A Abraham Lincoln rescued a turkey. That was supposed to be killed for Thanksgiving.
  B Abraham Lincoln rescued a turkey that was supposed to be killed for Thanksgiving.
  C Abraham Lincoln rescued a turkey it was supposed to be killed for Thanksgiving.
  D Correct as is

The second part of **A** is an incomplete sentence. **C** is a run-on sentence. **B** is correct because it combines two short, related sentences.

2 A Theodore Roosevelt's children taking a pony up in a service elevator.
  B Theodore Roosevelt's children had a pony that they once took up in a service elevator.
  C Theodore Roosevelt's children took a pony. Up in a service elevator.
  D Correct as is

A is an incomplete sentence. The second half of **C** is an incomplete sentence. **B** combines two short sentences correctly.

Apply the Strategies

Choose the best way to rewrite each underlined passage. If it needs no change, choose "Correct as is."

> An animal's tongue can be very useful. (1) A gecko wipes its eyelids with its tongue a giraffe's tongue strips leaves from a tree. (2) Some lizards scare their enemies with their tongues. The tongues are blue.

1 A A gecko wipes its eyelids with its tongue, a giraffe's tongue strips leaves from trees.
  B A gecko wipes its eyelids with its tongue but a giraffe's tongue strips leaves from trees.
  C A gecko wipes its eyelids with its tongue. A giraffe's tongue strips leaves from trees.
  D Correct as is

2 A Some lizards scare enemies with their blue tongues.
  B Some lizards. Scare enemies with their blue tongues.
  C Some lizards scaring enemies with their blue tongues.
  D Correct as is

Test Preparation Workshop 9

Writing Skills — Appropriate Usage

Strategies for Success

The writing sections of both national and Texas standardized tests require you to read a passage and answer multiple-choice questions about appropriate usage. Use the following strategies to help you answer such questions:

Use the Correct Form of a Word Some test questions will ask you to choose the correct part of speech, the appropriate form or correct case of a word, or a way to express a negative. Look at these examples:

1 The directions were very—

  A confusion   **C** confused

  B confusing   **D** confuse

An adjective is needed. **B** and **C** are both adjectives, but *confused* would mean the directions experienced confusion. **B** is correct.

2 This book encourages readers to think—

  A creative   **C** creatively

  B more creative   **D** most creatively

An adverb is needed to modify the verb *think.* **C** and **D** are both adverbs, but **D** is the superlative form, used only in comparisons. **C** is correct.

3 The Wilsons and _____ took a vacation.

  A us   **B** we   **C** ourselves   **D** ourself

The type of pronoun required in this sentence is part of a compound subject, so the answer is **B**.

4 It was so dark, I _____ see nothing.

  A couldn't hardly   **C** couldn't

  B could   **D** couldn't barely

A, **C**, and **D** make double negatives when combined with *nothing.* **B** is correct.

Use Correct Agreement A verb agrees with its subject in number. Don't be misled by singular indefinite pronouns like *anyone* and *everyone.*

A pronoun agrees with its antecedent in person, number, and gender. Look at these examples:

5 Everyone who _____ to go on this trip must have a signed permission slip.

  A want   **C** wants

  B are wanting   **D** have wanted

The verb must agree with the singular subject *everyone.* **C** is correct.

6 Students have not turned in _____ reports.

  A her   **B** their   **C** your   **D** our

The antecedent, *students,* is third person plural, so **B** is correct.

Use Correct Verb Tense and Form Some test questions will require you to choose the correct tense of a verb or the correct form of an irregular verb. Look at this example:

7 We _____ to the rodeo every June.

  A have gone **B** have went **C** is going **D** gone

The verb describes past action continuing in the present, so the present perfect tense is needed. *Gone* is the past participle of *go.* **A** is correct.

Apply the Strategies

Read the passage and choose the word or words that belong in each space.

    Everyone I know __(1)__ Helen Keller was an __(2)__ person. Although she __(3)__ her sight and hearing at the age of nineteen months, __(4)__ learned to communicate with the whole world. With the help of __(5)__ teacher, Anne Sullivan, Keller went to college.

1 A think **B** thinks **C** thinking **D** have thought

2 A amaze **B** amazement **C** amazed **D** amazing

3 A has lost **B** losed   **C** will lost **D** lost

4 A her   **B** she   **C** hers   **D** herself

5 A its   **B** their   **C** his   **D** her

Test Preparation Workshop 10

Writing Skills
Spelling, Capitalization, and Punctuation

Strategies for Success

The writing sections of standardized tests require you to read a passage and answer multiple-choice questions about spelling, capitalization, and punctuation. Use the following strategies to help you answer such questions:

Recognize Spelling Errors Check the spelling of each word in the passage. Pay special attention to homophones (*there, their, they're*), vowel sounds (*moan* not *mone*), double consonants (*worry* not *wory*), irregular verbs (*dealt,* not *dealed*), and words containing -ie- or -ei-.

Recognize Capitalization Errors Make sure that the first word in a sentence or a quotation is capitalized, that proper nouns are capitalized, and that no words are capitalized unnecessarily. All the words in a compound proper noun should be capitalized (Texas Education Agency).

Recognize Punctuation Errors Check end punctuation. Determine if commas are missing, misplaced, or unnecessary. Check for opening and closing quotation marks. Look at this example:

Read the passage and decide which type of error, if any, appears in each underlined section.

(1) <u>Windmills are old and new.</u> (2) <u>The first ones were used more then a thousand years ago in Persia.</u> (3) <u>Modern windmills called wind turbines convert wind energy into electricity.</u> (4) <u>some are powered by the wind produced by speeding cars.</u>

1 **A** Spelling error   **C** Punctuation error
  B Capitalization error **D** No error

2 **A** Spelling error   **C** Punctuation error
  B Capitalization error **D** No error

3 **A** Spelling error   **C** Punctuation error
  B Capitalization error **D** No error

4 **A** Spelling error   **C** Punctuation error
  B Capitalization error **D** No error

For question 1, there are no errors, so **D** is correct. For question 2, *then* should be *than,* so **A** is correct. For question 3, "called wind turbines" should be set off with commas, so **C** is correct. For question 4, *some* should be capitalized, so **B** is correct.

Apply the Strategies

Read the passage and decide which type of error, if any, appears in each underlined section.

(1) <u>Yellowstone national Park has something for everyone.</u> (2) <u>Hikers, boaters, skiers campers and photographers can all find lots of ways to have fun.</u> (3) <u>In 1872, Yellowstone became the country's first national park.</u> (4) <u>More than one hundred years later, it is still impresing visitors.</u>

1 **A** Spelling error   **C** Punctuation error
  B Capitalization error **D** No error

2 **A** Spelling error   **C** Punctuation error
  B Capitalization error **D** No error

3 **A** Spelling error   **C** Punctuation error
  B Capitalization error **D** No error

4 **A** Spelling error   **C** Punctuation error
  B Capitalization error **D** No error

Test Preparation Workshop 11

Research Skills — Using Information Resources

Strategies for Success

Some tests require you to review a packet of information resources and to respond to questions about how you would use these resources to gather information and plan a report on a given subject. Use these strategies:

Review the Packet of Information Skim through the packet to see what types of material are included, such as articles from encyclopedias and computer information.

Scan the Questions Look through the questions to see which types of information are required to answer the questions. Focus on each question separately. The questions are not necessarily related to each other. Locate the best example or piece of information in the packet to answer each question.

Use Correct Sentence Form Write responses to the short-answer questions in complete sentences and include key words. Look at these examples:.

Directions: Suppose that you are writing a report on the life and times of Thomas Alva Edison (1847–1931). Edison is one of the world's most important inventors.

This packet includes several information resources about Thomas Alva Edison:

- an excerpt from an encyclopedia article, "Inventions of the Nineteenth Century"
- a biographical dictionary entry
- *Thomas Alva Edison*, a biography of the inventor: a short excerpt, table of contents, and a list of key dates in Edison's life and career
- Computer screen: on-line index of library books about Thomas Edison

Excerpt from encyclopedia article: "Inventions of the Nineteenth Century"

A flood of inventions swept the United States in the late 1800's. By the 1890's Americans were patenting 21,000 new inventions a year. These inventions helped industry to grow and become more efficient. New devices also made daily life easier in many American homes.

Advanced Communication Some remarkable new devices filled the need for faster communication. The telegraph speeded communication within the United States. It still took weeks, however, for news from Europe to arrive by boat. In 1866, Cyrus Field ran an underwater telegraph cable across the Atlantic Ocean, bringing the United States and Europe closer together.

Thomas Edison In an age of invention, Thomas Edison was right at home. In 1876, he opened a research laboratory in Menlo Park, New Jersey. There, Edison boasted that he and his 15 co-workers set out to create "minor" inventions every 10 days and "a big thing every 6 months or so."

Biographical Dictionary

Edison, Thomas Alva A poor student, Thomas Edison grew up to invent the light bulb, the phonograph, and dozens of other devises. Edison once went without sleep for three days working on his phonograph. At last, he heard his own voice reciting "Mary Had a Little Lamb." Edison said, "Genius is one percent inspiration and ninety-nine percent perspiration."

Table of Contents from *Thomas Alva Edison*

Test Preparation Workshop 11

Research Skills — Using Information Resources (cont.)

Short Excerpt from *Thomas Alva Edison*

The key to Edison's success was his approach. He turned inventing into a system. Teams of experts refined Edison's ideas and turned them into practical inventions. Menlo Park became an "invention factory." The results were amazing. Edison became knows as the "Wizard of Menlo Park" for inventing the light bulb, the phonograph, and hundreds of other devices.

Lists of Key Dates
from *Thomas Alva Edison*

1847: Born in Milan, Ohio

1852: Moved to Port Huron, Michigan

1869: Was paid $40,000 for improvements to the stock ticker. Opened his first workshop in Newark, New Jersey

1874: Improved the typewriter

1877: Invented the phonograph

1879: Perfected the electric light

1887: Moved to West Orange, New Jersey. Worked on such inventions as the motion picture, a storage battery, a cement mixer, the Dictaphone, and a duplicating machine.

1931: Died at 84 in West Orange, New Jersey

Computer Screen

Library Online Catalog

Subject Search: Thomas Alva Edison

Line	Titles	Subjects
1	2	Edison, Thomas: Early Life
2	4	Edison, Thomas: Bibliography
3	1	Edison, Thomas: Biography

Sample Questions and Explanations

1 Which information given in the encyclopedia article would be LEAST useful for your report?
  A the number of patents in the 1890's
  B the date Edison opened his laboratory
  C Cyrus Field's contributions to communication
  D the description of Edison's workshop

The correct answer is **C.** Cyrus Field's contributions are not important to a report on Edison.

2 In which chapter of *Thomas Alva Edison* would you find information about Edison's schooling? ("Early Years" would provide the information.)

3 Which of these sources would you use to find books written about Thomas Alva Edison?
  A the encyclopedia article
  B the biographical dictionary article
  C computer screen
  D the biography Thomas Alva Edison

The correct answer is **C.** The other sources do not reference other books about Edition.

Apply the Strategies

4 Suppose you are going to write an outline of your report on the life of Thomas Alva Edison. What three main topics would you include?

5 State the main idea of your report.

6 In which source would you find detailed information about Edison's marriage?
  A the encyclopedia article
  B the biographical dictionary entry
  C the main body of the biography
  D the list of key dates from the biography

Test Preparation Workshop 12

Writing Skills — Proofreading

Strategies for Success

The writing sections of some standardized tests assess your ability to edit, proofread, and use other writing processes. You are required to look for mistakes in passages and then to choose the best way to correct them.

Check for Incorrect Verb Tense and Errors in Subject-Verb Agreement Check to see that the correct verb tense is used and make the verb agree in number with its subject. If the parts of the subject name more than one thing, use a plural verb. If the parts of the subject refer to the same thing, use a singular verb.

Correct Run-on Sentences Use an end mark and a capital letter to separate main clauses. Use a semicolon between clauses.

Correct Sentence Fragments Add a subject or verb to make a sentence fragment a complete sentence.

Use Supporting Details Effectively Avoid the use of details that interrupt the flow of the passage and that do not support the main idea.

Sample Passage and Questions:

Directions: A student wrote a paper about Alaska. There are mistakes that need correcting.

(1) Susan Butcher win the Iditarod dog-sled race several times. (2) A large strip of mountains cross Alaska. (3) Despite its challenges, the race attracts more and more racers every year. (4) In the years ahead, racers may come from such far-off countries as Sweden Norway and Denmark.

I Select the best way to write sentence 1.
   A Susan Butcher won the Iditarod dog-sled race several times.
   B Susan Butcher will win the Iditarod dog-sled race several times.
   C Susan Butcher would have won the Iditarod dog-sled race several times.
   D Best as it is

The correct answer is **A.** *Won* is the past tense of the irregular verb *win*.

2 Select the best way to write sentence 2.
   A A large strip of mountains crosses Alaska.
   B A large strip of mountains do cross Alaska.
   C A mountainous strip crosses Alaska.
   D Best as it is.

The correct answer is **A.** A large strip of mountains crosses Alaska. The subject is singular and requires a singular verb.

Apply the Strategies

(1) Secretary of State Seward bought Alaska from Russia the deal was mocked as "Seward's Folly." (2) Seward's $7.2 million purchase proved to be a bargain; gold deposits were discovered there three decades later. (3) My uncle told me about a trip he took to Alaska when he was only 12 years old. (4) Prospectors first struck gold in 1889.

I Which is the best way to write the underlined section in sentence one?
   A Secretary of State Seward bought Alaska from Russia. The deal was mocked as "Seward's Folly."
   B Secretary of State Seward bought Alaska from Russia, and the deal was mocked.
   C Secretary of State Seward bought Alaska. The deal was "Seward's Folly."
   D Best as it is

2 Which is the correct way to fix the flow of the passage?
   A Delete sentence 3
   B Move sentence 4 to the beginning.
   C Switch sentences 1 and 2
   D Move sentence 1 to the end.

Test Preparation Workshop 13

Writing Skills
Responding to Writing Prompts

Strategies for Success

The writing sections of many standardized tests require you to write an essay based on a writing prompt. Your essay usually is evaluated as a whole, on a 1–6 point scale from *outstanding* to *deficient,* and assessed for focus, content, organization, grammar, usage, and mechanics. Use the following strategies to help you with a writing assessment.

Read the Writing Prompt The writing prompt consists of two parts. The first part explains the topic you are asked to write about, or the writing situation. The second part provides specific instructions on how to respond to the prompt.

Look for Key Words As you examine the writing prompt, look for key words such as *define, explain, classify,* and *contrast.* These words indicate the purpose of your essay. It is essential that you keep these key words in mind as you develop your essay.

Budget Your Time When writing for a test, you need to be aware of how much time you have. Allow one quarter of your time for gathering ideas, half your time for writing your first draft, and one quarter of your time for revising.

Collect Your Ideas Before you begin writing, jot down key ideas and details that you plan to include. Then, review your ideas and decide on the best organization.

Draft Carefully Because you'll have less time to revise then you might in other writing situations, take care in the words and sentences you use as you draft your essay. Begin with an introduction that presents your main point. Follow with body paragraphs, each focusing on a single subtopic. End with a conclusion restating your point.

Use Transitions As you draft, use transitional words to indicate the connections between ideas. The following words show comparison-and-contrast relationships: *however, nevertheless, yet, likewise, in like manner, on the contrary, similarly, instead,* and *nonetheless.*

Proofread Make sure your descriptions are clear. Check that there are no errors in spelling, grammar, usage, or mechanics.

Key Strategies:

- Focus on the topic and do not include unnecessary information.
- Present the material in an organized manner.
- Provide supporting ideas.
- Write with sentence variety.
- Proofread your work.

Apply the Strategies

Practice the preceding strategies by writing an essay in response to the following prompt.

Sample Writing Prompt

Everyone looks forward to weekends and a break from the weekday routine. Think about one thing that you like to do on weekends and why. It could be a community activity, an opportunity to be by yourself to play video games or watch television, or sharing time with family members and friends.

Now explain in an essay why this event or activity is important to you. Support your ideas with examples and details.

Test Practice Bank

Reading Comprehension

Using Context Clues and Prefixes/Suffixes

Read the passage, and then answer the questions that follow. Mark the letter of your answer on a bubble sheet if your teacher provides one; otherwise, number from 1 to 6 on a separate sheet of paper, and write the letter of the correct answer next to each number.

> Cuisine in most hot climates features hot peppers because they cool people who eat them by making them perspire. Using peppers in food preparation can also delay spoilage. Peppers come in many varieties. Worldwide, there are more than 1,000 discrete kinds of hot peppers, although not all are piquant enough to make a person sweat. Peppers come in many degrees of hotness; for instance, the habañero (Scotch bonnet) is about 1,000 times hotter than the jalapeño. If you serve these peppers to guests without warning them, they will be disinclined to try your cooking again.

1 In this passage, the word *cuisine* means—
A sweating
B cooking
C gardening
D measuring

2 The word *spoilage* in this passage means—
F the prevention of spoiling
G the prevention of using peppers
H the act of using peppers
J the act of spoiling

3 In this passage, the word *discrete* means—
A similar
B popular
C separate
D unknown

4 In this passage, the word *piquant* means—
F spicy
G mild
H unpleasant
J widespread

5 From this passage, you can tell that a jalapeño is—
A a Scotch bonnet
B another word for habañero
C a person who likes spicy food
D a kind of pepper

6 The word *disinclined* in this passage means—
F happy
G hesitant
H eager
J able

Reading Comprehension

Following Written Directions

Read the passage, and then answer the questions that follow. Mark the letter of your answer on a bubble sheet if your teacher provides one; otherwise, number from 1 to 6 on a separate sheet of paper, and write the letter of the correct answer next to each number.

When you're making a personal or professional telephone call, begin by introducing yourself and stating your purpose. "Hello. My name is Lakota Sandford. I'm calling in response to your advertisement for a baby sitter." "Hi, Mrs. Martinez. This is Dave. Is Nick home?"

When calling for information or to order a product, it is not necessary to introduce yourself. If you're ordering something, you will be asked for personal information at the appropriate time.

If your listener keeps asking you to repeat yourself, you may need to speak more slowly and distinctly.

Repeating information ensures that you have heard the other person correctly. When you are receiving information, repeat it to verify its accuracy.

Be courteous on the phone. Say "please" and "thank you." Confirm any future contact. "Thanks for calling, Lakota. I'll meet with you Tuesday."

1 What is the first thing you should do when making a personal or professional phone call?
A Repeat information.
B Confirm future contact.
C Introduce yourself.
D Say "please" and "thank you."

2 It is NOT necessary to introduce yourself —
F when calling a friend
G when calling a professional
H when ordering a product
J when talking on the phone

3 How should you verify that your information is accurate?
A Repeat the information.
B Speak slowly and clearly.
C Introduce yourself.
D Call for information.

4 You should be courteous—
F when requesting information
G when on the phone
H when repeating yourself
J when making a professional call

5 Why is it important to speak clearly?
A to verify the accuracy of your information
B to keep from repeating yourself
C so your listener will not ask for your personal information.
D so your listener can understand

6 If your listener asks you to repeat yourself, you may—
F not have spoken clearly enough
G not have heard correctly
H not have introduced yourself
J not have confirmed future plans

Reading Comprehension

Identifying Main Idea; Identifying Best Summary

Read the passage, and then answer the questions that follow. Mark the letter of your answer on a bubble sheet if your teacher provides one; otherwise, number 1 and 2 on a separate sheet of paper, and write the letter of the correct answer next to each number.

Wetlands are areas of land where the water level remains near or above the surface of the ground for most of the year. Types of wetlands include bogs, fens, marshes, and swamps. Wetlands are home to many types of plants and animals, including several endangered species. They also help control flooding by holding large amounts of water. Although wetlands in the United States are protected by the Federal Clean Water Act and by various state and local laws, many environmentalists are asking for stronger laws to protect them.

---

1 What is the main idea of this passage?

A Wetlands are land areas in which water remains near or above the surface of the ground for most of the year.

B Wetlands are areas that are important for plants, animals, and people, and they may need special protection.

C Environmentalists are asking for stronger laws to protect wetlands.

D Wetlands are home to many plants and animals, including endangered species.

2 What is the best summary of this passage?

F Wetlands are important because they help control flooding.

G Wetlands are areas where the water is near or above the surface for most of the year, and they provide homes for endangered species.

H Wetlands are land areas where the water remains near or above the ground surface for most of the year. They provide homes for many plants and animals, some of which are endangered. Wetlands help control flooding. Although wetlands are currently protected by laws, stronger laws may be needed.

J Wetlands are areas where the water remains near or above the surface most of the year; wetlands can be bogs, fens, marshes, or swamps; wetlands are protected by the Federal Clean Water Act and by state and local laws, but many environmentalists want stronger laws.

Reading Comprehension

Arranging Details in Sequential Order

Read the passage, and then answer the questions that follow. Mark the letter of your answer on a bubble sheet if your teacher provides one; otherwise, number from 1 to 6 on a separate sheet of paper, and write the letter of the correct answer next to each number.

> Born in Galesburg, Illinois, in 1878, Carl Sandburg became one of the best-known American poets. Sandburg enlisted in the 6th Illinois Infantry when the Spanish-American War broke out in 1898. From 1910 to 1912, he was secretary to the mayor of Milwaukee. Sandburg moved to Chicago in 1913, where he became an editor of a business magazine and later became a staff member of the *Chicago Daily News*. *Poetry* magazine published a number of his poems in 1914, and his first collection, *Chicago Poems,* came out in 1916.
>
> Sandburg's epic poem, *The People, Yes,* was published in 1936. At that time, the United States was experiencing the Great Depression, a time of economic struggle that began in 1929 and continued into World War II (1939–1945). *The People, Yes* celebrates the common people and their courage in hard times.
>
> Sandburg won the Pulitzer Prize three times: in 1918, for his poetry collection, *Cornhuskers*; in 1940, for his biography of Abraham Lincoln; and in 1951, for his *Complete Poems.*

1 Carl Sandburg first won the Pulitzer Prize in—
A 1936 **B** 1918 **C** 1940 **D** 1951

2 Sandburg published *Chicago Poems*—
F during the Great Depression
G after World War II
H before publishing *The People, Yes*
J before *Poetry* magazine published some of his poems

3 Which of the following happened during World War II?
A *The People, Yes* was published.
B Sandburg won a Pulitzer Prize for his biography of Lincoln.
C Sandburg's poems were published in *Poetry* magazine.
D Sandburg won a Pulitzer Prize for his *Complete Poems.*

4 Sandburg moved to Chicago AFTER—
F working for Milwaukee's mayor
G publishing in *Poetry* magazine
H working at the *Chicago Daily News*
J publishing his first collection of poems

5 BEFORE becoming an editor, Sandburg had—
A won a Pulitzer Prize
B worked at the *Chicago Daily News*
C published his first poetry collection
D been in the 6th Illinois Infantry

6 The Great Depression began—
F after World War II
G after Sandburg moved to Chicago
H before the Spanish-American War
J before Sandburg was an editor

Reading Comprehension

Analyzing Information and Making Judgments

Read the passage, and then answer the questions that follow. Mark the letter of your answer on a bubble sheet if your teacher provides one; otherwise, number from 1 to 6 on a separate sheet of paper, and write the letter of the correct answer next to each number.

Enrique got home from school to find a list of instructions from his father.

1. Heat the oven to 350 degrees.
2. Take the casserole out of the refrigerator and put it in the oven.
3. Set the timer for 45 minutes.
4. When the timer goes off, remove the casserole and put it aside to cool.
5. Wash the breakfast dishes.
6. Vacuum the carpet in your room.
7. Do your homework.

Enrique heated the oven and put in the casserole. He looked for the timer but could not find it. Enrique vacuumed his room and then washed the breakfast dishes. He finished earlier than he thought he would, so he watched TV. After half an hour, he sat down at his desk to do his homework. After an hour, he smelled something burning. He ran to the kitchen and opened the oven door. The casserole was badly burned. Enrique turned off the oven and looked at the clock. His father would be home in a few minutes, and Enrique had burned dinner and had not finished his homework.

1 Which things did Enrique not do?
    A 1 and 3   **C** 3 and 4
    B 2 and 6   **D** 4 and 5

2 What did Enrique do that was not on the list?
    F remove the casserole
    G watch TV
    H wash the breakfast dishes
    J heat the oven

3 Enrique might have cooked dinner successfully if he had—
    A not watched TV
    B finished his homework earlier
    C washed the dishes first
    D set the timer

4 Enrique's father's instructions would have been more useful if they had included—

F the location of the timer
G instructions not to watch TV
H a description of the casserole
J vacuuming instructions

5 What would have helped Enrique complete his homework?
    A setting the timer
    B not watching TV
    C not vacuuming
    D removing the casserole

6 Which two tasks did Enrique perform in reverse order?
    F Heating the oven and putting in the casserole
    G Setting the timer and doing homework
    H Vacuuming and washing dishes
    J Doing homework and vacuuming

Reading Comprehension

Interpreting Diagrams, Graphs, and Statistical Illustrations

Read the passage, and then answer the questions that follow. Mark the letter of your answer on a bubble sheet if your teacher provides one; otherwise, number from 1 to 4 on a separate sheet of paper, and write the letter of the correct answer next to each number.

Charles Elder is taking a trip with his fourteen-year-old daughter, Melinda. The Elders live in a city called Cleaver and have decided to spend the weekend visiting historic places in Brady, a town located 200 miles away. Mr. Elder thought it would be a special treat if they could take the train instead of driving. It is summer, so Melinda is out of school, but Mr. Elder has to work Monday through Friday from 8:00 until 4:30 P.M. He is very busy, and so he has given Melinda the job of finding infor- mation about the train schedule and hotels. Melinda has received the following information from the Brady Chamber of Commerce.

TRAIN SCHEDULE

Train	Days	Departs Cleaver	Arrives in Nelsonville	Arrives in Brady
BRADY COMMUTER	Monday through Friday	7:00 A.M		10:00 A.M.
BRADY BULLET	Sunday through Friday	5:00 P.M.	6:30 P.M.	9:00 P.M.
BRADY EXPRESS	Monday through Saturday	7:30 P.M.		10:30 P.M.
BRADY FLYER	Daily	6:30 P.M.	8:00 P.M. (stays in Nelsonville for 30 minutes)	11:00 P.M.

1 If Mr. Elder works his normal day on Friday, which train would they have to take to arrive in Brady before the stores close at 10:00 P.M.?
   A Brady Commuter
   B Brady Bullet
   C Brady Express
   D Brady Flyer

2 If the Elders decided to spend the night in Nelsonville, how many trains could they take that would get them there in time to do some shopping before the stores close at 7:30 P.M.?
   F One
   G Two
   H Three
   J Four

3 If Mr. Elder has a meeting on Friday night that lasts until 9:00 P.M., what is the first train they could take the next day?
   A Brady Commuter
   B Brady Bullet
   C Brady Express
   D Brady Flyer

4 If the Elders waited until Saturday to leave, how many trains would they have to choose from?
   F One
   G Two
   H Three
   J Four

Reading Comprehension

Drawing Inferences and Conclusions; Making Generalizations

Read the passage, and then answer the questions that follow. Mark the letter of your answer on a bubble sheet if your teacher provides one; otherwise, number from 1 to 6 on a separate sheet of paper, and write the letter of the correct answer next to each number.

The day Professor Herbert started talking about a project for each member of our General Science class, I was more excited than I had ever been. I wanted to have an outstanding project. I wanted it to be greater, to be more unusual than those of my classmates. I wanted to do something worthwhile, and something to make them respect me.

I'd made the best grade in my class in General Science. I'd made more yardage, more tackles and carried the football across the goal line more times than any player on my team. But making good grades and playing rugged football hadn't made them forget that I rode a mule to school. . . .

—"A Ribbon for Baldy"
by Jesse Stuart

---

1 You can infer from the passage that the narrator wishes to—
 A become a great scientist some day
 B prove his worth to his classmates
 C become as good at science as he is at football
 D gain the confidence he needs to reach his goals

2 Which words best describe the narrator's feelings?
 F doubtful and afraid
 G depressed and hopeless
 H quick-tempered and fiery
 J determined and enthusiastic

3 You can conclude from the passage that the narrator will probably—
 A quit the football team
 B design an elaborate project
 C try to change science classes
 D let his classmates ride his mule

4 This passage was probably written to—
 F create a suspenseful mood
 G introduce the story's narrator
 H tell how a problem was solved
 J explain the effects of a decision

5 You can conclude from the passage that the setting is—
 A an imaginary place, in the future
 B a city, in the present
 C the country, in the past
 D a city, in the past

6 Which of these statements is a generalization based on the passage?
 F The narrator is competitive.
 G The narrator has never failed at anything.
 H The narrator prefers playing sports to studying.
 J The narrator has never been afraid of being teased.

Reading Comprehension

Identifying Cause and Effect

Read the passage, and then answer the questions that follow. Mark the letter of your answer on a bubble sheet if your teacher provides one; otherwise, number from 1 to 6 on a separate sheet of paper, and write the letter of the correct answer next to each number.

> "Last week he hurled the local blacksmith over a parapet into a stream, and it was only by paying over all the money which I could gather together that I was able to avert another public exposure. He had no friends at all save the wandering gypsies, and he would give these vagabonds leave to encamp upon the few acres of bramble-covered land which represent the family estate, and would accept in return the hospitality of their tents, wandering away with them sometimes for weeks on end. He has a passion also for Indian animals, which are sent over to him by a correspondent, and he has at this moment a cheetah and a baboon, which wander freely over his grounds and are feared by the villagers almost as much as is their master."
>
> —"The Adventure of the Speckled Band" by Arthur Conan Doyle

1 The man described in this passage is able to acquire Indian animals because of his friendship with—
   A nearby villagers
   B a local blacksmith
   C a group of gypsies
   D a correspondent

2 The man has left himself open to public attack because he has—
   F assaulted a blacksmith
   G purchased a large estate
   H misspent a friend's money
   J expressed fear of the villagers

3 What effect does the man's behavior have on the villagers?
   A They are afraid of him.
   B They feel pity for him.
   C They return his kindness.
   D They admire his generosity.

4 Why do the gypsies offer their tents to the man described in the passage?

   F He lets them camp on his estate.
   G He often guides them during their travels.
   H He shares their passion for Indian animals.
   J He gives them money.

5 Why is the man often absent from his estate?
   A He is arrested for his behavior.
   B He takes trips with the gypsies.
   C He travels overseas to purchase animals.
   D He has arguments with villagers.

6 How did the narrator prevent the man's assault on the blacksmith from being revealed?
   F by contacting a correspondent
   G by paying a large sum of money
   H by gaining the gypsies' cooperation
   J by appealing to the villagers' generosity

Reading Comprehension

Distinguishing Fact and Opinion

Read each passage, and then answer the questions that follow. Mark the letter of your answer on a bubble sheet if your teacher provides one; otherwise, number from 1 to 6 on a separate sheet of paper, and write the letter of the correct answer next to each number.

Dear Editor:

Don't call me lazy! In a May 19 article titled "The Trouble with Teens," the writer states that "typical teenagers do nothing but skateboard and hang out at the mall." I strongly disagree, and here's why. In a survey conducted by eighth graders at Hanover Middle School, 65 percent of the students said that they participate in an after-school club or play on a sports team. More important, though, there is no typical teenager, just as there is no typical adult. We are all individual and unique.

Sincerely,
13 and Proud of It

---

1 Which of the following expresses the writer's opinion?
A Sixty-five percent of students participate in after-school activities.
B A survey was conducted at Hanover Middle School.
C An article concerning teens appeared on May 19.
D There is no such thing as a typical human being.

2 In this passage, the writer states the fact that teenagers—
F are typical
G are unlike adults
H do after-school activities
J spend time at malls

3 The writer uses facts to support claims about—
A typical teenagers
B typical adults
C unique persons
D eighth graders

4 The writer uses a fact to support the opinion that—
F local teens are not typically lazy
G the writer is not typically lazy
H local adults are not typically lazy
J typical people do not exist

5 Which of the following does NOT express the writer's opinion?
A Typical teenagers do nothing.
B Every adult and teenager is unique.
C There are no typical teenagers.
D The article misrepresents teenagers.

6 In this passage, the writer's comparison of adults and teenagers is based on—
F fact
G opinion
H research
J surveys

Reading Comprehension

Recognizing Author's Point of View and Purpose

Read the passage, and then answer the questions that follow. Mark the letter of your answer on a bubble sheet if your teacher provides one; otherwise, number from 1 to 6 on a separate sheet of paper, and write the letter of the correct answer next to each number.

There are people who I have corresponded with on email for months before actually meeting them—people at work and otherwise. If someone isn't saying something of interest it's easier to not respond to their mail than it is not to answer the phone. In fact I give out my home phone number to almost no one but my email address is known very broadly. I am the only person who reads my email so no one has to worry about embarrassing themselves or going around people when they send a message. Our email is completely secure. . . .

—from "E-Mail from Bill Gates" by John Seabrook

---

1 How does the author of this passage feel about e-mail?
  A annoyed
  B cautious
  C enthusiastic
  D indifferent

2 The author's main purpose is to—
  F explain the process of sending e-mail
  G inform readers of the history of e-mail
  H describe a past experience sending e-mail
  J convince readers of the advantages of e-mail

3 What secondary purpose might the author have for writing this passage?
  A to convince readers that he is easy to contact
  B to entertain readers with a humorous incident
  C to describe his life before the development of e-mail
  D to present his own role in the development of e-mail

4 The author includes the first sentence of the passage to show that e-mail is—
  F convenient
  G inexpensive
  H problematic
  J time-consuming

5 The author says that people do not have to "worry about embarrassing themselves" while using e-mail in order to convince readers that e-mail—
  A can be sent anonymously
  B is used by almost everyone
  C cannot be secretly read by others
  D can prevent unintended mistakes

6 The author believes that communicating by telephone is—
  F more costly than using e-mail
  G more private than using e-mail
  H more personal than using e-mail
  J more adaptable than using e-mail

Combined Reading and Literary Skills

Read the passage, and then answer the questions that follow. Mark your answers to questions 1–9 on a bubble sheet if your teacher provides one; otherwise, number from 1 to 9 on a separate sheet of paper, and write the letter of the correct answer next to each number. Answer number 10 on a separate sheet of paper.

The truth is that computer networking is still in its infancy. Probably nothing illustrates this more clearly than the "ASCII[1] jail": 90% of network communications are still limited to plain old ASCII text—that is, the characters of the alphabet, the numerals 0 through 9, and the most basic punctuation marks. It's bad enough that multimedia communications have not been implemented in most of cyberspace.[2] Most of the time you can't even put a word in bold or italics!

Because people cannot see or hear you in cyberspace, you need to pay close attention to the style of your electronic communications if you hope to make a good impression there. The *style* of electronic communications encompasses everything about your correspondence except its content, from your use of network conventions like "smileys" and "sigs" to the number of characters per line in your email messages.

Style considerations are influenced by several rules of Netiquette, especially Rule 4, Respect other people's time, and Rule 5, Make yourself look good online. It doesn't matter how brilliant your messages are if they're formatted in such a way that no one can read them.

—"How to Be Polite Online"
from *Netiquette* by Virginia Shea

---

1. **ASCII:** Abbreviation of American Standard Code for Information Interchange, a standard computer code used to assist the interchange of information among various types of data-processing equipment.
2. **cyberspace:** Global communication performed through the use of computer technology.

---

1 In this passage, the word *implemented* means—
  A outlawed
  B recognized
  C reasoned with
  D put into effect

2 The word *encompasses* in this passage means—
  F imitates
  G includes
  H precedes
  J reverses

3 What example shows that computer networking remains in its early stages of development?
  A network conventions
  B multimedia style
  C ASCII text
  D Netiquette

4 What is the implied main idea of the first paragraph?
  F Network communication still has many basic problems.
  G Multimedia communications have

revolutionized cyberspace.

H People fear the use of ASCII text because it's so new.

J The use of ASCII text for networking was always a bad idea.

5 Why does the author refer to ASCII text as a "jail"?

A It is used by many people.

B It has very limited features.

C It is a relatively new method.

D It cannot be used in cyberspace.

6 The author believes that the style of an electronic message is—

F not limited by conventions

G enhanced by ASCII text

H as important as content

J of little consequence

7 Which of these is a FACT from the passage?

A Respecting others' time is an important rule of Netiquette.

B Ninety percent of network communications use ASCII text.

C Paying attention to style makes a good impression.

D Electronic messages should be clearly formatted.

8 The author's main purpose is to—

F protest rude behavior in cyberspace

G relate stories about cyberspace

H predict the future of network communication

J give advice about network communication

9 Based on the article, what is likely to happen to network communications in the future?

A The need for style guidelines will decrease.

B The use of bold and italic text will decrease.

C The use of multimedia in cyberspace will increase.

D The percentage of messages using ASCII will increase.

10 Why should style be an important consideration when you create an electronic message? Support your answer with evidence from the text.

Writing Skills

Sentence Construction

Read each passage, and then answer the questions that follow. Mark the letter of the answer on a bubble sheet if your teacher provides one; otherwise, number 1 to 6 on a separate sheet of paper, and write the letter of the correct answer next to each number.

> (1) Grandpa lived on a Sioux reservation, the Sioux once lived on the northern plains of North America. (2) They were famous for their bravery. (3) And their fighting skills. (4) Tension developed between: the Sioux and the U.S., in the 1800's.

1 How would you correct the underlined portion of sentence 1?
  A Grandpa lived on a Sioux reservation the Sioux once lived
  B Grandpa lived on a Sioux reservation. The Sioux once lived
  C Grandpa lived on a Sioux reservation: the Sioux once lived
  D Correct as is

2 How would you correct the structure of sentences 2 and 3?
  F They were famous for their bravery, And their fighting skills.
  G They were famous for their bravery, and their fighting skills.
  H They were famous for their bravery and their fighting skills.
  J Correct as is

3 How would you correct the structure of sentence 4?
  A Tension developed between, the Sioux and the U.S., in the 1800's.
  B Tension developed between the Sioux, and the U.S. in the 1800's.
  C Tension developed between the Sioux and the U.S. in the 1800's.
  D Correct as is

> (1) Isaac Bashevis Singer, came from a family of Jewish religious leaders. (2) He grew up in Warsaw which is Poland's capital. (3) Singer received a Jewish education before he decided to become a writer.

4 How would you correct the structure of sentence 1?
  F Isaac Bashevis Singer, came from, a family of Jewish religious leaders.
  G Isaac Bashevis Singer came from: a family of Jewish religious leaders.
  H Isaac Bashevis Singer came from a family of Jewish religious leaders.
  J Correct as is

5 How would you correct the underlined portion of sentence 2?
  A Warsaw, which is Poland's capital.
  B Warsaw; which is Poland's capital.
  C Warsaw. Which is Poland's capital.
  D Correct as is

6 How would you correct the structure of sentence 3?
  F Singer received a Jewish education; before he decided, to become a writer.
  G Singer received a Jewish education, before; He decided to become a writer.
  H Singer received a Jewish education; before, he decided to become a writer.
  J Correct as is

Writing Skills

Appropriate Usage

Read the passage, and choose the word or group of words that belongs in each space. Mark the letter of the answer on a bubble sheet if your teacher provides one; otherwise, number 1 to 6 on a separate sheet of paper, and write the letter of the correct answer next to each number.

John Steinbeck described the Badlands in South Dakota as "sculptured hills and ravines." The geologic formation of areas like this __(1)__ by water erosion, __(2)__ creates steep hills and deep valleys. __(3)__ geological areas are often found in very dry regions, where occasional flash floods __(4)__ gushing streams of water __(5)__ the surrounding rock and soil layers. Visitors __(6)__ come to the Badlands enjoy a variety of rock formations.

---

1 **A** caused
   B are caused
   C is caused
   D causes

2 **F** which
   G while
   H where
   J but

3 **A** What
   B This
   C That
   D These

4 **F** cause
   G causes
   H will causes
   J was caused

5 **A** erode
   B eroding
   C to erode
   D have eroded

6 **F** what
   G they
   H which
   J who

Writing

Spelling, Capitalization, and Punctuation

Read the passage, and decide which type of error, if any, appears in each underlined section. Mark the letter of your answer on a bubble sheet if your teacher provides one; otherwise, number from 1 to 6 on a separate sheet of paper, and write the letter of the correct answer next to each number.

Sporting events are big news. <u>People with a love of sports, and a</u>
<u>(1)</u>
flair for public speaking may want to pursue careers in sports reporting. <u>Some</u>

<u>sports reporter careers started with an interest in TV sports commentary,</u>
<u>(2)</u>
newspaper sports articles, or biographys of great athletes. <u>Still others began by</u>

<u>following player and team statistics.</u> <u>To understand what sports reporting</u>
<u>(3)</u> <u>(4)</u>
might involve focus on local sports activities. <u>Write an article about</u>

<u>a football game or a track meet,</u> <u>and submit it to your school newspaper;</u>
<u>(5)</u> <u>(6)</u>
Or consider writing a profile of an athlete.

---

1 **A** Spelling error
  B Capitalization error
  C Punctuation error
  D No error

2 **F** Spelling error
  G Capitalization error
  H Punctuation error
  J No error

3 **A** Spelling error
  B Capitalization error
  C Punctuation error
  D No error

4 **F** Spelling error
  G Capitalization error
  H Punctuation error
  J No error

5 **A** Spelling error
  B Capitalization error
  C Punctuation error
  D No error

6 **F** Spelling error
  G Capitalization error
  H Punctuation error
  J No error

Writing Tasks

The following activity is designed to assess your writing ability. The prompts will ask you to explain something. You may think of your audience as being any reader other than yourself.

Think of a game you enjoy playing. The game could be a board game, such as chess; a word game, such as twenty questions; or a physical game, such as charades or soccer. Write an essay explaining how to play the game or sport. Describe any special equipment that's needed to play. Explain in detail the rules and instructions of the game, so that the reader can clearly understand how to play it.

Recently technicians have found a way to use computers to manipulate a photograph by changing its color, size, shape, brightness, and clarity. Computer experts can even add, move, or delete parts of a photograph. Manipulated photographs can be informative and entertaining. However, altering photographs can also be deceptive and misleading; for example, a piece of evidence might be removed from the photograph of a crime scene. Some people think that laws should be passed to prevent photograph manipulation; others think that people should be free to express themselves. Still others suggest that all altered photographs should be labeled. As editor of your school newspaper, take a position for or against including a manipulated photograph in a news story. Explain your position.

There are advantages and disadvantages to being an only child, just as there are to having brothers and sisters. Choose one situation to describe. Either write an essay explaining the advantages and disadvantages of having brothers and sisters, or write about the pros and cons of being an only child. Support your personal essay with specific details and examples from your own experience, books, movies, or television shows.

Scoring Rubric

Use this scoring rubric to assess the composition you write in response to the prompts on the previous page. The scale runs from **0** (the poorest) to **4** (the best).

0	1	2	3	4
Blank paper	Vague or brief	Correct purpose, audience, and mode	Correct purpose, audience, and mode	Correct purpose, audience, and mode
In a foreign language	Poorly organized	Organization has lapses	Fair organization	Full, appropriate elaboration
Unreadable because of incoherence or illegibility	Wrong purpose, audience, or mode	Some elaboration and detail	Moderate elaboration and detail	Logical, effective organization
On wrong topic	Loses focus; rambles	Language control is limited	Clear, effective language	Fluent, clear, effective language
Content too scant to score	Lacks elaboration, detail, language control			

INDEX OF AUTHORS AND TITLES

LITERARY TERMS

READING STRATEGIES

GRAMMAR, USAGE, AND MECHANICS

STAFF CREDITS

The people who made up the *Prentice Hall Literature: Timeless Voices, Timeless Themes* team—representing design services, editorial, editorial services, managing editor, manufacturing and inventory planning, market research, marketing services, on-line services/multimedia development, permissions, product marketing, production services, and publishing processes—are listed below. Bold type denotes core team members.

Laura Bird, Betsy Bostwick, Pam Cardiff, **Megan Chill,** Rhett Conklin, Carlos Crespo, Gabriella Della Corte, Ed de Leon, Donna C. DiCuffa, **Amy E. Fleming, Holly Gordon, Rebecca Z. Graziano, William J. Hanna, Rick Hickox,** Jim Jeglikowski, John Kingston, **Perrin Moriarty,** James O'Neill, **Jim O'Shea, Maureen Raymond,** Rob Richman, Doris Robinson, Gerry Schrenck, Ann Shea, Melissa Shustyk, Annette Simmons, **Rita M. Sullivan, Elizabeth Torjussen**

ADDITIONAL CREDITS

Ernie Albanese, Robert H. Aleman, Diane Alimena, Michele Angelucci, Rosalyn Arcilla, Penny Baker, Anthony Barone, Rui Camarinha, Tara Campbell, Amy Capetta, Lorena Cerisano, Kam Cheng, Elizabeth Crawford, Mark Cryan, Paul Delsignore, Robert Dobaczewski, Irene Ehrmann, Kathryn Foot, Joe Galka, Catalina Gavilanes, Elaine Goldman, Joe Graci, Stacey Hosid, Leanne Korszoloski, Jan Kraus, Gregory Lynch, Mary Luthi, Vickie Menanteaux, John McClure, Frances Medico, Omni-Photo Communications, Inc., Photosearch, Inc., Linda Punskovsky, David Rosenthal, Laura Ross, Rose Sievers, Gillian Speeth/Picture This, Cindy Talocci, Mark Taylor, Lashonda Williams, Jeff Zoda

ACKNOWLEDGMENTS (continued)

Harcourt Brace & Company Excerpts from *The People, Yes* by Carl Sandburg, copyright 1936 by Harcourt Brace & Company and renewed 1964 by Carl Sandburg. "Choice: A Tribute to Dr. Martin Luther King, Jr." from *In Search of Our Mothers' Gardens: Womanist Prose,* copyright © 1983 by Alice Walker. "Forest Fire" from *The Diary of Anaïs Nin 1947–1955,* Volume V, copyright © 1974 by Anaïs Nin. From "For My Sister Molly Who in the Fifties" from *Revolutionary Petunias & Other Poems,* copyright © 1972 by Alice Walker. "Paul Bunyan of the North Woods" is excerpted from *The People, Yes* by Carl Sandburg, copyright 1936 by Harcourt Brace & Company and renewed 1964 by Carl Sandburg. Reprinted by permission of the publisher, Harcourt Brace & Company.

HarperCollins Publishers "Forgotten Language" from *Where the Sidewalk Ends* by Shel Silverstein. Copyright © 1974 by Evil Eye Music, Inc. "Brown vs. Board of Education" from *Now Is Your Time: The African-American Struggle for Freedom* by Walter Dean Myers. Copyright © 1991 by Walter Dean Myers. 3 lines from "The Falling Flower" by Moritake from *Poetry Handbook: A Dictionary of Terms* by Babette Deutsch. Copyright © 1974, 1969, 1962, 1957 by Babette Deutsch. "Why the Waves Have Whitecaps" from *Mules and Men* by Zora Neale Hurston. Copyright 1935 by Zora Neale Hurston. Copyright renewed 1963 by John C. Hurston and Joel Hurston. "Lights in the Night" from *An American Childhood* by Annie Dillard. Copyright © 1987 by Annie Dillard. Used by permission of HarperCollins Publishers.

Harvard University Press "Much Madness is divinest Sense—" (#835) and "If I can stop one Heart from breaking" by Emily Dickinson are reprinted by permission of the publishers and the Trustees of Amherst College from *The Poems of Emily Dickinson,* Thomas H. Johnson, editor, Cambridge, Mass.: The Belknap Press of Harvard University Press, Copyright © 1951, 1955, 1979, 1983 by the President and Fellows of Harvard College. "The Tell-Tale Heart" is reprinted by permission of the publisher from *The Collected Works of Edgar Allen Poe,* edited by Thomas Olive Mabbott, Cambridge, Mass.: Harvard University Press, Copyright © 1978 by the President and Fellows of Harvard College. Reprinted by permission of the publisher from *One Writer's Beginnings* by

Eudora Welty, Cambridge, Mass.: Harvard University Press, Copyright © 1983, 1984 by Eudora Welty.

Brook Hersey for the Estate of John Hersey "Not to Go With the Others" from *Here to Stay,* Copyright © 1962, 1987 by John Hersey, published by Alfred A. Knopf. Used by permission of Brook Hersey for the Estate of John Hersey.

Hill and Wang, a division of Farrar, Straus & Giroux, Inc. "Thank You M'am" from *Short Stories* by Langston Hughes, edited by Akiba Sullivan. Copyright © 1996 by Romana Bass and Arnold Rampersad. "The Story-Teller" from *Collected and New Poems 1924–1963* by Mark Van Doren. Copyright © 1963 by Mark Van Doren. Copyright renewed © 1997 by Dorothy G. Van Doren. Reprinted by permission of Hill and Wang, a division of Farrar, Straus & Giroux, Inc.

Holiday House, Inc. "January" from *A Child's Calendar* by John Updike. Copyright © 1965, 1999 by John Updike. All rights reserved. Reprinted by permission of Holiday House, Inc.

Henry Holt and Company, Inc. "The Road Not Taken" copyright 1916, 1923 by Holt, Rinehart and Winston, Inc. and renewed 1944, 1951 by Robert Frost from *The Poetry of Robert Frost,* edited by Edward Connery Lathem. "The Freedom of the Moon" from *The Poetry of Robert Frost,* edited by Edward Connery Lathem, Copyright 1956 by Robert Frost. Copyright 1928, © 1969 by Henry Holt & Company, reprinted by permission of Henry Holt and Company, Inc.

Evelyn Tooley Hunt and Negro Digest "Taught Me Purple" by Evelyn Tooley Hunt from *Negro Digest,* February 1964, © 1964 by Johnson Publishing Company, Inc. Reprinted by permission of Evelyn Tooley Hunt and *Negro Digest.*

Gish Jen "The White Umbrella" by Gish Jen. Copyright © 1984 by Gish Jen. All rights reserved. First published in *The Yale Review.* Reprinted by permission of the author.

Garrison Keillor "Something from the Sixties" by Garrison Keillor, from *The Talk of the Town,* published in *The New Yorker.* Used by permission of the author.

Daniel Keyes "Flowers for Algernon" (short story version) by Daniel Keyes. Copyright © 1959, 1987 by Daniel Keyes. Expanded story published in paperback by Bantam Books. Reprinted by permission of the author.

The Heirs to the Estate of Martin Luther King, Jr., c/o Writers House, Inc. as agent for the proprietor "The American Dream" by Martin Luther King, Jr. Copyright 1968 by Martin Luther King, Jr., copyright renewed 1996 by The Estate of Martin Luther King, Jr. Reprinted by arrangement with The Heirs to the Estate of Martin Luther King, Jr., c/o Writers House, Inc. as agent for the proprietor.

Alfred A. Knopf, Inc. "The Ninny" from *The Image of Chekhov,* Robert Payne, translator. Copyright © 1963 and renewed 1991 by Alfred A. Knopf Inc. "Mushrooms" from *The Colossus and Other Poems* by Sylvia Plath. Copyright © 1960 by Sylvia Plath. "Incident in a Rose Garden" from *New and Selected Poems* by Donald Justice. Copyright © 1995 by Donald Justice. "Harlem Night Song" and "Winter Moon" from *Selected Poems of Langston Hughes* by Langston Hughes. Copyright 1926 by Alfred A. Knopf, Inc. and renewed 1954 by Langston Hughes. "The Cyclone" from *Pecos Bill: Texas Cowpuncher* by Harold W. Felton. Copyright 1949 by Alfred A. Knopf, Inc. Reprinted by permission of the publisher, Alfred A. Knopf, Inc.

Barbara S. Kouts for Joseph Bruchac "Ellis Island" by Joseph Bruchac from *This Remembered Earth,* Geary Hobson, Editor, Red Earth Press, 1979. Used by permission of Barbara S. Kouts for Joseph Bruchac.

Amy Ling "Grandma Ling" by Amy Ling, originally published as "Grandma" in *Bridge: An Asian American Perspective*, Vol. 7, no. 3 (1980) by Amy Ling. Copyright © 1980 by Amy Ling. Used by permission of the author.

Little, Brown and Company "Sancho" from *The Longhorns* by J. Frank Dobie. Copyright © 1941 by J. Frank Dobie; © renewed 1969 by J. Frank Dobie. Reprinted by permission of Little, Brown and Company. Excerpt from *The Man Without a Country* by Edward Everett Hale (Little, Brown & Company).

Liveright Publishing Corporation "Those Winter Sundays," copyright © 1966 by Robert Hayden, from *Collected Poems of Robert Hayden* by Frederick Glaysher, editor. "love is a place," copyright 1935, © 1963, 1991 by the Trustees for the E.E. Cummings Trust. Copyright © 1978 by George James Firmage, from *Complete Poems: 1904–1962* by E.E. Cummings. Edited by George J. Firmage. Reprinted by permission of Liveright Publishing Corporation.

The LULAC National "The Other Pioneers" by Roberto Félix Salazar, published in *The LULAC News*, July 1939. Reprinted by permission of LULAC National.

Literary Trustees of Walter de la Mare, and the Society of Authors as their representative "Silver" from *Collected Poems 1901–1918* by Walter de la Mare. "All But Blind" by Walter de la Mare, from *The Complete Poems of Walter de la Mare*, Copyright 1969, 1970. Used by permission of the Literary Trustees of Walter de la Mare, and the Society of Authors as their representative.

N. Scott Momaday "New World" from *The Gourd Dancers* by N. Scott Momaday, copyright © 1976 by N. Scott Momaday. Reprinted by permission of the author.

Moon Publications Inc. From *Road Trip USA* by Jamie Jensen. Published by Moon Travel Handbooks. Text copyright © Jamie Jensen 1996. All rights reserved. Used by permission of Moon Publications Inc.

William Morris Literary Agency "Achieving the American Dream" by Mario M. Cuomo, Introduction from *The Italian Family Album*. Copyright © 1994 by Mario M. Cuomo. Reprinted by permission of William Morris Agency, Inc., on behalf of the author.

William Morrow and Company, Inc. "The United States *vs.* Susan B. Anthony" from *Women of Courage* by Margaret Truman. Copyright © 1976 by Margaret Truman Daniel. Reprinted by permission of William Morrow and Company, Inc.

Museum of New Mexico Press "Chicoria," translated by Rudolfo Anaya, is reprinted with permission of the Museum of New Mexico Press, from *Cuentos: Tales From the Hispanic Southwest* by José Griego y Maestas and Rudolfo A. Anaya, copyright 1980.

W. W. Norton & Company, Inc. "400-Meter Free Style" from *Selected Poems 1960–1990* by Maxine Kumin. Copyright © 1959 and renewed 1987 by Maxine Kumin. Originally published in *The Hudson Review*, Summer 1959. Reprinted by permission of W. W. Norton & Company, Inc.

W. W. Norton & Company, Inc., and Adrienne Rich "Prospective Immigrants Please Note," copyright © 1993, 1967, 1963 by Adrienne Rich, from *Collected Early Poems: 1950–1970* by Adrienne Rich. Reprinted by permission of the author and W. W. Norton & Company, Inc.

Naomi Shihab Nye "Hamadi" by Naomi Shihab Nye, copyright © 1993 by Naomi Shihab Nye. First published in *American Street*. Reprinted by permission of the author.

Harold Ober Associates Incorporated "Southern Mansion" by Arna Bontemps, published in *Personals*. Copyright 1949 by Arna Bontemps and Langston Hughes. Copyright renewed 1976 by Alberta Bontemps and George Houston Bass. "Christmas Day in the Morning" by Pearl S. Buck. Copyright © 1955 by Pearl S. Buck. Copyright renewed 1983 by Pearl S. Buck. Reprinted by permission of Harold Ober Associates Incorporated.

Pantheon Books, a division of Random House, Inc. "Coyote Steals the Sun and Moon" from *American Indian Myths and Legends* by Richard Erdoes and Alfonso Ortiz, editors. Copyright © 1984 by Richard Erdoes and Alfonso Ortiz. Reprinted by permission of Pantheon Books, a division of Random House, Inc.

Julio Noboa Polanco "Identity" by Julio Noboa Polanco from *The Rican, Journal of Contemporary Puerto Rican Thought,* copyright 1973. Reprinted by permission of the author.

Putnam Publishing Group "The Girl Who Hunted Rabbits" from *Zuñi Folk Tales,* translated by Frank H. Cushing with an introduction by J. W. Powell.

Random House, Inc. From *I Know Why the Caged Bird Sings* by Maya Angelou. Copyright © 1969 and renewed 1997 by Maya Angelou. "Raymond's Run" from *Gorilla My Love* by Toni Cade Bambara. Copyright © 1971 by Toni Cade Bambara. "Why Leaves Turn Color in the Fall" from *A Natural History of the Sense* by Diane Ackerman. Copyright © 1990. "Los New Yorks" from *Mainland* by Victor Hernández Cruz. Copyright © 1973 by Victor Hernández Cruz. Reprinted by permission of Random House, Inc. From *The Diary of Anne Frank* by Frances Goodrich and Albert Hackett. Copyright 1954, 1956 as an unpublished work. Copyright © 1956 by Albert Hackett, Frances Goodrich, and Otto Frank. Reprinted by permission of Random House, Inc. CAUTION: *The Diary of Anne Frank* is the sole property of the dramatists and is fully protected by copyright. It may not be acted by professionals or amateurs without written permission and the payment of a royalty. All rights, including professional, amateur, stock, radio broadcasting, television, motion picture, recitation, lecturing, public reading, and the rights of translation into foreign languages are reserved.

Reader's Digest and Robert MacNeil "The Trouble with Television" by Robert MacNeil (condensed from a speech delivered November 13, 1984, at the President's Leadership Forum, State University of New York at Purchase). Reprinted with permission from the March 1985 *Reader's Digest* and the author.

Marian Reiner "Elizabeth Blackwell" by Eve Merriam, from *Independent Voices* by Eve Merriam. Copyright © 1968 Eve Merriam. © Renewed 1996 Guy Michel and Dee Michel. Reprinted by permission of Marian Reiner.

Andrea Reynolds "The Adventure of the Speckled Band" from *The Complete Sherlock Holmes* by Sir Arthur Conan Doyle.

Wendy Rose "Drum Song" from *The Halfbreed Chronicles and Other Poems* by Wendy Rose. Copyright © 1985 by Wendy Rose. Reprinted by permission of the author.

Russell & Volkening as agents for the author "Harriet Tubman: Guide to Freedom" from *Harriet Tubman: Conductor on the Underground Railroad* by Ann Petry. Copyright © 1955 by Ann Petry, renewed 1983 by Ann Petry. Reprinted by the permission of Russell & Volkening as agents for the author.

St. Martin's Press, Inc., and Harold Ober Associates Inc. "Debbie" from *All Things Wise and Wonderful* by James Herriot.

ART CREDITS

(Art Credits continue on page 998.)

344: *Carl Sandburg,* Miriam Svet, The National Portrait Gallery, Smithsonian Institution, Washington, D.C./Art Resource, New York; **345:** Will Faller; **347:** *Paul Bunyan,* Rockwell Kent, The Granger Collection, New York; **351:** *July Hay,* Thomas Hart Benton, oil and egg tempera on composition board, 38" x 26 ¾", Signed and dated (lower left): Benton '43. The Metropolitan Museum of Art, George A. Hearn Fund, 1943. (43.159.1) Photograph copyright ©1982 By the Metropolitan Museum of Art/ ©T.H. Benton and R.P. Benton Testamentary Trusts/Licensed by VAGA, New York, NY; **352:** UPI/Corbis-Bettmann; **353:** Corel Professional Photos CD-ROM™; **354:** Corel Professional Photos CD-ROM™; **356–357 border:** ©The Stock Market/Jeff Gnass; **358–359 border:** Stephen J. Kraseman/DRK Photo; **361 l.:** Photo by South Dakota Tourism; **r.:** Photo courtesy of Jamie Jensen **364 l.:** Archive Photos; **m.t.:** Prentice Hall; **m.b.:** AP/Wide World Photos; **b.:** Thomas Victor; **365:** Corbis-Bettmann; **366:** Corel Professional Photos CD-ROM™; **368 t.:** Courtesy of the Governor; **b.:** Corel Professional Photos CD-ROM™; **371:** AP/Wide World Photos; **378:** Library of Congress; **380–381:** *USS Constitution and HMS Guerriere* (Aug. 19, 1812), Thomas Birch, U. S. Naval Academy Museum; **382–383:** *Prisoners,* from Iconographic Encyclopedia, Vol. 2, Div. VI, Naval Sciences, pl. 25, drawn by G. Heck, eng. by Henry Winkles, negative n. 72095, © Collection of the New–York Historical Society; **384–385:** *Row of Cannon,* from Iconographic Encylcopedia, Vol. 2, Div. VI, Naval Sciences, pl. 21 (detail), drawn by G. Heck, eng. by Henry Winkles, negative n. 72094, © Collection of the New–York Historical Society; **386–387:** *Officer of the Watch on the Horseblock,* Heck's Iconographic Encyclopedia, 1851, Collection of The New–York Historical Society; **388–389:** *Ship Plans,* from Iconographic Encylcopedia, Vol. 2, Div. VI, Naval Sciences, pl. 20 (detail), drawn by G. Heck, eng. by Henry Winkles, negative #. 72092, © Collection of the New York Historical Society; **392:** Chapman Billies Inc., Sandwich, MA; **397:** Chen Chi, *High Noon, New York,* 1986. Watercolor, 38" x 35", The Butler Institute of American Art, Youngstown, Ohio; **398 t.:** Russel Lee Photograph Collection, CN #03126, The Center for American History, The University of Texas at Austin; **b.:** Sonja H. Smith; **399–402:** Corel Professional Photos CD-ROM™; **405:** Renee Lynn/Photo Researchers, Inc.; **408 t.:** Jesse Stuart Foundation; **b.:** Prentice Hall; **409 t.:** ©The Stock Market/Gabe Palmer; **m.:** Richard Hutchings/PhotoEdit; **b.:** Bob Daemmrich/Stock, Boston; **411:** Jeff Greenberg/Omni-Photo Communications, Inc.; **412:** Fotopic/ Omni-Photo Communications, Inc.; **414:** *Girl in Car Window,* Winson Trang, Courtesy of the artist; **417:** Will Faller; **422 t.:** Pach/Corbis-Bettmann; **423:** Annie Griffiths/DRK Photo; **424:** *Hearth,* 1957, Loren MacIver, oil and plaster on masonite, H. 49 ⅝" W. 34 ⅝" The Metropolitan Museum of Art, Purchase, Maria-Gaetana Matisse Gift, 1993. (1993.280). Photograph copyright © 1994 by the Metropolitan Museum of Art **426–427:** image©Copyright 1997 PhotoDisc, Inc.; **430:** Robert Brennan/PhotoEdit; **435:** Bruce Forster/Tony Stone Images; **438–439:** *Les Memoires d'un saint, (The Memories of a Saint),* 1960, René Magritte, oil on canvas, 31 ½" x 39 ¼", Menil Collection, Houston, photographer: Hickey-Robertson, Houston, ©1998 C. Herscovici/Artists Rights Sociey (ARS), New York; **440:** Thomas Victor; **441:** Edward Holub/Photonica; **443:** Eric Perry/ Photonica; **445:** Joe Squillante/Photonica; **449:** *Spring,* ©1922, Georgia O'Keeffe, oil on canvas, 35 ½" x 30 ⅜", Frances Lehman Loeb Art Center, Vassar College, Poughkeepsie, New York, Bequest of Mrs. Arthur Schwab (Edna Bryner, class of 1907) 1967.31.15, ©2000 The Georgia O'Keeffe Foundation/Artists Rights Society (ARS), New York; **450 t.:** The Mark Twain House, Hartford, CT; **b.:** Janklow & Nesbit Associates, Photograph © by Jill Krementz; **451:** Steve & Dave Maslowski/Photo Researchers, Inc.; **452:** ©1994, Stan Osolinski/FPG International Corp.; **453:** image© Copyright 1997 PhotoDisc, Inc.; **454–455:** Martin and Sally Fox; **455:** image©Copyright 1997 PhotoDisc, Inc.; **456:** image©Copyright 1997 PhotoDisc, Inc.; **458–459 border:** L. West/ Photo Researchers, Inc.; **460:** The Image Bank; **460–461 border:** L. West/Photo Researchers, Inc.; **464 t.:** Photo by Dorothy Alexander; **m.:** ©Archive Photos; **b.:** Photo by William Lewis; **465:** Esbin Anderson/Omni-Photo Communications, Inc.; **466:** *Where to? What For? #3* ©1998 Nancie B. Warner, Courtesy of the artist; **467:** *Inspiration,* Daniel Nevins, SuperStock; **468:** *New York City—Bird's Eye View,* 1920, Joaquin Torres-Garcia, Yale University Art Gallery, Gift of Collection Societe Anonyme, ©1998 Artists Rights Society (ARS), New York/ADAGP, Paris; **472:** *Sir Arthur Conan Doyle* (detail), H. L. Gates, The National Portrait Gallery, London; **473:** Photofest; **475–489:** from *The Complete Adventures of Sherlock Holmes,* illustration by Sidney Paget; **496:** Kurt Wittman/Omni-Photo Communications, Inc.; **501:** *The Blank Signature (Carte Blanche),* 1965, René Magritte, oil on canvas, ©Board of Trustees, National Gallery of Art, Washington, D.C., Collection of Mr. and Mrs. Paul Mellon, ©2000 C. Herscovici/Artists Rights Society (ARS), New York; **502 t.:** Flannery Literary, photo © Ruth Wright Paulsen 1993; **m.t.:** AP/Wide World Photos; **m.b.:** Corbis-Bettmann; **b.:** AP/Wide World Photos; **503 b.l.:** Phil Dotson/Photo Researchers, Inc.; **r.:** *Brittle Willow, Brooklyn,* 1992, Anders Knutsson, 37"x 48", acrylic on linen (in the dark), Courtesy of the artist; **t.r.:** Merlin Tuttle/Photo Researchers, Inc.; **504–505:** *Brittle Willow, Brooklyn,* 1992, Anders Knutsson, 37" x 48", acrylic on linen (in the dark), Courtesy of the artist; **506:** Steve Kraseman/DRK Photo; **508–509:** Phil Dotson/ Photo Researchers, Inc.; **510:** Billy E. Barnes/PhotoEdit; **511:** Merlin Tuttle/Photo Researchers, Inc.; **516:** *Album of Virginia "Rockfish Gap and Mountain House,"* Edward Beyer, State Capitol, Commonwealth of Virginia. Courtesy The Library of Virginia; **518:** Culver Pictures, Inc.; **522:** *Variation IV,* Wassily Kandinsky, Russian Bauhaus Archive/SuperStock, **527:** Jonathan Nourok/PhotoEdit; **530–531:** *Mrs. Cushman's House,* 1942, N.C. Wyeth, Harriet Russell Stanley Fund, New Britain Museum of American Art, Conneticut, Photo by E. Irving Blomstrann; **533:** *Dinner at Haddo House,* Alfred Edward Emslie, National Portrait Gallery, London/SuperStock; **535:** Tim Flach/Tony Stone Images; **539:** *Fisherman's Family,* 1916, color woodcut with graphite, B.J.O. Nordfeldt, Amon Carter Museum, Fort Worth, Texas; **540:** Corbis-Bettmann; **541:** M. C. Escher "Self-Portrait" © 1998 Cordon Art B.V. Baarn-Holland. All rights reserved; **543–546:** Culver Pictures, Inc.; **551:** Courtesy National Archives; **552:** Library of Congress; **556 t.:** Thomas Victor; **b.:** Photo by Michael Nye; **557:** *Transfer to the #6,* Kathy Ruttenberg, Gallery Henoch; **558:** *Windows,* 1952, oil on canvas, 32" x 20 ¼", Charles Sheeler, Collection, Hirschl & Adler Galleries; **559:** Ken Karp; **562:** ©Ulf Sjostedt/FPG International Corp.; **564:** "The Prophet" a book by Kahlil Gibran; **567–568:** Bob Daemmrich/Stock, Boston; **572:** *The Tell-Tale Heart,* 1883, Odilon Redon, Charcoal on paper, 15 ¾" x 13 ⅛", Santa Barbara Museum of Art, Museum Purchase; **577:** *Moonwalk,* 1987, serigraph on paper, Andy Warhol, ©1999 Andy Warhol Foundation for the Visual Arts/Ronald Feldman Fine Arts, photograph by D. James Dee/ARS, NY; **578 t.:** *Paul Laurence Dunbar,* The Granger Collection, New York; **b.:** Prentice Hall; **579:** Corel Professional Photos CD-ROM™; **580:** Alan D. Carey/Photo Researchers, Inc.; **582:** *Farm Boy,* 1941, Charles Alston, Courtesy of Clark Atlanta University; **584:** image©Copyright 1997 PhotoDisc, Inc.; **586 b.:** UPI/Corbis-Bettmann **586–588:** Corel Professional Photos CD-ROM™; **590:** *Enoshima. Island at left with cluster of buildings among trees. Fuji in distance at right,* c. 1823. (detail), Katsusika Hokusai, The Newark Museum/Art Resource, NY; **594 t.:** The Granger Collection, New York; **b.:** Courtesy of the author; **595:** *Story Teller,* Velino "Shije" Herrera, National Museum of American Art, Washington, D.C./Art Resource, NY; **596:** *Stirling Station,* 1887, William Kennedy, Collection of Andrew McIntosh Patrick, UK/The Bridgeman Art Library International Ltd., London/New York; **601:** Lawrence Migdale; **602:** Courtesy of D. Alimena; **606–607:** ©The Stock Market/Tom Bean; **612:** Alan D. Carey/Photo Researchers, Inc.; **617:** David Young-Wolff/PhotoEdit; **620–621:** *Still Life #31,* 1963, mixed media construction with television, 48 x 60 x 10 ¾", Tom Wesselmann, Frederick P. Weisman Art Foundation, Los Angeles, CA., ©Tom Wesselmann/ Licensed by VAGA, New York, NY; **622:** Courtesy of the author; **623:** Pat & Tom Leeson/Photo Researchers, Inc.; **626:** Mike Mazzaschi/Stock, Boston; **627:** Tim Flach/Tony Stone Images; **631:** Vincent Van Gogh, *Portrait of Joseph Roulin,* (April 1889), Oil on canvas, 25 ⅜ x 21 ¾" (64.6 x 55.2 cm). The Museum of Modern Art, New York. Gift of Mr. and Mrs. William A. M. Burden, Mr. and Mrs. Paul Rosenberg, Nelson A. Rockefeller, Mr. and Mrs. Armand Bartos, Sidney and Harriet Janis, Mr. and Mrs. Werner E. Josten, and Loula D. Laskar Bequest (by exchange). Photograph ©2000 The Museum of Modern Art, New York; **632 t.:** Thomas Victor; **b.:** Arte Publico Press. Photo by Georgia McInnis; **633:** AP/Wide World Photos; **634:** Jean Paul Nacivet/Leo De Wys, Inc.; **636:** Mel Di Giacomo/ The Image Bank; **637:** Gottlieb/Monkmeyer; **638:** Michael Newman/ PhotoEdit; **646:** The Granger Collection, New York; **647:** Brown Brothers; **648:** The Granger Collection, New York; **649:** Courtesy of D. Alimena; **652 t.:** AP/Wide World Photos; **b.:** ©Archive Photos; **653:** *VII. Fuji in clear weather. One of the "Thirty-six Views of Fuji,"* Hokusai, © Copyright British Museum; **654:** *The Great Wave Off Kanagawa,* Katsushika Hokusai, From the series of Thirty-six views of Fuji, The Metropolitan Museum of Art, The H. O. Havemeyer Collection, Bequest of Mrs. H. O. Havemeyer, 1929, (JP 1847) Photograph © 1978 The Metropolitan Museum of Art; **656:** *The Watchtower,* 1942, watercolor on eggshell lacquered to wood, 5 ½ x 4", Savielly Schleifer, Musée d'Histoire Contemporaine, B.D.I.C., photo courtesy of ARCHIPEL; **658:** *The Unattainable,* Henri Pieck, by courtesy of Karrie Pieck, Holland, and Ineke Pieck, England; **662:** Capece/Monkmeyer Press; **665:** AP/Wide World Photos; **667:** *A Social History of Missouri,* (detail) 1936, Thomas Hart Benton, Courtesy Missouri Department of Natural Resources, photo by Greg Leech/©T. H. Benton and R. P. Benton Testamentary Trusts/Licensed by VAGA, New York, NY;

668 t.: John Wyand; **b.:** AP/Wide World Photos; **669:** AP/Wide World Photos; **670:** *Autumn Leaves,* 1994 by Ditz, Private Collection/Bridgeman Art Library International Ltd., London/New York; **673:** ©Robert Pearcy/Animals Animals; **675:** AP/Wide World Photos; **676–677:** Nathan Beck/Omni-Photo Communications, Inc.; **678:** *Untitled,* ©James Yang/Stock Illustration Source, Inc.; **684 t.:** Corbis-Bettmann; **b:** Library of Congress; **685:** Hazel Carew/Monkmeyer; **686:** Richard Hutchings/Photo Researchers, Inc.; **687:** Bob Daemmrich/Stock, Boston; **689:** Corbis-Bettmann; **695:** Reuters/Jay Gorodetzer/Archive Photos; **696:** Donna & Kent Dannen/ Photo Researchers, Inc.; **701:** Billy E. Barnes/PhotoEdit; **704–705:** *First Night,* oil on board, Mark Baring, Private Collection/The Bridgeman Art Library International Ltd., London/ New York; **707:** Theatre poster for the 1996 season for the McCarter Theatre in Princeton, NJ. Howard Levine/ David Meyhew, Art Directors, 7 x 11 acrylic, Wiktor Sadowski, Marlena agency; **708 t.:** UPI/Corbis-Bettmann; **711:** Joan Marcus Photography; **712:** UPI/Corbis-Bettmann; **714:** Copyright ANNE FRANK-Fonds, Basle/Switzerland; **717:** Copyright ANNE FRANK-Fonds, Basle/Switzerland; **720:** Jewish Historical Museum, Amsterdam; **727:** Copyright ANNE FRANK-Fonds, Basle/Switzerland; **733:** UPI/Corbis-Bettmann; **738:** The Granger Collection, New York; **743:** The Granger Collection, New York; **746:** Courtesy of Playbill; **747:** Joan Marcus Photography; **748–760:** Copyright ANNE FRANK-Fonds, Basle/Switzerland; **765 & 767:** The Granger Collection, New York; **773:** Peter Cunningham; **776:** Copyright ANNE FRANK-Fonds, Basle/Switzerland; **781:** *The Singer Faure as Hamlet,* Edouard Manet, Kunsthalle, Hamburg, Germany/ A.K.G., Berlin/SuperStock; **782:** *William Shakespeare,* (detail), Artist unknown, by courtesy of the National Portrait Gallery, London; **783:** Bonnie Kamin/PhotoEdit; **784:** Photofest; **786 l. & r.:** Photo by M. Marigold/ Photofest; **790 & 792:** Photofest; **796:** Title Page with a Portrait of Shakespeare, from *Mr. William Shakespeare's Comedies, Histories and Tragedies,* edited by J. Heminge and H. Condell, engraved by Droeshurt, 1623, British Library, London, UK/Bridgeman Art Library, London/New York; **801:** Tony Freeman PhotoEdit; **804–805:** *Man at the Edge of Paradise,* 1994, oil on canvas encased in lead, 60" x 84" x 2 ½", Adam Straus, Private Collection, Courtesy Nohra Haime Gallery; **806:** AP/Wide World Photos; **807:** *Nap in the Afternoon,* Kathleen Cook, Courtesy of the artist; **809 & 810:** Ken Karp; **813:** Marsden Hartley, *Birds of the Bagaduce,* 1939, oil on board, 28 x 22". The Butler Institute of American Art, Youngstown, Ohio; **814 t.:** *Henry Wadsworth Longfellow* (detail), Thomas B. Read, The National Portrait Gallery, Smithsonian Institution, Washington, D.C./Art Resource, New York; **b.:** Photo by Dorothy Alexander; **815:** *Benares,* Marshall Johnson, Courtesy, Peabody Essex Museum, Salem, Mass. Photo by Mark Sexton; **816:** *The Lookout—"All's Well,"* 1896, oil on canvas, 39 ⅞ x 30 ⅛" (101.3 x 76.5 cm.), Winslow Homer, Courtesy, Museum of Fine Arts, Boston, MA, Warren Collection; **820–821:** Shelley Rotner/Omni-Photo Communications, Inc.; **822:** *Horse in the Countryside,* 1910, canvas 33 ½ x 44 ½, Franz Marc, Museum Folkwang Essen, Essen, Germany; **826 t.:** New York Public Library; **m.t.:** *William Shakespeare,* (detail), Artist unknown, by courtesy of the National Portrait Gallery, London; **m.b.:** *E. E. Cummings* (detail), 1958, Self Portrait, The National Portrait Gallery, Smithsonian Institution, Washington, D.C./Art Resource, New York; **b.:** Dimitri Kessel/ Life Magazine; **827:** Bruce M. Esbin/Omni-Photo Communications, Inc.; **828:** *Relics,* Martin Lewis, Philadelphia Museum of Art: Bequest of Staunton B. Peck; **829:** Paul Hermansen/Tony Stone Images; **830:** *The Nest,* 1893, Constant Montald, Musées Royaux de Beaux-Arts de Belgique, Bruxelles-Koninklijke Musea voor Schone Kunsten van Belgie, Brussels, Belgium (photo Speltdom); **831:** Amos Zezmer/Omni-Photo Communications, Inc.; **834 t.:** Thomas Victor; **m.t.:** The Granger Collection, New York; **b.:** Photo by Victor Kumin; **835:** *View to Orchard,* Winter, Cerney House, Charles Neal, SuperStock; **836:** *The Magpie,* 1869, Claude Monet, Musée d'Orsay, Paris, ©Photo RMN; **837:** *Herons and Reeds,* hanging scroll, Japan, Asian Art Museum of San Francisco, The Avery Brunkage Collection, B65 D14, photo copyright © 1992 Asian Art Museum of San Francisco, CA. All Rights Reserved.; **838:** *Seashore at Palavas,* 1854, Gustave Courbet, Musée Fabre, Montpellier, France; **839:** Peter Terry/ Tony Stone Images; **845:** Hulton Gutty/Liaison Agency; **848:** Simon Battensby/Tony Stone Images; **853:** *Black Hat on a Yellow Chair,* 1952, Fernand Leger, University of Iowa Museum of Art, Iowa City, IA, Gift of Owen and Leone Elliott, ©2000 Artists Rights Society (ARS), New York/ADAGP, Paris; **854 t.:** ©Faber & Faber Ltd; **m.t.:** AP/Wide World Photos; **m.b.:** Pat Allen-Wolk; **b.:** The Granger Collection, New York; **855:** *Egrets in Summer,* 1940–45, oil on canvas, 82 ⅞ x 159", N. C. Wyeth, Courtesy of Metropolitan Life Insurance Company, Photograph © Malcolm Varon, New York, NY; **856:** Aram Gesar/The Image Bank; **858:** *Crawling Turtle II,* Barry Wilson, SuperStock; **859:** Jeff Greenberg/Omni-Photo Communications, Inc.; **862 t.:** Thomas Victor; **m.t.:** Photo by Kit Stafford; **m.b.:** NYT Pictures; **b.:** Thomas Victor; **863:** Liz Hymans/Tony Stone Images; **864 t.:** *Wallowa Lake,* Harley, Abby Aldrich Rockefeller Folk Art Center, Williamsburg, VA; **b.:** *Jack's Fireplace,* Jack Palance, 29" x 30", oil, photo©Ralph Merlino/ Shooting Star; **866:** ©Telegraph Colour Library/FPG International Corp.; **867:** David Young-Wolff/PhotoEdit; **868:** Mary Kate Denny/Tony Stone Images; **872 & 873:** Corel Professional Photos CD-ROM™; **874 t.:** Corbis-Bettmann; **m.:** *Philip Larkin* (detail), Humphrey Ocean, by Courtesy of the National Portrait Gallery, London; **b.:** Thomas Victor; **875:** Nathan Beck/Omni-Photo Communications, Inc.; **876:** *Red Hills, Lake George,* 1927, oil on canvas, Georgia O'Keeffe, Acquired 1945, The Phillips Collection, Washington, DC, ©2000 The Georgia O'Keeffe Foundation/ Artists Rights Society (ARS), New York; **878:** *China Roses, Broadway,* Alfred William Parsons, watercolor on paper, Christopher Wood Gallery, London, UK/The Bridgeman Art Library International Ltd., London/New York; **882:** Jack Finch/Photo Researchers, Inc.; **887:** David Young-Wolff/PhotoEdit; **890–891:** *Woodcutter,* 1891, Winslow Homer, Private Collection; **892:** Courtesy of Thomas Benét; **893 & 895:** The Granger Collection, New York; **899:** *His Hair Flows Like a River,* T.C. Cannon, Philbrook Museum of Art, Tulsa, Oklahoma; **900 t.:** © Peter Basch; **m.:** AP/Wide World Photos; **b.:** Mourning Dove (Humishuma) photo by John Lei/Omni-Photo Communications, Inc.; **901:** *Sunset in Memoriam* (detail), 1946, watercolor, 16 ⅞ x 23 ¹⁵⁄₁₆", Woody (Woodrow Wilson) Crumbo, Philbrook Museum of Art, Tulsa, Oklahoma, Gift of Clark Field (1946.45.5); **902:** *Cosmic Canine,* John Nieto, Courtesy of the artist; **905:** *Thunder Knives,* 1957, Pablita Velarde, Santa Clara, Museum of Indian Arts & Culture/Laboratory of Anthropology Collections, Museum of New Mexico, photographer: Blair Clark; **910 t.:** Chuck Slade; **m.t.:** Courtesy of the author; **m.b.:** Jackie Torrence from "Jackie Tales," (detail), published by Avon Books, 1998, Photograph by Michael Pateman; **b.:** Courtesy of the Estate of Carl Van Vechten, Joseph Solomon, Executor, The National Portrait Gallery, Smithsonian Institution, Washington, D.C./Art Resource, New York; **911:** Frederick Judd Waugh, *Breakers at Floodtide,* 1909, 35" x 40", The Butler Institute of American Art, Youngstown, Ohio; **912:** *Invitation to the Dance* (el convite), Theodore Gentilz, Gift, Yanaguana Society in memory of Frederick C. Chabot, Daughters of the Republic of Texas Library; **918:** *Wind and Geometry,* 1978, David True, Courtesy of the artist; **922:** NASA; **923:** AP/Wide World Photos; **926:** Tom Bean/Tony Stone Images; **931:** Courtesy of Westtown School, Westtown Pennsylvania 19395. Photograph courtesy of the Brandywine River Museum, Chadds Ford, PA; **932: t.** Carl Sandburg, Miriam Svet, The National Portrait Gallery, Smithsonian Institution, Washington, D.C./Art Resource, New York; **m.** Falls Village—Canaan Historical Society; **b.** Davey Crockett, Artist Unknown, The Granger Collection, New York; **933:** *Hammer in His Hand,* Palmer C. Hayden, Museum of African American Art, Palmer C. Hayden Collection, Gift of Miriam A. Hayden, Photograph by Armando Solis; Los Angeles, CA; **935:** *John Henry on the Right, Steam Drill on the Left,* 1944–47, Palmer Hayden, oil on canvas, 30 x 40", Collection of The Museum of African American Art, Los Angeles, CA, Palmer C. Hayden Collection, Gift of Miriam A. Hayden; **937:** *It's Wrote on the Rock,* Palmer C. Hayden, oil on canvas, 25 x 31 ⅞", Collection of The Museum of African American Art, Los Angeles, CA, Palmer C. Hayden Collection, Gift of Miriam A. Hayden; **940:** *Big Bend Tunnel,* 1944–45, Palmer Hayden, oil on canvas, 30 x 40", Collection of The Museum of African American Art, Los Angeles, CA, Palmer C. Hayden Collection, Gift of Miriam A. Hayden; **942:** *He Laid Down his Hammer and Cried,* 1944–47, Palmer C. Hayden, Museum of African American Art, Los Angeles, CA; **944:** UPI/Corbis-Bettmann; **947:** Eric Meola/The Image Bank; **951:** Superman and all related elements are trademarks of DC Comics ©1998. All rights reserved. Used with permission. **952:** Culver Pictures, Inc.; **956:** Photofest; **961:** Will & Deni McIntyre/Photo Researchers, Inc.